f the World

ENCYCLOPEDIA OF U.S. FOREIGN RELATIONS

ENCYCLOPEDIA OF
U.S. FOREIGN
RELATIONS

SENIOR EDITORS

Bruce W. Jentleson   Thomas G. Paterson

PREPARED UNDER THE AUSPICES OF THE

Council on Foreign Relations

SENIOR CONSULTING EDITOR

Nicholas X. Rizopoulos

VOLUME 2

Oxford University Press
New York   Oxford
1997

OXFORD UNIVERSITY PRESS

Oxford   New York
Athens   Auckland   Bangkok   Bogotá   Bombay   Buenos Aires
Calcutta   Cape Town   Dar es Salaam   Delhi   Florence   Hong Kong
Istanbul   Karachi   Kuala Lumpur   Madras   Madrid   Melbourne
Mexico City   Nairobi   Paris   Singapore   Taipei   Tokyo   Toronto

and associated companies in
Berlin   Ibadan

Published by Oxford University Press, Inc.,
198 Madison Avenue, New York, New York 10016

Oxford is a registered trademark of Oxford University Press

Library of Congress Cataloging-in-Publication Data
Encyclopedia of U.S. foreign relations / senior editors, Bruce W.
Jentleson, Thomas G. Paterson.
p. cm.
Includes bibliographical references and index.
1. United States—Foreign relations—Encyclopedias. 2. United
States—Relations—Encyclopedias. I. Jentleson, Bruce W., 1951-.
II. Paterson, Thomas G., 1941-.
E183.7.E53   1997   96-8159   327.73—dc20   CIP
ISBN 0-19-511055-2 (4-vol. set)
ISBN 0-19-511057-9 (vol. 2)

Printing (last digit): 9 8 7 6 5 4 3 2 1

Printed in the United States of America
on acid-free paper

DE GAULLE, CHARLES ANDRÉ JOSEPH MARIE

(*b*. 22 November 1890; *d*. 9 November 1970)

President of France (1945–1946, 1958–1969), whose relations with the United States were habitually strained. Born in Lille, the son of a teacher, de Gaulle graduated from the École Militaire at Saint-Cyr in 1912. He served in the infantry in World War I and was wounded and taken prisoner during the Battle of Verdun (1916). In 1923 de Gaulle became an instructor at the French army staff college and, beginning in the early 1930s, pleaded in vain for a reorientation of French military strategy around the tank and other modern weapons. Appointed a commander of an armored division at the outset of World War II, de Gaulle escaped to London after the fall of France in 1940 and organized French resistance as leader of the Free French government in exile. From the start his relations with President Franklin D. Roosevelt were rocky, in part because of U.S. ambivalence about the Vichy regime, the official French government in the occupied portion of France. In addition, Roosevelt distrusted de Gaulle personally and expressed a preference for a less assertive and less egotistical French leader. Roosevelt, however, underestimated de Gaulle's abilities and tenacity; in 1944, following the liberation of Paris, de Gaulle returned triumphantly to the French capital to head a new government. He resigned in early 1946, following disagreement over the constitution adopted by the postwar Fourth Republic.

A severe economic downturn in France and the growing crisis in Algeria brought de Gaulle back to the presidency in 1958. Resolving the North African problem became his immediate concern, which he settled in 1962 with the Evian Accords granting Algeria independence. His larger objective, however, was to restore to France some of the strength and international status it had lost since World War II. He accordingly continued the nuclear weapons development program initiated by his predecessors (France became the world's fourth nuclear power in 1960 with its first test explosion), rebuffed Anglo-American attempts to win Great Britain's admission into the European market in 1963 and 1967, and pushed for greater French influence over decision-making within the North Atlantic Treaty Organization (NATO). When that influence did not materialize, de Gaulle withdrew French military support for NATO in 1966. De Gaulle resented what he considered the military and political subordination of Western Europe to the United States, and he intended to have France take the lead in working toward a "European Europe" or a "Europe from the Atlantic to the Urals."

Outside of Europe, too, de Gaulle pursued policies that ran counter to U.S. wishes. For example, he encouraged Latin American nations to resist U.S. domination and to follow their own course, independent of the two superpowers. In the late 1960s he extended recognition to the People's Republic of China, despite strong objections from the U.S. Department of State. He also emerged as a leading international critic of the U.S. effort in Vietnam. De Gaulle concluded at an early stage that, despite its superior military power, the United States would not succeed in Vietnam where France had failed, because the struggle in Vietnam was fundamentally an internal conflict that demanded a political solution, and it was the Americans, not the North Vietnamese, who were the outsiders. In an age of decolonization, he believed, nationalism would prevail even over the superpowerful United States and the best that could be hoped for was some form of neutralization similar to that agreed upon for Laos in 1962.

These Gaullist initiatives resulted in growing U.S.-French friction as the 1960s progressed. De Gaulle was not anti-American in any simplistic sense. He voiced strong support for the Western alliance when the Soviets acted aggressively, as for example during the 1962 Cuban missile crisis and the Soviet invasion of Czechoslovakia in 1968. Taken altogether, de Gaulle's policies reflected a desire to keep France allied to the United States but not subordinated to it.

FREDRIK LOGEVALL

See also Algeria; Cuban Missile Crisis; Czech Republic; France; French Indochina; Laos; North Atlantic Treaty Organization; Vietnam; World War II

FURTHER READING

Costigliola, Frank. *France and the United States: The Cold Alliance Since World War II*. New York, 1991.

De Gaulle, Charles. *Memoirs of Hope: Renewal and Endeavor*. New York, 1971.

Hoffmann, Stanley. *Decline or Renewal: France Since the 1930s*. New York, 1974.

Lacouture, Jean. *De Gaulle: The Ruler 1945–1970*. Translated by Alan Sheridan. New York, 1993.

DE KLERK, FREDERIK WILLEM

(*b.* 18 March 1936)

President of the Republic of South Africa (1989–1994) who helped negotiate a political settlement between the white minority government and antiapartheid groups. Scion of an influential Transvaal political family, De Klerk was first elected to the South African Parliament in 1972. After seventeen years in Parliament he became leader of the ruling National Party on 2 February 1989 and president of South Africa in September of that year. Inheriting a nation torn by unrelenting demands for an end to apartheid, with an economy crippled by international sanctions, De Klerk in 1990 lifted the ban on antiapartheid organizations, including the African National Congress (ANC), and freed Nelson Mandela, an ANC leader imprisoned for twenty-seven years. In negotiations with Mandela and the ANC over the next four years, De Klerk accepted the idea of the nation's first nonracial elections, held in April 1994, thus ending three and a half centuries of white rule—and forty-six years of National Party rule—in South Africa. The voters chose Mandela as president, and De Klerk became second vice president. De Klerk and Mandela were jointly awarded the 1993 Nobel Peace Prize. De Klerk's administration brought to an end the long-standing U.S. dilemma of how to deal with explicitly racial discriminatory governments abroad.

THOMAS BORSTELMANN

See also South Africa

FURTHER READING

Arnold, Guy. *South Africa*. New York, 1992.
De Klerk, Willem. *F. W. de Klerk: The Man in His Time*. Johannesburg, 1991.

DE LÔME LETTER

See Spanish-American-Cuban-Filipino War 1898

DEMOCRATIC PARTY

One of the two major parties in U.S. politics since its formation under the leadership of Thomas Jefferson and James Madison in the early 1790s. Very broadly speaking, the Democratic party during much of its history has usually been the more internationalist of the major parties. Partly because of its attraction to internationalism, the Democratic party has often been more ideological in its foreign policy concerns than its major rival since the 1860s, the Republicans. In the late 1960s and the 1970s, the Democrats were torn by disputes over U.S. military involvements abroad, particularly in Southeast Asia. In the 1980s and 1990s changes in the economic interests of some major Democratic constituencies shifted some party representatives away from the traditional Democratic support for free trade.

During George Washington's first presidential term (1789–1793), differences over foreign policy played an important part in the emergence of national parties, which the framers of the Constitution had hoped to avoid. Although Jefferson served as Washington's first secretary of state, the administration's policies in foreign relations were strongly influenced by Alexander Hamilton, the secretary of the Treasury, who sought close association with Great Britain as a means for attracting foreign trade and investment. Jefferson, Madison, and their supporters preferred to maintain the alliance that had developed during the American Revolution with France, now engulfed by its own revolution. Outbreak of war between Great Britain and France in 1793 aggravated these differences.

Combined with disputes over domestic economic policy and the power of the federal government, disagreements over foreign policy produced a strong opposition in Congress, led by Madison, which took the name Republican party (not to be confused with today's Republican party, which was created in 1854). Jefferson resigned as secretary of state in 1793 and aligned himself with the pro-French Republicans, opposing Hamilton's Federalists. The war between Great Britain and France, Jefferson wrote to James Monroe in 1793, "kindled and brought forward the two parties, with an ardor which our own interests merely, could never excite." Election of Jefferson as president in 1800 raised his party to national dominance, which it was generally to maintain, although under the Democratic label after 1828, for the next sixty years. Before his election to the presidency Jefferson had argued for strict interpretation of the Constitution and narrow limitations on the powers of the presidency. When France offered to sell the vast Louisiana Territory to the United States in 1803, however, President Jefferson seized the opportunity and, with the support of his party in Congress, doubled the size of the young nation. The purchase of Louisiana proved extremely popular in the West, tipping the national political scales decisively in favor of the Jeffersonian party.

Continuing war between Great Britain and France, now led by Napoleon Bonaparte, contributed to growing tensions between the United States and Great Britain. Madison, who succeeded Jefferson as president in 1809, tried to steer clear of war, but provocative acts by Great Britain on the western frontier and the high seas generated prowar sentiment among the public. The congressional elections of 1811 brought to the House of Representatives a new generation of Republicans, known as War Hawks for their demand for belligerent action against Great

Britain. The War Hawks included Henry Clay of Kentucky, who was elected speaker of the House of Representatives, and John C. Calhoun of South Carolina. Partly propelled by hopes of acquiring Canada, the War Hawks pushed Madison into asking for a declaration of war against Great Britain in 1812. Although the war did not go particularly well for the United States, it reinforced the political supremacy of the party descended from Jefferson. The remnant of the Federalist party, some of whose members conspired to take New England out of the Union at the antiwar Hartford Convention in 1814, was completely discredited. The War of 1812 also made a national hero of General Andrew Jackson, winner of the Battle of New Orleans—fought two weeks after the peace treaty had been signed in Ghent but before word that the war was over had reached the United States.

Monroe succeeded to the presidency in 1817, and during his second term the old party system appeared to collapse. John Quincy Adams, son of the last Federalist president, had joined the dominant party and became Monroe's secretary of state, in which role he played an important part in the issuance in 1823 of the Monroe Doctrine, warning European powers not to intervene against the fledgling republics of the Western Hemisphere. In the competition to succeed Monroe in 1824, party designation was almost meaningless. Jackson, then supported by many former Federalists, led in the popular vote but fell short of a majority in the electoral college. Under the Constitution, the election went to the House of Representatives, with each state delegation having one vote. Clay, who had finished fourth in the popular vote, used his influence as speaker to secure the election of Adams, who had finished second. Adams made Clay his secretary of state—giving rise to charges of a deal that were to haunt both men for the rest of their political careers.

By 1828 the old Jeffersonian party had divided into a more conservative faction, called National Republicans, led by Adams and Clay; a more liberal faction, known as the Democratic-Republicans, led by Jackson; and a Southern faction, concerned chiefly with the defense of the institution of slavery, led by Calhoun. Jackson, strongly backed by most of the South and West, was elected president, with Calhoun as vice president. After Jackson's election, the winning party became generally known as Democratic, the title it has maintained ever since. During Jackson's first term, a crisis developed over the protective tariff enacted in 1828 at the behest of Northern manufacturers. The South, whose reliance on exports of cotton and other agricultural commodities gave it an interest in freer trade, demanded tariff reduction. In 1832 South Carolina, at the instigation of Calhoun, whose personal relations with Jackson for some time had been bad, declared the tariff null within its boundaries. Jackson, although no friend of the tariff,

threatened military action to enforce the national law. A compromise worked out by Clay, who had been the tariff's chief promoter, provided for a gradual tariff reduction that was acceptable to the South.

Manifest Destiny

National politics in the 1830s focused on struggles over domestic economic policy between the Jacksonian Democrats and a new conservative coalition, known as the Whigs, composed mainly of former Federalists and the more business-oriented faction of the old Republican party. In the 1840s political attention shifted to aspirations among many people in the United States to extend the nation's boundaries southward and westward. Expansionism was championed by many Jacksonian Democrats, including Senator Thomas Hart Benton of Missouri, coiner of the phrase "Manifest Destiny" to express the supposed inevitability of U.S. territorial growth; James K. Polk of Tennessee, elected president in 1844; Sam Houston, president of the Republic of Texas, which had seceded from Mexico in 1836 and sought annexation by the United States; and Jackson himself until his death in 1845. Southern Democrats were particularly eager to have the United States acquire not only Texas but the vast territories held by Mexico between Texas and California, seeing these as fertile areas for expansion of slavery to offset the growing populations of the Northern free states. The 1844 Democratic platform also promised acquisition of the entire Oregon Territory between California and Alaska, part of which was claimed by Great Britain. Faced by the possibility of war with Mexico, Polk agreed to settlement of the Oregon question by extension of the 49th parallel to the Pacific coast as the northern boundary of the United States. The War with Mexico erupted in 1846, the year after Polk accepted Texas into the Union, over the opposition of many Northern Whigs, thereby acquiring Texas, California, and the intervening western territories.

The party system that had emerged during the 1830s collapsed in the 1850s, first under the impact of nativist opposition to growing waves of immigration from Ireland and central Europe and then, more decisively, over the "irrepressible conflict" over slavery. The Democratic party, which had won the allegiance of most of the new immigrants, many of whom were Catholics, was a particular target for the nativist explosion that for a brief time dominated politics in the mid-1850s. Nativism, however, was soon succeeded by slavery as the dominant national issue, with even more dire effects for the Democrats. In 1860 the Democratic party divided into a Northern and a Southern wing, each running its own candidate for president, opening the way for the election of Abraham Lincoln and the accession of the newly formed Republican party.

During the Civil War, which began in 1861 when Southern states seceded from the Union in response to Lincoln's election, the Democratic party lost its entire Southern wing and also was reduced to minority status in most Northern states. Although many Northern Democrats loyally supported the Union cause, members of the party's "copperhead" faction favored a negotiated settlement with the Confederacy or were openly pro-Southern. After national reunification through Union victory in 1865, the Democrats continued to be shut out of power in much of the South, which was ruled by Republican governments backed by federal armies of occupation and supported by newly enfranchised African Americans. In most northeastern and midwestern states, Democratic strength was based mainly on city machines, such as Tammany Hall in New York, which organized the ever-growing legions of European immigrants, plus a few rural regions that had been pro-Southern during the Civil War or felt neglected by policies promoting industrial growth maintained by the nationally dominant Republicans.

After the end of Reconstruction in 1876, the Democrats regained power in most of the South, based largely on promises to maintain racial segregation and exclude African Americans from any share in government. The economic depression of the mid-1870s and revelations of corruption in Republican national and state administrations helped restore Democratic fortunes in parts of the North. The principal substantive issue between the major parties during this period was the protective tariff, which the Republicans supported as a means for fostering native industries, and the Democrats opposed, in part in response to the interest of Southern agriculture in freer trade, and in part through the influence of some Northern capitalists with ties to European financial interests who backed Democrats like Governor Grover Cleveland of New York. Cleveland's election as president in 1884 at last restored Democratic control of a national administration. Besides seeking lower tariff rates, Cleveland turned away from the aggressive intervention in Caribbean and Pacific island affairs that had characterized recent Republican administrations.

In the early 1890s both major parties were challenged by a new aggregation, the Populists, which grew from grievances among farmers in the West and South against Eastern-owned banks, railroads, and manufacturers. Populism expressed social and cultural as well as economic resentments, conveying fears among many rural Protestants that what they regarded as the American way of life was being supplanted by cosmopolitan habits and standards prevalent in big cities. The severe economic depression of the mid-1890s enabled forces sympathetic to populism in the Democratic party to achieve repudiation of Cleveland's second administration at the 1896 Democratic national convention and secure nomination

of their candidate for president, William Jennings Bryan of Nebraska. Bryan's defeat in the 1896 election by Republican William McKinley ushered in another period of Republican national dominance. Democrats in general supported the war against Spain waged by the McKinley administration in 1898, but many in the Populist wing of the party, which included pacifist as well as isolationist elements, opposed subsequent acquisition of the Philippine Islands as part of the peace settlement. Bryan, while attacking imperialism, advised approval of the peace treaty by the Senate, and enough Democrats voted in favor to secure ratification by one vote.

Benevolent Internationalism

The split of the Republican party in 1912 returned the Democrats to national power with Woodrow Wilson as president and large Democratic majorities in Congress. Although Wilson had previously been critical of the Populists, he made Bryan his secretary of state. With Wilson's approval, Bryan secured treaties with twenty-two nations calling for peaceful arbitration of international differences. In the general war that broke out in Europe in 1914, Bryan, a moderate pacifist, advised strict neutrality by the United States. Wilson, although sympathetic toward Great Britain, at first went along, but when Wilson insisted on an angry protest against the sinking of the British liner *Lusitania* by a German submarine in 1915, with 128 U.S. citizens killed, Bryan resigned.

Wilson successfully campaigned for reelection in 1916 on the claim that he had kept the United States "out of war." Relations with Germany, however, worsened. In April 1917 Wilson asked for a declaration of war "to make the world safe for democracy." Among the minority in Congress voting against the declaration was House Majority Leader Claude Kitchin of North Carolina, a Bryanite. In the controversy over entry by the United States into the League of Nations, which under Wilson's sponsorship had been made part of the peace treaty ending World War I, most Democrats in Congress supported approval. The Republicans, however, had won majorities in both houses of Congress in 1918. Wilson refused to accept reservations on the treaty to protect U.S. sovereignty, as demanded by the more moderate Republicans. Democrats in the Senate loyal to Wilson joined intransigent opponents of the League of Nations to reject approval of the treaty with reservations. In the 1920 election, the Democratic candidate for president, James Cox of Ohio, tried to play down international issues, but his running mate for vice president, Franklin D. Roosevelt of New York, who had served in Wilson's administration, ardently championed the League of Nations. When the Democratic ticket went down to overwhelming defeat, the question of U.S. participation in the League of Nations was regarded as settled. Out of national office during the 1920s, the Democrats offered only timid resistance in Congress to the protectionist policies of succeeding Republican administrations. When economic depression restored the Democrats to power under the leadership of Roosevelt in 1932, the new administration, guided by Secretary of State Cordell Hull, pressed successfully for reciprocal tariff reductions to encourage export of agricultural products.

The Roosevelt administration soon faced the rise of aggressive totalitarian powers in Europe and Asia. Reaction against participation in World War I had fed strong sentiments of isolationism in both major parties. Within the Democratic party, voters of Irish and German descent, reflecting the separate historical experiences of their respective lands of origin, particularly resisted any U.S. policy that could be construed as pro-British. Democratic leaders such as Senators Burton K. Wheeler of Montana and David Walsh of Massachusetts were among the most determined proponents of efforts to keep the United States isolated from international conflicts. Roosevelt, whose approach represented a combination of Wilson's benevolent internationalism with the more tough-minded nationalism of his Republican cousin, Theodore Roosevelt, did what he could during the late 1930s to use moral suasion against the totalitarian powers and prepare the nation for possible war. He was generally supported in these efforts by Southern Democrats, many of whom by the end of the 1930s were opposing the administration's New Deal domestic policies but were moved by economic interest and military tradition to be internationalists on foreign affairs. After World War II began in Europe in 1939, the small but influential Jewish bloc in the Democratic party also gave effective backing to Roosevelt's policy of assisting Great Britain and others in resisting Adolf Hitler by means short of war. (U.S. Jews nevertheless failed to persuade the Roosevelt administration to do much to help Jewish refugees.) Like Wilson in 1916, Roosevelt in 1940 campaigned for reelection on a promise to keep the country out of war. In the first year of his third term, he stepped up aid to Great Britain, and later to the Soviet Union, after the latter was invaded by German armies in the summer of 1941. Isolationists of both parties in Congress continued to resist. The issue was settled when Japan attacked Pearl Harbor on 7 December 1941.

Containment

After the end of World War II in 1945, Democratic party unity was disrupted by disagreement over response to the apparent expansionist intentions of the Soviet Union. Harry S. Truman, who had succeeded to the presidency after Roosevelt's death in 1945, took a hard line against what appeared to be a Soviet-supported communist insurgency in Greece and the perceived danger of communist parties taking over the war-ruined countries of western Europe. Truman's policies were strongly backed by Southern Democrats, including his secretary of state, former Senator James Byrnes of South Carolina, and by elected representatives of urban areas with large immigrant populations from countries of eastern Europe occupied by Soviet forces.

Henry Wallace, Truman's secretary of commerce, who had been vice president during Roosevelt's third term and had been dropped from the national ticket in 1944 at the insistence of conservative Democrats, in contrast favored continuation of wartime collaboration with the Soviet Union and accommodation of what he regarded as Joseph Stalin's reasonable aims. Wallace was vociferously supported by part of the Democratic party's left, particularly in New York City, southern California, and some labor unions. Following the advice of Byrnes, Truman in 1946 dismissed Wallace from his cabinet. Wallace bolted the Democratic party and in 1948 ran as the presidential candidate of a leftist coalition that took the name Progressive party (unrelated to Theodore Roosevelt's Progressives of 1912). Wallace's insurgency, plus the formation of a new states' rights segregationist party in the South to oppose the Truman administration's progressive civil rights policies, were thought to doom Truman's chances to win election to a full term in 1948. A plurality of voters, however, decided they preferred the incumbent president to his Republican opponent, Governor Thomas E. Dewey of New York, and Truman was elected in the biggest upset in U.S. political history.

In collaboration with his succeeding secretaries of state, George C. Marshall and Dean Acheson, Truman formulated the Cold War policies of containment of the Soviet Union and worldwide anticommunism that were to be pursued in one form or another by all administrations, both Democratic and Republican, for the next forty years. The Truman administration also firmly supported Israel, founded in 1948, reinforcing the loyalty of most Jews to the Democratic party. The Korean War, which began in 1950, helped erode public support for Truman and contributed to the election of Dwight D. Eisenhower in 1952 as the first Republican president in twenty years. During Eisenhower's two terms, Democrats in Congress, led by Speaker of the House Sam Rayburn and Senate Democratic Leader Lyndon B. Johnson, both of Texas, generally supported the administration's policy of cautious containment of the Soviet Union and other communist powers. Some of the Democratic left favored a more conciliatory international policy, but Senator Hubert H. Humphrey of Minnesota, the leader of the liberal Democrats in Congress, was among the staunchest of cold warriors.

In the 1960 presidential campaign, Senator John F. Kennedy of Massachusetts, the Democratic candidate, attacked the Eisenhower administration for having allowed a "missile gap" to open, allegedly giving the Soviets an advantage in nuclear arms. After Kennedy's election, the missile gap was quickly forgotten. The Kennedy administration continued the containment policy and in South Vietnam went beyond Eisenhower in giving military support to the pro-Western regime under attack by a well-armed communist insurgency. Kennedy also approved the 1961 Bay of Pigs invasion of Cuba, intended to overthrow the Marxist revolutionary government of Fidel Castro. Kennedy captured the altruistic side of the Democratic foreign policy tradition with such new programs as the Peace Corps and the Alliance for Progress to aid developing nations. The U.S. presence in Vietnam, continued and enlarged under Lyndon B. Johnson, who succeeded to the presidency after Kennedy's assassination in 1963, gradually became a divisive issue within the Democratic party. Against the belligerent if not bellicose anticommunism of Barry Goldwater, the Republican presidential candidate in 1964, Johnson was able to present a posture of prudent realism in foreign policy that satisfied liberal and moderate Democrats. Johnson initially had strong bipartisan support for his administration's Vietnam commitment, but as casualties mounted and the administration seemed unable to rationalize convincingly the U.S. mission, liberal, moderate, and even some conservative Democrats became increasingly critical. By 1968 differences over Vietnam had become so intense that Democratic "doves" were determined that Johnson should be opposed for renomination for a second full term. In the first presidential primary in New Hampshire, Johnson won only narrowly over his antiwar opponent, Senator Eugene McCarthy of Minnesota. Senator Robert Kennedy of New York, brother of the late president, now convinced that Johnson could be beaten, announced his own antiwar candidacy. McCarthy refused to step aside. Facing a deeply divided Democratic party, Johnson withdrew from the race. Vice President Hubert Humphrey, although he had himself developed reservations about the war, became the candidate of forces backing the administration. Early in June, Kennedy, after winning the presidential primary in California, was assassinated in Los Angeles by Sirhan Sirhan, an Arab who identified the Kennedys with the Democratic party's longstanding support for Israel.

The Democratic National Convention in Chicago in the summer of 1968 was torn by riots in the streets and passionate demonstrations by antiwar groups in the convention hall. Doves supporting McCarthy or Senator George McGovern of South Dakota, who had become the candidate of Kennedyites who could not bring themselves to back McCarthy, moved to repudiate Johnson's war policy in the Democratic platform. They lost by a three-to-two margin, with most Southern and city machine delegates supporting the administration. Humph-

rey was nominated to lead a badly split party. During the fall campaign, Humphrey cautiously edged away from Johnson's Vietnam policy. Ultimately he lost only narrowly to his Republican opponent, Richard M. Nixon, but the closeness of the election was only because the third-party candidacy of segregationist George C. Wallace of Alabama drained off many conservative votes.

Neo-Isolationism

In 1972, the Vietnam War having continued under Nixon, the doves had become the dominant force within the Democratic party. McGovern, running with solid dove support in the presidential primaries, trounced candidates representing the old Democratic establishment such as Humphrey and Senator Edmund Muskie of Maine. McGovern's platform went beyond opposition to the Vietnam War to a call for pullback from the degree of global resistance to communism maintained since the Truman administration. The theme of his acceptance speech at the Democratic National Convention in Miami, "Come home, America," harked back to the kind of Populist isolationism that had been expressed by Bryan within the Democratic party in the early years of the century. Despite the growing unpopularity of the war, the country was in no mood to accept McGovern's message and Nixon was easily reelected. Four years later, the Vietnam War having ended with U.S. withdrawal in 1975, most Democrats were prepared to bind up intraparty wounds. Gerald Ford, the incumbent Republican president who had succeeded Nixon following his resignation in 1974 as a result of the Watergate scandals seemed an easy target for defeat. Most Democrats longed for a presidential candidate who had in no way been associated with the national and party traumas of the past decade. Former Governor Jimmy Carter of Georgia seemed to fit the bill. Although almost unknown nationally at the beginning of 1976, Carter won the Democratic presidential nomination and in November narrowly defeated Ford. As president, Carter tried to combine relatively hard-line realism on foreign policy, represented within the administration by his national security adviser, Zbigniew Brzezinski, with increased emphases on promotion of human rights and reconciliation among nations as policy goals, represented by Secretary of State Cyrus Vance. He produced some successes, notably the achievement of peace between Israel and Egypt through the Camp David Accords in 1979, but the Soviet invasion of Afghanistan in 1979 and the captivity of fifty-two U.S. hostages in Teheran, Iran, contributed to the public impression by 1980 that the standing of the United States in the world had shrunk. This impression, combined with domestic economic troubles, helped cause Carter's defeat by Republican Ronald Reagan in the 1980 presidential election.

During the 1980s many Democrats in Congress and other positions of party leadership criticized the Reagan administration's posture toward the Soviet Union as overly bellicose and opposed its backing of right-wing anti-communist regimes and insurgencies in various parts of the world. The most controversial and partisan issues involved the administration's support for the Contra insurgency in Nicaragua, which most Democrats opposed, and the drive in Congress for sanctions against apartheid in South Africa, which the administration opposed and most Democrats favored. From the mid-1980s onward, the newly formed Democratic Leadership Council (DLC) gave expression to efforts by congressional Democrats, such as Senators Sam Nunn of Georgia and Albert Gore of Tennessee and Representative Les Aspin of Wisconsin, to formulate centrist foreign and defense policies. Some Democratic foreign policy hard-liners, including some who were quite liberal on domestic policy, reacting against what they regarded as the ascendancy of soft-liners within the Democratic party, crossed over to back Reagan for reelection in 1984 and his Republican successor George Bush in 1988. Dissatisfaction among hard-liners with Bush's foreign policy record, which, except for his leadership in the Gulf War of 1990–1991, they viewed as timid, helped produce relatively united Democratic support for Bill Clinton's presidential candidacy in 1992. Collapse of the Soviet Union and Western victory in the Cold War at the end of the 1980s freed Clinton, who had chaired the DLC, to make promotion of human rights and democracy major foreign policy goals. Clinton was faced with a shift among much of organized labor to a protectionist stance on foreign trade that caused many congressional Democrats to abandon the party's traditional free trade position. Clinton's successful drive in 1993 to win approval of the North American Free Trade Agreement (NAFTA), signed under Bush, was opposed by a majority of House Democrats, including much of the party leadership, but supported by a majority of Senate Democrats. After the Republicans won control of both houses of Congress for the first time in forty years in the 1994 elections, Clinton increasingly turned his attention to foreign policy. The administration was rewarded with significant, though perhaps impermanent, diplomatic successes in Haiti, the Middle East, Northern Ireland, and Bosnia. In the mid-1990s the Democratic party, in common with much of the nation, appeared to be groping for a new direction in foreign policy that would combine traditional internationalism with growing concern for protection of the national interest.

A. JAMES REICHLEY

See also Acheson, Dean Gooderham; Adams, John Quincy; Aspin, Leslie (Les), Jr.; Bipartisanship; Brzezinski, Zbigniew; Byrnes, James Francis; Calhoun, John Caldwell; Carter, James Earl; Clay, Henry; Clinton, William Jefferson; Hull, Cordell; Humphrey, Hubert Horatio; Jackson, Andrew; Jefferson, Thomas; Johnson, Lyndon Baines; Kennedy, John Fitzgerald; Kennedy, Robert Francis; Marshall, George Catlett, Jr.; McCarthy, Eugene; McGovern, George Stanley; Muskie, Edmund Sixtus; Nunn, Samuel; Polk, James Knox; Presidency; Republican Party; Roosevelt, Franklin Delano; Truman, Harry S.; Wallace, Henry Agard; War Hawks; Wilson, Thomas Woodrow

FURTHER READING

Cunningham, Noble E. *The Jeffersonian Republicans: The Formation of Party Organizations, 1789–1801.* Chapel Hill, N.C., 1957.
Divine, Robert A. *Foreign Policy and U.S. Presidential Elections, 1940–1964,* 2 vols. New York, 1974.
Epstein, Leon D. *Political Parties in the American Mold.* Madison, Wisc., 1986.
Goldman, Ralph M. *The National Party Chairmen and Committees: Factionalism at the Top.* Armonk, N.Y., 1990.
Hofstadter, Richard. *The Idea of a Party System.* Berkeley, Calif., 1969.
McCormick, Richard P. *The Second American Party System.* New York, 1966.
Parmet, Herbert S. *The Democrats: The Years After FDR.* New York, 1976.
Pomper, Gerald M. *Passions and Interests: Political Party Concepts of American Democracy.* Lawrence, Kans., 1992.
Reichley, A. James. *The Life of the Parties: A History of American Political Parties.* New York, 1992.
Schlesinger, Arthur M., Jr. *The Cycles of American History.* Boston, 1986.

DENG XIAOPING
(*b.* 1904)

Leader of the People's Republic of China since 1976. Born in Guangan, Sichuan province, Deng worked in France in the 1920s, where he joined the Chinese Communist Party, and later in the USSR, experiences that gave him an internationalist outlook. A Long March veteran, Deng joined the top rank of the party leadership in 1956. Over the next two decades, Deng twice survived disgrace at Mao Zedong's hand. Since Mao's death (1976), Deng has dominated China's politics but never occupied the top party and government posts himself, allocating them to protégés in an effort to regularize succession. After 1978, Deng launched reforms recasting China's economy onto market foundations and putting China's politics on a more institutionalized footing. These domestic reforms required a stable security context and a far broader interaction with the international economy, and Beijing's foreign policy under his leadership centered on these needs. Beijing normalized relations with Tokyo (1978), Washington (1979), and Moscow (1989). In dealing with Washington, Deng was the key

Chinese decision maker at all major junctures, including negotiations over normalization and the accord on U.S. arms sales to Taiwan (1982). Deng made his only visit to Washington in 1979.

The decision to suppress brutally the 1989 Tiananmen Square demonstrations was ultimately Deng's, and he guided Beijing's efforts to counteract international sanctions. Deng formally retired from his last post and stopped meeting with foreign visitors in 1990. Thereafter he made rare public appearances, though he remained the final arbiter in major foreign policy decisions. Former National Security Adviser Zbigniew Brzezinski described Deng as "bright, alert, shrewd...quick on the uptake, with a good sense of humor, tough, and very direct." Former Secretary of State George Shultz recalls that Deng "impressed me, as he did almost everyone who met him, with the strength of his intellect, his humor, his candor, and his ability to cut through to the essence of issues and talk bluntly about them."

H. Lyman Miller

See also China

FURTHER READING

Goodman, David S.G. *Deng Xiaoping and the Chinese Revolution: A Political Biography.* New York, 1994. Shambaugh, David, ed. "Deng Xiaoping: An Assessment." *The China Quarterly* No.135 (September 1993): 409–572.

DENMARK

A Scandinavian kingdom, bordering the North Sea on a peninsula directly north of Germany, that became a U.S. military ally in 1949. Official U.S.-Danish relations began in May 1791, when President George Washington sent merchant James Yard to the Danish West Indies to represent U.S. commercial interests there. Denmark awarded Yard the title of consul in September of that year, effectively extending formal recognition to the American republic. The United States established representation in the Danish capital of Copenhagen a year later, but full diplomatic relations were not established until a Danish minister arrived in Washington in 1801. The Danish envoy's initial mission was twofold: to ensure U.S. support for the shipping rights of neutral countries and, in the event of a Danish-British war, to maintain U.S. trade with Danish colonial possessions, particularly in the West Indies. In 1801, however, Denmark joined France in its war against Great Britain, and throughout the remainder of the war the Danish as well as the French navy regularly seized U.S. ships. Neither U.S.-Danish trade relations nor the question of compensation for seized American goods were normalized, nor was the question of compensation for seized American goods settled, until a treaty of commerce was signed in 1826, at which time Denmark agreed to pay the United States an indemnity of $650,000.

During the American Civil War, Washington negotiated with Copenhagen for the transfer of the Danish West Indies to the United States in order to better maintain its blockade of the Confederacy. However, the U.S. Senate blocked these efforts on the grounds that it was not in the interest of the United States to acquire overseas colonies. Negotiations continued intermittently for the next fifty years but both governments encountered domestic opposition. Conditions changed during World War I, however: Denmark, although it was neutral, suffered a significant disruption of its trade because of the war. By then the Danish West Indies had become a financial burden to Copenhagen and their people grew increasingly dissatisfied with Danish colonial rule. Denmark needed additional revenues, and the United States was determined not to allow the islands to fall into the hands of another European power, especially Germany. In 1917 the two countries signed an agreement whereby the United States purchased the islands of Saint Thomas, Saint Croix, Saint John, and sixty-five minor isles (now called the U.S. Virgin Islands) for $25,000,000, and in return renounced U.S. claims to parts of Greenland. In the period between the two world wars, U.S.-Danish relations remained friendly and cooperative. President Woodrow Wilson, upholding his principle of self-determination for peoples, supported Denmark's reacquisition of the northern half of German-held Schleswig-Holstein, which opted for Danish rule in a 1920 plebiscite.

The German invasion of Denmark in 1940 effectively placed the Danish government under Nazi control; in 1941, however, shortly before he was dismissed by Copenhagen under Nazi pressure, the Danish ambassador in Washington arranged for U.S. protection of Greenland in return for U.S. military stations on Greenland. After Denmark was liberated in May 1945, its parliament formally accepted the agreement on Greenland, and Danish-American military cooperation in Greenland began in 1951. Denmark was reluctant to join the North Atlantic Treaty Organization (NATO), since many Danes viewed membership as a radical departure from the Danish tradition of neutrality since the Napoleonic Wars. Denmark was eventually persuaded to become a founding member in 1949, after Norwegian plans for a neutral Scandinavian defense alliance failed to materialize. Danish public support for NATO membership fluctuated from a low of 27 percent in 1955 to a high of 69 percent in 1983, and left-wing elements in parliament have long called for a reevaluation of the country's commitment to NATO. The U.S. government criticized Copenhagen for cutting its defense expenditures in the 1970s and 1980s, but despite the disagreements over defense policy, the two countries have remained allies. Indeed, the United States has maintained uninterrupted diplomatic relations with Denmark (even during World War II) longer than with any other country.

Post–Cold War realities reduced the cohesion of what had been the usual parallel policies of the United States and its NATO allies. After Denmark committed troops to the UN peacekeeping effort in Bosnia-Herzegovina, it joined other NATO and European states participating in the operation to oppose U.S. initiatives to eliminate the arms embargo on Bosnia. In December 1995, however, Danish troops deployed to Bosnia-Herzegovina as part of the United Nations peacekeeping force were assigned to NATO Implementation Force's (IFOR) U.S. sector, coming under direct U.S. command.

DAVID P. AUGUSTYN

See also Danish West Indies, Acquisition of; Greenland; Napoleonic Wars; Neutral Rights; North Atlantic Treaty Organization; Virgin Islands

FURTHER READING

Soren, J. M. P. Fogdall. "Danish-American Diplomacy, 1776–1920." In *University of Iowa Studies in Social Studies*, Vol. VIII, No. 2, Iowa City, 1922.
Scott, Franklin D. *Scandinavia*. Cambridge, Mass., 1975.
Solheim, Bruce Olav. *The Nordic Nexus: A Lesson in Peaceful Security.* Westport, Conn., 1984.

DEPENDENCY

A concept of recent international political and economic history that sets out to explain persistent poverty in Latin America and other parts of the underdeveloped world. As is the case with theorists of imperialism, exponents of dependency theory (*dependentistas*) argue that poverty springs from the exploitation of some nations by others. But unlike theories of imperialism, which stress primarily the advanced capitalist nations themselves, dependency theory focuses on the histories, development processes, and economies of subject or "dependent" nations. During the 1960s and early 1970s, *dependentistas* directly challenged guiding tenets of twentieth-century U.S. foreign policy. They criticized U.S. policy for the long-term as well as ongoing consequences of dependence—brutal military take-overs in Latin America, unending poverty, and U.S. hostility toward any revolutionary changes. Enzo Faletto, Fernando Henrique Cardoso, and other dependency theorists rejected the views of modernization theorists—and exponents of the Alliance for Progress—who argued that Latin American countries would inevitably advance through a series of economic stages, leading ultimately to a wealthy consumer society. According to dependency theo-

rists, not only did many dependent countries not achieve wealth and development, but their continuing poverty was a consequence of the economic growth of dominant nations: through dependent trade relations that linked the interests of local elites and their metropolitan counterparts, rich nations extracted corporate profits, mineral resources, and the value of inexpensive labor from dependent nations.

Dependency theory gained a wide following in Latin America during the 1960s and 1970s. The Cuban revolution and increasing superpower intervention in the Western Hemisphere aroused a backlash against the United States. Although the works of Leland Jenks, William Appleton Williams, and other critics of U.S. foreign policy anticipated dependency theory, Walter LaFeber was the first prominent revisionist historian in the 1980s to make specific reference to dependency in a major work on U.S.-Latin American relations (*Inevitable Revolutions: The United States and Central America*, 1983). Since that time, many other scholars of U.S. foreign relations—including Bruce J. Calder, Louis A. Pérez, Jr., and Thomas D. Schoonover—have drawn upon dependency theory to analyze U.S. policy in Latin America. Other writers, however, have criticized dependency theory for its sweeping generalizations and lack of empirical evidence. Some have challenged the Marxist precepts of the *dependentistas*, while others argue that dependency's broad-brushed theoretical focus provides insufficient context for regional variations in U.S.–Latin American relations, and for questions of sex, race, and a range of other cultural and social problems in U.S. foreign policy.

DAVID SHEININ

See also Revisionism; Williams, William Appleman

FURTHER READING

Calder, Bruce J. *The Impact of Intervention: The Dominican Republic During the U.S. Occupation of 1916–1924.* Austin, Tex., 1984.
Cardoso, Fernando H., and Enzo Faletto. *Dependency and Development in Latin America.* tr., Marjory M. Urquidi. Berkeley, Calif., 1979.
Jenks, Leland. *Our Cuban Colony: A Study in Sugar.* 1928. Reprint, New York, 1970.
LaFeber, Walter. *Inevitable Revolutions: The United States and Central America.* Rev. 2nd ed. New York, 1993.
Pérez, Louis A., Jr. "Dependency," *Journal of American History*, 77, (June 1990), 133–142.
Schoonover, Thomas D. *The United States in Central America, 1860–1911: Episodes of Social Imperialism and Imperial Rivalry in the World System.* Durham, N.C., 1991.
Williams, William Appleman. *The Tragedy of American Diplomacy.* Rev. 2nd ed. New York, 1972.

DESTROYERS-FOR-BASES DEAL
(2 September 1940)

An agreement between the United States and Great Britain to exchange fifty overage U.S. Navy destroyers for long-term leases to strategically located bases in the Western Hemisphere. Great Britain's plight in summer 1940 against Nazi Germany led Prime Minister Winston S. Churchill to plead for U.S. aid, especially destroyers to replace British losses. When base rights in Newfoundland and British possessions in the Caribbean were offered, President Franklin D. Roosevelt concluded the terms were highly favorable to the United States. Nevertheless, he opted for an executive agreement rather than submit the arrangement to Congress, where isolationists might have impeded the deal. Following complicated negotiations over whether transfer of the destroyers should be linked explicitly to Great Britain's "gift" of base rights and whether the British government would offer a public statement about the future disposition of the British fleet, a formal agreement was reached. The destroyers-for-bases deal provided an immediate boost to British morale, but its larger significance was its contribution to U.S. security and as a milestone in America's journey from neutrality to active support of Great Britain and then to war.

THEODORE A. WILSON

See also Churchill, Winston Leonard Spencer; Isolationism; Roosevelt, Franklin Delano; World War II

FURTHER READING

Reynolds, David. *The Creation of the Anglo-American Alliance 1937–1941: A Study in Competitive Cooperation.* Chapel Hill, N.C., 1982.

DÉTENTE

A traditional diplomatic term for a relaxation of tensions between states. As the tensions of the Cold War began to attenuate, the term "détente" was widely used to describe the emerging East-West relationship. First applied by political figures on both sides to the situation in Europe in the mid-1960s, it also came to characterize the relationship between the United States and the Soviet Union in the period from 1972 through 1979 (although under increasing strain after 1975). Such relaxation of tensions between the two powers had, however, been advanced as early as 1969, and the period 1969–1979 is therefore often referred to as the decade of détente.

Leaders both in Washington and Moscow had much earlier come to realize the dangers and costs of unmitigated tension in the nuclear age. Although the term "détente" was not yet used, there were periods of reduced tension and renewed diplomatic engagement in the mid- and late 1950s, called the "spirit of Geneva" after the four-power summit in 1955 and the "spirit of Camp David" after Soviet premier Nikita Khrushchev's visit with President Dwight D. Eisenhower in 1959. In the mid-1960s, after heightened tensions over Berlin and

the Cuban missile crisis, a search for détente was revived but hopes were dashed by the escalation of the war in Vietnam. Only after 1969, when President Richard M. Nixon called for "an era of negotiations" to replace confrontation and later for building "a structure of peace," did détente become U.S. policy.

By the early 1970s Leonid I. Brezhnev and other Soviet leaders had also adopted a policy of détente. From the outset, however, there was a discrepancy between Soviet and U.S. conceptions of détente. Although both were grounded in the recognized supreme common interest in preventing the outbreak of nuclear war, they diverged from each other on key points. The U.S. conception of détente, articulated by President Nixon and head of the National Security Council, Henry A. Kissinger, called for U.S. manipulation of incentives and penalties in bilateral relations in order to serve other policy interests through what was called "linkage." Détente, in effect, was a strategy to provide U.S. leverage for managing the emergence of Soviet power by drawing the Soviet Union into the existing world order through acceptance of a code of conduct for competition that favored the United Sates. The Soviet conception of détente was one of peaceful coexistence, which would set aside direct conflict between the two superpowers, in order to allow socialist and anti-imperialist forces a free hand. The Soviet leaders thus saw their task as maneuvering the United States into a world no longer marked by U.S. predominance. This discrepancy led to increasing friction.

In the United States the policy of relaxing tensions and improving relations with the Soviet Union initially had popular appeal, but the pursuit of a strategy of détente had two serious shortcomings that eventually undermined public support. The first was an unjustified expectation that détente would mark an end of competition and conflicts of interest with the Soviet Union. Encouraged by the Nixon administration's use of such concepts as "building a structure of peace," many Americans confused détente with "entente," a French word referring to a close and cooperative relationship between states. When such a relationship did not emerge, disillusionment with détente followed. The second difficulty was that the Nixon-Kissinger concept of linkage—of "waging détente"—constituted a competitive strategy that increased tension. Moreover, the very effort to manage linkage led Nixon and Kissinger to secretive actions and conflicts with Congress, which often undercut the ability to provide either the incentives or the disincentives necessary to make the strategy work.

By the late 1970s the U.S. public and its leaders had become largely convinced that détente had failed. They believed that the Soviet Union had unfairly taken advantage of détente to build its own military power and to intervene in the Third World. The Soviet invasion of

Afghanistan in December 1979 was the last straw. Détente was abandoned by the administration of President Jimmy Carter. In 1980 Ronald Reagan was elected president on an avowedly anti-détente policy. Soviet leaders, for their part, continued to avow a desire for détente but believed that the United States had willfully jettisoned the policy. The decade of détente ended.

RAYMOND L. GARTHOFF

See also Brezhnev, Leonid Ilyich; Carter, James Earl; Cold War; Kissinger, Henry Alfred; National Security and National Defense; Nixon, Richard Milhous; Reagan, Ronald Wilson; Russia and the Soviet Union; Strategic Arms Limitation Talks and Agreements

FURTHER READING

Bell, Coral. *The Diplomacy of Détente: The Kissinger Era.* New York, 1977.
Garthoff, Raymond L. *Détente and Confrontation: American-Soviet Relations from Nixon to Reagan.* Revised. Washington, D.C., 1994.
Litwak, Robert S. *Détente and the Nixon Doctrine: American Foreign Policy and the Pursuit of Stability, 1969–1976.* New York, 1984.

DETERRENCE

A strategic concept with a long history in international politics that became central to U.S. Cold War strategy. Deterrence in the broadest sense involves an effort by one state to prevent another from doing something unwanted by threatening a harmful response. Although the unwanted action could be of almost any sort, deterrence is mainly used to refer to preventing an outright military attack by threatening either a defense or a retaliation the potential attacker finds unacceptably harmful. Deterrence is distinguished from "compellence," which means using force or threats to get another state to do, rather than not do, something. It also differs from persuasion via a reward for good behavior; deterrence is a stick, not a carrot.

When the United States assumed a central role in international politics after World War II, it was primed by recent experience to give considerable attention to deterrence. Officials believed the war began because of the failure of democracies to confront the Axis states with suitable threats in a timely fashion. Another grave threat—the Soviet Union—seemed to be emerging and, with the onset of the nuclear age, preventing another great war was the highest imperative of foreign policy. Even so, it took considerable time, debate, and resources to arrive at a designed deterrence posture, a deterrence strategy, and a full-blown theory of deterrence.

The Early Cold War Period

The initial step was to determine the role of nuclear weapons and deterrence in foreign policy. Debate emerged between those who believed it necessary to confront and contain the Soviet Union, largely by deterrence, and those who felt an accommodation was possible and feared that confrontation would poison the East-West relationship. The increasingly bitter Cold War struggle and growing evidence of the nature of the Soviet Union favored the former view and by 1950 it had triumphed. By then, this debate had become entangled in another about the role of nuclear weapons. Late in World War II, beginning with scientists who had worked on the atomic bomb and spreading to the highest levels of government, a view emerged that it would be best if nuclear weapons had no role in foreign affairs, if they were eliminated, and if steps were taken to prevent their redevelopment. A consensus initially emerged on the need to try to prevent others from developing nuclear weapons. As a result, wartime agreements with Great Britain to cooperate on nuclear weapons were canceled, efforts were made to control world supplies of uranium and thorium, and legislation was passed requiring that nuclear secrets be very closely held. In the Baruch Plan (1946) the United States proposed that an international agency control all aspects of nuclear energy; once it was in place, the United States would eliminate its own weapons. Soviet opposition prevented implementation of this plan.

As long as the United States had a monopoly on nuclear weapons, debate about their proper role continued and the idea of eliminating them began to fade. Deteriorating relations with Moscow and fear of Soviet military strength in Europe stirred interest in trying to use the atomic bomb for political leverage; alternative resources seemed too feeble. As U.S. military strength rapidly diminished after 1945, the Joint Chiefs of Staff began to count on nuclear weapons in a future war with the Russians, which pushed nuclear weapons toward the center of foreign policy as the ultimate basis of national security. As the State Department's George Kennan pointed out in opposing this, a heavy reliance on nuclear weapons was hardly compatible with eliminating them. Meanwhile, further development of nuclear weapons continued. The initial weapons, technically primitive, were replaced with more refined versions and the U.S. stockpile slowly expanded. The Soviet Union pursued a crash program on nuclear weapons, exploding its first nuclear device in 1949. This settled the debate, because it seemed that only nuclear deterrence could cope with Soviet nuclear weapons. Containment was now the heart of foreign policy, embodied in U.S. entry into the North Atlantic Treaty Organization (NATO) in 1949 for purposes of extending deterrence to protect Western Europe. Nuclear weapons became the central component of containment.

In 1946 Bernard Brodie, an academic expert on strategy, argued that the only real use of nuclear weapons was to deter future wars, but deterrence had received only limited attention in military strategic thinking. The armed forces focused more on planning to fight than on deterring a war with the Soviet bloc. They expected a repetition of World War II, in which a Soviet attack would overrun most of Europe, and the United States would mobilize huge forces and push it back until victory was achieved. Strategic bombing would be needed for this and nuclear weapons would make it much more effective, but large-scale ground fighting would still be necessary. Thus, the United States had arrived at a deterrence posture of sorts without a deterrence strategy to indicate what military forces should be maintained as the basis of deterrence or how to use them if necessary.

NSC-68, the Korean War, and a Global Alliance System

The first Soviet nuclear test in 1949, which ended the U.S. monopoly sooner than expected, stunned Washington. One response was that President Harry S. Truman in January 1950 ordered development of a thermonuclear, or hydrogen, bomb (the Soviet government did likewise); a bomb many times more destructive than atomic bombs. Both countries were to test such weapons by 1953. Another response was National Security Council Paper Number 68 (NSC-68), given to the president in June and the most comprehensive analytical and planning document of the day. It contended that nuclear weapons would soon be very difficult to use for fear of Soviet nuclear retaliation and that the Soviet bloc could then exploit its huge conventional forces in nonnuclear wars. NSC-68 called for a rapid buildup of U.S. and Western conventional forces because it envisioned East-West wars, even large wars, that would be nonnuclear. It warned that sole possession of the hydrogen bomb by the Soviets would be disastrous for U.S. foreign policy and that the United States had to proceed with its development as quickly as possible.

The Korean War, which began in June 1950, had a major impact on U.S. thinking. The common view in Washington was that the invasion of South Korea had been ordered by Moscow and demonstrated that the Soviets would exploit opportunities for using force to expand their sphere. Evidently U.S. nuclear forces alone were an insufficient deterrent, and this conclusion had far-reaching effects. The United States rearmed, not just to fight in Korea but to build sufficient conventional forces to deter or fight other wars elsewhere. The main concern was Europe, to which were sent six divisions. Western European rearmament was promoted through heavy U.S. military assistance, and, at U.S. insistence, West Germany was allowed to eventually rearm by joining NATO. NATO was converted from solely a political alliance into an elaborate force-in-being with a joint command structure. Elsewhere, the United States added

alliances with South Korea, Japan, and Taiwan; joined the Southeast Asia Treaty Organization (SEATO), and sponsored but did not join the Central Treaty Organization (CENTO) in the Middle East. This was the militarization of containment.

NSC-68 and the Korean War had another effect. NSC-68 contended that the Cold War, and therefore deterrence, was also a psychological contest. Therefore, Soviet perceptions of U.S. political will and willingness to fight were crucial to the effectiveness of deterrence. In this contest a loss anywhere was a loss everywhere, because it conveyed weakness or indecision. Korea seemed a good example. The United States had been losing ground in the Cold War, had publicly left South Korea outside the U.S. defense perimeter in Asia, and had only limited forces available; thus, the communists had attacked. From this perspective, deterrence commitments were highly interdependent—how the United States behaved in one case would determine the effectiveness of others. This applied to friends as well as enemies. If the U.S. image was one of weakness or lack of credibility, allies would melt away, shifting toward neutrality or deals with the other side. Such thinking shaped the decision to fight in Korea—failure to act there would undermine NATO and damage deterrence elsewhere.

U.S. leaders clearly perceived deterrence as American-centered. Other states could help but the United States was the key to success. The policy of containment had started as only partly an exercise in deterrence and mainly for Europe. Now it was primarily concerned with deterrence and pursued with fervor everywhere. The United States had turned from fostering balances of power in various places to containing threats (the original version of containment) and then to seeing itself as the prime contributor to those balances. This transformed deterrence from a facet of foreign policy to a distinctive basis for the structure and management of the international system, through which a catastrophic war could be avoided. To prevent such a war the United States relied on deterrence more than anything else during the next forty years.

The Doctrine of Massive Retaliation

The Korean War was also responsible for the first U.S. deterrence strategy. President Dwight D. Eisenhower's administration (1953–1960) rejected the view that nuclear weapons would soon be unusable and that the West must prepare for conventional wars. Korea was seen as demonstrating that conventional wars were far easier for communist states than democratic ones to start and fight, because they would play to the Soviet bloc's strengths and leave it too much of the initiative. The United States could not afford the forces to fight such wars all over the world. Deterrence had to be sustainable.

The answer was to rest deterrence on the threat of a prompt and massive nuclear retaliation, with the specific route to escalation of any lesser war left unspecified. For a nuclear attack there would be a nuclear response, and for a nonnuclear attack there might also be a nuclear response. It would likely be an all-out response and directed at the ultimate source of the trouble—the Soviet Union. This strategy brought important shifts in the deterrence posture. Conventional forces were reduced significantly, in keeping with the intent to escalate to the nuclear level at an early stage. The armed services prepared for early use of nuclear weapons in a war in Europe. As this was compatible with French and British plans to have nuclear weapons and was politically appealing to European allies who could not, it seemed, afford large conventional forces, NATO abandoned plans for huge conventional forces and became heavily dependent on nuclear deterrence. Many smaller (tactical and theater) nuclear weapons were sent to Europe for U.S. forces and the allies to use in a war.

The United States now constructed an enormous strategic arsenal, including thousands of thermonuclear weapons of vast destructive power. The Strategic Air Command (SAC) devised a deterrence posture that was closer to a preemptive strike than retaliation, a programmed massive blow designed to destroy Soviet nuclear forces before major damage was inflicted on the United States. The plan exploited the fact that, through overseas bases plus the intercontinental B-52, U.S. bombers could reach the entire Soviet bloc, while the smaller and less capable Soviet bomber force could not readily penetrate extensive North American air defenses. Thus, Soviet nuclear weapons need not deter U.S. nuclear retaliation.

The Theory of Mutual Deterrence

Flaws in massive retaliation as a strategy and defense posture quickly became apparent, which led to the development of a theory of mutual deterrence and to installation of a new strategy and posture. At the heart of these developments lay a series of problems with, or challenges to, deterrence. One was the problem of stability— the possibility that under certain circumstances the deterrence posture might make war with the Soviet Union more likely, the opposite of the intended effect. Another problem was that of credibility, initially raised in NSC-68. U.S. threats of retaliation had to be believable to deter enemies and reassure allies, but the threats could not easily be made believable. A third problem was political, in that deterrence, however it was practiced, had to remain politically acceptable at home and with the allies, which meant fending off concerns about its morality and keeping its costs down. These problems were interdependent; steps to deal with one often exacerbated

the others. The interaction of these problems shaped U.S. deterrence policy from then on.

Massive retaliation had a mixed political impact abroad. Europeans found it congenial for putting the Soviet Union at risk of destruction for even limited attacks on Europe but disliked the prospect that early use of nuclear weapons by NATO in a war would destroy much of their territory. Objections to the strategy really took hold with the first Soviet tests of intercontinental ballistic missiles (ICBMs) (1957), which meant the United States would soon be highly vulnerable to nuclear attack or retaliation. Many feared that the United States would be deterred from using nuclear weapons in retaliation (the credibility problem). In addition, it was widely believed—incorrectly—that the United States was significantly behind in missile development and faced an ominous missile gap. Deterrence could fail because the nation would be vulnerable to a preemptive missile attack that would wipe out its retaliatory forces (the stability problem).

The shifting strategic balance led officials and analysts in the late 1950s to develop a theory of mutual deterrence. It explained how deterrence forces could be configured to enhance deterrence stability, and how stability could be further reinforced by exploiting a mutual interest in avoiding a catastrophic war to inject a modicum of cooperation into the East-West rivalry. The mutual deterrence theory held that states in intense conflict and constantly fearful of attack from military forces that could wreak unimaginable destruction, had a mutual interest in deterring an all-out war. Deterrence required that forces to be used for a terrible retaliation, and the command system for using them, had to be able to survive the worst attack the enemy could mount, and the enemy had to know this. Assuming a rational opponent, such a deterrence posture could prevent an attack, but if one side's retaliatory forces could survive an attack and the other's could not, the latter would live in constant fear of attack that could lead it in desperation to attack first. Mutual deterrence thus seemed the most stable arrangement, the most likely to prevent a war. The relationship came to be termed the threat of mutual assured destruction (MAD).

The stability of mutual deterrence would be lost if one state then achieved, or seemed about to achieve, the ability to erase the other's retaliatory forces in an attack. That would be exceedingly dangerous—the other might be driven to attack first, before being preempted. Even worse would be a confrontation in which neither retaliatory capacity could survive the opponent's attack, because then each government would be under unbearable pressure to attack first. U.S. officials drew several conclusions that shaped their policies in the 1960s and 1970s. First, the ideal deterrence relationship would make both sides eager to avoid all-out war, keep wars as limited as possible, and keep crises from turning into war. Second, deterrence forces should be very destructive (for purposes of retaliation), not capable of destroying the opponent's retaliatory forces, and very difficult to destroy. Third, vigorous efforts to evade mutual deterrence by seeking an effective defense against the opponent's retaliatory forces or developing a preemptive attack capability (or a combination of the two) were destabilizing and should not be undertaken. Fourth, for purposes of deterrence stability, the two sides should cooperate to avoid destabilizing deterrence postures and strategies, moderate their arms competition, enhance their ability to control crises, limit nuclear proliferation, and avoid accidental nuclear exchanges.

The first of these conclusions confirmed that massive retaliation was unacceptable; it threatened rapid escalation when the object was to prevent this. Weakness at lower levels of combat, forcing the West to escalate to avoid losing a war, was dangerous; the goal was to be able to fight successfully, and thus deter attack, at any level. This called for the posture and strategy labeled "flexible response," which was adopted during the administration of President John F. Kennedy in 1961. Flexible response was an intent and ability to fight many kinds of wars, which applied even at the nuclear level. Fighting a geographically limited nuclear war or even a limited strategic nuclear war was better than escalating to an all-out war.

The second conclusion meant that retaliatory forces must be dispersed, hidden, hardened, mobile, and numerous. Bombers should be dispersed (they were concentrated on a few airfields well into the 1950s), missiles were more attractive than bombers if hardened (in silos) or hidden (on submarines), and strategic forces should be diverse and have redundant destructive capabilities in order to make a successful enemy surprise attack impossible. These features soon became characteristic of U.S. strategic forces. The third conclusion opposed developing missiles so accurate and with such large warheads as to be ideal for preemptive attack. U.S. missiles stayed within these bounds, for the most part, for years. This conclusion also disparaged efforts to develop an effective missile defense. Coupled with doubts about the effectiveness of any missile defense, concern about its destabilizing impact made any attempt at developing such a system controversial thereafter.

The fourth conclusion justified the hot line, the atmospheric test ban treaty (1963), and the nonproliferation treaty (1968), and constituted the conceptual basis for arms control via the Strategic Arms Limitation Talks (SALT) arms control—SALT I (1972), which included the Antiballistic Missile (ABM) Treaty, and SALT II (1979) agreements. Arms control was being used to institutionalize mutual deterrence, through MAD, as the bedrock of national security and global security management.

The theory of mutual deterrence and the various policies associated with the theory represented a profound response to the stability problem. Massive retaliation, however, was also criticized with regard to credibility and the strategy ran into various difficulties. The credibility problem ultimately derived from the assumption of rationality in deterrence theory and strategy. The trouble was that retaliation in the nuclear age, and especially in response to an attack only on one's allies, seemed likely to be so costly as to be irrational. Thus, a clever opponent need not be deterred because the threatened response, by a rational deterrer, was incredible, which applied at all levels. To answer an attack with nuclear weapons could provoke a terrible response—so why retaliate? On the other hand, to respond just on the conventional level could mean a war that escalated to nuclear weapons—who could promise it would not?—so why retaliate and take that risk? Even if the war stayed conventional, to respond would mean casualties, maybe huge casualties—so why retaliate? Deterrence required retaliatory credibility, but how could this be guaranteed?

Many solutions had already been tried or were now implemented. One emphasized treating commitments as interdependent, which, just as with Korea, was the central rationale for U.S. involvement in Vietnam. Credibility lay in sustaining one's reputation for upholding commitments by upholding them, but this came into conflict with keeping deterrence politically acceptable. Korea and Vietnam demonstrated that the American public's tolerance for costly limited wars was low, making threats to fight others in the future somewhat hollow. After the Vietnam War the credibility of U.S. commitments declined because of political constraints on the use of force (the Vietnam Syndrome), which lasted for years.

A solution already in use was to construct intimate links with allies. Credibility was the main reason for maintaining U.S. forces in Europe and Korea, putting them in harm's way in case of an attack to make it much more likely that the United States would fight. Similar thinking shaped the decision to place intermediate-range missiles in Europe in 1959–1960 and again in 1983. Hostilities in Europe could mean that these U.S. nuclear weapons would hit the USSR, directly involving the United States in the fighting. There were, however, serious political difficulties. Europeans and others liked having U.S. troops around for protection but not paying for them; Americans disliked paying so much to protect others. Burden-sharing disputes became an important factor in alliance politics, worrisome because of their potential effects on credibility. Keeping nuclear weapons in other countries or on visiting U.S. ships eventually became politically difficult in some countries.

A third solution was to make retaliation, even nuclear retaliation, virtually automatic by such means as a launch-on-warning (LOW) posture for strategic forces or giving local commanders the authority to use nuclear weapons. The 1950s practice of having bombers fly daily toward Soviet targets and turn back if the attack signal never arrived was close to a LOW posture. Deterrence theory condemned such steps as exacerbating the stability problem, and after 1960 this solution was abandoned.

Under the flexible response policy, resolving the credibility problem and the stability problem simultaneously was impossible. In seeking deterrence stability, U.S. officials wanted more options for any Western retaliation but only under strict central (that is, U.S.) direction in order to minimize chances of inadvertent war, control any escalation of a war, and enhance crisis stability. The fewer fingers on triggers, the better. As for credibility, having few options meant retaliation risked total catastrophe and that prospect would either paralyze American will or seem likely enough to do so as to induce the enemy to attack. Hence, from 1961 on Washington urged that NATO have larger (mainly European) conventional forces, retained the idea that a nuclear war might be contained to one theater, and adopted more elaborate menus for fighting a strategic nuclear war—all to enhance credibility.

European allies, however, tended to regard all this not as a solution to the credibility problem but as further evidence of it, displaying U.S. reluctance to enter into war with the Soviet Union on their behalf. Their responses consistently frustrated Washington. British and French nuclear forces were developed in case the Americans ever abandoned their commitment and as a way to trigger rapid escalation of a war in Europe to the nuclear level for both superpowers. U.S. analysts saw this as undermining the stability of deterrence in a future crisis. All European allies also complained about U.S. plans to limit a conventional or nuclear war just to their soil. They rejected this element of flexible response in their military contributions, leaving NATO unable to defend itself with conventional forces alone, which Americans saw as damaging NATO's deterrence credibility. The allies claimed, probably correctly, that the costs involved were politically unsustainable, but they also suspected that the more they could defend themselves, the less the United States would contribute to NATO, in peace or war, and thus the lower the credibility of U.S. deterrence. Steps that sustained credibility in the allies' view damaged both credibility and stability as seen from Washington.

Stability concerns recurred and had a major impact in the next three decades. Stability required that neither side gain the ability to destroy the other's retaliatory forces in an initial attack or via a robust defense, but it often seemed possible that one side might succeed in developing such a capability. There was an enormous incentive to try, especially for the military services. Charged with maintaining deterrence, military leaders also had to plan for the worst—a failure of deterrence and a nuclear war. In a nuclear war it would be ideal to have a preemptive attack capability to guarantee national survival. What was ideal for stability while deterrence held would be of little help once it broke down.

To all this was added the pressure of technological change, which periodically opened new possibilities for a capability that would nullify deterrence. New weapons and advances in surveillance increased the ability to detect and attack enemy weapons, even ballistic missile submarines, and strategic targeting became steadily more elaborate and precise. Missiles were faster than bombers and therefore all the better for surprise attack. Greater missile accuracy made enemy missiles, bombers, and command centers more vulnerable. Multiple, independently targeted reentry vehicle (MIRV) warheads on each missile made it possible to destroy more sites with fewer missiles. Some claimed, or feared, that new technology had made possible a robust defense against missiles.

Deterrence theory held that both sides should avoid such destabilizing steps. Technological change and the desire for survival said otherwise. Avoiding these steps was also politically difficult because leaders could be charged with neglecting national security. After all, who could say that deterrence would always work and a nuclear war would never occur? These factors produced recurring American fears of "gaps." In the mid-1950s it was the bomber gap—the Soviets were developing more intercontinental bombers than expected and might be able to launch a successful surprise attack. The 1960 presidential campaign brought accusations of a missile gap. In the 1970s debate arose over a possible MIRV gap—Soviet missiles could carry so many large warheads that all land-based U.S. forces were vulnerable to destruction. Later, fears emerged that a Soviet attack could disable the U.S. command system. By the 1980s there were charges of a missile defense and civil defense gap—the Soviets were said to be far better equipped to survive a nuclear war and thus less deterrable. (Russians had similar fears about U.S. missiles, MIRVs, and missile defense research.) Policymaking often turned on how seriously to take these alleged gaps and what to do about them. Stability remained the central preoccupation in the continuing strategic arms control negotiations but was also the main reason for criticisms of the SALT agreements. Avoiding the vulnerability of strategic forces was also a major motivation in arms research and deployment decisions.

A Partial Retreat from Mutual Deterrence

After 1972 the stability problem, amidst disillusionment with U.S.-Soviet détente, eventually incited an intense attack on mutual deterrence theory and the posture and strategy that flowed from it. According to critics, the belief that arms control efforts were producing stable deterrence was a dangerous illusion. Moscow was actually seeking to escape from mutual deterrence and win a nuclear war, using arms control negotiations to prevent an adequate U.S. response. The key to deterrence stability was to convince the Soviets they would lose the next war. The United States should downplay arms control, build forces that could promptly destroy Soviet forces, including defenses against Soviet missiles, and devise a strategy for winning even a nuclear war, which would bolster deterrence and ensure survival if deterrence failed. Anything less would be criminal. Opponents of this approach argued that this expanded defense program would not succeed—the Soviets would work desperately to nullify it—despite the huge U.S. effort that would be necessary. Such a program would, moreover, gravely threaten deterrence stability, and that could be suicidal.

The same concerns about stability arose for extended deterrence via theater or battlefield nuclear weapons and conventional forces, especially in Europe. Could deterrence be stable if the Soviet bloc had superiority in conventional forces, especially in forces good for a smashing attack? Americans tended to say "no"; the Europeans tended to say "yes" because NATO would use nuclear weapons. The Soviet bloc, however, had many nonstrategic nuclear weapons for deterring NATO's escalation or destroying NATO's weapons before they could be used, especially when, in the mid-1970s, the Soviets introduced much better theater nuclear weapons. Thus, said Americans, the conventional forces gap could cause deterrence to collapse. The usual answer, offered in both Europe and the United States, was that NATO clearly had enough forces to make any war started by the Soviet Union a very large one. If it was large, the chances of it becoming an all-out nuclear war were too high for the Soviet government to accept. Hence, deterrence was quite stable.

The U.S. posture and strategy also came under attack in the 1970s with respect to credibility. The solution to the credibility problem adopted in the late 1960s was to relax the assumption of rationality under the MAD conception of deterrence. While this way of thinking was only temporarily given official status in the late 1960s, it survived in U.S. politics, deterrence theory, and NATO's posture in Europe. Its essence was the suggestion that no government could be guaranteed to be rational in the heat of a major confrontation or war and that no amount of planning, no command system, could be a guarantee against escalation, especially once nuclear weapons were used. The United States and the West could therefore promise a retaliation that was irrational in terms of the potential consequences but was credible nonetheless because they might just do it anyway, and the Russians would be deterred because of the awful consequences if they did.

This made nuclear deterrence a fact of life, inescapably credible. Efforts to refine it by proliferating options—from

larger forces to war-fighting options to ballistic missile defenses—were unnecessary and would add nothing and, because they were unnecessary, the costs involved were excessive. They also invited undue confidence in how a war would go, a confidence that might erode mutual deterrence because the stability problem would be exacerbated. This explanation, however, had disturbing features. To relax the assumption of rationality to deal with the credibility problem reopened the stability problem at the highest level. Stability had been defined as a practical problem, a question of how deterrence strategies and postures, via their impact on the calculations and perceptions of governments, might make deterrence break down, particularly in a crisis, and might cause any initial military action to escalate. To say, however, that deterrence was credible because governments in a crisis could be foolish, passionate, confused, liable to losing control, was to suggest that mutual deterrence was unlikely to work indefinitely, that it was ultimately unstable.

This solution was also rejected, for quite different reasons, by many strategists and officials who argued that credibility could be maintained only if the United States was confident of prevailing in any war, even a nuclear war. It was asserted, with considerable justification, that this was how the Russians understood deterrence and how they designed their military posture and strategy. U.S. credibility required convincing Moscow that the West would win in a war, not that everyone would lose. The critics seemed at first to triumph when Ronald Reagan became president in 1981. They talked about prevailing in any war as the basis for credibility and pressed for the development of more, and more accurate, strategic forces of the sort previously considered highly destabilizing. They proposed plans to make all Soviet retaliatory forces, even ballistic missile submarines at sea, more vulnerable, and eventually became involved in efforts to develop a ballistic missile defense system, the Strategic Defense Initiative (SDI), or Star Wars. The Reagan administration showed little interest in arms control.

It proved impossible, however, to gain sufficient political support to completely overturn the prior U.S. approach to deterrence. The deterrence posture and strategy remained a hybrid of the two approaches, well short of a war-winning capability. The SDI was never sufficiently funded for full development of missile defenses. President Reagan had to announce that a nuclear war could not be won and should never be fought. Strong political pressures at home and from allies helped induce the administration to take up arms control negotiations again.

The entire debate about deterrence during the Reagan era did, however, lend considerable weight to two additional challenges to deterrence. One was in terms of morality. Nuclear deterrence was a mutual hostage relationship resting on the capacity and will to take millions of lives, perhaps even destroy all human life. For many Americans and Europeans, this could never be morally acceptable. For years there had been recurring pressure by morally concerned citizens against deterrence via campaigns for nuclear disarmament, opposition to civil defense programs, and objections to defense spending and new weapons systems. This opposition was only reinforced by the notion that governments were highly imperfect and might stumble into disaster and was reinvigorated by the Reagan military buildup. Such opposition could never be dismissed. Its persistence had much to do with the rapidity with which, once the Cold War began to evaporate, steps multiplied to deemphasize nuclear deterrence.

The other challenge came from proliferation, on the nuclear and conventional levels. The most telling objection to nuclear proliferation was that other governments would be irrational or unstable; in short, proliferation was a variant of the stability problem. The concern about irrationality, however, logically made the long-standing Soviet-U.S. nuclear deterrence questionable on the same grounds and led to the charge that the real U.S. concern was to avoid having to share the power and status provided by nuclear weapons. The proliferation problem constantly bedeviled foreign policy. The United States resisted British plans for nuclear weapons. It opposed French plans for a nuclear arsenal by political pressure and by trying to draw French (and British) nuclear weapons into a NATO pool over the use of which the United States would have a veto. Washington pressured other allies (Korea, Taiwan) into canceling nuclear weapons programs and helped devise the Nuclear Nonproliferation Treaty to limit, and the International Atomic Energy Agency to monitor, nuclear development. It developed the London suppliers club to curb transfers of nuclear-related technology. The United States also objected to India's nuclear test; tried to prevent South Africa, Pakistan, and North Korea from developing nuclear weapons; and would eventually squeeze Iraq's nuclear program.

The credibility problem, however, invited proliferation; allies suspected superpower guarantees were not credible and thus wanted their own deterrent. The stability problem invited flexible response, which called for larger conventional forces and thus led to their proliferation. This created the "doves dilemma": to discourage nuclear proliferation, states with serious security problems might need either U.S. security guarantees, which would mean more U.S. defense spending (more extended deterrence) or a greater ability to defend themselves, which would mean letting them have conventional weapons the United States preferred they did not have.

In any case, nuclear technology could not be con-

tained completely, given the incentives to acquire it and the nature of modern science. If friends or allies insisted on having nuclear programs, other political considerations often led to U.S. acquiescence. The United States learned to live with British and French nuclear weapons, looked the other way when Israel developed them, and tolerated Pakistan's nuclear program in exchange for Pakistan's help on Afghanistan. The United States became a major supplier, even the major supplier, of conventional weapons to maintain U.S. access to bases or intelligence sites vital for the deterrence posture, to sustain allies, and to maintain healthy defense industries to keep up its forces.

Deterrence After the Cold War

The demise of the Cold War raised a host of new or familiar concerns. Deterrence theory rested on the existence of a truly pervasive political conflict in which each side expected to be attacked if it ever lacked the capacity to deter. East-West rapprochement following the collapse of the Soviet Union in 1991 eliminated the viability of that assumption and thus the rationale for keeping nuclear deterrence as the centerpiece of U.S. national security. The impact on the deterrence posture was immediate. In 1987 the United States and the Soviet Union had agreed in the Intermediate Nuclear Forces (INF) Treaty to eliminate land-based missiles for nuclear weapons with a range of 500 to 3,000 kilometers and eventually decided to eliminate all land-based missiles of shorter range. In 1991 they were joined by Great Britain in an agreement to eliminate all nuclear weapons at sea except on ballistic missile submarines. Washington and Moscow also agreed to slash nuclear weapons carried by planes in Europe. In the Strategic Arms Reduction Talks (START I, 1991; START II, 1993) agreements they committed themselves to reduce strategic nuclear arsenals by roughly three-fourths, to 3,500 for the United States and 3,000 for Russia by the year 2003. They also agreed to take most strategic nuclear weapons off alert and to eliminate all MIRV packages on land-based missiles. They agreed in principle to further cuts in nuclear forces and, with other governments, entered into a moratorium on nuclear testing. Hence, nuclear deterrence moved from the center to the periphery of foreign policy, replaced by the pursuit of political accommodation. NATO did the same, announcing in 1991 that nuclear deterrence would now be a last resort, not a relatively early response, to attack. At the global level, deterrence faded—at least for the time being—as the crux of international system management, and efforts were made to marginalize the role of nuclear weapons in foreign policy.

However, U.S. officials now depicted their conventional forces, especially those based aboard, as a crucial contribution, in the form of deterrence, to regional peace and security. Hence, most classic concerns about deterrence remained. Without a Soviet threat, the stability problem was eased but still existed. Analysts noted that cuts in strategic forces could make it easier for Russia, if the Cold War returned, to achieve a preemptive-attack capability. Russian political and economic difficulties that inhibited ratification and implementation of START II were noted, and U.S. plans for its strategic forces included hedging against revival of a Russian threat.

Meanwhile, nuclear proliferation and the spread of ballistic missiles loomed as threats as the proliferation problem in all its guises survived the Cold War. The U.S. tried hard to dismantle Iraq's missiles and weapons of mass destruction (WMD) during and after the Gulf War. It mounted a strenuous campaign (including threats of military action) against North Korea's nuclear weapons program, eventually winning the North's acquiescence, in October 1994, by employing political and economic inducements as well. Washington harassed suppliers of WMD-related technology, led the way in securing extension of the Nuclear Nonproliferation Treaty in 1995, pressured and reassured the Ukraine into giving up nuclear weapons, and worried about possible nuclear war in South Asia. Such efforts were stimulated by the lurking suspicion that American deterrence, nuclear and conventional, was of uncertain reliability because Third World opponents had ever more powerful forces at their disposal and might be dangerously irrational. (The Gulf War was an example.) This invited renewed interest in defenses against ballistic missiles despite continuing objections that they could be destabilizing. The U.S. moved steadily toward development and deployment of limited missile-defense systems, while seeking cooperation with Russia and others to contain any threats this would involve to stability.

Credibility concerns remained as well. For America's allies, U.S. commitments seemed to have less credibility because, no longer facing the Cold War enemy, the American public was reluctant to bear significant costs in regional conflicts. This called into question the effectiveness of the alliances from the Cold War era. Debate continued about the interdependence of commitments in connection with U.S. inaction in Bosnia during both the administrations of Presidents George Bush and Bill Clinton and the U.S. withdrawal from Somalia in 1993–1994. The United States intervened militarily in Bosnia, in the end, primarily to sustain both its credibility and the alliance cohesion deemed vital for NATO's credibility.

Analysts in and out of government broached the idea of more reliance on collective deterrence through international organizations or a concert of major states, instead of primarily U.S. deterrence. This could provide an overwhelming threat of retaliation while spreading the costs and reducing any single state's ability to disrupt the stability of deterrence. It proved a daunting task, however, to get sufficient cooperation, particularly among democracies where citizens were reluctant to bear heavy defense burdens abroad, making it an elusive solution.

PATRICK M. MORGAN

See also Antiballistic Missile Treaty; Arms Control and Disarmament Agency; Arms Transfer and Trade; Baruch, Bernard Mannes; Central Treaty Organization; Flexible Response; Intermediate-Range Nuclear Forces Treaty; Korean War; Limited Nuclear Test Ban Treaty; Massive Retaliation; Mutual Assured Destruction; North Atlantic Treaty Organization; Nuclear Nonproliferation; Nuclear Weapons and Strategy; Russia and the Soviet Union; Southeast Asia Treaty Organization; Strategic Arms Limitation Talks and Agreements; Strategic Arms Reduction Treaties; Strategic Defense Initiative; Vietnam War

FURTHER READING

Ball, Desmond, and Jeffrey Richelson, eds. *Strategic Nuclear Targeting*. Ithaca, New York, 1986.

Bundy, McGeorge. *Danger and Survival: Choices About the Bomb in the First Fifty Years*. N.Y., 1988.

Clausen, Peter A. *Nonproliferation and the National Interest: America's Response to the Spread of Nuclear Weapons*. New York, 1993.

Cromwell, William C. *The United States and the European Pillar: The Strained Alliance*. New York, 1992.

Freedman, Lawrence. *The Evolution of Nuclear Strategy*. London, 1983.

Gaddis, John Lewis. *Strategies of Containment: A Critical Appraisal of Postwar American National Security Policy*. New York, 1982.

Gray, Colin. "Nuclear Strategy: The Case for a Theory of Victory." *International Security* 4 (Summer 1979): 63–87.

Hardin, Russell, et al., eds. *Nuclear Deterrence: Ethics and Strategy*. Chicago, 1985.

Herken, Gregg. *Counsels of War*. New York, 1987.

Jervis, Robert. *The Meaning of the Nuclear Revolution*. Ithaca, N.Y., 1989.

Morgan, Patrick M. *Deterrence: A Conceptual Analysis*, 2nd ed. Beverly Hills, Calif., 1983.

Schelling, Thomas, and Morton Halperin. *Strategy and Arms Control*, 2nd ed. Washington, D.C., 1985.

Schwartz, David N. *NATO's Nuclear Dilemmas*. Washington, D.C., 1983.

Snyder, Glenn H. *Deterrence and Defense: Toward a Theory of National Security*. Princeton, N.J., 1961.

Tyroler II, Charles, ed. *Alerting America: The Papers of the Committee on the Present Danger*. Washington, D.C., 1984.

Wohlstetter, Albert. "The Delicate Balance of Terror." *Foreign Affairs* 37 (January 1959):211–234.

DEUTCH, JOHN M.

(*b*. 27 July 1938)

Former chemistry professor and provost at the Massachusetts Institute of Technology (M.I.T.) and President Bill Clinton's top choice in 1995 to replace R. James Woolsey as Director of Central Intelligence (DCI)—the chief intelligence officer in the U.S. government. Born in Brussels, Belgium, to well-educated Jewish parents, Deutch became a U.S. citizen in 1945 and subsequently earned a B.A. in history and economics from Amherst College, followed by a B.S. in chemical engineering and a Ph.D. in physical chemistry from M.I.T.

Deutch initially declined Clinton's offer, preferring to keep his post as deputy defense secretary (the second highest position in the Department of Defense). The president's next choice, General Michael P. C. Carns, had to withdraw his candidacy, however, following revelations that he had violated immigration laws when he brought a Philippine domestic to the United States. Under strong pressure from the president, this time Deutch accepted, but insisted that the DCI position be elevated to Cabinet status.

Deutch already had been confirmed twice by the Senate for positions in the Department of Defense as deputy secretary and undersecretary. He also had served as a member of the president's Foreign Intelligence Advisory Board and in the Carter administration as undersecretary in the Department of Energy. While some senators raised concerns about placing the DCI in the Cabinet, Deutch assured senators that he would not allow a blurring of the line between objective intelligence reporting and policy advocacy.

Deutch came to the DCI position during a period of turbulence for U.S. intelligence agencies. The Sweeping global changes set off by the fall of the Soviet Union and the end of the Cold War, as well as demands for reform intensified by such controversies as the Aldrich Ames spy case and the allegations implicating the CIA in political murders by the Guatemalan military, led many to question what role the CIA should now play. In 1995 President Clinton and Congress established the bipartisan blue-ribbon Commission on the Roles and Capabilities of the United States Intelligence Community, chaired by former secreatries of defense Les Aspin and Harold Brown.

Along with the Aspin-Brown Commission's recommendations, Deutch brought to the DCI job his own agenda for reform, which included providing the best information possible to the president and other policymakers; ensuring reliable support to military operations; combating international terrorism, crime, and trade in narcotics; preventing the repetition of cases such as Ames's; and enhancing cooperation among the various intelligence agencies. Further, as a scientist interested in the technical aspects of intelligence collection, Deutch advocated a National Imagery Office (NIO) for the more efficient management of reconnaissance satellites. This initiative quickly ran into bureaucratic resistance. The National Photographic Interpretation Center, for example, preferred to remain within the CIA rather than

become part of a new and untried entity. An even more difficult task turned out to be Deutch's intention to revamp the Directorate of Operations (DO), which had given the CIA some of its worst blemishes, from the Bay of Pigs fiasco to the Iran-Contra Affair.

However, these and other efforts were hampered by serving under a president with limited interest in intelligence matters, and by the sprawling bureaucracy skilled in thwarting efforts to meddle in its affairs.

LOCH K. JOHNSON

See also Central Intelligence Agency; Clinton, William Jefferson; Intelligence

FURTHER READING
Parry, Robert. "The Spy Master." *Boston Magazine*, July 1995, 32–34, 55–56.
U.S. Senate. John Deutch statement, Confirmation Hearings, Select Committee on Intelligence (26 April 1995): 1–11.
———. John Deutch statement on "Worldwide Threat Assessment Brief," Hearings. Select Committee on Intelligence (22 February 1996): 1–23.

DEW
See Distant Early Warning (DEW) Line

DEWEY, GEORGE
(*b.* 26 December 1837; *d.* 16 January 1917)

Naval officer and hero in the Spanish-American-Cuban-Filipino War. Born in Montpelier, Vermont, Dewey graduated from the U.S. Naval Academy in 1858, did service during the Civil War, and later commanded ships and served in navy administrative posts. With the April 1898 outbreak of war between the United States and Spain, Commodore Dewey, as commander of the U.S. Asiatic Squadron, sailed from Hong Kong to the Philippines. On 1 May his ships sank the Spanish fleet in Manila Bay, thereby establishing a U.S. military presence in the Philippine Islands that eventually led to annexation. After securing Manila Bay, Dewey presided over the buildup of U.S. military forces. When neutral German naval ships violated Dewey's blockade rules, he protested vigorously, but he maintained harmonious relations with the British fleet. Dewey initially encouraged Filipino insurgent leader Emilio Aguinaldo to believe that the United States would cooperate with him in achieving independence, but when Dewey engineered the capitulation of Manila, he excluded Filipino insurgents from the city. In 1899 Congress promoted Dewey to admiral of the navy. Dewey eyed the presidency, but he could muster little support for a candidacy. From 1900 to his death Dewey served as president of the General Board of the Navy Department.

JOHN L. OFFNER

See also Aguinaldo, Emilio; Spanish-American-Cuban-Filipino War, 1898; Philippines

FURTHER READING

Sargent, Nathan. *Admiral Dewey and the Manila Campaign.* Washington, D.C., 1947.
Spector, Ronald. *Admiral of the New Empire: The Life and Career of George Dewey.* Baton Rouge, La., 1974.
Trask, David F. *The War with Spain in 1898.* New York, 1981.

DÍAZ, (JOSÉ DE LA CRUZ) PORFIRIO

(*b.* 15 September 1830; *d.* 2 July 1915)

President of Mexico (1876–1880, 1884–1911) who ended his country's decades-long civil and international wars. His dictatorship promoted economic growth and enabled Mexico to meet its international commitments. He maintained stable relations with the U.S. government and foreign business interests and resigned the presidency only in the face of a revolution in Mexico. In 1867 General Díaz's army captured Mexico City and overthrew the government of Emperor Maximilian, who had been installed by French troops in 1864. Díaz's troops restored Benito Pablo Juárez as Mexico's president. In 1876 Díaz seized power from Juárez's successor, Lerdo de Tejada, but in 1880 Díaz stepped aside for his ally, General Manuel González. Díaz returned to the presidency in 1884.

Under Díaz, Mexico encouraged foreign direct investment. In 1880 he awarded U.S. investors two concessions to build railroads between Mexico City and the U.S. border. In 1882 Mexico and the United States agreed to permit each other's armies to cross the border to punish raids by indigenous peoples. The next year the two governments signed a treaty to allow free trade in various products. U.S.-Mexican trade increased twelvefold between 1870 and 1910. In 1911 U.S. investments exceeded $646 million, about 40 percent of total foreign investments in Mexico. Díaz also sought to settle boundary disputes with the United States, and in 1884 the two countries signed a convention marking the border with greater precision. The U.S. government accepted Mexican ownership of the Guano islands off the Yucatán Peninsula (1886) and of Passion Island in the Pacific Ocean (1897). The only remaining border dispute was over the 600-acre Chamizal area. A change in course of the Rio Grande in 1864 had shifted this small parcel to the U.S. side. In 1899 the two governments created the International Boundary Commission to hear and settle future border disputes arising from the Rio Grande's changing course and to allocate water in common rivers.

Díaz differed with the United States mainly over Central America. In the early 1880s the U.S. government provided some support for Guatemalan claims on the Mexican state of Chiapas, which had belonged to the Guatemalan Captaincy General under the Spanish empire. In an attempt to balance U.S. influence in Central America, Díaz sent a warship in 1909 to assist Nicaraguan president José Santos Zelaya in fighting a rebellion supported by the U.S. government. In November 1910 Mexicans exiled in the United States launched a revolution to prevent Díaz's seventh reelection, and Díaz unsuccessfully demanded that the U.S. government arrest the conspirators. On 10 May 1911 the army garrison of Ciudad Juárez surrendered to the rebels. Although his army remained nearly intact, Díaz nonetheless resigned two weeks later. The ensuing revolution, which engulfed Mexico during the following decade, was fueled in part by the unhappiness of peasants dispossessed by Díaz's economic growth policies. Another contributing factor was opposition to his government's practice of granting generous concessions that allowed foreigners, especially U.S. firms, to exploit Mexico's natural resources.

JORGE I. DOMÍNGUEZ

See also Mexico; Nicaragua

FURTHER READING

Cosío Villegas, Daniel. *United States Versus Porfirian Mexico.* Lincoln, Nebr., 1963.
Vázquez, Josefina, and Lorenzo Meyer. *The United States and Mexico.* Chicago, 1985.

DIEGO GARCIA

A narrow ten and a half mile-long island located in southern Asia in the Indian Ocean, south of India halfway between Africa and Indonesia. Diego Garcia forms part of the Chagos Archipelago located in southern Asia in the Indian Ocean, south of India halfway between Africa and Indonesia, . Despite its isolated location, by the end of the 1970s Diego Garcia had become the strategic hub for U.S. military planning and power projection capabilities in the Indian Ocean region. Although the U.S. Navy considered developing an Indian Ocean infrastructure in the late 1950s, it was not until the mid-1960s that regional political developments permitted Washington to proceed with this plan. In 1965 Great Britain politically separated the British Indian Ocean Territories, including the Chagos Archipelago and several other island groups (but not the Seychelles). London's intent was to provide politically safe sites, not subject to foreign authority, on which Great Britain and the United States could construct military installations. On 30 December 1966, Washington and London signed a fifty-year lease (with the provision for a twenty-year extension) that granted the United States military rights to Diego Garcia. In 1971 the United States began dredging the lagoon and constructing a communications facility and a landing strip on Diego Garcia. Increased Soviet naval activity in the Indian Ocean in the early 1970s, however, coupled with the political fallout from the 1973 Arab-Israeli war, which restricted U.S. access to military facilities in the region, spurred military construction projects on the island.

In January 1980, under the aegis of the Carter Doctrine, Diego Garcia became the centerpiece of U.S. plans to develop a permanent strategic network in the Indian Ocean, especially as a site for pre-positioning supplies intended for the Rapid Deployment Force, which became the Central Command in 1983. During the 1987–1988 Kuwaiti reflagging operation and again during the 1990–1991 Desert Shield and Desert Storm operations against Iraq, Diego Garcia provided critical logistical support for U.S. military forces in the Persian Gulf. In 1991 U.S. B-52s based at Diego Garcia launched bombing missions against Iraqi forces in Kuwait. The U.S. military presence at Diego Garcia has sparked two political controversies. In the mid-1960s Great Britain depopulated the island by moving its 1,800 inhabitants, the Ilois, to Mauritius and the Seychelles. Although the Ilois received compensation, they have claimed the right of return and questioned the legality of Great Britain's lease of the island to the United States. In the 1970s and 1980s Diego Garcia became a target of proposals to turn the Indian Ocean into a nuclear-free zone and a zone of peace. Despite these continuing political-legal controversies, in the mid-1990s U.S. military planning for the Indian Ocean region remained centered on Diego Garcia.

JEFFREY A. LeFEBVRE

See also Carter Doctrine; Great Britain; Gulf War of 1990–1991; Middle East; Rapid Deployment Force

FURTHER READING
Bowman, Larry. *Mauritius.* Boulder, Colo., 1991.
Jawatkan, K.S. *Diego Garcia in International Diplomacy.* Bombay, India, 1983.
Larus, Joel. "Diego Garcia." In *The Indian Ocean: Perspectives on a Strategic Arena,* edited by William Dowdy and Russell Trood. Durham, N.C., 1985.
Wooten, James. *Regional Support Facilities for the Rapid Deployment Force.* Washington, D.C., 1982.

DIEM, NGO DINH

(*b.* 3 January 1901; *d.* 2 November 1963)

Prime minister of the State of Vietnam (1954–1955), president of the Republic of Vietnam (1955–1963), and ally of the United States. Diem was born into a Catholic family in the imperial capital of Hue, attended the prestigious National Academy, and took a law degree from the University of Hanoi. Entering the civil service upon

graduation, Diem rose rapidly through the ranks, becoming minister of the interior in the government of Emperor Bao Dai in 1933. He resigned a few months later in protest against French unwillingness to grant Vietnam greater autonomy and for the next two decades remained politically inactive. An ardent Catholic, Diem resolutely opposed communism, and in late 1945 he refused an offer from Ho Chi Minh to collaborate with the Vietminh. In 1950 he rejected Bao Dai's offer of the prime ministership in the proposed government of the Associated State of Vietnam. Instead, Diem embarked on a series of travels to Japan, Europe, and the United States, where he spent two years at the Maryknoll Seminary in New Jersey. This long hiatus from public life, coupled with his ascetic and reclusive lifestyle, made Diem an unlikely candidate for national leadership, but his name continued to carry considerable influence in Vietnam. While in the United States he made contacts with numerous influential Americans, including Francis Cardinal Spellman, Supreme Court Justice William O. Douglas, and Senators Mike Mansfield and John F. Kennedy. In the closing days of the 1954 Geneva Conference, Bao Dai appointed Diem prime minister. Although it would be incorrect to argue, as some have done, that Washington officials alone orchestrated the appointment, they certainly supported it; while mindful of Diem's flaws, they liked his strong anticommunism and fervent nationalism, and they hoped to use him to transform the south of Vietnam into a stable, noncommunist society. Diem pledged to work closely with the United States and moved swiftly to consolidate his power base in the south, suppressing opposition groups and refusing to hold the nationwide elections called for in the Geneva Accords.

Diem had numerous personal weaknesses, which over the next half dozen years dashed the hopes that Americans had for him. He alienated key groups in South Vietnamese society with policies that favored the country's minority Catholic population and with his refusal to follow through on a promised land reform program. He was prone to paranoia, which led him to refuse to delegate authority and to depend almost exclusively on his family for advice, in particular his brother Ngo Dinh Nhu, a shadowy figure who exerted great influence and was behind many of the regime's repressive policies against the Buddhists. Beginning in the late 1950s, social and political unrest, backed by North Vietnam, increased dramatically. In 1960 the National Liberation Front, composed of both communist and noncommunist elements and dedicated to overthrowing the Diem regime, came into existence. U.S. officials watched these developments with growing dismay, but they were not yet prepared to end their support of the Diem government. In the last half of 1963, however, U.S. policy toward Diem began to change, following a new round of repressive, Nhu-orchestrated government actions against the Buddhists and a further deterioration of the war effort. The administration of President John F. Kennedy demanded that Diem speed up reforms and listen to U.S. advice; when he did neither the administration became sympathetic to demands for his ouster. On 1 November 1963 a group of South Vietnamese generals, with the tacit and secret support of the Kennedy administration, staged a successful coup in which Diem and Nhu were killed.

Diem's regime has generated debate among students of the Vietnam War. To some, his repressive policies and his dependence on his brother Nhu seriously undermined the Republic of Vietnam, setting in motion the downward spiral that successors could never reverse. Others point to the weaknesses of those same successors and argue that Diem was the only strong anticommunist leader in South Vietnam. They argue that it was not his tenure but his overthrow that guaranteed its eventual defeat.

FREDRIK LOGEVALL

See also French Indochina; Kennedy, John Fitzgerald; Vietnam War

FURTHER READING

Anderson, David L. *Trapped by Success: The Eisenhower Administration and Vietnam, 1953–1961*. New York, 1991.
Karnow, Stanley. *Vietnam: A History*, rev. ed. New York, 1992.
Warner, Denis. *The Last Confucian*. New York, 1963.

DIEN BIEN PHU

A village in northwestern Vietnam, the site of the epic battle of the French-Indochina War (1946–1954). In a siege lasting fifty-five days in March–May 1954, the French garrison of 15,000 men was overwhelmed by four divisions of the Vietminh, communist forces under the leadership of Ho Chi Minh. The base was set up as bait to lure communist guerrillas into open battle, but the French had not counted on the Vietminh being armed with Chinese-supplied artillery. Quickly cut off from effective resupply, with a potential U.S. rescue effort scuttled and an inadequate relief force thirty miles away, the troops occupying the fortress surrendered on 8 May 1954. The defeat prompted the French to withdraw from all of Indochina in July 1954. Dien Bien Phu quickly became a symbol of the end of Western military invincibility. It directly inspired the Algerians in their war against the French, and, in the subsequent U.S. intervention in Vietnam, President Lyndon B. Johnson worried about a Dien Bien Phu situation arising at the military base at Khe Sanh during the Tet Offensive (1968). Although the Khe Sanh base held, in a symbolic sense all of Indochina became a Dien Bien Phu in the peninsula-wide communist triumphs of 1975.

TIMOTHY J. LOMPERIS

See also French Indochina; Geneva Conventions; Tet Offensive; Vietnam War

FURTHER READING

Fall, Bernard B. *Hell in a Very Small Place: The Siege of Dien Bien Phu.* Philadelphia, 1967.

DILLON ROUND

See General Agreement on Tariffs and Trade

DILLON, CLARENCE DOUGLAS

(*b.* 21 August 1909)

Ambassador to France (1953–1957), undersecretary of state (1958–1961), and secretary of the treasury (1961–1965). The son of a wealthy Wall Street banker, Douglas Dillon was born in Geneva, Switzerland. After completing his studies at the Groton School and Harvard University, Dillon began his financial career as a floor trader at the New York Stock Exchange and soon became vice president of his father's firm, Dillon, Read and Company. His career was interrupted by World War II navy service, where he rose quickly in rank from ensign to lieutenant commander. Dillon returned to double the firm's portfolio in six years. He was active in Republican politics and campaigned vigorously for Dwight D. Eisenhower in 1952 and Richard M. Nixon in 1960.

He began his career in government with an appointment as ambassador to France in 1953. He then served a four-year stint as an undersecretary of state. In this capacity he spearheaded the General Agreement on Tariffs and Trade (GATT) negotiations, which were dubbed the Dillon Round in his honor. Dillon was President John F. Kennedy's surprise choice for secretary of the treasury. By selecting Dillon the young president sent a signal that he took the need for "sound money" seriously and was willing to work toward that end in a bipartisan fashion. Given their similar social backgrounds, Dillon worked well with Kennedy. He helped focus Kennedy's attention on the troubling balance-of-payments deficit and the resulting need for conservative fiscal and monetary policies. He advocated Kennedy's tax cut proposal before Congress and won its passage after the 1963 assassination. He also lobbied successfully against a proposal to include the treasury secretary in the Federal Reserve Board—a move he felt would overly politicize monetary policy. When Kennedy died and Lyndon B. Johnson took over, the chemistry was gone. Dillon left the cabinet in 1965 but continued to press for responsible monetary policy. He returned to private life and served as head of the U.S. and International Securities Company, the Metropolitan Museum of Art in New York City, the Rockefeller Foundation, and the Brookings Institution. He also joined the Senior Adviser Group on Vietnam in 1968 to argue for a deescalation of the Vietnam War. Dillon was awarded the National Institute of Social Sciences Gold Medal in 1979 for humanitarian service and in 1989 received the Presidential Medal of Freedom.

KENDALL W. STILES

See also General Agreement on Tariffs and Trade; Kennedy, John Fitzgerald

DINGLEY TARIFF
See Tariffs

DIPLOMATIC METHOD

Or diplomacy, the formalized system of procedures or the process by which sovereign states, usually through ambassadors or other diplomatic representatives but sometimes through executive agents, conduct their official relations. Such relations are maintained bilaterally and, increasingly, multilaterally within international organizations or other multiparty arrangements, some of them involving nongovernmental actors. Diplomatic negotiation is usually considered the preferred method of resolving international disputes, taking precedence over the use of force (the "last resort") and even over the referral of issues to judicial tribunals.

Types of Diplomacy

There are several major types of diplomacy. Conventional intergovernmental diplomacy is carried out principally through embassies and foreign ministries in national capitals. Sometimes, for the sake of preserving confidentiality or for other reasons, surreptitious back channels are used, such as the one employed in 1969 by Henry A. Kissinger, as national security adviser to President Richard M. Nixon, and Anatoly Dobrynin, the ambassador of the Soviet Union in Washington. There are also various forms of conference diplomacy. The largest gatherings typically deal with complex regional or functional problems requiring the participation of technical experts as well as diplomatic representatives. Often representatives of nongovernmental organizations are also in attendance and offer information and advice. The United Nations Conference on Environment and Development, held in Rio de Janeiro in June 1992, was the largest such diplomatic conference ever held. Great-power contact groups, such as the one that helped arrange the independence of Namibia during the 1980s and the one dealing with the question of peace in Bosnia-Herze-

govina in the early 1990s, illustrate what has been termed "ad hoc multilateral diplomacy." Mediatory, or third-party, diplomacy, sometimes occasioning small conferences, may also be conducted by a single power, which serves as mediator between the parties directly involved, such as the good offices role played by President Jimmy Carter in bringing about the Camp David Accords between the leaders of Egypt and Israel in September 1978.

As air travel became easier and more common during and after World War II, heads of state or government increasingly met face to face "at the summit." Examples of adversarial and nonadversarial summitry include the bilateral conference between President Ronald Reagan and Soviet leader Mikhail Gorbachev at Reykjavík, Iceland, in October 1986, at which strategic nuclear armaments issues were discussed, and the multilateral meeting of leaders of the Asia Pacific Economic Cooperation group of nations in Bogor, Indonesia, in November 1994, where plans for a regional free-trade area by the year 2020 were discussed. The annual Economic Summits of the seven leading industrial democratic states (the Group of Seven), which were joined in the 1990s by the Russian Federation for discussion of politically related issues (making a Group of Eight), have been viewed, although with some exaggeration, as constituting a virtual global directorate.

There is also organizational diplomacy, in which permanent structures, such as the International Monetary Fund (IMF) and the World Bank, established by the Bretton Woods Conference in July 1944, are frameworks within which an institutionalized form of diplomacy, as well as ordinary bureaucratic negotiation, can take place. Multinational commercial diplomacy has been conducted within the context of the Geneva-based General Agreement on Tariffs and Trade (GATT), replaced at the beginning of 1995 by the new World Trade Organization (WTO). Multilateral diplomacy has taken on a parliamentary expression within the United Nations system, particularly in the General Assembly and to some extent the Security Council. In those bodies, permanent representatives and other delegates, mixing with international civil servants and accredited observers, form coalitions and lobby, debate, and vote resolutions in conformity with a constitution-like charter.

Persuasion, Compromise, Pressure

Whatever the framework of diplomacy, its methods do not fundamentally change, although they may be modified somewhat by the impact of technology (hot lines, teleconferencing, computer networking, and other innovative means of communication) and by cultural factors. There are essentially three methods—persuasion, compromise, and pressure. Persuasion consists of the marshaling of rational arguments, sometimes aided by appeals to emotion, for the purpose of inducing another party to agree, that is, genuinely to concur with the rightness, justice, or wisdom of a proposed measure. Compromise recognizes the frequent difficulty of coming to a full or even a degree of mutual agreement and, through the give-and-take process of exchanging material or other concessions, seeks to reach at minimum a settlement, or a convergence point that is acceptable, even if not truly agreeable, to both sides. The exercise of pressure makes clear to an opposing party, sometimes only tacitly, that more than words or rewards may be brought to bear and that physical or other coercion, including actual military force, might be employed. Such coercive diplomacy is exemplified by the so-called "Sarajevo ultimatum," the threat made by the North Atlantic Treaty Organization (NATO) in February 1994 to launch air strikes against Serbian artillery positions around the Bosnian city of Sarajevo if Serbian forces did not cease to attack it and their heavy guns were not withdrawn to a stated distance by a specified time.

The diplomatic art, as the international relations theorist Hans J. Morgenthau pointed out, consists of putting the right emphasis at any particular moment on each of these methods. All three usually are present to some degree in most international negotiations, especially between adversaries. Philosophical realists such as Morgenthau emphasize the primacy of power, especially the implicit possibility of the use of force (pressure). Idealists, on the other hand, place their trust in the efficacy of reason and dialogue (persuasion). Both realists and idealists recognize the need for one side in a conflict to understand and work through the other side's assessment of its own interests, thereby better to understand at what point an adjustment might be possible (compromise).

Linkage and Insight

Through linkage—the more or less explicit connection of different issues in a negotiation in order to make cooperation in one area conditional upon progress in another—diplomats can sometimes increase their overall influence. The basic strategic idea is that a strength, or assets, in one area can be used to compensate for a weakness, or deficits, in another. The delaying tactics used by Nixon and Kissinger in refusing to agree to a Moscow summit meeting with Leonid Brezhnev until May 1972 represented an indirect effort to gain leverage over the Soviet Union's ally, North Vietnam. Moscow wanted U.S. recognition, via the Strategic Arms Limitation Talks (SALT), of Soviet parity in the military field and also most-favored-nation trading rights. Washington wanted the Soviet leadership to put pressure, by denying further military aid, on the communist regime in Hanoi in order to force it to settle the Vietnam conflict on terms acceptable to the United States.

In diplomacy, the interrelatedness of linked issues often is expressed vaguely or even left entirely unspoken, at least in public discussion, lest the leverage seem too overt and a negotiator's pride be offended. Leaving such linkage implicit and unspoken may also be advisable when any substantive connection between the issues may be only tenuous or may not exist at all. One of the tasks of statesmanship, writes Henry Kissinger, himself an artist in the ambiguous formulation of diplomatic quid pro quos, is to understand which subjects are truly related, so that separate negotiations regarding them can be manipulated to reinforce each other. Accepting that it is reality and not policy that ultimately produces the interconnection of subjects in the world, Kissinger argues that the statesman's role is to recognize the relationship when it does exist, and that by seeing in advance the potential joining of issues, and then making the link, diplomats can weave a network of incentives and penalties.

Diplomacy is not, as the term "linkage" can misleadingly suggest, merely mechanical, dependent for its success on the application of external pressures. Insight and the projective imagination—intuition about individuals in their unique situations—are needed. The very word "diplomacy" connotes tact, consideration, and even a measure of empathy—the ability to see an issue from the other person's point of view, with some sensitivity to the other party's feelings as well as a basic knowledge of his or her beliefs. The difficulty of thus penetrating the mindsets of profound adversaries, including Joseph Stalin, Kim Il Sung, Mao Zedong, Ho Chi Minh, Fidel Castro, Ayatollah Khomeini, and Saddam Hussein, has been a major problem for U.S. leaders and officials inclined to favor negotiation. There is the constant risk of "mirror imaging," or assuming that the responses of such radical opponents are or would be the same as the responses of Americans in identical circumstances. In effect, such U.S. negotiation advocates may look at the faces of others and see only themselves. Especially during acute international crises, when the danger is great, the stakes are high, the time is short, and the facts are few, accurate intuition and insight into the thinking of an adversary can be crucial. One example of how valuable such knowledge can be is demonstrated by the insight into the mind of Soviet leader Nikita Khrushchev by Ambassador Llewellyn Thompson during the October 1962 Cuban missile crisis. Such insights are not always available, however, and it is in part to make up for a lack of such intimate knowledge and understanding that U.S. officials and scholars have developed generic models of crisis management.

Diplomacy as Limited Instrument

It must be acknowledged that diplomacy, even at its best, is a limited instrument. The United States practices diplomacy within a worldwide system that is conventionally defined, and legally as well as politically regulated, by the principle of reciprocity. In particular, interference in the domestic affairs of other states is forbidden, which can limit access to information and deny possibilities of influence. According to the Vienna Convention on Diplomatic Relations produced by the 1961 UN Conference on Diplomatic Intercourse and Immunities, the five main legitimate functions of any diplomatic mission are representation, or acting on behalf of a state in a legal sense as well as ceremonially and socially; protection of a state's interests and its nationals in a host country; negotiation, or conferring together in order to produce and prepare treaties or other formal agreements; observation, or ascertaining "by all lawful means" and duly reporting on the relevant conditions and developments in the host country; and the promotion of friendly relations, including cooperation and exchanges in the economic, cultural, and scientific fields.

It is only rarely that diplomacy can achieve all of the purposes that it may be expected to serve, foremost of which is the preservation of peace. Many U.S. commentators have considered the diplomatic craft, as historically developed by European diplomats, inadequate to this high task. President Woodrow Wilson, a liberal intellectual, launched a broad attack on traditional diplomacy, faulting it especially for its secrecy, hidden understandings, and tendency to arouse suspicion. He even considered it conducive to war. The first of his famous Fourteen Points, announced on 8 January 1918, proposed "open covenants of peace, openly arrived at, after which there shall be no private international understandings of any kind but diplomacy shall proceed always frankly and in the public view." Although Wilson himself, as head of the U.S. commission to the 1919 Paris Peace Conference, conducted numerous confidential negotiations in strictly closed sessions, he remained firm in his conviction that the fruits of all such discussions ought to be publicized and thereafter deemed part of the public law of the world. He proposed that all future treaties be registered with the League of Nations; virtually by definition, secret treaties would be invalid. Wilson's "new diplomacy," as it was then called, remains the most characteristically American attempt at diplomatic reform. Wilson's basic idea—that worldwide public opinion can be the support, and also the punitive sanction, for maintaining international order—is the essence of the modern theory of collective security.

Public Diplomacy and Parliamentary Diplomacy

Faith in the organized opinion of mankind, or the expressed will of the international community, also lies at the root of what the U.S. government and an increasing number of other governments now call public diplomacy. Such diplomacy is defined as the use by governments of press reportage, the electronic mass media, and other open channels of communication to reach both the influential elites and the general populations of foreign countries in order, directly if not indirectly, to cause their governments to modify their behavior in desired ways. The new technology of global communications, mostly commercially owned and directed, challenges the diplomatic craft. It can be used to extend the spatial and social scope of diplomacy, but because it is largely autonomous and beyond government control, it also threatens to make the practice of diplomacy irrelevant. For professional diplomats, information management is therefore arguably as important for success as the traditional art of negotiation.

No less significant for the continuing evolution of diplomatic method is another, even more distinctively Wilsonian concept: the legitimization of international decisions by passage through a world organization, initially the League of Nations, today the United Nations. This concept has produced what Dean Rusk, secretary of state from 1961 to 1969, was the first to call parliamentary diplomacy. A quasi-legislative procedure, combining the somewhat incongruous elements of debate and persuasion, parliamentary diplomacy produces not so much adjustments of immediate issues (decisions) as sets of rules, even entire systems (regimes) for long-term multilateral cooperation in various spheres.

In order to avoid the divisiveness of majority voting or use of the veto possessed by the United States and four other permanent members of the UN Security Council, a new diplomacy of consensus-building is being developed. Through the consensus procedure, joint conclusions are arrived at consultatively, among especially interested parties, and formal votes are not taken until a generally accepted, fully detailed accord emerges, frequently on the basis of a single negotiating text. This technique was demonstrated impressively during the negotiation of the UN Convention on the Law of the Sea (1982) and has often been employed subsequently. Some observers argue that, especially in the aftermath of the Cold War, with national security concerns and political-ideological differences reduced, consensus-building diplomacy and other cooperative negotiations establishing world order may become more dominant diplomatic methods.

ALAN K. HENRIKSON

See also Ambassadors and Embassies; Bosnia-Herzegovina; Bretton Woods System; Camp David Accords; Carter, James Earl; Coercive Diplomacy; Collective Security; Cuban Missile Crisis; Cultural Diplomacy; Earth Summit; Executive Agents; Fourteen Points; General Agreement on Tariffs and Trade; Gorbachev, Mikhail Sergeevich; Group of Seven; Helsinki Accords;

Hot Line Agreements; International Bank for Reconstruction and Development; International Monetary Fund; Law of the Sea; Kissinger, Henry Alfred; Morgenthau, Hans; Namibia; Nongovernmental Organizations; Reagan, Ronald Wilson; Serbia; Strategic Arms Limitation Talks and Agreements; Telecommunication Companies; United Nations; Wilson, Thomas Woodrow; World Trade Organization

FURTHER READING

Bailey, Thomas A. *The Art of Diplomacy: The American Experience.* New York, 1968.

Eban, Abba. *The New Diplomacy: International Affairs in the Modern Age.* New York, 1983.

Eldon, Stewart. *From Quill Pen to Satellite: Foreign Ministries in the Information Age.* London, 1994.

George, Alexander L. *Forceful Persuasion: Coercive Diplomacy as an Alternative to War.* Washington, D.C., 1992.

George, Alexander L., ed. *Avoiding War: Problems of Crisis Management.* Boulder, Colo., 1991.

Hampson, Fen Osler and Michael Hart. *Multilateral Negotiations: Lessons from Arms Control, Trade, and the Environment.* Baltimore, Md., 1995.

Henrikson, Alan K., ed. *Negotiating World Order: The Artisanship and Architecture of Global Diplomacy.* Wilmington, Del., 1986.

Iklé, Fred Charles. *How Nations Negotiate.* New York, 1964.

Karns, Margaret P. "Ad Hoc Multilateral Diplomacy: The United States, the Contact Group, and Namibia." *International Organization* 41 (Winter 1987): 93–123.

Kennan, George F. *American Diplomacy, 1900–1950.* Chicago, 1951.

Kissinger, Henry. *Diplomacy.* New York, 1994.

Morgenthau, Hans J. *Politics Among Nations: The Struggle for Power and Peace,* 6th ed. New York, 1985.

Nicolson, Harold. *Diplomacy,* 3rd ed. New York, 1963.

Putnam, Robert D. *Hanging Together: Cooperation and Conflict in the Seven-Power Summits.* Cambridge, Mass., 1987.

Quandt, William B. *Camp David: Peacemaking and Politics.* Washington, D.C., 1986.

DISTANT EARLY WARNING (DEW) LINE

A chain of radar installations within the Arctic Circle and across Alaska, Canada, and Greenland, erected in the 1950s to track incoming Soviet nuclear bombers. With the explosion of a Soviet thermonuclear device in 1953 and evidence that the Soviet Union was developing intercontinental jet bombers in 1954, the United States and Canada formed the North American Aerospace Defense Command and began developing a far-flung continental air defense system. The DEW line, completed in 1957, was the first line of detection in the U.S. air defense system, the first of three proposed main radar lines. It consisted of seventy-eight radar sites strung across the edge of the Arctic Ocean. The system reflected the belief, held by the administration of President Dwight D. Eisenhower, that defensive deployments would maintain U.S. strategic supremacy and preserve the credibility of the U.S. deterrent. Continental air defense

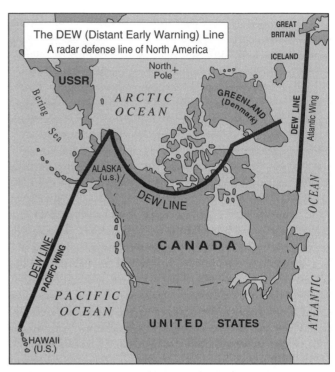

From "radar," Robert Morris Page. In *Merit Students Encyclopedia,* Volume 15. ©1991 by Macmillan Educational Company. Reprinted with permission of the publisher.

received a severe blow when the Soviet Union launched the satellite Sputnik in 1957. Defense against bombers meant little if the Soviet Union could attack the United States with intercontinental ballistic missiles. The effort to establish a system of continental air defense came to an end at the close of the 1950s, although many of its existing elements, like the obsolete DEW line, stayed in place. In the mid-1980s plans were initiated to replace the DEW line with a North Warning System, which would provide defense against cruise missiles and low-observable aircraft, and work in this area continued into the mid-1990s, although interest in the problem of vulnerability to an attack by cruise missiles was difficult to sustain with the end of the Cold War.

EMILY O. GOLDMAN

See also Canada; Greenland; Nuclear Weapons and Strategy; Sputnik I

FURTHER READING

Bruce-Briggs, B. *The Shield of Faith: A Chronicle of Strategic Defense from Zeppelins to Star Wars.* New York, 1988.

Carter, Ashton B., John D. Steinbruner, and Charles A. Zraket, eds. *Managing Nuclear Operations.* Washington, D.C., 1987.

Morenus, Richard. *DEW Line: Distant Early Warning, The Miracle of America's First Line of Defense.* New York, 1957.

DJIBOUTI

See Appendix 2

DODD, WILLIAM EDWARD

(*b.* 21 October 1869; *d.* 9 February 1940)

Noted historian of the American South and U.S. ambassador to Germany (1933–1937). Born in North Carolina, Dodd graduated from Virginia Polytechnic Institute in 1895 and received a Ph.D. in history from the University of Leipzig in 1900. He began his college teaching career at Randolph-Macon College in Virginia and accepted a professorship at the University of Chicago, where he specialized in the history of the American South. As a pioneer in this field, he wrote *The Cotton Kingdom: A Chronicle of the Old South* (1919), *Lincoln and Lee: Comparison and Contrast of the Two Greatest Leaders in the War Between the States* (1928), and *The Old South: Struggles for Democracy* (1937). His primary thesis was that the antebellum South had strayed from the democracy of Thomas Jefferson toward a society controlled by a planter aristocracy. Dodd was a political consultant to President Woodrow Wilson and became active in Democratic politics by the 1920s. In 1933 President Franklin D. Roosevelt hoped to capitalize on Dodd's German ties and appointed him ambassador to Germany. Although Dodd had admired Germany during his university days, he became highly critical, publicly and privately, of Adolf Hitler and the Nazi regime. Roosevelt hoped that Dodd would serve as an ameliorating influence on the Nazis, but Dodd warned the Roosevelt administration that Nazi Germany sought to dominate Europe and that Germany assumed that the United States would not intervene to prevent Nazi expansion. Dodd's criticisms of German policies, his difficulties with the Department of State over his undiplomatic position toward countries he considered undemocratic, and a host of embassy personnel problems resulting from his frugality, led to his recall in 1937.

LOUIS R. SMITH, JR.

See also Germany; Hitler, Adolf; Jefferson, Thomas; Roosevelt, Franklin Delano; Wilson, Thomas Woodrow

FURTHER READING

Dallek, Robert. *Democrat and Diplomat: The Life of William E. Dodd.* New York, 1968.
Offner, Arnold A. *American Appeasement: United States Foreign Policy and Germany, 1933–1938.* Cambridge, Mass., 1969.

DOLLAR DIPLOMACY

A term coined during the administration of President William Howard Taft (1909–1913) to describe efforts to advance U.S. objectives through the use of economic power. President Theodore Roosevelt laid the groundwork for this policy in 1905 with his Roosevelt Corollary to the Monroe Doctrine, which asserted a right of intervention in financially unstable Western Hemisphere nations that might be vulnerable to European control. The Taft administration extended that policy in both Latin America and China, supporting U.S. business expansion as a key instrument of U.S. influence and as a means of "substituting dollars for bullets." In Latin America dollar diplomacy was motivated by a desire to safeguard the Panama Canal as well as to promote U.S. financial predominance in the Caribbean region. The clearest example occurred in Nicaragua, which was of particular interest because of its potential as an alternative canal route. When the Nicaraguan government resisted demands to use U.S. rather than European banks to refinance its foreign debt, Washington helped engineer a successful rebellion and in 1910 negotiated a debt refunding with payment to be secured by a customs receivership under U.S. protection. Similar interventions also occurred in the Dominican Republic, Guatemala, Haiti, and Honduras. In China, the administration persuaded U.S. bankers to participate in the financing of railway construction projects in order to undercut Japanese and Russian influence and increase U.S. investment opportunities. Taft's dollar diplomacy fomented considerable resentment in Latin America and was formally repudiated by subsequent presidents, although the promotion of commercial interests and use of economic resources to attain political objectives remained enduring characteristics of U.S. foreign policy.

BENJAMIN J. COHEN

See also Nicaragua; Roosevelt, Theodore; Taft, William Howard

FURTHER READING

Munro, Dana G. *Intervention and Dollar Diplomacy in the Caribbean, 1900–1921.* Princeton, N.J., 1964.
Nearing, Scott, and Joseph Freeman. *Dollar Diplomacy: A Study in American Imperialism.* New York, 1925.

DOMINICA

See Appendix 2

DOMINICAN REPUBLIC

A nation located in the northern Caribbean Sea, about halfway between Cuba and Puerto Rico, occupying the eastern two-thirds of the island of Hispaniola (with Haiti occupying the western third). Its Spanish-speaking, predominantly Catholic and mulatto population of about 7.6 million shares a tenuous and oftentimes contested border with Haiti. Small in size but rich in natural resources, the Dominican Republic has been plagued by foreign meddling and intervention, political instability and corruption, and dictatorial or authoritarian rule throughout its history as an independent country. Since the middle of the nineteenth century, the United States has played a major, often determining, role in the fate of the Dominican people.

The First Republic and Spanish Annexation: 1844–1865

Living in a neglected Spanish colony, the Dominican people gained their independence almost by default in 1821. Within a few weeks, however, Haitian forces invaded the infant republic and reunified the island under Haitian rule until 1844, when various Dominican separatist movements coalesced to oust the Haitians. Following the Dominican declaration of independence on 27 February 1844, France remained the most aggressive nation in the quest for concessions and territorial rights in the struggling Dominican Republic.

During the early 1850s U.S. expansionism transformed and intensified the international rivalry over the Dominican Republic. The European powers continued to check each other's moves but became increasingly concerned with U.S. expansionist threats. While the British sought to preserve the status quo, which guaranteed them commercial domination over the Dominican Republic, France's policy became less aggressive and increasingly defensive, rejecting numerous Dominican offers to establish a protectorate. The year 1854 was a pivotal one. U.S. president Franklin Pierce embarked on two expansionist projects—seeking to acquire Cuba and territorial concessions in the Dominican Republic. In June Secretary of State William L. Marcy dispatched envoy William L. Cazneau with instructions to negotiate the recognition of the Dominican Republic in exchange for the cession of a coaling station in Samaná Bay, one of the hemisphere's finest bays. Cazneau's arrival in Santo Domingo caused immediate concern among European consular agents, who mobilized to block the proposed treaty, which they did through manipulation of racial fears.

The growing political crisis in the United States, which led to the Civil War, temporarily reversed the trend of growing U.S. influence over the Dominican Republic. The outbreak of the Civil War in 1861 moved the region's geopolitical clock back ten to twelve years, enabling the European naval powers once again to take the offensive in the Caribbean and Mexico. Ironically, the Spanish annexation of the Dominican Republic in 1861 found its greatest supporter in Dominican military leader Pedro Santana. Until the late 1850s Santana had been an ardent promoter of concessions to or annexation by the United States, but after 1859, when annexation to the United States was no longer plausible, he turned his attention to Spain. On 18 March 1861 Santana publicly declared his nation's annexation to Spain. Within two months, with war raging in the United States, Spain formally annexed the Dominican Republic, but Spain's intolerance, arbitrary government, and discrimination against Dominican nationals fueled an all-out rebellion against Spanish rule. Not coincidentally, on 3 March 1865, just a few weeks before the end of the U.S. Civil War, the queen of Spain issued a decree to abandon Santo Domingo.

The Second Republic: 1865–1916

The assassination of President Abraham Lincoln and the presidency of Andrew Johnson, a successor of lesser stature with a weak political base, obstructed the implementation of a coherent U.S. policy toward the Caribbean during the early years of Reconstruction in the United States. The Civil War, however, had made clear the importance of naval warfare, demonstrating that naval bases in the Caribbean could, in the future, determine the outcome of a confrontation with any of the European powers. Johnson, Secretary of State William H. Seward, and other expansionists focused on the acquisition of naval stations to protect commercial routes, particularly the projected isthmian route across Central America. This new brand of U.S. expansionism did not seek to annex or absorb large tropical territories and their populations; instead, Washington sought outposts for the protection of a commercial empire and eventually the establishment of corporate enclaves for the extraction of raw materials and the cultivation of tropical staples.

In the winter of 1866 Secretary of State Seward, the architect of the new global expansionism, toured the Caribbean in search of suitable locations for coaling stations and naval bases. He later sent his assistant, Frederick W. Seward, and Admiral David D. Porter to negotiate the purchase or lease of territory in the much-coveted Samaná Bay area. Dominican president Buenaventura Báez proved eager to swap a strip of Samaná for guns and cash, which he needed to fight an insurgent opposition. He was even willing to annex the entire country to the United States, but these efforts failed because of staunch congressional opposition in the United States and nationalistic opposition within the Dominican Republic. The United States finally recognized the Dominican Republic in 1866.

A new round of negotiations for the acquisition of territory in the Dominican Republic took place during the administration of President Ulysses S. Grant, but in 1870 and 1871 Congress rejected Grant's plans. His administration then proceeded to back the annexationist schemes of the Samaná Bay Company, a private speculative venture that successfully negotiated sovereignty over Samaná under a 100-year lease at $150,000 per year. Thus, as of 1 January 1873, Samaná became an unofficial

U.S. enclave. Later that year, however, anti-Báez insurgents took power and rescinded the lease.

During the seventeen years of iron-fisted rule and political dominance of General Ulises Heureaux (1882–1899), however, U.S. capital and commerce made significant inroads in the Dominican Republic, transforming its economy into one based predominantly on the export of sugar, and in the process displacing the republic's traditional European markets and sources of credit. Reciprocity treaties negotiated between the United States and the Dominican Republic in the 1880s and early 1890s reflected and supported the new commercial realities. In 1892 the New York–based San Domingo Improvement Company acquired control over Dominican customhouses previously held by a now-bankrupt Dutch company as security for Dominican debt. Heureaux was assassinated in 1899, leaving behind a country with a debt of $34.1 million, whose customhouses were liable to foreign control, and whose economy was increasingly part of North America's "new empire."

With their interests threatened by this new U.S. dominance, European bondholders pushed their governments to press for repayment. As a show of force, European warships were dispatched to Dominican waters in 1900 and 1903. In December 1904 the French government threatened to confiscate a portion of Dominican revenues by taking over the customhouses. President Theodore Roosevelt stood up to these challenges. Indeed, the situation in the Dominican Republic was a key factor in the 1904 Roosevelt Corollary to the Monroe Doctrine. In February 1905 an agreement was reached whereby Dominican customs would come under the direct control of U.S. officials, who would keep 55 percent of the receipts to make payments toward the Dominican debt and to run the customhouses and give the remaining 45 percent to the Dominican government for operating expenses. When the U.S. Senate rejected the agreement, Roosevelt bypassed the Senate in the name of "modus vivendi" and the treaty's provisions went into effect in April 1905. The modus vivendi further eroded Dominican autonomy, because it established that the Dominican government could not alter its tariff structure nor engage in new loan negotiations without the approval of the U.S. president.

In 1906 the U.S. government arranged for Dominican external and internal debts to be renegotiated, cut in about half, and consolidated under a new loan from Kuhn, Loeb, and Company of New York. In February 1907 the 1905 agreement was slightly modified, finally approved by the U.S. Senate, and elevated to treaty status, and Dominican customhouses came under the control of the U.S. Bureau of Insular Affairs. Much to the satisfaction of U.S. interests, Ramón Cáceres, who became president in December 1905, managed to establish a semblance of stability and economic prosperity, making considerable advances toward the payment of the national debt and the development of a national infrastructure. An assassin's bullet brought the Cáceres regime to a sudden end on 19 November 1911.

The state of political anarchy that followed Cáceres's demise threatened to dismantle the financial stability that U.S. pressures had secured since 1905. President William H. Taft ordered 750 troops landed in the Dominican Republic in September 1912, ostensibly to support a commission of peace negotiators, but political instability continued to plague the republic and became more intense as some local military leaders rallied in opposition to the U.S. military presence. President Woodrow Wilson's administration continued to pursue his predecessor's objectives of financial control with greater zeal, adding to the U.S. policy agenda the goal of establishing an effective, responsible, and, he hoped, democratic, government in the Dominican Republic. Facing the humiliating threat of large-scale deployments of U.S. troops, President Juan Isidro Jimenes stepped down in May 1916. Within a few days 700 more U.S. troops landed in Santo Domingo, gained control of the capital city and took charge of national finances. On 29 November 1916 Captain Harry S. Knapp, commander of the invading U.S. forces, declared U.S. military rule over the Dominican Republic.

The U.S. Occupation: 1916–1924

The occupation of the Dominican Republic was not an isolated event but part of a pattern of U.S. policies in the Caribbean that, not coincidentally, peaked during World War I, when secure access to the recently opened Panama Canal became of paramount commercial and military importance. The most immediate goal of the occupying forces was to pacify the republic and rid it of the strife caused by regional military leaders. The U.S. military government launched a disarmament campaign, in conjunction with an effort to train a professional, national military force that would not be susceptible to the ambitions of local military leaders. The occupied republic was eventually pacified and its population disarmed, but the goal of establishing an apolitical military failed, which would become painfully evident in the years following the withdrawal of U.S. troops.

The military government also made efforts to develop the country's infrastructure and to improve its educational and sanitary conditions. Considerable advances were made in the area of public works and infrastructure, including the construction of roads that linked the country's major cities. These projects were made possible by the extraordinary revenues entering the Dominican Republic during World War I, when the value of Dominican exports soared. The occupation government also had the capacity to finance such projects with loans previously unobtainable by Dominican governments. In the areas of education and sanitation, however, the military government had a mixed record and produced few long-term achievements. Many of its actions favored the sugar industry and commerce with the United States over other agricultural activities and exchange with other foreign markets. In 1920 a new tariff arrangement facilitated trade between the Dominican Republic and the United States by placing many items on the free trade list. Later that year an executive order effectively ended the ancient practice of access to common lands by requiring the surveying and titling of the Dominican territory. This measure further promoted the expansion of the sugar estates, an increasing number of which were U.S.-owned. During the eight years of occupation, U.S. capital came to control most of the sugar industry and about one-fourth of the agricultural land.

Opposition to the U.S. occupation came from two major sources: the *gavilleros*, peasant and sugar worker guerrillas; and the urban-based, nationalist intelligentsia. *Gavillero* resistance surfaced in the eastern provinces of El Seibo and San Pedro de Macorís, where U.S. agricultural capital and the new land tenure legislation threatened the subsistence of large segments of the traditional peasantry. Several instances of abuse and torture of *gavilleros* and civilians at the hands of U.S. servicemen were denounced and later confirmed in special hearings in the U.S. Senate. The opposition of the urban intelligentsia, which in the end led to the withdrawal of U.S. forces, unleashed an unrelenting domestic and international campaign denouncing the U.S. occupation. Nationalist agitation intensified in 1920, when, following several years of economic bonanza and high agricultural prices, the value of Dominican exports hit rock bottom in the postwar depression. At this point many of the military government's educational and sanitation programs came to a halt. On 24 December 1920 the military governor, Thomas Snowden, announced U.S. plans to withdraw its occupation forces.

In December 1920 the Wilson administration presented the first of several evacuation plans. Dominican leaders rejected it, fearing the vagueness of its terms. A year later they also rejected President Warren G. Harding's plan. Both the Wilson and the Harding plans insisted on the validation of the acts of the military occupation, including its contracts and loans. Nationalists still dominated the Dominican side of the negotiations and demanded a "pure and simple" withdrawal. Faced with this impasse, Dominican cabinet member Francisco J. Peynado and U.S. officials, including Secretary of State Charles Evans Hughes, negotiated in 1922 another withdrawal plan. The provisions of the Hughes-Peynado Plan were not too different from earlier ones, in that they validated the loans taken by the military government and

ratified the 1907 customs receivership. The plan also established the mechanisms for a transitional government and the eventual election of a constitutional president in 1924. While some nationalists remained opposed to the plan, Horacio Vásquez, Luis F. Vidal, Federico Velásquez, and other national leaders accepted the plan, which was signed on 19 September 1922. Within two years all U.S. troops were gone, Vásquez sat in the presidential palace, and the U.S.-created national military held a virtual monopoly on the use of force.

The Trujillo Era: 1930–1961

In the wake of the U.S. withdrawal, Rafael Leónidas Trujillo Molina, who had joined the new constabulary in 1918, became chief of the Dominican National Army, in which capacity he amassed a considerable personal fortune derived from a series of contracts to supply the armed forces under his own command and soon mounted a full-scale insurrection. When the U.S. government warned Trujillo that it would not recognize any government that reached power through the use of force, Trujillo got around this obstacle by winning a fraudulent election. Soon thereafter Trujillo vanquished his remaining opponents and received formal recognition from the United States.

Trujillo assumed dictatorial powers and expanded his fortune by granting lucrative state monopolies to himself and his relatives. In part because his personal finances and those of the state were so deeply intertwined, Trujillo assumed certain protectionist and nationalistic postures with regard to national finances and international trade. As early as 1931 he tried unsuccessfully to regain control of the customs and later raised tariffs to protect some incipient Dominican industries. In 1940–1941 Trujillo negotiated the Trujillo-Hull Treaty that terminated direct U.S. control over Dominican customs receipts. Some limitations to Dominican financial freedom remained, however, until 1947, when Trujillo paid off the country's foreign debt. His personal wealth continued to grow, reaching $800 million at the time of his death in 1961. Trujillo's relations with the United States were for the most part harmonious and cooperative. His regime fulfilled the role of a stable ally, but his orders to massacre thousands of Haitians along the Dominican-Haitian border in 1937 produced an international outcry that also drew protests from the Franklin D. Roosevelt administration. This genocidal episode was forgotten during World War II, when Trujillo proved a loyal and useful ally of the United States. During the early years of the Cold War, Trujillo's services became even more valuable to the presidencies of Harry S. Truman and Dwight D. Eisenhower.

The tentacles of Trujillo's bloody regime extended far beyond Dominican borders, as exemplified by the 1956 kidnapping in New York City of Jesús Galíndez, a Spanish-born Columbia University professor who was openly critical of Trujillo's rule. Galíndez was taken to the Dominican Republic and tortured and killed. This extension of Trujilloist terror to the streets of New York marked the internationalization of the dictator's political agenda. Trujillo came to view himself as the Caribbean's defender of traditional conservative values, which he believed were under assault from the region's so-called democratic left and, after 1959, from the socialist government of Cuba's Fidel Castro. On 14 June 1959 nearly 200 Dominican patriots invaded Dominican territory from Cuba with the support of Castro and Venezuela's President Rómulo Betancourt. They were immediately defeated by Trujillo's forces. Discovering a large opposition movement, Trujillo unleashed a brutal wave of torture and murder that moved the Catholic hierarchy, a long-time supporter of his regime, to criticize openly his escalating excesses. Feeling increasingly isolated and under siege, Trujillo plotted to assassinate Betancourt, which outraged other Latin American leaders and led to the imposition of economic sanctions by the Organization of American States (OAS).

By 1958 the Eisenhower administration had reevaluated its position toward Trujillo, who had overstepped the acceptable bounds of domestic and international behavior. The new thinking in the Eisenhower and later John F. Kennedy administrations was that rather than an ally against communism, Trujillo had become a threat that could lead to the establishment of another Fidel Castro in the heart of the Caribbean. According to information uncovered by Bernard Diederich and others, by 1958 the U.S. government began to support and arm conspirators seeking to overthrow the aging tyrant. Trujillo's propaganda machine attacked the United States, further souring U.S. relations, while Trujillo flirted with the communist bloc and threatened to nationalize the assets of U.S. firms. On the night of 30 May 1961 a small band of conspirators assassinated Trujillo. Their army contacts, however, failed to mobilize the anti-Trujillo forces into a position of control. The fallen dictator's oldest son and heir apparent, Ramfis, returned from Paris in an attempt to maintain the Trujillo regime. While Trujillo's agents tortured and killed scores of conspirators and suspects, Joaquín Balaguer served as the nominal chief executive under the direction of the military. Unable to maintain order and control over the situation, Ramfis and most of the Trujillo clan fled in late 1961. In February 1962 Balaguer sought asylum at the Papal Nunciature and later went into exile.

Civil War, U.S. Intervention, and Aftermath: 1965–1995

In the wake of Trujillo's fall, a myriad of political groupings sought power. The most influential of these was the Union Cívica Nacional (UCN), which represented the country's conservative elites. This organization dominated the Council of State that ruled after Balaguer. Not as powerful economically, but with mass support and better political organization, was the Partido Revolucionario Dominicano (PRD), led by long-time exile Juan Bosch. To the left of the PRD were various groups, among them the June 14 Movement, which advocated armed insurrection and had ties to Castro's regime. The momentarily obscured and somewhat moderated old Trujilloist bureaucratic sectors remained a political force under the leadership of Balaguer. Bosch's PRD defeated the UCN by a two-to-one margin in the December 1962 elections.

U.S. policymakers of John F. Kennedy and Lyndon B. Johnson's administrations paid very close attention to developments in the Dominican Republic, particularly in the light of Castro's consolidation of a socialist dictatorship in neighboring Cuba. U.S. warships were deployed near Dominican waters in the summer and fall of 1961 to intervene, if necessary, if the post-Trujillo transition degenerated into anarchy. Kennedy preferred to see a liberal and democratic government in the republic, but he was not optimistic about its chances of success. He was, however, adamantly opposed to the establishment of another Castro-type regime in the Caribbean and his advisers and envoys to Santo Domingo favored alternatives that were least likely to generate such an outcome. Upon taking office as president in February 1963, Bosch demonstrated a great degree of independence from U.S. advisers and did not show the anticommunist inclinations of his predecessors. On 25 September 1963 a military coup, with the backing of the UCN, the church, and business sectors, ousted Bosch. According to political scientist Howard J. Wiarda, there is some indication of U.S. involvement in the coup. In any case, following the assassination of Kennedy in November, President Johnson recognized the conservative triumvirate that succeeded Bosch. The triumvirate's leader, Donald Reid Cabral, enjoyed the support of the Johnson administration and the U.S. ambassador in Santo Domingo, William Tapley Bennett.

On 24 April 1965 a countercoup erupted when some divisions of the Dominican armed forces mobilized to reestablish Bosch as the constitutionally elected president. There was no real coordination, however, between the constitutionalist officers and the leaders of the PRD and the June 14 Movement. Entrepreneur Reid Cabral and the so-called loyalist military leadership called for U.S. troop deployments, apparently at the insistence of U.S. Ambassador John Bartlow Martin. On 28 April, following a major Constitutionalist victory under Colonel Francisco A. Caamaño Deñó, 500 U.S. Marines landed in Santo Domingo, ostensibly to protect U.S. lives and property. By then most of the principal PRD leaders had fled into exile or sought asylum, but the Constitutionalist forces had shown their military capacity and proven that they enjoyed popular support in the streets of Santo Domingo.

By sending in U.S. troops, President Johnson and his foreign policy team acted out of the conviction that communists were directing the Constitutionalist insurrection. On 2 May, Johnson announced further troop deployments and proclaimed what came to be known as the Johnson Doctrine: "The American nations cannot, must not, and will not permit the establishment of another communist government in the Western Hemisphere." By 24 May more that 20,000 U.S. troops and a token inter-American peace force had invaded Dominican territory and were fighting to bring the capital city under control.

On 3 September 1965 the U.S.-backed provisional government of Héctor García Godoy was in place, and elections for a new constitutional president were scheduled for 1 June 1966. Bosch remained an unacceptable option in the eyes of the Johnson administration, which perceived Balaguer as the best hope for stability. With U.S. troops still occupying their country, Dominican voters also viewed Balaguer as the candidate most conducive to peace, and he was elected president. With a blend of paternalism and authoritarianism, Balaguer ruled the Dominican Republic until 1978. During this period of relative political stability, U.S. corporate capital and military assistance grew exponentially. When the PRD's Silvestre Antonio Guzmán Fernández won the presidency in the 1978 elections, elements within the Dominican military seized scores of ballot boxes and threatened to block the PRD's ascent to power. Only after President Jimmy Carter used the threat of economic sanctions did the military allow for a peaceful governmental transition.

Guzmán and, to a much greater extent his successor, Salvador Jorge Blanco, also of the PRD, faced the combined crises of falling sugar prices and rising oil prices, along with increasing pressures from the International Monetary Fund (IMF). The situation worsened in 1985, when the United States cut the Dominican sugar quota by 48 percent. Following riots and other manifestations of popular unrest, Dominican voters returned Balaguer to the presidency in 1986 and reelected him in 1990. Between 1986 and 1994 he successfully promoted further foreign investment and expanded the incentives and facilities for foreign-owned manufacturing ventures. Despite charges of widespread electoral fraud, the eighty-seven-year-old Balaguer was reelected in 1994, although by a very small margin. The opposition PRD party and its leader José Francisco Peña Gómez challenged the results and the U.S. Department of State brought pressure for new elections. A few weeks into the crisis, Balaguer and Peña Gómez agreed to accept the results but to hold new presidential elections ahead of schedule in May 1996.

The economies of the Dominican Republic and the United States became increasingly intertwined and the links between the two countries more and more diversified. According to 1991 statistics, trade with the United States accounted for 46 percent of Dominican imports and 56 percent of exports. Sugar accounted for only a small portion of this trade. Another vital and growing link between the Dominican Republic and the United States consisted of the almost 1 million legal and undocumented Dominicans residing in U.S. territory, most of them in New York City and San Juan, Puerto Rico.

Luis Martínez-Fernández

See also Caribbean Basin Initiative; Cuba; Haiti; Inter-American Development Bank; International Monetary Fund; Johnson, Lyndon Baines; Kennedy, John Fitzgerald; Marine Corps, U.S.; Monroe Doctrine; Pan-Americanism; Trujillo Molina, Rafael Leónidas; Wilson, Thomas Woodrow

FURTHER READING

Calder, Bruce J. *The Impact of Intervention: The Occupation of the Dominican Republic During the U.S. Occupation of 1916–1924.* Austin, Tex., 1984.
Diederich, Bernard. *Trujillo: The Death of the Goat.* Maplewood, N.J., 1990.
Gleijeses, Piero. *The Dominican Crisis: The 1965 Constitutionalist Revolt and American Intervention.* Baltimore, 1978.
Kryzanek, Michael J., and Howard J. Wiarda. *The Politics of External Influence in the Dominican Republic.* New York, 1988.
Lowenthal, Abraham F. *The Dominican Intervention.* Cambridge, Mass., 1972.
Martínez–Fernández, Luis. *Torn Between Empires: Economy, Society, and Patterns of Political Thought in the Hispanic Caribbean, 1840–1878.* Athens, Ga., 1994.
Moya Pons, Frank. *The Dominican Republic: A National History.* New Rochelle, N.Y., 1995.
Vega, Bernardo. *Kennedy y los Trujillo.* Santo Domingo, 1991.
Welles, Sumner. *Naboth's Vineyard: The Dominican Republic, 1844–1924,* 2 vols. New York, 1928.
Wiarda, Howard J. *The Dominican Republic: A Caribbean Crucible,* 2nd ed. Boulder, Colo., 1992.

DOMINO THEORY

A term derived from President Dwight D. Eisenhower's comments at a press conference on 7 April 1954, when he gave the rationale for U.S. commitment to a noncommunist Vietnam. Eisenhower declared that if the United States did not block the communists there, a domino effect would result. "You have a row of dominoes set up," he said. "You knock over the first one, and what will happen to the last one is the certainty that it will go over very quickly. So you could have a beginning of a disintegration that would have the most profound influences." Eisenhower's infelicitous rhetoric did not result in his sending U.S. troops to Vietnam, but his conception of the need for the United States to prevent "dominoes" from falling throughout the world remained the standard response by U.S. policymakers from Eisenhower to President Richard M. Nixon as to why the United States intervened in Vietnam. The United States, some officials remarked, was the last domino.

Combined with the theory of containment, the domino theory resulted in a sustained belief that communism must be confronted at all costs and, consequently, that negotiations were either pointless or would lead to Munich-like appeasements. Throughout the early and middle stages of the Cold War, no presidential administration challenged these tenets, not only because they believed they were correct, but because they feared that their administrations might be accused of letting another country—like China in 1949—be lost to communism. In this sense, each administration feared that their most important domino might fall, that is, they might lose the White House to the opposition party.

The problem remains that while Eisenhower's statement is the classic summary of the "domino theory," it is an historically pinched reading of the origins and dynamics of the term. Eisenhower's last sentence in which he talked about "disintegration" points to issues that transcend the Vietnam War; it succinctly deals with the nature of U.S. foreign policy in the twentieth century. Variations of the domino theory abound in U.S. history. President Woodrow Wilson's belief that the United States had a moral duty to "make the world safe for democracy" led to U.S. interventions in the Mexican and Russian civil wars out of a fear that these were "bad" revolutions and would infect neighboring countries. In March 1947, when Dean Acheson, then an undersecretary of state, informed congressional leaders that the United States needed to come to the aid of Greece, he likened communism to "rotten apples" that would spread from one country to the next if the United States did nothing to prevent the process from starting. The key idea was both to preserve political states and economic systems conducive to U.S. interests and to challenge revolutionary or communist regimes. In the 1980s such thinking on the part of President Ronald Reagan's administration lay behind U.S. interventionist policies in Central America. Symptomatic of this historical problem is the question of language. Nation-states, and thus the people who lived in them, were being transformed into game pieces by American policymakers. Dominoes were just a crude analogy for this form of politics. The lasting power of the domino theory was in its power to communicate a complex foreign policy to the American people. An extremely easy image to understand, the domino theory proved attractive to U.S. policymakers when they proclaimed the whys and wherefores of U.S. actions abroad.

JONATHAN NASHEL

See also Cambodia; Communism; Containment; El Salvador; Greece; Laos; Nicaragua; Thailand; Vietnam

FURTHER READING

Ambrose, Stephen. *Eisenhower*, 2 vols. New York, 1983–1985.
Gelb, Leslie H., and Richard K. Betts. *The Irony of Vietnam: The System Worked*. Washington, D.C., 1979.
Gibbons, William Conrad. *The U.S. Government and the Vietnam War: Executive and Legislative Roles and Relationships*, 2 vols. Princeton, N.J., 1986.
Hogan, Michael J. and Thomas G. Paterson, ed. *Explaining the History of American Foreign Relations*. New York, 1991.

DONOVAN, WILLIAM JOSEPH

(*b.* 1 January 1883; *d.* 8 February 1959)

Army officer and founder and director of the World War II Office of Strategic Services (OSS). Born in Buffalo, New York, Donovan received his bachelor's (1905) and law (1912) degrees from Columbia University. His charisma and apparent fearlessness as a colonel in World War I earned him the nickname "Wild Bill," and he was awarded the Medal of Honor for his distinguished service in the war. He subsequently pursued a career in law and politics until the outbreak of World War II. In 1941 President Franklin D. Roosevelt chose Donovan to design and administer a new foreign intelligence agency, and Donovan created the OSS in 1942. Although OSS operations gathered valuable information on Axis troop movements and fortifications in southern France, inexperience and interagency rivalry limited the organization's effectiveness. Donovan recommended that the OSS be continued after the war, and although it was disbanded in September 1945, it laid the groundwork for covert action and the establishment of the Central Intelligence Agency (CIA). After the war, Donovan served under Supreme Court Justice Robert H. Jackson at the Nuremberg trials, and then returned to private law practice, followed by his appointment as U.S. ambassador to Thailand in 1953. Donovan left government service in 1954, but several of his protégés were founding members of the CIA.

CHARLES D. McGRAW

See also Central Intelligence Agency; Nuremberg, International Military Tribunal at; Office of Strategic Services; World War II

FURTHER READING

Brown, Anthony Cave. *The Last Hero: Wild Bill Donovan*. New York, 1982.
Dunlop, Richard. *Donovan: America's Master Spy*. New York, 1982.

DOUGLAS, LEWIS WILLIAMS

(*b.* 2 July 1894; *d.* 7 March 1974)

Influential diplomat in the early Cold War years. Born into a wealthy copper mining family, Douglas was raised in Arizona and educated at Amherst College. He saw combat as a first lieutenant during World War I, after which he entered politics and was elected as a Democrat to four terms in the U.S. House of Representatives (1927–1933). Douglas became budget director during the early New Deal (1933–1934) and served as deputy administrative director of the War Shipping Administration during World War II. As ambassador to Great Britain (1947–1950), Douglas enjoyed a close relationship with Secretaries of State George Marshall and Dean Acheson and helped shape the policy of containment during the early years of the Cold War. His reports from London highlighted the economic crisis in Europe after World War II and warned that western Europe, without U.S. assistance, might fall to communism. Considered an able and popular diplomat, he served as a principal spokesman for the European Recovery Program (Marshall Plan) during congressional hearings. While serving in London, Douglas had a significant role in negotiating the North Atlantic Treaty of 1949 and the subsequent formation of the North Atlantic Treaty Organization (NATO). He also championed a mutual defense treaty and the unification of East and West Germany. The loss of an eye in a fishing accident eventually forced his resignation in 1950.

After leaving government service, Douglas resumed his career as an insurance executive and served on the boards of numerous business, civic, and charitable organizations.

THOMAS G. SMITH

See also Acheson, Dean Gooderham; Cold War; Great Britain; Marshall, George Catlett; Marshall Plan; North Atlantic Treaty Organization

FURTHER READING

Browder, Robert P., and Thomas G. Smith. *Independent: A Biography of Lewis W. Douglas.* New York, 1986.

DRAGO DOCTRINE

(1902)

The principle advanced by Foreign Minister Luís M. Drago of Argentina that "the public debt cannot occasion armed intervention nor even the actual occupation of the territory of American nations by a European power." The doctrine was a response to the blockade and bombardment of Venezuela in December 1902 by Germany and Great Britain to persuade that republic to pay debts owed their investors. In a dispatch of 29 December 1902, Drago told the Argentine minister in Washington, Martin Garcia Mérou, to seek U.S. recognition of this principle in the spirit of the Monroe Doctrine. Both the Venezuelan blockade and Drago's note challenged the administration of President Theodore Roosevelt. In his 1901 annual message, Roosevelt had refused to "guarantee any state against punishment," as

long as there was no "acquisition of territory by any non-American power," but the blockade quickly became more formidable than expected by anyone in Washington. German and British ships bombarded Venezuelan ports and Italian ships joined the blockading squadrons. U.S. public opinion grew restive, and Roosevelt adjusted his policy, informing the blockading powers of his concern. Upon his recommendation, the German, British, and Italian governments consented to a settlement of their grievances by commissions and by referring the question of preference in the payment of claims to the Permanent Court of Arbitration at the Hague. When the Dominican government's default on its debts threatened another European intervention, Roosevelt in his annual message of December 6, 1904, warned that the United States would exercise "an international police power" in extreme cases of "wrong doing or impotence" in the Western Hemisphere. Under this policy—the Roosevelt Corollary to the Monroe Doctrine—the United States would forestall European interventions in the Caribbean by itself intervening on numerous occasions. The Drago Doctrine, however, continued to have a role in American diplomacy. At the 1906 Pan American Conference in Rio de Janeiro, Secretary of State Elihu Root assured Latin American delegates of the U.S. government's approval of the Drago Doctrine. At the Second Hague Peace Conference in 1907, U.S. delegate General Horace Porter called for adoption of a convention by which each signatory would pledge not to use force to collect contract debts until after rejection of an offer of arbitration. Drago, leading his country's delegation, objected that Porter's proposal was not in accordance with the Drago Doctrine, but the conference nevertheless accepted the proposal. In 1936, after the United States renounced its interventionist policies, the Pan American Conference in Buenos Aires adopted the Drago Doctrine as a fundamental principle for the Americas.

CALVIN D. DAVIS

See also Arbitration; Hague Peace Conferences; Pan-Americanism; Permanent Court of Arbitration (Hague Tribunal); Roosevelt Corollary; Roosevelt, Theodore; Root, Elihu; Venezuela

FURTHER READING

Davis, Calvin D. *The United States and the Second Hague Peace Conference: American Diplomacy and International Organization 1899–1914.* Durham, N.C., 1976
Langley, Lester D. *The United States and the Caribbean in the Twentieth Century,* 4th ed. Athens, Ga., 1989.
Perkins, Dexter. *The Monroe Doctrine 1867–1907.* Baltimore, Md., 1937.

DRUG ENFORCEMENT AGENCY

The federal agency responsible for implementing federal policy against narcotics. From its inception in mid-1973 within the Department of Justice, controversy accompanied the participation of the Drug Enforcement Agency (DEA) in the making and implementation of U.S. antidrug foreign policy. Both the DEA and its immediate predecessor, the Bureau of Narcotics and Dangerous Drugs (1968–1973), were created amid charges of lax administration and agent corruption. By the mid-1990s the DEA had offices and agents in nearly eighty countries. The DEA's mission at home was to stanch the flow of illegal drugs into the country and to apprehend traffickers. Abroad, the DEA's mission was theoretically limited to intelligence gathering and the training of foreign personnel, but the very nature of U.S. policy negated these limits. U.S. drug policy historically sought strict law enforcement, crop eradication, and interdiction, but even the DEA's best-known predecessor agency, the Federal Bureau of Narcotics (1930–1968), did not always define these goals as policy priorities, often deferring to broader security considerations. Ties in the 1970s and 1980s to Panamanian general Manuel Antonio Noriega, later a convicted trafficker, offer a recent example of this phenomenon. Interagency squabbles, disputes with governments in drug producing and shipping regions, and the vast technology at the disposal of global trafficking networks complicated the work of the DEA. The agency competed with the Customs Service, the Department of State, and the Department of Defense for budgetary allocations and authority in the policy-implementation hierarchy. Various plans to reorganize the federal bureaucracy by combining the DEA with other agencies could not alter the need for a DEA presence abroad. Drug officials made the case in the late 1980s and early 1990s for continuing DEA programs in the Andean countries of South America, Mexico, and the so-called Golden Triangle of Southeast Asia, where cooperation with U.S. policy was often less than ideal.

Through professionalization, DEA officials managed to shed the agency's image in Washington as a minor actor. Their success in doing so resulted from the maintenance of traditional drug control objectives, which withstood serious challenges in the 1990s. By the middle of the decade the DEA had come to play a more prominent role than before in the policy process.

WILLIAM O. WALKER III

See also Colombia; Justice, U.S. Department of; Mexico; Myanmar; Narcotics, International; Nigeria; Thailand

FURTHER READING

Musto, David F. *The American Disease: Origins of Narcotic Control,* rev. ed. New York, 1987.

Nadelmann, Ethan A. *Cops Across Borders: The Internationalization of U.S. Criminal Law Enforcement.* University Park, Pa., 1993.

Walker, William O., III. *Drug Control in the Americas,* rev. ed. Albuquerque, N.Mex., 1989.

Wilson, James Q. *The Investigators: Managing FBI and Narcotics Agents.* New York, 1978.

DRUGS

See Drug Enforcement Agency; Narcotics, International

DU BOIS, WILLIAM EDWARD BURGHARDT

(*b.* 23 February 1868; *d.* 27 August 1963)

A preeminent scholar with a Ph.D. from Harvard University, author of works on the history and status of African Americans, leader of the U.S. civil rights movement, founder of the National Association for the Advancement of Colored People (NAACP), and an African-American fighter for social justice and human rights at the international level. W. E. B. Du Bois was a pioneer in the African liberation movement and led four Pan-African Congresses between 1919 and 1927. By the beginning of the Cold War era, he had lost faith in American democracy and capitalism as means of achieving racial equality. In 1947 he petitioned the United Nations to pressure the United States to grant civil rights and equality to all of its nonwhite citizens, but to no avail. In 1951 he was indicted by the federal government, tried, and acquitted on charges of being an unregistered foreign agent. Du Bois joined the American Communist Party in 1961. In the same year, at the invitation of President Kwame Nkrumah of Ghana, Du Bois left the United States for that West African nation, where he began to compile the *Encyclopedia Africana.* He became a citizen of Ghana and never returned to the United States.

DONALD SPIVEY
JOYCE HANSON

See also Africa; Ghana

FURTHER READING

Aptheker, Herbert, ed. *The Writings of W. E. B. Du Bois in Non-Periodical Literature Edited by Others.* Millwood, N.Y., 1982.

Foner, Philip S., ed. *W. E. B. Du Bois Speaks: Speeches and Addresses,* 2 vols. New York, 1970.

Manning, Marable. *W. E. B. Du Bois: Black Radical Democrat.* Boston, 1986.

DULLES, ALLEN WELSH

(*b.* 6 April 1893; *d.* 29 January 1969)

Member of the Foreign Service (1916–1926), deputy director (1951–1953) and director (1953–1961) of the Central Intelligence Agency (CIA), and a major figure in the Cold War during his years with the CIA. Born in Watertown, New York, the son of Presbyterian minister Allen Macy Dulles and Edith Foster Dulles, Dulles graduated from Princeton University in 1914 and joined the diplomatic service in 1916. He was assigned posts in Vienna and Bern and learned about intelligence and espionage during World War I. Between the world wars he practiced law with his brother, John Foster Dulles, and served as legal adviser for several U.S. delegations at international conferences. From 1942 to 1945 Dulles served under William ("Wild Bill") Donovan in the Office of Strategic Services (OSS) as a spy-in-residence in the Bern Legation. He finished his war service as head of OSS-London and OSS-Germany, in which capacity he was responsible for securing delicate negotiations with the German high command to end the war. During World War II, Dulles suggested the need for a centralized intelligence function to inform the policy process concerning open-source and secret intrigues. This idea, reinforced by Donovan and others, was the guiding principle for the statutory charter of the CIA, the National Security Act of 1947.

In February 1953 President Dwight D. Eisenhower appointed Dulles director of the CIA, a somewhat controversial decision stemming from the president's appointment of John Foster Dulles as secretary of state. Allen Dulles presided over many covert actions in the 1950s, including the coup in Iran to unseat the government of Mohammed Mossadeq, the coup in Guatemala to unseat Jacobo Arbenz Guzman, the acquisition of Soviet premier Nikita Khrushchev's secret speech in 1956 acknowledging Joseph Stalin's reign of terror, and the U-2 aircraft overflights of the Soviet Union. His career came to an end as a result of his supervision in 1961 of the failed Bay of Pigs invasion of Cuba, an attempt to overthrow Fidel Castro's government. He resigned as CIA director that year but was awarded the Distinguished Service Medal by President John F. Kennedy a few days before his retirement. Dulles wrote several books, including *Germany's Underground* (1947), *The Craft of Intelligence* (1963), *The Secret Surrender* (1966), and, with Hamilton Fish Armstrong, *Can America Stay Neutral?* (1936). After he left the CIA he edited *Great True Spy Stories* (1968). His death was marked by a respectful pause by all the world's intelligence services, including the Soviet KGB.

JAMES D. CALDER

See also Bay of Pigs Invasion; Central Intelligence Agency; Donovan, William Joseph; Dulles, John Foster; Guatemala; Intelligence; Iran; Khrushchev, Nikita Sergeyevich; Mossadeq, Mohammed; Office of Strategic Services; U-2 Incident

FURTHER READING
Grose, Peter. *Gentleman Spy: The Life of Allen Dulles*. Boston, 1995.

DULLES, JOHN FOSTER

(*b.* 25 Feb. 1888; *d.* 24 May 1959)

U.S. secretary of state in the Eisenhower administration (1953–1959), who was often at the center of controversy because of his frankly stated views on Cold War issues. Those tracking his performance tended to see him as a striking embodiment of either the best or the worst features of U.S. foreign policies. In recent years, however, scholars have substantially tempered early Cold War caricatures. Passage of time has certainly encouraged a cooler perspective, but extensive access to archival records has been even more important to a more measured reappraisal. In particular, historians are now able to compare Dulles's sometimes simplistic public rhetoric with his often more sophisticated private views—and to appreciate subtleties and complexities once thought to be absent.

Early Life and Career

Although Dulles is primarily associated with the 1950s, his entire life deserves close attention: his family background and upbringing, earlier professional career, and evolving perspectives all tell much about the complex sweep of U.S. involvement with the twentieth century world.

Born in 1888, Dulles's youth coincided with the expansion of the U.S. role in the international arena—and family circumstances clearly nudged him toward a personal role in the process. His father, Allen Macy Dulles, was a Presbyterian minister in Watertown, New York, at the time of his first son's birth, but a man of cosmopolitan background and inclinations. He had received part of his education in Germany, for example, and took his children on extended annual trips to Europe; he had a strong intellectual bent as well and joined the faculty at Auburn Theological Seminary in 1904. Dulles's mother, Edith Foster Dulles, was the well-traveled daughter of John Watson Foster, an ambassador-turned-secretary of state who became a prominent international lawyer in turn-of-the-century Washington.

Although the family believed that Dulles would follow his father into the ministry after graduating from Princeton in 1908, he chose his grandfather's profession instead. He would always retain an interest in church affairs—and would eventually be criticized for being a policymaker with excessively religious preoccupations—but it was international law that dominated Dulles's life for almost forty years. He attended George Washington University Law School while living with his grandparents (just a short walk from the White House) and then found Foster's connections useful for entering the prestigious Wall Street firm of Sullivan & Cromwell in 1911.

War in Europe dramatically affected the young lawyer's career. Clients with primarily Caribbean business interests were rapidly joined by those facing complex transatlantic trading and insurance problems. These soon paved the way to government work, when encouraged by another well-placed relative, Woodrow Wilson's secretary of state Robert Lansing. Dulles spent a year as assistant to the chair of the War Trade Board and another nine months as a member of the U.S. delegation to the Paris Peace Conference. He worked primarily on "reparations" negotiations in Paris, helping to shape the more moderate U.S. alternatives to harsher European proposals. If Germany were treated in a traditional punitive manner, Woodrow Wilson and his counselors argued, the old cycle of war and peace would be repeated as the defeated enemy sought revenge. More immediately, miserable conditions within Germany would interfere with the revival of normal economic life throughout the continent, or serve as fertile ground for another outbreak of what was seen as the Bolshevik epidemic. Dulles actually drafted many of the reparation clauses included in the final Versailles treaty. His most important contribution was the conceptualization of the notorious "war guilt" clause, designed to offer the allies the psychological satisfaction of declaring Germany's general culpability in exchange for accepting pragmatic limits on actual indebtedness.

Dulles was indelibly marked by World War I and the Paris Peace Conference. For the rest of his life, there were few subjects that interested him more than transatlantic relations, especially the place of Germany and the role of economic transactions in the overall architecture of war and peace. Woodrow Wilson would cast long shadows through Dulles's life as well. As for many who had worked within the president's orbit, Dulles remained permanently convinced that U.S. efforts on behalf of liberal reform policies might eventually push the old imperial powers of Europe toward a new world order.

The Interwar Years

Dulles returned to Wall Street with exactly the kind of Washington and international experience that distinguished Sullivan & Cromwell. He rose rapidly within the firm and became its managing partner in 1926. Transatlantic business and banking now dominated his legal practice, as he took advantage of both accumulated technical expertise and a wide-ranging network of European contacts. He provided legal counsel to the Bank of New York, Morgan & Co., and other investment houses concerning international loans and securities issues during the 1920s and was associated with firms like International Nickel and the Belgian chemical giant Solvay & Cie.

Legal work very much affected the evolution of Dulles's perspective on foreign affairs. He was never anything but a staunch "internationalist," but his mood and specific concerns varied with the condition of the global business environment. At first, he was inclined to share some of the chagrin and pessimism expounded by his Paris associate John Maynard Keynes: there had been too many U.S. compromises on the reparations settlement and the added complications of large Allied debts

seemed likely to interfere with meaningful economic recovery. As U.S. prosperity took hold, however, Dulles grew more confident. He saw the Dawes Plan as having put the German debt problem on a more "business-like" basis, for example, and assumed European economic recovery was a direct result. He was especially impressed by the way U.S. bankers were wisely exercising new world leadership, utilizing billions of dollars of productive loans as their tools.

Darker thoughts returned during the Great Depression, of course, as massive unemployment, plummeting trade, and skyrocketing loan defaults plagued the United States and much of the rest of the world. The information garnered from his global travel and contacts moved Dulles toward grander-scale analysis of world affairs. As early as 1934, he wrote an article for the *Atlantic Monthly* in which he speculated about the way economic disasters could produce political and military sparks: he called it "The Road to War." As he grimly tracked the confirmation of his fears for the next five years, Dulles also demonstrated the staying power of his earlier Wilsonian impulses. He wrote and spoke extensively about the way international reform might ward off cataclysm, with emphasis on the value of liberalized trade and currency relationships.

By the late 1930s, just as he turned 50, Dulles began to place his analysis of economic crisis and conflict into a yet broader context. Interest in philosophy revived, yielding a book entitled *War, Peace, and Change* (1939). A study of what Dulles saw as the primordial struggle between "static" and "dynamic" forces, the work used history, political theory, ethics, and economics to argue the urgency of devising new mechanisms for "peaceful change." Simultaneously, religious impulses were rekindled as well. Dulles found himself especially attracted to the way some ecumenically minded Protestant leaders in North America and Europe were opting for an emphasis on international reform at a time when strident nationalism was more in fashion in the political arena.

For some time after the outbreak of World War II in Europe, in fact, Dulles was a staunch anti-interventionist because of his reform convictions. The twentieth-century world was experiencing systemic problems beyond the admittedly extreme villainy of Germany, Japan, and Italy, he believed. Why waste blood and treasure to restore a *status quo ante bellum* in which perpetually dangerous tendencies toward imperialism, militarism, and economic autarchy were central norms? Although his hesitancy about U.S. involvement in another world war had a measure of genuine intellectual integrity, it provoked accusations of quasi-fascist sympathies both during and after the 1930s. Some critics were distressed by what they saw as Dulles's readiness to treat the behavior of all great powers as essentially equivalent, and by his failure to recognize the important moral distinctions that sprang from various degrees of imperfection or evil in national misconduct. Others were suspicious about the role that Sullivan & Cromwell's substantial German business played in shaping its managing partner's aloof judgments. Evidence concerning the firm's Third Reich connections is too limited for definitive conclusions, but it does seem clear that Dulles's visits and professional efforts went on beyond the 1935 date he sometimes referred to when awkward questions were raised in later years.

World War II and the Truman Years

As with Woodrow Wilson before him, it was precisely a passion for reform that allowed Dulles to move toward interventionism. By late 1940, his evolving ecumenical interests led him to assume the responsibilities of chairing the Federal Council of Churches' "Commission to Study the Bases of a Just and Durable Peace," and it was this work that encouraged him to turn to postwar planning as a means of conceptualizing at least some meaningful compensation for the horrors of global conflict. Throughout World War II, by means of expansive public relations efforts, Dulles articulated the virtues of an updated Wilsonian agenda. He saw it as the "mission" of the United States to seek a "new world order": another international organization, buttressed by agreements encouraging commercial and financial cooperation, would allow an increasingly interdependent world to enjoy a more peaceful future.

World War II also saw Dulles moving more energetically into the U.S. political arena, adding a visible public role to the behind-the-scenes efforts he had invested since the 1920s. Friendship with rising Republican star Thomas E. Dewey proved especially important here. Dulles became the New York governor's primary foreign policy adviser in the 1944 campaign, playing a key role in steering the Republican Party away from the "isolationist" image that often hung over it. Dewey-Dulles support for a "United Nations Organization" and for international economic mechanisms made it easier for Franklin D. Roosevelt and Cordell Hull to maintain enthusiasm for "bipartisanship."

Following Roosevelt's death, Harry Truman and many of his advisers continued in this direction, generally seeing Dulles and Senator Arthur H. Vandenberg as their key political partners. In Dulles's case, ongoing bipartisanship would translate into attendance at numerous international conferences (including sessions of the Council of Foreign Ministers and the United Nations General Assembly) as well as regular consultation on key issues (such as the Marshall Plan and North Atlantic Treaty Organization [NATO]).

Like many around him in the early Truman administration, Dulles became a vigorous Cold Warrior. He moved more slowly in this direction than his later reputation might suggest, however. Where George Kennan and others had retained strong suspicions of the Soviet Union all through World War II, Dulles had been either relatively indifferent to fears of a communist menace or inclined to urge the need to calmly work out inevitable disagreements concerning the shape of the postwar world. Beginning with a lengthy *Life* magazine article in June 1946—symptomatic of what was becoming a close Dulles–Henry Luce relationship by that date—his public rhetoric heated up dramatically. Highly threatening communist expansionism, coordinated from Moscow, became a constant theme in his discussions of the issues and crises dominating the headlines of the period: the establishment of a Soviet control structure in Eastern Europe, a peace settlement with Germany (and the 1948–1949 Berlin Crisis), the rehabilitation of Western Europe, among others. A commitment to "containment" policies went hand-in-hand with such a perspective. Dulles offered enthusiastic support to the Marshall Plan, for example, and consistently urged strong U.S. leadership with respect to keeping Germany from falling behind the "Iron Curtain."

As important as anticommunism was to Dulles's evolving thoughts on international affairs, other concerns were also prominent. Both publicly and privately during the Truman years, he made it clear that his *pre*–Cold War concerns remained of central significance as well. His support for the Marshall Plan, for example, was always explained in a way that linked old and new problems. In particular, he believed large-scale U.S. aid might be used to coax European integration—an enthusiasm he shared with his old friend Jean Monnet. And integration, he explicitly argued, would serve a multiplicity of significant ends: it would increase the Continent's ability to withstand communist aggression and subversion; it would reduce the potential for conflict inherent in traditionally autarchic trade and commercial practices; and it would provide a solid institutional structure within which Germany's vast potential could safely be tapped for the benefit of the entire transatlantic community. So concerned was Dulles with the complexities of post-1945 problems, in fact, that he was initially hesitant about the birth of NATO, although a military pact might be helpful for "containment" purposes; that is, he was fearful that it would lull Europeans into a false sense of security and make them less willing to undertake the reforms necessary to solve very old problems distinct from the rising Soviet threat.

In 1948 Dulles came very close to acquiring a substantial measure of personal control over foreign policymaking. When Dewey made a second try for the presidency, an almost unanimous chorus of pundits and pollsters predicted victory, and it was widely assumed that his chief foreign affairs adviser would soon be heading the Department of State. Confidence made it easier for both men to reject a strident campaign strategy, with "statesmanlike" emphasis being placed instead on the virtues of bipartisan internationalism. In the midst of the Berlin crisis, however—and with any number of domestic issues being debated, as well—this approach did not prove as persuasive with voters as hoped.

In the aftermath of Dewey's defeat, Dulles tried to find a partial substitute for his anticipated foreign policy role. When Dewey appointed him to fill out the last months of an unexpired Senate term in New York, he made the decision to run for the seat in his own right in the fall of 1949. His stature actually allowed him to play a meaningful role during his days in the Senate—particularly during debates on NATO and the Military Assistance Program—but neither he nor the New York Republican party had enough clout to defeat Democrat Herbert Lehman.

The New York Senate race was bitterly and distastefully fought, all around, but both Dulles and the Truman administration were willing to separate campaign politicking from more fundamental convictions concerning the need for bipartisan foreign policies. Soon, Dulles was drawn back to Washington: in April 1950 he was appointed "counselor" to Secretary of State Dean Acheson. The two men never developed a close relationship, and each would give vent to acerbic partisan swipes in later years. Nevertheless, Acheson's appreciation for Dulles's effective handling of a few specialized tasks allowed them to work together comfortably enough for a year and a half.

While earlier work with the Truman team had kept Dulles firmly on familiar ground—via an almost total emphasis on European issues—he was now turned toward Asia. His formal responsibility became the supervision of negotiations for a Japanese peace treaty, which quickly led to regular involvement in deliberations concerning the Korean conflict and China policy as well. This was very tricky territory for a Republican, given the whirlwind raised by Joseph McCarthy and others during precisely this period. Dulles's overall attachment to bipartisanship, however, as well as his interest in the particular Asian policies he was helping to design, kept him firmly in the Truman administration until the end of 1951.

In some respects, Dulles's involvement with the Japanese peace treaty took him in significant new directions. As an old Wilsonian and international lawyer, to be sure, he had long followed developments in many corners of the world. Now, like other U.S. policymakers, he began to dramatically expand his formal attentiveness to areas beyond the Europe that had been his primary preoccupation. New responsibilities helped to substantively

globalize Dulles's foreign policy thinking, preparing him for yet further evolution during the Eisenhower years.

In other respects, however, Dulles's new work simply expanded the geographical boundaries of old concerns. Normalization of relations with Japan and a series of complementary security agreements with countries like Australia and the Philippines were seen as vitally necessary in order to halt communist expansion in Asia—a "containment" goal very much transposed from calculations regarding Europe. Dulles also developed a staunch Cold War perspective on other Asian problems swirling around his peace treaty work. He immediately urged a forceful response to the June 1950 invasion of South Korea, for example, and was an early advocate for the extension of U.S. protection to the Chinese Nationalists' last-stand bastion on Taiwan. (Apparent support for Jiang Jieshi won Dulles a good deal of support from the so-called "China lobby" in the early 1950s and he enjoyed friendly relations with Congressman Walter Judd, Senator H. Alexander Smith, and others in spite of his official status in the Truman administration.) And there were echoes of Dulles's interwar as well as Cold War preoccupations in his work on the Japanese peace treaty. His attentiveness to the economic terms of the settlement, in particular, revealed a thoroughly consistent desire to maximize regional opportunity—and to minimize autarchic trade and currency restrictions.

Dulles received widespread praise for more than a year of arduous and imaginative effort when the Japanese Peace Treaty was signed in the fall of 1951, and Harry Truman soon asked him to serve as ambassador to Tokyo. Maneuvering for another presidential election had already begun, however, and appointment as secretary of state seemed a more appealing objective. This was not a fanciful calculation, given the beleaguered state of the Democrats *and* Dulles's ability to straddle the divisions among Republicans. Traditional ties with the Republican party's "eastern internationalist" wing made for comfortable connections with late-blooming candidate Dwight D. Eisenhower, exemplified by a shared commitment to strong transatlantic ties and fiscal responsibility. Recent interest in Asia, however—as well as feverish frustration over too many lost elections—also gave Dulles genuine links with Robert Taft and other firebrands often inaccurately labeled as "isolationists." It was Taft who actually coaxed Dulles to serve as chief foreign affairs adviser for the 1952 Republican platform.

Although Eisenhower won the nomination, he and Dulles were both ambitious and pragmatic enough to pay a price for the maintenance of party unity. In spite of occasional signs of discomfort, they waged a campaign whose foreign policy messages were shriller and more demagogic than either would have preferred—or than

Dulles had advocated in 1948. Melodramatic but vague calls for "liberation" were offered as an alternative to "immoral" containment, for example, while the Democrats were castigated for putting all of Asia at risk with weak or traitorous policies toward China and Korea.

The Eisenhower Years: 1953–1954

That both Eisenhower and Dulles campaigned in a fashion somewhat at variance with deeper personal inclinations was a foretaste of the partnership that developed between them after a stunning election victory. While it was once believed that a somewhat lazy and grandfatherly president allowed his arrogant secretary of state to dominate foreign policymaking, the long-closed records of the 1950s now reveal a more complex relationship. More often than not, Eisenhower and Dulles shared strikingly similar goals and policy preferences. Each played relatively distinct roles between 1953 and 1959, but each also acted in a way that revealed a conscious and comfortable symbiosis. The secretary of state proffered analyses and proposals, for instance, while the president generally waited for and utilized this advice in order to reach final decisions. Dulles's ability to play the initiating role in this multistage process was not harmed by the fact that his brother served as director of the Central Intelligence Agency (CIA). The Dulleses were in touch almost daily, by phone or in person, both formally and informally: this gave the secretary of state especially sure access to intelligence information and intimate insights into the "covert operations" options that Eisenhower regularly found appealing.) Dulles also sometimes served as something of a lightning rod when it came to the enunciation of controversial policies, leaving to Eisenhower the more congenial role of calm and grandfatherly statesman. For Dulles, of course, such designated roles were part of a familiar pattern: a clear extension of the dynamics of his decades of work as a corporation lawyer. And if he had needed any additional encouragement with respect to the virtues of combining power and deference, he had only to recall the bitter collapse of his uncle Robert Lansing's relationship with Woodrow Wilson.

If Dulles never exercised the kind of control once imagined, some of the other images that quickly sprang up around him had at least some substance. Given the information available to the media and the public at the time, in particular, it is easy to see how the secretary of state's early actions generated his reputation as a rabid and rigid Cold Warrior. In the Foggy Bottom corridors under his jurisdiction, McCarthy-like scourings resulted in the deaccession of countless books in U.S. libraries abroad and controversial personnel departures (including "China Hands" like John Carter Vincent). In turn, a strafed Department of State seemed likely to execute only the harshest policies. Joseph Stalin's death in March 1953 appeared to be treated as a non-event, given studied disinterest in the possibility of détente with a Kremlin consistently denounced as the seat of godless and atheistic communism. In Asia, nuclear sabres were rattled in order to bring a long-delayed end to the war in Korea. This seemed to be an early example of two concepts soon linked with Dulles's name: "brinkmanship," denoting a readiness to go to war—or toward major escalation—in order to deter an enemy from making it necessary to actually do so; and "massive retaliation," the shorthand label often used to sum up a new Republican emphasis on the cost-saving potential of nuclear weapons.

Some of the toughness associated with Dulles's early initiatives as secretary of state significantly shifted U.S. foreign policy. "Massive retaliation" and the overall "new look" within which it had found its home, for example, certainly altered the Truman-Acheson grand strategy captured in the famous NSC-68 policy paper—in particular, by substituting a "long haul" sensitivity to burgeoning defense budgets for an open-ended optimism that any and all costs could safely be borne by the U.S. economy. But the changes encouraged by Dulles (and, always, by Eisenhower) should not distract attention from plentiful evidence of fundamental consistency. More often than not, the secretary of state remained faithful to both the broad impulses of the Truman years and his own deep-rooted preoccupations.

Earlier policies that had garnered bipartisan support certainly remained high on the agenda of Dulles's priorities. Transatlantic relationships were never anything but a paramount concern, with intense efforts during 1953–1954 on behalf of the European Defense Community (EDC) being a key early example. Nor did moves in Eastern Europe actually shift into a dramatically higher gear, whatever the rhetoric of "liberation" might have suggested. Even in Asia, the basic watchword remained "containment"—of both the Moscow and the Beijing varieties of "communism." The Korean War ended only with an armistice, after all, with the *status quo ante bellum* essentially rigidified in the end. In subsequent months, as well, Acheson-like policies that aggravated Republican hawks like Senator William Knowland emerged in Indochina. There was continued support for France's efforts to crush a nationalist revolution, for example, but it was support that stopped short of acceding to Paris's pressure for the use of atomic weapons during the 1954 Dien Bien Phu crisis. This was the beginning of a Vietnam variation on the "limited war" theme that had characterized Democratic policies in Korea—and was neither more nor less immoderate an approach as a result.

Dulles matched faithfulness to bipartisan essentials with consistency regarding pre-Cold War concerns that had been of great significance to him. EDC, for example, was his belief that it would tap West Germany's military strength while building a multinational structure that would make it safe to do so: there was passion here for what can be dubbed "dual containment," tying post-1945 and much earlier problems. As well, an essential goad to Dulles's now consistently high appraisal of Asian issues was his long-gestating conviction that global economic relationships required careful tending and development: the reintegration of a recovering economic giant like Japan and the security of Southeast Asia's vast raw materials, among other things, were never far from his mind after 1953.

If Dulles's inclinations remained essentially consistent in 1953–1954, it should be noted that their geographical boundaries did expand. In particular, the Middle East and Latin America now found their way into month-to-month calculations—just as Asia had become a complement to Europe in 1950–1951. This was partially a function of a secretary of state's overall responsibilities, of course, but also the result of Dulles's own sensitivity to the increasingly integrated global environment of the 1950s. It did not *seem* as farfetched as it actually was to discuss the nationalist or reform policies of Iranian and Guatemalan leaders in the context of a worldwide struggle against communism, for example, or to let "domino theory" logic spawn the covert operations that would overthrow unpalatable governments. And Dulles's career-long attentiveness to international economic linkages made it easy to add on yet more layers of concern: if United Fruit found itself vulnerable in Guatemala, how would this affect the security of U.S. investments in many other quarters? If petroleum profits went more regularly into Middle Eastern treasuries, how much damage would be done to valued European allies?

1955–1956

For some months in mid-1955—after more than two years of energetic service as secretary of state—Dulles must have felt that foreign policies combining consistency with a dash of innovation were beginning to pay major dividends. Satisfying earlier conclusions to varied crises or problems seemed to have accumulated sufficiently to augur a period of more general calm and stability in the international arena. In Europe particularly, Moscow gave the impression that the dreaded West German adherence to NATO (April 1955) had actually cajoled more conciliatory policies overall. An endlessly delayed Austrian peace treaty was signed in May, for example, and the first "summit" conference since Potsdam was held with great fanfare in Geneva in July. Elsewhere too, encouraging signs were evident. In Asia, for instance, the relative Indochina calm that had been ushered in by 1954's Geneva conference and accords had extended into another year. A pro-

longed and especially threatening crisis in the Taiwan Strait had also settled down by the spring of 1955: faced with the U.S. Seventh Fleet and explicit hints of nuclear retaliation, Beijing had backed away from pressing its campaign to end Jiang Jieshi's control of offshore islands like Jinmen (Quemoy) and Mazu (Matsu).

But appearances proved deceptive—and momentary. Even in 1955, Dulles never reached a point where his reading of international difficulties allowed the genuine relaxation of full-fledged satisfaction. Sometimes this was because new or ongoing problems were so profound and complex as to defy easy solution. Sometimes, alternatively, the resources or control capabilities available to the United States proved to be too limited—at least relative to the ambitious goals that an intellectually subtle Dulles was nonetheless tempted toward in practice.

The "spirit of Geneva" that emanated from the mid-1955 summit conference, for example, had some potential for generating détente. Continuing negotiations made it clear that German reunification was not going to be achieved, but few outside Germany itself were distraught about this—certainly not a Dulles who had finally managed to get a truncated "Federal Republic of Germany" bridled into NATO. Instead of enjoying modest calm in a long-volatile area, however, Dulles (and Eisenhower) decided to continue pressing a presumably beleaguered Moscow. Eastern European "satellites" were seen as especially vulnerable targets. There was no let up in established "psychological warfare" efforts like the broadcasts of Radio Free Europe, for example, and questions have often been raised about the way in which the highly colored propaganda delivered by émigré broadcasters may have contributed to the explosions and tragedies of 1956. Given his brother's position, the secretary of state would also have known about "Red Sox/Red Cap" preparations; though hard evidence remains classified, this CIA project was designed to prepare paramilitary units for covert operations in Eastern Europe.

Elsewhere too, in 1955–1956, opportunities were neglected or spurned. In Indochina, optimism led Dulles (and Eisenhower) to continually undercut the settlement possibilities inherent in the 1954 Geneva accords: aid and military advisers flowed to U.S. client Ngo Dinh Diem and all-Vietnam elections were obstructed in order to sculpt a separate South Vietnamese state into existence. While such moves became part of a slow U.S. dance toward disaster in Southeast Asia, promising developments detonated more quickly in the Middle East. By 1955, Dulles had sought to strengthen U.S. standing in the Arab world via steps like pressing the British to surrender their traditional imperialist role in Egypt and by agreeing to support construction of the Aswan dam. He had also become enthusiastic about "Project Alpha," a complex mix of diplomacy and "carrots" designed to defuse bitter Arab-Israeli tensions. In July 1956, however, Dulles reneged on the Aswan dam offer—partially because of suspicions that Cairo's vaunted "neutrality" was beginning to tilt too much toward the communist camp, partially because of some pressure from Capitol Hill concerning the way potentially burgeoning Egyptian cotton crops might create problems for U.S. producers once the new dam had worked its wonders. When Egypt's leader, Gamal Abdel Nasser, angrily retaliated by nationalizing the Suez canal, the stage was set for one of the worst crises of the Eisenhower years.

Dulles's decision to back away from the imaginative Aswan project has often been seen as symptomatic of larger problems developing in U.S. policies toward the so-called "Third World"—including those directed at Indochina. There has been particular emphasis on the way Cold War fears (or phantoms) distorted Washington's perceptions of complex nationalist impulses within recently independent societies or revolutionary movements. In a way, Nasser did bite the hand that was feeding him, for instance, by buying arms from Czechoslovakia and recognizing the People's Republic of China: this gave rise to spiraling speculation about his role as a Moscow puppet in the vital Middle East—and a sharp rethinking of previous efforts to woo him. Ongoing research suggests that such calculations were not always crudely simplistic, though they certainly were so at times. For all of their melodramatic rhetoric, for example, experienced leaders like Dulles and Eisenhower increasingly recognized that the world was not besieged by a strictly monolithic communist conspiracy. They might continue to oppose a Ho Chi Minh, that is, but they could do so while appreciating signs of strain between Moscow and Beijing—or between Moscow and any number of nascent Titos in Eastern Europe and elsewhere.

Another noteworthy complexity in Dulles's (and Eisenhower's) apparently hamhanded approach to Asian/African/Latin American developments by the mid-1950s was his fire and brimstone anticommunism that sometimes served as a convenient and politically useful shorthand for explaining antagonisms actually spurred by more complex nationalist or radical policies. Nasser, for example, could seem much more like a regionally ambitious Mosaddeq than a Moscow pawn—a charismatic Arab likely to cause problems all on his own unless he was carefully checked. What Dulles demonstrated in the Third World, that is, was an attraction to the kind of "dual containment" that was at the heart of his policies in Europe: Cold War calculations in tight tandem with a consciousness that not all problems were exclusively connected to "communism."

1956–1959

The midpoint of the Eisenhower presidency came at a time of dramatic developments that must have blended the satisfying and the problematic for Dulles. One almost purely positive feature was the president's stunning re-election triumph in November 1956, a clear indication of broad public support for the foreign policies with which the secretary of state was so intimately associated. Although Adlai Stevenson won some points by criticizing established Republican foreign policies—such as hesitancy to limit nuclear testing—most voters opted for more of the overall package Eisenhower and Dulles had been offering. The joy of reelection was heavily shadowed, however, by a series of public and personal crises unfolding at just this point. Under any circumstances, for example, it would have been difficult to deal with the Middle East after Great Britain, France, and Israel actually began their secretly planned military action against Egypt. How much worse to have to navigate this "Suez crisis" at precisely the moment when Moscow unleashed brutally repressive moves against growing unrest in Hungary and Poland. And to compound the strain yet further, Dulles found himself hospitalized during the worst days of the double explosion—struggling through a first battle with the cancer that would end his life in May 1959.

Such an admixture of successes and problems—with a heavy tilt toward the negative—would weigh on Dulles for the two years and some months that remained in his career as secretary of state. Old problems would simply not go away and new ones continually raised their heads; old policies did not yield desired results and yet new ones were not easily or successfully devised.

A Soviet Union that had seemed on the verge of collapse or on the way to significant change in 1955, for example, continued to distress Dulles and other Americans. Moscow's bloody reassertion of power in Eastern Europe was followed by a clutch of material and diplomatic successes, ranging from impressive military and technological advances like the launch of Sputnik to an escalation of visibility and respectability in Asia, Africa, and Latin America. In the very last months of Dulles's life, as well, yet another Berlin crisis was ignited by renewed Soviet and East German maneuvers.

In Asia, the apparent promise of 1955 was also mocked. Normal relations with the People's Republic of China remained as distant as ever. Dulles continued close ties with Jiang Jieshi, in spite of private talk about a "two Chinas" policy, and struggled through another "JinJinmen-Mazu crisis" in 1958. The fundamental problems inherent in Washington's gameplan for Indochina also became increasingly apparent, with mounting signs of both the Ngo Dinh Diem regime's inadequacies and the instability of conditions in Laos and Cambodia. And a full list of the region's problems—as Dulles would have listed them—would go on and on, ranging from internal strains in South Korea and the Philippines, to more blatantly threatening unrest in Indonesia, to the tensions caused by a prolonged U.S. military presence in Japan.

In the Middle East, the "Eisenhower Doctrine" was dramatically unveiled in 1957 in an effort both to assert U.S. leadership in the aftermath of the Suez crisis and to separate Dulles and the president from any vestiges of anachronistic European colonialism (an extension of the logic that had unfolded in Indochina). It proved easier to declaim than to act effectively, however. When U.S. Marines landed on the beaches of Lebanon in 1958, for example, few in Washington or elsewhere believed that this move to support the controversial government of Camille Chamoun was either a brilliant success or a necessity. Meanwhile, even a presumably safe Latin American backyard became a troubled neighborhood. Richard Nixon encountered fiery anti-Americanism in Paraguay, Peru, and Venezuela in 1958, for example, while other threatening problems began to develop in Panama and Cuba.

Only in Western Europe did Dulles enjoy some genuine satisfaction as his work neared its end. Of greatest significance to him was the way in which the Federal Republic of Germany became more and more firmly tied to its continental neighbors and its transatlantic friend. An expanded NATO and the birth of both Euratom and the Common Market were greatly prized by Dulles as giant steps toward solving a multiplicity of German and continental problems. Yet even in Western Europe, the late 1950s brought developments that must have gnawed on Dulles's equanimity. The Suez crisis was not easily forgotten in London or Paris, for example, and some of Charles de Gaulle's moves toward making France more independent of NATO were at least partial examples of fallout. European economic rehabilitation and integration also turned out to be two-edged swords, helping to engender troublesome currency and trade issues for the U.S. by 1959.

Conclusion

The uneven record of Dulles's final years can probably be seen as symbolic for any appraisal of his lifelong work in the realm of foreign affairs. He had strengths and achievements often ignored by vigorous critics, but flaws and failures untallied by admirers as well.

A progression of attributes deserves emphasis on one side of the ledger. First, it is clear that Dulles could shrewdly analyze many of the complex global issues confronting the United States. To some degree, this shrewdness was the product of decades of experience in day-to-day legal and economic affairs, but it is also obvious that he had the kind of innate intellectual skills that allowed him to gain that experience in the first place. Second, his analytical abilities regularly translated into technical problem-solving. He had a brilliant lawyer's tactical imagination and sometimes used it to devise ingenious routes through his clients'—and his country's—problems. Third, he had enormous energy. Permeating both private life and public service, this made it that much more possible for him to turn his analytical and tactical skills into concrete results. And fourth, he was often able to make those results satisfying to those who hired him as a lawyer or to those citizens who supported him as secretary of state.

The other side of a hypothetical ledger would have to list the ways in which Dulles's attributes could be limited, or distorted by other traits. His analytical shrewdness could founder on the shoals of knee-jerk reactions, for example. In Southeast Asia, the Middle East, and Latin America, certainly, moments of acumen regarding the complex nature of problems and crises were regularly overpowered by sweeping anticommunist preconceptions. Faulty diagnoses, of course, could then undercut the appropriatness and effectiveness of apparently skillful prescriptions. Dulles and Eisenhower could both feel some pride in the "nation-building" policies adopted for Vietnam, for instance, but this did not prevent a deteriorating situation from being passed on to John Kennedy and Lyndon Johnson.

Even Dulles's energy had its problematic face—in the sense that more subtlety and moderation might have made for more solid achievements. Sometimes an excess of exuberance was the source of no more than essentially stylistic problems. Dulles's public declarations could be rather crudely aggressive, for example, with public and scholarly misunderstanding spinning off of such phrases as "massive retaliation" and "liberation." But more fundamental difficulties are involved as well. On any number of occasions, a less thrusting approach to predicaments might have improved the chances of progress as opposed to stalemate or crisis. This is a possibility that at least begs for debate with respect to the potential for a measure of U.S.-Soviet détente in Central Europe—or some modicum of normalcy in U.S.-China relations. Was there a point at which a driving Washington pursuit of maximum goals translated into counterproductive and dangerous arrogance?

Dulles's flaws were certainly not unique. To allow preconceptions to hamper analysis, to seek ambitious objectives in a way that might prevent achievement of moderate ones, and so on, these are failings common to many U.S. policymakers—and many average Americans—especially in the aftermath of World War II. They are also typical of the behavior of other "Great Power" leaders in virtually any era. But to recognize Dulles's place in a broad continuum, of course, is only to reinforce the conclusion that his is a life with much to tell about the history of U.S. foreign policy.

RONALD W. PRUESSEN

See also Brinkmanship; Cold War; Dawes Plan; Dien Bien Phu; Dulles, Allen Welsh; Eisenhower Doctrine; Eisenhower, Dwight David; Guatemala; Iran; Jinmen-Mazu Crisis; Lebanon; Massive Retaliation; McCarthyism; North Atlantic Treaty Organization; Nuclear Weapons and Strategy; Suez Crisis

FURTHER READING

Brands, H.W. Jr. *Cold Warriors: Eisenhower's Generation and American Foreign Policy.* New York, 1988.
Dulles, Eleanor Lansing. *John Foster Dulles: The Last Year.* New York, 1963.
Dulles, John Foster. *War, Peace, and Change.* New York, 1939.
Grose, Peter. *Gentleman Spy: The Life of Allen Dulles.* Boston, 1994.
Guhin, Michael A. *John Foster Dulles: A Statesman for His Times.* New York, 1972.
Hoopes, Townsend. *The Devil and John Foster Dulles.* Boston, 1973.
Immerman, Richard, ed. *John Foster Dulles and the Diplomacy of the Cold War.* Princeton, 1990.
Marks, Frederick W., III. *Power and Peace: The Diplomacy of John Foster Dulles.* Westport, Conn., 1993.
Pruessen, Ronald W. *John Foster Dulles: The Road to Power,1888–1952.* New York, 1982.
Toulouse, Mark G. *The Transformation of John Foster Dulles: From Prophet of Realism to Priest of Nationalism.* Macon, Ga., 1985.

DUMBARTON OAKS CONFERENCE

(1944)

A meeting of representatives of the United States, Great Britain, the Soviet Union, and China at a private estate in Washington, D.C., to draft proposals for the constitution of a general international organization, the United Nations, to supervise the peace after World War II. As suggested by the U.S. Department of State, the conference proceeded in two separate phases. Negotiations were first conducted between the U.S., Soviet, and British delegations between 21 August and 28 September 1944; a second set of discussions was held among the U.S., British, and Chinese delegations from 29 September to 7 October. This arrangement enabled representatives of the Soviet Union, which was still neutral in the war with Japan, to avoid meeting the Chinese. The conference results, published as "Proposals for the Establishment of a General International Organization," set out the purposes and principles of the organization, its membership and organs, and arrangements to maintain international peace and security and to promote international economic and social cooperation. Some issues remained to be resolved at the Yalta Confer-

ence in February 1945, notably the voting procedure of the proposed Security Council (especially the veto) and questions of membership. (The Soviet Union wanted each of its sixteen constituent republics to have a seat in the proposed General Assembly.) The Dumbarton Oaks Proposals nevertheless laid the substantive foundation for the United Nations Charter, which was subsequently adopted at the San Francisco Conference in October 1945.

CHRISTOPHER C. JOYNER

See also League of Nations; Peace Movements and Societies, 1914 to Present; United Nations; Yalta Conference

FURTHER READING:

Hilderbrand, Robert C. *Dumbarton Oaks: The Origins of the United Nations and the Search for Postwar Security.* Chapel Hill, N.C., 1990.
Russell, Ruth B., and Jeanette E. Muther. *A History of the United Nations Charter: The Role of the United States, 1940–1945.* Washington, D.C., 1958.

DURBROW, ELBRIDGE

(*b.* 21 September 1903)

Career Foreign Service officer and ambassador to South Vietnam. Born in San Francisco, Durbrow graduated from Yale University in 1926 and later attended Stanford University, the University of Dijon in France, and several other European universities. He began his Foreign Service career as vice-consul in Warsaw, Poland, in 1930 and was among the first to receive special schooling in Soviet affairs. In 1932 he moved to Bucharest, Romania, and in 1934 he was assigned to Moscow as an economic expert. He disliked the Soviet regime, believing it unprincipled, uncivilized, and undemocratic. Durbrow was transferred to Naples, Italy, in 1937 and moved to Rome in 1940. He returned to the United States the following year and became assistant chief of the Division of Eastern European Affairs in the Department of State. He hoped that closer diplomatic and economic ties with the Allies would motivate the Soviet Union to temper its territorial ambitions, but as Soviet armies liberated Eastern Europe from Nazi control, he warned that the Soviets would use popular-front governments to fulfill their territorial aspirations and to win influence in Eastern Europe. In 1944 he became chief of the Division of Eastern European Affairs and steadfastly opposed recognition of Hungary, Romania, and Bulgaria because of their undemocratic governments.

In 1946, as the Cold War developed, he replaced George F. Kennan as counselor at the U.S. embassy in Moscow. Once again he warned of Soviet expansionist goals and of the USSR's efforts to drive a wedge between the United

States and Great Britain. In 1948 he returned to Washington, serving in two State Department administrative posts before being posted to Rome in 1950 as minister counselor. In 1955 he became minister and consul general to Singapore, and in 1957 he was named ambassador to South Vietnam. He supported Ngo Dinh Diem's regime until the fall of 1960, when he reported that Diem's control over South Vietnam was slipping and that unless steps were taken to reform the government, Diem would likely be overthrown in a coup or lose power to the Vietcong. He believed that Diem should be replaced. Increasingly dissatisfied with Durbrow, Diem and Colonel Edward G. Lansdale recommended that he be transferred, and in 1961 he was recalled by President John F. Kennedy. From 1961 to 1965 Durbrow served as alternate representative to the North Atlantic Council, a division of the North Atlantic Treaty Organization (NATO). He was an adviser to the commander of the Air University at Montgomery, Alabama, until he retired in 1968.

JAMES L. GORMLEY

See also Cold War; Eastern Europe; Vietnam War

FURTHER READING

DeSantis, Hugh. *The Diplomacy of Silence: The American Foreign Service, the Soviet Union, and the Cold War, 1933–1947*. New York, 1980.

Halberstam, David. *The Best and the Brightest*. New York, 1972.

E

EAGLEBURGER, LAWRENCE SYDNEY

(*b.* 31 August 1930)

Diplomat, ambassador to Yugoslavia (1977–1981), deputy secretary of state (1989–1992), and secretary of state (1992–1993). A graduate of the University of Wisconsin, Eagleburger joined the Foreign Service in 1957 and served in various posts in Washington, in the Departments of State and Defense and the National Security Council, and abroad, with a particular focus on Yugoslavia, where he was posted in 1962–1965 and later served as ambassador. He subsequently served as undersecretary for political affairs (1982–1984). He retired from the Foreign Service in 1984 to become president of Kissinger Associates, Inc., but returned to government four years later as deputy secretary of state and became secretary of state in 1992. Experienced, pragmatic, frank, and widely respected as a tough-minded problem solver, Eagleburger's tenure as secretary of state was tested by the post–Cold War era's unstable chaos, which he had predicted earlier. Criticized for moving slowly on Bosnia, for example, he acknowledged misjudging Serbian President Slobodan Milosevic, whom he subsequently said should be tried for crimes against humanity. Steadfastly opposed to military intervention against the Serbs in Bosnia and Herzegovina, he nonetheless supported the United Nations–approved no-fly zone over Bosnia to prevent expansion of the Balkan conflict. Essentially a caretaker after Secretary of State James A. Baker stepped down to concentrate on President George Bush's 1992 reelection campaign, Eagleburger grappled with a range of intractable issues for which no lasting solutions were found.

BRUCE R. KUNIHOLM

See also Bosnia-Herzegovina; Bush, George Herbert Walker; Croatia; Serbia; Yugoslavia

EARMARKING

An increasingly important mechanism that Congress uses in legislation to require, prohibit, or condition particular actions by the executive branch in carrying out the nation's foreign or domestic policy. A country, a group, or a particular activity are specifically mentioned in legislation and then directives are set out regarding that entity. When "earmarks" are used, the executive branch has virtually no discretion in the implementation of congressional policy decisions. While earmarking is employed in a wide array of legislation on both domestic and foreign issues, the foreign aid appropriation bills are perhaps best known for placing restrictions on how some funds may be used or in specifying how other funds must be used. In the area of foreign aid, earmarks are used both to compel aid to particular countries and to set exact levels of assistance. For almost two decades, for example, legislation has specified exact levels of funding that must be given to Israel and Egypt. It has also identified a series of other countries that must receive aid and specified their dollar amounts as well. Indeed, in 1990 Congress earmarked about 88 percent of all Economic Support Fund assistance and 96 percent of military assistance for specific countries. In the post-Cold War era, this practice has continued with even some former republics of the Soviet Union having aid amounts designated to them in foreign assistance appropriations legislation.

Earmarks also can serve to constrain, condition, or even prohibit actions of the executive branch. Any military assistance to Nicaraguan Contras was strictly prohibited by Congress for a two-year period in the 1980s. Some countries may be explicitly prohibited from receiving any U.S. aid. Beginning in the 1970s, continued foreign assistance was made conditional on the recipient government not engaging in a "consistent pattern of gross human rights violations." Also in the 1970s aid to Argentina and Chile was prohibited because of human rights violations by the regimes then in power. The continuation of aid to a number of countries, such as El Salvador, was at various times made conditional on their regular improvement in human rights conditions. Between 1975 and 1978, U.S. aid to Turkey was forbidden because of its use of U.S. weapons in its 1974 invasion of Cyprus in 1974. At later times both aid to and trade with Iran and Iraq were prohibited by congressional action. The president's granting of most-favored-nation trade status to any country was made conditional upon its having a free emigration policy, although in this case the president was given some discretion. In 1993 the continued funding of U.S. operations in Somalia was made conditional on, and restricted to, its use to protect American personnel there and to maintain the flow of relief supplies to needy people. These restrictions precluded its use to support or oppose any of the political factions. In sum, earmarking has become a major technique through which Congress can shape foreign policy and can restrict or determine the extent of presidential discretion in its execution.

JAMES M. McCORMICK

See also Congress; Foreign Aid; Human Rights; Iran-Contra Affair; Johnson Act; Most-Favored-Nation Principle; Presidency

FURTHER READING

"Most Aid Earmarked." *Congressional Quarterly Weekly Report* (20 January 1990): 198.
Cloud, David S. "'Earmarking' Squeezes Technology Agency." *Congressional Quarterly Weekly Report* (18 January 1989): 165–166.
Felton, John. "Dole Takes on Israeli Lobby, Proposes Cutting U.S. Aid." *Congressional Quarterly Weekly Report* (20 January 1990): 196–198.

EARTH SUMMIT, RIO DE JANEIRO

(1992)

Formally known as the United Nations Conference on Environment and Development (UNCED), this grand event of June 3–14, 1992 at Rio de Janeiro represented a major shift in the international community's response to environmental problems since the United Nations Conference on the Human Environment, held in Stockholm in 1972. UNCED focused on socioeconomic and other problems that related to both environment and development and attempted to place both of these domains on "an equal footing." Extensive preparatory work in both governmental and nongovernmental forums preceded the conference, as did the large-scale mobilization of a wide range of "stakeholders" along all issue-areas of relevance. The term "stakeholders" refers to organized groups (governmental and nongovernmental) who defined themselves in terms of some form of "interest." UNCED was the largest meeting on environment ever convened by the international community. The pre-UNCED process consisted of consensus-building (most notably that converging around the final text of Agenda 21), extensive intergovernmental constitutions, and a wide range of nongovernmental forums for expression of views among stakeholders. All of these preparations greatly strengthened the substantive, political, and diplomatic significance of the meeting, which nonetheless was contentious. At Rio, the intergovernmental meeting was accompanied by a parallel process involving nongovernmental entities (of all types and from almost every country). The major products of UNCED include the Framework Convention on Climate Change, the Convention on Biological Diversity and on Agenda 21. As a global statement of intent and strategy, Agenda 21 represents the international community's general consensus about global "problems" as well as general "solutions." One of the most significant outcomes of UNCED was the formal incorporation of the concept of "sustainable development" as the main objective steering the development activities of the international community. This concept posited a model of "sustainability" (referring to resilience of social and environmental conditions) juxtaposed against (perhaps even replacing) the conventional models of growth that focused mainly on expansion of economic output that had shaped international thinking in the post–World War II era. In organizational terms, UNCED stipulated the establishment of the United Nations Commission on Sustainable Development (UNCSD) to oversee the follow-up activities of the general accords of Rio and directed the establishment of similar commissions (or councils) at the national level. In the United States, the Presidential Council on Sustainable Development represents the formal response of the United States to the UNCED directives. At Rio, the U.S. delegation, representing the views of the Bush administration, was quite reserved on the subject of biodiversity (in fact, the United States refused then to sign that convention on the grounds that private industry would be hampered) and gave only modest support to Agenda 21. As of June 1996, the United States still had not ratified the Convention on Biological Diversity that grew out of the Earth Summit at Rio. A formal international review of the post-Rio activities, scheduled for 1997 (five years after UNCED) provided a target date for a major international evaluation and assessment of intent and of actions.

NAZLI CHOUCRI

See also Environment; United Nations Environment Program

FURTHER READING

Choucri, Nazli, ed. *Global Accord: Environmental Challenges and International Responses.* Cambridge, Mass., 1993.
Council on Environmental Quality. *United States of America National Report.* Washington, D.C., 1992.
United Nations Conference on Environment and Development. *Agenda 21: Programme of Action for Sustainable Development.* New York, 1992.

EASTERN EUROPE

The region that came to be known as Eastern Europe was defined in large part by political, rather than traditional geographic, criteria. From 1948 to 1989, it included those states in the region that were ruled by communist governments: Poland, East Germany, Czechoslovakia, Hungary, Bulgaria, Romania, Albania, and Yugoslavia. Since the end of communist rule, citizens in the region, particularly in Poland, Czechoslovakia (and its successors, the Czech and Slovak Republics) and Hungary, see their countries as part of central Europe. Among American analysts and policymakers, several terms including Central Europe, East Central Europe, South East Europe, and the Balkans have been used to define all or parts of the region. Most recently, officials in the U.S. Department of State have decided to refer to all of the countries in the region as part of central Europe.

U.S. relations with the countries of central and eastern Europe have been influenced by the political upheavals and changes that have occurred in the area in the twentieth century. They have also reflected the generally low priority U.S. policymakers have given to relations with countries in the region.

The Interwar Period

The countries that were referred to as Eastern Europe during the communist period differed greatly from each other prior to the institution of communist systems. Located at the heart of Europe, they were subject to a wide variety of cultural, economic, and religious influences. They were also often part of or ruled by larger outside powers. As a result, the ethnic groups in the region developed very different religious and political traditions, and achieved different levels of economic development. Tensions between the region's various ethnic groups have often led to political instability and armed conflict.

Following the demise of the Austro-Hungarian Empire at the end of World War I, independent states were created in the area. All of these states were republics or constitutional monarchies. However, only in Czechoslovakia was it outside actors who brought down democracy. In the rest of the region, democratic liberties were restricted, and monarchs, or coalitions of military officers, traditional land-owning elites and representatives of the new industrial and bureaucratic elites came to dominate increasingly authoritarian regimes.

The demise of democracy in all but Czechoslovakia can be attributed in part to the lack of social conditions favorable to democracy. With the exception of Czechoslovakia, all of the countries in the region were agrarian societies with underdeveloped economies. Early efforts to industrialize met with some success. Growth rates in Poland and Romania, for example, were higher in the 1920s than those in most West European countries. However, the impact of the great depression was devastating throughout the region. Unemployment levels soared, as did social misery, particularly in the cities.

In Albania, Romania, and Bulgaria, seventy-five to eighty percent of the population remained dependent on agriculture in the 1930s. Yugoslavia was also predominantly agrarian society, although development levels varied greatly within the country. In Poland and Hungary, sixty and fifty percent of the population, respectively, was still dependent on agriculture in 1930. Only in Czechoslova-

kia, which had accounted for seventy to ninety percent of the industry of the Austro-Hungarian Empire, and those sections of Germany that later became the German Democratic Republic (GDR), did development levels and social structures approximate those found in more developed western European countries.

Literacy rates and educational levels followed similar patterns. In Czechoslovakia, there was near universal female as well as general literacy by 1921. Literacy rates in Hungary and Poland approximated those in the more developed western European countries by the early 1930s. In the Balkan countries, from one third to one half of the adult population, and far larger percentages of women, were illiterate at this time. Political leaders expanded educational opportunities throughout the region. However, since the national economies could not absorb the large numbers of university graduates produced, universities became hotbeds of political unrest. They also became recruiting grounds for extremist movements on both left and right.

Communist parties were established throughout the region in the early 1920s. The party was strongest in Czechoslovakia, where it gained from ten to thirteen percent of the vote in free elections and remained legal until the German occupiers banned all political parties. Communists also did well in Yugoslavia and in Bulgaria, where they drew on a radical peasant tradition, until the party was banned. In the rest of the region, however, right wing extremists posed the greatest danger to political stability.

Groups such as the Arrow Cross in Hungary and the Iron Guard in Romania played on popular dissatisfaction and became major forces in political life. In Bulgaria, the extreme nationalist Internal Macedonian Revolutionary Organization (IMRO), came to rule parts of the country.

The actions of political leaders and citizens' lack of experience with pluralistic and egalitarian forms of government also contributed to the demise of democracy. There were political leaders dedicated to the principles of democracy in each of these countries. However, with the exception of Czechoslovakia, where Tomá G. Masaryk, the country's first president, and other leaders were fervent defenders of democratic values, many of the traditional elites in Eastern European countries had little real faith in democracy and did whatever possible to subvert it.

The persistence of democracy in Czechoslovakia reflected the fact that the country enjoyed far better conditions, particularly in the Czech lands, for the maintenance of democratic government. The actions of the country's leaders also helped to sustain democracy. Under Masaryk and Eduard Beneš who succeeded him as President in 1935, the leadership enacted progressive social and labor policies. However, although they were more successful than many of their counterparts elsewhere in the region in incorporating the growing working class into politics and defusing discontent, Czechoslovakia's leaders were not as successful in dealing with the country's various ethnic groups. The dissatisfaction of the Sudeten Germans with their loss of status as members of the ruling group under Austria and with their economic situation provided the pretext for Hitler's annexation of the Sudetenland and occupation of Bohemia and Moravia. Similarly, resentment of what many perceived to be their secondary status led many Slovaks to welcome the creation of a Slovak state under Hitler's tutelage in 1939.

As the interwar period progressed, internal strife, coupled with the need to rely on external capital and expertise, led to the increasing penetration of most of these countries by Italy and Germany. It was the actions of outside powers that eventually brought about the end of the interwar state system. However, internal forces weakened these governments and facilitated penetration by outside actors.

Ethnic conflicts and the legacy of Versailles hindered efforts at cooperation within the region and led the leaders of the new states to look to outside allies to provide security. The impact of these factors was particularly evident in the foreign policy objectives of interwar Hungary. Defeated in World War I, Hungary lost two-thirds of its prewar territory and one-third of its ethnically Hungarian prewar population as the result of the Treaty of Trianon. Many of those who remained outside Hungary's borders were not ethnic Magyars. However, approximately three million Magyars ended up in other states. Efforts to regain lost territories and population dominated Hungary's political agenda and poisoned relations with the country's neighbors. Irredentist sentiment also created support for closer relations with Germany, with its promises of territorial gain for Hungary.

Conflicting interests, ethnic antagonisms, and border disputes also hindered cooperation among other states in the region. Czechoslovakia, Yugoslavia, and Romania created the Little Entente to guard against Hungarian irredentism, but other forms of regional cooperation were slow to develop. Instead, each state sought to ensure its security primarily by relying on international bodies such as the League of Nations and on outside powers.

In Poland, political leaders looked to the League of Nations and treaties with France to ensure their security. They also sought to maintain good relations with Romania. The Treaty of Locarno of October 1925, which weakened France's commitment to its eastern allies, threatened this strategy. Poland signed a non-aggression treaty with the Soviet Union in 1932 and a Declaration of Non-Aggression with Germany in 1934, neither of which prevented Germany and the Soviet Union from invading Poland in 1939. The German attack of 1 September 1939 was followed by an invasion by Russian troops and the flight of Poland's president and government on 17 September.

Leaders of Czechoslovakia relied on their treaty with France and on good relations with Great Britain to guarantee Czechoslovakia's security. A member of the Little Entente, Czechoslovakia also played an active role in the League of Nations. Czechoslovakia signed a treaty with the Soviet Union in 1935 under which the Soviets were obligated to aid Czechoslovakia only if France honored its commitment to do so.

In the immediate post-World War I period, Italy was the main power active in the region besides France. Relations with Italy became important in Hungary, as well as in Albania and Bulgaria. Germany, already the main trading partner of the countries in the region by the early 1920s, made good use of the lack of interest of most other western countries to increase its economic and political influence in the region. As Germany recovered from its defeat in World War I, German influence grew. Economic agreements concluded in the mid-1930s bound many of these countries closely to Germany for markets and trade. German and Italian investment was a leading source of capital in much of the region. Hungary and the Balkan countries were particularly receptive to German overtures.

U.S. relations with the new states in the region predated their establishment. Woodrow Wilson was originally hesitant to support the urging of leaders from the region that independent states be created to replace Austria-Hungary. As World War I progressed, however, he became convinced of the impossibility of resurrecting Austria-Hungary after the war's end. U.S. support for independent states in the region was reflected in several of Wilson's Fourteen Points, and the United States rapidly recognized the new states. However, although the United States ranked third among the region's trading partners during the interwar period, central and eastern Europe did not figure prominently in U.S. foreign policy calculations. As the United States withdrew from Europe to focus on areas closer to home after World War I, U.S. leaders came to view relations with the central and eastern European countries as low level concerns.

World War II

The United States did not recognize the results of the Munich agreement in 1938 or the German and Soviet invasions of Poland in 1939. The U.S. government recognized the Czechoslovak and Polish governments in exile and provided support for missions abroad. However, active U.S. involvement in support of the efforts of those governments to liberate their countries came only after U.S. involvement in World War II.

U.S. policy toward the other countries in the region reflected their status as belligerents or non-combatants. Originally neutral, Romania moved closer to the Axis powers in 1939 and early 1940. Forced to cede Bessarabia to the Soviet Union in June 1940, Romania nonetheless requested and received German guarantees after accept-

ing the loss of part of Transylvania to Hungary and the Southern Dobruja to Bulgaria. The growth of German influence in the region was evident in the admission of Hungary, Romania and Slovakia to the Tripartite Pact in November 1940. Bulgaria and Yugoslavia signed the Tripartite Pact on 25 March 1941. Although the new government installed in Belgrade in reaction to this move did not renounce Yugoslavia's adherence to the Pact, mass demonstrations in support of the United States and Britain were among the factors that led to Hitler's plan to defeat and dismember Yugoslavia.

Under German pressure, Bulgaria, Romania, Slovakia, Hungary, and Croatia declared war on the United States and Britain in December 1941. The United States declared war on Bulgaria, Hungary, and Romania in June 1942.

The shape of post-World War II central and eastern Europe was influenced decisively by the way in which the war ended. As the war drew to a close, differences in the perspectives of the leaders of the United States, Britain and the Soviet Union became evident. U.S. leaders looked to a peace conference at the end of the war to determine boundaries and resolve territorial issues. They were particularly sensitive to the future status of Poland, given the large number of Polish-Americans. However, apart from the issues of Poland and Germany, central and eastern Europe remained low priority issues for U.S. policymakers.

Many central and eastern Europeans charge Roosevelt and Churchill with agreeing to give the Soviet Union a free hand in the region through secret agreements reached in meetings such as those that occurred between Stalin, Roosevelt, and Churchill in Teheran in late November and early December 1943, in Moscow between Churchill and Stalin in October 1944, and at Yalta in February 1945. While documented evidence of Churchill's and Stalin's discussion of a specific division of influence in the Balkans in 1944 exists, similar evidence for Roosevelt's acquiescence to Soviet domination of part of the region is not available. However, it is clear that little was done to ensure the realization of the principles of the Yalta Declaration, which pledged the allies to help create conditions in which elections could be held to allow people to choose their form of government and to work to restore self-government to groups deprived of it by force. As a result, much of central and eastern Europe fell within the Soviet Union's sphere of influence after World War II. The course of the war in Europe helped cement Soviet control of the region. U.S. troops liberated part of Germany, and part of western Czechoslovakia. However, Soviet troops played the major role in liberating much of the rest of the region. In Yugoslavia, Soviet troops helped to liberate Belgrade, but the largest share of the fighting was done by Tito and the partisans with support from the United States and Britain.

The Communist Era

As the Cold War developed, U.S. policy reflected the growing hostility between the Soviet Union and the Western Allies. U.S. policy toward central and eastern Europe came to be dominated by consideration of its impact on U.S.-Soviet relations. With some modifications, this orientation prevailed until the end of communist rule in the region in 1989.

The Soviet rejection of the Marshall Plan, the cornerstone of the U.S. approach to aid economic recovery in Europe, signaled the breakdown of the World War II alliance and presaged the decrease in economic ties between East and West in Europe. Several of the central and eastern European countries, including Czechoslovakia, expressed interest in the Marshall Plan but yielded to Soviet pressure to withdraw from the process.

U.S. measures to restrict trade with communist countries began in early 1948. The Export Control Act of 1949 prohibited exports judged related to national security to communist states. The Coordinating Committee on East-West Trade Policy (COCOM) was created in November 1949 to coordinate decisions regarding trade in strategic goods. Further acts restricting trade were passed in the early 1950s. Thus, the Battle Act (1951) prohibited American assistance to any state that shipped strategic goods to the Soviet Union or countries it dominated, and the Trade Agreement Extension Act (1951), removed most-favored-nation status (MFN) from the Soviet Union and the central and eastern European states.

The primary exception to U.S. efforts to isolate central and eastern European countries was Yugoslavia. U.S. leaders were initially suspicious, but Yugoslavia's expulsion from the socialist commonwealth was followed by U.S. aid, including military assistance and loans from the Export-Import Bank.

Efforts to emulate certain aspects of Soviet experience began in several central and eastern European countries as soon as they were liberated by the Red Army. However, between 1944 and 1948, central and eastern European communist leaders, at Soviet urging, gave lip service to the need to adapt the Soviet model to the specific conditions of their countries. Although the Communist Party had a number of advantages that were not shared by their opponents, other political forces were allowed to operate during this period, and political life reflected each nation's particular history and traditions.

This toleration of diversity ended abruptly in 1948, following Tito's expulsion from the socialist commonwealth in 1947 and the intensification of hostility between the Soviet Union and its wartime allies. After the February 1948 coup by communist leaders in Prague brought Czechoslovakia firmly under communist control, copying the Soviet model of political organization, economic development, and social transformation began in earnest.

As the result of these policies, the organization of political, economic, and social life in central and eastern Europe came to resemble that of the Soviet Union to a large degree. Central and eastern European leaders also emulated Soviet approaches in areas as diverse as cultural policy and science. Censorship of information and the outlawing of any effective political opposition made it difficult for opponents of the regime to articulate alternatives. As the Stalinist system was consolidated, purges and show trials similar to those held in the Soviet Union also took place.

The negative effects of this model were soon evident. When political conditions allowed, central and eastern European citizens protested and worked to change the system. Much of the forty-odd years of communist rule in central and eastern Europe can be understood as a clash between the demands of a uniform model and the peculiarities of individual central and eastern European countries.

Worker protests in Czechoslovakia and East Germany after Stalin's death in March 1953 were quickly repressed by the authorities. However, the process of destalinization set in motion by Soviet leaders was to have serious repercussions in Poland and Hungary in 1956.

In both cases, cautious steps to remove some of the worst excesses of the Stalinist system led to growing divisions within the party leadership and a growth of nonconformist activities outside the party. When Khrushchev's secret speech at the 20th congress of the Soviet Communist Party unleashed another, more ambitious round of destalinization in 1956, popular pressure for change outran the ability of the Hungarian and Polish leaderships to control it. In retaliation for growing demands in Hungary for a multiparty political system and withdrawal from the Warsaw Pact, Soviet troops suppressed the Hungarian revolution. In Poland, the Soviets agreed to rely on Wladyslaw Gomulka, previously placed under house arrest for his support of national communism, to reassert the party's control.

Although Gomulka later adopted more conservative policies and condoned a new round of officially sponsored anti-Semitism in 1968, the loosening of political control that occurred early in his tenure as head of the Polish party was to have lasting repercussions in Poland. Riots and strikes by workers in 1970 and 1976 brought about change in government policies and Gomulka's replacement. They also served as dress rehearsals for the massive strikes that led to the formation of Solidarity, the first officially recognized free trade union in the communist world, in 1980. Solidarity was forced to go underground when General Wojciech Jaruzelski declared martial law in December 1981. However, its legacy helped to set the stage for the negotiated end of communism in Poland in 1989.

Political developments also took an unorthodox turn in Hungary. After restoring the communist party's control in Hungary, Janos Kadar presided over a process of economic reform that led to the introduction of many market elements. His rule was also characterized by a gradual broadening of the limits of debate and decrease in restrictions on the activities of intellectuals. Leaders in both Poland and Hungary took steps to increase the economic and other ties of their countries with non-communist European countries and with the United States.

In the rest of the region, communist rule was much harsher during most of the communist period. In Czechoslovakia, the effort to create socialism with a human face in 1968 was brutally crushed by Soviet and Warsaw Pact troops. Led by Gustáv Husák, the communist party reasserted its control, re-instituted strict censorship and control of intellectual life, and removed supporters of reformist party leader Alexander Dubček from their positions in intellectual and economic life as well as from political power. The economic and cultural stagnation that resulted was broken only in the late 1970s by the appearance of Charter 77 and VONS, the Committee for the Defense of the Unjustly Persecuted. Efforts to increase contacts with the West were renounced, and Czechoslovakia remained highly integrated in the socialist bloc for the remainder of the communist era. The East German regime was similarly conservative. Under Walter Ulbrecht and then Eric Honccckcr, the leadership developed a special economic relationship with West Germany. But ties to other Western countries were strictly limited.

In Bulgaria, Romania, and Albania, destalinization remained a largely formal process that had very little impact on the way the political systems operated. Harsh penalties coupled with economic development kept the open expression of discontent to a minimum in all three. But, although the political system continued to be very repressive in all three countries, their foreign policies diverged in important ways. Along with East Germany and Czechoslovakia, Bulgaria remained the most loyal ally of the Soviet Union in the region. Trade and economic ties were concentrated almost exclusively in the socialist world, and contact with the United States and with non-communist European countries was very limited.

In Romania, the highly repressive regime of Nicolae Ceausescu relied heavily on the security forces to remain in power. In the 1960s, reluctance to follow Khrushchev's plans to encourage specialization within the Council on Mutual Economic Assistance (CMEA) led Romania's leaders to develop greater independence in foreign policy. Romania became the first communist country to recognize Israel after the Cold War and refused to participate in the invasion of Czechoslovakia in 1968. However, these steps were not accompanied by any liberalization at home. Rather, the policies of the Ceausescu regime, particularly toward Romania's sizable Hungarian minority, became increasingly erratic in the 1970s and 1980s.

Albania's communist leaders followed a consistently hard-line policy both domestically and in foreign policy until the late 1980s. In 1948, Albania's leaders renounced their close relationship with the Yugoslav Communist Party in favor of the Soviet Union. After breaking with the Soviet Union in 1956 over the issue of destalinization, they turned to China as a patron and example. Albania experienced its own cultural revolution in the 1970s. However, Albanian-Chinese relations soured after the beginning of warmer U.S.-Chinese relations in the early 1970s. After the death of Enver Hoxha in 1985, Ramiz Alia began to lessen Albania's extreme isolation. The country's extremely xenophobic policies were altered, and the leadership pursued better relationships with its neighbors, particularly Italy.

U.S. policies toward central and eastern Europe during the communist period were determined by consideration of the impact of actions there on developments in the Soviet Union and by the importance of the region for the security of Western Europe. These policies also varied with changes of U.S. administrations as well as with developments within the region.

In the late 1940s and early 1950s, U.S. relations with the states of central and eastern Europe reflected the development of the Cold War and the doctrine of containment of communism. Economic ties and trade were restricted, and cultural and other contacts decreased. As central and eastern European leaders sought to insulate their populations from exposure to western ideas, tourism and travel to the region by U.S. citizens also declined.

The more ambitious goal of rollback or liberation of the countries of central and eastern Europe received some support in the United States during the late 1940s and early 1950s. However, the concept of rollback had a limited impact on U.S. policy. The U.S. failure to come to the aid of the revolutionaries in Hungary in 1956 illustrated the empty nature of these slogans.

Under the Kennedy and the Johnson administrations, the United States adopted a more flexible approach to the region. Spurred by Poland's efforts to develop a form of communism more adapted to Polish conditions after 1956 and by Polish requests for economic assistance, the new policy sought to weaken the ties of central and eastern European countries to the Soviet Union by increased economic and other contacts. Often referred to as peaceful engagement, and under Johnson, as bridge building, this approach reflected the overall U.S. goal of fostering gradual transformation in the region while not directly challenging Soviet interests in the area. Despite the reservations of Congress, export controls were relaxed and economic contacts with those central and eastern European countries that deviated most from the Soviet line increased modestly.

This policy of differentiation in U.S. treatment of particular communist countries according to the extent to which they pursued autonomous policies at home or abroad led to preferential treatment for Yugoslavia, Poland, and due to its efforts to assert some independence in foreign policy, Romania. The Johnson administration also took steps to increase economic contact with other communist countries.

The 1968 invasion of Czechoslovakia and growing concern over the war in Vietnam led to greater Congressional restrictions on the granting of MFN status and other aspects of trade with the region in the mid- to late-1960s. However, the effects of these measures were temporary. Under Nixon, the United States redoubled its efforts to increase economic links to central and eastern Europe. Controls on exports to the region declined, and the Export-Import Bank was once again permitted to finance projects in the region. This orientation was given added impetus by detente with the Soviet Union.

In the early 1970s, high level visits to central and eastern Europe were accompanied by efforts to eliminate trade restrictions and establish trade offices. Differentiation continued to be evident in U.S. policy toward particular countries. In 1973, a National Security Decision Memorandum specified the conditions and timing of U.S. overtures and responses to countries in the region. It made improved economic relations contingent on countries' stands on issues involving U.S. interests, specifically on movement toward resolving bilateral issues including U.S. claims for the nationalization of property and the protection of U.S. citizens. In 1974, congressional concern about human rights violations prompted the passage of the Jackson-Vanik amendment, linking MFN status for communist states with progress toward free emigration.

Under the Carter administration, differentiation continued to guide U.S. policy, but the rigid rank ordering of 1973 was replaced by a de facto division of the region into two groups. The first group, which included Romania, Poland, and Hungary, was to be favored. Countries in the second group, which included the rigid, hard-line regimes in Bulgaria, Czechoslovakia, and the GDR, were accorded less favorable treatment. Expansion of U.S. economic links to the region reflected the eagerness of several governments, particularly those in Poland and Hungary, for loans, credits and increased trade with the West. U.S. trade with the region increased greatly in the last half of the 1970s but continued to be far less important that that of western European countries. The United States provided credits and agricultural guarantees to the Polish government in 1979. In 1980, it extended such programs after the Polish government's agreement with Solidarity.

The dramatic changes in U.S. policy toward central and eastern Europe many feared with Ronald Reagan's election as President in 1980 did not take place. Although Reagan's supporters included those who wanted to cut all aid to central and eastern Europe in order to force the Soviet Union to come to the region's aid, this orientation was not reflected in official policy. After the imposition of martial law and the suppression of Solidarity in December 1981, the United States revoked Poland's MFN status and imposed economic sanctions on both Poland and the Soviet Union. However, under pressure by Polish-American groups, dissidents and the Church in Poland, the administration began to lift the sanctions in 1984. The remaining sanctions were lifted in 1986 after the Polish government declared a general amnesty for political prisoners.

Contacts with the GDR and Czechoslovakia also increased modestly during the 1980s, the first in recognition of the GDR's economic importance in the bloc and the second as the result of the resolution of American claims related to the nationalization of American assets after World War II. Concern with human rights violations led to successful U.S. pressure on Romania to rescind the tax imposed on emigrants in 1983. However, in 1988, the increasingly personalistic and erratic Ceausescu leadership renounced its interest in renewing its MFN status in the face of likely congressional action to rescind it.

The Post-Communist Era

In 1989 and 1990, communist governments collapsed in all of the countries of the region. The end of communist rule in central and eastern Europe opened the way to overcome the post-World War II division of Europe. It also opened a new chapter in U.S. relations with the countries of the region.

The process by which communist regimes fell varied. In Poland and Hungary, communist leaders negotiated themselves out of power in roundtable discussions with the opposition. In both cases, the roundtables culminated a lengthy process of change within the party and in the broader societies. In the former GDR, Czechoslovakia, and Romania, mass demonstrations by thousands of citizens brought about the sudden, unanticipated collapse of what were among the most repressive regimes in the region. In Bulgaria and Albania, the transfer of power to a non-communist government took place in two stages: first to reform communist leaders and then to non-communist political forces.

The end of communist rule led to far-reaching changes in the government, economies, and foreign relations of the countries in the region. Efforts to create or re-create democratic political systems, reintroduce market economies, and rejoin Europe proved to be more demanding than anticipated at the outset of the transition from communist rule. In Yugoslavia and Czechoslovakia, the framework of the state was itself a casualty.

Czechoslovakia escaped the tragedy of civil war that accompanied the break-up of Yugoslavia. However, as in other countries in the region, the costs of dealing with the disruptions, economic hardships, and uncertainty created by the transition were great for many citizens. The election of governments that included successors to the communist parties in Poland in 1993 and Hungary in 1994, and the success of Vladimir Mečiar's anti-market rhetoric in Slovakia in the 1994 elections illustrated that for many citizens, the economic hardships associated with the move to the market led to a desire for a return to some of the guarantees of the past system if not to its political features.

Although they differed in the speed with which they pursued market oriented reforms, the post-communist governments in the region shared a Western orientation in foreign policy. Thus, all took steps to reorient trade patterns and integrate their countries into Western political and economic institutions. All expressed a desire to join the European Union as well as NATO.

U.S. policy toward central and eastern Europe since 1989 reflected the changed political reality in the region. U.S. leaders welcomed the change of regimes and pledged U.S. assistance for the effort to create stable democracies and market economies. Early assistance for Hungary and Poland was extended through the Support for East European Democracies Act (SEED) of 1989 even as non-communist governments were established in other countries. Enterprise funds to support the establishment of private businesses were supplemented by programs of technical and other assistance in areas as diverse as assistance to deal with the ecological consequences of communist rule and the training of local government leaders. The United States also supported stabilization and other loans to countries in the region by the IMF and the World Bank. Trade relations were normalized, and MFN status extended to those countries that previously did not have it. Investment and commercial treaties were signed. Tourism and cultural and educational exchanges also increased.

As during the interwar period, U.S. economic interests in central and eastern Europe were limited. Trade with the countries of the region accounted for a relatively small proportion of all U.S. trade. Trade with the United States increased significantly for many of these countries, but remained secondary to trade with other European countries. Many central and eastern European leaders and citizens saw U.S. investment as a necessary counterbalance to German influence in the region, and U.S. investment grew significantly.

The issue of new security arrangements for the region proved problematic for U.S. policymakers. As in the case of the region's economic links, this issue brought to the fore differences in the perspectives of the United States and some of its European allies. These were most evident in the case of Bosnia and other parts of former Yugoslavia. In late 1994, for example, U.S. support of a coordinated response to continued aggression by the Bosnian Serbs was hampered by congressional unwillingness to appropriate funds to support a continued arms boycott of the Bosnian Muslims.

The question of NATO membership for the countries of the region was similarly problematic. Russian opposition to the inclusion of the central and eastern European countries in NATO was one of the factors that led to the elaboration of the Partnership for Peace in 1993. Designed to allow the gradual integration into NATO of the military forces of formerly communist countries, including Russia and other successors of the Soviet Union, the Partnership for Peace was controversial in central and eastern European countries. Although all became signatories, many countries regarded it as a poor substitute for the security guarantees of NATO membership. Many also regarded it as evidence that the subordination of central and eastern European interests to the demands of the U.S.-Soviet relationship that characterized U.S. relations with the countries of the region during the communist era survived the collapse of both communism and the Soviet Union.

President Clinton's January 1994 statement that it was a question of when, not if, the four countries of the Visegrad grouping (Poland, the Czech Republic, Slovakia, and Hungary) would become NATO members was welcomed by those countries. However, many central and eastern Europeans remained skeptical, particularly in light of continuing Russian opposition to any expansion of NATO.

SHARON L. WOLCHIK

See also Albania; Bulgaria; Cold War; Czech Republic; Hungary; North Atlantic Treaty Organization; Poland; Romania; Russia and the Soviet Union; World War I; World War II; Yugoslavia

FURTHER READING

Byrnes, Robert F. *U.S. Policy: Toward Eastern Europe and the Soviet Union.* Boulder, Colo., 1989.

Dawisha, Karen. *Eastern Europe, Gorbachev, and Reform: The Great Challenge.* 2nd ed. New York, 1990.

Duignan, Peter, and L.H. Gann. *Eastern Europe: The Great Transformation, 1985-1991.* Stanford, Calif., 1992.

Gati, Charles, ed. *The International Politics of Eastern Europe: Studies of the Institute on East Central Europe and Research Institute on International Change.* New York, 1976.

Gati, Charles. *The Bloc That Failed: Soviet-East European Relations in Transition.* Bloomington, Ind., 1990.

Garrett, Stephen A. *From Potsdam to Poland.* New York, 1986.

———. "Eastern Empire Ethnic Groups and American Foreign Policy." *Political Science Quarterly* 93 (Summer 1978): pp. 301-23.

Gordon, Lincoln. *Eroding Empire: Western Relations with Eastern Europe.* Washington, D.C., 1987.

Kovrig, Bennett. *The Myth of Liberation: East-Central Europe in U.S. Diplomacy and Politics Since 1941.* Baltimore, Md., 1973.

Kovrig, Bennett. *Of Walks and Bridges: The United States and Eastern Europe.* New York, 1991.

Lundestad, Geir. *The American Non-Policy Towards Eastern Europe, 1943-1947.* Tromsø, Norway, 1978.

Roberts, Henry L. *Eastern Europe: Politics, Revolution & Diplomacy.* New York, 1970.

Rothschild, Joseph. *East Central Europe Between the Two World Wars.* Seattle, Wash., 1974.

Seton-Watson, Hugh. *Eastern Europe Between the Wars, 1918-1941.* 3rd ed. rev. New York, 1967.

Simons, Thomas W. *Eastern Europe in the Postwar World.* 2nd ed. New York, 1993.

Swain, Geoffrey, and Nigel Swain. *Eastern Europe Since 1945.* New York, 1993.

EAST TIMOR

Located on the island of Timor in Southeastern Asia between Malaysia and Australia, a former Portuguese colony which was invaded by neighboring Indonesia in December 1975, shortly after the Portuguese withdrawal and the outbreak of civil war. U.S. interest in East Timor was small when it was under Portuguese rule, but the issues of the invasion and subsequent annexation, and the authoritarian nature of Indonesian rule over East Timor, continued to affect U.S. foreign policy towards Jakarta in the 1980s and 1990s. In general, Washington adhered to policy guidelines formulated at the time of the invasion, which accepted Indonesian sovereignty over East Timor, but rejected the legitimacy of the annexation and criticized human rights abuses by the Indonesian government. A number of members of Congress, as well as other critics, called for much greater U.S. pressure on Indonesia to allow Timorese self-determination and independence. Criticisms and condemnation of human rights violations also came from the European Community and the United Nations. The Carter administration and its successors, however, gave priority to avoiding a major dispute that would disrupt U.S.-Indonesian relations. Official policy was thus confined to seeking to influence the Indonesian government's physical treatment of the people of East Timor and persuade Jakarta to open the territory to international relief agencies, journalists, and officials. On 12 November 1991, Indonesian military units opened fire and killed a large number of anti-Indonesian demonstrators in East Timor, prompting renewed attention to the issue in Washington. The Bush administration reacted by calling for the Indonesian government to punish the military personnel responsible and by reaffirming the "access policy," while stressing the broad range of U.S. interests in Indonesia. Congress, however, passed resolutions calling for Timorese self-determination and terminated the International Military

Education Training program for Indonesia as of fiscal year 1993. Criticism of Indonesia's human rights violations in East Timor led President Bill Clinton to block Jordan's proposed sale of U.S.-built F-5 fighters to Indonesia in 1993 and to help secure passage in the UN Human Rights Commission of a resolution critical of human rights violations in East Timor.

ROBERT G. SUTTER

See also Human Rights; Indonesia; Mandates and Trusteeships; United Nations

FURTHER READING

U.S. House Committee on Foreign Affairs. *Recent Dvelopments in East Timor: Hearing before the Subcommittee on Asian and Pacific Affairs*, 97th Congress, 2nd Sess. Washington, 1982.

U.S. Senate Committee on Foreign Relations. *Crisis in East Timor and U.S. Policy Toward Indonesia: Hearing before the Committee on Foreign Relations*. 102nd Congress, 2nd session. Washington, 1992.

ECONOMIC ASSISTANCE

See Foreign Aid

ECONOMIC SANCTIONS

A frequently used tool of diplomacy, which for historical and philosophical reasons the United States has particularly favored. Indeed sanctions constituted an important U.S. weapon even before the thirteen colonies achieved their independence. During the twentieth century the United States has utilized sanctions for both economic and political reasons. Yet the history of economic sanctions illustrates that invoking them in order to convince a target country to change its political behavior often represents the triumph of hope over experience.

Economic sanctions fall into two categories. The first is the withdrawal of special government-granted privileges such as loss of most-favored-nation (MFN) status, access to special government loan guaranties, or the ending of foreign aid. In the second category lie the punitive actions the actor nation can take against the target country, such as the freezing of assets, denial of the right to purchase certain specified (and usually sensitive) goods, and the prohibition of access to capital markets or the curtailing or ending of all trade (an "embargo"). If the actor country imposes a blockade on the target nation, that is an act of war and, as such, is not within the ambit of this article. By their nature economic sanctions are imposed by the actor government but may be carried on by the private sector which often suffers in consequence.

Economic sanctions may be used for economic or political reasons. The withdrawal of preferential trade sta-

tus because the target country has been dumping goods (selling them below cost) in the actor nation's markets is a typical example of the use of sanctions for economic reasons. This usage is less controversial than the implementation of economic sanctions in response to a target country's political or military actions. Clearly identifying the goal of a particular instance of sanctions is fundamental to a proper evaluation of their utility and success.

The first use of economic sanctions by the United States occurred prior to independence. In response to the British government's attempt, after 1763, to impose new taxes, merchants in Boston and New York adopted a policy of "non-importation," a voluntary embargo on the purchase of non-essential British products. In 1775 the thirteen colonies, on the verge of declaring their independence, expanded this policy into one of non-importation, non-exportation, and non-consumption.

The merits of coercion without recourse to war particularly appealed to Thomas Jefferson. The Napoleonic Wars gave him the opportunity to put his beliefs into practice as president. By 1806 both Great Britain and France had instituted blockades against one another. Because Great Britain controlled the seas after the destruction of the French fleet at the Battle of Trafalgar in 1805, Great Britain's Orders in Council, which almost entirely ended U.S. trade with the European continent, were more onerous than the French Continental System. The United States, as a neutral, was caught in the middle. Warships of the Royal Navy forcibly stopped and searched U.S. cargo ships, a tactic which led to the death of three U.S. seamen and the wounding of eighteen in the *Chesapeake* case of June 1807. In response to the blockade and the escalating crisis, Jefferson, now president, obtained congressional approval in December 1807 for an Embargo Act which banned all U.S. ships from going to foreign ports and prohibited U.S. merchants from using foreign ships to transport U.S. goods. The effect of the act was detrimental but not determinative to the British and French war efforts; it was catastrophic for U.S. commerce. In March 1809 the Non-Intercourse Act, prohibiting trade with Great Britain and France, replaced the Embargo Act. The French government revoked the ban on U.S. shipping with Great Britain in April 1812 and London repealed the Orders in Council on 23 June 1812, four days after the United States had declared war on Great Britain. While the first major instance of economic sanctions since the Republic's founding had been disastrous for the United States, the idea of economic sanctions as a substitute for military action remained firmly rooted in the U.S. consciousness.

Wilson and the League of Nations

Woodrow Wilson, president of the United States during World War I, had at the heart of his concept of a brave new world a League of Nations which would harness both moral and military authority in defense of world peace. Article 16 of the League's Covenant declared that "if any member state utilized military action in contravention of the covenant, it shall *ipso facto* be deemed to have committed an act of war against all other members of the League, which hereby undertake immediately to subject it to the severance of all trade and financial relations." Faith in the efficacy of economic sanctions had grown in direct proportion to the carnage of World War I. Diplomats claimed that in the complex modern world, states were so dependent on trade that any interference with it would cause them to renounce political or military objectives. The growth of mass democracy also made the use of sanctions more popular. The need to convince a voting citizenry of the need for a war which could result in the loss of civilian life encouraged the prior usage of diplomatic tools short of armed conflict. The devastating carnage of World War I reinforced this trend.

That the League's one significant use of economic sanctions proved a signal failure did little to challenge faith in the efficacy of this tool of diplomacy. In 1935, responding to Italian dictator Benito Mussolini's decision to invade Abyssinia (now Ethiopia), the League embargoed the sale of arms, rubber, certain minerals and transport animals, imposed financial sanctions, and prohibited Italian imports. But the sanctions exempted the key items of coal, oil, and steel. Further blunting their impact was the fact that they were not applied by Germany and the United States, neither of which belonged to the League, nor by Italy's neighbors, Austria, Hungary and Switzerland. Italy's quick victory over Abyssinia, therefore, did not vitiate the faith of the proponents of sanctions in their efficacy but simply illustrated how not to apply them.

For its part, the U.S. government encouraged a "moral embargo" which failed miserably: U.S. oil supplies to Italy jumped from 6.5 to 17.8 percent during 1935. At the same time the United States had enacted two types of economic sanctions. The first, enshrined in the Johnson Act of 1934, prohibited U.S. private loans to any country that had failed to repay its World War I debts to the United States. During the next three years Congress passed and the president signed into law a series of neutrality acts which prohibited loans to belligerents, placed a mandatory embargo upon shipments of arms to belligerents, and forbade U.S. citizens to travel on ships of belligerents. These pieces of legislation illustrated the continuing U.S. faith both in the importance of economic diplomacy and in the ability of any given country to short circuit military action.

The period 1937 to 1941 also saw the growing U.S. use of economic weapons against Japan. In 1937, following the commencement of a full-scale Japanese onslaught against China, the Roosevelt administration refused to "find a war" in the Far East, thereby circumventing the provisions of the neutrality acts and allowing Washington to avoid embargoing China while furnishing aid for that beleaguered nation. In July 1940, Congress passed an "Act for Strengthening the Nation's Defense" which gave the president power to restrict the export of any war material required for U.S. defense or license its export to friendly nations. Roosevelt thereafter slowly began restricting exports of strategic materials including prohibiting the sale of scrap iron to Japan. (The prohibitions operated against all exports but in practice only affected Japan as Washington granted export licenses to friendly nations.) One year later the U.S. government, somewhat inadvertently, prohibited all petroleum exports to Japan. Far from preventing Pearl Harbor and the U.S. entry into World War II in December 1941, these decisions, as historians have since debated, may have hastened the coming of the conflict.

Economic Sanctions During the Cold War

The bipolar conflict greatly encouraged the use of economic sanctions. Articles 39, 41, and 42 of the United Nations Charter provided a mechanism for the multilateral implementation of this tool of statecraft. Furthermore, once the borders of the bipolar world had been set, a battle ensued for the hearts and minds of the growing number of uncommitted states. In this contest economic sanctions, however slim the chances of their actually affecting a target country's actions, had an important role to play: they proved to skeptical audiences that the United States objected to certain behavior and was willing to take some action, albeit far short of war, to demonstrate its distaste.

The Cold War directly motivated the longest running implementation of U.S. sanctions—the attempt, coincident with the Cold War, to impose economic hardships on the Soviet Union and its satellites. The Export Control Act of 1949 was passed as the primary legislative basis for embargoing exports to the Soviet Union and its allies and COCOM was established as the basis for a multilateral embargo also involving most of NATO and Japan.

The Battle Act, enacted in 1950, linked continuation of Marshall Plan and other foreign aid to the recipient countries's acceptance of anti-Soviet sanctions. A counterpart mechanism (CHINCOM) targeted the People's Republic of China. The most important example of the United States's use of economic sanctions during the 1950s came during the Suez crisis which began when Egyptian president Gamel Abdel Nasser nationalized the Suez Canal. In the period from October 1956 through March 1957 the United States used the threat of economic sanctions against all four actors: Great Britain,

France, Israel and Egypt. The Eisenhower administration cut off economic aid to Egypt and froze the dollar deposits of the Egyptian government and of the Suez Canal Company. It denied loans to Great Britain and blocked British borrowings from the International Monetary Fund, while preventing oil shipments to Great Britain and France. American aid stopped flowing to Israel and the administration threatened to forestall any dollars, public and private, from reaching the Jewish state.

In its last year in office the Eisenhower administration also used economic sanctions against Cuba. After the accession to power of Fidel Castro on 1 January 1959, Washington drastically reduced the sugar quota which exempted Cuban production from U.S. tariffs. In 1960, responding to the Cuban expropriation of U.S. property, Washington prohibited all exports to Cuba except for food and medicine. President John Kennedy continued his predecessor's policy which became a regional one once the Organization of American States (OAS) imposed collective sanctions on Cuba from 1964 through 1975. The United States maintained its own embargo past the end of the Cold War. In 1965 the United States and Great Britain, together with the United Nations, implemented sanctions, which most importantly included oil, against the white settler state of Rhodesia which unilaterally had declared its independence.

The United States itself became the victim of economic sanctions during the next decade when the Arab oil producer states instituted a boycott of the United States in retaliation for U.S. support and resupplying of Israel during the Yom Kippur War of 1973. Notable examples of the U.S. use of sanctions during the 1970s included their utilization against Idi Amin's regime in Uganda, and their imposition against Iran in reaction to the seizure of U.S. hostages in Tehran in November 1979. This latter episode broke new legal ground because the United States asserted that it had jurisdiction over dollar accounts in foreign branches of U.S. banks, a claim which ran directly contrary to everything the U.S. government and U.S. legal experts had asserted since the creation of the Eurodollar offshore market for the trading of dollars twenty years earlier. The Soviet invasion of Afghanistan in December 1979 brought a host of U.S. economic sanctions against the Soviet Union. Among other things, the United States ordered the suspension of U.S. grain sales to the Soviet Union and ensured that U.S. athletes would not attend the 1980 Moscow Olympic games.

The battle over U.S. governmental sanctions against South Africa during the 1980s illustrated the way in which sanctions can become a major issue in domestic politics. The Reagan administration proved highly resistant to the use of economic weapons, preferring to let private U.S. companies doing business in South Africa

follow their own consciences or the voluntary Sullivan principles. Ultimately public and congressional pressure for stiff government sanctions prevailed. As a result, Washington imposed a steadily growing series of economic sanctions on the white-dominated regime. These remained in force until President F.W. de Klerk led the Pretoria government through the dismantling of the system of apartheid and the termination of minority control over the government.

The second half of the Cold War witnessed the increasing use by the United States of economic sanctions for economic purposes, specifically to improve the U.S. domestic economy. Motivating this use of sanctions was the decline of the U.S. economy relative to that of other major Western economies, especially the increasing U.S. trade deficit which began in 1971. This response to trade difficulties was in part made possible by the growing number of rules which the free trade regime spawned after the end of World War II. Most-favored-nation status, quotas (voluntary and otherwise), and economic penalties for activities such as dumping and illegal subsidies created privileges and exceptions which could be withdrawn and penalties which could be imposed against a country which seemed to be violating the letter or spirit of the free trade regime and in particular, was seen to be impeding U.S. access to its own market. Japan became the most noticeable target of this form of sanctions, as its massive trade surplus with the United States, together with its sheltered and rule-bound home market, increasingly raised U.S. hackles. The end of the Cold War only increased the attractiveness of economic sanctions as a tool of diplomacy. In the wake of the Iraqi invasion of Kuwait in August 1990 the U.S. government immediately imposed stiff economic sanctions in order to isolate Saddam Hussein's regime. The United Nations adopted these sanctions and imposed further ones until the economic wall around Iraq was as complete as anything previously constructed (Resolution 661 of 6 August 1991). Economic sanctions, however, failed to persuade Saddam Hussein to withdraw from Kuwait. Only the multilateral Desert Storm military operation could accomplish this goal. Thereafter the United Nations voted to retain economic sanctions on Iraq until Saddam Hussein disclosed and destroyed his nuclear, biological, and chemical weapons and made restitution to the victims of the Kuwaiti invasion (Resolution 687 of 2 April 1991).

Beginning in 1992, Serbian aggression in the former Yugoslavia provided the occasion for a series of United Nations sanctions on Serbia. They remained in effect until the Dayton Accords were signed on 21 November 1996. At the same time the United States and other nations imposed an arms embargo on all three combatant states in that conflict: Croatia, Serbia, and Bosnia-Herzegovina. The Clinton administration also oversaw the international attempt to topple the Haitian regime led by General Raoul Cedras by the use of ever more stringent sanctions. However, while their economic impact was felt, in none of these cases did the sanctions achieve any significant results in strictly political terms.

The Relative Inefficiency of Economic Power

The frequent use of economic sanctions might suggest that their use during the Cold War era had proved effective. Actually the reverse is true. Sanctions rarely affect a target country's political or military decisions. Three reasons explain this phenomenon. The first is that the target country usually does not have a vital need for the embargoed item. Contrary to generally held assumptions, most imported products are not strictly necessary to a country's survival and the continuance of its war effort. Additionally, sanctions often encourage import substitution programs which spawn domestic industries that replace imports. In regimes headed by dictators, generally the target of sanctions, the issue of need is further vitiated because only the government and military must be supplied with the items subject to sanctions. For example, the United States, together with Great Britain and France, cut off most of Egypt's access to hard currency during the Suez crisis. Yet Egypt, as a developing nation, had little actual need for foreign exchange and could survive for years without access to these frozen deposits.

The second explanation lies in the fact that most target countries can find alternative sources of supply. Rhodesia made do with oil from South Africa after the imposition of United Nations sanctions prohibited oil shipments to the UDI government. The Soviet Union got grain from Argentina. The sanctions imposed in 1990 impeded but did not end Iraq's receipt of supplies through Jordan, Iran, and Turkey. While clandestine stocks may be more costly and less frequently delivered than normal ones, they are usually sufficient to keep the target country's economy functioning. The same phenomenon operates with regard to exports. Countries subject to embargoes generally remain able to sell their trade commodities, albeit at stiff discounts. Iraqi oil, prohibited from sale by United Nations resolutions, still finds its way to market as did Rhodesian products earlier.

The most important determining factor, however, is the depth of commitment of the target country in respect to the objectionable action. In all cases of sanctions in response to political or military behavior, the target has taken an action which violates the norms of international behavior. It has taken this weighty action because its government and (in the case of democracies) population believe that the political or military goal is crucial to its national interest. That being the case, the target will not abandon its decision simply because of economic hardship. Two-thirds of white Rhodesians voted for UDI. As these settlers believed that black majority rule was anathema, sanctions could not change their minds. Saddam Hussein, Iraq's dictator, intended to make Kuwait his own. He explicitly rejected lesser actions which would have enriched his country's coffers without so completely offending the norms of international conduct. Having chosen to attempt a full scale annexation of Kuwait, Saddam Hussein could not be deterred by economic hardship. The Serbian government and its Bosnian Serb allies initially believed that it was essential to possess and control much of Bosnia-Herzegovina. Moreover, economic sanctions may have the perverse effect of strengthening the target country's government. It can blame economic difficulties on outside forces and use patriotic and xenophobic emotions to rally its citizens in continuing the political or military struggle.

The case of Great Britain during the Suez crisis of 1956 provides a striking example of the truth of these remarks. Great Britain needed money—the embargoed item—and lacked an alternative source of supply. As a democracy, any consequent hardship would need to be justified to its electorate. Of greater importance, the goal was not one which the target government believed constituted a vital national interest. Economic disaster for the sake of a canal license which had only twelve years to run was peripheral to Great Britain's national interest. For these many reasons, sanctions did prove effective in changing the British government's actions. To achieve this constellation of factors simultaneously is nevertheless extremely difficult; the absence of these elements explains why economic sanctions are almost always ineffective to affect political or military decisions.

This is not to say that economic sanctions should never be used. Repeatedly U.S. administrations have successfully resorted to sanctions in order to demonstrate their bona fides at home and abroad. Sanctions showed that the United States opposed racial prejudice in Rhodesia and South Africa. They proved that the Eisenhower administration and its successors would not easily tolerate a communist regime in Cuba. Of equal importance, as the case of Iraq demonstrated, the imposition of sanctions and their failure to alter the target country's conduct demonstrates to critics of military action that all options short of force have been exhausted. The political advantages of the rhetorical support of the recourse to sanctions, not least as a shield by the U.S. government against domestic and foreign criticism, will no doubt ensure their continued use although, as British Prime Minister Neville Chamberlain noted, more often than not they fail to prevent war, fail to stop war, and fail to save the victims of aggression.

DIANE B. KUNZ

See also Cold War; Coordinating Committee for Multilateral Export Controls; Cuba; Export Controls; Extraterritoriality; Human Rights; League of Nations; Napoleonic Wars; Organization of Petroleum Exporting Countries; Suez Crisis; World War II

FURTHER READING

Adler-Karlson, Gunnar. *Western Economic Warfare 1947–1983.* Stockholm, 1968.

Hufbauer, Gary Clyde, Jeffrey J. Schott and Kimberly Elliot. *Economic Sanctions Reconsidered.* 2nd ed., Washington D.C., 1990.

Kunz, Diane B. *The Economic Diplomacy of the Suez Crisis.* Chapel Hill, N.C., 1991.

Jentleson, Bruce W. *Pipeline Politics: The Complex Political Economy of East-West Energy Trade.* Ithaca, N.Y., 1986.

Leyton-Brown, David, ed. *The Utility of International Economic Sanctions.* New York, 1987.

Miyagawa, Makio. *Do Economic Sanctions Work?* New York, 1992.

Renwick, Robin. *Economic Sanctions.* Cambridge, 1981.

Weintraub, Sidney, ed. *Economic Coercion and U.S. Foreign Policy.* Boulder, Colo., 1982.

ECUADOR

Republic located in Western South America, bordering the Pacific Ocean at the Equator between Colombia and Peru. Relations between Ecuador and the United States for most of the nineteenth century were informed by the distance between the two countries and by a general mutual ignorance that gradually broke down in the twentieth century. Since its independence in 1830, Ecuador's foreign policy has been largely directed at maintaining the integrity of its borders, especially in the face of competing Peruvian and Colombian claims to large portions of Ecuador's territory in the Amazon. In 1941 Ecuador and Peru went to war over a boundary dispute that erupted once again in 1995.

In these border conflicts, the United States has historically sided with Peru, a position Ecuadorians believed to be unjust. The United States, for example, was the principal power in promoting the Río Protocol, which ended the fighting between Peru and Ecuador in 1942. In this settlement, Ecuador gave up its claim to a large amount of territory in the Amazon region, including access to the Amazon River. The Ecuadorian government believed that it had been coerced by the United States into signing this agreement. The United States, on the other hand, argued successfully that peace in the Western Hemisphere was necessary for victory in World War II and did in fact push Ecuador into signing an agreement that it later repudiated.

Since the mid-nineteenth century, Ecuador has suspected that the United States had designs on the Galápagos Islands. The islands were then thought to be an important source of guano, a cheap fertilizer rich in nitrogen, used by U.S. planters to restore vitality to soils depleted by overintensive cultivation of tobacco and cotton. In 1855 an aggressive American ship captain, Julius de Brissot, reported rich guano deposits on the islands. He made a deal to extract guano from the islands with José de Villamil, who held the rights to colonize and exploit the islands. This arrangement aroused tremendous opposition in Ecuador when it became public knowledge. Ecuadorians asserted that the United States was accused of trying to create a protectorate over the islands and that the next step would be the occupation and eventual acquisition. In reality, the Galápagos proved to be a poor source of guano, and, in any event, the United States did not wish to acquire them.

Early in the twentieth century, the suspicions of Ecuadorians were once again raised by a renewed interest in the islands on the part of the United States. This time some U.S. strategic planners envisioned the islands as a defensive naval station for the Panama Canal, which was completed in 1914, and in 1910 negotiations took place between the government of President Flavio Eloy Alfaro and the United States. Eloy Alfaro welcomed a U.S. presence in the Galápagos. U.S. payments would provide an additional source of income for Ecuador; more important, some Ecuadorians hoped that the United States would guarantee Ecuador's territory in the face of Peruvian aggression. Other powerful Ecuadorians, however, especially the political enemies of Eloy Alfaro, denounced the negotiations as treasonous. In the end, the talks failed, and the Galápagos never became a U.S. protectorate or naval station. During World War II, the United States built a number of air bases in Ecuador, among them bases on the Galápagos Islands and at Salinas on the Pacific coast near Guayaquil. Ecuador's production of rubber and balsa proved important for the U.S. war effort, and Ecuador's border dispute with Peru temporarily quieted down.

U.S. entrepreneurs, such as Archer Harman, who built the Guayaquil to Quito Railroad (completed 1907) linking the coast with the highlands, played an important role in advancing U.S.-Ecuadorian relations. Harman brought capital and technology to bear in modernizing Ecuador. The banana industry, which boomed in the 1950s and 1960s, also benefited from access to U.S. investments and U.S. markets. Ecuador has generally welcomed U.S. capital and technology, which have been valuable in helping exploit the country's natural resources. An oil boom that began in the 1960s attracted U.S. companies, such as Gulf and Texaco, which helped develop the petroleum industry and made oil the country's major export by the 1970s. The United States has been Ecuador's principal trading partner since World War II, further reinforcing the economic ties between the two nations.

Differences have marred relations on occasion. The refusal of Ecuador to accept the Río Protocol of 1942—guaranteed by the United States—as binding continued to be a source of friction in the 1990s. In the early 1960s Ecuador openly sympathized with Cuba for a short while as a way to demonstrate its independence of the United States and its displeasure with the continuing U.S. backing of the Río Protocol. Other major differences surfaced in the 1950s and 1960s. Ecuador, like several other Latin American nations, claimed that its territorial rights extended 200 miles out to sea. This claim created a conflict with U.S. tuna boat operators, who openly ignored the Ecuadorian claims. Ecuadorian naval vessels periodically seized U.S. tuna boats and brought them into Guayaquil for adjudication; boat owners were fined, bringing diplomatic protests by the United States and legislation passed by Congress protecting U.S. interests from Ecuadorian "depredations." In the 1980s, however, the United States accepted the 200-mile limit as the international standard, and the "tuna wars" between Ecuador and the United States passed into history.

In the 1980s and 1990s Ecuadorian indigenous groups of the Amazon region have taken the lead, with the support of U.S. conservationists and other Indians rights activists, in protecting their habitats against threats to their culture and their way of life. The Protestant Pentecostal movement that mushroomed in the United States has very successfully evangelized in Ecuador, spreading Protestantism and North American religious values widely. The "Voice of the Andes," the radio station HCJB (Heralding Christ Jesus's Blessings), was established in 1931 and became the most powerful station in Ecuador. By 1956 its message was being heard around the world, tying Protestantism, the United States, and Ecuador more closely together in the minds of its listeners.

LAWRENCE A. CLAYTON

See also Cuba; Latin America; Peru

FURTHER READING

Isaacs, Anita. *Military Rule and Transition in Ecuador, 1972–1992.* Pittsburgh, Pa., 1993.

Martz, John D. *Politics and Petroleum in Ecuador.* New Brunswick, N.J., 1987.

Pike, Fredrick B. *The United States and the Andean Republics: Peru, Bolivia, and Ecuador.* Cambridge, Mass., 1977.

Schodt, David W. *Ecuador: An Andean Enigma.* Boulder, Colo., 1987.

EDEN, ROBERT ANTHONY,
1st Earl of Avon

(*b.* 12 June 1897; *d.* 14 January 1977)

British foreign secretary (1935–1938; 1940–1945; 1951–1955) and prime minister (1955–1957). After leaving

Oxford University with a first-class degree, Eden entered Parliament in 1923 as a Conservative. He joined the cabinet as minister without portfolio for League of Nations affairs in 1935 and was named foreign secretary in December of that year. In 1938 Eden resigned, in the process garnering a largely unjustified reputation as an ardent foe of appeasement. In reality, Eden's actions were motivated by fury at Prime Minister Neville Chamberlain's failure to consult him before first rejecting a secret diplomatic proposal from President Franklin D. Roosevelt and then conducting secret diplomacy aimed at Italy's Benito Mussolini. In 1940 Prime Minster Winston Churchill appointed Eden foreign secretary. As foreign secretary, member of the war cabinet, and leader of the House of Commons, Eden became a key member of Great Britain's wartime coalition government. He remained optimistic about the possibility of close cooperation with the Soviet Union far longer than Churchill did and proved much more enthusiastic about opening a "second front" against Nazi forces in Europe than did the prime minister. Eden's involvement in the repatriation of Soviet soldiers who had fought with the German army proved especially controversial, although the decision to return these men to the Soviet Union against their will was made by the war cabinet as a whole.

Eden's experiences dealing with the increasingly dominant U.S. members of the Anglo-American partnership nurtured a growing distrust of Washington, to which Eden increasingly gave voice. At San Francisco in 1945 he unsuccessfully opposed the U.S. idea of protecting the Monroe Doctrine by including a provision for regional organizations under the United Nations Charter. Dean Acheson, secretary of state during President Harry S. Truman's administration, found Eden far less impressive than he had imagined and a difficult negotiating partner. Eden's clashes with John Foster Dulles, who became secretary of state in 1953, during the negotiations over the Japanese peace treaty in 1951 permanently soured their relations. Eden considered the U.S. policy of nonrecognition of the People's Republic of China dangerously provocative. He sparred with Dulles during the Geneva Conference of 1954 on Indochina. Eden also was appalled by the way the United States in 1954 prevented the complaint of Jacobo Arbenz Gúzman's government of Guatemala that it had been driven from power by a U.S.-engineered attack from being heard by the Security Council.

After leading his party to victory in elections in May 1955, Eden proved an inept prime minister. Although he lacked ministerial experience in domestic affairs, his government foundered on an issue of foreign policy: the Egyptian nationalization of the Suez Canal on 26 July 1956. After diplomatic efforts led by Secretary of State Dulles failed to undo Egypt's action, Eden abandoned any effort to work with the United States and instead sought a military attack on Egypt. On 29 October, Israel attacked the Sinai Peninsula and the Gaza Strip; two days later France and Great Britain attacked Egypt. Strong U.S. opposition to the strike combined with U.S. economic pressure forced a humiliating withdrawal of British and French forces from Egypt on 22 December. By that time Eden's fate had been sealed; someone had to pay the price for the embarrassment to Great Britain. Ill health only compounded Eden's political problems. He resigned from office on 9 January 1957, then spent the next two decades attempting to vindicate his actions during the Suez crisis. In particular, Eden untruthfully maintained that he had never authorized British military cooperation with Israel during the Suez invasion.

DIANE B. KUNZ

See also Appeasement; Churchill, Winston Leonard Spencer; Dulles, John Foster; Great Britain; Suez Crisis

FURTHER READING

Carleton, David. *Anthony Eden: A Biography*. London, 1981.
Eden, Anthony. *Memoirs*, 3 vols. Boston, 1960–1965.
Rhodes, James Robert. *Anthony Eden*. London, 1986.

EGYPT

Located in Northeastern Africa, bordered by the Mediterranean Sea, the Red Sea, Sudan, Libya, and Israel, it is the most populous nation in the Middle East and historically the leader of the Arab world. From the nineteenth century to World War II, Egypt was a quasi-independent protectorate, first of the Ottoman Empire and then the British Empire, and its relationship with the United States was limited to generally amicable, non-official contacts. After 1945, the relationship evolved dramatically, involving interactions between a global superpower and a regional giant.

From 1945 to 1952, U.S. policies toward the British presence in Egypt and toward Israel (established in 1948) generated friction. Despite a brief improvement following the Egyptian Revolution of 1952, tension and animosity continued until 1973. In the early 1970s, however, the two powers enjoyed a remarkable rapprochement, and in the decades that followed they forged a partnership on a number of key issues.

In the nineteenth century, private U.S. citizens established informal cultural and economic links with Egypt. Evangelical Christian missionaries began proselytizing there in the 1820s. By the 1880s more than thirty missionaries presided over a college and a network of local schools and churches, and in 1920 their successors founded the American University in Cairo. (The completion of the French-built Suez Canal in 1869 spurred U.S. advo-cates of a transisthmian canal in Central America.) U.S. firms established modest commercial ties in the late nineteenth century, notably to purchase Egyptian oil and to sell weapons to the *khedive*, the ruling Turkish viceroy. Prior to the British occupation of Egypt in 1882, dozens of Americans enlisted as advisers and officers for the *khedive's* army. Washington established diplomatic relations with Egypt in 1922, but during the periods of Ottoman rule and British dominance, the United States identified few political or strategic interests in a land that seemed so remote and exotic.

During the Great Depression of the 1930s, officials in the Department of State encouraged private firms to challenge British commercial supremacy in Egypt. This attitude changed when World War II broke out, at which point the United States supported British control of Egypt on strategic grounds. The Suez Canal and a vast network of British military facilities were vital to the defeat of the Axis powers, all the more so since pro-Axis sentiment was found among high-level Egyptian officials. In February 1942, President Franklin D. Roosevelt signaled his approval of Great Britain's dominance when he implicitly endorsed the British decision to force a reluctant King Farouk to appoint a pro-British prime minister. U.S. refusal to provide Lend-Lease aid to Egypt or purchase surplus Egyptian cotton, and unfavorable coverage of Farouk in the U.S. press, further damaged wartime relations between Roosevelt and Farouk. In 1946, however, the Department of State and the Egyptian Foreign Ministry agreed to raise their legations to embassy status.

Until the overthrow of the monarchy in 1952, several issues soured relations with Egypt. As the Cold War emerged, Western defense strategists considered access to Egypt's military facilities, especially its air bases, to be essential. The British refused to leave Egypt until their right of return in the event of war was guaranteed. Contrary to its stated anti-colonial ideals, Washington supported the British position and refused to endorse Egypt's demand for full independence. In 1947, U.S. support for the creation of Israel, over the objections of Egypt and other Arab states, alienated both the Egyptian government and populace. When Israel militarily defeated Egypt in 1948–1949, anti-U.S. passions soared in Cairo. In 1950–1951, Egyptian nationalists forced Cairo to reject a U.S.-British proposal to establish a multilateral defense pact, the Middle East Command, in the Suez Canal Zone.

The Nasser Era

The Egyptian revolution of 1952 opened a brief period of more amicable relations. In 1952–1954, a coalition of military officers led by Gamal Abdel Nasser ousted King Farouk and took power. Allegations that the Central Intelligence Agency encouraged the officers to rebel remain unproven by available records, but it is clear that Washington warmly welcomed Nasser as a fresh alternative to Farouk's corrupt and incompetent monarchy. U.S. officials brokered a compromise Anglo-Egyptian base treaty that ended British occupation of Egypt while preserving Western strategic interests, and Washington prepared to provide Cairo extensive military and economic aid to ensure its pro-Western orientation. After 1954, however, U.S.-Egyptian relations took a sharply negative turn. The United States sought to include Egypt in a new security pact called the Middle East Defense Organization, and to resolve permanently the Arab-Israeli conflict, beginning with an Egyptian-Israeli peace treaty. Egypt, by contrast, embraced a new foreign policy based on opposition to Western influence in the Middle East, neutrality in the Cold War, cooperation with (but not subservience to) the Soviet Union, the expansion of Egyptian political influence in Arab, African, and Muslim states, and outspoken hostility to the state of Israel. As a result, Nasser's prestige and influence soared among anti-colonial and anti-Zionist nationalists in Arab states and elsewhere in the Third World, while Washington viewed him with growing and deep suspicion.

The Nasser regime refused to make the compromises suggested in the Alpha Plan, a major Anglo-U.S. blueprint for Israeli-Egyptian peace publicized in 1955. In fact, after a devastating Israeli raid at Gaza in February 1955, tensions along the Egyptian-Israeli border mounted steadily until they exploded outright in the Suez War of October 1956. Nasser adamantly refused to join the Baghdad Pact, and eventually emerged as a chief critic of the pact and its Arab member, Iraq. In September 1955, Egypt purchased a substantial quantity of Soviet arms over the vigorous objections of U.S. officials, who viewed the deal as a blatant Soviet attempt to penetrate the heartland of the Middle East and North Africa.

In late 1955 the administration of President Dwight D. Eisenhower tried to woo Egypt away from Moscow by offering to finance the construction of a high dam on the Nile River at Aswan. Nasser had revived a plan, first considered in Farouk's reign, to build a high dam that would control flooding, generate electricity, and stimulate industry and agriculture. Of the total estimated cost of $1. billion, Egypt needed $400 million in foreign currency. After exhaustive financial negotiations, the World Bank agreed to loan Egypt $200 million and the United States and Great Britain pledged to provide $70 million and to consider sympathetically subsequent requests for the remaining $130 million. However, Egypt refused to submit to the conditions included in the British and U.S. aid offer, and continued to negotiate with Soviet Russia, the People's Republic of China, and other communist regimes. Washington thereupon decided, under the top secret Omega Policy, gradually to reduce Nasser's prestige and influence in the Middle East. Consistent with the Omega Plan, the Eisenhower administration rescinded the Aswan Dam aid offer in July 1956. Nasser promptly retaliated by nationalizing the British- and French-owned Suez Canal Company, announcing that he would use its revenues to finance the dam. Egypt defied British and French demands to return the canal company (despite a veiled threat of Anglo-French force); rejected the request of an international committee to relinquish control of the canal to an international entity; and refused U.S. and United Nations efforts to resolve the dispute by compromise. In late October war erupted when Israeli, French, and British forces attacked Suez. The Egyptian Army blocked the canal with debris. Eisenhower's decision to force Great Britain, France, and Israel to halt the operation and withdraw was applauded in Cairo, but Egyptian officials were angered by Washington's decisions to suspend aid to Egypt, freeze Egyptian assets in the United States, and involve itself in the question of control of the canal and the terms under which it would be cleared of debris and then reopened.

U.S.-Egyptian relations continued to decline. Egypt interpreted the Eisenhower Doctrine of early 1957, officially a declaration of intent to resist the spread of communism in the Middle East, as a hostile measure meant to contain Nasser's revolutionary appeal in the region. Cairo condemned Eisenhower's applications of the doctrine in Jordan and Syria in 1957 and Lebanon in 1958. When Egypt and Syria joined to form the United Arab Republic (February 1958 to September 1961), Washington viewed the union as a manifestation of Egyptian expansionism and blamed Nasser for stimulating the bloody revolution that ended the pro-Western monarchy in Baghdad in July 1958. Nasser accepted Soviet aid for the Aswan Dam in late 1958 despite quarrels with Moscow over political developments in Iraq and Syria.

President Eisenhower secured a brief rapprochement between the United States and Egypt when he decided to exploit the political rivalry that emerged between Egypt and the new regime in Iraq. In 1959, Washington found Egypt eligible for food aid, and in 1960 the U.S. supplied two-thirds of Egyptian grain imports. U.S. officials convinced Egypt to put its conflict with Israel "on ice," so as to avoid discussions of the issue that was a major source of tension in U.S.-Egyptian relations. A September 1960 meeting arranged between Eisenhower and Nasser in New York was seen as a symbol of mutual respect. President Kennedy followed up with such friendly gestures as appointing Arab expert John Badeau as ambassador to Cairo and initiating personal correspondence with Nasser. In October 1962 Kennedy granted Egypt a three-year, $432 million food aid deal. By the middle 1960s, however, this rapprochement had faded. In 1962, Egypt intervened in a civil war in Yemen, where

Egyptian troops engaged guerrilla forces backed directly by Saudi Arabia and indirectly by the United States. In June 1963, Cairo signed another arms agreement with Moscow, in order to support its extensive deployment in Yemen, which had reached 70,000 troops by 1964.

President Lyndon B. Johnson, dismayed by Cairo's apparent dependence on the Soviets and hostile rhetoric toward Israel, discontinued Kennedy's efforts at maintaining a friendly relationship with Nasser. In late 1964, a mob protesting U.S. policy in the Congo burned down the United States Information Service Library in Cairo, and the Egyptian Air Force shot down the private airplane of oil prospector John Mecom, a friend of Johnson, when it flew off course. When Washington protested these incidents, Nasser told Johnson to "drink from the sea." Insulted, Johnson thereupon acceded to the demands of several members of Congress and suspended the three-year food aid package in January 1965. After Egypt modified its behavior later in 1965, Washington briefly resumed aid but halted shipments a second time in 1966 when Cairo increased its anti-U.S. and anti-Israeli propaganda.

Escalating Arab-Israeli tensions further complicated the U.S.-Egyptian relationship because Egypt moved closer to Moscow and Israel moved toward greater dependence on Washington. Cairo condemned U.S. weapons shipments to Israel, even as it accepted Soviet arms and military advisers, and deplored what it viewed as pro-Israel attitudes in the U.S. Congress and White House. In late spring 1967, a series of Egyptian threats and military moves, and Egypt's eviction of the U.N. peacekeeping buffer force from Sinai, prompted Israel to launch what it saw as a preemptive strike against the Egyptian air force on 5 June 1967, starting the Six Day War, in which Syria and Jordan joined Egypt. Israel captured the Sinai and Gaza along with Syrian and Jordanian territory, dealing a severe blow to Nasser's prestige. Egypt accused the United States of participating in Israel's military operations, closed the Suez Canal, and severed diplomatic relations with Washington.

The relationship between Washington and Cairo remained cold through 1973. From 1967 to 1970, Egyptian and Israeli forces along opposite banks of the Suez Canal engaged each other in an escalating war of attrition. Egypt increasingly relied on Soviet arms and advisers, and Soviet pilots and artillery crews operated combat aircraft and anti-aircraft missiles used against Israel in 1970. Much to Egypt's embitterment, the United States made sure that Israel received adequate arms to defend its position. In 1970 Secretary of State William P. Rogers brokered a deescalation of the war of attrition, but he failed to convince Egypt and Israel to make peace. The war of attrition continued sporadically after Nasser's sudden death in late 1970.

The Sadat Era

Anwar Sadat, who succeeded Nasser to the presidency of Egypt, became uncomfortable with the extensive Soviet military presence in his country. When he failed to obtain from Moscow the quantities of weapons he needed to continue the war of attrition, he decided to lessen his country's dependence on Moscow by expelling Soviet military advisers in July 1972. Washington misinterpreted this act as a conciliatory signal to the United States, when in reality Sadat wanted the freedom to resume hostilities against Israel without Soviet restraints. In October 1973, Egypt joined Syria in attacking Israel. In addition to recovering occupied territory, Sadat sought to destroy the myth of Israeli invincibility, escape the debilitating stalemate along the canal, and force the United States to take renewed interest in the regional conflict.

The seeds of a major U.S.-Egyptian rapprochement were planted during the 1973 war. At first, Nixon administration officials hurriedly delivered weapons to a beleaguered Israel and delayed a U.N. cease-fire resolution until Israeli forces restored equilibrium along the Egyptian-Israeli front. Secretary of State Henry Kissinger then impartially negotiated Egyptian-Israeli ceasefire agreements and disengagement accords and in 1974 convinced Sadat to restore diplomatic relations with Washington. Egyptian officials applauded Kissinger, Nixon, and his successor, Gerald R. Ford, for even-handed treatment of Arab-Israeli issues. Nixon and Ford rewarded Sadat's moderation with substantial sums of economic aid, surpassing $1 billion per year by 1977.

President Jimmy Carter tried to build on Kissinger's handiwork by organizing an international summit in Geneva to settle the Arab-Israeli conflict. In part because he feared Soviet influence at Geneva, Sadat seized the initiative by making an historic trip to Israel and opening bilateral talks, and Carter assumed the role of arbitrator. At Camp David, the presidential retreat in Maryland, in August and September 1978, and in ventures to Jerusalem and Cairo in March 1979, Carter helped resolve deadlocks in the Egyptian-Israeli negotiations. He hosted the signing of a formal peace treaty at the White House on 26 March, for which President Sadat and Israeli Prime Minister Menachem Begin were later jointly awarded the Nobel Peace Prize. The treaty established peace between the two states, returned the Sinai to Egypt, and opened the Suez Canal to Israeli shipping. Egypt was castigated and ostracized by other Arab states, and Sadat was assassinated in October 1981 by a fanatical nationalist who opposed the peace treaty. Washington rewarded Egypt's peacemaking with substantial economic and military aid. Hosni Mubarak, Sadat's successor as president, affirmed the peace treaty with Israel and moved Egypt toward a partnership with the United

States, providing military base rights and cooperating with U.S. plans in the early 1980s to construct an anti-Soviet network in the Middle East.

Since then, the U.S.-Egyptian relationship has remained on the whole friendly and cooperative, although not without occasional disagreements. Once Egypt recovered the Sinai, cemented its peace with Israel, and renewed its membership in the Arab community, Washington came to rely on it as a facilitator of regional peace negotiations. Egypt endorsed U.S. efforts to promote peace agreements between Israel and other Arab states and between Israel and the Palestinian people. Egypt received $23 billion in military and economic aid between 1981 and 1990 and some $2.3 billion per year in the early 1990s.

During the Persian Gulf War of 1990–1991, U.S. and Egyptian interests converged. Determined to oppose Iraq's bid for political aggrandizement through aggression, Egypt provided crucial political, logistical, and military support for the U.S.-organized operations that helped expel Iraqi forces from Kuwait. To reward this support, the United States cancelled Egypt's military debt of $7 billion in late 1990.

Tensions still lingered in the U.S.-Egyptian relationship. Once it had restored ties with other Arab states, Egypt occasionally sided with them against the United States. Cairo complained about Washington's apparent tolerance of Israeli aggression against Lebanon and its arms sales to Iran. In 1985, Egypt tried to shelter from the United States the hijackers of the cruise ship *Achille Lauro* who had murdered a U.S. citizen. In the early 1990s Egypt opposed U.S. plans to use force to resolve serious disputes with Libya. Some Egyptians criticized the level of devastation the United States inflicted on Iraq in 1991 and complained that the destruction of Iraqi power would enhance the strength of Israel. So strident did the criticism become that President Mubarak felt compelled to explain that he endorsed the war to promote Egyptian and pan-Arab interests, not simply to please the United States. While grateful for U.S. economic aid, Egyptian officials complained that Israel received more assistance and on better terms, even though its population was one-tenth that of Egypt. Minor trade disputes also generated tension. In 1990, Egypt's net foreign debt reached $50 billion, including $12 billion owed to the U.S. government, making it relatively one of the most indebted states in the world.

For their part, U.S. officials became uncomfortable with the rising tide of religious fundamentalism in Egypt, manifest in secret cells such as the "Islamic Group." Fundamentalists openly protested liberal social policies of the secular government and secretly tried to overthrow it with terrorist attacks on police and army officials. When Mubarak ordered government crackdowns that resulted in hundreds of deaths and thousands of arrests, fundamentalists retaliated by targeting foreign tourists and residents for violence. Egyptian fundamentalists were implicated in the February 1993 bombing of the World Trade Center in New York. Such actions notwithstanding, many analysts believe that it would be a mistake to see the unrest in Egypt strictly as manifestations of extremism. The Mubarak government was also being opposed by more moderate groups disillusioned with the state of the economy, official corruption, and political repression. Thus, while still strongly supportive of Mubarak, the Clinton administration had begun to push for greater internal reforms.

There also were signs of change in the foreign policy agenda. While Egypt and Mubarak personally continued to play a key role in the peace process, the Israel-Palestinian accords and Israel-Jordan treaty meant that Egypt no longer stood alone in being at peace with Israel. Its role in the peace process thus was becoming less central. At the same time, issues such as Egypt's refusal to join the Chemical Weapons Convention and its resistance in 1995 to indefinite extension of the Nuclear Nonproliferation Treaty without Israeli accession continued to strain U.S.-Egyptian relations.

PETER L. HAHN

See also Camp David Accords; Cold War; Gulf War of 1990–1991; Israel; Middle East; Nasser, Gamal Abdel; Nuclear Nonproliferation; Sadat, Anwar El-; Suez Crisis

FURTHER READING

Aftandilian, Gregory L. *Egypt's Bid for Arab Leadership: Implications for U.S. Policy.* New York, 1993.

Burns, William J. *Economic Aid and American Policy toward Egypt, 1955–1981.* Albany, N.Y., 1985.

Hahn, Peter L. *The United States, Great Britain, and Egypt, 1945–1956: Strategy and Diplomacy in the Early Cold War.* Chapel Hill, N.C., 1991.

Quandt, William B. *The United States and Egypt: An Essay on Policy for the 1990s.* Washington, D.C., 1990.

———. *The Peace Process: American Diplomacy and the Arab-Israel Conflict Since 1967.* Washington, D.C., 1993.

EINSTEIN, ALBERT

(*b.* 14 March 1879; *d.* 18 April 1955)

The most prominent and important physicist of the twentieth century, born in Ulm, Germany, raised in Munich, and educated in Switzerland. Although never an outstanding student, in 1905, only five years after graduating from the Zurich Polytechnic, and while working in the patent office in Bern, Einstein published three brilliant scientific papers on "Light Quanta," "Brownian Motion," and the "Special Theory of Relativity." Demonstrating that time was relative, and that mass and energy were equivalent and could be converted, the "special theory" revolutionized physics and our understanding of nature. In 1914, Einstein was appointed professor in the Prussian Academy of Sciences and director of Kaiser Wilhelm Institute for Physics in Berlin. In 1916 he published the "General Theory of Relativity," and in 1921 was awarded the Nobel Prize in physics. Einstein became a committed and outspoken social activist, deeply concerned about the social implications of science, the problems of war, and the plight of the Jewish people. His active support for pacifism and Zionism made him the target of Germany's growing anti-Semitic movement during the 1920s and early 1930s. When German dictator Adolph Hitler came to power in 1933, Einstein accepted a professorship at the newly formed Institute for Advanced Study in Princeton, N.J., and took up permanent residency in the United States. In 1941 he became a U.S. citizen. Fear that Nazi Germany might take advantage of the discovery of nuclear fission led Einstein to put aside his pacifist principles and sign a letter, written by a former student, physicist Leo Szilard, in the summer of 1939, warning U.S. President Franklin D. Roosevelt of nuclear fission's military implications. But the U.S. atomic destruction of Hiroshima and Nagasaki in 1945, and the ensuing nuclear arms race, led Einstein to regret this modest contribution to initiating the development of the atomic bomb, and to work fervently for nuclear disarmament and world government. He also actively opposed the suppression of political freedom during the McCarthy period. In 1952 he turned down an offer to become the president of the new state of Israel.

MARTIN J. SHERWIN

See also Hiroshima and Nagasaki Bombings of 1945; Nobel Peace Prize; Nuclear Weapons and Strategy; Peace Movements and Societies, 1914 to present; Science and Technology

FURTHER READING

Clark, Ronald. *Einstein: The Life and Times*. New York, 1971.
French, A. P., ed. *Einstein: A Centenary Volume*. Cambridge, Mass., 1979.
Nathan, O., and H. Norden. *Einstein on Peace*. New York, 1960.

EISENHOWER, DWIGHT DAVID

(*b*. 14 October 1890; *d*. 28 March 1969)

Thirty-fourth president of the United States (1953–1961). Dwight D. Eisenhower's years in the White House marked a highly significant period in the history of twentieth-century international relations. This period encompassed the end of the Korean War, the Geneva accords on Indochina, the first "summit" conference (Geneva) after Potsdam, the Suez Crisis, Fidel Castro's revolution in Cuba, and a second Berlin tangle, among many other developments. For some time, questions have been raised about Eisenhower's personal role in this dramatic period. A World War II military hero, Eisenhower made a successful transition to the political arena and then retained an impressive measure of popularity throughout his presidency. But did broad public enthusiasm emerge more from the smiling and grandfatherly congeniality he exuded in the 1950s than from recognition of dynamic or effective leadership? Speculation has abounded, for example, about the way the president's penchant for leisurely pastimes like golf and fishing translated into minimal supervision of Secretary of State John Foster Dulles's activist globe trotting. Critics have assessed Eisenhower's foreign policy record as a relatively sorry one. For some observers, problems sprang primarily from the rigidity of U.S. thinking during the "Ike Age"—with simplistic Cold War preconceptions hampering efforts to deal with a Soviet Union climbing out from under the burdens of Stalin's power or a "Third World" seething with anti-imperialist nationalism. Others saw difficulties more in the softness or fiscal conservatism of the elderly president's final years in office, when *Sputnik* and the "missile gap" seemed to suggest a loss of U.S. vigor. In more recent years, many of these criticisms have themselves been called into question.

Debate continues over the balance between achievements and failures, but vast archival records have made it abundantly clear that Eisenhower's thoughts and deeds powerfully influenced international affairs in the 1950s. Eisenhower emerges as a far more complex figure than once imagined. On the one hand, his management style was considerably more purposeful and sophisticated than critics believed. He subtly combined behind-the-scenes delegation and supervision with masterful media and public-relations skills to produce what the scholar Fred I. Greenstein has indelibly labeled "hidden-hand" leadership. On the other hand, Eisenhower's intellectual and analytical abilities were more impressive than tongue-tied press conference performances sometimes suggested. Eisenhower's "New Look" military impulses, for example, revealed a sensitivity to the limits of U.S. power in sharp contrast to the sometimes Herculean assumptions of the Harry S. Truman years. There would be uneven translation of shrewd abstract insights into concrete policy decisions, to be sure, but historians with an eye on the broad sweep of Cold War developments often note Eisenhower's distinctive ability to keep the United States essentially at "peace" between 1953 and 1961.

Early Life and Career, 1890–1945

Eisenhower's often subtle and complex views on international affairs—as well as his leadership style—

evolved slowly through decades of experience. In some ways, his background was unusual relative to the formative life and career patterns of other Americans who would become prominent Cold War leaders. But his route to foreign policymaking was neither inappropriate nor unique (George C. Marshall would be an important counterpart example). Compared to Dulles, for instance, Eisenhower's earliest life experiences did not seem likely to yield a globally oriented future. Dulles did spend his childhood in a small town not so different from Abilene, Kansas, Eisenhower's hometown, but family ties regularly took Dulles to Washington and Europe. More narrow horizons predominated through Eisenhower's education and early career. Princeton and law school brought Dulles to clients involved in international business and then to government work under Woodrow Wilson (at the War Trade Board and the Paris Peace Conference). The future president, on the other hand, went from undistinguished days at the U.S. Military Academy at West Point (1911–1915) to an initial assignment training troops in San Antonio, Texas. Throughout the year and a half of U.S. participation in World War I (1917–1918), indeed, he was unable to persuade Department of War superiors to transfer him to European duties.

But wider horizons and opportunities soon opened. A posting in Panama (1922–1925) was followed by advanced training at the Command and General Staff School at Fort Leavenworth and the Army War College in Washington (1925–1926, 1927–1928). Work with General John J. Pershing on the Battle Monuments Commission led to a one-year assignment in Paris and then to duties as assistant to Army Chief of Staff Douglas MacArthur. When MacArthur was given the responsibility of creating a new Philippine army, he took Eisenhower with him to Manila for a four-year tour of duty (1935–1939). While following a different path than Dulles, who was building himself a lucrative career with a prestigious Wall Street law firm and spending extended periods of time in Europe, Eisenhower's experiences were more relevant, given the foreign-policy issues that would confront both men in the 1950s. In their own way, extended postings on the edges of the U.S. empire inculcated a visceral awareness of the way the wider world had become a fundamental ingredient in his country's affairs. The future president would also become accustomed to playing a personal role in that wider world, essentially coming to take for granted the ways in which U.S. power, and the responsibilities that could come with power, shaped-day-to-day behavior.

The outbreak of war in Europe in 1939 had a dramatic impact on Eisenhower's military career, pushing him toward the kind of status and expertise that would make an important foreign policymaking role a distinct possi-

bility for the first time. Initial involvement in Army training and expansion at Fort Sam Houston, Texas, was soon followed by new Washington assignments: in December 1941 he was put in charge of the Philippines and Far Eastern section of the War Plans Division; in March 1942 he became commanding officer of the entire structure, now renamed the Operations Division. By June 1942 General George Marshall had chosen him to command the European Theater of Operations. From his base in London, Eisenhower oversaw the important Mediterranean operations of 1942–1943 and the preparations for the vital "Overlord" assault on Normandy, which he in due course directed. Germany's defeat turned Eisenhower into a celebrated war hero—and gave him experiences that would color his approach to international affairs for the rest of his life. Like so many of his generation, for example, he took from World War II a fundamental conviction regarding the need for an activist U.S. role in the global arena: if Americans tried to retreat to some kind of "isolationist" posture, he categorically believed, grave threats to national interests and world peace were bound to resurface as they had in the 1930s; if Americans chose to accept the responsibilities thrust upon them by history, however, dangers would either be stymied before they gathered steam or effectively controlled through the application of necessary power. Eisenhower's wartime experiences also clearly affected his views on the *manner* in which the United States should exercise world leadership. Confidence in U.S. power, for example, went hand-in-hand with strenuous emphasis on the need for allies: finite physical and mental resources meant that the United States would inevitably have to share wartime and postwar responsibilities with other nations. Eisenhower believed, in turn, that partnerships required hard work and careful tending. In a 1942 letter to his wife, he described his duties in a way that well captured his sense of demanding complexities: coordinating the Anglo-American war effort meant that he had to be "a bit of a diplomat—lawyer—promoter—salesman—social hound—*liar* (at least to get out of social affairs)—mountebank—actor—Simon Legree—humanitarian—orator—and incidentally...a soldier!"

It bears noting that some have argued that Eisenhower could be too open to the less savory aspects of his role, for example, the notorious "Darlan Deal" in North Africa, where an early Anglo-American offensive involved cooperation with one of Vichy's enthusiastic Nazi collaborators. Usually, however, he is given a real measure of credit for the Allied cooperation that helped produce victory. He was astute enough to recognize the diplomatic necessities of his role—and intuitively tactful enough to carry them off; he had a capacity for strenuous work and could shrewdly channel some of his energies into nurturing both personal ties and public relations.

Eisenhower and the Emerging Cold War, 1945–1952

Long before his formal move into the political arena, Eisenhower had ample opportunity to apply wartime lessons or convictions to postwar foreign policy. A succession of military posts from 1945 to 1952 put him close to the center of both discussions and decisions regarding the postwar U.S. role. After some months in Frankfurt immediately following Germany's defeat, he was appointed Army Chief of Staff. He held this position until becoming president of Columbia University in mid-1948, but quite quickly returned to government service after Truman asked him to serve as the first supreme commander of the North Atlantic Treaty Organization (NATO) in late 1950. Even while at Columbia, Eisenhower traveled to Washington about once a week for meetings with Secretary of Defense James Forrestal and others.

A quick glance might suggest that the future president became a typically vigorous and engaged Cold Warrior during these years. Certainly his views shifted away from an initial, Roosevelt-like faith in the potential for Washington-Moscow cooperation. In the spring of 1945, for example, in spite of changing military circumstances and pressure from British leader Winston Churchill and others, Eisenhower had favored sticking to wartime agreements concerning Soviet moves into Berlin and Prague. By 1947, the year of the Truman Doctrine, however, he was writing that "Russia is definitely out to communize the world." An expansion of U.S. military power seemed an inevitable corollary to such changing perceptions and General Eisenhower became a highly vocal supporter of Universal Military Training, the development of global bases, and an atomic arsenal, among other programs. Though every inch a military man, for example, he quickly developed a strong belief in the need for multifaceted responses to post-1945 problems. Economic programs became a particularly regular concern—perhaps because of wartime sensitivity to the crucial relevance of his homefront's resources—and he became an early proponent of aiding in the rehabilitation of both Western Europe and its crucial German core through the Marshall Plan. Nor was this a policy preference rooted in some narrowly defined reading of security needs. A widening circle of highly placed friends in the world of business and finance persuaded him—if he needed persuasion—that the broad national interest required expansive trade and investment opportunities. By 1951, he could write to a defense contractor executive that "From my viewpoint, foreign policy is, or should be, based primarily upon one consideration...the need for the United States to obtain certain raw materials to sustain its economy...and to preserve profitable foreign markets for our surpluses." Nor did Eisenhower embody early Cold War

clichés even when dealing with more precisely military matters. Unlike many Truman administration stalwarts, for example, he developed serious qualms about the skyrocketing defense spending that began in 1950–1951. He was dismayed by the many Washington policymakers who failed to "understand that national security and national solvency are mutually dependent...." Such concern for fiscal responsibility, in fact, was one of the factors that led him to his role as NATO supreme commander. Sharing heavy European responsibilities with trusted allies, he believed, would make it less dangerous for the United States to shoulder the burden of full-fledged *global* leadership: he was willing to serve as a NATO "Moses" in order to encourage U.S. support for a strengthening of the alliance.

From 1947 on, the World War II hero had been urged to enter the political arena by both Republicans and Democrats. Even Eisenhower's most thorough biographers tend to be unsure whether his initial refusal to move in this direction resulted from genuine reluctance or from a calculated desire to whet public interest. By late 1950, however, several factors were overcoming any hesitance. Eisenhower was convinced that it was time for a change in Washington: aside from the fact that the Democrats had domestic priorities he did not support, he saw the Truman administration's combination of exorbitant defense spending and an inability to end the war in Korea as especially reprehensible. Yet, the most visible Republican leaders of the day offered less than palatable alternatives. A late 1950 meeting during which Senator Robert Taft of Ohio, the leading aspirant for the Republican 1952 presidential nomination, voiced ambiguous sentiments regarding NATO generated particular anxiety. Would resurgent Republican "isolationism" threaten deeply valued transatlantic ties? Coaxed by Thomas E. Dewey and other "internationalist" Republicans—as well as by his own ego and ambitions to at least some degree—Eisenhower gradually came to believe that he could serve as the best and safest candidate in 1952.

Foreign policy issues figured prominently in Eisenhower's drive for the White House, and his campaign provided revealing previews of both the substance and style of his presidency. At times, the candidate could show himself as the forthright leader of a sophisticated team. There were cool discussions of issues that would remain high on a list of real administration priorities: the need for reductions in defense spending and tariffs, for example, or the desirability of reintegrating Germany and Japan into the international community. More extreme and even demagogic behavior was also prevalent, however. Some of this emerged from the Republican party more than from its standard bearer: running-mate Richard Nixon's blasting Democratic nominee Adlai Stevenson as a graduate of Dean Acheson's "Cowardly

College of Communist Containment" or the platform's castigation (drafted by Dulles) of the way the Yalta accords and "traitors to the nation in high places" had aided "communist enslavement." But Eisenhower himself also regularly got caught up in more rabid campaigning, hoping to rally the Republican right wing that had been longing for a Taft candidacy. In his great "crusade," the general said on various occasions, he would work to uproot any "subversive or pinkish influence" in Washington and to lift the "yoke of Russian tyranny" from Eastern European satellites. In spite of widely reported antipathy, he even tiptoed around Senator Joseph McCarthy, whose charges of communist infiltration of the U.S. government were proving wild and unsubstantiated. To the chagrin of some admirers, Eisenhower refrained from an anticipated defense of McCarthy target George Marshall while campaigning in Wisconsin.

In the end, it was probably a policy vagary that did more to ensure victory than the political red-baiting bellicosity. Eisenhower's 24 October declaration that "I shall go to Korea" is often said to have definitively clinched the election for him. He had been avoiding sensationalist promises regarding the conflict that had generated such intense frustration and anger. Biting Republican party platform criticisms of Truman's "loss" of China and "immoral containment" had suggested that a Republican victory might bring a sharp escalation of the war effort. But Eisenhower repeatedly urged caution on this front and was explicitly critical of those urging a widening of the war. Such temperateness failed to tap the dramatic potential of the Korean issue, however, and the pledge to investigate personally was designed to grab headlines without incurring risks. As a campaign ploy, it worked splendidly; many concluded that they could put their faith in this military hero's ability to figure out the right thing to do—even if he did not yet seem to know what that would be. In a way that would become typical of his eight-year presidency, Eisenhower enjoyed a distinctly personal triumph in 1952: he won 55.1 percent of the popular vote while the Republicans behind him squeaked through to an eight-vote majority in the House of Representatives and a tie for control of the Senate.

The Search for Balance and Moderation: The Presidency, 1953–1955

The nature of Eisenhower's victory is indicative of the way he was to be the central figure in U.S. foreign policy between 1953 and 1961. Others played significant roles, to be sure, but no one was ultimately either equally or more important than the president. This was partially the result of political realities in the 1950s: Eisenhower's electoral success—repeated in 1956—made him fundamentally necessary to the efforts of others. It was also a function of the president's self-perceptions and style.

Never just a vote-gathering figurehead, he had his own emphatic foreign-policy agenda; he was also enough of an intuitive, master politician to breathe real life into it. Eisenhower's White House years saw nuanced and sometimes stunning performances—even if substantive results could be mixed or problematic.

One of the most basic components of Eisenhower's approach to foreign policy by 1953 was a search for balance and moderation. (This had its counterpart in his effort to shape "modern Republicanism" in the domestic sphere as well.) Time and again—either consciously or instinctively, with respect to both processes and goals—he seems to have sought the middle ground between more extreme possibilities. He was not always successful in imposing restraint—even on himself—but the fundamental impulse was clearly there. The policymaking system that took shape in 1953–1954 is certainly a case in point. On the one hand, Eisenhower was true to lifelong military experience in delegating substantial responsibility for dealing with foreign affairs. Secretary of State Dulles was given a particularly weighty role in analyzing problems and proposing responses, but others were allowed to become prominent players as well: Joint Chiefs of Staff Chairman Arthur Radford, Central Intelligence Agency (CIA) director Allen Dulles, and Secretary of Defense Charles Wilson, for example. On the other hand, the president usually expected and received deferential consultation on important policy matters. He also treated the National Security Council as an important venue for freewheeling debate—although he always ultimately conceived of it as an advisory body rather than one in which tallies of views would determine direction. A related kind of give-and-take characterized Eisenhower's approach to policy input from beyond the executive branch as well. Certain concessions were made to the Republican "Old Guard," for example, sometimes relatively unpalatable ones involving hot rhetoric concerning "Red China" or tongue-biting concerning McCarthyism. At the same time, however, there were limits to the price the administration was willing to pay for right-wing support: the president's own calculations of what common sense required could pull him back, as did the pragmatics of maintaining a desirable measure of bipartisan cooperation with Congressional Democrats.

Balance and moderation were high priorities for substantive as well as procedural matters and Eisenhower came into office with the clear intention of correcting some of what he saw as the policy excesses of the Truman years. In this respect, there is testimony to the seriousness and sophistication of the new president's approach to leadership responsibilities in the fact that he immediately moved to reevaluate the very fundamentals of U.S. diplomacy. In a series of high-level and extended exercises often referred to as "Operation Solarium" (after the White House room where some sessions were held), key administration leaders considered the basic nature of the U.S. role in world affairs: what dangers and/or responsibilities required attention? How could these most effectively be addressed? The New Look policies that emerged did wind up conforming to many of the essentials of Truman's policies, but important changes resulted as well. While there was no doubt about a continuation of global leadership efforts, there was also emphasis on the need for fiscal caution: "long haul" calculations would require some trimming of expenditures in order to maintain both economic health and security. The New Look's search for a more responsible foreign policy ironically generated its own perceptions of extremism. Eisenhower was quickly associated with a strategy that seemed to favor presumably inexpensive nuclear weapons over conventional force: some quipped that the new administration wanted "more bang for the buck." Secretary of State Dulles used the chilling phrase "massive retaliation" in this respect, while the president himself eventually made it clear that he was prepared to use at least "tactical" atomic weapons "just exactly as you would use a bullet...." In fact, however, neither the New Look's design nor its execution were as unbalanced as contemporary opinion sometimes had it. Eisenhower and his advisers did certainly work to build a grand-scale nuclear arsenal: the United States had 18,000 atomic weapons by 1960, three times as many as in 1953. They could also be careless in their rhetoric about its potential utility—or purposely fiery, in the hope of intimidating and thereby deterring antagonists. Nevertheless, the administration simultaneously developed a full range of additional foreign-policy tools. The president was enthusiastic about "covert operations," for example, seeing psychological warfare and Central Intelligence Agency (CIA)-assisted coups as cost-effective—and plausibly deniable—means of dealing with difficult situations. Military and economic aid programs were also of considerable importance, as were energetic diplomatic efforts via the United Nations (UN) and regional security organizations such as NATO and the Southeast Asia Treaty Organization (SEATO). Even Eisenhower's thinking about reducing conventional military forces had its balancing ingredient: a clear assumption that the manpower of allies such as Great Britain, the Federal Republic of Germany, and the Republic of China would allow the U.S. to concentrate on air and naval power without at all adversely affecting total "Free World" strength. In the end, any number of New Look components produced unpalatable or problematic results—but via a more complex route than quick "massive retaliation" images suggest.

Complexity—and a mixed record—are evident in Eisenhower's early decisions about the use of his arsenal as well as its design. While he clearly sought moderation

and balance in his policies, he regularly veered off toward extremism and hamhandedness. The result was an awkward counterpoint that continues to divide scholarly judgments about the quality of presidential leadership. This issue became especially evident in Eisenhower's approach to dealing with "enemies" of the United States. On the one hand, for example, it is true that the predominant tone of policies toward the Soviet Union was not determined by the presidential campaign's "crusade" and "liberation" rhetoric. On the other hand, Eisenhower (and Dulles) long resisted anything that smacked of compromise or détente. Joseph Stalin's death in March 1953 was certainly not seen as an immediate opportunity for a Cold War thaw: change in Moscow's behavior might come, it was believed, but only if steady pressure were maintained on the new Soviet leaders. In a passive sense, this view translated into the president's adamant resistance to Winston Churchill's call for a summit conference. More active policies were also pursued: the targeting of Eastern European satellites for psychological warfare efforts (radio broadcasts and leaflet drops by balloons), for example, or strong support for the rearmament of West Germany (via a European Defense Community) in spite of extreme Soviet sensitivity on this front.

By spring 1955, Eisenhower seemed to believe that the moment for a relaxation of tensions might actually have come. In spite of the fact that the Federal Republic of Germany was about to become a member of NATO, Moscow offered accommodating gestures—most notably, completion of a long-delayed Austrian Peace Treaty. The July summit conference in Geneva saw the president enthusiastically cultivating a peacemaker's image, and the media made much of the way his smiling congeniality contrasted with Dulles's dour reserve. In fact, Eisenhower was really only flirting with the notion of détente. Pressures for reform and liberation in Eastern Europe, for example, helped to push the Soviets away from the slight degree of flexibility that may have been part of their approach to the key issue of German reunification. And when dealing with disarmament—the other high-profile item on the agenda—the president opted for what seems to have been a grand propaganda flourish more than a serious initiative: an "Open Skies" proposal that stood no chance of acceptance by Moscow. The so-called "Spirit of Geneva" quickly faded.

Eisenhower's approach to the People's Republic of China (PRC) also tilted more toward belligerence than balanced moderation. Although he and several key advisers recognized early on that Mao Zedong and Zhou Enlai were far from being Kremlin puppets, a policy of pressure was chosen again, partially as a means of more speedily driving a wedge between Soviet and Chinese "Reds," partially in order to force what would have been defined as better Beijing behavior in any event. In the very first days of his presidency, Eisenhower decided to lift Truman-imposed limitations on Taiwan's freedom of maneuver: a so-called "unleashing" of Jiang Jieshi to demonstrate the new administration's determination to flex U.S. muscles in Asia. This was quickly followed by an important episode of "brinkmanship"—hints of a readiness to use nuclear weapons to end the Korean conflict if a satisfactory armistice were not rapidly signed. After Beijing did cooperate in bringing the bitter war to an end, in July 1953, Eisenhower's impulses were clearly torn. While an ongoing relaxation of tensions was sometimes attractive, so was a continuing use of power to further cajole a strongly nationalistic Chinese Communist regime. In 1954, for example, Eisenhower walked a problematic tightrope regarding Indochina. Even in the face of France's obvious inability to suppress Ho Chi Minh's communists in Vietnam, the president held back from any formal commitment of U.S. force—much less the use of nuclear weapons suggested by some within his administration during the Dien Bien Phu crisis. At the same time, he fully supported the creation of SEATO as a multilateral mechanism for checking further Beijing or communist expansion in the vicinity of Vietnam. Using an image that would echo throughout the Cold War era, he argued that the tumbling of the Indochina "domino" would set off a dangerous chain reaction. A similar admixture was evident in Eisenhower's response to the prolonged "offshore islands" crisis that stretched from September 1954 through April 1955. Chinese Communist efforts to take tiny Nationalist-held strongholds like Jinmen (Quemoy) and Mazu (Matsu) never really seemed a sufficient justification for war to Eisenhower: "those damn islands," he called them. While he moved cautiously for some months, however—even negotiating a defense treaty with Jiang that theoretically made it easier for Washington to control his bellicose actions—the president never considered simply giving up the positions and eventually rattled his nuclear sabres once again. Beijing backed off—until 1958—but going to the brink a second time over the islands seemed absurd and dangerous to many Eisenhower admirers and critics alike.

When dealing with lesser enemies, Eisenhower might be said to have kept enough sense of balance to avoid dramatic and costly actions—but not enough to lead him to modify extreme objectives. Support for the CIA's covert operations in Iran and Guatemala certainly seem to reveal this kind of uneven pattern. Helping to topple Mohammad Mosaddeq's government in Teheran in 1953 and Jacobo Arbenz's in Guatemala City in 1954 involved relatively inexpensive and even "plausibly deniable" maneuvers. The determination to undertake such measures in the first place, however, revealed either melodramatic thinking and/or excessive control ambitions—with scholarly judgment somewhat divided about the exact

proportions in this unpalatable mix. Some appraisals emphasize the way Mosaddeq's nationalization plans and Arbenz's labor and tax reforms were seen as dangerous signs of the Kremlin's ever-searching tentacles. Others speculate about the way Cold War rhetoric was used to rationalize moves to eliminate essentially nationalist threats to U.S. and European oil interests and investments in the Third World overall.

Eisenhower came closest to both reasonable moderation and achievement in his first years in office when dealing with issues that did not involve sharply etched antagonists. He generally developed effective and productive relationships with close European allies, for example. There were rocky moments—as when resentment and concern were generated by the administration's December 1953 threat to undertake an "agonizing reappraisal" of transatlantic relations if there were further delays in vivifying the European Defense Community (EDC). More often, however, Eisenhower got what he wanted from key NATO partners. With Great Britain, he managed to balance serious consultation and support with sometimes pointed skepticism. This posture made it easier for London to coordinate policies with respect to Moscow and German rearmament, even while straining somewhat under U.S. pressure to reform Britain's Middle Eastern relationships. Ties with France were more fragile, but still regularly cooperative. Eisenhower's willingness to offer verbal sympathy and substantial aid was initially designed to serve double duty: to support Paris's efforts in Indochina while securing cooperation regarding the EDC. Disaster on both counts did seem to threaten in mid-1954: on the one hand, because of the essential collapse of the French campaign in Southeast Asia following Dien Bien Phu and the Geneva Conference; on the other, because of a French National Assembly vote defeating the EDC treaty. The president and other policymakers moved fairly quickly beyond anger, however—if only temporarily. A direct U.S. role in Vietnam actually began to seem preferable to reliance on a French proxy—and new London-aided negotiations produced a "Western European Union" mechanism that won Paris's support for West Germany's rearmament and NATO membership by the spring of 1955.

Foreign Crises in the Third World and Eastern Europe: The Presidency, 1956–1959

The foreign-policy patterns established during Eisenhower's first two years in the White House had considerable staying power. Approaches to specific issues such as relations with Moscow or Beijing remained quite consistent—as did more overarching characteristics such as the president's uneven ability to follow through on an abstract commitment to common sense moderation. Such steadiness proved to be a dubious virtue, however.

The global arena of the mid- and late 1950s was extremely volatile: constant tremors were produced by developments as diverse as breakthroughs in nuclear technology (involving widespread production of missiles and forays into space) and the leaps and bounds away from colonialism that saw the emergence of dozens of new African and Asian states. Eisenhower's performance that had initially been mixed at best became steadily more questionable as he proved unable or unwilling to adapt. For a period of some months, to be sure, it looked as if Eisenhower would not actually have an opportunity to develop further his foreign policies in any direction. He suffered a serious heart attack while on vacation in Colorado in September 1955 and did not return to Washington and normal routines until the end of the year. There is testimony to his popularity and political clout, however—as well as to his stamina, sense of duty, and ego—in the fact that he moved surely and easily to renomination. There were flurries of additional concern about an ileitis attack and major surgery in June 1956, but Republicans spent far more time bickering over the possibility of dumping Vice President Richard Nixon from the ticket than rallying round the man who would head it. This proved true for voters in general as well. Democratic candidate Stevenson renewed his efforts against Eisenhower and highlighted a number of foreign policy concerns, most notably when he criticized both the president's openness to nuclear testing and his limited expenditures on missile development. These were not particularly consistent attacks, however, and Eisenhower managed to project a more "hard sense" approach to military and international affairs than the "pie in the sky" Democrats, as he put it. Election day saw him double his 1952 margin of victory.

The president had far more trouble abroad than at home during the campaign—though in the end, two international crises may have actually increased the number of people who wanted to stick with the leader they knew. In both the Middle East and Eastern Europe, problems that had been brewing for years exploded in the summer and fall of 1956. Egypt was at the heart of the first explosion, though it would not be unreasonable to say that the Suez Crisis actually sprang from a fundamental conflict between rising Arab nationalism and Western imperialism. In the early years of Eisenhower's presidency, there had been at least some positive signs regarding transition to a relatively cooperative, postcolonial order. London's slow but real movements had been coaxed and supplemented by Washington, to the point where Eisenhower had agreed to contribute substantially to Gamal Abdel Nasser's Aswan Dam development project. But Washington's potential for clumsy performance in these years was typified by a July 1956 decision to renege on this offer: agitation from groups more sympathetic to Israel and from cotton districts fearing longterm

Egyptian competition had helped change administration minds, as had Cairo's readiness to buy Czech arms and recognize the PRC.

Nasser's seizure of the Suez Canal—in order to raise substitute funds for development—prompted sharply different policies on the two sides of the Atlantic. Eisenhower and Dulles favored extended multinational negotiations with Egypt in order to avoid burning all bridges to the Middle Eastern nationalists sitting on top of vast oil reserves—and to avoid the construction of new bridges between Moscow and the Arabs. London and Paris, on the contrary, opted for the use of old-fashioned force. To compound the potential significance of their disagreement, they kept Washington totally in the dark about elaborate plans being concerted with Israel. When military operations began in the week before election day in the United States, Eisenhower grew livid. He immediately declared his opposition to the moves against Egypt and had his administration take the lead in organizing a U.N. effort that soon forced old allies to a humiliating retreat.

When it came to dealing with the other major crisis that year, it was Washington that had to retreat—away from the "liberation" rhetoric that had often flown when Eisenhower and other policymakers discussed Eastern Europe. Nikita Khrushchev's February 1956 denunciation of Stalinism, at the twentieth Communist Party Congress, had intensified the hopes of major transformations first spawned by new Moscow leaders in 1954–1955. In Poland and Hungary, in particular, protests and backstage maneuvers soon led to promising liberalization on the economic and political levels. Moscow's seeming acceptance came to a shocking end in October, however, and bloody repression in the streets of Budapest signalled a reassertion of tighter Soviet controls.

Eisenhower had regularly insisted that he favored U.S. support for the effort to peacefully "roll back" Soviet power in the satellites, but he had also allowed the sending of many mixed messages. Voice of America and Radio Free Europe broadcasts, leaflet drops to stir discontent with the Soviets, planning for the organization of resistance groups and the placement of arms caches for them—these among other flourishes suggested that the president was enthusiastic about propaganda pressure on Moscow and at least open to the possibility of applying his appetite for covert action. In the face of the full-fledged Hungarian explosion, however, he backed away from a direct U.S. role that would have risked war. This was clearly a sensible and painful decision, but there might have been less suffering for Eastern Europeans if their hopes for U.S. support had not been encouraged in the first place.

Both the Suez crisis and the Hungarian uprising had long-term consequences for Eisenhower's second term as president and for U.S. foreign relations. The Middle East certainly became an increasingly important quarter for direct U.S. activism. As with the Indochina tangle in 1954–1955, Washington began to see a need to leapfrog over inept or recalcitrant European proxies. Costs and frustrations mounted in the process, however, as new layers were added to already well-established linkages with Israel and Saudi Arabia. The "Eisenhower Doctrine," for example, approved by Congress in January 1957, gave advance approval to the use of U.S. troops in the Middle East if the president believed it necessary to deal with aggression supported by "International Communism." In mid-1958, this served as the foundation for a Marine landing in Beirut, Lebanon. The pro-Western, Christian government of Lebanon was actually under threat from Arab nationalist and pro-Nasser factions, but Cold War clichés about Moscow machinations were trotted out for public-relations purposes. The transparency and clumsiness of the operation—as well as the barrage of criticism it generated at home and abroad—may have given Eisenhower a taste of what London and Paris had experienced at the time of Suez.

Although Eastern Europe did not similarly become a region of increasing U.S. activity, the Soviet repressive muscle-flexing in 1956 created a steady series of new problems for the Eisenhower administration. Khrushchev and other Moscow leaders clearly refused to skulk away from the international arena in the wake of bitter criticisms of their intervention in Hungary. In a way which prompted rueful chagrin in Washington, in fact, they went on apparently to gain in stature as a result of diplomatic and economic offensives. Eisenhower felt compelled, for example, to expand U.S. aid programs to countries such as India in order to limit Soviet inroads: Washington contributions to the developing world climbed to almost 90 percent of the foreign-aid budget in the late 1950s. Moscow also seemed especially determined to show itself as part of the wave of the future when it came to technological progress. Americans were certainly dealt a traumatic shock by the double-barreled breakthroughs after the Soviet testing of an intercontinental ballistic missile in August 1957 and the "Sputnik" satellite launch two months later. Criticisms of Eisenhower's budget limitations and overall New Look strategies mounted—in the Ford Foundation–sponsored "Gaither Report" and the writings of Henry Kissinger among other places. Although U-2-flight and other intelligence persuaded the president that there was no serious "missile gap" or "bomber gap" confronting the United States, he gradually increased defense expenditures during his last years in office.

The impact of continuing problems in the Middle East and U.S.-Soviet relations was certainly not eased by developments in Asia. In this region too, Eisenhower found himself confronting a steady flow of predicaments and frustrating results. To no one's real surprise, for example, SEATO proved to be too limited a tool to solve the Indochina conundrum: it might help ward off external interventions—except for Washington's own—but it had no real relevance to the internal problems of political factionism that were the most serious challenges. Between 1955 and 1957, the president made a clear end-run around the Geneva Accords by building a direct U.S. role in South Vietnam. Increasing U.S. aid, the dispatching of U.S. military advisers, and Washington's spurning of Vietnam-wide elections were designed to nurture a viable Saigon partner. While Vietnam smoldered, Eisenhower himself was forced to deal with another dramatic engagement with the PRC. When direct talks with U.S. representatives began in Geneva after the calming down of the 1954–1955 offshore-islands crisis, Beijing may have hoped they would lead to a gradual normalization of relations. They did not—given Washington's studied resistance to agreements that might undercut ties with Jiang or increase Chinese Communist stature in Asia. Prolongation of U.S.-sponsored economic restrictions against China, the transfer of missiles to Taiwan, and the continuing augmentation of Nationalist forces on the coastal islands helped push the PRC toward its own attempt at brinkmanship: renewal of the bombardment of Jinmen and Mazu in September 1958. Eisenhower was sure enough of U.S. military superiority to tough out this challenge—and Beijing did quickly back off once again, although the Asian arena of the Cold War remained as troubled as ever.

The Last Presidential Years: 1959–1961, and the Eisenhower Record

In some ways, Eisenhower was at the top of his form as his leadership neared its end. Dulles's death in May 1959 saw the president take on a more thoroughly front-and-center role in foreign affairs. The power that had always been his now became more obvious than his hidden hand style had sometimes suggested. He traveled a great deal, for instance, and sometimes found huge, cheering crowds in far corners of the globe such as India and North Africa. People admired him for his performance at home as well, particularly during the slow-boil process that seemed to threaten a new Berlin crisis. Eisenhower's instinctive desire to remain calm found an initial match in Khrushchev's tactics. The Soviet leader allowed threatening ultimata to fade through 1959, especially after an exuberant visit to the United States, where meetings at Camp David seemed to relax tensions and demonstrate Eisenhower's capacity for mature statesmanship.

The Cold War did not relent, however. In the spring of 1960, Khrushchev refused to attend a Paris summit conference after the Soviet downing of a U-2 spy plane over

Soviet territory and the capture of the American pilot. Eisenhower had initially tried to deny U.S. espionage in this case—and had been careless in allowing the flights to continue during the time before the summit in the first place. Still, this particular disaster did not demonstrably undercut the president's stature during his last months in office. Americans genuinely liked and admired Eisenhower enough to forgive certain failings. The Farewell Address of early 1961, in which he highlighted the dangers of a politically powerful "military industrial complex" at home, can be seen as another example of the same pattern: as the name attached to it suggests, this speech generated the kind of respect reserved for historical icons such as George Washington—in spite of the fairly self-evident fact that Eisenhower had played a major role in creating the very problem he described. The president's personal popularity did not keep headlines from revealing many serious problems, however. Nor did it keep the Republican Party in power once party leadership had been transferred to Nixon, who lost the 1960 presidential election to John F. Kennedy. In some areas, the news seemed particularly bleak. After years of U.S. neglect and exploitation, for example, Latin America became an explosive arena. Vice President Nixon's stormy and even dangerous 1958 tour sounded alarm bells, as did anti-U.S. student rioting in Panama the following year. An extended crescendo rang ever more jarringly after Castro's revolution in Cuba began in 1959. Eisenhower shifted gears slightly: following the advice of brother Milton Eisenhower and others, for example, he created an Inter-American Development Bank. But there was greater reliance on older tools, as with restrictions on trade with Cuba to slow the radicalism of revolution and the preparations made to apply the Guatemalan psychological warfare script to Castro's radical regime in Havana. In early 1960 the president also ordered the CIA to train Cuban exiles for a possible invasion of the island—the genesis of the 1961 Bay of Pigs invasion.

In Asia, meanwhile, any positive vibrations emanating from another lull in struggles with Beijing over the offshore islands were greatly offset by other sparks and timebombs. Old ally Syngman Rhee in South Korea was forced from office by popular protests in 1960—and Eisenhower himself was forced to cancel a visit to Japan because of anti-U.S. demonstrations there over renewal of a military security pact. Neither of these signs of troubling times proved to be as quickly or profoundly disturbing as the tremors building in Indochina. In the middle of his tenure, the president had hoped to design a process by which he could simultaneously promote peace, the containment of communism, and a U.S. leadership role in Asia. By the time he left office, however, these hopes were being ever more steadily mocked. Ngo Dinh Diem's regime in South Vietnam continued to twin

corruption with resistance to economic and political reform—and made no substantive progress toward nation-building as a result. And Eisenhower policies in Laos had contributed substantially to nation-destabilization, via CIA and military support for the rightist forces that plagued the nationalist/neutralist efforts of Souvanna Phouma.

Aside from the view offered during farflung motorcades during his final years in the White House, Eisenhower could take some fuller measure of satisfaction only from transatlantic relations. Eastern Europe remained a sore subject after the 1956 disasters, to be sure, as a certain amount of shamefaced awkwardness seasoned ritualistic denunciations of Soviet imperialism. But developments in western and central Europe offered significant antidotes. The president had worked hard to encourage the Federal Republic of Germany's membership in the European Coal and Steel Community and NATO earlier in the 1950s—and he very much saw the creation of Euratom and the Common Market as extremely valuable supplementary steps after mid-decade. On the one hand, these building blocks of European integration were valued as effective tools for preventing any further revival of a German menace in the twentieth century: they contributed to what has been called a "dual containment" policy that allowed a major German contribution to Cold War strength without risking independent German power. On the other hand, Eisenhower satisfaction with continental integration also sprang from what might be termed "triple containment" logic. Like Dulles, the president believed there was a historical European tendency to conflict—not just a German one—and that this could be tamed by way of functional cooperation, particularly at the economic level.

Even in the realm of transatlantic relations, however, serious problems arose in the late 1950s. Fallout from Suez was not easily sloughed off, for example. British Prime Minister Harold Macmillan managed to move London toward a restoration of cooperative ties with Washington fairly quickly, but some resentment lingered. French attitudes toward the United States—and vice versa—were yet more delicate. Charles de Gaulle's return to power, in particular, saw greater emphasis on French amour propre—and a corresponding diminution of cooperation in NATO and on other issues. In general, as well, the process of integration helped lift western and central Europe to higher levels of economic success by the late 1950s. Although Eisenhower certainly remained enthusiastic about this development, his last years in the White House also gave him a taste of its potential downside: shifting commercial and investment patterns forced him to confront balance of trade and "dollar gap" problems that were a far cry from the prevalent economic concerns when he entered office.

In every quarter, in fact, the world had witnessed dramatic changes during the eight years of Eisenhower's presidency—and seldom for the better as far as the exercise or enjoyment of U.S. power was concerned. The United States was still far and away the most powerful single state in the international arena, but the huge chasms that had elevated it above the economic and military resources of others had clearly begun to close. Western Europe had recovered from the devastation and dislocations of World War II, Japan was beginning its economic "miracle," and the Third World was shedding colonialism and gaining independence while beginning to form an international bloc. As a result, Eisenhower increasingly found himself confronting complex world problems that were greater than the capacities of his seemingly awesome New Look arsenal. Eisenhower's personal equanimity and continued popularity at the time of his retirement were not enough to make his legacy a fully satisfying or positive one. His capacity for realistic or common sense statesmanship had had its limits throughout his presidency—not the least in the way it was regularly overpowered by his own aggressive definitions of U.S. interests and needs. If the more positive attributes of his approach to international affairs could not thoroughly dominate even the Eisenhower administration's policies, they were even less likely to have a meaningful impact on the self-consciously vigorous assertiveness of his 1960s heirs.

After retirement, Eisenhower went to his farm at Gettysburg, Pennsylvania, near the famous battlefield. He wrote his memoirs, published in 1963 and 1965 as the two-volume *The White House Years*, dedicated in 1962 the Eisenhower presidential library in Abilene, Kansas, and received CIA briefings on major foreign-policy questions. Eisenhower also consulted with Kennedy during the Cuban missile crisis in the fall of 1962, warning the young president not to let the Soviets prolong the negotiations. During the Lyndon B. Johnson Administration's escalation of the war in Vietnam, Eisenhower publicly supported a hawkish policy, including expanded bombing of North Vietnam, in order to achieve victory. He communicated regularly with President Johnson on Vietnam tactics and strategy, sharing with Johnson a disdain for the rising antiwar sentiment in the United States but telling the president that he should abandon a "war of gradualism" in favor of a declaration of war against North Vietnam; the United States, said Eisenhower, should "take any action to win," including, perhaps, use of nuclear weapons. Eisenhower was greatly disappointed when Johnson halted the bombing of the north in early 1968.

When Eisenhower died of heart failure a year later, Americans remembered him as a selfless public servant. "I like Ike" still resonates in the public consciousness.

RONALD W. PRUESSEN

See also Austria; Bay of Pigs Invasion; Berlin; Brinkmanship; Central Intelligence Agency; China; Cold War; Containment; Covert Action; Cuba; Dien Bien Phu; Domino Theory; Dulles, Allen Welsh; Dulles, John Foster; Eisenhower Doctrine; European Defense Community; Germany; Great Britain; Guatemala; Hungary; Iran; Isolationism; Jiang Jieshi; Jinmen-Mazu Crises; Korean War; Laos; Lebanon; Marshall, George Catlett; Massive Retaliation; McCarthyism; National Security Council; Nixon, Richard Milhous; North Atlantic Treaty Organization; Nuclear Weapons and Strategy; Open Skies; Presidency; Russia and the Soviet Union; Southeast Asia Treaty Organization; Sputnik I; Suez Crisis; Taft, Robert A.; Taiwan; Third World; U-2 Incident; Vietnam War; World War II

FURTHER READING

Ambrose, Stephen E. *Eisenhower: Soldier, General of the Army, President-Elect, 1890–1952.* New York, 1983.

———. *Eisenhower: The President.* New York, 1984.

Bischof, Günter, and Stephen Ambrose, eds. *Eisenhower: A Centenary Assessment.* Baton Rouge, La., 1995.

Brendon, Piers. *Ike: His Life and Times.* New York, 1986.

Cook, Blanche Wiesen. *The Declassified Eisenhower.* Garden City, N.Y., 1981.

Divine, Robert. *Eisenhower and the Cold War.* New York, 1981.

Eisenhower, Dwight D. *The White House Years: Mandate for Change, 1953–1956.* Garden City, N.Y., 1983.

———. *The White House Years: Waging Peace, 1956–1961.* Garden City, N.Y., 1963.

Greenstein, Fred I. *The Hidden-Hand Presidency: Eisenhower as Leader.* New York, 1982.

Melanson, Richard A., and David Mayers, eds. *Reevaluating Eisenhower: American Foreign Policy in the 1950s.* Urbana, Ill., 1987.

Pach, Chester J., Jr., and Elmo Richardson. *The Presidency of Dwight D. Eisenhower.* Lawrence, Kans., 1991.

EISENHOWER, MILTON STOVER

(*b.* 15 September 1899; *d.* 2 May 1985)

Government official and presidential adviser on Latin America noted for his successful tenures as the president of Kansas State, Penn State, and Johns Hopkins Universities. Born in Abilene, Kansas, Milton S. Eisenhower began his lengthy government career in the foreign service in 1924. He spent most of the interwar years in the Department of Agriculture, but after the attack on Pearl Harbor, President Franklin D. Roosevelt made him responsible for relocating Japanese Americans from the California coast, an assignment in which he received a painful education in the prejudices and misperceptions that afflicted U.S. foreign relations. These lessons were reinforced when he became associate director of the Office of War Information (OWI), and again when his brother, President Dwight D. Eisenhower, appointed him as his personal envoy to Latin America. Pivotal to the evolution of the Alliance for Progress in the 1950s was Milton Eisenhower's 1963 book arguing that the antidote to communism in Latin America was U.S. assistance to liberal reformers in the Western Hemisphere. Until his death he advised presidents of both parties.

RICHARD H. IMMERMAN

See also Alliance for Progress; Eisenhower, Dwight David; Latin America; Propaganda; Race and Racism

FURTHER READING

Ambrose, Stephen E., and Richard H. Immerman. *Milton S. Eisenhower: Educational Statesman*. Baltimore, Md., 1983.
Eisenhower, Milton S. *The Wine is Bitter: The United States and Latin America*. Garden City, N.Y., 1963.
———. *The President is Calling*. Garden City, N.Y., 1974.

EISENHOWER DOCTRINE

A statement of policy set forth by President Dwight D. Eisenhower in a speech on 5 January 1957 and approved by Congress two months later. This statement and its implementation sought to combat recent Soviet inroads in the Arab world. The Eisenhower Doctrine authorized the president to provide up to $200 million in economic aid and to dispatch American military forces to any Middle Eastern state requesting assistance against "overt armed aggression from any nation controlled by international communism."

After the Soviet bloc agreed to sell arms to Egyptian president Gamal Abdel Nasser in September 1955, the Eisenhower administration became convinced that the Kremlin intended to make the Middle East a central arena of the Cold War. During the next year the United States worked closely with Great Britain to block Nasser's anti-Western nationalism and to curb Soviet influence in Damascus and other Arab capitals. After Great Britain, France, and Israel orchestrated a tripartite attack on Egypt during the Suez Crisis in late 1956, however, the Eisenhower administration moved toward a unilateral American policy in order to avoid being tarred with the brush of imperialism. Although couched in anticommunist rhetoric, the Eisenhower Doctrine did not evoke universal support in early 1957. Some critics, like Arkansas Senator J. William Fulbright, worried that Eisenhower and Secretary of State John Foster Dulles were confusing Arab nationalism with international communism. Others, like Minnesota Senator Hubert H. Humphrey, complained that the White House was seeking "a predated declaration of war" that would weaken congressional control over foreign policy. But few on Capitol Hill wished to be held responsible for "losing" the oil-rich Middle East to the Soviets, and the Eisenhower Doctrine sailed through Congress in March 1957.

It evoked a mixed reaction from the nations of the Middle East. Egypt and Syria denounced it as imperialism pure and simple. Pro-Western regimes in Iraq and Saudi Arabia welcomed American economic assistance but feared that military intervention would backfire, playing into the hands of Arab radicals. Israeli leaders doubted whether they would receive U.S. military assistance under any circumstances. Only Jordan and Lebanon embraced the Eisenhower Doctrine enthusiastically.

President Eisenhower came close to invoking the doctrine twice during 1957. When Palestinian radicals and pro-Nasser officers attempted to overthrow King Hussein of Jordan in April, the president moved the U.S. Sixth Fleet into the eastern Mediterranean and hinted that he might airlift U. S. troops into Amman. When Syria announced plans to buy arms from the Kremlin in August, he warned that the Syrian attack on Turkey or any other neighboring pro-Western regime would prompt swift American military intervention. Not until the summer of 1958, however, did the president actually send troops to the Middle East, and even then he did not invoke the Eisenhower Doctrine. On 14 July, pro-Nasser officers in Baghdad sent shock waves through the Arab world by toppling the Iraqi monarchy in a bloody coup. Within hours, Lebanese president Camille Chamoun, a pro-Western Maronite Christian, formally requested American military help against Muslim rebels backed by Egypt. With a flourish of Cold War rhetoric, Eisenhower dispatched 14,000 U.S. Marines to Beirut the next day. Because he could not prove that Lebanon was threatened by "a nation controlled by internation communism," the president cited his prerogatives as commander in chief, not the Eisenhower Doctrine, to justify his decision to intervene. After helping restore stability in Lebanon, the Marines returned home in November 1958. Before the year was out, however, the president had largely replaced the Eisenhower Doctrine by approving National Security Council (NSC) 5820, which emphasized an accommodation with Arab nationalism rather than military intervention as an effective means of containing the Soviet Union in the Middle East.

DOUGLAS LITTLE

See also Cold War; Containment; Egypt; Eisenhower, Dwight David; Lebanon; Middle East; Nasser, Gamal Abdel; Suez Crisis; Syria

FURTHER READING

Brands, H. W., Jr. *The Specter of Neutralism: The United States and the Emergence of the Third World, 1947-1960*. New York, 1990.
Divine, Robert A. *Eisenhower and the Cold War*. New York, 1981.
Dowty, Alan. *Middle East Crisis: U.S. Decision-Making in 1958, 1970, and 1973*. Berkeley, Calif., 1984.
George, Alexander L. and Richard Smoke. *Deterrence in American Foreign Policy: Theory and Practice*. New York, 1974.

Lesch, David W. *Syria and the United States: Eisenhower's Cold War in the Middle East.* Boulder, Colo., 1992.

Paterson, Thomas G. *Meeting the Communist Threat: Truman to Reagan.* New York, 1988.

Stivers, William. "Eisenhower and the Middle East." In *Reevaluating Eisenhower: American Foreign Policy in the 1950s,* edited by Richard A. Melanson and David Mayers. Chicago, 1987.

ELECTIONS AND FOREIGN POLICY

The impact of foreign policy on elections is controversial, with some analysts assessing it as standing roughly on a par with domestic policy in many post–World War II elections, with others seeing politics stopping "at the water's edge" and finding a foreign policy to have had very little impact, outside of war elections.

Foreign policy can affect voters only if they care about foreign policy, only if they have some minimal information about such policy, and only if the political parties and their candidates present sufficiently distinct stances on foreign policy. While the extent of public concern and information about foreign affairs has long been debated, all agree that when there has been an absence of party and candidate differences the impact of foreign policy in the voting booth has been attenuated. The deciding factor is whether the public has cared to make a choice partly based on foreign affairs, when alternatives are clear, or whether the public is uninterested or incapable of considering foreign policy under all but the most extreme conditions.

Political Parties

From the founding of the nation until World War II, political parties were divided over foreign policy concerns. With the United States assuming a position of world leadership after World War II, a bipartisan foreign policy consensus took effect.

Until World War II, public debate in the United States over foreign affairs was primarily episodic, because the oceanic divide made it possible to ignore foreign policy concerns and because the U.S. economy was relatively closed for its first two centuries. Still, many believe that foreign policy played a key role in the emergence of the first two political parties, the Federalists and the Democratic-Republicans, in the late 1790s. While these parties grew out of divisions over domestic policies, such as Secretary of the Treasury Alexander Hamilton's fiscal proposals, their positions solidified when they extended their reach to include foreign concerns. Most notable were divisions over relations with Great Britain and France, revealed through such specifics as Jay's Treaty, the XYZ Affair, and the Alien and Sedition Acts. Many mark the demise of the Federalists, in turn, by being on the wrong side of the "War Hawk" election of 1810, preceding the War of 1812.

While foreign affairs were of great concern to the governing elite throughout the nineteenth century, these debates were cast, in public forums such as elections, in critical but episodic fashion or in a "domesticated" version or in symbolic terms with little substance. The two most regularly recurring foreign issues of the nineteenth century were the tariff and immigration, but both were mostly debated in public in terms of their domestic consequences. The tariff debates, for example, were commonly over the use of the revenues so generated. Should they be used to balance the budget and reduce pressure for other sources of national governmental revenue, or should they be used for domestic improvements, such as building roads, canals, or harbors? Similarly, immigration was most often addressed in public campaigns in terms of the impact of the new arrivals and their role in this democracy, and, except for the brief life of the nativist American or Know-Nothing party in the 1850s, these issues were mostly debated at the local level.

To be sure, diplomacy and foreign military concerns, from the Monroe Doctrine on, continued, and foreign trade was important from the founding, but these took second place to domestic priorities unless there was a critical episode. Slogans such as "54–40 or Fight," "Remember the Maine," and William Randolph Hearst's cable prior to the Spanish-American-Cuban-Filipino War, "You provide the pictures Stop I'll provide the War Stop," are illustrative. By the end of that century and the beginning of the twentieth century, such episodes became increasingly common, due in part to the growing international reach of U.S. interests. "Twisting the lion's tail," referring to tweaking the British Empire, was a common, if primarily symbolic, campaign refrain at the end of the nineteenth century, similar to the Republicans "waving the bloody shirt" in reference to the Civil War. By 1900 the question of a U.S. empire was consequential in the presidential campaign, signaling not only the success of U.S. industrialization but also the competition for foreign markets with other empires of the day. Isolation that had for long been so felicitous was harder to maintain by the beginning of the twentieth century, and some were arguing that the United States should choose to end that isolation, at least economically. Isolation, however, remained possible. President Woodrow Wilson's successful reelection in 1916 rested in large measure on avoiding entanglement in World War I, and he recognized this publicly with the oft-repeated campaign slogan, "He kept us out of war." By 1920, however, events had changed, and he had hoped to make the 1920 presidential election a "solemn referendum" on the League of Nations. Isolation was chosen, however, and the United States not only held no such solemn referendum but retreated from further active engagement in diplomatic and military affairs, as signified by the Kellogg-Briand Pact.

World War II and the emergence of the United States as a world power meant that the choice of isolation was no longer possible, diplomatically, militarily, or economically. Coincident with this emergence was the era of a bipartisan consensus in foreign policy, especially over superpower competition with the Soviet Union. Former Republican isolationism effectively ended, as best exemplified by the conversion of Senator Arthur H. Vandenburg of Michigan to an internationalist position. This combined with efforts of the Democratic party to distance itself from domestic communism, to invoke the policy of containment, to fight in Korea against communist aggression, and to seek to avoid the label as the party that "lost China." The result was that there were at most modest differences between the centers of the governing elites of the two parties on foreign affairs. With good systematic polling data available at the time, it was possible to seek an understanding of the role of foreign policy in elections. The effect of foreign policy on public opinion and on voting behavior was found to be negligible, but it could not be judged whether this was attributable to public ignorance and indifference or to the lack of distinctive alternatives offered by the parties and their candidates. The breakdown of the bipartisan consensus over Vietnam and into the 1970s and 1980s provided, at last, the ability to disentangle these possibilities.

Voting Behavior

Analysts, armed at last with high quality survey data, began in earnest to study the public, its views, and the basis of its political choices. The first two decades after World War II were marked primarily by the discovery of how little structure there was to the public's views, confirming the concerns of such thinkers as Walter Lippmann, who in the 1920s worried about the ability of the public to play their allotted role in democracy. These analysts found a public with little information, interest, and sophistication about politics, especially public policy. Their characterization seemed even more true about foreign than domestic policy.

Scholars at the University of Michigan, especially with the publication of *The American Voter* (1960) by Angus Campbell et al., presented a social-psychological view of public opinion and voting behavior that dominated the field for the next fifteen years or more. Their central concept for understanding voting behavior was party identification. This was an affective loyalty to one party or the other that, for most citizens, was forged early in life, endured over the life cycle for many, and shaped partisan views of candidates and issues. Issues were, in this view, a relatively less important determinant of choice than party or even candidate evaluations. The positions voters took on issues were shaped by affective partisan ties; the public was not well informed about policy, held relatively incoherent views, and the positions they did hold were unstable over time. The public was, overall, relatively unsophisticated on these matters, lacking for the most part even the most rudimentary structure to their views or were, in a common catchphrase, "ideologically innocent."

While such findings indicated little role for issues of any kind in public choice, the public's understanding of foreign policy trailed even that of domestic policy. In an influential early study, *The American People and Foreign Policy* (1950), Gabriel A. Almond summarized this position: "Foreign policy attitudes among most Americans lack intellectual structure and factual content. Such superficial psychic states are bound to be unstable since they are not anchored in a set of explicit value and means calculations or traditional compulsions." While the next decades would reveal modification of these views of the public's opinions, the overall assessment of foreign policy beliefs would be largely unaffected. As Deborah Welch Larson put it in *Origins of Containment* (1985): "The public's attention span to foreign affairs is strictly limited; elections are not decided on foreign policy issues." Shortly thereafter, analysts began to find a more consequential role for foreign policy, and although foreign policy may now be more consequential than originally believed, no one can dispute one central finding of Almond and Larson. The public does have very little factual content about foreign affairs. Thus, changing views are about their "value and means calculations [and] traditional compulsions." It is also in part the dearth of factual content that makes public concerns and evaluations about foreign affairs so dependent upon the debate among political elites.

By the end of the 1960s and into the 1970s, this early account of public opinion was revised, especially in terms of issue voting. The 1950s, especially the 1956 and 1960 presidential elections on which the earliest views were based, were especially quiescent politically. The civil rights movement, Great Society programs, and Vietnam War made the 1960s and early 1970s a much more turbulent political period. This richer policy environment stimulated greater public interest in and attention to policy. In addition, the differences between the stances of presidential candidates Lyndon B. Johnson and Barry Goldwater in 1964 and Richard M. Nixon and George S. McGovern in 1972, for example, not only heightened these public controversies, but also presented the public with much clearer choices on policy.

The most influential study of this period was entitled *The Changing American Voter* (1976). The authors of this study found that voter awareness of and concern about policy had increased, that the public's policy opinions displayed greater structure and increased ideological sophistication, and that the public saw more clearly the increased cleavages between the parties and candidates.

Issues were, therefore, more potent in affecting voter choice. If anything, however, the surprise in this "revisionist" view, given the tumultuous nature of the times, was in how modest these increases were. This revised view applied with equal strength to foreign and to domestic concerns, but the dominance of the Vietnam War and its dramatic impact on the public made it unclear whether the increased public interest would continue into more peaceful times.

Public understandings changed dramatically in the next fifteen years. One important development was the increased appreciation of what is called "retrospective" voting. This marked a turn from seeing the voter as making assessments of the campaign platforms and promises of the candidates to seeing the voters as evaluating the performance of the incumbent party—that is determining how successful the incumbent had been in achieving peace, prosperity, and tranquility—perhaps in conjunction with expectations about the performance of the opposition. Given the political circumstances of the 1970s and 1980s, economic performance was an especially important basis of retrospective evaluations (underlying, for example, presidential candidate Ronald Reagan's famous question in 1980, "Are you better off today than you were four years ago?"). The complex nature of foreign affairs made it another important source of retrospective evaluations. Complex, ambiguous, and even classified information meant that, even should the voters have desired, they would have been unable to judge the appropriate policy means. They could, however, judge how successful the president had been in making war or in keeping peace.

A second major change was in rethinking the nature of public opinion in general and on policy in particular. Earlier studies had implicitly measured public opinion against the standard of a voter who was well informed, reasonably sophisticated, and able to judge dispassionately among alternative policy options. Actual voters fall well short of such an ideal. Newer studies, however, portray a citizen with a more fragmented, but possibly richer, understanding of public policy. Instead of holding global belief systems such as liberal or conservative ideology, the public was found to have more specific clusters of opinions. Relatively static stances emerging from affective and durable partisan loyalties were replaced by more dynamic interactions. Thus, for example, partisan identification was found to be affected by issue evaluations. Scholars found that the public draws from a range of considerations to determine their preferred policy position, and the range of considerations and individual uses differ over time and circumstance. Instead of holding fixed attitudes largely immune to media and political campaigns, the specific positions voters prefer change over time, as different considerations are evoked by the media, candidates, or acquaintances. Scholars found that both the media and campaigns of the candidates "prime" the public, bringing the most heavily debated issues to the top of voters' concerns.

Impact of Foreign Policy

While these developments found a more central role for issues in general, foreign policy in particular was found to be even more consequential than previously believed. One set of scholars found that retrospective evaluations loomed large in all elections from 1972 to 1992. Economic evaluations have always been substantial components, but retrospective evaluations of foreign affairs have often, but not always, been consequential. Another series of studies demonstrated that public opinion on foreign policy is better articulated than previously believed, but it (and especially attitudes toward the Soviet Union) falls in a number of clusters of opinions rather than dichotomous global evaluations, such as "hawk" or "dove." As an example, analysts found that, with only a few exceptions, foreign affairs was highly salient to the public since the late 1950s. Such attitudes were as accessible for use by voters as domestic issues in many elections. The effect of foreign policy on elections is strong only when candidates emphasize foreign policy issues and present clear choices on those issues. In those circumstances its impact on voting is comparable to that of domestic policy. Clearly presented foreign and domestic policy considerations together are as effectively important as party and candidate evaluations.

The Public and the Candidates, 1970s to 1990s

The clarity of candidate choices increases the awareness of foreign policy and provides a basis of choice. The bipartisan consensus on foreign policy, from the end of World War II to Vietnam, largely precluded the public from choosing on the basis of foreign policy. Indeed, it made sense to pay little heed to candidate appeals to foreign policy because they were so often similar. Foreign policy was much discussed in the 1960 campaign, but the slight differentiation on the issues between Kennedy and Nixon prevented the public from selecting a candidate based on foreign policy considerations. With increasing public concern and greater clarity between Johnson and Goldwater, foreign policy played a larger role in 1964. The subsequent breakdown of the bipartisan consensus led to regular partisan cleavage.

The end of the bipartisan consensus had a great effect on the parties and candidates as well. The Republicans were seen as the party better able to handle foreign policy. From McGovern's relatively extreme stance on Vietnam in 1972 through George Bush's effective characterization in 1988 of Michael S. Dukakis as one "who had never met a weapons system he liked," the Democrats were seen as less effective on foreign policy in general and in handling competition with the Soviet Union in particular. One significant component of the Republican advantage in presidential elections from 1972 to 1988 was their popularly perceived position as the party better able to stand up to what Reagan described as the "evil empire" of the USSR.

The impact of foreign policy on elections from 1952 (the first with high quality survey data) to 1988 can be summarized by considering the interaction between the public and political elites. Public concern about foreign affairs was high (albeit varyingly so) in all elections from 1952 through 1972, quite low in 1976, and then relatively high again in the three elections of the 1980s. Almost invariably, this concern reflected some aspect of bipolar competition, although focused, of course, on the wars in Korea in 1952 and in Vietnam in 1968 and 1972. In 1980 the seemingly endless Iranian hostage crisis and the Soviet invasion of Afghanistan provided two other areas of foreign policy focus, reflecting both genuine concern about the plight of the hostages and a perception of U.S. weakness in the face of Soviet aggression.

The key, then, to understanding the effect of foreign affairs on the vote was the differentiation between the two parties and their respective nominees. From 1952 (and presumably 1948) to 1968, the bipartisan consensus meant that foreign concerns had relatively little electoral relevance or impact. The two exceptions were 1952 and 1964, but these were the exceptions that demonstrate the point. The Korean War had a discernible impact on voting in 1952, but the question was who was better able to manage the war. In 1964 Johnson's firm but moderate stance enabled him successfully to portray Goldwater as someone not to be trusted to manage superpower competition and nuclear weaponry, thus indirectly influencing foreign policy through negative assessments of Goldwater's capabilities. In 1968, in contrast, the relative similarity (and high ambiguity) of the two parties' nominees on the Vietnam War meant that, as highly concerned as most were, there was no basis of choice on which to vote.

With the bipartisan consensus broken by 1972, the Republican party was perceived as more capable of keeping U.S. defenses strong and of dealing effectively with the Soviet Union. Perhaps more accurately, Republicans were seen to continue their stance from the earlier period, while the Democrats were seen to have changed to a position more isolationist, weaker on defense, and weaker in confrontation with the Soviet Union. This perception was reinforced by the succession of Democratic nominees, from McGovern in 1972 to Dukakis in 1988. With relatively high concern and relatively clear choice, the public based its vote, to some substantial measure, on foreign policy. This was clearly true in 1972 and only

somewhat less true in 1980, 1984, and 1988. Only in 1976, with the fallout from the Watergate scandal, high concern about genuine economic woes, and an era of détente, were foreign concerns more modest and candidate cleavages more muted. As a result, foreign policy played little role in that election.

One might have expected George Bush in 1992, victorious in the Persian Gulf War and presiding during the collapse of the USSR, to have benefited in comparison to Bill Clinton, a candidate with little foreign policy experience and vulnerable to charges of draft avoidance. Such was not the case. The 1992 election marks a wholly new era, one in which our understandings of the role of foreign policy in elections must once again be reconsidered. The 1992 election was an exception. Foreign affairs was a low priority, and the candidates, especially Clinton and H. Ross Perot, spoke very little about it. The main reason this was politically possible was that 1992 was the first presidential election after the collapse of the Soviet Union and the Warsaw Pact alliance.

The end of the Cold War has three direct consequences for understanding the role of foreign policy in elections. First, it has greatly diminished the public's perceptions of the threat of war involving the United States. This reduction in the perceived threat of war, in turn, removes one of the major, and certainly what had been the most consistent, cause of concern in the public about foreign affairs. Second, bipolarity had provided a relatively clear set of principles by which the public could make sense of world affairs, and it also offered a standard for assessing when U.S. interests were at stake. Third, the clear distinction between the parties that had emerged in and after the Vietnam War had, in turn, frayed considerably, so that the pubic had begun to see less differentiation between the two parties on foreign policy. One example of the impact of these three consequences is that two of President Clinton's major legislative victories, passage of the NAFTA and GATT treaties, were possible only because of bipartisan support in a Congress where bipartisanship was extremely rare. In sum, without clear policy objectives, meaningful principles, direct threats to public welfare, and clarity of partisan choice in foreign affairs, the 1992 elections, and conceivably those of the future, may be even better characterized than those of the 1940s and 1950s as primarily domestic, in which voting did, indeed, end at water's edge.

Clinton's domestic-centered presidency was short lived, however. From raising the issue of "gays in the military" and of confronting such issues as Haitian refugees and the role of U.S. troops in Somalia (that he had inherited from President Bush), Clinton could not, and often chose not to, avoid foreign affairs in office as he had minimized them on the campaign trail. Perhaps ironically, his successful initiatives in Haiti, the Middle East, and the former Yugoslavia have helped counteract such domestic policy failures as his health care proposal. Whatever the consequence for the immediate elections, his presidency emphasizes that no U.S. leader can ignore foreign affairs, either those that are currently episodic, or those of a more persistent nature, such as economic policy making in a world economy.

The new questions to ask about the impact of foreign affairs on elections in the late 1990s are how the public will assess foreign concerns, judge U.S. interests, and make sense of a complex, no longer bipolar, world. Will each crisis be unique and therefore uniquely evaluated, or will there be a set of principles, meaningful to the public, that can be employed in the way the public employs bipolarity? The answers to these questions will come from U.S. political leadership and their reaction to events and to the possibilities these events offer for elections and for governance.

John H. Aldrich

See also Democratic Party; Public Opinion; Republican Party

FURTHER READING

Abramson, Paul R., John H. Aldrich, and David W. Rohde. *Change and Continuity in the 1992 Elections.* Revision. Washington, D.C., 1995.

Aldrich, John H., John L. Sullivan, and Eugene Borgida. "Foreign Affairs and Issue Voting." *American Political Science Review* 38 (March 1989): 123–141.

Almond, Gabriel A. *The American People and Foreign Policy.* New York, 1950.

Campbell, Angus, Philip E. Converse, Warren E. Miller, and Donald E. Stokes. *The American Voter.* New York, 1960.

Holsti, Ole R. "Public Opinion and Foreign Policy." *International Studies Quarterly* 36 (1992): 439–466.

Hurwitz, Jon, and Mark A. Peffley. "How are Foreign Policy Attitudes Structured? A Hierarchical Model." *American Political Science Review* 81 (December 1987): 1099–1120.

———. "Public Images of the Soviet Union." *Journal of Politics* 52 (February 1990): 3–28.

Larson, Deborah Welch. *Origins of Containment.* Princeton, N.J., 1985.

Lippmann, Walter. *Public Opinion.* New York, 1922.

Nie, Norman H., Sidney Verba, and John R. Petrocik. *The Changing American Voter.* Cambridge, Mass., 1976.

EL SALVADOR

Located in Central America and bordering the North Pacific Ocean between Guatemala and Honduras, a nation long troubled by internal strife and, in the 1980s, by U.S. military intervention. Had the United States accepted El Salvador's request for annexation in 1823, when the new nation sought protection against Guatemalan ambitions, or had Salvadoran President Maximiliano Hernández Martínez accepted a U.S. gunship's offer of support during the 1932 peasant revolt, El Salvador's history might read more like that of Nicaragua, where the United States intervened on numerous occasions. But the United States in 1823 ignored El Salvador's overture, and Hernández proved more than capable of putting down the 1932 uprising, killing 30,000 suspected rebels in the Salvadoran "matanza" or massacre.

In the 1960s, the United States promoted El Salvador as an example of the possibilities for development within the Alliance for Progress. But despite impressive economic growth rates and diversification, Salvadorans remained among the poorest of the world's populations, suffering above all from a dramatic concentration of wealth in a tiny propertied class engaged principally in coffee production—the oligarchic "Fourteen Families." Determined to redress the preponderance of power and property in the country, radicals, social democrats, and the rural poor began mobilizing for change in the 1970s. When right-wing military leaders displaced a reformist coup in 1979, resistance to El Salvador's political alliance of army and oligarchs exploded into civil war. Taking its name from the most prominent martyr of the 1932 "matanza," the Farabundo Martí Front for National Liberation (FMLN) vowed to put an end to government by extremists and to avenge the 24 March 1980 assassination of Archbishop Oscar Arnulfo Romero by a right-wing death squad.

The FMLN launched an ambitiously named "final offensive" in 1981. This revolutionary campaign coincided with Ronald Reagan's assumption of the presidency in the United States and his vow to defeat "communism" everywhere. Determined to prevent "another Nicaragua," a reference to the victory of the radical Sandinistas, and despite evidence (including the murders of three North American nuns, a social worker, and two Agency for International Development agricultural advisers) of army complicity in terrorism against the Salvadoran populace, the Reagan administration funneled unprecedented levels of arms, aid, and advisers to the Salvadoran government—at an average of $739.5 million per year during Reagan's two terms. Emboldened by North American backing, the military and the right-wing "death squads" pursued their campaign of violence against suspected subversives, killing an estimated 30,000 civilians in the first three years of the conflict in a grisly replay of the 1932 matanza. In 1983, over strong Reagan administration opposition, Congress tied Salvadoran military aid to improvements in human rights. This provision had some positive impact, including some strengthening of efforts by Christian Democratic President José Napoleón Duarte to rein in the military.

Vowing that in the fight against communism, "Central America is the most important place in the world," Reagan administration officials refused to recognize the military stalemate which existed in the civil war after 1984. Duarte faced a challenge from Roberto d'Aubisson Arrieta, leader of the extremist right-wing ARENA party and himself closely associated with the death-squads. Reagan officials worked for d'Aubisson against Duarte in the 1984 Salvadoran election, which the FMLN boycotted. Duarte defeated d'Aubisson, but the civil war continued as Duarte, for whom Congress removed restrictions on U.S. aid, proved incapable of controlling the army.

The 1989 assassination by a death squad of six Jesuit priests provoked an international outcry and jarred the new administration of George Bush. Pressure mounted against the Salvadoran government to negotiate with the rebels. The peace agreement reached between the FMLN and ARENA President Alfredo Cristiani on 31 December 1991 promised to put an end to El Salvador's long war. Under United Nations supervision, the rebel army disbanded and reconstituted itself as an opposition political party. The ARENA-led government then struggled to reduce the size of the armed forces and to bring to justice the perpetrators of the thousands of murders, disappearances, and other atrocities of the past decade. The 1993 UN Truth Commission report condemned high-ranking military and government officials, and by implication the U.S. policies which had strengthened and sustained them.

LeeAnna Y. Keith

See also Alliance for Progress; Human Rights; Latin America; Nicaragua; Reagan, Ronald Wilson

FURTHER READING

Bologna, Enrique A. *El Salvador in Transition.* Chapel Hill, N.C., 1982.
Coatsworth, John H. *Central America and the United States: The Clients and the Colossus.* New York, 1994.
Diskin, Martin, and Kenneth Sharpe. *The Impact of U.S. Policy in El Salvador, 1979–1986.* Berkeley, Calif., 1986.
LaFeber, Walter. *Inevitable Revolutions: The United States in Central America.* New York, 1993.
Webre, Stephen. *José Napoleón Duarte and the Christian Democratic Party in Salvadoran Politics, 1960–1972.* Baton Rouge, La., 1979.

EMBARGOES

See Economic Sanctions; Export Controls

EMBASSIES

See Ambassadors and Embassies

ENERGY, U.S. DEPARTMENT OF

The department of the executive branch that exercises control over research and development in energy technol-ogy, energy conservation and regulation, the distribution of federal power resources, and the nuclear weapons program. The Department of Energy (DOE) traces its origins back to 1942 and the Manhattan Project of the Army Corps of Engineers, which developed the atomic bomb. In 1946, Congress instituted civilian control in this field by establishing the Atomic Energy Commission. In the early 1970s, during the worldwide energy crisis resulting from an Arab oil embargo, President Nixon installed a Federal Energy Office in the White House and Congress set up the federal Energy Administration, the Nuclear Regulatory Commission, and the Energy Research and Development Administration. Congress established the DOE in the fall of 1977, thereby consolidating at the cabinet level various federal government energy functions that had emerged over the years. The responsibilities transferred to the new department included those of such earlier agencies as the federal Energy Administration, the Federal Power Commission, and the regional power administrations, along with certain functions of the Interstate Commerce Commission and of the Departments of Commerce, Housing and Urban Development, the Navy, and the Interior. The Nuclear Regulatory Commission, however, remained an independent agency. In 1993 the department had an annual budget of $10.4 billion, with eight field operations offices, two naval reactor development centers, and three regional power distribution headquarters. It directly employed approximately 20,000 people, most of them in Washington, in addition to a network of forty-three research laboratories and other experimental facilities staffed largely by contract personnel.

The department views its mission as bearing broadly on energy questions; on defense; on cleanup and waste management; and on science, technology, and the national laboratories. It is responsible for reducing U.S. energy vulnerability to international developments, maintaining a secure capability in the field of nuclear weapons, providing safe solutions for problems of military nuclear waste, and supporting the U.S. defense posture. Several senior positions carry duties bearing specifically on U.S. foreign relations. The assistant secretary for congressional, intergovernmental, and international affairs coordinates energy programs with U.S. foreign policy and with cooperative international programs, including such organizations as the International Atomic Energy Agency (IAEA). The assistant secretary for defense programs supervises U.S. nuclear weapons development, testing and production, and the management of defense-related nuclear waste. Within the defense programs section, the Office of Intelligence and National Security provides research expertise to the intelligence community, administers DOE research in arms implementation and compliance, and oversees international safeguards research in support of nonproliferation agreements. The assistant secretary for policy, planning, and program evaluation formulates international policy development and ensures the U.S. energy goals conform to treaty obligations. Two other bureaus have responsibilities with international implications: the Office of Nuclear Energy reports to the assistant secretary for energy efficiency and renewable energy and advises on nonproliferation issues, and the office of Science Education and Technical Information, which reports to the under secretary, represents the United States in the multilateral information exchange programs of the IAEA and the International Energy Agency, as well as those under other international agreements.

HENRY E. MATTOX

See also Atomic Energy Commission; Atoms for Peace; International Atomic Energy Agency; Manhattan Project; Nuclear Nonproliferation; Oil and Foreign Policy; Oil and World Politics; Oil Companies; Organization of Petroleum Exporting Countries

FURTHER READING

U.S. Department of Energy, Office of the Executive Secretariat, History Division. *The Department of Energy's Heritage.* Washington, D.C., March 1993.
———, Office of Science and Technology Adviser. *Capsule Review of DOE Research and Development Laboratories and Field Facilities.* Washington, D.C., September 1992.

ENVIRONMENT

The collection of flora, fauna, and natural resources that composes the biosphere and supports human life has been a sporadic but significant issue in U.S. foreign relations throughout the twentieth century. Environmental protection, which is usually a domestic concern, has become more of an international concern as people have come to recognize that the biosphere is a global commons that transcends national boundaries. While diplomats have often made it an important issue, the place of environmental protection on the diplomatic agenda has often depended on grass-roots support from the U.S. public.

The scope of environmental diplomacy has changed dramatically over the course of the century. In 1895, U.S. Attorney General Judson Harmon informed Mexico that the United States could do what it pleased with water from the Rio Grande, reflecting the widespread attitude that natural resources belonged to those who had the power to control them. In the first half of the twentieth century, U.S. diplomats took the lead in promoting cooperative solutions to specific trans-border problems with Canada and other neighboring nations. By the late-twentieth century, the United States encouraged the negotiation of huge multilateral agreements dealing with almost insolvable global problems. Many of the crises that seem so pressing in the late-twentieth century have antecedents from the first half of the century; efforts to resolve those earlier disputes still have value as precedents and foundations for today's solutions.

The Progressive Era

In a sense, environmental diplomacy is very old, as nations have often clashed over rights to contested natural resources. For example, beginning with the negotiations that led to the Treaty of Paris of 1783, U.S. diplomats made fishing rights in the waters off Newfoundland a high priority. Similarly, U.S.-Canadian land disputes, whether in the Aroostook Valley of Maine, the Oregon Territory, or the Alaskan boundary, usually came down to access to something of value, be it fertile soil or gold. Until the twentieth century, then, the diplomacy of natural resources mainly involved attempts by each nation to gain something at its competitors' expense.

A major change in natural resources diplomacy came with the ascendancy of Theodore Roosevelt to the presidency in 1901. Roosevelt certainly was capable of using threats to win resources, as he demonstrated in the Alaskan boundary dispute, but he also had a sense that natural resource conservation required international cooperation. In proposing a North American conference on conservation he wrote that "it is evident that natural resources are not limited by the boundary lines which separate nations, and that the need for conserving them upon this continent is as wide as the area upon which they exist." As the only president to give high priority to protection of natural resources, Roosevelt helped to boost the growing conservation movement into a national political force. With that power, conservationists were able to influence U.S. foreign policy after Theodore Roosevelt left office.

The Progressive Era conservation movement consisted of two diverse, overlapping wings—preservationism and utilitarianism. Preservationists held as their prime goal the protection of natural beauty, including appealing species and impressive geological formations. In contrast, utilitarians concentrated on the need for rational management of economically important natural resources, such as timber. In the early part of the century, utilitarians held sway to the extent that preservationists felt compelled to justify their causes with utilitarian arguments. Although the preservationist impulse dominates contemporary environmentalism, U.S. citizens still seek utilitarian reasons to protect natural resources.

The first natural resource treaty to emphasize conservation, the disastrous Inland Fisheries Treaty of 1908, suggested that the new cooperative approach needed

MAJOR UN EFFORTS TO PROTECT THE ENVIRONMENT

1949   Scientific Conference on the Conservation and Utilization of natural Resources marks the first time the United Nations addressed the environment.

1957   International Geophysical Year leads to 1959 Antarctic Treaty.

1958   UN Conference on the Law of the Sea (UNCLOS) begins to address oceanic pollution.

1960   UNCLOS II codifies the move to claim expanded territorial waters.

1968   The Biosphere Conference spurs a UN plan to hold a general conference on the human environment.

1972   UN Conference on the Human Environment (UNCHE) meets in Stockholm

1973   Convention on International Trade in Endangered Species (CITES) is signed and placed under control of the UN Environmental Program (UNEP)

       UNCLOS II begins a heated nine-year debate on seabed mining and the general concept of "the common heritage of mankind."

1985   UNEP overseas the negotiations of the Vienna Convention for the protection of the Ozone Layer.

1987   UNEP builds upon the Vienna Convention with the Montreal Protocol on substances that Deplete the Ozone Layer.

1992   The UN Conference on Environment and Development convenes in Rio de Janeiro.

some refinements. Roosevelt's secretary of state, Elihu Root, opened negotiations with the British ambassador in 1906 to protect the dwindling fresh-water fisheries along the U.S.-Canadian border. The treaty established a two-member scientific commission to create joint regulations that would end destructive fishing techniques and pollution. Under the leadership of renowned scientist David Starr Jordan, the commission crafted visionary rules to protect the fisheries. Diplomats and scientists alike assumed that the rising conservationist tide would ensure compliance on both sides of the border.

To their surprise, the most vocal response came from angry fishermen on both sides of the border who feared that they were surrendering their rights to foreign competitors. Working through their senators, U.S. fishermen gutted the treaty regulations. Jordan attempted to save the spirit of the agreement, but he had very little help. The average conservationist did not care much about fish from a utilitarian or preservationist standpoint. In 1914, the two sides agreed that the treaty was finally dead.

Conservationists learned from this otherwise forgettable treaty that natural resource diplomacy often harmed the economic interests that were causing the environmental degradation in the first place. Fishermen on the Great Lakes and in the state of Washington were

hardly a political juggernaut, but they mobilized far more effectively than did the scientists who recognized the danger from overfishing. Diplomats would not challenge such interests unless they were sure of strong public support. But such support depended on educating the general public that international cooperative restrictions best served long-term national interests. Success would only come if conservationists could generate more power than the economic actors whose businesses were at stake.

The treaty's failure also revealed the greatest international obstacle to successful environmental protection diplomacy—a fear of lost sovereignty. Environmental protection, whether domestic or international, requires the establishment of regulations that usually deprive citizens of economic rights. Although controversy often accompanies these regulations, few doubt that some level of government has the sovereignty to take such action. Opponents of international regulations, however, have often claimed that they grant foreign diplomats and bureaucrats the authority to establish rules in the United States. Such claims almost always have no basis, because the U.S. government enters, and may exit, the agreements freely. Still, the specter of foreign control of internal policy has been sufficient to hinder environmental protection diplomacy.

The first successful conservation agreement was the Boundary Waters Treaty of 11 January 1909 between the United States and Great Britain. The two nations established the International Joint Commission (IJC), a bilateral organization with three members from each side of the U.S.-Canadian border with primary authority to regulate the use, obstruction, and diversion of the boundary waters and their tributaries. The IJC also received jurisdiction over the entire frontier between the two countries. Despite the broad scope of its power, the IJC usually served as an arbiter of last resort or as an agency to manage scientific research, but not as an aggressive regulator.

While the IJC succeeded in controlling the use of waterways, it was unable to deal with the abuse thereof, especially pollution. Perhaps spurred on by the findings of the ichthyologists working on the Inland Fisheries Treaty, in 1912 the two governments called on the IJC to study the problem of water pollution along the entire border. After six years, the commission reported that all of the rivers and lake shore waters were too polluted to drink, and some were dangerous by any measure. With the support of both governments, the IJC drafted a treaty that would have committed both sides to pass clean-up legislation. But, like the streams of pollutants heading from the cities, the idea slipped below the surface, not to gain the public's attention until the 1970s.

Soon after the two countries worked out the Boundary Waters Treaty, they turned their attention to the long-standing dispute over sealing in the North Pacific Ocean. The majority of North Pacific fur seals use the Pribilof Islands in the eastern Bering Sea as summertime rookeries, although on average each seal spends about three-quarters of its life in international waters. After purchasing Alaska in 1867, the U.S. government leased the right to harvest seals on the Pribilofs to a private company. During the 1880s, Canadians began to harvest the seals on the high seas (known as pelagic sealing), sparking a conflict between Great Britain and the United States over legal rights to an animal species that wandered between U.S. territory and international waters. After twenty years of failed confrontational diplomacy, in 1909 the two sides finally agreed to discuss joint conservation efforts.

By then, the Russians and Japanese had become deeply involved, forcing all four powers to compromise before the North Pacific Fur Seal Convention of 1911 could become reality. The convention stipulated that all sides would outlaw pelagic sealing and allow the United States to manage scientifically the Pribilof seal herd in exchange for a division of the profits. Protecting the seals was quite popular in the United States, because seal conservation had both utilitarian and preservationist appeal. The herd had declined from more than two million seals to about 150,000, but cooperative international action finally had saved the species.

While fur seal conservation presented fairly straightforward challenges, the fur seal convention was still important for setting the agenda for future natural resource treaties. Many factors encouraged their protection; they were a single species concentrated in a remote part of the world; they faced overhunting, not pollution or habitat damage; as cute, furry mammals, they appealed to the general public; and finally regulators could control the market for seal fur easily. Although unusually favorable, the sealing controversy had at its heart the basic question of environmental diplomacy: how do diplomats determine who holds rights to common property, be it fur seals or clean air? The answer would become far more complex with the global crises of the late-twentieth century, but the question would remain the same.

Common property, which no one owns but many use, is at the center of most, if not all, international environmental crises. One country cannot manage or own a resource, such as the seals, that does not confine itself to national boundaries. Over time, citizens from different nations will be drawn to the resource, often creating fierce competition. Biologist Garrett Hardin described the results of such competition as "the tragedy of the commons," a situation in which rational economic actors destroy common property through overuse. Because no government is willing to restrict unilaterally the activities of its citizens, environmental diplomacy succeeds only when all of the users of common property agree to sacrifice short-term national interests for longer-term concerns.

Conservationists won another important victory in 1916 with the completion of the Migratory Bird Treaty (MBT) between the United States and Great Britain (for Canada). For centuries, North Americans had taken an aggressive attitude towards shooting birds for fashion, the table, or sport. Late in the nineteenth century, the fledgling preservationist movement began to coalesce around bird protection. The economic interests behind commercial bird hunting were not especially strong, but most governments did not make bird protection a priority. After years of propaganda and efforts to change local laws had produced only minimal results, conservationists determined that the only way to protect birds was through a treaty that would force the U.S. and Canadian national governments to restrict hunting. Department of State officials expressed skepticism that birds were a matter of international concern, but under pressure from President Woodrow Wilson and conservationists they consented. Opponents challenged the legality of the treaty in the courts, leading to the Supreme Court decision *Missouri* v. *Holland*, in which Justice Oliver Wendell Holmes established the federal government's right to regulate the environment.

Like the seal convention, the MBT was as important for the precedents it set as for the protection it provided.

The treaty is still the basis of federal protection statutes, and many species owe their continued existence to the treaty's provisions. The treaty's success depended largely on the hard lobbying of the National Association of Audubon Societies, the first broadly-based non-governmental organization (NGO) to concentrate on environmental policy. As a strategy, Audubon combined the basic preservationist appeal of wild birds with the utilitarian argument that birds protected crops from the ravages of highly-reproductive insects. Finally, the MBT was the product of years of public education through Audubon-sponsored school programs and the writings of great authors such as John Burroughs. In sum, preservationists succeeded because they created an atmosphere of public support for strong bird protection measures.

In the aftermath of these early successes, conservationists imagined a host of possible conservation treaties that the U.S. government might initiate. Some suggested multinational efforts to save whales, walruses, and other sea mammals that spend their time in international waters. Others wanted to extend the terms of the Migratory Bird Treaty to Latin America, recognizing that many U.S. birds wintered south of the Rio Grande. They saw local opportunities to resolve outstanding fishing and pollution issues with Canada and global opportunities to discuss conservation strategies. Their dreams were large, but their influence was waning.

The Interwar Years

In the 1920s and 1930s, U.S. conservationists continued their efforts to promote international conservation, but they found that the problems were far more complex. For instance, U.S. efforts to spread migratory bird protection eventually yielded two more treaties that appeared to have great value, but in fact were not very effective. As early as 1913, some conservationists advocated focusing international bird conservation efforts on Mexico, because that country lacked environmental safeguards. Even as Congress was passing the enabling legislation for the MBT in 1918, conservationists called for negotiations with Mexico. Over time their idea gathered momentum, and U.S. diplomats opened negotiations with the Mexican government in the 1920s.

They quickly learned, though, that Latin America was not the fertile soil for the treaties that they imagined. First, little reliable scientific evidence existed about bird populations or migration habits south of the Rio Grande. Researchers from the Smithsonian Institute and the U.S. Bureau of Biological Survey were just beginning to explore the region, and until they answered some basic questions there could be no scientific basis for negotiations. Second, unlike Canada and the United States, Mexico had no powerful official or private conservation organization. Conservationists came largely from middle-class progressives, who were a rare breed outside of the industrial democracies. Finally, revolutionary fervor had created an air of distrust between Mexico City and Washington. Presidents Woodrow Wilson and Warren Harding refused to recognize any Mexican government that sanctioned the nationalization of U.S. oil companies, and U.S. diplomats feared that bird protection negotiations would confer diplomatic legitimacy upon the Mexican government.

Sporadic discussions between the two governments and U.S. conservationists finally brought some results in the 1930s. In conjunction with Franklin Roosevelt's Good Neighbor Policy, U.S. diplomats sought to find common ground with their Mexican counterparts. While they made progress towards a migratory bird treaty, Mexican authorities emphasized that they considered such an agreement to be part of a larger effort to resolve natural resource disputes, especially regarding fishing rights. In 1936, the two sides finally agreed to a bird protection treaty that was not much of an advance beyond the 1916 accord between Great Britain and the United States. Conservationists praised the treaty, but they realized that it had not substantially improved the lot of U.S. birds that migrated below the Rio Grande.

After three years of rumination, conservationists came up with an important breakthrough—a multilateral convention to protect natural resources throughout the hemisphere. U.S. scientists wanted to take action to prevent the kind of destruction in Latin America that had been so widespread in the United States. But they also realized that U.S. power in the region could harm their cause; Latin Americans receiving any such proposal from Washington might suspect an ulterior motive. The scientists solved their problem by working through the Pan American Union (PAU), the forerunner of the Organization of American States. The PAU voted to appoint a committee of experts—none from the United States—to study the matter, and it came back with a draft treaty remarkably similar to ideas that U.S. scientists had outlined.

Through the June 1940 Convention on Nature Protection and Wild Life Preservation in the American Republics, the United States tried to export conservationism to Latin America. The signatory nations agreed to take all practicable steps to establish national parks, national reserves, nature monuments, and wilderness reserves, as well as to protect migratory birds and endangered species. Except for the endangered species clause, each of these features had a counterpart in U.S. law. The convention required very little from the United States other than maintenance of existing programs. But few of the PAU governments were prepared to undertake such far-reaching proposals. In many cases, they needed the assistance of scientists from the United States to begin the planning. Despite this hindrance, by 1942 most of the PAU members had signed the convention.

In many ways, the Convention on Nature Protection resembled more modern, multilateral environmental treaties. Like its more recent counterparts, it brought together many nations in a joint effort to solve a complex problem. Opponents argued that national land policy was not an international problem, but supporters argued that preservation of nature was of interest to all mankind. The preservationist impulse inspired the scientists and diplomats who forged the agreement, but there was a strong element of utilitarian reasoning. Finally, as with many modern treaties, the United States took the lead in molding the agreement.

Although the treaty was generally well structured, it had important flaws common to many more recent conventions. Foremost among them was the absence of an enforcement mechanism. Individual governments had only their consciences to encourage compliance with the treaty. No sanctions existed to punish nations that did not adhere to its terms. To compound the problem, the cultural and economic gap that separated the United States from the other signatory nations suggested that U.S. citizens were attempting to prevent poorer nations from pursuing U.S.-style development. Whereas many citizens of the Latin American countries doubtless believed that the convention might slow economic development by hindering the free use of resources, U.S. scientists and diplomats thought they were sharing their wisdom in an effort to prevent unnecessary abuses of nature.

These two great flaws insured that the Convention on Nature Protection never reached its potential. A few Latin American countries, especially Costa Rica, worked hard to fulfill their obligations. But most governments could not afford to take thorough steps in that direction, especially if the United States was not willing or able to help bear the costs. Environmental issues had become a matter of diplomatic concern, but they were not yet important enough for governments to undertake coercive action.

Running parallel to the negotiations with Mexico, Canada and the United States set a precedent for dealing with air pollution in the Trail Smelter case. In the 1920s, a private company began operating a nickel smelter in Trail, British Columbia, just north of Washington state. The plant's twin smokestacks produced sulfur dioxide that drifted across the border and caused extensive damage, especially to agriculture. Laws on both sides of the border left U.S. farmers with no legal standing on the issue; therefore they pressured the U.S. government to negotiate with the Canadian government. After more than a decade of fruitless negotiations, the two sides agreed to submit the case to arbitration. In 1941, the arbitration panel ruled that Canada had to pay damages and prevent future transboundary harm from the smelter.

The Trail Smelter case represented an important step forward in three respects, although by contemporary standards it seems inadequate. First, the decision suggested that governments had an obligation to consider the broader impact of pollution. Second, it established a precedent for international law, even if it had no direct impact on any other dispute. Third, by submitting to arbitration, the two nations expressed a willingness to resolve the dispute on an equitable basis in an atmosphere of trust.

Although an important advance at the time, the Trail Smelter ruling had three important limitations. First, because the pollution came from a single source, the ruling did not set a precedent for the more complex air pollution problems of the late-twentieth century. Second, the tribunal of arbitration indicated that the damage had to be "serious" to warrant international intervention, which limited its later usefulness as a precedent. And third, the case did not provide any insights on controlling the pollution of international water or airspace.

Whaling

The interwar years brought U.S. participation in one more effort to protect the environment through international efforts to regulate whaling. People had hunted whales for centuries, but in the early-twentieth century new technology and increasing demand for whale oil drove the industry to unsustainable efforts. People found many uses for whale parts, including dog food, soap, and, most importantly, margarine. Meanwhile, whaling companies shifted from remote whaling stations or lone vessels to the modern factory ship, a huge vessel with a flotilla of smaller catcher ships. With these increased resources, whalers had almost no limits on where, when, and how much they could catch. The industry's growth brought chaos on the high seas and wild fluctuations in the market for whale products—and disaster for the whales.

With the whaling industry in disarray, in 1930 the League of Nations convened negotiations to create uniform regulations for whaling. Negotiators believed that they could craft moderate rules that would sustain the whales, and therefore the whaling industry, in perpetuity. The resulting Geneva Convention for the Regulation of Whaling, like the other agreements of the time, was an important step forward, even though it seems wholly inadequate today. After taking effect in 1935, it required all whaling vessels to be licensed, protected all calves and nursing females, discouraged indiscriminate slaughter, and called for more scientific research. Most noticeably absent were enforcement mechanisms and means of luring rogue nations, such as Germany and Japan, to join the twenty-six signatory powers.

The absence of those two nations, especially in a time of international tension, revealed the central limit of environmental protection diplomacy. As much as a nation such as the United States might wish to protect whales, it had limited ability to coerce another nation into compliance. If, for instance, U.S. economic or diplomatic retaliation could not roll back the Japanese invasion of China, then certainly the United States was not going to dictate whaling policy to Japan. Even if protecting whales had been more important to the United States than protecting its interests in China, it could do little to stop Japan from pursuing its own short-term interests. If anything, using the "tragedy of the commons" paradigm, rogue nations benefited by avoiding regulations to which other nations adhered.

Recognizing that the 1931 agreement failed to stabilize the industry, the whaling nations met again in London in 1937 to tighten the regulations. Because each nation wanted to guard its own rights, the delegates could agree to outlaw only those practices that none of them pursued, such as hunting the nearly extinct Antarctic race of the humpback whale. Thus, by the end of the 1930s, the whaling nations had produced the skeleton of international conservation without actually fleshing out the regulations to the point of viability.

By the time, then, that World War II absorbed all diplomatic energy, the environment had gained a position as a low-level priority for U.S. foreign policy. The nation's diplomats would address pollution and conservation when doing so fit in with general national objectives, although those issues always were subordinate to political, economic, and military concerns. Despite the secondary status of environmental protection, conservationists and scientists had done well to force it onto the diplomatic agenda. In the years after 1945, when parts of the world community became much more serious about the environment, they found a solid foundation on which to build.

Because the Cold War dominated the years immediately after 1945, the environment remained for a time a secondary concern of U.S. foreign policy. The threat of nuclear war, combined with U.S. faith in technology and desire for unchallenged economic growth, deterred people from worrying about the long-term impact of pollution or natural resource depletion. In the 1940s and 1950s, environmental issues remained on the U.S. diplomatic agenda only when they served Cold War interests.

In 1946, the United States led another effort to restore order to the whaling industry. Meeting in Washington, delegates created the International Whaling Commission (IWC) to protect whales and oversee the industry. Though well-intentioned, the IWC had very little power. As in previous agreements, the delegates took steps that were years too late. The two most innovative measures—the global quota system and the call for scientific input—inadequately addressed the causes of the whales' decline. There were no strong constituencies of private citizens in any of the countries lobbying for strict controls of the industry, so the delegates let the whalers set the rules.

U.S. diplomats did allow their Cold War concerns to dictate one policy, the readmission of Japan to the whaling community. Whalers in the Allied nations had looked forward to seas free from German and Japanese competition. Instead, U.S. diplomats, led by Dean Acheson, pushed Japan back into the whaling business. Fearing that food shortages might push that country closer to communism, U.S. diplomats overruled conservationist and nationalistic impulses in their effort to put more food on Japanese tables. The move haunted the IWC years later, but it clearly demonstrated the place of conservation in the Cold War.

Strangely, the very successful move to protect Antarctica emerged in the depths of the Cold War. Decades before, in a fit of optimism or foolishness, several nations had staked claims to the ice-bound continent. After World War II, improving technology suggested that people might be able to tap the continent's resources, which were unknown but potentially vast. In response to the International Geophysical Year (1957–1958), the nations with claims or interests in Antarctica began to consider an international regime to protect the continent. In 1959, twelve nations agreed to the Antarctic Treaty, which set aside the continent as a research reserve free from commercial exploitation. To complete the agreement, in 1964 the treaty nations signed a set of Agreed Measures for Antarctic Fauna and Flora. The Antarctic agreements provided the basis for two more conventions that extended international protection in the southern seas. In 1972, the signatory nations agreed to the Convention for the Conservation of Antarctic Seals; in 1980, they accepted the Convention on the Conservation of Antarctic Marine Resources.

As with many other environmental treaties, the 1959 treaty requires unanimity among the members to make changes—a measure that reveals the problems and promise of international environmental protection. Environmentalists often complain, accurately, that the necessity of securing a unanimous vote prevents the adoption of radical reforms. For instance, the 1980 agreement leaves open the harvesting of krill, a tiny crustacean that serves as a basic component of the food web. Despite complaints from protectionists, the signatory powers have been unable to agree on amendments to regulate this potentially damaging practice. On the other hand, in 1988 France and Australia killed a proposal that the other nations had accepted that would have loosened the restrictions on mineral exploration. If the necessity of unanimous consent had not stopped it, the 1988 agreement might have undermined the advances of the previous three decades.

The Rising Involvement of the United Nations

While the twenty-five years after World War II were relatively quiet, in the 1970s the environment moved to a position of international prominence. The widespread celebration of Earth Day in April 1970 signalled a growing global acknowledgement that many environmental problems required international cooperation. As part of the general unrest that spread through the Western democracies in the late 1960s, a grass-roots environmental movement emerged that demanded that nations set aside their rivalries in order to reverse the deterioration of the earth. Although many of these people thought of themselves as pioneers, they were able to build upon decades of work by predecessors.

The United Nations emerged as the logical focal point for two reasons. First, in the midst of the Cold War, the UN had some credibility as a neutral body that tried to avoid taking sides in most controversies. It was not perfect, but it presented the best available international forum. Second, as part of the post-Earth Day awakening, it became clear that the most pressing environmental problems were global and, therefore, required the cooperation of dozens of nations. The UN had already drawn these nations together into one organization.

The history of UN activities in global conservation reflects changing global attitudes towards the environment. In 1949, the United Nations sponsored the Scientific Conference on the Conservation and Utilization of Resources. Despite efforts by a few conservationists in the United States to broaden the conference's scope, delegates focused solely on techniques for better management of resources. In 1968, responding to scientific advances, the United Nations sponsored the Biosphere Conference, held in Paris, which focused on the planet's flora and fauna. Delegates passed twenty resolutions calling for action by governments and the United Nations, suggesting that they now grasped the extent to which human damage required corrective action.

These early conferences led the United Nations in 1968 to accept a Swedish proposal to hold "an international conference on the problems of human environment." The wide support in the General Assembly indicated that environmental awareness had reached an all-time high, but debate revealed important splits among the various nations. Western, industrialized nations framed the debate, but Third World and Soviet bloc countries often offered different opinions as to the causes of and solutions to the crisis. Thus, some leaders suspected that the Western nations were using the state of the global environment as a means to prevent economic progress in developing countries. This tension, which harkens back to the 1940 Western Hemisphere convention, is still one of the central impediments to global agreement on tough regulations.

In the dozens of prepatory meetings between 1969 and 1972, during which the United States took a strong leadership role, delegates made three crucial decisions. First, they chose Canadian Maurice Strong as secretary-general of the conference, and he provided powerful direction. Second, they produced a broad, six-point agenda that covered everything from traditional natural resource management to newer links between culture and environment, giving the conference an extremely wide mandate and appeal. Third, they chose not to invite East Germany, which was not a member of the United Nations. The Soviet bloc countries boycotted, noting that West Germany, which also was not a member, had received an invitation. The boycott limited participation, but it also lessened East-West tension.

In the summer of 1972, the UN Conference on the Human Environment (UNCHE) convened in Stockholm with delegates from 114 countries and representatives from more than 500 non-governmental organizations (NGOs). The private citizens held their own Environmental Forum that ran parallel to the official meetings, and they had occasional access to Strong, delegates, and the general sessions. Never had so many nations gathered together to discuss the environment, and never had a conference taken such an inclusive approach. The broad agenda and wide attendance made it possible to imagine a truly global perspective on the environment.

The conference ran into an obstacle when delegates split over the nature of the world's environmental problems. One group believed that they had to focus on the human impact by combatting pollution and conserving natural resources. The other argued that environmental problems arose from the imbalance of economic and social development around the world. The two sides combined their opinions in the suggestion that sound development and environmental protection were linked. This tenuous compromise still dominates, but tension between industrial and developing countries threatens to destroy it.

During the conference, Third World nations took the opportunity to attack the West and the colonial legacy as the sources of their environmental problems. They pointed to poverty as the root of their difficulties and called for more equitable distribution of natural resources. The Western nations generally agreed in principle. At the Environment Forum, where the radical left dominated, representatives adopted a more strident tone in challenging capitalism and Western leadership.

In the end, the UNCHE produced three important results. First, its very existence strengthened the place of the environment on the international diplomatic agenda. Even the most traditional minds had to accept that environmental concerns had a place in international relations. Second, the delegates produced a number of important documents that provided guidelines for the next several years. The Declaration on the Human Environment and the Declaration of Principles established the tone that still dominates discussion about the biosphere. The 109 Recommendations for Action set national, regional, and international goals that governments are still trying to attain. Third, in response to the conference the UN General Assembly created the UN Environment Program as a central coordinating agency within the secretary-general's office. Demonstrating its commitment to the Stockholm principles, the United States provided the most funding for the UNEP.

Beyond official pronouncements and public debates, the Stockholm conference opened the way for three major developments in protecting the environment. First, it restored NGOs to the prominent position that they had not really held since the early 1900s, even in the United States. Since 1972, every attempt to solve international environmental crises has included input from private citizens claiming to speak for overlooked public interests. Second, diplomats have moved beyond the bilateral agreement to the unwieldy but more realistic multilateral conference. The success of the UNCHE demonstrated that dozens of nations can work together, so that once insurmountable global problems might now be manageable. Third, at Stockholm diplomats and bankers, for the first time, accepted the notion that environmental protection had to be incorporated into economic development plans.

Protecting Endangered Species

Out of the Stockholm conference came a strong movement finally to end whaling. The conference's emblem had been a whale, because the decline of the great sea mammals demonstrated clearly the damage to the biosphere. Among the Resolutions of Action was one calling for a ten-year moratorium on whaling, followed by a thorough study of whale populations. Environmentalists pointed out that whale products were peripheral to the world's economy and that whales ranked among the most advanced species on earth. They argued that killing whales no longer had even a shred of respectability. The United States favored the moratorium and worked to make it a reality. The IWC, meeting later in 1972, voted six to four (with four abstentions) against it. In response to environmentalist pressure, though, moratorium opponents proposed changes that they claimed, once again, would stabilize whaling stocks.

While the U.S. government and mainstream conservationists worked through traditional channels to create the ban on whaling, a new, more radical organization sprang to life—Greenpeace. While Greenpeace was by no means the only organization to take up the "Save the Whale" banner, it did become the most renowned.

Through its bold actions and clever use of television, Greenpeace roused world opinion against continued whaling. By the middle of the 1970s, only a few countries, particularly Japan, Norway, and the USSR, allowed whaling, and even they were feeling the pressure.

In 1982, the U.S. effort to ban whaling finally met success, when the IWC voted twenty-five to seven for a moratorium to begin in 1986. Under IWC rules, the countries that voted against the ban had the right to exempt themselves from it, which was just one of the many flaws of the IWC structure. The Russians, Japanese, and Norwegians have vacillated since then, claiming from time to time the need to collect whales for research purposes. On occasion, the United States has moved under the Packwood-Magnuson Amendment to the 1972 Marine Mammal Protection Act to punish whaling nations by excluding their citizens from fishing in U.S. waters. The international reaction may have been too late to save some species, such as the blue whale, but it demonstrated how environmental protection could became an international priority under the right conditions.

Also building on the momentum of the Stockholm conference, in 1973 the United States organized the Convention on International Trade in Endangered Species of Wild Fauna and Flora (CITES). In the early 1960s, the prestigious International Union for the Conservation of Nature and Natural Resources had proposed international action to stop the trade in endangered species. The idea languished until 1969, when the U.S. Congress passed the Endangered Species Act, which provided impetus to the proposal. Approximately 100 nations have ratified the treaty.

CITES shows both the successes and failures of the drive to attain international protection of the environment. On the positive side, the convention lists endangered species—now about 1,000—and imposes restrictions, usually bans, on trade in them. The UNEP manages the agreement on a scientific basis and holds biannual meetings, in which many NGOs participate, to discuss modifications of the rules. CITES stands out as one of the few broadly based organizations that can effectively implement economic sanctions against offenders. Its rapid ratification led to other agreements such as the 1976 convention protecting polar bears and the 1979 Convention on Conservation of Migratory Species of Wild Animals.

On the negative side, CITES has flaws common to most other environmental treaties. As with any convention with teeth, opponents worked to lessen its impact. First they held up the agreement throughout the 1960s until public pressure became too great, but by then some species certainly had passed into extinction. Then some of the worst offenders simply refused to sign, much as Japan withheld accession until 1980. Finally, signatory powers had the right to proclaim exemptions for themselves, thus freeing their citizens from unpopular but necessary measures. But perhaps the most revealing facet of CITES is its emphasis on vertebrates. The absence of plants, which form the basis for life on earth, and invertebrates, which outnumber and outweigh vertebrates, demonstrates that even this advanced agreement was based more on popular opinion than sound science.

The Oceanic Commons

The concerted effort to save the whales helped to drive home the point that the international waters and the resources in them were common property in need of joint regulation. Throughout the century, diplomats had found occasion to resolve disputes among nations about the use of contested waters, but beginning in the 1970s the disputes became more complex and the solutions more innovative. Three issues, all driven by improving technology, dominated the diplomacy of the oceanic commons: mineral rights, fishing, and pollution.

Up to the 1970s, the United States had usually been able to resolve its occasional fishery disputes—which usually involved Canada—with little controversy. Most nations accepted the standard rules, created by Hugo Grotius in 1609, of a three-mile territorial limit and freedom of the high seas. Nations that had disputes about fishing rights usually established joint fishery commissions to set rules and arbitrate disputes. After World War II, many governments decided that the three-mile limit was obsolete in the face of improved fishing and mineral extraction technology. As nations began to claim territorial waters out to twelve miles, the United States followed suit. In most cases, the primary goal of such an extension was to gain control over more fishing grounds. The old fishery commissions struggled to keep up, but still the United States generally found itself free of controversy.

In the 1970s, Ecuador and Peru claimed 200-mile territorial limits in the Pacific Ocean, sparking conflict with the United States over tuna fishing. U.S. fishermen refused to recognize these new limits, both because they had no historical precedent and the tuna were a highly migratory species. To avert a brewing "tuna war," the American Pacific Coast nations formed the Inter-American Tropical Tuna Commission, with jurisdiction over the tuna industry. To complicate matters, in the early 1970s, it became public knowledge that tuna fishing in the region resulted annually in the deaths of thousands of porpoises, which had a poorly understood association with the tuna. Thus, while the government was trying to protect U.S. tuna fishers, NGOs were organizing boycotts against them for killing porpoises.

The post-1945 efforts to extend territorial limits, as well as pollution and fishing disputes, led the United Nations to call a Conference on the Law of the Sea (UNCLOS) in 1958. This meeting produced four separate agreements, three of which dealt with pollution. While a step in the right direction, these agreements did not address questions of oil spills and ocean dumping.

In 1960, UNCLOS II met to discuss territorial limits. By then, most coastal nations had extended their limits beyond the traditional three miles. The United States joined those that had adopted a twelve mile buffer, with a 200-hundred mile Economic Exclusion Zone. Such partitioning of the seas harmed fisheries management, but nations could not afford to let competitors have an advantage. The real domino effect of the 1940s and 1950s was the rush of nations to push their dominion as far as possible into the high seas. The conferees had no choice but to codify what most of the world's nations had already done.

With jurisdictional and mineral-rights issues still in flux, UNCLOS III met in 1973 and worked for the next nine years. Delegates focused on the establishment of a regime for harvesting minerals from the seabed. The ocean floors have nodules of valuable metal ores, such as nickel and manganese, scattered unevenly. Mining them will be difficult and may be unprofitable; only a few developed nations have the technology and capital to do so. The developing nations, which controlled the voting through their sheer numbers, argued that these nodules were "the common heritage of mankind." Therefore, they advocated the creation of an International Seabed Authority that would oversee any seabed mining operations and distribute the fees to the poorer countries.

In 1982, UNCLOS III finished a treaty that encompassed most of the developing world's ideas regarding seabed mining. Businesses of any nation that signed the Law of the Sea Convention that wished to pursue the nodules would have to turn over most of their profits and share their technology with other countries' businesses. Over one hundred nations signed the treaty in the first few months, but the United States, the United Kingdom, West Germany, Japan, and France all declined. It will not take effect until sixty nations actually ratify it.

Just as the law of the sea negotiations stumbled on economic differences, so to did attempts to control oil pollution on the high seas. Throughout history, people have used the oceans as a dump, figuring that their vast size would disperse pollutants. Only in the last few decades has scientific study refuted that idea. The means of polluting water are innumerable, but dumping and spilling oil have always been among the most damaging and noticeable. While accidents involving supertankers have garnered the most attention, the bulk of oil pollution comes from routine ship operations, such as pumping ballast water from holds. Massive or sustained oil pollution can damage fish, wildlife, and coastal economic activity.

The United States usually has led efforts to control oil pollution. In 1926, the United States proposed a ban on dumping oil at sea by ships. Few other nations expressed interest, and the idea languished until 1954, when increased demand for petroleum led to greater oceanic traffic of oil tankers. In that year, diplomats in London agreed to the International Convention for Prevention of Pollution of the Sea by Oil, which prohibited oil discharge in certain protected coastal zones. Since then, the treaty parties have revised it or developed separate agreements several times; most recently, in 1979, they produced a convention that provided additional compensation to people harmed by oil spills.

While each revision of the oil pollution conventions has added to the protection of the oceanic environment, environmentalists believe that the rules are still inadequate. The oil industry succeeded in blunting the most stringent regulations by convincing governments that they were unnecessary and costly. But the most significant problem has been the refusal of certain nations, such as Panama and Liberia, to join such conventions. Each ship must be registered to some nation, and that nation has sole responsibility for enforcing regulations for that ship. Panama and Liberia use very lax shipping laws as a way of attracting foreign vessels to fly their flags, and they will not agree to any convention that might cost them their advantage. Under such pressures, the oceanic commons will continue to decline.

The Atmospheric Commons

Just as nations began to see the high seas as joint property after 1945, so too did they start to think of the earth's atmosphere as a common resource in need of protection after 1972. Other than the Trail Smelter case of 1941, nations had done little to control trans-border air pollution; but a combination of more pollution and increased awareness of the risks sparked major controversies in the 1970s and 1980s over acid rain and depletion of the ozone layer. In both cases, the United States found itself in the middle of a complex battle over economics and scientific certainty.

The acid rain dispute between the United States and Canada began in the late 1970s, when Canadian scientists reported that sulfuric dioxide (SO_2) in rain and snow was destroying the pH balance in lakes throughout eastern Canada. Approximately half of that chemical in the Canadian atmosphere came from the United States, especially coal-burning power plants in the Great Lakes region. The potential damage from acid rain included not only the death of aquatic life, but also the decimation of the vast northern forest, which formed an important part of the Canadian economy. Canada suffered from the geography and winds that brought the pollution, as well as from the geology that left most of the country with no

natural limestone buffer against increased acidity. Thus by 1980, most Canadians knew about acid rain, feared its consequences, and blamed the United States for not preventing it.

The two countries had faced off over air and water pollution before, and it seemed that a solution would be easy to find. In the 1960s, the United States had proposed to send oil tankers and naval vessels through the Arctic Ocean; the Canadian government protested that the risk of oil pollution was too great and demanded that Washington reconsider. The two sides reached a compromise that pleased neither but preserved harmony. In the 1970s, the two nations agreed to tackle pollution in the Great Lakes, an issue which they had skirted since the creation of the International Joint Commission in 1909. In 1972, they signed the Great Lakes Water Quality Agreement, which served to reduce the flow of pollutants into the lakes. Over the next two decades, they strengthened the rules three more times. While critics claim that the diplomats are still avoiding the underlying problems, supporters point out that the region's water is much cleaner than it was in 1969, when the Cuyahoga River caught fire.

Despite this background of success, Canada and the United States were unable to resolve the acid rain dispute quickly because the U.S. government hesitated. Only a small percentage of U.S. citizens—mostly from the northeast, which had geology and precipitation similar to Canada—knew about the issue. Many mid-westerners feared that gains in reducing acid rain would mean economic losses in the region, and they fought against concessions to Canada. In 1980, Canada and the United States agreed to the Acid Rain Memorandum of Intent, which called for both sides to reduce acidic emissions and urged further negotiations.

In the United States, the incoming Reagan administration (1981–1989) downplayed concern about acid rain. U.S. officials emphasized that confusion reigned in both the scientific and policy communities about the sources, amount, and impact of acid precipitation. For instance, some environmentalists argued that the 1977 Clean Air Act caused acid rain by encouraging the construction of tall smoke stacks on mid-western power plants. The administration argued that the act reduced acid rain because it had cut down on the production of SO_2. Arguing that acid rain was not an issue, in 1982 the U.S. government terminated talks with Canada on the subject.

The arrival in Ottawa of Brian Mulroney and his more conservative government in 1984 helped to bring acid rain back to the bargaining table. Perhaps because Mulroney took a more moderate stance on acid rain than his liberal predecessor, he prevailed upon his ideological soul mate Ronald Reagan to reconsider his position. In 1986, Reagan admitted that acid rain might be a problem, and in 1987 the two nations signed a treaty authorizing joint research into the problem. The U.S. government did not take any official action until the passage of the Clean Air Act of 1990 mandated reduction of SO2 emissions.

In the middle of the 1980s, another, more global, atmospheric crisis arose, with the discovery of a hole in the ozone layer over Antarctica. Ozone, an unstable collection of three oxygen atoms, exists in small amounts in the upper atmosphere, where it serves to block harmful ultraviolet radiation from reaching the earth. For more than a decade, scientists had been investigating the possibility that chlorofluorocarbons (CFCs), complex molecules used in refrigerants, styrofoam, and aerosol propellants, could cause damage to the ozone layer. When originally synthesized in the 1930s, CFCs seemed to be the perfect chemicals because they were non-toxic, non-flammable, stable, cheap, and extremely useful. As research continued, though, scientists found that when CFCs reached the upper atmosphere they caused chain reactions that broke down ozone. The stability of the compounds was now a curse, because individual molecules might last decades in the ozone layer, eroding the earth's shield against ultraviolet radiation.

As it turned out, the research of the early 1980s had been worrisome enough to warrant the calling of an international conference before the announcement of the ozone hole over the south pole. In 1985, twenty nations, including the leading producers of CFCs, signed the Vienna Convention for the Protection of the Ozone Layer, which put UNEP in charge of further research on and monitoring of the ozone. The treaty's vague language reflected the difficulties in obtaining a consensus from the various negotiators. They agreed to take appropriate measures to protect the ozone layer, although the convention did not specify any such measures or even list specific chemicals to control. Still, the agreement gave momentum to efforts to study and protect the ozone layer. So far, more than seventy nations have signed the agreement.

At the Vienna meeting, the United States pushed through a resolution requiring that the treaty powers agree to a binding set of regulations within two years. In general, Japan and Western Europe opposed U.S. efforts to move more quickly against CFCs because U.S. industry was in a better position to adapt to new rules. In fact, U.S. industrialists played the biggest role in convincing the Reagan administration that the Vienna convention was a worthy exception to the administration's opposition to more regulation.

In 1987, delegates from sixty nations met in Quebec to finalize terms for what became known as the Montreal Protocol on Substances that Deplete the Ozone Layer. They agreed on a list of chemicals, especially CFCs, that caused harm and pledged to cut production in half by 1999. Although a major breakthrough, critics pointed out some of the many flaws. China, India, and Brazil refused to sign, arguing that the rules punished developing nations who needed cheap CFCs to catch up to the technologically advanced nations; no method existed to transfer technology or financial assistance to help these countries overcome this legitimate complaint. Several European nations described the terms as too stringent, although many environmentalists thought they were too lax. Also, representatives from NGOs and U.S. industry worried about the lack of an enforcement mechanism to ensure compliance.

In response to the criticism, the signatory powers reconvened in Helsinki in 1989 and London in 1990 to tighten up the rules. Further research suggested that the problem was worse than expected; therefore, the eighty-one nations that met at Helsinki called for a total ban on CFCs by 2000. Addressing the concerns of developing nations, they also called on the industrial powers to provide financial assistance to poorer countries in order to implement the agreement. At the London conference, the delegates devised systems to make both proposals reality. In 1992, President George Bush announced that, because of technological advances, the United States would end CFC production by 1995.

Reforming Economic Development

Another important derivative of the Stockholm conference was a budding awareness that international development schemes were creating environmental damage. Since 1945, wealthy nations had found it in their interest to loan money to encourage economic development in other countries. Whether through direct foreign aid programs, such as the U.S. Agency for International Development (USAID), or multilateral development banks (MDBs), such as the World Bank, by the late 1970s industrialized nations were distributing tens of billions of dollars annually around the world. In addition to providing direct loans and contributions, these agencies' decisions influenced private lenders by giving legitimacy to certain countries or projects. Beginning in the 1970s, private citizens, especially in the United States, pressured these lenders to consider the environmental impact of the various development projects.

The first important step towards making the environment a priority came in the middle of the 1970s, when the Natural Resources Defense Council and the Sierra Club, with help from other organizations, lobbied USAID to be more environmentally responsible in its foreign aid programs. Over the years, USAID had made a number of controversial decisions, including subsidies for the export of pesticides that were illegal in the United States. When USAID proved unresponsive, the NGOs filed lawsuits to force government foreign aid agencies to prepare environmental impact statements for all projects. In 1979, President Jimmy Carter issued an executive order that satisfied some of the demands. When President Reagan scaled back Carter's measure, the NGO's persuaded Congress to force the USAID to spend a percentage of its budget on protecting the environment.

The NGOs then turned their attention to the World Bank and other MDBs. For years, the MDBs had loaned money to developing nations in support of large, central projects that facilitated exports on the theory that exports provided the best means to raise the per capita GNP in a non-industrialized country. Environmentalists believed that these programs destroyed the environment in two ways. First, the MDBs did not count extraction of natural resources or ecosystem damage on national balance sheets, so the numbers did not accurately reflect the environmental costs of development. More critically, loans required repayment. In the drive to acquire foreign currency, governments often encouraged their citizens to ignore environmental consequences of economic actions. Thus, farmers and ranchers moved onto marginal lands, prospectors invaded remote regions, and industrialists overlooked pollution in their efforts to make money.

The NGOs wanted to change the way the MDBs did business, and they saw the U.S. government, which had power in many of the MDBs, as the best place to start. The Reagan administration was not especially sympathetic, so environmentalists turned their attention to Congress. In 1983, Congress began to hold hearings on the environmental impact of World Bank policies. After hearing testimony from U.S. and foreign NGOs, a bipartisan consensus emerged in 1986 that the United States should use its influence to reform the World Bank's lending process. Congress ordered the U.S. delegate to the World Bank to take into consideration the environmental impact of projects when voting on loans. Under such pressure, the World Bank undertook major reforms in 1987 that led to a better environmental record. The other major MDBs followed suit. Despite the progress, though, environmental groups and development agencies still are often at odds.

While the changes in lending institutions pleased environmentalists, they perceived a need to establish a separate program to reverse the destruction of tropical forests. For decades citizens of tropical countries had slowly nibbled away at the fringes of the vast rain forests, such as the Brazilian Amazon. As medical and agricultural revolutions cut mortality rates in these countries after 1945, the population began to grow rapidly. The demand for land went up accordingly, which increased pressure on the forests. Poor farmers moved from marginal plot to marginal plot, often practicing slash-and-burn agriculture. At the same time, many rain forest countries witnessed a boom in cattle ranching, which brought even more pressure to clear the forests.

In past decades, both European and North American countries had exploited their resources in similar manners, but the destruction of tropical forests caused a great deal of concern around the world. Not only do tropical forests contain untold thousands of species of plants and animals, but also it became clear that their very presence stabilized the earth's climate. As part of photosynthesis, plants convert carbon dioxide (CO_2) into oxygen, thus helping to scrub the air of a widespread pollutant. At the same time, the burning of forests annually adds to the atmosphere more than two billion tons of CO_2, plus untold methane and nitrous oxide. Scientists reported that the these chemicals, known as greenhouse gases, could be causing a gradual warming of the planet. No one knew what climate change might bring, but most people agreed that it was best to work for stability by protecting the world's forests.

Therefore, in 1985, the World Bank, the World Resources Institute, and the UN Development Program joined forces to create the Tropical Forestry Task Force. After much study and input from NGOs around the world, the task force produced the Tropical Forestry Action Plan (TFAP). Supporters believed that previous financial aid had only encouraged the destruction of forests, and they hoped to bring a new attitude to forestry, including watershed rehabilitation and sustainable logging. For a variety of reasons, though, the TFAP came under the jurisdiction of the UN Food and Agriculture Organization, which held to traditional methods. By 1990, the TFAP had a budget of $1.3 billion and seventy member nations. It is fair to say, though, that it has not reversed the problem of deforestation.

Many people saw the connection between deforestation and the debt loads caused by excessive borrowing, and they worked to break the cycle. The most innovative approach became known as the debt-for-nature swap, in which NGOs, and sometimes Western governments, purchase and cancel the debt of developing countries in exchange for strengthened environmental protection. Instead of encouraging environmentally harmful activities that generate foreign currency necessary to pay off the debt, governments can reduce foreign debt by agreeing to spend domestic currency on environmental protection. Although such transactions have been quite successful, the size of Third World debt, especially compared to NGO resources, makes the debt-for-nature swap a limited tool.

Cold War Legacies

In the fall of 1986, the world learned about the worst nuclear accident in history, the near meltdown at the Chernobyl nuclear power plant in the Ukraine. In the fire and explosion that destroyed part of the power station, a large radioactive cloud escaped and drifted over eastern and northern Europe. The Soviet Union tried to cover up the incident, but Scandinavian scientists detected the radiation and forced the Soviets to disclose at least some of the truth. Within months, many nations signed two agreements pledging to provide full disclosure and help one another in case of another nuclear accident. Many in the anti-nuclear movement—which had been tightly linked to the environmental movement—saw in the Chernobyl incident the confirmation of their worst fears, that nuclear power or nuclear weapons would cause irreparable damage to the biosphere.

As Mikhail Gorbachev's reforms allowed for the opening of Eastern Europe and the Soviet Union to westerners, they discovered that Chernobyl was also a symbol of the general environmental disaster that communism had wrought. In their race to catch up with the Western economies, socialists in Eastern Europe had abandoned environmental protection in the name of increasing gross national product. In the process, they had unleashed air and water pollution that destroyed forests and rivers, lowered the water levels in the inland lakes and seas, and caused health problems for people of all ages. The poor environmental records, in conjunction with political chaos in the former Soviet Union, caused concern about the safety of nuclear weapons and power in Eastern Europe. In November 1992, Senators Sam Nunn and Richard Lugar tied Soviet nuclear disarmament to the Chernobyl disaster, the outbreak of ethnic tensions, and nuclear non-proliferation. Fearing that the collapse of the Soviet Union might lead to a nuclear accident, they proposed to link foreign aid to the republics of the former Soviet Union with the republics' willingness to centralize control of their nuclear stockpiles in Moscow. Since then, the United States has made some effort to tie its foreign aid to Eastern Europe to nuclear safety and environmental clean up.

The Earth Summit

As recognition of the wide range of global environmental problems mounted—in part because of the end of the Cold War, the UN was preparing for its second meeting on the subject, the UN Conference on Environment and Development (UNCED). The Earth Summit, as most people called it, met in June 1992 in Rio de Janeiro with a broad mandate to discuss issues affecting the biosphere. Representatives from 170 nations attended. William Reilly, the administrator of the Environmental Protection Agency, led the U.S. delegation, which also included a congressional contingent led by Senator Al Gore, Democrat of Tennessee. While Reilly presented the official positions from the administration, Gore played an unusual role by acting as a vocal critic from

within the delegation. On paper, the United States maintained its position as one of the leaders of international environmental reform, but two controversial decisions prompted many observers, especially Gore, to charge that the nation had surrendered that leadership.

Two official agreements came out of the UNCED, led by the Framework Convention on Climate Change, which 150 nations signed. Most of the delegates agreed that human economic activity was threatening the stability of the climate and that international agreement was necessary; indeed, the UN had endorsed such a convention as early as 1989. Negotiations revealed two splits in the comity of nations. While industrialized countries called for stricter controls on air pollution, developing nations pointed out that pollution had been the price of western economic development. To them, pollution controls were reasonable, but the industrialized nations should compensate them for some of the economic costs. At the same time, the United States split from the other industrialized countries in opposing national pollution targets. In part, the U.S. government was acting on scientific uncertainty, but the Bush administration also was concerned about maintaining national sovereignty over the economy. This controversial stand helped to create a convention that many regard as too vague.

The second major agreement was the Convention on Biological Diversity, which also garnered more than 150 signatures. The United States had first proposed such a convention years before, but the negotiations carried it out of U.S. control. The final text required the signatory powers to take action to protect biodiversity internally and established a mechanism for channeling money for such steps to the developing world. Despite intense pressure at home and abroad, the United States refused to sign. The administration criticized the convention's vague language on intellectual property rights and regulation of biotechnology. President Bush argued that the U.S. government already did more than any other country to protect biodiversity, so therefore nothing was lost. In April 1993, President Bill Clinton signed the convention after working out an interpretive statement with business and environmental leaders.

In addition, the countries agreed to two sets of recommendations. First, they compromised on a declaration of forest management principles. The United States had led the push for a forestry convention, but many developing nations strenuously objected to surrendering their control over such a basic resource. Second, they produced a 900-page document, known as Agenda 21, as an unofficial action plan for protecting the global environment. The agenda was not binding, but like other UN declarations, on human rights for instance, it had a certain moral authority.

The urgency evident in many of the delegates reflected a growing conviction that the environment has become an important international security concern. By many estimates, the world's population will soon reach eight billion, and the global economy will continue to expand rapidly. The growing economy and population may combine to exacerbate shortages and unequal distribution of resources, which could, in turn, lead to conflict. Some fear that resource scarcity, especially in developing countries, might lead to authoritarianism, disintegration of nations, or aggression against neighboring states. Competition for resources has long been a cause of political instability and strife, but the wave of environmental degradation in the mid–1990s seemed to be unprecedented. The mood at the Earth Summit suggested that many governments and NGOs now see environmental protection as a central concern for their national security.

The Bush administration's stance at the Earth Summit made explicit the modern tension between environmental protection and economic nationalism, especially in times of economic restructuring. That tension took a strange turn in the debates about the North American Free Trade Agreement (NAFTA) in 1993 and the General Agreement on Tariffs and Trade (GATT) in 1994. NAFTA's opponents argued that the agreement would allow U.S. companies to move to Mexico to take advantage of its weaker environmental laws. Those who opposed GATT complained that the newly-formed World Trade Organization would have the authority to weaken U.S. environmental laws. In both cases, then, some environmentalists found themselves linked with the economic nationalists who often fought U.S. participation in international environmental accords. Supporters of freer trade helped to secure congressional approval of both measures by promising to maintain strong U.S. laws.

The Earth Summit, the links between the environment and national security, and the debate over free trade demonstrated that the environmental issues on the diplomatic agenda had become much more complex over the course of the century, and diplomats from around the world were much more receptive to the whole idea of discussing environmental disputes. But the same basic challenges remained from the Progressive Era. It is still difficult to regulate a common property resource. Nations still fear yielding their sovereignty. Economic actors still respond to their short-term interests rather than the long-term good of the nation, region, or planet. Private citizens still play a vital role in determining the positions of their governments. Finally, although shaken at Rio, the United States still maintains its position as the leading initiator of environmental diplomacy.

KURK DORSEY

See also Antarctica; Canada; Earth Summit; Environmental Protection Agency; Law of the Sea; Rio de Janiero; United Nations; Whaling

FURTHER READING

Benedick, Richard. *Ozone Diplomacy: New Directions in Safeguarding the Planet.* Cambridge, 1991.

Caldwell, Lynton Keith. *International Environmental Policy: Emergence and Dimensions.* 2nd ed. Durham, N.C., 1990.

Carroll, John, ed. *International Environmental Diplomacy.* Cambridge, 1988.

Chacko, Chirakaikaran Joseph. *The International Joint Commission Between the United States of America and the Dominion of Canada.* New York, 1968.

Dahlberg, Keith, et al. *Environment and the Global Arena: Actors, Values, Policies, and Futures.* Durham, N.C., 1985.

Francis, Daniel. *A History of World Whaling.* New York, 1990.

Hardin, Garrett. "The Tragedy of the Commons," *Science.* vol. 162, 13 December 1968.

Hayden, Sherman. *The International Protection of Wildlife.* New York, 1942.

Hollick, Ann. *United States Foreign Policy and the Law of the Sea.* Princeton, N.J., 1981.

Homer-Dixon, Thomas. "Environmental Scarcities and Violent Conflict: Evidence from Cases," *International Security.* vol. 19, Summer 1994.

Hurrell, Andrew and Benedict Kingsbury, eds. *The International Politics of the Environment: Actors, Interests, and Institutions.* Oxford, 1992.

Lythle, Mark. "An Environmental Approach to American Diplomatic History." *Diplomatic History* (Spring 1996).

Mathews, Jessica, ed. *Preserving the Global Environment: The Challenge of Shared Leadership.* New York, 1991.

Mott, Richard. "The GEF and the Conventions on Climate Change and Biological Diversity." *International Environmental Affairs.* vol. 5:4, Fall 1993.

Sand, Peter, ed. *The Effectiveness of International Environmental Agreements: A Survey of Existing Legal Instruments.* Cambridge, England, 1992.

ENVIRONMENTAL PROTECTION AGENCY

An independent agency of the U.S. government charged with the preservation of the environment. It was founded in 1970 in response to a growing environmental awareness in the United States. Its general mission has been to curb pollution and environmental hazards. Although it is a domestic policy agency, the EPA has recently taken on a role as a source of scientific information and advice for U.S. diplomats.

Since 1970, the United States has participated in a number of treaties and conferences to protect the international environment. In most cases, diplomats have not had the necessary expertise to best represent the national interest. Often, the EPA has provided that expertise, although diplomats have not always used it. The ability of the agency to influence international policy has depended both on the willingness of U.S. diplomats to accept scientific input and on the agency's willingness to insert itself into the fray.

The EPA first made an impact on U.S. diplomacy in the negotiations that led to the 1987 Montreal Protocol on

Substances that Deplete the Ozone Layer. The agency had laid the groundwork for the protocol by establishing tough domestic anti-pollution regulations, including some designed to reduce the emission of chlorofluorocarbons, which scientists believed to be especially damaging to the ozone layer. Such rules encouraged U.S. business leaders and diplomats to support efforts to abolish ozone-depleting substances worldwide. Throughout the negotiations, the EPA produced volumes of scientific evidence to support the U.S. position both at home and abroad.

The agency has also found itself at odds with the official White House and Department of State position. In 1992, EPA director William Reilly led the U.S. delegation to the Earth Summit in Rio de Janeiro. The Bush administration, however, was not willing to base its policy entirely on the recommendations of the agency. Thus, although Reilly received international acclaim for his leadership, he was unable to translate the agency's expertise into a U.S. diplomatic agenda.

After Bill Clinton won the 1992 presidential election, he chose Carole Browner to be the new director of the EPA. In April 1993, Clinton signed the biodiversity agreement after the EPA helped to draft an interpretive statement that satisfied some of the concerns of the business community. Under the Clinton administration, the EPA has become much more involved in international pollution prevention and habitat protection. In addition, the agency provides advice to developing nations on a wide range of environmental protection issues.

KURK DORSEY

See also Environment; Law of the Sea; United Nations

FURTHER READING
Benedick, Richard E. *Ozone Diplomacy: New Directions in Safeguarding the Planet.* Cambridge, Mass., 1991.

EPA

See Environmental Protection Agency

EQUATORIAL GUINEA

See Appendix 2

ERITREA

Located in Eastern Africa, bordering the Red Sea between Djibooti and Sudan, a nation which was formerly part of Ethiopia. On 24 May 1993 Eritrea formally seceded from Ethiopia and became an independent state under the control of the Eritrean People's Liberation Front (EPLF), which in February 1994 became the People's Front for Democracy and Justice (PFDJ). During the preceding four decades the United States opposed Eritrean independence, but following a UN-supervised referendum in April 1993 in which the Eritrean people voted overwhelmingly in favor of independence, Washington granted diplomatic recognition of the new Eritrean state.

The United States first became interested in this former Italian colony during World War II, establishing a communications facility, Radio Marina (which in the 1950s was renamed Kagnew Station), near the Eritrean town of Asmara in early 1943. Because of the strategic value of this facility, in 1950 Washington supported a UN-sponsored plan calling for a ten-year federation between Ethiopia and Eritrea, which took effect in December 1952. Washington, which did not want to jeopardize its base rights in Ethiopia, acquiesced when Ethiopia's emperor Haile Selassie annexed Eritrea in 1962. Over the next fifteen years Washington provided military and counterinsurgency aid to Ethiopia which was used by Addis Ababa in an unsuccessful effort to suppress a secessionist rebellion that had erupted in Eritrea in the fall of 1961.

Even after U.S.-Ethiopian military relations were terminated in April 1977, following the overthrow of Haile Selassie by a pro-Soviet Marxist regime led by Colonel Mengistu Haile Mariam, Washington refused to support the Eritrean insurgents (at least overtly), and remained publicly opposed to Eritrean independence. Concern about the leftist ideological orientation of the dominant EPLF, coupled with the Department of State's fear of alienating friendly African governments who faced separatist and ethno-nationalist problems of their own, resulted in a hands-off approach. U.S. policy changed when the Mengistu regime in Ethiopia began to crumble in the spring of 1991. At the end of May 1991, the Bush administration assisted the emergence of an independent Eritrea by helping to broker an agreement providing for the transfer of power in Addis Ababa to the Ethiopian People's Democratic Liberation Front (EPDLF) and a two-year transition period for Eritrea, after which the Eritrean people were allowed to exercise the right of self-determination. In the mid-1990s, U.S.-Eritrean relations have become quite close despite Washington's past record of opposition to and non-support for Eritrean nationalism. The United States provides economic and small amounts of military aid to Eritrea. Washington also has been supportive of Asmara as part of a regional campaign to isolate the National Islamic Front (NIF) government in Sudan which since 1992 has been supporting the Eritrean Islamic Jihad Movement (EIJM). The United States refused to side with Eritrea during the December 1995 war with Yemen over the Hanish Islands in the Red Sea, and called for international mediation.

JEFFREY A. LEFEBVRE

See also Africa; Ethiopia

FURTHER READING

Connell, Dan. *Against All Odds: A Chronicle of the Eritrean Revolution.* Trenton, N.J., 1993.

Iyob, Ruth. *The Eritrean Struggle for Independence: Domination, Resistance, Nationalism, 1941–1993.* New York, 1995.

LeFebvre, Jeffrey A. *Arms for the Horn: U.S. Security Policy in Ethiopia and Somalia, 1953–1991.* Pittsburgh, Pa., 1991.

——. "Post-Cold War Clouds on the Horn of Africa: the Eritrea-Sudan Crisis." *Middle East Policy* Vol IV, 182 (1995): 34–49.

ESPIONAGE

The secret method of obtaining information that the holder wishes to conceal, also known as spying. Espionage is but one source of intelligence information, which supplies government decision-makers with strategic estimates required for foreign policy, planning, and action. Because espionage is by definition an illegal method of gathering information, it requires deception and the highest degree of secrecy. In common usage the terms "intelligence," "espionage," "counterintelligence," and "covert action" are often used inaccurately or interchangeably. Intelligence, in the context of foreign relations, means evaluated and usually secret information needed for strategic success in government decisions. Espionage is one method—secret and illegal—of gathering information. Counterintelligence protects secret information and personnel, and tries to identify, neutralize, and exploit espionage by adversaries. Covert action, often performed by the same officers and agents involved in espionage, is political action that aims to influence foreign behavior and events.

Spying as an instrument of policy over the centuries has been associated with deception, seduction, passion, and money. More than 2,000 years ago Sun-tzu, a Chinese strategist, suggested in *The Art of War* that wars might be unnecessary if military leaders possessed accurate information on the secret battle plans and strength of an enemy. He suggested that leaders and commanders who hired the most intelligent spies would be most successful. Queen Elizabeth I commanded her foreign minister to recruit foreign spies to provide information enabling the preemption of enemies of England. As a prime tool in foreign relations, espionage increased in use with the rise of the nation-state. The need for an ever-expanding variety of secret information grew apace with the growing complexity of society, governmental institutions, and advancing technology.

In the struggle for independence from Great Britain, American colonial revolutionaries sought information through espionage. Intelligence historians refer to George Washington as "America's first spymaster." General Washington's war account book contains an entry of $333 to pay a spy to enter Boston to report on British

capabilities and intentions. Information obtained by espionage was an important factor in the success of the revolution. The U.S. westward expansion in the first half of the nineteenth century and the later pursuit of Manifest Destiny involved a variety of forms of strategic deception, including espionage against both foreign colonials and Native Americans.

Before the turn of the century and into the twentieth century, espionage became well established in governments, particularly in nations with expansionist foreign policies. In the United States, however, government intelligence organizations with cadres of professional spies developed slowly. In wartime, intelligence systems were organized but abolished or sharply reduced in size in postwar years. When the United States entered World War I in 1917, the army chief of staff, General Peyton C. March, had an intelligence staff consisting of two officers and two clerks. Expansion and contraction of espionage resources reflect the isolationist impulse in U.S. foreign relations. The belief prevailed that the United States, protected by the two great oceans, need not be concerned in peacetime with the affairs of distant nations. Except in war, spies were not regarded as essential to national security. Furthermore, spying was not easily squared with U.S. ethical values. The expansionist policies of Italy, Germany, and Japan in the 1930s, however, stimulated an interest and growth in espionage activities worldwide. Concern about foreign spies or "fifth columns" of the Fascist powers prompted reactive growth of espionage capabilities among the democracies. The United States, however, was the last to react. During that time the U.S. Army and Navy developed capabilities with foreign codes and ciphers. The notorious Black Chamber, an army code-breaking establishment under Herbert O. Yardley, was abolished after World War I on the premise that reading other persons' confidential communications was dishonorable.

As war in Europe approached in the late 1930s, the U.S. Department of War bolstered its Signal Intelligence Service as money and staff were increased for codebreaking. Led by William F. Friedman, army chief cryptanalyst, work began on breaking Japan's diplomatic ciphers, termed the "Purple" code. Friedman's team was successful in August 1940 and the product was known as "Magic." Even with such a significant intelligence asset, the bombing of Pearl Harbor on 7 December 1941 was a total shock. Although controversy abounds regarding the Pearl Harbor surprise, no extensive network of spies and no central organization existed for collating information gathered in the field.

The United States entered World War II with little espionage capability. Dean Acheson, as undersecretary of state, told Congress in 1945 that prior to the war the Department of State's "technique for gathering information differed only by reason of the typewriter and telegraph from the techniques which John Quincy Adams was using in St. Petersburg and Benjamin Franklin was using in Paris." Nonetheless, five months before the Pearl Harbor attack, President Franklin D. Roosevelt requested that William J. Donovan draft a plan for a new intelligence service designed to fight a global war. This assignment ultimately resulted in the creation in June 1942 of the Office of Strategic Services (OSS). Among its other functions, the OSS, under the supervision of the Joint Chiefs of Staff, became the vehicle for espionage in pursuit of total victory in the war. The OSS was the first large-scale U.S. secret operations institution. It made significant contributions to victory but was quickly dismantled at war's end.

The OSS nonetheless set the foundation for what became a vast postwar intelligence bureaucracy. Some OSS leaders were dominant figures in the postwar Central Intelligence Agency (CIA), which was established by Congress in 1947 after two years of internecine bureaucratic warfare over the future of a U.S. intelligence organization. Attempting to apply the lessons of wartime experience, the original concept of a postwar intelligence agency was as a coordinator of information gathered by various military and department intelligence units to aid presidential foreign policy decision-making. The principal work of the CIA in its original conception was analysis in a social science mode. Eventually the CIA was assigned the task of Cold War espionage, psychological warfare, and secret political action, focusing primarily on targets in the Soviet Union, Eastern Europe, and selected Third World nations.

Intelligence analysis requires data, and as the Cold War evolved, data from crucial parts of the world was inaccessible by open means because of repressive security regimes. Consequently, espionage became an increasingly utilized instrument. Indeed, an espionage war became a major feature of the East-West conflict from 1950 to 1990. Frequent East-West spy scandals were a feature of these Cold War years. Somewhere along the line hostility developed within the U.S. intelligence system between the professional covert operators of an elite clandestine service responsible for espionage and the analysts who believed that systematic research was the most reliable road to the foreknowledge sought by political decision-makers. Ultimately, clandestine operations became the main focus of media, congressional, and public attention with periodic scandals attending disclosures of some covert actions. Within the career intelligence system, however, clandestine operations became the dominant CIA culture. In its first twenty years, two-thirds of the highest CIA executive positions were filled by officers from the clandestine service. It was not until the 1990s that a career analyst was appointed director of central intelligence.

Two kinds of secret operations were carried out by the Operations Directorate, which was the locus for the conduct of foreign espionage. Besides the illegal search for secret information, secret operators were assigned covert action missions, efforts to influence by secret means political outcomes in foreign target areas. Covert action is officially defined by the CIA as "special activity abroad in support of foreign policy such that the role of the U.S. Government is neither apparent nor publicly acknowledged." Under this rubric elections were manipulated, secret monetary aid was dispensed, psychological warfare waged, and governments overthrown in favor of U.S.-preferred leaders. Indeed, assassination plots were attempted. In effect the CIA was a major instrument for implementing foreign policy in the Cold War years. Bolstered by prematurely judged "successes" in Iran, 1953, and Guatemala, 1954, hundreds of covert action projects were undertaken, aimed mostly at perceived similar activities by the Soviet Union. Problems arose within the intelligence system from combining intelligence gathering with policy implementation. When those committed to a given foreign policy were also tasked with gathering and analyzing information about operational feasibility, a blindness to reality was a risk. Operational failure was not uncommon. The U.S.-sponsored attempted invasion of Cuba at the Bay of Pigs in 1961 is a prime example. A more general problem was the politicization of intelligence estimates that sometimes resulted in misleading estimates designed to please decision-makers.

Espionage Methods

Most agent espionage, labeled HUMINT, is conducted by second party individuals, that is, a foreign national who has been hired by an intelligence officer. Professional intelligence officers, called "case officers" by the CIA, usually recruit citizens within target countries. These are termed agents, who have been induced to steal secret information or disloyally to disclose government information to which they have access. Other sources of information are termed "contacts" or "occasional sources." These may be "witting" or "unwitting," depending on their knowledge of who is seeking the information. Sources of this sort are categorized as "untested," "tested," "reliable," or "unreliable."

Espionage sources are variously motivated. Greed or financial need is often a prime motive. Other incentives, such as ambition, political ideology, blackmail often associated with sexual involvement, or nationalistic idealism often figure in particular cases. Believing that the West must be warned of war danger, for example, Colonel Oleg Penkovsky, a highly placed Soviet military officer, provided important secret information to Western intelligence officers during 1961 and 1962. Some have credited Penkovsky with supplying President John F. Kennedy with information crucial to avoiding nuclear war in the Cuban missile crisis in 1962. H. A. R. (Kim) Philby, a British diplomat, worked as a spy for the Soviet Union in the 1940s and 1950s on ideological grounds, narrowly escaping to the Soviet Union in 1963 before apprehension. Most exposed U.S. spies, particularly in the 1980s, were motivated by financial greed. More than a dozen Americans were uncovered as major spies for the Soviet bloc in the 1980s, notably John Walker, Jr., Ronald Pelton, Edward Lee Howard, and James Hall III. While ideology once seemed the dominant motive of U.S. spies in the early Cold War period, financial reward was the prime motive in later years. A dramatic example is Aldrich Ames, a career CIA officer for thirty-one years, who supplied the Soviet Union and Russia with thousands of secret CIA documents from 1985 until his arrest in 1994. His treachery caused the execution of ten of the CIA's Soviet sources and compromised scores of U.S. covert operations. The KGB, the Soviet intelligence agency, had paid him more than $2 million. In 1994 he was sentenced to life in prison without parole. Later it was revealed that highest U.S. officials wittingly received, and made decisions based upon, tainted Soviet information derived from Ames's treachery.

Some foreign spies must be seduced into cooperation, while others volunteer. The latter are termed "walk-ins" or "defectors." These must be handled with extreme caution because "double agents" sometimes appear among the volunteers. Some spies pretend to be disloyal but sometimes secretly maintain their primary loyalty, hoping to deceive their new masters, or alternatively, to benefit from double payments. Counterintelligence staffs maintain a skepticism about defectors, subject them to careful interrogation, including polygraph testing, and restrict their use for positive intelligence purposes. Internal controversies about the bona fides of defectors have rocked the U.S. intelligence system, particularly during the regime of James J. Angleton, CIA counterintelligence chief from 1948 to 1974. Many believe that bureaucratic reactions to Angleton's presumed paranoia explain a subsequent security laxity, allowing Aldrich Ames to operate undetected for nearly a decade. The most valuable source of all is the "agent-in-place," commonly called a "mole," who remains in a sensitive position of trust with access to important secret information but who has been recruited by a foreign intelligence service. Penkovsky and Ames are examples.

With the evaporation of East-West Cold War tensions, high-priority worldwide espionage targets shifted to industrial-technological secrets. A post-Cold War debate, inconclusive at this writing, began over whether the United States should employ industrial espionage against foreign areas including friendly nations. Terrorism, drug trafficking, and the spread of weapons of mass destruction also became major concerns. If leadership in such developments can be detected by espionage, foreknowledge may be useful in deterrence or international controls. Spying is justified with the argument that only by espionage can terrorism and other threats be deterred.

Forms and Techniques

All forms and techniques of espionage are aided by an accelerating technology of communications and a variety of computing, measuring, sensing, and photographic devices. Tiny cameras and microfilm have long made it easier for persons to photograph secret documents and conceal the film. Space satellites supplementing high altitude and drone aircraft have also increased dramatically the ability to keep under surveillance military weapons, installations, and movements. Advanced technology has also fostered worldwide undersea surveillance systems. Details of the most advanced high-technology devices normally are secret, but it is known that telephones can be tapped without wires, rooms can be monitored with electronic listening devices without entry, and photographs can be made at night. Similar technology can be used for countermeasures, and competition constantly escalates between those seeking secret information and those protecting it. In sensitive locations within certain foreign embassies, confidential discussions occur within plastic bubbles surrounding secure rooms as an antiespionage measure. In the late 1980s the construction of a new U.S. embassy in Moscow was abandoned because Soviet intelligence had implanted listening devices secretly within the walls of the new building. Security of communications remains under constant assault by spies using a variety of techniques.

Espionage in International Law

Espionage is universally treated as a serious crime in national laws. The United States outlawed spying in the Espionage Act of 1917, enacted by Congress two months after entry into World War I. The law was broadened by the Espionage and Sabotage Act of 1954, which authorized the death penalty in peace or war and required foreign agents to register. A further change in 1958 covered U.S. citizens spying against the United States overseas. In international law, the status of espionage remains ambiguous. Legal distinctions exist between spying in peacetime and wartime military espionage. Modern diplomatic protocol granting privileges and immunities to accredited foreign service officers in foreign countries prohibits spying. Numerous examples over the years can be cited of diplomats expelled rather than imprisoned for alleged espionage. Nonetheless, embassies and legations provide cover for espionage activities. Even so, professional distinctions must be made between spies and diplomats. One reason for the growth of the CIA's functions is that diplomatic rules prohibit spying.

But what are the outer limits of national sovereignty when a growing amount of intrusive surveillance occurs from space reconnaissance satellites that are commonly called "spy stations"? How far up does sovereignty go? What constitutes peacetime territorial intrusion? International law provides no clear answers. The pragmatic answer is that if a nation has the capability to prevent intrusive surveillance and chooses to apply it, aggressive interdiction can result. Although President Dwight D. Eisenhower publicly proclaimed the right and necessity to send spy planes over the Soviet Union in the late 1950s, U-2 pilot Gary Powers was shot down, tried, and convicted by a Soviet court in 1960. He was freed in 1962 in exchange for Rudolf Abel, a Soviet agent imprisoned in the United States for espionage. The posture of the United States has been that national sovereignty does not extend beyond the earth's atmosphere. Thus, surveillance of foreign territory from space is seen as legally permissible. The Soviet Union took the contrary position that space surveillance of its territory violated international law.

Strategic arms limitation agreements between the United States and the Soviet Union, beginning in the 1960s, witnessed a mutually tacit agreement about space surveillance. Leaders of the two nations adopted euphemisms to refer to peacetime reconnaissance from space, such as mutual verification of arms control agreements by "national technical means." The Strategic Arms Limitation Treaty (SALT II) signed by the United States and the Soviet Union on 18 June 1979 seemed to represent mutual acceptance of space surveillance for verification, but the wording of the SALT II treaty remained ambiguous: "Each party shall use national technical means of verification at its disposal in a manner consistent with generally recognized principles of international law." Such principles, however, remained vague.

In wartime a spy was generally viewed by the target state as simply one form of military soldier. The Declaration of Brussels, drawn up at a fifteen-member European conference in 1874 on the laws of war, acknowledged espionage. It was stipulated that a spy, if caught, would be tried according to the laws of the army capturing him. This was a precursor to later Hague and Geneva conventions refining espionage rules in wartime, which stated that a spy, when taken in the act, was not to be punished without trial. The Geneva Convention of 1949 and protocols of 1977 further adjusted standards, mandating for spies trial with counsel, an appeal process, and a six-month waiting period before execution. In essence, military spying in wartime was viewed as a component of military operations. Peacetime espionage on the other hand is not a breach of, and is not governed by, interna-

tional law. Severe national penalties are imposed in an effort to deter espionage.

Ramifications

Espionage has been practiced because information is a crucial element of power in relations among nations. One attribute of state sovereignty is the ability to protect certain kinds of information from unwanted disclosure. As nations pursue national interests, espionage will remain a feature of international relations. In wartime, information becomes of critical strategic as well as tactical importance. Military success or failure can be determined by espionage. From colonial times forward, the United States has mobilized espionage resources against wartime enemies. In interwar years such resources were largely neglected. The Cold War generated the creation and expansion of large bureaucracies for espionage by the United States and other major powers.

Costs or benefits of espionage in foreign relations are difficult to assess in the absence of full details, even though a vast and growing body of documents and literature exists. If espionage in some cases has been demonstrably a determinant of diplomatic or military success, in other cases espionage attempts have impaired the chances of diplomatic success or provoked an adversary into unwanted political or military conflict. In 1960 the shooting down of a U.S. spy plane deep within the Soviet Union destroyed President Eisenhower's hope for détente with the Soviet Union. Russian President Boris Yeltsin in the summer of 1992 disclosed that the Soviet Union had shot down dozens of U.S. aircraft during the Cold War. These planes were engaged in what the Soviet Union viewed as espionage. Incidents in the Gulf of Tonkin in 1964, which resulted in a grant of presidential authority to escalate the Vietnam War, exemplify aggressive U.S. naval espionage operations.

Espionage by both the CIA and the KGB during the Cold War contributed to mutual perceptions of aggressive intent, which fostered suspicions and intensified the Cold War. Espionage arguably had a negative net effect on reducing international tensions during this period. It is more difficult to demonstrate the benefits than the costs of espionage, especially in peacetime. This is in part because of persisting secrecy, but also because the reasons that unwanted events did not occur or that foreign policies succeeded are often impossible to demonstrate. Given its long history, however, espionage as a tool of statecraft will continue. Information tends to gain in importance with advancing technology, and knowledge and power will become increasingly interrelated. While most information can be gained by legal, nonsecret methods, international economic competition will stimulate searches for essential elements of information. The continuation of state sovereignty bolstered by competitive political and religious ideologies, and economic nationalism, accompanied by advancing technology, will spawn political, military, and industrial secrets that other nations will covet and seek to discover by spying. The end of the Cold War, and intelligence scandals in the years 1994–1996, placed the U.S. espionage system under microscopic study by a Presidential Commission and by the Congressional intelligence committees. Proposals ranged from the abolition of the CIA to reforms in its organization, role, and functions. The end of the twentieth century will likely see a remodeled espionage system.

HARRY HOWE RANSOM

See also Ambassadors and Embassies; Central Intelligence Agency; Cold War; Cryptology; Hiss, Alger; Intelligence; National Security and National Defense; Office of Strategic Services; Russia and the Soviet Union; Strategic Arms Limitation Talks and Agreements; U-2 Incident; Verification

FURTHER READING

Ameringer, Charles D. *U.S. Foreign Intelligence: The Secret Side of American History.* Lexington, Mass., 1990.

Andrew, Christopher. *For the President's Eyes Only: Secret Intelligence and the American Presidency from Washington to Bush.* New York, 1995.

Constantinides, George C. *Intelligence and Espionage: An Analytical Bibliography.* Boulder, Colo., 1983.

Dulles, Allen W. *Great True Spy Stories.* New York, 1968.

Godson, Roy, ed. *Intelligence Requirements for the 1980s*, vol. 5 of *Clandestine Collection.* Washington, D.C., 1982.

——— , Ernest R. May, and Gary Schmitt, eds. *Intelligence at the Crossroads: Agendas for Reform.* Washington, D.C., 1955.

Grose, Peter. *Gentleman Spy: The Life of Allen Dulles.* Boston, 1994.

O'Toole, G. J. A. *Honorable Treachery: A History of U.S. Intelligence, Espionage, and Covert Action from the American Revolution to the CIA.* New York, 1991.

——— . *The Encyclopedia of American Intelligence and Espionage: From the Revolutionary War to the Present.* New York, 1988.

Richelson, Jeffrey. *America's Secret Eyes in Space.* New York, 1990.

———. *A Century of Spies: Intelligence in the Twentieth Century.* New York, 1955.

Schweizer, Peter. "The Growth of Economic Espionage." *Foreign Affairs.* Vol. 75, No. 1. (Jan.-Feb. 1996) pp. 9–14.

Shulsky, Abram N. *Silent Warfare: Understanding the World of Intelligence.* Washington, D.C., 1991.

Smith, Myron J., Jr. *The Secret Wars: A Guide to Sources in English.* vol. 2 of *Intelligence, Propaganda and Psychological Warfare, Covert Operations.* Santa Barbara, Calif., 1981.

Stanger, Ronald J., ed. *Essays on Espionage and International Law.* Columbus, Ohio, 1962.

Volkman, Ernest. *Espionage: The Greatest Spy Operations of the 20th Century.* New York, 1995.

between leftist rebels and conservative governments in Guatemala and El Salvador and between counterrevolutionary forces (Contras) and the revolutionary Sandinista government of Nicaragua. Convinced that the Sandinista-led government in Nicaragua and the rebels in El Salvador and Guatemala were Soviet-oriented communists, the Reagan administration aimed for the victory of the Contras in Nicaragua and of the two friendly governments over their rebel challengers, rather than for negotiated settlements. Washington repeatedly frustrated efforts by eight Latin American countries (the Contadora and the Contadora Support Groups) to craft a peace agreement. With U.S. policy in the region in temporary disarray following the Iran-Contra scandal, the presidents of the five Central American countries seized the initiative; they began negotiations in Esquipulas, Guatemala, in 1986, and signed a "Procedure for a Strong and Lasting Peace in Central America" in Guatemala City on 7 August 1987. Crafted by Costa Rica's President Oscar Arias Sánchez, it provided for national reconciliation; cessation of hostilities; democratization; free elections; and an end of assistance to irregular forces and to the use of one nation's territory by irregular forces attacking other states; and it provided for balanced international and internal verification. Arias won the 1987 Nobel Peace Prize for his efforts. Washington, responding to international opinion, endorsed the accord but raised questions almost exclusively concerning Nicaragua's compliance. While its northern neighbors failed to comply with many of their obligations, Nicaragua implemented the accord, held an internationally-supervised election in 1990, and, after a surprise victory by an anti-Sandinista coalition, accepted the results. The Contras formally disbanded that June. After the end of the Cold War, the Bush administration reversed policy and promoted negotiations in Guatemala and El Salvador. In 1992, a UN-brokered peace within the framework of Esquipulas was achieved in El Salvador.

THOMAS W. WALKER

See also Contadora Group; Contras; El Salvador; Guatemala; Iran-Contra Affair; Nicaragua; Nobel Peace Prize; Reagan, Ronald Wilson

FURTHER READING

Goodfellow, William and James Morrell. "From Contadora to Esquipulas to Sapoá and Beyond." In *Revolution and Counterrevolution in Nicaragua.* Thomas W. Walker, ed. Boulder, Colo., 1991.

Office of Public Diplomacy, U.S. Department of State. *Negotiations in Central America: 1981–1987* (Revised Edition). Washington, D.C., 1987.

ESQUIPULAS II

A 1987 agreement of Central American governments creating a framework for peace in the region. During the 1980s, Central America was racked by violent conflict

ESTONIA

The most northerly and smallest of the three Baltic states bordering the Baltic Sea, Latvia, and the Russian

Federation. Of all the former Soviet republics, Estonia is the closest to the West both in its culture and its current economic structure. This is due to longstanding historical traditions, to the independence of Estonia between 1919 and 1940, and to Estonia's proximity to Finland. The United States, and to a greater or lesser degree the West in general, gave qualified support to the Estonian desire for independence from the Soviet Union, and are now strongly committed to help maintain that independence. In September 1992, Estonia held parliamentary elections under a new democratic constitution, which led to a strongly pro-free market government under Prime Minister Mart Laar, which governed until defeated in elections in 1995. Estonia has close and friendly relations with the United States, which contains a small but influential Estonian-American community. Estonia is a small country of 45,215 square kilometers lying on the eastern shore of the Baltic Sea, and the southern shore of the Gulf of Finland. Its population numbers a mere 1.57 million, of whom barely one million are ethnic Estonians. Most of the rest are Russian. Until the thirteenth century, the Estonians lived independently in a loose confederation of tribes and worshiped their own pagan religion. Thereafter they passed under German and Swedish rule before being annexed to Russia in 1721. During World War I, the province of Estonia was occupied by the advancing German army. In November 1918, when the Germans collapsed, Estonian national leaders were able to declare and establish independence in the face of an invasion from Soviet Russia.

A key role in securing Estonian independence was played by the British Royal Navy, which landed guns and supplies for the Estonians and, more importantly, prevented the powerful Russian navy from making a landing on the coast. The U.S. role was limited to moral support and some humanitarian aid. Formal Western recognition of Estonian independence was delayed by a desire not to anger and weaken the White Russian forces, or to infringe on the sovereignty and territory of imperial Russia, which had been the ally of the Western powers in World War I. White Russian leaders like General Anton Denikin were passionately opposed to losing any of what had been Russian imperial territory. By 1922, however, Estonia had been recognized by the United States and the other Western powers and had become a member of the League of Nations. In June 1940, with the way prepared by the Molotov-Rubentrop pact between Nazi Germany and the Soviet Union, Estonia was invaded and subsequently annexed by Stalin's forces. The United States protested strongly against this move, which it declared counter to the charter of the League of Nations of which the Soviet Union was a signatory. The United States never recognized the Soviet annexation of Estonia and the other Baltic States, and this refusal was con-

firmed by repeated votes of the U.S. Congress and statements by successive U.S. administrations. The Estonian flag continued to hang in the U.S. Department of State, and independent Estonia continued to be represented by consulates in Washington and New York.

For more than forty years, this seemed no more than a meaningless gesture on the part of the United States and other Western powers; but this legal stand was to be of great importance during the Baltic movements for independence between 1988 and 1991. Moreover, Estonians were continually reminded of their de jure independence by the Estonian Service of Radio Free Europe/Radio Liberty (RFE/RFL), the American radio station based in Munich. RFE/RFL also reminded Estonians of the atrocities committed against Estonians under Stalin, and of continuing human rights abuses by the Soviet regime. Another big factor was the small but highly dynamic and nationally-aware Estonian-American community which had grown dramatically since 1945, and which played a key role in reminding American politicians of Estonia's right to independence. Since 1991, several Estonian Americans have played an important part in the reborn state. The U.S. Embassy in Tallinn contains a number of Estonian-American diplomats. This has furthered understanding between Estonia and the United States, but has led to some criticism from local Russians, who feel that the diplomats concerned may be too committed to Estonia and may be insensitive or even hostile to the local Russian minority.

The rise of the Baltic independence movements at the end of the 1980s confronted the Bush administration with a dilemma. On the one hand, the United States was clearly morally committed to Estonian independence. On the other, Washington was desperately anxious not to do anything to weaken Mikhail Gorbachev in the face of increasing attacks from Soviet hardliners. American policy in essence was therefore to stress U.S. recognition of de jure independence while declaring that the conditions were not present for de facto recognition and the reestablishment of diplomatic links. Estonia avoided the direct military response from the Soviet Union that Lithuania endured in January 1991, largely because its leaders moved toward independence more slowly and with greater openness to negotiations. The failure of the anti-Gorbachev coup of August 1991 and the ensuing collapse of the Soviet Union removed the last obstacle to full U.S. recognition of the Baltic states. The United States moved rapidly to set up a substantial embassy in Tallinn. U.S. aid has been very considerable in proportion to the small size of Estonia, though from 1996 this was to be scaled down. Economically speaking, Estonia has amply justified Western confidence and support. The Estonian government has pursued a firm policy of free market reform, and in 1993, after sinking deeply for several years, the economy grew by four percent a year. The main political concern of U.S. diplomacy in Estonia has been the desire to reduce the threat of conflict between Estonia and Russia, over two linked issues: the treatment of the Russian minority within Estonia and the withdrawal of Russian troops from the country. In 1993, Washington's desire not to irritate Russia unnecessarily was shown when a retired U.S. officer of Estonian descent, Colonel Alexander Einseln, accepted an invitation to become commander in chief of the Estonian army. The U.S. administration reacted by stripping him of his pension, though this was later overturned by a vote of Congress. The United States in general, like other Western powers, pursued a policy of steady public pressure on Russia to withdraw its troops, coupled with more discreet diplomatic pressure on the Estonian government not to go too far in restricting the civil rights of non-Estonians who immigrated into Estonia under Soviet rule. On 31 August 1994, the last Russian troops withdrew from Estonia. Under Western pressure, Estonian government modified the most objectionable aspects of its citizenship and residency requirements. A lesser cause of tension has been the Estonian legal claim to the small Russian territories given to Estonia by the Treaty of Tartu, and transferred to Russia by Stalin. Washington disapproves of this claim, but has not criticized it publicly. Early in 1994, Estonia acceded to the NATO "partnership for peace." Estonians regard this as a vastly inadequate substitute for full NATO membership; but U.S. diplomats have made clear that in view of Estonia's exposed position, this is not for the moment in the cards. A direct Russian intervention in the Baltic States would, however, undoubtedly totally disrupt U.S.-Russian relations, and result in severe economic and diplomatic sanctions from Washington.

ANATOL LIEVEN

See also Latvia; Lithuania; Russia and the Soviet Union; Stalin, Joseph

FURTHER READING

Flint, David. *The Baltic States—Estonia, Latvia and Lithuania.* Brookfield, Conn. 1992.

Hider, John, and Patrick Salmon. *The Baltic Nations and Europe.* London, 1991

Lieven, Anatol. *The Baltic Revolution: Estonia, Latvia, Lithuania and the Path to Independence.* New Haven, Conn., 1993.

ETHICS

The process of moral reasoning by which decisions are made on right and good conduct. When Socrates (469–399 B.C.) asked the first question of ethics—How should one live?—he introduced the concept of the examined life. In the context of U.S. foreign relations, ethics begins with the idea that the international arena is an arena for moral choice. In terms of foreign policy, ethics is about reconciling moral imperatives (what ought to be done) with political and practical realities (what can be done). The consideration of ethics as an element of U.S. foreign policy inevitably leads to a related concept, American exceptionalism, the idea that because of its unique geography, history, and culture, the United States is a nation with a special mission. How one conceives of the proper role of ethics in U.S. foreign policy is in large part based on how one interprets the idea of exceptionalism. Does the United States operate by principles unlike those of any other nation? If indeed it does, should it act purely as an exemplar or, conversely, as a missionary?

The early New England colonists saw their "errand into the wilderness" as an attempt to build a model society. As John Winthrop explained in his famous sermon of 1639, the new community was to be like "a city upon a hill," a beacon for the rest of the world, and a departure from the corrupted ways of Europe. Winthrop's sentiments were later echoed in various manifestations by statesmen from George Washington to Ronald Reagan. The early phases of U.S. diplomatic history were heavily influenced by the exemplar approach. This inward-looking approach was reflected in Washington's warning to avoid foreign entanglements and the destructive ways of European statecraft. John Quincy Adams, who served both as secretary of state (1817–1825) and as president (1825–1829), continued this line of thought with his statement that the United States "goes not abroad in search of monsters to destroy....[She] is champion and vindicator only of her own." Diplomats as recent and as distinguished as George F. Kennan have adhered to this isolationist-exemplar line, arguing that Americans should reserve their high and praiseworthy moral standards for themselves and not seek to determine what is right or wrong for other nations.

An equally influential strain of exceptionalism arose in the early twentieth century, after periods dominated by the concepts of Manifest Destiny and imperial adventure. It was embodied in the thought and policies of Woodrow Wilson, whose exceptionalism set the tone for the emergence of the United States as a world power and challenged the isolationist-exemplar approach. Wilson (and others, including Franklin D. Roosevelt, John F. Kennedy, Jimmy Carter, and Ronald Reagan) infused the idea of exceptionalism with universal, internationalist, and, some might say, messianic qualities that it previously had lacked. Wilson maintained that the United States in the twentieth century should not only lead by example but provide moral leadership by promoting universal values around the world and supporting institutional mechanisms that would serve this purpose.

This change from an isolationist exceptionalism to an internationalist exceptionalism had momentous consequences for Wilson's era and the rest of the century. Forty years after Wilson, Kennedy pledged in his oft-quoted inauguration address that the United States would "pay any price, bear any burden, meet any hardship, support any friend, oppose any foe to assure the survival and the success of liberty." Twenty years after Kennedy, Reagan echoed these sentiments as he led a global struggle against the Soviet "evil empire" and proclaimed the Reagan Doctrine "to nourish and defend freedom and democracy" by supporting anticommunist insurgencies.

The idea of exceptionalism has not gone unchallenged, and countervailing views have been expressed by realists of every period, most notably John Quincy Adams, Theodore Roosevelt, and Henry Kissinger. Even the strongest opponents of exceptionalism, however, would agree with the assessment of Arthur M. Schlesinger, Jr., that the Anglo-Saxon and Calvinist roots of U.S. culture have given Americans a strong desire to see that their exercise of power is morally virtuous. Americans have never accepted traditional European notions of raison d'état and realpolitik as applicable to U.S. statecraft. This may help to explain why these terms have no commonly used English equivalent and maintain their original French and German forms.

After exceptionalism, the second great debate in ethics and foreign policy concerns the application of abstract principles to specific cases. The polar positions frequently are cast as realism versus idealism. Realists follow in the tradition of Niccolò Machiavelli, Thomas Hobbes, and Hans J. Morgenthau. In addition to their emphasis on the ubiquity of egoism, conflict, and insecurity, they are deeply skeptical of the utility of universal normative principles as guides to policymaking. Idealists take the opposite tack and begin with the idea that universal principles offer a path to a harmonious social order. For idealists like the Abbé de Saint-Pierre, Immanuel Kant, and Woodrow Wilson, there is no animus domanandi (will to power) that is not subject to the ameliorating effects of universal, rationally derived moral principles.

While there are great differences in the worldviews and assumptions of realists and idealists, many scholars note that the differences are often overdrawn. A common caricature of ethics and U.S. foreign policy pits a naive and crusading moralism against a ruthlessly amoral cynicism. Moralism is usually represented by the "Kantian" Woodrow Wilson; cynicism is generally represented by the "Machiavellian" Theodore Roosevelt. The most incisive critique of this paralytic stereotype is suggested by Kenneth W. Thompson, who warns against thinking of ethics and foreign policy as destined to either self-righteous moralism on the one hand or hopeless cynicism on the other. Arguing against those who imply that ethics in

foreign policy is an oxymoron, Thompson notes that even the most ardent realists do not adhere to Thucydides's aphorism that "the strong do what they will, and the weak do what they must." Even archrealists such as Nicholas Spykman concede that appeals to a "higher good" do have some positive effects on the worst instincts of humanity, even if these effects are difficult to classify or predict with any regularity. As the analyst Fareed Zakaria points out, it is no coincidence that today's most prominent realists—from the statesman Kissinger to the scholar Kenneth Waltz—have seriously studied the work of the archetypal idealist Kant. In a similar vein, Joseph S. Nye, Jr., develops a notion of "soft power" to show how ideals can be functional to, and not necessarily in competition with, power.

Just as dangerous as nihilism, according to Thompson, is its opposite, moralism, or the tendency to apply principles without regard to power, context, or consequences. Moralism is characterized by its indiscriminate nature and the hubris of those who believe they have an exclusive insight into what is truly moral. Moralism lacks the basic components of ethical reasoning: an honest assessment and weighing of competing moral claims and the consideration of principles in close connection to consequences. Thompson goes on to suggest an Aristotelian approach that holds that principles by themselves mean very little; it is the application of principles—and the concurrent evaluation of competing moral claims—that characterize the ethical approach.

In all periods of U.S. diplomatic history, abstract doctrines have been imbued with moral weight. These doctrines have been put forth for reasons both rhetorical and practical and to serve as guides for decision-making. Whether or not these doctrines have warranted stature as moral pronouncements is another area for debate and discussion. For example, no U.S. leader in the late twentieth century would defend William Howard Taft's proclamation of 1912: "The day is not far distant when the Three Stars and Stripes at three equidistant points will mark our territory: one at the North Pole, another at the Panama Canal, and the third at the South Pole. The whole hemisphere will be ours in fact as, by virtue of our superiority of race, it already is ours morally." In assessing such a statement, one obviously must consider the weight of historical and cultural assumptions and the perennial possibilities of cultural blindness.

Here the study of history is of supreme relevance. As Paul Nitze suggests, a historical approach can assist us in "winnowing out and eliminating those value systems that have in the past encouraged repellent results," while also helping us "to find systems of values that promise to encourage or produce more generally satisfactory results." Many studies suggest that annunciated principles—whether in terms of formal doctrines or in more informal formulations such as "appeasement" or "containment"—need to be measured against traditions of morality. The traditions of morality are as old as civilization itself and include sources that are religious and secular, deontological and utilitarian, absolutist and pragmatic. In the United States, the most prominent fonts of morality are the Judeo-Christian religious tradition and the Greco-Roman philosophical tradition that emphasizes character, virtue, and law.

In philosophical terms, some traditions are "rule-oriented," others "consequence-oriented." Rule-oriented traditions are deontological, meaning that they are concerned primarily with duties (moral imperatives). Consequence-oriented traditions focus on the results of actions, usually employing some utilitarian calculus as the basis for judgment. All of these traditions have in common bases for judgment that transcend the vicissitudes of national self-interest and the exigencies of immediate political situations. At its core, ethics in the context of U.S. foreign policy is about determining moral principles, examining these principles in light of religious or philosophic traditions, and analyzing the resulting policy accordingly.

Realists and idealists alike recognize that policy must be subjected to tests of moral validity—validity that is established independent of political expediency. For all their emphasis on "national interest," most realists do not deny the existence of moral values that transcend national imperatives. While a basic premise of realism is that such moral values have limited utility in statecraft, most realists understand that there are values above raison d'état and that ideas such as freedom and order or power and justice need to be considered together. Idealists, on the other hand, give primacy to universalizable principles that they take to be eminently useful in statecraft. These principles are in fact moral values that combine with the national interest to become the guideposts for a "moral" foreign policy.

When looking at principles and policy together, one needs to give attention to questions of agency, that is, if ethics is about choice, then who are the actors, and what is the context for action. Traditionally, distinctions have been made between individual ethics and social ethics. Individual ethics focuses on duties and choices, as well as on the role of conscience and the cultivation of individual virtue. Social ethics focuses on community or societal standards. Because individuals must act within a social structure, the two are organically related. Even with this organic link, however, it is useful to linger over this distinction because it enables one to address issues ranging from human rights to abortion in terms of individual judgment (what is good for oneself) as well as of social views (what is good for society).

For foreign policy analysts, the most interesting question has been whether the affairs of states can and should be judged by the same standards as individual behavior. The statement of Italian leader Camillo Benso, Conte di Cavour, "what rogues we would be if we did for ourselves what we do for our country," is frequently invoked in this context, as is the title of Reinhold Niebuhr's treatise on the subject, *Moral Man and Immoral Society*, which suggests a natural bifurcation. There has been great ambivalence on this issue, with much contradiction arising from realists and idealists alike. Thomas Jefferson, in attempting to distinguish U.S. statecraft from European, wrote that there is "but one system of ethics for men and for nations—to be faithful to all engagements under all circumstances, to be open and generous, promoting in the long run the interests of both." Niebuhr, in opposition, wrote that "group relations can never be as ethical as those which characterize individual relations." Niebuhr, along with Winston Churchill and a long line of realists, held that "Sermon on the Mount" ethics might be relevant for individuals but were of little use to statesmen who had to act on behalf of their constituents.

This potential chasm between individual and social ethics (particularly as it relates to foreign policy) has led analysts to look diligently for bridges, and some have been found. John Herz, for example, focuses his brand of realism not on the animus domanandi posited by Morgenthau or the fact of "man's sinful nature" as posited by Niebuhr. Rather, Herz posits a "security dilemma" that he defines as a "social constellation that befalls any group (such as nation-states) that lacks superior authority." According to Herz, it is not that individual ethics and the ethics of statecraft are different; it is the unique characteristics of the international system that threaten the balance. Morgenthau was sympathetic to that view, expressing in the wake of the Nuremberg war crimes trials his opinion that any society that maintained a dual standard of ethics would not long survive. Officers "just following orders" were convicted by the tribunal; by implication, raison d'état itself was found to be morally deficient.

The overwhelming trajectory of American thought has supported the idea of a continuum between individual and social ethics—not a sharp break. Even Kennan, who has written that state behavior is not a category fit for moral judgment, has also spent a career explaining and exhorting that foreign policy must reflect the ideals and aspirations of the American people. Without this moral authority, policies will lack legitimacy and therefore be bound to fail. The Vietnam War—and its perceived illegitimacy, which grew as months and years went by— stands as the preeminent modern example.

Of course, not all principles or standards are internally generated. There is indeed an international system that has developed "rules of the game" that must be accounted for in philosophical, political, and historical context.

Hedley Bull coined the oxymoronic phrase "anarchical society," which suggests that the international milieu is not wholly Hobbesian (where life is characterized by the war of each against all). Numerous international relations theorists have pointed out that an international society does exist and that certain norms and mores, including and exceeding those codified by law, are operative.

International moral norms are the prescriptive principles of desirable behavior to which most nations can and do agree. Many such norms are codified in documents such as the United Nations Charter, the Universal Declaration of Human Rights, and the Geneva Conventions. Others exist as tacit understandings between and among states. The evolution of international moral norms includes principles such as the sovereign equality of states, the presumption of nonintervention, the recognition of human rights, and the right of self-determination. As Dorothy V. Jones points out, these principles have not been created in a vacuum; they have arisen out of the hard-won lessons of war and peace throughout world history, and particularly the twentieth century.

It becomes apparent in virtually every discussion of ethics and foreign policy that the role and resonance of international moral norms cannot be reduced solely to a discussion of international law. The difference between law and ethics—between what is codified as legal principle, or ethics past, and what is required today in terms of right and good conduct—often varies according to circumstance and interpretation. Terry Nardin explains that "international law is a source as well as an object of ethical judgments" and that "the authority of international law is determined by criteria internal to the institution of international law, not by exogenous tests of moral validity." As a result, according to Nardin, "international legal obligation is independent of moral obligation." Clearly, law and ethics are intimately related and even reinforcing, as Daniel Patrick Moynihan illustrates in his book *On The Law of Nations*, but, as Nardin and others have shown, the two are not interchangeable.

Legal codes are an important touchstone for ethical thinking, but such codes, like codes of ethics in the professions (e.g., business, medicine), cannot answer the hardest questions of moral choice. The examined life demands more: it demands a level of reflection that exceeds what is lawful, procedurally correct, or generally agreed upon by a professional group or community. In demanding reflection on what is right and good, ethics exceeds the moral minimum implied by law and reaches for the virtuous resolution.

Laws, norms, and mores change and evolve not because they are inherently weak or hopelessly "relativistic" but because the societies that produce them hold them up to constant scrutiny and endless reflection. The challenge for those considering ethics in the context of U.S. foreign policy is to consider how well U.S. foreign policy has reflected the best of its own moral traditions, as well as those of the rest of the world. Have its words and rhetoric matched its deeds? In facing a world of moral ambiguity and uncertainty, where has the United States succeeded in terms of conducting a "moral" foreign policy, and where has it failed? The history—filled as it is with both hypocrisy and triumph—reveals what kind of a nation the United States is and what kind of a nation it wants to be.

By definition, there is no closure on the idea of the examined life; it goes on in perpetuity. Even after death, lives are examined by successive generations seeking to understand the past, the present, and their prospects for the future. This does not, however, mean that ethical reasoning and reflection are irrelevant to policy and best left to academics and philosophers who live far from the policy arena. The end of the Cold War opened a new era of hard choices that will assuredly evoke moral dilemmas. Without the evils of communism or capitalism as self-justifying foils, and without a dire bipolar balancing of terror dominating the geopolitical calculus, moral principles beyond old "necessities" will receive renewed attention from scholars, citizens, and statesmen alike.

Morgenthau once said that in the field of political philosophy, novelty is not a virtue. Circumstances change but essential truths do not. For those who have studied ethics and foreign policy, the key has been to examine essential truths in light of new knowledge and social change. Unlike so many fields in international studies that have been left in disarray in the wake of the Cold War, there is no need to rethink the essential premises of ethics and foreign policy. The choices will be as difficult as ever, but the pathways are well marked.

JOEL H. ROSENTHAL

See also Ethnic Groups; Human Rights; Idealism; Isolationism; Kennan, George Frost; Morgenthau, Hans; Realism; Roosevelt, Theodore; Wilson, Thomas Woodrow

FURTHER READING:

Kegley, Charles W., Jr., ed. *Controversies in International Relations Theory: Realism and the Neoliberal Challenge.* New York, 1995.

Kennan, George F. "Morality and Foreign Policy." *Foreign Affairs* 64 (Winter 1985–1986): 205–219.

Morgenthau, Hans J. *Politics Among Nations*, 6th ed. New York, 1985.

Moynihan, Daniel Patrick. *On the Law of Nations.* Cambridge, Mass., 1990.

Nardin, Terry. "International Ethics and International Law." *Review of International Studies* 18 (1992): 19–30.

Nardin, Terry, and David R. Mapel, eds. *Traditions of International Ethics.* Cambridge, Mass., 1992.

Niebuhr, Reinhold. *Moral Man and Immoral Society.* New York, 1932.

Nitze, Paul H. *Tension Between Opposites: Reflections on the Practice and Theory of Politics.* New York, 1993.

Nye, Joseph S., Jr. *Bound to Lead: The Changing Nature of American Power*. New York, 1990.

Schlesinger, Arthur M., Jr. "National Interests and Moral Absolutes." In *The Cycles of American History*. Boston, 1986.

Smith, Michael Joseph. *Realism from Weber to Kissinger*. Baton Rouge, La., 1986.

Thompson, Kenneth W. *Traditions and Values in Politics and Diplomacy*. Baton Rouge, La., 1992.

Zakaria, Fareed. "Is Realism Finished?" *National Interest* 30 (Winter 1992–1993): 21–32.

ETHIOPIA

Republic located in Eastern Africa bordering the Red Sea, Dijbouti, Kenya, Ethiopia, and Sudan has been ruled in the late twentieth century by a pro-West, transitional conservative monarchy (until September 1974); a Marxist-Leninist military government backed by the Soviet Union and Cuba (until May 1991), and then by a pro-West, transitional democratic government. Although economic relations between the United States and Ethiopia developed at the end of the nineteenth century, Washington did little to foster increased trade with Ethiopia. Diplomatic relations between Ethiopia and the United States were established on 27 December 1903 with the conclusion of a treaty of commercial relations. Washington's low level of interest in Ethiopia was reflected in the fact that the United States first opened a U.S. legation in Addis Ababa only in 1928 and did not establish an embassy in Ethiopia until the end of World War II. The U.S. legation was closed in 1936 following the Italian invasion and occupation of Ethiopia, which Washington never recognized, a fact that gained it the long-lasting appreciation of Ethiopian Emperor Haile Selassie. Following the liberation of Ethiopia from Fascist control in 1943, Washington reopened the U.S. legation in Addis Ababa and declared Ethiopia eligible to receive Lend-Lease assistance, which amounted to very little given Ethiopia's limited military capabilities.

Despite U.S. dismissal of Ethiopia's ability to contribute to the war effort, during World War II the United States developed a strategic interest in Ethiopia. In 1943 the United States established a radio communications station (Radio Marina) near the town of Asmara in the former Italian colony of Eritrea, then under British military occupation. On 13 February 1945 Haile Selassie met with President Franklin D. Roosevelt on the Great Bitter Lake, at which time the emperor explained Ethiopia's need for direct access to the Red Sea and expressed a desire to control Eritrea. Although sympathetic to Ethiopia's plight, Roosevelt made no commitment. By the end of the 1940s, however, U.S. defense planners placed a high priority on maintaining access to Radio Marina, whose potential strategic value was just starting to be realized and exploited. In 1950, when the fate of Eritrea was placed in the hands of the United Nations, Washington exerted behind-the-scenes pressure that resulted in the passage of a UN resolution calling for a ten-year federation between Ethiopia and Eritrea. In May 1953, five months after the Ethiopia-Eritrea federation was implemented, Washington and Addis Ababa signed a twenty-five-year arms-for-bases accord that guaranteed the United States access to Radio Marina, renamed Kagnew Station after the Ethiopian contingent that had fought in the Korean War.

The May 1953 agreement laid the foundation for a long security relationship between the United States and Ethiopia. From 1953 through 1974, funding for the U.S. military assistance program (MAP) in Ethiopia totaled $197 million, making Ethiopia the leading U.S. MAP recipient in sub-Sahara Africa. Subsequent agreements, which represented "rent" for Kagnew, committed the United States to help build a modern Ethiopian air force (1958), train and equip a 40,000-man army (1960), and provide Ethiopia with a squadron of F-5 jet fighters (1966). While U.S. arms flowed into Ethiopia, Kagnew Station became a crucial part of the U.S. Strategic Communications (STRATCOM) and Defense Satellite Command (DSC) systems. Among other functions, Kagnew was used as a link in the U.S. worldwide defense communications system, to gather intelligence in the Middle East and Africa, to communicate with Polaris nuclear submarines in the Indian Ocean, and to help in the development of ballistic missiles.

By the early 1970s, however, Kagnew's strategic value had diminished as a result of advances in satellite technology and the development of naval communications facilities on the Indian Ocean island of Diego Garcia. Moreover, the escalating war in Eritrea between the central government and Arab-backed rebel forces made Kagnew a growing political liability regionally and domestically. In the aftermath of the October 1973 Arab-Israeli War the United States was trying to improve relations with the Arab world; moreover, some leading members of Congress feared that the United States might be drawn into another Vietnam War–type situation in Ethiopia. Evidence of Ethiopia's diminishing strategic value was provided in May 1973 when the administration of President Richard M. Nixon rejected Haile Selassie's request for several hundred million dollars' worth of military aid to purchase sophisticated U.S. weapons systems; with Congress reducing funding for the U.S. military assistance program worldwide, Addis Ababa was forced to buy arms from Washington on a cash-and-carry basis.

In September 1974 Haile Selassie was deposed by the Ethiopian military, which established a secret Provisional Military Administrative Council (PMAC), also known as the *dergue* (the committee). Washington initially adopted a wait-and-see attitude toward the revolutionary government, but relations became strained over the *dergue's* radical and hard-line domestic policies, especially the nationalization of U.S. businesses and its insistence on seeking a military solution to the war in Eritrea. In early February 1977 a shootout between rival factions within the PMAC elevated to the top position Colonel Mengistu Haile Mariam, a hard-line radical who favored prosecuting the war in Eritrea, brutally suppressing domestic political opponents, and strengthening ties with the Soviet Union. President Jimmy Carter's administration responded by suspending U.S. security assistance to Ethiopia on human rights grounds. At the end of April 1977 Mengistu ordered the closure of Kagnew Station and expelled the U.S. military mission from Ethiopia. Washington retaliated by terminating the security assistance program (SAP).

The Carter administration believed that Addis Ababa's realignment with Moscow was only a temporary setback and therefore sought to avoid actions that might create a permanent breach in U.S.-Ethiopia relations. Despite the urgings of friends and allies in the Middle East, the United States refused to provide arms to the Somali government during the 1977–1978 Ogaden War between Ethiopia and Somalia. The Eritrean insurgents were similarly shunned by Washington. Following the seizure of the U.S. embassy in Tehran, Iran, in November 1979 and the Soviet invasion of Afghanistan at the end of December, however, President Carter agreed to provide "defensive" weapons to Somalia and to seek to gain access to Somali military facilities. In August 1980 the United States signed an arms-for-access accord with Somalia, making that country part of the U.S. strategic network developed in the Indian Ocean during the 1980s under the aegis of the Carter Doctrine. Ethiopia's alignment with Libya and South Yemen, both Soviet arms clients, in the summer of 1981 did not sit well with the globalist-minded administration of Ronald Reagan. Throughout the 1980s the U.S. policy toward Ethiopia was one of encirclement, as the United States armed Somalia, Kenya, and Sudan.

As the Cold War came to an end and Moscow began disengaging militarily from Ethiopia, Mengistu sought to repair relations with Washington. In order to attract U.S. aid and to repay Israel, which once again had begun to supply arms to Ethiopia, in November 1990 Mengistu announced that all Ethiopian Jews (the Falashas) would be free to emigrate to Israel. During the 1990 crisis in Kuwait that led to the Persian Gulf War, Ethiopia, which was on the UN Security Council, voted with the United States to condemn the Iraqi invasion of Kuwait and to impose sanctions against Baghdad. Ethiopia also supported Security Council Resolution 678, authorizing the use of force against Iraq. The United States tried to repay the favor by agreeing to mediate an end to the Ethiopian-

Eritrean war, but by the spring of 1991 the war had turned decisively against Ethiopia. At the end of May the administration of President George Bush helped to broker an agreement that allowed Mengistu to get out of Ethiopia and for the Ethiopian People's Revolutionary Democratic Front (EPRDF), which was allied with the Eritrean People's Liberation Front (EPLF), to take power in Addis Ababa. At the same time, the Ethiopian war effort in Eritrea collapsed, allowing the EPLF to take power in Asmara. In May 1993 Eritrea formally declared its independence from Ethiopia. After the downfall of the Mengistu government, diplomatic relations between Washington and Addis Ababa assumed a more normal and friendly course. With the end of the Cold War and the diminished strategic value of Africa for Washington, U.S. interests in Ethiopia in the 1990s were predominantly of a political and humanitarian nature and, as such, were pursued through modest economic and security assistance programs. Nonetheless, when the Clinton administration submitted its FY 1996 Foreign Assistance budget to the U.S. Congress in the spring of 1995, Ethiopia ranked second among U.S. aid clients in Sub-Saharan Africa, behind only South Africa. Moreover, the United States has been supportive of Addis Ababa as part of a regional campaign to isolate the National Islamic Front (NIF) government in Sudan which is perceived as attempting to disrupt the region.

JEFFREY A. LEFEBVRE

See also Africa; Eritrea; Somalia

FURTHER READING

Korn, David. *Ethiopia, the United States, and the Soviet Union*. Carbondale, Ill., 1986.

LeFebvre, Jeffrey A. *Arms for the Horn: U.S. Security Policy in Ethiopia and Somalia, 1953–1991*. Pittsburgh, Pa., 1991.

———. "Post-Cold War Clouds on the Horn of Africa: The Eritrea-Sudan Crisis," *Middle East Policy* Vol IV, Nos. 1 & 2 (1995), pp. 34–49.

Marcus, Harold. *Ethiopia, Great Britain, and the United States, 1941–1974*. Berkeley, Calif., 1983.

ETHNIC GROUPS

Since colonial times, racial and ethnic concerns—terms of varied definition but used herein as common among historians in the cultural rather that the biological sense—have influenced U.S. foreign policy. On the mainland, white settlers produced a society they regarded as English and rarely shed the ethnic or racial antagonisms they had inherited from their mother country. These hatreds led many of them to view conflict with Native Americans, Spaniards, and French settlers as ethnoracial. Benjamin Franklin stands as the most articulate colonial representative of this attitude. For example, he regarded the French and Indian War (1756–1763) as a struggle between Anglo-Saxons and Latins.

This kind of emotion carried over into the American Revolution, making it difficult for some of the colonists to overcome their harsh feelings toward France when it became their ally against Great Britain. This distrust also roiled the peacemaking at Paris in 1783 as well as the foreign relations of the federal government launched six years later. The nation's founders identified an evolving Americanism with Englishness, but the new nation was multiethnic and multiracial, containing, in addition to numerous Native and African Americans, six major white ethnic groups—English, Scot, Irish, French, German, and Dutch. None constituted a majority but among the Europeans about half were English in origin.

The Anglo-American group set the standard that governed national loyalty, political behavior, and foreign relations. It ignored diversity, especially as represented by racially identifiable outsiders such as Native and African Americans. This affinity of the founders for people of their own kind expressed itself in the formation of the nation's first national political parties that shaped foreign policy. Although the Anglo-American elite dominated both the Federalist and Republican parties, it split over foreign policy. Republicans, who retained more of the wartime hostility toward Great Britain than the Federalists, generally favored holding on to the old alliance with France, but the Federalists did not, largely for ethnic and economic reasons. They made a close relationship with Great Britain a fundamental principle. In 1797 their pro-British policies aggravated the crisis that brought the country into the Quasi-War with France. Extreme Federalists agitated to enlarge it by exploiting a popular Francophobia.

The Nineteenth Century

When the Quasi-War ended in 1800, most Americans who followed the course of the Napoleonic Wars cheered Great Britain, largely because of a shared ethnicity. Because of maritime grievances, however, the United States in 1812 chose war against the mother country, and as a whole, Americans fought loyally for the stars and stripes. Still, the bond with Great Britain did not weaken. Some New Englanders again pledged themselves to the Union Jack, while Anglo-Americans as a group could not stop speaking of England as the nation of "common blood."

In the next two decades, immigrants from Western Europe brought more diversity to the nation. Their ethnicity, religions, and customs sparked friction but did not change the thrust of foreign policy. In the confrontation with Spain over the fate of Florida in 1819, for example, Americans denounced their adversaries with the same anti-Spanish and anti-Catholic biases they had expressed since the colonial era. These prejudices, coupled to simplistic notions of exceptionalism and mission, spilled over into relations with the new Mexican nation. When Anglo-American settlers precipitated a revolution in Texas in 1835, the many Americans who despised Mexicans as a mongrel people viewed the clash as racial. They despised Mexicans as belonging to an inferior, mongrel "race." They talked constantly of the ethnoracial affinity between themselves and the white Texans, stressing that both belonged to the "Americo-Anglo-Saxon race."

After the Texans won independence the agitation for its annexation, a financial depression, a xenophobia directed against non-British newcomers, and a confrontation with Great Britain over the Oregon Country formed the background for the presidential election of 1844. Expansionists spoke out against the British but rarely with ethnic slurs. Many Americans appeared loath to battle "Anglo-Saxon brethren." Rather quickly, the bond of kinship between the U.S. and English elites helped resolve the Oregon dispute peacefully.

America's leaders hardly paused, however, over the prospect of shedding Mexican blood to acquire Texas and California. Many spoke of an ordained right to conquer racial inferiors. As the abolitionist poet James Russell Lowell put it, to U.S. Expansionists "Mexicans worn't human beans," just the "sort o' folks a chap could kill an' never dream on 'it arter." This low regard for Mexicans contributed to the animosities that led to war in May 1846. The overwhelming victory over Mexico seemingly confirmed the ill-founded assumptions of Anglo-Saxon superiority implicit in the popular notion of Manifest Destiny.

In 1848, as the War with Mexico ended, a potato famine in Ireland set in motion events that would impact U.S. politics and foreign relations. The blight impelled thousands of Catholic Irish to migrate to the United States. Their presence, added to that of kinfolk who had migrated earlier, rekindled a white nativist hatred of outsiders expressed frequently in the following decade in antiforeign political agitation. This encounter with anti-Catholic and ethnic prejudice, as well as the desire to help kin in the old homeland, drew increasing numbers of Irish into the politics of foreign policy. Before the decade faded, the sectionalism and other concerns that led to the American Civil War eroded the power of antiforeign politics.

Historians usually viewed the Civil War from the perspective of the white belligerents, characterizing it as a brother's war, but meaningful aspects of foreign policy during its course revolved around race. For years, Southerners had blocked recognition of Haiti and Liberia because their peoples were black. Following secession in 1861, Southerners could no longer exercise a veto in foreign policy. Thus, President Abraham Lincoln's government extended diplomatic recognition to both countries. It was not until Lincoln issued the Emancipation Proclamation in January 1863, however, that his government admitted openly that it was battling racial slavery. That admission moved British statesmen, who, as the *Times* of London explained, deplored the mutual killing of men "from a race...from which we are also sprung," and other European leaders to side with the Union cause.

When the war ended, a revived antiforeignism attracted adherents in part because of the activities of the Irish-American Fenian Brotherhood, which tried to interject an anti-British bias into U.S. foreign policy. Fenians hoped to exploit the anti-British sentiment deriving from the civil conflict to foment war between the United States and Great Britain with the goal of gaining independence for Ireland. By 1870 this plan had failed, substantially because Irish-American politicking could not overcome the power of the Anglo-Americans who stood against the Fenian agitation because it menaced peace with Great Britain.

These Anglos still formed the only group with sufficient political clout to give direction to foreign policy, but they did not view themselves as belonging to an ethnic group, as did later arrivals. They regarded themselves as the truest of Americans who in matters of foreign policy worked solely for the national interest, which they defined. In the 1880s they perceived danger to their dominance mainly in the influx of Southern and Eastern European immigrants. They and other white nativists joined the Ku Klux Klan, the American Protective Association, and other hate organizations to attack the newcomers, as well as previously settled African Americans, Jews, and Catholics. Despite the popularity of these societies, they could not halt the social transformation brought about by the new immigrants. The nativists succeeded, however, in blocking the flow of Chinese to the Pacific Coast. Treaty arrangements and legislation restricted Chinese immigration so effectively as to shut it off. Other than a negative impact, as in the Chinese case, the influence of the rising minorities on the politics of foreign policy remained slight.

Change came slowly, as in minority response to incidents at the end of the 1880s. In 1888 German-Americans upset with President Grover Cleveland's policy in Samoa that clashed with German interests there, claimed credit for contributing to his defeat in a bid for reelection. Three years later, ethnic animosities in New Orleans led to the lynching of eleven Italians and Italian Americans who had just been acquitted of murder. Italy severed diplomatic relations while jingoists talked of war. Italian-American groups turned to politicking to ease the confrontation. When the president in effect apologized and the United States indemnified the families of the victims, the crisis passed but not the popular animosity toward non-Anglo ethnoracial groups.

This antagonism expressed itself in part in the Anglo-Saxon racism that peaked at the turn of the century. Its disciples filled the ranks of such nativist societies as the American Restriction League, founded in 1894. These organizations lobbied to stem the influx of Southeastern Europeans, Asians, and others. Nativist intellectuals, such as historians John Fiske and George Bancroft and politician Henry Cabot Lodge, stressed racial stock as crucial in the conduct of foreign policy. They and other restrictionists assumed that in world affairs the United States could be great only if Anglo-Saxons, "the elect race," remained in command. Such a perspective stands out in the actions of the Anglo-American elite that in April 1898 plunged the nation into war with Spain. A vague concept of a new Manifest Destiny, hatred of Spaniards and Catholics, claims of exceptionalist virtue, and the misconceptions of social Darwinism, whipped up popular support while dehumanizing Spaniards, Cubans, and Filipinos.

Following Spain's defeat, the United States annexed the Philippines under the guise of assuming a white man's burden. It led to a war against poorly armed Malays that both sides regarded as racial. In three years of combat (1899–1902), marked by atrocities on both sides, 18,000 Filipino "insurgents" and 100,000 civilians died; American deaths numbered 4,000. While other governments criticized this U.S. conquest, the British elite applauded it. In turn, the Anglo-American elite, despite a contrary sentiment, supported the British in the Boer War, in large measure out of ethnic solidarity. This close relationship between the elites, often called a rapprochement, had a greater impact on foreign policy than virtually anything else at the time. As Secretary of State John Hay said, "The one indispensable feature of our foreign policy should be a friendly understanding with England." So close did the British and U.S. elites feel that they founded the Anglo-American League and the *Anglo-Saxon Review* and spoke of cementing this special relationship with a "racial alliance."

The Twentieth Century and Two World Wars

At the beginning of the twentieth century, minorities, such as Irish Americans and American Jews stepped up their involvement in the politics of foreign policy. The Jews were to prove more successful than the Irish. In 1902 Jews who recently had fled pogroms in Russia, along with established Jewish Americans from earlier immigration, pressured Washington to take action against the anti-Semitism of Czarist Russia. President Theodore Roosevelt responded positively, as much because he had an eye on potential Jewish votes in approaching congressional elections as for humanitarian reasons. After another series of brutal anti-Jewish pogroms in Russia, Congress, out of compassion and in response to ethnic lobbying, voted unanimously to abrogate the 1832 Russian-American treaty of amity and commerce. On 12 December 1912 President William H. Taft endorsed this protest by terminating the treaty and withdrawing the U.S. ambassador.

Racial concerns also helped mold relations with Japan. When the Japanese started immigrating to the West Coast in the 1890s, as had the Chinese, they encountered discrimination. In 1906 this antipathy, exploited by a Japanese and Korean Exclusion League, produced the segregation of Asian schoolchildren in San Francisco and brought on a crisis with Japan. President Theodore Roosevelt defused the confrontation, but with difficulty. In other instances, however, Roosevelt, as a believer in Nordic superiority and Anglo assimilation, sanctioned discrimination, particularly against non-Anglo groups he regarded as disloyal. He denounced them, "the hyphenated American—the German-American, the Irish-American," for not cherishing allegiance only to the United States "pure and simple." Roosevelt, Woodrow Wilson, and other leaders who took up the hyphenate slur preached, in the words of historian John Higham, "100 percent Americanism," which they defined usually in terms that made it an extension of Anglo-Saxonism.

African Americans, of course, had no place in the Anglo-Saxon credo. They were descended from African ethnic groups as varied as those from Europe but they did not have the same bond to specific ancestral homelands as did European Americans. Even after African Americans shed slavery and acquired the privilege of voting, racism, poverty, and lack of cohesion prevented them from exerting effective pressure to advance their own interests, let alone those of kin abroad. For these and other reasons, policymakers rarely took into account African-American wishes in matters of foreign policy. It was not until the twentieth century that concerned African Americans came together as part of a single ethnoracial group. In 1910, with the formation of the National Association for the Advancement of Colored People (NAACP), African Americans could lobby for their own causes at home and abroad. Following the U.S. military takeover of Haiti in 1915, the NAACP protested the racial injustices in occupation policy. This lobbying contributed ultimately to a softening of the harsh treatment of Haitians.

When World War I erupted in Europe in 1914, Anglo Saxonists turned hyphenism into a reason for national alarm. They cast suspicion on the loyalty of the 32 out of 92 million people who were either foreign-born or first-generation Americans. President Woodrow Wilson and the Anglo-American elite deplored the connections of immigrant groups with the Central Powers while they openly favored the Allied side. Wilson condemned Irish Americans and others for trying to influence foreign poli-

cy to benefit their land of origin while he courted select ethnic groups. Although the reasons for the U.S. decision to enter the war are complex, Wilson's widely shared concern for the bond between the governing elites in the United States and Great Britain contributed significantly to the desire to intervene in 1917. Immediately after intervening, the U.S. government exploited ethnic emotion. It sponsored Loyalty Days designed to inculcate an Anglo-American patriotism among immigrants. This type of flag waving stirred up local vigilantes, who tarred and feathered German Americans while the government officials impaired their civil rights with forms of censorship. Leaders of other ethnic groups, however, hailed Wilson as a great humanitarian for proclaiming self-determination a foremost goal of U.S. foreign policy.

At the Paris Peace Conference of 1919, Wilson's version of self-determination disappointed those it excluded. Irish Americans, for example, embraced the concept as a means of gaining independence for Ireland. When he rebuffed them in deference to the English bond, they turned against him, the Treaty of Versailles, and the League of Nations. Others deplored Wilson's killing of a clause within the League of Nation's covenant sponsored by the Japanese upholding racial equality. This action, among others, persuaded peoples of color that the politicians at Paris had produced an "Anglo-American peace" governed by racism.

Among the non-Anglo groups involved in foreign policy lobbying, the Polish Americans achieved the most notable success. Their politicking helped recreate an independent Poland because the Wilson administration wanted Polish-American voters to remain Democratic. Similarly, Italian-American pressure groups sought favorable treatment for the objectives of their homeland. They failed, however, to obtain backing for Italy's takeover of Fiume on the Dalmatian coast, a move lobbied against by Slovenes, Croats, and Serbs in the United States. Jewish Americans elicited administration support for Zionism, or a national homeland in Palestine, in part because of well-organized ethnic lobbying.

When the Treaty of Versailles came before the Senate in 1919, political reality suggested that the administration balance its close relationship with Great Britain with concern for the views of a diverse electorate. Minorities previously disparaged as hyphenates now voted their interests in larger numbers than in the past and formed lobbies for influencing foreign policy. Although most politicians remained committed to the desires of the Anglo-Americans, they could no longer readily dismiss the wishes of other constituents. For this and other reasons the Senate defeated the treaty. Wilsonians were convinced that vengeful hyphenates killed it.

These ethnic clashes over foreign affairs exacerbated the xenophobia fueling the postwar Americanization movement. Nativists again pressed to repair perceived damage to the nation's Anglo stock by the supposedly flawed genetic endowment of outsiders. The nativists set the tone for a restructuring of the immigration laws that would have a negative impact on foreign policy. Under the illusion that the collective identity of Americans could be stabilized, Congress in 1921 and 1924 legislated restrictive quotas for immigrants. It created a system of preference that placed the British on top, peoples from Western Europe just below them, those from Southeastern Europe next in line, and excluded those from Asia and other lands of color. The stigmatized peoples, especially the Japanese, whose Gentlemen's Agreement was abrogated by the legislation, protested, but to no avail.

During the next two decades this legislated bigotry injured the conduct of foreign policy. It also affected colonial policy, as in 1934, when in response to nativist demands to block further Filipino immigration, Congress granted the Philippines autonomy. In the following year, as Italy and Ethiopia verged on war, ethnoracial concerns exerted a heavier pressure on foreign relations. In an unprecedented display of unity, African Americans politicked for a pro-Ethiopian policy. They clashed with Italian-American groups that lobbied for policies favorable to their ancestral homeland. The African-American campaign appeared more successful because Franklin D. Roosevelt's administration used it to oppose Fascist Italy's aggression.

A comparable mix of ethnoracial, ideological, and power considerations shaped U.S. attitudes toward the belligerents of World War II. In 1939 foreign-born whites constituted 8.5 percent of the population, while those born of immigrant parents formed another 17.5 percent. All concerned ethnoracial groups took a position toward the war. Some desired intervention to aid previous homelands under attack, while others opposed U.S. entry because they feared having to fight ethnic kin. The most ardent interventionists were old-stock Anglo-American Protestants.

Old biases injured various ethnoracial groups associated with the Axis countries, but especially Japanese aliens and Japanese Americans. In December 1941, when the Japanese attacked Pearl Harbor, 127,000 people of Japanese ancestry lived in the United States, with nine out of ten residing on the Pacific coast. In the spring of 1942 the government interned citizens of Japanese ancestry as well as aliens on the theory that their "racial characteristics" drew them to Japan and made them disloyal. German and Italian aliens suffered less, partially because their U.S. relatives had acquired political clout. Both sides regarded the Pacific war as racial. The Japanese, who portrayed themselves as pan-Asian patriots battling white colonialists, denounced, with some propaganda effect abroad, the racism in U.S. society. To offset these

charges, President Franklin D. Roosevelt exaggerated the importance of China as an ally. He also urged Congress to overturn the exclusion law that for sixty-one years had stigmatized the Chinese as undesirable, which the legislators did in the fall of 1943.

The concern of U.S. Jews and others over a more vicious racism contributed to the hardening of policy toward Adolf Hitler's Germany. Nazi anti-Semitism led to the mobilizing of Jewish groups within the United States to press Washington to protest the mistreatment of their kin in Germany and to open doors to those who tried to flee. The Roosevelt administration protested, condemned the Nazi pogroms, and received a substantial number of persecuted Jews as refugees. With this influx and mobilization, the United States replaced Europe as the center of world Zionism. Even so, the anti-Semitism in the Department of State, in Congress, and in the public sidetracked liberalization of the immigration laws that would have permitted the entry of more Jews. Later, the government also reacted slowly to the horror of genocide. In all, Jews and others believed that the United States could have done more to prevent the destruction of European Jewry.

The Cold War Era

At the end of World War II in 1945, as in 1919, the lobbying of ethnic groups modified details, if not the basic structure, of the peacemaking. For example, before the Yalta Conference in February 1945, Roosevelt asked Soviet leader Joseph Stalin to accept the resurrection of a Poland the Nazis and Soviets had destroyed so that he could strengthen his position with Polish-American voters in his campaign for reelection. Roosevelt's effort contributed to the recreating of Poland. Still, Poles and other Americans of Eastern European ancestry urged opposition to regimes the Soviets imposed on their ancestral lands. These lobbyists could not change the reality of communist control but they exerted enough pressure on Washington to reinforce its nonrecognition of the Soviet absorption of Latvia, Lithuania, and Estonia. Even defeated Italy benefited from the rising influence of offspring in the United States. Roosevelt and Harry S. Truman both responded to a limited degree to the politicking of Italian Americans for lenient treatment of Italy. Consequently, Italy escaped the harsher terms in the occupation and peacemaking desired by others, such as the British. In 1946, when Truman and his advisers feared that Italy's electorate might vote communists into power, they turned to the Italian-American community for assistance. Italian Americans responded with a flood of letters to relatives in Italy, an intervention that apparently contributed to the defeat of the communists.

In the postwar years, even though the children and grandchildren of southeastern European immigrants had moved into mainstream culture, they and other minority groups still suffered discrimination, especially in immigration legislation. This statutory bias injured the nation's foreign relations, often with allies. The Soviets, for example, countered attacks on their own oppressive policies by citing the record of racism in the United States. Nevertheless, the preoccupation of the foreign policy establishment with anticommunism made changes in the immigration laws a matter of low priority.

Despite this Cold War obsession, ethnoracial groups politicked for change but with mixed results. In the McCarran-Walter Act of 1952, Congress defeated major reform. It did, nonetheless, liberalize aspects of immigration and refugee policy. It also gave Asians a small quota and allowed them to become citizens. U.S. Jews, most of whom had now become Zionists, politicked more effectively for a homeland in Palestine. Stirred by the Jewish suffering in the Holocaust, the U.S. public responded favorably, but Department of State advisers and others warned President Harry S. Truman that a pro-Zionist policy would injure the national interest by alienating Arabs. After Zionist lobbyists, members of Congress, and political advisers pressured him, he disregarded his foreign policy advisers. In October 1946, on the eve of congressional elections, he endorsed the idea of a Jewish state, later contributed to its creation, and, when it came to life on 14 May 1948 as the state of Israel, promptly accorded it de facto recognition. Although scholars debate the extent of Jewish political influence on Truman's decision, most regard it as crucial, but not necessarily singular. In later years Jewish lobbying helped to funnel U.S. aid to Israel to keep it alive against Arab efforts to destroy it, and even in permitting it to expand.

During these early postwar years, as colonies became independent countries and Africa acquired a new prominence in world affairs, African Americans began mobilizing more effectively to influence foreign policy. Partially in response to those efforts, in 1956 the Department of State established a separate office of African Affairs, upgrading it two years later to bureau status. African Americans pressed for more. Beginning in 1960 they sought to influence policy toward the Congo (Zaire). They also urged Presidents John F. Kennedy and Lyndon B. Johnson to help destroy apartheid in South Africa by isolating its white regime. Both presidents responded favorably, but the antiapartheid movement did not acquire meaningful strength until after the passage of the Civil Rights Act of 1964. African Americans organized support for blacks in South Africa much as other ethnic groups lobbied for assistance to kin in their old homelands. Thereafter no administration could ignore the plight of the majority black peoples in southern Africa.

Beginning in August 1964, U.S. leaders paid far more attention to the war in Vietnam than to African issues.

Initially, much of the public viewed the intervention in Vietnam as it had the Korean War, as part of the anticommunist crusade. Seemingly, race or ethnicity had little to do with the U.S. involvement. As the world once more witnessed whites, or other Asians armed by Americans, slaughter Asians, however, most peoples of color, and even many white, yellow, and black Americans, such as Martin Luther King, Jr., characterized the war as racial. The racial impact reached something of a peak in March 1968, when U.S. soldiers killed or brutalized at least 347 Vietnamese civilian men, women, and children in the village of My Lai.

At times a widespread antiwar movement intertwined with the civil rights assault on racism. This civil rights agitation also contributed to a recasting of immigration policy. With the Immigration Act of 1965, Congress phased out the national origins quota system. It thus eliminated an ethnoracial discrimination that had embittered aspects of foreign relations for forty-one years. In addition, the civil rights movement stimulated among many Americans a greater consciousness of their roots. Writers and others no longer characterized minorities pejoratively as "hyphenates" but as less offensive "ethnics." Politicians of both major parties continued to fish for ethnic votes but, because of the ethnic resurgence, with a more obvious sense of answerability than before.

African Americans benefited with political gains that in the 1970s made possible the formation of the congressional Black Caucus. Although it focused primarily on domestic issues, its members also concerned themselves with foreign policy, especially as it pertained to African nations. In May 1972 the caucus organized the first African-American National Conference on Africa, designed particularly to influence foreign policy in matters concerning race and southern Africa. In 1982 prominent African Americans launched TransAfrica, Inc., the first national African-American lobby dedicated to influencing foreign policy toward African and Caribbean countries. It quickly acquired a membership of more than 10,000 and became the main conduit for African-American concerns in foreign relations.

TransAfrica followed the example of the Israeli lobby, composed of various groups, many of which in 1958 had become the American Israel Public Affairs Committee (AIPAC), in its methods of pressuring Congress and presidents. Both Kennedy and Johnson courted Israel in order to obtain the backing of Jewish-American organizations. Just before the Six-Day War in June 1967, Johnson assured the Israelis they would "not be alone." He backed these words up with substantial aid when Israel launched a preemptive war and quickly triumphed against another Arab effort aimed at her destruction. During the Yom Kippur War in October 1973, when Israel's battle against Egypt and Syria at first went badly, U.S. Jews mobilized more effectively than in previous foreign affairs crises. Although President Richard M. Nixon felt no obligation to Jewish voters, he did respect the power of the Israeli lobby in influencing Congress and public opinion. For this reason, as well as because of the Cold War ramifications and possible Soviet direct involvement, the Nixon administration backed Israel with massive amounts of military aid that proved crucial to its victory.

Despite the pro-Arab influence of officials in major oil companies and of officials in the State Department, American Jews exercised such power for numerous reasons. No other important ethnic or religious group challenged them; they had support from the public at large; and Arab Americans had no community behind them strong enough to compete with the Israeli lobby. At this point the community started building influence with the National Association of Arab Americans (NAAA), founded in 1972. It and other critics accused U.S. Jews, in their concern for Israel, of dual loyalty. This charge rang hollow because these Jews operated well within the American political experience. In their politicking they followed a pattern set by Anglo Americans, Irish Americans, and others.

In the 1970s the status of Northern Ireland reactivated foreign policy politicking among Irish Americans. Militants became deeply concerned when British troops in 1969 entered Ulster to suppress communal violence between Catholics and Protestants. In using force, primarily against Catholics, the soldiers soon became part of the problem. In April 1970 concerned Irish Americans organized the Irish Northern Aid Committee (NORAID) to help Catholics in Ulster. Prominent Irish-American senators and others charged the British government with acquiescence in violations of human rights. They appealed for a united Ireland that the British would not support because of deference to Ulster Protestants. Irish Americans failed to change foreign policy on this issue but their lobbying did place strain on the special relationship with Great Britain.

An analogous problem arose in 1974, when longstanding animosities between Greeks and Turks erupted into violence over who should control Cyprus. Greek Cypriots engineered a coup that brought intervention by Turkish troops, who occupied the northern third of the island. Repercussions quickly spilled over into ethnic politics in the United States. Greek Americans mobilized a lobby, the American Hellenic Institute, that persuaded Congress to embargo arms against Turkey with the aim of pressuring it to evacuate Cyprus. The clout of three million Greek Americans, in contrast to the opposition of 45,000 Turkish Americans, thus gave direction to an aspect of foreign policy that affected the U.S. role in world affairs. Instead of giving in to the pressure, Turkey forced Americans, for a time, to evacuate a number of military bases and listening posts in that country.

All the while demographic changes had clouded the traditional perception of the United States as basically white. In 1968, when the new immigration legislation went into effect, a new surge of immigrants transformed the nation's ethnoracial mix. Within a decade an estimated 12 million legal and illegal newcomers crowded into the country, with two arriving from Asia and Hispanic America for every one from Europe. The United States ceased to fit the metaphor of a melting pot of Europeans who shared a core culture. The most numerous of the colored arrivals, the Mexicans, had been trekking into the American Southwest in quest of economic opportunity for more than one hundred years. Beginning in the 1960s, as Mexico's birthrate soared, more and more of its people poured into the United States and became the second largest ethnoracial minority. Slowly they mobilized their resources for ethnic politicking, creating their first lobby, the National Council of La Raza, in 1968. As immigration became the foremost issue in the relationship between the United States and Mexico, Mexican-American lobbies focused on the subject. They worked against proposals to restrict immigration, an effort endorsed by successive Mexican governments.

The Hispanic lobbyists achieved their first major success on a foreign policy issue in 1984 when they helped defeat the Simpson-Mazzoli bill, which was aimed at changing immigration policy with tighter federal controls, especially over the border with Mexico. Two years later, however, when Congress passed a revised version of Simpson-Mazzoli, the victory lost some of its luster. Mexican-American groups denounced the new law as racist. The law, however, took their feelings into account by offering important concessions to undocumented workers. In subsequent years, as the legislation clearly failed to curb illegal entries, the border crossing became the nation's most explosive domestic issue affecting foreign policy. Hispanic lobbies had their hands full in combating a flurry of proposals for ending the influx of illegals and tightening refugee and immigration laws. The most dramatic battle occurred in California over a measure called Proposition 187. It denied illegal immigrants in the state educational and other benefits. Mexican Americans and others denounced it as racist, mounted a massive campaign against it, and elicited support from high officials in Mexico. Even President Bill Clinton opposed it, saying it would harm relations between the two countries. Nonetheless, in November 1994 the voters approved it. The courts blocked enforcement but the law became a model for similar legislative efforts on a national scale.

This pitting of ethnoracial groups against each other, as in this instance of Hispanics versus Euro-Americans, over immigration and other foreign policy issues, happened often. It occurred when African Americans attributed some of their problems to cold war foreign policy expenditures that they believed could have been used to help them. They denounced in particular the federal benefits for Cuban refugees as racially biased. The Cuban influx had started in January 1960, six months after Fidel Castro had seized power in their homeland. Encouraged by cold-war warriors in Washington these Cubans arrived in three or more waves. More than eighty-two per cent were white and most were educated.

To a greater extent than in most ethnic groups' foreign policy concerns, a hatred of Castro and of communism shaped the political outlook of Cuban Americans. They formed the heart and guts of the disastrous Bay of Pigs invasion of Cuba in April 1961. Thereafter they operated as a kind of pressure group that backed virtually all hard-line, anti-communist initiatives, especially anything that could overthrow or harm the Castro regime, such as the complete economic embargo the United States imposed on Cuba in October 1960. In 1966 Congress passed the Cuban Adjustment Act that allowed virtually unlimited Cuban immigration. Between 1961 and 1971 the federal government spent more than $730 million on Cuban immigrant aid programs such as job training, housing, and education. No other refugee group received such extensive taxpayer bounty. Even other Hispanics, such as Mexican-American activists, complained about the discriminatory nature of the program. Political strategists, particularly in the Republican party, catered to the Cuban Americans, most of whom had settled in the Miami area, because Florida enjoyed rapid growth in electoral votes and in its congressional delegations.

Between 26 April and September 1980 nearly 125,000 Cubans fled to the United States in the "Marial Boatlift." A number of them were criminals Castro had let out of his jails. When this third wave arrived pent-up African American anger in Miami exploded. Race riots erupted in 1980, 1982, 1984, and 1989. Their causes were complex but African Americans often cited as one reason for the violence their feeling of being cheated by the privileges accorded the Cubans. At the same time the coming of the Marielitos marked a change in public attitude toward Cuban Americans and in government policy. Late in 1980 Congress passed the Refugee Act that restricted the number of Cubans who could legally enter the country. Political refugees declined and by the end of the decade the great migration had ended. With the passing of the Cold War the Cuban-American community also lost some of its political clout.

Into the mid-nineties the Cuban Americans remained the most visible politically of all Hispanic groups, though not because of their numbers. In all, about one million had migrated. After forty-five years of ethnic politicking over foreign policy issues they still retained influence out of proportion to their numbers because of their economic success, their cohesiveness, their strategic location, and a

political activism more intense than in most other immigrant groups. Even though they often disagreed among themselves over local issues, most clung to their anti-communism and still lobbied to maintain the embargo against Cuba. As one observer noted, "Miami is likely the only city in the United States where anti-communism is a municipal issue."

The clashing of ethnic groups over foreign policy happened again when African Americans such as Jesse Jackson, who sought the Democratic presidential nomination in 1988, publicly empathized with Palestinians and supported the Palestine Liberation Organization (PLO), despite its continual terrorism. Jewish leaders struck back in anger. Most African Americans, however, stood behind Jackson's candidacy because of race as well as his program calling for more aid to African nations in the manner of assistance to Israel. This behavior of Hispanics, Jews, African Americans, and other minorities to influence foreign policy alarmed old-line nationalists, as had the efforts of "hyphenates" earlier in the century. The ultra-patriots also accused these recent minority lobbyists of placing loyalty to foreign lands above allegiance to the United States. Ironically, many of those who pointed fingers belonged to the Anglo-American establishment that had long practiced what their opponents and others regarded as a comparable divided allegiance. For example, in 1983 during the Falkland Islands War between Great Britain and Argentina, President Ronald Reagan's administration aided the British while publicly claiming a policy of neutrality. U.S. leaders realized that this assistance, just short of direct involvement in the hostilities, would provoke anti-U.S. bitterness throughout Latin America. The United States took the risk not only because Great Britain was its closest ally and Argentina was the aggressor, but because they valued the closeness of the connection with Great Britain, especially what some called the "blood ties." Again the ethnic bond between the elites gave significant direction to foreign policy.

This Anglo-American identification with a far-removed homeland after more than 200 years of U.S. nationhood illustrated the toughness of ancestral bond. It cast doubt on the assimilationist hypothesis that as the children of immigrants moved into mainstream culture the ethnic identification would disappear. Instead, in some parts of the country where ethnoracial groups became virtually permanent lobbies for their original homelands, the ethnic politics of foreign policy became a component of the governing process. Nonetheless, many in Great Britain and the United States deplored U.S. demographic changes as a danger to the special relationship between their countries. The British element in the U.S. population had been declining steadily until in the 1990s it no longer formed even the largest single minority. Elites in both countries feared that the traditional domination of foreign policy by the Anglo-American establishment would erode. Actually, the Anglo standard of Americanism stood virtually unchanged. It remained the model for assimilating immigrants and still set the goals in most areas of foreign policy. From the 1980s to the mid-1990s, the relationship with Great Britain remained at the heart of U.S. foreign policy, or, in the words of Secretary of State James A. Baker III, it was "extraordinarily special." All the while the breakup of the Soviet Union left the United States as the world's only superpower. As such, the repeated use of U.S. force against people of color alarmed those who viewed such actions through the prism of race or ethnicity.

The Post-Cold War Period

Presidents George Bush (1989–1993) and Bill Clinton (1993–1997) encountered similar charges in dealing with thousands of impoverished Haitians who fled their island nation and braved the seas in flimsy boats, fundamentally with the hope of finding a better life in the United States. Both administrations repatriated these generally illegal and unwanted immigrants. African-American spokesmen attacked this policy as racist because it treated the Haitians much less generously than it had the Cuban, Jewish, and Southeast Asian refugees of the Cold War years. African-American leaders also wanted the government to restore to power Jean-Bertrand Aristide, Haiti's first democratically elected president, ousted in September 1991 by a bloody military coup. After pressure from the congressional black caucus, TransAfrica, and other constituents, Clinton agreed to use force to remove the repressive military regime. Despite considerable public opposition, he defended this policy, as had his Republican predecessors in their interventions. U.S. troops, he said, would protect human rights, restore democracy, and block the refugee flood. Neither the president nor congressional politicians spoke forthrightly about the racial ingredient in this policy, although it was a crucial element, especially to African Americans.

Never before in the nation's history had African-American lobbyists been so obviously successful in giving guidance to foreign policy. This achievement seems remarkable because in the 1990s assimilationists still regarded ethnoracial politics as a danger to national cohesion. They condemned single-issue groups because ostensibly their politicking neglected the common interests of all Americans, but pressure based on ethnicity had been a part of policymaking in foreign relations since the founding of the Republic. Only in specific instances, however, has non-Anglo ethnic politics been the decisive driving force. Overall, only the scale and diversity of such politicking had changed. As long as old loyalties survived and the United States received immigrants, such politics seemed destined to continue. Why not, pluralists asked, accept such politicking in foreign policy as a proper ingredient of a democratic

society? In the mid-1990s acceptance remained difficult because traditional assimilationists, and pluralists too, had not yet confronted squarely the reality that since its founding, the United States had changed drastically. Through immigration it had become a polyglot, or "world nation," whose rainbow citizenry retained ties to peoples scattered over the globe. These connections increasingly influenced, or had the potential of influencing, foreign policy to a degree greater than in the past.

ALEXANDER DeCONDE

See also Congress; Elections and Foriegn Policy; Ethics; Fenians; Immigration; Manifest Destiny; Race and Racism; Refugees

FURTHER READING

Bailey, Thomas A. *The Man in the Street: The Impact of American Public Opinion on Foreign Policy.* New York, 1940.
DeConde, Alexander. *Ethnicity, Race, and American Foreign Policy.* Boston, Mass., 1992.
Dower, John W. *War Without Mercy: Race and Power in the Pacific War.* New York, 1986.
Drinnon, Richard. *Facing West: The Metaphysics of Indian-Hating and Empire Building.* Minneapolis, Minn., 1980.
Gerson, Louis L. *The Hyphenate in Recent American Politics and Diplomacy.* Lawrence, Kans., 1964.
Horsman, Reginald. *Race and Manifest Destiny: The Origins of American Racial Anglo-Saxonism.* Cambridge, Mass., 1981.
Howe, Russell W., and Sarah H. Trott. *The Power Peddlers: How Lobbyists Mold America's Foreign Policy.* New York, 1975.
Hunt, Michael. *Ideology and U.S. Foreign Policy.* New Haven, Conn., 1987.
Lauren, Paul G. *Power and Prejudice: The Politics and Diplomacy of Racial Discrimination.* Boulder, Colo., 1988.
Plummer, Brenda G. *Rising Wind: Black Americans and U.S. Foreign Affairs 1935 to 1960.* Chapel Hill, N.C., 1996.
Said, Abdul Aziz, ed. *Ethnicity and U.S. Foreign Policy.* New York, 1977.
Shepard, George W., Jr., ed. *Racial Influences on American Foreign Policy.* New York, 1970.
Westin, Reuben F. *Racism in U.S. Imperialism: The Influence of Racial Assumptions on American Foreign Policy, 1893–1946.* Columbia, S.C., 1972.

EU

See European Union

EUROPEAN BANK FOR RECONSTRUCTION AND DEVELOPMENT

The European Bank for Reconstruction and Development was the first international organization created in the post-Cold War era. Established in May 1990 following the dramatic political events of 1989, including Czechoslovakia's Velvet Revolution and the fall of the Berlin Wall, the EBRD was proposed by French President François Mitterand to assist the countries of Eastern and Central Europe with their transitions to multiparty democracy and market economies. The EBRD differs from other multilateral development banks, such as the Asian and Inter-American Development Banks and the World Bank, in membership, voting procedures, and its overtly political purpose. The EBRD makes loans only to those governments committed to constitutional reforms and to the principles of laissez-faire economics. The EBRD agreement also contains a unique mandate for private sector development and environmental protection and restoration.

Both states and other international organizations, specifically the European Union (EU) and the European Investment Bank (EIB), are members of the EBRD. Of the forty signatory states, thirty-one were European (the twelve members of the European Community, the predecessor of the EU; eleven other European countries plus Israel; and eight recipient countries); nine (Japan, the United States, Canada, Australia, New Zealand, Egypt, Korea, Morocco, and Mexico) were non-European. With the dissolution of the Soviet Union in 1992, all the former Soviet republics became EBRD members and potential recipients.

The EBRD Agreement requires close cooperation with other international agencies in addition to the EU and the EIB, including the International Monetary Fund (IMF), the World Bank (IBRD), the International Finance Corporation (IFC), the Multilateral Investment Guarantee Agency (MIGA), the Organization for Economic Cooperation and Development (OECD), and the United Nations and its specialized agencies.

The tripartite organizational structure of the EBRD is identical to that of other multilateral development banks. The institution has a board of governors that includes representatives of all member states; a twenty-three member board of directors responsible for establishing policies and making decisions on loans, guarantees, investments, borrowing, and technical assistance; and officers. The members of the European Union, the EU itself, and the EIB control 51 percent of the votes on the board of directors, which are allocated on the basis of subscribed shares in capital stock.

The operating priorities for the EBRD include supporting infrastructure for private sector development (transportation, telecommunications, energy, municipal services, housing, environmental management); financial sector reform; development of small and medium-size private companies; restructuring of industrial enterprises; stimulation of foreign direct investment; and environmental rehabilitation. It can operate through providing loans; making equity capital investments; providing technical assistance; facilitating access to capital markets; underwriting the equity issues of securities; or deploying Special Funds. Between its creation and the end of 1992 the EBRD had undertaken fifty transactions, committing $1.5 billion for projects primarily in Hungary, Poland, and Czechoslovakia.

The original capitalization for the EBRD was set at ten billion ECU (European Currency Units, the value of which is equal to the sum of fixed amounts of EU members' currencies in the "basket"). The United States pledged a ten percent share to be paid over five years, or $1.21 billion, $363 million of which was to be paid in and $847 million of which was to be available in callable funds. It fought hard to ensure that contributions were not limited to ECUs but could be made in dollars and yen.

The United States was skeptical about creating yet another multilateral funding institution and also was concerned that Soviet demands for loans would divert resources from Eastern Europe. It therefore sought limits on lending to "any potential recipient country" and sought to emphasize private sector development by limiting public sector lending to forty percent.

The early development of the EBRD was clouded by controversy over the leadership of Jacques Attali, its first president. Attali gained a reputation for lavish spending on the Bank's headquarters in London, his own travel, and a large staff. He stepped down in June 1993 amid charges of bad management that led the U.S. Congress to withhold part of the U.S. contribution.

MARGARET P. KARNS

See also Eastern Europe; European Union; Inter-American Development Bank; International Bank for Reconstruction and Development

FURTHER READING

Menkveld, Paul A. *Origin and Role of the European Bank for Reconstruction and Development.* London, 1991.
Shihata, Ibrahim F. I. *The European Bank for Reconstruction and Development: A Comparative Analysis of the Constituent Agreement.* London, 1990.
Symposium on the Role of International Financial Institutions in Central and Eastern Europe. *Journal of Comparative Economics.* February 1995.
Weber, Steven. "Origins of the European Bank for Reconstruction and Development." *International Organization* 48 (Winter 1994): 1-38.

EUROPEAN COMMUNITY

See European Union

EUROPEAN DEFENSE COMMUNITY

A proposal to create an integrated defense force consisting of France, Germany, Italy, and the Benelux nations, designed to "rearm the Germans without rearming Germany." After the outbreak of the Korean war, U.S. officials believed the defense of Western Europe was impossible without German participation. At the September 1950 meeting with foreign ministers, U.S. officials proposed the creation of ten German divisions in return for the dispatch of additional U.S. forces and the appointment of a U.S. Supreme Commander to the North Atlantic Treaty Organization (NATO). The French opposed German rearmament bitterly, but under pressure for an alternative they proposed the Pleven Plan, authored by Jean Monnet, to create a genuine European army integrated at the level of battalions. Though some in the United States believed the French were merely trying to prevent German rearmament, Monnet insisted that their intention was to prevent the creation of an independent German army. German chancellor Konrad Adenauer insisted that West Germany could not rearm unless granted sovereignty and equality with other nations. U.S. leaders became convinced that the only way to rearm Europe was through an integrated European force in a politically unified continent. With the enthusiastic support of NATO Commander General Dwight D.Eisenhower, the Pleven Plan was transformed into the European Defense Community and made militarily practical, with German units integrated at the division level. The treaties creating the European Defense Community, along with treaties ending the occupation of Germany, were signed in May 1952.

Though the United States was not a member of the European Defense Community the Eisenhower administration strongly urged its ratification and threatened an "agonizing reappraisal" if the European Defense Community failed to be approved. Despite this pressure, the French Assembly rejected the proposal in August 1954. Though the European Defense Community was not approved, it helped Europeans come to terms with the issue of Germany's rearmament. West Germany was admitted into NATO and restored to sovereignty in May 1955.

Thomas A. Schwartz

See also European Union; North Atlantic Treaty Organization

FURTHER READING

Large, David Clay. *Germans to the Front: West German Rearmament in the Adenauer Era.* Chapel Hill, N.C., 1995.
Schwartz, Thomas Alan. *America's Germany: John J. McCloy and the Federal Republic of Germany.* Cambridge, Mass., 1991.
Wall, Irwin M. *The United States and the Making of Postwar France, 1945–1954.* New York, 1991.

EUROPEAN RECOVERY PROGRAM

See Marshall Plan

EUROPEAN UNION

Since 1993 the successor name for the European Community (EC) and, prior to that, the European Economic Community (EEC). The EU represents continuing movement toward the economic and political integration of Western Europe—but is by no means the final stage. Issues related to further integration, including monetary union and common foreign and security policies, and to the broadening of the membership to include additional European states, including formerly communist ones, remain to be resolved.

History

Today's EU may be traced back to the 1951 Paris Treaty, in which six Western European states (Belgium, Italy, France, Luxembourg, the Netherlands, and West Germany) formed the European Coal and Steel Community (ECSC). The idea of the French wine merchant Jean Monnet, the ECSC was designed to integrate the coal, steel, and iron industries of the member states into a customs union (that is, to eliminate internal tariffs and to set up a common external tariff) in order to reap economies of scale; to take wartime industries out of the hands of national governments to reduce their capability to make war again; to begin a process of Franco-German reconciliation that was expected to lead to permanent peace; and to strengthen Western Europe as a bulwark against communism. The ECSC was empowered to set prices and production levels and to regulate import, export, and internal trade. The United States played a key role in helping allay French and German fears over cooperation; an attempt in 1952 to complement the economic community with a European Defense Community (EDC) failed when the French Parliament rejected it in 1954. The ECSC states expanded their efforts toward economic integration when they ratified the Treaty of Rome in 1957, which created the European Economic Community (EEC) and the European Atomic Energy Community (EURATOM). The EEC extended the customs union to agriculture and other industrial sectors (except defense). EURATOM brought the members' nuclear industries under common rules to ensure safety and nonproliferation. In 1967 the institutions of the ECSC, the EEC, and EURATOM were merged under a single organizational rubric, the European Community (EC). In 1970 the EC members formed an intergovernmental forum for foreign policy cooperation known as European Political Cooperation (EPC). In 1987 the founding treaties were amended by the Single European Act, which committed members to complete the task of setting up a common market and achieving free movement of goods, services, capital, and labor in the so-called 1992 project. The Single European Act also brought EPC closer to the treaty rubric and committed members to consult and coordinate on foreign policy issues of mutual concern, including the political and economic aspects of security. The Maastricht Treaty on European Union (TEU), which went into effect on

1 November 1993, created three "pillars" to support the new union. The first pillar was the EC and the plan for economic and monetary union (EMU); the second was the Common Foreign and Security Policy (CFSP), which subsumes and strengthens EPC and opens the door to a future common defense policy; and the third was cooperation within the union in such areas as police functions, immigration, and judicial affairs. The treaty designated the 1948 Western European Union (WEU), a collective self-defense pact of most of the EU states, as the future security arm of the European Union. The EU has enlarged its membership four times. Denmark, Ireland, and the United Kingdom joined in 1973, Greece in 1981, Spain and Portugal in 1986, and Austria, Finland, and Sweden in 1995. Switzerland, Turkey, Cyprus, and Malta have applied for membership, as have ten Central and Eastern European countries (Poland, Hungary, Slovakia, the Czech Republic, Romania, Slovenia, Bulgaria, Estonia, Latvia, and Lithuania). To be eligible for membership, states must be practicing democratic market economies in Europe.

Structure and Decision-Making

The EU is neither a state nor a traditional international organization. It is a new kind of international structure whose bodies have certain powers that exist concomitantly with those of the constituent members. The interlocking of national and EU administrations and the symbiotic decision-making relationship between EU and national institutions is what many scholars refer to as a system of "cooperative federalism." The core problem for the EU and its member governments is how to find a balance between European-wide and national interests and between the two contending approaches to decision-making: integration and intergovernmentalism. The integration approach to European cooperation stresses a major role for central institutions, decision-making by qualified majority voting, and a loss of some degree of state sovereignty for the good of the whole. The intergovernmental approach stresses the central, indeed primary, role of governments in deciding on common actions on the basis of consensus, with central institutions playing a less significant role.

Of all the EU bodies, the European Court of Justice (ECJ) and the European Commission, by virtue of their constitutional mandates, are most committed to the integration approach. The ECJ, the EU's supreme court, interprets treaty law, delivers opinions, passes judgments, and levies fines. It has furthered European integration as many of its decisions have expanded the purview of the EU bodies and laws into new areas of cooperation. When conflict has arisen between national and EU laws, the ECJ has often ruled that EU law takes precedence. The Commission's constituency is "Europe," rather than individual states. Commission staff work for the EU and the commissioners themselves, who divide up the various portfolios of the agency's workload, are expected to advance the cause of European integration. The Commission's chief powers are the initiation and execution of legislation. The guardian of the treaties, the Commission not only has key oversight, investigatory, and enforcement powers, it also negotiates for the EU in international trade negotiations. The Commission has a staff of 17,000 employees who are dependent on national bureaucracies to help in the formulation and implementation of EU policies. The Commission cannot make laws, but it has important discretionary power in the way it crafts and implements them. It proposes agricultural support prices each year; its power to impose price, production, and import controls on steel products under certain circumstances exceeds that of the president of the United States in relation to the U.S. steel industry; and it administers the aid program to Central and Eastern Europe of twenty-four industrialized democracies. Jacques Delors, president of the Commission until 1995, was a driving force behind the passage and implementation of the Single European Act, but his influence and that of the Commission suffered in the 1990s as member governments sought to reestablish their dominance by strengthening the relative power of the Council of Ministers (as they had done in the mid-1960s). Despite the ups and downs in the Commission's relationship with the member governments, the latter continue to rely on the Commission's expertise, resources, institutional memory and continuity, and the presence in the EU's capital, Brussels, all despite public statements to the contrary.

Unlike the Commission, the Council of Ministers consists of representatives from national governments who are pursuing state interests and who are answerable to their heads of government. The Council enacts legislation and is the locus of power in the EU. The Council can ask the Commission to initiate policy proposals. Membership in the Council varies according to the nature of the policy being discussed; when EU farm prices are being set, the members' agriculture ministers meet, and when economic or financial policy needs to be addressed, the economic and finance ministers meet. Among its tasks, the Council votes on the Commission's budget proposals, gives the Commission mandates to conduct international trade negotiations, and decides how to craft and implement joint foreign policy actions. Since 1975 the EU heads of government (and the French head of state) have met biannually as the European Council to set guidelines and priorities for the EU, make appointments to EU bodies, and attempt to work out problems that cannot be solved at lower levels of decision-making. In the early 1980s, for example, when the British government demanded changes in the way its contribution to the EU budget was calculated, it took the European Council to work out a compromise; in October 1993 the European Council sent guidelines to the Council of Ministers on new areas of joint foreign policy action. The presidency of the European Council rotates among the membership, with each member having a six-month term. The European Parliament has the final right to approve or reject the EU's budget in full; it also has important decision-making authority in certain areas of foreign policy (accepting new members into the EU and authorizing association accords with nonmembers) and of the internal market (issuing directives on harmonization of product standards). The European Parliament has the power to confirm the European Council's nominees (as a set group, not individual nominees) for the European Commission. Since the European Parliament is the only democratically elected EU body, it reflects European public opinion, although many of its members are disappointed that the Parliament still does not have the power to legislate. The truth of the matter is that neither the EU nor the member governments are omnipotent. They constrain as well as strengthen each other. The EU has grown in importance because its member governments recognize that some of their key interests are best pursued in a European context. In reality, a "pooling" rather than an "erosion" of state sovereignty has occurred. Members enhance their sovereignty within a larger universe. The supranational vision of a united Europe espoused by Jean Monnet and his followers has been replaced by a more pragmatic and realistic vision: while state interests are served in the EU, the EU also plays a role in forging compromises that advance its members' common interests. European interests may be advanced as individual states bargain with one another to seek common policies; despite the strong national control of the EU, bargains are struck, and what is lost individually may be gained collectively. The United States is more concerned about the need for the EU to be more cohesive and effective in dealing with European and international problems than it is about the contending approaches to European integration and the infighting among the EU institutions. For the United States, what matters is not how but when common policies are devised.

Issues of Concern to U.S. Foreign Policy

The successful conclusion in 1994 of the Uruguay Round of negotiations on the General Agreement on Tariffs and Trade (GATT) resolved a number of trade issues in U.S.-EU relations, but trade will continue to be a source of tension between the two. The Round did not resolve such key trade issues as aircraft subsidies, film and entertainment products, and trade in telecommunications and several other service sectors. These and other "post-GATT" issues are being taken up in U.S.-EU bilateral

consultations as well as in other multilateral fora including the World Trade Organization (WTO), successor to the GATT. The EU's goal of achieving a monetary union by the end of the century has been sorely tested by the crisis in the European Monetary System in the early 1990s and subsequent sluggish economic growth and loss of political momentum. However, there is still a possibility that several EU members will meet the criteria for joining the EMU. The impact on U.S. interests could be significant if the "Euro," as the new currency will be called, rivals the dollar as an international reserve currency. Monetary cooperation still falls outside the orbit of U.S.-EU bilateral consultations since finance ministers on both sides of the Atlantic have preferred to limit such discussions to the purview of the group of seven. The TEU also commits the members to develop joint foreign policy actions as part of the goal of a CFSP. Such actions are expected to have a high political profile, represent the highest political commitment on the part of the member governments, better link EU economic resources with political goals, and thus carry more weight abroad. The European Council has laid out guidelines for joint actions in several areas for which the Council of Foreign Ministers has gone on to implement: dispatch of election monitors to Russia and South Africa; dispatch of humanitarian aid to the former Yugoslavia and the setting up of a civil administration for the city of Mostar; provision of substantial aid for the Palestinian Authority; active diplomatic support for the extension of the Nuclear Nonproliferation Treaty; export controls on dual-use goods; and controls on antipersonnel land mines. On the whole, the EU's progress in developing a CFSP has been very slow. Members differ over the scope and frequency of joint actions and over developing the WEU as the EU's defense arm. The TEU called for the convening of an intergovernmental conference of the member governments in 1996 to review the workings of the CFSP and other areas of the TEU. Although no panacea for all the EU's problems is envisaged, the members are expected to make some modest, pragmatic changes to decisionmaking that could improve the functioning of the CFSP. The United States, which supports a more active EU role in international affairs, has a deep stake in the success of the CFSP. The more the EU is capable of participation in international problem solving, the more the United States has a partner and interlocutor with whom to share the burden. The 1990 "Transatlantic Declaration" provided the consultative framework within which the United States and EU share information and compare policy positions. The 1995 "New Transatlantic Agenda and Action Plan" enables the United States and EU to move from the habit of consultation to that of policy coordination and joint action in a wide array of regional and global functional and security-related issues, humanitarian assistance, combating disease, and police cooperation. Ultimately, the EU will have to decide if it can muster the political will to make CFSP a reality. If the EU can improve its capacity to act internationally, then the prospects for U.S.-EU foreign policy coordination increase exponentially.

The EU is committed to the expansion of its membership to include up to twelve new states in the Mediterranean and in Central and Eastern Europe. These countries are most anxious to join the EU. If, however, the EU widens before it deepens (improves/streamlines decision-making structures), enlargement could dilute or even reverse European political integration, turning the EU into a loose free trade area. The intergovernmental conference of 1996 is expected to produce some needed improvements in the functioning of the EU in advance of enlargement, although many maintain that wholesale change, which is needed, will not occur. The United States has a deep stake in the EU's widening and deepening exercises. Widening will be instrumental in stabilizing the nascent democracies of the former Soviet bloc and bringing them into the European mainstream, and—if handled carefully—will be complementary to NATO's own outreach to the East. However, if the EU widens before it deepens, and consequently reverses the progress made to date in political integration, the United States will not have the kind of international partner it needs to help share the burden of regional and global problem solving. Thus the United States supports deepening and widening but with the former preceding the latter.

ROY H. GINSBERG

See also Agriculture; European Defense Community; International Trade and Commerce; Monnet, Jean; Schuman, Robert

FURTHER READING

European Commission. *General Report on the Activities of the European Communities, 1995.* Luxembourg, 1996.
Featherstone, Kevin, and Roy H. Ginsberg. *The United States and the European Union in the 1990s; Partners in Transition.* London, 1996.
Hackett, Clifford. *Cautious Revolution: The European Union Arrives.* Westport, Conn., 1995.
Rhodes, Carolyn, and Sonia Mazey, eds. *The State of the European Union: Building a European Polity?* Boulder, Colo., 1995.

EVARTS, WILLIAM MAXWELL

(*b.* 6 February 1818; *d.* 28 February 1901)

Attorney general (1868–1869), secretary of state (1877–1881), and U.S. senator. Born in Boston, Evarts graduated from Yale University (1837) and attended Harvard Law School (1838–1839). He practiced law in New York City and served as assistant U.S. attorney for the Southern District of New York from 1849 to 1853. Returning to private practice, he remained active in Republican party politics and served on special missions to Europe for Secretary of State William Seward during the Civil War. In 1868 Evarts was chief counsel to President Andrew Johnson during Johnson's impeachment trial and then served as U.S. attorney general. Evarts was appointed secretary of state in 1877 by President Rutherford B. Hayes. In that position, Evarts opposed attempts by a French company to construct a canal across Panama but failed in his efforts to secure a new agreement to replace the Clayton-Bulwer Treaty of 1850. He took a strong stand to defend U.S. lives and property during a turbulent revolution in Mexico, although the administration eventually recognized and established friendly relations with the rebel government headed by Porfirio Díaz. His efforts led to the improvement of the consular reporting system and the negotiation of treaties with China to regulate commerce and immigration. Following his tenure as secretary of state, he served as a delegate to the International Monetary Conference in Paris (1881) and as a U.S. senator from New York (1885–1891).

MICHAEL J. DEVINE

See also American Civil War; Clayton, John Middleton; Díaz (José de la Cruz), Porfirio; Hayes, Rutherford Birchard; Mexico; Panama and Panama Canal

FURTHER READING

Barrows, Chester L. *William M. Evarts: Lawyer, Diplomat and Statesman.* Chapel Hill, N.C., 1941.
Dyer, Brainerd. *The Public Career of William M. Evarts.* Los Angeles, 1933.

EVERETT, EDWARD

(*b.* 11 April 1794; *d.* 15 January 1865)

Minister to Great Britain (1841–1845) during the Harrison-Tyler administration and secretary of state (1852–1853) during the last four months of the Fillmore administration. Everett succeeded his friend and supporter Daniel Webster, who died during his second term as secretary of state. Everett dealt with the Perry mission to "open" Japan and worked on resolution of a dispute over the Guano Islands with Peru. On behalf of the United States he rejected a British-French proposal that the three powers permanently disavow any intent to acquire Cuba. The United States had no intention to obtain the island, he said, but he could not rule out its annexation in the future. Near the close of the Fillmore administration he helped obtain passage, as part of the 1853 appropriation bill, of a measure creating the office of assistant secretary of State.

KENNETH R. STEVENS

See also Cuba; Fillmore, Millard; Japan; Perry, Matthew Calbraith; Peru

FURTHER READING

Stearns, Foster. "Edward Everett, Secretary of State, November 6, 1852, to March 3, 1853." In *The American Secretaries of State and Their Diplomacy*, edited by Samuel Flagg Bemis et al., Vol. 6, 114–141. New York, 1958.

Varg, Paul. *Edward Everett: The Intellectual in the Turmoil of Politics.* Selinsgrove, Pa., 1992.

EXECUTIVE AGENTS

The United States Constitution vests in the president the power to nominate and appoint ambassadors and consuls provided "two-thirds of the senators present concur" (Article II, Section 2). This provision, linked to the requirement that treaties with foreign governments also demand a two-thirds vote of approval in the Senate, was designed to restrict the president's capacity to act alone. By withholding approval the Senate could in theory delay or block policies and interfere with the president's negotiations with other governments. Hearings on formally nominated individuals could be both time consuming and irritating from the president's point of view. Strong presidents, beginning with George Washington, were impatient with this provision. They had no choice but to respect it when making formal diplomatic appointments, but when they wanted fast action they made special appointments without Senate approval of executive agents, individuals reporting directly to the president, often without any involvement of the department or the secretary of state. The use of executive agents gave the president some direct control over foreign policy without interference from either Congress or the bureaucracy.

Executive agents have been used most often for specific purposes, for instance opening discussions with a government not recognized by the United States, or negotiating a settlement whether by treaty or executive agreement. John Jay, while serving as chief justice of the Supreme Court, was an executive agent of President Washington in negotiating the 1795 treaty with Great Britain. President Woodrow Wilson sent a succession of executive agents to Mexico between 1913 and 1916 when the United States did not recognize a Mexican government. The most important executive agents have served a president over a period of years on a range of important issues. Colonel Edward M. House, Wilson's intimate adviser on foreign affairs from 1913 to 1919, both anticipated the role of the modern assistant to the president for national security affairs, and was an envoy entrusted with the most sensitive issues of war and peace. A man of independent wealth, he received no salary until he took on the official assignment of member of the U.S. delegation to the Paris Peace Conference of 1918–1919. Harry Hopkins, a principal architect of Franklin D. Roosevelt's domestic programs in the 1930s, was Roosevelt's agent during World War II, traveling to England and to the Soviet Union in spite of poor health. His last mission, in May 1945, was to call on Joseph Stalin as executive agent for President Harry S. Truman.

The mission of an executive agent can be secret when the president wishes to avoid publicity or desires to avoid embarrassment should the mission fail. In 1919 President Wilson sent William Bullitt on a secret assignment to the Bolshevik regime in Russia to see if some accommodation could be reached. The mission failed in part because Wilson chose not to pursue the opening Bullitt claimed to have discovered. A more spectacular and successful secret mission was that of President Richard Nixon's national security adviser, Henry A. Kissinger, to the People's Republic of China in July 1971. The Kissinger mission led to President Nixon's trip to Beijing in February 1972 and the end of the hostile isolation of the two countries toward each other. On other occasions executive agents are appointed with great fanfare in order to signal a president's deep interest in an issue or divert political pressure. Thomas Jefferson sent James Monroe to Paris in 1803 to deal with the problem of the pending French move into Louisiana. In 1994 President Bill Clinton, when under fire for lacking a clear policy toward a turbulent situation in Haiti, appointed William Gray, a former member of Congress and prominent African-American, as special adviser on Haiti.

The multiplicity of channels of communication available for the conduct of foreign policy had by the mid-twentieth century reduced the importance of ambassadors and other officers approved by the Senate and correspondingly enhanced the role of executive agents. By the end of the century scarcely an important issue existed that did not see the use of one or more executive agents.

GADDIS SMITH

See also Bullitt, William Christian; Hopkins, Harry Lloyd; House, Edward Mandell; Jay, John; Kissinger, Henry Alfred; Monroe, James

FURTHER READING

Seymour, Charles. *The Intimate Papers of Colonel House.* 4 vols., Boston, Mass., 1926–1928.

Sherwood, Robert. *Roosevelt and Hopkins.* New York, N.Y., 1950.

Wriston, Henry M. *Executive Agents in American Foreign Relations.* Baltimore, Md., 1929.

EXECUTIVE AGREEMENTS

Agreements made by the president or his representative with another country. They are distinct from treaties in that the advice and consent of the Senate is not required for executive agreements, although the Supreme Court has held in several cases (for example, *United States* v. *Belmont* and *United States* v. *Pink*) that they have the same force of law, and they cannot overrule or displace conflicting laws. The use of executive agreements draws upon two sources of authority: the constitutional power of the president (the powers granted in Article II of the Constitution) and statutory authorizations or treaties (powers granted by congressional actions). While executive agreements have been used by presidents since the beginning of the Republic, their use increased dramatically after World War II, making them an important source of the growth of presidential dominance over foreign policy. Indeed, some analysts report that by the mid-1990s executive agreements made up ninety-five percent of all foreign policy commitments, dwarfing treaties as the major instrument for making U.S. commitments abroad. Many important foreign policy commitments of the post–World War II era, such as the Offensive Arms Pact of the Strategic Arms Limitation Treaty (SALT I) of 1972 and the 1973 agreement that ended the Vietnam War, have assumed this form. A series of congressional hearings in the late 1960s and early 1970s revealed the existence of a number of important executive agreements involving military and intelligence operations that had been concluded with other countries and kept secret, even from Congress. In light of these revelations and in the aftermath of the Vietnam War, Congress sought to place some controls on the use of executive agreements in making international commitments. It passed the Case-Zablocki Act (1972), requiring that before an executive agreement could be implemented, the president must report it to Congress within sixty days, but it failed to enact a series of other measures that would have afforded Congress the use of the legislative veto over executive agreements that it found objectionable. As a result, executive agreements remain an important instrument of presidential foreign policymaking.

JAMES M. MCCORMICK

See also Case-Zablocki Act; Congress; Legislative Veto

FURTHER READING

Fisher, Louis. *Constitutional Conflicts Between Congress and the President.* Princeton, N.J., 1985.

Johnson, Loch, and James M. McCormick. "Foreign Policy by Executive Fiat." *Foreign Policy* 28 (Fall 1977): 117–138.

———. "The Making of International Agreements: A Reappraisal of Congressional Involvement." *Journal of Politics* 40 (May 1978): 468–478.

Nelson, Michael, ed. *Congressional Quarterly's Guide to the Presidency.* Washington, D.C., 1989.

EXECUTIVE PRIVILEGE

The president's claim of a constitutional right to withhold information from both the legislative and the judicial branches. The basis for this executive claim, which was first asserted in 1958, is the separation of powers, as outlined in the U.S. Constitution and historical precedent. The claim is made that the president has the right to exercise his policy judgment independently and that he must be able to engage in confidential communications with aides to arrive at such decisions. Not all observers accept that the claim of executive privilege is legitimate. One writer, Raoul Berger, has asserted that executive privilege is a myth. He contends that the concept is nowhere mentioned in the Constitution, that it is not necessarily protected by either the separation of powers or historical precedent, and that its operation is ultimately harmful to the U.S. system of government. Congress and the public, he maintains, need to be aware of all presidential information if they are to perform their functions in a democracy. Other constitutional analysts do not accept such a blanket dismissal of executive privilege, but they do note its limitations. When impeachment of an executive or a legislative official or possible administrative malfeasance are at issue, the courts—and even presidents—have acknowledged that it is inappropriate to claim executive privilege. In such cases Congress should have access to confidential executive information. Full disclosure of such privileged communications to Congress, however, is not required under specific circumstances. A matter that is the "exclusive province" of another branch, an investigation solely within the executive branch, and certain kinds of information that involve trade secrets or commercial advantages may be withheld from disclosure under particular circumstances.

In *United States* v. *Nixon* (1974), the Supreme Court acknowledged the existence of executive privilege, based upon the separation of powers within the Constitution, but noted that there is no absolute right of executive privilege. When criminal matters require access to such privileged communications, the executive must yield such information. Executive privilege claims involving "military, diplomatic, or sensitive national secrets" are more likely to be constitutional, although the right is not absolute, as revealed in the Pentagon Papers case (*New York Times Company* v. *United States* 1971).

JAMES M. MCCORMICK

See also Congress; Presidency

FURTHER READING

Berger, Raoul. *Executive Privilege: A Constitutional Myth.* Cambridge, Mass., 1974.

Fisher, Louis. *Constitutional Conflicts Between Congress and the President.* Princeton, N.J., 1985.

Smith, Jean E. *The Constitution and American Foreign Policy.* St. Paul, Minn., 1989.

EXIMBANK

See Export-Import Bank

EXPORT CONTROLS

The Export Control Act of 1949 (amended in 1969 and 1979 and renamed the Export Administration Act) authorizes the executive branch to restrict exports to any destination for reasons of national security, foreign policy, or short supply. Controls for reasons of national security usually have been applied to exports that could enhance the military capabilities of an actual or potential adversary. Foreign policy–based controls have been prompted by policies or actions by other states that threaten U.S. values or interests. Short-supply controls have been more economic in nature, seeking to ensure domestic supplies of potentially scarce products and to prevent inflationary pressures that short supplies could set off.

Export controls were used during the Cold War primarily to deny products and technologies of potential military significance to members of the Warsaw Pact. These controls were coordinated with other Western states in the Coordinating Committee-Consultative Group (COCOM). The United States also has employed unilateral controls on trade against numerous countries including Cuba, North Korea, Syria, Iraq, Iran, and Libya to promote human rights, punish terrorism, discourage nuclear proliferation, or signal disapproval of the government.

The utility of U.S. export controls has been debated for decades. Some scholars view them as an effective instrument of statecraft, while others claim that the economic costs of employing them outweigh any political benefits. The issue has divided the U.S government, with the State, Defense, and Commerce departments and members of Congress often taking divergent positions. In a number of instances diplomatic controversy has resulted because of political pressure exerted by the United States on other governments to match its controls, and U.S. claims of the authority to apply its national controls beyond its borders, in defiance of international law. For example, the extraterritorial application of U.S. sanctions prompted a major conflict between the United States and West European governments over energy trade with the Soviet Union in 1982. There also have been recurring conflicts between the U.S. government and industry; the latter claim that unilateral and overly comprehensive controls earn U.S. firms reputations as unreliable suppliers and place them at a disadvantage in international trade competition. One major case was the 1980 grain embargo against the Soviet Union in response to the invasion of Afghanistan.

With the end of the Cold War, the export controls directed against the Soviet Union were significantly relaxed, and COCOM was disbanded in 1994. However, countries suspected of developing weapons of mass destruction have become the main targets of U.S. controls. The United States and twenty-seven other countries agreed in 1995 to create a successor regime to COCOM, called the Wassenaar Arrangement, to restrict the export of dual-use technologies and conventional weapons to pariah states such as Libya and Iran. The U.S. government also continues to coordinate controls on weapons of mass destruction with other governments through such other multilateral arrangements as the Nuclear Suppliers Group, the Missile Technology Control Regime (ballistic missiles), and the Australia Group (chemical weapons).

The domestic debate over the economic costs versus the national security or foreign policy benefits of export controls has persisted after the Cold War. For example, between 1991 and 1996 a political stalemate between the executive branch and Congress prevented the renewal of the Export Administration Act. The latest version of that act lapsed at the end of 1990, leaving the executive to administer controls under the authority of the International Emergency Economic Powers Act (IEEPA).

MICHAEL MASTANDUNO

See also Cold War; Economic Sanctions; Nuclear Nonproliferation

FURTHER READING
Jentleson, Bruce, W. *Pipeline Politics: The Complex Political Economy of East-West Energy Trade.* Ithaca, N.Y., 1986.
Long, William. *U.S. Export Control Policy: Executive Autonomy vs. Congressional Reform.* New York, 1990.
Mastanduno, Michael. *Economic Containment: CoCom and the Politics of East-West Trade.* Ithaca, N.Y., 1992.

EXPORT-IMPORT BANK

An independent agency of the U.S. government that aids in the financing of U.S. exports. The bank was established in 1945 as the successor to the Export-Import Bank of Washington, founded in 1934. Impetus for establishing the Export-Import Bank derived from the fact that many other countries provide financial support to their exporters; failure by the U.S. government to do so might have been seen as putting U.S. exporters at a competitive disadvantage. The Export-Import Bank can be viewed as providing a subsidy for U.S. exporters, a subsidy intended to offset the effects of similar subsidies maintained by competing nations. Despite its independence, the bank has often been used as an instrument of U.S. foreign policy, providing assistance for trade with countries favored by the United States and withholding it as a mild form of sanction to nations out of favor. The Export-Import Bank maintains four major programs. Working Capital Guarantees involve direct

AUTHORIZATIONS BY MARKET

Country	Loans	Guarantees	Medium Term Insurance	Total	Exposure 9/30/95
Argentina	$7,153,086	$147,636,035	$34,005,041	$188,794,162	$2,048,251,535
Chile	165,437,658	10,275,000	6,636,429	182,349,087	342,666,090
China (Mainland)	495,776,668	308,479,290		804,255,958	2,930,354,843
Ecuador	806,388	20,537,499	16,207,389	37,551,276	104,120,175
El Salvador	2,663,537	81,083,783	7,463,478	91,210,798	135,348,306
India	32,245,049	33,621,413	2,420,724	68,287,186	1,459,300,896
Indonesia	586,934,109	625,886,594	3,485,000	1,216,305,703	2,792,015,145
Kenya	3,822,673			3,822,673	78,390,788
Lithuania	17,860,200	7,998,606		25,858,806	25,858,806
Mexico	15,655,022	824,618,113	481,988,460	1,322,261,595	5,975,306,414
Pakistan	103,949,650	122,843,329		226,792,979	293,035,185
Philippines	131,705,718	315,046,290	1,275,000	448,027,008	2,214,493,997
Sri Lanka	6,329,235			6,329,235	12,511,506
Trinidad and Tobago	22,840,165			22,840,165	178,331,036
Turkey	5,132,363	317,754,702		322,887,065	2,070,083,804
Total of Countries	1,598,311,521	2,815,780,654	553,481,521	4,967,573,796	20,660,068,526
Total Authorizations	1,598,311,521	2,815,780,654	553,481,521	4,967,573,796	20,660,068,526

Source: Export-Import Bank of the United States

loans to small and medium-size U.S. businesses to develop products for export. Export Credit Insurance is designed to reduce the risk of nonpayment for U.S. exporters who offer short-term commercial credit on export sales. The bank also provides loan guarantees to banks that lend money to foreign purchasers of U.S. goods and makes direct loans to purchasers of U.S. exports. As of September 1992 Export-Import Bank exposure under these programs totaled $41.8 billion.

ROBERT M. DUNN JR.

See also Most-Favored-Nation Principle

FURTHER READING

Export-Import Bank of the United States. *Annual Reports.*
Rodriguez, Rita. *The Export-Import Bank at Fifty: The International Environment and the Institution's Role.* Lexington, Mass., 1987.

EXTRADITION

The legal process whereby, in accordance with a request from the competent authorities of the requesting state, a person is transferred from the jurisdiction of the requested state to face criminal proceedings in the requesting state. In the 1980s the United States made an average of 100 such requests per year to foreign states and received approximately 300 requests annually from countries seeking extradition of people from the United States.

U.S. law generally does not permit extradition from the United States unless a valid extradition treaty exists between the United States and the requesting state. Most extraditions to the United States are also pursuant to treaty, although some countries permit extradition without treaties on the basis of reciprocity or comity. The United States has extradition treaties with more than 100 foreign states. U.S. international extradition practice is governed by somewhat antiquated federal legislation and by these extradition treaties, which are generally self-executing and form part of U.S. law. Requests for extradition from the United States are made through federal authorities; U.S. attorneys may seek provisional arrest warrants and often represent the requesting state in extradition proceedings. A person whose extradition is sought is entitled to a hearing before a federal examining magistrate to contest such matters as identity, adequacy of the evidence adduced, and compliance with the relevant treaty. If certification of extradition is granted, extradition is at the discretion of the secretary of state.

Extradition treaties typically define extraditable offenses; set forth substantive requirements, such as that the act by the accused person be criminal under the law of each state if committed there (the principle of double criminality) and that the requesting state proceed against the accused only for offenses related to those specified in the extradition request (the principle of specialty); set forth procedural requirements for extradition; and specify exceptions under which extradition is nonobligatory or impermissible. The political offense exception began to appear frequently in international extradition law after 1833, but the definition of "political offenses" has varied considerably, and increasingly states have circumscribed the exception to avoid providing impunity for heinous acts. In the late 1970s U.S. courts began to use the political offense exception to prevent extradition to the United Kingdom of a few alleged members of the Provisional Irish Republican Army; in 1986 the United States and the United Kingdom signed a supplementary treaty excluding from the category of political offenses several crimes associated with terrorism. This agreement was accompanied by relaxation of the traditional practice by which U.S. courts do not inquire into the anticipated treatment of the extradited person in the requesting state (the rule of noninquiry). Increasingly, extradition is prohibited where there are substantial grounds to fear that prosecution, punishment, or prejudicial treatment in the requesting state will be based on race, religion, nationality, or political opinion. Other exceptions to extradition in some treaties relate to the death penalty, humanitarian considerations, certain military or fiscal offenses, and the practice of many states (not including the United States) of refusing to extradite their own nationals. Most states whose constitutions prohibit extradition of their nationals to other countries are in theory able to prosecute their nationals for crimes committed anywhere, whereas the United States and other common-law countries do not assert such expansive criminal jurisdiction over extraterritorial conduct of nationals other than for hijacking, terrorism, and other special categories of offenses.

Extradition is an important element of international cooperation in criminal law enforcement. It can be a slow and cumbersome process, and law enforcement agencies on occasion resort to other devices, including informal cooperation to transfer custody at borders, abduction, and exclusion or expulsion of aliens to other states under immigration laws. An alternative to transfer of custody is for the alleged offender to be tried where found. This option is embodied in multilateral treaties dealing with specific offenses, such as drug trafficking and crimes against aircraft; these treaties provide that states must either prosecute or extradite suspects.

BENEDICT W. KINGSBURY

See also International Law; Terrorism

FURTHER READING
Bassiouni, M. Cherif. *International Extradition: United States Law and Practice*, 2nd ed. New York, 1987.
Nadelmann, Ethan. *Cops Across Borders: The Internationalization of U.S. Criminal Law Enforcement.* Philadelphia, 1993.

EXTRATERRITORIALITY

The application of national law to transactions beyond the borders of the nation; it can be exercised in such varied business and regulatory sectors as banking, securities and foreign exchange, trade and export controls, shipping, aviation, taxation, and telecommunications. The most notable example of extraterritoriality in U.S. history was the right granted by treaty from 1844 to 1943 to try U.S. citizens accused of crime in China in U.S. courts.

The United States has often applied U.S. law to business transactions beyond its borders. Such extraterritorial application of national law has had significant impact upon U.S. foreign policy and relations.

Because extraterritorial application of national laws can have an adverse impact on other countries, such application often creates tensions in foreign relations. For example, the U.S. Department of Commerce successfully promulgated export controls in 1981 on US. goods and technologies intended for use in constructing the Urengoi gas pipeline in the Soviet Union. When the government attempted in 1982 to impose those export controls extraterritorially to U.S. affiliates and subsidiaries in Europe, there was sharp European reaction. The British government invoked its Protection of Trading Interests Act to prohibit its companies and U.S. subsidiaries in the Great Britain from complying with the extraterritorially imposed U.S. controls. The European Community and other countries acting individually, including Germany and France, formally protested the extraterritorial application of U.S. controls, and U.S.-European relations deteriorated significantly. In reaction to the European protests and worsening relations, and with the realization that its policy was having little effect on European involvement in the pipeline, the U.S. government lifted the extraterritorial export controls on 13 November 1982.

Another often cited example of the application of U.S. law beyond the borders of the United States is the 1976 decision of the Ninth Circuit Court of Appeals in *Timberlane Lumber Company* v. *Bank of America*. Timberlane alleged that the Bank of America and others conspired to prevent Timberlane from milling lumber in Honduras and exporting it to the United States. "The intent and result of the conspiracy, they [Timberlane] contend, was to interfere with the exportation to the United States, including Puerto Rico, of Honduran lumber for sale or use there by the plaintiffs, thus directly and substantially affecting the foreign policy of the United States." Initially, the defendants argued that there had been no substantial effect on U.S. commerce and that jurisdiction over actions taking place outside U.S. territory was lacking. On these grounds the case was dismissed in district court. The circuit court reversed the Timberlane dismissal and recommended the case to trial. In the decision the circuit court maintained, "There is no doubt that American antitrust laws extend over some conduct in other nations."

In 1996 the Helms-Burton Amendment, a piece of U.S. legislation directed against Cuba, extended U.S. law extraterritoriality in ways that infuriated U.S. allies. The European Union, Japan, Canada, Mexico, Australia, and others took sharp exception to U.S. efforts to extend U.S. laws beyond its national jurisdiction. For example, Title IV of the Amendment "directs the [U.S.] Secretary of States to deny a visa to, and the Attorney General to exclude from the United States, aliens [e.g., Europeans, Canadians, etc.]...involved in the confiscation of property, or the trafficking of property [in Cuba], owned by a U.S. national." Some countries enacted blocking legislation and threatened to place trade sanctions on the United States if this and other provisions were implemented.

GARY K. BERTSCH

See also Export Controls

FURTHER READING

Dallmeyer, Dorinda G. "The Problem of Extraterritoriality in U.S. Export Control Policy." In Gary K. Bertsch and Steven Elliott-Gower, eds., *Export Controls in Transition*. Durham, N.C., 1992.

Lange, Dietr, and Gary Born, eds. *The Extraterritorial Application of National Laws*. New York, 1987.

F

FAIRBANK, JOHN KING

(*b.* 27 May 1907; *d.* 14 September 1991)

A leading force in modern Chinese studies and U.S. relations with China for more than half a century. Born in Huron, South Dakota, and educated at Exeter Academy, the University of Wisconsin at Madison, and Harvard and Oxford universities, Fairbank taught Chinese history at Harvard from 1936 to 1977. He also served in the Office of Strategic Services and Office of War Information in Washington, Chongqing (Chungking), and Shanghai from 1941 to 1946. The author of sixty-five books and 450 articles or reviews, Fairbank studied late Ch'ing diplomatic history, modern China's social revolution, and China's relations with the West, especially the United States. He directed the East Asian Research Center at Harvard from 1956 through 1972, and at Harvard and nationally he promoted a distinctly American approach to understanding China, one in which area studies were conceived of as directly contributing to the successful U.S. engagement in Asia. His students went on to teach at more than 125 universities in the United States and abroad.

As policy analyst, he became an early supporter of U.S. intervention against Japan in the 1930s, of halting aid to the Nationalist government after World War II, and of expanding contact with the People's Republic of China after 1949. Well known in policy and academic circles, he came to national attention during the period of McCarthyism, when he was attacked because of alleged procommunist sentiments and writings. Denied permission to enter Japan in 1951, he voluntarily appeared before the Senate Internal Security Committee (the McCarren Committee) in 1952 when it was investigating alleged communist infiltration of the Institute of Pacific Relations. He publicly defended several U.S. diplomats, including John Stewart Service and John Paton Davies, Jr., and academics, principal among them Owen Lattimore, in their loyalty and security hearings. Later, as an academic organizer, he helped bridge the divide in the China field created by the "who lost China" debate.

In the 1960s and 1970s Fairbank advocated expanding relations with the People's Republic of China and, after 1966, opposed U.S. intervention in what he believed to be a civil war in Vietnam. After retiring from Harvard, he devoted himself to completing eleven books on Chinese history and editing the *Cambridge History of China* and commenting on U.S.-China relations for the media. Throughout his life, Fairbank argued that recurrent tensions between China and the United States represented not merely a clash of state interests but a collision of civilizations. He believed that cultural differences can create international conflict and that an informed understanding of these differences, rather than cultural convergence, is a starting point for managed coexistence.

PAUL M. EVANS

See also China; China Hands; Davies, John Paton, Jr.; McCarthyism; Vietnam War

FURTHER READING

Evans, Paul M. *John Fairbank and the American Understanding of Modern China.* New York, 1988.
Fairbank, John K. *The United States and China*, 4th ed. Cambridge, Mass., 1979.
———. *Chinabound: A Fifty-Year Memoir.* New York, 1982.

FALKLAND ISLANDS

Located in the South Atlantic Ocean, off the southern coast of Argentina and 300 miles northeast of Cape Horn, this group of sparsely populated islands is known in Argentina as the Malvinas. Occupied by the British since 1833, they are also claimed by Argentina. On two occasions the United States has sided with Great Britain in a confrontation with Argentina over title and control. In the eighteenth century Great Britain and Spain squabbled over the islands but neither established a permanent settlement. In 1820, however, newly independent Argentina, heir to the Spanish claim, established a small colony. In 1831, when the Argentine governor seized three U.S. vessels on a charge of illegal seal hunting, the officer in command of a U.S. Navy frigate landed a small force, seized the governor and his men, and expelled them from the islands. The British, without objection from the United States, then established their own colony. Argentina protested both the U.S. action and the British occupation but had no power to do more. The United States chose not to consider the British occupation a violation of the noncolonization principle of the recently proclaimed Monroe Doctrine. In the great age of commercial sailing ships, the Falkland harbor of Stanley was a welcome refuge for vessels battered in the Cape Horn passage. In 1914, at the outset of World War I, the British defeated a German navy squadron at the Falklands and kept possession. The opening of the Panama Canal in the same year put an end to the strategic and commercial importance of the Falklands.

After World War II the Argentine government opened a political and diplomatic drive to regain the islands. The United States refused to take sides on the question of sovereignty and said only that territorial disputes should be settled without resort to force. The British settlement then numbered about 1,800 people, most of whom were engaged in sheep raising. U.S. neutrality supported that status quo. The United States also had no desire to irritate Great Britain, its closest European ally, by favoring a government with which Washington had seldom had good relations. Argentine efforts from the 1940s through the 1970s to negotiate a British withdrawal or gain effective support from the United States or the Organization of American States (OAS) were unavailing.

On 2 April 1982 the governing military junta of Argentina captured the Falkland Islands with a surprise attack against a minuscule defending force. The junta believed, correctly, that the reoccupation would be popular among the Argentine people, but it was catastrophically wrong in its assumption that the United States would either support Argentina or remain truly neutral. The junta may have expected a reward for cooperating with the United States in preparing the Contra insurgent forces in Nicaragua. Instead, the United States led the United Nations Security Council in passing a resolution calling for immediate Argentine withdrawal. Secretary of State Alexander M. Haig, Jr., set new records for long-distance shuttle diplomacy by flying between Washington, London, and Buenos Aires in a failed effort to secure Argentine withdrawal or prevent a war between Great Britain and Argentina. Meanwhile, the British dispatched an armada to retake the islands. British public opinion backed the uncompromising stand of Prime Minister Margaret Thatcher. American public and political opinion was almost completely behind Great Britain and against the Argentine junta, whose reputation suffered from its record of severe human rights violations.

As the British prepared to counterattack, the United States provided them with intelligence and logistical support. After hard fighting in May 1982 and serious losses on both sides, the British prevailed. The Argentine forces on the Falklands surrendered on 14 June. The war cemented a close personal relationship between Prime Minster Thatcher and President Ronald Reagan. Latin American criticism of the United States for siding with a European power was widespread but did not last. In Argentina, the discredited junta was replaced in October 1983 by a freely elected president, Raul Alfonsin, and the Falklands remained a British possession.

GADDIS SMITH

See also Argentina; Contras; Great Britain; Haig, Alexander Meigs, Jr.

FURTHER READING

Freedman, Lawrence, and Virginia Gamba-Stonehouse. *Signals of War: The Falklands Conflict of 1982*. Boston, 1990.
Haig, Alexander M. *Caveat: Realism, Reagan, and Foreign Policy*. New York, 1984.
Thatcher, Margaret, *The Downing Street Years*. New York, 1993.

FEDERALIST PAPERS

Essays written in 1787–1788 by Alexander Hamilton, John Jay, and James Madison and published to support ratification of the Constitution. Often reprinted in book form, these essays form the classic exposition of the new structure for a federal government, including the power to defend the nation's interests in international affairs. During the 1780s major issues in U.S. foreign policy went unresolved. Because the Articles of Confederation left the important government powers of raising taxes and regulating trade in the hands of the states, the federal government could not pay its foreign debts and the European powers regarded the new nation with contempt. Only the states could make commercial arrangements with foreign powers. The U.S. army was so weak that it could not protect new western settlements nor end British and Spanish control of frontier areas and waterways on U.S. soil.

The framers of the Constitution in 1787 took these problems into consideration and included several provisions to strengthen greatly the central government's hand in the conduct of foreign policy, including an independent executive department and a two-house Congress with power to tax and to regulate commerce with foreign nations. The Constitution also retained and, in some cases, redefined certain delegations of government power from the Articles of Confederation, such as the right to declare war and make peace, to make treaties with the advice and consent of two-thirds of the Senate, to send and receive ambassadors and other ministers and consuls, to coin money, and to regulate Indian affairs.

During the fall and spring of 1787–1788, special conventions met to consider ratification of the Constitution. The public debate became heated and Alexander Hamilton, a lawyer, delegate to the Constitutional Convention from New York, and strong defender of the document, became alarmed by the number of articles in the press expressing fear of a stronger central government. Believing a written rebuttal necessary, he secured help in the enterprise from John Jay, a fellow New Yorker and secretary for foreign affairs, and James Madison, a delegate to the Constitutional Convention from Virginia and one of its most articulate supporters. In all, they published eighty-five articles between 27 October 1787 and 28 May 1788 in such New York newspapers as the *Independent Journal, New York Packet, Daily Advertiser, and New York Journal and Daily Patriot Register.* Hamilton wrote fifty-one of the articles, Madison twenty-nine, and Jay, who was ill during the period, only five.

A number of the articles dealt with foreign policy issues. Madison (Numbers 14, 41, and 42) and Jay (Numbers 3, 4, and 5) argued that a stronger central government could protect the United States from attacks from the sea or from either British, Spanish, or Indian instigated hostilities on its western borders. It could better repel threats to its commerce as a result of the closing of the Mississippi River to U.S. ships by Spain and U.S. exclusion from navigation of the St. Lawrence River by Great Britain. A more energetic government would command respect abroad and be able to resolve treaty violations short of war. If it had a strong national government, moreover, the United States would not invite war through weakness but would discourage it through strength. All three authors stressed that an independent executive department would manage foreign relations more efficiently and could negotiate and enforce treaties more effectively. Jay (Number 64) and Hamilton (Numbers 69, 72, and 75) defended the power of the executive to make treaties with the consent of two-thirds of the Senate. They maintained that treaties were not simply laws but contracts with foreign powers that derived their force of law from the obligations of good faith between nations. To operate as law, treaties should be negotiated by the executive and approved by the Senate, thus gaining the respect of foreign powers.

Hamilton was the most ardent defender of congressional power to regulate foreign commerce and provide for a strong national defense (Numbers 11, 22–25, and 34). He asserted that given the new U.S. efforts to regulate international trade, the European powers would be worried about commercial competition from the United States. With U.S. control over foreign imports, European nations would be more likely to relax their own trade restrictions to prevent their exclusion from lucrative U.S. markets. Like Madison and Jay, Hamilton feared attacks from Native Americans, the Spanish, or the British along the western frontier. A strong and efficient central government could raise both an army and a navy competent to protect its commerce and territory from foreign threats.

The *Federalist Papers* first appeared in book form in June 1788 and served as an invaluable source of the Fed-

eralists' arguments in the pivotal ratifying conventions held in Virginia in June and New York in July. Today, the *Federalist Papers* rank as the nation's greatest classic of political thought.

REBECCA G. GOODMAN

See also Articles of Confederation; Constitution; Hamilton, Alexander; Jay, John; Madison, James

FURTHER READING

Elkins, Stanley and Eric McKitrick. *The Age of Federalism, The Early American Republic, 1788–1800.* New York, 1993.
Marks, Frederick W., III. *Independence on Trial: Foreign Affairs and the Making of the Constitution,* 2nd ed. Baton Rouge, La., 1986.
Morris, Richard B. *The Forging of the Union, 1781–1789.* New York, 1987.
Ostrom, Vincent. *The Political Theory of a Compound Republic: Designing the American Experiment.* Lincoln, Nebr., 1987.
Quinn, Frederick, editor. *The Federalist Papers Reader.* Washington, D.C., 1993.
Rossiter, Clinton. *Alexander Hamilton and the Constitution.* New York, 1964.

FEDERALIST PARTY

An early political faction that controlled the U.S. government from 1789 to 1801 and opposed the presidencies and states' rights policies of Thomas Jefferson and James Madison (1801–1817). Federalists championed a strong central government at home, and in foreign policy they sought accommodation with Great Britain.

President George Washington hoped that the new constitutional government that succeeded the Articles of Confederation in 1789 would be spared the political factionalism that might jeopardize his chances of creating a strong and stable government. In reality, however, partisan bickering and political alliances had been the hallmarks of the English colonies and the American states in rebellion. To Washington's dismay—but surely not to his surprise—history repeated itself: political wrangling became the order of the day in the nation's first capitals of New York and Philadelphia, and political parties were born.

While questions such as the president's discretionary power caused divisions from the beginning, a fundamental reason for the rise of the Federalist Party was the financial program supported by Alexander Hamilton. Hamilton, the intellectually gifted secretary of the treasury, believed that the United States had to have both good credit and reliable revenue. Toward these ends, he called for the creation of a national debt, the establishment of a national bank, and tariffs on imports. Like-minded individuals, Washington included, embraced Hamilton's vision.

On the other hand, critics led by Congressman James Madison argued that the Constitution did not sanction a national bank and maintained that speculators would be the chief beneficiaries of Hamilton's debt design. Madison and Secretary of State Thomas Jefferson expressed concern that Great Britain's domination of the new republic's trade would give the island kingdom excessive influence in the United States. These Virginians, who led the Republican faction, agreed that the United States should seek a balance between Great Britain and France by encouraging Franco-American commerce.

With Washington's assistance and with compromise, Hamilton's ideas generally became law: a national debt was created, the Bank of the United States was chartered, and trade with the French never successfully challenged Great Britain's stranglehold on the U.S. market. Indeed, to preserve peace with Great Britain and to assure the continuance of Anglo-American commerce—that is, to provide the government with the bulk of its revenue—the Washington administration subordinated U.S. interests to Great Britain in the Jay Treaty of 1794 in order to keep Anglo-American relations peaceful. While placating the British, Jay's treaty infuriated the French and led directly to the XYZ Affair which, in turn, sparked the Quasi-War with France from 1797 to 1800.

The Federalists's successes proved their undoing. Although it became law, the widely unpopular Jay Treaty crystallized opposition to the emerging Federalist Party, and the taxes levied to finance the undeclared war with France provoked further resentment. Finally, the Quasi-War split Federalist ranks when more moderate Federalists sided with President John Adams's peace policies and more bellicose Federalists attempted to undermine a peaceful resolution of Franco-American differences. In the election of 1800, having proved themselves their own worst enemies, the Federalists and Adams still lost only narrowly to Jefferson and the Republicans. The Federalists, however, never regained control of the presidency or the Congress.

As Jefferson and his party won the support of more Americans, the Federalists, once identified with New England rather than with the nation, steadily lost influence and the voters' allegiance. With the election of 1816, the party passed into history. Still, the Federalists had left their imprimatur on the United States: Hamilton's financial program remained largely intact; the national judiciary rested in the Federalists's hands; and the Federalists could point with pride to the peaceful political transition to the Republicans that had occurred in 1801.

CLIFFORD L. EGAN

See also Adams, John; French Revolution; Hamilton, Alexander; Jay's Treaty; Jefferson, Thomas; Madison, James; Republican Party; XYZ Affair

FURTHER READING
Ammon, Harry. *The Genet Mission*. New York, 1973.
Banner, James M., Jr. *To the Hartford Convention: The Federalists and the Origins of Party Politics in Massachusetts, 1789-1815*. New York, 1970.
Elkins, Stanley, and Eric McKitrick. *The Age of Federalism*. New York, 1993.
Fischer, David Hacket. *The Revolution of American Conservatism: The Federalist Party in the Era of Jeffersonian Democracy*. New York, 1965.
Rose, Lisle A. *Prologue to Democracy: The Federalists in the South, 1789-1800*. Lexington, Ky., 1968.

FEDERAL RESERVE BANK OF NEW YORK

The most important of twelve federal reserve banks which, along with the Board of Governors in Washington, make up the Federal Reserve System. That system was founded as a result of the Federal Reserve Act of 1913. The unique importance of the New York Fed (as it is commonly known) lies in the fact that New York is the scene of almost all large-scale trading in financial assets in the United States; this means that, between meetings of the Federal Open Market Committee, the New York Fed manages open market policy, which is the core of monetary policy. (Open market policy is the purchase or sale of U.S. Treasury securities by the New York Fed, with the goal of increasing or decreasing the U.S. money supply). Since foreign exchange trading is also concentrated in New York, foreign exchange market operations of the Federal Reserve System and of the U.S. government are also carried out through the New York Fed. The New York Fed has a large international research division and maintains day-to-day contact with major foreign central banks. It also provides deposit and custodial facilities through which foreign central banks hold exchange reserves in the form of dollars. The New York Fed has been centrally involved in many international financial crises. During the early 1930s, for example, it made loans to European countries in an attempt to sustain the gold standard. At the beginning of the 1960s, the vice president of the New York Fed, Charles Coombs, was primarily responsible for negotiating the creation of the Central Bank Reciprocal Currency Arrangement (generally known as the Federal Reserve Swap System), which allows the central banks of various industrialized countries to borrow foreign exchange reserves from each other.

ROBERT M. DUNN, JR.

See also Balance of Payments and Balance of Trade; Bretton Woods System; British Loan 1946; Dillon, Clarence Douglas; European Bank for Reconstruction and Development; Foreign Direct Investment; Gold Standard; Group of Seven; International Bank for Reconstruction and Development; International Monetary Fund; Monnet, Jean; New International Economic Order; Treasury, U.S. Department of

FURTHER READING

Board of Governors of the Federal Reserve. *The Federal Reserve System: Purposes and Functions.* 7th ed. Washington, D.C., 1984.
Federal Reserve Bank of New York. *Annual Report.*

FENIANS

A secret society of Irish revolutionaries founded in Paris in 1858 and named for the mythical warriors of the legendary third-century Irish leader Finn MacCool. In Ireland they were organized as the Irish Republican Brotherhood and in the United States as the Fenians. The Fenians sought to end British rule in Ireland. The "to Canada" policy split the American Fenians movement into irreconcilable factions. The Fenians hoped to secure territory in Canada for a Fenians Republic, exacerbate U.S.-British tensions, and improve the prospects for a successful revolution in Ireland by embroiling British forces in Canada, possibly in a war with the United States. Fenians attacks launched at Campobello, New Brunswick, from Vermont, and at Fort Erie, Ontario, from Buffalo, New York, in 1866, 1870, and 1871, ended as melancholy failures.

Fenians success depended on their hope that President Andrew Johnson, and later President Ulysses S. Grant, would not enforce U.S. neutrality laws, which outlawed raising armies that might be used against another nation. Although Johnson and Secretary of State William Seward were both ardent annexationists, including Canadian annexations, they chose to enforce the neutrality laws, thereby dooming Fenians hopes. Both men procrastinated about enforcing these laws because President Johnson's political survival was linked to continued support in New York State, which had a large and well organized Irish-American community that Johnson believed supported the Fenians strategy. By enforcing these neutrality laws, however, the United States improved its chances of negotiating other outstanding issues with Great Britain, including the *Alabama* Claims, which dealt with damages inflicted by British-built Confederate ships on U.S. ships during the Civil War. The Fenians continued to play an active role in Irish-American politics and in Ireland, not only in the 1867 uprising in Ireland, but in the Easter uprising in 1919, the War against England in 1920–1922, and the subsequent Civil War in Ireland.

JOHN MCLEAN

See also Alabama Claims; Canada; Ireland; Seward, William Henry

FURTHER READING

Castel, Albert. *The Presidency of Andrew Johnson.* Lawrence, Kans., 1979.
Jenkins, Brian. *Fenians and Anglo-American Relations During Reconstruction.* Ithaca, N.Y., 1969.
Stuart, Reginald. *U.S. Expansion and British North America, 1715–1871.* Chapel Hill, N.C., 1988.

FIJI

See Appendix 2

FILIBUSTERS

Nineteenth century adventurers who operated outside U.S. and international law and against public declarations of U.S. presidents. Sometimes from U.S. ports, they planned and launched military invasions of nations, especially in Latin America, that were at peace with the United States. Activities by filibusters were never successful over the long-term. Their ventures heightened sectional tensions over the expansion of slave territory and created foreign relations problems for the United States, Spain, England, France, and countries in Central and South America. At the peak of their activity in the 1850s, filibuster expeditions prompted U.S. army and navy counterattacks.

In the decade before the Civil War, thousands of U.S. citizens launched expeditions against Canada, Cuba, Ecuador, Hawaii, Honduras, Mexico, and Nicaragua. The excitement, adventure, and considerable newspaper coverage of the filibuster operations captured the attention and won the sympathy of many U.S. citizens. The motives of filibusters varied, ranging from ideological to fanciful. Some filibusters were committed to the expansion of slavery into new territory. Others wished to spread democracy and republican government, and some wished to demonstrate racial and political superiority. A number of filibusters hoped to satisfy dreams of glory and wealth.

In 1806 Francisco de Miranda, a Venezuelan expatriot aided by U.S. volunteers and financing, attempted twice, unsuccessfully, to spark a democratic revolution in Venezuela. The same year, Aaron Burr's poorly planned attempt to gain control of Mexico failed to spread beyond U.S. territory. A Venezuelan-born Cuban aristocrat, Narciso Lopez, supported by Mississippi Governor John A. Quitman, led expeditions to Cuba in 1850 and 1851 with the intention of freeing Cuba from the Spanish empire and annexing the island to the United States. Spain's capture and subsequent killing of Lopez temporarily halted filibuster activity against Cuba. Mexico became the new object of filibustering when José Carvajal conducted a raid on the northeastern part of the country in the fall of 1851. William Walker, the most famous of all filibusters, first led hapless attacks against Mexico in 1853 and 1854. Two years later, he achieved short-lived success after gaining control of Nicaragua and appointing himself president. His autocratic rule, which included the legal restoration of slavery, lasted only months and ended when the U.S. Navy forced his surrender. Walker's attempt in 1860 to capture Honduras also failed, and he was killed by a Honduran firing squad.

Filibustering was not an aberration but, rather, a part of U.S. territorial expansion and belief in manifest destiny. Because filibustering became associated with proslavery elements, controversy surrounding the expeditions intensified sectionalism in U.S. political discourse.

BRUCE D. MACTAVISH

See also Burr, Aaron; Cuba; Manifest Destiny; Mexico; Slave Trade and Slavery; Walker, William

FURTHER READING

Brown, Charles Henry. *Agents of Manifest Destiny: The Lives and Times of the Filibusters.* Chapel Hill, N.C., 1980.
May, Robert E. *The Southern Dream of a Caribbean Empire, 1854–1861.* Baton Rouge, La., 1973.
———. "Young American Males and Filibustering in the Age of Manifest Destiny: The U.S. Army as a Cultural Mirror." *Journal of American History* 78 (December 1991): 857–886.

FILLMORE, MILLARD

(*b.* 7 January 1800; *d.* 8 March 1874)

Thirteenth president of the United States (1850–1853). Born in Locks, N.Y., he was admitted to the bar in 1823 and began his political career as an Anti-Mason. In 1834, Fillmore joined the Whig Party. Serving in Congress from 1833 to 1835 and again from 1837 to 1843, he became the Whig leader in the House of Representatives. As chairman of the Ways and Means Committee, he drafted a tariff bill in 1842 raising import duties on manufactured products. Two years later, Fillmore ran unsuccessfully for the governorship of New York. To satisfy the Henry Clay wing of the party, which wanted a tariff to fund internal improvements to aid trade and commerce, the Whigs selected Fillmore in 1848 as their vice presidential candidate to run with General Zachary Taylor. When President Taylor died of typhoid fever on 9 July 1850, Fillmore became president. He moved quickly to appoint a new cabinet, which included Daniel Webster as secretary of state (1850–1852). Although Taylor had not supported Clay's compromise bill of 1850, designed to end the sectional disputes over the extension of slavery into the territories acquired through the Mexican War, Fillmore did, and he signed it into law. Fillmore's enforcement of the Fugitive Slave Act, however, cost him support with the anti-slavery wing of his party.

Fillmore's foreign policy was largely restrained. The most significant event in foreign affairs during his presidency was Commodore Matthew C. Perry's first visit to Japan, which led to the opening of relations with that country. Generally, however, Fillmore was preoccupied with domestic issues, which were increasingly fractious in the years that led to the Civil War. He did not support the filibustering expeditions launched from U.S. soil against Latin American countries. He and Webster expressed sympathy toward Hungary's attempt to gain its independence from Austria, but when the exiled Hungarian patriot Louis Kossuth visited the United States in 1851 looking for support, the Fillmore administration informed him that it would not interfere in the affairs of Europe. Due to the split between the slavery and anti-slavery factions within the party, the Whigs declined to renominate Fillmore as their presidential candidate in 1852. In 1856 he was the presidential candidate of the American "Know-Nothing" Party, but he ran a poor third. After this loss, Fillmore returned to Buffalo, N.Y., where he lived until his death.

LOUIS R. SMITH, JR.

See also Clay, Henry; Filibusters; Hungary; Japan; Perry, Matthew Calbraith; Presidency; Taylor, Zachary; Webster, Daniel

FURTHER READING

Grayson, Benson Lee. *The Unknown President: The Administration of President Millard Fillmore.* Washington, D.C., 1981.
Perkins, Bradford. *The Cambridge History of American Foreign Relations: The Creation of a Republican Empire, 1776–1865.* New York, 1993.
Smith, Elbert B. *The Presidencies of Zachary Taylor and Millard Fillmore.* Lawrence, Kans., 1988.

FILM COMPANIES

See Broadcast and Film Companies

FINLAND

Located in northern Europe, bordering the Baltic Sea between Russia and Sweden. The United States recognized Finland and established relations with Helsinki in 1919, two years after it achieved independence from Russia. Finland was convulsed in a vicious civil war shortly after independence, at which time the United States provided food relief. By the 1930s the Finnish economy had a favorable balance of trade and Finland was able to honor its debts; it was highly regarded in the United States.

The American public sympathized with Finland during its brutal Winter War against the Soviet Union in 1940–1941, and Washington maintained friendly relations despite Finland's growing alliance with Nazi Germany. When Finland resumed hostilities against the Soviets, however, in concert with the German invasion of the Soviet Union in the summer of 1941, President Franklin D. Roosevelt's administration assessed that U.S. strategic interests had shifted and U.S.-Finnish relations had become strained. As early as August 1941 U.S. Secretary of State Cordell Hull had repeatedly warned Helsinki that German-Finnish cooperation could result in a severing of relations. When the United States entered World War II, the Allies pressured Washington to act against Finland. Finnish consulates in the United States were closed in August 1942, but in September, Finnish President Risto Ryti told Secretary Hull that Finland was determined to follow its pro-German policy. Another warning by Hull in 1943, when the tide of war had turned against Finland (and its German ally), raised a flurry of debate in Finnish political circles over approaching the Soviets for peace. In June 1944, however, President Ryti personally pledged to Adolf Hitler that his country would not make a separate peace with Moscow. In response, Washington broke diplomatic relations and recalled its ambassador but did not resort to a declaration of war. Finland's geostrategic status proved to be a diplomatic asset as that country was chosen to be the host for the Cold War deliberations in the 1970s, which culminated in the signing of the Helsinki Final Act and the creation of the Conference on Security and Cooperation in Europe (CSCE) in 1975. The CSCE established a brake on East-West rivalry in Europe by laying down the first formal recognition of Europe's postwar borders.

Washington and Helsinki resumed diplomatic ties after the war, and the United States offered assistance in 1947 through the European Recovery Plan (ERP). Despite Finland's dire economic situation, its government rejected participation in the ERP because of objections from Moscow. Finland, however, was able to secure substantial loans from the U.S. Export-Import Bank, receiving $200 million to help rebuild its industrial base and repair its war-ravaged economy. Finland's World War II defeat at the hands of the Soviets had placed the country firmly in Moscow's sphere of influence. In 1948 Helsinki felt compelled to sign a treaty with the USSR that imposed neutrality on Finland and limited Finnish sovereignty in foreign relations and defense matters. This pattern of indirect Soviet dominance—as opposed to direct military and political manipulation in Eastern Europe—came to be known as "Finlandization."

Because of the geopolitical realties of the Cold War, the United States soon came to recognize Finland's precarious position between the two superpowers and accepted Finland's officially neutral status. The U.S. government embarked on a policy of refraining from disrupting the delicate Finno-Soviet relationship, while upholding Finnish sovereignty and independence and expanding Finnish contacts with the West. However, Finland's proximity to Scandinavian members of the North Atlantic Treaty Organization (NATO) in effect provided the country with a measure of security in that the United States would not allow Soviet aggression in a strategically important region. Some U.S. policymaking circles were critical of Finland's professed neutrality, while it, in their view, benefited as a "free rider;" "Finlandization" soon became a disparaging term in the Cold War lexicon for countries who insisted on being "fence-sitters." But given the reality of the situation, successive U.S. administrations accepted Finland's status as necessary for that country's strategic well-being.

During the Cold War period, the cordiality of U.S.-Finnish relations gave rise to increased economic cooperation. Finland borrowed extensively from U.S. financial institutions for investment in its infrastructure, agriculture, and industry. The number of Finnish firms investing in the United States expanded from five in 1970 to 350 by 1992, making the United States the second-largest recipient (after Sweden) of Finnish investments. The collapse of the Soviet Union in 1991 allowed Finland to pursue a more independent defense policy. In 1992 Finland finalized a deal with the United States for the acquisition of U.S. fighter planes, and in 1994 it opted to join NATO's Partnership for Peace program. In December 1995, Finnish troops in Bosnia-Herzegovina as part of the United Nations peacekeeping force came under U.S. command as part of NATO's Implementation Force (IFOR).

DAVID P. AUGUSTYN

See also Helsinki Accords; Russia and the Soviet Union; Self-Determination; War Debt of World War I; World War I; World War II

FURTHER READING

Kirby, D. G. *Finland in the Twentieth Century*, Minneapolis, Minn., 1979.
Meditz, Sandra W., and Eric Solsten. *Finland: A Country Study*. Area Handbook Series. Washington, D.C., 1990.
Rinehart, Robert. *Finland and the United States: Diplomatic Relations Through Seventy Years*. Washington, D.C., 1993.
Scott, Franklin D. *Scandinavia*. Cambridge, Mass., 1975.
Solheim, Bruce Olav. *The Nordic Nexus: A Lesson in Peaceful Security*. Westport, Conn., 1984.

FISH, HAMILTON

(*b.* 3 August 1808; *d.* 6 September 1893)

Politician and secretary of state, 1869–1877. Born into a socially prominent New York family and named for his father's friend Alexander Hamilton, Fish graduated from Columbia University in 1827 and was admitted to the bar in 1830. A conservative Whig, he served in Congress (1843–1845), and was later elected lieutenant governor (1847–1848) and governor (1849–1851) of New York. He favored internal improvements and public education. As a U.S. senator (1851–1857), he opposed the extension of slavery and with the collapse of the Whig Party, reluctantly joined the new Republican Party in 1856. During the Civil War, Fish served on the Union Defense Committee and as U.S. Commissioner for the Relief of Prisoners of War. After the war, he befriended General Ulysses S. Grant, leading to his appointment as secretary of state when Grant became president.

As secretary of state (1869–1877), Fish became the dominant figure in Grant's cabinet; his extensive diary, now in the Library of Congress, provides important insights into the inner workings of the Grant administration. Although he was not experienced in foreign affairs, Fish was an able administrator of the Department of State and an even-tempered diplomatist. Exasperated by the importunities of office seekers, he eventually instituted written examinations to cull out unqualified candidates seeking consular appointments. Although expressing mild reservations, Fish supported Grant's attempts in 1869 and 1871 to annex the Dominican Republic, which led to a bitter dispute with Massachusetts Senator Charles Sumner, chairman of the Senate Foreign Relations Committee. Fish convinced Grant not to recognize Cuban belligerency in 1869 in its struggle for independence, and played a key role in avoiding war four years later when Spain seized the *Virginius*, a ship flying the U.S. flag and carrying volunteers to fight against the Spanish in Cuba. He failed in efforts to win rights from Colombia and Nicaragua to build a canal across the isthmus. Fish's greatest success came in negotiations with Great Britain to settle the *Alabama* claims issue arising from British failure to prevent the Confederacy from obtaining warships in Great Britain during the Civil War. The result was the Treaty of Washington (1871), which significantly reduced tensions between the United States and Great Britain. In 1870, Fish sought to prevent the extension of the Franco-Prussian War to Asia, while demonstrating his hostility to revolutionary change by opposing the Paris Commune uprising that followed in 1871. In the Pacific, Fish maintained American treaty rights in China and negotiated a significant treaty of commercial reciprocity with Hawai'i (1875). He retired from public life in 1877.

DAVID L. WILSON

See also Alabama Claims; Colombia; Cuba; Dominican Republic; Grant, Ulysses Simpson; Hawai'i; Panama and Panama Canal; Spain; Sumner, Charles

FURTHER READING
Chapin, James B. "Hamilton Fish and American Expansion." In Merli, Frank J. and Theodore A. Wilson, eds., *Makers of American Diplomacy*. vol. 1, pp. 223–251, New York, 1974.
Nevins, Allan. *Hamilton Fish: The Inner History of the Grant Administration*. New York, 1936.

FISHERIES

Sites of commercial fishing activity and often beyond the control of government, which have been a source of diplomatic conflict throughout U.S. history. Perhaps the most lengthy dispute centered on access to the great cod fisheries off Newfoundland, but technological advances, changes in international law, and increasing international competition have caused many other crises over access to fisheries throughout the twentieth century.

In negotiations leading to the Treaty of Paris of 1783, John Adams of Massachusetts worked hard to protect the rights of his fellow New Englanders to fish freely off Newfoundland. He won the "right" of access to the high seas that fishers of both countries frequented and the "liberty" of U.S. citizens to fish within a three-mile territorial limit. In practical terms, the treaty preserved the status quo, but in later years definitions of the terms, rights, and liberties would cause contention.

Anglo-American rivalry in the early 1800s insured that access to Newfoundland's fisheries would remain on the diplomatic agenda. Negotiators of the Treaty of Ghent, which ended the War of 1812, failed in their effort to restore U.S. liberty to fish in Canada's inshore waters, and New England fishing boats were seized. To prevent escalation of the dispute, Great Britain and the United States agreed in the Convention of 1818 to grant the right to fish certain inshore areas forever and to revoke other rights. In addition, U.S. fishers won the right to land in certain areas to dry and cure fish. The rules drafted during that convention were in force for most of the century.

In the 1850s, British diplomats offered new interpretations of the terms of the Convention of 1818 that threatened to restrict U.S. liberties. In the ensuing negotiations leading to the Marcy-Elgin agreement of 1854, the British agreed to restore all U.S. liberties to inshore waters in return for a reciprocal trade agreement with Canada. The United States revoked the treaty in 1866 in retaliation for presumed British support of the Confederacy.

The confederation of most of the British colonies, excepting Newfoundland, into the Dominion of Canada in 1867 led to a showdown between Canada and the United States over access to Canada's inshore fisheries. In the Treaty of Washington in 1871, the United States and Great Britain agreed to restore reciprocity on fish exports and some fishing rights for ten years in exchange for a cash payment that an arbitration panel set at $5,500,000. Congress was not pleased with this arrangement, and in 1885 the United States abrogated the treaty, leaving U.S. fishers clamoring again for access to these rich Canadian waters.

Under pressure to reach an accommodation, in 1888 the Bayard-Chamberlain Treaty emerged from the Joint High Commission. This exhaustive agreement settled a number of disagreements that had lingered since 1818, if not since 1783, including procedures and territorial limits that U.S. fishers had to obey, and it granted Canadians access to U.S. territorial waters. The treaty allowed U.S. fishers more rights inshore in Canada if Congress removed tariffs on Canadian fish products. In the midst of a presidential election campaign, the Republican Senate killed the treaty, partly to spite President Grover Cleveland. In the interim, Bayard had established a modus vivendi that prevailed for many years.

In 1905, years of frustration finally culminated in the retaliation by Newfoundland against the United States for congressional dismantling of a commercial reciprocity treaty. The colony's new rules made fishing uneconomical for New Englanders, but the U.S. government was powerless to retaliate. With such a wide gulf between them, in 1907 the United States and Great Britain pledged to arbitrate their dispute before the Permanent Court of Arbitration at the Hague, and they signed a formal agreement to that effect in 1909. In September 1910, the tribunal authored a compromise that resolved most outstanding disagreements and granted Britain the right to enact reasonable regulations. All parties accepted the ruling, which finally removed this impediment to better Anglo-American relations.

The twentieth century brought many more fisheries into diplomatic agendas. Turning to the Pacific, Canada and the United States agreed to regulate the halibut fishery in 1922 and salmon fishery in 1929. After World War II, improved technology and greater demand encouraged fishers to travel great distances, which sparked more crises, many of which were multilateral. Seeking to protect their fishing industries, many countries claimed 200-mile coastal fishery zones and the right to regulate the passage of foreign vessels through them. The United States often opposed such infringements, as the "tuna wars" of the 1970s with Peru and Ecuador demonstrated. The United States established a 200-mile zone around its borders, however, and withheld access to the zone as a diplomatic tool, especially in matters of environmental protection. As environmental awareness grew, many nations joined forces to stop destructive practices such as dolphin capture in tuna nets. It became apparent that fisheries faced destruction from a lack of cooperative regulation. This threat became clear in the spring of 1995, when Canada accused Spain of rapacious fishing just beyond Canada's 200-mile zone. Despite international law weighing on its side, Spain eventually ceded to Canada, but the brush with war spurred the United Nations to oversee the completion in August 1995 of a global agreement on fisheries just beyond or straddling the 200-mile zones.

KURK DORSEY

See also American Revolution; Canada; Environment; Freedom of the Seas; Great Britain; Law of the Sea; Whaling

FURTHER READING

Innis, Harold. *The Cod Fisheries: The History of an International Economy.* New Haven, Conn., 1940.
Sand, Peter H., ed. *The Effectiveness of International Environmental Agreements: A Survey of Existing Legal Instruments.* Cambridge, England, 1992.

FIVE-POWER TREATY

See Washington Conference on Limitation of Armaments

FLETCHER, HENRY PRATHER

(*b.* 10 April 1873; *d.* 10 July 1959)

A career diplomat and official of the Republican Party who advocated U.S. overseas investments as beneficial to all peoples. He served in China, in various Latin American posts, and as ambassador to Mexico, Belgium, and Italy. A conservative and internationalist, Fletcher urged "dollar diplomacy" in Latin America and Asia, and he believed that the United States had the right to intervene in the affairs of Latin American nations to protect U.S. interests and to maintain stability in the Western Hemisphere. Of his twin careers in foreign policy and national Republican Party politics, Fletcher stated, "Diplomacy is just practical politics on an international plane; I find lots of similarities between the two fields." Born in Greencastle, Pennsylvania, he became a court reporter, read law, and was admitted to the bar in 1894. In 1898, he became a private in Theodore Roosevelt's Rough Riders and served in Cuba during the war with Spain. Fletcher also served in the Philippines during the war of 1899–1901. President Theodore Roosevelt appointed him second secretary to the legation in Havana (1902–1903). He filled the same post in Peking from 1903 to 1905, was secretary of the legation to Portugal from 1905 to 1907, and was chargé d'affaires in Peking from 1907 to 1909. An ardent advocate of U.S. investments abroad, Fletcher developed lasting associations while serving in China with Wall Street barons such as Edward H. Harriman, Thomas Lamont, and J. P. Morgan.

Fletcher was named minister to Chile in 1909 and, despite his solid Republican credentials, was reappointed ambassador by President Woodrow Wilson. During his Chilean tenure (1909–1916), Fletcher helped the Guggenheim interests and Bethlehem Steel achieve dominant positions in the copper and steel industries. In 1916 Fletcher was appointed ambassador to Mexico where he disagreed with President Wilson's cautious policies toward the Carranza government. He resigned from diplomatic service after a brief stint as head of Latin American Affairs in the State Department, saying, "I wasn't particularly keen about the League of Nations." When Republicans returned to the White House, Fletcher served as undersecretary of state (1921–1922), ambassador to Belgium (1922–1924), and ambassador to Italy (1924-1929). Fletcher was frustrated by Benito Mussolini's fascist government because of two issues: procrastination on payment of war debts, and what Fletcher viewed as the "systematic impressment" into the Italian armed forces of Italian Americans, who were visiting friends and relatives in Italy. In 1925 Fletcher participated in negotiations leading to the Volpi-Mellon agreement for refinancing Italian war debt, and, while uneasy about the Italian dictator's style, Fletcher believed Mussolini to be friendly toward the United States and a positive, stabilizing force in Italy.

Fletcher headed the U.S. delegation to the Fifth Pan-American Conference (1923), served on the delegation to the Sixth Pan-American Conference (1928), and led the delegation to the International Conference for the Protection of Library and Artistic Property in Rome (1928). In November 1928 he toured Latin American capitals on a goodwill tour with President-elect Herbert Hoover as a confidential adviser, and in 1930, Hoover appointed Fletcher to the Commission on Conditions in Haiti, headed by W. Cameron Forbes. The Forbes Commission made recommendations that led to an agreement in 1932 that eventually ended U.S. military occupation of Haiti. Fletcher faulted his government for a "lack of foresight as far as 'Haitianization' is concerned." Fletcher chaired the U.S. Tariff Commission (1930–1931) and served as Chairman of the Republican National Committee (1934–1936). He remained general counsel of the party until 1944. He acted as a special adviser to the secretary of state in July 1944 and participated as a delegate to the Dumbarton Oaks Conference that year.

MICHAEL J. DEVINE

See also Chile; Haiti; Harriman, Edward Henry; Hoover, Herbert; Italy; League of Nations; Mexico; Roosevelt, Theodore

FURTHER READING

DeConde, Alexander. *Half Bitter, Half Sweet: An Excursion into Italian-American History.* New York, 1971.
Fletcher, Henry P. "Quo Vadis, Haiti?". *Foreign Affairs* 8 (1930): 533–548.
Schmitz, David F. *The United States and Fascist Italy, 1922–1940.* Chapel Hill, N.C., 1988.
Spector, Robert M. *W. Cameron Forbes and the Hoover Commission to Haiti, 1930.* Washington, D.C., 1985.

FLEXIBLE RESPONSE

The basic strategic concept of the North Atlantic Treaty Organization (NATO) after 1967. A strictly defensive doctrine, it calls for a flexible range of military responses, both conventional and nuclear, to all levels of aggression or coercion aimed at members of the NATO alliance. These responses are intended first to deter aggression and preserve peace; but if deterrence fails, they should also maintain the security of the NATO area by defeating an attack at whatever level it occurs. During the Cold War, the strategy of flexible response sought primarily to deter a Soviet-led Warsaw Pact invasion of Western Europe—particularly after Moscow's nuclear build-up appeared to undermine the credibility of the U.S. extended nuclear deterrent. NATO's conventional forces contributed to war prevention by ensuring that no potential attacker could hope to achieve easy conquest or territorial gains. At the same time, the deployment of U.S. tactical (and later, intermediate-range) nuclear weapons in Western Europe, along with the presence of U.S. troops near the East-West border as a potential "trip wire," meant that any conventional conflict had the inherent potential for nuclear escalation—up to and including general nuclear war—making the risks of any type of aggression appear incalculable and hence unacceptable to a rational adversary. In this way, flexible response combined two mutually reinforcing deterrent threats: the threat to deny an aggressor's war aims by conventional means, backed up with the threat to inflict severe (nuclear) punishment if an initial conventional attack proved successful.

Flexible response also served as the basis of the transatlantic security bargain. It was tacitly understood that if deterrence were ever to fail, the United States and its West European allies would have divergent strategic interests, with Washington seeking to delay nuclear escalation as long as possible and the Europeans favoring the early use of nuclear weapons to halt an attack and thus preclude the devastating consequences of a protracted conventional war. These tensions threatened to fracture the alliance. Flexible response offered a way out of this dilemma by not spelling out the circumstances under which NATO would resort to nuclear weapons in the event of a Warsaw Pact invasion. While the alliance would defend initially against an attack with conventional means, the aggressor would face a finite risk of nuclear escalation if NATO's conventional defenses were overrun. This inherent ambiguity served deterrence by increasing the uncertainty in the mind of a potential adversary; it also enhanced alliance cohesion by allowing the United States and its European allies to interpret the doctrine in ways each found most reassuring. As a result, flexible response functioned successfully both as a military strategy aimed at war prevention and as a political device for managing sensitive and divisive issues of shared nuclear risk.

The dramatic events of 1989–1990, when Soviet control over the Warsaw Pact nations crumbled, prompted

NATO to adapt the doctrine of flexible response to the transformed European security environment. Meeting in London in July 1990, allied leaders launched a comprehensive review of NATO strategy that culminated in the adoption of a new "Alliance Strategic Concept" at the November 1991 Rome Summit. This document concluded that while NATO still required a small nuclear deterrent force based in Europe to "provide an essential political and military link between the European and North American members of the Alliance," the circumstances under which any use of nuclear weapons might have to be contemplated had become "even more remote." The revision of flexible response permitted a substantial reduction of NATO's substrategic nuclear forces. All nuclear artillery shells and short- and intermediate-range nuclear missiles were removed from Europe, so that the only U.S. nuclear weapons remaining were gravity bombs carried on dual-capable aircraft. Given the lack of a near-term military threat to NATO, these weapons play a largely political and symbolic role in reinforcing the transatlantic security partnership.

JONATHAN B. TUCKER

See also Cold War; North Atlantic Treaty Organization; Nuclear Weapons and Strategy

FURTHER READING

Cordier, Sherwood S. *The Defense of NATO's Northern Front and U.S. Military Policy*. Lanham, Md. 1989.

Killebrew, Robert B. *Conventional Defense and Total Deterrence: Assessing NATO's Strategic Options*. Wilmington, Del., 1986.

FLORIDA

Admitted to the Union as a state in 1845 but a significant region prior to that year as a peninsula occupying a strategic location along the eastern boundary of the Gulf of Mexico, separated from the island of Cuba by a narrow waterway known as the Straits of Florida. For centuries the Floridas (as they were then known) were crucial to the Spanish colonial empire in the New World. In the early years of the Republic, they also became vital to the interests of the United States, both as a natural appendage to its territory and as a haven for runaway slaves and marauding Indians who attacked U.S. settlements and then returned to the safety of Spanish territory. Some in the United States believed that France had included West Florida—the panhandle section of Florida extending westward from the Apalachicola River to the Mississippi—in the Louisiana Purchase. Unable to resolve that question through negotiations, the United States occupied much of West Florida in 1810 and annexed it in 1812. Concerned with growing British interest in both East and West Florida, in 1811 Congress

Modified from *A History of American Foreign Policy,* Alexander DeConde, Volume I. ©1963, 1971, 1978 Charles Scribner's Sons. Used by permission of Charles Scribner's Sons, an imprint of Simon & Schuster Macmillan.

passed the No-Transfer Resolution, which stipulated that the United States would not allow Spain to cede any portion of the Floridas to another nation. During the War of 1812, the United States also seized East Florida, but subsequently returned it to Spain. A crisis was precipitated in 1818 when U.S. troops again entered East Florida, this time led by Major General Andrew Jackson. Spain's difficulty in controlling its New World colonies, many of which were then seeking independence, encouraged the Spanish to negotiate. The Adams-Onís Treaty, signed by representatives of the United States and Spain in 1819, included, among other provisions, a resolution of the Florida controversy. In that agreement, the United States returned East Florida to Spain, who then ceded it back to the United States. Spain also recognized the earlier annexation of West Florida by the United States. As part of the settlement, the United States agreed to pay up to $5 million in claims of United States citizens against the Spanish government.

RICHARD C. ROHRS

See also Adams-Onís Treaty; Jackson, Andrew; Louisiana Purchase; No-Transfer Principle; Spain; War of 1812

FURTHER READING

Brooks, Philip Coolidge. *Diplomacy and the Borderlands: The Adams-Onís Treaty of 1819*. Berkeley, Calif., 1939.

Cox, Isaac J. *The West Florida Controversy, 1798–1813: A Study in American Diplomacy*. Baltimore, Md., 1918.

Jahoda, Gloria. *Florida: A Bicentennial History*. New York, 1976.

Perkins, Bradford. "The Creation of a Republican Empire, 1776–1865." Vol. 1 of *The Cambridge History of American Foreign Relations*. Warren I. Cohen, ed. 4 vols. New York, 1993.

Waciuma, Wanjoni. *Intervention in Spanish Floridas, 1801–1813: A Study in Jeffersonian Foreign Policy*. Boston, Mass., 1976.

FOOD AND AGRICULTURAL COMPANIES

Great empires and nations historically have measured their strength not only by their weaponry, but also by their self-sufficiency and wealth in agriculture. The more productive a country was in agriculture, the more resources it could release to support industry and commerce. For the most part, only a small portion of what was produced locally was traded, although agricultural trade was common enough for the early nineteenth-century economist David Ricardo to use, as his example of comparative advantage, the trading of Portuguese wines for English cloth. Countries fought over land and agricultural resources. The desire to avoid such hostilities and ensure access to staple food supplies was a principal motivation for establishing trade rules.

Today, agricultural markets are being opened up to international trade as never before. This liberalization of agricultural trade works in favor of the United States, which has abundant resources of land and technology to produce food. Surplus-producing countries, such as the United States, gain power to purchase industrial and other products and may also use food as a weapon to achieve specific foreign policy objectives. Conversely, countries experiencing food shortages, shortfalls, or structural deficits in agricultural production are placed in positions of relative powerlessness in international relations. Developing countries with dense urban populations that cannot feed themselves have to use scarce foreign exchange to import food. Even a highly developed country like Japan may be vulnerable to marked disruptions caused by food shortages or embargoes.

The vast resources of the United States have historically made it a rich agricultural nation. It evolved into a major exporter of agricultural commodities and the world's residual supplier of basic food and foodstuffs. The agricultural economy of the United States initially grew with the integration and expansion of its domestic economy. The next surge of growth in American agriculture came with the emergence of multinational agribusinesses. These companies enhanced trade and internationalized U.S. agriculture through foreign direct investment. Through technological advances and integrated commercial management, farm production capacities in the United States reached a stage where they exceeded domestic utilization requirements. In the mid-1990s, twenty-seven percent of all bulk sales of agricultural commodities went into exports. Higher value products (HVP) which are semi-processed and processed agricultural products, such as fruits, vegetables, animal feeds, flour, and breads, were thirteen percent and climbing every year as the structure of trade for U.S. agricultural products changed.

While the trade ratio of U.S. agriculture increased as the economy matured, trade alone was no longer sufficient to secure foreign market sales. It also became necessary to invest in foreign markets and U.S. companies took the plunge. These companies became the leading industries in global food and agricultural merchandising markets. A typical example was Cargill, Inc., based in Minnesota, which began as the owner and operator of rural grain elevators in the Midwest and emerged as the largest privately owned multinational in the world. Archer Daniels Midland (ADM) was once an Illinois-based farm supply company that was transformed into a multinational agribusiness of enormous proportions. Pillsbury, once a family-owned flour milling company, became a multinational subsidiary of its British parent, Grand Metropolitan. In the mid-1990s General Mills, another U.S. corporate landmark, set up a joint venture with Nestlé, the giant Swiss multinational food manufacturer, to establish Cereal Partners Worldwide, the second largest cereal company outside North America.

As these examples indicate, American farming had become corporatized and U.S. agriculture had become internationalized. By the 1990s American companies dominated bulk and processed food markets worldwide. U.S.-based food companies with affiliate networks overseas had high ratios of intraaffiliate trades. These in-house transactions accounted for an increasing share of total U.S. agricultural exports. As in other industries, foreign direct investment has become a bridgehead for U.S. agricultural exports.

Agricultural Roots of Foreign Policy

This evolution in the structure of American agricultural wealth has had clear and inevitable ramifications for U.S. foreign policy. During the colonial period and the early years of the Republic, the link between agriculture and foreign policy seemed remote and indirect. American agricultural policy was focused then on ensuring production and introducing impartial regulatory mechanisms to ensure fair prices to farmers. Food policies centered on maintaining uninterrupted access to supplies at fair and stable prices, allowing the public to have access to abundant and safe basic agricultural products. Apart from such early export crops as tobacco, cotton, and modest amounts of wheat, corn, and oilseeds, agricultural products were produced for the home market and enjoyed broad protection against foreign imports. In key respects, free trade ran counter to the agricultural growth and development policies of the federal government in those early years. When U.S. agriculture graduated to a phase of surplus production during World War II, it was time to abandon trade restrictions and move to a closer approximation of free trade. U.S. agriculture in general depends heavily on exports to boost demand for its product. In agriculture, as in other sectors of the maturing economy, the growth and greater efficiency of domestic markets led logically to aggressive export and investment strategies.

By the 1950s the country was awash in grain. Inevitably, a succession of rich harvests coupled with a wealthier consumer base and changing consumer preferences transformed U.S. agriculture. Structural surpluses created a more intensive search for new markets outside the United States. The grain basket of the Great Plains became a new element in U.S. foreign policy leadership. U.S. food resources served as collateral for the European Recovery Program (ERP) after World War II. With U.S. exports declining after World War II, ERP assured export markets for U.S. agricultural products, marrying economic self-interest with foreign policy objectives for Europe. During the Cold War, food surpluses were used as a tool to counter the Soviet Union and as aid to influence development and foreign policies in the Third World. In 1980 the United States embargoed grain exports to the Soviet Union as a direct result of the USSR's earlier invasion of Afghanistan. The purpose of the embargo was not to force the Soviets to withdraw from Afghanistan, but only to state that as long as they were there, the United States would halt grain sales to them.

Notwithstanding the sharp demarcation of the Iron Curtain, reinforced by the U.S. policy of containment of communism, in the 1980s U.S. agriculture saw the Soviet Union as a country with a need to import agricultural products (wheat and corn), with the U.S. as the only available supplier. They were rightly viewed as an enormous market. The administration of President Richard Nixon was faced in the early 1970s with burdensome surpluses that had been temporarily siphoned off to developing countries through Food for Peace programs. Sagging domestic farm prices, politics, and strategic considerations made a formidable alliance, and in 1973 inspired the establishment of the first special credit sale program for the Soviet Union in the name of détente. Soviet leaders also were prepared to ignore ideology to ensure stable supplies of food and feed products for livestock throughout the Soviet empire. The United States so readily filled Soviet needs that within ten years, the Soviet Union was a major market for U.S. agricultural exports. From 1970 to 1980, the Soviet Union changed in the eyes of the United States from that of a country we would prefer not to trade with, to one of a valued customer, accounting for eleven percent of total U.S. exports of wheat and coarse grains.

Just as American agriculture helped underwrite U.S. advancement to the role of a global superpower, major U.S. economic and foreign policy initiatives after World War II served to internationalize its agribusiness and the entire agricultural economy. U.S. farms and agribusinesses were producing for the world market. Next to money, agricultural products are perhaps the most fungible items in international trade. Therefore, it was a logical progression for the Midwestern grain belt to become the catalyst for a new global outlook in U.S. foreign and economic policy.

Beginning in the mid-1970s foreign buyers and competing food suppliers grew less than accepting of the dominant position of the United States in global food markets. Traditional markets like Japan and developing countries, suffering from protracted periods of food deficits, attempted to reduce their dependency on imports for political as well as economic reasons. Japan invested heavily in food security, by bolstering their own stocks, and carefully managing their imports and exports, in order to insulate its people from food shortages. Developing countries, under the guidance of donor institutions such as the World Bank and AID, have tried to aim for self-sufficiency and cut down on food imports. These policies are based on a fear that without free trade in agricultural products, political issues and trade policies could send food costs skyrocketing. U.S. foreign policy interventions, such as the soybean embargo of 1973, which targeted Japan, or the grain and oilseed embargo of January 1980, aimed at the Soviet Union, raised international concerns about the reliability of the United States as a supplier. Although the suspension of soybean export sales was a response to a run-up in domestic prices and the 1980 embargo was a response to the Soviet invasion of Afghanistan, both embargoes had the same net effect of destabilizing world commodity markets and embodied the food weapon strategy. Food-importing countries and food aid recipients alike interpreted them as a warning of the perils of food dependency.

Competing suppliers, mainly the European Union (EU), Canada, Australia, and Argentina, anxious to sell their own surpluses, were quick to fan these anxieties and write their own export contracts. The result of improved production technologies and government support programs, these surpluses had quickly become sufficiently burdensome to convince EU policy makers that they were a wasteful economic drain that could not be sustained indefinitely. Export promotion offered an immediate, temporary solution. Eventually, however, aggressive national export campaigns fueled incipient trade wars with a host of foreign policy ramifications. By the 1980s the food and agricultural policies were as complicated and as fragile as a spider's web.

Within the United States there was similar uncertainty. Shrinking export markets, idle agricultural capacity, and unsuccessful food-weapon strategies left U.S. leaders uncertain about how to integrate their foreign policy objectives with agricultural interests. The changing structure of the U.S. and world agricultural economy itself had altered the traditional equation in which agricultural surpluses were a source of power. An expansion of the agribusiness portfolio overseas had brought a diffusion of agricultural interests and discontinuities in farm and food policies.

The Role of Agribusiness

By the 1980s U.S. agribusiness—a catch-all term for commercial, generally multinational, agro-industries—had consolidated its domestic base and established a network of global corporate alliances. According to the U.S. Census Bureau, in 1987, ten percent of U.S. farms accounted for eighty percent of total crop sales; fifty U.S. processing companies accounted for forty-eight percent of total sales; and fifty food wholesalers accounted for seventy-one percent of total sales. With concentration came vertical and horizontal integration. Vertically speaking, although food processors, for example, often remained one step removed from production, they were likely to have production contracts with growers. They also were likely to have their own packaging, shipping, and warehousing facilities as well as processing plants. On the horizontal side, their integrated operations often made them information providers, futures brokers, and a resource for working and investment capital. In effect, their size and level of integration had introduced a new set of assumptions and changing conditions for the marketplace. They were frequently not only major sources of demand for products, but also catalysts for the development of new products to satisfy specialized consumer requirements.

The same phenomenon has occurred in the most economically advanced foreign markets, thereby facilitating a new level of globalization and competition in the food industries. When the EU was a fledgling common market in the 1950s, the strategy for most food companies was to export commodities and finished products into these markets. As governments attempted to restrict access to their markets so as to bolster their own agro-industries, U.S. companies came to rely increasingly on foreign direct investment to penetrate such markets. Representatives of multinational food firms indicated that their companies established foreign affiliates not only to overcome trade barriers but also to reduce transportation costs, secure access to local transportation and distribution networks, and to satisfy specialized buyer requirements in the foreign country.

Another complementary strategy was the establishment of global alliances or links with foreign companies. These new relationships could take several forms but principally involved licensing and joint ventures. The level of globalization in the food industry was so successful that by the mid-1990s the majority of trade in food products took the form of interaffiliate trades rather than exports from U.S.-based companies. Moreover, this new pattern of trade was two-sided, involving U.S. imports as well as exports. U.S. companies provided technology and ingredients for their processed product internationally. They were marketing their products less on the basis of where the raw materials originated and more on the basis of a combination of market factors.

The agribusiness cycle of foreign direct investment, by then in full swing in newly industrialized and postindustrial economies, was considerably less advanced in developing countries and former socialist countries. Companies were often reluctant to assume the risks of direct investment exposure in countries with a history of political uncertainty or instability. Moreover, surveys of multinational company investment and marketing strategies showed that these countries did not offer the commercial infrastructure and differentiated consumer requirements necessary to justify a direct corporate presence. Equally important was the regulatory environment, which was often extremely costly and discriminatory for a foreign firm. Many U.S. companies opted for a regional strategy in such cases. For example, U.S. agribusinesses exporting to Indonesia and Malaysia often routed their product through an affiliate in Singapore. One alternative strategy was to move gradually toward establishing a local production facility by first establishing a connection with a local partner to introduce international brands alongside well-established local brands. Another alternative was to buy a local facility already in operation and produce locally during the initial growth and development phase.

Whatever their strategy, integrated and internationalized agro-industries had become a magnetic force for change. Criticism of multinationals was directed at their influence in developing inappropriate lifestyles and consumer preferences, which their critics considered to be inordinate. They were also accused of causing environmental damage and taken to task for repatriating profits at the expense of much-needed local revenue. On the other hand, these companies frequently provided invaluable technologies, training, assets, and foreign capital.

Foreign Policy Implications

Remarkable new conditions were created by U.S. and foreign agribusinesses. U.S. public policies, including foreign policies, lagged in appreciating the consequences and potential ramifications created by these dynamic changes. The General Agreement on Tariffs and Trade (GATT) of 1995 (the Uruguay Round) appeared likely to effectively reduce previous agricultural abuses of international trading regulations. It required participating countries to reduce levels of trade-distorting support, export subsidies, and import protection. The agreement's measures were expected to virtually double U.S. gross farm sector income and to triple savings from reduced federal government payments by the year 2005. This was an extremely positive step, but the new agreement ignored many essential trade-related questions arising from the newly globalized structure of agribusinesses and the food industry in general.

Foreign policy makers had yet to grapple with this phenomenon, even though industry and government had created these new conditions together, sometimes inadvertently. For example, the U.S. government sponsored or contributed public monies to private sector research in agricultural biotechnologies in an effort to retain a competitive advantage for U.S. agribusinesses. U.S. companies were jump-started for new biotechnological products and then began to license their production internationally. The net result was a much-needed boost in earnings for U.S. agribusinesses and the beginning stages of global technology transfer. The new age of production technologies could further change the historical zero-sum nature of food politics. Biotechnological breakthroughs might justify the reduction of food imports for many countries, rich and poor, on straight economic grounds. In a world of bioagriculture, for example, a country like Japan, which is rich in capital and technological resources, could eventually become a net exporter of processed foods.

With rapid dissemination of agricultural biotechnologies, traditional U.S. foreign and trade policy assumptions about U.S. agribusiness interests clashed with the new realities. With less home-based production and intensive intracompany or alliance patterns of trade, conventional export promotion programs could boomerang in favor of foreign competitors. A policy of trade and investment sanctions to induce political change could undermine direct U.S. agribusiness interests up and down the marketing chain. It might also counteract the contributions of the private sector to the desired direction of political change embraced by U.S. policymakers.

The food embargoes against the Soviet Union made this point quite dramatically. For example, cutting across existing export contracts in an effort to punish the Soviets for invading Afghanistan was, as U.S. critics noted, nothing more than shooting ourselves in the foot. It imperiled U.S. farmers and merchandisers who depended on grain sales to the Soviet Union. It may have even served to harden the Soviet position on Afghanistan as well. Conversely, rewarding policy initiatives with food assistance may no longer pack the political punch it was thought to have in the 1950s. As early as the 1960s, when President Lyndon Johnson tried to cut off Food for Peace deliveries to India or Egypt to induce them to change particular policies, he was rebuffed; and when aid was resumed, their leaders failed to deliver policy changes desired by the United States. U.S. food assistance for humanitarian purposes may have remained extremely beneficial in alleviating short-term famines, but as an instrument to induce policy changes in Haiti or Bosnia, it proved to be of little political value.

In the case of Japan, the U.S. government endorsed a spectrum of confrontational tactics designed to promote U.S. agricultural and other industry interests. Undoubtedly, policymakers assumed that the level of Japan's food imports made that country dependent to a significant degree on access to U.S. agricultural exports. It is not clear to what extent policymakers took into account the ownership structure of agricultural trade with Japan, where a majority of the product is moved to Japan through affiliates located and incorporated in the United States. Moreover, the fact that growers would be severely affected by any interruption in trade with Japan proved to be a real drawback to overly assertive policies toward Japan. International alliances between U.S. and Japanese companies undoubtedly further complicated U.S. policy initiatives in the 1993–1994 negotiations undertaken by President Bill Clinton's administration.

Russia afforded still another example of an emerging dichotomy between private sector interests and public policy goals. Congress, like the executive branch, was extremely concerned about the direction of economic change and the future of democracy under President Boris Yeltsin. As a result, bilateral and international funding assistance to Russia was delayed and food assistance was directed to targeted organizations that seemed to offer the best prospects for the advancement of democracy. At the same time, however, the U.S. Department of Agriculture, with congressional backing, awarded Russia new and larger tranches of export credits fully guaranteed by the U.S. government so that they would buy more U.S. commodities. In short, the credit window for agricultural exports was opened at the same time the larger window for balance of payments was shut. As a result, Russia's economic condition was not improved nor did U.S. agricultural interests benefit under the circumstances.

Most indicators suggested that the efforts of makers of foreign policy to enlist agricultural interests to advance foreign policy objectives had become an almost futile exercise. These interests had become extremely diverse, depending as much, if not more, on the level of integration or internationalization, as on the range of crops or products. Agricultural wealth had taken on new meaning. It continued to contribute significantly to U.S. economic prosperity, but in all probability it could not successfully be called upon to define or support any specific foreign policy. Rather, it had become useful in defining the limits of power itself.

RICHARD GILMORE

See also Agriculture; European Union; Export Controls; Food for Peace; Foreign Aid; Foreign Direct Investment; General Agreement on Tariffs and Trade; Hoover, Herbert; Humanitarian Intervention and Relief; International Commodity Agreements; Japan; Multinational Corporations; Russia and the Soviet Union; Somalia; Ukraine

FURTHER READING

Allen, Kristen. *Agricultural Policies in a New Decade, Part 3.* Washington, D.C., 1990.
Cotterill, Ronald. *Competitive Strategy Analysis in the Food System.* Boulder, Colo., 1993.
Gilmore, Richard. "World Agriculture Without GATT." *Choices* (second quarter 1991).
———. *A Poor Harvest. The Clash of Policies in the Grain Trade.* New York, 1982.
Goodwin, Geoffrey. "Appendix B: Wheat and Coarse Grains—Stabilisation or Status Quo." In *A New International Regime,* edited by Geoffrey Goodwin and James Mayall. London, 1979.
Knutson, Ronald D. *Agricultural and Food Policy,* 2nd ed. Englewood Cliffs, N.J., 1990.
Pinstrup-Andersen, Per. *The Political Economy of Food and Nutrition Policies.* Baltimore, 1993.
Schertz, Lyle P., and Lynn M. Daft. *Food and Agricultural Markets: The Quiet Revolution.* Washington, D.C., 1994.
Tweeten, Luther G. *Agricultural Trade: Principles and Policies.* Boulder, Colo., 1992.

FOOD AND AGRICULTURE ORGANIZATION

See United Nations

FOOD FOR PEACE

The Food for Peace program, also known as PL 480, is the primary instrument used by the United States to provide food aid to developing nations. It was created in 1954 in order to use surplus farm commodities to help both relief and development efforts overseas. It attempted to achieve several goals simultaneously: to protect the economic stability of U.S. agriculture by keeping domestic prices insulated from excess production; to promote agricultural exports by increasing the demand for U.S. commodities overseas; to dispose of surpluses which otherwise largely go to waste; and to assist developing nations. As of 1994, the program consisted of three separate programs, or "titles," which were required by law to be integrated with the U.S. development assistance program to a specific country, with special emphasis on activities that increase nutritional impact or child survival. Title I, administered by the Department of Agriculture, provided for concessional sales of U.S. agricultural commodities to developing countries. Recipient

governments had to agree to take steps to expand their own food production and improve food storage and distribution facilities. In addition, there was a special concern that these concessional sales should not reduce regular commercial sales from the U.S. and its allies. This usually meant that recipient nations had to commit themselves to purchasing a given amount of commodities at commercial prices in addition to the commodities they receive through the Food for Peace Program.

Titles I and II were coordinated by the Agency for International Development (AID). Title II programs provided grants of food for two main purposes: (1) emergency and disaster relief, (which is the major occasion for U.S. emergency food aid) and (2) programs run by private voluntary organizations, cooperatives, and intergovernmental organizations such as the World Food Program. Title III provided grant food assistance to the poorest developing countries.

The Food for Peace program was the subject of considerable debate, largely focusing on the extent to which its various goals were mutually compatible. Among the most important issues raised were the following: (1) Providing food at concessional prices might solve food shortage problems in a developing country in the short term, but it could make matters worse in the long term by depressing local food prices; this might reduce the incentive for local farmers to grow food and thus increase the dependency on food imports. (2) The program might succeed in encouraging people in developing nations to develop a preference for U.S. goods and boost U.S. exports, but that might not be in the interest of the developing nation. For example, there might be other, indigenous crops more appropriate for the national diet and equally or more nutritious. Shifting tastes to U.S. products therefore not only might increase dependency on imports, but also might actually reduce the nutrition levels in the country. (3) Contrarily, some critics charged that when food aid programs are used to encourage the production of food in developing nations, such programs might not only reduce the demand for U.S. products, but in some cases might lead to the creation of direct competition, making the status of the American farmer even more precarious.

STEVEN H. ARNOLD

See also Agriculture; Agency for International Development; Foreign Aid; Humanitarian Intervention and Relief

FURTHER READING

Morrison, Elizabeth, and Randall B. Purcell, eds. *Players and Issues in U.S. Foreign Aid.* West Hartford, Conn., 1988.
International Trade and Development Education Foundation. *The United States Food for Peace Program, 1954–1984.* Arlington, Va., 1985.
Ruttan, Vernon. *Why Food Aid?* Baltimore, Md., 1993.

FORD, GERALD RUDOLPH

(*b.* 14 July 1913)

Thirty-eighth president of the United States (1974–1977). Born in Omaha, Nebraska, Ford grew up in Grand Rapids, Michigan, won All-American football honors at the University of Michigan in the 1930s, and was a founder of the Isolationist American First Committee while at Yale Law School. Ford served in the navy during World War II and was first elected to Congress as a Republican in 1948. As a protégé of Senator Arthur H. Vandenberg, he supported internationalist policies during the 1940s and 1950s, most notably opposing cutbacks in foreign aid sought by conservatives. House minority leader after 1965, Ford accused the administration of President Lyndon B. Johnson in 1965 of "shocking mismanagement" of the Vietnam War and urged intensive military measures to end the war quickly.

Appointed vice president in 1973 by President Richard M. Nixon after the resignation of Spiro T. Agnew, Ford became president when the Watergate scandal and the threat of impeachment forced Nixon's resignation in August 1974. One month later, Ford pardoned Nixon for all federal crimes he might have committed while in office, a move that generated significant controversy. By retaining Henry Kissinger as secretary of state, Ford signaled his intent to continue the foreign policy of his predecessor. Popular support for those policies continued to diminish; however, especially unpopular was the continuing war in Indochina, where Congress banned further military intervention and cut back military aid. The short-lived euphoria over recovery of the *Mayaguez*, a U.S. merchant vessel seized by the Cambodians in May 1975, could not offset U.S. defeat in Southeast Asia. Congress, in Ford's words, also "pulled the plug" in December 1975 on U.S. covert aid to anticommunist forces in Angola. Even conservatives lambasted Ford's efforts to extend détente, criticizing negotiators at the Strategic Arms Limitation Talks for acquiescing on Soviet missile superiority and claiming that the Helsinki Accords (1975) legitimized East European regimes and boundaries in return for hollow human rights pledges.

Criticized for his failure to invite the Soviet dissident Aleksandr Solzhenitsyn to the White House, Ford banned the term "détente" from political discourse during the 1976 presidential campaign. Ford's claim during a televised campaign debate that the people of Poland did not "consider themselves dominated by the Soviet Union" was considered by many a political gaffe that caused him to lose the election to Jimmy Carter. After leaving office, Ford wrote his memoirs, *A Time to Heal* (1979) and contributed to public discussions on foreign policy through symposia and publications sponsored by the Ford Presidential Library in Ann Arbor, Michigan.

J. GARRY CLIFFORD

See also Détente; Helsinki Accords; Presidency; Vietnam War

FURTHER READING

Cannon, James. *Time and Chance: Gerald Ford's Appointment with History.* New York, 1994.

Firestone, Bernard J., and Alexei Ugrinsky. *Gerald R. Ford and the Politics of Post-Watergate America.* Westport, Conn., 1993.

Greene, John Robert. *The Presidency of Gerald R. Ford.* Lawrence, Kans., 1994.

Schapsmeier, Edward L., and Fredrick H. Schapsmeier. *Gerald R. Ford's Date with Destiny: A Political Biography.* New York, 1989.

FORDNEY-MCCUMBER TARIFF

See Tariffs

FOREIGN AID

An instrument of statecraft, which, in the narrowly defined sense of voluntary state-to-state resource transfers extended by a donor government to promote its foreign policy objectives, is one of diplomacy's oldest tools. Before the birth of Christ, for example, such interstate subventions figured in the creation and maintenance of alliances of the diverse governments around the Mediterranean, providing the cement to coalitions especially in times of war. Such military aid was a feature of wartime diplomacy for the European nation-state; Americans accepted this form of foreign aid during the Revolutionary War, and the United States government dispensed it on a massive scale during the World Wars I and II. Indeed, the U.S. military aid program for its World War II Allies, known as the Lend-Lease program, supplied—at today's prices—the equivalent of over $200 billion worth of goods and material to the Allies; these provisions were critical to the victory over the Axis powers.

Although military aid and security aid—foreign assistance for explicitly political purposes, such as influencing the international posture of the recipient government—have continued to account for a major portion of U.S. foreign aid allocations since the end of World War II, the term "foreign aid" itself has taken on a very different connotation. In its common usage today, the term "foreign aid" typically refers to economic aid or assistance—monies provided by a donor government in hope of promoting economic recovery, material advance, or poverty alleviation in the recipient state.

The notion of foreign aid as economic aid *per se* is a very modern one, and reflects two of the important new realities of international relations: first, that changes in a nation's economic capabilities can now very rapidly shift the balance of power between countries, or alter the scope and nature of their commercial interactions; second, that

U.S. FOREIGN AID
(grants and loans, economic and military) by Region, 1946-1994

Region	Total (in millions of US dollars)
Near East	117,243.9
Sub-Saharan Africa	23,200.3
Latin America	35,476.5
Asia	101,430.1
Europe	79,150.5
New Independent States	3,468.4
Oceania and Other	1,266.3

Source: *U.S. Overseas Loans and Grants.* Office of Budget in the Bureau for Management of the U.S. Agency for International Development.

existing technological possibilities and administrative techniques now offer governments in low-income countries the possibility of effectuating dramatic economic transformations of the territories under their direction.

After World War II, the United States pioneered the concept, and application, of economic diplomacy through foreign aid. The earliest, and still most acclaimed, of these postwar U.S. exercises was the Marshall Plan—formally, the European Recovery Program (1948–1952)—through which the United States expended the equivalent (in today's prices) of over $60 billion to foster economic reconstruction in war-devastated Western Europe. By the end of the Marshall Plan, most of the beneficiary countries had indeed reached, or nearly reached, their prewar levels of output and productivity; subsequently, of course, Western Europe has enjoyed continuing material advance.

In 1949, in President Harry S. Truman's inaugural address to Congress, what is now commonly described as "foreign aid" was initially proposed. Originally called "technical assistance," this form of economic diplomacy is now known as "development assistance" or "development aid."

Unlike Marshall Plan aid, the focus of development aid was regions and countries where productivity, and per capita incomes, had never been high. While its particulars have evolved and its scope has greatly broadened since its inception, all development aid policies provide resources to recipient governments with the intention of hastening the local pace of material advance and (directly or indirectly) raising local living standards.

Since the advent of the United States's "technical assistance" program in 1950, development aid programs have been devised and underwritten by virtually every industrialized democracy. (Development aid also has been offered, at various junctures, by other governments as well, including the Communist regimes in China and the former Warsaw Pact, some Organization of Petroleum Exporting Countries (OPEC) states, and a few of the economically successful East Asian governments.) While virtually all "developing countries" receive at least some amount of development aid at present, the weight of development assistance efforts has shifted between regions, and countries, over the past four and a half decades. In the early 1950s, for example, non-communist Asia obtained a large proportion of available development aid; in the 1980s, sub-Saharan Africa emerged as a priority area for development assistance; and in the 1990s, with the collapse of Soviet-bloc communism, the governments of Eastern Europe and the so-called "Newly Independent States (NIS)" have become significant aid recipients. In the early 1990s, on a global basis, roughly $60 billion a year was disbursed in official development assistance; of that total, roughly $10 billion a year came from the United States.

Foreign Aid Policies: Mechanisms and Objectives

The taxonomy of foreign aid policies begins, in an administrative or bureaucratic sense, by distinguishing bilateral aid from multilateral aid. The former are programs provided and funded by a single government, and received by a single government. In the United States, bilateral development aid has been managed by a succession of official institutions: principally, the Economic Cooperation Administration (ECA) from 1950–1953; the International Cooperation Administration (ICA, 1953–1961); and, since 1961, the U.S. Agency for International Development (USAID).

The multilateral aid programs are funded by, and dispensed to, a multiplicity of governments, usually through some mediating international organization. Today the principal institutions administering multilateral aid are the World Bank (which began operations in 1946); the regionally-focused "multilateral development banks" for Asia, Latin America, Africa, and Eastern Europe/NIS; and the United Nations (through such subsidiaries as the United Nations Development Program (UNDP), the Food and Agriculture Organization (FAO), and the United Nations Children's Fund (UNICEF), among others). The United States was instrumental in establishing each of these multilateral agencies, and is typically the largest single funder in each to this day. In the early 1990s, multilateral aid accounted for roughly one-third of total global development assistance outlays; bilateral programs, roughly two-thirds.

A second administrative distinction within the aid taxonomy separates grants from "soft" loans. Grants are outright donations, whether they occur in the form of cash payments or resource transfers (such as food aid); "soft" loans, by contrast, are funds or resources lent with the expectation that they be paid back—but at highly favorable interest rates, so that the loan amounts in part to a concessional transfer. Multilateral aid today is mainly conducted through soft loans; the balance between grants and soft loans is a little more even in bilateral aid.

Over the past four and a half decades, the types of development aid described above have been used to finance a shifting locus of developmental priorities and objectives. In the 1950s and 1960s, the emphasis in most aid programs was on "infrastructural development:" dams, roads, and major production facilities that required major expenditures to execute, but that were expected to contribute substantially to the productivity and growth prospects of the local economy. In the 1970s, in the United States and elsewhere, the emphasis shifted to "basic human needs"—that is to say, to improving the living standards of poor and vulnerable elements within a recipient country's population directly (through expanded social services) instead of indirectly (through the "trickle-down" effects of economic growth). In the 1980s, "structural adjustment" or "policy reform" aid became financially significant: these programs proposed to underwrite a shift by governments in low-income countries to economically responsible—but unpopular or potentially destabilizing—domestic and international policies. In the early 1990s, a new priority in development aid is known as "sustainable development;" under this rubric come programs intended to protect the environment from various forms of degradation.

Prospects For U.S. Foreign Aid Policies

The United States has experimented with, and devoted considerable resources to, diverse forms of foreign aid in the more than fifty years since the end of World War II. Aid programs can be examined in terms of a wide variety of sometimes conflicting criteria: "realist vs. idealist;" security interests, commercial interests or humanitarian interests, and so on. Yet no matter what framework one chooses for evaluating foreign aid policies of the United States, the postwar record of performance is likely to look decidedly mixed.

In part, this impression may arguably derive from the inherent ambiguities in assessing the success or failure of particular foreign aid policies. Military and security aid policies, for example, may be judged a failure if they fail to prevent a coup or an insurgency—yet they may seem "wasteful" or unnecessary if they actually forestall unwelcome events and underwrite a measure of stability in the recipient country. By the same token, assessing the actual economic impact of development aid in a recipient country, for its part, is an exceedingly difficult task under the best of circumstances, considering the great multiplicity of factors that must be taken into consideration when accounting for any country's economic performance.

Even in its broadest outlines, however, the postwar foreign aid story is suggestive of the possibility that U.S. aid may have "worked" in some places, and fared very poorly in others. "Success stories" would look to include Taiwan and South Korea, where major U.S. aid commitments were eventually followed by very rapid and ultimately self-sustaining growth; conversely, the experience in sub-Saharan Africa, where stagnation and decay have been prevalent in the 1980s and 1990s despite major and growing donor commitments, suggests a very different sort of verdict. In the final analysis, all aid donors must grapple with an inescapable dilemma: government-to-government resource transfers permit the leaders of the recipient government to pursue their preexisting intentions with fewer constraints, no matter what those preexisting intentions may happen to be.

On the subject of foreign aid, U.S. public opinion polls have consistently reported what appears to be a profound paradox. On the one hand, poll after poll indicates that the U.S. public sees ending world hunger and analogous objectives as worthy and important priorities. On the other hand, those same public opinion polls show a deep—and possibly growing—public hostility toward official U.S. foreign aid programs, and evidence strong—possibly growing—support for cutbacks in U.S. foreign aid spending.

Foreign aid, of course, is not likely to be eliminated from the U.S. budget, or from the U.S. foreign policy toolkit. Economic diplomacy, and its diverse instruments, are required for the conduct of foreign relations by all capable modern governments—all the more so by great powers. Coping with the ambiguities and frustrations of foreign aid policy, however, promises to be an enduring challenge for U.S. policymakers in the years to come.

NICHOLAS EBERSTADT

See also Agency for International Development; Alliance for Progress; Arms Transfer and Trade; Cold War; Food for Peace; Lend-Lease; Marshall Plan; Point Four

FURTHER READING
Brown, William J., and Opie Redvers, Jr. *American Foreign Assistance*. Washington, D.C., 1953.
Cassen, Robert and Associates. *Does Aid Work?* New York, 1994.
Eberstadt, Nicholas. *Foreign Aid and American Purpose*. Washington, D.C., 1988.

FOREIGN BROADCAST INFORMATION SERVICE

A part of the National Technical Information Service, the Foreign Broadcast Information Service (FBIS) monitors, translates and publishes selected information from news services outside the United States. FBIS reports are prepared for use by other agencies of the federal government and also are made available to the public. Reports are published in regional editions according to the sources covered—for example, Western Europe, Latin America, the Near East and South Asia, or sub-Saharan Africa. Major research libraries maintain subscriptions to the daily and weekly FBIS reports, which are compiled and indexed as permanent reference resources. While related to the intelligence services and nominally an element of the Central Intelligence Agency, FBIS differs in that it collects its material from open public sources and, with minimal exceptions of copyrighted material, noted below, makes it available to the public. Most FBIS material is taken from domestic and international broadcasts in countries outside of the United States. Some comes from news agencies and other open media sources. Although FBIS material is occasionally marked "Official Use Only" and restricted to government agencies, this is not a security classification; it is rather an administrative marking made necessary when the source material is copyrighted because FBIS does not honor copyright restrictions or pay to use material.

FBIS material is not an exhaustive compilation of news content, nor is it a representative sample of material broadcast in various countries. Monitors respond to requests for information on specific topics, and also apply their own assessment of what is important and useful. Selected material typically emphasizes government policy statements, statistics, and current events, which are likely to be of immediate interest to FBIS customers. While FBIS does not analyze or interpret its reports, it is a valuable source for analysts in the Departments of State and Defense, the National Security Council and other agencies, members of Congress, and scholars and researchers. FBIS can be compared with the BBC Monitoring Service, which also monitors foreign broadcasts and distributes translations to government and private customers. Major news agencies also monitor local and competing media, but few operate on as large a scale as the BBC or FBIS. FBIS should not be confused with the National Security Agency (NSA), which also monitors foreign broadcasts as part of a broader mission to collect electronic intelligence, or with similar activities of the CIA itself or military intelligence agencies.

ROBERT L. STEVENSON

See also Intelligence

FURTHER READING

Hester, Al and Kristina White (eds.) *Creating a Free Press in Europe.* Athens, Ga., 1994.

FOREIGN CORRUPT PRACTICES ACT

A 1977 law which grew out of the Watergate scandal during the Nixon administration. During its investigation of illegal contributions to the Nixon reelection campaign, the Securities and Exchange Commission discovered "improper payments" made to foreign officials in the Netherlands, Korea, and Japan by American corporations. The case of Lockhead, which had bribed Japanese officials to secure the sale of its Tristar L-1011 aircraft, received the most notoriety; the scandal led to the resignation and prosecution of the Japanese prime minister, Kankuie Tanaka. By mid-1974, the extent of bribery abroad became clear as more than one hundred U.S. firms acknowledged such payments. The Foreign Corrupt Practices Act amended the Securities Exchange Act of 1934. The new act made it illegal for corporations to bribe foreign officials and required firms to keep stricter account of their transactions, to prevent the use of hidden slush funds to finance illegal payments. The Department of State, some members of the business community, and academics criticized the act. Businesses argued that the law did not clearly define the difference between illegal "bribes" (payments made to influence foreign officials) and legal "gratuities" (payments that merely accelerated actions which would have eventually been carried out in any case). Critics from the business community also maintained that the Foreign Corrupt Practices Act prevented them from competing equally with foreign companies not subject to such constraints. Studies since the act's passage, however, have failed to discover any significant loss of business. In fact, the act probably forced U.S. firms to become more aware of local laws and culture, thereby helping to create more reliable bonds between the host countries and U.S. corporations.

The Department of State worried that disclosure of the activities of foreign government officials in lawsuits could undermine friendly regimes. Though bribery scandals occasionally have led to the downfall of governments, since most investigations of corruption have been undertaken by the government in power, most anticorruption movements have not fueled radical nationalist or leftist movements. Some academics argued that the law constituted "moral imperialism," but this argument was based on the unwarranted assumption that the United States had higher ethical standards. In fact, foreign governments have shown an equal desire to combat corruption. Despite predictions that few would be prosecuted under the act, there have been several convictions. In 1978 the U.S. Customs Service fined Control Data Corporation $1,381,000 for making "illegal" payments in order to secure business in Iran. In the late 1980s, the multinational advertising firm of Young & Rubicam was found guilty of bribing Jamaica's minister of tourism. The Omnibus Trade Act of 1988 addressed the ambiguities of the Foreign Corrupt Practices Act, clarifying which payments were legal and to whom these payments could be made.

MICHAEL A. RENO

See also Foreign Direct Investment; Japan; Watergate

FURTHER READING

Cruver, Donald R. *Complying with the Foreign Corrupt Practices Act: A Guide for U.S. Firms Doing Business in the International Marketplace.* Chicago, 1994.

Greanias, George C., and Duane Windsor. *The Foreign Corrupt Practices Act: Anatomy of a Statute.* Lexington, Mass., 1982.

FOREIGN DIRECT INVESTMENT

The primary, but not the only mode, by which multinational corporations (MNCs) extend their activities outside of home markets. Foreign Direct Investment (FDI) is a balance of payments concept of accounting. FDI flows, as reported in a nation's balance of payments accounts, are increases in the book value of the net worth of investments in one country held by investors from another, where investments are under the managerial control of the investors. Most such investments are subsidiaries of MNCs and the investors are the parent organizations of these firms.

FDI is directed either inward or outward. The former represents investments by foreign-based MNCs in subsidiaries established or acquired in the nation, and the latter represents investments by locally based MNCs in subsidiaries established or acquired abroad. Most nations use a low threshold of the percentage of total equity held by an investor in a subsidiary to determine whether the investor holds "managerial control." The United States, for example, uses a threshold of 10%. Unfortunately, no international standard exists for such thresholds, and individual nations are not consistent in their use, resulting inter alia in inconsistencies across nations in the reporting of total FDI.

Despite problems of definition associated with FDI, it is the best measure of the extent of the internationalization of business. Viewed this way, the numbers reported in the 1990s are impressive; annual flows of FDI have been approximately $175 billion. This figure represents increases in the net worth of the overseas affiliates of MNCs and says nothing about total assets under their control. This latter number is significantly higher than the total stock of FDI. Accurate aggregate figures are not available for total assets under the control of MNCs, but estimates can be derived as follows: According to the United Nations (UNCTAD 1994), the top 100 MNCs held about $3.4 trillion in total assets at the end of 1992, of which about $1.3 trillion was held outside their home countries. These firms, however, accounted for only about one-third of total outward FDI of their home countries. If the ratio of total assets to outward FDI for all MNCs based in these countries was the same as for the top 100, total assets of all such MNCs would have been $10.2 trillion at the end of 1992, of which $3.9 trillion would have been outside their home countries.

Trends in FDI between the late 1950s and 1990s are indicated in Chart 1, which shows flows of FDI from the G7 countries (United States, Japan, Germany, France, Italy, United Kingdom, and Canada) from 1967 through 1993. Flows from the United States and the remaining six nations are indicated separately. FDI from the G7 nations only is shown because figures for most other nations over this period are incomplete. The G7 nations accounted for the overwhelming majority of outward FDI over the period. The share of FDI of the G7 declined from over ninety percent of total reported flows at the beginning of the period to slightly under eighty percent at the end. Part of the apparent decline may be the result of more complete reporting of balance of payments information from non-G7 countries in later years.

The chart clearly shows two important pieces of information. First, that U.S. share of the indicated flows was fifty percent or more in most years from 1967 to 1979 but fell after 1979, reaching a low of just over seventeen percent in 1990. The extremely low flow of FDI out of the United States in 1982 was the result of an adjustment in the valuation of stock of U.S. direct investment abroad by the Commerce Department. U.S. share recovered sharply in subsequent years, reaching over thirty-nine percent in 1993. Second, total flows of FDI from the G7 nations underwent a "minisurge" during the late 1970s and early 1980s, then fell sharply following 1981 and grew steadily, with growth becoming spectacular following 1985.

Much of the surge of FDI of the 1980s took place among industrialized nations. Considerable two-way direct investment took place between North America and Europe during the decade, and considerable one-way direct investment from Japan to North America and Europe, but not from Europe or North America to Japan. Intra-European direct investment flows were substantial. Beginning in 1990 the percentage of total world direct investment flows to developing countries began to rise substantially, most of which were directed to a few rapidly growing nations such as China, other dynamic developing economies in East Asia, and a handful of other rapidly growing developing nations.

Just as there is a major difference between FDI and total assets under the control of MNCs, there is an important distinction between FDI, which is a financial investment, and the economic concept of real investment. Note that from the perspective of a subsidiary under the control of a foreign parent, FDI is a *source* and not a *use* of funds. From this perspective, FDI represents funds generated from the sale of new equity to the parent organization or from internal cash flow (retained earnings). These are two possible sources of funds; others can include (1) debt raised from local or international lenders other than the parent; (2) equity capital raised

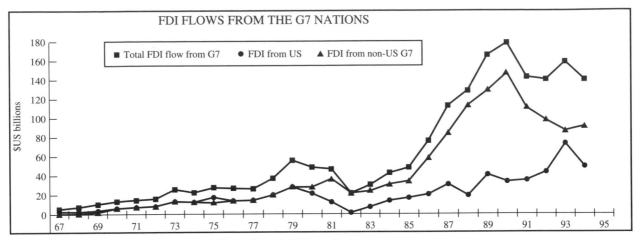

Source: Compiled from various issues of *International Financial Statistics*. International Monetary Fund.

from local minority shareholders; and (3) trade debt. By contrast, capital expenditures of the subsidiary, which correspond to economic investment, are *uses* of funds. FDI flows do not necessarily correspond to real capital formation generated by subsidiaries of MNCs. Such capital expenditures can be financed from sources other than FDI, and FDI can be used to fund expansion of assets other than capital assets. For U.S.-based MNCs, capital expenditures abroad have consistently exceeded recorded outward direct investment during the last quarter of the twentieth century. That FDI does not correspond exactly to investment in the economic sense is a point, nonetheless, that often is not demonstrated in economic models that attempt to capture the effects of FDI.

The meaning of these distinctions is that foreign direct investment is merely one way to measure activity of MNCs.

EDWARD M. GRAHAM

See also Group of Seven; Multinational Corporations

FURTHER READING

Graham, Edward M. "Foreign Direct Investment in the World Economy." In *World Economic Outlook, Supplementary Staff Studies*, International Monetary Fund, July 1995.

———, and Krugman, Paul R. "The Surge of Foreign Direct Investment in the 1980s." In *Foreign Direct Investment*, edited by Kenneth Froot. Chicago, 1993.

United Nations Conference on Trade and Development (UNCTAD), *World Investment Report 1994: Transnational Corporations, Employment, and the Workplace*. New York and Geneva, United Nations Publication, 1994.

FOREIGN INTELLIGENCE ADVISORY BOARD

Created in 1956 as the President's Board of Consultants of Foreign Intelligence Activities in response to the 1955 Hoover Commission report on intelligence activities. In

May 1961, following the failed Bay of Pigs invasion of Cuba, President John Kennedy renamed it the President's Foreign Intelligence Advisory Board (PFIAB). This highly secretive member panel advised presidents from Eisenhower to Carter on intelligence matters and organization. Composed of distinguished former corporate, government, military and scientific leaders, and thinkers such as James R. Killian, General James H. Doolittle, Edwin H. Land, George Schultz, Edward Teller, and Les Aspin, its original purpose was to advance the role of science and technology in the intelligence process. In contrast to its limited role during the Eisenhower administration (for example, in the development of the U-2 spy aircraft), the responsibilities of the PFIAB were later expanded to include assessment of the overall effectiveness of the intelligence community. Following several public disclosures of allegedly illegal CIA activities in the 1970s, President Jimmy Carter abolished the organization in May 1977. In part, Carter was responding to disclosures of Senator Frank Church's investigative committee and the Rockefeller Commission, each of which inquired deeply into CIA misdeeds which, when added together, indicated an agency that Church labeled "a rogue elephant." The PFIAB, some believed, had failed to inquire into suspected unlawful CIA actions, thus raising questions about its ability to reveal possible violations of law within the intelligence community.

Explanations for Carter's decision to abolish the PFIAB have varied. Some scholars have concluded that Carter wanted more control over the CIA in order to redirect intelligence policy implementation. Others have suggested that he believed the Board was overly confident that covert action plans could achieve certain foreign objectives. Carter insisted on the need for separate alternative intelligence analyses from competitive agencies, and for greater technological advances. President Ronald Reagan reinstated the PFIAB in October 1981 to review the intelligence community's effectiveness in information collection, analysis, and dissemination, but reduced its size from twenty-one to sixteen members in 1985. The Board survived in the administrations of Presidents George Bush and Bill Clinton, but its size was further reduced to six members, each of whom has direct experience in intelligence matters.

JAMES D. CALDER

See also Bay of Pigs Invasion; Church, Frank Forrester III; Central Intelligence Agency; Cuba; Intelligence; Science and Technology; Shultz, George Pratt; Teller, Edward; U-2 Incident

FURTHER READING

Andrew, Christopher. *For the President's Eyes Only: Secret Intelligence and the American Presidency from Washington to Bush* New York, 1995.

Jeffreys-Jones, Rhodri. *The CIA and American Democracy*. New Haven, Conn., 1989.

FOREIGN POLICY ASSOCIATION

The Foreign Policy Association (FPA) was founded by a group of internationalists in New York City in 1918 for the purpose of promoting U.S. entry into the League of Nations and was originally called the League of Nations Association. When the U.S. Senate failed to approve the Treaty of Versailles, the name was changed to Foreign Policy Association. The FPA since has acted primarily as a nonpartisan educational organization dedicated to enlightening the public on matters of U.S. foreign policy and world politics. Headquartered in New York City with a staff of thirty people, and reliant on the financial support of corporations and foundations, it sponsors a "Great Decisions" program involving thousands of participants in local discussion groups throughout the country; offers a variety of publications; works closely with community groups, colleges, universities, and schools; and arranges conferences and special programs on world affairs. Meetings of the Foreign Policy Association are often used by prominent individuals, including administration officials, as forums for delivering major foreign policy addresses.

JEREL A. ROSATI

See also Public Opinion

FURTHER READING

Foreign Policy Association. *Annual Report*. New York

FOREIGN SERVICE

The component of the federal government, administered largely by the Department of State, that staffs U. S. embassies and consular offices abroad, and other posts such as missions to international organizations in the United States and abroad, mostly with career professionals. Foreign Service (FS) personnel are also assigned to the Department of State and other foreign affairs agencies in Washington on a rotating basis. The Foreign Service through the years has had its definition, role, responsibilities, and operating procedures spelled out in a number of laws, most recently by the Foreign Service Act of 1980 (Public Law 96-465). Under the terms of that act, the service consists of the following categories: ambassadors (that is, chiefs of diplomatic missions) and ambassadors at large, neither of which category is necessarily made up of careerists; members of the administratively distinct Senior Foreign Service (those holding the four highest career ranks); Foreign Service officers (FSOs), the largest group of professional diplomatic and consular officers; and specialists (employees who provide needed technical skills, such as doctors and nurses, clerks, and communications technicians). Locally-hired foreign national employees (FSNs), who fill administrative and specialist positions in posts abroad, and consular agents (a designation now seldom used) make up final categories.

History

The modern Foreign Service of the United States has antecedents dating before the establishment of the Republic. In March 1776, the Continental Congress appointed one of its members as "commercial agent" in France, with a view toward initiating talks on aid. Only weeks after the colonies declared their independence, the Congress named two additional "commissioners" to France, instructing them to seek the support of King Louis XVI. Foremost among those first American diplomats was the redoubtable Benjamin Franklin, who took a leading role in negotiating two crucial U. S.-French treaties. The alliance thus arranged came into effect in February 1778 and proved to be instrumental in the new nation's long struggle for liberty. In 1783, Franklin, assisted by John Adams and John Jay, negotiated with London the treaty which acknowledgedU.S. independence. Consular appointments, too, began early in the history of the new nation. In 1780, the first U.S. consul named died at sea en route to Paris; Thomas Barclay replaced him the next year. Six years later, the Congress sent another consul abroad, this time to Canton, China. By then, Thomas Jefferson had replaced Franklin as minister to France and John Adams had become the first U.S. envoy to Great Britain. At the end of the 1780s, posts overseas totalled two diplomatic missions, London and Paris, and ten consulates. In 1800, the total had risen to fifty-eight, most of them consular offices. From then on, the United States maintained a significant overseas diplomatic and consular presence, at least in terms of the number of posts.

Envoys in Europe during the first decades of the Republic included not only statesmen of the caliber of

Franklin, Jefferson, Jay, and Adams, but such luminaries as James Monroe, John Quincy Adams, Gouverneur Morris, and Robert R. Livingston. Political appointees expecting to take up their duties for only limited periods of time, they were nonetheless men of substance and talent. During the first half of the nineteenth century, as the United States expanded its diplomatic relations, the number of representatives increased substantially. By 1850, the United States had twenty-seven missions abroad headed by appointees with the rank of minister and 197 consular posts (the first full-fledged embassies with chiefs of mission at the ambassadorial level were established only in the 1890s). At the turn of the twentieth century, the numbers had risen to forty-one diplomatic and 318 consular posts. Political appointees filled all ranks, and with few exceptions came and went with the changes of political administrations, despite the fact that by this time other industrialized nations had established career services. Although U.S. representatives abroad included numerous competent individuals, all too many exhibited the drawbacks of inexperience, lack of training, haphazard administration, and lack of continuity brought about by the politicized nature of appointments.

The major turning point toward reform of the system came in 1924 when Congress passed the Rogers Act, which put the Foreign Service on a professional, administratively coherent, merit-oriented basis for the first time. The Rogers Act combined the hitherto distinct consular and political branches into the unified Foreign Service, a corps of officers numbering a few hundred. The Act established a career cadre interchangeable subject to diplomatic or consular assignments. Following up on sporadic earlier reforms, it required competitive examinations for officer appointments below the level of minister, provided for promotion based on merit, and set forth new salary, retirement, and allowances schedules.

During the interwar years, other agencies also became involved with international affairs. The onset of World War II prompted their incorporation into the Foreign Service; over the course of the war foreign affairs agencies proliferated. Many of these were dismantled amidst postwar demobilization, but the Soviet challenge spurred recognition by the leadership of the Foreign Service and the Department of State that change was needed to meet post-war demands. The result was the Foreign Service Act of 1946, which provided the organizational framework for expansion over the next several decades. Starting in early 1950, the effectiveness and morale of the Foreign Service received a profound setback as a result of the demagogic communist-hunting campaigns of Wisconsin's Senator Joseph R. McCarthy. Over the next four years (during which the United States fought the Korean War) McCarthy smeared, among others, numerous Foreign Service professionals with accusations of conspiracy, subversion and treason. Particularly hard hit were the "China hands," a group of specialists with enormous expertise on China, whom McCarthy blamed for the communist victory in China in 1949. It would be decades before the Foreign Service could rebuild its expertise on China. Moreover, virtually across the board, the Department of State was forced to exercise extreme if not excessive caution in selections, appointments, and promotions in the Foreign Service. Junior officer and other recruitment were curtailed until the Senator finally went into eclipse following a vote of censure by the Senate in late 1954. After this unfortunate interlude, the Foreign Service soon more than doubled in size, partly because hundreds of Department of State personnel were integrated into it between 1954 and 1957, and partly because of increased junior officer recruitment.

During this period several other agencies and programs concerned with foreign affairs were established: the Central Intelligence Agency (CIA) and other intelligence organizations with overseas interests. In some respects these played complementary roles but in others they became competing centers of expertise and creativity. The Department of Treasury assigned attachés abroad, as did the Federal Bureau of Investigation. By 1961, a succession of foreign aid agencies evolved into the Agency for International Development (AID). The U.S. Information Agency (USIA, which is designated the U.S. Information Service, USIS, abroad) was created in 1953, the Foreign Agricultural Service (FAS) in 1954, and the Foreign Commercial Service (FCS) in 1979. In addition, Congress established the Peace Corps and the Arms Control and Disarmament Agency. Differing personnel structures were stretched to cover the differing requirements of various agencies. The career status of many appointees and their relationship to the Foreign Service system remained unclear. To some extent this is still the case; the personnel of some federal agencies with international concerns do not form part of the Foreign Service.

It was in this context that the Congress passed the 1980 Act rationalizing the overseas personnel systems of the Department of State and four directly affected agencies. The 1980 Act empowers not only the Department of State, but also the secretaries of Agriculture and Commerce, and the directors of the International Communications and International Development Agencies, to use the Foreign Service personnel system. The law thereby brings under the Foreign Service umbrella the Department of Agriculture's FAS and Animal and Plant Health Inspection Service, the Department of Commerce's FCS, plus USIA and AID. These parent organizations, along with the Department of State, make up the Foreign Service's five "home" agencies in Washington.

Organization and Titles

The career Foreign Service recruits on a highly selective basis. Applicants for junior FSOs must pass searching written and oral examinations. As many as 15,000 applicants take the written test, usually given annually; those who pass this first hurdle, must then go through a rigorous screening procedure, including oral examinations and background checks, whether they are potential FSOs or specialists. At most about 300 are eventually selected for appointment. Members of the service hold personal FS (Foreign Service) pay-grade ranks, ranging from the lowest level at FS-9 up to FS-1, and then further upward in the Senior Foreign Service through the four career ranks of counselor, minister-counselor, minister, and ambassador; promotion is made on the basis of formal merit-based evaluation procedures. Locally-hired FSNs employed abroad have pay scales based on local compensation rates.

Senior FSOs, and some specialists, hold both personal ranks and diplomatic and/or consular titles particular to their assignments abroad. The highest diplomatic title is ambassador (formally ambassador extraordinaire and plenipotentiary), the designation of the President's personal representative to the head of state in the nation to which he or she is assigned. By law and presidential directive, ambassadors are in charge of all official American personnel except U.S. military theater commanders in the countries to which they are assigned. This is in an effort to bring order into the direction of the sometimes numerous burcaucratic programs in a given country. Below rank of ambassador, diplomatic titles are, in descending order of prestige: minister, minister-counselor, counselor, and first, second, and third secretaries of embassy. On occasion, specialists assigned to embassies are accorded one of those diplomatic titles or that of attaché, a more specialized diplomatic designation. The title "chargé d'affaires ad interim" is given to an officer of whatever rank and title officially named to head an embassy in an ambassador's absence from the country of assignment. Consular officers are primarily concerned with the protection of U.S. citizens and their property abroad, commercial affairs and some general reporting, and with the issuance of visas and other documents to foreigners wishing to visit the United States. Consuls general head large consular establishments; consuls rank lower and are in charge of smaller posts, followed by vice consuls.

Embassies are located in capital cities. Consulates general often are associated with embassies, but in addition they also may be located in important provincial and port cities. Consulates, which have the same functions as consulates general, are located in smaller cities. Most Foreign Service personnel are assigned abroad to embassies or consular offices; other assignments include a limited number of missions to international organizations, such as the United Nations in New York or Geneva, and special purpose USIA (USIS) or AID posts. Career Foreign Service personnel are subject to assignment anywhere around the globe. In addition to many offices in Washington, by the mid-1990s, they staffed some 250 posts in nearly all of the countries of the world. Slightly more than one-half of these offices are embassies; most of the remainder are consulates general and consulates. Decades ago, the Foreign Service had far more posts overseas than today, partly because consulates formerly handled shipping documentation requirements that have since been eliminated. In 1920, for example, there were 410 posts, many of them only small consular outposts. At the end of 1995, the Foreign Service numbered slightly more than 11,000 U.S. citizens, both in the United States and abroad, and almost 9,000 FSNs overseas (plus more than 13,000 FSNs employed on contract). Of these, almost 8,100 of American employees reported to the Department of State (as did most of the FSNs). The others were employed by the Department of Agriculture (about 180), the Department of Commerce (about 240), USIA (approximately 1,100), and AID (some 1,450). Roughly one-half of the U.S. citizens were senior officers or FSOs; the remainder were technical or administrative specialists.

Neither law nor regulation obliges the president to name professionals to the highest Foreign Service positions. Indeed, throughout much of American history, all envoys and virtually all other diplomatic and consular officers were amateurs. The senior ranks of the Foriegn Service have included both political appointees and careerists of varying qualifications, competence, and success. Outstanding non-professional ambassadors in the years after World War II included David K.E. Bruce (envoy five times between 1949 and 1975) and Ellsworth Bunker (seven ambassadorial assignments, 1951 to 1973). Examples of the first-rate ambassadors from the career Foreign Service are George F. Kennan (ambassador to the Soviet Union in 1951 and to Yugoslavia, 1961 to 1963), Walter J. Stoessel (envoy to Poland, the Soviet Union, and the Federal Republic of Germany between 1968 and 1982), and Loy W. Henderson (ambassador to Iraq, India, Nepal, and Iran between 1943 and 1954). During the latter half of the twentieth century, careerists customarily have made about two-thirds of the United States's diplomatic envoys and the great majority of its consuls general. The continuation of political ambassadorial appointments frequently occasions controversy, especially when a contributor to a presidential campaign with scant qualifications in the field of foreign affairs receives a prestigious post.

Responsibilities

The men and women of the Foreign Service, under the policy direction of the secretary of state, represent the interests of the United States with respect to foreign nations and multinational agencies, assist in the conduct and formulation of foreign affairs-related programs, and, as needed, undertake activities for all government agencies, including the legislative and judicial branches. This in fact covers a multitude of duties. Traditional tasks overseas directed by the Department of State fall into the areas of political, economic, consular, and administrative affairs. FSOs assigned those responsibilities make presentations to and negotiate with host governments; they collect information on issues and events in their country of assignment, analyze it, and report it to Washington; they provide protection and passport services to traveling Americans and issue (or deny) U.S. visas to foreigners; and they meet the many operational requirements of posts abroad. Broader world responsibilities after World War II led to increased involvement in such fields as the environment, nuclear proliferation, arms control and disarmament, refugees, human rights, and the environment. In other foreign affairs areas, USIA is concerned with public and media information and cultural presentations. AID focuses on economic development assistance. The Departments of Agriculture and Commerce promote U.S. exports and advise American businessmen in their fields of competence. When on assignment in Washington, Foreign Service personnel help formulate policies and instructions for programs implemented abroad.

For long periods of time in American history the Foreign Service has been virtually ignored by the public, the press, and the politicians. On other occasions, however, it has been the subject of public and partisan criticism for executing unpopular or unsuccessful foreign policies formulated in Washington and derided as "striped pants cookie-pushers." Nonetheless, as dramatically demonstrated by the embassy hostage crisis in Iran, (1979–1981), and as is far less spectacularly shown on many other occasions, the Foreign Service merits the designation of America's peacetime "first line of defense," a phrase used in 1946 by Dean Acheson, the secretary of state. The uncertainties of the post–Cold War world, however, has posed new challenges. The movement to reduce the size of government began to affect the Foreign Service through major cutbacks in personnel and fewer opportunities both for entry by young applicants and for advancement at senior levels. This occurred at a time when the nature of American interests and the threats the United States faced were going

through historic changes, calling for as much professionalism as possible in how it conducts its foreign affairs.

HENRY E. MATTOX

See also Agency for International Development; Agriculture; Ambassadors and Embassies; China Hands; Commerce, U.S. Department of; Diplomatic Method; McCarthyism; State, U.S. Department of; United States Information Agency

FURTHER READING

American Foreign Service Association. *American Diplomacy and the Foreign Service.* Washington, D.C., 1989.

American Foreign Service Association and Diplomatic and Consular Officers, Retired. *The U.S. Foreign Service: A Global Mission.* Washington, D.C., 1992.

Kennedy, Charles Stuart. *The American Consul: A History of the United States Consular Service, 1776–1914.* New York, 1990.

Steigman, Andrew L. *The Foreign Service of the United States: First Line of Defense.* Boulder, Colo., 1985.

FORMOSA

See Taiwan

FORMOSA RESOLUTION

Passed on 28 January 1955 by overwhelming margins in both the Senate and the House, during an ongoing crisis with China. The Formosa Resolution was one of the broadest discretionary grants of war powers ever made by a congress to a president, in this case Dwight D. Eisenhower. A crisis had erupted between the People's Republic of China (PRC) and the Nationalist Chinese government of Jiang Jieshi (Chiang Kai-shek) based on Taiwan—or Formosa, as it was commonly referred to in those days. What had been continuing tensions and threats had escalated in late 1954 to military skirmishes and PRC attacks on the Nationalist-controlled islands of Jinmen and Mazu (Quemoy and Matsu), located in the Formosa Straits not far from the Chinese mainland. In December, the Eisenhower administration signed a defense treaty with Taiwan, providing it with a U.S. security guarantee. The PRC considered this a provocation and interference in its internal affairs (China claimed Taiwan as Chinese territory); and it thereupon increased its shelling of the offshore islands. On 24 January 1955, President Eisenhower sent a special message to Congress requesting explicit authority to take military action in this crisis if he decided the situation warranted it. By votes of 410 to 3 in the House and 83 to 3 in the Senate, the Congress passed the Formosa Straits Resolution authorizing the president "to employ the armed forces of the United States as he deems necessary" to defend Taiwan and the offshore islands. Congress supported the president's position that such advance and broad authorization was necessary to deter the PRC. But in so doing, Congress established a powerful precedent further eroding the importance of the constitutional provision giving it the power to declare war. The same pattern was repeated three years later in the Middle East with the Eisenhower Doctrine, part of whose wording was strikingly similar in its "as he deems necessary" grant of authority to use military force. The precedent also would hold, this time with far more serious consequences, in the authorization granted President Lyndon Johnson "to take all necessary action" in Vietnam in the Tonkin Gulf Resolution of 1964.

BRUCE W. JENTLESON

See also China; Congress; Constitution; Eisenhower Doctrine; Eisenhower, Dwight David; Jinmen-Mazu Crises

FORRESTAL, JAMES VINCENT
(*b.* 15 February 1892; *d.* 22 May 1949)

Secretary of the navy (1944–1947) and secretary of defense (1947–1949) during World War II and the early years of the Cold War. Born in Matteawan (now part of Beacon), New York, Forrestal worked as a reporter and city editor before attending Dartmouth College in 1911. He transferred to Princeton University in 1912 and became editor of the prestigious *Daily Princetonian*. His classmates voted him Most Likely to Succeed, as well as The Man Nobody Knows. Forrestal mysteriously withdrew from Princeton weeks before graduation, ostensibly because he was lacking a course credit.

In the fall of 1916, after a short stint in journalism, he joined the prestigious Wall Street brokerage firm of Dillon, Read, as a bond salesman. In 1917, during World War I, Forrestal enlisted in the department of the Navy, was promoted to lieutenant in 1918, and resigned in 1918, after which he returned to Dillon, Read.

In 1926, Forrestal married Josephine Ogden, a *Vogue* editor and Ziegfeld Follies dancer. After a rapid rise to partnership at Dillon, Read, Forrestal became president in the 1930s. In June 1940, he was at the peak of his career, a multimillionaire and prominent figure on Wall Street with wide connections in national and international business. Recommended by Supreme Court Justice William O. Douglas, Forrestal accepted an appointment as a $10,000-a-year personal assistant to president Franklin D. Roosevelt. He specialized in Latin American affairs, but though possibly not aware of it, Forrestal was one of many bankers, industrialists, business people, and lawyers whom the administration was recruiting for prominent roles in the war preparedness effort.

Shortly after Forrestal and his wife arrived in Washington, D.C., in 1940, Josephine suffered a breakdown that was diagnosed as schizophrenia. Forrestal kept his wife's illness a secret and tried to pretend nothing had happened. Her illness became a large factor in his own breakdown years later.

On 22 August 1940, after only six weeks as Roosevelt's personal assistant, Forrestal was designated first undersecretary of the Navy, a post newly created by Congress. He was given total responsibility for procurement, which he quickly systematized as well as for establishing integrated planning for the first time in the history of the navy. From 1940 to June 1945, the inventory of the naval fleet grew from 1,099 to 50,759 vessels; its ranks of officers and sailors grew from 160,997 to 3.4 million. His success in expanding the navy was so great that by the end of World War II he had turned it into a larger organization than the combined fleets of the rest of the world.

When Secretary of the Navy Frank Knox died unexpectedly in mid-1944, Roosevelt chose Forrestal to succeed him. The press, public, and navy approved unanimously and Forrestal became the principal spokesman for the navy during the war.

In August 1945, Forrestal contributed decisively to ending the war with Japan. With Harry Truman now president and the second atomic bomb having been dropped on Nagasaki, a Tokyo broadcast expressed Japan's readiness to accept unconditional surrender as detailed in the Potsdam Declaration, provided they "did not prejudice the prerogatives of his Majesty as a Sovereign Ruler." Most of Truman's advisers argued for accepting the condition, but Secretary of State James F. Byrnes thought U.S. citizens would not accept this concession. Forrestal suggested they accept the Japanese condition, but call it unconditional surrender anyway. Truman and Byrnes agreed, and the Japanese war came to an end.

After the Japanese surrender, Forrestal expected to leave government. He wished to publish a newspaper or found a magazine of serious political commentary, but concerns about national security held him back. Perceiving a new threat posed by the Soviet Union, Forrestal advocated the containment of Soviet influence long before it was promulgated in the Truman Doctrine of 1947. Strongly opposing measures designed to reduce Germany and Japan to impotence, Forrestal supported economic aid to turn those countries into effective barriers against Soviet expansion. In 1946, he stood behind the decision to send a U.S. warship to Greece and Turkey, both of which appeared to be under communist threat. Forrestal opposed the creation of the state of Israel in 1948 on the grounds that it would alienate oil-producing states in the Arab world and lead to a Soviet foothold in the Middle East.

In the fall of 1945, President Truman's sudden push for "military unification" caught the navy and Forrestal off-guard. Believing the navy "politically dumb" and in need of help to defend its independence, he found another reason to stay in office. He fought for greater unity of the armed services but not complete integration. After much debate the final compromise was largely Forrestal's work. The National Security Act, adopted on 26 July 1947, effected the reorganization that created a single Department of Defense, with the secretary of defense given cabinet rank.

When in September 1947 Secretary of War Robert Patterson declined Truman's proffered appointment as secretary of defense, the president turned to Forrestal, a surprising choice. Forrestal had zealously argued against the president's plan of military unification and was in an awkward position to oversee the entire armed forces. Truman probably reasoned that if Forrestal remained secretary of the navy, he would make the job of the secretary of defense more difficult, whereas if he were secretary of defense, he would make the system work. Forrestal accepted the job and sought a balance of services that had previously operated separately as navy, army, and air force. A battle began between the three, however, and air power advocates in the air force and Congress were determined the air force should receive the lion's share of the military budget.

While this battle was being fought, U.S.-Soviet relations deteriorated. Forrestal recommended a modest military buildup, which placed him at odds with Truman, who insisted on a balanced budget. Forrestal's compromise budget figure of $16.9 million was overridden by Truman's ceiling of $15 million. The strains of Forrestal's position began to take their toll and his confidence began to erode due to fatigue and a mounting sense of failure to bring order and harmony to the military establishment and to convince the president to support an enlarged military budget. Forrestal became increasingly concerned about the activities of the Communist party and began to support extreme-right political causes. He believed Israeli secret agents were following him. Years later, Israeli sources admitted that agents had been following him to discover whether he was secretly negotiating with representatives of Arab countries.

By the late fall of 1948, Forrestal had lost standing with President Truman. After his surprising reelection, Truman announced several cabinet changes. In March 1949, and in the wake of growing reports of Forrestal's irrational behavior, Truman asked Forrestal to resign. Shortly afterward, Forrestal was diagnosed as suffering from "reactive depression." He was admitted to Bethesda Naval Hospital in Maryland, where on 22 May 1949 he committed suicide by leaping from a window.

DOUGLAS BRINKLEY

See also Cold War; Containment; Defense, U.S. Department of; Israel; Kennan, George Frost; National Security Act; Navy, U.S. Department of; Truman, Harry S.; Truman Doctrine; World War II

FURTHER READING

Dorwart, Jeffrey. *Eberstadt and Forrestal: A National Security Partnership, 1909–1949*. College Station, Tex., 1991.
Greenhalgh, Robert, and Robert Howe Connery. *Forrestal and the Navy*. New York, 1962.
Hoopes, Townsend, and Douglas Brinkley. *Driven Patriot: The Life and Times of James Forrestal*. New York, 1992.
Millis, Walter, ed. *The Forrestal Diaries*. New York, 1951.
Rogow, A. Arnold. *James Forrestal: A Study of Personality, Politics, and Policy*. New York, 1983.

FORSYTH, JOHN

(*b.* 22 October 1789; *d.* 21 October 1841)

Secretary of state from 1834 to 1841. Forsyth served as Republican congressman from Georgia from 1813 to 1818 and chaired the House Foreign Relations Committee. He entered the U.S. Senate briefly in 1818, but resigned to accept the post of U.S. Minister to Spain, which he held from 1819 to 1823. He was ill suited for the mission. He secured Spanish ratification of the 1819 Adams-Onís Treaty but wrote several intemperate diplomatic notes that angered the Madrid government and led to his recall as soon as the treaty was approved. On his return to the United States, Forsyth reentered state and national politics. He served one term in Congress from 1823 to 1827, one term as governor of Georgia from 1827 to 1829, and another term in the U.S. Senate from 1829 to 1834. During this period he aligned himself with the developing Jacksonian Democrats.

In 1834 Andrew Jackson appointed Forsyth secretary of state, a post he held to the close of Jackson's term and through the Martin Van Buren administration from 1837 to 1841. During his tenure as secretary Forsyth upheld Jackson's bellicose position when the French government reneged on its agreement to pay spoliation claims to the United States in accordance with an 1831 treaty. Forsyth strenuously resisted British claims for the right to visit and search U.S. vessels suspected as slave traders off the coast of Africa. In the Amistad case of 1839, in which Spanish-owned slaves bound between Cuban ports seized control of the ship carrying them and landed in the United States, Forsyth conceded that the slaves should be returned to Spanish jurisdiction. He was overruled by a federal district court (and ultimately the U.S. Supreme Court) which freed the slaves. Forsyth's other involvements included U.S. recognition of Texas independence, accomplished in 1837, and efforts to join Texas to the United States, which failed.

While Forsyth was secretary of state, the United States rejected Britain's proposal to compromise over the disputed Maine-Canada boundary, primarily because of Maine's intransigence. A dangerous moment in Anglo-American relations occurred in December 1837 when British and Canadian forces attacked the U.S. steamboat *Caroline*, which was assisting Canadians who were rebelling against their government. New York officials arrested a Canadian on a charge of murder for his participation in the raid. Forsyth was a capable, if lackluster, secretary of state who was a loyal servant to Presidents Jackson and Van Buren.

KENNETH R. STEVENS

See also Adams-Onís Treaty; Amistad Affair; Caroline Affair; France; Jackson, Andrew; Slave Trade and Slavery; Spain; Van Buren, Martin

FURTHER READING

Duckett, Alvin L. John Forsyth, *Political Tactician*. Athens, Ga., 1962.

McCormac, Eugene I. "John Forsyth, Secretary of State, July 1, 1834 to March 3, 1837." In *The American Secretaries of State and Their Diplomacy*, vol. 4, edited by Samuel Flagg Bemis. (New York, 1928): 299–343.

FOSTER, JOHN WATSON

(*b.* 2 March 1836; *d.* 15 November 1917)

Minister to Mexico (1873–1880), minister to Russia (1880–1881), minister to Spain (1883–1885), and secretary of state (1892–1893); Foster was noted for his negotiating skills and his writings on American diplomacy. Born in Pike county, Indiana, he graduated from the University of Indiana (1855), spent a year at Harvard Law School, and, after clerking for a lawyer in Cincinnati, was admitted to the Indiana bar in 1857, and practiced law in Evansville, Indiana, where he became prominent in Republican party politics. After serving in the Union Army during the Civil War, Foster returned to Evansville where he published the Daily Journal and rose to the chairmanship of the Republican state committee. In his first foreign experience of any kind, he served with extraordinary competence as minister to Mexico (1873–1880), where he persuaded a reluctant administration in Washington to recognize the government of Porfirio Diaz. Following relatively uneventful tenures as minister to Russia and Spain, he established a successful international law practice in Washington, D.C., where his clients included the governments of China, Russia, and Chile. During President Benjamin Harrison's administration, Foster was made special plenipotentiary to negotiate reciprocity agreements (1890–1891) and special agent for Fur Seal Arbitration (1892–1893), and was appointed secretary of state in June 1892 following the abrupt resignation of

James G. Blaine. As secretary, Foster led an unsuccessful effort to annex Hawai'i and negotiated a peaceful settlement of the "*Baltimore* Affair" with the government in Chile.

In 1895, at the request of Chinese Viceroy Li Hung, he travelled to Japan to assist the Chinese government in negotiating the Treaty of Shimonoseki. In the brief Sino-Japanese War, the Chinese forces had been crushed and at Shimonoseki the Chinese were forced to recognize Korean independence; cede Formosa, the Pescadores Islands, and the Liaotung Peninsula to Japan; pay Japan a heavy indemnity; and open four additional Chinese ports to Japanese traders. Only the intervention of European powers prevented the Japanese from implementing all the terms of the treaty. Named ambassador for a special mission to Great Britain and Russia in 1897, Foster sought unsuccessfully to arrange a four-power conference to resolve disputes related to the harvesting of Bering Sea fur seals. In 1903 he represented the United States before the tribunal in London arbitrating the demarcation of the Alaska-Canada border. In 1907, accompanied by his nineteen-year-old grandson, John Foster Dulles, Foster counseled the Chinese delegation at the Second Hague Conference.

An advocate of U.S. expansion in the Pacific (especially Hawai'i), and of the wider use of arbitration and international law by the nations of the world, Foster urged a greater U.S. involvement in world affairs including the support of Christian missionary efforts, expanded trade through reciprocity agreements, and a more professional diplomatic corps. He wrote *A Century of American Diplomacy, 1776 to 1876* (1900), *American Diplomacy in the Orient* (1904), and numerous other works on U.S. foreign policy. His candid two-volume *Diplomatic Memoirs* (1909) presents valuable information on, and analysis of, the individuals and events of his era. He helped found the American Society for International Law in 1906 and the Carnegie Endowment for International Peace in 1910. Foster was influential in launching the early careers of two secretaries of state: those of his son-in-law, Robert Lansing (secretary of state, 1915–1920), who began his international career in Foster's law firm, and of his grandson, John Foster Dulles (secretary of state 1953–1959), whose education, training, and first employment opportunities in diplomacy and law were carefully arranged by his proud grandfather. Scholarly, nationalistic, and deeply religious, Foster believed that the United States had a special mission to bestow the benefits of democracy and Christianity on the less enlightened people of the world. He believed this could for the most part be achieved peacefully, through Christian moral leadership, legalistic organizations devoted to world peace, and American investments in the world's non-industrial nations. Although Foster frequently proclaimed himself a pacifist, he fought in the

Civil War because of his anti-slavery convictions and approved of the U.S. entry into World War I as an unavoidable means of halting German aggression.

MICHAEL J. DEVINE

See also Alaska Boundary Dispute; Arbitration; Blaine, James Gillespie; Carnegie Endowment for International Peace; Chile; China; Diaz (Jose de la Cruz), Porfirio; Dulles, John Foster; Harrison, Benjamin; Hawai'i; International Law; Lansing, Robert; Mexico; Missionaries; Sealing; Sino-Japanese War

FURTHER READING

Devine, Michael J. *John W. Foster: Politics and Diplomacy in the Imperial Era, 1873–1917.* Athens, Ohio, 1981.

FOUR-POWER TREATY

See Washington Conference on Limitation of Armaments

FOURTEEN POINTS

President Woodrow Wilson's statement of U.S. objectives in World War I, stated in an 8 January 1918 address to Congress. The Fourteen Points were crucial in persuading Germany to seek an armistice, outlined Wilson's vision for a new world order, and influenced American thinking and policies for decades. They were simultaneously a response to an immediate crisis during World War I, an interpretation of the causes of World War I in particular and all wars in general, and a reflection of deep currents in the U.S. diplomatic tradition.

The German crisis was both military and political. German forces at the beginning of 1918 were stronger than at any time since the beginning of the war in 1914. Bolshevik revolutionaries had concluded an armistice with Germany on 15 December 1917, allowing the transfer of German forces from Russia to the western front in preparation for a spring offensive aimed at winning the war. Exhausted British and French armies suffered low morale. Italy, their ally, had been decisively defeated at the battle of Caporetto in the autumn of 1917 by German and Austrian forces. The U.S. Army was still training and would not arrive for combat in Europe for another six months.

The political crisis of 1918 flowed from the Bolshevik appeal of 22 November 1917, for a peace to be determined by the peoples of the warring powers against their imperialist governments. To underline the wickedness of governments, the Bolsheviks published texts of secret treaties found in archives and concluded earlier in the war among the powers at war with Germany. The treaties demonstrated the governments' cynicism, plans to divide the spoils of victory, and alleged moral bankruptcy. The selfish objectives, combined with vengeful Allied rhetoric, supported German advocates of complete victory as the only alternative to the extreme terms the Allies intended to impose.

President Wilson deplored the objectives of the treaties and wished to disassociate the United States from them. He feared that war-weary people would be persuaded by the Bolshevik appeal, would stop fighting, and would hand victory to Germany. Another dire possibility was that Bolshevik revolutionary doctrine would spread beyond Russia and subvert the liberal constitutional democracy on which Wilson's political faith was founded. When Wilson's confidential envoy Colonel Edward M. House failed to persuade the European governments associated with the United States in the war with Germany to renounce their selfish aims and thereby answer the Bolshevik appeal, Wilson decided the United States had to act unilaterally. Working with Colonel House and drawing on studies prepared by a group of academic experts on war aims, known as "The Inquiry," he prepared a public statement. The president hoped that four audiences would heed his words and react in desirable ways: (1) the U.S. people, who would be inspired by the clarity and ideals of the nation's war aims; (2) the people of Great Britain and France, who would insist their governments adopt unselfish objectives; (3) the people of Russia, who would repudiate the Bolsheviks and return to the war against Germany; and (4) liberals in Germany, who would realize that Germany could occupy an honorable place in the community of nations by accepting reasonable terms.

The first and last of the points were the most important, the bookends holding the others in place. The first called for "open covenants of peace openly arrived at" and the permanent abolition of private (that is, secret) international agreements. This point echoed Wilson's 1917 speech calling for "peace without victory," condemning secret diplomacy and implying an offer of a negotiated peace rather than one imposed by the victors on the vanquished. Open diplomacy implied that democratic governments had to be accountable to the people to be reliable preservers of peace and, conversely, that the old system of secret maneuvering for selfish advantage by a small number of officials unaccountable to the people was itself a cause of war. Open diplomacy was rooted in the U.S. Constitution, which required that treaties had to be presented to the Senate and approved before ratification.

The fourteenth point stated the necessity of creating "a general association of nations...for the purpose of affording mutual guarantees of political independence and territorial integrity onto great and small states alike." This point evolved into the League of Nations, predecessor to the United Nations. It was Wilson's formula for preventing war and aggression through collective security, and it reflected both a proposal for an inter-American security pact advanced in 1914 and the advocacy of a citizens group known as the League to Enforce Peace.

The second point, calling for freedom of navigation on the seas in peace and war, was a response to U.S. disagreement during 1914–1917 with Great Britain over the rights of neutrals and, above all, to the conflict with Germany over the use of the submarine. The innovation was in the qualification in the final clause of the point: freedom of seas "except as the seas may be closed in whole or in part by international action for the enforcement of international covenants." The qualification expressed Wilson's hope that the "general association of nations" would use blockades enforced at sea as punishment of international blockades as a deterrent to aggression or punishment in cases of aggression.

The third point called for equality of trade conditions among all parties to the peace, with the lowest possible tariffs. This was a combination of traditional U.S. support of free and unfettered trade (the "open door") and Wilson's belief that trade rivalries and economic discrimination contributed to hostility among nations. The point was an offer to Germany designed to counteract threats from Great Britain and France that Germany might be faced with an economic "war after the war," denied a market for its goods, and subject to punitive economic arrangements.

The fourth point called for reduction of national armaments under adequate guarantees from the general association of nations. In the chicken-or-the-egg argument over whether insecurity produced arms races or arms races produced insecurity and led to war, Wilson gave priority to arms. By reducing arms by guaranteed international agreement, Wilson believed all nations would find security and less threat of war.

The fifth point reflected the idea that colonial rivalries caused war and that native peoples needed protection against exploitation. This point dealt specifically with the issue of what would happen to Germany's colonies in Africa and the Pacific, not with all colonies. Wilson was not advocating independence for non-white peoples. Instead, the point merely asked that the interests of the population (not their opinions) be considered when colonial territory was assigned to one power or another. Wilson shared the impression that German colonial practice had been brutal, and this principle assured against returning colonies to Germany.

The sixth and longest point called for the Germans to withdraw from all Russian territory, and for all nations to deal sympathetically with the plight of that politically unstable country. Wilson asked that Russia be accorded the right to determine its own future "under institutions of her own choosing" with "assistance also of every kind that she may need and may herself desire." Behind these benign generalities lay a tangle of controversy. Was Bolshevism freely chosen by the Russian people or was it imposed on them with assistance from the German enemy, the antithesis of democracy? To whom in Russia should assistance be granted and for what purposes? Wilson did not have answers to those questions and by the middle of 1918 had reluctantly agreed to U.S. participation in military intervention on Russian territory.

Other points called for evacuation and restoration of occupied Belgium (7); the return of invaded territory to France and the restoration of Alsace-Lorraine acquired by Germany in 1871 (8); changes in the frontiers of Italy along "clearly recognizable lines of nationality" (9); autonomy for the peoples of the Austro-Hungarian empire (10); a settlement of Balkan issues "along historically established lines of allegiance and nationality" (11); the breakup of the Ottoman Empire (12); and independence for Poland (13).

The address did not achieve its immediate objectives. Russia descended into civil war and did not rejoin the fight against Germany. Nor did German public opinion demand peace. British prime minister David Lloyd George agreed with Wilson's aims, but French prime minister Georges Clemenceau was skeptical and derogatory. In the fall of 1918, the German military high command asked for an armistice and a peace to be negotiated on the basis of the Fourteen Points and other Wilsonian statements. Colonel House returned to Europe and won qualified French and British approval for an armistice followed by a peace conference based on the Fourteen Points. House was assisted in this effort by an interpretation of the points written largely by Walter Lippmann and approved by Wilson. The armistice was signed and went into effect 11 November 1918. The ensuing Versailles peace treaty written at the Paris Peace Conference both violated and fulfilled parts of the Fourteen Points. The spirit was violated in that the treaty was negotiated by the victors and presented, take it or leave it, to Germany. Changes made at Germany's request were minimal. The exclusion and ostracism of Russia and the failure to establish effective arms limitations also violated Wilson's points. Furthermore, when the U.S. Senate failed to approve the treaty, the League of Nations lacked U.S. membership. A number of specific territorial aims, however, mentioned in the Fourteen Points were achieved.

GADDIS SMITH

See also Blockade; Freedom of the Seas; House, Edward Mandell; League of Nations; Lippmann, Walter; Neutral Rights; Open Door Policy; Russia and the Soviet Union; Submarine Warfare; Wilson, Thomas Woodrow; World War I

FURTHER READING

Gelfand, Lawrence E. *The Inquiry: American Preparations for Peace, 1917–1919*. New Haven, Conn., 1963.

Knock, Thomas J. *To End All Wars: Woodrow Wilson and the Quest for a New World Order*. New York, 1992.

Mayer, Arno J. *Political Origins of the New Diplomacy, 1917–1918*. New Haven, Conn., 1959. Revised edition, *Wilson vs. Lenin*. New York, 1964.

Trask, David F. *The United States and the Supreme War Council: American War Aims and Inter-Allied Strategy, 1917–1918*. Middletown, Conn., 1961.

Walsworth, Arthur. *America's Moment: 1918, American Diplomacy at the End of World War I*. New York, 1977.

FOX, CHARLES JAMES

(*b*. 24 January 1749; *d*. 13 September 1806)

British statesman who influenced policy toward the American colonies and the nascent United States. A liberal reformer and early supporter of Lord North (with whom he nevertheless quarreled intermittently), Fox was a popular member of Parliament, an extraordinary orator, an occasional cabinet official, and eventually foreign secretary. Fox's prominence in the Whig party, his well-deserved reputation as a libertine, and his bitter invective against King George III and leading conservative statesmen generally resulted in his exclusion from the most powerful cabinet positions. On two occasions, however, Fox had a significant impact on the United States and its foreign relations.

For four critical months in 1782, Fox, as foreign secretary in a coalition government reluctantly accepted by the king, tried to shape Britain's peace overtures to the new United States at the close of the American Revolution. A decade earlier, he had broken with the North ministry over the handling of the colonial crisis that led to the revolutionary war. Throughout the war Fox blasted the cabinet's attempts to hold the empire together by force. The clamor for peace brought Fox and other opposition leaders to power in March 1782. Fox pressed for an immediate recognition of American independence, even before the signing of the peace treaty. Every step to improve Anglo-American relations, he argued, would help to secure for Great Britain the benefits it had once enjoyed from its colonies. Divisions within the new ministry, particularly the conflict over American policy between Fox and William Petty, the Earl of Shelburne, defeated this policy, leading Fox to resign in July 1782.

For the next twenty-four years, Fox served as head of the Whig party in Parliament, emerging as the inveterate enemy of William Pitt, while championing a wide range of domestic reforms opposed by the king and the conservative majority. In January 1806, however, Fox returned to the cabinet amidst the renewed crisis of the Napoleon-

ic Wars. Given his earlier stance, Fox's appointment as foreign secretary imbued the American minister to London, James Monroe, with hopes of progress on the vexatious issues of neutral rights and impressment. Early discussions between them suggested that Great Britain might restore the broken-voyage loophole in its enforcement of the Rule of War of 1756 (that neutrals could not engage in a trade during war that they were excluded from in time of peace), effectively nullifying the restrictions of the 1804 *Essex* decision on continuous voyage and opening trading opportunities for U.S. merchants. Expecting the arrival of William Pinckney as envoy extraordinary, however, Fox and Monroe postponed their negotiations. In May a new Order in Council included slight concessions on the carrying trade, but announced an unacceptable paper blockade. Before the negotiations could resume, Fox was on his deathbed.

JAMES E. LEWIS, JR.

See also American Revolution; George III; Great Britain; Impressment; Monroe, James; Monroe–Pinkney Treaty; Napoleonic Wars; Neutral Rights; Orders in Council; Pitt, William

FURTHER READING

Ayling, Stanley. *Fox: The Life of Charles James Fox*. London, 1991.

Mitchell, L. G. *Charles James Fox*. New York, 1992.

Perkins, Bradford. *Prologue to War: England and the United States, 1805–1812*. Berkeley, Calif., 1961.

FRANCE

Located in Western Europe, bordering the North Atlantic Ocean between Spain and Germany. Without doubt, there exists between France and the United States a certain sentimental bond, one that conjures up hallowed names and events from more than two centuries of contact: Benjamin Franklin charming the philosophes in Paris, the Marquis de Lafayette rallying to the U.S. cause during the American Revolution, the French gift of the Statue of Liberty in 1886, U.S. doughboys fighting in trenches "over there" in World War I, and again on the beaches of Normandy in 1944. Despite these cherished images, the history of Franco-American diplomatic relations is one of fierce division, bitter quarrels, misunderstanding, and conflict. Such has been the mutual suspicion between the two countries that were it not for the presence of common enemies—Great Britain in the eighteenth and nineteenth centuries, Germany and the Soviet Union in the twentieth—France and the United States might themselves have become warring rivals rather than the reluctant allies they have been off and on for more than two hundred years.

Establishment of the United States, 1763–1815

The first alliance of the United States with a foreign power was signed with France in 1778. The diplomatic origins of this treaty lay in the outcome of the Seven Years' War (1756–1763). France, defeated by an Anglo-Prussian alliance, lost nearly all of its North American territories to Great Britain and Spain in the Treaty of Paris (1763). With the exception of the small islands Saint Pierre and Miquelon off Newfoundland, France ceded all of Canada to Great Britain, as well as the lands stretching south and west toward the Mississippi River. Spain, a French ally, received all of Louisiana Territory west of the Mississippi in return for agreeing to an immediate peace and the cession of Florida to Great Britain. This humiliating expulsion from North America was a severe blow to French imperial pretensions, and almost immediately, the French king's principal minister, Étienne François, Duc de Choiseul, began to plot revenge. In an effort to isolate Great Britain in Europe, Choiseul tried to improve France's relations with Spain and Austria and made overtures to Prussia. In the meantime, he carefully watched for signs of strain in the relationship between Great Britain and its North American colonies, in the hopes of exploiting any rift.

This strategy proved quite shrewd, for Choiseul perceived that in the eyes of the American colonists, Great Britain and not France now stood as the chief threat to the burgeoning, expansive American colonies. Differences between Great Britain and the colonies, previously masked by the French menace, now flourished. In the decade following the Treaty of Paris, Great Britain attempted to consolidate its hold on the colonies, primarily in order to secure revenue to pay for the staggering costs of the Seven Years' War—a war ostensibly fought, in large part, to defend the American colonies from French incursions—and to cover the costs of maintaining troops in North America. The resistance with which these measures were met signaled to French observers that a possible breach between Great Britain and its colonies might yet provide an opportunity for France to return to North America. Sure enough, on 29 November 1775, the Continental Congress authorized the Committee of Secret Correspondence to seek the aid of foreign nations, particularly France, in the struggle for independence.

The evidence of insurrection in the colonies was keenly noted by the new French foreign minister, Charles Gravier, Comte de Vergennes. Like his predecessor Choiseul, Vergennes hoped to profit from a break between the colonies and Great Britain, and in August 1775 sent a secret messenger, Julien-Alexandre Achard de Bonvouloir, to meet with the Continental Congress. Upon his arrival in Philadelphia in December 1775, Bon-

vouloir met with the Committee of Secret Correspondence, and informed his interlocutors, Benjamin Franklin and John Jay among them, that France was favorably disposed to the colonial uprising and would sell the Americans arms and supplies. Following these discussions, the committee instructed Silas Deane, a former congressional delegate from Connecticut, to travel to France to purchase arms and uniforms for 25,000 soldiers.

Bonvouloir's report to Vergennes informing him of the American desire for French aid provided the minister with the opportunity for which France had been waiting since 1763. Vergennes presented the new young King Louis XVI with a memorandum setting out the advantages of assisting the American rebels. Great Britain's wealth and naval power, he asserted, rested upon Great Britain's monopoly of the American trade; if that monopoly were broken, so too would be the British dominance. These arguments persuaded Louis XVI in May 1776 to authorize an appropriation of one million livres to aid the rebels. Over the next seven years, France provided some 35 million livres in loans and 10 million in grants to the American revolutionaries. Thus, even before Deane's arrival in Paris in July and before the Declaration of Independence, the French monarchy had decided to assist the American colonists in breaking Great Britain's hold over North America.

In order to avoid providing Great Britain with a causus belli, however, Vergennes intended to keep France's subsidies to America secret. To this end, he employed the clever dramatist Pierre Augustin Caron de Beaumarchais as the head of a fictitious trading company named Roderigue Hortalez et Compagnie, which received the government funds, purchased arms and supplies, and sold them to the Americans on credit. The weapons delivered through this ruse proved vital to the triumph of the Continental army over the British forces of General John Burgoyne at Saratoga in October 1777.

Following the Declaration of Independence, Congress appointed a joint diplomatic commission to France, whose purpose was to seek a treaty of amity and commerce, and to secure military supplies, through loan or purchase. The commission that gathered in Paris in December 1776 consisted of Silas Deane, already in Paris, Benjamin Franklin, and Arthur Lee, a former colonial agent for Massachusetts, then serving in London. The commissioners had been supplied with a model treaty, devised by John Adams, along with instructions to secure a commercial treaty while carefully avoiding any military connection and any territorial trade-off with France in return for aid. Adams was asking France to risk war with Great Britain without any assurance that the Americans would support France or provide territorial spoils. Vergennes welcomed the commissioners, but he refused an alliance on these terms, not least because

MINISTERS AND AMBASSADORS TO FRANCE

MINISTER	PERIOD OF APPOINTMENT	ADMINISTRATION
Benjamin Franklin[1]	1778–1785	Continental Congress
		Confederation Congress
Thomas Jefferson	1785–1789	Confederation Congress
		Washington
William Short	1790–1792	Washington
Gouverneur Morris	1792–1794[2]	Washington
James Monroe	1794–1796	Washington
Charles Cotesworth Pinckney[3]	1796	
William Vans Murray[4]		
James A. Bayard[5]		
Robert R. Livingston	1801–1804	Jefferson
John Armstrong[6]	1804–1810	Jefferson
		Madison
Jonathan Russell	1810[7]-1811	
Joel Barlow	1811–1812	Madison
William H. Crawford	1813–1815	Madison
Albert Gallatin	1815–1823	Madison
		Monroe
James Brown	1823–1829	Monroe
		J. Q. Adams
William C. Rives	1829–1832	Jackson
Levett Harris	1833	Jackson
Edward Livingston	1833–1835[8]	Jackson
Lewis Cass	1836–1842	Jackson
		Van Buren
		W. H. Harrison
		Tyler
Henry A. Wise[9]		
William R. King	1844–1846	Tyler
		Polk
Charles J. Ingersoll[10]		
Richard Rush	1847–1849	Polk
William C. Rives	1849–1853	Taylor
		Fillmore
John Y. Mason	1854–1859	Pierce
		Buchanan
Charles J. Faulkner	1860–1861	Buchanan
William L. Dayton	1861–1864	Lincoln
John Bigelow	1865–1866	A. Johnson
John A. Dix	1866–1869	A. Johnson
Elihu B. Washburne	1869–1877	Grant
Edward F. Noyes	1877–1881	Hayes
Levi P. Morton	1881–1885	Garfield
		Arthur
Robert M. McLane	1885–1889	Cleveland
Whitelaw Reid	1889–1892	B. Harrison
T. Jefferson Coolidge	1892–1893	B. Harrison

(table continues on next page)

AMBASSADOR	PERIOD OF APPOINTMENT	ADMINISTRATION
James B. Eustis	1893[11]–1897	Cleveland
Horace Porter	1897–1905	McKinley
		T. Roosevelt
Robert S. McCormick	1905–1907	T. Roosevelt
Henry White	1907–1909	T. Roosevelt
Robert Bacon	1909–1912	Taft
		Wilson
Myron T. Herrick	1912–1914	Taft
		Wilson
William G. Sharp	1914–1919	Wilson
Hugh Campbell Wallace	1919–1921	Wilson
Myron T. Herrick	1921–1929	Harding
		Coolidge
Walter E. Edge	1929–1933	Hoover
Jesse Isidor Straus	1933–1936	F. Roosevelt
William C. Bullitt	1936–1940[12]	F. Roosevelt
William D. Leahy	1941–1942[13]	F. Roosevelt
Jefferson Caffery	1944–1949[14]	F. Roosevelt
		Truman
David K. E. Bruce	1949–1952	Truman
James C. Dunn	1952–1953	Truman
C. Douglas Dillon	1953–1957	Eisenhower
Amory Houghton	1957–1961	Eisenhower
James M. Gavin	1961–1962	Eisenhower
Charles E. Bohlen	1962–1968	Kennedy
		L. Johnson
R. Sargent Shriver, Jr.	1968–1970	L. Johnson
		Nixon
Arthur K. Watson	1970–1972	Nixon
John N. Irwin, II	1973–1974	Nixon
Kenneth Rush	1974–1977	Ford
Arthur A. Hartman	1977–1981	Carter
Evan Griffith Galbraith	1981–1985	Reagan
Joe M. Rodgers	1985–1989	Reagan
		Bush
Walter J. P. Curley	1989–1993	Bush
Pamela C. Harriman	1993–Present	Clinton

[1]Commissioned also to negotiate a treaty with Sweden.
[2]Morris was still at his post when his successor presented credentials.
[3]Proceeded to post, but was not recieved by the Directory; left post, 5 Feb. 1797. Nomination was confirmed by the Senate, but no record has been found of a new commission following confirmation.
[4]Not commissioned; nomination superseded by a nominiation of Murray and two others to serve on a joint commission. Received his commission about 13 Feb. 1811; was not isseud a letter of credence, but continued his official relaitons with the Govt. of France begun in Sept. 1810 as Chargé d' Affiares ad interim.
[5]Did not serve under this appointment.
[6]Nomination was confirmed by the Senate, but no record has been found of a new commission following confirmation.
[7]Commission not of record, but enclosed with an instruction of this date.
[8]Thomas P. Barton served as Chargé d' Affiares ad interim until 8 Nov. 1835, when he closed Legation Paris, having been recalled.
[9]Not commissioned; nomination rejected by the Senate.
[10]Not commissioned; nomination rejected by the Senate.
[11]Took oath of office, but did not proceed to post in this capacity.
[12]Near the end of Bullitt's term of service, Anthony J. Drexel Biddle, Jr., acted as Deputy Ambassador to France, 13-25 June 1940.
[13]S. Pinkney Tuck was serving as Chargé d' Affaires ad interim when France severed diplomatic relations with the U.S., 8 Nov. 1942.
[14]Embassy Paris was opened to the public 1 Dec. 1944 with Ambassador Caffery in charge pending presentation of his letter of credence.

Sources: *Principal Officers of the Department of State and United States Chiefs of Missions.* ©1991 by Office of the Historian, Bureau of Public Affairs, Washington, D.C.; *The U.S. Government Manual*, Annual. Washington, D.C.

France's naval rearmament was far from complete, and he could not yet risk war with Great Britain. Still, he did procure for them an additional grant of two million livres from the French treasury. Throughout 1777, with the American war effort stalled, the commissioners in France tried unsuccessfully to secure a French alliance. Although the French treasury kept up a steady supply of loans and grants to pay for shipments of arms, uniforms, and supplies, the ailing Continental army hardly made an appealing alliance partner against the formidable British.

In December 1777, however, American fortunes improved. News arrived in Paris of the American victory over Burgoyne at Saratoga, providing the commissioners with great bargaining power to apply against Vergennes. Now, the commissioners could threaten to conclude a compromise peace with Great Britain, leaving France without any return on its investment in the rebel cause, and leaving British power in North America intact. Great Britain, however, was not prepared to offer unconditional independence, and the American commissioners much preferred a French alliance with which to prosecute the war rather than a compromise with Great Britain to end it. Vergennes also saw the moment had come for decisive action: French naval rearmament had been completed and, with the British briefly on the defensive, France's prospects in the war appeared good. In any case, two years of French aid to the rebels had badly soured relations with Great Britain and the two nations were drifting toward war.

On 6 February 1778 France concluded two treaties with the United States, one a treaty of amity and commerce based on the freedom of the seas, the other a treaty of alliance in case recognition of the United States should bring war with Great Britain—which, of course, it did. The alliance provided that neither party would strike a separate peace with Great Britain without the other's consent. There would be no peace until the independence of the United States was secured by treaty, after which France would guarantee the independence of the United States. In return, the United States would guarantee the possession by France of its West Indian islands.

Within two months, France dispatched a dozen ships of the line to New York, in the hopes of destroying Admiral William Howe's fleet and blockading British-held New York into submission. The French fleet failed, however, and Vergennes realized only a combined Franco-Spanish fleet could defeat the British. In order to gain Spanish entry into the war, France paid a heavy price, offering Spain support for its designs on Florida, assistance in taking Gibraltar, and a promise to undertake a joint invasion of Great Britain itself. France's alliance with Spain, signed on 12 April 1779, had direct consequences for the United States. Together, the French and Spanish fleets established superiority over the outnumbered British, making possible the Franco-American victory over Gen-

eral Charles Cornwallis at Yorktown, Virginia, in October 1781. Meanwhile the Spanish armies fought very successfully against the British in Florida, forcing them to divert scarce resources from the north. In short, French diplomacy, as well as French military and financial aid, proved crucial to the success of the American War of Independence.

The early life of the Franco-American alliance consummated during the American Revolution was by no means a smooth and amicable one. United by a common antipathy to the British presence in North America, the two countries were nonetheless divided over military and diplomatic strategy. In setting out the war aims of the Americans, for example, Vergennes's minister in America, Conrad Alexandre Gérard, fought the demands of New England congressmen to include Canada, Nova Scotia, and the Newfoundland fisheries in the American desiderata. While Gérard claimed that he did so in order to avoid prolonging the war, his actions raised the suspicions of certain factions in Congress that France did not have America's true interests at heart. By 1780, as the military fortunes of the Americans worsened and the financial situation bordered on the catastrophic, American leaders were forced to place nearly all diplomatic and military authority into the hands of the French for, despite the aspersions some Americans cast upon the French war effort, France remained the only hope for a favorable outcome of the war. Such was American dependence upon France that in 1781 Gérard's successor, Anne-César, Chevalier de la Luzerne, was able to force the Congress to form a peace commission whose actions were to be wholly subject to French approval. Congress in effect turned over its own powers to negotiate treaties to a foreign government—an act of submission unique in the annals of American diplomatic history. The victory at Yorktown, however, gave Americans renewed confidence that a favorable conclusion to the war could be secured.

Suddenly fearful that France might try to strike a deal with Great Britain and Spain at the expense of the United States, John Adams, John Jay, and Benjamin Franklin entered into peace negotiations with Great Britain. The new Shelburne ministry, eager for peace, agreed to recognize American independence. It also granted generous boundaries, including the eastern bank of the Mississippi and rights to the Newfoundland fisheries. On 30 November 1782, the American negotiators came to terms with the British without prior approval from Vergennes. This preliminary agreement broke the spirit if not the letter both of Congress's instructions and of the 1778 alliance. Vergennes was not unduly disturbed, however, for the British-American agreement provided him with enough leverage to bring his other ally, unrequited Spain, to the negotiating table. A final treaty of peace was signed in Paris on 3 September 1783. France had certainly been crucial to the success of the American Revolution, although she gained little for her efforts.

In the decades following independence, the United States remained dependent on trade with Great Britain and vulnerable to British economic manipulation. France had done nothing to curb British power by supporting the rebellion of the colonies. Instead, France incurred enormous debts, the burden of which the state could not bear. Further, the alliance of 1778—the centerpiece of France's North American policy—came under heavy strain soon after the conclusion of the Treaty of Paris.

In 1785 Thomas Jefferson began a three-year term as U.S. minister to France, a position from which he hoped to strengthen Franco-American trade relations as a means of weakening Great Britain's mercantile stranglehold over the young Republic; but Jefferson's vision of a strong Franco-American relationship designed to counter British economic manipulation was strongly opposed by Treasury Secretary Alexander Hamilton. Hamilton argued that Anglo-American commercial relations were so important to the economic health of the United States that certain sacrifices had to be made to keep this trade intact, even if it meant overlooking the terms of the 1778 treaty of amity and commerce with France. By the time Jefferson became secretary of state in 1789, France was embroiled in revolution and appeared likely to go to war with Great Britain.

President George Washington's administration had little cause to believe that aiding France against Great Britain would advance the national interest. On the contrary, trade with both belligerents might serve American mercantile interests very nicely. When in 1793 revolutionary France declared war on Great Britain, Holland, and Spain, President Washington issued a proclamation of neutrality, which came as a blow to the French government because it had expected at the very least sympathy from the United States toward the French cause. Paris received such sympathy both from Jefferson and from much of the American public, but not in great enough quantities to counterbalance the Hamiltonian determination to do nothing to harm Anglo-American trade relations.

After 1793, as the French Revolution veered away from its liberal, reforming path and lurched toward violence and cataclysm, President Washington adhered to Hamilton's anglophile principles in foreign policy. The French minister to the United States, Edmond Charles Genêt, only worsened relations between the two countries by behaving as if the neutrality proclamation were not in effect. Not only did Genêt outfit French privateers in U.S. ports, he revealed his country's interest in reacquiring Spanish-held Louisiana. The prospect of a new French empire in North America raised immediate concern in Washington's cabinet and reinforced the president's suspicions of French motives.

Franco-American relations went from bad to worse when, in 1794, Hamilton persuaded Washington to send Jay to London to obtain a treaty regulating Anglo-American wartime commercial relations. The resulting Jay's Treaty gave the British the right to seize French goods on neutral American ships, at a time when France was bound by treaty to resist doing the same to American ships carrying British goods. The French government, now in the hands of the Directory, claimed that Jay's Treaty was a de facto Anglo-American alliance, and a breach of the 1778 accord. In July 1796 the Directory decreed that France would treat neutral shipping the same way the British did, that is, by disregarding the "free ships, free goods" principle that had heretofore applied to American shipping. U.S. ships now had to contend with French as well as British depredations on the high seas.

So disillusioned had President Washington become with the French that in September 1796, upon declaring his decision to leave office at the end of his term, he warned future generations of Americans "to steer clear of permanent alliances with any portion of the foreign world." From the alliance of 1778, Americans drew the lesson that their best interests lay in carefully avoiding any involvement in the diplomacy of the Old World. As if to provide direct evidence of the kind of interference in America's affairs that Washington denounced, the new French minister to the United States, Pierre Adet, lent public support to Jefferson against John Adams in the election of 1796, sponsoring editorials in newspapers denouncing the Federalists. Adams triumphed anyway and even tried to improve Franco-American relations by sending a mission to Paris in 1797. His emissaries, however, were met by three secret agents of Foreign Minister Charles Maurice de Talleyrand-Périgord. These three men, later referred to as X, Y, and Z in official accounts of the affair, demanded a "loan" to France of more than $12 million, in addition to a bribe of $250,000, as a condition for negotiations to improve Franco-American relations. When news of the French effrontery reached the United States in early 1798, war fever broke out. Talleyrand was burned in effigy, while Federalist patriots and orators damned the French. In the spring of 1798, Congress ordered increases in naval armaments and authorized the U.S. Navy to seize French ships. In July, Congress declared an embargo on all commercial transactions with France.

During this Quasi-War, the U.S. Navy succeeded in protecting American shipping in the Caribbean, where most French depredations occurred, and thereby demonstrated U.S. resolve to confront France if necessary. The navy took as prizes some eighty-five French armed vessels—a small number compared to the 1,853 instances of spoliation suffered by Americans at the hands of French warships in the years 1793 to 1800. The Quasi-War, however, did not erupt into a full-blown conflagration. The Directory was hardly eager for war with the United States, fearing the possibility of an Anglo-American alliance, and the threat of such a pact on French possessions in the West Indies, especially the lucrative Saint Domingue (Haiti) colony. Hostilities would also provide American hawks such as Alexander Hamilton an excuse to undertake a campaign of conquest in Florida or Louisiana, denying to France what it hoped to gain from Spain, its weakened ally. Furthermore, the British had sunk much of the French fleet off the coast of Egypt in August 1798, and so French naval strength was at a low ebb. When in November 1799 Napoleon Bonaparte overthrew the Directory and became first consul, he wanted to improve relations with the United States in the hopes of resurrecting the French empire in North America and building a maritime coalition against Great Britain. Talleyrand, who retained his post under Bonaparte, therefore sought to defuse the crisis.

President Adams also shrank from forcing a war with France. The ferocity of the opposition to war by Jeffersonian Republicans made him fearful of leading a divided country into a conflict with a great military power. After an initial wave of anti-French sentiment, most Americans declared their hope that war could be avoided. Upon receiving assurances from France that U.S. envoys would be welcome in Paris to discuss a settlement of the dispute, Adams dispatched William Vans Murray, U.S. minister at The Hague, Chief Justice Oliver Ellsworth, and former North Carolina governor William R. Davie to negotiate a new foundation for Franco-American relations. The Americans did not receive the $20 million they asked as compensation for French spoliations, but Napoleon did agree to recognize the free ships, free goods principle. The parties also agreed to declare the 1778 treaty defunct. In the Convention of 1800, signed on 30 September at Château Môrtefontaine, the U.S. negotiators freed their country from its first, and now wholly undesired, entanglement in European affairs.

No sooner had the United States declared its independence from Old World imbroglios, however, did the long arm of European diplomacy reach across the ocean once again. The very day after the Convention of 1800 was signed, France and Spain concluded a secret treaty retroceding Louisiana to France. For almost a decade, French governments had been contemplating the retrieval of this vast province from Spain, chiefly as a means of supplying the French Caribbean islands with foodstuffs but also as a way of assuring French influence over the United States. The return of imperial France to North American soil, just when France had agreed to peace with Great Britain, presented the new U.S. president, Thomas Jefferson, with the greatest test of his administration. U.S. westward expansion, in which Jefferson fervently believed, might now be blocked by French control of the entire Mississippi Valley. Jefferson responded quickly to this threat. First, he dispatched a private emissary, Franco-American merchant Pierre S. du Pont de Nemours, to inform the French that should they come into possession of New Orleans, the United States would surely be thrown into an alliance with Great Britain, but, on the other hand, the United States might be willing to buy New Orleans and West Florida from France. Jefferson then empowered his minister in France, Robert R. Livingston, and James Monroe, as minister extraordinary, to negotiate for the purchase of these territories, offering as much as $10 million. The envoys were told that if France refused, they should cross the channel and sign an alliance with Great Britain.

To the astonishment of the American interlocutors, Napoleon did not refuse and offered not only New Orleans and West Florida, but the entire Louisiana Territory as well. Three factors informed this decision. First, Louisiana had been intended as a satellite of the French sugar islands, but François-Dominique Toussaint-L'Ouverture's insurrection in Saint Domingue had so compromised French control of the island that the sugar trade was imperiled. Without control of that colony, Louisiana became unnecessary as well. Second, by the fall of 1802, France had not yet taken control of the port of New Orleans—the key to the entire Louisiana Territory—and Napoleon learned that Jefferson was intending to oppose by force a French takeover of the port. When Napoleon's invasion fleet was immobilized in Dutch ports by ice, the assault became impossible. Finally, and most importantly, the fragile Peace of Amiens between Great Britain and France broke down in 1803, and Napoleon decided to sell to the United States the vast territory that Great Britain might take from him by force once hostilities resumed. Thus, after swift negotiations, France agreed in April 1803 to cede the territory for payment of $15 million.

Jefferson and Secretary of State James Madison believed that after the Louisiana Purchase, France and the United States could coexist amicably. With Great Britain and France engaged in war, the United States turned its neutrality to its advantage, increasing its commerce with both belligerents. The United States had no power to enforce European respect for neutral rights, however, and as the conflict between France and Great Britain increased in intensity, each nation sought to deny the other any advantage, especially with regard to trade. With Great Britain pursuing a naval blockade of the European continent, Napoleon in turn barred continental trade with Great Britain. U.S. maritime commerce inevitably suffered. Jefferson recoiled from war with any European power and hoped to use economic coercion to attain respect for neutral rights. His embargo efforts failed, however, to produce British or French respect for U.S. neutrality.

Inexplicably, Napoleon consistently failed to exploit the Anglo-American rift. Despite the Convention of 1800, French ships harassed U.S. vessels just as doggedly as did the British. Napoleon dismissed the United States as a naval and military power and thought that the country did itself great shame by not repelling more zealously British depredations on the high seas. Further, his engagements in central and eastern Europe occupied his mind far more than the United States. Nonetheless, Napoleon proved his clever skills of manipulation in 1810, when he offered to comply with Macon's Bill Number 2, a piece of legislation passed by the U.S. Congress offering the imposition of trading sanctions against either France or Great Britain should the other modify its maritime restrictions against the United States. Napoleon did not in fact abide by the terms of the bill; French ships continued to raid U.S. traders, especially those shipping grain to the Iberian peninsula, where France was fighting the British, Portuguese, and Spanish. Nonetheless, Napoleon had demonstrated his sympathy with the U.S. position, and Congress in 1811 therefore imposed nonintercourse restrictions against Great Britain. Within a year, the United States and Great Britain were at war.

Napoleon cleverly used Macon's Bill to his own advantage, but he had not tricked the United States into going to war with Great Britain. The *Chesapeake-Leopard* Affair of 1807 had given the United States adequate grounds to declare war against Great Britain, and since that time, British abuses had been more visible and obnoxious than French ones. Further, Great Britain possessed a valuable U.S. war aim, Canada, a fact that gave an added incentive to war.

Although the United States and France were now at war with a common enemy, they were not allies or associates, nor did they coordinate their war efforts. The Madison administration was keen to limit its war to Great Britain and avoid hostilities against other enemies of France. Nevertheless, Napoleon's debacle in Russia left Madison anxious, and the emperor's fall in 1814 proved most alarming: Great Britain would now be free to throw all its weight against the United States. Furthermore, following the Bourbon restoration, King Louis XVIII was obliged to deny the access to French ports that U.S. vessels had used to stage attacks on British ships. Great Britain, however, did not want a lengthy war on U.S. soil and granted a generous peace, restoring the status quo ante bellum in December 1814.

Franco-American Relations and U.S. Expansion, 1815–1914

After 1815 France and the United States present a study in contrasts. In France, the Bourbon monarchy was not absolute, but affected to be so; its character was reactionary, Catholic, and backward-looking. Although France

benefited economically from the calm brought to international relations following the Congress of Vienna, the Bourbon Restoration could not provide political stability, particularly after the succession of Charles X to the throne in 1824. In 1830 he was toppled by a brief, bloody uprising from a populace wholly unwilling to see the authority of the Catholic church and the aristocracy restored. Events in the United States could not have been less similar. The War of 1812 boosted American manufacturing; the Constitution had weathered the storm of war and now the political parties embarked upon an "era of good feelings"; and westward expansion—the fulfillment of the United States's Manifest Destiny—began in earnest. The Old World never seemed less relevant to the aspirations of the New. Consequently, France occupied a far less important role in U.S. foreign relations during the nineteenth century than it had done in the eighteenth; and where the two nations came into contact, the issue was usually related to the dramatic expansion of U.S. influence, commercial power, and territorial boundaries.

Between 1815 and 1830 relations between the two countries focused on Latin America. France looked longingly to the Spanish provinces of this continent as suitable territories for the transplant of new Bourbon princes, to be raised by careful French cultivation. Thus, the recognition in 1822 by the United States of the independence of the Latin American nations came as a blow to French pretensions, as did the opposition of Great Britain to any plan of French hegemony in the region. It was with France in mind, among others, that Secretary of State John Quincy Adams penned for President Monroe the principles the latter announced in 1823, and which became the Monroe Doctrine—that the United States would not tolerate the interposition of European powers anywhere in what Adams called "the American Continents."

The other major issue in Franco-American relations during the Bourbon monarchy and its successor, the Orleanist constitutional monarchy of Louis-Philippe, was U.S. claims for damages done to U.S. interests during the wars of 1803–1815. American claimants sought some $12 million from France for violations of the Convention of 1800, which purported to recognize the free ships, free goods principle. Albert Gallatin, the U.S. minister to France from 1816 to 1823, brought these claims to the French government, but they were never settled. After Andrew Jackson became president in 1828, he demonstrated his new style of forceful leadership by demanding the prompt settlement of the claims. In 1831 Jackson's envoy, William C. Rives, signed an agreement for 25 million francs, less than half the sum sought by claimants, but the French Chamber of Deputies delayed payment. An angry President Jackson asked Congress for legislation allowing the seizure of French property as recompense. France took umbrage at Jackson's tactics and proceeded to break off diplomatic relations. The young and fragile French monarchy could not support the strain of hostilities with the United States and agreed to interpret certain soothing remarks by President Jackson as an apology for his threats. By 1836 France began payments of the sum demanded.

The increasing ability of the United States to behave as it wished, without the consideration of the European powers, was demonstrated again in the dispute over the annexation of Texas by the United States in 1844–1845. France had recognized the independence of Texas in 1839 and opposed its annexation. France and Great Britain had even offered to secure Mexican recognition of Texas if it would agree not to join its northern neighbor. Although there was no likelihood of Anglo-French intervention to keep Texas from doing so, the linkage of Texas to the United States meant one less region in the New World on which pressure could be exerted by the Old. The U.S. minister to France in 1846, William R. King, acknowledged this when he told Secretary of State James Buchanan that French influence in U.S. affairs could be regarded as "insignificant."

When the revolution of 1848 failed to establish a stable republic in France, the door was opened to the enterprising Louis Napoleon Bonaparte, a nephew of his namesake, who was elected president in 1848, only to establish the French Second Empire via a coup d'etat in 1851. Napoleon III, as he styled himself, ruled until 1870 and proved on numerous occasions to be a thorn in the side of American diplomats. Although roundly condemned in the United States for his dismantling of the short-lived Second Republic, Napoleon III nonetheless had the support of France's commercial classes, and his reign was characterized by economic growth, internal stability, and a foreign policy of "grandeur." He involved France in the Crimean War of 1854–1856; he went to war with Austria in 1859, ostensibly on behalf of the Kingdom of Piedmont; and he extended French colonial influence in Algeria, Senegal, Indochina, Syria, and, via the Suez Canal, the Red Sea.

During the American Civil War, Napoleon III's foreign adventures came to threaten the United States. Southern leaders expected that France and Great Britain would extend recognition to their cause chiefly because of the importance of cotton to the European textile industry, and secondarily because the Civil War offered a means of hobbling the expansive, acquisitive American republic. While Napoleon III inclined toward the South, however, and contemplated recognition of the Confederacy, France never did abandon its strict neutrality during the conflict. Great Britain determined to stay out of the war, and without Great Britain, Napoleon would not act.

Instead, Napoleon III hoped to profit from America's turmoil by intervening in Mexico, with the aim of estab-lishing a French-backed monarchy there. Napoleon's Mexican debacle had its origins in an Anglo-French-Spanish debt-collecting expedition sent to Mexico in 1862. When the other two powers withdrew, France alone sent troops to Veracruz, where they were defeated by a force under President Benito Juarez. French reinforcements eventually captured Mexico City and placed a Habsburg prince, Archduke Maximilian, on the throne of Mexico. The Civil War prevented the United States from responding to this glaring challenge to the Monroe Doctrine, although Secretary of State William H. Seward and Congress made strong representations to France. French ineptitude and Mexican guerrilla warfare undid the enterprise, and by 1867 French troops had evacuated Mexico and left Maximilian to be shot by firing squad. Thus, having alienated southern opinion by denying recognition to the Confederacy, and angering the North by his well-known sympathies for the South and his antipathy to republicanism, Napoleon earned the wrath of the United States as a whole by his precipitous imperial adventure in Mexico. Consequently, the United States was not sorry to see Napoleon III's reign come to an end in 1870, when the emperor was defeated by Prussia in a war he had done much to provoke.

During the early years of the Third Republic (1870–1940), Franco-American relations tended to center on colonial affairs, for these were the years not only of the United States' great push for expansion but also of the scramble among the Europeans for imperial spoils in Africa and Asia. In the Western Hemisphere, the United States continued to observe with concern French efforts to restore or shore up influence in such states as Haiti, Venezuela, Brazil, and Argentina; France sent four times as many exports to Argentina as it did to the United States. In particular, the U.S. government remonstrated against a French-financed Panama Canal, an effort which began in 1881 only to be defeated by engineering problems and malaria. In Africa, where the United States had far less at stake than in Latin America, the United States nonetheless frowned on France's aggressive colonial expansion in the Congo, Madagascar, and North Africa. In Asia, President William McKinley's secretary of state, John Hay, fought, with only moderate success, to keep China open to U.S. trade by discouraging the creation of closed trading spheres favored there by Germany, Russia, and France. In any case, however, France's colonization of Indochina ensured a leading role for France in Asia.

The U.S. war with Spain over Cuba in 1898 seemed likely to damage Franco-American relations. France was a Latin and Catholic country like its old ally, Spain, and was Spain's largest trading partner. The power of the United States, however, looked far more imposing than Spain's, and there could be no question of France opposing the United States in the conflict. French Foreign

Minister Gabriel Hanotaux made a genuine but unsuccessful effort to mediate between the two powers, and proclaimed France's neutrality when war broke out. France hosted the postwar peace conference, at which Spain ceded Cuba, Puerto Rico, Guam, and the Philippines to the United States, but relations with the brash new world power—now clearly an imperialist rival—remained cool.

Franco-American Relations Through Two World Wars

When war broke out in Europe in August 1914, there existed no special bond that might propel the United States into war on France's side. President Woodrow Wilson believed all the belligerents equally guilty for the outbreak of hostilities and planned to maintain a strict neutrality in the conflict. While it is true that France and the United States shared certain sentimental attachments—in this period the name of Lafayette was ceaselessly invoked as emblematic of French aid for the American War of Independence—these were superficial. In 1916 Wilson ran for reelection on an antiwar platform and sent his close aide, Colonel Edward M. House, to Europe to try to negotiate a peace on the basis of status quo ante bellum. These overtures were poorly received in France, a country that claimed to be fighting for the liberation of its territory, including Alsace-Lorraine, from German invasion. Furthermore, Wilson's high-minded denunciations of Old World diplomacy, secret treaties, and balance-of-power politics struck the French leadership as irrelevant, Delphic utterances, totally out of step with the complexities of the European situation.

The German resumption of unrestricted submarine warfare in January 1917 dramatically changed U.S. attitudes toward the war and led to an immediate strengthening of Franco-American relations. The United States entered the war in April 1917 to a hail of acclaim from France. The U.S. flag was hoisted above the Eiffel Tower; more prosaically, the exhausted French treasury could now borrow from the U.S. government. It was not until June 1917 that the first U.S. troops arrived in France, under the command of General John J. Pershing. By January 1918 only 161,000 American troops had landed on French soil, but U.S. troops then began pouring into France. By the end of July more than 1 million American soldiers were serving there; by the end of the war in November, that number had doubled.

The deployment of these troops presented a problem initially. Marshal Ferdinand Foch, the supreme allied commander, wanted to see the U.S. troops amalgamated into the existing Allied divisions. Pershing rejected this scheme and insisted on maintaining control of his own troops. Thus, U.S. troops, outfitted almost entirely with French ammunition, field guns, tanks, and aircraft, fought under their own commanders. The Americans made their greatest impact in the war after the spring of 1918, at Belleau Wood, where they were instrumental in preventing a German advance on Paris; at Saint-Mihiel; and in the Meuse-Argonne sector.

U.S. military and financial support provided the crucial margin of victory for the Allied powers, but France, and Europe, naturally had to pay a price for this U.S. assistance. Wilson's popularity in postwar Europe, evident when he traveled to Paris to participate in the peace conference, was based both on his role as leader of the military power that had come to the assistance of the Allies and on the broad appeal of his moral vision. Wilson's war aims, which included a rejection of secret treaties and advocated freedom of the seas, free trade, disarmament, self-determination, and a League of Nations, were the principles on which the postwar settlement was to be predicated. However, French Premier Georges Clemenceau shared little of Wilson's vision. After the war France still faced a German neighbor with a larger population and a larger economy; with its old ally Russia in the hands of the Bolsheviks, containing Germany appeared more difficult than ever. For France, security from future German invasion was paramount. Clemenceau insisted that the left bank of the Rhine be occupied by the Allies and that Germany be made to pay war reparations. He also wanted to see Germany's coal- and iron-producing regions under French control, regardless of the economic consequences for Germany.

Throughout the Paris negotiations, French demands for economic and military security clashed openly with Wilson's generous if naive vision of international relations. Only in March 1919, when Wilson offered a Franco-American security treaty guaranteeing French borders, did Clemenceau relent, agreeing to limit his demands to the temporary occupation of the Rhineland, and this as a bargaining chip to enforce German payment of reparations. Clemenceau also conceded to Wilson that the Saar—a coal-rich region just inside Germany's border with France—would not be annexed by France but administered by the League of Nations for fifteen years.

The rejection by the U.S. Senate of the Treaty of Versailles in 1920 was a shock to French diplomacy. Not only would the United States not become a member of the League of Nations, but the all-important Franco-American security guarantee ceased to exist as well. French security now depended on a weak alliance system of Eastern European states—Poland, Czechoslovakia, Yugoslavia, and Romania—and on vigilant application of the Versailles Treaty, the aim of which was the economic hobbling of Germany. This latter issue dominated the diplomacy of the 1920s.

At the end of the war, France owed the United States some $4 billion, a sum it could not possibly pay off unless Germany in turn paid reparations to France. Germany, exhausted by the war, could not—or would not—pay its reparations, so France initially tried to get the United States to diminish or even cancel French war debts. The United States refused to do so under four successive administrations, those of Wilson, Warren G. Harding, Calvin Coolidge, and Herbert Hoover. France also could not easily earn dollars by selling goods to the United States because of the immense tariff walls built up during the 1920s and because prohibition eliminated the export of spirits, a traditional French product, to the United States. Instead, economically depleted countries, with no foreign currency reserves, were asked to pay off enormous debts before reestablishing their economic health. Germany's efforts to pay reparations boosted inflation and led to a suspension of payments in 1922. This violation of the Versailles Treaty gave France cause in 1923 to cross the Rhine and occupy Germany's industrial heartland, the Ruhr Valley, in order to extract the reparations by force. This occupation, undertaken by the government of Raymond Poincaré, was roundly condemned by the United States, and President Harding withdrew U.S. troops that had been aiding in the occupation of the demilitarized Rhineland. The Ruhr occupation poisoned the international atmosphere in Europe and, because it completely disrupted German manufacturing and trade, led to the financial ruin of Germany. The Harding government suspected Poincaré of wanting to establish French control of the German coal and steel industry, followed by French hegemony in Europe. U.S. intervention in the crisis resulted in the promulgation of the Dawes Plan of 1924, which reduced and restructured Germany's reparations bill and provided for U.S. investment in German reconstruction. This in turn aided the French in repaying their war debts until 1930, when the international economic crisis put an end to international payments.

The entire issue of war debts created distrust and bitterness between France and the United States. France felt that its sacrifices in the period 1914–1918 deserved to be rewarded with generosity by the American people, not usurious demands for repayment, while Americans blamed France for its obsessively Germanophobic policies and its apparent disdain for international financial obligations.

On disarmament, the other major issue of the 1920s, France and the United States found few areas of agreement. At the Washington Arms Limitation Conference of 1921–1922, France felt slighted when Secretary of State Charles Evans Hughes placed the French navy on the same level with that of Italy—well behind the U.S., British, and Japanese navies—in suggesting limitations on naval expansion. After 1925, however, when Aristide Briand became foreign minister, France proved more willing to participate in global disarmament efforts. Briand garnered international acclaim for his participation in the Locarno Conference of October 1925, which marked a distinct improvement in Franco-German relations. In 1928 he concluded the curious Kellogg-Briand Pact with Secretary of State Frank Kellogg. This agreement had initially been intended by Briand to serve as a means of improving Franco-American relations by declaring both nations' intention never to go to war with each other, but Kellogg was reluctant to sign a pact with France that smacked of a special relationship and proposed that the agreement be open to any signatory willing to renounce war as an instrument of national policy. This toothless pact generated much praise and not a little sarcasm. In general, France, a country woefully vulnerable to invasion and seeing potential enemies in every direction, found it difficult to accept advice on disarmament from a nation that enjoyed wealth, power, and total security. President Herbert Hoover's proposal in 1932 for a reduction of the world's navies and armies by one-third seemed particularly preposterous in France in light of the growth of National Socialism in Germany, and Adolf Hitler's accession to power in 1933.

In the last six years before the outbreak of World War II, Franco-American relations were virtually dormant. President Franklin D. Roosevelt, preoccupied with domestic economic recovery and committed to a policy of isolationism, offered only weak moral support to the governments in Europe that appeared most threatened by German militarism. Hitler's 1933 rearmament efforts, his introduction of compulsory military service in 1935, his remilitarization of the Rhineland and alliance with Italy's Benito Mussolini in 1936, all established a pattern that alarmed Americans and Frenchmen alike but produced negligible responses in both countries. French diplomats tried to shore up alliances with the Soviet Union, Great Britain, and the Eastern European states and to coax Italy away from Germany; these measures proved ineffective in inhibiting Hitler. The U.S. Congress, meanwhile, tied Roosevelt's hands by passing neutrality legislation, ensuring that the United States would not be able to aid belligerents in a European war. French leaders welcomed Roosevelt's 1937 "quarantine" speech, but were bitterly disappointed when its implication—that fascism must be opposed—was not followed by action. Despite the frequent pleas from U.S. Ambassador William C. Bullitt for American support to France, Roosevelt maintained his distance from European affairs, and supported the policy of appeasement that France and Great Britain pursued at the Munich Conference of 1938. In late 1938 Roosevelt did, however, approve the sale to France of advanced U.S. military aircraft, although few planes had been delivered when Germany invaded France in May 1940.

France's collapse before the German blitzkrieg signaled to many Americans the end of France as a great power. When an obscure French general, Charles de Gaulle, broadcast an appeal from London calling on the French people to resist Germany, the U.S. government was not impressed and preferred to court the aged French leader, Marshal Henri Philippe Pétain, to whom the fleeing French government had turned over power. The new U.S. ambassador, Admiral William Leahy, believed Pétain, a hero of World War I, would resist German demands to turn over the French fleet and colonies, underestimating the willingness of Pétain's regime, now established in the resort town of Vichy, to collaborate with Germany. Despite de Gaulle's clear determination to oppose at all costs the German occupation of France, the U.S. government kept him at arm's length, working instead with Pétain and his associates, such as Admiral François Darlan, the commander of Vichy's navy and briefly prime minister. This policy paid off during the U.S. invasion of North Africa in November 1942. When Pétain ordered Vichy forces to resist the invasion, Darlan, by chance in Algiers, countermanded Pétain's orders. Having jumped to the Allied side, Darlan then acted as the French leader in North Africa, until his assassination in December 1942.

After Vichy was overrun by the Germans in retaliation for the U.S. invasion, Pétain was reduced to little more than a German puppet. The United States needed to find an appropriate leader to act as a rallying point for French resistance. Roosevelt supported the innocuous General Henri Giraud, preferring to limit the power of de Gaulle, who had already made a nuisance of himself by claiming to be the sole voice of Free France. Despite Roosevelt's efforts to prop up Giraud, de Gaulle consolidated his authority as leader of the resistance throughout 1943–1944, effectively outmaneuvering Giraud as de facto leader of the French opposition to Hitler.

Roosevelt consistently opposed de Gaulle not just on personal grounds—he was deemed difficult and unreliable—but because the president wanted as free a hand as possible in reshaping the postwar world. De Gaulle's vision of a strong, influential France, possessing a colonial empire and a seat at international conference tables, contradicted Roosevelt's ideas. In practical terms, however, the United States needed de Gaulle's help, particularly as the plans for the invasion of France were laid. General Dwight D. Eisenhower, the supreme Allied commander, respected de Gaulle's control over the French resistance and appreciated that he would be an effective opponent of revolution in France following a German withdrawal. The Americans, however, resisted giving de Gaulle real power. He was not consulted about the Normandy invasion and his proclamation of a provisional government was not recognized by the United States until October 1944. De Gaulle, all too aware of the need for politically symbolic victories, followed the Allied advance across France in June and July 1944, finally ordering General Philippe Leclerc, the commander of the French First Division, to liberate Paris from the Germans. Despite Eisenhower's orders for a joint Franco-American force to take the city, Leclerc's troops reached the capital a day before the Americans and proclaimed Paris liberated by French arms. This pattern of French resistance to U.S. direction of the war reappeared throughout the winter campaign of 1944–1945, as de Gaulle sought to win back prestige for the French military, often disobeying Eisenhower's orders.

The Cold War Era

Postwar relations between France and the United States remained acrimonious, although characterized by an element of mutual dependence. De Gaulle knew, although he resented it, that France had to rely on the United States for economic, military, and political support during the period of reconstruction. Likewise, the administration of President Harry S. Truman, preoccupied with the overall strategic goal of containing communist expansion in Europe, had to rely on France, a nation with a large empire and strategic location. Thus, while the United States clearly dominated the bilateral relationship, France maintained some bargaining power.

After de Gaulle's resignation from the presidency in January 1946, his successors during the short-lived Fourth Republic (1946–1958) tried to maintain France's independence from the United States, but France's undeniable weaknesses, especially economic, forced a large degree of compliance with U.S. leadership in the early Cold War. Indeed, Franco-American relations were totally transformed in the decade following World War II. The two countries had not been so intimately involved with each other since 1778, although now France was the dependent partner. Just as some Americans had chafed under French leadership in the eighteenth century, U.S. economic and military power, although a lifeline for postwar France, created resentment among the French.

Three areas demonstrate this pattern of dependence and resistance—economic policy, planning for postwar Germany, and security issues. Between 1944 and 1952 the United States pumped $5.5 billion into the French economy, about $2.9 billion coming through the Marshall Plan. French governments, however grateful for this support, nonetheless resisted U.S. economic advice on how best to use the money. Jean Monnet, France's chief economic planner, designed an investment plan that aimed to rebuild the French steel, manufacturing, and agricultural sectors. Although successful in jump-starting French reconstruction, the Monnet Plan also boosted inflation. U.S. officials fought bitterly with French governments about how best to limit inflation in this period and restore stability to the French currency.

Similarly, France and the United States clashed violently on policy in Germany. French leaders, especially Georges Bidault and Robert Schuman, two Christian Democratic leaders who dominated French foreign policy until the mid-1950s, sought to place restrictions on German economic growth, demanded a federal political structure with strong regional governments and a weak executive, and insisted on keeping Germany's armed forces completely neutered. France used its position as an occupying power to veto Anglo-American proposals for swift economic and political reconstruction so often that General Lucius Clay, commander of the U.S. zone of occupation, thought the French more difficult to deal with than the Russians. Despite U.S. assurances that democratic West Germany was different from its militarist predecessor, Franco-German rapprochement proved hard to build.

In security affairs, France welcomed U.S. willingness to keep troops in Europe and ardently supported the creation of the North Atlantic Treaty Organization (NATO), but France diverged from the United States on certain key strategic issues. First, should Germany be rearmed? France thought not and suggested fusing German troops into a European army, designed to profit from German manpower while keeping French officers in positions of authority. This idea, although initially considered unsound by the United States, garnered support when it was seen as a means of bringing Germany into the fold of the Western alliance. In the end, however, the European Defense Community was stillborn because even the prospect of moderate German rearmament was unacceptable to the French public. The second strategic issue that produced acrimony was the French colonial war in Indochina. Since 1945 France had been fighting the Vietminh in an effort to regain control over its Southeast Asia colonies. The outbreak of the Korean War in 1950, however, altered U.S. perceptions of France's Indochina war; it now was seen by Washington as part of a global campaign to contain communist expansion. As U.S. interest in—and funding of—the French military effort expanded, so did Washington's frustration with France grow, because the French never prosecuted the war vigorously enough for U.S. tastes. France's decision to withdraw in 1954 after the major defeat of French forces at Dien Bien Phu only worsened U.S. perceptions of the value of France as an ally. There was a European dimension to the Indochina affair as well, because France's war effort in Asia depleted the French forces in Europe. The United States thought this situation an argument for German rearmament, but Paris cried foul, claiming that while French troops were shedding blood in Asia, the Western allies should not be rearming France's old enemy Germany.

In some areas, France and the United States did find common ground. American desires to see Europeans coordinate their economic policies squared with French thinking that Germany, if integrated with its neighbors, could be more easily controlled and contained. Thus, the Schuman Plan of 1950 to fuse the coal and steel production of France and Germany was immediately supported by the United States, even though the plan grew from French desires to see Germany's industrial capacity monitored by an international organization. The Schuman Plan laid the foundations of the European Economic Community (EEC) and proved to be one of the most constructive acts of French statesmanship in the twentieth century.

These successes could not hide major areas of conflict in the bilateral relationship. Franco-American relations suffered over the fate of France's colony, Algeria. Secretary of State John Foster Dulles hoped to gain international acclaim for the United States by supporting decolonization across the globe—creating serious friction between Paris and Washington. France considered Algeria French soil, and the NATO alliance recognized it as such, but the United States did not want to become committed to a French colonial war as it had in Indochina and gave only lukewarm support over the issue. When, in October 1956, France, angered at Egypt's support for the Algerian rebels, joined Great Britain and Israel in invading the Suez Canal zone in the hopes of toppling Egyptian President Gamal Abdel Nasser, President Eisenhower threatened serious reprisals, undercutting the invasion. France was humiliated by the response, despite pursuing what the French government believed was a policy beneficial to French and Western interests, namely, opposing Arab nationalism. The rift in Franco-American relations led French leaders to the conclusion that Washington could not be trusted and that France should possess its own nuclear deterrent. France stepped up its atomic weapons program in direct response to the events of the Suez Crisis.

The Algerian War, meanwhile, intensified in the wake of the botched Suez invasion and threatened to spread to newly independent Tunisia and Morocco. When in 1958 the United States offered to mediate in the war, the weakened, almost defeated French government accepted. The French military, angered over civilian lack of backbone, staged a coup in Algiers, called for the return of General de Gaulle, and threatened Paris itself with invasion. De Gaulle, widely seen in France as the only man who could control the army, became the last premier of the Fourth Republic, promptly dissolved it, and was then elected president of the Fifth Republic under a new constitution that gave far more power to the executive. The old nemesis of the United States had returned.

Although de Gaulle realized Algeria was a lost cause and soon granted independence, he concluded that the time had come for a complete reassessment of Franco-American relations. During his years in the political wilderness, he had criticized the Fourth Republic for its timidity with regard to Washington. He proposed instead a foreign policy of "grandeur," that is, one which demonstrated independence and resolve on behalf of French interests. While de Gaulle demonstrated his basic loyalty to the Western alliance during the two most serious standoffs in the East-West rivalry—the Berlin Crisis of 1958–1961 and the Cuban Missile Crisis of 1962—his long-term strategic thinking led to friction and acrimony with the United States.

On strategic and nuclear issues, for example, de Gaulle demanded much greater influence in NATO and called for the creation of a tripartite command structure through which the United States, Great Britain, and France could dominate the alliance. He did not get his way, however, because the United States balked at any plan that might raise French status within the alliance while angering other European nations. Nor did France develop the close nuclear partnership with the United States that Great Britain enjoyed. Because de Gaulle adamantly refused to allow the United States to control missiles that were deployed on French soil, the Eisenhower and John F. Kennedy administrations both denied France nuclear technology. De Gaulle, undeterred, moved forward with France's nuclear-weapons program. In 1960 France tested its first atomic weapon and in 1968 detonated a hydrogen bomb. The United States had not blocked the development of a French nuclear arsenal.

De Gaulle's European policies also alarmed the U.S. government. In 1963 de Gaulle signed a friendship treaty with Germany and surprised the world by revealing a strong personal affinity toward German Chancellor Konrad Adenauer. At the same time, he vetoed Great Britain's application to enter the EEC. Both gestures were aimed at promoting France's position as the dominant European power, leading an economic and political bloc that might act as a pivotal "third force" between the United States and the Soviet Union. Such thinking challenged U.S. conceptions of Cold War strategy, in which power lay chiefly in Washington. After 1965 de Gaulle redoubled his efforts to weaken the U.S. hold over the alliance. He began a campaign to weaken the federalist aspect of the EEC, which he saw as an American-inspired plan to reduce the power of individual European nation-states, and called instead for a "Europe des patries." He began to reach out to the Soviet Union in hopes of launching an East-West détente, and in 1966 he withdrew France from the integrated command of NATO. His intention was to create a strong, independent France, speaking for a loosely integrated Europe of sovereign states, one not bound to the dictates of the United States and willing to engage in independent initiatives toward the Eastern bloc. De Gaulle's strategy never succeeded—the Germans were too wary of any weakening of U.S.-German ties to follow de Gaulle's footsteps—but his policies did seriously alienate France from the United States.

The Vietnam War only worsened the bilateral relationship. De Gaulle publicly lambasted the Southeast Asia policy of President Lyndon B. Johnson's administration. In this he spoke for his country; the war was unpopular with the French public and fed French perceptions of the United States as a nation willing to risk global conflagration on behalf of a misguided obsession with communism. De Gaulle told Washington that war would not lead to democracy in Vietnam. Johnson meanwhile was infuriated with de Gaulle's warm relations with Ho Chi Minh, his recognition of Communist China, and his constant calls for U.S. withdrawal from the war. Although these declarations did little to impede Johnson's policies in Asia, they boosted de Gaulle's image as a leader who, while committed to the Western alliance, would speak out against the United States.

Economic relations were as strained as political and military ones. De Gaulle's government, ever on the lookout for signs of U.S. trespasses on French independence, opposed the massive U.S. investments being made in France and Europe during the 1960s. De Gaulle also began to cash in large amounts of dollars for gold, in an attempt to weaken the dollar as a world currency. This kind of economic nationalism angered U.S. officials who simply could not comprehend de Gaulle's particular animus toward the United States. In the wake of the violent student protests in May 1968, de Gaulle's confidence in his mandate began to wane somewhat; in 1969, following the defeat in a national referendum of a measure for political reform that de Gaulle favored, the aged general resigned from office. His departure gradually allowed some improvement in Franco-American relations, but his legacy in foreign policy endured for many years after his death in 1970. Subsequent French governments have taken pride in France's strategic and nuclear independence and have demonstrated consistent willingness to take initiatives not sanctioned—and even directly opposed—by Washington. This stance has emerged as a national consensus on foreign policy and remains one of de Gaulle's most lasting legacies.

President Richard Nixon, working with de Gaulle's successor, President Georges Pompidou, tried to improve relations with France but ultimately failed to do so. The United States was pleased when Pompidou lifted de Gaulle's long-standing veto on British entry into the EEC. The United States also began a covert program to share nuclear technology with France, but economic problems continued to sour relations. The Nixon administration's abandonment of the Bretton Woods currency exchange system in 1971—a move that made European exports more expensive—triggered much hostility in France. The unilateral U.S. action was widely seen as a declaration of economic war on other industrialized countries that had large dollar holdings. One result of U.S. policy was to spur the creation of the Common Agricultural Policy, a European system of agricultural subsidies that would ultimately threaten to undermine America's traditional dominance of world agricultural markets. The Nixon administration tried to undo some of the damage by declaring 1973 the "Year of Europe"—a misguided and transparent effort to shore up the alliance and reassert U.S. hegemony over Europe. The Year of Europe was marred not least by continued French criticism of U.S.-Soviet bilateral summit diplomacy in which Europeans were not represented.

U.S.-French relations were further strained by conflicting policies in the Middle East. France had become a chief supplier of arms to Libya, Algeria, and Iraq, while maintaining an arms embargo on Israel as a mark of disapproval of Israel's annexations of Arab territory following the Six-Day War in 1967. Thus, when President Pompidou visited the United States in 1970, he encountered violent protests by Jewish groups in Chicago and New York. When the Yom Kippur War of October 1973 broke out, the United States strongly backed Israel, while France—dependent upon imports of Middle East oil—did not and indeed impeded U.S. efforts to resupply the Israeli military by denying U.S. aircraft the use of French airspace. (Of all the European allies, only Portugal acquiesced in allowing U.S. flyovers). France continued arms deliveries to Libya and Saudi Arabia. In the wake of the war, French Foreign Minister Michel Jobert hoped to strengthen French ties with the Arab world by leading a European front that would bargain directly with the Organization of Petroleum Exporting Countries (OPEC), isolating the United States. Secretary of State Henry Kissinger would have none of it and demanded the establishment of a U.S.-dominated International Energy Agency that would coordinate U.S., Japanese, and European energy policy with regard to OPEC. Jobert, belligerent and hostile, bitterly criticized his European colleagues for acceding to U.S. leadership, but in the end, the United States revealed the large influence it could still exert upon Europe, especially in times of crisis.

Pompidou's sudden death in 1974 brought Valéry Giscard d'Estaing to the French presidency. Giscard, a conservative but not a Gaullist politician, was urbane, multilingual, and an economic wizard. He improved French relations with West Germany, which had been making France nervous by opening up talks with East Germany and the Soviet Union. Germany and France pledged to work toward closer economic links and even laid the groundwork for military cooperation. While Giscard wanted to improve relations with Washington as well, one of his major goals was to strengthen the Paris-Bonn axis so that Europe could speak with a united voice in international affairs. Giscard continued the French pattern of staying out of America's particular feuds. When U.S.-Soviet relations deteriorated following the Soviet inva-

sion of Afghanistan in 1979, France resisted efforts by President Jimmy Carter's administration to impose sanctions on the Soviet Union; French athletes attended the Moscow Olympics in 1980, which was boycotted by the United States; and France did not place an embargo on Iran during the U.S. hostage crisis.

During the 1980s Franco-American relations gradually improved, even though conservative president Ronald Reagan had very little in common with France's new socialist president François Mitterrand. In certain crucial respects, Mitterrand proved a far more valued ally than many of his predecessors. Under Mitterrand's leadership, France worked closely with NATO, thereby improving French relations with the Western alliance. Mitterrand also supported the United States during the controversy over the Reagan administration's effort to deploy Pershing and cruise missiles—or intermediate nuclear forces (INF)—in Western Europe. The INF plan triggered a wave of pacifism and antinuclear sentiment, especially in Germany. France, however, remained steadfast in its support of the U.S. nuclear deterrent, confident in the knowledge that the missiles would not in any case be deployed on French soil. Mitterrand viewed the missiles as an added measure of assurance that Germany, then under the leadership of the Social Democratic Party (SPD), would not drift toward neutralism and accommodation with the Soviet Union. So firm was Mitterrand's belief that when he traveled to Bonn to celebrate the twentieth anniversary of the Franco-German Treaty of Friendship in 1983, he publicly criticized the SPD leadership for backing away from the deployment of INF missiles. In a striking departure from the norm, a French leader had openly supported a U.S. policy despite opposition within Europe. Precisely because Mitterrand so strongly valued the U.S. deterrent as a means of assuring French national security, he opposed the Reagan administration's proposal for the Strategic Defense Initiative (SDI), an antiballistic missile system that would shield the United States from a Soviet attack. Mitterrand feared that SDI would leave France outside the U.S. nuclear umbrella. Similarly, when Reagan and reformist Soviet leader Mikhail Gorbachev agreed in 1987 to eliminate the INF missiles, Mitterrand fought the treaty, arguing that it could lead to a denuclearized Europe and a neutralist German foreign policy toward Moscow.

While Mitterrand demonstrated solidarity with Washington in the area of nuclear weapons policy, other issues continued to bedevil Franco-American relations. In 1982 the United States objected to the European sale to the Soviet Union of technology for building a natural gas pipeline. The French went ahead despite strong U.S. complaints. In 1986 France refused to let U.S. jets into French airspace to bomb the residence of Libyan leader Moammar al-Qaddafi, even though French officials privately hoped to see the Libyan toppled. Trade disputes also continued to damage relations, as the U.S. government complained that French subsidies to farmers unfairly undercut U.S. exports. Nonetheless, France and the United States in the 1980s had grown ever more interdependent. French people appeared to welcome American food, films, and products in ways unimaginable just two decades earlier. The opening of Euro-Disney, a $4 billion theme park near Paris built by the Walt Disney Company, underscored the degree to which French and American consumer cultures had converged.

The Post Cold War Era

The fall of the Berlin Wall in 1989 suddenly changed the strategic landscape of Europe. Overnight, the prospect of German reunification placed in jeopardy the carefully calibrated balance of power between Bonn and Paris that had been in place since 1950. West German leader Helmut Kohl promptly took advantage of the collapse of East Germany by calling for the integration of the two states—on terms largely determined by Bonn. Kohl's willingness to act as a latter-day Otto von Bismarck—the unifier of the German peoples—naturally created anxiety in Paris, and Mitterrand worked closely with the administration of President George Bush to secure guarantees from Kohl (and Gorbachev) that a united Germany would remain locked into NATO and the European Community. The appearance of a powerful, united German state pushed the French and the Americans closer together, but it also threatened to create a bidding war, as both nations sought to improve their "special relationship" with Germany.

France and the United States cooperated closely in the Gulf War of 1990-1991. France sent 10,000 troops to serve under U.S. command in the war with Iraq, although Mitterrand angered the United States by attempting to negotiate a last-minute deal for the Iraqi evacuation of Kuwait. However, if the Gulf War brought France and the United States together as comrades-in-arms, the war among the successor states of Yugoslavia had precisely the opposite effect. When war broke out in the spring of 1992 in Bosnia-Herzegovina between Bosnians, Muslims, and Serbs, the latter backed in their nationalist ambitions by the Serbian leadership in Belgrade, the NATO alliance failed to arrive at an adequate response. Subsequent debate about policy toward the war in Bosnia provoked the worst crisis in NATO since the 1956 Suez invasion, and France and the United States were the principal antagonists.

The United States, keen on avoiding any troop commitments in Bosnia, argued that since the Serbs were the clear aggressors in the war, the Muslims ought to be supplied with arms so as to improve their chances on the battlefield. Further, the Serbs should be threatened with NATO air-strikes unless they ceased their war against the Bosnians.

But the French, with over 6,000 peace-keeping troops on the ground in the former Yugoslavia, proposed a different solution. Air strikes on the Serbs and weapons shipments to the Bosnians, they believed, would only serve to prolong the war and prompt Serb reprisals against French troops. The French claimed that a diplomatic solution, involving the partition of Bosnia into ethnic enclaves, provided the best means to secure peace. French policy was ardently opposed by the Bosnian government, which appealed to the United States for aid in fighting the Serbs. Americans were not comfortable with the French position, and the U.S. Congress demanded that President Bill Clinton take a more forceful stand in favor of the Bosnians. Yet since the United States had no troops on the ground and had repeatedly urged the Europeans to take the leading role in resolving the conflict, the Americans could not prevail in having their policy adopted. Between 1992 and 1995, as NATO and UN credibility fell to an all-time low, French and Americans publicly criticized each other in tones rarely heard between allies, even these two nations so often at odds.

Following a series of particularly gruesome Serbian war crimes—including the systematic murder of some 7,000 Muslim citizens of Srebrenica in July 1995—NATO finally pulled together to deliver a sustained air campaign against Serb positions. Faced with NATO resolve to use force, the Serbs signalled their intention to halt the war. A few months later the Dayton Accord was signed and the NATO Implementation Force (IFOR) of about 50,000 troops was sent to Bosnia to seek to keep the peace. Observers were left to wonder whether three years of Franco-American debate over the use of air power against the Serbs had prolonged the war needlessly.

Bosnia was not the only area of French-American conflict in the 1990s. In trade relations, the two countries fought bitterly, especially as the Uruguay Round of international trade discussions about the General Agreement on Tariffs and Trade (GATT) neared collapse in late 1993. France insisted on maintaining traditional subsidies for farmers, which to American eyes gave French agriculture unfair advantages in world markets. Heavy pressure and a tense war of words finally resulted in a last-minute deal. French unilateral intervention in 1994 in the African nation of Rwanda, in which a grisly civil war had prompted much international condemnation but no action, garnered France not praise but the criticism of the American public, which believed that France was concerned more with its image as a great power than with the fate of the Rwandan people. In March 1995 France took delight in giving a warm welcome to Cuban leader Fidel Castro, an old nemesis of the United States, thus reasserting its willingness to act independently of U.S. policies. The election of Jaques Chirac to the Presidency of France in May 1995 briefly served to heal the rift in Franco-American relations which Bosnia had caused. It was Chirac, in fact, who had shifted France's policy in favor of NATO air strikes against the Serbs, and who had called for a far more vigorous NATO role in the conflict. Chirac also announced, in the wake of the Bosnian war, that France would return to certain key military bodies in the NATO alliance from which de Gaulle had withdrawn in 1996. Yet just as Chirac won U.S. plaudits for his forcefulness in Bosnia, he shattered this honeymoon by revealing that France planned to carry out a series of nuclear weapons tests, in violation of the nuclear test-ban treaty which France had signed in 1992, and which the Clinton administration strongly supported. U.S. public opinion violently criticized Chirac's decision, and when the French president visited Washington in February 1996, after the French tests had been completed, numerous Congressmen boycotted his speech to a joint session of Congress.

Thus, as the twentieth century was coming to an end, U.S.-French relations remained much as they had been for more than two hundred years—close, at times intimate, but often hampered by conflicting strategic, economic, and political priorities.

WILLIAM I. HITCHCOCK

See also American Revolution; Beaumarchais, Pierre Augustin Caron de; Canada; Clemenceau, Georges; Colonialism; Convention of 1800; Dawes Plan; Deane, Silas; de Gaulle, Charles André Joseph Marie; Dien Bien Phu; Franklin, Benjamin; French and Indian War; French Indochina; French Revolution; Haiti; Imperialism; Jay, John; Kellogg-Briand Pact; Lafayette, Marie Joseph Gilbert Motier, Marquis de; Louisiana Purchase; Mitterrand, François; Monnet, Jean; Napoleon Bonaparte; Napoleonic Wars; Neutral Rights; North Atlantic Treaty Organization; Paris Peace Conference of 1919; Pershing, John; Saint Pierre Miquelon Affair; Schuman, Robert; Suez Crisis; Talleyrand, Charles Maurice; Vergennes, Charles Gravier de; Versailles Treaty of 1919; War Debt of World War I; World War II; XYZ Affair

FURTHER READING

Blumenthal, Henry. *France and the United States: Their Diplomatic Relations, 1789–1914*. Chapel Hill, N.C., 1970.
——— . *Illusion and Reality in Franco-American Diplomacy, 1914–1945*. Baton Rouge, La., 1986.
Case, Lynn M., and Warren F. Spencer. *The United States and France: Civil War Diplomacy*. Philadelphia, 1970.
Cogan, Charles G. *Oldest Allies, Guarded Friends: The United States and France Since 1940*. New York, 1994.
Costigliola, Frank. *France and the United States: The Cold Alliance Since World War II*. New York, 1992.
Dull, Jonathan R. *A Diplomatic History of the American Revolution*. New Haven, Conn., 1985.
DeConde, Alexander. *The Quasi-War: The Politics and Diplomacy of the Undeclared War with France, 1797–1801*. New York, 1966.
Duroselle, Jean-Baptiste. *France and the United States: From the Beginnings to the Present*. Chicago, 1978.
Egan, Clifford. *Neither Peace nor War: Franco-American Relations, 1803–1812*. Baton Rouge, La., 1983.
Grosser, Alfred. *The Western Alliance: European-American Relations Since 1945*. New York, 1982.
Harrison, Michael M. *The Reluctant Ally: France and Atlantic Security*. Baltimore, Md., 1981.
Hurstfield, Julian G. *America and the French Nation*. Chapel Hill, N.C., 1986.
Kaplan, Lawrence S. *Colonies into Nation: American Diplomacy, 1763–1801*. New York, 1972.
Kuisel, Richard. *Seducing the French: The Dilemma of Americanization*. Berkeley, Calif., 1993.
Schuker, Stephen A. *The End of French Predominance in Europe: The Financial Crisis of 1924 and the Adoption of the Dawes Plan*. Chapel Hill, N.C.,1976.
Stinchcombe, William C. *The American Revolution and the French Alliance*. Syracuse, N.Y., 1969.
Wall, Irwin. *The United States and the Making of Postwar France, 1945–1954*. New York, 1991.

FRANCO, FRANCISCO

(*b.* 4 December 1892; *d.* 20 November 1975)

Spanish general and military ruler of Spain (1939–1975). Born at El Ferrol in northern Spain, Franco was educated at the National Military Academy in Toledo and rose to prominence during the 1920s, when he led Spanish troops to victory over Moroccan guerrillas seeking independence from Madrid. Deeply troubled by the political and economic changes wrought by the liberal revolution that toppled King Alfonso XIII in 1931, Franco led a military rebellion against the Spanish Republic in July 1936 that triggered a bloody civil war, from which he emerged victorious three years later with the help of German weapons and Italian troops. Although Franco's ties with Adolf Hitler's Germany and Benito Mussolini's Italy worried many in Washington, the United States quickly recognized his regime in April 1939. During World War II, President Franklin D. Roosevelt wooed Franco with modest amounts of oil, cotton, and silver, helping to ensure Spanish neutrality at a time when unimpeded passage through the Straits of Gibraltar was critical to the success of the U.S. campaign in the Mediterranean. The earlier association with the Axis powers haunted Franco after the war, however, when President Harry S. Truman blocked his bid to join the United Nations and excluded Spain from the North Atlantic Treaty Organization (NATO). By the early 1950s, however, the U.S. quest to contain the Soviet Union and Franco's staunch anticommunism encouraged a rapprochement between Washington and Madrid. Eager to bolster its strategic position in the western Mediterranean, the administration of President Dwight D. Eisenhower concluded a treaty with Franco in 1953 (the Pact of Madrid) which granted the United

States a seventeen-year lease for naval and air bases at Rota, Torrejon, and Seville in exchange for $226 million in economic and military aid. After renewing the lease on schedule during President Richard M. Nixon's administration, Franco surprised many Americans by preparing Spain for the transition to a constitutional monarchy and membership in NATO, which eventually followed after his death.

DOUGLAS LITTLE

See also Spain

FURTHER READING

Beaulac, Willard. Franco: *Silent Ally in World War II.* Carbondale, Ill., 1986.

Crozier, Brian. *Franco.* Boston, 1968.

Feis, Herbert. *The Spanish Story: Franco and the Nations at War.* New York, 1948.

Payne, Stanley. *Politics and the Military in Modern Spain.* Stanford, Calif., 1967.

Preston, Paul. *Franco: A Biography.* New York, 1994.

FRANKLIN, BENJAMIN

(*b.* 17 January 1706; *d.* 17 April 1790)

Printer, author, inventor, scientist, philanthropist, leader in the American Revolution, and diplomat who negotiated the 1783 peace treaty with Great Britain. Franklin's ideas on diplomacy and international relations were first shaped through his experiences in defending colonial Pennsylvania against frontier French and Indians and through his active concern to prevent a breach between Great Britain and its North American colonies. Franklin moved to Philadelphia from his home in Boston in 1723. By hard work, sound business practices, a rare ability to make friends in high places, and skillful self-promotion, he became the owner in 1730 of a printing business, which included ownership of the Pennsylvania Gazette. He came to be known as a person of sound views and commendable public spirit through writings he published in his newspaper, publication of pamphlets on public issues, his exceptional success in establishing institutions to serve the public, and his activity in the Pennsylvania colonial assembly. His self-improvement projects included study of the French, Italian, and Spanish languages. At the age of forty-two Franklin, by then a public personality, determined that he had financial sufficiency and decided to devote his time to public affairs and to science, then called natural philosophy.

The eighteenth century provided a policy school for colonial Americans on local, regional, and international questions. Great wars and contests for empire among the European states provoked colonials to consider their place in these contests. Competing ideas about the nature of empires, the real and illusionary components of national power, and what the constituent parts within the British Empire owed to each other raised profound issues that were widely discussed in the American colonies. Franklin was introduced to aspects of these central issues in part because of his discontent with the Penn Family, proprietors of Pennsylvania, who resisted having their assets taxed to support public endeavors. In thinking through the role of the Penn family in governing Pennsylvania, much discussion occurred about the nature of the British Empire, imperial governance, French and Indian threats to the western borders, and the economic role of the colonies within the larger imperial mosaic.

King George's War (1740–1748), one of the European wars of the eighteenth century, became the occasion for Franklin's first pamphlet on foreign affairs. In *Plain Truth, or, Serious Considerations on the Present State of the City of Philadelphia, and Province of Pennsylvania* (1747), he called to account those who refused to do their duty to protect Philadelphia against French and Spanish privateers because many pacifist Quakers, whom the nondefenders despised, refused to take up arms. He then chastised the ruling Quakers, suggesting they relinquish political power during times of crisis so that those willing to defend Pennsylvania could do so. Clearly no pacifist himself, Franklin urged that unity in the face of external danger be the order of the day. He actively assisted in building defenses for Pennsylvania, brought guns from Boston, and helped enlist 10,000 volunteers. Maintaining unity against external threats was the earliest and the most extended theme in his long career of diplomacy. Franklin credited the Six Nations of the Iroquois Confederacy for his early emphasis on unity. He admired the Six Nations and actually began his career in diplomacy when he concluded a treaty with this confederacy on behalf of Pennsylvania in 1753.

French and Indian threats from the western country, where English and French imperial ambitions clashed ever more directly in the 1750s, stimulated Franklin to think beyond Philadelphia and Pennsylvania. Given the relaxed imperial governing style of Great Britain and the great distance of the colonies from England, he reasoned that security for the colonial frontier against the French and Indians was possible only if the colonies united in some common union for protection. At the Albany Congress of 1754, called to discuss colonial security questions, Franklin proposed his "Plan of Union." Although not well received either in the colonies or in London, the Albany Plan nonetheless showed Franklin's maturing thinking about security questions. In the Albany Plan he pointed the colonies toward cooperation on a basis of equality and enlightened self-interest. These concepts became part of his thinking about all political relationships—security through unity, equality of peoples and political units within the imperial system, and all parties acting on the basis of enlightened self-interest. The proposal for colonial union also reflected his profound belief that "God helps those who help themselves."

The trans-Appalachian West especially caught Franklin's imagination during the 1750s. The value of that vast area to the British, to the colonies, and ultimately to an independent United States was a topic on Franklin's agenda for decades. Franklin's interest in the West was certainly stimulated by his own extensive land speculations, but for Franklin the West became an obsession. Franklin, not Thomas Jefferson, was the first great American imperialist who looked west, first for colonial security and later for national domestic political fulfillment. Franklin thought agriculture the most useful of all occupations and saw the West as a beckoning area where vast wealth could be produced and where farm families could double the population every twenty to twenty-five years. He initially envisioned this population increase as the shield of empire before which the French or Indians must retreat. French encirclement could be resisted by sheer human productivity and strategic territorial advances.

When questions arose in London about the potential for such a wealthy and well-populated area remaining loyal to England, and with its citizens willing to forgo establishing manufacturing enterprises, Franklin reassured the worriers. With land plentiful, he argued, farmers with large families would not willingly move to urban centers where misery and poverty prevailed. Because manufacturing seemed to flourish only in squalid urban centers, one could rest assured that Americans in the West would happily provide agriculture and raw materials for England and be content to purchase the products of its manufacturers. Mutuality and enlightened self-interest could be served and the British Empire would find its bonds strengthened in a greater West. To pen up the Americans, he argued, certainly meant crisis for the British Empire.

Franklin's romance with the whole concept of American expansionism became more pronounced during the Great War for the Empire (1756–1763), also called the French and Indian War or the Seven Years' War. In 1757 he went to London to represent the interests of Pennsylvania in its contest with the Penn family and remained in England during most of this major war, whose central players were Great Britain, France, Prussia, Austria, and Spain. He thus heard the debates in Parliament and read them in the press over possible terms of the peace and involved himself in arguing what constituted the true muscle of empire. Franklin was especially disturbed to hear some claim that the West Indian sugar island of Guadeloupe was more important to acquire than Canada at the end of the war.

To counter what he considered myopic views, Franklin published a pamphlet entitled *The Interest of Great Britain Considered with Regard to Her Colonies and the Acquisition of Canada and Guadeloupe* (1760), in which he argued that the security of the American colonies demanded the removal of the French from Canada. Franklin believed that with the expulsion of France from Canada the American colonies would become the center of the British Empire. He was also convinced that a French-free Canada would become another vast area of settlement for the North American colonists. When the Great War for the Empire ended in 1763 and Great Britain expelled France from Canada, Franklin concluded that the future of the American colonies was now assured.

Toward Independence

Events were soon to prove right those who suspected the Americans would be ungrateful and even more difficult to govern once the French left North America. The British government faced financial crisis because of the war's cost and decided that it must secure greater revenues from its American colonies. The effort met American coldness and even assertions that the colonies owed Great Britain nothing as a result of its exertions in the Great War for the Empire. Great Britain, the colonists declared, had been seeking only its own selfish advantage.

In the Stamp Act crisis of 1765 Americans refused to sell revenue-producing stamps that, they argued, infringed on their rights. Franklin was in England at the time. He had returned to America in 1762 but was sent back to London almost immediately to represent Pennsylvania in its tax dispute with the Penn family. Surprised by the American reaction, Franklin was called before the House of Commons in February of 1766 to be examined on American views of what constituted acceptable taxation by Parliament. He outraged certain members of Parliament and pleased the Americans colonials by asserting that the Great War for the Empire had been entirely a mercantilist war designed to enhance British domestic and trading interests, and that the Americans had participated in the war in a spirit of disinterested helpfulness. He hoped to persuade Parliament that it must proceed carefully in levying taxes on Americans. Franklin believed in a mercantile empire, united for protection and trade, but with the limitation that all within the empire have equal opportunity to prosper.

Following repeal of the Stamp Act in 1766, Franklin intended to return to Philadelphia, but Pennsylvania reappointed him its agent, as did Georgia in 1768, New Jersey in 1769, and Massachusetts in 1770. His duties in representing these colonies kept him abreast of both European and American developments, but he failed in several missions, including gaining greater autonomy for Pennsylvania from the Penn family. His active courtship of the great for support, very painful indeed to a onetime poor boy who prized his independence, was an experience he did not repeat in France. Franklin came to view

English political life as debased, with statesmanship and well-crafted imperial policies being the chief casualties of this environment. Colonial policies were shaped, he gradually became convinced, by a Parliament sensitive primarily to the interests of British merchants or corrupt American colonial officials.

At first blaming only Parliament, Franklin came in the early 1770s to believe that the king was also a primary source of bad advice and ill will toward Americans. What had gone wrong? It was English pride, Franklin believed, a ruinous pride and passion that made it ever easier for English politicians to ignore the wider interests of empire as they focused on greasing local interests for immediate political purposes. His own denouement came when he admitted that he had forwarded to his friends in America confidential letters of former Governor Thomas Hutchinson of Massachusetts, written in 1768–1770, letters in which Hutchinson had argued that public order demanded the curtailment of certain colonial rights. Following publication of the letters in Boston, Franklin was called before the Privy Council in January 1774, where he was ridiculed, denounced as a common thief, and held up for public scorn. In 1775 he wrote to a friend: "When I consider the extream Corruption prevalent among all Orders of Men in this old rotten state, and the glorious publick Virtue so predominant in our rising Country, I cannot but apprehend more Mischief than Benefit from a closer Union."

Revolutionary Diplomat

Franklin returned to Pennsylvania in May 1775, now aged sixty-nine, with mature views on diplomacy, nation-state relations, and the course for America to follow in its great political crisis with England. He fully understood the role of military power in shaping interstate relations, but he believed that economic strength was the best harbinger of a nation's future. Committed to the concepts of mutuality, equality, and enlightened self-interest in relations between nations, Franklin had grown to hate war and spoke of armies as "devouring monsters." He also believed that nations should seek to be self-reliant, not placing their fortunes within the power of others.

Franklin moved toward American independence, having had his fill of England and its politicians, monarch, and imperial policies. He argued that help would be sent to America by those powers who believed, as he did, that great risks were fully justified to secure American trade for the future. Military alliances seemed unnecessary to gain this assistance because of the awesome value of American trade. Franklin believed European political culture so debased that America should minimize political connections with Europe.

Upon his return to Philadelphia, Franklin was immediately chosen a member of the Continental Congress.

He also sat on a commission of three to induce the Canadians to join America in armed resistance to Great Britain, but the mission was a failure. The French Catholics of Quebec, whatever their aversion to Great Britain, had no intention of placing their fate in the hands of Protestants who had reviled them as a popish menace when England had moved to accommodate their interests in the Quebec Act of 1774. Franklin was sharply disappointed in their response because he had long seen Canada as the northern wing of the American colonial West. Almost boisterously confident in the future of an independent America, he was nevertheless aware that the Americans were unlikely to win independence from Great Britain unaided if the independence movement evolved into full-scale war. The colonials had not a single ship of the line to oppose Great Britain. American willingness to tax themselves to support a war was uncertain, for Americans by now had long practice in viewing centrally imposed taxation as unjust. With a significant percentage of the population opposed to independence and many others indifferent, it seemed clear that the new American government stood in need of major foreign assistance.

France stood as the great foreign hope of the Congress. As chair of the Committee of Secret Correspondence (the State Department in embryo), Franklin wrote the instructions for Connecticut merchant Silas Deane's mission to ask France to enter into a treaty with the new nation, whether for commerce or defense or both. France had been considering how best to seek revenge on Great Britain since the end of the Great War for the Empire. Not only had France been humiliated but its influence in Europe had been sharply diminished since 1763. The French court, and particularly its foreign minister, Charles Gravier, Comte de Vergennes, eagerly sought to encourage the Americans to break their connection with Great Britain, to direct American trade into French channels, and thus to reconfigure the balance of power between England and France in France's favor. In fact, France had committed itself to assisting the Americans through secret aid two months before the Declaration of Independence, when Vergennes granted funds to the dummy company Roderique Hortalez et Compagnie, created by Pierre-Augustin Caron de Beaumarchais to aid clandestinely the American revolt.

Partly to encourage a positive response for assistance from all nations, Congress opened American ports to all on 6 April 1776 and voted for independence on July 2. Franklin and his colleagues on the Committee of Secret Correspondence prepared "model treaties" that American agents might use in negotiating agreements with foreign nations. The revolutionary leaders anticipated no pressing need to offer a military alliance to France or to any other power in exchange for its aid. It was thought quite sufficient to offer France and others the golden opportunity to gain U.S. commerce now and in future years. Franklin hoped to see the United States trading with all nations but having intimate political relationships with none.

Encouraged by reports from Deane in France, the Congress decided in September 1776 to send a commission of three to negotiate a commercial treaty. Franklin, Deane, and Arthur Lee of Virginia were appointed. Franklin, who once said that his policy on public appointments was "never ask, never refuse, nor ever resign," consented to this new task despite his age and growing infirmity. He arrived in France early in December 1776. No diplomat from North America had ever received the public welcome accorded Franklin. Already a member of the distinguished French Academy, the learned Franklin had achieved fame as a scientist, philosopher, and philanthropist. Several of his works had been translated and widely disseminated in France, including *Poor Richard's Almanac* (1732–1757). The French entertained ideas that in the New World humankind had made a fresh and wonderful start. Franklin, a shrewd public relations person, knew that effective diplomacy stood on more than one leg and therefore presented himself wearing modest clothing, topped by a fur cap and loose-fitting spectacles, and nodded in kindly fashion as he passed through adoring crowds waiting to see him. John Adams, no great friend of Franklin, was astonished at the enormity of his reputation. Even the coachmen, chambermaids, and kitchen scullions, Adams marveled, knew about Franklin and considered him a friend to humanity.

In his role as commissioner of the United States, Franklin soon found himself happier with the French court than with the American Congress. He grew dismayed that Congress sent inexperienced agents to the courts of Europe, seeking aid and treaties even before those courts had consented to receive the American commissioners. This amateurish militia diplomacy provoked Franklin, because he believed in negotiating from strength. Americans must first prove they could fight effectively and tax themselves for the cause of liberty. Aid from abroad must certainly then follow in due course. A desperate Congress ignored his advice. Military engagements early in the war were not encouraging and the weak authority of the central government made the levying of heavy taxes impossible. Furthermore, the credit of the new government had not been established and ruinous inflation threatened. To succeed, the United States cause had to have ever greater amounts of aid from France.

Franklin and his two colleagues purchased blankets and gunpowder to assist the war effort, arranged credit to meet endless bills, made provisions to sell American tobacco, met with military officers who hoped to receive high appointments in the American army, and tried to serve as naval affairs counselors to American merchants or to privateers. Franklin, Lee, and Deane miscued badly in 1777 by encouraging American privateers to make use of French ports and personnel in ways that threatened to bring France prematurely into the war. This effort led to a sharp rebuke from the French government. Vergennes expressed his outrage and for a time refused even to meet with the commissioners. Franklin also got caught up in a vicious quarrel between his fellow commissioners when Lee accused Deane of graft and dishonest practices while purchasing or transmitting French goods to American shores through Hortalez et Compagnie. Lee's confrontational and accusatory style, and his determination to ruin Deane in American circles, caused Franklin acute distress. Lee also questioned Franklin's attention to duty and his honesty.

Acting on instructions from Congress, Franklin and his colleagues early raised the possibility of a commercial alliance with France. The French, however, were not eager to move precipitously toward a war with Great Britain until their family ally, Spain, agreed to join the effort and before their own navy was ready. For months Vergennes did his best to persuade Spain to sign on, but in the meantime, France was actively making naval preparations to enter the war in 1778. The successful conclusion of the long Saratoga campaign in October 1777 provided France with a public justification to enter the war in 1778, because the American victory underlined to the French court that the United States had staying power. In addition, following Saratoga, Franklin and Deane alarmed Vergennes when Deane held discussions with Paul Wentworth, a British negotiating agent. Might the Americans decide to abandon the war? France decided to take no chances. Victory now dictated French entrance into the war with or without Spain. Franklin and his colleagues had been instructed only to negotiate a commercial treaty; France wanted a military alliance as well.

Between December 1777 and February 1778 Franklin and his colleagues negotiated two treaties with France, and Franklin marveled that France treated his country so generously. The Treaty of Amity and Commerce contained a number of provisions, including most-favored-nation status and concessions on neutral rights, that were normally found only in treaties between nations of equal stature. Reciprocity and mutual advantage were its undergirding principles. This treaty also served notice that France had recognized the United States as an independent nation. In the Treaty of Alliance, France promised to fight Great Britain until the "independence absolute and unlimited of the United States" had been secured. France also promised the United States the right to retain conquered British territory outside the thirteen states in North America or the islands of Bermuda, although an opening was made for Spain to retake the

Floridas from Great Britain. The alliance was to last "forever." It is difficult to name any treaties in modern history where nations of such disparate resources concluded treaties with provisions suggesting equal status and power between the parties. Despite growing congressional dissatisfaction with Franklin for his failure to submit systematic reports, he was appointed sole plenipotentiary to France in September 1778.

Franklin's work for the next two years was less dramatic but no less strenuous and vexatious. He suffered agonies when Congress repeatedly instructed him to seek new loans from France but then failed to wait for news of his successful application. In the meantime, Congress proceeded to make purchases, drawing upon the credits that Franklin had supposedly secured from France. Franklin was repeatedly compelled to ask France to honor bills for which it had received no proper notice and had no obligation to pay. Furthermore, American militia diplomats, rejected at the various courts of Europe, invariably turned up in Paris, wanting to offer advice and becoming offended if their advice was not sought or was ignored. Franklin was also pressed by Americans seeking letters of recommendation to Frenchmen, or by Frenchmen soliciting letters to advance their interests in America. He likewise negotiated for the return of American prisoners of war. American ship captains petitioned for funds to outfit their ships or to help in the disposition of merchandise. As Franklin noted, the very sound of carriage wheels rolling into his residence at Passy struck terror into his heart.

Franklin had to bear the snide and unjust comments of colleagues who found his relentlessly upbeat attitude toward the French court and French assistance to be naive if not indicative of bad judgment. He also had to bear fairly biased reproaches for being disorderly with mission records, a matter not improved until Adams replaced Deane. The American mission likewise provided a lively source of information for a succession of British spies. Franklin's tendency to trust others was badly misplaced as head of mission, but his temperament craved a convivial and relaxed atmosphere.

Negotiating Peace with Great Britain

The Battle of Yorktown in October 1781 propelled Great Britain toward negotiating peace with the United States. The war for independence had been a long and exasperating one for both nations. Franklin believed that Great Britain's prosecution of the war against America had been cruel and rapacious. A true and long-lasting peace therefore demanded that Great Britain go far beyond normal acts of reconciliation.

The American Congress, which did not trust any single person to negotiate a peace treaty with Great Britain, decided to send a commission of three. Franklin, appointed reluctantly by Congress, was joined by John Jay of New York and John Adams. Under the influence of the French minister, Congress instructed the peace commissioners to follow the advice of the French court and submit to French advice on all points relating to the negotiations. Such instructions were absurd and humiliating, going far beyond the provision of Article VIII in the Treaty of Alliance. In that article, both parties promised not to sign a separate peace.

Despite his initial support for the binding instruction from Congress, Franklin in April 1782 opened the negotiations for peace independently of France. Richard Oswald, a personal agent of the British colonial affairs secretary, William Petty, Earl of Shelburne (soon to be prime minister), found Franklin persuasive in presenting terms that Franklin labeled "necessary" and "advisory." Necessary items concerned recognition of American independence, withdrawal of all British troops, boundary settlements between loyal colonies and the United States, adjustment of Canadian boundaries to pre-1774 lines, and freedom for Americans to fish on the Newfoundland Banks. By the time Adams and Jay had joined the peace negotiations, Franklin had outlined the chief concerns and staked out the American positions. Nevertheless, Jay and Adams brought added vigor and some needed caution concerning French objectives. Serious and formal negotiations began in October 1782. Franklin, ill during much of the final negotiation, supported Jay and Adams in taking initiatives to bring matters to a conclusion with Great Britain without consulting or informing France. Both men had recent diplomatic experiences—Jay in Spain and Adams in Holland—which convinced them that nations acted out of self-interest and had no real concern for America. France, itself desperate for an end to this ruinous war, did not intervene to prevent the American delegation's negotiations.

Franklin placed his own stamp on the negotiations for peace. Through Oswald, he tried early to persuade the British cabinet to cede all of Canada to the United States, explaining that true reconciliation could come only if Great Britain took unusual steps to appease American anger. Canada was one of his "advisory" items. Franklin hinted that if Canada remained in British hands, hostility between Great Britain and the United States must continue, thus forcing the United States to cling to its French alliance. His effort to obtain Canada as well as Nova Scotia faltered. Franklin's argument for a peace of true reconciliation seemed to center around Great Britain yielding enormous land tracts to the United States.

Franklin also took a very decided interest in the disposition of the claims of loyalists. He was normally a conciliatory person, going halfway to meet the political needs of the other side. He knew there was firm support in the Parliament not to abandon those loyalists in America who had stood with the Crown and whose property in the new nation had been confiscated. Justice must be done, Parliament insisted, for those who had remained loyal to the empire. On this issue, however, Franklin proved unyielding. His own son, a former colonial governor, had chosen the loyalist side, a decision which cut Franklin to the heart. Also, he believed that the loyalists had supported or were responsible for many acts of needless cruelty during the war, including inciting Indians to attack and scalp frontier peoples who backed the Revolution. Where Adams and Jay might have agreed on some middle way on the loyalist issue, Franklin insisted that justice argued for no compromise, although he did suggest that the loyalists receive land in Canada if Great Britain ceded the huge area to the United States. In November 1782 he lashed out at Oswald: "Your ministers require that we should receive again into our bosom those who have been our bitterest enemies, and restore their properties who have destroyed ours; and this while the wounds they have given us are still bleeding." The peace treaty provided only that Congress "earnestly recommend" to the states that they give due consideration to the financial claims of the loyalists. The loyalists received little of substance, provoking outrage in the House of Commons and contributing to the fall of the Shelburne government in February 1783.

Franklin also wanted Great Britain to acknowledge its war guilt, even to paying reparations to those who had suffered at British hands. Here again Franklin's general philosophy of reconciliation was at work; one should build a permanent peace and such a peace will happen only when equity and justice are observed. Because he believed that Great Britain was totally responsible for this terrible fratricidal war, with its hands "red, wet, and dripping with the Blood of my Countrymen, Friends and Relations," it was up to the British to make the gestures necessary for true reconciliation. Franklin, the genuinely outraged nationalist, seemed unwilling or unable to recognize the shared responsibility for the outbreak and cruelties of the revolutionary war.

During the peace negotiations Franklin, trying to be loyal to France, was concerned less than he should have been that France was unlikely to support the American desire to expand to the Mississippi River. Vergennes was committed to American independence but not necessarily to a settlement that gave the United States a title of land to the Mississippi or American rights to navigation of the river. Such a settlement could not only make the new nation independent of France but a threat as well to Spain, which feared for its possessions in the Floridas. On one point, however, Franklin was adamant: the United States must never cede or surrender its right of access to the Mississippi River. As he said to Jay, "A neighbor might as well ask me to sell my street door."

The final settlement, arguably, was shaped more by British war weariness and the Shelburne government's desire to end the war in a way that detached the United States from its French connection than by the skills of Franklin, Adams, and Jay. Preliminary terms were agreed to in November 1782 without the concurrence of France, a technical violation of the Treaty of Alliance. The Treaty of Paris was signed on 3 September 1783. Final terms constituted a stunning victory for the United States.

Franklin's work in France was now largely finished, although he secured a new loan of six million livres from France despite French displeasure with the peace commission's independent diplomacy. In all, he had assisted in procuring forty million livres in assistance from France, more than $80 million in contemporary purchasing power. Franklin received his welcome notice of congressional recall in May 1785. His mission had been a triumph both for public and traditional diplomacy and for his country. Elected to the Constitutional Convention of 1787, Franklin, now quite infirm and always an unwilling oral debater, contributed little to the discussions on foreign relations.

Characteristics of Franklin's Diplomacy

Franklin's diplomacy and his ideas concerning international relations flowed from a lifetime of experience, observation, and wide reading. His actions in foreign relations were characterized by his intense desire to have a meeting of minds; he never lost faith that reasonable persons could arrive at mutually agreeable decisions from which good could result for both sides. He seldom used legal arguments to win his point. He did not, for example, support his urgent wish for the western lands or Canada with Oswald on the basis of old claims or land surveys. Reason and reconciliation were his polestars. He believed, moreover, that nations should honor treaties, pay their debts, and respond with gratitude and fidelity to those who supported them.

Franklin contended that justice rested with one side or another in a war. He considered nations that made war for trade or dominion bandit gangs bent on plunder. Franklin did not accept the contemporary concept that different codes should guide the behavior of nations and individuals. He insisted that vigorous preparation for war was one of the most effective ways to avoid it. With all his aversion to war, he nonetheless believed war to be a legitimate exercise of power when a nation was threatened with destruction. His sympathies in war were with the innocent sufferers. Gaining the release of prisoners of war constantly concerned him during the American Revolution. He hoped to see the day when innocents were not attacked during wars.

He also opposed the practice of privateering. These ideas on prisoners of war and privateering he incorporated into a treaty of amity and commerce signed with Prussia in July 1785, shortly before he returned to Philadelphia.

Franklin was a supporter of free trade, and his understanding of human pride and the deep human desire to dominate others prevented him from adopting a view widely held by French rationalists that right-ordered economic relations between nations would greatly reduce the occurrence and ferocity of wars. His hopes that humanity would act in reasonable ways toward one another were constant but his expectations were modest.

Always a newspaperman, Franklin understood the value of carefully crafted public diplomacy. He was notably discreet in conducting negotiations and believed in the usefulness of secret diplomacy. While most students of international affairs of his century concerned themselves primarily with calculations of power and dynastic rivalries, Franklin kept his focus on ensuring the freedom and well-being of individuals. This objective kept his attention centered on the need for expansion in North America. Indeed, his concern for expansionism served as a harbinger of the Manifest Destiny of the next century. His conviction that the United States should distance itself from European political entanglements in ordinary circumstances became fundamental postulates of the new nation.

Marvin R. Zahniser

See also Adams, John; American Revolution; Beaumarchais, Pierre Augustin Caron de; Canada; Colonialism; Continental Expansion; Deane, Silas; France; French and Indian War; Great Britain; Imperialism; Jay, John; Loyalists; Manifest Destiny; Mississippi River; Vergennes, Charles Gravier

FURTHER READING

Bemis, Samuel F. *The Diplomacy of the American Revolution.* Bloomington, Ind., 1957.

Crane, Verner W., ed. *Benjamin Franklin's Letters to the Press.* Chapel Hill, N.C., 1950.

Dull, Jonathan R. *Franklin the Diplomat: The French Mission.* Philadelphia, 1982.

Hanna, William S. *Benjamin Franklin and Pennsylvania Politics.* Stanford, Calif., 1964.

Kaplan, Lawrence S. *Colonies into Nation: American Diplomacy, 1763–1801.* New York, 1972.

Ketcham, Ralph L. *Benjamin Franklin.* New York, 1965.

Labaree, Leonard W., et al., eds. *The Papers of Benjamin Franklin*, 30 vols. New Haven, Conn., 1959–1993.

Lemay, J.A. Leo, ed. *Reappraising Benjamin Franklin: A Bicentennial Perspective.* Newark, Del., 1993.

Morris, Richard B. *The Peacemakers: The Great Powers and American Independence.* New York, 1965.

Smyth, Albert H., ed. *The Writings of Benjamin Franklin*, 10 vols. New York, 1905–1907.

Stinchcombe, William C. *The American Revolution and the French Alliance.* Syracuse, N.Y., 1969.

Stourzh, Gerald. *Benjamin Franklin and American Foreign Policy.* Chicago, 1954.

Tucker, Robert W., and David C. Hendrickson. *The Fall of the First British Empire.* Baltimore, 1982.

Van Doren, Carl. *Benjamin Franklin.* New York, 1938.

Van Doren, Carl, ed. *Benjamin Franklin's Autobiographical Writings.* New York, 1945.

Wharton, Francis, ed. T*he Revolutionary Diplomatic Correspondence of the United States*, 6 vols. Washington, D.C., 1889.

FREEDOM OF INFORMATION ACT
(6 September 1966)

Requires the executive branch to release official records to applicants upon request, unless the information sought is privileged under one or more of the exclusions set forth under the law. Enacted in 1966 to become effective 4 July 1967, the Freedom of Information Act (FOIA) went virtually unnoticed by the public at the time. The act was based, in the words of President Bill Clinton more than a quarter of a century later, "upon the fundamental principle that an informed citizenry is essential to the democratic process." Almost anyone has the legal right to apply for access to agency-held information, and FOIA sets forth procedures and requirements and provides for judicial review of refusals.

With respect to U.S. foreign relations, the principal area of information that may be withheld by federal agencies consists of properly classified records that a particular agency determines should be kept secret in the interest of national defense or foreign policy. Another eight exemptions, each specifically and narrowly drawn, range from internal agency rules and practices to trade secrets obtained on a privileged basis to geological and geophysical data to personnel and similar files, the release of which would constitute an invasion of personal privacy. (The Privacy Act of 1974, effective September 1975, further protects the confidentiality of personal information held in executive branch files but specifically gives the right of access to certain records that contain information about the person who is applying.) None of these exemptions directly concerns foreign relations. In 1986 three exclusions concerning law enforcement records were added to the basic law.

The legislative history of the FOIA includes a housekeeping statute dating back to 1789, the provisions of which were incorporated in the Administrative Procedure Act of 1946. That law authorized executive branch departments to keep records confidential "for good cause" if in the public interest or if bearing solely on their internal management. Only "persons properly and directly concerned" could petition for agency records. Those provisions were interpreted for many years as not requiring, or even permitting, the release to the public of information upon request. An initial effort to liberalize this restrictive stand, the Moss-Hennings Act of 1958, set forth a right of access to agency files but had little practical effect. After years of debate among congressmen, agency officials, public interest spokesmen, and the press, the FOIA became law as an amendment to the public information section of the 1946 law. A revision of the FOIA adopted in 1967 made it explicit that agencies might refuse to release information if secrecy were required in the public interest or if the information sought pertained solely to internal administrative matters. In 1974 Congress passed an especially important amendment, which compelled agencies to declassify information if at all feasible. Other modifications followed in 1976, 1978, and 1984, culminating with the Freedom of Information Reform Act of 1986, but the legislative and judicial branches of the federal government remained unaffected.

Despite the law's intent to further openness, the FOIA has engendered controversy in the field of foreign affairs. Scholars and journalists have complained about the pace and extent of compliance with their requests for information, especially with regard to policies during the Vietnam era and those pertaining to Central America during President Ronald Reagan's administration. Especially pointed was the debate over whether the executive branch had routinely overclassified much documentation; under the law, government agencies often simply decline to release any information that is privileged because of its classification or release only documents with heavily censored portions. Under the best of conditions, the process can be time-consuming and can end in failure to obtain the desired records and can occasion an appeal or a lawsuit. Petitioners desiring information, normally submitting their requests by letter, must describe the material needed as specifically as possible; the particular agency then generally has ten working days to respond. If the agency can identify the information and determines the request can be met at least partially, the agency charges fees according to Office of Management and Budget guidelines, amounting at most to the actual cost of searches and the duplication of materials. If the agency denies the request, the applicant has up to forty-five days to appeal, after which time he or she may bring a FOIA lawsuit in a U.S. district court. The government department concerned under the law has the burden of proof that the information may not be released. The Department of Justice, which is responsible for coordinating administration of the act and for encouraging agency compliance, has since 1993 defended government departments in court against such suits only if those departments can show not only that the information sought is excluded by law but also that its release would cause "foreseeable harm" in the category of exclusion.

The volume of requests since the late 1970s to executive branch agencies under the FOIA has been substantial. No central compilations are made, but department and agency figures reported annually to Congress indicate that in calendar year 1991, a total of about 589,000 applications was received. The Department of State received 5,309 that year; the Central Intelligence Agency (CIA), 4,563, including applications for information processed under the Privacy Act or the mandatory declassification review; the Department of Defense, 129,437, many of which concerned defense contracts; the Treasury Department, 56,017, including inquiries to the Internal Revenue Service; the Department of Agriculture, 63,775, mostly crop production and commercial inquiries; and the Department of Justice, 71,265, many of which were requests to the Federal Bureau of Investigation (FBI) for information on personal files. The cost of FOIA compliance in 1991 for these five departments and one agency amounted to an estimated $60 million. The Department of State's FOIA workload increased from 4,780 requests received in 1989 to 5,683 in 1993; during that same period, application cases that were closed—applications that were met at least partially, or if denied, not appealed or litigated—declined from 5,966 to 5,399 as a backlog was reduced. Figures on the CIA are comparable: in 1989 requests for CIA information totaled 4,519; by 1993, this number had risen to 6,555. Requests met by the CIA numbered 4,178 in 1989 and 5,705 in 1993. Defense Department totals were higher, given the size of the agency and the commercial nature of much of the information requested. In 1989 the Department of Defense received 119,492 requests and 18,651 in 1993, in which year 89,631 applications were granted in full or in part and 1,798 requests were denied in full.

After a slow start, only grudging bureaucratic compliance in the years following its enactment, and controversy surrounding executive branch classification procedures, indications in the mid-1990s were that the FOIA, while still sometimes involving an extended procedure, would function reasonably effectively in permitting popular access to the immense store of information and knowledge contained in the voluminous files of the U.S. government's executive branch. State secrets concerning foreign policy and national defense remained closed under the law.

HENRY E. MATTOX

FURTHER READING

Adler, Allan Robert. *Step-by-Step Guide to Using the Freedom of Information Act.* Washington, D.C., 1992.

Franklin, Justin D., and Robert F. Bouchard, comps. *Guidebook to the Freedom of Information and Privacy Acts.* New York, 1986.

Hernon, Peter, and Charles R. McClure. *Public Access to Government Information: Issues, Trends, and Strategies.* Norwood, N.J., 1988.

FREEDOM OF THE SEAS

A fundamental principle of international law whereby all states have the right to use the high seas with due regard for the interests of other states. The origins of this principle are usually associated with Dutch jurist Hugo Grotius, whose work *Mare Liberum* ("The Free Sea," 1609) defended freedom of the seas against Portuguese usurpations. His essay prompted rebuttals defending the lawfulness of claims to sovereignty over the high seas, among which *Mare Clausum* ("The Closed Sea," 1635) by the Englishman John Selden is best known. State practice during the nineteenth century affirmed general acceptance of the doctrine that no state could assert a legal right to bar other members of the international community from the use of any portion of the high seas. Freedom of the seas is generally construed to mean freedom of navigation, which presumes the absence of territorial sovereignty on the high seas. The principle, as initially codified in Article 2 of the 1958 Geneva Convention on the High Seas, corresponded to customary international law. A similar interpretation was incorporated into Article 87 of the 1982 United Nations Convention on the Law of the Sea, which enumerates certain freedoms of the high seas, including freedom of navigation, overflight, laying of submarine cables and pipelines, constructing artificial islands and installations, and fishing and scientific research. Exercise of these freedoms presupposes that states engage in activities on the high seas on objects (ships) linked together by a legal connection, namely those objects flying the flag of a state. The essence of the principle is that ships of one state have the right of noninterference on the high seas by ships of other states. No state may subject any part of the high seas to its sovereignty, and rules on high seas freedoms make no distinction between coastal or land-locked states. Since World War II the principle of freedom of the seas has been eroded by creeping national jurisdiction into ocean space. Most coastal states have expanded territorial waters from three to twelve miles seaward, and some claim up to 200 miles. Adoption during the 1970s by countries of the 200-mile exclusive economic zone concept put forty percent of the high seas under national jurisdiction.

CHRISTOPHER C. JOYNER

See also International Law; Law of the Sea; Neutral Rights

FURTHER READING

Churchill, R. R., and A. V. Lowe. *The Law of the Sea*, 2nd rev. ed. Manchester, England, 1988.
Hollick, Ann L. *U.S. Foreign Policy and the Law of the Sea*. Princeton, N.J., 1981.
Van Dyke, Jon M., Durwood Zaelke, and Grant Hewison, eds. *Freedom for the Seas in the 21st Century: Ocean Governance and Environmental Harmony*. Washington, D.C., 1993.

FREE SHIPS, FREE GOODS
See Neutral Rights

FREE TRADE

A concept according to which governments should not regulate, tax, or otherwise interfere with international commerce. This position, in opposition to the earlier policy of mercantilism, was put forward by Adam Smith in *The Wealth of Nations* (1776) under the rubric of "absolute advantage" and in a more compelling form by David Ricardo in *Principles of Political Economy and Taxation* (1817) under the rubric of "comparative advantage." Under the mercantilist policies prevailing when Smith and Ricardo wrote, the government regulated most aspects of the economy, but particularly tried to discourage imports in order to maintain a surplus in the balance of trade. Ricardo's arguments were quite persuasive and were a major reason for the United Kingdom's shift to a policy of free trade in the middle of the nineteenth century.

The dominant argument for free trade is that it encourages each country to specialize in the production of those goods in which it has the greatest relative or comparative efficiency. If all countries pursue such specialization, productive factors (land, labor, and capital) in each of them will be used with the greatest possible efficiency, and the output of all goods can be increased, thus increasing total real incomes. Most international economists find this argument to be convincing. Although it is clear both from the relevant theory and from historical experience that these efficiency improvements do result from free trade, this policy has powerful opponents in most countries. Those industries that must compete with lower cost imports and their employees are understandably unimpressed by this approach. In the United States most large companies in technologically advancing industries support free trade, whereas it is opposed by most labor unions and industries with relatively static technologies. Virtually every country, except Hong Kong, has some limits or taxes on imports in order to protect domestic import-competing industries. Less than perfectly competitive markets can result in nongovernmental barriers to trade, such as when Japanese firms collude and agree not to purchase imported goods, even if they are less expensive than those available from domestic suppliers.

ROBERT M. DUNN, JR.

See also Balance Payments and Balance of Trade; General Agreement on Tariffs and Trade; Hull, Cordell; Most-Favored-Nation Principle; Tariffs

FURTHER READING

Baldwin, Robert, and Anne Krueger. *The Structure and Evolution of Recent U.S. Trade Policy*. Chicago, 1984.

Dunn, Robert M. Jr., and James C. Ingram. *International Economics*. 4th ed. New York, 1996.

Taussig, Frank. *The Tariff History of the United States*. New York, 1988.

FRELINGHUYSEN, FREDERICK THEODORE

(*b.* 4 August 1817; *d.* 20 May 1885)

U.S. senator (1866–1869, 1871–1877) and secretary of state (1881–1885). A graduate of Rutgers College in 1836, Frelinghuysen became a leading corporation attorney and served as attorney general of New Jersey (1861–1866) before being elected to the Senate, where he was associated with the Stalwarts (proponents of President Ulysses S. Grant) wing of the Republican party. Succeeding James G. Blaine, leader of the Half-Breed (or anti-Grant) wing, in the Department of State, Frelinghuysen replaced activism with caution.

In Latin America, Frelinghuysen undercut Blaine's efforts to mediate disputes between Chile and Peru (the War of the Pacific) and between Mexico and Guatemala. In August 1882 he withdrew Blaine's invitations to a Pan-American conference, an initiative designed in part to reduce tensions between Chile and Peru. Like Blaine, he attempted to abrogate the Clayton-Bulwer Treaty (1850), an agreement that recognized British rights over any canal built through Central America, but Frelinghuysen suffered a British rebuff. On 1 December 1884 Frelinghuysen negotiated a treaty with Lorenzo Zavala, Nicaragua's former president, by which the United States would become co-owner of any canal constructed in Nicaragua. In the process the agreement established a virtual U.S. protectorate over that nation. On 29 January 1885 the Frelinghuysen-Zavala Treaty failed to win Senate approval and was withdrawn by President Grover Cleveland. Frelinghuysen also turned down protectorate offers made by Haiti in May 1883 and by Venezuela that October.

In Europe, Africa, and Asia, Frelinghuysen enjoyed few successes. To little avail, he continued Blaine's efforts to end French and German discrimination against importing U.S. pork, and he protested against British coercive measures that curbed the rights of Irish Americans during British efforts to quell protests led by the Home Rule for Ireland Party. In May 1881 a trade agreement was made with the Hova tribe, which ruled much of Madagascar, but in October 1884 he refused Hova pleas that the United States intervene in their conflict with the conquering French. He sought ratification of the Berlin agreement of 25 February 1885, which formally recognized Belgian King Leopold II's Congo Free State, but the treaty was withdrawn after Cleveland entered the White House. It was only in Korea that Frelinghuysen could claim a modicum of success. In May 1882 the United States signed the Treaty of Chemulpo, an agreement that acknowledged the independence of Korea (which was, in reality, dominated by China), gave the United States most-favored-nation status and extraterritorial rights in Korea, and permitted the exchange of diplomats. Frelinghuysen also promoted commercial reciprocity agreements with Mexico (January 1883), with Spain concerning Cuba and Puerto Rico (November 1884), with the Dominican Republic (December 1884), and with Hawai'i (December 1884), but all were undercut by Congress and remained stillborn.

JUSTUS D. DOENECKE

See also Arthur, Chester Alan; Blaine, James Gillespie; Ireland; Korea; Nicaragua

FURTHER READING

Doenecke, Justus D. *The Presidencies of James A. Garfield and Chester A. Arthur*. Lawrence, Kans., 1981.

Pletcher, David A. *The Awkward Years: American Foreign Policy Under Garfield and Arthur*. Columbia, Mo., 1961.

FRÉMONT, JOHN CHARLES

(*b.* 21 January 1813; *d.* 13 July 1890)

Soldier, explorer, and agent of continental expansion. Born in Savannah, Georgia, and raised in Charleston, South Carolina, Frémont studied engineering at the College of Charleston, served briefly in the navy, and joined the Army Topographical Corps in 1838 as a second lieutenant. In 1841 he married Jessie Benton, daughter of influential Missouri Democratic Senator Thomas Hart Benton. Between 1842 and 1846 Captain Frémont led three separate government expeditions to explore the Oregon Trail, the Great Basin between the Rocky and Sierra mountain ranges, and the Sierra Nevada in Mexico's California province. He reported favorably on northern California's agricultural potential. On the eve of the war with Mexico, in early 1846, Frémont and his armed party of sixty-two men were in Mexican territory. Frémont's precise role in detaching California from the Mexicans remains murky. His mission was purportedly under orders to ascertain the best passage into California, but prior to the declaration of war he had challenged Mexican authority. After an angry rebuff from Mexican military officials in Monterey, the expedition withdrew into Oregon and received new instructions from Washington in May, just as the Bear Flag Revolt of American settlers broke out in northern California. The actual instructions delivered in those dispatches have been the subject of historical debate, but Frémont soon reentered California and aided the revolt. When he received word of the outbreak of the Mexican War in July, Frémont participated in occupying the province and served briefly as its governor.

A dispute between Frémont and his superior, General Stephen Kearny, resulted in Frémont's court-martial and dismissal from the army. Although President James K. Polk canceled the dismissal, Frémont resigned and eventually turned to politics. He represented the new state of California as senator from 1850 to 1851 and became the Republican party's first presidential nominee in 1856. In a remarkably strong showing against James Buchanan, the Frémont campaign carried all but five northern states, suggesting that a sectional antislavery party could eventually win the White House. Frémont returned to the U.S. Army during the Civil War, engaged unsuccessfully in railroad ventures afterward, and served as governor of the Arizona Territory from 1878 to 1883. He died in New York City.

PAUL R. GRASS

See also California; Mexico, War with

FURTHER READING

Egan, Ferol. *Frémont: Explorer for a Restless Nation*. Garden City, N.Y., 1977.
Goetzmann, William H. *Exploration and Empire: The Explorer and the Scientist in the Winning of the American West*, 2nd ed. New York, 1972.
Nevins, Allan. *Frémont: Pathmarker of the West*. New York, 1939; repr. Lincoln, Nebr., 1992.
Rolle, Andrew. *John Charles Frémont: Character as Destiny*. Norman, Okla., 1991.

FRENCH AND INDIAN WAR

(1754–1763)

Also called the Great War for Empire and the Seven Years' War, it was the last of four wars fought between Europe's imperial powers that involved the British North American colonies during the century before independence. Each of the earlier wars had followed a similar pattern—beginning in Europe, spilling over into the colonies, and producing few territorial changes in North America. The French and Indian War, on the other hand, started in the colonies, sparked a war that ultimately included each of Europe's great powers, and ended by redrawing the political map of North America.

The origins of the French and Indian War derived from a three-way contest for control of the Ohio River valley. The Indian occupants, particularly the Iroquois Confederation, sought to safeguard this area from European intrusion. The French saw the valley as the natural link between their colonies in Louisiana and Canada. As the French erected posts in this region in the early 1750s, the British colonists worried that they would be confined east of the Appalachian Mountains. During the summer of 1754 the British colonists initiated two approaches to removing the French threat. In Albany, New York, representatives of seven northern colonies met with Iroquois chiefs in a vain attempt to secure their assistance. In the backcountry, Virginia militia under George Washington marched on Fort Duquesne, the French outpost at the forks of the Ohio, but in early July, Washington surrendered his hastily constructed fort and retreated toward Virginia. The French threat to westward expansion, it seemed, could only be met with British aid.

When the colonists called on London for assistance, the British cabinet responded quickly. During the summer of 1755 a British army under Major General Edward Braddock renewed the offensive against Fort Duquesne, but failed. In May 1756 Great Britain and France formally declared war on each other. The war continued badly for the British in the next two campaigns. By 1758, however, British Prime Minister William Pitt had assumed personal control of the worldwide British war effort. Assigning the war in the colonies the highest priority, Pitt selected the officers to prosecute it, provided them with men, resources, and naval support, and called for increased assistance from the colonists. The capture of Louisbourg in July 1758 swung the war in Great Britain's favor. In September 1759 any prospect of French victory disappeared as the British under General James Wolfe captured Quebec, cutting the supply lines of the remaining French forces and driving their Indian allies into neutrality. The surrender of Montreal a year later ended the fighting in North America.

In February 1763 the Treaty of Paris concluded a war that had involved all of the major European powers and had been fought in North America, Europe, Africa, the Caribbean, the Philippines, and India. The treaty conferred upon Great Britain all of the French and Spanish territory east of the Mississippi River. Spain ceded the Floridas, but received Louisiana from France as compensation. Only a handful of islands remained of France's New World empire. As Pitt had recognized, the changes in North America gave Great Britain a commanding position in the European balance of power, but the war entailed heavy costs for Great Britain as well. Burdened with debt, it redefined the imperial relationship to shift some of the costs of empire onto the colonists. The crisis that ensued culminated in the American Revolution. Just two decades after the first, another Treaty of Paris marked the dissolution of Great Britain's North American empire.

JAMES E. LEWIS, JR.

North America After the French and Indian War

UNEXPLORED

RUSSIANS

HUDSON BAY

HUDSON'S BAY COMPANY

OREGON
Disputed by
Russia and Spain

LOUISIANA

Mississippi R.

RESERVE

QUEBEC

NEWFOUND-LAND

ST. PIERRE & MIQUELON
(France)

NOVA SCOTIA

NEW ENGLAND

THE THIRTEEN COLONIES

VIRGINIA

CAROLINAS

EAST FLORIDA

WEST FLORIDA

GULF OF MEXICO

INDIAN

PACIFIC OCEAN

N E W   S P A I N

CUBA

BRITISH HONDURAS

HAITI
(France)

HISPANIOLA

ATLANTIC OCEAN

CARIBBEAN SEA

NEW GRANADA

England

Spain

Proclamation Line of 1763

0   1000 Miles
0   1000 Kilometers

See also Canada; Florida; France; Great Britain; Louisiana Purchase; Native Americans

FURTHER READING

Bird, Harrison. *Battle for a Continent.* New York, 1965.
Ferling, John. *Struggle for a Continent: The Wars of Early America.* Wheeling, Ill., 1993.
Jennings, Francis. *Empire of Fortune: Crowns, Colonies, and Tribes in the Seven Years' War in America.* New York, 1988.
McKay, Derek, and H. M. Scott. *The Rise of the Great Powers, 1648–1815.* London, 1983.

FRENCH INDOCHINA

The Southeast Asian countries of Vietnam, Cambodia, and Laos, which became French colonies in the nineteenth century. The colonization began in 1850 when French naval forces attacked the Vietnamese port city of Da Nang, and Vietnam became a French colony in 1867. France established protectorates over Cambodia in 1863 and Laos in 1893. U.S. interest in these French colonies was minimal until World War II, when the United States sought to defeat the Japanese and forestall its territorial ambitions, ones that included France's colonies. During the war the U.S. Office of Strategic Services (OSS)—forerunner of the Central Intelligence Agency—began to cooperate with the Vietminh, the leading nationalist-communist movement in Vietnam. Believing that the United States was in favor of dismantling colonialism, the Vietminh cooperated with the Americans and helped locate U.S. airmen who had been shot down over the Vietnam-China border during their multiple battle with the Japanese. Relations between the OSS and the Vietminh leader, Ho Chi Minh, reached a point where Ho was designated OSS agent 19, code name "Lucius."

Between 1941 and 1945 U.S. policy toward French Indochina changed. Initially, the administration of President Franklin D. Roosevelt had sought the end of colonial empires, including French control over Indochina, but by the time of Roosevelt's death in 1945, the United States generally acquiesced to French rule, stipulating nothing more than vague pronouncements that independence was a future goal. This transformation of policy was the direct result of the Cold War. Because U.S. interests were now predicated on combating communism and maintaining Western unity, French control over its former colonies was deemed far more acceptable to the United States than supporting the Vietminh. This anticommunist policy continued throughout the administration of President Harry S. Truman and prevented the United States from recognizing Ho's government, the Democratic Republic of Vietnam (later commonly known in the West as North Vietnam). The Truman administration put primary emphasis on Ho's communism and acquiesced in the return of French jurisdiction over Indochina. In December 1946 the French Indochina War broke out when French naval forces reasserted their control over their former colony by bombarding Haiphong and killing thousands of Vietnamese civilians. The U.S. response was to aid monetarily the French in what American officials perceived as a battle between the West and international communism. By 1954 more than seventy-five percent of France's war effort in Indochina was being funded by the United States—more than $4 billion between 1950 and 1954. This effort, along with the stationing of more than 300 U.S. military personnel in Vietnam, furthered U.S. interests in this region.

During the siege at Dien Bien Phu in 1954, the administration of President Dwight D. Eisenhower seriously considered France's request for nuclear weapons to salvage its military position. Although this plan was eventually rejected—after the British refused to be a partner to any major military action—U.S. policy continued to deny the Vietminh control over Vietnam. France's defeat by the Vietminh led to the 1954 Geneva Conference and the signing of the Geneva Accords. France agreed to leave Vietnam. While the United States was not a signatory to these agreements, its representative pledged that the United States would not interfere in scheduled elections to unify Vietnam. In contradiction to this pledge, the United States immediately set about creating the anticommunist state of South Vietnam under the rule of Ngo Dinh Diem. After the conference, Laos and Cambodia received nominal independence. Cambodia's leader, Prince Norodom Sihanouk, tried to manage his country's interests by declaring a neutrality between the French, the South Vietnamese, the communists, and the growing U.S. presence in the region. He failed, and Vietnamese forces used his country as a staging ground for their attacks against noncommunist forces; in 1971 Sihanouk was overthrown in a U.S.-sponsored coup. In Laos, independence in 1954 meant little; it was unable to control its borders or govern its people because of the ever-expanding Vietnam War. Thus, while the French gradually relinquished their interests in Indochina the area became the center of renewed conflicts.

JONATHAN NASHEL

See also Cambodia; Colonialism; Diem, Ngo Dinh; France; Ho Chi Minh; Imperialism; Laos; Vietnam; Vietnam War

FURTHER READING

Duiker, William J. *Sacred War: Nationalism and Revolution in a Divided Vietnam.* New York, 1995.

Fall, Bernard. *The Two Viet-Nams: A Political and Military Analysis,* rev. ed. New York, 1967.

Huỳnh Kim Khánh. *Vietnamese Communism, 1925–1945.* Ithaca, N.Y., 1982.

Kahin, George McT. *Intervention: How America Became Involved in Vietnam.* New York, 1987.

Ngo Vinh Long. *Before the Revolution: The Vietnamese Peasants Under the French.* Cambridge, Mass., 1973.

Patti, Archimedes. *Why Vietnam? Prelude to America's Albatross.* Berkeley, Calif., 1980.

FRENCH REVOLUTION
(1789–1799)

An event with wide-ranging international consequences that began with the fall of the Bastille, a royal prison and symbol of despotic tyranny, and ended with the accession of Napoleon Bonaparte as first consul. The abolition of privilege, the establishment of a republic, and the wars that came in the wake of the revolution transformed life not only in France but worldwide. The United States intersected with the French Revolution in many ways. U.S. political parties arose in part because of the issues generated by the revolution, U.S. foreign commerce fell victim to harassment, and debate surrounded the status of the Anglo-French alliance of 1778 for the United States.

One of the primary stimuli to the revolution was an economic crisis, aggravated by French support for the American Revolution at a cost of approximately 1,000 million livres. The French government raised these funds by subscribing long-term loans, followed by short-term notes to cover the interest payments on the principal. By 1788 expenses exceeded revenues by twenty percent (more than 100 million livres), and most of the government's annual income went to cover interest payments on the loans. Raising taxes would have meant revising tax practices that exempted the privileged classes of France, and cutting expenses would have reduced the patronage of the monarchy. Neither alternative prevailed, provoking a loss of confidence in the government, especially among property owners and the expanding bourgeoisie. Peasant discontent swirled not around the fiscal crisis of mounting debts so much as around the increasing price of bread, which in normal times consumed one-third to one-half of an urban worker's wages and perhaps ninety percent of an agricultural worker's income. By the time the Bastille fell on 14 July 1789 and King Louis XVI had been taken from Versailles to Paris on 6 October, few people in France mourned the fall of absolutist monarchy, cornerstone of the ancien régime.

Many people in the Americas cheered Louis XVI's fall, none more so than slaves in the French colony of Saint Domingue (Haiti), where a slave rebellion in 1791 undermined French control. In the United States, Thomas Jefferson, who had returned from France after serving as U.S. minister from 1785 to 1789, was one of many who applauded French moves toward the establishment of a constitutional monarchy. The execution, however, of Louis XVI in January 1793 and of more than 16,000 people from October 1793 to July 1794 led to concerns that the revolution had degenerated into anarchy. More disturbing to Americans than the political changes in France was the open warfare between France and Great Britain that began after February 1793. These wars proved especially divisive in the United States as Americans chose sides between the two belligerents and provoked a crisis in President George Washington's second administration. There was also concern that the two treaties signed in 1778 between France and the United States—one of perpetual alliance, the other of amity and commerce—might obligate the United States to help the French. In any case, strict adherence to the treaties would certainly provoke British anger and possible retaliation against the United States. Other questions that arose were whether the treaties continued between nations when governments changed and whether the movement of French troops outside its borders invalidated the defensive treaty of alliance.

After intensive discussions within the cabinet, President Washington announced that the treaties with France remained in effect, but his Proclamation of 1793 required U.S. citizens to remain impartial toward the two warring nations. Within Washington's cabinet, profound disagreements developed over the meaning of neutrality. Secretary of the Treasury Alexander Hamilton argued that neutrality should favor the British. Hamilton feared that pro-French policies would jeopardize U.S. access to British investments and markets, on which was hinged the success of his domestic financial program. He expected the United States to eventually surpass the British economically and militarily but feared that in the short run U.S. military weakness made the nation dependent upon British naval power. Secretary of State Thomas Jefferson, however, wanted to use the French alliance to break the nation's dependence on British trade. Failing that, he would have the British pay for U.S. neutrality by agreeing to develop favorable trade relations with British West Indian colonies or to remove troops from British forts in the Northwest Territory. Jefferson, who worried that the British would use the European wars to further U.S. economic dependence or even embark upon a plan for recolonization, believed that U.S. agricultural exports gave the nation a powerful advantage.

During 1793 and 1794, Jefferson's fears seemed well-founded as the British seized cargoes, searched ships for deserters from the British navy, and commandeered (impressed) sailors as dictated by the wars with France, rather than international law. In the hope of resolving differences with the British, Hamilton succeeded in having Supreme Court Chief Justice John Jay sent to England to try to work out differences between the two nations and liberalize trade relations. Instead, Jay's Treaty (1794) further divided the United States between French and English partisans, added additional fuel to the emerging two-party system that swirled around Hamilton and Jefferson, and sorely tested the nation's cohesiveness. Although Jay's Treaty settled none of the outstanding problems with Great Britain, it ushered in a period of exceptional prosperity for U.S. shipping interests. A lively reexport trade, also known as the carrying trade, with colonies in the West Indies developed between 1793 and 1801, and the establishment of friendly relations with Great Britain may have caused Spain to open trade on the Mississippi River to Americans in 1795 through Pinckney's Treaty. The price for achieving better relations with the British was a deterioration of relations with revolutionary France. The French minister to the United States, Pierre Adet, worked with Republican senators to block approval of Jay's Treaty and to secure the election of Jefferson as Washington's successor in 1796. In reprisal for making a treaty with Great Britain, during the administration of John Adams (who succeeded Washington to the presidency), France ignored U.S. insistence on freedom of the seas, pressed a U.S. delegation for a humiliating loan (the XYZ Affair), and moved to the brink of war with the United States in 1798. Only Adams's stubborn resistance to bowing to Hamilton's desire for a war with France kept the two nations at peace and paved the way for a partial settlement of differences between the two countries in the Convention of 1800, which ended the Franco-American alliance.

By 1800, however, new problems faced the United States. Following the failure of a succession of governments since 1789, in 1799 Napoleon came to power dedicated to restoring order and preserving the revolution. As the Napoleonic Wars quickly demanded the entire resources of both Great Britain and France, neither country saw any reason to respect the rights and interests of a weak nation caught in the balance between the two leviathans. Such was the legacy of the French Revolution for the United States.

RONALD L. HATZENBUEHLER

See also Adams, John; Convention of 1800; France; Haiti; Hamilton, Alexander; Impressment; Jay's Treaty; Jefferson, Thomas; Napoleonic Wars; Pinckney's Treaty; XYZ Affair

FURTHER READING

Doyle, William. *The Oxford History of the French Revolution.* New York, 1989.
Horsman, Reginald. *The Diplomacy of the New Republic, 1776–1815.* Arlington Heights, Ill., 1985.
Kaplan, Lawrence. *Colonies into Nation: American Diplomacy, 1763–1801.* New York, 1972.
Sutherland, D. M. G. *France, 1789–1815: Revolution and Counterrevolution.* New York, 1986.
Vovelle, Michel. *The Fall of the French Monarchy*, translated by Susan Burke. Cambridge, 1984.

FULBRIGHT, JAMES WILLIAM

(*b.* 9 April 1905; *d.* 9 February 1995)

U.S. senator from Arkansas (1945–1975) who sponsored the Fulbright scholarships, led Senate critics of the Vietnam War as chairman of the Foreign Relations Committee, and advocated détente with the Soviet Union.

Born in Sumner, Missouri, Fulbright grew up in the university town of Fayetteville, Arkansas, where his father, Jay Fulbright, became the foremost civic and financial leader and his mother, Roberta, who exercised a profound influence on her son, became an outspoken columnist and scourge of corrupt politicians through the family-owned newspaper, the *Northwest Arkansas Times.* J. William Fulbright graduated with a bachelor's degree from the University of Arkansas in 1925. He performed creditably in his studies and outstandingly in football. Awarded a Rhodes Scholarship, he saw Washington, D.C. and New York for the first time en route to Oxford University, where he received another B.A. in 1928 and an M.A. in 1931, the latter conferred automatically without further study. He studied history for three years at Oxford and played rugby and lacrosse. The Rhodes experience, followed by a year of travel in Europe, became the gestation for the Fulbright scholarships. Fulbright returned home to attend George Washington University law school, from which he graduated in 1934. After a brief period as an attorney in the Anti-Trust Division of the U.S. Department of Justice and another year teaching law at George Washington University, Fulbright returned with his wife, Betty, to Fayetteville in 1936. There he taught law at the university and helped manage his family's enterprises.

In 1939, at age 34, Fulbright became president of the University of Arkansas. During his brief tenure in that position, he instituted modest educational reforms while speaking out forcefully and repeatedly against U.S. isolationism in the face of Nazi Germany's early victories in World War II. In June 1941, for political reasons having at least as much to do with Fulbright's mother and her reformist activities as with Bill Fulbright himself, Governor Homer Adkins fired Fulbright from the university presidency.

In 1942 Fulbright ran for and was elected to the U.S. House of Representatives. During his single term, he gained national attention, first by challenging what he called the "imperialist arguments" of Congresswoman Claire Booth Luce (who had denounced proposals for a new system of international cooperation as "globaloney" and advocated a strategy of U.S. preeminence in global aviation), then by securing enactment of the Fulbright Resolution, which pledged congressional support for a world peacekeeping organization. This endorsement, of the future United Nations, was gratefully received by the Roosevelt administration.

In 1944 Fulbright was elected to the U.S. Senate, where he would serve for thirty years. In 1946 he secured enactment of the Fulbright Act, which established what came to be known as the Fulbright scholarships, later characterized by Fulbright as "a modest program with an immodest aim—the achievement in international affairs of a regime more civilized, rational and humane than the empty system of power of the past." The Fulbright scholarships, providing for annual exchanges of students and scholars between the United States and numerous foreign countries, are still the largest exchange-of-persons program in world history. In 1946, Fulbright, an advocate of parliamentary democracy, incurred the animosity of President Harry S. Truman by suggesting, after the Democrats lost control of both houses of Congress, that Truman appoint a Republican secretary of state (the office then next in line for the presidency) and that Truman himself resign. In 1951 Fulbright strongly supported President Truman when he removed the enormously popular General Douglas MacArthur from his command of United Nations forces in Korea.

Appointed to the Senate Foreign Relations Committee in 1949, Fulbright became increasingly active and outspoken on foreign policy issues (as well as certain domestic issues such as federal aid to education) during the 1950s. Outraged and disgusted by the excesses of Senator Joseph McCarthy's charges of communist infiltration of the U.S. government, Fulbright cast the single vote in the Senate against funding McCarthy's investigative subcommittee in 1954 and then drew up the censure resolution that, as amended, was subsequently introduced by Republican Senator Ralph Flanders of Vermont and approved by the Senate. Fulbright raised objections to aspects of the Eisenhower administration's foreign policy, including the abrupt cancellation of U.S. support for the Aswan Dam in Egypt in 1956 and the "Eisenhower doctrine" of 1957. The doctrine authorized the president to use armed force against "communist" aggression in the Middle East. Fulbright criticized the "sanctimonious moralism" of Secretary of State John Foster Dulles.

In 1959, with strong support from Senate Majority Leader Lyndon B. Johnson, Fulbright became chairman of the Foreign Relations Committee, a position he would hold until he left office in 1974, the longest tenure of the chairmanship in Senate history. In 1959, at the request of the State Department, Fulbright presided at a special meeting of the Foreign Relations Committee with Nikita Khrushchev when Speaker of the House John McCormack refused to allow the Soviet leader to address a joint meeting of Congress. In 1960 the Foreign Relations Committee held extended closed-door hearings in which Fulbright took the Eisenhower administration to task for its handling of the U-2 spy plane incident. In later years Fulbright would take a more charitable view of Eisenhower, commending his decision not to intervene militarily at the time of the French defeat at Dien Bien Phu in Indochina in 1954.

Considered but not chosen secretary of state (a position he did not want) by president-elect John F. Kennedy in 1960, Fulbright as floor leader strongly supported Kennedy's reformed foreign aid program of 1961, which largely reoriented U.S. foreign assistance to less developed countries. He strenuously objected to Kennedy's plans for the ill-fated landing of Cuban exiles at the Bay of Pigs. This opposition elicited Kennedy's later observation, "Well, you're the only one who can say I told you so." In the 1962 Cuban missile crisis Fulbright preferred an armed landing in Cuba over direct naval confrontation with the Soviet Union. Thereafter, Fulbright encouraged Kennedy to move toward détente and in 1963 led in the debate to secure Senate consent to the Limited Nuclear Test Ban Treaty.

Fulbright's relations with President Lyndon B. Johnson, close and cordial at the outset, were shattered by their differences over the Vietnam War. To his subsequent regret, and on the basis of what he later recognized as misinformation, Fulbright sponsored the Gulf of Tonkin Resolution in the Senate in August 1964. He proceeded thereafter, through private communications, including a memorandum dated 5 April 1965, to try to dissuade President Johnson from large-scale military intervention in Vietnam. In a Senate speech on 15 September 1965, Fulbright voiced strong objection to U.S. military intervention in the Dominican Republic and in early 1966, having failed at private persuasion, initiated the public hearings that would make the Senate Foreign Relations Committee a forum of debate and dissent throughout the Vietnam war. During that period the Committee also held far-ranging public hearings on U.S. relations with China, in which Fulbright called for recognition of the People's Republic of China, as well as recognition on a wide range of other topics including Soviet-U.S. détente, which he strongly supported, the Atlantic Alliance, and the psychological aspects of international relations. Fulbright's strong views on U.S. foreign policy, including the Vietnam war, were spelled out in *The Arrogance of Power* (1966), in which he stated that the Vietnam war was a manifestation of the historical tendency of great powers to extend their commitments beyond their resources and, by so doing, jeopardize their preeminence and stability. The book became a best seller.

Fulbright experienced a mixed relationship with the Nixon administration between 1969 and 1974. He continued to raise strong objections to the Vietnam war, but he strongly supported Nixon's "opening" to China and his policy of détente toward the Soviet Union, serving as floor manager for the Anti-Ballistic Missile Treaty (1972). Fulbright developed a cordial working relationship with Secretary of State Henry A. Kissinger on these issues and backed Kissinger's initiatives toward Middle East peace. Fulbright, in a Senate speech in August 1970, called for Israeli withdrawal from the territories occupied in the 1967 war in return for a security treaty with the United States, a proposal he reiterated several times. This position elicited vehement criticism among Israel's supporters. These and other thoughts on U.S. foreign and domestic policy were elaborated in another book, *The Crippled Giant* (1972), which stressed the inseparability of foreign and domestic policy and the "dangerous obsoleteness of traditional power politics in the nuclear age."

Challenged by a popular incumbent governor, Fulbright was defeated in his reelection bid in the Democratic primary in Arkansas in 1974. In 1975 he joined the Washington, D.C. law firm of Hogan and Hartson, where he served "of counsel," while continuing to travel, speak, and write on U.S. foreign policy. In 1989 he published *The Price of Empire*, a collection of commentaries and reminiscences. In May 1993 Fulbright was awarded the Medal of Freedom by President Bill Clinton.

SETH P. TILLMAN

See also Antiballistic Missile Treaty; Bay of Pigs Invasion; China; Cold War; Congress; Cuban Missile Crisis; Détente; Dien Bien Phu; Dominican Republic; Dulles, John Foster; Eisenhower Doctrine; Foreign Aid; Fulbright Program; Isolationism; Israel; Kennedy, John Fitzgerald; Kissinger, Henry Alfred; Limited Nuclear Test Ban Treaty; MacArthur, Douglas; McCarthyism; Truman, Harry S.; U-2 Incident; Vietnam War

FURTHER READING

Berman, William C. *William Fulbright and the Vietnam War: The Dissent of a Political Realist.* Kent, Ohio, 1988.
Brown, Eugene. *J. William Fulbright: Advice and Dissent.* Iowa City, Ia., 1985.
Fulbright, J. William. *Prospects for the West.* Cambridge, Mass., 1963.
———. *Old Myths and New Realities.* New York, 1964.
———. *The Pentagon Propaganda Machine.* New York, 1971.
———, and Seth P. Tillman. *The Price of Empire.* New York, 1989.
Powell, Lee Riley. *J. William Fulbright and His Time.* Memphis, Tenn., 1996.
Woods, Randall B. *Fulbright.* New York, 1995.

FULBRIGHT PROGRAM

A government-sponsored educational program for the exchange of faculty lecturers, researchers, professionals, and graduate students between the United States and the rest of the world. Established after World War II in order to further international understanding, the Fulbright Program by 1994 had awarded more than 200,000 grants to facilitate the international exchange of scholars between the United States and 130 countries. The program currently makes nearly 5,000 new grants each year to Americans for study, lecturing, or research abroad, and to foreign scholars for similar purposes in the United States. This total includes the U.S. Scholar Program, which sends almost 1,000 scholars and professionals a year to more than 125 countries; the Student Program, which offers 600 graduate school–level fellowships annually in some 100 nations; and the Teacher Exchange Program, which involves more than 200 U.S. educators, mainly from secondary schools, in 35 countries abroad. Additionally, the Fulbright international exchange effort facilitates the establishment of partnerships between U.S. and foreign universities, and since 1979 has included the Hubert H. Humphrey Fellowship Program, which sponsors training in the United States for mid-level professionals from developing nations.

Launched with little fanfare and scant congressional notice shortly after World War II, the program came into being through the efforts of Arkansas Senator J. William Fulbright, a former Rhodes Scholar at Oxford University. On 1 August 1946 President Harry S. Truman signed into law the Fulbright Act (Public Law 79-584), under which surplus nonconvertible currencies, generated by the sale abroad of surplus U.S. war matériel under the Surplus Property Act of 1944, were made available to fund an exchange program administered by the Department of State. A serious lack of hard currency needed to implement the program was alleviated somewhat through the cooperation of American universities and private foundations, but the breakthrough came in January 1948 with the passage of the U.S. Information and Educational Exchange Act (the Smith-Mundt Act), which authorized the appropriation of dollar funds, however limited, for international exchange. That fall, participants from the United States, China, Burma, and the Philippines inaugurated the program.

Over the years, U.S. government funding increased, and contributions from foreign governments as well as private foundations became a significant source of support. In the mid-1980s U.S. government funding averaged $20 million annually, to which thirty other participating countries added another $9 million or more. By fiscal year 1990, the congressional appropriation had risen to $91.3 million, while binational commissions were contributing an additional $20.6 million. The legislative history of the Fulbright Program was completed with the passage of the Mutual Educational and Security Exchange Act of 1961, also called the Fulbright-Hays Act (cosponsored by Fulbright and Representative Wayne Hays of Ohio). The act consolidated previous laws, retaining the main points of the program, adding new features and authorizing support for foreign language and area studies under the Department of Education. In 1978 responsibility for administering the program's other functions was transferred from the Department of State to the U.S. Information Agency. The U.S. Department of Education directs a portion of a program supporting non-Western foreign language and area research and training abroad.

Between the academic years 1948–1949 and 1990–1991, a total of 99,333 grants were awarded to Americans to travel abroad—50,830 for travel to Europe, 13,967 to the Middle East and South Asia, 11,947 to East Asia and the Pacific, 8,380 to the American Republics, and 4,209 to Africa. During the same period, 117,518 foreign nationals received grants for study in the United States, of whom 66,956 were from Europe, 17,049 from East Asia and the Pacific, 16,692 from the Americas, 5,076 from the Middle East and South Asia, and 1,816 from Africa.

Grant recipients are chosen through an application process involving a number of government and private organizations. Most U.S. citizens going abroad engage in teaching or educational seminars, whereas most foreign nationals undertake university study in the United States. The grant periods generally run from two months to a full academic year. During the 1993–1994 academic year, awards under the American Scholar Program, the activity perhaps most familiar to the public, numbered more than 1,000. The faculty members and professionals chosen to go abroad represented disciplines ranging from agriculture to the theater. That year, more American grantees went to lecture or conduct research on American literature than in any other field, with political science and education close runners-up. Overall, in 1993-1994 the American Scholar Program chose 852 American scholars from the humanities and social sciences, eighty-five from the physical sciences, and eighty-two from the life sciences.

The Fulbright Program over the years has afforded large numbers of individuals the opportunity to become acquainted with the people of other nations. The stature of the grantees in many cases has been extraordinarily high. Overseas Fulbright Program alumni include prime ministers, cabinet ministers, members of national legislatures, Supreme Court justices, university presidents, and senior business executives. American alumni of the program have gone on to become members of Congress, university deans and presidents, influential journalists and writers, prominent composers, ambassadors, and include at least a dozen Nobel Prize winners in several fields.

The wording of the 1961 Fulbright-Hays Act indicates clearly that the program's goal from its inception has been to assist in the development of friendly, sympathetic, and peaceful relations between the United States and the other countries of the world. In 1976 Senator Fulbright told a biographer: "It was my thought that if large numbers of people know and understand the people from nations other than their own, they might develop a capacity for empathy, a distaste for killing other men, and an inclination to peace."

HENRY E. MATTOX

See also Fulbright, James William; United States Information Agency

FURTHER READING

Brown, Eugene. J. *William Fulbright: Advice and Dissent.* Iowa City, Iowa, 1985.
Council for International Exchange of Scholars. *Fulbright Scholar Program: Grants for Faculty and Professionals.* Washington, D.C., 1994.
J. William Fulbright Foreign Scholarship Board. *Forty Years: The Fulbright Program 1946–1986.* Washington, D.C., 1986.
———. *The Fulbright Program 1990.* Washington, D. C., 1991.
Johnson, Walter, and Colligan, Francis J. *The Fulbright Program: A History.* Chicago, 1965.

FUR TRADE

The commerce in the pelts of fur-bearing mammals was especially prevalent in North America from the colonial period to the early twentieth century. Whereas in Mexico and South America the Spanish found precious metals, in North America the French, British, Dutch, Russians, and Americans found fur-bearing mammals, such as beaver, seal, otter, fox, deer, bison, and bear. The pelts of these animals, available in great numbers, became very valuable export commodities, and for much of American history the fur trade was on the leading edge of landed and commercial expansion.

In colonial America, the dynamics of the fur trade encouraged the expansion of European empires, especially along rivers that offered access to the interior. Both the French and British realized that trading beaver pelts could be very profitable, and competition for that resource was one cause of the French and Indian War. With superior skill, Native Americans, such as the Iroquois, captured the animals, and traders offered the Indians European goods in exchange for the pelts. Early European settlers and explorers believed that the vast regions of North America contained an unlimited abundance of natural resources. This erroneous assumption led to the systematic destruction of fur-bearing animals throughout North America. Even many of the Native American tribes that had previously maintained something of a balance with their environment participated in overhunting. As fur-bearing mammals declined under hunting pressure, European fur traders had to go deeper into the western and northern wilderness, often hundreds of miles from white settlement.

After the United States gained independence, the fur trade continued to be an important part of international relations. Beginning in the 1780s, American merchant ships traveled to the northwest coast of the continent—where they struggled with Russian and British traders for influence—to collect sea-otter pelts for shipment to China. This lucrative trade helped to establish U.S. power in the region, open trade with the Orient, and destroy the otter population. As U.S. settlements spread westward, fur traders were often in the vanguard, if only because fur-bearing animals were more plentiful in the remote regions of the continent. President Thomas Jefferson used the Lewis and Clark Expedition (1804–1806) in part as a means to promote the fur trade in the new Louisiana Territory. In order to best exploit the opportunity there and in the Oregon country and to combat the powerful Hudson's Bay Company, John Jacob Astor formed the American Fur Company in 1808. In addition to beginning a series of fortified outposts in the West, Astor instituted the practice of relying on white trappers instead of Indians.

The decline of the sea otters eventually led to one final confrontation over the fur trade in North America. In the mid-1800s U.S. fur traders turned their attention north to the fur seal herds of Russian America. The general success of Yankee merchants in penetrating the region encouraged the Russians to sell Alaska to the United States. Fierce competition for seal fur among U.S. citizens, Canadians, and Japanese raged from the 1880s to 1911, when all parties to the controversy agreed to a convention that regulated the harvesting of the valuable fur seals.

KURK DORSEY

See also Alaska Purchase; Astor, John Jacob; Canada; Continental Expansion; Lewis and Clark Expedition; Native Americans; Sealing; Wildlife

FURTHER READING

Brown, Jennifer S., ed. *The Fur Trade Revisited*. East Lansing, Mich., 1991.

Busch, Briton. *The War Against the Seals*. Montreal, 1985.

Laut, Agnes C. *The Fur Trade of America*. New York, 1921.

Phillips, Paul C. *The Fur Trade*. Norman, Okla., 1961.

G

GABON

See Appendix 2

GADSDEN PURCHASE

(1853)

Centerpiece of the Gadsden Treaty between the United States and Mexico. The treaty, named for the U.S. minister to Mexico, James Gadsden, resolved a dispute over the boundary between the United States and Mexico drawn in the 1848 Treaty of Guadalupe Hidalgo. Gadsden's instructions from Secretary of State William L. Marcy had been to purchase a large slice of northern Mexico, but the cash-strapped Mexican dictator Antonio López de Santa Anna would sell only the area around the disputed Mesilla Strip. To gain what would become the last piece of the lower forty-eight states, the United States paid $10 million for the 29,142,000 acres that now form the southern portions of Arizona and New Mexico. The United States purchased these millions of acres of arid land in order to gain a route for a southern transcontinental railroad. At the time, however, many abolitionists saw the hand of the slavocracy behind this additional southward expansion.

KURK DORSEY

See also Mexico

FURTHER READING

Faulk, Odie. *Too Far North . . . Too Far South*. Los Angeles, 1967.
Garber, Paul Neff. *The Gadsden Treaty*, repr. ed., Gloucester, Mass., 1923.

GALBRAITH, JOHN KENNETH

(*b*. 15 October 1908)

Economist and ambassador to India (1961–1963). Born in rural Ontario, Canada, Galbraith graduated from Ontario Agricultural College (Guelph University), earned an M.A. and Ph.D. from the University of California at Berkeley, and did postdoctoral work at Cambridge University. He taught economics at Harvard and Princeton universities and wrote in the liberal tradition of Thorstein Veblen and John Maynard Keynes. Galbraith's best-known writings, including *American Capitalism: The Concept of Countervailing Powers (1952)* and *The Affluent Society* (1958), examine and praise the productivity and social benefits of postwar welfare state capitalism in the United States. He is also a leading authority on Third World economic development. Galbraith served in the wartime Office of Price Administration, and after the war worked in the State Department's Office of Economic Security Policy. During the 1950s he became active in Democratic party politics. A participant in John F. Kennedy's presidential campaign, Galbraith served as ambassador to India during that administration. In that post he oversaw a large economic aid program to that country and challenged Cold War orthodoxy by advocating tolerance for New Delhi's nonaligned foreign policy. Following a trip to Saigon in November 1961, Galbraith also expressed skepticism to President Kennedy about the growing U.S. involvement in Vietnam. After leaving his ambassadorship, Galbraith became a leading voice in the anti–Vietnam War movement. He resumed his career in academe and wrote a number of books, both scholarly and popular, on economic policy and American society. He remains a prominent and respected figure in intellectual, political, and policy circles.

DENNIS MERRILL

See also India; Vietnam War

FURTHER READING

Galbraith, John Kenneth. *Ambassador's Journal: A Personal Account of the Kennedy Years*. Boston, 1969.
——— . *A Life in Our Times: Memoirs*. Boston, 1981.
——— . *The Culture of Contentment*. Boston, 1992.
McMahon, Robert J. *The Cold War on the Periphery: U.S. Relations with India and Pakistan, 1947–1965*. New York, 1994.
Merrill, Dennis. *Bread and the Ballot: The United States and India's Economic Development, 1947–1963*. Chapel Hill, N.C., 1990.

GALLATIN, ALBERT

(*b*. 29 January 1761; *d*. 12 August 1849)

Republican party leader, member of Congress (1795–1801), secretary of the treasury (1801–1813), member of the peace commission that negotiated an end to the War of 1812, and minister to France (1816–1823). Born in Geneva, Switzerland, Gallatin settled in Fayette County, Pennsylvania, and became active in state politics prior to serving in the U.S. House of Representatives. A critic of

Alexander Hamilton's Federalist fiscal policies, he helped create the House Ways and Means Committee. In the debate surrounding Jay's Treaty, Gallatin not only opposed it, but upheld the principle that Congress had the right to review treaties. As U.S. relations with France deteriorated in the 1790s, Gallatin opposed Federalist efforts to prepare for war and the Alien and Sedition Acts of 1798.

When Republican Thomas Jefferson won the presidential election of 1800, the new president named Gallatin secretary of the treasury. Convinced that he was brought into the cabinet to undo Federalist policies of the Washington and Adams administrations, Gallatin sought to reduce governmental expenditures and eliminate the national debt incurred by the Federalists. From the beginning, he approached his tasks with a doctrinaire zeal that surpassed even Jefferson's. He clashed with other cabinet members, primarily Secretary of the Navy Robert Smith, who believed Gallatin's call for a significant reduction in the army and navy threatened the nation's defenses and foreign policy, particularly when the United States was at war with Tripoli, and when relations with Great Britain, France, and Spain were strained.

When James Madison succeeded Jefferson as president in March 1809, his first choice for secretary of state was Gallatin. Personal and political opposition to Gallatin among certain Republicans, however, forced the president to keep Gallatin in the treasury position and to make Robert Smith secretary of state. Gallatin's resentment of Smith compelled the treasury secretary to support various schemes of Smith's opponents calculated to drive him from office. In March 1811, with Gallatin threatening to resign unless Smith was dismissed, Madison fired Smith.

During the War of 1812, Gallatin resigned as secretary of the treasury and was appointed to a diplomatic mission to Russia, where Czar Alexander I had offered to mediate an end to the war between Great Britain and the United States. Although the British refused the czar's offer of mediation, they signalled their willingness, in November 1813, to negotiate directly with the United States. The U.S. peace commission included Henry Clay, Speaker of the House of Representatives; Jonathan Russell, former U.S. chargé in London and present minister to Sweden; Federalist Senator James A. Bayard; and U.S. minister to Russia, John Quincy Adams. Gallatin and the other Americans met a British delegation in Ghent in August 1814 to begin negotiations.

The U.S. delegation was composed of strong-willed, independent thinkers, and Gallatin's tact helped hold the commission together. On 24 December 1814, representatives of Great Britain and the United States agreed to accept the status quo ante as the basis for ending the war, and signed the Treaty of Ghent. Building on the momentum produced by the successful negotiations at Ghent, on 3 July 1815, John Quincy Adams, who had been made

minister to England, joined Clay and Gallatin in concluding a convention with the British which freed U.S. and British trade from discriminatory tariffs, and renewed it in key areas, as had existed before the war.

In 1816, Gallatin was appointed U.S. minister to France, a post he held until 1823. Although these were the most pleasurable years of his long career in public service, they were the least productive. Receiving $7 million in spoliation claims incurred by U.S. shippers under Napoleon's Berlin, Milan, and other decrees, and securing a satisfactory commercial treaty with France were his primary objectives. On both issues, his efforts proved futile. In 1818, while minister to France, he was again appointed special commissioner to negotiate a trade treaty with Britain and to settle outstanding issues between the nations. The result of these talks, which included Richard Rush, Adams's replacement as minister to London, was the Convention of 1818. The agreement established the boundary of the United States and British Canada along the 49th parallel, from the Lake of the Woods to the Rocky Mountains, and provided for joint occupation of the Oregon country for ten years. Other provisions dealt with slaves taken by the British during the War of 1812, resolution of the fisheries controversy off the coast of British North America, and renewal of the Anglo-American commercial convention of 1815 for ten years. In 1831, after a long and distinguished public career, Gallatin retired from public service.

THOM M. ARMSTRONG

See also Adams, John Quincy; Alien and Sedition Acts; Clay, Henry; Ghent, Treaty of; Great Britain; Jay's Treaty; Jefferson, Thomas; War of 1812

FURTHER READING

Adams, Henry. *A History of the United States During the Administrations of Thomas Jefferson and James Madison*. 9 vols. New York, 1889–1891.

———. *The Writings of Albert Gallatin*. 3 vols. 1879. Rpt. New York, 1960.

Armstrong, Thom M. *Politics, Diplomacy and Intrigue in the Early Republic: The Cabinet Career of Robert Smith, 1801–1811*. Dubuque, Montana, 1991.

Walters, Raymond, Jr. *Albert Gallatin: Jeffersonian Financier and Diplomat*. New York, 1957.

GAMBIA

See Appendix 2

GANDHI, INDIRA PRIYADARSHINI

(*b.* 19 November 1917; *d.* 31 October 1984)

Prime minister of India (1966–1977, 1980–1984). The daughter of India's first prime minister, Jawaharlal Nehru,

Gandhi was born in the city of Allahabad in the state of Uttar Pradesh in northern India. Having adopted her husband's surname, Gandhi became prime minister in 1966 following the death of her father's successor, Lal Shastri. Under her stewardship India maintained its policy of nonalignment in the Cold War but increasingly relied on Soviet military and diplomatic support against Pakistan, a development that displeased U.S. officials. She incurred the wrath of President Lyndon Johnson when in 1966 she publicly criticized the U.S. bombing of North Vietnam. The U.S. Agency for International Development nonetheless worked with the Gandhi government during the 1960s and 1970s to introduce high-yielding varieties of wheat and rice that eventually made India self-sufficient in food grains. In 1971, when India went to war with Pakistan, a U.S. ally, to help secure the independence of Bangladesh (formerly East Pakistan), President Richard Nixon sent U.S. aircraft carriers to the Bay of Bengal as a warning to India not to press the war to the point of threatening Pakistani survival. Nixon and his national security adviser, Henry Kissinger, sought to preserve a South Asian balance of power while using friendship with Pakistan to facilitate improved U.S. relations with China. In 1975 an Indian court found Gandhi guilty of violating elections laws. She refused to resign, instead declaring a state of emergency and ruling repressively. She was defeated in the 1977 elections but returned to power in 1980.

Although Gandhi spoke out against increased U.S. aid to Pakistan after the Soviet invasion of Afghanistan in 1979, she worked with the administration of President Ronald Reagan to improve Indo-American relations through military and economic cooperation. Gandhi was assassinated by two of her security guards who were members of the Sikh religious community. They sought revenge for Gandhi's use of Indian troops to evict a band of armed Sikh separatists from the sacred Golden Temple in Amritsar, the capital city of the state of Punjab; she was succeeded as prime minister by her son, Rajiv Gandhi.

DENNIS MERRILL

See also Bangladesh; India; Nonaligned Movement; Pakistan; Vietnam War

FURTHER READING

Ali, Tariq. *An Indian Dynasty: The Story of the Nehru-Gandhi Family.* New York, 1985.

Hess, Gary R. "Accommodation Amid Discord: The United States, India, and the Third World." *Diplomatic History* 16 (Winter 1992): 1–22.

Masani, Zareer. *Indira Gandhi: A Biography.* London, 1975.

Merrill, Dennis. *Bread and the Ballot: The United States and India's Economic Development, 1947–1963.* Chapel Hill, N.C., 1990.

Wolpert, Stanley. *Roots of Confrontation in South Asia: Afghanistan, Pakistan, India, and the Superpowers.* New York, 1982.

GARFIELD, JAMES ABRAM

(*b.* 19 November 1831; *d.* 19 September 1881)

President of the United States (1881). Born in Cuyahoga County, Ohio, Garfield attended Western Reserve Eclectic Institute (later Hiram College) in Hiram, Ohio, and graduated from Williams College in 1856. He was a teacher (1856–1861), an Ohio state senator (1859–1861), an officer in the Union Army (1861–1863), and a Republican member of the House of Representatives (1863–1880). An advocate of commercial expansion, he championed reciprocal trade, reminding Congress in 1876 that "we want all fair chances that the markets of the world can give us for selling our surplus supplies." In particular, Garfield warned against Great Britain's penetration of the "great tropical world" of Latin America, an area that he believed the United States should look to for new markets. With the acquisition of Alaska in 1867 and the completion of the transcontinental railroad in 1869, the United States seemed destined to become "the arbiter of that sea, the controller of its commerce and chief nation that inhabits its shores." In 1876 Garfield strongly supported the new commercial treaty with Hawai'i, hoping that economic influence might obviate the need for political domination. Except for Canada, he repudiated territorial expansion, mentioning Cuba and the West Indies by name. During the 1870s he also backed arbitration of the Alabama Claims issue and the Canadian fisheries dispute.

Elected to the Senate in 1880, he never took his seat, because he was nominated for president at the Republican convention. In his inaugural address, Garfield called for U.S. "supervision and authority" over any canal built across the Isthmus of Panama, but he left much of his foreign policy in the hands of his truculent secretary of state, James G. Blaine. During Garfield's brief presidency, the United States intervened on the side of Peru in its war against Chile (the War of the Pacific, 1879–1883), supported Guatemala in a border dispute with Mexico, sought to alleviate European concerns over the quality of U.S. pork imports, and protested against European efforts to guarantee Colombia's sovereignty over a neutralized Isthmus of Panama. Garfield was assassinated by Charles J. Guiteau, a disgruntled office seeker, barely six months into his presidency.

JUSTUS D. DOENECKE

See also Blaine, James Gillespie; Chile; Panama and Panama Canal; Peru

FURTHER READING

Doenecke, Justus D. *The Presidencies of James A. Garfield and Chester A. Arthur.* Lawrence, Kans., 1981.

Peskin, Allan. *Garfield.* Kent, Ohio, 1978.

Pletcher, David M. *The Awkward Years: American Foreign Relations Under Garfield and Arthur.* Columbia, Mo., 1962.

GARVEY, MARCUS MOZIAH

(*b.* 17 August 1887; *d.* 10 June 1940)

Jamaican-born black nationalist leader. While living in London from 1911 to 1914, Garvey associated with many members of the political left and developed a vision of an Africa liberated from white imperialists and of a union of people of African descent. To promote his dream of an "Africa for Africans," In 1914 Garvey formed the Universal Negro Improvement Association (UNIA) in Jamaica; two years later he moved the headquarters of the organization to Harlem in New York City. Through the pages of his publication *Negro World*, he spread his ideas for African repatriation and for the establishment of an independent and powerful black capitalist nation in Africa, specifically the West African Republic of Liberia. Garvey founded the Black Star Steamship Line to transport the repatriates, but the line folded as a result of fraud, mismanagement, and, possibly, sabotage. Arrested in 1923 and convicted on charges of mail fraud in 1925, Garvey was sent to federal prison. President Calvin Coolidge commuted his sentence in 1927, but Garvey was deported to Jamaica upon his release. Although his movement declined, Garvey continued to lecture throughout the world on behalf of African liberation and race solidarity for the remainder of his life.

DONALD SPIVEY
JOYCE HANSON

See also Liberia

FURTHER READING

Garvey, Amy Jacques, ed. *Philosophy and Opinions of Marcus Garvey, or Africa for the Africans*, 2nd ed. London, 1967.
———. *Garvey and Garveyism*. Kingston, Jamaica, 1963.
Hill, Robert A., ed. *The Marcus Garvey Papers*, 7 vols. Berkeley, Calif., 1983.
Martin, Tony. *Race First: The Ideological and Organizational Struggles of Marcus Garvey and the Universal Negro Improvement Association*. Dover, Mass., 1976.
Vincent, Theodore. *Black Power and the Garvey Movement*. San Francisco, 1971.

GATES, ROBERT MICHAEL

(*b.* 25 September 1943)

Director of the Central Intelligence Agency (CIA) from November 1991 through January 1993. Born in Wichita, Kansas, Gates graduated from the College of William and Mary (B.A., 1965), and Georgetown University (Ph.D., 1974). He joined the CIA in 1966 as a Soviet specialist and rapidly rose thorough the agency's ranks to become deputy director under William Casey (1986–1987). Throughout the 1980s Gates advocated policies that fit the rigid anticommunist agenda of President Ronald Reagan's administration. In 1986 Reagan nominated Gates to replace Casey as CIA director, but evidence that Gates knew and kept secret from Congress details of the Iran-Contra affair impeded his confirmation. Although Gates denied knowledge of the arms for hostages deal, he withdrew his nomination on 2 March 1987 and continued serving as deputy CIA director. In 1988 President-elect George Bush named Gates to the concurrent post of deputy national security adviser under National Security Adviser Brent Scowcroft, a position Gates used to promote further hard-line anti-Soviet policies.

Bush renominated Gates to become CIA director in 1991, and, despite lingering suspicions about his role in Iran-Contra, Gates won confirmation in November. In this capacity, Gates appeared to modify his staunch Cold War views. Reacting to criticism that the CIA had failed to predict the collapse of Soviet power in 1991, Gates advocated thawed U.S.-Russian relations in the form of joint offensives against nuclear proliferation, organized crime, and international drug trafficking. He also approved an "openness task force" to improve the CIA's public image and oversaw declassification of some CIA documents dating from the 1960s and before. These gestures, however, belied Gates's continued wariness of Moscow. He contested widespread claims that the CIA had become irrelevant in the post–Cold War world and called for increased expenditures for intelligence, especially in the economic realm, where he claimed other nations had achieved an advantage over the United States. Gates also qualified his stated vision of overhauling the CIA to make it more efficient by claiming that he sought "evolutionary," not sweeping, changes for the agency. He continued endorsing traditional CIA tactics, as when he conferred with Middle Eastern leaders in 1992 on how to remove from power Iraqi President Saddam Hussein, a leader troublesome to U.S. interests in the Persian Gulf.

Gates ordered investigations into the Banca Nazionale del Lavorno scandal, wherein the Bush administration allegedly supplied covert loans to Iraq prior to its 1990 invasion of Kuwait, then tried to conceal the evidence. Documents withheld by the CIA, however, helped prevent prosecutors from bringing indictments against either the agency or the Bush administration for their possible complicity in the affair. After stepping down from the directorship in January 1993, Gates joined Scowcroft, Deputy Secretary of State Lawrence S. Eagleburger, and Trade Representative Carla A. Hills to found the Forum for International Policy, a nonprofit foreign policy research group. Upon learning of the indictment in 1994 of CIA spy Aldrich Ames, who had sold U.S. secrets to Moscow throughout the 1980s and early 1990s, Gates asserted that the case proved that Russia still could not be trusted.

DEBORAH KISATSKY

See also Casey, William Joseph; Central Intelligence Agency; Cold War; Eagleburger, Lawrence Sydney; Hussein, Saddam; Iran-Contra Affair; Iraq; Narcotics, International; Nicaragua; Nuclear Nonproliferation; Scowcroft, Brent

FURTHER READING

Draper, Theodore. *A Very Thin Line: The Iran-Contra Affairs.* New York, 1991.

Gates, Robert M. *From the Shadows: The Ultimate Insider's Story of Five Presidents and How They Won the Cold War.* New York, 1996.

Persico, Joseph E. *Casey: From the OSS to the CIA.* New York, 1990.

Woodward, Robert. *The Commanders.* New York, 1991.

GATT

See General Agreement on Tariffs and Trade

GENERAL AGREEMENT ON TARIFFS AND TRADE

Agreement containing the basic rules guiding the international trade regime. The GATT was not an organization in the formal sense. Nor did any legislative body formally ratify the agreement. Instead, selected countries were invited to sign what was considered a legally binding protocol, and their official status was "contracting parties," not members.

While once a free-standing international agreement, the contents of the GATT were incorporated in their entirety as a component of the World Trade Organization (WTO) created at the start of 1995. As a result of this shift, the interpretation and enforcement of what officially still is referred to as the GATT has become the responsibility of the WTO.

The trade rules in the GATT were originally part of the International Trade Organization (ITO), agreed to in the Havana Charter of 1948. The U.S. Congress, however, failed to ratify U.S. membership in the ITO, in part because of opponents who argued that its powers infringed on U.S. sovereignty. Opponents also felt that the ITO contained too many provisions that tacitly would allow discrimination against U.S. exports. As an interim measure, the ITO's charter was modified and became operational as the GATT in January of 1948. Once it was clear that the ITO proposal was defunct, the GATT emerged as a permanent second-best effort (in lieu of a formal organization) to promulgate and enforce a multilateral code of conduct for the pursuit of a more liberal trading system.

U.S. adherence took the form of an executive agreement. The Congress officially never recognized the existence of the GATT, and U.S. law still takes precedence in domestic court cases over any commitment taken in connection with the GATT.

GENERAL AGREEMENT ON TARIFFS AND TRADE (GATT) ROUNDS		
Round	Date	Location
Geneva	1947	Switzerland
Annecy	1949	France
Torquay	1950-1951	England
Geneva	1955-1956	Switzerland
Dillon	1960-1962	Switzerland
Kennedy	1964-1967	Switzerland
Tokyo	1973-1979	Japan, Switzerland
Uruguay	1986-1994	Uruguay, Switzerland

The WTO secretariat (prior to 1995, the GATT secretariat), at its headquarters building in Geneva, Switzerland, acts on behalf of the contracting parties by monitoring trade policies and flows, as well as by supporting multilateral trade liberalization negotiations and forums for bilateral dispute settlements. In operational terms, the GATT has served the international community and U.S. trade policy objectives in three broad respects: (1) It provides a set of rules and principles governing the conduct of trade which is to be followed by contracting parties. The United States and other adherents often find it convenient to point to GATT provisions as justification for rejecting a domestic interest group's request for import protection. (2) It has served as a negotiating forum for an ongoing series of multilateral trade negotiations designed to progressively reduce official barriers to the flow of international trade. (3) It provides a neutral forum for trade dispute settlements among contracting parties.

Major Provisions

The GATT's rules are enshrined in thirty-eight articles and a series of annexes, all of which are written in vague language not always clear even to experienced lawyers. The high propensity for ambiguous wording reflects partly the difficult issues at hand and partly the need to find a least common denominator approach to often divisive economic issues among the original negotiators. The agreement does not seem to have been drafted with the intention of producing a strong, definitive set of binding rules and procedures. Instead, it offers a flexible, loosely defined framework that relies on the common interests of contracting parties. Procedurally, contracting parties at GATT meetings made decisions on a consensual basis; that is, the formal objection of one country could block an agreement.

Four fundamental concepts are clearly recognized, the GATT's ambiguity notwithstanding. The first is the most-favored-nation principle proclaiming that trade should be conducted on a nondiscriminatory basis: duties applied by one country on an imported product should be applied equally to all other contracting parties. Second, the preamble of the GATT agreement establishes a basic philosophy that links the pursuit of rising standards of living and real incomes and the most efficient use of the world's resources to the reduction of trade barriers. It also calls for the general elimination of quantitative restrictions (quotas), on the grounds that these restrictions represent greater distortions to trade because they make price competition between domestic and imported goods irrelevant. Third, once a tariff concession is negotiated, this rate is fixed, or "bound" by GATT principles at the lower rate; it cannot be rescinded without the offer of compensation to affected trading partners. Other forms of import protection cannot be implemented to circumvent new trade concessions.

The final fundamental concept is that bilateral trade conflicts involving GATT provisions should first be addressed through consultation, not unilateral action. If the parties cannot resolve their dispute, they can refer it to the WTO secretariat which arranges for a panel of neutral trade experts. In accordance with the established dispute settlement process, the panel issues a finding, which is sometimes years in coming and is not absolutely binding. The GATT's provisions dealing with the dispute settlement process were modified by the Uruguay Round agreement and transferred to the WTO. Countries no longer can block the report from being officially adopted. However, the losing country still has the option of refusing to comply with the ruling and either providing compensation (in the form of reduced trade barriers elsewhere) to the winning country or accepting trade retaliation by the winning country.

Another significant provision in the GATT Articles of Agreement is the provision for national treatment, which ensures that the same legal, regulatory, and tax treatment given to locally produced products will be applied to other contracting parties' imported goods. In what is the major exception to the lowering of import barriers, Article XIX, or the safeguard provision, states that contracting parties may take temporary restrictive measures when increasing imports "cause or threaten serious injury" to domestic producers of like products. (In U.S. law, this provision is known as the "escape clause.") Various articles define two principal forms of unfair trade practices: dumping (sales of imports at less than fair value) and government subsidies to exporting companies. General rules also are laid out to govern the imposition of retaliatory actions—anti-dumping and countervailing duties—to negate the margin of unfair pricing of imports. If certain conditions are met, contracting parties may extend preferential treatment to fellow members of a free-trade area or

customs union and remain in conformity with GATT rules. The conditions include the elimination of barriers on all substantial trade and calculations that import barriers imposed on an overall basis by a free-trade or customs union on a nonmember's goods will be no higher after formation of the trade bloc than they were before. This arcane article has played a significant role in relations between the United States and the European Union (EU) because the U.S. government on a couple of occasions demanded and received compensation when new member countries adopted the EU's common external tariff and common agricultural policy.

Liberal trade advocates, while usually sympathetic to the GATT's limited power to prevent adoption of protectionist measures by a determined country, strongly criticized the GATT for what they considered an excessive number of exemptions and loopholes legitimizing adoption of import barriers and discriminatory trade treatment. Above and beyond the aforementioned safeguard mechanism and provision for regional trading blocs, GATT sanctions the imposition of import barriers in cases of balance-of-payments emergencies and, to accommodate developing countries, in cases where needed to promote official assistance to "economic development." Articles XX and XXI lay out a number of other specific non-economic justifications for trade restrictions, such as protection of national security and protection of human, animal, and plant life and health.

The United States and the EU have frequently exploited a major loophole in GATT provisions which discourages import but not export restraints. In lieu of restricting imports, these countries have persuaded Japan and certain developing countries (mainly in East Asia) to "voluntarily" restrain their exports of sensitive goods. Orderly marketing agreements, as they are known, are not in legal terms an import restraint, but in economic terms they are the equivalent of a quantitative import barrier.

U.S. Policies and Objectives

U.S. trade policy since 1934 has been heavily influenced by two philosophies. The first is belief in the economic proposition that the world trading system will achieve maximum efficiency and therefore maximum output through an international specialization of labor whereby countries produce goods in which they have a competitive advantage and import goods they cannot produce efficiently. The second is the political philosophy espoused by Cordell Hull, secretary of state under President Franklin Roosevelt, that an open trading system induces increased cooperation and harmonious political relations among countries, while a system of relatively closed markets provokes strains and conflicts among nations. The world had a bitter experience in the 1930s with the mutually harmful recourse to "beggar thy neighbor" policies. A global escalation of trade barriers was triggered by the highly protectionist U.S. Smoot-Hawley Tariff of 1930 and then by the unemployment problems associated with the subsequent spread of the worldwide depression.

The United States helped usher in a new era in global trade relations in 1934. The Reciprocal Trade Agreements Act was passed by the Congress in that year, in large part due to the exhortations of Hull. For the first time in history, the president was given substantial authority to negotiate bilateral reciprocal tariff-cutting agreements, and soon after the bill passed, U.S. trade negotiators initiated the world's first systematic effort to reduce trade barriers.

At the conclusion of World War II, the United States sought to establish a liberal international trading order— a relatively open, market-based system with a minimum of official barriers. The GATT became the major vehicle for this quest. When the Cold War developed, a national security calculation was added to the U.S. ideological predilection that markets should be allowed to operate as free as possible from governmental controls. As part of the priority foreign policy goal of promoting the quick recovery of the economies of Western Europe and Japan as a means to the end of containing the expansion of Soviet influence, the United States sought to enhance the export performance of its allies by making the U.S. market readily accessible to their imports.

The unexpected speed with which the economies of Western Europe and Japan recovered, in part due to U.S. assistance, led to a relative decline in U.S. economic strength and competitiveness. The result was a fundamental shift in the priorities of U.S. foreign trade policy beginning in the late 1960s. The U.S. became less tolerant toward protectionist measures maintained by its major trading partners, especially as U.S. competitiveness deteriorated due to relatively high U.S. inflation. Trade policy in general and the GATT in particular became more of a venue to defend American commercial interests and less of an instrument to promote national security priorities. The U.S. government used the GATT's dispute settlement facilites on several occasions to press for the easing of restrictive measures adopted by the EU and Japan in violation of the spirit of the agreement.

There has been one constant in U.S. policy toward the GATT from its inception through the early 1990s: the United States has consistently been the lead country in the ongoing multilateral effort to dismantle official barriers and distortions and thereby increase the flow of international trade.

Trade Liberalization Process

The GATT had no regular meeting schedule, no formal administrative machinery, and no enforcement powers. Nevertheless, it had a marked impact on the global order through its main accomplishment—sponsorship of an ongoing series of multilateral trade negotiations (MTNs). The purpose of these talks, often referred to as rounds, is the progressive reduction of national barriers to trade and the implementation of additional rules of national behavior to deal with new trends in an ever-changing system of international commercial transactions. The ultimate motivation of countries participating in these talks is constant: belief that the economic benefits of expanded export opportunities created by global trade liberalization will outweigh the inevitable domestic social and economic dislocations associated with increased imports.

Since 1947, there have been eight rounds of MTNs. The first four were held from 1947 through 1956 and can be classified as "minirounds" in that they produced agreements restricted to relatively moderate reductions on a relatively limited range of manufactured goods. Aided by an economy largely invulnerable to import competition, U.S. trade negotiators were relatively generous in reaching agreements on reciprocal tariff cuts with other countries. The fifth round was held from 1960 through 1962 and marked the debut of the EU as a collective negotiator, replacing representatives from its individual member countries. The most significant result of the so-called Dillon Round (named for Douglas Dillon, the U.S. under secretary of state in 1960) was a series of unilateral trade concessions by the EU to bring its internal free trade and common external tariff arrangements into conformity with GATT rules dealing with free trade areas and customs unions. In every subsequent trade round, the two most influential and forceful participants have remained the EU and the United States.

The genesis of the sixth trade round was a fundamental policy dilemma faced by the incoming administration of President John F. Kennedy. On the one hand, the cultivation of a new, closer partnership of equals with Western Europe in the Atlantic Community was a priority foreign policy goal. On the other hand, the erection by the EU of a Common External Tariff and a Common Agricultural Policy loomed as a clear and present threat to the continued access of U.S. goods to their largest overseas market. It was decided that the best way to reconcile the situation was to negotiate major reductions in trade barriers and thus foster closer, more harmonious U.S.-EU relations. In the Trade Expansion Act of 1962, Congress granted unprecedented negotiating authority to the president to lower trade barriers. The successful conclusion of the Kennedy Round of trade negotiations in 1967 resulted in the deepest (about 35 percent on average) and most numerous tariff reductions in history.

The United States would play the principal role in the initiation of the next round of trade negotiations for a different reason: the belief that its trading partners imposed a greater degree of protectionism than did the United States and that this discrimination was a major contributing factor to the deteriorating U.S. trade balance in the early 1970s. When the Tokyo Round commenced in 1973, its expanded agenda represented a major change in trade liberalization efforts. The success of the Kennedy Round and its predecessors had lowered tariffs in the industrial countries to an average of about 8 percent, a low enough level that they were superseded by nontariff barriers (e.g., quotas and discriminatory health and safety standards) as the principal restraints to the flow of trade. An effort to do nothing but reduce tariffs would have been largely a waste of time. The Tokyo Round broke new ground in dealing with nontariff barriers and in confronting the special trade problems of the less developed countries (LDCs). Up to this point the GATT had been accused of being concerned only with the interests of the industrialized countries.

The Tokyo Round agreement in 1979 produced a number of innovative measures above and beyond the usual reductions in tariffs (which were reduced further to an average range of 5 to 6 percent among the industrialized countries). The agreement included elaborate codes of conduct to address nontariff barriers. Governments agreed to make their procurement processes more transparent and less biased against bids submitted by foreign bidders. Similarly, another code mandated more open, nondiscriminatory procedures for setting technical standards for products by subjecting imported goods to the same specifications and testing requirements as domestically produced products. Another code differentiated between those domestic subsidies which were acceptable, and those which were classified as unacceptable export subsidies. Other codes dealt with methods of customs valuation (how goods are classified for assessing tariffs), and with import licensing systems.

The so-called enabling clause, of the Tokyo Agreement legitimized "special and differential" trade policy treatment for LDCs. This measure authorized favorable discriminatory treatment for LDCs such as duty-free treatment of some of the LDCs' manufactured exports and a reduction in the obligation of LDCs to provide reciprocal reductions in trade barriers to industrialized countries.

The agenda of GATT negotiations was broadened even further in the eighth round, the longest and most complicated ever held. The Uruguay Round spanned eight years, starting in the fall of 1986 and ending in December 1993. The launching of the new round was mainly the result of yet another U.S. government initiative, this time reflecting trade officials' beliefs that there was a threefold rationale for another multilateral trade negotiation: (1) the need to deal with unfinished business of the Tokyo Round; (2) the need to arrest an increasing worldwide recourse to protectionism and trade distortions; and (3) the need to draft and apply common rules of national conduct to several new trade situations not yet covered by international agreement, such as agriculture and services.

The ambitious nature of the Uruguay Round was reflected in the complexity of the negotiating process: fourteen separate working groups focused on liberalization and the making of rules for merchandise goods, while a separate negotiating group dealt with services (insurance, transportation, tourism, financial markets, etc.) for the first time ever in international trade. Despite the burden of overcoming numerous political obstacles and the sheer physical difficulty of reaching consensus among the record 117 countries participating in the round, every negotiating group was successful. The provisional version of the final agreement consists of forty separate agreements stretching over 500 pages.

Improved market access was provided through three separate agreements: further reductions in tariffs (to an average of about 3 percent in industrial countries), further strengthening and clarification of the codes of conduct dealing with nontariff barriers produced in the Tokyo Round, and a ten-year phaseout of the Multifiber Arrangement. Initiated in 1974, the Multifiber Arrangement had established the framework for imposing quantitative limits on the annual exports of textiles and apparel from LDCs to industrial countries.

A second category of agreements consists of efforts to strengthen existing trade rules. Refinements were made in international agreements pertaining to unfair trade practices, such as pricing imports at less than fair value (dumping). More consistency and transparency were introduced into the safeguard provisions (providing temporary restrictions on imports that injure or threaten serious injury to domestic producers).

A major achievement of the Uruguay Round was the establishment of rules in three aspects of trade relations where countries' behavior had previously been unconstrained. First, an initial set of rules were agreed upon to limit barriers to international transactions in services, the fastest-growing element in trade. The General Agreement on Trade in Services imposes such measures for liberalizing service sectors as improved market access, national treatment (domestically owned and foreign firms are to be treated identically by the local government), and most-favored-nation treatment for imports of services. Second, the agreement on Trade Related Intellectual Property Rights establishes common rules for protecting patents, trademarks, copyrights, industrial designs, etc., and strengthens enforcement provisions. Third, the Trade Related Investment Measures agreement seeks to reduce the trade-distorting effects of domestic regulations affecting foreign direct investment. Among other measures, the agreement prohibits imposition of export performance or local content requirements specifically on foreign owned corporations.

From a political perspective, the most significant and difficult-to-reach agreement of the Uruguay Round concerned agriculture. Never before had there been anything more than token trade liberalization in this politically "untouchable" sector, a reflection of intense pressure by farmers everywhere for the retention of high production subsidies and high import barriers. An agreement on agriculture was made possible largely because the U.S. government made it a nonnegotiable demand for agreeing to any final trade package. This initiative was the culmination of years of frustration over lack of progress in lowering foreign agricultural trade barriers, especially those of the EU's Common Agricultural Policy, which limited exports of efficiently produced U.S. crops.

The agriculture package called for reductions of 36 percent in export subsidy outlays on a country-by-country basis and 21 percent in the quantities of agricultural goods exported with subsidies. These reductions were to be phased in over a six-year period for developed countries and a ten-year period for developing countries. Internal support programs, which distort trade, were to be reduced by 20 percent. Nontariff barriers to agricultural imports were to be converted into tariffs (a process called tariffication), and then the tariffs were to be gradually reduced by an average of 36 percent. In addition, a formula was agreed upon to assure minimum market access (measured in terms of market share accounted for by imports) for all protected agricultural products. Rules were established to allow countries to determine their national standards for health and safety measures related to animals and plants, as long as they were based on scientific principles and not disguised efforts to ban imports.

The final agreement of significance to come out of the Uruguay Round held significant institutional implications for the GATT. The World Trade Organization (WTO) was to be created as the world's first formal international trade organization. It was to oversee arrangements for the enforcement of three categories of agreements. In addition to the GATT agreement dealing with merchandise trade, the WTO administers directly new agreements on services and on trade-related intellectual property rights, both of which were outside the scope of the GATT's articles of agreement. In effect, the structure of the WTO (also to be headquartered in Geneva) will be imposed on top of the existing GATT operation.

The WTO was designed to administer a new, all-encompassing Dispute Settlement Understanding. The new dispute settlement mechanisms strengthened the old process in several ways. For example, the new rules accelerated the timetable for investigations and prohibit the losing party in a dispute from blocking panel decisions. Furthermore, the WTO was expected to institutionalize regular reviews of the trade policies of member countries and issue annual reports on the operation of the trading system.

From a legal standpoint, two GATT agreements will coexist: the original 1947 agreement and the new 1994 version of the GATT agreement, which includes the Uruguay Round's new liberalization measures and the new trade-related investment measures agreement. Countries were required to decide whether to remain a contracting party to the older, more limited agreement or to join the newer, expanded version of the GATT by becoming a member of the WTO. (The incentives were such that all existing GATT member countries selected the WTO option.)

The old, original GATT has been replaced by a trade organization having a stature commensurate to the International Monetary Fund and the World Bank. On the one hand, the GATT was monumentally successful in supervising a multilateral reduction of trade barriers without precedent in world history. On the other hand, sovereign countries regularly took advantages of its loopholes or ignored the articles of agreement when national interests dictated. Furthermore, some have suggested the basic concept of trade policy multilateralism is dying, the victim of increasing recourse to regional trade blocs such as the EU and the North American Free Trade Agreement.

The institutional demise of the GATT in favor of the WTO suggested, however, that the multilateral movement is still alive and well. The new organization should expedite the process by which new global rules are applied to the seemingly never-ending growth and diversification of world trade. No matter how innovative the Uruguay Round, its agreements will neither end trade frictions nor prevent new issues, like the environment and the absorption of formerly communist economies into the world trading system, from causing the need for further multilateral trade negotiations. The only real change in the offing is that instead of the GATT, the WTO will be the host of the new multilateral trade agenda.

STEPHEN D. COHEN

See also Most-Favored-Nation Principle; Reciprocal Trade Agreements Act; World Trade Organization

FURTHER READING

Dam, Kenneth W. *The GATT.* Chicago, Ill., 1970.

Evans, John W. *The Kennedy Round in American Trade Policy.* Cambridge, Mass., 1971.

Hudec, Robert. *The GATT Legal System and World Trade Diplomacy.* New York, 1975.

Jackson, John H. *The World Trading System.* Cambridge, Mass., 1992.
———. *World Trade and the Law of GATT.* Indianapolis, Ind., 1969.
Nau, Henry R. *Domestic Trade Politics and the Uruguay Round.* New York, 1989.
U.S. Congressional Budget Office. *The GATT Negotiations and U.S. Trade Policy.* Washington, D.C., 1987.

GENERALIZED SYSTEM OF PREFERENCES

The program by which the United States and other industrialized countries extend duty-free tariff treatment on a nonreciprocal basis to manufactured goods made in and exported from less-developed countries (LDCs). The Generalized System of Preferences (GSP) emerged in the early 1970s from the so-called North-South dialogue, which discussed the utility of creating a new international economic order. The policy of providing preferential access to the markets of the industrialized countries is based on the principle that stimulating the growth of the domestic manufacturing sectors of LDCs through increased exports from the South to the North is more efficient than foreign aid as a means of accelerating economic development. Preferential tariff treatment was a specific response to the LDC arguments that while a flourishing industrial sector is critical to elevating a country out of poverty, most LDC internal markets were too small to foster competitive industries. Hence, the expansion of production through rising exports of manufactured goods was seen as a critical element in the development process (as well as a benefit to consumers in the industrialized countries).

The U.S. GSP program was originally authorized for a limited period in the Trade Act of 1974 and was renewed several times. The legislation authorizes the president to grant duty-free treatment to specified imports under specified limitations to countries declared to be eligible for the program. The U.S. version of GSP in the early 1990s was extended to more than 140 countries and territories, and it applied to more than 4,300 tariff categories. Goods valued at $16.7 billion entered the United States duty-free under GSP in 1992 (as compared with total imports of $110 billion from eligible countries and $523 billion in total imports from all countries). A significant unforeseen characteristic of the GSP program has been the disproportionate benefits accruing to a relatively few advanced developing countries that possess the most competitive manufacturing sectors. The four "little dragons"—Korea, Hong Kong, Singapore, and Taiwan—so dominated the U.S. program (as a group, they eventually were shipping more than 50 percent of the goods entering the United States under GSP) that in 1989 they were involuntarily "graduated," that is, the U.S. government

removed them from eligibility. Since that time a different group of countries has become dominant. In 1992, for example, the top five beneficiary countries (Mexico, Malaysia, Thailand, Brazil, and the Philippines) accounted for 71 percent of GSP imports into the United States. The U.S. GSP program expired at the end of July 1995; legislateive action to renew it was still pending in mid–1990.

STEPHEN D. COHEN

See also General Agreement on Tariffs and Trade; New International Economic Order; Third World

FURTHER READING

Office of the U.S. Trade Representative. *A Guide to the U.S. Generalized System of Preferences.* Washington, D.C., 1991.
Organization of American States. *United States System of Generalized Preferences.* Washington, D.C., issued annually.

GENEVA CONVENTIONS

Four fundamental treaties adopted in 1949 setting forth principles and rules of the modern international law of war. They have been accepted as legally binding by virtually all states, including every major military power. The United States ratified them in 1955. The conventions were negotiated by states on the basis of drafts prepared by the International Committee of the Red Cross (ICRC)—based in Geneva, Switzerland—which, like the national Red Cross and Red Crescent societies, has a special role in the implementation of these and other international humanitarian law conventions. Formally, most of the provisions in the 1949 Geneva Conventions apply only to armed conflicts between two or more state parties, although there are a few provisions relating to peacetime activities. Common article 3 applies to noninternational armed conflicts, listing important minimum protections for civilians and for combatants no longer taking an active part in hostilities.

Geneva Convention I for the Amelioration of the Conditions of the Wounded and Sick in Armed Forces in the Field amplifies and supersedes the 1864, 1906, and 1929 Geneva conventions on this subject. It requires respect for and protection of the wounded and sick, medical personnel and related units, and humanitarian emblems such as the red cross. Geneva Convention II makes comparable provision for the protection and rescue of the wounded, sick and shipwrecked at sea, and for the marking and protection of hospital ships. The rules contained in these conventions have been reasonably widely respected. Geneva Convention III Relative to the Treatment of Prisoners of War (POWs) revised the 1929 Geneva convention on POWs in light of experience in World

War II. The rules against execution, violence, medical experimentation, reprisals and intimidation in relation to POWs, the general obligations to provide food, shelter, medical help, and protection to POWs, and some of the more specific duties concerning camp discipline, labor, religious freedom, correspondence, and other matters have been fairly widely accepted in the practice of states, although there also have been serious abuses. Major problems arise where states fail to repatriate prisoners after the conclusion of hostilities (e.g., the 1971 Indo-Pakistani War and the 1980–1988 Iran-Iraq War), and where prisoners do not want to be repatriated to their countries of origin (e.g., the 1950–1953 Korean War and the 1990–1991 Gulf War).

Geneva Convention IV Relative to the Protection of Civilian Persons in Time of War builds upon provisions in the 1899 and 1907 Hague Regulations and other instruments, but it is distinctive in focusing exclusively on the law concerning civilians. Most of its rules apply to civilians in the hands of a state of which they are not nationals—conduct of states toward their own nationals is regulated by other bodies of international law concerning human rights, crimes against humanity, and cognate issues. All alien civilians are covered by prohibitions of collective punishment, reprisals, hostage-taking, pillage, murder, torture, rape, corporal punishment, and other forms of violent or inhumane treatment. Further specific provisions apply to alien civilians in the territory of an enemy state (usually those living in or visiting another state when war breaks out), in territory occupied by a foreign state, and in internment. In 1949 many states had bitter memories of recent occupation, whereas the larger victorious powers were in military occupation of the defeated states, and there were great difficulties in agreeing on a realistic but humane balance between the competing interests of occupiers and occupied, particularly where civilians of the occupied state mount passive or active resistance. Convention IV permits various measures of punishment and internment by occupiers for security purposes, while in other ways restricting the occupier's freedom to act. States' parties to Convention IV have not always been willing to acknowledge its applicability in pertinent cases, but it has been an influential source of standards and a basis for some ICRC humanitarian activity, as with regard to Israel in the West Bank. Military occupation is one of several situations where the model of war as a conflict between readily identifiable national military forces does not cover the practical problems. In World War II many occupied states were proud of their partisans, resistance forces, and other irregulars, while occupiers waged war against these forces through brutal measures against innocent and not-so-innocent civilians. The 1949 Conventions strike a bal-

ance between lawful and unlawful (or privileged and unprivileged) combatants in Geneva Convention III, which extends POW status to members of militias and other volunteer groups provided they have responsible command and fixed distinctive emblems, carry arms openly, and conduct operations in accordance with the laws and customs of war. The conventions require that states punish individuals responsible for grave breaches.

Further development of the 1949 Conventions was undertaken in the two Protocols adopted in 1977. Geneva Protocol I deals with international armed conflict, supplementing and extending many of the 1949 provisions. It is innovative in combining protection of victims with control of means and methods of warfare. Several of its most important provisions seek to strengthen protection of civilians and civilian objects. Starvation of civilians, damage to the natural environment, and attacks on dams, dikes, and nuclear power stations are prohibited or severely restricted. The civilian population may not be the object of attack. Attacks and reprisals may be directed only at "military objectives," meaning those objects which make an effective contribution to military action and whose capture or destruction offers a definite military advantage. The use of weapons and methods causing unnecessary suffering is prohibited. Precautions are required of attackers and defenders to minimize damage to civilians. A general principle of proportionality is espoused to limit "collateral damage" and other civilian misery. These provisions have potential implications for weapons of mass destruction, some of which (including poisons, gas, chemical, bacteriological, and biological weapons) are dealt with in other treaties. The U.S. position, contested by others, is that Protocol I has no bearing on the use of nuclear weapons. The most controversial aspect of Protocol I is the Western perception that it legitimizes wars of decolonization and other causes then favored by Third World states, especially in the provision that wars of self-determination "in which peoples are fighting against colonial domination and alien occupation and against racist regimes" are to be treated as international armed conflicts under the 1949 Geneva Conventions. This, and concern that other provisions conferred excessive advantages on guerrillas, overly restricted aerial bombardment, or otherwise inhibited U.S. military operations while aiding adversaries, led successive U.S. administrations not to ratify Protocol I, although the spirit of many of its provisions has been incorporated into U.S. military law and policy. Geneva Protocol II deals with noninternational armed conflicts between the military forces of a state party and organized armed groups under responsible command controlling enough territory to conduct sustained military operations and to implement the Protocol. It does not apply to riots or other internal disturbances. It prohibits attacks by government and antigovernment forces against civilian populations and civilian foodstuffs, drinking water, and agricultural areas. It requires basic humanitarian protections for those who do not, or no longer, participate in hostilities, and for the wounded, sick, and shipwrecked. Although formally invoked by the ICRC in a few conflicts, for example the El Salvador civil war in the 1980s, it has had little impact in such cases, and has been ignored by the parties in many other conflicts. The United States has not ratified Protocol II, although it has no major objections. Roughly half the states of the world have become party to one or both of the 1977 Protocols.

Implementation remains a more intractable problem than lawmaking. Major principles of the Geneva Conventions and Protocols are institutionalized in operational doctrine and in domestic law such as the U.S. Uniform Code of Military Justice. Since the war in Indochina, U.S. military forces have become increasingly well trained in laws of war issues. In some cases, humanitarian standards have been applied voluntarily where formally inapplicable or where, as with certain operations authorized or conducted by the United Nations after 1990 (e.g., in Somalia and Haiti), the formal legal position is complex. Significant problems of implementation arise even for the strongest and best-disciplined military powers, and this is all the more true where discipline and accountability is weak or where the parties lack a common interest in respecting particular international rules. The involvement of entire economies and societies in war, changes in military technology and methods, and the frequency of guerrilla or militia actions, have made the central distinction between combatants and noncombatants an increasingly difficult one to define and maintain. In many international conflicts one or more of the parties has ignored or repeatedly violated some if not all of its obligations. The increased international concern with applying international law to conflicts that are wholly or partly internal involves severe political and legal problems of implementation. The establishment of the United Nations international criminal tribunals to try war crimes and other atrocities committed in the former Yugoslavia and Rwanda was a bold if risky enforcement initiative, but it is unlikely to culminate in any general solution to problems of implementation.

BENEDICT W. KINGSBURY

See also International Law; International Red Cross and Red Cross and Red Crescent Movement

FURTHER READING

Best, Geoffrey. *War and Law Since 1945*. Oxford, U.K., 1994.
Pictet, Jean S., ed. *Commentary on the Geneva Conventions of 12 August 1949*, 4 vols. Geneva, 1952–1960.
Roberts, Adam, and Richard Guelff, eds. *Documents on the Laws of War*, 2nd ed. Oxford, U.K., 1989.
Sandoz Yves, et al., eds. *Commentary on the Additional Protocols of 8 June 1977*. Geneva, Switz., 1987.

GENOCIDE CONVENTION

Adopted in 1948 in response to the massive loss of human life incurred during the Holocaust of World War II. The Convention defines "genocide" as the infliction of certain specified acts "with intent to destroy, in whole or in part, a national, ethnical, racial or religious group, as such...." Prohibited acts include "killing members of the group;... causing serious bodily or mental harm to members of the group;...deliberately inflicting on the group conditions of life calculated to bring about its physical destruction in whole or in part;...imposing measures intended to prevent births within the group;.... forcibly transferring children of the group to another group." States which become parties to the Convention engage to change their domestic legal systems to penalize individuals who commit a number of specifically prohibited acts. Although many states ratified the Convention shortly after its execution, the United States delayed until 1988.

With the end of the Cold War, ethnic and national groups within many states have engaged in unconstrained hostilities, perpetrating acts of brutality reminiscent of those that motivated the drafters of the Genocide Convention. In this context, questions remain about the efficacy of a convention that depends on governmental legal obligations when national officials may have lost control over subgroups within their territories or where state authorities may have committed banned acts.

Early in World War II, the Allied powers learned that Nazi forces had begun a massive, ruthless, brutal program of systematic extermination of Jews and other racial, ethnic, religious and social minorities. U.S. president Franklin D. Roosevelt and British Prime Minister Winston Churchill issued pledges in 1941 to conduct war crimes trials at the end of the conflict. With the signing of the Declaration on German Atrocities in Occupied Europe in London in 1943, the United States, United Kingdom, and Soviet Union began preparing for the trial of German officials involved in "war crimes," "crimes of aggression," and "crimes against humanity." The Charter of the International Military Tribunal, signed in London on 8 August 1945, defined "crimes against humanity" as "murder, extermination, enslavement, deportation, and other inhumane acts...or persecutions on political, religious, or racial grounds...whether or not in violation of the domestic law of the country where perpetrated." Indictments of 185 individuals were issued pursuant to the charter, with subsequent trials conducted before international tribunals in Nuremberg and elsewhere. Death sentences for over a dozen defendants resulted, and prison sentences for 120. Although none of the defendants were convicted of committing genocide specifically, many of their verdicts reflected all the criteria of genocide.

The international military tribunals established important new legal norms. The authorship and application of those principles by military victors, however, and the unique, horrendous nature of the crimes raise doubts about their applicability. Some observers were concerned that defendants accused of similar crimes in the future could argue the Nuremberg principles to be inapplicable as laws relevant only to the the Holocaust. In an effort to establish general principles that could be applied prospectively as a general international resolution of such mass killings, Raphael Lemkin, a Polish international lawyer who lost 50 family members during the Holocaust, coined the term "genocide." Lemkin's initiative provoked the newly formed United Nations to undertake the establishment of new legal principles. On 11 December 1946, the General Assembly passed resolution 96(I), which declared that "genocide is a crime under international law which the civilized world condemns and for the commission of which principals and accomplices are punishable." Almost two years later, on 9 December 1948, the General Assembly unanimously adopted the Convention on the Prevention and Punishment of the Crime of Genocide. On 12 January 1951, the Convention entered into force after ratification by twenty states.

The Convention obligates any party state to adopt legislation imposing criminal punishment upon any act of "genocide," "conspiracy to commit genocide," "direct and public incitement to commit genocide," an "attempt to commit genocide," or "complicity in genocide." States must hold any individual committing these to be punishable without regard to official or private status.

Individuals who have committed prohibited acts within the territory of party states must be brought to trial before a competent tribunal of that state. If that state has accepted the jurisdiction of an international penal tribunal, then violators may be tried before that tribunal. At the time of the adoption of the treaty, no international tribunal existed, although the International Law Commission, a subsidiary organ of the General Assembly, had been mandated to draft a code of "offenses against the peace and security of mankind ...." Progress was made in the 1990s toward the establishment of a permanent international criminal tribunal.

States party to the Convention must comply with lawful requests for extradition of individuals accused of prohibited acts. Those states may not deny extradition on the grounds that the accused was justified by political motivation, a contention that can preclude extradition. Any dispute about interpretation of the Convention or the responsibility of a state for violations are to be resolved before the International Court of Justice upon the request of any party to the Convention.

A total of 121 states had ratified the Genocide Convention as of March 1996. The United States signed two days after its adoption by the General Assembly, and President Harry S. Truman quickly submitted it to the Senate for final ratification. The Senate delayed immediate action because of concerns about the consistency of the proposed criminal sanctions with the Constitution and its desire to protect U.S. racial segregation laws and other domestic laws pertaining to ethnic and racial groups from formal international scrutiny. During the Cold War, some members of national ethnic minorities attempted to describe discriminatory treatment as genocide according to the meaning set forth by the Convention. For example, some radical commentators characterized attempts to promote birth control among African-American teenagers as a form of genocide. Similar claims were made regarding the living conditions of native Hawaiians and of Native Americans. After the end of official segregation, constitutional doubts and debates over infringements on U.S. sovereignty persisted. U.S. ratification of the Convention took place in 1988, with the addition of several reservations, understandings, and declarations. Each of these conditions limits the commitment of the United States under the treaty. First, the U.S. obligation to appear before the International Court of Justice to resolve disputes involving the Convention was reduced to cases in which it has specifically agreed to litigate in that forum. Second, the Constitution is to take precedence over any provision that, in the judgment of the United States, is inconsistent with the Constitution. Third, the United States will limit provisions of the treaty defining genocide as including infliction of mental harm to permanent damage in mental functioning. Finally, individual acts may fall within the definition of genocide only when the individual has a specific intent to destroy an ethnic or racial group "in whole or in substantial part."

The systematic killing of hundreds of thousands of Cambodians in the 1970s provided fresh evidence that genocide remained a present horror. With the growing number of violent conflicts between ethnic groups following the end of the Cold War, calls for the enforcement of norms against genocide have increased. While there has been general consensus among governments, multilateral bodies, and nongovernmental organizations that these instances of large-scale killing should be recognized as genocide, existing legal norms posed problems.

For example, many states initially argued that Article 2(7) of the United Nations Charter prohibited states from interfering in the internal affairs of other states. While those prohibitions have been significantly weakened, difficulties remain for states and international organizations seeking to fashion responses to ethnic violence within other states. In reaction, resolutions of the U.N. Security Council have authorized collective responses to internal conflicts which have led to patterns of mass killings. For example, the U.N. Protective Force (UNPROFOR) was authorized by Resolution 836 (1993) to use necessary force to protect civilian safe havens in Bosnia. Member states also have begun legal action to clarify the applicability of the norms of the Genocide Convention. In 1993, Bosnia-Herzegovina brought a claim in the International Court of Justice asserting that the Federal Republic of Yugoslavia should be held responsible for acts of genocide committed in Bosnia-Herzegovina.

While claims by states against states provide the traditional remedies in international law, new mechanisms have been established to deal with modern crimes involving mass killings. These mechanisms differ in that they seek punishment of individuals. In Resolution 827 (1993), the U.N. Security Council authorized the establishment of the Ad Hoc International War Crimes Tribunal for the former Yugoslavia. In July 1995, the prosecutor of that tribunal delivered indictments charging two leaders of the Bosnian Serb faction with genocide. Actions against some leaders have not been pursued as vigorously as might have been hoped in order to reach settlement. Similar proceedings were initiated in response to disturbances in Africa. In 1994, early reports of mass killings of Tutsis by Hutus in Rwanda grew to indicate killings taking place on an enormous scale at appalling speed. Few observers hesitated to characterize the killings as genocide. Security Council response was dilatory, and insufficient to stop the killings. It did adopt Resolution 955 (1994), however, which authorized the establishment of the International Criminal Tribunal for Rwanda to pursue punishment of the perpetrators. Investigations continue.

Though full judicial proceedings may provide the best response to specific acts of genocide, they are not always possible. But even when full application of the Convention's prohibitions proves difficult for political reasons, formal international repudiation may provide an important sanction against individuals and groups that seek acceptance. In addition, groups within states which resist genocide can point to the principles of the Convention to justify actions which might otherwise be characterized as treasonous. Finally, evidence of violation of the Convention can provide incentives for states and international organizations to provide political and other assistance to people struggling to endure extreme danger and suffer-

ing. In this manner, the Genocide Convention can play a positive political role whether or not formal judicial proceedings succeed.

EDWIN M. SMITH

See also Bosnia-Herzegovina; Cambodia; Holocaust; International Law; Nuremberg, International Military Tribunal at; Rwanda; World War II

FURTHER READING
Kuper, Leo. *The Prevention of Genocide*. New Haven, Conn., 1985.
Lemkin, Rafael. *Axis Rule in Occupied Europe*. Washington, D.C., 1944.
Lifton, Robert Jay. *The Nazi Doctors: Medical Killing and the Psychology of Genocide*. New York, 1986.
Merron, Theodor. "Comments: War Crimes in Yugoslavia and the Development of International Law." *The American Journal of International Law*, 88 (January 1994): 78.
Post, Jennifer A. "The United States and the Genocide Treaty: Returning Genocide to Sovereign Concerns." *Suffolk Transnational Law Journal*, 13 (Spring 1990): 686.

GENTLEMEN'S AGREEMENTS
(1900, 1907, 1908)

Understandings reached between the United States and Japan limiting the emigration of Japanese workers to the United States. "Gentlemen's agreement" as a generic phrase refers to an informal understanding between nations, short of a formal treaty. Following the San Francisco earthquake and fire of 18–19 April 1906, the schools that reopened in October segregated Asian children. On 25 October the Japanese government objected to the policy on the grounds that this exclusion violated the 1894 treaty between Japan and the United States that granted Japan most-favored-nation status. The immigration to the United States of unskilled Japanese workers had become an increasing source of friction, especially in California, during cyclical economic declines when the number of lower-paying jobs decreased. In the first Gentlemen's Agreement (August 1900), Japan had agreed not to issue passports to laborers. As part of a compromise in which President Theodore Roosevelt secured the desegregation of San Francisco's schools, Japan, in its note of 24 February 1907, consented not only to stop Japanese labor emigration but to recognize the right of the United States to exclude Japanese labor immigrants with other foreign passports. Another Japanese note, of 18 February 1908, reconfirmed this new Gentlemen's Agreement. Roosevelt sent a group of U.S. warships, called the Great White Fleet, on a world cruise to demonstrate that the United States had not settled its differences with Japan because it feared Japanese naval power. The exclusion of all Japanese immigrants by an act of Congress in 1924 abrogated the Gentlemen's Agreements. The abrogation contributed to the deterioration of relations, a trend that ultimately led to war in 1941.

RICHARD H. COLLIN

See also Immigration; Japan; Most-Favored-Nation Principle

FURTHER READING
Daniels, Roger. *The Politics of Prejudice: The Anti-Japanese Movement in California and the Struggle for Japanese Exclusion.* Berkeley, Calif., 1962.
Neu, Charles E. *An Uncertain Friendship: Theodore Roosevelt and Japan, 1906–1909.* Cambridge, Mass., 1967.
Rodman, Paul W. *The Abrogation of the Gentlemen's Agreement.* Cambridge, Mass., 1936.

GEORGE III

(*b.* 4 June 1738; *d.* 29 January 1820)

British monarch (1760–1820) at the time the North American colonies broke away from the British Empire and formed the United States of America. George III was the first son of Frederick, Prince of Wales (1707–1751), and the grandson of George II (1683–1760). Once thought to be mentally retarded as well as a believer in royal absolutism, he is now regarded by most historians as a man of at least average intelligence, although one probably afflicted with the hereditary metabolic disease porphyria, and as a ruler who respected parliamentary government. Assuming the throne in 1760, George III was determined to be an active monarch, but he usually accepted the judgment of his ministers concerning the management of British North America. He successfully urged repeal of the Stamp Act (1765), as well as retention of an elected, instead of appointed, council in Massachusetts until 1774. The king nevertheless believed that the colonies were subordinate to parliamentary authority; he approved the policy of Lord North Frederick, prime minister from 1770 to 1782, enforcing imperial control and refusing to grant concessions in response to protests by the North American colonists.

The North American settlers viewed George III as the symbol of British authority, rather than as the originator of policies that they considered economically and politically oppressive. The Declaration of Independence, however, blamed him for almost all the colonists' grievances. Even though the Declaration distorted the facts, its long indictment of the king proved emotionally powerful and bolstered the rebel position that the British Parliament had no authority over the colonies. As titular head of the British armed forces, George III picked seasoned military men for command but accepted Parliament's control of the war effort. Always confident of

imperial victory, he opposed but did not block Parliament's vote in February 1782 to end military operations in America. When Lord North resigned in the wake of the American victory, George III considered abdication. The king reluctantly accepted the final peace treaty in December 1783. After the loss of the North American colonies, the king reasserted his authority by forcing his ministers to resign and dissolving Parliament. George III then supported the rise to power of William Pitt the Younger in 1784. A Tory generally aligned with the king, Pitt led the British government in the war against revolutionary France from 1793 to 1801 and from 1804 to his death in 1806. During this period George III's mental stability progressively declined. In 1788 he suffered the first of four breakdowns. Almost blind by 1806, he became progressively violent and was declared certifiably insane at the end of 1810. The lengthy controversy over the naming of the Prince of Wales as regent delayed parliamentary discussion of the repeal of certain Orders in Council that interfered with U.S. neutral trade. These events, among others, ultimately led the United States to declare war on England in June 1812.

REBECCA G. GOODMAN

See also American Revolution; Great Britain; Napoleonic Wars; Pitt, William; War of 1812

FURTHER READING
Ayling, Stanley. *George III.* New York, 1972.
Brooke, John. *George III.* New York, 1972.
Clark, John Charles. *The Life and Times of George III.* London, 1972.
Watson, J. Steven. *The Reign of George III, 1760–1815.* Oxford, 1960.

GEORGIA

See Appendix 2

GERMANY

The major central European country, bordering France, Poland, the Czech Republic, Austria, Switzerland, Belgium, Luxembourg, the Netherlands, and Denmark. Gremany contributed heavily to immigration to the United States in the nineteenth century, and its relations with the United States have ranged from aloofness to warfare to close-knit alliance. The basic although not the sole determinant of U.S. policy toward Germany has been the historic U.S. interest in a stable, balanced European political order.

Relations Through World War II

Leaders in the United States recognized quite early the geopolitical imperative of opposing the hegemony of any

U.S. MINISTERS AND AMBASSADORS TO GERMANY[1]

MINISTER	PERIOD OF APPOINTMENT	ADMINISTRATION
John Quincy Adams	1797–1801	J. Adams
Henry Wheaton	1835–1846	Jackson
		Van Buren
		W. H. Harrison
		Tyler
		Polk
Andrew J. Donelson	1846–1849	Polk
		Taylor
Edward A. Hannegan	1849–1850	Taylor
Daniel D. Barnard	1850–1853	Fillmore
		Pierce
Peter D. Vroom	1853–1857	Pierce
		Buchanan
Joseph A. Wright	1857–1861	Buchanan
		Lincoln
Norman B. Judd	1861–1865	Lincoln
		A. Johnson
Joseph A. Wright	1865–1867	A. Johnson
George Bancroft	1867–1874	A. Johnson
		Grant
J. C. Bancroft Davis	1874–1877	Grant
		Hayes
Bayard Taylor	1878	Hayes
Andrew D. White	1879–1881	Hayes
		Garfield
A. A. Sargent	1882–1884	Arthur
John A. Kasson	1884–1885	Arthur
		Cleveland
George H. Pendleton	1885–1889	Cleveland
Murat Halstead[2]		
William Walter Phelps	1889–1893	B. Harrison
		Cleveland

AMBASSADOR

Theodore Runyon	1893–1896	Cleveland
Edwin F. Uhl	1896–1897	Cleveland
		McKinley
Andrew D. White	1897–1902	McKinley
		T. Roosevelt
Charlemagne Tower	1902–1908	T. Roosevelt
David Jayne Hill	1908–1911	T. Roosevelt
		Taft
John G. A. Leishman	1911–1913	Taft
		Wilson
James W. Gerard	1913–1917[3]	Wilson
Ellis L. Dresel	1921–1922	Harding
Alanson B. Houghton	1922–1925	Harding
		Coolidge

(table continues on next page)

AMBASSADOR	PERIOD OF APPOINTMENT	ADMINISTRATION
Jacob Gould Schurman	1925–1930	Coolidge
		Hoover
Frederic M. Sackett	1930–1933	Hoover
William E. Dodd	1933–1937	F. Roosevelt
Hugh R. Wilson	1938	F. Roosevelt[4]
James B. Conant	1955–1957[5]	Eisenhower
David K. E. Bruce	1957–1959	Eisenhower
Walter C. Dowling	1959–1963	Eisenhower
		Kennedy
George C. McGhee	1963–1968	Kennedy
		L. Johnson
Henry Cabot Lodge, Jr.	1968–1969	L. Johnson
Kenneth Rush	1969–1972	Nixon
Martin J. Hillenbrand	1972–1976	Nixon
		Ford
Walter J. Stoessel, Jr.	1976–1981	Ford
		Carter
Arthur F. Burns	1981–1985	Reagan
Richard R. Burt	1985–1989	Reagan
Vernon A. Walters	1989–1991	Bush
Robert M. Kimmitt	1991–1993	Bush
Richard C. Holbrooke	1993–1994	Clinton
Charles E. Redman	1994–Present	Clinton

[1]Representatives from Adams to Bancroft (second commission) were commissioned to Prussia; resident at Berlin. Bancroft (third and fourth commissions) and Davis were commissioned to the German Empire. Representatives from Taylor to Wilson were commissioned to Germany; those from Conant to date have been commissioned to the Federal Republic of Germany.
[2]Not commissioned; nomination rejected by the Senate.
[3]Gerard left post, 10 Feb. 1917.
[4]During the period 1938-1941 each of the following officers served as Chargé d' Affaires ad interim for more than a year; Alexander C. Kirk, May 1939-Oct. 1940; Leland B. Morris, Oct. 1940-Dec. 1941. Morris was serving as Chargé d' Affaires ad interim when Germany declared war on the U.S., 11 Dec. 1941.
[5]The Embassy in Germany was reestablished 5 May 1955 with Ambassador-designate Conant (who had been serving as High Commisisoner) in charge except for a brief temporary absence pending confirmation of his nomination, commissioning, and presentation of his letter of credence.

Sources: *Principle Officers of the Department of State and United States Chiefs of Missions.* ©1991 by Office of the Historian, Bureau of Public Affairs, Washington, D.C.; *The U.S. Government Manual*, Annual. Washington, D.C.

one European state, a necessity spoken of by the founders of the Republic and indirectly reflected in the Monroe Doctrine, but feared entangling alliances. Instead, during the nineteenth century the United States relied on Great Britain to protect the common interest in a Continental equilibrium of power. Throughout the nineteenth century relations between the United States and Germany, although sustained in the area of immigration and commerce, were of secondary political importance to both countries and acquired a somewhat episodic and fractured quality. Prior to its unification in 1871, "Germany" was a politically dispersed geographical expression, and the United States, preoccupied first with westward expansion and later with the antecedents and the reverberations of the Civil War, had no significant transatlantic political reach. The United States was politically disengaged from the loosely associated German states, and the interests of Washington and the various German capitals were connected only indirectly through the diplomacy of intermediaries, such as Great Britain and France.

After 1871 Germany became the predominant European power and began to pursue aspirations beyond the European continent in the Atlantic and Pacific, where German ambitions confronted those of the United States, which also conducted a foreign policy of expanding scope and energy. This led to frictions, primarily naval and economic rivalries, that erupted in periodic minor contretemps, as in Manila Bay, Samoa, Beijing, and Venezuela, and ultimately escalated to full enmity during World War I. Germany's unrestricted submarine warfare against merchant shipping eventually forced the United States to enter the war and restore the European balance, something the continental powers had been unable to accomplish on their own, even when aided by the maritime power of Great Britain.

The United States sought a lenient peace for Germany at the Paris Peace Conference of 1919, in part because it feared Bolshevik encroachment in Central and Eastern Europe, and in part because the new German political system turned away from monarchic autocracy and held out the prospect of democracy. Nevertheless, the U.S. Senate rejected both the Versailles Treaty and U.S. membership in the League of Nations, and during the interwar period the United States largely abandoned Wilsonian principles of internationalism and withdrew into political isolationism. Although the United States extended most-favored-nation status to Weimar Germany and eased the burdens of German war reparations with the Dawes Plan (1924), it abandoned the political task of helping to pacify Europe, leaving a resentful and only temporarily weakened Germany to become again the dominant European power in the 1930s. This time, under the Nazi leadership of Adolf Hitler, Germany's rampant expansionism and espousal of an odious ideology challenged U.S. interests on both geostrategic and moral grounds.

During the 1930s the administration of President Franklin D. Roosevelt, hampered by an isolationist Congress and public opinon, had done little to encourage British and French resistance to Hitler's determination to upset the European order. After Germany's 1939 invasion of Poland, however, and the consequent British and French declaration of war, Roosevelt moved as fast as he could, given the political restraints in the United States, to assist the Allies at war with Germany. By 1941, with Western Europe under German control and Germany bent on the attempted conquest of Russia, there was an undeclared naval war between the United States and Germany in the Atlantic—with U.S. warships protecting convoys with supplies for Great Britain and Russia from attacks by German U-boats. The U.S. government's determination to do everything possible to secure Germany's defeat was intensified by the fact that Germany and Japan were formal allies, as well as by a fear of spreading Nazi influence in Latin America. On 8 December 1941, the day after the Japanese attack on Pearl Harbor, the United States declared war on Japan but not on Germany. On 11 December, however, Adolf Hitler relieved President Roosevelt of the necessity of decision by declaring war on the United States.

Thus, the United States fought again in World War II to restore the European balance of power. A justified fear of Germany's formidable land forces, however, led Great Britain and the United States to postpone the cross-channel attack until June 1944, while Russia bore the brunt of fighting and very heavy casualties. Partly in order to reassure the Russians and partly to avoid repetition of the post–World War I situation, in which Hitler claimed that Germany had been betrayed into putting down its arms by false promises, Roosevelt and British Prime Minister Winston Churchill insisted on Germany's unconditional surrender. Roosevelt, who believed that a propensity for war was ingrained in the German national character, toyed with the idea of the permanent dismemberment of Germany and the destruction of all heavy industry, as envisaged in the Morgenthau Plan (1944). Under criticism from advisers, he backed away from such schemes.

The Post-World War II Era

After World War II the United States was again confronted with an unbalanced European system of states, this time unhinged by the Soviet Union. Moscow controlled Eastern Europe; held sway in its zone of occupation in Germany, which later became the German Democratic Republic, or East Germany; and hindered the joint administration of the four zones of occupation established at the end of the war. These disagreements, mostly about the political and economic management of Germany, were an important factor in the origins of the Cold War in Europe. Germany, although defeated, remained at the epicenter of European politics, a major geopolitical prize sought by East and West.

The U.S. occupation policy for its zone was sometimes unclear, although its general thrust was to eliminate all traces of Nazi influence, introduce democratic institutions, and assure that industry was used only for peaceful purposes. The International Military Tribunal at Nuremberg tried, convicted, and sentenced to death or imprisonment several Nazi leaders for "crimes against humanity." In January 1947 the British and U.S. zones were fused into "Bizonia," and in 1948 the Western powers embarked on German economic revival with an infusion of Marshall Plan aid and currency reform to curb inflation. In June 1948 the Soviet Union sought to disrupt the political consolidation of the Western zones by imposing a blockade of Berlin—a city divided, like all of Germany, into four occupation zones controlled by the United States, Great Britain, France, and the Soviet Union. The United States responded with a successful air lift that demonstrated the commitment of the Western allies to sustain their sphere of influence in Europe.

The movement toward formation of a West German government, under Western supervision, continued apace, and in May 1949 the Federal Republic of Germany (West Germany) was established. The Germans chose Bonn as their provisional capital, the former military governors became high commissioners, and the new German government, elected in August and led by Chancellor Konrad Adenauer, quickly agreed to make a military contribution to the Western defense effort.

The Bonn government's freedom of action in both domestic and foreign affairs was limited and revocable. The Western powers reserved for themselves sweeping rights over the future economic and political direction of the new German state until a fuller measure of sovereignty was granted in 1955, when the Federal Republic joined the North Atlantic Treaty Organization (NATO) and when the high commissioners became ambassadors. In particular, the Western powers retained for themselves—as well as for the Soviet Union—the four-power rights stemming from the victory in World War II to deal with Berlin and questions pertaining to all of Germany. These rights remained in effect until the reunification of Germany in 1990.

The central intention of U.S. foreign policy toward the Federal Republic of Germany in the postwar period was to make the West Germans free with respect to the personal liberties and constitutional safeguards that are the essence of a democratic political order, but not free to formulate and implement an independent foreign policy. The restraint of West Germany through international organizations and treaties was at the core of Washington's postwar European policy of double containment—the containment of the Soviet Union at arm's length and of West Germany with an embrace. Every major event in the postwar history of Europe followed from this policy, including the establishment, rearmament, and economic reconstruction of West Germany within the restraints of such international organizations as NATO, the Western European Union (WEU), the European Coal and Steel Community (ECSC), and the European Economic Community (EEC); the development of NATO from a loosely organized mutual assistance pact into an integrated military alliance; U.S. support for West European economic integration; and the partition of Germany and Europe, until it was overcome with the breakup of the Soviet empire in the late 1980s and early 1990s.

The double-pronged effectiveness of the U.S. containment policy was supplemented in the military sphere. In the 1950s sizable U.S. troops were stationed in Germany. The United States was still invulnerable and could therefore enunciate a credible doctrine of nuclear deterrence that both restrained the Soviet Union and met the security and reassurance needs of West Germany. Throughout the 1950s political containment and strategic deterrence complemented one another, and their respective double functions—containing the adversary as well as the partner, deterring the opponent as well as reassuring the ally—were interlocking and mutually supportive. Integrative transatlantic and West European institutions, military as well as political and economic, bound the Federal Republic of Germany to the West while also laying the foundation for a concerted Western containment effort against the East.

The West Germans understood that rearmament was the price for the restoration of German sovereignty, although even incomplete after 1955, and for the commitment of the Western powers to support the reunifica-

tion of Germany. Reunification, however, was acceptable to the United States only if all of Germany enjoyed free elections and was included in a Western political sphere. Because the Soviet Union would not accept such terms, holding out instead the prospect of a united, neutral Germany, reunification was not possible as long as the Cold War lasted.

Rearmament was not popular in West Germany, however, and was severely contested. The German Social Democratic Party (SPD), the major voice of opposition, attacked rearmament and membership in NATO and WEU on the grounds that they would deepen the division of Germany, revive militarism, and create a framework for developing Germany's politics, economics, and society along conservative lines. The Social Democrats were encouraged by the famous Joseph Stalin notes of March 1952, which seemed to offer German reunification in return for German neutrality in the Cold War. They were thus deeply disappointed when the Bonn government and the Western powers dismissed the offer as a Soviet ploy to delay or derail the rearmament of West Germany and its attachment to the West. When NATO began deploying nuclear weapons on West German soil in the mid- and late 1950s, the SPD and its supporters strongly objected, arguing that Germany could become a nuclear battlefield. This issue was to burden U.S.-West German relations for decades.

The developing U.S.-West German partnership became especially durable because it went beyond geopolitical and military considerations and encompassed economic policy and cultural bonds as well. Washington impressed upon the West German government the need for free markets and liberalized trade and provided, through the Bretton Woods monetary system, generous liquidity with U.S. balance of payments deficits. The Bonn government, especially its minister of economics, Ludwig Erhard, also subscribed to the principles of a free market economy. The German commitment to low inflation rates, budgetary discipline, and the liberalization of domestic and foreign trade complemented U.S. policies. The Bretton Woods international monetary system came into full fruition at the end of the 1950s with the free convertibility of currencies and ushered in a period of growth, in which an overvalued dollar, based on fixed exchange rates, permitted an export boom in West Germany and Japan, which was further aided by the liberal trade practices of the United States and the economic effects of the Korean War. The rapid economic reconstruction of West Germany—the so-called "economic miracle"—secured its democracy, invigorated its diplomacy, and cemented its attachment to the Western alliance.

By the mid-1950s the Soviet Union was contained within the political and geographic sphere of influence it had gained at the end of World War II, and the Federal Republic of Germany was firmly anchored in the Western alliance. The U.S. policy of double containment had succeeded. The German Democratic Republic, which was also established in 1949 and became a member of the Warsaw Pact in 1955, was equally attached to its own alliance. Both German states became the most important and loyal members of their respective alliances. Any significant change in this status and in the relationship between the two German states was viewed in Washington with caution and suspicion. Thus, in the early 1970s, when West German Chancellor Willy Brandt initiated a more dynamic Ostpolitik, or in the 1980s, when "Genscherism" (named after West German foreign minister Hans-Dietrich Genscher) seemed to portend a looser German attachment to NATO, the United States reacted negatively. In the wake of détente and inter-German reconciliation, the United States finally recognized East Germany in 1974. Although this shift did not imply a fundamental improvement of U.S.-East German relations, it did reflect the fact that the United States, as well as East Germany and the Soviet Union, shared an interest in a stable if divided European political order.

The Waning of Double Containment

In the 1950s and 1960s many Germans became convinced that both the United States and the Soviet Union, as well as their respective allies, regarded the partition of Germany as an element of stability in Europe, and that neither had a genuine interest in overcoming it. The government of the Federal Republic of Germany was faced with a dilemma. On the one hand, it saw how the Cold War had divided the country, but it also feared, especially during the later years of Chancellor Adenauer's tenure in power (1949–1963), that a relaxation of tensions might lead to an East-West accommodation on the basis of the permanent and legitimized partition of Germany. The Germans were disappointed by the acquiescent U.S. response to the building of the Berlin Wall in 1961, which they viewed as a further indication that the United States was not interested in furthering German unification and was merely paying it lip service.

The U.S.-West German security compact was also eroding, aggravating the tensions that afflicted U.S. policy of double containment. In the 1960s, as the United States gradually became vulnerable to nuclear attack, largely the consequence of the buildup of Soviet intercontinental ballistic missiles (ICBMs), West Europeans lost some confidence that the United States would risk its own destruction for the sake of the alliance. Again, West Germany was the most affected, as it was dependent upon the United States for its security; legally and politically precluded from obtaining its own national nuclear deterrent; and handicapped by its unique political, geographical, and historical position in Europe and the alliance. Some in the Federal Republic saw themselves obliged to pay increasing political and economic costs for decreasing strategic benefits. This issue was at the core of the U.S.-West German frictions that developed in the 1960s over a wide range of issues in the area of security policies, which revolved essentially around the question of how the credibility of the U.S. nuclear commitment to Western Europe could be sustained now that the United States was running the risk of self-destruction.

Moreover, the administrations of Presidents John F. Kennedy and Lyndon B. Johnson adopted the doctrine of "flexible response," which required higher German defense expenditures while simultaneously decreasing the likelihood that Washington would initiate nuclear war to protect an ally. It was in this context that U.S. conventional troops on German soil took on their additional significance. Their presence enhanced the credibility of extended nuclear deterrence, both because the troops served a "hostage" function that ensured the prompt engagement of the United States in the early stages of a European conflict, and because they enlarged NATO's capacity for nonnuclear defense of the central front, thereby raising the nuclear threshold to a more credible level. Nonetheless, the Germans also began to tire (especially in the 1970s) of Washington's periodic threats to reduce American troops in Germany and viewed Washington's emphasis on the inherent deterrent value of conventional forces as a transparent attempt to compensate for diminishing American nuclear commitments.

The security partnership between the United States and West Germany became the backbone of NATO after France withdrew from NATO in 1966. Nevertheless, the security interests of the United States and West Germany were no longer as compatible as they had appeared to be in the 1950s. Bonn found itself diplomatically isolated when the Kennedy and Johnson administrations gave precedence to arms-control arrangements with the Soviet Union, such as the Nuclear Nonproliferation Treaty in 1968, and when President Johnson canceled the Multilateral Nuclear Force scheme, thwarting West Germany's aspirations for nuclear comanagement and creating significant domestic political problems for West German Chancellor Ludwig Erhard. While Washington sought arms control arrangements to stabilize the military and political balance, the West Germans resisted such action because some of the arrangements would have made East Germany a signatory and thus given it the de facto international recognition Bonn was determined to deny it.

U.S.-West German relations were clouded by personality conflicts. President Kennedy grew exasperated with West German remonstrations on the proper course of

Western policy on the German question; and President Johnson, preoccupied with Vietnam and uncomfortable with European affairs, proved a distant diplomatic partner. The West German government found it difficult to adjust to the new style of U.S. diplomacy, which was significantly different from that of the Eisenhower years.

In West Germany, the political landscape had changed as well. Beginning in the late 1950s, the Social Democrats jettisoned their Marxist ideology and by the early 1960s began to see themselves as the true defenders of NATO against the pro-Gaullist wing of the Christian Democrats. In 1966 they joined the Christian Democrats in the so-called grand coalition, which paved the way for SPD Chancellors Willy Brandt (1969–1974) and Helmut Schmidt (1974–1982), who governed with the Free Democratic Party in coalition governments. A partial but significant consensus emerged in West Germany on some major foreign policy issues, such as the importance of close relations with the United States, the future of Western European integration, and resignation on the question of German unification.

The disputes between Washington and Bonn were briefly alleviated by East-West détente during the administration of President Richard M. Nixon but reemerged sharply during the administrations of Carter and Reagan. The Germans grew resentful when they saw the East-West détente of the early and mid-1970s (which they had themselves supported with their innovative Ostpolitik) threatened by renewed East-West tensions in the late 1970s and throughout the 1980s. Bonn's expectations of enlarged and intensified human contacts between the Federal Republic and the German Democratic Republic were at least partly fulfilled, and the Germans hoped to secure and broaden these benefits, while both the United States and the Soviet Union were disappointed with the results of détente and suspended it periodically.

Throughout the 1970s and 1980s the conflicting pulls of Bonn's security interests, which tied them closely to the West, and détente interests, which demanded a dialogue with the East, put a severe strain on U.S.-German relations. The two countries responded to different geostrategic imperatives. The United States had the perspective of a global power, Germany that of a regional power. Washington saw itself challenged by Moscow everywhere and on everything—in Central and South America, in Southeast Asia, in Africa, in the nuclear arms race—whereas the Germans took a narrower and more limited view of the Soviet threat. They chafed at having to follow a confrontational American diplomacy and security policy when their own interests called for a more conciliatory stance. Washington's waffling on the neutron bomb project, its criticism of West German exports, nuclear technology, and, above all, the problem of

deploying new intermediate-range nuclear forces in Europe burdened the relationship. The West German chancellor was deeply concerned about the extensive build-up of Soviet intermediate-range nuclear missiles aimed at Western Europe, which he considered a political as well as military threat. The NATO "double-track" decision of December 1979—to begin deploying U.S. cruise missiles in several countries and Pershing II intermediate-range missiles in West Germany by 1983 while simultaneously seeking an arms control agreement with Moscow—put the U.S.-West German security relationship to a severe test. When the administration of President Ronald Reagan, in its first term, showed no interest in arms control arrangements with the Soviet Union, the West German government was left in the lurch, forced to implement the deployment of nuclear missiles in the face of heated opposition and mass demonstrations. The government of Chancellor Helmut Kohl saw deployment as a test of loyalty to the alliance, but the U.S.-West German security compact remained strained until 1987, when new Soviet leadership and the Reagan administration's interest in arms control made possible an agreement to eliminate intermediate-range missiles.

In general, the Germans began to sense that American security policies continued to serve Washington as an instrument to curtail German diplomatic flexibility. Although the fear of Soviet military aggression diminished substantially over the decades, the singular nuclear status of the Federal Republic—full of nuclear weapons, devoid of nuclear control—remained unchanged. Paradoxically, the advent of strategic parity between the United States and the Soviet Union (and their corresponding willingness to accept the principle of Mutual Assured Destruction and to stabilize their relations through arms control and détente) enlarged rather than narrowed the opportunities to use nuclear diplomacy for the purposes of alliance management. Their extensive nuclear arsenals obtained the two superpowers little political advantage in their direct contest with one another, but they provided powerful diplomatic leverage over countries, such as the Federal Republic, whose security depended on the United States and who needed to follow the strategic guidelines and deployment decisions of NATO.

The nuclearization of American diplomacy toward the Federal Republic was fraught with risk. It fueled neutralism in West Germany and thus eroded political support for the Western alliance; it inevitably emphasized the different security interests of the allies; and it underlined their nuclear or nonnuclear status. Nuclear diplomacy became divisive diplomacy.

In the 1980s the geostrategic complementarity that had in the early postwar decades connected the politics of containment with the strategies of deterrence was itself called into question. Containment and deterrence, each weakened by its own infirmities, appeared to be drifting apart. Like all its predecessors, the Reagan administration entered office reaffirming the American commitment to the historic policy of containment and the necessity of implementing it with an engaged American presence in Europe. At the same time, however, a tempting set of contradictory calculations began to form the administration's strategic thinking. There developed in Washington a sense that the American nuclear commitment to the defense of Europe had grown into more of a liability than an asset and that present and future American interests might be better served by a more detached and qualified strategic association with Europe, coupled with a political and economic tilt toward the Pacific and an appropriately supportive maritime strategy. Political containment, however, clearly required a deep and sustained American engagement in the affairs of Europe, whereas on the military-strategic level an equally plausible rationale seemed to call for a measure of disengagement from Europe and perhaps a return to unilateralism.

The incipient unilateralism that some West Germans saw in the Reagan administration's plans for the Strategic Defense Initiative (SDI) was another principal source of tension and consternation. The prospect of placing a technologically complex defensive shield over the United States implied to some a U.S. disengagement from Europe. Although dutiful in its support of SDI, the Kohl government saw in the program the reversal of the principle of extended deterrence, a major obstacle to East-West arms control and détente, and, in any event, a distraction from more pressing problems. After government spokespeople had initially voiced strong opposition to SDI, the Bonn government avoided airing its concerns in public. Chancellor Kohl had gained office in 1982 at least in part with the promise of improved U.S.-West German relations, which he sought to protect from yet another divisive issue.

Behind the specific disputes over weapons and strategies lay the larger question of whether the security of the United States would remain linked to the security of West Germany and Western Europe as a whole. The ease with which President Reagan was ready to trade away central and historic elements of NATO strategy at the Reykjavík summit in 1986 was deeply worrisome to Western Europe, especially to West Germany. It demonstrated to some West Germans how their country had been excluded from consultations, how little their basic security concerns seemed to matter to the U.S. president, how relatively insignificant the Euro-strategic nuclear issue was to the East-West military balance, and how centrally important it was to the political balance in Europe.

Economic Tensions

Relations between the United States and West Germany also suffered over the decades from a slow but steady erosion in the area of economics. Beginning in the 1960s, chronic frictions developed over monetary policy since the United States and Germany interpreted the ground rules of the Bretton Woods international monetary system in different ways. The United States enjoyed a privileged position in the system, which allowed it to create money without the normal restraints on countries with chronic balance-of-payments deficits. The German position was ambivalent. On the one hand, West Germans continued to enjoy the benefits of an undervalued and thus export-boosting deutsche Mark (DM), which had helped them achieve their so-called economic miracle in the 1950s. The West Germans were becoming prosperous under the auspices of the international monetary system, accumulated large foreign currency reserves through substantial and chronic balance-of-payments surpluses, and gradually developed an attitude about their economic prowess amounting to a form of "economic nationalism." On the other hand, the fixed-parity and free-convertibility principles of the Bretton Woods regime opened West Germany to massive capital inflows that threatened domestic price stability—the central principle of West Germany's economic culture—and reduced the effectiveness of West Germany's counter-cyclical fiscal and monetary policies. Throughout the 1960s and early 1970s, huge monetary movements forced the West German central bank to create new money, although there was no corresponding contraction of the money supply in the United States, the major originating country. From the West German perspective, the adjustment process of the Bretton Woods system became cumbersome. It placed the major burden of dealing with inflation on surplus countries rather than deficit countries and curtailed the West Germans' capacity to retain a measure of national independence on issues that they regarded as vital to their economic welfare.

Nevertheless, the West Germans shied away from the responsibility of bringing down Bretton Woods; indeed they helped support it. The myth that Bretton Woods still worked could be sustained only because the West German Bundesbank stopped converting dollars into gold and otherwise refrained from shaking the regime, as the French did with great relish. The United States, in turn, was induced by its chronic balance-of-payments deficits to apply strong pressures on the Federal Republic to carry a larger burden of NATO's defense costs. What developed was a relationship of mutual dependence. The United States supplied the West Germans with security benefits, which Washington considered a major source of its balance-of-payments problem, and insisted on repayment in the form of "offset" payments, military purchases in the United States, and other burden-sharing arrangements within NATO.

But even though West Germany made greater efforts in the 1960s and early 1970s than any other country to cushion the monetary system against constant onslaughts of the dollar, in effect helping to postpone the demise of Bretton Woods, differences between Bonn and Washington over monetary matters were serious and fundamentally irreconcilable, for they stemmed from opposing views of what constituted responsible monetary practices. Following the closing of the "gold window" by the Nixon administration in 1971 and the elimination of the fixed-rate exchange mechanism of the international monetary system, the fluctuations of exchange rates turned out to be much more severe than anticipated, aggravated by the oil-price shock of 1973–1974. Money markets responded to the differences between U.S. and West German fiscal and budgetary policies, and the deutsche Mark was becoming the "counterpart-currency" of the dollar. For decades, a strong deutsche Mark went hand in hand with a weak dollar, and vice versa; rarely did the currencies rise or fall together. From the European perspective, the dollar continued to play a volatile and disruptive role. In 1978 German Chancellor Helmut Schmidt and French President Valéry Giscard d'Estaing created the European Monetary System, which, aside from moving the European Community closer to monetary union, was also intended to serve as a monetary shield against Washington's policy of benign neglect toward the dollar.

Fundamentally, the shift of U.S. policies toward Europe and the European Community in the 1970s, initiated by the Nixon administration and carried through by the administrations of Presidents Gerald Ford and Jimmy Carter, signaled the abrogation of an implicit but important postwar transatlantic compact. The essence of this compact was that the United States, secure in its hegemonic economic and monetary position, would be willing to make economic sacrifices in return for political privileges. During the 1970s both sides pushed for altering the postwar economic and political framework. The growing monetary strength of Europe and Japan made the Bretton Woods arrangement seem obsolete, and the United States, rather than curtail its domestic economic autonomy, abandoned Bretton Woods for its own reasons.

The world monetary crises of the early 1970s revolved essentially around the economic, strategic, and political role of the United States in world affairs and what part the European allies, especially Germany, were willing and able to continue financing. By the late 1970s the changes in the basic postwar understanding between the United States and Germany concerning security policies and arms control, monetary policies, and East-West détente had led to a significant erosion of the U.S.-West German partnership, inducing Bonn to intensify its European ties and seek an even closer Franco-German partnership.

The situation did not improve in the 1980s. The economic partners of the United States criticized high U.S. interest rates as a way to attract foreign capital, allowing U.S. overconsumption, military overextension, and budgetary irresponsibility. The West Germans began to attribute their own economic problems of the early 1980s, which included zero growth, rising unemployment, a current-account deficit, and a weak deutsche Mark, to U.S. economic policies, arguing in essence that the United States was living beyond its means.

Schmidt's successor, Helmut Kohl, and the new center-right coalition over which he presided, entertained the same misgivings about U.S. economic policy, although they expressed them less forcefully. The United States, in turn, viewed the West German preoccupation with monetary stability and fiscal responsibility as an obstinate and irrational economic obsession, detrimental to U.S. national interests and to the health of the global economy at large. The West Germans, noting that Washington refused to raise taxes and sought to pass on to its economic partners the burdens of U.S. profligacy, shied away from playing the role of locomotive, which had weakened the West German economy during the Carter years. Bonn also resisted the obligation to prop up exchange rates with massive interventions, fearing adverse consequences for West Germany's price stability and for the probity of the West German central bank.

In contrast to monetary issues, trade issues had only rarely burdened U.S.-West German economic relations directly, yet they began to be an indirect irritant during the administration of President George Bush, when the constant and acrimonious disputes between the European Community and the United States during the Uruguay Round of the General Agreement on Tariffs and Trade (GATT) negotiations led Washington to seek West German help, especially in dealing with France, placing Bonn in an uncomfortable diplomatic position.

The End of the Cold War and German Reunification

The revolutionary European events of 1989–1990 led quickly to German reunification. The fall of the Berlin Wall in November 1989 was followed by monetary union, political union within the constitutional framework of the Federal Republic's Basic Law, and all-German elections in December 1990. German unity was accomplished less by the focused diplomatic efforts of Bonn or Washington than by the disintegration of the Soviet empire, Moscow's decision to condone the emergence of a new Europe without resort to arms, and the sudden and unstoppable surge of the East Germans' discontent and anger in the streets of Leipzig. Nonetheless, the achievement of German unity and the collapse of the Soviet empire removed a large burden from the German-U.S. relationship. After an initial period of hesitation, Washington lent full political and diplomatic support to the cause of German unity, putting to rest long-standing German concerns about the sincerity and reliability of the U.S. commitment to support it. The intricate negotiations that accompanied the process of reunification—the internal and external ones between the two German states and the four postwar occupying powers—clearly demonstrated that Bonn could rely primarily on the support of Washington and the assent of Moscow, both of which (but especially Moscow) needed to be persuaded that it was an isolated Germany, not a united one, that had in the past inflicted such misfortunes on others and on itself. The dissolution of the Warsaw Pact and the Soviet Union dramatically underlined how the threat to German security had waned, how the salience of nuclear and conventional deterrence had diminished, and how the transatlantic security connection apparently had become less important. Nonetheless, NATO's historic function of containing not only the Soviet Union but also Germany was again revealed with a somewhat embarrassing clarity during negotiations leading to German unification: precisely because NATO had lost its military-strategic purpose, its political purpose of binding Germany to the West moved to the foreground. The West sought to make membership of a united Germany in NATO palatable to Moscow and the Eastern European capitals by emphasizing the common interest of all Europeans, East and West, to see a united Germany securely anchored and contained in an integrative security system. The reassurance that NATO had always extended to its members—to guarantee security not only for Germany but also from Germany—was now in effect also offered to the former opponents in the East. After strong initial opposition, Moscow accepted the Western premise, assented to the continuing membership of Germany in NATO and thus removed the last obstacle to German reunification.

From the perspective of the United States, the continuing membership of Germany in NATO became the indispensable transatlantic link that assured an institutionalized U.S. presence in Europe. NATO remained the symbol of the transatlantic compact and held out the hope that the loss of Moscow's influence in Eastern Europe did not mean a corresponding loss of Washington's influence in Western Europe. NATO, however, quickly found itself having to cope with the problems that afflicted Europe in the post-containment era, especially in its inability to fashion an effective, coordinated response to the breakup of Yugoslavia. The new threats to security in Europe, driven by unresolved historic grievances, ethnic and religious strife, and bellicose nationalism, were not responsive to the traditional security principle of deterrence, the governing strategic posture during the Cold War, but required the potential intervention (or at least interposition) of troops. The German-American connection within NATO was among those that became frayed in dealing with the conflicts in the former Yugoslavia. Following what the United States considered a premature German recognition of Slovenia and Croatia, the Germans retreated to a passive position, justifying their inaction with constitutional prohibitions and the burdens of past German misdeeds.

By the time the Clinton administration entered office in early 1993, it appeared as if German-American relations were in some kind of suspended state, each side preoccupied with internal problems, unprepared to engage the other in a common effort to deal with the issues of the new Europe or to lend to NATO the vitality that only its two most important members could supply. There were muted but deep disagreements over the future membership of NATO, which the United States preferred to remain limited, but which the Germans were ready to extend to central and east European countries. The administration of President Bill Clinton initially was very wary, with its eye to the possible effect it might have of feeding the ultranationalist movement in Russia. The initial decision made at the January 1994 NATO summit was to create the Partnership for Peace program as something of a compromise, establishing military cooperation with former Warsaw Pact states, but stopping well short of actual NATO membership. Above all, the Germans perceived in the Clinton administration, driven by economic and domestic political considerations and a readiness to leave such intractable problems as Bosnia and Herzegovina in European hands, a disquieting orientation toward the Pacific and away from Europe.

Following the July 1994 Group of Seven (G-7) summit in Naples, Italy, Clinton visited Germany. His visit coincided with two events that had profound implications for Germany's changing international role. One was the deactivation of the final U.S. military brigade in Berlin. After almost fifty years, and multiple crises, the U.S. military presence in Berlin had ended. The second critical event was the ruling by the German Supreme Court that it was constitutional for Germany to deploy its troops beyond Europe as part of UN peacekeeping forces. While only an extremely liberal interpretation of the ruling could draw precedent for anything other than participation in multilateral peacekeeping forces, it nevertheless marked a major change in Germany's international role.

The Transformation of the German-American Partnership

The problems that burdened U.S.-German relations over the decades following World War II were the result both of objective conditions and changing subjective attitudes. By the 1990s only older Germans had personal recollections of U.S. diplomacy in the postwar period and of the remarkable rapport between U.S. and German policymakers in the late 1940s and throughout the 1950s. The subsequent generation of Germans was informed by a less benevolent image of the United States. Whereas the Germans had managed to reach a centrist position on most foreign policy issues, the United States was moving away from a significant measure of consensus in the 1950s toward a pronounced fragmentation in the subsequent decades. The Vietnam War, economic and political pressures, and demographic shifts rent the bipartisan base of U.S. foreign policy and sharpened the divergence of viewpoints between the United States and West Germany. But changing German perceptions of the United States were not primarily the result of subjective change in successive generations. Beyond the question of image, appearance, and "generation gaps," a new reality emerged. By the 1960s and 1970s it had became apparent that German and U.S. economic, monetary, military-strategic, and political interests, while hardly conflictual, were no longer as congruent as they had been earlier. Both countries were committed to a democratic political order, but their dissimilar socioeconomic conventions, historical experiences, and national temperaments inclined them toward divergent domestic and foreign policies. The Germans (as well as other Western Europeans) had become more self-confident and more critical of their transatlantic partner. This attitude was reciprocated in the United States, where a certain weariness with the burdens of alliance set in, accelerated by the end of the Cold War and the diminished security threat to the West.

In the 1990s there remained in both Germany and the United States a large measure of goodwill toward one another, but the translation of these sentiments into practical policies required of both sides a larger understanding of the deeper geostrategic tides that had sustained the partnership between the United States and Germany in the postwar era. Should the United States perceive a self-equilibrating European order, which would permit a less intense U.S. engagement, and should the enlarged Federal Republic of Germany perceive its diplomatic fortunes as less dependent on the United States, the common interests that sustained U.S.-German relations from the end of World War II to the end of the Cold War would diminish and rest on less secure foundations.

WOLFRAM F. HANRIEDER

See also Adenauer, Konrad; Austria; Berlin; Brandt, Willy; Bretton Woods System; Cold War; Containment; Dawes Plan; Détente; Eastern Europe; Hegemony; Hitler, Adolf; Holocaust; Kohl, Helmut; Marshall Plan; Monroe Doctrine; Morgenthau Plan; North Atlantic Treaty Organization; Russia and the Soviet Union; Samoa, American; Schmidt, Helmut; Strategic Defense Initiative; Versailles Treaty of 1919; World War I; World War II

FURTHER READING

Calleo, David. *The German Problem Reconsidered: Germany and the World Order, 1870 to the Present.* New York, 1978.
Dehio, Ludwig. *Germany and World Politics in the Twentieth Century.* New York, 1959.
Feis, Herbert. *The Diplomacy of the Dollar, First Era, 1919–1932.* New York, 1966.
Friedländer, Saul. *Prelude to Downfall: Hitler and the United States, 1939–1941.* New York, 1967.
Gatzke, Hans W. *Germany and the United States. A "Special Relationship?"* Cambridge, Mass., 1980.
Gimbel, John. *The American Occupation of Germany: Politics and the Military, 1945–1949.* Stanford, Calif., 1968.
Hanrieder, Wolfram F. *Germany, America, Europe: Forty Years of German Foreign Policy,* 2nd ed. New Haven, Conn., 1991.
Jonas, Manfred. *The United States and Germany: A Diplomatic History.* Ithaca, N.Y, 1984.
May, Ernest R. *The World War and American Isolation, 1914–1917.* Cambridge, Mass., 1959.
Nelson, Keith L. *Victors Divided: America and the Allies in Germany, 1918–1923.* Berkeley, Calif., 1975.
Ninkovich, Frank. *Germany and the United States: The Transformation of the German Question Since 1945.* New York, 1995.
Offner, Arnold A. *American Appeasement: United States Foreign Policy and Germany, 1933–1938.* Cambridge, Mass., 1969.
Trommler, Frank, and Joseph McVeigh, eds. *America and the Germans: An Assessment of a Three-Hundred-Year History.* 2 vols. Philadelphia, Pa., 1985.

GHANA

A coastal country in Western Africa that borders Côte d'Ivoire, Togo, Burkina Faso, and the Gulf of Guinea. Prior to its independence in 1957, Ghana was known as the Gold Coast, having earned that name as a source for gold during the sixteenth century. The most prominent of the early polities of Ghana was the Asante or Ashanti kingdom, which dates back to roughly 1680. The Asante quickly expanded and established themselves as major suppliers of slaves during the eighteenth and early nineteenth centuries. The British, the eventual colonizers of Ghana, moved into the area primarily to suppress the slave trade. After several decades of skirmishes, the British established firm control over the Asante kingdom in 1876 and the colony of the Gold Coast began to assume its final form.

Ghana began to move toward independence after World War II under the leadership of Kwame Nkrumah, who had attended college in the United States and earned a law degree in England. Upon returning to Ghana, he founded the Convention People's Party (CPP), and in 1951 the CPP won the Gold Coast elections, and Nkrumah was asked by the British to form a cabinet. By 1954 Ghana was granted home rule, independence was formally gained in 1957, and in 1960 Nkrumah was elected its first president.

Whereas other African leaders of his generation tended to be more sanguine about U.S. intentions, Nkrumah took a much more cautious and at times hostile view. He was among the most ardent and active African leaders in the global Third World and Nonaligned movements. He also was a strong advocate of Pan Africanism. In 1966, however, Nkrumah was deposed in a military coup while he was on a state visit to the People's Republic of China, in part because of his increasingly repressive and corrupt rule. The main problems between the United States and Ghana, both under Nkrumah and other Ghanaian leaders, have revolved around the tendency of Ghanaian governments to seek active roles in the Nonaligned and Pan Africanist movements. The earliest examples of such conflicts developed before Ghana even attained its independence. In 1956 there was extensive correspondence between the government of Prime Minister Nkrumah and President Dwight D. Eisenhower over the guest list of the Ghanaian independence ceremony. Specifically, the United States tried its utmost to dissuade Ghana from inviting representatives of communist countries to the program. The United States also expressed displeasure over the fact that the People's Republic of China had been invited while Taiwan was ignored. In response to U.S. criticism, Nkrumah's government repeatedly stated that as a nonaligned country, Ghana would not involve itself in East-West rivalries. Another concern for the Eisenhower administration was the fact that U.S. civil rights leader Martin Luther King, Jr., was an honored guest at the independence ceremony along with Vice President Richard Nixon. This was in keeping with Nkrumah's Pan Africanist philosophy and also reflected his personal knowledge of segregation and discrimination within the United States.

During the administration of President John F. Kennedy, U.S. intervention in the Belgian Congo and the assassination of Patrice Lumumba drew severe criticism from Ghana. Although Nkrumah openly stated that he did not want the new government in the Congo to be too heavily influenced by the Eastern Bloc, he was apparently comfortable enough with the government to lend it his support and to send in troops like a number of other African nations did to aid Lumumba. The Ghanaians saw the combined U.S.-European intervention as a worrisome, even if temporary, resurgence of colonialism.

In the thirteen years following Nkrumah's rule, Ghana went through a number of other military coups, culminating in the 1979 coup led by Lieutenant Jerry Rawlings, whose government executed many of its leading opponents, precipitating criticisms from, and tensions with, the administration of President Jimmy Carter. With but brief intervals, Rawlings continued to rule Ghana into the mid-1990s, and human rights issues were a source of tension between the United States and Ghana throughout the decade.

ANTHONY Q. CHEESEBORO

See also Africa; Nonaligned Movement

FURTHER READING

Fage, J. D. *A History of West Africa*. Cambridge, Mass., 1969.
Jackson, Robert H., and Carl G. Rosberg. *Personal Rule in Black Africa: Prince, Autocrat, Prophet, Tyrant*. Los Angeles, Calif., 1982.
Jeffries, Richard. *Ghana: The Political Economy of Personal Rule* in *Contemporary West African States*, edited by Donald O'Brien, John Dunn, and Richard Rathbone. Cambridge, Mass., 1989.
Marable, Manning. *African and Caribbean Politics: From Kwame Nkrumah to the Grenada Revolution*. London, 1987.
U.S. Department of State. *Foreign Relations of the United States*. "Africa." Edited by Stanley Snaloff. 89th Cong., 2nd sess. Washington, D.C.: Government Printing Office, 1989.

GHENT, TREATY OF
(1814)

Agreement between Great Britain and the United States that ended the War of 1812. Sometimes called the Peace of Christmas Eve, because it was signed on 24 December, the treaty was negotiated in Ghent, Belgium, by a U.S. commission consisting of John Quincy Adams, Henry Clay, Albert Gallatin, James A. Bayard, and Jonathan Russell and a British delegation consisting of William Adams, Admiral James Gambier, and Henry Goulburn. Although Great Britain held the military advantage during the negotiations, the British were exhausted by their long wars with France and preoccupied with the Congress of Vienna; their envoys at Ghent seemed no match for the more talented U.S. delegation, agreeing to a peace that did not require the United States to surrender either honor or territory. The treaty made no reference to the Orders in Council, impressment of seamen, or any of the other maritime issues over which the United States had declared war in 1812, and it did not mention any of the territorial concessions and other demands made by Great Britain at the beginning of the negotiations. It simply restored the conditions that had prevailed prior to the war (status quo ante bellum). Both sides agreed to return all conquered territory, to establish peace with the Native American tribes and restore all rights and privileges the tribes had enjoyed in 1811, and to strive to end the slave trade, which Great Britain had outlawed in 1807 and the United States in 1808. The treaty also established three commissions to resolve disputes over portions of the U.S.-Canada boundary. The Treaty of Ghent helped legitimize the United States as a nation. Although the War of 1812 had ended in a draw, it also demonstrated that the young republic would fight to defend its rights. On 11 February 1815 the Senate unanimously approved the treaty.

DONALD R. HICKEY

See also Adams, John Quincy; Clay, Henry; Gallatin, Albert; Great Britain; Impressment; War of 1812

FURTHER READING

Engelman, Fred L. *The Peace of Christmas Eve.* New York, 1962.
Perkins, Bradford. *Castlereagh and Adams: England and the United States, 1812–1823.* Berkeley, Calif., 1964.
Updyke, Frank A. *The Diplomacy of the War of 1812.* Baltimore, Md., 1915.

GIBSON, HUGH SIMONS

(*b.* 16 August 1883; *d.* 12 December 1954)

Senior career diplomat active in humanitarian relief efforts and pre-World War II disarmament efforts. Born in Los Angeles, Gibson studied with private tutors before completing academic work in 1907 at the École Libre des Sciences Politiques in Paris. His European education and personal knowledge of the Continent prepared him for a forty-five-year diplomatic career, much of it spent in Europe. Beginning in 1908 Gibson served in diplomatic posts across Europe and the Americas, from Great Britain, Belgium, Luxembourg, Switzerland, and Poland to Honduras, Cuba, the Dominican Republic, and Brazil.

Gibson's greatest contributions to U.S. diplomacy were made in Europe. He was the U.S. representative to the Preparatory Commission for Disarmament Conference (1926–1927), an international body whose role was to plan for general disarmament discussions. In 1927 he was appointed ambassador to Belgium (until 1933) and in the same year headed the U.S. delegation at the Geneva Conference for Limitation of Naval Armaments, a follow-up to the Washington Naval Conference of 1921–1922. Gibson's diplomacy helped to keep talks going despite the discord among the three major naval powers—Great Britain, Japan, and the United States. During the presidency of Herbert Hoover (1929–1933), Gibson attempted to revive naval arms negotiations with the president's ardent backing. He proposed a "yardstick" approach for disarmament that would have measured different categories of ships by taking into account such factors as the ages of the ships and gun calibers rather than the tonnage ratios approach adopted at the Washington Conference. This approach reopened the way to arms discussions, but the effort was unsuccessful, in part because of continuing disagreement over how to measure different types of cruisers. Later efforts at the London Naval Conference in 1930 and at the General Disarmament Conference at Geneva in the early 1930s, where Gibson again played key roles, failed to advance disarmament.

Gibson achieved better results with relief programs. Early in World War I, while posted in Brussels, he helped organize the Commission for Relief in Belgium. After the war he assisted Herbert Hoover as director general in the American Relief Administration, aiding destitute people across Europe who might otherwise have been attracted to the appeals of revolutionaries. As part of his diplomatic service in Poland (1919–1924), Gibson assisted with a variety of relief programs. During World War II he was director general for Europe of the Commission for Polish Relief and the Commission for Relief in Belgium. In his last diplomatic assignment, from 1952 until his death in 1954, Gibson directed the Intergovernmental Committee for the Movement of Migrants from Europe.

STEPHEN KNEESHAW

See also Belgium; Humanitarian Intervention and Relief; London Naval Conferences of 1930 and 1935–1936; Poland; Washington Conference on the Limitation of Armaments

FURTHER READING

Ellis, L. Ethan. *Republican Foreign Policy, 1921–1933.* New Brunswick, N.J., 1968.
Gibson, Hugh. *The Road to Foreign Policy.* Garden City, N.Y., 1944.
Hall, Christopher. *Britain, America, and Arms Control, 1921–1937.* New York, 1987.
Hoover, Herbert, and Hugh Gibson. *The Problems of Lasting Peace.* Garden City, N.Y., 1942.

GLOBAL WARMING

See Environment

GOLD STANDARD

The international financial and balance of payments adjustment system that prevailed in the major industrialized countries in the period before World War I. The United States was on the gold standard after 1879. Populists such as William Jennings Bryan opposed this system because it implied a considerably tighter monetary policy than wanted by his rural supporters, most of whom were debtors. The gold standard was suspended at the beginning of World War I, and most exchange rates floated in the immediate postwar period. The United States returned to gold in 1922, as did the United Kingdom in 1925. By 1928 forty-five countries were on gold, but they started to leave as the Great Depression began, in order to gain more control over domestic monetary policy.

Under the classical gold standard system, national governments promised to buy or sell gold at a fixed price, the relative price of gold thereby determining par exchange rates. Market exchange rates could move only within a narrow band, which was determined by the costs of shipping gold between national financial centers. This cost was about 0.6 percent of the value of the gold for London and New York. All payments, deficits, and surpluses were settled in gold, meaning that deficit countries lost gold and surplus countries increased their gold holdings. Because gold was also the backing for the local currency, a country with a balance of payments deficit was supposed to reduce its money supply, and a country with a surplus to allow its money supply to grow. Monetary contraction in deficit countries and a parallel monetary expansion in the surplus countries was supposed to produce automatic payments adjustment, that is, a movement from disequilibrium back to payments equilibrium. In the deficit country a declining money supply would raise interest rates, attracting capital inflows from abroad and would reduce both prices and income growth, which would improve trade account performance. This balance of payments adjustment mechanism was first described by David Hume in 1752 and is known as the specie flow process, where specie is money that consists of precious metal. The system was subject to shocks from the gold mining industry, such as major discoveries of new ore, which could be inflationary. The gold standard failed in the 1930s, in part because the surplus countries refused to play by the rules—they refused to allow their money supplies to expand as the system required, which produced extreme deflationary pressures on the deficit countries.

The gold-exchange standard of the post–World War II era was quite different from the classical gold standard. The dollar was tied to gold, and the United States stood willing to sell gold to foreign central banks at that dollar price, but there was no commitment to sell to private parties and no commitment to manage monetary policy in response to disequilibriums in the balance of payments. In August 1971 President Richard M. Nixon suspended the gold exchange standard because of heavy gold losses by the United States. There was some discussion of returning to the classical gold standard in the late 1970s and early 1980s, but interest in such a return to gold faded quickly.

ROBERT M. DUNN, JR.

See also Balance of Payments and Balance of Trade; Bretton Woods System; Nixon, Richard Milhous; Roosevelt, Franklin Delano

FURTHER READING

Eichengreen, Barry, ed. *The Gold Standard in Theory and History.* New York, 1985.

Gowa, Joanne. *Closing the Gold Window: Domestic Politics and the End of Bretton Woods.* Ithaca, N.Y., 1983.

Triffin, Robert. "The Myths and Realities of the So-Called Gold Standard." In Robert Triffin, ed., *Our International Monetary System: Yesterday, Today, and Tomorrow.* New York, 1968.

GOLDWATER, BARRY

(*b.* 1 January 1909)

Outspoken conservative U.S. senator (1953–1965, 1969–1987) and Republican presidential candidate (1964) noted for his strong anticommunist views. Born in Phoenix, Arizona, Goldwater became a businessman and a staunch anti–New Deal conservative. First elected to the U.S. Senate in 1952, he received the Republican nomination for the presidency in 1964 but lost by a wide margin to the Democratic candidate, President Lyndon B. Johnson. Goldwater championed toughness against international communism, supporting direct U.S. involvement in the 1961 Bay of Pigs operation in Cuba and urging an offensive military commitment in Vietnam. Democrats attacked him as a "radical right" hawk who was willing to drop "small" tactical nuclear weapons in Vietnam, claims that scared voters and contributed to his 1964 electoral defeat. Goldwater was a long-standing critic of foreign aid programs and of the United Nations. In the 1970s, heading the Senate Select Committee on Intelligence, he criticized congressional liberals for curbing the activities of the Central Intelligence Agency (CIA) and thus diminishing U.S. capabilities abroad. In 1984 he condemned the illegal mining of Nicaraguan harbors by President Ronald Reagan's administration as a violation of the trust between the executive and the legislative branches. Goldwater's activist anticommunism always undergirded his political positions, but he was always a staunch believer in adhering to the principles enunciated in the Constitution. His critics thought him reckless, but they respected his personal integrity.

THOMAS W. ZEILER

See also Bay of Pigs Invasion; Central Intelligence Agency; Nicaragua; Republican Party; Vietnam War

FURTHER READING

Goldwater, Barry. *The Conscience of a Conservative.* New York, 1960.

———, and Jack Casserly. *Goldwater.* New York, 1988.

McDowell, Edwin. *Barry Goldwater: Portrait of an Arizonan.* Chicago, 1964.

GOOD NEIGHBOR POLICY

One of the main features of President Franklin D. Roosevelt's Latin American policy, designed to improve the image and relations of the United States in the region and especially to ameliorate the Latin American environment for trade and investment after decades of accumulated ill-will. The concept of the "good neighbor" had been employed earlier by such prominent statesmen as Elihu Root, Charles Evans Hughes, and President Herbert Hoover. The development and significance of Roosevelt's Good Neighbor Policy can only be understood against the background of the previous century of U.S. relations with Latin America. Prior to the articulation of the notion of a Good Neighbor approach to inter-American relations, U.S. foreign policy toward Latin America was most commonly associated with the Monroe Doctrine, the various corollaries to that doctrine, and the U.S. military interventions that occurred in the Caribbean and Central America from the administration of Theodore Roosevelt (1901–1909) through the 1920s. U.S.-Latin American policy in the nineteenth and early twentieth centuries derived from the twin sources of the Monroe Doctrine and the Pan-American ideas of hemispheric alliances that originated with Simón Bolívar, Latin American statesman and revolutionary leader. The Monroe Doctrine, initially defensive in orientation, acquired a more aggressive reputation over the course of the nineteenth century through the Olney Doctrine of 1895 during the Venezuelan crisis and the police power notion of the Roosevelt Corollary of 1904. At the same time, however, the United States took the lead after 1889 in establishing the Pan-American institutions that provided the context within which a Good Neighbor concept could emerge in the 1930s. Military intervention, as well as the dollar diplomacy that emerged during the late Roosevelt and William H. Taft presidencies, had by the 1920s led to an increasingly tense environment in inter-American relations, which made essential a shift in policy away from interventionism and toward a Good Neighbor Policy.

The first decisive step was the official repudiation of the linkage between the Monroe Doctrine and the Roosevelt Corollary. The initiative to separate the two came late in Calvin Coolidge's presidency. The effort was directly linked to the spirit of the Kellogg-Briand Pact of 1928, which renounced war as an instrument of policy. However impracticable that pact later became, the United States had initiated it, and all of the Latin American countries except Argentina, Uruguay, and El Salvador were signatories to the agreement. The contradictions between the interventionism of the Roosevelt Corollary and adherence to the Kellogg-Briand Pact were evident to the Coolidge administration. As a result, Undersecretary of State J. Reuben Clark, Jr., prepared a memorandum in which he concluded that the Roosevelt Corollary was not justified under the Monroe Doctrine. The Hoover administration reluctantly agreed to the publication of Clark's *Memorandum on the Monroe Doctrine* and

during 1929 negotiated a series of inter-American treaties of conciliation and arbitration. As president, Hoover also moved in the direction of reform, although there remains debate among scholars over the extent of the debt Franklin Roosevelt owed his predecessors. The Clark Memorandum, combined with the arbitration treaties, Hoover's goodwill tour of Latin America between his election and inaugural, and his withdrawal of U.S. troops from Nicaragua and Haiti all improved relations with the other Latin American republics but support for tariff protectionism undermined much of that early goodwill.

As early as the 1928 presidential campaign, Franklin Roosevelt critically assessed the dollar diplomacy and interventionist aspects of U.S.-Latin American policy and suggested that U.S. intervention in the affairs of the other American republics should take place only in concert with the other regional powers. Roosevelt identified several objectives that would feature prominently in his administration: the desire to improve the U.S. image in Latin America; the linkage between that improved relationship and expanded economic relations; a willingness to work as part of the inter-American system, rather than unilaterally; and a shift away from involvement in the internal affairs of the other American republics. In his first inaugural address in March 1933, President Roosevelt expressed the sentiments that formed the basis of the Good Neighbor Policy: "I would dedicate this nation to the policy of the good neighbor—the neighbor who respects his obligations and respects the sanctity of his agreements in and with a world of neighbors." In that address, as well as in the policies pursued subsequently by his administration, Roosevelt stressed the reciprocal nature of U.S. policy, whether in political, economic, or military affairs.

The Roosevelt administration applied the Good Neighbor Policy in a number of instances. The most consistent application of the policy during the 1930s and World War II years was the discontinuation of military intervention. The administration went further than any of its predecessors in formally accepting the principle of nonintervention in the internal affairs of the other American states. Secretary of State Cordell Hull signed the Convention on the Rights and Duties of States concluded at the Montevideo conference in 1933 as well as the protocol on nonintervention drafted at the 1936 Inter-American Conference in Buenos Aires. The official U.S. interpretation of these conventions is critical to an understanding of what the Roosevelt administration meant by the "good neighbor" and nonintervention. At no time did the administration yield its right to protect its nationals and U.S. corporations operating in Latin America, and that dimension was as important to Latin Americans as direct military intervention. To U.S. officials, "intervention" meant the use of armed force; "internal affairs" meant the domestic politics of the American states; and "directly or indirectly" meant only military, not diplomatic, pressure.

Developments in Cuba in the 1930s provided one example of the gradual shift in U.S. policy, but it was one replete with ambiguities. Since the first decade of the century, the United States had exercised a virtual protectorate over Cuba under the terms of the Platt Amendment (1901), which provided the United States with both a right and an obligation to maintain Cuban sovereignty, life, property, and individual liberty. In 1933 Cuba's apparent stability was threatened by the rise of more effective political opposition after years of strong-arm rule by the repressive Gerardo Machado (1924–1933). In August 1933 President Roosevelt approved the recommendation of his friend and personal representative in Havana, Sumner Welles, that Machado had to be compelled to resign. Although there was no U.S. military intervention to effect that objective, Machado departed and was replaced by a short-lived government under Carlos Manuel de Céspedes, Welles's choice for president. When a combination of university students and professors, workers, and young military officers led by Ramón Grau San Martín quickly ousted Céspedes, Welles and Roosevelt refused to extend recognition, despite vigorous criticism in the Latin American press and diplomatic community that the United States was interfering in Cuban domestic politics. The issue became moot when a sergeants' revolt overthrew Grau in 1934 and established the rule of Fulgencio Batista, which continued until he was overthrown in 1959 by Fidel Castro. The Roosevelt administration was highly vulnerable to critical cries of interventionism throughout the Cuban episode. The United States did not land troops, but U.S. naval forces remained in Cuban waters during much of the crisis.

Nevertheless, throughout the Roosevelt years the United States did not deploy troops to Latin America to resolve diplomatic disputes, alter governments, change Latin American government policies, or combat nationalism. To some members of the private U.S. business sector, this new direction of policy was undesirable, even unacceptable, especially to oil company officials whose properties were nationalized in Bolivia in 1937 and in Mexico in 1938. For several years Venezuela appeared to be moving in a similar direction but effective diplomacy curtailed the initiative. The Bolivian and Mexican nationalizations were successful, in part because the United States accepted the principle of nationalization with adequate compensation but also because the Roosevelt administration sought the cooperation of other hemispheric nations in the late 1930s as Europe and Asia disintegrated into world war.

It is always difficult to assess the relative importance of single individuals in the development of a foreign policy. In the case of the Good Neighbor Policy, there is little

dispute that Franklin Roosevelt himself, as president, provided critical leadership. Although Secretary of State Hull's relationship with the president was never close, Hull provided important pressure on the administration to move toward trade liberalization as one means to avert international conflict. His influence was evident in the 1934 Reciprocal Trade Agreements Act, which enabled the administration to negotiate a number of such agreements in Latin America. After the failure of his interventionist stance in Cuba, Welles became one of the more conciliatory and respected voices in Latin American affairs, first as assistant secretary of state and then as undersecretary. Laurence Duggan, chief of the Department of State's Latin American Division, was a major figure in the development and application of a modified policy toward Latin America. Duggan convinced Welles in 1936 that U.S. diplomats in Central America be instructed to act toward the governments to which they were accredited as they would toward any major power in Latin America or elsewhere; U.S. representatives in Central America were instructed not to give advice or take any action on issues of domestic politics in those nations. Assistant Secretary of State Adolf A. Berle, Jr., was also firmly committed to the policy of nonintervention and the application of reason and common sense throughout the decade. Although a noncareer diplomat, Josephus Daniels, Roosevelt's personal friend and former secretary of the navy in Woodrow Wilson's administration, had a major impact on U.S.-Mexican policy as ambassador during the critical years of the oil nationalization crisis. In a spirit of renewed progressivism, Nelson A. Rockefeller, coordinator of inter-American affairs in the late 1930s, pursued a loosely defined agenda to improve hemispheric relations by enhancing private enterprise and technical development in Latin America, combating subversives on the left and right, and attempting to improve cultural understanding.

The emphasis that the Roosevelt administration placed on abstaining from military intervention and on reciprocity in relations with Latin America was the essence of the Good Neighbor Policy. The administration continued to attempt to shape Latin American economic, political, social, and diplomatic policies along lines acceptable to the United States and American interests, whether the issue was favorable to foreign investment legislation, adherence to private enterprise, the democratization of government processes, restraint on radical Latin American labor organizations, trade liberalization to facilitate the export of U.S. products, or the containment of Latin American leanings toward either communism or fascism.

In the final analysis, therefore, the main contribution of the Good Neighbor Policy was to move the United States toward a more multilateral and less military approach to Latin American issues. That approach did not subsequently compromise either the right of self defense or the capacity of the United States to use its political and diplomatic power, as evidenced by events in Guatemala in 1954, Cuba after 1959, the Dominican Republic in 1965, Chile in 1970–1973, Central America in the 1980s, or Panama in 1989. The Good Neighbor Policy did not survive during the Cold War, but the notion of international reciprocity that lay at the heart of the policy has demonstrated more resilience.

STEPHEN J. RANDALL

See also Berle, Adolf Augustus, Jr.; Bolívar, Simón; Bolivia; Clark Memorandum; Coolidge, Calvin; Cuba; Daniels, Josephus, Jr.; Dollar Diplomacy; Hoover, Herbert Clark; Hull, Cordell; Kellogg-Briand Pact; Latin America; Mexico; Monroe Doctrine; Oil and Foreign Policy; Oil Companies; Olney, Richard; Pan-Americanism; Platt Amendment; Rockefeller, Nelson Aldrich; Roosevelt, Franklin Delano; Roosevelt Corollary; Venezuela; Venezuela Boundary Dispute; Welles, Benjamin Sumner

FURTHER READING

Cobbs, Elizabeth A. *The Rich Neighbor Policy: Rockefeller and Kaiser in Brazil*. New Haven, Conn., 1992.
Gellman, Irwin F. *Good Neighbor Diplomacy: United States Policy in Latin America, 1933–1945*. Baltimore, Md., 1979.
Green, David. *The Containment of Latin America: A History of the Myths and Realities of the Good Neighbor Policy*. Chicago, 1971.
Randall, Stephen J. *The Diplomacy of Modernization: Colombian-American Relations, 1920–1940*. Toronto, 1977.
Wood, Bryce. *The Dismantling of the Good Neighbor Policy*. Austin, Tx., 1985.
——— . *The Making of the Good Neighbor Policy*. New York, 1961.
Woods, Randall Bennett. *The Roosevelt Foreign Policy Establishment and the "Good Neighbor": The United States and Argentina, 1941–1945*. Lawrence, Kans., 1979.

GORBACHEV, MIKHAIL SERGEEVICH

(*b*. 2 March 1931)

Soviet leader whose reforms, intended to save the Soviet Union from economic and political collapse, led, with surprising speed, to the breakup of the communist bloc in Eastern Europe, to the dissolution of the Soviet Union, and to the end of the Cold War. In 1985 Gorbachev, at age fifty-four, became the youngest Communist party secretary-general in Soviet history. He inherited an increasingly inefficient economy strained to the breaking point by the country's arms race with the United States. Gorbachev realized that communism as an ideological force and the Soviet Union as a global political power were both at risk of self-destructing. He made his top priorities a drastic reduction of defense spending, an equally dramatic overhaul of the economy (perestroika), and a liberalization of the rules governing the personal and political lives of Soviet citizens (glasnost). Over the next six years, Gorbachev also transformed Soviet foreign policy, replacing Cold War confrontation with a commitment to détente and superpower cooperation. His own charm and the elegance of his wife, Raisa, also improved the image of Soviet leadership.

Gorbachev graduated from Moscow University in 1955 with a degree in law. He joined the Communist party while at the university and by the age of forty had become party chief of the agriculturally important Stavropol region and had earned a second degree from the Stavropol Agricultural Institute. He went to Moscow in 1978 as the Central Committee Secretariat's agricultural expert and, as a protégé of Yuri Andropov, the powerful head of the Soviet secret police, the KGB, soon became a full member of the Politburo. After Gorbachev became secretary-general of the party, his rhetoric, demeanor, and obvious interest in disarmament won rapid acceptance in Europe. In Ronald Reagan, however, he faced a U.S. president who had revived Cold War rhetoric, had launched the Strategic Defense Initiative (SDI), and had openly supported anticommunist freedom fighters around the globe. Beginning in 1985 Gorbachev and Reagan held annual summits, in Geneva, Reykjavík, Washington, and Moscow, during which they developed a personal friendship. At Reykjavík in 1986 Gorbachev offered to eliminate all nuclear weapons; in return, he asked Reagan to abandon SDI, but the president refused. Acrimony over SDI, among other issues, temporarily delayed any agreement on arms reduction. The Intermediate-Range Nuclear Forces Treaty, signed in Washington in 1987, provided for the removal and then the destruction of one class of nuclear weaponry. During his stay in the United States, Gorbachev captivated the American public.

Gorbachev won international approval for his announcement, in a 1988 address to the United Nations, that he would unilaterally decrease the number of Soviet ground troops by 500,000. In 1989 he withdrew Soviet troops from Afghanistan. That same year, he openly rejected the Brezhnev Doctrine and refused to intervene as, one after another, the Soviet Union's former Eastern European allies ousted their communist leaders and moved toward democracy, opening their borders and markets to the West. After some hesitancy, Gorbachev even sanctioned German reunification and Germany's continued membership in the North Atlantic Treaty Organization (NATO). In naming Gorbachev the man of the decade in its 1 January 1990 issue, *Time* magazine acknowledged his pivotal role in ending the Cold War. Gorbachev's international initiatives, which earned him the 1990 Nobel Peace Prize, were matched in magnitude, if not in popularity, by reform efforts at home. He embarked on radical economic programs of decentralization and even privatization, endorsed political and personal freedoms, and granted increased autonomy to Soviet republics. These moves were criticized by Soviet conservatives, who feared any change, and by Soviet liberals unhappy with the slowness of that change.

As the Soviet economy continued its downward slide, domestic opposition to Gorbachev's reforms increased, and the West did not deliver enough financial support to ease the country's transition to a more open, free-market society. By 1990 Boris Yeltsin, the bombastic but popularly elected liberal president of the Russian Republic, was openly challenging Gorbachev's leadership. With Yeltsin's help, Gorbachev survived an August 1991 coup attempt by conservative forces, but pressure from the republics led to the Soviet Union's dissolution later that year. Gorbachev resigned on 25 December 1991. Shortly after leaving office, Gorbachev founded an international think tank. In May 1992 he delivered an address at Westminster College in Fulton, Missouri—the site of Winston Churchill's "iron curtain" speech forty-six years earlier—and attributed the origins of the Cold War to misunderstandings by both the United States and the Soviet Union. In a talk to members of Congress, Gorbachev pleaded for more economic aid for Russia and predicted that the U.S. response to Russia's transitional crisis would set the groundwork for Russia's response to the United States once that crisis was over. By 1992 Gorbachev's country no longer existed, he himself held no official post, and the outcome of the reforms he had set in motion remained unclear.

LINDA KILLEN

See also Afghanistan; Brezhnev Doctrine; Cold War; Nuclear Weapons and Strategy; Reagan, Ronald Wilson; Russia and the Soviet Union; Strategic Defense Initiative; Yeltsin, Boris Nikolayevich

FURTHER READING

Beschloss, Michael R., and Strobe Talbott. *At the Highest Levels: The Inside Story of the End of the Cold War.* Boston, 1993.
Garthoff, Raymond. *The Great Transition: American-Soviet Relations and the End of the Cold War.* Washington, D.C., 1994.
Gorbachev, Mikhail S. *The August Coup: The Truth and the Lessons.* New York, 1991.
———, et al. *Perestroika, Global Challenge: Our Common Future.* Nottingham, England, 1988.
Whelan, Joseph G. *The Moscow Summit, 1988: Reagan and Gorbachev in Negotiation.* Boulder, Colo., 1990.

GRADY, HENRY FRANCIS

(*b.* 12 February 1882; *d.* 14 September 1957)

Government official, ambassador to India (1947), Greece (1948), and Iran (1950–1951), and a leading advocate of U.S. aid to Southeast Asia and the Near East. Born in San Francisco, Grady received his doctorate in economics from Columbia University in 1927. He entered government service in 1918 as a specialist in the Bureau of Planning and Statistics of the U.S. Shipping Board. He then worked for the U.S. embassies in London (1919–1920) and Holland (1920) and for the Bureau of Foreign and Domestic Commerce (1921). A long-time proponent of reduced international tariffs as a means to foster U.S. prosperity and global peace, Grady in 1934 helped the U.S. government develop the reciprocal trade agreements program. After spending seven years in various government posts working to implement his global free-trade goals, Grady became head of American President Lines and oversaw the transport of strategic defense materials from Asia to the United States (1941–1947). He also led the American Technical Mission to India (1942) and served in the Economic Section of the Allied Control Commission in Italy (1942–1943). With the onset of the Cold War, Grady concluded that U.S.-sponsored economic development of the Near East and Asia could help contain communism. He also argued that the United States should offer Third World nationalist movements political support and foreign aid to prevent their leaders from seeking alliances with the Soviet Union. Grady began advocating Near East development in Greece, where he headed the U.S. branch of the Allied Mission for Observing the Greek Elections (1945–1946). As India's first U.S. ambassador he then supported increased U.S. aid to Prime Minister Jawaharlal Nehru's government. As ambassador to Greece, where he helped implement the Truman Doctrine and the Marshall Plan. Grady also pressed for expanded U.S. assistance to Iran. While ambassador to that country he advised the administration of President Harry S. Truman increase economic and military aid to the Tehran government and to back Prime Minister Mohammad Mosaddeq's efforts to nationalize the Abadan oil refinery. Fearful of alienating a U.S. ally, Great Britain, and less apprehensive than Grady that the popular Iranian leader might pursue a Soviet alliance, Truman provided Mosaddeq's government with only token support. Grady retired from the foreign service in 1951.

DEBORAH KISATSKY

See also Cold War; Foreign Aid; Greece; India; Iran; Marshall Plan; Truman Doctrine

FURTHER READING

Cottam, Richard. *Iran and the United States: A Cold War Case Study.* Pittsburgh, 1988.
Merrill, Dennis. *Bread and the Ballot: The United States and India's Economic Development, 1947–1963.* Chapel Hill, N.C., 1990.
Wittner, Lawrence S. *American Intervention in Greece, 1943–1949.* New York, 1982.

GRANT, ULYSSES SIMPSON

(*b.* 27 April 1822; *d.* 23 July 1885)

Eighteenth president of the United States (1869–1877) and Civil War general. Born in Ohio, Grant graduated from the U.S. Military Academy in 1843 and served in the Mexican War (1846–1848). In 1854 he resigned from the army and moved to Missouri. Following the outbreak of the Civil War in April 1861, Grant was appointed a colonel in an Illinois volunteer regiment and promoted two months later to brigadier general. In March 1864 he was put in command of all the Union armies and eventually forced the surrender of Confederate forces at Appomattox, Virginia, on 9 April 1965. Grant won the Republican nomination for president in 1868, was elected, and reelected in 1872. President Grant's foreign policy derived from his military experience. He sought territorial expansion to enhance national security and resolve domestic issues, and he worked toward the resolution of disputes with Great Britain. Grant employed former Union army comrades as diplomatic agents, especially in pursuit of his expansionist goals, which failed largely because of allegations of scandal. Aided by an outstanding secretary of state, Hamilton Fish, with whom he enjoyed a relationship of trust, Grant achieved a major settlement with Great Britain that laid the basis for the most important U.S. international relationship.

Grant sought to annex the Dominican Republic for its strategic location and harbor at Samaná Bay and as a haven for settlement of freedmen, thereby providing an example for the emancipation of slaves in Spanish Cuba. In January 1870 Grant thought he had obtained the support of Republican Senator Charles Sumner, chairman of the Foreign Relations Committee. Sumner, however, an ardent wartime abolitionist, feared that the neighboring black nation of Haiti would lose its independence if the United States annexed the Dominican Republic. He also objected to Grant's use of his private secretary, General Orville E. Babcock, to negotiate the annexation treaty; Sumner suspected corruption because of Babcock's association with private investors interested in profits in the Dominican Republic. Rumors of a "Dominican job," involving commercial franchises and leases at Samaná, had circulated since the administration of President Abraham Lincoln and recent Alaska scandals were fresh in mind. The Foreign Relations Committee investigated Babcock's negotiation, delayed, and reported adversely; Sumner spoke at length against the treaties, which failed by a vote of 28 to 28. Grant immediately removed Sumner's friend John Lothrop Motley, who had long been disobedient to Secretary of State Fish, as minister to Great Britain. Bitter controversy ensued. Sumner insinuated publicly that Grant was involved in Dominican real estate deals, which enraged Grant, who was innocent. Grant's Senate supporters removed Sumner as chairman of the Foreign Relations Committee in March 1871.

This action cleared the way for a major foreign policy victory. Sumner had insisted that Great Britain owed $125 million for wartime damages and $2 billion more for recognizing Confederate belligerency, and he wanted Canada ceded to the United States as payment. These excessive demands had frustrated negotiations over U.S. claims. Sumner's removal allowed Fish, who kept Grant fully informed, to negotiate the Treaty of Washington, an extraordinary arbitration agreement with Great Britain. The treaty dealt with the difficult Alabama Claims by establishing rules of due diligence as a basis for subsequent financial arbitration—which the administration also managed brilliantly—and skillfully calmed Canadian fisheries, trade, and boundary issues as well.

Grant abandoned his Dominican goals but dispatched another Union army veteran, Colonel A. B. Steinberger, as commissioner to Samoa, which had a valuable harbor. Steinberger unwisely involved himself in native politics; he became premier, halted the liquor traffic, and quarrelled with British officials, who deported him in April 1876 and revealed his correspondence with Babcock. Simultaneous disclosure of Babcock's entanglement with the St. Louis Whisky Ring and the Washington Safe Burglary Conspiracy Case created scandal, forcing Grant to discharge his secretary and ending Grant's Samoan ventures.

Hindsight has created the impression that Grant's presidency was a time when Americans turned from foreign ventures to development of the West, but this impression ignores the understanding of the importance of foreign affairs by prominent statesmen in the Lincoln, Andrew Johnson, and Grant administrations and their continuing interest in territorial expansion.

PAUL S. HOLBO

See also Alabama Claims: Dominican Republic; Fish, Hamilton; Great Britain; Presidency; Sumner, Charles

FURTHER READING

Campbell, Charles S., *The Transformation of American Foreign Relations*, New York, 1976.
Carpenter, John A., *Ulysses S. Grant*, New York, 1970.
Holbo, Paul S., *Tarnished Expansion: The Alaska Scandal, the Press, and Congress, 1867–1871*, Knoxville, Tenn., 1983.

GREAT BRITAIN

The Western European island nation, commonly referred to today as the United Kingdom, bordered by the North Atlantic Ocean, the English Channel, and the North Sea. The American colonies, very much a part of the British Empire for more than one and a half centuries, formally gained their independence from the mother country in 1783. Since that time, the United States has maintained a relationship with Great Britain marked first by war, and then by territorial conflict, commercial competition, diplomatic rapprochement, partnership, and outright alliance.

The Anglo-American relationship is the most significant one in the history of U.S. foreign relations. Great Britain not only established the first commercial colonial settlements on the East Coast of North America, but it also provided the primary language, customs, and institutions for the thirteen British colonies that became the United States of America in 1776. The United States emerged from the War for Independence as a country molded by its cultural and economic ties to the mother country. Because of Great Britain's substantial trade with and capital investment in the United States, the large flow of British immigrants to the United States, and the military partnership and alliance cemented in the two world wars (and in the North Atlantic Treaty Organization since 1949), the two nations have been bound together in what some have called a "special relationship." Still, Great Britain and the United States fought each other during the American Revolutionary War and the War of 1812, clashed over Canada in the nineteenth century, and differed over a host of international issues in the twentieth century—including neutral rights, U.S. nuclear-weapons policy, relations with the People's Republic of China, British colonialism, and Middle Eastern policies. Friction developed, too, from the concomitant decline of British power and the rise of U.S. power, especially after World War II.

The British American Colonies

Great-power competition for trade and colonies became the impetus for Great Britain's imperial policies in North America during the late sixteenth and early seventeenth centuries. The government also used colonization to alleviate social and political pressures caused by overpopulation and unemployment. The crown issued charters for colonial settlement along the Atlantic coast of North America between 1606 and 1732. In 1606, King James I conferred a charter on the Virginia Company which established the first successful colony the following year at Jamestown.

British colonists survived the early years through their own resourcefulness combined with crucial assistance from a group of Algonquian Indians and with supplies shipped from England. Relying on Indian expertise, Virginia developed its first successful export crop (tobacco) in 1612. Tobacco cultivation quickly transformed Jamestown into a labor-intensive plantation economy dependent on a steady supply of indentured servants from England. Virginia Company mismanagement caused the crown to revoke its charter and place the colony under royal control in 1625. Jamestown later developed its own representative assemblies under the guidance of a royal governor.

The Puritans, reformist dissidents from the Anglican Church, founded Plymouth colony in 1620 in present-day Massachusetts to practice their own brand of Calvinism without interference from the Church of England. As head of the Anglican Church, James I was unwilling to permit Puritans to establish a colony for religious reasons; however, he did allow the Virginia Company to issue them a patent to set up plantations on the Atlantic coast north of Jamestown. Like the Jamestown colonists, Puritans received critical assistance, especially food supplies, from local Indians.

The success of the Plymouth settlement encouraged another group of Puritans to leave England. Although Charles I assumed that the Massachusetts Bay Company would be headquartered in London when he chartered it in 1629, company leaders intended to govern the colony and the company from New England. When the Puritans chose to settle in Massachusetts Bay, they did so with the intention of establishing a new society and government based on religious principles—a society and government independent from England. By 1652 the colony became a commonwealth.

Unlike Jamestown colony, the Puritan colonies adopted a township system of government and settlement. Townships were laid out providing for a town hall, school and church. The poor New England soil and short growing season forced colonists to turn from agriculture to other commercial pursuits, especially fishing, fur trading, timber harvesting, and, later on, manufacturing. Some Puritan colonists chose to leave established settlements and to found new ones in Rhode Island, New Hampshire, Connecticut and Maine.

Most of the other British colonies established along the Atlantic coast in the seventeenth century were proprietary colonies. The first of these was Maryland. George Calvert, the first Lord Baltimore, approached Charles I in 1632 to request a land grant in the Chesapeake Bay area north of Jamestown in order to found a colony as a refuge for Catholics. Lord Baltimore died before he could realize his dream, so his sons Cecilius and Leonard established Maryland with the king's grant. Due to the introduction of tobacco cultivation, the colony adopted a plantation economy dependent on slave labor.

The other proprietary colonies, namely New York, New Jersey, Pennsylvania (including Delaware), and North and South Carolina, were either founded or fell under British rule through Charles II's colonial policies during the Stuart Restoration (1660 to 1685). Charles II used colonial land grants as a means of retiring debts the Stuarts incurred during their exile, when Puritans ruled Great Britain (1649 to 1660), and as means of expanding British possessions in North America. The Stuarts returned to power when Charles II became king in 1660. By "giving" his brother James, the Duke of York, the Dutch colony of New Netherland, Charles planned to strike a blow at England's arch commercial rival, the

Netherlands, by depriving it of a valuable colony and increasing control over the colonies by eliminating the profitable trade between English and Dutch colonies in North America.

Shortly after James received the charter for New Netherland in March 1664, he took steps to seize the colony, which was renamed New York. He also implemented liberal administrative policies such as the retention of local customs and the Dutch legal system. It was certainly the most cosmopolitan of the colonies Great Britain acquired, considering its diverse population of Dutch, Walloon, French, German, and Swedish settlers, Africans brought in as slaves, and Indians.

In 1680, William Penn approached Charles II to claim part of his inheritance, namely a large royal debt owed his father. Penn received a charter for territory, including most of present-day Pennsylvania and Delaware. He founded his colony based on Quaker beliefs. Using the British system as a model, Penn established a representative government elected through a liberal suffrage policy. He also cultivated good relations with the Delaware Indians by paying them for land granted to him by the crown. Thanks to Penn's wisdom and liberal policies, Pennsylvania soon became one of the most prosperous and cosmopolitan British colonies.

The Glorious Revolution of 1688 marked the rise of parliamentary power in Great Britain and caused the colonies to demand self government. James II's usurpation of parliamentary power precipitated this revolution, which brought William III and Mary to the throne by invitation of Parliament, and also undermined James's colonial policy of exercising greater control over the colonies by converting them into royal provinces, like Virginia and New York. Inspired by Parliament's successful bid for power, the colonies, too, demanded representative government. As a result, the British government adopted a system of royal provinces which provided for colonial assemblies elected by the people but subordinate to the crown. The growth of parliamentary power served as a model and a justification for a representative system of government in the colonies. The English example ultimately furnished a rationale for revolution on the other side of the Atlantic.

British Relations with North American Colonies Deteriorate

During the period from 1689 to 1763, the colonies drew further apart from England due to the effect of wars involving England that extended to the American colonies. The wars also caused Great Britain to alter its relationship with the colonies by taxing them in the 1760s and 1770s. Great Britain and its archrival France, fought on opposite sides in both the European and American theaters of these wars in their struggle to determine the balance of power on both sides of the Atlantic.

The French and Indian War (1754 to 1763) redefined the balance of power between France and Britain, and also marked an acceleration in the deterioration of Great Britain's relations with the American colonies. Westward expansion by English colonists served as the catalyst for the war, which began over land in the Ohio valley claimed by both the French government and English colonists. It ended in 1763 with the destruction of the French Empire in North America. France ceded its possessions east of the Mississippi River (including its Canadian territory) to Britain, while French possessions west of the Mississippi went to Spain.

The expulsion of France from North America paradoxically exacerbated tensions between Great Britain and American colonists—first, over westward expansion and, then, over imperial rule. Colonists saw the French defeat as an opportunity to move into the rich Ohio valley—a move that the British knew would cause conflict with the Indians and jeopardize the lucrative fur trade. In fact, conflict with Indians in 1763 resulted in a major Indian uprising and the death of whites living on the frontier. British troops crushed the revolt. King George III issued the Proclamation of 1763, designating the Appalachian Mountains as the boundary between colonial settlements along the seaboard and Indian lands west of the mountains, which were closed to settlement. Nevertheless, colonists continued to move west in defiance of British law.

War debts incurred in prosecuting wars between 1689 and 1763 depleted British coffers, so the government adopted, for the first time, colonial taxation policies to cover administrative and defense expenditures for the American colonies. In short, the British government decided to tax the colonies to pay for their own administration. The government retained taxation policies adopted during the Grenville ministry, from 1764 to 1765, until the Revolutionary War broke out in 1775. These tax laws were the American Revenue Act of 1764 (frequently called the Sugar Act); the 1765 Stamp Act, which provided tax stamps on printed material (legal documents, newspapers, and the like); the Townshend Acts of 1767, which provided for import taxes on lead, paper, and tea; and the Tea Act of 1773.

Colonists protested against taxation policies starting with the passage of the 1765 Stamp Act, when colonists mounted demonstrations throughout the colonies. This protest movement articulated its opposition to government policies through the Stamp Act Congress of 1765. The Congress asserted that colonists were entitled to all the rights and privileges of Englishmen, yet it demanded rights reflecting an American rather than English experience. The colonists insisted that Great Britain adapt its

U.S. MINISTERS AND AMBASSADORS TO GREAT BRITAIN

MINISTER	PERIOD OF APPOINTMENT	ADMINISTRATION
John Adams[1]	1785–1788	Confederation Congress
Thomas Pinckney	1792–1796	Washington
Rufus King	1796–1803	Washington
		J. Adams
		Jefferson
James Monroe	1803–1807	Jefferson
William Pinkney[2]	1808–1811	Jefferson
		Madison
Jonathan Russell	1811[3]–1812	Madison
John Quincy Adams	1815–1817	Madison
Richard Rush	1818–1825	Monroe
Rufus King	1825–1826	J. Q. Adams
Albert Gallatin	1826–1827	J. Q. Adams
James Barbour	1828–1829	J. Q. Adams
		Jackson
Louis McLane	1829–1831	Jackson
Martin Van Buren[4]	1831–1832	Jackson
Aaron Vail	1832–1836	Jackson
Andrew Stevenson[5]	1836–1841	Jackson
		Van Buren
		W. H. Harrison
		Tyler
Edward Everett	1841–1845	Tyler
Louis McLane	1845–1846	Polk
George Bancroft	1846–1849	Polk
		Taylor
Abbott Lawrence	1849–1852	Taylor
		Fillmore
Joseph R. Ingersoll	1852–1853	Fillmore
		Pierce
James Buchanan	1853–1856	Pierce
George M. Dallas	1856–1861	Pierce
		Buchanan
Charles Francis Adams	1861–1868	Lincoln
		A. Johnson
George B. McClellan[6]		A. Johnson
Reverdy Johnson	1868–1869	A. Johnson
J. Lothrop Motley	1869–1870	Grant
Frederick T. Frelinghuysen[7]	1870	Grant
Oliver T. Morton[8]	1870	Grant
Robert C. Schenck	1870–1876	Grant
Richard H. Dana, Jr.[9]		
Edwards Pierrepont	1876–1877	Grant
		Hayes
John Welsh	1877–1879	Hayes
James Russell Lowell	1880–1885	Hayes
		Garfield
		Arthur

(table continues on next page)

MINISTER	PERIOD OF APPOINTMENT	ADMINISTRATION
Edward J. Phelps	1885–1889	Cleveland
		B. Harrison
Robert T. Lincoln	1889–1893	B. Harrison

AMBASSADOR

Thomas F. Bayard	1893–1897	Cleveland
John Hay	1897–1898	McKinley
Joseph Choate	1899–1905	McKinley
		T. Roosevelt
Whitelaw Reid	1905–1912	T. Roosevelt
		Taft
Walter Hines Page	1913–1918	Wilson
John W. Davis	1918–1921	Wilson
George Harvey	1921–1923	Harding
		Coolidge
Frank B. Kellogg	1923–1925	Coolidge
Alanson B. Houghton	1925–1929	Coolidge
Charles G. Dawes	1929–1931	Hoover
Andrew W. Mellon	1932–1933	Hoover
Robert Worth Bingham	1933–1937	F. Roosevelt
Joseph P. Kennedy	1938–1940	F. Roosevelt
John G. Winant	1941–1946	F. Roosevelt
W. Averell Harriman	1946	Truman
O. Max Gardner[10]	1946–1947	Truman
Lewis W. Douglas	1947–1950	Truman
Walter S. Gifford[11]	1950–1953	Truman
Winthrop W. Aldrich	1953–1957	Eisenhower
John Hay Whitney	1957–1961	Eisenhower
David K. E. Bruce	1961–1969	Kennedy
		L. Johnson
Walter H. Annenberg	1969–1974	Nixon
		Ford
Elliot L. Richardson	1975–1976	Ford
Anne Legendre Armstrong	1976–1977	Ford
Kingman Brewster, Jr.	1977–1981	Carter
John J. Louis, Jr.	1981–1983	Reagan
Charles H. Price, II	1983–1989	Reagan
Henry E. Catto, Jr.	1989–1991	Bush
Raymond G. H. Seitz	1991–1994	Bush
		Clinton
William J. Crowe, Jr.	1994–Present	Clinton

[1] Accredited also to the Netherlands.
[2] Originally commissioned as MP at the court of His Beitannic Majesty and given a letter of credence as such, 12 May 1806—on the same day that he and Monroe were accredited jointly as Commissioners Plenipotentiary and Extraordinary on a special mission. When Monroe was preparing to leave London, he informed the Foreign Secretary that Pinkney would succeed him in the ordinary duties of the Legation; the British authorities declined to accept Pinkney's 1806 letter of credence, but dealt with him informally until he was recommissioned and reaccredited.
[3] Commission (issued during a recess of the Senate) not of record, but enclosed with an instruction of this date.
[4] Nomination later rejected by the Senate.
[5] Nomination of 20 May 1834 rejected by the Senate; nomination of 1 Feb. 1836 confirmed.
[6] Not commissioned; nomination rejected by the Senate.
[7] Declined appointment.
[8] Declined appointment.
[9] Not commissioned; nomination rejected by the Senate.
[10] Took oath of office, but died in the United States before proceeding to post.
[11] Did not serve under this appointment.

Sources: *Principal Officers of the Department of State and United States Chiefs of Missions.* ©1991 by Office of the Historian, Bureau of Public Affairs, Washington, D.C.; *The U.S. Government Manual,* Annual. Washington, D.C.

institutions to accommodate colonial institutions and customs. The British government, however, was unable to reconcile its own traditions with American customs. London repealed the Stamp Act in 1766 for pragmatic reasons—because of widespread protest, particularly the boycott of British goods.

Charles Townshend continued Grenville's short-sighted policies with the Townshend Acts and the renewal of the Quartering Act of 1765, requiring the colonies to furnish housing for British troops. Townshend underestimated the extent of resentment toward British policies, and British authorities were unable to enforce the taxes due to widespread colonial resistance. After the 1770 Boston Massacre, the North ministry repealed the import taxes, save the tax on tea, in order to restore amicable relations. Relations with the colonies remained peaceful until 1773, even though neither side abandoned its position on imperial policies.

The uneasy peace unraveled completely over the Tea Act of 1773; colonists responded to the tax on tea with the Boston Tea Party. Public outrage in England over the destruction of the tea tipped the balance in favor of hard-line imperialists in the North ministry who wanted to crush colonial resistance. Toward the end, Parliament passed the Coercive Acts in March and April 1774. Because Massachusetts led the rebellion, the Coercive Acts placed the colony under royal administration and closed the port of Boston until its citizens paid for the destroyed tea. The North ministry assumed that it could force Boston to accept these measures. But the Coercive Acts, alongside the Quebec Act, alienated even more moderate colonists. Such policies obviously drove Great Britain and the colonies farther apart.

The American Revolution

British policies of suppressing the rebellion in the mid-1770s united the colonists against Great Britain and played into the hands of radicals, who advocated independence. The other colonies supported Massachusetts through the First Continental Congress, which convened in September 1774 to formulate a unified response to Great Britain. Many colonists believed that the other colonies would probably share Massachusetts's fate at the hands of the British government. The Congress approved the Declaration of Rights and Grievances which called for the repeal of the Coercive Acts and the Quebec Act and for colonial self-government in domestic affairs. The Congress also agreed to boycott British goods if the grievances were not resolved. Lord North responded with a compromise designed to reassert British authority, but since its terms did not address the colonial grievances, it was rejected.

The North ministry acted on the perception that the empire still could be preserved through force when, in April 1775, it ordered military authorities to put down the rebellion and arrest its leaders. Even the first shots fired on Lexington Common failed to unite colonists against Great Britain. When the Second Continental Congress met in May, there was little support for independence. The decisions to prosecute the war and the adoption of the Olive Branch Position, reflected the absence of a consensus among colonial leaders. But George III had decided that the conflict could only be resolved through force; therefore, he refused to receive the Olive Branch Petition, the last colonial peace initiative. In doing so, he unwittingly aided the independence movement by forcing moderates into the radical camp, which advocated independence.

Thomas Paine's radical pamphlet, "Common Sense" (1776), coalesced public opinion behind the independence movement by simplifying complex issues so that they appealed to a broad constituency. By proclaiming the Declaration of Independence, the Continental Congress assumed both leadership of the independence movement and responsibility for creating a new nation state. The Congress realized that the United States of America could not ensure its independence from Great Britain without assistance from abroad and, therefore, turned to France. As the defeated power of the French and Indian War, France stood to gain more than any other European power in the event that Great Britain lost its American colonies.

The United States negotiated with the French government for diplomatic recognition of the United States and for treaties of amity and commerce. France hesitated, at first, to support the United States, for to do so meant war with Great Britain, and there was no assurance that the new Continental Army was any match for seasoned British troops. But French perceptions changed dramatically with the American victory at the Battle of Saratoga in 1777. The Franco-American Treaty of Alliance, concluded "forever" on 6 February 1778, proved crucial to the American struggle for independence. The United States, undoubtedly, could not have secured independence without French military and financial assistance. The war ended when combined American and French forces defeated British troops at the Battle of Yorktown in 1781.

The Rockingham ministry opened peace negotiations directly with the French government. American negotiators Benjamin Franklin, John Jay, and John Adams chafed at instructions requiring them to work through the French foreign minister, the Count de Vergennes, because they realized that Vergennes would be willing to sacrifice American interests to benefit France. Once they discovered that Vergennes had no intention of defending the United States's land claims west of the Appalachian Mountains, Franklin, Jay, and Adams decided to violate their instructions and the terms of the Franco-American alliance by concluding a separate peace treaty with Great Britain. London was delighted with the opportunity to disrupt the Franco-American alliance. Under the generous terms of the 1783 Treaty of Paris, Great Britain formally recognized the United States as an independent nation state bounded by the Mississippi River to the west, Canada to the north, and Spanish Florida to the south. In addition, the United States gained navigation rights on the Mississippi and continued access to Newfoundland fisheries. The United States would not have obtained such a settlement through French diplomacy. French prestige rose because Great Britain had lost the American colonies.

Anglo-American Differences, 1783–1815

Anglo-American relations only temporarily improved after the war. The wars of the French Revolution soured these relations by 1793 and then pulled the two nations into war against one another in 1812. The United States commissioned John Adams as the first minister to Great Britain in 1785; however, Great Britain did not send its first representative to the United States for another six years. British negotiations with the United States for commercial treaty foundered over American demands for reciprocity in the 1780s. Even so, Anglo-American trade increased because of well-established commercial ties important to the debt-ridden new nation. Like France, Great Britain hoped to transform the United States into a client state. The United States was saved from such schemes by the outbreak of the French Revolution in 1789, which led to another Anglo-French war beginning in 1793, and which upset the balance of power in Europe and necessarily forced the major powers to focus on European issues. Still, as a major maritime nation, the United States was caught in the cross fire of British and French commercial warfare—a strategy adopted to end the wars and determine the fate of France.

President George Washington reckoned that the United States could not survive another war so soon after obtaining independence, so he heeded the advice of his Anglophile secretary of the treasury, Alexander Hamilton, by setting aside the Franco-American alliance and steering clear of the European war. Instead of responding to the call for assistance issued by the French minister, Citizen Genêt, Washington announced the Neutrality Proclamation of 1793. The president knew that the French Revolution had divided his administration and the country as a whole between pro-French and pro-English factions. For these reasons, he wisely charted a neutral course—a course continued by his successors until 1812, when James Madison asked Congress to declare war on Great Britain over long-standing maritime and frontier grievances.

Anglo-American maritime disputes focused on Great Britain's use of the Rule of 1756 (first used during the French and Indian War), on the paper blockade, and on impressment into the Royal Navy of British and American seamen serving on U.S. merchant ships. Great Britain implemented these measures to curtail French commerce and thereby force France to sue for peace. In the process, Great Britain interrupted America's highly profitable trade with Europe and the Caribbean. London used the Rule of 1756, the British maritime policy prohibiting imperial powers from opening colonial trade (closed in peacetime) to neutral carriers in wartime, to prevent France from relying on neutral American merchant ships to conduct French colonial trade in the Caribbean. To interdict French transatlantic trade, Great Britain employed the paper blockade; therefore, British men-of-war seized neutral cargoes on the high seas if such cargoes were enroute to France or ports under French control. The blockade conflicted with "free ships, free goods," a fundamental principle of American diplomacy embodied in the "Plan of 1776," which stipulated that neutral goods carried on neutral vessels were free from confiscation in time of peace and war. The British government also relied on impressment policies to maintain a seasoned navy, a crucial element in commercial warfare.

While this commercial warfare harassed American shipping, frontier settlers became convinced that friction with Indians, resulting in heavy loss of life, was caused by the presence of British troops west of the Appalachian Mountains. Although Great Britain agreed in 1783 to dismantle its frontier fortifications, it realized that to do so would not only jeopardize amicable relations with the Indians and the profitable fur trade, but also would encourage the establishment of settlements. British interests would be served (as much as they were in 1763) by creating an Indian buffer state in the interior, which might discourage both westward immigration and national expansion.

In 1794, President Washington tried to resolve Anglo-American disputes through negotiation by appointing a leading Federalist, Supreme Court Chief Justice John Jay, to negotiate with Great Britain. Jay's efforts were undermined by Hamilton, who provided the British with privileged information because he feared that tough negotiations would threaten Anglo-American trade relations and the American economy, thus jeopardizing Hamilton's financial system. Jay's Treaty shocked the U.S. government because Great Britain conceded so little—just the evacuation of western forts, as it had promised in 1783. That Great Britain continued to violate American maritime rights by seizing American ships and cargoes and impressing American merchant sailors into the British navy contributed to public outrage over the treaty. Jay did not obtain a commercial treaty and an agreement for compensation of confiscated American property, yet public anger over the treaty terms intensified anti-British sentiment in the United States. Nonetheless, Jay's Treaty may have prevented a war, and it fostered a temporary Anglo-American rapprochement.

Thomas Jefferson's election as president in 1800 ushered in a long period of Republican rule and deteriorating Anglo-American relations. His francophilism did not—as Great Britain had feared—prevent him from maintaining America's neutrality. His use of economic measures to compel France and Great Britain to respect American neutral rights backfired by destroying U.S.-European trade without obtaining concessions from either nation. Jefferson's successor, James Madison, did little to provide a consensus for either the country or the Republican party which were divided over disputes with Great Britain and France. He failed to resolve disputes and bungled negotiations with the two nations.

Dominated by "war hawks" in 1811, Congress demanded respect for national honor and assumed a leadership role, especially after the battle with Shawnee Indians at Tippecanoe in Indiana territory. War hawks incorrectly attributed the Indian revolt to British agitation rather than to treaty violations by settlers. American suspicions, dating back to the Revolutionary War, that Great Britain used Canada as a base for hostile operations in the United States were heightened to the point where responsible leaders again debated the feasibility of seizing Canadian territory in order to protect U.S. borders. By the time militants demanded war with Great Britain over maritime and frontier issues, Madison had also decided that war could force Great Britain to respect American rights. He failed to consider the consequences of war with Great Britain for a minor power like the United States.

The U.S. declaration of war in June 1812, caught Great Britain by surprise. Preoccupation with the Napoleonic Wars had prevented Spencer Perceval's ministry from recognizing the seriousness of American grievances. Perceval's death and the more conciliatory Liverpool ministry came too late to preserve peace. The war proved disastrous for the United States. By 1814, the British blockade had devastated the American economy; British troops had invaded American territory, and American attempts to conquer Canada had failed. Anglo-American peace talks took place at Ghent. The 1814 Ghent treaty restored the status quo ante bellum without mention of neutral rights or impressment. Despite the United States's defeat by superior British land forces from 1812 to 1814, important American victories late in the war strengthened the U.S. bargaining position at Ghent. U.S.-British relations improved, once again, with the reestablishment of peace.

Great Britain and U.S. Western Expansion

The peace provided the United States with the opportunity to expand westward and southward, and yet the westward movement also caused friction with Great Britain. By the 1850s, the movement had divided the new nation over the extension of slavery and pulled it toward civil war. Great Britain and the United States settled some issues through negotiation, as demonstrated by the mutual demilitarization of the Great Lakes in the Rush-Bagot Agreement of 1817 and the establishment of the U.S.-Canadian border for Louisiana Territory at the forty-ninth parallel in the Convention of 1818. Other issues, however, including territorial claims (primarily along the U.S.-Canadian border) and the adoption of spheres of influence in the Western Hemisphere, complicated Anglo-American relations during much of the nineteenth century.

American nationalism expressed by the acquisition of Spanish Florida in 1819 by the Adams-Onís Treaty was clearly at odds with the conservative Congress system established in Europe and designed to preserve the status quo of monarchical states fashioned at Vienna in 1815. But when Spain's King Ferdinand VII requested that the major powers restore both his throne and his American colonies in 1823, Great Britain (a Congress member) and the United States became alarmed. British Foreign Secretary George Canning suggested that London and Washington issue a joint statement that Spanish-American colonies were closed to future colonization. Monroe was favorably impressed with the proposal until he consulted Secretary of State John Quincy Adams, who persuaded him that America's best interests lay in issuing a unilateral statement recognizing Latin American countries as independent nation states. The United States, Adams believed, must be free to expand into these new areas, and Canning's joint declaration would have renounced this opportunity while providing for future British expansion.

Adams argued that the United States should adopt a policy discouraging all European states from fulfilling their imperial ambitions in the Western Hemisphere. He pointed out that this approach would address Russian claims in the Pacific Northwest, concern by European powers over the Latin American independence movement, and Great Britain's desire to exercise greater influence in the hemisphere. The United States should continue George Washington's policy of avoiding European alliances while promoting American expansionist interests independently of Great Britain. Yet Adams counted on British naval power to support these policies—a fact he acknowledged implicitly by stating that, if Canning's proposal were adopted, the United States would "come in as a cock-boat in the wake of a British man-of-war." Adams realized that the United States alone could not enforce the Monroe Doctrine of 1823, with its warnings against future European colonization and intervention in the affairs of independent nations in the Western Hemisphere, and with its announcement of the two-spheres policy—a policy of isolating the hemisphere from involvement in European affairs.

The Monroe Doctrine became a fundamental principle of American diplomacy and, as such, had important implications for Anglo-American relations. Its announcement constituted a rejection of Canning's overture for an Anglo-American rapprochement, which Adams deemed an act of self-denial that would have blocked America's westward expansion. The British had argued that the joint statement would have served both countries by deterring European powers from absorbing remnants of the Spanish empire while Spain and newly-independent Latin American nations were preoccupied with chaotic internal affairs. But the Liverpool ministry reckoned that improved U.S. relations would allow Great Britain to discourage American expansionism and foster growing British commercial interests in Latin America. The British government was aware of anti-British elements in the Monroe Doctrine, for the Liverpool ministry recognized the role of Anglo-American political and commercial rivalry as a motive for adopting the doctrine. Rivalry for Latin American markets continued into the twentieth century. Thus, Great Britain and the United States charted parallel but not always compatible Latin American policies after 1823.

By the 1840s, Anglo-American relations had deteriorated to the point that the two nations seemed on the verge of war over a number of disputes, particularly the ill-defined northeastern Canadian-American boundary established by the 1783 Peace of Paris. The Webster-Ashburton Treaty of 1842 successfully resolved the most serious of these disputes with the northern boundary settlement, provisions for Anglo-American cooperation in curtailing the African slave trade, and an extradition agreement for crimes of violence and crimes against property. Secretary of State Daniel Webster and (the special commissioner) British Lord Ashburton delineated the northeastern boundary for Maine, New Hampshire, Vermont, New York, and Wisconsin Territory by establishing the Maine boundary along the St. John River and by placing Rouses Point on Lake Champlain and the Connecticut River within American borders. Webster also agreed to renounce American claims to some 5,000 square miles in northern Maine in exchange for territory between Lake Superior and the Lake of the Woods, where rich iron deposits were subsequently discovered.

American refusal to assent to an international agreement (concluded in 1818 at Aix-la-Chapelle) to suppress the African slave trade nearly destroyed the Webster-Ashburton negotiations. Without American cooperation, Great Britain and other European nations could not legally search vessels suspected of transporting slaves if they flew the American flag. So slave traders frequently used the American flag to evade capture. Although the United States had moved toward outlawing the slave trade in 1808, it had rejected British proposals for cooperation because of serious problems posed by British maritime and impressment policies until the end of the War of 1812 and because American proslavery forces would not support such a proposal. Webster and Ashburton struck a compromise, which addressed American concerns over national sovereignty, by agreeing that Great Britain and the United States would maintain separate naval patrols off the African coast to enforce the ban against slave trading. America's reluctance to provide adequate funding for these patrols irritated the British, but the agreement did ease tensions between the two nations.

Great Britain tried to block American expansion by supporting independence movements in Texas and California and by instructing Hudson's Bay Company officials in the Oregon territory to refuse assistance to American settlers in the Pacific Northwest. In 1824, Hudson's Bay Company established a huge fur trading operation in the Willamette Valley with authority, granted by the British government, over territory extending into present-day British Columbia and western Montana. Few Americans lived in the Pacific Northwest when the United States began to press its claim to the region under an Anglo-American Joint Occupation Treaty of 1827. President James K. Polk's aggressive expansionism undercut British plans to contain the United States. First, he pressured Britain to relinquish claims to the Oregon territory under threat of war. Partly because of Canadian discontent over colonial policies, the Peel ministry pushed for a compromise, which it obtained with the 1846 Oregon Treaty establishing the forty-ninth parallel as the Canadian-American boundary. Secondly, Polk acquired California, Texas, and the Southwest through war with Mexico. Because Great Britain knew that it could not prevent the United States from taking these territories from Mexico, the British government made no attempt to do so. By 1848, it looked as though the United States might tear itself apart over westward expansion and the issue of slavery, thereby denying itself future great power status—a status Great Britain consistently opposed.

Anglo-American competition extended to Central America, where both nations vied with one another over commercial and transit rights. Even though Great Britain had been unsuccessful in containing the United States's westward expansion, London planned to contain U.S. expansion into Central America and the Caribbean. Unstable European politics, however, motivated Great Britain to resolve differences with the United States via the Clayton-Bulwer Treaty of 1850, which provided for joint administration of an isthmian canal—a significant project for both governments because of the importance of Pacific commerce.

The American Civil War

After the Confederate States of America seceded from the Union in 1861, Great Britain declared neutrality and recognized the existence of a state of war. Complex relations with the North and South persuaded British leaders to maintain neutrality throughout the war. Although the Palmerston ministry privately claimed that the disintegration of the United States would serve British interests, more perceptive leaders in London saw dangers because of profitable commercial relations with both the North and South. These considerations, and bellicose Northern threats that Great Britain should not recognize the Confederacy, convinced Palmerston that neutrality was the best option. The Lincoln administration found that such threats were an effective means of depriving the Confederacy of critical European support and assuring compliance with its naval blockade of southern ports.

The British attempted to preserve relations with the North without alienating the South, which they thought might actually succeed in securing independence. Caught between northern King Corn and southern King Cotton diplomacy, the British government discovered that domestic requirements for grain far exceeded the textile industry's demand for cotton, since its warehouses stored a surplus of cotton. National interests necessarily favored the North because Great Britain had proclaimed neutrality, and Great Britain also had a greater demand for northern rather than southern goods. Nevertheless, tensions over the blockade and U.S. Navy Captain Charles Wilke's seizure of Confederate diplomats from the British steamer *Trent* nearly raised tensions to the breaking point. And Foreign Secretary Lord John Russell's failure to halt construction in Liverpool shipyards of ironclad naval ships purchased by the Confederacy further strained relations with Washington. U.S. minister to Britain Charles Francis Adams's skill in handling these and other difficult issues helped preserve peace between the two nations. On the whole, Palmerston tolerated the northern blockade, a paper blockade, precisely because it was based on British precedents used against the United States in the Revolutionary War and the War of 1812 (see the War of 1812 above). As the premier naval power, Great Britain intended to avail itself, in the future, of American precedents—particularly in expanded use of the Doctrine of Continuous Voyage, which provided for the seizure of contraband at any point in transit. The outbreak of World War I in 1914 provided just such an opportunity to use these Civil War precedents against American merchant ships to cut off trade with Germany.

The Battle of Antietam in 1862 followed by Lincoln's announcement of the Emancipation Proclamation, which declared slaves free in territory under Confederate control, caused Great Britain to postpone recognition of the Confederacy. Palmerston cautiously entertained French emperor Louis Napoleon's call for great power mediation of the American Civil War prior to Antietam. General Robert E. Lee's retreat into Virginia, however, cast doubt on Confederate prospects for victory. Even though Palmerston and Russell interpreted the Emancipation Proclamation as an act of military expediency rather than moral principle, they perceived that popular support for Lincoln's antislavery policies, especially among British working classes, made it more difficult to recognize the Confederacy because of its retention of slavery. The issue of intervention, particularly mediation, divided Palmerston's cabinet by November 1862, but during the next year, the prime minister's policy of neutrality prevailed over Russell's arguments for mediation. Decisive Union victories at Vicksburg and Gettysburg in July 1863 convinced the British government that neutrality served national interests.

Toward Rapprochement

The Confederate defeat in 1865 signaled a fundamental change in Anglo-American relations because the United States became more politically cohesive and militarily powerful as a result of the Union victory. That Great Britain could no longer challenge the power of the United States in North America marked a shift in the balance of power on the continent. The postwar period was colored by bitter anti-British feelings in the United States over destruction caused by British-built Confederate commerce destroyers such as the *Alabama*. After much wrangling, Washington and London finally settled Civil War damage claims in Washington's favor with the Treaty of Washington in 1871. Anti-British passions were kept alive by millions of Irish immigrants, who fled the potato famine and British rule to settle in the United States. In the struggle for independence from Great Britain, the Irish nationalist Fenian Brotherhood even staged an invasion of Canada from Buffalo, New York, in 1866. More important, Irish-American voters remained a formidable force in American politics into the twentieth century. Great Britain withdrew from North American affairs partly because it granted Canada self-government by establishing a federation in 1867, and partly because of European political considerations, especially the German and Italian nationalist movements. Nevertheless, Great Britain maintained great-power status in Central America and the Caribbean throughout the nineteenth century despite competition from the United States.

American competition for influence ultimately forced the British government to reduce its role in the Western Hemisphere in order to maintain amicable relations with Washington while London focused on foreign crises elsewhere. One such crisis, over the Samoan Islands, complicated Anglo-American relations to the breaking point by

1889, but both nations resolved their differences with each other and with a third rival, Germany, by establishing a tripartite protectorate over the islands in 1889. The United States contested British claims to protectorates in Belize (British-Honduras) and the Mosquito Coast. From 1894 to 1895, the United States used the Clayton-Bulwer Treaty and the Monroe Doctrine to pressure Great Britain out of Nicaragua. Nicaraguan appeals to the United States for assistance against British intervention on the Mosquito Coast arrived in Washington when President Grover Cleveland was embroiled with yet another dispute with London.

In 1895, Cleveland's Secretary of State, Richard Olney leveled a "twenty-inch gun" blast by asserting the Monroe Doctrine and demanding that the Salisbury ministry settle the Venezuela-British Guiana boundary dispute through arbitration. Olney claimed U.S. supremacy in the Western Hemisphere. Preoccupation with more pressing affairs in Africa and East Asia prevented Salisbury from recognizing the urgency of Cleveland's demands, and even then he took for granted solid relations with the United States, despite anti-British statements by leading politicians. By early 1896, however, Salisbury agreed to arbitration while rejecting Cleveland's interpretation of the Monroe Doctrine. When faced with dangerous imperial rivalries in Africa and elsewhere, Great Britain chose to forge sound relations with the United States.

Cleveland's assertion of U.S. power became firmly etched in Salisbury's mind, as Cleveland's successor, William McKinley, took the United States into the Spanish-American-Cuban-Filipino War of 1898. Although British sympathies lay with Queen Victoria's niece, Spanish Queen-Regent Maria Cristina, neutrality best served national interests in view of crises in East Asia and in South Africa over the establishment of spheres of influence by the major powers and the need for Anglo-American cooperation, especially in Asia. Germany's acquisitions in the Pacific and in East Asia caused concern in London. Great Britain knew that Spain was no match for the United States and, therefore, concluded that it might as well recognize America's great-power status—albeit a status built on the ruins of the Spanish empire. With victory, the United States attained supremacy in the Western Hemisphere. America's acquisition of Guam and the Philippines, American Samoa (1899), and the annexation of Midway (1867), the Hawaiian Islands (1898), and Wake (1899) made the United States a Pacific power.

For these reasons, Great Britain cultivated closer relations with the United States as a prelude to an Anglo-American alliance beneficial to British interests in the Pacific and East Asia. The British government needed allies to deal effectively with international rivalries, especially rivalry with Germany; therefore, London hoped that the United States would enforce the American Open Door policy in East Asia, since it closely complemented British commercial objectives at a time when the Boer War in South Africa drained national resources. U.S. neutrality eased Great Britain's isolation during this war. After the United States rejected Great Britian's overtures for an alliance because it would compromise American sovereignty, the British government concluded, first, the 1902 Anglo-Japanese Alliance and then the Anglo-French Entente to ensure British interests in East Asia and other regions. In time, Washington saw the Anglo-Japanese Alliance as detrimental to American interests in the Pacific and took steps to break it.

Great Britain's desire for Anglo-American cooperation, combined with its decision to withdraw from Latin America to concentrate on Asian policies, led Salisbury to conclude the Hay-Pauncefote Treaty (1901) which abrogated the Clay-Bulwer Treaty and conceded, in effect, North American naval and military supremacy to the United States. Both governments acknowledged the strategic importance of an isthmian canal, but Great Britain was willing to concede construction and control of the canal to the United States in exchange for assurances of free access in time of peace and war. President Theodore Roosevelt's enthusiasm for the project motivated him to acquire the canal zone through "gunboat diplomacy" and negotiation so that construction could begin without delay. Great Britain retained only token naval and military forces in the Caribbean by 1906. Despite Roosevelt's aggressive Latin American policies, Great Britain realized that he supported an Anglo-American rapprochement. The Balfour ministry was pleased that Roosevelt's belief in balance-of-power politics caused him to favor the Japanese during his mediation of the Russo-Japanese War of 1904–1905. For similar reasons, London knew that it could count on Roosevelt's support against German imperialist claims in Morocco at the Algeciras Conference in 1906.

Rapprochement, Partnership in World War I, and Versailles

Shared history, language, cultural heritage, and close commercial relations reinforced Anglo-American political ties by the turn of the century. Twentieth-century U.S.-British relations have been characterized more often by mutual interests than dissension in an age of international conflict—especially two world wars and the Cold War. Such mutual security interests provided the basis for alliances during both world wars and for what historians have called the Anglo-American "special relationship" after 1945.

If bitter international rivalries and the dangerous Anglo-German naval arms race drew Great Britain closer to the United States by 1906, the outbreak of the Great

War in 1914 persuaded the Asquith ministry that Great Britain needed American friendship more than ever. The Anglophile Woodrow Wilson administration viewed Germany's invasion of Belgium in defiance of international law as proof of German perfidy. Wilson declared neutrality in "thought and action" in 1914, and, throughout the war, he protested violations of neutral rights by both Great Britain and Germany. Wilson ascertained that the British blockade of Germany would be accomplished by controlling European trade. On 30 March 1915, he protested the blockade as an unprecedented violation of neutral rights. London's redefinition of contraband, which provided a justification for the seizure of more goods enroute to Germany, also exacerbated tensions with Washington. But Wilson ultimately distinguished between German and British violations of neutral rights because German submarine warfare destroyed lives—for which there could never be adequate compensation—not just property. So the president was willing to tolerate British violations of U.S. neutral rights because they could be adjudicated after the war. In any case, Anglo-American legal precedents going back to Revolutionary times provided the basis for British blockade measures, including the paper blockade, lists of contraband goods liable to seizure, and the Doctrine of Continuous Voyage. The war also dramatically increased Great Britain's economic dependence on the United States, since Great Britain became both America's most important trading partner and its greatest debtor. U.S. loans to and trade with the Allied Powers greatly exceeded U.S. commerce with and loans to Germany.

Unlike Secretary of State William Jennings Bryan, Wilson and top foreign policy advisers, Edward M. House and Department of State counselor Robert Lansing, were more sympathetic to Great Britain's wartime objectives than to those of Germany because of their Anglophilism and because they recognized that a German victory would diminish U.S. power and influence. The president privately acknowledged that a German-dominated Europe would be detrimental to U.S. interests in the postwar world. Still, he realized that the American people were divided along ethnic lines and would not support war against Germany. Large immigrant groups, especially Irish Americans and German Americans, were not sympathetic to the British cause.

German-American relations began to deteriorate after 7 May 1915, when a German submarine sank the *Lusitania*, a British passenger liner, causing the death of 1,198 people, including 128 Americans. Secretary Bryan resigned over Wilson's insistence that German submarines observe international laws of naval warfare because Bryan predicted that the policy would draw the United States into war against Germany. Wilson believed that the United States could ensure its historic policy of freedom of the seas only by holding Germany to "strict accountability" for its submarine warfare and violations of neutral rights. Despite assurances given by the German government that its submarines would observe international law, other submarine attacks against the *Arabic* and *Sussex*, and the revelation of an espionage ring in the United States run by German naval attaches, convinced Wilson and his advisers that Germany could not be trusted to honor its agreements.

The United States severed diplomatic relations with the German government immediately after Berlin's 1 February 1917 declaration of unrestricted submarine warfare. Wilson believed that Americans would not go to war for selfish reasons, and so, even though he cited grievances against Germany (especially submarine warfare), he asked the country to wage war for peace. Wilson emphasized that American participation in the war would ensure a German defeat, and it would also enable the United States to assist in the establishment of a new world order in which peace would be preserved through a league created by democratic nations. To distinguish American war aims from those of the Allied Powers (France and Great Britain) who had territorial ambitions and sought a punitive peace settlement, the United States entered the war as an Associated rather than Allied power. Wilson preserved this distinction by refusing to integrate American forces with those of the Allied Powers; thus, U.S. armies retained their own command and only fought against German forces in Western Europe. Despite such differences, Great Britain cooperated with the United States in economic and political matters.

Wilson's call for a new League of Nations grew from close Anglo-American cooperation on a public and private level dating from the early years of the war. Two effective political pressure groups, the British League of Nations Society and the American League to Enforce Peace, began work independently on the league concept soon after the war began, as did Wilson and his special adviser, Colonel House. House and British Foreign Secretary Sir Edward Grey discussed the concept within the context of a peace settlement. Indeed, British and American league proposals introduced at the Versailles Peace Conference in 1919 were the product of Anglo-American cooperation by both governments working closely with British and American League pressure groups. Although the league concept had broad international support at Versailles, British and American policymakers fashioned the most comprehensive league proposal considered by the conference.

British prime minister David Lloyd George and President Wilson found that their respective national interests coincided more frequently than not at Versailles. In general, they readily agreed over European issues (for example, Polish boundaries and Danzig, German disarmament, and demilitarization of the Rhineland). They were in substantial agreement over French territorial claims in Europe but found it more difficult to resolve Japanese claims in Asia and the Pacific. Lloyd George, however, sided with French Premier Georges Clemenceau over German war reparations and indemnities. Wilson reluctantly acceded to the Anglo-French position because he assigned a higher priority to international acceptance of the League, which he hoped would preserve the postwar peace. But since the U.S. Senate rejected the Versailles Treaty and League membership, Wilson never had the chance to assist in the preservation of the peace settlement, which he had, in part created.

The Road to World War II

Unlike Great Britain, the United States greatly limited its international engagement in the postwar period. President Franklin D. Roosevelt, for example, declared neutrality when war broke out in 1939. Still, the United States remained an economic power in the world with considerable influence in the Western Hemisphere. Anglo-American relations were strained due to massive British war debts of approximately $4 million owed to the United States. Throughout the 1920s and 1930s, British governments pressed for debt cancellation or reduction because of the tremendous cost of the war and because it had destroyed the European economy. American presidents Warren G. Harding, Calvin Coolidge, and Herbert Hoover were more sympathetic to American taxpayers' demands for repayment than to British arguments that the debts caused severe economic hardship and jeopardized international commerce, since British monies were allocated to debt repayment rather than to rebuilding the national economy and international trade. U.S. agreements to reduce interest rates and to reschedule debt payment did nothing to ease British resentment over the debts or to address other serious problems such as German reparations, which amounted to $33 billion. American bankers provided Germany with loans and rescheduled reparation payments through the Dawes Plan in 1924 and then through the Young Plan in 1929. Neither Great Britain nor other allied debtor nations (France, Italy, and others) were able to continue their payments to the United States during the Great Depression. American loans to Germany ceased after the U.S. stock market crash in 1929, and then the following year, U.S. trade with European countries fell sharply after Congress passed the Smoot-Hawley tariff, which raised tariff rates by an average of 59 percent.

Despite tensions over economic issues, Great Britain and the United States found common ground for agreement at international arms limitations conferences. Even though the United States did not join Great Britain in League membership, it sent an observer to League meetings and participated in international arms-control conferences designed to prevent another deadly arms race. President Harding hosted the 1921–1922 Washington Conference out of concern for world peace, national security, and a desire to end the Anglo-Japanese Alliance, which he perceived as antithetical to U.S. interests in the Pacific. Britain shared these objectives due to the increasingly burdensome defense expenditures of an unnecessary alliance. Adoption of the Four-, Five-, and Nine-Power pacts by Britain, the United States, France, Italy, and Japan at Washington served Anglo-American interests especially in East Asia and the Pacific. While arms-control treaties and the 1928 Kellogg-Briand Pact outlawing war demonstrated Anglo-American cooperation to maintain peace during the interwar period, they did not necessarily address the national concerns of Germany, Japan, and Italy—powers which decided to change the world order to assure their own great-power status in the 1930s. When these nations launched their imperialist wars in Asia, Europe and Africa, League members discovered that they had neither the political consensus nor the enforcement powers to preserve peace or to prevent a second world war. Germany's invasion of Poland in 1939 caused Great Britain to declare war against Germany for the second time in twenty-five years to fulfill treaty obligations guaranteeing international borders.

Because most Americans supported a policy of nonintervention in the war, the United States declared neutrality once again. But President Roosevelt soon came to the same conclusion in 1939 that Wilson had reached in 1914; German victory would be detrimental to American interests and, in fact, would diminish U.S. power considerably. Unlike Wilson, however, Roosevelt insisted that, in Secretary of State Cordell Hull's words, "even a neutral cannot be asked to close his mind or his conscience." The British sought another Anglo-American alliance to meet the Axis threat. Between 1939 and 1941, Roosevelt obtained adjustments in neutrality legislation, which restricted American rights to trade with and travel to belligerent countries, so that the United States could aid Great Britain. The British government solicited aid because it needed war material and the military alliance that would most certainly develop out of such a relationship. The destroyers-for-bases deal which provided Great Britain with destroyers in exchange for military base sites, Lend-Lease shipments of war matériel, and the Anglo-American alliance defined in the Atlantic Charter changed the United States's status from that of a neutral to that of a pro-British non-belligerent by the summer of 1941—a status German dictator Adolf Hitler privately acknowledged but chose to tolerate until Germany defeated the Soviet Union. During their meeting at Argentia, Newfoundland, on 12 August 1941, Roosevelt and British prime minister Winston Churchill agreed to mutual wartime and postwar objectives in the Atlantic Charter, including the establishment of a postwar collective security organization. This alliance also provided for the integration of British and American naval forces in joint convoy operations which resulted in an undeclared naval war between the United States and Germany in the Atlantic Ocean prior to the Japanese attack on Pearl Harbor in December 1941.

The Grand Alliance: Cooperation and Rift

The Grand Alliance of the United States, Great Britain, and the Soviet Union defeated the Axis Powers (Germany, Italy, and Japan) because the Allies coordinated strategic operations in Europe, Asia, North Africa, and the Pacific. Great Britain received a total of $13.5 billion in Lend-Lease supplies from the United States—a greater amount of supplies than any other Allied Power. Lend-Lease shipments began arriving in the Soviet Union after German troops crossed Soviet borders in June 1941. But the wartime conferences, especially Tehran, Yalta, and Potsdam, allowed the Allies to establish common wartime and postwar objectives, despite divergent national priorities. Soviet leader Joseph Stalin, the only ally locked in combat with Axis ground forces on home territory, was deeply suspicious of Anglo-American intentions. Stalin consistently pressed for an early cross-channel invasion of Allied forces into France to relieve Soviet forces in the East, but the Anglo-Americans postponed the Normandy invasion, until June 1944, to prepare for the assault against formidable German fortifications. Churchill's concern over heavy casualties in France led him to advocate other options, especially the invasions of North Africa and Italy. Roosevelt agreed to the North African and Italian invasions as a way to confront the Axis powers prior to the Normandy invasion—the most effective way to prosecute the war. Nevertheless, combined Anglo-American forces won the Battle of the Atlantic, defeated the Japanese navy in the Coral Sea and at Midway, swept Axis troops from North Africa, and invaded Italy by July 1943. Coordinated strategic operations allowed Allied forces to launch simultaneous attacks on different fronts, as was the case, in November 1942, when Russian troops attacked German positions at Stalingrad while Anglo-American forces invaded Morocco and Algeria in North Africa, or when Russian offensives in eastern Europe coincided, first, with the Normandy invasion and, later, with the Anglo-American drive to capture Berlin in 1945.

Wartime cooperation enabled the Allied Powers to win, even as tensions within the alliance contributed to the emergence of the Cold War. Stalin's distrust of his Anglo-American allies over their delays in the invasion of German-occupied France and disagreement among the Allies over postwar policies, particularly over the makeup of the Polish government and the partition of Germany, caused the rift between Stalin and the Anglo-Americans. Different national priorities, which had been suppressed so that the war could be prosecuted effectively, emerged most prominently when the Allies turned to the postwar world order. Although Roosevelt and Churchill had defined broad Anglo-American policies in the Atlantic Charter, including self-determination of peoples and the establishment of a postwar collective security organization, Stalin did not share their vision of the postwar world. The Allies thus disagreed over the sort of peace they fought to secure. Stalin argued that Soviet security requirements must take precedence over Anglo-American promises of free elections in eastern Europe because German troops had crossed eastern Russian borders twice in twenty-five years. Roosevelt and Churchill realized that such security requirements would be used to justify Soviet domination of eastern Europe—an objective which Churchill had long opposed as antithetical to British interests. Compromises on Polish elections and the partition of Germany made at Tehran, Yalta, and Potsdam, satisfied no one, but, as Roosevelt later explained to a state department official, it was "the best" that could be done given the position of Soviet troops at the end of the war. In an effort to maintain a postwar peace, Roosevelt and Churchill helped establish a new collective security organization modeled on the League, the United Nations. At the Bretton Woods Conference (1944), they also created the World Bank and the International Monetary Fund (IMF) to promote international trade and economic stability.

An atomic, or nuclear, Anglo-American "special relationship" developed cautiously, first, because of British reluctance to collaborate with the United States on atomic technology that Britain had pioneered from 1939 to 1941, and, later, because America's Cold War policy of preserving a monopoly on atomic technology. When the American Manhattan project surpassed British efforts by 1942, Britain perceived that existing agreements to exchange information were inadequate, and it became amenable to an earlier American offer of a joint atomic project. But by that time, the United States was unwilling to collaborate. Britain finally obtained American cooperation, and the Quebec Agreement of 1943 established Canada as the site of the Anglo-American atomic project. However, the British had participated as a junior partner, because the United States more or less defined their role. Although both countries continued to consult each other on atomic policy from 1946 to 1956, they no longer collaborated as they had in the last two years of the war due to America's decision to maintain a monopoly on atomic power.

If wartime cooperation strengthened Anglo-American relations, Great Britain's reluctance to relinquish the empire, particularly in Asia, produced friction within the alliance. The United States had long criticized British imperialism, and Roosevelt initially believed that British colonies should be replaced by independent self-governing nations after the war. Roosevelt's refusal to fight for the preservation of the British Empire caused serious differences between himself and Churchill, despite the president's assurances of loyalty to the Grand Alliance. By 1945, the United States faced a fait accompli when British, French, and Dutch Allied military operations reclaimed their Asian colonies from Japanese occupation forces. Nationalist forces ultimately succeeded in the struggle against European colonialism so that India, Burma, Malaysia, Indonesia, and other nations achieved their independence in the next few years.

The Cold War and After

The victorious powers built the new world order on the ruins of empires carved out by the Axis Powers. This new order and the superpower competition between the United States and the Soviet Union, which characterized the Cold War, provided a context for international affairs for the next five decades. Europe and Asia suffered massive devastation and loss of life, as most of the fighting took place on those continents. Approximately forty-five million people died in the war. If the war almost destroyed France and the Soviet Union, it succeeded in destroying both the French and British Empires. The United States was the only Allied Power unscathed by the war; moreover, its enormous industrial power and its possession of the atomic bomb made it the premier world power. In contrast, the Soviet Union had suffered the greatest losses—more than twenty million deaths—and the most damage of any of the Allies, but its huge reconstruction program and its production of the atomic bomb in 1949 enabled it to challenge America's predominance. By the 1950s, the United States and the Soviet Union had become superpowers that dominated the postwar world. The emergence of a bipolar world with competing Soviet and American spheres of influence, defined by wartime responsibilities within the Grand Alliance, itself, necessarily aligned Great Britain with the United States. Thus, British foreign policy did not change even when Clement Attlee succeeded Churchill as prime minister in 1945.

Since Great Britain had historically opposed Russian influence in Europe and the eastern Mediterranean due to British commercial and strategic interests, the government in London largely supported American policies of containing the Soviet Union, particularly in Europe, during the Cold War. In his "Iron Curtain" speech of 5 March 1946, former Prime Minister Churchill popularized the term "special relationship" to characterize close Anglo-American relations that developed during World War II and that, he believed, were essential to counter aggressive Soviet East European policies. The following year, when Great Britain informed the United States that it could no longer afford to assist Greece (a British client state), President Harry S. Truman secured military and economic aid for Greece and Turkey under the Truman Doctrine. This allowed the British-backed Athens government to defeat a leftist insurgency and Turkey to resist Soviet pressure for access to the Mediterranean Sea. British foreign minister Ernest Bevin also encouraged the United States to adopt the Marshall Plan for the economic recovery of Europe and Great Britain and to create the North Atlantic Treaty Organization (NATO). Bevin's support for the programs helped ensure their success and reinforced the "special relationship;" Great Britain received the largest share of Marshall aid funds, $3.2 billion. Anglo-American cooperation in implementing the containment policy amounted to a reversal of the relationship the two nations had developed since 1783, with the United States providing assistance to its former mother country now in decline.

Washington and London, however, frequently disagreed over the Middle East. The Attlee ministry suspected the Truman administration of challenging the British sphere of influence in the Middle East, particularly after the United States supported the creation of the state of Israel in British-controlled Palestine in 1948, and then supplanted the British in Iran by the early 1950s.

The United States assumed Great Britain's role as the predominant Western power in the Middle East and in the Pacific, especially in Southeast Asia, where American governments, from 1945 to 1956, supported the French against Nationalist Vietnamese forces led by Ho Chi Minh. As historian Paul Kennedy has pointed out, America's global strategic commitments presented problems similar to those faced by the British during the nineteenth century: strategic commitments which exceeded its military capabilities and huge military expenditures which jeopardized its domestic economy and international trade.

After 1945, Great Britain and the United States more readily forged common policies in Europe and Asia than in the Middle East. The Truman and Attlee governments agreed on support for West Berlin against the Soviet Union during the crisis of 1948, on the establishment of West Germany in 1949, and on the commitment of United Nations's forces to Korea in 1950, because these crises pitted the British and Americans against Communist nations. But unlike the United States, Great Britain had opened diplomatic relations with the Communist People's Republic of China (PRC). After Chinese troops invaded North Korea in November 1950, Attlee became alarmed over the possibility that the United States might use the bomb against the PRC, because such action might escalate the conflict into a wider war. Anglo-American relations deteriorated due to the Suez crisis of 1956, which occurred when Egyptian president Gamal Abdel Nasser nationalized the British-and-French-controlled Suez Canal after the United States canceled aid to Egypt. British, French, and Israeli troops invaded the canal area to regain the canal and to oust Nasser, who was the leader of the pan-Arab movement. The Eisenhower administration curtailed British and French oil supplies and financial support to force the withdrawal of Anglo-French-Israeli troops from the Suez Canal area.

In 1957, mutual security interests, intensified by the Russian *Sputnik* satellite, drew Great Britain and the United States together in a new nuclear partnership. The two countries had already signed treaties providing for the peaceful use of nuclear power and then concluded a series of defense agreements, from 1958 to 1962, according Great Britain exclusive access to American nuclear technology. This so-called "special relationship" entailed the exchange of information on nuclear defense technology and of nuclear materials, as well as the sale of nuclear weapons (the Skybolt missiles in 1960 and the Polaris missiles in 1962) to Great Britain, which permitted the United States to establish military bases in the British Isles and to deploy nuclear weapons there. This arrangement nearly went awry when the Kennedy administration canceled the Skybolt program for technical reasons in 1962. Because of American reticence to share nuclear technology until 1958, the Macmillan ministry suspected that Washington never intended to deliver the missiles. Kennedy dispelled these suspicions by substituting the Polaris missiles. The United States established nuclear policies through international arms limitations or reduction treaties from 1960 to the early 1990s, and Great Britain accepted these policies—U.S.-Soviet arms limitations agreements such as the Antiballistic Missile (ABM) Treaty of 1972 and the Strategic Arms Limitations Treaties (SALT) of 1972 and 1979. None diminished British defense systems. The international nuclear disarmament movement, with its British and American counterparts, gave impetus to U.S.-Soviet Strategic Arms Reductions Talks (START) from 1985–1991, producing the Intermediate-Range Nuclear Forces (INF) Treaty of 1987 and the START Treaty four years afterward. Again, Anglo-American interests coincided, inasmuch as Great Britain remained dependent on the United States for its nuclear force and faced considerable pressure from the British antinuclear movement. British loyalty also translated into support for America's Strategic Defense Initiative (SDI).

For the most part, Great Britain has been a loyal ally of the United States throughout the twentieth century. America's containment policy tended to strengthen ties with Britain—except in the case of Vietnam from 1954 to 1973. Anglo-American relations cooled during the Viet-nam War because Great Britain's best interests were served by remaining on the sidelines—thereby intensifying America's isolation from the international community over the war. Great Britain confronted more pressing problems elsewhere, especially in its Asian and African colonies where independence movements caused the further disintegration of the empire. Severe financial problems, the need to focus on European affairs, and a war against Malaysian Communists from 1948 to 1968, also prevented Great Britain from providing the United States with little more than sympathy and offers to mediate the Vietnam conflict. British-American relations warmed up again after the Vietnam War, particularly when the Conservative Thatcher ministry and the Republican administration of Ronald Reagan were in power. The two governments cooperated on many levels because they had adopted similar economic and foreign policies. Reagan provided British military forces with crucial assistance, including military intelligence, Sidewinder missiles, and military base facilities in the south Atlantic, during the Falklands War between Great Britain and Argentina in 1982. Thatcher was the only European leader to support Reagan's 1986 bombing raid on Libya, which was executed in retaliation for alleged terrorist attacks.

The collapse of the Soviet Union in 1991 and its earlier loss of its sphere of influence in Eastern Europe ended both the Cold War and the stability offered by the bipolar world thus altering the basis for Anglo-American relations. The use of United Nations forces against Iraq in the 1991 Persian Gulf War, however, demonstrated continued Anglo-American cooperation to preserve peace. The reunification of Germany in 1990, the role of the new Germany in European politics, and the status of Eastern European nations and former Soviet republics continues to affect relations between the United States and Great Britain vis-à-vis Europe. As a member of the European Union and the European Parliament, Great Britain necessarily wants to play a major role in shaping twenty-first-century Europe, especially given EU's goal of an integrated market in the 1990s. Both Great Britain and the United States have encouraged the establishment of democratic governments in Eastern Europe and the former Soviet republics. Despite London's rejection of Washington's proposal to lift the arms embargo against Bosnian Muslims, the two governments have tried to use NATO as a stabilizing influence in the region—for instance, in Bosnia from 1994 to 1996—with some success. In addition, Great Britain remains one of the United States's major trading partners, and one with which the United States maintains a favorable balance of trade.

JANET M. MANSON

See also Adams, Charles Francis; Adams, John; Alabama Claims; American Revolution; Atlantic Charter; Canada; Churchill, Winston Leonard Spencer; Cold War; Destroyers-for-Bases Deal; European Union; Fenians; French and Indian War; George III; Ghent, Treaty of; Impressment; Jay's Treaty; Kellogg-Briand Pact; Lloyd George, David; Marshall Plan; Monroe Doctrine; Napoleanic Wars; Neutral Rights; Neutrality Acts of the 1930s; North Atlantic Treaty Organization; Open Door Policy; Oregon Question; Paris Peace Conference of 1919; Potsdam Conference; Roosevelt, Franklin Delano; Rush-Bagot Agreement; Suez Crisis; Thatcher, Margaret; Trent Affair; Truman Doctrine; United Nations; Venezuelan Boundary Dispute; War Debt of World War I; War of 1812; Washington Conference on the Limitation of Armaments; Webster-Ashburton Treaty; Wilson, Thomas Woodrow; World War I; World War II; Yalta Conference

FURTHER READING

Allen, Harry Cronbrook. *Great Britain and the United States: A History of Anglo-American Relations (1783-1952).* New York, 1955.

Bartlett, C. J. *"The Special Relationship:" A Political History of Anglo-American Relations Since 1945.* New York, 1992.

Beer, George Louis. *The Origins of the British Colonial System, 1578-1660.* Gloucester, Eng., 1959.

Bourne, Kenneth. *The Foreign Policy of Victorian England, 1830-1902.* Oxford, 1970.

———. *Britain and the Balance of Power in North America, 1815-1908.* Berkeley and Los Angeles, 1967.

Campbell, Charles S. *From Revolution to Rapprochement: The United States and Great Britain, 1783-1900.* New York, 1974.

Christie, Ian R. *Crisis of Empire: Great Britain and the American Colonies, 1754-1783.* New York, 1966.

Feis, Herbert. *Churchill Roosevelt Stalin: The War They Waged and the Peace They Sought.* Princeton, N.J., 1957.

Hathaway, Robert M. *Great Britain and the United States: Special Relations Since World War II.* Boston, 1990.

Jones, Howard. *The Webster-Ashburton Treaty: A Study in Anglo-American Relations, 1783-1843.* Chapel Hill, N.C., 1977.

———. *Union in Peril: The Crisis over British Intervention in the Civil War.* Chapel Hill, N.C., 1992.

Kennedy, Paul. *The Rise and Fall of the Great Powers: Economic Change and Military Conflict, 1500 to 2000.* New York, 1987.

Louis, Wm. Roger, and Hedley Bull, eds. *The "Special Relationship" Since 1945.* Oxford, 1986.

McNeill, William H. *America, Britain & Russia: Their Co-operation and Conflict, 1941-1946.* New York, 1970.

Nicholas, H. G. *The United States and Britain.* Chicago, 1975.

Perkins, Bradford. *Castlereagh and Adams: England and the United States, 1812-1832.* Berkeley and Los Angeles, 1964.

———. *The First Rapprochement: England the United States, 1795-1805.* Berkeley and Los Angeles, 1967.

———. *Prologue to War: England and the United States, 1805-1812.* Berkeley and Los Angeles, 1961.

Reynolds, David. *The Creation of the Anglo-American Alliance, 1937-41: A Study in Competitive Co-operation.* Chapel Hill, N.C., 1982.

Stuart, Reginald C. *United States Expansionism and British North America 1775-1871.* Chapel Hill, N.C., 1988.

Watt, D. Cameron. *Succeeding John Bull: America in Britain's Place, 1900-1975.* Cambridge, 1984.

GREECE

The southernmost Balkan state, bordered by the Ionian, Mediterranean, and Aegean Seas, Albania, Yugoslavian Macedonia, Bulgaria, and Turkey. With its many islands extending deep into the eastern Mediterranean, it has traditionally served as the crossroads between Europe, Asia, and Africa. Although modern Greece is a relatively young state, its recorded history dates to the Neolithic age of the six millennium B.C. Almost 80 percent of its land area (totaling 51,000 square miles) is mountainous and barren, forcing its people (approaching 11 million) to turn to the sea, commerce, and foreign ventures for their livelihoods. The ancient Greeks (Hellenes) were the builders of a series of impressive civilizations culminating in the golden age of Athens in the fifth century B.C., whose achievements are the fountainhead of Western civilization. Following Alexander the Great's Hellenistic but multinational empire, which extended across Persia to the Hindus River, Greece became a minor outpost of the Roman Empire. Later, Greek language, culture, and rulers were dominant elements of the Byzantine Empire and especially its capital, Constantinople, until its fall to the Ottoman Turks in 1453.

Early Relations

The Greek nation's struggle to gain its freedom from Ottoman rule (1821–1829) attracted much sympathy in the United States, where classical Greece had many admirers, including Thomas Jefferson. Although the administration of President James Monroe (1817–1825) kept its distance from the conflict, Americans supported the insurgents privately, and some traveled to Greece to take part in the war. The infant Greek state was recognized by the United States in 1833, and a commercial treaty was signed four years later. For the next eighty years, as Greeks in large numbers sought their fortune in the New World, bilateral relations remained rudimentary.

In 1918 the United States joined Great Britain and France in providing the breakaway government of Eleutherios Venizelos, in power since the previous year, with a large loan that brought Greece actively into World War I on the side of the Entente powers. At the Paris Peace Conference of 1919 President Woodrow Wilson approved Allied plans permitting Greece to land troops in Asia Minor in May 1919. When in 1922, following the Kemalist counteroffensive, Turkish forces expelled the Greeks, U.S. officials sought to avert wholesale slaughter, and the U.S. Navy rescued many fleeing Greeks. A refugee settlement commission under Henry Morgenthau and private American relief agencies helped Greece cope with the enormous problems caused by the influx of more than a million destitute refugees from Turkey. In

GENERAL DISTRIBUTION OF GREEK AMERICANS IN THE LATE 1980S	
First Generation	250,000
Second Generation	400,000
Third Generation	250,000
Fourth Generation	100,000
Total	1,000,000

From *Greek Americans: Struggle and Success*, Charles C. Moskos. ©1989 by Transaction Publishers. Reprinted with permission of Transaction Publishers. All rights reserved.

the interwar period U.S. construction companies were involved in major public works in Greece, and the United States became one of that country's principal trade partners. Otherwise, with the exception of the extradition case of the Chicago financier Samuel Insull, who was charged with embezzlement and larceny and fled to Athens hoping to avoid prosecution (1932–1934), the United States took little interest in Greece. This attitude did not change during the years of the Ioannis Metaxas dictatorship (1936–1941), particularly since the new regime was careful not to hinder private American commercial and construction activities in Greece.

During World War II, U.S. officials accepted Great Britain's primary responsibility for Greek affairs but questioned London's interventionist policies, not least in Cairo, where the Greek government-in-exile was based, and support for the Greek monarchy. At the First Quebec Conference (August 1943) President Franklin D. Roosevelt joined Prime Minister Winston S. Churchill in formally endorsing the intention of King George II to return to Greece at the earliest opportunity and submit to a referendum the question of the monarchy's future sometime after the war. In December 1943, alarmed by the growing anti-monarchy sentiment among Greeks, British officials sought to pressure the king to declare that he would return only after a referendum had invited him back. Although the Department of State had already communicated to the king its support of the British proposal, at a meeting in Cairo Roosevelt encouraged him, to reject it and complained that the plan would "deprive the king of his crown." In December 1944 U.S. vessels transported British troops from Italy to Athens, which helped suppress a leftist uprising. Several months later Roosevelt's suggestion for a U.S.-British-Soviet mission to supervise postwar reconstruction in Greece was rejected by Churchill, who opposed any Soviet role in Greek affairs. In March 1946 U.S., British, and French observers monitored the first parliamentary elections in Greece since 1936, and strong American support in the Foreign Ministers Council assured the transfer to Greece from

Italy of the Dodecanese islands (formally carried out in February 1947); but otherwise the United States refused to become actively involved in Greek problems.

Truman Doctrine, U.S. Aid, and Cyprus: 1946–1964

President Harry S. Truman's administration began to take serious interest in Greece in mid-1946, in the context of the emerging global conflict with the Soviet Union. U.S. officials perceived the communist insurgency in Greece (1946–1949) as a major component of Moscow's strategy to expand its control to the eastern Mediterranean and beyond. In December 1946 American officials supported the Greek government in its complaint at the United Nations that the insurgency was fomented by Greece's communist northern neighbors. To contain the further spread of Soviet power the Truman Doctrine (March 1947) provided Greece and Turkey with substantial economic, military, and diplomatic assistance. A formal agreement, signed on 20 June 1947, defined the terms of assistance and granted American officials a controlling influence over virtually all major activity of the Greek state. A Joint U.S. Military Advisory and Planning Group (JUSMAPG) provided overall support, advice and supervision to the Greek government forces in their efforts to defeat the communist insurgency. On its recommendation the Truman administration decided (January 1948) that until the insurgents had been defeated military assistance would have priority over all other forms of American support. Under the command of Lt. Gen. James A. Van Fleet, a World War II combat veteran, the American military mission played a crucial role in the preparation and implementation of all major operations against the insurgents and American field officers were assigned to Greek units at the division and corps levels. The Greek armed forces were supplied with a variety of weapons and equipment which proved effective against the communist guerrillas. American economic and military assistance during 1946–1949 exceeded one billion dollars. In May 1949, Soviet feelers for a peaceful settlement of the Greek crisis were treated with skepticism and the insurgency was soon crushed by the government's superior forces.

Following the end of the civil war in 1949, Washington continued to play an important role through programs of economic and military aid and through its influence over Greek conservatives, the security forces, and the palace. Supported by the United States, Greece and Turkey became members (October 1951) of the North Atlantic Treaty Organization (NATO), sent troops to the Korean conflict, and were generally integrated in the anti-Soviet alliance. A 1953 agreement on military facilities granted the United States far-reaching privileges in Greece,

GREEK IMMIGRATION TO THE UNITED STATES			
Era		Approximate Total	Approximate Annual Average
Early Migration	1873–1899	15,000	500
Great Wave	1890–1917	450,000	25,000
Last Exodus	1918–1924	70,000	10,000
Closed Door	1925–1946	30,000	1,300
Postwar Migration	1947–1965	75,000	4,000
New Wave	1966–1979	160,000	11,000
Declining Migration	1980–1989	25,000	2,500

From *Greek Americans: Struggle and Success*, Charles C. Moskos. ©1989 by Transaction Publishers. Reprinted with permission of Transaction Publishers. All rights reserved.

including extraterritoriality status for its military personnel and their dependents. Under the conservative prime ministers Alexandros Papagos (1952–1955) and Konstantinos Karamanlis (1955–1963), Greek authorities spared no effort to accommodate U.S. interests, and bilateral relations remained close, even as Greece's economic dependence on the United States was gradually curtailed. Efforts to bring about the union of Cyprus, a British colony, with Greece caused serious tension not only in Greek-British and Greek-Turkish relations (about one-fifth of the Cypriots are Moslem Turks, and the island was once part of the Ottoman Empire), but also in U.S.-Greek relations as American officials became concerned that the Cyprus dispute was damaging NATO. In August 1953 the Papagos government solicited U.S. assistance in dissuading the Greek Cypriot leader, Archbishop Makarios, from bringing the Cyprus problem to the United Nations. In his response Secretary of State John Foster Dulles indicated that the United States had no wish to become involved, particularly since Makarios could not be trusted to cooperate with western diplomatic efforts. Although the Karamanlis government endorsed the Eisenhower Doctrine (May 1957), American diplomats concluded that "We can no longer be as certain as we have been in the past that we shall have Greece's support in foreign policy matters that are critical to us." In July 1958 Karamanlis warned Washington that unless American pressure was exerted on Britain concerning Cyprus, the Greek public would react against the West. In December 1959 on an official visit to Athens, President Dwight D. Eisenhower promised Greece continued economic and political support but carefully avoided the Cyprus issue. In April 1960, following Soviet threats that Greece would suffer if it accepted American missiles, Secretary of State Christian Herter visited Athens and reaffirmed American commitment to protect Greece. A year later President John F. Kennedy honored Karamanlis

at the White House and the Greek prime minister addressed the House of Representatives, where he appealed for more economic assistance. The United States welcomed the establishment of Cyprus as an independent republic in 1960.

Rifts: 1964–1990

The electoral defeat of the conservatives in 1964 and the rise of the centrists-liberals under Georgios Papandreou ushered in a new and more difficult era in U.S.-Greek relations. The political climate, which reflected in part a growing anti-American and anti-NATO sentiment, appeared to undermine the power of conservative elites, the military, and the monarchy, all of whom had been particularly receptive to U.S. concerns. Furthermore, renewed friction between Greece and Turkey over Cyprus and assorted Aegean problems threatened to paralyze NATO's southern flank and on several occasions brought the two neighbors to the brink of war. In 1964 Turkey was restrained from invading Cyprus when President Lyndon B. Johnson bluntly warned that such action would have dire consequences for Turkey. In turn, while on a visit to Washington (June 1964), Papandreou was told that unless the Cyprus problem was settled promptly, American assistance to Greece would be terminated and that if Turkey resorted to war Greece would be defeated. Under Washington's persistent pressure, Greek-Turkish talks on the Cyprus dispute resumed and a plan prepared by former Secretary of State Dean Acheson, which would have given most of the island to Greece, was briefly discussed before it was rejected by the Greek side at the insistence of Cyprus President Archbishop Makarios, who wished to preserve the republic as an independent state. The rejection of the Acheson plan, Greece's refusal to participate in NATO exercises, and anti-West statements by members of the Papandreou government (including the prime minister's son, Andreas) intensified the growing rift in U.S.-Greek relations. In 1967, when Turkey threatened once more to intervene in Cyprus by force, the situation was again defused through U.S. efforts; this time the envoy, Cyrus R. Vance, convinced the Greek government to withdraw most of the troops it had stationed in Cyprus. Nevertheless, the Cyprus controversy remained the principal bone of contention between Athens and Ankara, damaging U.S. relations with both its allies across the Aegean.

Under these circumstances U.S. officials were neither surprised nor unhappy when a group of middle-rank army officers (mostly colonels), intent on preventing the electoral victory of a left-center coalition, seized power in Athens in April 1967. Although Central Intelligence Agency (CIA) operatives are known to have been in close contact with the principal conspirators, there is no concrete evidence of U.S. complicity in the coup. After perfunctory statements that democracy should be restored, and a brief embargo on heavy weapons, the United States easily accommodated itself to the colonels' dictatorship, which was eager to please Washington. The administration of President Richard M. Nixon focused its attention on considerations of global strategy and was not concerned with what Secretary of State Henry Kissinger called the theology of complaints regarding violations of human rights and democratic rule in Greece. Accordingly, the military junta was restored to the status of a valued ally, and high-level U.S. officials bestowed lavish praise upon it. Simultaneously, U.S. officials made no secret of their dislike for the independent-minded president of Cyprus, Archbishop Makarios, whose feuding with the Greek government threatened to plunge the island republic into violence once again.

In 1974, despite clear signs that the Greek junta was plotting to overthrow Makarios, the Nixon administration made no serious attempt to avert disaster in Cyprus. When the Athens-engineered coup toppled Makarios, who barely survived assassination, the United States temporized. Undersecretary of State Joseph Sisco traveled to Athens and Ankara with, in his words, a "virtually empty attaché case, a smile, and a shoeshine." This time Turkey invaded Cyprus and occupied the island's northern region, uprooting nearly 200,000 Greek Cypriots; in Athens the junta disappeared under the weight of its own ineptitude and disgrace. Henceforth, United States policy would, in essence, accept the Turkish view that the two ethnic communities in Cyprus could coexist and the republic survive only under a confederal regime, a solution that was unacceptable to the Greek side. Thus, the Cyprus problem continued to aggravate relations between Washington and Athens.

Following the reestablishment of democracy in 1974 under Karamanlis's conservative New Democracy party,

Greece withdrew its military personnel from all NATO headquarters, although they returned in October 1980 following protracted negotiations, and abrogated the U.S. Navy's homeporting agreement, as a wave of anti-American demonstrations swept over the country that was punctuated by acts of vandalism against U.S. property. The CIA chief of station in Athens, Richard S. Welch, who was serving under diplomatic cover, was assassinated soon after his identity was revealed in the press. Negotiations to renew the bilateral agreement on defense and economic cooperation became stalled. The U.S. Navy lost access to the Eleusis naval base and Karamanlis announced his intention to negotiate the placing of all NATO and U.S. bases in Greece under Greek command. On the other hand, in January 1975 Defense Minister Evangelos Averoff informed parliament that the government was asking the administration of President Gerald Ford to restore military assistance programs which had been drastically curtailed during the years of military dictatorship. And U.S. plans to remove from Greece aging nuclear warheads were placed on hold at the request of Greek officials who feared that the move might be interpreted as favoring Turkey. In April 1977, Averoff announced that of the seven major United States bases in Greece four would remain, and several months later the two governments initialed a new four-year defense cooperation agreement under which the United States would provide Greece with $700 million in military assistance in exchange for the continued use of the four bases. Although he was determined to avoid an open rupture with the United States, Karamanlis sought to reduce Greece's reliance on Washington through a variety of new diplomatic ventures, including membership in the European Community. For its part, despite promises to seek a "just and durable" solution to the Cyprus problem, the administration of President Jimmy Carter failed to break the impasse, and when it lifted its arms embargo against Turkey (September 1978) it incurred the anger of Greeks everywhere. Until the conservatives' defeat in October 1981, U.S.-Greek relations remained cool, and, despite their partnership in NATO, the interests of the two appeared to diverge increasingly.

The emergence of a socialist government, the first in Greek history, did not augur well for U.S.-Greek relations. Its leader, Andreas Papandreou, a U.S. citizen and one-time economics professor at the University of California, had made criticism of the United States, NATO, and capitalism the key themes of his political career since the 1960s. His neo-Marxist theories, neutralist orientation, confrontational style, and inflamed nationalist-populist rhetoric promised to put Greece on a collision course with U.S. policies. Indeed, through his first tenure as prime minister (1981–1989), Papandreou regularly irritated Washington with his obstreperous tactics in NATO, criticism of U.S. policies, cordial relations with the Soviet bloc and radical Arab elements, as well as with his brinkmanship in Greek relations with Turkey. To dramatize its defiance of U.S. and NATO strategy in the Balkans, the Papandreou government declared a new national defense doctrine (1985) designed to protect the country specifically against a Turkish threat, a pact of friendship and cooperation was concluded with Bulgaria (1986), and military talks were held with Yugoslavia and Romania.

In the end, the socialist government could not change the fact that, ideological considerations notwithstanding, Greece's vulnerability in the Aegean and elsewhere required the continuation of U.S. support. Accordingly, beneath the anti-American posturing, care was taken to prevent a breakdown in bilateral relations. In 1983 a new defense and economic cooperation agreement was signed, which allowed the U.S. bases to remain in Greece. For its part, the Ronald Reagan administration undertook to help maintain the existing balance of military power between Greece and Turkey by providing them with defense assistance on a 7–10 ratio. Less important irritants, including requests for the extradition of suspected terrorists, the status of the Voice of America's (VOA) relay stations in Greece, and Greek votes in the United Nations, remained unresolved. A travel advisory concerning alleged shortcomings of antiterrorist measures in Greece, issued by Washington in July 1985, prompted angry responses in Athens. When the scandal-plagued socialists lost the election of June 1989, a difficult era in U.S.-Greek relations came to a close.

The 1990s

During their brief return to power (1990–1993), the conservatives under Prime Minister Konstantinos Mitsotakis sought to improve the tenor of U.S.-Greek relations. A new eight-year agreement was concluded on the bases which, in a general reorganization of U.S. forces overseas, had been reduced to two, and Greece participated in NATO exercises designed to secure sea communications in the Mediterranean. In June 1990 Mitsotakis visited the United States and renewed several economic and trade agreements and was hosted by President George Bush who accepted an invitation to visit Greece. Despite domestic opposition the Greek government decided to take part in the U.N.-mandated war against Iraq by contributing one frigate to the multi-national naval force in the Red Sea. Clearly pleased, the Bush administration reiterated that it was fully committed to the security of Greece and accepted in principle a Greek request for Patriot missiles. President Bush paid a two-day visit to Greece in July 1991 and in his address to the parliament

praised the Greeks for their dedication to Western ideals and to NATO. The visit helped soothe somewhat the Greeks' irritation with the Department of State's annual report on human rights which referred to the existence in northern Greece of a "Slavo-Macedonian" minority. In addition to the festering problems of Cyprus and Greek-Turkish disputes, relations between Washington and Athens were burdened by a new development—the elevation of Yugoslavian Macedonia to the status of independent state in 1991. Against a background of conflict and antagonism between Greeks and Slavs in the Balkans, Greeks professed to find proof of irredentist aspirations aimed at Greek Macedonia in the new republic's national symbols of the constitution, the flag, maps, and so on. Accordingly, Greece strenuously opposed the recognition of the new state under the name of Republic of Macedonia by the international community and imposed on it an economic embargo. On the other hand, the United States sought to insure the survival and internal stability of Yugoslavian Macedonia as a barrier to further ethnic conflict in the Balkans. Thus, following the socialists' return to office in 1993, U.S. relations with Greece were troubled by the twin clouds of Macedonia and the Athens-Ankara feud. In April 1994 an official visit to Washington by Prime Minister Papandreou, chastened and in poor health, symbolized his reconciliation with U.S. authorities but otherwise produced little of substance. In an attempt to satisfy Athens and placate the energetic Greek-American community, the administration of President Bill Clinton promised to intensify its efforts to mediate in Greece's disputes with Macedonia and Turkey. On the other hand, the United States supported the admission of the new state under the name Former Yugoslav Republic of Macedonia into the United Nations in 1993, and recognized it in February 1994, but it refrained from exchanging ambassadors.

In September 1995 behind the scenes U.S. diplomacy assisted in the conclusion of a bilateral agreement under which Athens lifted its embargo on Yugoslavian Macedonia while Skopje pledged to change its flag and remove from its constitution certain passages which the Greeks had found objectionable; talks on the new republic's official name were to continue. American diplomats also assisted Greece and Albania to diffuse a number of problems which threatened to damage relations between the two Balkan neighbors. And in January 1996 Washington's strong admonitions, including telephone calls from President Clinton, succeeded in averting a new military confrontation between Greece and Turkey, this time over an uninhabited islet in the Aegean. Shortly before this latest crisis the replacement of the ailing Papandreou by one of his younger and more pragmatic socialist colleagues, Costas Simitis, offered some promise that relations between Greece and the United States might now be conducted in a more constructive atmosphere. The Clinton administration lost no time in inviting the new Greek prime minister to Washington. While breaking no new ground, the working visit of Prime Minister Simitis in April paved the way for a more productive dialogue in bilateral relations and was followed by the visit of the President of the Hellenic Republic, Costis Stephanopoulos, to whom the Clinton administration and the Greek American community extended a cordial welcome. But while American officials listened sympathetically, there were no signs that on the foreign policy and security issues of greatest concern to Greece the United States was prepared to side with Athens.

In the mid-1990s relations between the United States and Greece were unencumbered by serious bilateral problems and had largely recovered from the poisonous effects of their patron-client mode of the Cold War era. At the same time, the end of East-West divisions ushered in a new era of instability and conflict which tends to accentuate the divergence in Greek and U.S. interests. In the Bosnian crisis, Greek traditional sympathies for the Serbs and fear that the Moslems' cause would expand Turkey's power across the Balkans turned the Greek officials into sullen critics of U.S. policies in the region. Greece agreed to contribute to the NATO forces sent to enforce the peace agreement in Bosnia at least in part so as to match Turkey's enthusiastic participation in the effort. More significant, in Washington's view, the end of the Cold War diminished Greece's role as a barrier to Soviet aggression while problems with its neighbors have denied Greece the opportunity to become a constructive influence and regional leader. On the other hand, the value of Turkey for American interests in the Middle East and central Asia, and in the Moslem world generally, has been enhanced. As a result, in its regional conflicts, including those with Albania, Yugoslavian Macedonia, and Turkey, Greece was not likely to receive the unqualified support of the United States.

JOHN O. IATRIDES

See also Containment; Cyprus; Macedonia, former Yugoslav Republic of; North Atlantic Treaty Organization; Overseas Military Bases; Truman Doctrine; Turkey

FURTHER READING

Couloumbis, Theodore A. *The United States, Greece, and Turkey: The Troubled Triangle.* New York, 1983.
Couloumbis, Theodore A., and John O. Iatrides, eds. *Greek-American Relations: A Critical Review.* New York, 1980.
Iatrides, John O. "Greece and the United States: The Strained Partnership." In *Greece in the 1980s,* edited by Richard Clogg. New York, 1983.
———. "Beneath the Sound and Fury: US Relations with the PASOK Government." In *Greece, 1981–89, The Populist Decade,* edited by Richard Clogg. New York, 1993.
———, ed. *Ambassador MacVeagh Reports: Greece 1933–1947.* Princeton, N.J., 1980.
Jones, Howard. *A New Kind of War: America's Global Strategy and the Truman Doctrine in Greece.* New York, 1989.
Stearns, Monteagle. *Entangled Allies: U.S. Policy Toward Greece, Turkey, and Cyprus.* New York, 1992.
Stern, Laurence Marcus. *The Wrong Horse: The Politics of Intervention and the Failure of American Diplomacy.* New York, 1977.
Wittner, Lawrence S. *American Intervention in Greece, 1943–1949.* New York, 1982.

GREENLAND

Located in the North Atlantic ocean between Norway and Canada, it is the largest island in the world. An autonomous but integral part of the kingdom of Denmark, Greenland's foreign policy is directed by Copenhagen. In 1979 it was granted home rule and achieved full internal self-rule by 1981, giving the government in Godthåb political clout in its dealings with the United States over the sometimes controversial U.S. military presence. Relations between the United States and Greenland began with the whaling trade around Davis Strait in 1732. A U.S. strategic interest in Greenland was first articulated by William H. Seward, secretary of state under President Abraham Lincoln, who was interested in acquiring the island. During the nineteenth century Greenland was a base of operations for U.S. Arctic explorers, the most famous of whom was Rear Admiral Robert E. Peary, who launched his ambitious expedition to the North Pole from Greenland. Under the terms of a 1917 treaty with Denmark, the U.S. government renounced all claims to territory discovered by Peary.

Prior to World War II, Greenland did not play a vital role in Washington's commitment to North Atlantic security. In 1941, one year after the German occupation of Denmark, the Danish ambassador in Washington signed an agreement with Secretary of State Cordell Hull permitting the United States to establish military bases in Greenland. In return for this wartime protectorate, the United States reaffirmed Danish sovereignty over the island. After the war, and especially after the outbreak of hostilities in Korea in 1950, Washington sought to keep its military facilities in Greenland as part of a hemisphere defense plan. The 1951 Defense of Greenland Agreement with Copenhagen laid the basis for continued U.S. military presence on the island as a function of collective security under the North Atlantic Treaty Organization (NATO) and established Greenland as a vital link in the Greenland-Iceland-United Kingdom (GIUK) and Distant Early Warning (DEW) defense lines. Controversy over the U.S. military bases arose after Greenland was granted home rule in 1979. In 1986 Washington agreed to reduce the sizes of the bases at Thule and Søndre

Strømfjord by one-half and to return the land to native Inuit Greenlanders who had been dislocated by the military buildup. In March 1987 Greenland's prime minister, Aqqaluk Lynge, demanded a parliamentary inquiry into U.S. defense plans to build a new radar system in Thule. He contended that the system violated the 1972 Antiballistic Missile Treaty between the United States and the Soviet Union, but the U.S. government insisted that it was simply upgrading an old system. Control of the Søndre Strømfjord radar installation was transferred to the Greenland government in September 1992 under an agreement signed the year before.

DAVID P. AUGUSTYN

See also Denmark; Distant Early Warning (DEW) Line; Overseas Military Bases

FURTHER READING

Scott, Franklin D. *Scandinavia*. Cambridge, Mass., 1975.
Solheim, Bruce Olav. *The Nordic Nexus: A Lesson in Peaceful Security*. Westport, Conn., 1984.
Sundelius, Bengt, ed. *Foreign Policies of Northern Europe*. Boulder, Colo., 1982.

GRENADA

Located in the eastern Caribbean Sea, north of Trinidad and Tobago, and the southernmost of the Windward Islands in the West Indies, Grenada achieved independence from Great Britain in 1974. Since then there have been considerable shifts in the Caribbean microstate's relations with the United States. Although the United States has a long history of interest in the Caribbean, prior to the mid-1970s that concern was not focused on the British West Indies. Rather, it was Great Britain, the colonial power, that exerted primary external influence over Grenada. During the 1950s and 1960s that influence extended to creating a federation scheme for the West Indies, including Grenada, which failed in the early 1960s, and creation of the Oxford plan, which granted the Caribbean territories statehood in association with Great Britain as of 1967. Five years later Grenada's government, under the leadership of Premier Eric Gairy, sought full independence from Great Britain and achieved that status on 7 February 1974.

The years immediately following independence were difficult ones for Grenada. One of the least developed states in the Caribbean Basin, Grenada's agriculturally based economy, dependent on the export of bananas, nutmeg, and cocoa, was mismanaged by the government of Prime Minister Gairy. Further problems stemmed from the corrupt and repressive nature of the government, which was pro-Western in its stance. A nearly bloodless coup on 13 March 1979 led to suspension of the independence constitution and the establishment of a People's Revolutionary Government (PRG) under the leadership of Prime Minister Maurice Bishop. Despite the PRG's socialist orientation and the overthrow of an elected government, the United States, among other states, recognized the new government. Nevertheless, the administration of President Jimmy Carter grew concerned about Grenada's seemingly radical foreign policy shift, which included diplomatic and economic ties with the Soviet Union and other Eastern bloc countries and an extensive military assistance relationship with Cuba.

Aware of these factors, and worried about the possible military potential of an international airport being constructed in Grenada, the administration of President Ronald Reagan exerted pressure on the island in an effort to isolate the country and thwart what it saw as growing communist expansion in the Caribbean. To that end Grenada was excluded from economic assistance programs, such as the Caribbean Basin Initiative, and Reagan refused to accept the credentials of the country's ambassador to the United States. In addition, during early 1982 the United States staged three military exercises in the Caribbean during a single eight-week period. One of these, code named Amber and the Amberines, apparently was perceived by the PRG to be a rehearsal for an attack on the island.

Despite these tensions between the United States and the PRG, Grenada appeared to be relatively stable. However, dissatisfaction within the Central Committee of the ruling New Jewel Movement led to Prime Minister Bishop's being placed under house arrest on 13 October 1983. This prompted discussions among the United States and a number of other Caribbean states regarding a military operation in Grenada, although at first it was unclear whether the purpose of such an operation was to rescue U.S. nationals, primarily medical students on the island, or to rescue Bishop. The latter's murder on 19 October led to more intense exchanges between the United States and the Caribbean states and a decision by Reagan to divert a naval task force en route to Lebanon to Grenada, in case there was a need to evacuate U.S. citizens. In a meeting held on 21 October the heads of government of the members of the Organization of Eastern Caribbean States (OECS) agreed to impose a package of political and economic sanctions on Grenada's newly formed Revolutionary Military Council (RMC). Although it was not revealed until later, a decision was made at the same meeting to remove the RMC through the use of force. Four days later, on 25 October, Operation Urgent Fury was initiated with the landing of U.S. Marines on the island. It was not until 28 October that the approximately 6,000 U.S. troops in Grenada succeeded in eliminating all resistance by the People's Revolutionary Army and hundreds of Cuban construction workers. The 300 members of the Commonwealth Caribbean force, who did not take part in the fighting, later initiated a policing role.

In the aftermath of the invasion, the Reagan administration emphasized that military action had been justified as part of an effort to protect U.S. nationals abroad, because it constituted collective action under a regional arrangement (OECS) and because it was aimed at restoring law, order, and democratic institutions in Grenada. With respect to the latter factor, the country returned to democratic government through elections held in 1984. Although international reaction to the intervention was negative, the U.S. public supported the action, which was rapid, relatively inexpensive, and conclusive. Grenada also was of foreign policy significance to the United States in that it was the first direct U.S. military intervention after the Vietnam War and constituted a demonstration by the Reagan administration of the resolve to use force in an activist manner in the foreign policy realm.

CAROLINE A. HARTZELL

See also Caribbean Basin Initiative; Great Britain; Organization of American States

FURTHER READING

Burrowes, Reynold A. *Revolution and Rescue in Grenada: An Account of the U.S.- Caribbean Invasion.* New York, 1988.
Davidson, Scott. *Grenada: A Study in Politics and the Limits of International Law.* Brookfield, Vt., 1986.
Gilmore, William C. *The Grenada Intervention: Analysis and Documentation.* New York, 1984.
Schoenhals, Kai P., and Richard A. Melanson. *Revolution and Intervention in Grenada: The New Jewel Movement, the United States, and the Caribbean.* Boulder, Colo., 1985.

GRENADA INVASION

(1983)

A U.S. operation designed to oust a Marxist government from the Caribbean island of Grenada. On 25 October 1983 U.S. troops invaded Grenada, the first U.S. military intervention in the Caribbean since the Dominican crisis in 1965. The administration of President Ronald Reagan justified the incursion by citing the danger to 1,000 U.S. citizens from the ruling Marxist dictatorship. The invasion stemmed from rising tensions between the United States and the Soviet Union, alarm in Washington over the success of the Nicaraguan revolution, and reports that Cuba was building a runway on Grenada that could serve as a base for military aircraft. The invading forces brought down the government within a week. All U.S. troops were withdrawn by the end of 1983. Costing some $75 million, the intervention successfully toppled a hostile regime, brought about a return to elected government, and marked an important military triumph for

President Reagan. The strategic and legal arguments for the action, however, seemed moot. U.S. actions violated Articles 15 and 17 (the nonintervention principle) of the Rio Pact of 1947. Moreover, the claims of the Reagan administration that Grenada was being readied as a major Soviet bloc military base proved to be exaggerated. Beyond the cost in lives to Americans (eighteen dead), Grenadians (forty-five dead), and Cubans (twenty-four dead), the U.S. action alienated Latin American allies troubled about a revival of U.S. military intervention in the Caribbean and heightened political opposition in Europe to the deployment there of U.S. strategic missiles. When the United Nations Security Council condemned the invasion of Grenada, the United States vetoed the resolution.

DAVID SHEININ

See also Grenada; Reagan, Ronald Wilson; Rio Treaty

FURTHER READING

Dunn, Peter M., and Bruce W. Watson, eds. *American Intervention in Grenada.* Boulder, Colo., 1985.
MacDonald, Scott B., Harald M. Sandstrom, and Paul B. Goodwin. *The Caribbean After Grenada.* New York, 1988.
Schoenhals, Kai P., and Richard A. Melanson, eds. *Revolution and Intervention in Grenada: The New Jewel Movement, the United States, and the Caribbean.* Boulder, Colo., 1985.

GRESHAM, WALTER QUINTIN

(*b.* 17 March 1832; *d.* 28 May 28 1895)

Secretary of state (1893–1895). Born in Indiana, Gresham was educated in a log schoolhouse before attending the Corydon Seminary and Indiana University. He read law with a local attorney and was admitted to the Indiana bar in 1854. Gresham helped organize the Indiana Republican party in 1856 and was elected to the Indiana House of Representatives in 1860. After rising to the rank of major general of Indiana Volunteers during the Civil War, he returned to law and politics and was appointed federal district judge for Indiana in 1869. He was briefly postmaster general (1883) and secretary of the Treasury (1884) and then was named circuit judge for the seventh judicial district, where he gained a reputation for his fearlessness in ruling on controversial railroad matters. Unsuccessful in his attempts to secure the Republican nomination for the presidency in 1884 and 1888, he supported the candidacy of the Democratic nominee, Grover Cleveland, in 1892. After Cleveland's victory, Gresham became secretary of state. Although firm, independent, and fair, Gresham had little previous experience with foreign policy issues. He advised the president not to resubmit to the Senate a treaty for the annexation of Hawai'i negotiated following a coup in

Honolulu during the final weeks of President Benjamin Harrison's administration; Gresham's efforts to return the Hawai'ian Queen Liliuokalani to her throne proved embarrassing. Opposed to expansionist policies, Gresham helped settle a dispute between Great Britain and Nicaragua, cautiously monitored events surrounding the Sino-Japanese War, and negotiated with German and British representatives to resolve disputed issues concerning Samoa. He died in office.

MICHAEL J. DEVINE

See also Cleveland, Stephen Grover; Hawai'i

FURTHER READING

Calhoun, Charles W. *Gilded Age Cato: The Life of Walter Q. Gresham.* Lexington, Ky., 1988.

William, Matilda. *The Life of Walter Quintin Gresham, 1832–1895,* 2 vols. Chicago, 1919.

GREW, JOSEPH CLARK

(*b.* 27 May 1880; *d.* 25 May 1965)

Ambassador to Japan (1932–1941). Beginning his diplomatic career in 1904, Grew represented the United States in Denmark, Switzerland, and Turkey. Grew also served as undersecretary of state (1924–1927), in which capacity he helped create the United States Foreign Service (1924) as an organization of professionals with more opportunities for secure tenure and promotion based on merit. Grew exemplified, however, an older style of U.S. diplomat—conservative, dignified, and socially prominent with independent financial means. As ambassador to Japan, Grew became popular with Japan's civilian diplomats, because they realized that the ambassador sought to avert conflict between the two nations. For example, Grew generally opposed the imposition of economic sanctions against Japan advocated by officials in Washington, D.C., such as Stanley K. Hornbeck, Henry Morgenthau, Jr., Harold L. Ickes, and Dean Acheson. Although opposed to Japanese expansionism, Grew argued that sanctions would not deter the Japanese but would so exacerbate U.S.-Japanese tensions that the Japanese might attack the United States. Early in 1941 Grew even warned that the Japanese might strike at Pearl Harbor if the escalating conflict continued. Failing to prevent war, Grew returned to the Department of State in 1942 (he was repatriated in a wartime exchange of diplomats between the two belligerents). He became undersecretary of state (1944–1945), helping to formulate postwar policy toward Japan. Grew successfully argued that the United States should allow the Japanese to retain their imperial institution, transformed into a constitutional monarchy similar to that of Great Britain, and to keep their current emper-

or. After his retirement in September 1945, Grew wrote his memoirs and continued to advocate close U.S.-Japanese relations.

BARNEY J. RICKMAN III

See also Foreign Service; Japan

FURTHER READING

Grew, Joseph Clark. *Ten Years in Japan: A Contemporary Record Drawn from the Diaries and Private and Official Papers of Joseph C. Grew, United States Ambassador to Japan.* New York, 1944.

———. *Turbulent Era: A Diplomatic Record of Forty Years, 1904–1945,* edited by Walter Johnson, 2 vols. Boston, 1952.

Heinrichs, Waldo H., Jr. *American Ambassador: Joseph C. Grew and the Development of the United States Diplomatic Tradition.* Boston, 1966.

Iriye, Akira. *Across the Pacific: An Inner History of American–East Asian Relations.* New York, 1993.

———. *The Origins of the Second World War in Asia and the Pacific.* New York, 1987.

Iriye, Akira, and Warren I. Cohen, eds. *American, Chinese and Japanese Perspectives on Wartime Asia, 1931–1949.* Wilmington, Del., 1980.

Nakamura, Masanori. *The Japanese Monarchy: Ambassador Joseph Grew and the Making of the "Symbol Emperor System," 1937–1991.* New York, 1992.

Prange, Gordon William. *At Dawn We Slept: the Untold Story of Pearl Harbor.* New York, 1981.

GREY, EDWARD
Grey of Fallodon, 1st Viscount

(*b.* 25 April 1862; *d.* 7 September 1933)

British statesman and baronet (better known to American readers as Sir Edward Grey), created Viscount Grey of Fallodon in 1916, who served as a Liberal party member of Parliament from Berwick (1885–1916), undersecretary for foreign affairs (1892–1895), and foreign secretary (1905–1916). From 1904 onward Grey advocated a close Anglo-French relationship to balance the rising power of Germany. Although the Anglo-French Entente of 1904 had been negotiated by a Conservative government, Grey made it clear to the Germans and French in 1905 that the policy would continue under the Liberals. As foreign secretary he concluded an Anglo-Russian Entente in 1907 and authorized conversations between the British military staff and their French and Belgian counterparts, which continued until 1914. In 1911 he secured a renewal of the Anglo-Japanese alliance of 1902 (to 1923) to strengthen Great Britain's position in Asia. During the Balkan crisis of 1912–1913 he urged mediation on the contending states, and he renewed the proposal following the assassination of Austrian Archduke Francis Ferdinand on 28 June 1914, but his efforts at peacemaking proved futile.

When the Germans invaded Belgium, Grey insisted in Parliament on 3 August 1914 that Great Britain declare war against Germany. His main task thereafter was to manage relations with the United States so that British interference with neutral trade would not lead to a break in relations. His remarkable success in this difficult task was demonstrated on 22 February 1916, when he and Colonel Edward M. House, President Woodrow Wilson's friend and informal agent in Europe, signed the House-Grey Memorandum, declaring that if Germany refused to come to a peace conference, the United States would probably enter the war on the British side. Rapidly losing his eyesight and believing that the British government was committing itself to extreme war aims that would prevent the establishment of a lasting peace after the war, he left office in December 1916, when David Lloyd George became prime minister. In 1919 Grey returned to service as a special ambassador to the United States in an unsuccessful effort to win U.S. ratification of the Treaty of Versailles. During the 1920s his declining health prevented him from taking part in politics, but he completed two volumes of memoirs.

KENDRICK A. CLEMENTS

See also Great Britain; House, Edward Mandell; World War I

FURTHER READING

Grey, Viscount, of Fallodon, Edward. *Grey: Twenty-five Years, 1892–1916*, 2 vols. New York, 1925.
Hinsley, Francis Harry, ed. *British Foreign Policy Under Sir Edward Grey.* London, 1977.
Robbins, Keith. *Sir Edward Grey.* London, 1971.
Steiner, Zara S. *Britain and the Origins of the First World War.* New York, 1977.
Williams, Joyce. *Colonel House and Sir Edward Grey: A Study in Anglo-American Diplomacy.* Lanham, Md., 1984.

GROMYKO, ANDREI ANDREYEVICH

(*b.* 18 July 1909; *d.* 2 July 1989)

Soviet diplomat and statesman who served as ambassador to the United States (1943–1946), United Nations Security Council representative (1946–1948), foreign minister (1957–1985), Politburo member (1973–1988), and chairman of the Supreme Soviet of the USSR (1988–1989). Born in Byelarus (Belorussian Soviet Socialist Republic) to a poor peasant family, Gromyko had no prerevolutionary past and owed his career to Joseph Stalin and his successors. He began his diplomatic career as the youngest Soviet ambassador to the United States, then served as the permanent Soviet representative on the UN Security Council. Gromyko inherited much from the geopolitical preferences and outlook of his predecessors Vyacheslav Molotov and Andrei Vyshinsky, but, unlike them, strongly believed in peaceful coexistence with the capitalist great powers. His priority was international recognition of the geostrategic status quo in Europe through détente with the United States.

During the Cuban missile crisis in 1962, Gromyko knew of the presence of Soviet missiles in Cuba but denied the fact during his meetings with President John F. Kennedy and Secretary of State Dean Rusk. Although he did not oppose the Soviet military build up, he actively promoted U.S.-Soviet cooperation on strategic arms limitation, including support for the Antiballistic Missile Treaty of 1972 and the Strategic Arms Limitation Treaties of 1972 and 1979. He also advocated a positive response to West Germany's Ostpolitik (1971) and the signing of the Helsinki Accords (1975). Gromyko regarded the People's Republic of China as a growing threat in the East and was a vocal critic of U.S. attempts to play the "China card" against the Soviet Union. He paid much less attention to growing U.S.-Soviet competition in the Third World and went along with those in the Soviet Politboro who favored military assistance to the progressive regimes and movements of national liberation. As Soviet leader Leonid Brezhnev became increasingly out of touch in the late 1970s, Gromyko became part of a national security troika with Dimitri Ustinov and Yuri Andropov. In December 1979 Gromyko, persuaded that U.S.-Soviet détente was stalled, supported his government's decision to invade Afghanistan, and his efforts toward improvement of U.S.-Soviet relations during President Ronald Reagan's first administration (1981–1985) were unsuccessful. Gromyko's workaholic and low-key diplomatic style had endeared him to Joseph Stalin, lacked appeal for Stalin's successor, Nikita Khrushchev, but gained the respect of Brezhnev. Western diplomats regarded Gromyko as one of the most professional diplomats in Soviet history, one who persistently sought to win world recognition for the Soviet Union as a superpower.

VLADISLAV M. ZUBOK

See also Cuban Missile Crisis; Khrushchev, Nikita Sergeyevich; Russia and the Soviet Union; Stalin, Joseph

FURTHER READING

Craig, Gordon A., and Francis L. Loewenheim. *Diplomats, 1939–1979.* Princeton, N.J., 1994.
Garthoff, Raymond L. *Détente and Confrontation: American-Soviet Relations from Nixon to Reagan*, rev. ed. Washington, D.C., 1994.
Gromyko, Andrei Andreyevich. *Memoirs.* New York, 1989.

GROUP OF SEVEN

The largest seven industrialized countries (United States, Japan, Germany, Great Britain, France, Italy, and Canada), whose representatives meet to coordinate macroeconomic and international economic policies. Also known as the Summit 7, because the heads of the seven governments meet annually (usually in July) to discuss policies of common interest. These meetings usually do not produce major advances in economic policies but they attract considerable political and media interest. The G-7 meetings sometimes give impetus to policies, and the sessions held by technical experts and subcabinet-level officials that precede the meetings of the heads of state are often quite successful in dealing with economic issues. The G-7 was used for consultations on how to handle the economic and financial impacts of the Organization of Petroleum Exporting Countries (OPEC) price increases during the 1970s and for discussions leading up to the GATT Uruguay Round in the early and mid-1980s. Unlike the International Monetary Fund or the Organization for Economic Cooperation and Development, the G-7 does not have a formal organizational structure, headquarters, or founding charter. It is an informal group, designed in part to provide a small negotiating forum in which the large industrialized countries can deal with issues by themselves, without the involvement of smaller countries or those with different interests. The G-7 meetings began in Rambouillet, France, in 1975 to discuss the financial difficulties resulting from the oil price increases of OPEC in 1974. Sessions since the collapse of the Soviet Union in 1989 have included discussions on the integration into the world economy of the former Soviet Republics. Boris N. Yeltsin, head of the Russian government, joined the group in the early 1990s, at which time the G-7 became the G-7 plus one. A subgroup known as the G-5 (the seven minus Italy and Canada) often coordinates international monetary policies, as at the Plaza Conference in 1985 and the Louvre Conference in 1987. In 1985, for example, the G-5 finance ministers decided at the Plaza meeting that the exchange rate for the dollar was too high and that it needed to decline, which it did during the next two years. At the Louvre meeting in 1987, they decided that exchange rates were approximately correct. Monetary and exchange market intervention policies were used in the attempts to reach these goals.

ROBERT M. DUNN, JR.

See also International Monetary Fund; Organization for Economic Cooperation and Development

FURTHER READING

Putnam, Robert D., and Nicholas Bayne. *Hanging Together: Cooperation and Conflict in the Seven-Power Summits*, rev. ed. Cambridge, Mass., 1987.

Spero, Joan Edelman. *The Politics of International Economic Relations*, 4th ed. New York, 1990.

GUADALUPE-HIDALGO, TREATY OF

See Mexico, War with

GUAM

See Pacific Island Nations and U.S. Territories

GUAM DOCTRINE

See Nixon Doctrine

GUATEMALA

Located between Honduras and Mexico, Guatemala is the largest and most populous of the Central American republics. U.S. economic interests have exerted a strong influence on the country, and the United States has intervened militarily to protect those interests and to eliminate perceived security threats. Even after the Cold War, the violence and instability of the political life of the country and the poverty of the majority of Guatemala's people kept U.S. attention focused on the country.

A Spanish crown colony for nearly three centuries, Guatemala attained its independence on 15 September 1821, was annexed the following year by Mexico, and became independent again in 1823. In that year Guatemala and the other newly independent countries of Central America formed the United Provinces of Central America. At the same time, a power struggle emerged between the Liberal and Conservative parties in Guatemala, with the Liberals in power from 1831 to 1838, the latter year marking the demise of the United Provinces confederation. The Conservatives held the reins from 1839 to 1871, followed by nearly continuous Liberal rule until 1944.

The first few decades following Guatemala's independence saw scant change in the social and economic orders of the colonial era. The Creole elite continued to exert control over a captive indigenous labor force that was used to produce such exports as cacao, indigo, and cochineal dyes. Although Great Britain replaced Spain as the dominant external commercial player in the region, Guatemala's status as primarily a single-export (cacao) economy remained constant. Significant changes in the country's social and economic structure took place only after the country shifted to the production of coffee for export during the latter part of the nineteenth century. The large amounts of land required to produce coffee led to the concentration of land ownership in the hands of a few, as well as the incorporation within the dominant class of propertied ladinos (Spanish-speaking and culturally westernized Guatemalans whose racial heritage is both Creole and Indian). Coffee production also generated a need for a larger pool of cheap labor than that required for producing indigo and cochineal. The export of coffee also made necessary the development of an infrastructure to facilitate its storage and transportation.

As a result of these needs, Indian lands were expropriated or otherwise acquired by the Guatemalan oligarchy. The state, which during this period was ruled by four dictators (Rafael Carrera, 1838–1865; Justo Rufino Barrios, 1871–1885; Manuel Estrada Cabrera, 1897–1920; and Jorge Ubico Castañeda, 1931–1944), played a more significant role in the economy by providing material support for private enterprise and by encouraging foreign investments. The state also mobilized cheap Indian labor for the coffee plantations by passing forced-labor laws, debt servitude, and stringent vagrancy laws.

By the early twentieth century, three large monopolistic U.S. companies were exerting great influence in Guatemala. The United Fruit Company (UFCo), at first primarily a shipper and exporter of bananas, eventually monopolized banana production and became Guatemala's largest landowner. Transport facilities came to be dominated by International Railways of Central America (IRCA), a subsidiary of UFCo. Electric Bond and Share (EBS) controlled all of Guatemala's electrical facilities. The extent of investments in Guatemala initially gave the United States a significant degree of leverage and influence within the country. Relations between the Guatemalan oligarchy and U.S. business interests further solidified the positions of the three companies. For example, Ubico had once worked closely with the Rockefeller Foundation in the United States, where his bid for the Guatemalan presidency was looked upon favorably. Later, during his dictatorship, UFCo and IRCA contract revisions were made on terms very favorable to their interests.

The stable relationship between Guatemala and the United States began to change with the October Revolution of 1944. Following a series of strikes and protests, Ubico was forced to resign from office in July 1944 and was replaced by a military triumvirate, which was ousted in October by armed students, workers, and dissident junior officers. Open elections, held under an interim junta, brought Juan José Arévalo Bermejo to office in 1945. Under his leadership a progressive new constitution was put into effect, freedom of speech and freedom of the press were guaranteed, and workers and peasants were encouraged to organize. Arévalo weathered a number of military revolts and attempted coups during his five-year term in office and turned the presidency over to Colonel Jacobo Arbenz Guzman in 1950.

Arbenz, a key figure in the October Revolution, espoused a program of furthering the revolution's social reforms, promoting economic development along independent rather than dependent capitalist lines, and redistributing income. His government constructed a hydroelectric plant, a highway system, and a new port, projects meant to break the IRCA and UFCo monopolies through direct competition. Arbenz's policies also included an agrarian reform program that was enacted in 1952, put into effect in 1953, and generated resistance on the part of U.S. interests, especially UFCo. With 85 percent of its landholding not in use, UFCo not only faced expropriation of vast amounts of land but also the prospect of a low rate of compensation by the Guatemalan government for seized property, because UFCo had consistently undervalued its land for tax purposes. The U.S. State Department became involved and made compensation claims for U.S. property on behalf of UFCo. The U.S. position on this issue was affected in part by the personal interests of some members of the administration of President Dwight D. Eisenhower, including Secretary of State John Foster Dulles and his brother, Central Intelligence Agency (CIA) Director Allen Dulles, both of whom had been members of a New York law firm with ties to UFCo.

Of even greater significance to U.S.-Guatemalan relations, however, was the Cold War anticommunist position of the United States. Arbenz's agrarian reform program and the presence in his government of members of the newly recognized Communist party led to claims that Guatemala under Arbenz's leadership constituted a "communist threat" to the United States. This claim and Arbenz's purchase of arms from Czechoslovakia prompted a series of actions on the part of the Eisenhower administration, including an attempt to pressure members of the Organization of American States (OAS) to take collective action against Guatemala as an agent of the Soviet Union. When OAS members resisted naming Guatemala specifically in the declaration that followed the Tenth Inter-American Conference in Caracas (1954), the United States decided to employ covert action under CIA auspices. An invasion force of a few hundred Guatemalan exiles was organized under the leadership of Carlos Castillo Armas and provided with some fighter planes to attack the capital, Guatemala City. Unnerved by the attack, Arbenz resigned on 27 June 1954, and Castillo Armas was installed as president on 8 July. His administration, among others, was looked upon favorably by the United States, which gave the Castillo Armas government some $80 million in aid. Relations between the two countries were further solidified when the administration of Miguel Ydígoras Fuentes (1958–1963) allowed anti-Castro Cuban exile forces to train in Guatemala prior to the Bay of Pigs invasion.

Much of the history of Guatemala since 1954 has been one of government-directed counterrevolution and military counterinsurgency. During the twelve-year period following Arbenz's resignation, political parties, labor organizations, and peasant movements were repressed; the Agrarian Reform Law was revoked and lands were returned to their previous owners; and thousands of people were jailed and killed. During these years, while the military ruled the country, a number of rebel groups formed in reaction to political, social, and economic injustices. Chief among them were the Revolutionary Armed Forces and the 13th of November Revolutionary Movement, groups that were later joined by Indian-based guerrilla organizations protesting the massacres of indigenous peoples and seeking some degree of autonomy for their communities. The use of guerrilla warfare by these groups and their adoption of Marxist-Leninist ideology prompted the United States to escalate military aid to the Guatemalan armed forces. Despite such aid, military operations against the guerrillas were to prove ineffective for several years.

The levels of repression that met the actions of guerrilla groups, university students, unions, and the urban poor in the latter part of the 1970s prompted the U.S. State Department during the administration of President Jimmy Carter to criticize Guatemala's human rights record. Guatemala's response was to continue to accept economic assistance but refuse further military aid from the United States. During the 1980s many of President Ronald Reagan's Central American policies—a mixture of military operations against rebel groups, the substitution of civilian governments by military governments, and reformist programs—were put into effect in Guatemala. Although the United States continued to provide the country with economic aid, U.S. participation in these policies was relatively low in contrast to the level of U.S. efforts expended in Nicaragua and El Salvador under the Reagan administration. Despite Guatemala's political reforms of the 1980s and what its military considered to be the short-term successes of its counterinsurgency strategy, in the 1990s Guatemala remained an unstable country troubled by violence. In May 1993, in the wake of demonstrations following the breakdown of peace talks aimed at ending the country's long-running civil war, civilian President Jorge Serrano Elias reacted by conducting a "self-coup," dissolving the congress and the supreme court. President Bill Clinton condemned Serrano Elias's antidemocratic maneuver, suspended U.S. military and economic aid, and threatened broader economic sanctions. Forced from office on 19 June by the military and business groups fearful of threatened sanctions, Serrano Elias was succeeded by Ramiro de Leon Carpio, a leader known for his support of democracy and human rights.

The behavior of the Guatemalan military became the focus of world attention in 1995 when Jennifer Harbury, an American lawyer, publicly protested the murder by the Guatemalan army of her husband, Efraín Bámaca Velásquez, a Guatemalan guerrilla leader. Subsequent claims of CIA involvement in the case by Democratic Congressman Robert Torricelli led President Clinton to order an inquiry into CIA links with the case, as well as

the 1990 murder by the Guatemalan army of hotelier Michael DeVine. An internal CIA probe into the agency's conduct in Guatemala concluded that its officers there had failed to disclose clandestine activities to Congress and to the agency and determined that agents had broken no laws in connection with the death of Bámaca and DeVine. The Guatemalan military suffered a further blow with the 7 January 1996 victory, in a run-off election, by rightist candidate for the presidency Alvaro Arzú Irigoyen. President Arzú Irigoyen, who had promised to curtail the privileges of the military, removed most of the army high command within a week of taking office.

Caroline A. Hartzell

See also Central Intelligence Agency; Dulles, John Foster; Human Rights; Latin America; Organization of American States

FURTHER READING

Booth, John A., and Thomas W. Walker. *Understanding Central America*. Boulder, Colo., 1989.

Glejeses, Piero. *Shattered Hope*. Princeton, N.J., 1991.

Hamilton, Nora, Jeffry A. Frieden, Linda Fuller, and Manuel Pastor, eds. *Crisis in Central America: Regional Dynamics and U.S. Policy in the 1980s*. Boulder, Colo., 1988

Immerman, Richard. *The CIA in Guatemala*. Austin, Tx., 1982.

Jonas, Susanne. *The Battle for Guatemala: Rebels, Death Squads, and U.S. Power*. Boulder, Colo., 1991.

LaFeber, Walter. *Inevitable Revolutions: The United States in Central America*. New York, 1993.

GUERRILLA WARFARE

The term "guerrilla," which means small war in Spanish, dates from the popular resistance to French forces following Napoleon's conquest of Spain in 1808, but guerrilla warfare has always been a popular strategy, as ancient by sources such as the Bible, and especially the Book of Maccabees indicate. Guerrilla warfare is often a tool of the weak against the strong but also may be supported as a lower-risk, cost-effective national security strategy by powerful nations. Historically, guerrillas are usually defeated by their adversaries, albeit often at great cost to the society at large. When successful, guerrillas have effectively complemented conventional military efforts, forced social and political concessions, and, occasionally, either by expanding to include conventional forces or by precipitating a successful rebellion, overthrown regimes.

Guerrillas commit sabotage, temporarily sever lines of communication, and attempt to deplete an adversary with surprise attacks and ambushes. The guerrilla uses superior agility to concentrate quickly and disperse as necessary, avoiding at all costs direct, sustained encounters with larger conventional forces that have superior firepower and logistical support. The less external support, the more the guerrilla must rely on popular support and a strategy of protracted conflict, hoping to exhaust the adversaries morally and physically. The effectiveness of a covert support structure among the population, which may be coerced in part as well as provided willingly, often is the key factor in the success or failure of guerrillas, because it provides security, recruits, intelligence, funds, and logistical support.

Distinguishing guerrillas, who fight for political objectives, from bandits, who seek pecuniary gain but employ guerrilla tactics and propaganda, can be difficult. During the U.S. occupation of Haiti in 1915, U.S. Marines had to deal with bandits who eventually acquired politically motivated leadership that led them in guerrilla warfare. Pancho Villa, a Mexican revolutionary who frequently resorted to banditry, precipitated General John J. Pershing's expedition into Mexico to punish Villa's raid on Columbus, New Mexico. Irregular raiding forces also may be difficult to distinguish from guerrillas. Raiders, such as Mosby's Rangers in the American Civil War, can operate independently behind enemy lines using guerrilla tactics and assistance from sympathetic irregular forces. If such raiding activity is closely tied to conventional operations and removed from the vast majority of the civilian population, it may not properly qualify as guerrilla warfare.

Practitioners of guerrilla warfare are sometimes distinguished as partisans or insurgents. The term "partisan" is often used in reference to guerrillas fighting a foreign occupation, especially prior to and during World War II, whereas the term "insurgent" is generally applied to guerrillas fighting their own government or a colonial regime. A questionable distinction occasionally attributed to partisans and insurgents is that partisans require external assistance and thus can be fought by cutting their sources of support, whereas insurgents, who can subsist on the support of the population alone, must be countered with a combination of political, social, and military programs designed to woo and intimidate the population into abandoning support for the insurgency.

The U.S. experience in fighting, supporting, and using guerrillas includes diverse examples of success and failure. The colonials who declared their independence from England used guerrilla warfare to good effect throughout the American Revolution to harass and seriously diminish British forces as a prelude to the victory at Saratoga, New York, in 1777 and more systematically, in Nathanial Greene's southern campaigns, to set up the decisive American victory at Yorktown in 1781. Between the revolutionary war and World War II the United States had no need to resort to guerrilla warfare, but it found several occasions to consider support for guerrillas. In its efforts to win West and East Florida from the Spanish, the United States supported a few brief insurgent actions against Spanish garrisons in the early 1800s. The United States was more circumspect with official support for Spanish-American revolutionaries, not wanting to bring down the wrath of European monarchies, but it generally looked away when private initiatives were undertaken on their behalf. Despite some public sentiment in favor of support of the Boer guerrillas fighting the British in South Africa, the U.S. government also remained aloof from that struggle.

Much more frequent and noteworthy during the nineteenth century and early twentieth century were the occasions when the United States had to mount counterinsurgency operations. In the American Civil War, some of the Indian wars, its subjugation of the Philippines, and its Caribbean interventions in Nicaragua and Haiti, the United States encountered numerous guerrilla adversaries, all of whom were eventually vanquished during military campaigns. When the most resourceful and determined of guerrilla opponents, for example, confederate raiders and the Seminoles could not be brought to bay by a combination of military force and political stratagem, U.S. forces resorted to the time-honored but most merciless counter-guerrilla strategy short of indiscriminate murder and genocide, by systematically destroying the livestock, crops, and habitations of the populations supporting the guerrillas.

The World War II Period

During and shortly after World War II, the United States again found some value in guerrilla warfare. Following the lead of the British and Soviets, the United States made good use of partisan forces, in both the European and Far Eastern theaters. Following the war, when it became apparent that the West could not match Soviet conventional forces in Europe and before the North Atlantic Treaty Organization (NATO) fully integrated nuclear weapons into its arsenal to compensate for its conventional inferiority, the United States trained Army Special Forces to organize partisan resistance and conduct guerrilla war in the event of a Soviet invasion of Europe. Encouraging resistance to Soviet domination in Eastern Europe during peacetime was another option explored. Ultimately, the United States abandoned support for those resistance movements that lingered on after World War II in the Baltic States, the Ukraine, and Albania and refused to offer more than moral support to rebellions that flared up in East Germany and Hungary in the 1950s. Similarly, U.S. support for pro-Nationalist Chinese raids into Communist China from Burma in the early 1950s was ineffectual and soon abandoned.

More important to the United States was the dilemma posed by liberation movements using guerrilla warfare around the globe. These movements were principally directed against European colonial administrations or their loyal allies, but they frequently espoused Marxist ideology and accepted support from the Soviet Union or its proxies. U.S. policy had to balance an ideological distaste for European colonialism with fear of growing Soviet power. Depending on the circumstances, U.S. policy also had to account for the limited ability of the United States to affect the outcome of such struggles at costs commensurate with the interests at stake. Given its own revolutionary origins on the one hand and its support for the principle of sovereignty on the other, the decision to aid guerrillas or counter-guerrilla operations always was an especially delicate foreign policy issue for the United States. Set against the backdrop of a global geopolitical struggle with the Soviet Union, guerrilla warfare became a major U.S. foreign policy and defense issue during the Cold War.

The United States repeatedly weighed in against guerrilla movements when not doing so appeared likely to expand the communist sphere of influence. Following the announcement of the Truman Doctrine in 1947, the United States offered diplomatic, economic, and military support to governments fighting communist guerrillas, starting with Greece in 1947 and then the Philippines, Indochina, Guatemala, and other Latin American counties. President John F. Kennedy, confronted with foreign policy crises in Cuba, the Congo, Laos, and Vietnam involving communist-supported guerrillas and challenged by Soviet leader Nikita Khrushchev's January 1961 speech justifying communist support of wars of national liberation, was particularly concerned with developing countermeasures to guerrilla war. Kennedy urged every general officer to read Khrushchev's speech, enjoined every U.S. Marine to master the art of fighting the guerrilla, and gave special attention and support to the U.S. Army Special Forces as the nation's premier counterinsurgency warriors.

On occasion during the Cold War, when it calculated it would be to its strategic advantage, the United States distanced itself from counterinsurgency efforts, especially if the insurgent cause seemed just and their Soviet ties questionable. For example, the United States slowly distanced itself from the French counterinsurgency war in Algeria in the early 1960s and abandoned the Anastasio Somoza Debayle regime in Nicaragua in the late 1970s. The United States also found opportunities to support guerrillas who served anti-Soviet purposes, especially as Soviet influence and pro-Soviet regimes spread. In Vietnam, U.S. Special Forces trained Montagnards and Hmong tribesmen in guerrilla warfare and directed them against the Vietcong and North Vietnamese. In the early 1970s the United States supported Kurdish insurgents as a means of curbing the adventurism of the pro-Soviet government in Iraq but later withdrew the support as part of an agreement with the shah of Iran. In the 1980s,

President Ronald Reagan extended support to anti-Soviet or pro-Western guerrilla movements in Angola, Nicaragua, Afghanistan, and Cambodia. Such support for anticommunist insurgencies came to be known as the Reagan Doctrine.

Guerrilla warfare has been variously described by military historians and practitioners as either a mere nuisance or a critical problem. Many believe that the political impact of partisan warfare is greater than its military consequences, because it helps to restore the self-respect of a defeated nation and instills a spirit of resistance to occupying authority. In any case, it is generally acknowledged that the type of partisan warfare that pinned down and chewed up substantial portions of Napoleon's army, the Japanese in China, and the Axis powers in central Russia and the Balkans is most effective when complemented by an ascendant allied conventional force. Of greater consequence and controversy, at least as far as the United States is concerned, is the importance of guerrilla warfare in insurgency and how to fight it.

While the causes of insurgency are complex, including diverse combinations of socioeconomic, cultural, and political factors, the operational dimensions are less so. The conventional wisdom is that a revolutionary insurgency passes through three phases: a period during which the insurgents use propaganda, subversion, terrorism, and political agitation to build support for their cause; a period of guerrilla warfare during which they extend and exhaust the government's security forces while building their own conventional capabilities; and the final stage during which a combination of guerrilla and conventional operations succeed in overthrowing the government. Counterinsurgency, then, requires a patient, restrained, well-coordinated, and sustained application of political, informational, judicial, and military power to isolate the insurgents from the population. An alternative strategy is a ruthless combination of relentless military pressure on the insurgents and merciless economic warfare against the insurgents' popular sustainment base, which may lead to the destruction of a sizable portion of the indigenous population. When U.S. forces have followed one of these two approaches, they have been successful in preventing an insurgent victory or in destroying the insurgency altogether.

The unsatisfactory experience in Vietnam did not put an end to U.S. counterinsurgency efforts, as demonstrated by the lengthy and expensive support for El Salvador's counterinsurgency during the 1980s. The Vietnam War, however, influenced U.S. foreign policy and the U.S. approach to counterinsurgency. Vietnam convinced many Americans that the character of the United States is particularly ill-suited for counterguerrilla warfare. It reinforced an American predilection for decisive, overwhelming force whenever the military is employed on behalf of limited political objectives. Democracy, in general, is handicapped in fighting a well-organized insurgency by limited and divided governmental authority, slow and deliberative procedures, and restrictions on intrusive police actions. Otherwise laudable American characteristics, such as reliance on technology and firepower, a proclivity to separate military from political functions, a desire to exert leadership, and an eagerness to obtain decisive results, it is argued, make the United States a poor counterinsurgency partner for governments struggling with insurgency. More generally, despite the fact that, historically, insurgencies are rarely successful against governments that are not divided or distracted, the Vietnam experience has inclined U.S. leadership to believe that guerillas with broad popular support cannot be defeated. Thus, the practical result of Vietnam, as articulated in the Nixon Doctrine and subsequently codified in numerous national security documents, is a broad consensus that U.S. troops should not be directly employed to fight insurgents and that any U.S. assistance should be limited to advice and security assistance to the host nation's government.

Guerrilla Warfare and Urbanization

Rapid urbanization of the world's populations and the demise of the Soviet Union raised the question of whether guerrilla warfare was a diminishing concern for U.S. policy. The developing world's urban population was projected to grow to almost double that of the industrialized world by the year 2000. To overthrow a government, guerrillas must eventually control cities, and the question as the twentieth century draws to a close is whether they will operate in rural areas to build themselves into conventional forces capable of the task or mobilize an urban population that will rise up in rebellion en masse or both. Urban insurrections can succeed, as in Paris in 1830 and 1848 and Iran in 1979, when the armies refused to shoot down citizens, but they are rare, and many students of the subject consider the subversion that precipitates these rebellions to be a different phenomenon than guerrilla warfare. They argue that the relative inaccessibility and expanse of rural areas are what afford the guerrilla safety and mobility in comparison with more heavily armed and supported conventional forces, and that urban guerrilla warfare is a misnomer.

In contrast, it can be argued that the shantytowns around major cities in the developing world may be nearly as impenetrable to conventional security forces as jungles and mountains and thus provide the guerrilla similar protection. Moreover, guerrilla warfare in an urban environment may only alter its character by putting a greater emphasis on decentralized command and control and small units of four or five guerrillas who conduct more sniping, sabotage, and acts of terrorism than ambushes of security forces. Terrorism, frequently a concomitant of rural insurgency used to extract cooperation from an ambivalent or uninterested population, does play a greater role in urban operations, in which it disrupts normal routine more effectively and achieves greater propaganda value. However, one might classify urban guerrillas, their activities, and the means to counter them as especially brutal and complicated, because they inescapably mix combatants and noncombatants. As a result, involvement in urban insurgency is an especially unattractive option for the United States.

More generally it should be observed that absent a Soviet global, coordinated, and geopolitical threat, many of the local conflicts involving guerrilla war will be of less interest to the United States, which reinforces the post-Vietnam tendency to remain aloof from internal struggles. A quick survey of contemporary U.S. foreign policy problems, however, illustrates that neither urbanization nor the demise of the Soviet Union will eliminate guerrilla warfare as a potential foreign policy and defense problem for the United States. Guerrilla warfare in the 1990s, as represented in the Kurdish resistance in Turkey, the Islamic insurgents in the Philippines and Algeria, and various guerrilla movements on the periphery of the former Soviet empire, such as the Muslim rebels in Tajikistan, present difficult foreign policy decisions for the United States. To the extent that the United States remains a global power with global interests, it often will be forced to make the difficult decision of whether it should support guerrillas or those fighting them, diplomatically and otherwise.

In Caribbean confrontations with the leaderships of Haiti and Cuba, the U.S. reluctance to assume the full costs of prevailing with direct military power has led some commentators to argue that the principal responsibility for removing dictators resides with the people themselves, and that the United States should only assist the process, possibly through support for a guerrilla movement. The continuing relevance of guerrilla warfare is also suggested more directly by the U.S. experience in Somalia in the 1990s, where U.S. forces in support of a United Nations humanitarian relief operation were confronted by Somali warlords using guerrilla tactics, and in Bosnia, where the United States contemplated engaging Serbian forces. The fact that it is expensive to fight guerrillas, and that the United States, because of self-imposed limitations, finds it difficult to do so, probably means that U.S. adversaries will continue to find guerrilla warfare an attractive means of pursuing objectives contrary to U.S. interests.

CHRIS LAMB

See also American Revolution; Haiti; Spanish-American-Cuban-Filipino War, 1898; Vietnam War; Villa, Pancho

FURTHER READING

Asprey, Robert B. *War in the Shadows: The Guerrilla in History.* Garden City, N.Y., 1975.

Cable, Larry E. *Conflict of Myths: The Development of American-Counterinsurgency Doctrine and the Vietnam War.* New York, 1986.

Ellis, John. *A Short History of Guerrilla Warfare.* New York, 1976.

Laqueur, Walter. *Guerrilla: A Historical and Critical Study.* Boston, 1976.

Shultz, Richard H., Jr., Robert L. Pfaltzgraff, Jr., Uri Ra'anan, William J. Olson, and Igor Lukes. *Guerrilla Warfare and Counterinsurgency: U.S.-Soviet Policy in the Third World.* Lexington, Mass., 1989.

Taw, Jennifer Morrison, and Bruce Hoffman. *The Urbanization of Insurgency: The Potential Challenge to U.S. Army Operations.* Santa Monica, Calif., 1994.

GUINEA

See Appendix 2

GUINEA-BISSAU

Located in Western Africa, bordering the North Atlantic Ocean between Guinea and Senegal, a republic formerly known as Portuguese Guinea, and one of the world's poorest countries. Since the area's contact with Europe in the sixteenth century, it has had a turbulent history. Until the eighteenth century the region was a significant source of slaves bound for Latin America, and during the latter part of the nineteenth century, the British and the French challenged Portuguese control of the territory, subsequently settling these claims by negotiation. In 1961 a nationalist movement, the African Party for the Independence of Guinea and Cape Verde (PAIGC), directed by Amílcar Cabral until his assassination in 1973, initiated guerrilla warfare aimed at securing the territory's independence from Portugal. Although the rebels received some support in the form of Cuban trainers located in neighboring Guinea and Soviet and Chinese arms, the revolution came to a successful end only with the overthrow of the conservative military regime in Portugal in April 1974. Guinea-Bissau's independence was recognized on 10 September 1974, and the country has since been dominated by a single political party. The country, which relies on agriculture for subsistence, has received assistance in the form of aid and grants from Portugal, the United States, and other countries and the World Bank.

CAROLINE A. HARTZELL

See also Africa

FURTHER READING

Chabal, Patrick. *Amílcar Cabral: Revolutionary Leadership and People's War.* Cambridge, Mass., 1983.

Rudebeck, Lars. *Guinea-Bissau: A Study of Political Mobilization.* Uppsala, Sweden, 1974.

GULF OF TONKIN RESOLUTION

See Vietnam War

GULF WAR OF 1990–1991

The first major war of the post–Cold War era, precipitated by Iraq's invasion of Kuwait on 1 August 1990. The war took place between Iraq, led by President Saddam Hussein, and a United Nations coalition led by the United States. The fighting began on 17 January 1991 and ended on 1 March 1991. The war lasted only forty-three days but involved the most intensive air and armored operations since World War II, and the widespread use of new military technologies ranging from Stealth attack aircraft to modern tank-fire control systems with thermal-imaging sights.

The U.N. coalition achieved its major objectives of defending Saudi Arabia against a possible invasion by Iraq and of liberating Kuwait. The war did not remove Saddam Hussein from power, but it did deprive Iraq of much of its military power. A cease-fire at the end of the war allowed the UN to destroy most of Iraq's weapons of mass destruction and deny it imports of arms and military technology. For the first time since World War II, the United States and Russia cooperated in a major military operation. Another first was the broad coalition between Western and Arab states, demonstrating the potential ability of cooperative defense to repel aggression and execute peace enforcement.

Historical Context of the Iraqi Invasion

Iraq invaded Kuwait in order to establish regional hegemony in the Persian Gulf and because of a growing internal economic crisis. This crisis was caused by a combination of problems: the cost of repaying the foreign debts incurred during its 1980–1988 war with Iran, and the expense of funding massive new arms purchases and major economic development projects. The Iraqi regime had bought more than $60 worth of arms during the Iran-Iraq War, as much as one-third of its gross domestic product. By 1990 Iraq was $80 billion to $100 billion in debt and unable to meet its debt repayment costs. Despite these problems, Iraq was spending additional billions on missiles and biological, chemical, and nuclear weapons and ambitious civil development projects, such as the reconstruction of the ports of Basra and Fao.

Iraq provoked a political crisis during the months before the invasion. It charged Kuwait and the United Arab Emirates with over-producing oil and violating the quotas set by the Organization of Petroleum Exporting Countries (OPEC). As the crisis progressed, Iraq deployed several divisions near its border with Kuwait and demanded de facto control of Bubiyn and Warbah—

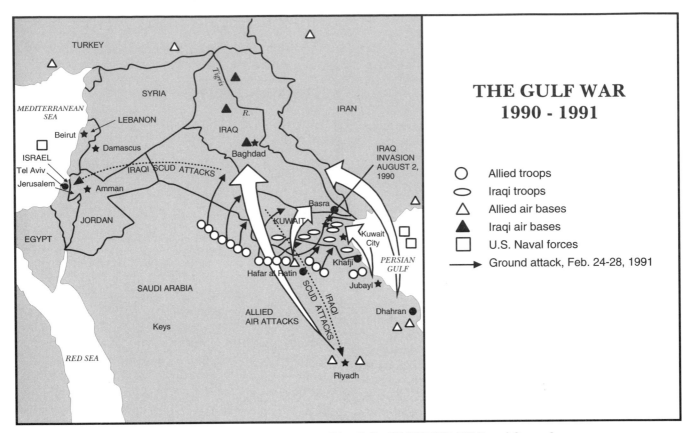

THE GULF WAR 1990 - 1991

- ○ Allied troops
- ⬭ Iraqi troops
- △ Allied air bases
- ▲ Iraqi air bases
- ☐ U.S. Naval forces
- → Ground attack, Feb. 24-28, 1991

From *The American Age: U.S. Foreign Policy At Home and Abroad*, Walter LaFeber, 2nd Edition, Volume II, *Since 1986.* ©1994,1989 by W.W. Norton & Company, Inc. Reprinted with permission of W. W. Norton & Company, Inc.

two Kuwaiti islands near Iraq's port of Umm Qasr that face Iraq's only channel to the Persian Gulf that does not border on Iran.

It is unclear whether Saddam Hussein intended to seize all of Kuwait when he first deployed troops at the border. Before the invasion he repeatedly told other Middle East leaders that the crisis could be avoided without a war and made no preinvasion claim to Kuwait. These statements led the United States, other Western nations, and the leading Arab states to respond to the crisis by trying to negotiate a settlement between Iraq and Kuwait. They believed that Saddam Hussein would accept a reasonable economic settlement and that any ultimatums or declaration on their part might provoke rather than deter Iraqi military action. They saw the worst-case threat as limited to demonstrative military action or an Iraqi attempt to expand control over its access to the Persian Gulf. The United States thus failed to send a clear signal to Iraq that the U.S. government would consider using military force if Iraq attacked Kuwait. This failure to react to Iraqi military capabilities, as distinguished from estimates of its intentions, may have influenced Hussein's behavior, although it seems just as likely that he would have disregarded such signals,

as he apparently believed that neither the United States nor any combination of nations would risk fighting a major war in the region.

In the end, Kuwait was completely unprepared when Hussein ordered his troops to invade the country on 2 August 1990. Iraqi forces met with only token resistance from Kuwaiti military forces and seized the entire country in less than two days. At the time of the invasion, Iraq claimed to be acting in support of an uprising by prodemocratic Kuwaiti forces and stated that Iraqi forces would soon withdraw. Within a week of seizing Kuwait, however, Iraq announced that it would annex Kuwait as its nineteenth province. Iraq justified these actions by claiming it was "liberating" territory stolen by Great Britain, but, in reality, Iraq lacked any serious claim to Kuwait. Ottoman control of the territory was historically uncertain and disputed, and Iraq was not a legitimate successor to the Ottoman Empire, having been created by Great Britain at the end of World War I out of part of the territory of the Ottoman Empire. In 1899 Kuwait had signed a comprehensive agreement with Great Britain, and its boundary had been demarcated by the Anglo-Turkish Convention of 1913. By 1921, when Iraq was created as a distinct state, Kuwait had existed for more than two decades as a small independent Bedouin settlement.

The real reasons behind Iraq's invasion concerned hegemony, not history. Control over Kuwait relieved Iraq of a major part of its debt payments and gave it potential access to more than 8 percent more of the world's oil reserves, massive Kuwaiti holdings of money and gold, and a deep-water port on the Persian Gulf. When Iraq stated it had annexed Kuwait, Kuwait's Fund for the Future had investments worth more than $100 billion. Kuwait was capable of adding at least 2 million barrels of oil a day to Iraq's exports of roughly 3.5 million, and offered the opportunity to increase Iraq's total oil reserves from 100 billion to 198 billion barrels (a total of nearly 20 percent of the world's reserves). The invasion also allowed Iraqi forces to deploy near the most vulnerable area in Saudi Arabia, from where they could intimidate or invade the other southern Persian Gulf states. Iraq deployed a full corps of armored and mechanized forces in an attack-ready position near Kuwait's southern border with Saudi Arabia, where the only opposition Iraq faced was fewer than two Saudi brigades and limited amounts of Saudi and U.S. offensive air power. Although Iraq may not have planned to attack Saudi Arabia, this strategic position gave Iraq immense political and military leverage over Saudi Arabia and potential control over an additional 28 percent of the world's total oil reserves.

Forging an International Military Coalition

Saddam Hussein seems to have gambled on Saudi Arabia and the other southern Persian Gulf states accepting his invasion as a fait accompli, and that the United States would either fail to mobilize an effective effort to force Iraq to retreat or would be unwilling to go to war. This calculation proved wrong in every respect. Saudi Arabia immediately gave the Kuwaiti government in exile its full support. The Saudi and Kuwaiti governments were backed by their partners in the Gulf Cooperation Council—Bahrain, Oman, Qatar, and the United Arab Emirates. King Fahd of Saudi Arabia asked for U.S. military support the same day he was shown that Iraq had moved its divisions to the Saudi border and into positions where they could invade. President George Bush acted quickly and firmly in response to the Saudi request for help. On 7 August 1990 the United States announced it would send land, air, and naval forces to Saudi Arabia and began to deploy air units less than a week after the first Iraqi troops entered Kuwait. Despite its prior hostility to the southern Persian Gulf states and the West, Iran supported Kuwait, and most of the Arab world proved equally firm. On 3 August 1990 the Arab League Council voted to condemn Iraq and demand its withdrawal from Kuwait. Egypt and Syria strongly opposed Iraq and along with Algeria and other Arab states later sent military

forces to defend Saudi Arabia and liberate Kuwait. The only Arab political powers to support Iraq after its invasion of Kuwait were Jordan, Libya, Mauritania, the PLO, the Sudan, and Yemen.

Great Britain, France, and other nations of Western and Central Europe, along with Japan and the Soviet Union also condemned the Iraqi invasion. The Soviet condemnation proved to be particularly decisive. Although President Mikhail Gorbachev tried to maintain Soviet influence in the region and conducted his own negotiations to persuade Iraq to withdraw from Kuwait, the Soviet Union consistently supported the United Nations and the United States. The end of the Cold War and the new climate of relations between the United States and the Soviet Union allowed the United Nations to play a major role in fighting aggression for the first time since the Korean War. One day after the invasion the Security Council voted 14 to 0 (Resolution 660) to demand Iraq's immediate and unconditional withdrawal from Kuwait. In the months that followed, the Security Council took every measure short of war to force Iraq to leave Kuwait. It adopted resolutions that ordered a financial and trade embargo against Iraq; declared Iraq's annexation of Kuwait null and void; called on Iraq to free the foreign hostages it had taken; established an international naval blockade; halted air cargo shipments; and made Iraq liable for war damages and economic costs.

The United States and other members of the UN coalition built up the military forces necessary to defend Saudi Arabia in a campaign known as Operation Desert Shield. In late October U.S. leadership realized that political and economic pressure would not persuade Iraq to leave Kuwait, and the military buildup increased in size toward 400,000 troops and changed in character. Under the leadership of U.S. General H. Norman Schwarzkopf, the UN command shifted its mission from defending Saudi Arabia to liberating Kuwait, and the United States and its allies began to deploy additional forces toward this end.

Throughout this period, the Bush administration clearly understood that the UN's effort to persuade Saddam Hussein and the Ba'ath Party elite to withdraw from Iraq might fail. Many of the military planners evaluating Iraq's actions concluded that Iraq was continuing a major military buildup and planned to either wait out the UN coalition or defeat it through a strategy of attrition. Moreover, Iraq continued to systematically terrorize the Kuwaiti people and loot the country's wealth. On 29 November 1990 the Security Council, with the United States leading the way, authorized the nations allied with Kuwait "to use all necessary means" if Iraq did not withdraw from Kuwait by 15 January 1991.

Major debate broke out in the United States over the use of force to liberate Kuwait. On 13 November 1990 leaders in Congress announced that the key committees in the House and Senate would hold hearings in December. Many leaders of both parties believed that any such use of force required the support of Congress. Forty-five members of the House filed suit on 20 November 1990 to require President Bush to seek congressional approval. The debate intensified once Congress held hearings on whether to use force or wait to see if prolonged sanctions and an embargo would force an Iraqi withdrawal.

On a practical level, the United States and its allies were confronted with the reality that they could not sustain a major offensive force in Saudi Arabia indefinitely and that by mid-spring the weather, longer days, and higher temperatures would present problems. Because of these concerns, President Bush sought approval from Congress on 8 January 1991 to use "all necessary means" of force. The House authorized the use of force (250 to 183) on 12 January, and the Senate followed suit (52 to 57) after rejecting a motion to rely on sanctions. Although public opinion polls produced many contradictory results during this period, about 60 percent of the American people seemed to have supported the president by January 1991.

The United States, Great Britain, France, Jordan, Russia, and a number of other countries made repeated efforts to persuade Iraq to withdraw peacefully from Kuwait before the UN deadline. Although Iraq continued to negotiate and freed the Western and Arab civilians it had taken hostage, Baghdad seemingly calculated that either the UN would not attack or that Iraq could defeat UN forces. Several last-minute efforts were made to avoid war, including a meeting between Secretary of State James Baker and Iraqi Foreign Minister Tariq Aziz in Geneva in early January and direct negotiations between Tariq Aziz and Soviet President Gorbachev in Moscow. Iraq continued to insist that it would only consider withdrawing if Israel withdrew from all its occupied territories. Iraq continued to expand its armed forces and defenses along Kuwait's coast and southern border, stepped up its efforts to convert Kuwait to an Iraq province, and persecuted Kuwait citizens. The UN Security Council thereupon voted on 15 January 1991 to reject a French proposal to accept an Iraq offer to set up a peace conference.

By this time the UN Command had deployed the forces General Schwarzkopf and the other coalition military leaders thought necessary to liberate Kuwait. The United States expanded its forces to 527,000 personnel, more than 110 naval vessels, 2,000 tanks, 1,800 fixed-wing aircraft, and 1,700 helicopters. Great Britain, France, Saudi Arabia, Egypt, Pakistan, and Syria also made significant military contributions. Other allied nations, including Canada and Italy, supplied air and naval forces; Oman, Qatar, and the United Arab Emirates deployed a significant portion of their small forces. At the same time, Iraq built up its military forces in Kuwait to a massive theater-wide force of 336,000 troops, 3,475 battle tanks, 3,080 other armored vehicles, and 2,475 major artillery weapons. Its total combat air strength in Kuwait and Iraq totaled 819 aircraft.

The UN coalition not only had a significant advantage in numbers, it also had a near monopoly in advanced electronic warfare, night combat capabilities, and advanced intelligence systems. Iraq was organized to defend against a slow moving, land-oriented enemy of the kind it had faced in Iran. It instead encountered a fast-maneuvering and air-oriented opponent with a far higher tempo of combat operations than Iraq could sustain twenty-four hours a day.

The Course of the Fighting: "Desert Storm"

The Gulf War began at 3:00 A.M. on 17 January 1991, when the UN coalition launched the offensive known as Operation Desert Storm. A series of devastating U.S. air attacks hit Iraqi command and control facilities, communications systems, air bases, and land-based air defenses. AH-64 Apache attack helicopters knocked out Iraq's forward radar system, sea-launched cruise missiles hit critical communications targets, and F-117 Stealth attack fighters struck Iraq's most heavily defended targets with precision weapons. UN coalition air forces were so superior that Iraq failed to win a single air-to-air engagement. By 20 January the coalition air forces achieved enough air superiority to broaden their targets from Iraq's air defenses to key headquarters, civil and army communications, electric power plants, and Iraq's facilities for the production of weapons of mass destruction. By 24 January Iraq ceased active resistance in the air, and Iraqi aircraft began to flee to Iran. The UN coalition then used long range air-to-surface weaponry, including the U.S. F-177 Stealth fighter and cruise missile, electronic warfare and other countermeasures, and antiradiation missiles to counter Iraq's ground-based air defenses, and was able to strike Iraqi ground targets with comparative impunity for the rest of the war.

From this point on until 24 February, UN air forces focused on destroying Iraqi ground forces in the Kuwaiti theater of operations, Iraq's elite Republican Guards units, its air bases and sheltered aircraft, and its hardened command and control facilities. They struck at Iraq's military supply depots and biological, chemical, and nuclear warfare facilities.

Iraq's ability to retaliate was limited to launching modified Scud missiles against targets in Saudi Arabia and Israel. Iraq launched its first missiles on the second day of the war and was able to continue launching them until the war ended, despite a massive "Scud hunt" that involved thousands of UN sorties. These Scud strikes had considerable propaganda value, but they failed to intimidate Saudi Arabia or provoke Israel into striking at Iraq—an action that might have alienated the Arab members of the UN coalition. The United States immediately assured Israel that it would take every possible military action to suppress Iraq's Scud launch capabilities and rushed Patriot air defense missiles to both Israel and Saudi Arabia. The rapidly deployed Patriots, which had not been fully modified to act as missile defense systems, had serious technical limits. There also were problems in how the Israeli government deployed them. Nevertheless, the weapons provided a vital boost in public confidence that helped keep Israel from joining the war.

The land phase of the war began at 4:00 A.M. on 24 February, when UN forces attacked along a broad front ranging from Khafaje on the Persian Gulf to positions north of Rafha on the Iraqi-Saudi border. The attack involved some 100,000 U.S. and 50,000 Allied troops, with 50,000 U.S. troops in reserve. The UN coalition launched a concentrated armored advance and achieved its major objectives in half the time originally planned. It attacked a gravely weakened Iraqi army. The U.S. and British ground troops which led the advance employed an Air-Land battle strategy originally developed to meet the Warsaw Pact armies, as demoralized Iraqi forces attempted to defend themselves using tactics more similar to those of World War I and without being able to employ air power. While some Republican Guard units fought well, the bulk of the Iraqi army consisted of poorly trained conscripts with poor morale and little motivation. Many fled after putting up only brief resistance, and others were taken prisoner.

By 26 February 1991, the UN coalition forces had effectively liberated Kuwait. U.S. forces in the Seventh and Seventeenth Corps had reached positions outside Basra in a surprisingly short time and destroyed the key Republican Guard divisions holding the area just north of the Kuwaiti border. Other UN forces, including the First and Second Marine divisions, had reached positions on the edge of Kuwait City and begun fighting for control of the international airport. These advances took place despite record rainfalls, which created substantial amounts of mud and severely limited the coalition's ability to provide air support.

Baghdad radio announced at 1:00 A.M. on 26 February that all Iraqi forces would withdraw from Kuwait in compliance with UN Resolution 660—although Saddam Hussein declared Iraq was withdrawing in the face of aggression from thirty countries. On 27 February President Bush announced that the United States would halt military operations at 8:00 A.M. on 28 February. During the brief period between the president's announcement and the cease-fire, the U.S. Seventh Corps shattered the remainder of the heavy Republican Guard divisions in the theater. The Seventeenth Corps moved closer to Basra, British and U.S. Army forces liberated northern Kuwait, Saudi and other Arab forces liberated Kuwait City, and U.S. Marines secured the southern and western outskirts of Kuwait City.

The war ended with the total defeat of Iraq's forces in the south, but the conflict ceased before UN forces could encircle and cut off all of the Iraqi forces and before the air campaign could destroy the retreating Iraqi forces around Basra. The war also was terminated in a way that met the UN's objectives in liberating Kuwait, but made no attempt to broaden the objective by supporting the Kurdish and Shi'ite uprisings that followed or by forcing the replacement of Saddam Hussein's Ba'ath government with a new, more democratic, and more friendly regime. Consequently, there has been considerable debate over the decision to end the war, and some critics have argued that even a few days of additional armored and air warfare would have proved decisive in overthrowing Hussein. Defenders of Bush's decision argue that a longer war would have killed more Iraqis and destroyed more equipment but that it would have required weeks of air offensives to destroy the remaining Iraqi ground forces outside the Kuwait theater of operations. Moreover, attacking and bombing the retreating Iraqi forces around Basra might have involved the UN in a prolonged battle in an inhabited area and killed thousands of additional Iraqis without altering the Iraqi regime.

The Political, Military, and Strategic Impact of the War

The Gulf War of 1990–1991 had several major strategic impacts. It was one of the most decisive military victories in history, and marked a revolution in warfare. The use of the Air-Land battle strategy demonstrated new concepts of air warfare and a combination of improved targeting systems and air munitions that made air power far more effective against ground forces than ever before. Massive physical damage was inflicted on the enemy with relatively limited losses. The land battle involved the longest and most rapid sustained armored advance in history and the largest heliborne assault. The assault demonstrated that armored forces could fight as well, if not better, at night and could advance at record rates of maneuver for twenty-four hours a day without stopping. The speed, precision, and intensity of this new tempo of warfare made previous concepts of warfare virtually obsolete.

In political terms, the Gulf War achieved virtually all of the objectives originally sought by the United States and authorized by UN resolutions before the conflict. On 2 March the UN Security Council approved Resolution

686, which set out the Allies' conditions for a cease-fire. The resolution called on Baghdad to accept the Council's twelve previous resolutions against Iraq and demanded that Iraq renounce its annexation of Kuwait, agree to pay reparations, release all prisoners, help remove mines, and return stolen property to Kuwait. The resolution required Iraq to cease hostile acts against other countries and parties, including missile attacks and flights of combat aircraft. Iraq accepted the UN terms on 3 March.

Kuwait was liberated, Iraq's military ability to threaten the region was sharply reduced, and a UN special commission and the International Atomic Energy Agency were able to supervise the destruction of most of Iraq's remaining long-range missiles and its capability to build and use weapons of mass destruction. The war did not, however, create a more liberal and moderate regime in Iraq or permanently remove the threat Iraq posed to other Persian Gulf states. The various uprisings that followed the war did not overthrow Saddam Hussein. Between 1991 and 1993 Hussein was able to put down the Shi'ite rising in the south that took place immediately after the war, draining the marshes in southern Iraq and using military pressure to destroy the last remnants of Shi'ite resistance. Only UN authorization of Operation Provide Comfort and U.S. and Allied military action prevented Iraqi forces from overrunning the Kurdish areas in northern Iraq after a similar uprising.

Despite its losses during the war, Iraq retained the largest army in the Persian Gulf region, plus 100 to 200 long-range missiles, some ability to deliver chemical weapons, and most of its prewar biological weapons capability. Although Iraq lost its nuclear facilities, it retained much of its nuclear weapons technology. Iraq continued terrorist activities against its neighbors and the UN mission in Iraq, including the attempted assassination of former President Bush during his visit to Kuwait on 14–16 April 1993.

The war left several major issues for U.S. policy unresolved, including whether it would have been better for the United States to continue military action against Saddam Hussein until Iraq's ruling Ba'ath elite was removed from power and how the United States should deal with the problem of nuclear proliferation and missile attacks in future conflicts.

ANTHONY H. CORDESMAN

See also Bush, George Herbert Walker; Hussein, Saddam; Iraq; Kuwait; Middle East; United Nations; Organization of Petroleum Exporting Countries; Powell, Colin; Russia and the Soviet Union; Saudi Arabia; United Nations

FURTHER READING

Atkinson, Rick. *Crusade: The Untold Story of the Gulf War.* Boston, 1993.

Cohen, Eliot, ed. *Gulf War Air Power Survey.* Washington, D.C., 1993.

Cordesman, Anthony H. *The Gulf War.* Boulder, Colo., 1996.

——— and Abraham R. Wagner. *The Lessons of Modern War Volume IV: The Gulf War.* Boulder, Colo., 1996.

De La Billiere, Peter. *Storm Command.* London, 1992.

Freedman, Lawrence, and Efraim Karsh. *The Gulf Conflict, 1990–1991.* London, 1993.

Gordon, Michael R., and General Bernard C. Trainor. *The General's War: The Inside Story of the Conflict in the Gulf.* Boston, 1995.

Granbard, Stephen R. *Mr. Bush's War.* New York, 1992.

Hallion, Richard P. *Storm Over Iraq: Air Power and the Gulf War.* Washington, D.C., 1992.

Jentleson, Bruce W. *With Friends Like These: Reagan, Bush, and Saddam, 1982–1990.* New York, 1994.

Murray, Williamson. *Air War in the Persian Gulf.* Baltimore, Md., 1995.

Nye, Joseph S., Jr., and Roger Smith. *After the Storm: Lessons from the Gulf War.* Madison, Wisc., 1992.

Pagonis, William G., and Jeffery L. Cruikshank. *Moving Mountains.* Cambridge, Mass., 1992.

Scales, Robert H., ed. *Certain Victory: The U.S. Army in the Gulf War.* Washington, D.C., 1993.

Schwarzkopf, H. Norman. *It Doesn't Take a Hero.* New York, 1992.

U.S. Department of Defense. *Conduct of the Persian Gulf War: Final Report to Congress.* Washington, D.C., 1992.

Woodward, Bob. *The Commanders.* New York, 1991.

GUNBOAT DIPLOMACY

The political application of limited naval force as a supplement to diplomacy and an alternative to war in order to either secure an advantage or avert a loss in an international dispute or conflict with foreign nationals. Gunboat diplomacy should be distinguished from mere naval visits that need not convey any specific message nor imply any exercise of pressure. It should also be distinguished from a full-scale military intervention and occupation. Indeed, while in some instances such full-scale interventions and occupations have taken place, in certain situations naval forces have distinct advantages over land-based units: they can intervene, disengage, and withdraw more easily and rapidly, and they are less disruptive psychologically and less offensive diplomatically because they can be assembled and ready for intervention but not be committed.

The region in which the United States has most frequently resorted to gunboat diplomacy has been Latin America. In no fewer than twenty instances, mostly in the early twentieth century, the United States intervened in such Latin American and Caribbean states as Mexico, Cuba, the Dominican Republic, Haiti, and Nicaragua. While each case had its own issues and circumstances, in general the exercise of gunboat diplomacy in Latin America and the Caribbean represented the convergence of the Monroe Doctrine of 1823, including the Roosevelt Corollary of 1904, warning the imperial European powers to stay out of the Western Hemisphere; the economic drive and ideological attitude of an expansionist United States, known as Manifest Destiny to some and deemed imperialism by others; the drive for national greatness through naval power; and the strategic importance of the then-new

Panama Canal. In some instances—for example, Haiti in 1915–1943 and Nicaragua in 1912–1933—what began as limited interventions became long-term military occupations. President Franklin D. Roosevelt's Good Neighbor Policy marked a break with gunboat diplomacy, although the United States again frequently intervened in Latin America and the Caribbean during the Cold War, albeit more often by other methods, such as covert action.

The United States also frequently employed gunboat diplomacy in China. It established a Yangtze River patrol in 1921 to protect U.S. interests, lives, and property; sent warships along with other nations to Canton in 1923 to protect the foreign administration of Chinese customs; and, along with Japan and other European navies, sent thirty-five warships to Shanghai in 1927 to protect foreign economic interests during the Chinese civil war between nationalists and communists.

During the Cold War the United States used gunboat diplomacy in a variety of circumstances. In 1946, as the Cold War began to heat up, naval units were permanently stationed in the Mediterranean to promote U.S. policy and diplomacy. When President Harry S. Truman sought congressional authorization for aid to Greece against its communist insurgency in 1947, he announced that strong naval squadrons would visit Greek ports. Other instances of the use of U.S. naval forces included patrolling the Taiwan Straits in 1950 to prevent a communist invasion of Formosa; harassing British and French warships in 1956 in disapproval of their intervention at Suez; deployment to the Gulf of Siam during the Laotian crisis of 1961–1962; blockading Cuba in 1962 during the missile crisis; reinforcing the U.S. presence in the eastern Mediterranean in 1970, in response to the outbreak of civil war in Jordan and to counter Syrian intervention and deter Soviet and Egyptian military involvement; and attempting to influence the course of the 1971 Indo-Pakistani War. Since the end of the Cold War, the principal uses of limited naval force by the United States have involved the enforcement of economic sanctions, as against Iraq, Haiti, and Serbia. Gunboat diplomacy has not disappeared, but it has shifted in its primary forms and purposes.

A number of forces have affected both the frequency and utility of gunboat diplomacy over time. Political considerations, like nationalism, have heightened the will of governments to deter, resist, and retaliate against the use of limited naval force. International opinion has prejudiced attitudes against outside intervention. The bipolarity of the Cold War increased the ability of weak states to withstand the exercise of limited naval force and raised the risk of naval opposition. Technological developments in weaponry such as cruise missiles, bomber aircraft, coastal submarines, and modern mines offer potential victims new means of deterrence, defense, and counter-attack. Nevertheless, limited naval force is still effective on the high seas for escort, convoy, interception, capture, blockade, surveillance, and harassment, while the conduct of inshore operations has merely changed requiring more political preparation, more elaborate naval planning, and a larger task force than a mere gunboat.

EMILY O. GOLDMAN

See also Blockade; China; Coercive Diplomacy; Cold War; Latin America; Navy, U.S. Department of; Preventive Diplomacy

FURTHER READING

Blechman, Barry M., and Stephen S. Kaplan, eds. *Force Without War: U.S. Armed Forces as a Political Instrument.* Washington, D.C., 1978.

Cable, James. *Gunboat Diplomacy, 1919–1991.* New York, 1994.

Healy, David. *Gunboat Diplomacy in the Wilson Era: The U.S. Navy in Haiti, 1915–1916.* Madison, Wisc., 1976.

GUYANA

See Appendix 2

H

HABIB, PHILIP CHARLES

(*b.* 25 February 1920; *d.* 25 May 1992)

Ambassador to the Republic of Korea (1971–1974), assistant secretary of state for political affairs (1974–1976), undersecretary of state for political affairs (1976–1978), and skilled negotiator, especially on Middle East issues. Habib joined the Foreign Service in 1949 and was posted to Canada, New Zealand, and Washington. He served with the rank of minister in Saigon at the height of the Vietnam War and was a member of the U.S. delegation to the Paris peace talks (1968–1971). Together with David K. E. Bruce, Habib became what Secretary of State Henry Kissinger termed President Richard Nixon's "Paris negotiating team." As ambassador to the Republic of Korea, Habib became known as one of the Department of State's leading experts on Southeast Asian issues. After suffering the first of a series of heart attacks, Habib officially retired from the State Department in 1978 but became a special adviser to Secretary of State Cyrus R. Vance the next year. Habib helped conduct the Camp David negotiations between Israel and Egypt in 1978, and he had the difficult task of explaining to the sultan of Oman why President Jimmy Carter's administration had used Oman without prior consultation as a base for the aborted U.S. hostage operation against Iran in April 1980. After the June 1982 Israeli invasion of Lebanon, Habib negotiated a cease-fire that permitted Palestine Liberation Organization (PLO) forces to leave West Beirut; he then helped mediate a cease-fire between Lebanon and Israel. Habib ended his service in the Middle East in 1983. Three years later, as President Ronald Reagan's envoy to the Philippines, Habib played a key role in convincing President Ferdinand Marcos to resign his position and leave Manila. In 1987 Habib helped negotiate a cease-fire and free elections in Nicaragua; in August of that year he finally retired from diplomatic service.

During Habib's retirement he served as a trustee of the American University in Beirut (1983–1992) and chaired the Pacific Forum of Honolulu (1980–1991). He also remained an active alumnus of the University of Idaho, where he created the Philip Habib Endowment for the Study of Environmental Issues and World Peace. Habib's ebullient personality, quick wit, and friendly manner contributed to his high reputation as a superb negotiator. Kissinger described Habib as "one of my heroes" and stated that Habib was "every secretary of state's idea of a great Foreign Service officer." To Secretary of State George Shultz, Habib was "America's top diplomatic pro" with a style that was "direct, forceful, no-nonsense."

DIANE B. KUNZ

See also Camp David Accords; Carter, James Earl; Korea; Lebanon; Middle East; Nicaragua; Philippines; Vietnam War

FURTHER READING

Shultz, George P. *Turmoil and Triumph: My Years as Secretary of State.* New York, 1993.
Spiegel, Steven L. *The Other Arab-Israeli Conflict: Making America's Middle East Policy from Truman to Reagan.* Chicago, 1985.

HAGUE PEACE CONFERENCES

(1899, 1907)

Called to consider issues of war and peace, the conferences began the first world organization of independent nations. Such an organization was not, however, the objective of the initiator of the conferences, Czar Nicholas II of Russia. In a circular note of 24 August 1898, often called the "Peace Rescript," he called on all governments with diplomatic representatives at his court to participate in a conference to consider limitations on armaments. His foreign minister issued a second circulars on 11 January 1899 that in eight points called for consideration of the armaments problem, improvements in the laws of war, and improvements in procedures for international arbitration. The idealistic language of the circulars caught the imagination of leaders of peace groups in Europe and the United States, and these leaders dubbed the proposed meeting a peace conference. The Russian government made it clear, however, that the conference would not discuss current international political problems.

The Russian invitation arrived in Washington a few days after the signing of an armistice ending hostilities between the United States and Spain. President William McKinley's administration accepted at once but told the Russians that the U.S. Army and Navy were too small to meet the nation's responsibilities and that the United States was not interested in limitations. When the conference opened at The Hague on 18 May 1899, noted naval historian Alfred Thayer Mahan and army Captain William Crozier, coinventor of the Buffington-Crozier disappearing machine gun carriage, representing the United States, opposed any measure requiring limits on U.S. armed forces. None of the great powers except Russia sought such limitations, and even Russian interest had waned since the Peace Rescript. The conference did agree upon declarations against expanding bullets, poison gas, and projectiles thrown from balloons. The conference also completed the work of earlier conferences on the laws of war. A convention on land warfare incorporated much of the unratified Brussels Declaration of 1874, a code based in part upon *General Orders No. 100*, the Union government's Civil War code for land warfare. Another new convention extended the 1864 Geneva Convention's rules governing treatment of the sick and wounded on land to those at sea in accordance with an unratified agreement of 1868. The chairman of the U.S. delegation, Andrew D. White, suggested that private property at sea be declared immune from capture. The British were opposed to this proposal and without their support it died.

The conference had its most notable successes with arbitration, framing a convention defining principles for both mediation and voluntary arbitration and creating the Permanent Court of Arbitration. Defeat in the U.S. Senate in 1897 of the Olney-Pauncefote Treaty, which called for obligatory arbitration with Great Britain, and U.S. disregard of Spanish suggestions for arbitration had weakened U.S. claims to be an advocate of arbitration. Secretary of State John Hay saw the peace conference as an opportunity for the United States to appear once again as an exponent of arbitration and recommended establishment of an international court modeled on the U.S. Supreme Court. Fearful that such a court might interfere with enforcement of the Monroe Doctrine, the U.S. delegates did not present Hay's plan but joined with the chairman of the British delegation, Sir Julian Pauncefote, in presenting a plan that would require each signatory power to name qualified persons to a list from which judges could be chosen for arbitrations. The proposal passed—the conference had taken a hesitant step toward a world court. The U.S. delegates gained some prestige by their efforts, but their reservations became clear when Mahan noted that Article 27 of the arbitration convention stated that signatory powers had the duty of reminding quarreling governments of the Permanent Court. He warned of trouble over the Monroe Doctrine. White thereupon made a declaration to a plenary session of the conference that the United States in signing the arbitration convention was not departing from its traditional policies. Everyone present knew that this statement meant that the United States had no intention of involving itself in European international politics and that it would continue to oppose European attempts to extend political control in the Americas.

Despite White's declaration, the United States supported the Permanent Court until the outbreak of World War I. At the suggestion of President Theodore Roosevelt, the Permanent Court in 1902 took as its first case a dispute between Mexico and the United States over the ancient Pious Fund of the Californias. It was also at Roosevelt's suggestion that the court in 1904 decided the question of preferential payment of claims, after Germany, Great Britain, and Italy blockaded Venezuela to force payment of the claims of their nationals. The Roosevelt administration had less success winning Senate approval of treaties calling for obligatory arbitration, treaties through which Secretary Hay hoped to strengthen the court. The Senate approved the Hay treaties but added amendments requiring that a special agreement be submitted for each arbitration; believing that the Senate was putting roadblocks in the way of arbitration, Roosevelt withdrew the treaties.

The Hague Conference of 1899 also recommended that another conference continue its work, and peace groups frequently urged that another conference be convened. In 1904 Roosevelt promised the visiting Interparliamentary Union that he would call one. The Russian government, upon conclusion of the Russo-Japanese War in 1905, asked Roosevelt to step aside; Nicholas II, initiator of the first conference, wished to call the second conference. Roosevelt agreed at once. It was expected that the conference would meet in 1906, but a U.S. request that all Latin American republics be included made postponement until 1907 necessary, because few of the republics had enough experts to take part in both a Hague conference and the third Pan-American Conference, already scheduled for 1906 at Rio de Janeiro.

When the Second Hague Peace Conference convened on 15 June 1907, forty-four governments were represented, compared to twenty-six in 1899. The new conference came closer to being a conference of the world than any earlier conference. The original purpose of the first conference, consideration of limitations on armaments, received even less attention in 1907 than it had at the first conference. The Russians listened to objections voiced by the German representatives and kept the topic off the program, although delegates applauded a British resolution, supported by the United States, that recognized the seriousness of the armaments question. The conference made only minor revisions in the 1899 land warfare convention but incorporated its articles regulating internment of belligerent personnel and care of the wounded into a convention defining the rights and duties of neutral states and persons. The conference also renewed the declaration against throwing projectiles from balloons.

The conference gave the laws of maritime warfare careful study. The problems neutrals faced at sea during the Russo-Japanese War had been so numerous that even Great Britain welcomed these negotiations. The British and Germans separately proposed the creation of an international prize court to make decisions about captured ships. The United States supported the idea and urged compromise between the two plans. The conference framed a convention to establish a court at The Hague that would be appointed by the great powers. It was apparent, however, that few governments could accept the convention, for the conference could not agree on definitions of contraband and blockade—both essential elements of the prize law the court would interpret. The British also quietly let it be known that they would invite the maritime powers to a special conference. The peace conference concluded nine other conventions concerning naval warfare, many of them reflecting the experiences of conference participants during the Russo-Japanese War. It also concluded a convention requiring signatories to issue a formal declaration before beginning a war, a move spurred by Russian resentment over the surprise Japanese attack on Port Arthur in 1904.

The conference revised and improved the arbitration convention, but U.S. efforts to establish more ambitious arbitral institutions fell short. The Germans defeated a proposal for a worldwide obligatory arbitration convention. The U.S. representatives, however, were more concerned about the failure of their proposal for a court of arbitral justice, which would have established a court always organized and ready to hear cases. This proposal became the basis of a draft convention but failed because of disagreement over representation on the court. The Brazilians, backed by other Latin American delegations, demanded representation for all sovereign states, but the United States argued that so large a body could not possibly become the kind of court the world needed. Irritation over Latin American reactions to their proposal notwithstanding, U.S. delegates considered issues concerning Latin America among their primary concerns. They secured approval of a convention prohibiting armed intervention to collect debts until arbitration had been offered and refused. This agreement hardly resembled the Drago Doctrine that inspired it, but it was a warning to European powers of U.S. opposition to armed expeditions undertaken to collect debts. At the close of the conference there was yet another U.S. statement of special interest in the Americas; the chairman of the American delegation, Joseph H. Choate, repeated White's 1899 declaration about the U.S. intention to adhere to its traditional policies with regard to Europe and the Americas.

U.S. delegates considered the continuation of the Hague Conferences of the utmost importance. Choate secured a resolution calling for a third conference within a period corresponding to that between the first two conferences and creating a committee to begin collecting information two years before the new conference. The resolution effectively ended Russian sponsorship of the conferences and opened new opportunities for constructive U.S. diplomacy. Americans participated actively in the London Naval Conference of 1908–1909 and through quiet negotiations tried to secure authority for the projected prize court to act as a court of arbitral justice. These aspirations came to nothing when the British House of Lords blocked ratification of the Declaration of London. U.S. representatives nonetheless pursued other policies intended to strengthen the Hague system. The Root Arbitration Treaties (1908–1909), although they referred each arbitral agreement to the Senate, advanced the idea that arbitration was a concern of many nations, but broader treaties proposed by President William Howard Taft were abandoned in the face of objections by the Senate. Despite this setback, the Taft and Woodrow Wilson administrations exerted pressure on European governments to prepare for the Third Hague Peace Conference, tentatively set to convene in 1915.

The outbreak of war in 1914 ended the Hague Peace Conferences, but their influence continued. The unratified Declaration of London and the Hague conventions on warfare on land and sea provided important guidelines throughout World War I. After the war the newly created League of Nations founded the Permanent Court of International Justice on the basis of the 1907 draft convention for a court of arbitral justice. The Permanent Court of Arbitration continued to exist and received authority to nominate judges for the new court. When the United Nations replaced the League of Nations, the court became the International Court of Justice, and the Permanent Court of Arbitration retained its nominating functions.

Secretary of State Charles Evans Hughes recalled the initiative of Nicholas II concerning armaments limitations when he opened the Washington Conference on Limitation of Armaments in 1921, but the Hague Conferences provided little inspiration for progress in that area, for the Washington Conference or for the many others that followed. Far more important have been the Hague conventions on the laws of war, which are still integral parts of the international law of war and the subject of several international conferences since World War I.

CALVIN D. DAVIS

See also Arbitration; Drago Doctrine; London Naval Conferences of 1930 and 1935–1936; Mahan, Alfred Thayer; Monroe Doctrine; Peace Movements and Societies to 1914; Permanent Court of Arbitration (Hague Tribunal); Permanent Court of International Justice; Washington Conference on the Limitation of Armaments

FURTHER READING

Davis, Calvin D. *The United States and the First Hague Peace Conference*. Ithaca, N.Y., 1962.

———. *The United States and the Second Hague Peace Conference: American Diplomacy and International Organization 1899–1914*. Durham, N.C., 1976.

Kuehl, Warren F. *Seeking World Order: The United States and International Organization to 1920*. Nashville, 1969.

Scott, James Brown. *The Hague Peace Conferences of 1899 and 1907*. 2 vols. Baltimore, 1909.

HAGUE TRIBUNAL

See Permanent Court of Arbitration (Hague Tribunal)

HAIG, ALEXANDER MEIGS, JR.

(*b.* 2 December 1924)

Career military officer, foreign policy adviser, and secretary of state (1981–1982). A graduate of the U.S. Military Academy and a veteran of the Korean War, Haig served in the Pentagon in the 1960s before becoming national security adviser Henry Kissinger's deputy on the National Security Council (NSC) in 1969. In Kissinger's words, "Haig...disciplined my anarchic tendencies and established coherence and procedure in an NSC Staff of talented prima donnas." Haig became President Richard M. Nixon's chief of staff in 1973 and played an indispensable role in persuading Nixon to resign following the Watergate scandal. Supreme Allied Commander in Europe for the North Atlantic Treaty Organization (NATO) during President Jimmy Carter's administration, Haig was appointed secretary of state by Ronald Reagan in 1981. Known for his polysyllabic vocabulary and tangled syntax, Haig purported to be the "vicar" of a new foreign policy that would restore U.S. prestige by presenting a tough face to the Russians, taking an aggressive anticommunist stance in Central America, and dramatically escalating the arms race. Bureaucratic in-fighting and international crises limited Haig's tenure as secretary of state to less than eighteen months. Reagan took responsibility for crisis management away from Haig and assigned it to Vice President George Bush. White House staffers resented Haig's apparent ambition for the presidency; the secretary also clashed with United Nations Ambassador Jeane Kirkpatrick, who adopted a pro-Argentine position during Haig's effort to mediate the Falklands War between Great Britain and Argentina (although the president supported Haig's pro-British posture). Haig was also overruled on the sale of airborne warning and command aircraft (AWACs) to Saudi Arabia and on lifting the grain embargo against the Soviet Union, both of which he opposed privately but defended publicly. The final break came during the Israeli invasion of Lebanon in June 1982, when White House aides interfered with Haig's instructions to Ambassador Philip Habib, who was trying to negotiate a diplomatic settlement to the conflict. When Haig complained to Reagan, the president, in Haig's words, accepted "a letter of resignation I had not submitted." After leaving office, Haig ran unsuccessfully for the Republican nomination for president in 1988. He also wrote op-ed pieces on U.S. foreign policy and served as an adviser to major corporations, such as the defense contractor United Technologies.

J. GARRY CLIFFORD

See also Bush, George Herbert Walker; Falkland Islands; Kirkpatrick, Jeane Duane; Kissinger, Henry Alfred; Lebanon; National Security Council; Nixon, Richard Milhous; Reagan, Ronald Wilson; Russia and the Soviet Union; Saudi Arabia

FURTHER READING

Haig, Alexander Meigs. *Caveat*. New York, 1984.

———. *Inner Circles*. New York, 1992.

Morris, Roger. *Haig: The General's Progress*. New York, 1982.

Schultz, George P. *Turmoil and Triumph*. New York, 1993.

HAITI

Island republic located in the northern Caribbean Sea southwest of Cuba, occupying the western part of the island of Hispaniola. A long history of distrust, tension, and conflict, rooted in political and cultural differences, characterizes U.S. relations with Haiti. These include disagreements over U.S. hemispheric interests and, in the view of many scholars, elements of racism in U.S. policy. U.S. relations with Haiti originated in colonial commerce. Eighteenth-century Saint Domingue, as the French colony was known, offered attractively priced tropical staples to the North American market. Trade expanded during the American Revolution when France funneled munitions to the American rebels through Saint Domingue. The upheavals of the French Revolution spurred a slave rebellion in 1791 which contributed to the breakdown of French rule in the colony in the succeeding decade. By 1799, freedman François-Dominique Toussaint L'Ouverture gained military control and secured the cooperation of the French. He restored some order to the territory but Napoleon Bonaparte turned against him, capturing him in 1803 and sending forces to restore direct rule. Haitian rebels nevertheless defeated the French, and on 1 January 1804 General Jean-Jacques Dessalines declared the independence of Haiti (reclaiming the original Indian name), making it the second oldest republic in the Western Hemisphere.

Despite its trade with Haiti and support of the Haitian revolutionists, the United States did not recognize the new nation; racism and fear that diplomatic recognition might cause a slave revolt in the United States impeded normalization of relations until 1862, when the United States was in the midst of the Civil War. Washington paid scant attention to the Caribbean republics until after the Spanish-American-Cuban-Filipino War, when interest in an isthmian canal across Central America led to renewed attention in the region. Concerned that Haiti's chronic poverty might precipitate extrahemispheric intervention, the administration of President William Howard Taft induced Haiti to accept a major loan and other concessions in 1910.

This stabilizing strategy failed. After a mob assassinated President Vilburn Guillaume Sam in July 1915, President Woodrow Wilson sent marines to Haiti to restore order. Wilson argued that Haiti had no legitimate government and suggested that foreign powers might use World War I as an excuse to gain a foothold there. The military intervention forced the Haitian legislature to elect a president and authorize a treaty making Haiti a U.S. protectorate, giving the United States control over Haiti's finances. The Haitian legislature refused to approve the corresponding constitutional changes, and in 1917 U.S. authorities adjourned the legislature and kept it adjourned for the next thirteen years.

The occupation regime revived forced labor, enacted press censorship, removed restrictions on land ownership by foreigners, and introduced overt racial segregation. These unpopular policies contributed to a peasant rebellion in 1919–1920 that was suppressed by the marines. A subsequent U.S. Senate investigation impelled Washington to make administrative changes and to introduce some reforms without fundamentally affecting Haiti's underdeveloped economy. Direct control of the Haitian government proved costly to the United States, while provoking resentment and proving an imperfect instrument for conflict resolution. In 1930 Americans began training Haitians to carry out civil, military, and police functions, and in 1934 the occupation was terminated. The United States resumed normal relations with Haiti at the ministerial level and in 1943 raised its legation to embassy status. The United States also initiated economic assistance to Haiti in 1944 and became the only country to maintain a resident aid mission there.

The Haitian army became a key political actor soon after the withdrawal of the marines. François ("Papa Doc") Duvalier, elected in 1957 with military support, gradually undermined his benefactors, creating a patronage machine and using state power to profit his family and associates. Appropriating voodoo theology and black nationalism, Duvalier marshaled the resentments of the impoverished majority to fortify his rule, ruthlessly suppressing opposition through a secret police force, the Tonton Macoutes.

Concerned about the brutality of the Duvalier regime, as well as allegations that Duvalier was blatantly misappropriating aid money and intended to misuse a Marine Corps mission to Haiti to strengthen the Tonton Macoutes, the administration of President John F. Kennedy terminated most U.S. assistance to Haiti in 1963. Duvalier, who refused to accept Washington's demands for strict accounting procedures as a condition of aid renewal, renounced all aid from Washington. As a result, Haiti did not participate in the Alliance for Progress. After Kennedy's death in November 1963, U.S. pressure on Duvalier relaxed. Because of Haiti's strategic location near Cuba, the site of a 1959 revolution, Washington adopted a policy of unenthusiastic acceptance of the Duvalier regime. Although embarrassed by the human rights violations of the Haitian government, the administration of Lyndon B. Johnson extended military aid to the country. Duvalier, newly confident, declared himself president for life in 1964. U.S.-Haitian relations were reinforced in the late 1960s when President Richard Nixon, who was supportive of Duvalier's anticommunist stance, reintroduced economic assistance to Haiti. Shortly before Duvalier died in 1971, he named his nineteen-year-old son, Jean-Claude Duvalier, as his successor.

Jean-Claude Duvalier faced a challenge from U.S. President Jimmy Carter, who linked assistance for dependent governments to progress toward democracy. As part of the Carter administration's fiscal year 1979 budget, for example, U.S. aid to Haiti, which was considered to have a relatively repressive government, was redesigned to reach only the neediest social sectors in the country. The administration's 1980 military aid request, in turn, led to Haiti's being dropped from the list of foreign military sales recipients, although it kept its international military education training programs. Such changes were, in large measure, the result of U.S. congressional initiatives, but they took place within the context of an administration that was more sympathetic to such initiatives than previous U.S. administrations. Under such pressure, Duvalier made ineffectual concessions to demands for free speech and a free press that merely fed mounting demands for change. A light assembly export industry developed in Haiti during this time. Manufacturers profited from Haitian proximity to the United States, the low wage scales, and the confidence that labor unrest would be suppressed. The Haitian government closed its eyes to labor exploitation in the off-shore manufacturing sector. Its permissiveness here, and with regard to such ventures as drug trafficking, helped buy the cooperation of wealthy Haitians and of foreigners.

In 1980 the Carter administration also had to cope with the beginning of a major refugee crisis as Haitian "boat people" sought refuge in the United States. Many Haitians, reacting to economic distress and repression, entered the United States, legally or illegally, in the 1980s.

Immigration authorities considered undocumented aliens economic rather than political refugees and refused them asylum. This treatment contrasted markedly with that accorded Cubans, who routinely were deemed political refugees and given asylum. Many of the Haitians, who set sail in all sorts of unseaworthy crafts, died en route; other vessels were intercepted by the U.S. Coast Guard and repatriated. Haitians fortunate enough to arrive safely in the United States remained in legal limbo. The AIDS pandemic also affected Haitian refugees. The Centers for Disease Control considered Haitian immigrants a special risk because of the large proportion of Haitians suffering from AIDS. Although it revised this view in 1985, the public perception of Haitians as carriers persisted, and the stereotype was one of the factors limiting Haitian entry into the United States.

Following food riots in Haiti in 1985, the Department of State threatened to withhold assistance pending reforms. Whereas in his first term President Ronald Reagan had given virtually unqualified support to almost any dictator who was staunchly anticommunist, in his second term he began to shift away from repressive figures like Duvalier, Chile's General Augusto Pinochet, and the Philippines' Ferdinand Marcos. There was no U.S. help this time, and Duvalier could not quell the unrest. On 7 February 1986 he fled into exile aboard a U.S.-provided aircraft. Popular celebration greeted Duvalier's abdication. The most brutal members of the secret police were lynched and symbols of Duvalier's rule were destroyed. The dictator's departure nevertheless left intact the Haitian military, which had been trained and supplied by the United States, and the secret police. With the Duvaliers gone, these elements struggled to appropriate the enterprises they had controlled and coveted the old regime's despotic authority over the populace. Haitians termed the subsequent repression "Duvalierism without Duvalier."

The army-dominated provisional government that replaced Duvalier approved a constitution and enacted token reforms, but the government found itself confronted with a newly politicized citizenry. With U.S. approval, elections were scheduled for 29 November 1987. On election eve and day, terrorists (who according to many observers included members of the feared Tonton Macoutes as well as active members of the army) destroyed property in the capital city of Port-au-Prince and shot and hacked voters to death at a polling site. The government then suspended the voting. In response, the Reagan administration discontinued nonhumanitarian aid.

Few Haitians dared participate in elections rescheduled for January 1988. Presidential candidate Leslie F. Manigat won with assistance from the provisional government but lost credibility with much of the Haitian population because of this collaboration. When he defied the powers that put him in office, they deposed him on

20 June. An army junta then assumed visible control, suppressing dissidence and blocking new elections. The United States provided some support for the junta, withholding some aid but continuing military assistance.

Renewed pressure from President George Bush's administration led to the naming of Ertha Pascal-Trouillot, a civilian and Haiti's first woman chief of state, as provisional president in March 1990. This did not mean, however, that the military was powerless. Army and police elements resolutely sabotaged efforts toward democratization and launched an attack on an advisory group of influential citizens in June. Washington carefully supervised the December 1990 election in which Haitians chose a former priest, Jean-Bertrand Aristide, as president with 70 percent of the vote. Aristide subscribed to the radical Christianity and antiestablishmentarianism of *ti egliz*, the Haitian popular church. He was an avowed enemy of Duvalierism, had been expelled from the Salesian order, and survived several assassination attempts.

Aristide was the champion of the impoverished majority of Haitian society, and tensions with both the military and the elite were apparent from the very beginning of his presidency. A military coup that began 29 September 1991 overthrew Aristide the following day, less than a year after his election. Many Aristide supporters were killed in this rebellion led by General Raoul Cédras. Thousands fled in boats even more unseaworthy than those used in the 1980 exodus. Aristide was forced into exile, first in Venezuela and then in the United States.

The Bush administration imposed trade sanctions both unilaterally and through the Organization of American States (OAS) in an effort to improve human rights in Haiti, restore democracy there, and stop drug smuggling, but these were only partial sanctions, and poorly enforced ones, and they ended up imposing further suffering on the masses of the Haitian people without providing significant leverage over the Cédras regime. Meanwhile, the refugee crisis worsened, with almost 40,000 Haitians being intercepted by the U.S. Coast Guard in the year following the coup. The Bush policy of forced repatriation for many of these people came under sharp criticism, including from the 1992 Democratic presidential candidate, Bill Clinton. Clinton also accused Bush of not being sufficiently committed to the restoration of democracy in Haiti.

After Clinton's victory, the dominant expectation was that he would reverse the policies he had so forcefully criticized, but he did not. With his memories of the domestic political fallout he had faced as governor of Arkansas from the 1980 Cuban boat-people refugee influx, he largely continued the Bush policy of forced repatriation. There was a ray of hope in mid-1993 when, through the diplomatic mediation of the Clinton administration in conjunction with the United Nations and the OAS, the Governor's Island agreement (named for the island in New York Harbor where the negotiations took place), outlining the terms and the timetable for Aristide's return was signed by General Cédras and President Aristide. The agreement collapsed, however, before it was fully implemented.

From the verge of a seeming diplomatic triumph, the Clinton administration's Haiti policy degenerated into one of its major foreign policy problems. Efforts were made to tighten economic sanctions, but again these were halfhearted at best, with limited cooperation from other countries and less than a full and credible commitment even from the United States. In October 1993 the administration was intimidated by riotous crowds on the docks of Port-au-Prince and ordered the USS *Harlan County*, which was carrying military and police trainers to Haiti, to turn around and steam home.

Through most of 1994 the Clinton administration found itself the focus of bipartisan criticism. Some, such as Senate minority leader Robert Dole, questioned U.S. support for Aristide and argued vigorously against a military invasion. Others, such as pro-Aristide Senator Edward M. Kennedy and the congressional Black Caucus, advocated intervention. When the Cédras regime intensified its repression, President Clinton, spurred also by complaints that his foreign policy showed "weakness" and "inconsistency," declared on 15 September his intention to invade Haiti unless Cédras stepped down. The next day, a last-minute mission led by former President Jimmy Carter went to Haiti and negotiated an agreement that called for the resignation of the Cédras regime and the return of Aristide. Some 23,000 U.S. troops were deployed to Haiti beginning on 19 September and took up their positions without significant resistance. Aristide returned to Haiti on 15 October 1994 and reassumed the presidency the following month.

Haiti then faced the task of national reconstruction. The country suffered from staggering poverty and deep political divisions. Though fortified by some $1.2 billion dollars in credits and grants, Aristide had to assure international donors and lenders that he could run a competent and fair administration. He also had to keep populist promises to his constituents. Washington held Aristide to a strict constitutionalism. The United States government and private voluntary organizations, some of them funded by trade unions and foundations, expressed great interest in the forthcoming legislative elections, scheduled for June 1995. U.S. sources made money available for voter education and helped finance the organization of the electoral process. All parties, including those that had supported the junta, were eligible to participate. Candidates loyal to the Aristide government won the majority of legislative and mayoral posts in races marked by low voter turnout. Other political priorities for the new Haitian administration included public order and the restoration of the legal system. Although the new Interim Public Security Force was to replace the former brutal police apparatus, many of its officers had served under past regimes. Haitians expressed concern that persons known to have committed terrorist acts remained armed and at large, and that groups associated with the junta retained large weapons caches.

The political climate in the United States influenced the Clinton administration's policy toward Haiti. The sweeping Republican victory in the 1994 congressional elections strengthened the position of those who had originally opposed U.S. support for Aristide. The administration sought to counter the depiction of Aristide as an irresponsible radical by putting strong pressure on Haiti to follow conservative economic policies. It cooperated with international lenders to urge the Haitian government to divest its holdings in such state enterprises as the electricity utility and to cut the public payroll. This became a source of contention. Some of the state enterprises were lucrative and could provide badly needed revenues to a reform government. The international community also wished the Aristide administration to end subsidies to local agricultural producers and permit the free flow of imports. Insistence on greater privatization and austerity by the International Monetary Fund and major powers on one hand, and local objections on the other, led to the resignation of Prime Minister Smarck Michel in October 1995. According to the Governor's Island agreement, Aristide had to agree not to run for a second term and to permit new presidential elections to take place. His successor, René Préval, was elected on February 7, 1996. Préval had been prime minister and largely continued the policies associated with Aristide.

U.S. relations with Haiti remained tense. Many Haitians acknowledged the U.S. contribution to the restoration of democracy but did not agree with U.S. methods of rehabilitating the country. The United States military began a phased withdrawal from Haiti in March 1995, giving increased responsibility for peace keeping to multinational UN forces. The refugee problem continued. Soon after Aristide's return, some 4,000 Haitians were forcibly repatriated from the U.S. base at Guantanamo, Cuba. "Boat people" continued to leave the impoverished island. The Haitian government took significant steps at reform, which included the provision of thousands of government scholarships, urban renewal in Port-au-Prince, and tentative efforts to bring terrorists to justice. It was hampered in these projects by its lack of leverage and the strict oversight of the international community, which, as in the past, continued to place fiscal stability ahead of social reform.

BRENDA GAYLE PLUMMER

See also Clinton, William Jefferson; Latin America; Organization of American States

FURTHER READING

Plummer, Brenda Gayle. *Haiti and the United States: The Psychological Moment.* Athens, Ga., 1992.

Schmidt, Hans. *The United States Occupation of Haiti, 1915–1934.* New Brunswick, N.J., 1971.

Trouillot, Michel-Rolph. *Haiti, State Against Nation: The Origins and Legacy of Duvalierism.* New York, 1990.

HAMILTON, ALEXANDER

(*b.* 11 January 1755; *d.* 12 July 1804)

Revolutionary leader, coauthor of the *Federalist Papers*, and first secretary of the Treasury (1789–1795). Few played a more significant role in shaping the early U.S. Republic under the Constitution. Born in the West Indies in 1755 or 1757, Hamilton made his way to Boston in 1773, and then to New York City, where he attended King's College (now Columbia University).

During the American Revolution, Hamilton served as a lieutenant colonel and aide de camp to General George Washington. This service laid the foundation for their close relationship. In December 1780, Hamilton married Elizabeth Schuyler, daughter of General Philip Schuyler, a prominent New York politician. Admitted to the bar in 1782, Hamilton became a delegate to the second Continental Congress. After the Revolutionary War he practiced law, but it was in finance that he demonstrated genius. Certain that the new nation needed a sound banking system, he founded the Bank of New York in 1784.

Hamilton criticized the weakness of the federal government under the Articles of Confederation. As one of the principal activities for convening the Annapolis Convention of September 1786, he authored an influential report that partly led to the Constitutional Convention in Philadelphia in May 1787.

Throughout the Constitutional Convention, Hamilton demonstrated that he was foremost a nationalist, an advocate for strong central government with a strong executive branch. Although the Constitution did not provide for a government as strong as Hamilton would have liked, he nevertheless threw himself into the ratification process in New York. Along with John Jay and James Madison, Hamilton helped write the *Federalist Papers*, eighty-five newspaper essays which explained the theory behind the Constitution and countered arguments against it.

When Washington became the nation's first president in 1789, he selected Hamilton as secretary of the Treasury, a post he held until his resignation in January 1795. Hamilton's administrative brilliance became evident in the series of reports he made to Congress beginning in January 1790. Attempting to establish the United States as a respected world power and place the country on sound financial footing, Hamilton sought to use economic means to accomplish his primary political goal, governmental stability produced by tying interests of the wealthy to the success of the government. Of his four major reports to Congress, none was as controversial as the proposal to create a national bank.

The clash over the federal government's constitutional authority to create a bank contributed to the beginning of political parties in the United States: the Federalists, who supported Hamilton's views, and the Democratic-Republicans (or simply Republicans), who were more in line with Jefferson and Madison.

In addition to differences regarding Hamilton's plan, philosophy of government, and vision for the United States, the outbreak of the French Revolution and related events contributed significantly to the origins of political parties. To Hamiltonians, perceived excesses of the French Revolution, such as the execution of Louis XVI in 1793, were to be deplored. Mob rule, according to Hamilton, had replaced legitimate rulers. To Jefferson and his followers, one could not expect a country like France to be transformed overnight and without bloodshed. To Hamiltonians, such a position was anathema. They saw Great Britain as the last hope for stability and order, particularly after France declared war on Great Britain in February 1793, thrusting the major powers of Europe into world wars that would last for more than two decades. Hamilton's close relationship with Washington afforded him influence over economic and foreign policy. He was pro-British and anti-French in his sympathies.

For Washington, the French Revolution and wars that followed created a dilemma. What would happen if France called on the United States to adhere to its treaties with France dating back to 1778, when the United States fought its revolution for independence from Great Britain? Hamilton advised the president that the treaties were no longer binding because they were signed with the government of Louis XVI, which no longer existed. Jeffersonians, however, argued that the treaties had been signed with the French nation and remained in force. Although Washington sided with his secretary of state, he sought to prevent the United States from involvement in the European conflagration. He pursued neutrality in his Neutrality Proclamation, issued 22 April 1793.

Events linked to the French Revolution posed the greatest challenge to Washington's government. His first diplomatic crisis originated over Nootka Sound, on the west coast of Vancouver Island. During the summer of 1789, several British ships attempting to establish a trading post were seized by Spanish authorities who claimed the territory for Spain and placed it off limits to foreigners. If war erupted, Hamilton, with his pro-British sympathies, was willing to let the British cross U.S. soil from Canada to strike at Spanish territories in Louisiana, Florida, and New Orleans. Jefferson, not trusting the British, cautioned against this. Fortunately, the crisis of 1789–1790 did not lead to war.

In early 1792, in an attempt to change Great Britain's discriminatory trade policies toward the United States, Jefferson, along with Madison and other friends in Congress, used his influence to secure the introduction of several bills that would impose discriminatory duties on British goods, and threatened Great Britain's important commerce with the United States. Hamilton blocked Jefferson's plan out of fear that such measures would endanger his financial plan, which was predicated on revenues from trade with Great Britain. When the British finally decided to send their first duly accredited minister to the United States in October 1791, Jefferson's efforts to elicit concessions from Great Britain were undermined by Hamilton's machinations: he secretly informed the British minister that Jefferson's anti-British views did not necessarily reflect the sentiments of the administration. Increasing alienation with the Washington administration's policies and resentment at Hamilton's interference in foreign affairs prompted Jefferson to resign as secretary of state the last day of 1793.

When the representative of revolutionary France, Citizen Edmond Genet, arrived in the United States in April 1793, he received a warm reception. Soon, however, his activities angered Washington and Hamilton. Determined to test the administration's neutrality, Genet and the Hamiltonians clashed over the terms of the 1778 Treaty of Alliance, which, Genet argued, allowed for the outfitting of French privateers in U.S. ports for the purpose of preying on British merchant ships. Having arrived in the United States with little money with which to hire privateers, Genet was instructed to ask for complete repayment of the debt to France for loans incurred during the American Revolution. The money would be used to recruit Americans and pay for Genet's privateering schemes against British shipping, as well as for the food supplies he purchased. Hamilton opposed payment, and the president agreed with him. They also considered the outfitting of French privateers a violation of U.S. neutrality. When Genet sought to appeal to the American people over the head of the president, Washington demanded the recall of the "burned-out comet," as Hamilton referred to Genet. He was replaced in 1794 by Joseph Fauchet.

The administration succeeded in establishing rapprochement with England that culminated in the signing of Jay's Treaty in 1794, but a direct outgrowth of the Treaty was increased tensions with France. Although

Federalists such as Hamilton wanted to avoid war with Great Britain at almost any cost, the continuing intransigent position of the British, compounded by their perceived arrogance, made war a distinct possibility. Hoping to avert war and resolve some of the outstanding issues, which included confiscation of U.S. ships and cargoes, impressment of U.S. seamen into the Royal Navy, incitement of Native Americans in the Northwest, failure to remove troops and forts from U.S. territory, and the removal of slaves, the president dispatched a special envoy to England. Hamilton had been Washington's first choice, but because of Hamilton's unpopularity with the Jeffersonians, the president sent Chief Justice John Jay of New York, a staunch Federalist, instead.

Jay's one bargaining chip was the possibility that if the British proved intractable, he could negotiate with Danish and Swedish ministers in London about joining a group of neutrals being formed to resist Great Britain's high-handed maritime practices. Hamilton secretly informed British Minister George Hammond that the United States would not join the Armed Neutrality because the Washington administration intended to avoid European entanglements. Hamilton's act constituted a gross betrayal of duty by an official of the U.S. government. As a direct consequence, Great Britain knew it had nothing to fear if it refused U.S. wishes. Jay signed the treaty that bears his name on 19 November 1794. For the first time, Great Britain had signed a commercial treaty with the United States, though a limited one. The only immediate concession in the treaty was the British promise to evacuate northwest forts. Great Britain had already agreed to evacuate them in the Treaty of Paris of 1783. The northeastern boundary issue, prerevolutionary debts, and spoliation claims for British maritime seizures were referred to an arbitration commission for resolution.

Aware that the treaty would be unpopular with many Americans, especially those who perceived it as pro-British and a betrayal of the French alliance, the Senate voted to keep the treaty's provisions secret during its debate. Neither Washington nor Hamilton, who had left government in January 1795 to practice law in New York City, thought the treaty ideal. Nevertheless, the former secretary of the treasury recommended the Senate approve it, and after two weeks of debate, Federalists in the Senate pushed it through by a bare minimum of votes. When terms of the treaty were leaked, many Americans and Frenchmen were outraged. Hamilton, who had attempted to speak in support of the treaty, was stoned from a platform in New York. After much deliberation and with ambivalent feelings, the president decided to sign the treaty. With serious political divisions developing in the nation, disputes with Indians in the West, a hostile Spain on the southwest border, and Hamilton's financial plan threatened, Washington calculated that going to war with England would jeopardize survival of the young republic.

By 1796, the pressures of office and abuse from Republicans and from the French helped convince Washington to retire from politics. After confiding his intention to Hamilton, the former cabinet member persuaded the president to delay formal announcement of his retirement until three months prior to the actual gathering of electors who would cast their votes for president. In what became known as Washington's Farewell Address of 1796, Hamilton's influence was obvious. Hoping to swing the 1796 election to the Federalists, in a race where the leading Republican candidate was Thomas Jefferson, Hamilton had transformed the address into a partisan political campaign statement. Denouncing the evils of political party development, Washington cautioned against permanent alliances with foreign governments, a clear reference to the French alliance. So influential was the admonishment against permanent alliances that Washington's words became the cornerstone of U.S. "isolationist" policy for 150 years.

Although no longer holding a governmental post, Hamilton remained active in Federalist politics by exercising considerable influence over cabinet members such as Timothy Pickering, secretary of state in the administration of John Adams. When public disquiet over the Quasi-War (1798–1800) with France led to Federalist demands for a larger army in the event of seemingly certain war, Hamilton expected to become inspector general of the army. Suspicious of Hamilton's motives, Adams agreed that the former secretary could be second in command to George Washington, who consented to come out of retirement, if necessary, to assume command of the army. In 1799, after receiving overtures from the French government that suggested an interest in resolving the crisis with the United States, Adams changed his mind about full-scale war and sent a delegation to France that was headed by the U.S. minister at The Hague, William Vans Murray. The result of the negotiations was the signing of the Convention of 1800 (also known as the Treaty of Mortefontaine) on 30 September 1800, which ended the Quasi-War with France and extricated the United States from its treaties of 1778 and 1788.

Adams's decision to seek peace with France incensed Hamilton and other so-called High Federalists. They viewed full-fledged war with France as a way to use the army to conquer Spanish Florida and Louisiana, destroy the Republicans politically, and help establish the powerful central government that Hamilton preferred. Adams's actions split the Federalist party in the election of 1800, as Hamilton and other High Federalists supported Charles Cotesworth Pinckney of South Carolina over Adams, helping tilt the election to the Republicans. When the two Republican candidates, Thomas Jefferson

and Aaron Burr of New York, each received the same number of votes in the Electoral College, Hamilton worked behind the scenes to influence the vote in the House of Representatives in favor of Jefferson over Burr, an arch rival and fellow New Yorker. Although Hamilton and Jefferson had disagreed on many issues over the years, Hamilton believed Jefferson to be a man of principle. For Burr, he only had contempt. In February 1801, the tie vote in the House of Representatives was broken, and Jefferson became president, while Burr became vice president.

In 1804, when Burr sought the governorship of New York, Hamilton opposed his candidacy. Hamilton denounced Burr, asserting that he was a man of "unsatiable ambition...who ought not to be trusted with the reins of government." When Burr lost the election, he challenged Hamilton to a duel with pistols. On 11 July 1804, Burr mortally wounded Hamilton in Weehawken, New Jersey. The man who had played such a key role in U.S. politics for two decades died the following day.

THOM M. ARMSTRONG

See also Adams, John; Articles of Confederation; Burr, Aaron; Federalist Papers; Federalist Party; France; French Revolution; Great Britain; Jay, John; Jay's Treaty; Jefferson, Thomas; Madison, James; Nootka Sound Affair; Pickering, Timothy; Washington, George; Washington's Farewell Address

FURTHER READING

Boyd, Julian P. *Number 7: Alexander Hamilton's Secret Attempts to Control American Foreign Policy.* Princeton, N.J., 1964.

Cooke, Jacob E. *Alexander Hamilton.* New York, 1982.

Deconde, Alexander. *Entangling Alliance: Politics and Diplomacy Under George Washington.* Durham, N.C., 1958.

McDonald, Forrest. *Alexander Hamilton: A Biography.* New York, 1979.

Stourzh, Gerald. *Alexander Hamilton and the Idea of Representative Government.* Stanford, Calif., 1970.

Syrett, Harold C. et al., eds. *The Papers of Alexander Hamilton.* 25 vols. New York, 1961–1977.

HAMMARSKJÖLD, DAG HJALMAR AGNE CARL

(*b.* 29 July 1905; *d.* 18 September 1961)

Secretary-general of the United Nations (1953–1961). Born in Jönköping, Sweden, the son of a former Swedish prime minister, Hammarskjöld earned a doctorate in economics from the University of Uppsala. He served in the finance ministry (1936–1947) before joining the foreign ministry, where he served as head of Sweden's delegation to the Organization of European Economic Cooperation (OEEC) and vice chair of OEEC's executive committee (1948–1949). He was appointed Sweden's deputy foreign minister (1951) and became a member and chief of the Swedish delegation to the UN (1952). On 17 April 1953 he was named to succeed Trygve Lie as secretary-general of the UN. His reputation was that of an economic expert and technician, not a diplomat or politician.

In 1954–1955 Hammarskjöld successfully mediated the release of eleven U.S. airmen under the UN Command in Korea who were imprisoned by the Chinese—the only direct conflict between Western and communist states that he sought to settle peacefully. In articulating principles for preventive diplomacy and peacekeeping, Hammarskjöld argued that the UN could be most effective in dealing with disputes that were not within or between the East-West blocs. Thus, when crises in the Middle East or elsewhere threatened to involve the superpowers, he sought to remove the Cold War elements in order to reduce the possibility of intervention and the threat of larger conflict. Because of his activist program, however, Hammarskjöld clashed with both the United States and the Soviet Union.

During the 1956 Suez Crisis, Hammarskjöld oversaw the creation of the first UN peacekeeping force—the United Nations Emergency Force (UNEF)—to facilitate the withdrawal of Israeli, French, and British forces that had invaded the Suez Canal Zone. UNEF supervised a cease-fire between Egypt and Israel for the next eleven years. U.S. and Soviet acquiescence, as well as the use of contingents from countries other than the five permanent members of the Security Council, were keys to UNEF's success. By contrast, the Hungarian Revolution, which occurred almost simultaneously with the Suez Crisis, demonstrated the impotence of the UN and its secretary-general in the face of a powerful member state's opposition. When Soviet troops crushed the rebellion, Hammarskjöld and other UN members could do little but condemn the Soviet intervention.

Hammarskjöld took significant initiatives in the Middle East in 1958, Laos in 1959, and the Congo in 1960. He helped defuse tensions raised by the 1958 coup in Iraq and subsequent U.S. military intervention in Lebanon. In Laos, Hammarskjöld, faced with evidence of U.S. covert involvement and communist-supported guerrilla activity, sought ways to gather unbiased information and to conciliate among the Laotian parties, which made him a target of criticism from both East and West. After President John F. Kennedy took office in 1961, the United States shifted toward a policy of neutralizing Laos consistent with Hammarskjöld's efforts. Settlement was actually achieved outside the UN framework, however, through the 1961 Geneva conference. In 1960 the UN sent a peacekeeping force, UN Operation in the Congo (ONUC), to the newly independent Congo to maintain order and facilitate the withdrawal of Belgian

forces. ONUC inevitably became involved in the political rivalries among internal factions, and the UN was perceived by the Soviet bloc and many African states as favoring the Western-supported factions. Efforts to prevent the secession of Katanga province took the ONUC forces beyond the traditional peacekeeping role to one of enforcement. The Soviet Union demanded Hammarskjöld's resignation and replacement by a tripartite executive or troika. A number of member states, including the Soviet Union, withheld contributions for the peacekeeping expenses. Hammarskjöld lost his life in a plane crash while trying to mediate the Katangan situation. As a result of the controversy over the Congo operation, the UN faced a major funding crisis.

Throughout his service as secretary-general, Hammarskjöld advocated the importance of an impartial international civil service, reflecting convictions rooted in his Swedish upbringing. This was a necessary response to the Soviet charges of bias brought against his predecessor and implicit in the troika proposal. It also brought him into conflict with the United States over investigations of U.S. members of the UN Secretariat during the McCarthy era of anticommunist campaigns. Critics also charged that Hammarskjöld tried to carve out a role for the secretary-general independent of UN member states. The consensus of most analysts, however, is that Hammarskjöld based his actions on the principles enunciated in the UN Charter and that he established important precedents for the resolution of conflicts and the development of the UN. He is best remembered as the secretary-general who articulated the concepts of preventive diplomacy and peacekeeping. He was posthumously awarded the Nobel Peace Prize in 1961. His book *Markings* (1964) reflects his deep religious beliefs as well as his literary interests.

MARGARET P. KARNS

See also Congo Crisis; Suez Crisis; United Nations

FURTHER READING

Foote, Wilder, ed. *Servant of Peace: A Selection of the Speeches and Statements of Dag Hammarskjöld, Secretary-General of the United Nations 1953–1961.* New York, 1962.
Urquhart, Brian. *Hammarskjöld.* New York, 1972.
Zacher, Mark W. *Dag Hammarskjöld's United Nations.* New York, 1970.

HAMMER, ARMAND
(*b.* 21 May 1898; *d.* 10 December 1990)

Businessman and philanthropist who strongly influenced U.S.-Soviet relations. Born in New York City, Hammer visited Moscow in 1921 as a young physician and met Vladimir Ilyich Lenin, the Soviet leader, who persuaded him to use his entrepreneurial skills to attract foreign capital. Lenin rewarded Hammer's efforts with asbestos mining and pencil manufacturing concessions. Hammer avidly fostered personal contacts with all subsequent Soviet leaders except Stalin, whom he once described as "not a man with whom you could do business." After acquiring Occidental Petroleum in 1956, Hammer became prominent in international business and energetically worked to improve Soviet relations with the West. Beginning in 1972, at the behest of Prime Minister Golda Meir of Israel, he championed the cause of Jews who wished to emigrate from the Soviet Union to Israel. He often acted as an unofficial emissary between U.S. and Soviet leaders and claimed credit for arranging the 1985 summit conference between President Ronald Reagan and Soviet leader Mikhail Gorbachev, a claim disputed by many historians who doubted that Hammer played a central role in forging U.S.-Soviet détente. Hammer nonetheless kept open channels of communication during the Cold War, reducing ignorance and fostering improved trade relations. Reacting to his death, Gorbachev described Hammer as "associated with one of the most remarkable pages" in the U.S.-Russian relationship, a man who "was very close in many ways to the Soviet Union and to Russia."

T. MICHAEL RUDDY

See also Détente; Lenin, Vladimir Ilyich; Russia and the Soviet Union

FURTHER READING

Epstein, Edward J. *The Three Lives of Armand Hammer.* New York, 1996.

Hammer, Armand, and Neil Lyndon. *Hammer.* New York, 1987.

Weinberg, Steve. *Armand Hammer: The Untold Story.* Boston, 1989.

HARDING, WARREN

(*b.* 2 November 1865; *d.* 2 August 1923)

Republican president of the United States from 1921 to 1923 and U.S. Senator from 1915 to 1921, known for his efforts to restore "normalcy" after World War I. Harding exerted considerable influence on U.S. foreign policy during his brief tenure as president. Born in Blooming Grove, Ohio, Harding became owner-editor of the *Marion Star* in 1884. He entered the Ohio State Senate in 1900 and was elected to the U.S. Senate in 1914.

During his term in the Senate, Harding followed the party line and showed little initiative in legislation. A "strong reservationist" during the debate on the League of Nations and the Versailles Treaty that ended World War I, Harding did not totally reject a U.S. role in that new world organization, though he opposed the Wilsonian plan on a partisan basis.

Harding's presidential election win over James B. Cox in 1920 by one of the largest popular majorities in U.S. history (61 percent) mirrored the nation's rejection of progressive reform and diplomatic and military commitments in Europe and Latin America which had characterized the administrations of Theodore Roosevelt, William Howard Taft, and Woodrow Wilson.

In domestic policy, Harding reflected a national mood of exhaustion, prudence, reduction of government programs, and a pro-business attitude, presiding over U.S. policy during an era of financial retrenchment in government spending. These attitudes included the rejection of broad, moralistic objectives, particularly in foreign policy. His administration focused on empowering business and bringing business methods into government through measures such as raising tariffs and establishing the Budget Bureau. Harding's domestic record was overshadowed by the Teapot Dome Scandal and other evidence of corruption.

Harding's presidential style was that of chairman of the board, setting basic policy, and leaving the details and implementation to subordinates, particularly cabinet members. His term coincided with a Senate dominated by strong figures seeking to promote legislative power. Accepting this situation, Harding advocated cooperation between the executive and legislative branches, viewing himself as facilitator and compromiser. He devoted considerable attention to establishing basic policies, but let his cabinet design and conduct the actions within the broad basis he outlined. In the case of foreign policy this practice left wide discretion to Secretary of State Charles Evans Hughes. While Harding worked closely with Hughes to set broad policy directions, and constantly requested information and copies of correspondence, Hughes was responsible for implementation.

Relations with Europe were dominated by the postwar atmosphere and the dispute over the payment of reparations by the defeated powers and loan payments by the Allies. Harding supported the establishment of a commission of experts to deal with the reparations issue. The United States hosted the Washington Conference of 1921–1922, which resulted in an agreement reducing naval armaments in the Pacific by establishing ratios limiting capital ships (battleships and cruisers) among the five principal naval powers (the United States, Great Britain, France, Italy, and Japan). Harding unsuccessfully supported a proposal for separate U.S. membership in the Permanent Court of Justice (World Court), without the commitment of full membership in the League of Nations.

Harding's greatest contributions were in Latin America. Considerable U.S. presence there was the legacy of military interventions of his predecessors. Harding initiated a new direction in U.S.-Latin American relations, launching the process of terminating previous military interventions. Though a strong supporter of U.S. business and investment, Harding focused on good will as the basis for an economic relationship with hemispheric neighbors. He lobbied to secure Senate approval of agreements involving such longstanding questions as terminating U.S. occupation of the Isle of Pines and its return to Cuba, a legacy of the Spanish-American-Cuban-Filipino war, and a 1914 canal treaty with Colombia providing compensation for the 1903 U.S. seizure of Panama.

Harding set a significant precedent by establishing that U.S. military interventions in the Caribbean presented questions of foreign policy. Breaking a deadlock between competing cabinet secretaries, Harding directed the transfer of supervision of U.S. troops in the Caribbean from the Department of the Navy (which often functioned as if it were the U.S. colonial ministry and was referred to as such by Latin Americans) to the Department of State. This shift was significant because the Department of State advocated terminating the occupations and the Department of the Navy invariably found reasons to extend military presence. Implemented in the Dominican Republic, Haiti, and Cuba through the dispatch of presidential commissioners reporting to the Department of State, this action effectively substituted political for military control in the occupied nations and laid the basis for military withdrawal. Arrangements to end occupation of the Dominican Republic only, however, were completed during Harding's tenure. The installation of a Dominican provisional government on 21 October 1922 initiated steps toward elections leading to the withdrawal of U.S. troops in 1924.

Harding played a pivotal role in the initial rapprochement between the United States and the revolutionary governments of Mexico, through the Bucareli Conference, which established the basis for settling the vexing oil-claims issue. To achieve this agreement, Harding established direct communication with his Mexican counterpart through intermediaries outside regular diplomatic channels. In this instance and others, Harding set a tone of conciliation that reflected both his style and the prevailing mood of the nation.

KENNETH J. GRIEB

See also Bucareli Agreements; Hughes, Charles Evans; Latin America; Mexico; Panama and Panama Canal; Washington Conference on the Limitation of Armaments

FURTHER READING

Murray, Robert K. *The Harding Era: Warren G. Harding and His Administration*. Minneapolis, Minn., 1969.

———. *The Politics of Normalcy: Governmental Theory and Practice in the Harding-Coolidge Era*. New York, 1971.

Downes, Raldolph C. *The Rise of Warren Gamiel Harding: 1865–1920*. Columbus, Ohio, 1970.

Grieb, Kenneth J. *The Latin American Policy of Warren G. Harding*. Fort Worth, Tx., 1976.

Cohen, Warren I. *Empire Without Tears: America's Foreign Relations, 1921–1933*. Philadelphia, Pa., 1987.

HARRIMAN, EDWARD HENRY
(*b*. 20 February 1848; *d*. 9 September 1909)

Financier and railroad executive notable for his aggressive effort to extend U.S. investment control over transportation systems overseas. Born in Hempstead, Long Island, N.Y., he left school at fourteen and worked as an office boy on Wall Street. With borrowed money he bought a seat on the stock exchange at the age of twenty-one. Harriman moved into transportation by purchasing a small boat that operated on the Hudson River between New York City and Newburgh. Following his marriage in 1879 to Mary Williamson Averell, the daughter of a banker and railroad president, Harriman began his rise among the nation's railroad barons. He rebuilt bankrupt railroads, beginning with the Lake Ontario Southern, and in 1883 gained a substantial interest in the Illinois Central Railroad. In 1897 he became chairman of the moribund Union Pacific, restoring the outdated system and acquiring the Oregon Railroad and Navigation Company to provide his line with an outlet to the Pacific. He owned large interests in many railroads and in 1901 acquired the gigantic Southern Pacific Railroad. His huge financial empire included banks, insurance companies, and the Pacific Mail Steamship Company, which operated in ports in East Asia. Harriman envisioned a worldwide transportation system under U.S. ownership, and at the conclusion of the Russo-Japanese War in 1905 he tried to establish an enormous railroad enterprise in China. At the invitation of the U.S. minister to Japan, Lloyd C. Griscom, he met with Japanese officials and briefly visited China and Korea. Political and diplomatic complexities, however, kept him from acquiring the South Manchuria Railway. Harriman's large stock purchases in various railroads, in particular the Chicago, Burlington, and Quincy Railroad (over which he tried to gain control in an unsuccessful struggle with James J. Hill), led to an investigation by the Interstate Commerce Commission (1906–1907) and to public criticism of his business practices.

MICHAEL J. DEVINE

See also China

FURTHER READING

Kennan, George. *E. H. Harriman: A Biography*. 2 vols. Boston, 1922.

Klein, Maury. *Union Pacific: The Rebirth, 1894–1969*. New York, 1990.

HARRIMAN, WILLIAM AVERELL
(*b*. 15 November 1891; *d*. 26 July 1986)

International businessman, diplomat, expert on Soviet affairs, and governor of New York. Born into great wealth, which he augmented through business and banking ventures, W. Averell Harriman offered his services to every president from Franklin D. Roosevelt to Ronald Reagan, gaining national and international recognition for his efforts to reduce East-West tensions during the Cold War. Although Harriman usually adopted hard-line positions toward the Soviet Union, he never failed to receive an audience in the Kremlin, where Soviet leaders accepted him as an eminent representative of the capitalist ruling class and as a man who could be trusted to relay accurately their views to U.S. leaders.

The eldest son of the Gilded Age railroad mogul E. H. Harriman, W. Averell Harriman was born in New York City and attended preparatory school at Groton before entering Yale University. He graduated in 1913, having distinguished himself in rowing. Harriman avoided service in World War I, a decision for which he was criticized and that he later regretted. In 1920 he used his inherited wealth to found an investment banking firm (which merged with Brown Brothers in 1931) and invested in the railroad and shipbuilding industries in the United States, Poland, Germany, and—increasingly the focus of his attention—the Soviet Union. When not engaged in business in the 1910s and 1920s, Harriman improved his skills as a polo player and socialite.

Harriman first entered public service as an administrator for the National Recovery Administration. He soon developed a close relationship with Franklin D. Roosevelt and quit the Republican party to affiliate with the Democrats. Attending the Atlantic Conference in 1941, he served as Roosevelt's point man for Lend-Lease aid to both Great Britain and the Soviet Union. After U.S. entrance into World War II, Roosevelt sent Harriman as his special envoy to conduct sensitive negotiations with the Soviet premier, Joseph Stalin, and with the British prime minister, Winston Churchill. It fell to Harriman to reassure Stalin, who had grown bitter over the Allies' delay in opening a second front against Nazi Germany, and to shore up the Grand Alliance.

While serving as ambassador to the Soviet Union from 1943 to 1946, Harriman at first provoked the resentment of professional diplomats in the U.S. Foreign Service who served under him in Moscow. Many of them considered Harriman, who never learned the Russian language, little more than a well-connected dilettante, but he gradually won the respect of experts on the Soviet Union, including George F. Kennan, and reciprocated by paying increasing attention to their views. During the wartime alliance, Roosevelt and Harriman counted on Stalin to help establish a postwar order based upon U.S.-Soviet cooperation. Soviet refusal to aid Polish freedom fighters in the 1944 Warsaw uprising against the Nazis, however, convinced Harriman that the Soviets could not be trusted. When Stalin moved to recognize a pro-Soviet regime in postwar Poland and to carve out an Eastern European

sphere of influence, Harriman warned against a potential "barbarian invasion of Europe." After Roosevelt's death in April 1945, Harriman's views influenced the hard-line stance adopted by the administration of Harry S. Truman at the onset of the Cold War.

The tense East-West relationship remained at the core of Harriman's diplomatic activity for the rest of his career. After serving briefly in 1946 as ambassador to Great Britain, Harriman joined Truman's cabinet as commerce secretary. In that capacity, he helped coordinate the European Recovery Program, or Marshall Plan, which was designed to revive the Western European economy and to contain the Soviet Union. Thereafter, Harriman became Truman's special assistant for foreign affairs. From 1951 to 1953 he also served as U.S. representative to the North Atlantic Treaty Organization and as director of the Mutual Security Agency.

Although Harriman never failed to offer his advice about the Soviet Union, he had defined himself as a New Dealer and thus was not asked to serve in any formal capacity during the Eisenhower presidency. Instead, he turned his attention to domestic politics, winning election as governor of New York in 1954. Despite that victory, Harriman was a poor politician (he had trouble remembering names), and his great wealth seemed to work as much against him as for him in politics. He failed twice in bids for the Democratic nomination for president, in 1952 and 1956, and was defeated by the Republican candidate, Nelson Rockefeller, in his bid for reelection as New York governor in 1958. Harriman longed to return to diplomacy and still dreamed of serving as secretary of state, a post he often said he would prefer to the presidency.

The New Frontiersmen of the administration of John F. Kennedy considered Harriman something of a New Deal relic and showed no interest in offering him a prominent position. In typical fashion, however, Harriman repeatedly proffered his services and eventually became a key member of Kennedy's diplomatic team. Appointed first as a roving ambassador, Harriman served Kennedy effectively in such Cold War trouble spots as the Congo, Laos, and South Vietnam. Harriman advised Kennedy to avoid choosing sides in the postcolonial turmoil in the Congo. Concerned about the communist threat to Laos in 1961, Harriman urged Kennedy to send U.S. troops, advice that the president rejected in favor of a neutralist solution. In South Vietnam, Harriman encouraged the overthrow of the ineffectual leader Ngo Dinh Diem. Harriman also served in the Kennedy administration as assistant secretary of state for Far Eastern affairs and as undersecretary for political affairs. During the October 1962 Cuban missile crisis, Harriman urged Kennedy to find a way to live with the Soviet missiles in Cuba, arguing that the Soviet premier, Nikita S.

Khrushchev, had been pressured by hard-liners in his own government to install the missiles in Cuba and was looking for a face-saving way out of the impasse. Harriman achieved perhaps the high point of his diplomatic career when he successfully negotiated the 1963 Limited Nuclear Test Ban Treaty with the Soviet Union.

President Lyndon Johnson distrusted Harriman as a Kennedy man, but the veteran diplomat gradually overcame the new president's doubts. Johnson called on Harriman's negotiating skills near the end of his presidency, which fell into disarray as the United States appeared unable to realize its promises of victory in Vietnam. After the tumultuous domestic fallout from the Tet offensive by the communist North Vietnamese in 1968, Johnson moved to deescalate the war and asked Harriman to lead his negotiating team in Paris. Long a hawk on Vietnam, Harriman agreed with Johnson that the United States could not afford to compromise South Vietnamese independence. As a result, Harriman's formal diplomatic career ended in failure, as the Paris talks went nowhere.

Harriman served in no formal capacity during the Nixon, Ford, Carter, and Reagan presidencies, but he continued to nurture his image as a Soviet expert through frequent trips to Moscow. Harriman was one of a tiny minority of Westerners to have held discussions with every Soviet leader from Stalin to Yuri Andropov. Upon returning home from these periodic visits to Moscow, Governor Harriman, as he preferred to be called, invariably offered to report to the White House on his findings.

Throughout his career Harriman prided himself on his willingness to serve presidents as a "special envoy" to all points of the globe. Keeping a suitcase packed so that he could leave the country at a moment's notice, Harriman coveted a reputation as a tough and tireless negotiator. If he was vain, restless, and ambitious, as critics and associates often charged, he never refused to serve his country in a diplomatic capacity.

In 1982 Harriman donated $10 million to Columbia University's Russian Institute, which was renamed in his honor. It was an appropriate legacy for a man who built a reputation for expertise on the Soviet Union. Harriman's third wife, Pamela, continued the Harriman diplomatic legacy, becoming ambassador to France in 1993.

WALTER L. HIXSON

See also Ambassadors and Embassies; Cold War; Congo Crisis; Cuban Missile Crisis; Harriman, Edward Henry; Kennedy, John Fitzgerald; Laos; Limited Nuclear Test Ban Treaty; Marshall Plan; Mutual Security Act; North Atlantic Treaty Organization; Poland; Russia and the Soviet Union; Stalin, Joseph; Vietnam War; World War II

FURTHER READING

Abramsonson, Rudy. *Spanning the Century: The Life of W. Averell Harriman, 1891–1986*. New York, 1992.

Harriman, W. Averell. *Peace with Russia?* New York, 1959.
——— , and Elie Abel. *Special Envoy to Churchill and Stalin, 1941–1946*. New York, 1975.

HARRIS, TOWNSEND
(*b.* 3 October 1804; *d.* 25 February 1878)

U.S. businessman, traveler, negotiator of the first commercial treaty (Harris Treaty) between the United States and Japan (1858), and first accredited U.S. minister to Japan (1859–1862). Born in Sandy Hook, New York, he received little formal education but read extensively and learned several European languages. As an early teen Harris and his mother moved to New York City to join Harris's older brother's mercantile business. Harris devoted himself to public service, including a term as president of the New York City Board of Education, where he helped found the Free Academy (later The College of the City of New York).

In 1849, following the death of his mother and a disagreement with his brother, Harris left New York and travelled for six years in China and Southeast Asia. He engaged in some trading while learning the culture and customs of the region. In 1855, shortly after the forcible opening of Japan by Commodore Matthew C. Perry, Harris used his contacts in the New York Democratic Party (especially with Secretary of State William L. Marcy and Senator William H. Seward) to be appointed first U.S. consul general to Japan. In August 1856 he arrived in Shimoda, Japan, with the challenge of securing a full commercial treaty with a nation closed to western trade since the seventeenth century.

Harris began fourteen months of negotiations, all stalled, and he was permitted to talk only with lower palace officials. At last, in December 1857, he was granted an audience with the Tokugawa shogunate at Edo Castle, where he presented a letter from President Franklin Pierce requesting a commercial treaty. In arguing his case Harris referred to a variety of developments in Asia that included the British and French attack on China (Arrow War of 1858) and assertive actions of Denmark in Asia. In February both sides approved a draft treaty and on 29 July 1858, the Harris Treaty, or Japanese-American Treaty of Amity and Commerce, was signed by Harris and Japanese tairo Il Naosuke (effective July 1859). The treaty, borrowing from earlier U.S.-Siam and U.S.-China agreements, established trade relations with Japan and signaled a fundamental opening of the country. Specific provisions included broadening commercial privileges; establishing consuls in all ports of trade (Nagasaki, Kanagawa, Niigata, Hyogo, Shimoda, and Hakodate); exchanging diplomatic representatives, setting tariffs, and extraterritoriality. The treaty was favorable to the United States and served as a model for other U.S. agreements with Japan and Denmark, Russia, Great Britain, and France. The rapid increase in trade brought more westerners to Japan and precipitated a monetary crisis and inflationary spiral that combined to fuel challenges to the shogunate. Harris remained in Japan until 1862, when he returned to New York City and retired from public life.

BRUCE D. MACTAVISH

See also Extraterritoriality; Japan; Marcy, William Learned; Perry, Matthew Calbraith; Pierce, Franklin; Seward, William Henry

FURTHER READING

Harris, Townsend. *The Complete Journal of Townsend Harris, First American Consul General and Minister to Japan.* Garden City, N.Y., 1930.

HARRISON, BENJAMIN

(*b.* 20 August 1833; *d.* 13 March 1901)

Twenty-third president of the United States (1889–1893). He was born in North Bend, Ohio, the grandson of William Henry Harrison, the ninth president of the United States (1841). After attending private schools and graduating from Miami University (Ohio) in 1852, he read law and opened a practice in Indianapolis, Indiana. Like many prominent politicians of his generation, he became a Union officer during the Civil War. His path to the presidency included a successful law practice and six years in the U.S. Senate (1881–1887). Harrison defeated the Democratic nominee, Grover Cleveland, for the presidency in 1888, despite losing the popular election by 100,000 votes. Having reluctantly appointed James G. Blaine as secretary of state, Harrison directed foreign policy personally and relied for advice on foreign policy issues from Secretary of the Navy Benjamin Tracy and from John W. Foster, an experienced diplomat, international lawyer, and fellow Indianan who succeeded Blaine in June 1892. Harrison believed that the nation should pursue a more assertive foreign policy. He promoted the rebuilding of the U.S. Navy with steel-hulled ships, sought to secure the harbor of Môle Saint Nicholas in Haiti, negotiated an agreement with Great Britain and Germany concerning the governance of Samoa, and ordered the seizure of Canadian vessels harvesting Alaskan fur seals. Following an attack on sailors from the *USS Baltimore* by a Chilean crowd in 1891, Harrison rejected Blaine's moderate policy and demanded an apology and reparations for what he considered an "insult to the U.S. uniform of the United States sailors." In the final months of his administration, Harrison worked

unsuccessfully with Secretary Foster to annex Hawai'i after a coup in Honolulu by white planters overthrew the government of Queen Liliuokalani. In 1892 Harrison was defeated by Cleveland in his bid for reelection and returned to his law practice. Harrison authored a widely used text on U.S. government, *This Country of Ours* (1897), and represented Venezuela before an international arbitration tribunal in Paris in 1899, winning a favorable settlement for his clients in their border dispute with Great Britain.

MICHAEL J. DEVINE

See also Chile; Haiti; Hawai'i; Presidency; Venezuela

FURTHER READING

Socolofsky, Homer E., and Allan B. Spetter. *The Presidency of Benjamin Harrison.* Lawrence, Kans., 1987.
Spetter, Allan B. "Harrison and Blaine: Foreign Policy, 1889–1893." *Indiana Magazine of History* 65 (1969): 214–227.

HARRISON, WILLIAM HENRY

(*b.* 9 February 1773; *d.* 4 April 1841)

Ninth president of the United States (1841). Born in Charles City County, Virginia, Harrison attended Hampden-Sydney College. He pursued a military career and became a national hero through his battlefield victories, against the Shawnee at Tippecanoe in 1811 and against the British in the Battle of the Thames in 1813. As governor of the territory of Indiana from 1800 to 1812, Harrison had negotiated treaties with Native Americans that resulted in the acquisition by the United States of millions of acres of land. While serving as U.S. minister to Colombia in 1819, he aroused the hostility of President Simón Bolívar by indiscreetly associating with Bolívar's political enemies.

In 1840 Harrison became the first successful Whig candidate for the presidency; however, the cold that Harrison caught on 4 March 1841 as he delivered the longest inaugural address in U.S. history developed into pneumonia, and on 4 April he became the first president to die in office. During his short term as president Harrison had no discernible impact on foreign policy. He was succeeded by Vice President John Tyler, linked to Harrison in the campaign slogan "Tippecanoe and Tyler Too."

KENNETH E. SHEWMAKER

See also Bolívar, Simón; Continental Expansion; Native Americans; Presidency; Tyler, John; War of 1812

FURTHER READING

Goebel, Dorothy Burne. *William Henry Harrison: A Political Biography.* Indianapolis, Ind., 1926.
Peterson, Norma Lois. *The Presidencies of William Henry Harrison and John Tyler.* Lawrence, Kans., 1989.

HARTFORD CONVENTION
(15 December 1814–5 January 1815)

Conclave held in Hartford, Connecticut, by New England Federalists to deal with issues raised by the War of 1812 and to air their long-term grievances. Twenty-six delegates took part. The report of the convention, largely the work of Harrison Gray Otis of Massachusetts, recommended that the states nullify federal proposals to conscript militia and to enlist minors, and that they seek authority to divert federal tax money to pay for state and local defense. The convention's report also recommended seven constitutional amendments to prevent a renewal of policies that many Federalists believed had damaged New England's interests during the previous decade. These amendments called for requiring a two-thirds vote in Congress to declare war, interdict trade with a foreign nation, or admit new states to the Union; imposing a sixty-day limit on embargoes; ending the practice of counting slaves (who were counted as three-fifths of a person) for the purpose of apportioning representation in Congress; barring naturalized citizens from holding federal office; and prohibiting presidents from serving more than one term or the election of a president from the same state twice in succession. Although the state governments of Massachusetts and Connecticut approved the amendments and sent delegates to Washington to negotiate for authority to divert federal tax money to the states, their mission coincided with the arrival of news of the Battle of New Orleans and the signing of the Treaty of Ghent, which ended the War of 1812. Hence nothing came of their mission.

The Hartford Convention marked the climax of Federalist opposition to the War of 1812 and demonstrates both the potentially disruptive effect of disagreements over foreign policy on national unity and the impact of domestic political differences on foreign policy. The convention also was an important episode in the history of federal-state relations. Because the report of the convention did not recommend secession or a separate peace with Great Britain, it was generally considered a triumph of moderation. (At the time, New England Federalists did not know that Great Britain was prepared to offer New England a separate peace if the United States did not ratify the Treaty of Ghent.) In the end, the notoriety of the Hartford Convention contributed to the decline of the Federalist party after the War of 1812.

DONALD R. HICKEY

See also Ghent, Treaty of; War of 1812

FURTHER READING

Hickey, Donald R. *The War of 1812: A Forgotten Conflict.* Urbana, Ill., 1989.

Morison, Samuel Eliot, ed. *The Life and Letters of Harrison Gray Otis, Federalist, 1765–1848*, 2 vols. Boston, 1913.

HAVEL, VÁCLAV
(*b.* 5 October 1936)

Playwright and president of the Czech Republic (1990–1992). Havel was born into a wealthy Prague family, but due to the fact that the strategy of the communist leadership was to reduce the power of the old elite by making it difficult for their children to pursue an education, he was forced to complete high school by taking night courses while working as a laboratory assistant. After studying briefly at a technical university, he finished his studies at the theater department of the Academy of Arts as an correspondent student. Havel began his career working as a stagehand at the ABC Theater. He soon moved to the Theater on the Balustrade, Prague's main avant-garde theater. His plays *The Garden Party* (1963), *The Memorandum* (1967), and *The Increased Difficulty of Concentration* (1968) contributed to the theater of the absurd in Prague. During the intellectual ferment of the 1960s, Havel worked with other writers in the Writers' Union to press for intellectual freedom in Czechoslovakia. The invasion of Czechoslovakia by Warsaw Pact troops in August 1968 ended Havel's official literary career. Although they could not be performed in Czechoslovakia, Havel's plays, including *The Conspirators* (1971), *The Beggar's Opera* (1972), *The Mountain Hotel* (1974), *Protest* (1978), *Largo Desolato* (1984), *Temptation* (1985), and *Slum Clearance* (1988), were very well received abroad. His books *Living in Truth* (1986) and *Letters to Olga* (1983), written to his wife from prison, documented his increasing concern with political issues.

Havel was one of the founders of Charter 77, Czechoslovakia's principal human rights organization, and the Committee for the Defense of the Unjustly Persecuted. Arrested numerous times for his activities in the opposition, Havel was sentenced to four and a half years in prison in 1979; he was released in March 1983. In early 1989 Havel was once again imprisoned for several months for his participation in a peaceful demonstration to commemorate the death of Jan Palach, a Czech student who immolated himself in January 1969 to protest the August 1968 invasion of Czechoslovakia.

In November 1989, when police brutality toward peaceful student demonstrators led Czechs and Slovaks to take to the streets, Havel quickly became the symbol of his country's hopes for a democratic future. He was elected president of Czechoslovakia in December 1989 by a parliament still dominated by Communist party officials. As president of Czechoslovakia (from 1993, the Czech Republic), Havel devoted a good deal of attention to foreign policy. Under his leadership the government took steps to restore Czechoslovakia's sovereignty and to normalize its relations with its neighbors. With Jiří Dienstbier, foreign minister of Czechoslovakia from 1989 to 1992, Havel worked to restore Czechoslovakia to its place on the European stage. He succeeded in obtaining membership in the Council of Europe and an association agreement with the European Community (later the European Union) and pressed for full membership in the EC. Originally an advocate of a pan-European security system, he came to support full membership for Czechoslovakia in the North Atlantic Treaty Organization. Havel also worked to restore Czechoslovakia's traditionally warm relationship with the United States, and visits to the United States in 1990 and 1993 generated much goodwill toward the Czech Republic.

An unorthodox politician who has sought to infuse politics with morality, Havel often airs controversial views. He continues to call upon the United States and other democracies to recognize their responsibility to act in defense of Western values and to realize the connection between the fate of Central and East European countries and their own well-being. Havel's stature as an international figure remained high even as he proved unable to stem the movement that led to the breakup of Czechoslovakia. He resigned as president of Czechoslovakia in July 1992 after the Slovak government adopted a resolution declaring Slovakia's sovereignty and was elected president of the newly created Czech Republic in February 1993.

SHARON L. WOLCHIK

See also Czech Republic; Eastern Europe; European Union; North Atlantic Treaty Organization

FURTHER READING

Havel, Václav. *Letters to Olga: June 1979-September 1982.* New York, 1989.
———. *Living in Truth: Twenty-two Essays Published on the Occasion of the Award of the Erasmus Prize to Václav Havel.* London, 1987.
Kriseová, Eda. *Václav Havel: The Authorized Biography.* New York, 1993.

HAWAI'I

A chain of eight main islands located in the north central Pacific Ocean about 2,400 miles southwest of San Francisco. The Hawai'ian Kingdom was formally recognized as an independent nation by the United States in 1849, annexed in 1898, and incorporated as its fiftieth state in 1959.

In August 1789 the *Columbia*, a Boston trading ship, took on supplies during a three-week stay and thus made the first U.S. contact with the Sandwich Islands (English, French, Spanish, and Russian ships had earlier visited Hawai'i.) A flourishing trade in fur and sandalwood during the first two decades of the nineteenth century brought a rapid increase in U.S. trading ships in Hawai'ian ports. The 1820 arrival of New England Congregational missionaries and the first official representa-

tive of the U.S. government bolstered these economic ties. Hawai'i signed its first international agreement in 1826, a treaty of navigation and friendship with the United States. (The U.S. Senate failed to approve the treaty because it did not want to recognize Hawai'ian independence, but Hawai'i chose to abide by it nonetheless.) By 1842, in the midst of a three decade-long boom in the Pacific whaling industry, U.S. ships accounted for eighty percent of all foreign traffic in Hawai'ian ports. Reflecting this dominant U.S. economic presence and the expanding religious, cultural, and political influence of Protestant missionaries, U.S. Secretary of State Daniel Webster warned that his government would oppose any other nation's attempt to annex the Hawai'ian islands. The settling of the U.S. West Coast brought increased attention to the islands' strategically important location, and in August 1849 the United States formally recognized the Hawai'ian Kingdom by agreeing to a friendship treaty that also established closer commercial ties.

In 1854 King Kamehameha III, with minimal support from the native Hawai'ian population, applied for U.S. statehood. He was responding to the recurring acquisitive actions of France and Great Britain, the weakened state of his political power, and strong pressure from U.S. merchants and sugar planters (sugar cane was now the island's dominant export crop). The United States blocked Kamehameha's scheme so as not to antagonize France, and Kamehameha's death late in the year ended this effort. In 1855 and 1867 the United States and Hawai'i signed reciprocity agreements, but the U.S. Senate rejected the first in response to pressure from Louisiana sugar planters and the second in response to fears over a loss of tariff revenues. Renewed efforts by King Kalakaua's representative Henry A.P. Carter and U. S. Secretary of State Hamilton Fish produced the Hawai'ian Reciprocity Treaty, approved by the Senate on 18 March 1875 by a 51 to 12 vote. The agreement extended U.S. commercial and economic influence in the islands by allowing the free trade of goods while preventing Hawai'i from leasing or disposing of any port, harbor, or territory to another nation. (The United States itself coveted Pearl Harbor.) The United States regarded the treaty as a means for blocking European expansion in the Pacific while protecting its own interests. The treaty was renewed in early 1887 with the United States then gaining the exclusive right to Pearl Harbor as a naval station.

During a sugar boom and rising native Hawai'ian nationalism, a powerful bloc of sugar planters gained control of the Hawai'ian government by forcing the so-called Bayonet Constitution on King Kalakaua in July 1887. This new constitution greatly reduced the powers of the monarchy and added a property ownership requirement for eligible voters. The native Hawai'ian population now faced a series of successive problems: vast tracts of land in the hands of white sugar planters; economic domination by the United States (in 1890, ninety-nine percent of Hawai'ian exports went to the United States and seventy-six percent of imports came from the United States); influx of thousands of Japanese and Chinese contract laborers; disfranchisement; and a weakened voice in politics. The McKinley tariff bill, approved 1 October 1890, multiplied these problems by creating an economic depression. The tariff bill ended the Hawai'ian sugar boom by removing the duties on all raw sugar bound for the United States (thus ending Hawai'i's advantage over other foreign producers) and granting U.S. producers a two cent per pound bounty. The effects were felt immediately; sugar prices fell thirty-eight percent on the day the tariff went into effect, property values declined, wages were cut, and unemployment rose.

In 1891, Queen Liliuokalani inherited the throne and began to take back Hawai'i for its peoples. Her efforts culminated on 14 January 1893 with a request to her cabinet to approve a new constitution that would give natives, especially the monarch, more political power at the expense of the *haole* (foreigners). Two days later came the response from sugar planters and other white residents who felt threatened economically and politically. In Honolulu, Queen Liliuokalani was overthrown by a small group of whites from the Annexation Club. U.S. minister John L. Stevens conspired with the revolutionists, and 150 sailors from the U.S. cruiser *Boston* surrounded the royal palace. Stevens extended recognition to the newly declared government and a delegation went to Washington, D. C. to gain annexation. Queen Liliuokalani was confined to her quarters for months. President Benjamin Harrison, two weeks before his term expired, quickly sent an annexation treaty to the Senate. The new president, Grover Cleveland, however, because he opposed forced annexation, withdrew the treaty and, following the findings of his special commissioner, James H. Blount, condemned the revolutionists and the role of Minister Stevens and made futile efforts to restore the queen. A stormy public and congressional debate followed with anti-imperialists able to stop annexation. The election of pro-expansionist William McKinley in 1896 and the start of war with Spain in 1898 solidified support for annexation.

The Hawai'ian Islands became U.S. territory through a joint resolution of Congress on 7 July 1898 and McKinley's signing the annexation measure a day later. McKinley used the method of a joint resolution because he did not think he could get the two-thirds vote required in the Senate. Hawai'i became the United States's fiftieth state on 21 August 1959. Statehood was delayed for six decades primarily because conservative members of the U.S. Congress refused to accept the islands' nonwhite population as deserving of equal status as U.S. citizens.

BRUCE D. MACTAVISH

See also Cleveland, Stephen Grover; Fish, Hamilton; Harrison, Benjamin; McKinley, William; Tariffs; Webster, Daniel

FURTHER READING

Kuykendall, Ralph S. *The Hawai'ian Kingdom*. 3 vols. Honolulu, 1938, 1963, 1967.
Liliuokalani. *Hawai'i's Story by Hawai'i's Queen (1898)*. Reprint. Honolulu, 1990.
Osborne, Thomas J. *Empire Can Wait: American Opposition to Hawai'ian Annexation, 1893–1898*. Kent, Ohio, 1981.
Stevens, Sylvester K. *American Expansion in Hawai'i, 1842–1898*. Harrisburg, Pa., 1945.
Tate, Merze. *The United States and the Hawai'ian Kingdom: A Political History*. New Haven, Conn., 1965.

HAY, JOHN MILTON

(*b*. 8 October 1838; *d*. 1 July 1905)

Secretary of state (1898–1905) under Presidents William McKinley and Theodore Roosevelt. Born in Salem, Indiana, Hay grew up in Illinois, graduated from Brown University in 1858, then returned to Springfield, Illinois, to study law. When fellow Springfield lawyer Abraham Lincoln became president, he brought John Hay and John G. Nicolay with him to Washington to serve as his private secretaries. The two men later coauthored a ten-volume biography of Lincoln published in 1885. Hay also published poetry and novels, and he occasionally worked as a journalist. He held a number of minor diplomatic posts after Lincoln's death and served as assistant secretary of state from 1878 to 1881. A staunch lifelong Republican, Hay was selected by McKinley to serve as U.S. ambassador to Great Britain in 1897, where his literary prominence and urbanity made him a popular emissary. When Secretary of State William R. Day resigned to serve on the delegation to negotiate an end to the Spanish-American-Cuban-Filipino War, McKinley recalled Hay to Washington to become secretary of state.

Most effective at implementing policies that the presidents he served or the flow of events had already largely determined, Hay's most famous action was the issuance of the Open Door notes in 1899 and 1900. These messages to the great powers forcefully articulated the traditional U.S. desire to preserve access for U.S. traders in Chinese markets. The Open Door Policy required frequent reiteration but no significant U.S. military action, owing to the balance of power among the European nations and Japan in east Asia. The Open Door Policy formed the basis of U.S. policy in the region well into the 1930s.

Hay's other major achievement was a series of diplomatic moves that facilitated the building of the Panama Canal. He began by seeking to obtain from British

Ambassador Julian Pauncefote a release from pledges the United States had made to Great Britain in the Clayton-Bulwer Treaty of 1850. The first Hay-Pauncefote Treaty (1900) permitted the United States to build an isthmian canal without prior British approval but left in place the earlier treaty's prohibition against fortifications, a provision the U.S. Senate would not accept. The second Hay-Pauncefote Treaty (1901) lifted all restraints on U.S. action. The secretary of state immediately opened discussions with Tomás Herrán who represented the Colombian government that ruled Panama as a province, but the Colombian senate refused to ratify the Hay-Herrán Treaty in 1903. A brief and successful U.S.-assisted Panamanian revolution followed. Hay immediately negotiated a virtually identical treaty with French entrepreneur Philippe-Jean Bunau-Varilla, who had helped engineer the revolt, clearing the way for the United States to begin digging the canal.

Hay also stoutly defended U.S. claims in the Alaska boundary dispute with Great Britain that culminated in an agreement favorable to the United States in 1903. He played a secondary role in other major initiatives, however, such as the Platt Amendment and the Roosevelt Corollary. President Roosevelt exercised a strong personal influence in diplomatic affairs, and his energy and impatience were not always compatible with Hay's more gentlemanly and contemplative style. Although Roosevelt did not consider Hay a great secretary of state, he recalled him fondly as "the most delightful man to talk to I ever met."

JOHN M. DOBSON

See also Alaska Boundary Dispute; Lincoln, Abraham; Open Door Policy; Panama and Panama Canal; Roosevelt, Theodore

FURTHER READING
Clymer, Kenton J. *John Hay*. Ann Arbor, Mich., 1975.
Dennett, Tyler. *John Hay*. New York, 1933.

HAYES, RUTHERFORD BIRCHARD

(*b.* 4 October 1822; *d.* 17 January 1893)

Nineteenth president of the United States (1877–1881). Born in Delaware, Ohio, and graduated from Kenyon College in 1842, Hayes studied law at Harvard Law School and began to practice law in Lower Sandusky (later Fremont), Ohio, in 1845. In 1850 he moved his practice to Cincinnati, becoming active in local Republican party politics. In 1864, while serving as a brigadier general in the Union army during the Civil War, Hayes won election to the U.S. House of Representatives. He was reelected in 1866 but resigned his seat in 1867 when

nominated for governor of Ohio. He was elected by a narrow margin and reelected in 1869. He declined the opportunity to seek a third term in 1871 but was persuaded to seek the governorship again in 1875. His election victory catapulted him to national prominence, and he became the Republican candidate for president in 1876. His inauguration in 1877 followed a difficult campaign against Democrat Samuel J. Tilden. An election controversy was settled by an Electoral Commission only after a deal was struck in which Hayes agreed to remove federal troops from the South.

Hayes's administration faced few serious foreign policy issues. His competent secretary of state, William M. Evarts, improved the consular reporting system and successfully opposed efforts by a French company to construct a canal across the Isthmus of Panama. Evarts also played a key role in normalizing relations with Mexico. Raids by bandits and Indians on U.S. settlements near the Mexican border had been exacerbated when Mexican rebels, led by General Porfirio Díaz and using Brownsville, Texas, as their base, crossed the Rio Grande and attacked Mexican government forces. Following the overthrow of the Mexican regime by the rebels, Hayes was reluctant to recognize the Díaz government until convinced by Evarts and John W. Foster, U.S. minister to Mexico, that despite his nationalistic rhetoric, Díaz was friendly toward the United States and willing to cooperate in ending hostilities along the U.S.-Mexican border.

In 1879 Hayes vetoed the Fifteen Passenger Bill that would have allowed only fifteen Chinese immigrants per vessel. Hayes saw the bill as a clear violation of the Burlingame Treaty of 1868, but he understood that mounting pressure from Californians would force modifications in the treaty's immigration provisions. On 17 November 1880 Hayes signed a new treaty with China, which enabled the United States to legislate against the immigration of Chinese laborers. The Chinese government agreed to the restrictions on Chinese immigration to the United States in return for assurances that Chinese residents in the United States would receive government protection. Hayes served for one term and spent his final years in retirement in Fremont, Ohio, where he became active in philanthropic endeavors.

MICHAEL J. DEVINE

See also China; Díaz, (José de la Cruz) Porfirio; Evarts, William Maxwell; Foreign Service; Mexico; Panama and Panama Canal

FURTHER READING
Hayes, Rutherford Birchard. *Diary and Letters of Rutherford Birchard Hayes*, 5 vols., edited by C. R. Williams, 1922–1926.
Hoogenboom, Ari Arthur. *The Presidency of Rutherford B. Hayes*. Lawrence, Kans., 1988.

HEARST, WILLIAM RANDOLPH

(*b.* 29 April 1863; *d.* 14 August 1951)

Owner of the *New York Journal* and proponent of war with Spain in 1898. California-born Hearst acquired the *New York Morning Journal* in 1895 and began a circulation battle with Joseph Pulitzer's *New York World*. Hearst enthusiastically embraced yellow journalism, featuring banner headlines, lurid stories, and sensational pictures. During the Cuban insurrection against Spain, Hearst championed the Cuban cause, railed against the cruelty of Spanish officials, accused Spain of the *Maine* explosion, and demanded U.S. military intervention. *Journal* circulation soared. Although Hearst's views reached a national audience, his impact is problematical. Hearst followed rather than led public opinion. Many newspaper editors disliked Hearst's journalistic practices and delighted in exposing fabricated *Journal* stories. Moreover, as a Democrat, Hearst was ignored by the administration of President William McKinley. After the Spanish-American-Cuban-Filipino War, Hearst served in the House of Representatives from 1903 to 1907, but he failed in his bids to become mayor of New York City, governor of the state, and the Democratic party's nominee for president. Although Hearst's newspapers made him a millionaire, following his political setbacks, they had little influence on U.S. foreign policy. At the start of World War I, Hearst was pro-German and anti-British. He opposed entering the war and also objected to President Woodrow Wilson's League of Nations. Hearst later became a bitter critic of President Franklin D. Roosevelt and the New Deal at a time when his newspaper, magazine, and film empire fought to stave off bankruptcy.

JOHN L. OFFNER

See also Journalism and Foreign Policy; League of Nations; Spanish-American-Cuban-Filipino War, 1898; World War I

FURTHER READING

Mugridge, Ian. *The View From Xanadu: William Randolph Hearst and United States Foreign Policy.* Toronto, 1995.
Swanberg, W. A. *Citizen Hearst.* New York, 1961.
Winkler, John K. *William Randolph Hearst.* New York, 1955.
Wisan, Joseph E. *The Cuban Crisis as Reflected in the New York Press.* New York, 1934.

HEGEMONY

The economic, military, and political dominance of a great power in world affairs. Hegemony constitutes unrivaled leadership, with the capacity to influence the world in the direction of a nation's own international image. For example, a hegemon might use its power to create an open international economy, as did the United States after World War II. Alternatively, it might create a command, managed international economy, as did the Soviet Union in Eastern Europe.

The concept of hegemony was popularized by the economist Charles Kindleberger in the early 1970s, although the term had been used previously by realists, such as E. H. Carr, and radicals, such as Antonio Gramsci. Drawing on the history of U.S. policy during the Great Depression and the post–World War II periods, Kindleberger characterized hegemony as a farsighted, even altruistic, approach by a great power to create an international system in which all can prosper. He attributed the better economic performance of the post–World War II period to the role of the United States. In contrast to its insular posture of the 1930s, which had exacerbated global protectionist tendencies, the United States after World War II established an open, liberal world economic order. A stable world currency, relatively free access to the large U.S. market, and investment capital for purposes of reconstruction and development were provided, as exemplified in the Marshall Plan. Realists and radicals, on the other hand, see the policies of the hegemon as inherently myopic and self-aggrandizing. Realists applaud the stabilizing influence of a dominant power (even if motivated by self-interest), but radicals deplore the imposition of the hegemon's economic system (for example, exploitative capitalism) on others. Gramsci emphasizes the subtle power of the hegemon as a source of social and cultural values in the international system, with nations submitting to it naturally, often without recognizing their dependence.

Interest in hegemonic stability increased as the United States appeared to lose its dominance in the 1970s. The U.S.-spawned Bretton Woods System of fixed exchange rates collapsed under the weight of U.S. budget deficits and oil price increases, while the war in Vietnam discredited U.S. leadership. Policymakers and scholars alike wondered whether the apparent passing of the hegemon would lead to a less stable world. Two critical issues arose. Was the United States in an irreversible secular decline? Was the decline of a hegemon always followed by growing international economic, political, and eventually military conflict?

The debate about decline revolves around U.S. competitiveness and its superpower role in the post–Cold War world. Declinists point to the relative decline of U.S. output and finance relative to European and Asian upstarts since World War II; antideclinists stress the improvements in U.S. manufacturing productivity in the 1980s, the dominance of U.S. service industries, and its military and diplomatic credibility as shown in the Persian Gulf War. Although theories of hegemonic decline offer rather dire predictions that conflict increases as the hegemon declines, other studies contend that the institutions created by the hegemon live on beyond it. The North Atlantic Treaty Organization, the General Agreement on Tariffs and Trade, and the United Nations, for example, provide important vehicles for creative problem-solving in the post–Cold War world and enjoy the support of virtually all nations, including many former communist countries.

How should the hegemon respond to its decline? Some analysts urge a turn toward multilateralism and power sharing, as identified with the administration of President Jimmy Carter (and perhaps that of President Bill Clinton). Others call for retrenchment, a tougher trade regime toward Europe and Japan, and more focus on domestic problems. Still others urge a reassertion of hegemonic leadership and U.S. support for political freedom, open markets, and the rule of law in the post–Cold War order—policies in effect during the administrations of Presidents Ronald Reagan and George Bush. Hegemony and its consequences thus underlie a good deal of the debate over U.S. foreign policy in the post–Cold War era.

KENDALL N. STILES

See also Balance of Power; Bretton Woods System; New International Economic Order; Realism

FURTHER READING

Kennedy, Paul M. *The Rise and Fall of the Great Powers.* New York, 1987.
Keohane, Robert O. *After Hegemony, Cooperation and Discord in International Politics.* Princeton, 1984.
Kindleberger, Charles P. *The World in Depression, 1929–1939.* Berkeley, Calif., 1973.
Nye, Joseph S. *Bound to Lead: The Changing Nature of American Power.* New York: Basic Books, 1990.

HELMS, JESSE ALEXANDER, JR.

(*b.* 18 October 1921)

U.S. senator (1974–) and major foreign policy spokesman for conservative Christian fundamentalists. Although Helms lacked a strong background in international affairs, he demonstrated a talent for generating publicity as an arch-anticommunist who frequently opposed presidential nominations to diplomatic posts and within the Department of State. Born in Monroe, North Carolina, Helms attended Wake Forest University, but never graduated. After a career in journalism and broadcasting, he served as administrative assistant to the archconservative Senator Wallis Smith. He was himself elected to the Senate in 1973. Helms's influence on foreign policy came as the ranking Republican minority member of the Senate Foreign Relations Committee, where he became a voice of extremist and conspiratorial theories. During the 1980s he championed the defense buildup, supported apartheid in South Africa, and continued his bitter oppo-

sition to the Soviet Union and communism, including a vote against the 1987 Intermediate Nuclear Forces Treaty. In 1995, after the Republicans won the 1994 congressional elections, Helms became chair of the Senate Foreign Relations Committee and continued to grab headlines through his blunt utterances.

MARK H. LYTLE

See also Intermediate Range Nuclear Forces Treaty; Republican Party

FURTHER READING

Applebome, Peter. "Pit Bull Politician." *New York Times Magazine* (28 October 1990).
Ferguson, Ernest B. *Hard Right: The Rise of Jesse Helms.* New York, 1986.
Horner, Charles. "The Senator They Love to Hate." *Commentary* 93 (January 1992): 51–53.

HELMS, RICHARD MCGARRAH

(*b.* 30 March 1913)

Director of the Central Intelligence Agency (1966–1973) and ambassador to Iran (1973–1977). Born in St. David's, Pennsylvania, Helms graduated from Williams College in 1935, then worked as a journalist for the United Press and the *Indianapolis Times.* Conversant in German and having traveled in Europe, Helms was introduced to Adolf Hitler in 1936; he later wrote two articles about the experience. Named advertising manager for the *Times* in 1941, Helms ended a brief career in journalism shortly thereafter. He served as a navy lieutenant commander early in World War II and was recruited for intelligence work with the Office of Strategic Services. OSS service took him to Washington, New York, London, Luxembourg, and Berlin.

After the war and his service with such luminaries of espionage as William J. Donovan and Allen W. Dulles, Helms returned to Washington in 1945. Two years later he was fully immersed in organizational developments at the newly formed Central Intelligence Agency (CIA). From 1947 to 1966 Helms climbed the career ladder through the ranks of deputy assistant director for special operations, assistant deputy director for plans, deputy director of plans, deputy director of central intelligence, and director of the CIA. Appointed to the latter position by President Lyndon B. Johnson, Helms was admitted to the inner circle of the president's "Tuesday luncheon" briefing sessions.

Throughout his career at the CIA, Helms was known as an administrator with a penchant for action and loyalty to his superiors, in particular Presidents Johnson and Richard M. Nixon. As CIA director, his service tended to favor operations over intelligence analysis. He placed the protection of the agency's operations and its employees high on a list of professional priorities. In the long run, however, Helms and the agency were seen as instruments of excessive executive branch secrecy regarding the Vietnam War and a number of covert operations.

Beginning in 1967 Helms was ordered by Johnson to develop plans to conduct domestic counterintelligence against anti–Vietnam War groups, operations that later evolved into Operation Chaos. Believing he had White House authorization even though he knew such activities violated the CIA charter, Helms continued the counterintelligence operations until 1970. The next few years brought several congressional inquiries into CIA operations, including covert activities in Chile and involvement in the Watergate affair. Helms was called to Camp David by Nixon in December 1972 and informed that he would be appointed ambassador to Iran. Helms, however, was convinced that the real reason he was being fired from the CIA was for failing to aid the president during the Watergate scandal.

In October 1977 Helms was indicted on charges that he had failed to give complete and accurate testimony in 1973 to the Senate Foreign Intelligence Committee regarding CIA operations against Chilean dictator Salvador Allende Gossens. He received a $2,000 fine and a suspended jail sentence, believed by some to have been a political method for redressing alleged CIA abuses of authority. President Ronald Reagan awarded Helms the National Security Medal in 1983 in recognition of Helms's dedication to service. That same year he served as a member of the Scowcroft Commission on U.S. strategic forces.

JAMES D. CALDER

See also Central Intelligence Agency; Covert Action; Watergate

FURTHER READING

Colby, William, and Peter Forbath. *Honorable Men: My Life in the CIA.* New York, 1978.
Powers, Thomas. *The Man Who Kept Secrets: Richard Helms and the CIA.* New York, 1979.
Prados, John. *Presidents' Secret Wars.* New York, 1986.
Ranelagh, John. *The Agency.* New York, 1986.

HELSINKI ACCORDS

On 1 August 1975 in Helsinki, Finland, thirty-five states (including all the countries of Europe except Albania, plus the United States and Canada) adopted the Final Act of the Conference on Security and Cooperation in Europe (CSCE). The Helsinki Final Act (or Helsinki Accords as it is commonly called), was a central symbol of détente in the 1970s. It also introduced the issue of human rights into the official mainstream of East-West relations.

World War II concluded without a formal peace treaty to ratify the territorial changes in Central and Eastern Europe. In return for formal international recognition of the postwar partition of Europe, the Soviet Union and its allies were willing to engage in ongoing dialogues on security and cooperation. Human rights were included on the CSCE agenda at Western European insistence, under the novel notion of domestic security for citizens. Given these multiple concerns and objectives, it is not surprising that the Final Act's ten "Principles" and three "Baskets"—dealing with political and military issues (especially frontiers and nonintervention), economic relations, and humanitarian relations—were held together in a delicate political balance.

The provisions with the greatest political impact, much to the surprise of most participants and initial observers, proved to be Principle VII ("Respect for human rights and fundamental freedoms.") and Basket III ("Co-operation in Humanitarian and Other Fields"). Human rights occupied center stage at the follow-up meetings in Belgrade (1977–1978), Madrid (1980–1983), and Vienna (1986–1989), which provided an official forum for the West to pressure the Soviet bloc states to improve their human rights practices. Even more importantly, the CSCE process encouraged and legitimated dissident activity in the Soviet bloc. For example, the Moscow Helsinki Group, founded in May 1976, was the leading dissident group in the Soviet Union in the late 1970s. In Czechoslovakia the coming of the Belgrade follow-up meeting helped to spur Charter 77, a manifesto signed by 242 people, including Vàclav Havel (who in 1990 became the first elected president of newly democratic Czechoslovakia). In many respects, the Helsinki Final Act began to lay the organizational basis for the revolutions of 1989.

The initial impetus for CSCE came from West Germany, especially Chancellor Willy Brandt, and from the Soviet Union. U.S. participation, however, was essential, and without the general trend toward détente the CSCE would not have been possible. In addition, the United States played a leading role in the follow-up meetings.

JACK DONNELLY

See also Brandt, Willy; Détente; Human Rights; Organization on Security and Cooperation in Europe

HENDERSON, LOY WESLEY
(*b.* 28 June 1892; *d.* 24 March 1986)

Staunchly anticommunist U.S. career diplomat. Born in the hills of Arkansas and educated at Northwestern University, Henderson went overseas with the Red Cross during World War I; the experience whetted his taste for life abroad, prompting him to enter the Foreign Service in 1922. Early posting to Riga, Latvia, and training in Washington under Robert Kelley, the State Department's noted anti-Soviet expert, prepared him to be named second secretary of the newly opened U.S. embassy in Moscow in 1934. His experiences there, often as acting chief of mission, confirmed his distrust of Soviet leader Joseph Stalin. In 1938 he returned to Washington to take charge of the State Department's Eastern Europe desk but went back to Moscow in 1942 as counselor of the embassy and chargé d'affaires. He acted as an intermediary between President Franklin D. Roosevelt and Stalin until complaints from the Kremlin and Washington liberals about his suspicions of Stalin's designs forced him out of U.S.-Soviet relations. In 1943 he was assigned to Iraq, where he spent two uneventful years as minister in Baghdad. He was recalled to Washington in 1945 to take charge of the State Department's Division of Near Eastern and African Affairs.

With the postwar breakdown of relations between Washington and Moscow, Henderson found his anti-Soviet sentiments again in fashion. He successfully advocated a firm U.S. response to Soviet machinations in Iran in 1946 and played a crucial backstage role in the 1947 formulation of the Truman Doctrine, which sent aid to Greece and Turkey to help those countries resist perceived communist and Soviet pressure, but once more Henderson's refusal to bend to political realities caused him political trouble. He opposed U.S. support for the 1948 creation of Israel, arguing that U.S. backing for the Zionist state would alienate the Arabs, open the region to Soviet adventurism, and might disrupt the flow of oil to the West. When partisans of Israel in Congress and in the White House demanded Henderson's head, they got it.

In 1948 Henderson was named ambassador to India, where he tried vainly to convince Prime Minister Jawaharlal Nehru of the demerits of nonalignment in the Cold War. He was appointed ambassador to Iran in 1951, and there his anti-Soviet inclinations were put to better use. He gradually became convinced that Prime Minister Mohammed Mossadeq was leading Iran to anti-Western ruin, and he advocated strong action to right the situation. With others, he persuaded President Dwight D. Eisenhower to launch the 1953 Central Intelligence Agency operation that helped topple Mossadeq and reinstate the pro-U.S. shah of Iran.

Henderson returned to Washington in 1954 as deputy undersecretary for administration to help reorganize the State Department. With the exception of occasional overseas journeys—to Egypt during the 1956 Suez Crisis, to the Congo in 1960—he remained in Washington until his retirement in 1961. Afterward he taught at American University in Washington and began writing his memoirs; at the time of his death his autobiography remained unfinished.

H. WILLIAM BRANDS

See also Cold War; India; Iran; Israel; Kelley, Robert; Mossadeq, Mohammed; Nehru, Jawaharlal; Nonaligned Movement; Russia and the Soviet Union; Truman Doctrine

FURTHER READING

Brands, H. W. *Inside the Cold War*. New York, 1991.

Henderson, Loy W. *A Question of Trust: The Origins of U.S.-Soviet Diplomatic Relations: The Memoirs of Loy W. Henderson.* Edited by George W. Baer. Stanford, Calif., 1986.

HERITAGE FOUNDATION

A conservative, Washington-based think tank, founded in 1973, that specializes in producing reports on current policy topics for members of Congress, appointees to federal offices (especially Republican ones), and journalists. The Heritage Foundation has sought to influence conservative law makers on issues ranging from federal tax policy and health care reform to strategic defense and aid to former communist nations. In 1973, Paul Weyrizh and Edwin J. Feulner, Jr., members of the conservative Republican study committee, a task force composed of congressional aides, received a $250,000 grant from beer manufacturer Joseph Coors to found a conservative think tank on the model of the liberal Brookings Institution. Under Feulner's leadership, the Heritage Foundation grew quickly as donations came in from other individuals and foundations and became, during the Reagan and Bush administrations, the flagship of the conservative intellectual movement.

The Heritage Foundation produces some 200 publications each year—single sheet "executive memorandums," ten- to twenty-page "backgrounders," monographs, and the journal *Policy Review*. The foundation also sponsors conferences, symposia, and research fellowships. While a number of prominent politicians have been Distinguished Fellows of the foundation—Jack Kemp, Richard Allen, Edwin Meese—most of the foundation's work is carried out by young, graduate-student-age scholars. The foundation is better known for its ideological zeal and the ability to articulate conservative opinions than for traditional scholarly studies, though most of the foundation's publications are well researched and thoroughly documented. The Heritage Foundation has been a consistent and vocal advocate of free market, supply-side economics, federal tax cuts, a strong national defense, and the creation of a North American free trade zone.

The best known of the foundation's publications is *Mandate for Leadership* (1980), a 1093-page review of government operations delivered to the Reagan transition team soon after the 1980 presidential election. *Mandate* provided a blueprint for a complete overhaul of the federal government. The Heritage Foundation's notable foreign policy recommendations have included early advocacy of the Strategic Defense Initiative for ballistic missile defense, staunch support of Israel, support of anti-communist "freedom fighters" in Nicaragua, Afghanistan, Angola, and Ethiopia, and constant economic and military pressure on the Soviet Union during the Cold War. The foundation has been critical of the United Nations and was instrumental in the Reagan administration's decision to withdraw from the United Nations's Educational, Scientific, and Cultural Organization (UNESCO). Since the collapse of the Soviet Union, the Heritage Foundation has advocated rapid conversion of Eastern Europe into free market states.

THOMAS MICHAEL SLOPNICK

See also Bush, George Herbert Walker; Cold War; Israel; Reagan, Ronald Wilson; Strategic Defense Initiative; Think Tanks; United Nations

FURTHER READING

Ricci, David M. *The Transformation of American Politics: The New Washington and the Rise of Think Tanks.* New Haven, Conn., 1993.
Smith, James Allen. *The Idea Brokers: Think Tanks and the Rise of the New Policy Elite.* New York, 1991.

HERTER, CHRISTIAN ARCHIBALD

(*b.* 28 March 1895; *d.* 30 Dec. 1966)

U.S. secretary of state in the latter part of the second Eisenhower administration (April 1959–January 1961). This appointment culminated a long career in international affairs. Born in Paris, the child of expatriate artists, Herter attended Howard University (A.B., 1915). In 1916 he entered the foreign service. Postings in Berlin and Bern were followed by work on the League of Nations Covenant at the Paris Peace Conference in 1919. After helping Herbert Hoover to organize the American Relief Administration, he also served as Hoover's assistant in the globally active Department of Commerce (1921–1924).

At this point in his life, Herter seems to have developed ambivalent feelings about an ongoing career in Washington—or even in government. After some years in publishing (as editor of *The Independent,* for example), he did return to politics as a representatives in the Massachusetts state house. National affairs reattracted him in 1942, when he began ten years of service as a member of Congress. In 1952, however, he returned to state politics, waging the first of two successful campaigns for the governorship.

Even during his Boston-based years, Herter maintained an interest in foreign-policy issues. Widely recognized as part of the "eastern internationalist" wing of the Republican party, he became an enthusiastic supporter of initiatives such as the Marshall Plan and of a bipartisan foreign policy. His foreign-policy views made it easy for him to support Thomas E. Dewey and Dwight D. Eisenhower in the 1948 and 1952 presidential elections. In 1956, in fact, Herter was briefly thrust into the limelight as a potential running mate for Eisenhower—via the efforts of some Republican liberals to dump Richard Nixon. Herter himself showed little interest in a place on the GOP ticket, though there was some speculation that his indifference was encouraged by the promise of a senior Department of State appointment.

Two years as undersecretary of state (1957–1958) gave Herter a thorough familiarity with the broad range of international issues. He developed a comfortable working relationship with Secretary John Foster Dulles. When the secretary's cancer reached a critical stage in early 1959, it was only Herter's own health problems (severe arthritis, requiring the use of crutches for walking) that caused even momentary doubts about his designation as successor.

Herter faced a barrage of problems as furious as any evident earlier in the Eisenhower presidency, including ongoing tangles regarding Berlin and the complex choreography of negotiations with Soviet Premier Nikita Khrushchev; the Soviet downing of the U.S. U-2 spy plane and the collapse of the Paris summit conference; the early stages of Washington's efforts to curb Fidel Castro's Cuban revolution; and explosive developments in the Congo, where in mid-1960 a civil war erupted after independence. The secretary of state's approaches to those difficulties closely matched the president's, allowing Eisenhower at least a rough approximation of the smooth partnership he had been used to with Dulles. Herter could be as patient and moderate as the president, for example, and the two men reinforced each other's inclinations to emphasize calm negotiation as a response to Moscow's sometimes bellicose flourishes regarding Berlin. As with Dulles before him, however, Herter's moderation could also be counterpointed by more aggressive and demanding impulses—mirroring Eisenhower in this respect as well. Openness to discussion of Berlin problems did not translate into a willingness to make concessions on German matters. Nor was Herter at all adverse to the harshly anti-Castro policies developed by the Eisenhower administration.

After leaving the Department of State, Herter continued as a public servant. In 1961–1962 he chaired the blue-ribbon committee on foreign affairs personnel. In 1962 he became the president's special representative for trade negotiations, serving until his death.

RONALD W. PRUESSEN

See also Berlin; Castro, Fidel; Cuba; Dulles, John Foster; Eisenhower, Dwight David; Hoover, Herbert

FURTHER READING

Noble, G. Bernard. *Christian A. Herter*. New York, 1970.

HIJACKING

See Terrorism

HIROHITO

(*b.* 29 April 1901; *d.* 7 January 1989)

The emperor of Japan, 1926–1989. For centuries, Japan had an emperor who reigned and a shogun who ruled. In the middle of the nineteenth century, young samurai and courtiers persuaded dissident lords to depose the shogun and "restore" power to the emperor. By December 1926, when Hirohito assumed the throne, Japanese officials had created an imperial cult: Shinto became a state religion, and the emperor a deity. Hirohito's reign was designated Shōwa, or "bright peace."

Though his power was absolute, the emperor still did not rule. In his meetings with his government, the emperor mostly listened. He offered no initiatives. He rarely rejected advice. He did not quell ministries fighting to control one or another of his powers. These fights often immobilized government. That encouraged the army and the navy to pursue their own strategies in expanding the Japanese Empire before World War II. With reluctance, Emperor Hirohito approved the Japanese cabinet's plan in 1941 to expand beyond China into French Indochina, risking war with the United States. In September of that year, he broke his customary silence in a meeting with army and navy leaders by reading a poem for peace written by his grandfather. In early December, the emperor sat silently as an imperial conference of key leaders decided on war against the United States. The Japanese attack on Pearl Harbor soon followed. Some four years later, on 10 August 1945, after U.S. atomic bombs blasted Hiroshima and Nagasaki, the emperor broke tradition and made the personal decision that Japan must surrender, subject to the preservation of his own sovereignty. Three days later, however, he accepted U.S. terms that he could remain on the throne but that his "authority" would be "subject to the supreme commander of the Allied powers." After the war, Secretary of the Treasury Henry Morgenthau said both Hirohito and Germany's Adolf Hitler should have been tried as war criminals. Joseph Grew, the last prewar ambassador to Japan, said that he knew Hirohito to be a man of peace. General Douglas MacArthur, responsible for the postwar occupation of Japan, concluded that the emperor could do for him what he had done for other shoguns: provide legitimacy for U.S. rule.

Hirohito renounced his divinity. He campaigned throughout the country in support of an American-inspired constitution that said sovereignty resided with the people, made the legislature the supreme organ of state, and described the emperor as a symbol, with no powers of governance. He continued to pursue his interest in marine biology, about which he wrote a number of books. In a poll taken throughout Japan shortly after Hirohito's death, 82 percent of the respondents expressed satisfaction with a symbolic emperor.

NATHANIEL THAYER

See also Hiroshima and Nagasaki Bombings of 1945; Japan; MacArthur, Douglas; Pearl Harbor, Attack on; World War II

FURTHER READING

Behr, Edward. *Hirohito: Behind the Myth*. New York, 1990.
Crump, Thomas. *The Death of an Emperor: Japan at the Crossroads*. New York, 1991.
Large, Stephen S. *Japan: a Political Biography*. New York, 1992.

HIROSHIMA AND NAGASAKI BOMBINGS OF 1945

Atomic bomb attacks by the United States against Japan near the end of World War II. At 8:15 on the morning of 6 August 1945, the *Enola Gay*, a B-29 named after pilot Paul Tibbett's mother, released a uranium-based atomic bomb over the center of the Japanese city of Hiroshima. The blast and fire are estimated to have immediately killed 65,000 civilians and a few thousand military personnel. Approximately 60,000 more people are reported to have died in the ensuing months from injuries and radiation poisoning. Three days later, another B-29, *Box Car*, dropped a plutonium-based atomic bomb over Nagasaki and missed its target, the residential center of the city, because of cloud cover. Approximately 30,000 civilians were killed immediately and an equal number are estimated to have died later from radiation. The motivation of these surprise atomic attacks against cities of little military consequence, and their effect on the timing of the end of the war, have been fiercely debated ever since.

Soon after the attack, President Harry S. Truman announced that the bomb had been used to end the war quickly to save the lives of U.S. citizens. Historical research has challenged this statement. The most compelling evidence for an alternative explanation emerged in the 1960s when Secretary of War Henry L. Stimson's diary became available to researchers. Entries such as "troubles with Russia...[are connected] to the future of S-1 [the atomic bomb]" appear in his diary in 1944 and then more frequently and pointedly throughout 1945. On 6 June 1945, he recorded that the president postponed the Potsdam Conference to coincide with the scheduled test of an atomic device at Alamogordo, New Mexico, and that the president said he thought the atomic bomb would serve as "a quid pro quo" in seeking a settlement with the Soviets with regard to "the Polish, Rumanian, Yugoslavian, and Manchurian problems." Furthermore, General Leslie R. Groves, the most influential advocate of the bomb's use against Japan, stated that, "There was never from about two weeks from the time I took charge of this project [1942] any illusion on my part but that Russia was our enemy and the project was conducted on that basis." The accumulation of such evidence has led historians to conclude that one motivation for bombing Hiroshima was to demonstrate to the Soviet Union the power of the new weapon. The debate among these historians is whether or not "troubles with Russia" was the primary reason for the attack.

It is debated that those responsible for the project used the weapon because of the significant human and material resources it commanded, and the $2 billion spent on it. If the bomb were used successfully, a senior official of the Department of War noted in the spring of 1945, no one in Congress would investigate. If not, Congress would investigate nothing else. The warning expressed by many prominent Manhattan Project (atomic bomb) scientists that a postwar nuclear arms race was to be avoided at all costs appears to have contributed to the atomic bombings of Hiroshima: "If the bomb were not used in the present war," University of Chicago Metallurgical Laboratory Director Arthur Compton wrote to Stimson, "the world would have no adequate warning as to what was to be expected if war should break out again."

Scholars and others, including Dwight D. Eisenhower, Admiral William D. Leahy, and General Curtis LeMay, have questioned whether the bombing of Hiroshima and Nagasaki was necessary to end the war quickly, as President Truman claimed. By May 1945, Japanese specialists in the department of state had come to believe that the doctrine of "unconditional surrender" was the primary obstacle to peace. Japan would surrender, they concluded, if assured that the emperor and the imperial dynasty would not be jeopardized. Based on daily readings of Japan's diplomatic messages, which the United Sates had been intercepting and decoding throughout the war, this conclusion was passed on to President Truman at the end of the month by Joseph C. Grew, acting secretary of state and former ambassador to Japan. Truman informed Stimson, who noted in his diary that Grew was not aware of the atomic bomb.

The Japanese continued to insist on guarantees after the two atomic bombs had destroyed their targets and the Soviets had entered the war. They would surrender, they announced on 10 August, on condition that the Potsdam Declaration "does not compromise any demand which prejudices the prerogatives of His Majesty as Sovereign Ruler." In response to assurances that the emperor would continue to occupy the throne, Japan surrendered on 14 August. Reflecting on Grew's proposal in his autobiography, Stimson wrote, "History might find that the United States, in its delay in stating its position [on unconditional surrender terms] had prolonged the war." What Stimson did not say was that the availability of nuclear weapons caused the delay. Until the atomic bombs were used, until their power had been demonstrated, the nuclear option precluded modifying unconditional surrender, "the only obstacle to peace," as was noted in an intercepted message of 13 July 1945, from Foreign Minister Shigenori Togo to Ambassador Naotake Saro in Moscow.

MARTIN J. SHERWIN

See also Japan; Manhattan Project; Potsdam Conference; Truman, Harry S.; World War II

FURTHER READING

Bernstein, Barton J. "The Atomic Bombings Reconsidered." *Foreign Affairs*. Vol. 74, No. 1 (1995).
Sherwin, Martin J. *A World Destroyed: Hiroshima and the Origins of the Arms Race*. New York, 1985.
Lifton, Robert Jay, and Greg Mitchell. *Hiroshima in America: 50 Years of Denial*. New York, 1995.

HISS, ALGER

(*b*. 11 November 1904)

A controversial government official and public figure because of persisting charges against him that he had spied for the Soviet Union. Hiss was born in Baltimore and was educated at Johns Hopkins University and Harvard Law School. The jurists Felix Frankfurter and Oliver Wendell Holmes became the first of many influential mentors that later included such members of the foreign relations establishment as Secretaries of State Edward R. Stettinius, Jr., and Dean G. Acheson. In 1936 Hiss, an ardent New Dealer, began service in the Department of State. He served as secretary of the Dumbarton Oaks Conference (October 1944); attended the Yalta Conference (February 1945), where he was responsible for UN matters; and became temporary secretary-general of the UN organizing conference in San Francisco (April 1945).

By late 1945 several former Soviet spies had secretly informed the Federal Bureau of Investigation (FBI) that Hiss was a Soviet agent. FBI Director J. Edgar Hoover soon conducted a covert campaign to discredit him. In January 1947 Hiss left government to become president of the Carnegie Endowment for International Peace. On 3 August 1948 senior *Time* magazine editor Whittaker Chambers, testifying before the House Un-American Activities Committee, alleged that Hiss had been a communist. In later statements Chambers charged that from 1934 to 1938 Hiss had been an agent in Chambers's Soviet-controlled spy ring and had passed to Chambers State Department cables and reports. In dramatic confrontations the debonair Hiss, seen by many as one of the best and brightest of his generation, denied the charges made by the rumpled, tortured Chambers, who was seen by Hiss's admirers as representing the totalitarian threat to Western civilization.

The statute of limitations prevented the government from indicting Hiss for espionage. In 1949 he was tried for perjury, but the jury deadlocked. In January 1950 a second jury convicted Hiss of perjury. He served forty-four months in a federal prison. For decades thereafter Hiss fought for vindication. He failed in court, but claimed victory when in 1992 a high Russian official announced that a partial review of KGB documents convinced him that Hiss had not been a Soviet agent. Nonetheless, the debate on Hiss's guilt continued. The scholarly community remained divided, with much of the evolving debate stemming from Allen Weinstein's 1978 study *Perjury: The Hiss-Chambers Case*, which argued that Hiss was guilty of perjury and that Whittaker Chambers had told the truth. The spy case overshadowed Hiss's achievements, including his leadership in helping to establish the United Nations. The Hiss controversy damaged Secretary of State Acheson after he publicly defended Hiss, and it fueled McCarthyism. The Hiss case lingers as one of the mysteries, and perhaps tragedies, of the Cold War era.

WILLIAM E. PEMBERTON

See also Acheson, Dean Gooderham; Carnegie Endowment for International Peace; Cold War; Dumbarton Oaks Conference; McCarthyism; United Nations; Yalta Conference

FURTHER READING

Hiss, Alger. *In the Court of Public Opinion.* New York, 1957.
———. *Recollections of a Life.* New York, 1988.
Weinstein, Allen. *Perjury: The Hiss-Chambers Case.* New York, 1978.

HITLER, ADOLF

(*b.* 20 April 1889; *d.* 30 April 1945)

Führer (leader) of the German Nazi Party and Reich Chancellor (1933–1945) who led Germany during World War II. He was born at Braunau am Inn, Austria, son of Alois Hitler and Klara Pölzl. His father was an official of middling rank in the Austrian Imperial Customs Service, and the young Hitler grew up in relative comfort. An undisciplined student at the Realschule in Linz, two years after his father's death in 1905 Hitler dropped out of school. He moved to Vienna in 1907 and failed to be admitted to the prestigious Academy of Fine Arts. After his mother died in 1908 he lost his last means of support and lived in poverty. As he drifted from one municipal housing facility to another, he grew to hate the imperial upper-class establishment and non-German elements in Vienna, especially Jewish immigrants from the East.

In 1913, Hitler moved from Austria to the German city of Munich. When war broke out in 1914, he eagerly joined a Bavarian infantry regiment assigned to the French front. At last, the rootless drifter had found a home. He fought bravely and was committed to the German cause. Although twice wounded and twice decorated, once with the Iron Cross, First Class, he never rose above the rank of Corporal. No German was more dismayed than Hitler by the defeat of his adopted country in November 1918. He heard the news in a hospital near Berlin, where he was recovering from exposure to a British gas attack. Even though it was German commanders who had capitulated, Hitler became convinced that Germany was "stabbed in the back" by its civilian leaders, the socialists, Bolsheviks, and Jews.

Hitler nursed bitter feelings after returning to his regiment in Munich, a city unsettled by recent left-wing revolution and right-wing repression. In 1919, the army assigned Hitler to attend and report on a meeting of the German Workers Party (DAP). He found himself agreeing with its Völkisch (racist) nationalism, resolute anti-Semitism, and militant rejection of the Versailles Treaty. Sensing this group could be of use to him, Hitler joined the DAP.

By 1920, Hitler had renamed, remodeled, and mastered the DAP. It became the National Socialist German Worker's Party (Nazi Party). Using his newly discovered and remarkable ability as a beer hall orator, Hitler attracted increasing numbers to the party. Eventually he outmaneuvered his partners to become undisputed party leader, or Führer. In November 1923, pressed by those in the party who demanded a national revolution and following his gambler's instinct, Hitler ordered an armed revolution, the Munich Beer Hall Putsch. The rebellion proved a disaster, Hitler was imprisoned, and the party went into disarray.

Always an opportunist, Hitler used his time in prison to compose his political testament, *Mein Kampf* (*My Struggle*, vol. 1, 1925). Grounded in the most brutish form of Social Darwinism, Hitler claimed that "...he who does not want to fight in this world...has no right to exist." He depicted the Aryan "race" as the "founders of culture," destined to win Lebensraum (living space) in Eastern Europe, and the Jewish "race" was the destroyer of culture, an enemy that Germany must "root out."

In 1925, Hitler set about rebuilding his party on more conventional lines, as Germany entered a period of growth and stability. The Nazis remained a minor party until the Great Depression swept Germany in the early 1930s. Confronted with the crisis, the coalition of parties ruling Germany split. Chancellor Heinrich Brüning was forced to enact legislation by decree. Taking advantage of the political paralysis, Hitler led his party relentlessly in numerous elections. In the Reichstag elections in July 1932, the Nazis took 37 percent of the vote, becoming Germany's largest party. In the November elections, however, the total shrank to 33 percent. It appeared the power of the Nazis had peaked and was receding. Then suddenly, as a result of the calculations of the political elite of the Weimar Republic, Hitler was swept into power.

The conservative German leadership had never accepted the legitimacy of the Weimar Republic and hoped to use economic collapse and civil disorder as an excuse to rid Germany of the Republic. They expected to use Hitler's populist legions as a means to restore elite rule. On 30 January 1933, President Paul von Hindenburg appointed Hitler Reich Chancellor. When, in February, a deranged Communist set fire to the Reichstag building, Hitler suspended civil rights and called for new elections. When the new Reichstag assembled in late March, Hitler demanded and received total legislative power. Dictatorship had replaced Weimar democracy.

Between 1933 and 1938 Hitler's popularity grew. In 1934, he tilted in favor of the conservative elite by ordering the bloody elimination of the S.A. (storm trooper) leadership that had demanded violent social revolution and that rivaled the armed forces. He restored German industry, expanded employment, ended street violence, and reestablished Germany as a European power. These achievements were accompanied by the centralization of authority in the form of an absolute police state. By early 1938, Hitler was sufficiently confident to turn against the conservative elite. He ousted the establishment leaders from the Ministries of Foreign Affairs, Defense, and Economics, and replaced them with Nazi loyalists. Next he turned to war as a means to consolidate power.

Hitler thought it his destiny to destroy communist Russia and win "living space" for Germany in the east. He was also determined to strike against his "racial" enemy, the Jewish people. Combining these ideas, Hitler proclaimed it his mission to destroy "Jewish Bolshevism." After the early 1920s, Hitler had become so committed to these views that he strove to position himself to attack Judaism in Europe and Bolshevism in Russia. Nonetheless, to achieve and maintain power, Hitler had

to make numerous decisions unrelated to his presumed ultimate goal. Hitler, the ultimate gambler, took advantage of the unpredictable and disjointed politics of the 1930s and the weakness of his opponents to move toward European war and an attack on Judaism.

Internally divided and fearful of war, England and France failed to challenge Hitler's remilitarization of the Rhineland and subsequent expansion to the east, when he moved into Austria and Czechoslovakia and challenged Poland. On 1 September 1939, a week after signing the Nazi-Soviet Pact, Hitler attacked Poland. He assumed that, without Russia as an ally, England and France would maintain neutrality. He was shocked when the two powers declared war on Germany. For Hitler, World War II began as the "wrong war," in that he became allied with Bolshevik Russia against the western powers. Nevertheless, by June 1940, Hitler's blitzkrieg, joined at the last minute by Benito Mussolini's Italy, had defeated France. Hitler's mastery of continental Europe seemed nearly complete; he could only curse an England that refused to accept German victory.

Hitler, the irrepressible gambler, soon began to squander his dominant position in Europe. On 22 June 1941, he returned to his original design by attacking his Soviet ally. No doubt he calculated that by striking swiftly he could succeed, and a quick victory would dash British hopes of eventual Soviet assistance. The German army drove deep into Russia. In December, however, the Wehrmacht offensive stalled outside Moscow and a Russian counteroffensive forced the Germans back. In the summer of 1942, Hitler renewed his offensive, seeking to divide Russia by cutting deep into the Ukraine. As winter descended, the German Sixth Army became trapped at Stalingrad. The Führer's rigidity contributed to massive defeat. By 1943, the Russians had gained the initiative.

Hitler made two even more brutal—and irrational—military decisions. The first was on 11 December 1941, after the Japanese attack on Pearl Harbor, when he declared war on the United States. German-American relations were already near the breaking point. The steady stream of U.S. supplies across the Atlantic helped sustain England; and, on 11 September 1941, President Franklin D. Roosevelt had ordered U.S. destroyers to "shoot on sight" when they spotted German submarines. Hitler dismissed U.S. military potential but ordered his navy to avoid provocation because his efforts were centered on Russia. Recklessly, he encouraged the Japanese to attack the United States in the Pacific. Only if Japan was attacked, however, were the Germans bound by treaty to assist their ally. Thus, Hitler's declaration of war on the United States was not based on reasoned strategy, but, more likely, on his delusion of personal invincibility.

His second mistake was made in January 1942, when at the Wannsee Conference, Hitler's henchmen, on his direct orders, made definite plans to proceed with the Final Solution of the Jewish Question, the extermination of all European Jews. By the first decision he brought it on himself to challenge the overwhelming industrial and military power of the United States, virtually assuring Germany's defeat. By the second, he won eternal infamy for himself and his followers. His program of genocide focused primarily on Jews, but Slavs and gypsies were also victimized. Moreover, the Polish people were to be "reduced to a remnant of substandard beings," their lands seized for German "living space." The Jews were efficiently and brutally herded into extermination camps, located primarily in Poland. By war's end, some 5 to 6 million European Jews had been murdered.

In late 1944, although it was clear that Germany had lost the war, Hitler determined to continue fighting. Prolonging the war led to the deaths of vast numbers of German soldiers and civilians and the further devastation of German cities. As U.S. forces fought across Germany from the west and Soviet units closed in from the east, Hitler hoped blindly for a change of fortune. News of Roosevelt's death on 12 April 1945, brought momentary elation. Hitler's propaganda chief, Joseph Goebbels, humored him, arguing that this turning point for Germany's fortunes was "written in the stars." On 30 April 1945, as Russian forces were penetrating Berlin, Hitler committed suicide in his bunker beneath the Reich chancellery. Germany capitulated to the Allies a week later.

EDMUND S. WEHRLE

See also Germany; Holocaust; Russia and the Soviet Union; World War I; World War II

FURTHER READING

Bullock, Alan. *Hitler and Stalin: Parallel Lives.* New York, 1992.
Carr, William. *Hitler: A Study in Personality and Politics.* New York, 1979.
Compton, James V. *The Eagle and the Swastika: Hitler, the U.S.A. and the Origins of World War II.* Boston, 1967.
Fest, Joachim C. *Hitler.* New York, 1974.
Kershaw, Ian. *The Hitler Myth: Image and Reality in the Third Reich.* Oxford, 1985.

HOAR, GEORGE FRISBIE

(*b.* 29 August 1826; *d.* 30 September 1904)

Member of the House of Representatives (1869–1877), U.S. senator (1877–1904), and noted anti-imperialist. Born into a prominent New England family in Concord, Massachusetts, Hoar practiced law in Worcester until his election to the U.S. House of Representatives in 1869. He moved to the Senate in 1877 and served there until his death. A lifelong Republican, Hoar became the most prominent dissenter from his party's imperial policy in

the late nineteenth and early twentieth centuries. After reluctantly approving annexation of Hawai'i in 1898 as strategically necessary to the war with Spain, he was one of only two Republicans in the Senate to vote against the annexation of the Philippines. Hoar pronounced the annexation unconstitutional and immoral, a violation of the principles of the Declaration of Independence. He contended that the United States should not govern others without their consent and predicted that the islands would be a strategic and economic liability.

JOSEPH A. FRY

See also Hawai'i; Spanish-American-Cuban-Filipino War, 1898

FURTHER READING

Beisner, Robert L. *Twelve Against Empire: The Anti-Imperialists of 1898–1900.* Chicago, 1992.
Hoar, George Frisbie. *Autobiography of Seventy Years,* 2 vols. New York, 1903.
Welch, Richard E. *George Frisbie Hoar and the Half-Breed Republicans.* Cambridge, Mass., 1971.

HO CHI MINH

(*b.* 19 May 1890; *d.* 2 September 1969)

Vietnamese communist leader who presided over North Vietnam in its war with South Vietnam and the United States (1959–1969). He led his countrymen to independence against the French (1954) and subsequently forced the United States to withdraw from Vietnam, handing Washington its sharpest post–World War II foreign-policy defeat. Born in central Vietnam to an impoverished Mandarin family, Ho left his country in 1911, and visited Europe, North Africa, and the United States, where he came face to face with capitalism, colonialism, and, through voracious reading, Western ideals. He settled in France in 1917 and became a leader of the Vietnamese community. Inspired but quickly disillusioned by President Woodrow Wilson's Fourteen Points, Ho discovered the writings of Vladimir I. Lenin and underwent a Damascus-road like conversion to communism.

As a budding revolutionary, Ho became a charter member of the French Communist party in 1920 and was sent to Moscow for training. He was then dispatched to China, where in 1930 he founded the Indochinese Communist party. In May 1941 he convened a meeting of the party in Vietnam to launch his revolution. In the war against the French (1946–1954) Ho drew on his peasant origins and his internationalist career to display both diplomatic flexibility and grass-roots political savvy. While his military forces were building up, Ho temporized with the French. When the fighting came to a stalemate in 1950, both sides internationalized the war. Despite a resounding military victory at Dien Bien Phu in 1954, Ho, worried about U.S. intervention, settled for a compromise peace that partitioned the country. Ten years later, despite the strong U.S. military intervention on behalf of South Vietnam, Ho and his confederates waged a concerted people's war, with Soviet and Chinese help, to wear down the U.S. will to continue. Notwithstanding enormous losses, the North Vietnamese succeeded, although Ho did not live to see the final victory. An enigma to Westerners, his austere life and single-minded patriotism made Ho a revered figure in Vietnam. In the United States, hawks insisted he was above all a communist ideologue, while doves praised him as a genuine nationalist. He was, in fact, undeniably both.

TIMOTHY J. LOMPERIS

See also Dien Bien Phu; French Indochina; Vietnam War

FURTHER READING

Duiker, William J. *The Communist Road to Power.* Boulder, Colo., 1981.
Halberstam, David. *Ho.* New York, 1987.

HOFFMAN, PAUL GRAY

(*b.* 26 April 1891; *d.* 8 October 1974)

President of the Studebaker automotive company who left his successful career to promote and help administer U.S. foreign aid programs. A lifelong Republican and symbol of bipartisan foreign policy, he served on several advisory and fact-finding committees that focused on international economic reconstruction following World War II. President Harry S. Truman appointed him to head the Economic Cooperation Administration, the agency charged with implementing the Marshall Plan. From April 1948 until he resigned in January 1950, Hoffman won strong support from Congress and successfully negotiated with European governments by promoting the benefits of economic reconstruction and integration for both the United States and Western Europe. Moving beyond Cold War anticommunism, he later became a prominent advocate of U.S. and international foreign aid to assist poor countries in their development. From 1959 until he retired in 1971, he administered what became the United Nations Development Program, raising and distributing money for world development projects.

ALAN R. RAUCHER

See also Cold War; Marshall Plan; United Nations

FURTHER READING

Hoffman, Paul Gray. *Peace Can Be Won.* Garden City, N.Y., 1951.
Hogan, Michael J. *The Marshall Plan.* New York, 1987.
Raucher, Alan R. *Paul G. Hoffman.* Lexington, Ky., 1985.

HOLOCAUST

(1933–1945)

Nazi Germany's systematic mass killing of European Jews in the years 1941–1945. No clear overview of the Holocaust is possible, however, without first examining the Nazi anti-Jewish actions that preceded their mass murder. The term "Holocaust," as used in this context, thus encompasses a two-stage historical event: from 1933–1940, a policy of persecution, with the objective of pressuring Jews to emigrate from Germany and German-held territory; and from 1941–1945, a policy of systematic extermination, with the objective of annihilating European Jewry (the so-called Final Solution). About 5.5 million of Europe's 9 million Jews were killed. The exact number of victims cannot be determined; the frequently cited 6 million was the estimate available at the Nuremberg Trials, held by the Allied powers shortly after World War II to prosecute German war criminals.

The Holocaust grew out of an obsessive hatred and fear of Jews by Adolf Hitler and other leading Nazis, who came to power in Germany in 1933. Hitler's *Mein Kampf* and Nazi ideology expressed these anti-Jewish sentiments. These attitudes built on nearly 2,000 years of anti-Semitism in Western society. Both the Catholic and Protestant branches of the Christian church had carried and nurtured a hatred of Jews for many centuries, thereby ingraining it deeply into Western culture. During the nineteenth and twentieth centuries, the focus of anti-Semitism shifted from the old religious hatred of Jews to new, supposedly "scientific" racial and political theories. Social scientists maintained that the Jews constituted an inferior race, characterized by inborn physical and moral degeneracy and filth. Anti-Semitic political leaders argued that the Jews wielded vast, frequently secret, international economic and political power. The most widespread version of this theory was the myth of a hidden Jewish conspiracy to take over the world through the Jews' supposed control of the capitalist system as well as of the Soviet Union and the international communist movement. Racial, political, and some degree of religious anti-Semitism influenced not only the Nazis and others in Germany and across Europe who collaborated in the Holocaust, but also the bystanders, those in Axis Europe and in the outside world who failed to try to help the Jewish victims.

Nazi Persecution, 1933–1938

The Nazi assault on the Jews began immediately after Hitler took power in Germany in January 1933. The early measures struck at educational and economic opportunity and also began a process of forced transfer of all Jewish-owned businesses to non-Jewish hands ("aryanization"). Although not as yet officially government-

ESTIMATED JEWISH LOSSES IN THE HOLOCAUST

Country	Initial Jewish Population	Minimum Loss	Maximum Loss
Austria	185,000	50,000	50,000
Belgium	65,700	28,900	28,900
Bohemia and Moravia	118,310	78,150	78,150
Bulgaria	50,000	0	0
Denmark	7,800	60	60
Estonia	4,500	1,500	2,000
Finland	2,000	7	7
France	350,000	77,320	77,320
Germany	566,000	134,500	141,500
Greece	77,380	60,000	67,000
Hungary	825,000	550,000	569,000
Italy	44,500	7,680	7,680
Latvia	91,500	70,000	71,500
Lithuania	168,000	140,000	143,000
Luxembourg	3,500	1,950	1,950
Netherlands	140,000	100,000	100,000
Norway	1,700	762	762
Poland	3,300,000	2,900,000	3,000,000
Romania	609,000	271,000	287,000
Slovakia	88,950	68,000	71,000
Soviet Union	3,020,000	1,000,000	1,100,000
Yugoslavia	78,000	56,200	63,300
Total	9,769,840	5,596,029	5,860,129

From *Encyclopedia of the Holocaust*, Israel Gutman, Editor in Chief, Volume IV, Appendix, Section 6. ©1990 Macmillan Publishing Company. Reprinted with permission of Macmillan Reference, USA, a division of Simon & Schuster.

sponsored, some violent assaults took place. In 1935 the Nuremberg Laws stripped Jews of their basic citizenship rights. It was well understood in foreign diplomatic circles as well as in Germany itself that the objective of the persecution was to make life for the Jews in Germany so harsh that they would emigrate. By the end of 1937, however, only about 25 percent of Germany's Jews had left. Emigration was very difficult in a world beset by depression, and many Jews still believed that Germany, a highly cultured society, would not tolerate such persecution for very long.

In March 1938 Germany annexed Austria and in September 1938 it absorbed part of Czechoslovakia. The German government's anti-Semitic decrees of the previous five years were applied overnight in these newly occupied areas, setting off a rush of Jews attempting to emigrate. Increasing persecution in Germany itself during 1938 reached a climax in November with *Kristallnacht* (the Night of Broken Glass), a nationwide outburst of violence and looting directed against the Jews and surreptitiously sponsored by the government. Nearly 100

Jews were killed, 30,000 were incarcerated in concentration camps, Jewish property was smashed, and almost every synagogue in the country was burned. Drastic government decrees rapidly followed. A huge fine was levied on the German Jews, all remaining Jewish-owned businesses now had to be transferred to non-Jewish hands, and Jews were entirely excluded from public schools. With virtually no economic base left and with major violence now an ever-present possibility, the Jews could no longer remain in Germany.

Obstacles to Jewish Emigration

After *Kristallnacht* the German Jews joined those of Austria and Czechoslovakia in the rush to get out. Jews lined up for blocks at foreign consulates hoping to obtain visas to emigrate to any safe haven. Immigration-quota waiting lists built up for years ahead. Tens of thousands did manage to clear the world's immigration barriers and reach Palestine, the United States, France, Great Britain, and other countries, but most did not get out, for the world closed its doors in 1939, 1940, and 1941. Before 1938, the outflow of Jews from Germany, which had averaged under 26,000 per year, had been small enough to be absorbed by countries in western Europe and overseas. After Germany took over Austria, however, the heavy pressure on Jews to leave that country, added to the increasing level of persecution in Germany itself, had turned the refugee problem into a major crisis. President Franklin D. Roosevelt initiated a conference of thirty-two democratic nations that met at Évian, France, in July 1938, but hopes that the world would open its doors went unfulfilled. Led by the United States and Great Britain, nation after nation explained at the Évian Conference that they could accept few additional refugees. Before adjourning, the conference did create a permanent Intergovernmental Committee on Refugees and charged it with seeking places for refugees to settle and persuading the German government to permit fleeing refugees to take a portion of their property with them. The committee, however, failed to locate places where refugees could go. It negotiated an arrangement for the removal of some Jewish property from Germany, only to see that plan collapse when war broke out, in September 1939. From that point on, the Intergovernmental Committee became virtually inactive.

Three developments in the spring of 1939 further illustrate the closing of world boundaries. The Wagner-Rogers Children's Bill, introduced in the U.S. Congress, would have permitted 20,000 German refugee children to come to safety in the United States without being counted against the small but by then overcrowded immigration quota. This was to be a one-time exception to the quota limits. With no support from the administration of President Franklin D. Roosevelt, however, the legislation failed even to reach the floor of Congress. In the same weeks, a German steamship, the *St. Louis*, arrived at Havana, Cuba. More than 900 of the refugees on board were forbidden to land because the Cuban government had canceled their permits. The ship wandered for days off the coasts of Cuba and Florida. The Cuban government would not relent, appeals to President Roosevelt went unanswered, and the *St. Louis* returned to Europe. Third, in May 1939 Great Britain, which governed Palestine as a League of Nations mandate, responded to Arab pressures by cutting Jewish immigration to the region—an important haven to fleeing Jews—to 15,000 per year. As it turned out, the British authorities did not even allow that small quota to be filled.

Systematic Extermination, 1941–1945

From 1939 to 1941 Germany seized Poland, overran France and much of the rest of western Europe, and invaded the Soviet Union. These conquests brought under German rule millions of additional Jews whom the Nazis were determined to be rid of. The Nazi changeover from a policy of forced emigration to one of genocide

(the systematic extermination of an entire people) occurred in connection with Germany's attack on the Soviet Union in June 1941. In planning that invasion, the decision was made to send special mobile killing units (*Einsatzgruppen*) directly behind the advancing German armies. The *Einsatzgruppen* were charged with clearing the newly conquered areas of the hundred of thousands of additional Jews who now fell into German hands. For the most part, the method used was mass gunfire, carried out at ditch sites. Between June 1941 and the end of 1942, the Einsatzgruppen killed more than 1.3 million Jews who lived in Poland, Lithuania, Latvia, and the western Soviet Union.

The decision to extend the policy of systematic annihilation to all the Jews of Europe was probably made during summer 1941; it was certainly reached by October 1941. For the Jews outside the eastern European regions where the Einsatzgruppen operated, killing centers were established and equipped with large gas chambers. Six killing centers had become active by spring 1942, all of them located in Poland (Auschwitz, Belzec, Chelmno, Lublin/Majdanek, Sobibor, Treblinka). During the next three years, Jews from all across Europe were deported, mostly by freight train, to these killing centers. Approximately 3 million Jews died in them.

A Tepid Western Response

Only bits and pieces of information about the mass killings filtered out to the West until June 1942, when a careful report from the Polish Jewish underground reached London. It estimated 700,000 Polish Jews had already been killed in what its authors had concluded was an ongoing German campaign to "annihilate all the Jews in Europe." Soon afterward, confirmation that a full-scale genocide was in fact under way came to Switzerland from a highly placed source in Berlin. This report reached London and Washington in August 1942. The U.S. Department of State remained skeptical until 24 November 1942, by which time additional evidence was so compelling that Undersecretary of State Sumner Welles authorized the foremost U.S. Jewish leader, Rabbi Stephen Wise, to make the terrible news public. At the same time, the reality of genocide was independently confirmed and made public in Great Britain and in Palestine. Two weeks later, on 8 December 1942, U.S. Jewish leaders conferred with President Roosevelt and found him already well aware of the extermination program. In the U.S. mass media, the confirmed news of extermination, now amply documented, received minimal notice. That pattern continued throughout the war; consequently, those in the United States who hoped to build public pressure for government action to help the European Jews had first to find ways to bring the Holocaust to the public's attention.

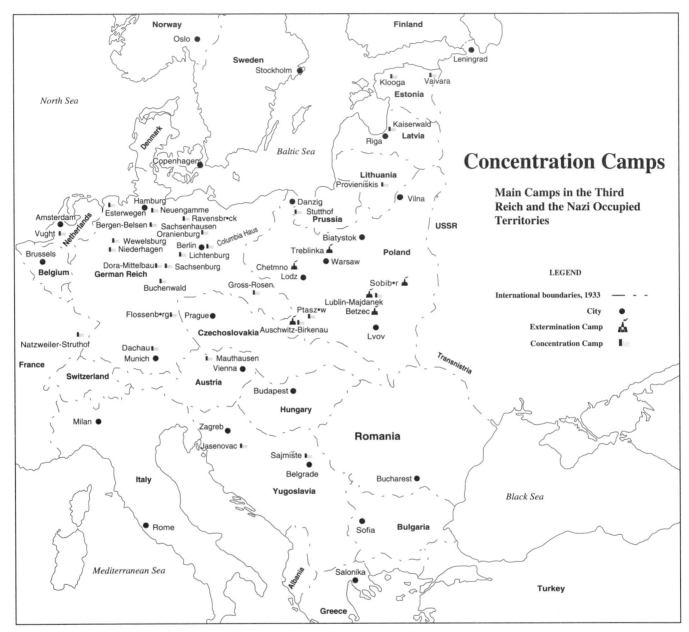

Concentration Camps

Main Camps in the Third Reich and the Nazi Occupied Territories

LEGEND

International boundaries, 1933	— - -
City	●
Extermination Camp	🏭
Concentration Camp	∎

From *Encyclopedia of the Holocaust*, Israel Gutman, Editor in Chief, Volume I. ©1990 Macmillan Publishing Company. Reprinted with permission of Macmillan Reference, USA, a division of Simon & Schuster.

On 17 December 1942 Great Britain, the United States, the Soviet Union, and the governments-in-exile of eight German-occupied countries issued an Allied War Crimes Declaration. It condemned Germany's "bestial policy of cold-blooded extermination" of the Jews and affirmed that the perpetrators would be brought to retribution. The declaration came about largely because of pressures that had arisen in Great Britain, where leaders of the Christian church and many members of Parliament had joined with Jewish groups in calling for action to

help the Jews of Europe. These pressures continued in Great Britain well into the spring of 1943. In the United States, pressures for government rescue measures also developed during early 1943, but they were weaker than in Great Britain, partly because of indifference toward the plight of the Jews on the part of U.S. Christian churches and most members of Congress.

Despite their official condemnation of Germany's extermination program, neither the British Foreign Office nor the U.S. State Department was willing to seek ways to rescue Jews. The British realized that any sizable outflow of Jews from Axis Europe would put immense pressure on them to reverse their tightly restrictive policy concerning Jewish immigration to Palestine, a policy to which they were adamantly committed. The State Department also feared the exit of tens of thousands of Jews from Nazi Europe because that would place pressure on the United States to open its gates to some extent. For both governments, the policy, unofficial and unannounced, was the avoidance of rescue.

In a move calculated to undermine public pressures for rescue action, the British Foreign Office and the U.S. State Department held a twelve-day conference on the refugee problem at Bermuda in April 1943. To avoid public pressure and to control the flow of information, the conference was kept inaccessible to all outsiders except five closely controlled news correspondents. The results of the Bermuda Conference were kept secret, but the two governments announced afterward that all possibilities had been studied and a number of recommendations for action sent forward. In reality, the conference recommended virtually nothing of use to the Jews of Europe. Its objective had been fulfilled, however, because, unknown to the public, it had been held not to find ways to rescue Jews but to dampen the pressures for rescue action that had built up since late 1942.

Despite the Bermuda Conference, the struggle for a U.S. government rescue program continued. By late summer 1943 the leadership in this effort had shifted to a group of activists led by Peter Bergson, also known as Hillel Kook. Bergson and some of his closest collaborators were Palestinian Jews who had reached the United States in 1939 and 1940. Secretly they were connected with the Irgun, a Jewish armed underground in Palestine. Utilizing full-page newspaper advertisements, pageants, and mass meetings, the Bergson groups sought to publicize the Holocaust and stress the need for a U.S. government rescue program. In October 1943 they successfully organized a march on Washington by 400 Orthodox rabbis, and in November, drawing on months of lobbying on Capitol Hill, they managed to have a resolution introduced in Congress. It called on President Roosevelt to establish a government rescue agency independent of the inert Department of State. Substantial support for the resolution was building in Congress as 1943 closed.

Meanwhile, in an independent series of events, Treasury Department officials had discovered that the State Department not only had attempted virtually nothing for rescue, but it had even obstructed the limited rescue efforts that U.S. Jewish groups were trying to undertake on their own. Treasury officials also learned that the State Department, led by Assistant Secretary of State Breckinridge Long, had quietly arranged to keep immigration to less than 10 percent of the legally available quotas, had moved in early 1943 to cut off the flow of Holocaust information from Europe, and had sent altered documentation to the Treasury Department in an attempt to cover up the information stoppage. These and other findings were summarized by the Treasury officials in a detailed report to Secretary of the Treasury Henry Morgenthau, Jr., entitled "Acquiescence of This Government in the Murder of the Jews." Morgenthau took the information to President Roosevelt on 16 January 1944. Roosevelt, aware that he was facing a nasty scandal and also aware that the State Department's record on rescue would be debated within days when the Senate took up the rescue resolution, decided to head off the building crisis. He agreed to Morgenthau's suggestion that he issue an executive order establishing a government rescue agency charged with doing everything possible, consistent with the war effort, to rescue the victims of Germany's genocide program. The agency was called the War Refugee Board.

Inadequately funded and barely supported by the president and his administration, the War Refugee Board became largely a Treasury Department operation. Nor did it receive any assistance from Great Britain or the Soviet Union. Collaborating closely with Jewish organizations in the United States and overseas, and sponsoring the important rescue work carried out in Budapest by the Swedish diplomat Raoul Wallenberg, the War Refugee Board did, however, play a crucial role in saving about 200,000 Jews and at least 20,000 non-Jews. Nonetheless, as the board's director, John Pehle, summarized it years later: "What we did was little enough….Late and little, I would say."

The Legacy of the Holocaust

One-third of the world's Jewish population was purposely destroyed by the Nazi Holocaust. But one important outcome in the aftermath of the slaughter was the extension of international law at the Nuremberg and other postwar trials to include "crimes against humanity." Similarly, a crucial factor in the emergence of the state of Israel in 1948 was the Western world's realization of the vast dimensions of the Jewish catastrophe in the Holocaust. World sensitivity to the terrible plights of all refugees increased somewhat after the 1940s, and in a few cases, including the United States and Germany, more generous policies concerning the granting of refugee asylum have been attempted. Still, the world has been unable or unwilling to develop means of responding effectively when massive persecution and violence are imposed on civilian populations, including in Biafra, Uganda, Cambodia, the former Yugoslavia, and Rwanda.

DAVID S. WYMAN

See also Genocide Convention; Germany; Hitler, Adolf; Morgenthau, Henry, Jr.; World War II

FURTHER READING

Gutman, Israel, ed., *Encyclopedia of the Holocaust*, 4 vols. New York, 1990.

Hilberg, Raul. *The Destruction of the European Jews*, 3 vols., rev. ed. New York, 1985.

Marrus, Michael R. *The Holocaust in History*. Hanover, N.H., 1987.

Wyman, David S. *The Abandonment of the Jews: America and the Holocaust, 1941–1945*. New York, 1984.

——— . *Paper Walls: America and the Refugee Crisis, 1938–1941*. Amherst, 1968.

HONDURAS

Located in Central American between Nicaragua and Guatemala, a poor republic that endured U.S. economic and political pressures, including military interventions, during the early part of the twentieth century. In later years, however, because Honduras became relatively calm and violence-free, it did not attract the degree of U.S. attention that other Central American countries— namely El Salvador, Nicaragua, and Guatemala—did. With the exception of the early decades of the twentieth century, U.S. policies toward Honduras consisted of a series of "half measures"—until the advent of the 1980s, when Honduras became a central player in U.S. policy toward the region.

Honduras's level of relative stability derived in large measure from the country's pattern of economic and political development. Like El Salvador, Guatemala, and Nicaragua, Honduras was colonized by Spain early in the sixteenth century, gained independence in 1821, and became part of the short-lived federation of the United Provinces of Central America. During the period of Spanish control, because the mountainous and geographically isolated land did not yield a product that could profitably be exported over the long term, the colony fell into a state of rural isolation and poverty. The country's subsistence economy persisted until the end of the nineteenth century. At that time the Honduran elite, concerned about the country's lack of development, sought to attract foreign investment by providing generous concessions to investors. The elite's efforts were rewarded by the move to the country of a number of foreign-owned banana companies. The economic and political effects these companies had on the nation made it a quintessential "banana republic."

The banana industry, which included major U.S. companies, such as Standard Fruit and United Fruit, did not have some of the initial adverse social and economic impacts in Honduras that it did in other Central American countries. Because the banana industry settled on the thinly populated northern coast, few peasants were displaced or indigenous communal holdings appropriated. On the other hand, Honduras became very dependent on banana exports as a source of economic growth,

failing to develop other viable export commodities, such as coffee and cotton, until after 1950. The country's reliance on the banana industry also inhibited the development of an independent entrepreneurial class. The activities of the banana companies in the nation's political and economic life included sponsorship of a revolutionary expedition launched from the United States during the first decade of the twentieth century in an effort to topple President Miguel Dávila, who it was feared might favor new banana growers. The U.S. government failed during the same period to establish a U.S. protectorate over Honduras, but the United States did free Honduras from British influence, and U.S. military interventions (six by 1925) protected lives and property in Honduras. The banana companies also engaged in bribes and payoffs to politicians and military officials. The most obvious instance of this occurred in the mid-1970s, when President López Arellano was ousted after the "bananagate" scandal, which involved bribes of more than a million dollars paid by United Brands to members of the administration to lower taxes on banana operations. The scandal was uncovered in 1975 by a U.S. Senate investigation of the activities of U.S. multinational corporations in the Third World.

In the category of labor relations, foreign ownership of the banana companies meant that Honduran governments were not inclined actively to try to keep the wages of banana workers down and were generally unwilling to repress strikes with force. Because of this political space, Honduras developed a larger organized labor force than did its neighbors. In addition, because there was not much of a local oligarchy for it to protect, and because it generally was not used to quell working class protests, the army in Honduras remained fairly weak into the twentieth century.

Conditions in Honduras began to change in the middle of the twentieth century. The contest for power between the National and Liberal political parties, rivals since the latter part of the nineteenth century, was interrupted by the military's seizure of power in 1956. Withdrawing from political rule after only nineteen months, the military turned power over to Liberal Ramón Villeda Morales. In exchange, the new constitution of 1957 gave the military autonomy from direct presidential control. During his tenure as president, Villeda Morales initiated social reforms, including social security and labor and agrarian reform laws. Honduras also became a member of the newly formed Central American Common Market (CACM) at this time. Washington, fearing that a regional bloc would discriminate against U.S. economic interests, did not extend support to the Common Market during the 1950s. During the 1960s, concluding that the CACM fit into Alliance for Progress objectives, the United States gave CACM nearly $20 million for projects and loaned the Central American Bank for Integration more than $180 million.

The military overthrow of Villeda Morales in 1963 signaled the Honduran military's decision to continue to play a central role in national politics, whether through direct rule or behind-the-scenes influence of civilian politicians. Several factors influenced this decision. One was the Cold War environment. As part of its regional strategy of containment, the United States, under a military defense assistance agreement of 1954, began training Honduran armed forces. Honduran officers received training from the U.S. Army School of the Americas. Despite the absence of guerrilla activity in Honduras, the bulk of the training consisted of counterinsurgency tactics. U.S. military assistance to the country also increased substantially during this period, rising from $2.6 million for 1950–1963 to $4.6 million for 1964–1967. Another factor contributing to the buildup of the military in Honduras was the so-called "soccer war" of 1969 with El Salvador. The presence in Honduras of vast numbers of land-hungry Salvadorans, combined with perceived disadvantages on the part of poor and virtually nonindustrialized Honduras in its trade relations with such CACM countries as El Salvador, led to increased tensions between the two countries. During World Cup soccer play between the two nations, El Salvador invaded Honduras. The seventy-two hour war, which claimed 2,000 lives, augmented the size of the Honduran military thereafter.

By the late 1970s pressure was being exerted on the military to remove itself from political power. Worsening economic conditions, calls by civilian politicians for their return to power, and corruption scandals undercut military rule. The administration of President Jimmy Carter pressed the regime of General Policarpo Paz García for some reform measures and elections. This pressure, however, did not include cutting off military aid to Honduras. In fact, U.S. foreign military aid to the country soared from a total of $19.6 million for 1970–1979 to $9 million in 1981 and peaked at $77 million in 1984. U.S. economic assistance also grew, rising from $36 million in 1981 to $168 million in 1984. After winning the presidential election of 1981, Liberal Roberto Suazo Córdova became Honduras's first popularly elected civilian ruler in a decade.

Once President Ronald Reagan assumed office in 1981, the United States raised the stakes in Honduras. As part of its policy to remove the Sandinistas from power in Nicaragua and eliminate leftist guerrillas in El Salvador, the Reagan administration pressed Honduras to become the staging ground for U.S. operations in the region and the site of U.S.-built military bases and for U.S. training of Salvadoran troops. Honduras also embarked on joint military exercises with the United States. One such exercise, Big Pine II, included more than 10,000 troops and took place close to the Nicaraguan border. The long exercise stretched from August 1983 to March 1984. The U.S. ambassador to Honduras, John Negroponte, was significant in making Honduras a haven for the Nicaraguan Contras.

U.S. policies and activities disrupted Honduran society. The financial largesse it received permitted the military to further expand in size and power. Death-squad and guerrilla activity, both of which had been virtually absent in the country, cropped up in the early 1980s. Human rights violations multiplied. Economic conditions deteriorated and poverty deepened after U.S. aid decreased with the end of the conflicts in Nicaragua and El Salvador. The withdrawal of all but about 1,000 U.S. troops from the country undermined one of the economy's few sources of growth. Although Honduras has had democratic elections since 1981, relations between civilian governments and the military were still strained in the mid-1990s. Contributing to these tensions was the creation of a special commission by President Rafael Leonardo Callejas (1990–1994) to investigate human rights abuses by the armed forces. A decline in resources available to the military also caused friction. The reduction of U.S. assistance to Honduras prompted armed forces commander in chief General Luis Alonso Discua to announce in April 1994 that the armed forces wanted to end the 1954 military assistance treaty with the United States.

CAROLINE A. HARTZELL

See also Contras; El Salvador; Latin America; Nicaragua; Reagan, Ronald Wilson

FURTHER READING

Blachman, Morris J., William M. LeoGrande, and Kenneth E. Sharpe, eds. *Confronting Revolution: Security Through Diplomacy in Central America.* New York, 1986.

Booth, John A., and Thomas W. Walker. *Understanding Central America,* 2nd ed. Boulder, Colo., 1993.

Coatsworth, John H. *Central America and the United States: The Clients and the Colossus.* New York, 1994.

LaFeber, Walter. *Inevitable Revolutions: The United States in Central America,* 2nd ed. New York, 1993.

Rosenberg, Mark B., and Philip L. Shepherd, eds. *Honduras Confronts Its Future: Contending Perspectives on Critical Issues.* Boulder, Colo., 1986.

HONG KONG

A British dependency in East Asia on the South China Sea that will revert to Chinese sovereignty in 1997. Declared a free port in 1841, Hong Kong developed as a warehousing and distribution center for British trade with southern China. It later declined in size and importance relative to Shanghai, the most cosmopolitan city on the China coast and focal point of U.S. operations there. It was not until 1949 that Hong Kong developed into the leading manufacturing, commercial, and communications center it is today.

U.S. interest in and interaction with Hong Kong was extensive in the post–World War II period. Following the lead of the British as administrator of the territory, U.S. businesses, government, and not-for-profit organizations used it as an important base for operations throughout East Asia. Hong Kong began its rise to prominence as a commercial center in East Asia after Shanghai was taken by communist forces in 1949. The large number of people from the People's Republic of China (PRC) who sought refuge in Hong Kong and the subsequent cutoff of much entrepôt trade between China and the West, a result of the embargo during the Korean War (1950–1953), led to the development of textile and other light manufacturing industries in Hong Kong, many of which exported to the U.S. market.

Once Great Britain withdrew most military forces east of the Suez Canal during the 1960s, Hong Kong's security rested much more on Chinese restraint and goodwill than on the very limited power of British forces in the colony. In the late 1960s violence associated with the most radical phase of "Red Guard diplomacy" during China's Cultural Revolution threatened to spill over and jeopardize stability in the colony. As Maoist influence faded, however, increasingly cordial, practical, and extensive ties developed between the colony and the PRC. Transportation markedly improved and visits increased, encouraged by official representatives of both sides. The British governor of Hong Kong made his first trip to the PRC in March 1979, and Chinese leader Deng Xiaoping told him that investors in Hong Kong should put their hearts at ease over Chinese intentions toward the colony. Americans used Hong Kong as an important base for operations to take advantage of new commercial opportunities then opening in mainland China.

In the early 1980s the United States remained Hong Kong's largest investor and trading partner. By mid-1983, according to official U.S. statistics, U.S. investment in Hong Kong reached $2.7 billion, but the actual figure was thought to be much higher, estimated at around $4 billion. The United States was the major foreign direct investor in Hong Kong's manufacturing sector with 47 percent of total investment, followed by Japan with 30 percent. Out of Hong Kong's total two-way trade of $44.5 billion in 1982, $8.6 billion was with the United States. The United States absorbed 38 percent of Hong Kong's total domestic exports that year. In 1983 Hong Kong's trade value jumped by more than 20 percent, and the United States absorbed 42 percent of Hong Kong's exports. As a supplier, the United States ranked third, after China and Japan; the U.S. share of Hong Kong's import market was 11 percent in 1982 and 1983.

In 1984 Great Britain and China signed an agreement returning Hong Kong to PRC control by 1997. The agreement adhered to China's plan that Hong Kong would retain considerable autonomy and its capitalist economic system for fifty years after 1997, thereby giving some reassurance to investors and others interested in Hong Kong's future. The U.S. government remained an interested bystander in the negotiations. Neither London nor Beijing showed much public interest in U.S. support or involvement. Nevertheless, the 1984 agreement preserved the commercial, financial, and legal structures important to U.S. business. The next several years saw continuous Chinese-British interchange under the framework established by the 1984 agreement. Incremental progress was made toward incorporating the various Chinese reassurances and promises into the PRC basic law passed in 1990 that was to govern the administration of Hong Kong after 1997. Perhaps of more importance for the future of Hong Kong was the rapid development of a very close and interdependent economic relationship between Hong Kong and the newly opened regions of coastal China, especially neighboring Kwangtung Province. The level and scope of Hong Kong's trade and foreign exchange earnings with China grew rapidly, far surpassing the considerable growth rate of the Chinese economy as a whole. China's post–Mao Zedong "open door" to economic investment provided opportunities for Hong Kong entrepreneurs and for foreign investors—including many Americans—working through Hong Kong companies. Sixty to 70 percent of external investment in mainland China came from Hong Kong.

The developing pattern of economic interdependence and political accommodation (especially by the British side) might have continued in a steady way toward 1997 had it not been for the political crisis in mainland China posed by the 1989 Tiananmen Square incident, which began as a peaceful prodemocracy demonstration by students in Beijing and ended with more than 1,000 dead. In the wake of that incident, Great Britain, the United States, and others recalculated the importance of their relationship with Beijing in the post–Cold War world. In fact, however, Tiananmen did little to upset the broad trend of economic interconnectedness. Trade, investment, and other such interchange—including a growing role for U.S. businesses based in Hong Kong—continued to grow vigorously. The events laid the groundwork for a serious political crisis and Sino-British confrontation in the 1990s, however, over the future course of governance in Hong Kong. The United States showed strong sympathy with London during the crisis. The Tiananmen Square incident saw a crackdown on dissent, which led to more than one million Hong Kong citizens demonstrating against the PRC government's action. People in the territory were influential in supporting dissidents in the PRC and in smuggling out political critics and information that proved to be damaging to the standing of the Beijing regime at home and abroad.

British and Chinese calculations over Hong Kong thus changed in several ways. For the British, the so-called politically apathetic Chinese people in Hong Kong had shown a keen interest in politics. Many pressed for more support from London to establish better safeguards against possibly capricious and repressive PRC government action toward Hong Kong after 1997. The increasingly important middle class of professionals and businesspeople in the colony called for the strengthening and expanding of representative government in Hong Kong. For China, the demonstrations and subsequent action of people in Hong Kong raised a major security concern. They heightened PRC sensitivities over any action by the British or others that could be seen as fostering political or other conditions in Hong Kong that were at odds with Beijing's definition of stability.

U.S. politicians and media commentators supported initiatives to strengthen democracy and representative government in Hong Kong by Governor Christopher Patten in 1992. Among other things, the initiatives called for more elected members of Hong Kong's Legislative Council. The U.S. Congress passed a law on U.S.–Hong Kong relations that registered U.S. concern that Beijing not take steps that would upset stability and undercut Hong Kong's nascent democratic institutions. Other legislation recorded Congress's antipathy with what was seen as Beijing's heavy-handed approach to Hong Kong affairs. Subsequently, the U.S. posture on Hong Kong moderated along with a more general moderation in U.S. policy toward mainland China. There was little congressional attention to Hong Kong in 1994, for example. Although Beijing continued to attack Patten strongly and pledge to undo any political reforms in 1997, U.S. officials followed the advice of Hong Kong officials in avoiding confronting Beijing over the issue.

ROBERT G. SUTTER

See also China; Deng Xiaoping; Great Britain

FURTHER READING

Ching, Frank. *Hong Kong and China: For Better or For Worse.* New York, 1985.
Miners, Norman. *The Government and Politics of Hong Kong.* Hong Kong, 1991.
Rafferty, Kevin. *City on the Rocks: Hong Kong's Uncertain Future.* New York, 1991.
Vogel, Ezra. *The Four Little Dragons: The Spread of Industrialization in East Asia.* Cambridge, Mass., 1991.

HOOVER, HERBERT

(*b.* 10 August 1874; *d.* 20 October 1964)

An engineer, humanitarian, secretary of commerce, and thirty-first president of the United States (1929–1933),

born in West Branch, Iowa. Orphaned a decade later, Hoover spent his teenage years in Oregon with an uncle and aunt. In 1891 he entered the first class of Stanford University, where he studied mining and graduated in 1895. As a consulting metallurgical engineer for the next two decades, he became a millionaire working in Australia, China, Burma, Russia, and Mexico, actually circling the globe five times in the years 1902–1907.

Public Service to 1929

Hoover first came to public attention in 1914 when, from London, he helped organize the rescue and evacuation of thousands of U.S. citizens stranded in Europe at the outbreak of World War I. For the next three years he directed the Commission for Relief in Belgium (CRB), later described by Hoover as "the greatest job Americans have undertaken in the cause of humanity." Food came from private donors and governments; indeed, the United States, Great Britain, France, and other nations subscribed four-fifths of the $300 million that fed seven million Belgians and two million French. Hoover and his assistants dealt directly with all the governments involved, including German army and civilian officials, as if the CRB were a quasi-sovereign entity. After a wartime stint as U.S. food administrator, the "great engineer," as he had become known, headed the American Relief Association (1918–1922), which sent some $5 billion in U.S. food and medical supplies to alleviate famine and disease in postwar Europe. During the huge famine in Soviet Russia in 1921–1923, Hoover, a fervent anti-Bolshevik, negotiated with the new communist regime to make sure that his own representatives would supervise distribution.

Humanitarian achievements brought Hoover fame, political appointment, and a philosophy of public service that emphasized volunteerism. His notion of cooperative association, practiced in his relief activities and exemplified throughout the United States by groups such as the Red Cross, community chests, YMCAs, granges, and settlement houses, comprised what he called the American System. In contrast to bureaucracy, "cooperation appraises its methods and consequences step by step and pays its bills as it goes," thus constituting a form of "self-government outside of political government," in Hoover's words. He joined with others in seeking a world order of peace and prosperity by having private experts in business, finance, labor, and agriculture cooperate with government officials in what has been called a system of "corporatism."

As secretary of commerce under Presidents Warren G. Harding and Calvin Coolidge (1921–1928), he tried to act on these ideas. Inheriting a miscellany of divisions and bureaus, Hoover quickly reorganized them, notably changing the small bureau of foreign and domestic commerce into virtually a second Department of State. He expanded its budget, multiplied its expert personnel, increased its offices abroad from twenty-three to fifty-eight, and appointed the Harvard economist Julius Klein to run the bureau. Despite complaints about poaching from Department of State consular officials, Hoover's department scored its biggest success by encouraging business and investors to gain dominance over Latin American markets through cartels and special trading arrangements. Harding called Hoover "the smartest 'geek' I know," while Coolidge complained that he "has offered me unsolicited advice for six years. All of it bad."

Hoover as President

Elevated to the White House in 1929, Hoover projected a balance between the United States's traditional isolationism and internationalism. An enthusiastic early supporter of Woodrow Wilson, he had initially favored membership in the League of Nations without reservations, but reluctantly accepted Henry Cabot Lodge's reservations as politically necessary. He supported an "open door" for trade internationally, but valued access to raw materials higher than he did expanding export markets; he also accepted high tariffs and thought in terms of economic self-sufficiency with the Western Hemisphere. A practicing Quaker, he preferred the "club of public opinion" and moral suasion over economic sanctions and military force. Hoover emphasized nonmilitary means—treaties, arbitration, conferences, disarmament, economic and financial arrangements—in his lifelong quest for world order. "We can never herd the world into paths of righteousness with the dogs of war," he warned. He espoused what one scholar has called "independent internationalism"—active on an international scale, but independent in practice. He was isolationist only in the sense of avoiding war, scaling down military interventions, and preserving the freedom to make independent choices. The new president put his personal stamp on diplomacy. Following a ten-week tour of Central and South America, Hoover pledged in his inaugural address a policy on nonintervention and, in 1930, issued a memorandum by Undersecretary of State J. Reuben Clark repudiating the Roosevelt Corollary to the Monroe Doctrine. Despite debt defaults and Latin American resentment against the Hawley-Smoot Tariff Act of 1930, no further military interventions occurred; under Hoover's direction, U.S. marines evacuated Nicaragua and committed to leaving Haiti. Hoover's department of state helped settle the long festering Tacna-Arica dispute between Peru and Chile and the Leticia incident between Peru and Colombia in 1932.

In the realm of disarmament, Hoover achieved a modicum of success at the London Naval Conference of 1930 by working out a "yardstick" agreement beforehand with British Prime Minister Ramsay MacDonald whereby a rough equivalency was reached between the U.S. Navy's "heavy" eight-inch gun cruisers of 10,000 tons and Great Britain's six-inch gun "light" cruisers. This understanding enabled the United States, Japan, and Great Britain to extend the 10:6 naval limitation ratio to cruisers and submarines, notwithstanding an escape clause that permitted any of the three powers to suspend the agreement if threatened by a nonsignatory nation. Hoover did send a delegation in 1932 to the General Disarmament Conference in Geneva, but the economic crisis of the Great Depression prevented him from following the deliberations closely. At one juncture he asked all nations to make an across-the-board reduction of 30 percent in all armaments, an impractical request because some countries, such as Germany, wanted to rearm and would have been delighted to see their erstwhile enemies reduce their armaments toward Germany's already low level. Only the Soviet Union, with few friends in Western capitals and still denied formal diplomatic recognition from the United States, supported the president's demarche. Hoover also recommended a distinction between defensive and offensive weapons, thus eliminating the latter, but again his categorization proved impossible to make (all weapons being defensive in the rationale of their possessors).

Hoover's aversion to military methods emerged most conspicuously in his response to the seizure of China's Manchurian province by Japanese armies. Once the fighting began outside Mukden in September 1931, Secretary of State Henry L. Stimson urged the Chinese and Japanese to cease hostilities. Fearful that the international community would "dump" the "Manchurian baby" in Washington's lap, Hoover and Stimson sent a diplomat to Geneva to monitor the League of Nations deliberations. While the League debated and appointed an investigatory commission, Japanese forces quickly overran Manchuria. What to do? Hoover ruled out U.S. military intervention, and when Stimson suggested, in December, that the United States cooperate in imposing economic sanctions against Japan, the president again said no—it would be like "sticking pins in tigers." Hoover privately judged that Japan's aggression did "not imperil the freedom [or] the economic or moral fiber of our people. I do not propose to sacrifice American life for anything short of this."

Thus, Hoover chose nonrecognition. The secretary of state issued what came to be known as the Stimson Doctrine; his political fortunes on the wane, Hoover wanted it called the Hoover Doctrine. Citing tradition and international law, Stimson pledged not to recognize any arrangements in China that might impair U.S. treaty rights, violate the Open Door policy, or subvert the Kellogg-Briand Pact. Defiantly, the Japanese assaulted Shanghai three weeks later. A combative Stimson persuaded Hoover to reinforce the U.S. military garrison in the Chinese city. Hoping to bluff Japan without its knowing that it had no reason to be afraid, Stimson sent a public letter in February to the chairman of the Senate Foreign Relations Committee that hinted at sanctions and threatened to fortify Guam and build up the U.S. Navy in the Pacific if Japan did not halt its aggression. The secretary hoped the public letter would "encourage China, enlighten the American public, exhort the League, stir up the British, and warn Japan." The ploy failed. Any chance that Japan might be deterred was eliminated when Hoover instructed Undersecretary of State William R. Castle, Jr., to announce that in resolving international disputes the United States would always employ peaceful means. Although eventually endorsed by the League of Nations, nonrecognition did not prevent Japan from quitting the League, negotiating a truce with China, and reconstituting Manchuria as the puppet state of Manchukuo.

Also in 1930 Hoover declared a one-year moratorium on debt payments dating from World War I, but thereafter only Finland paid its debts to the United States, forever winning a place in the hearts of U.S. citizens. Debtors defaulted, Germany stopped paying reparations, and the world settled into the Great Depression of the 1930s.

The Post-White House Years

Upon departing the presidency, Hoover spent his remaining thirty-one years out of public office, except for short appointments by Presidents Harry S. Truman and Dwight D. Eisenhower to survey world food resources and assist in reorganization of the federal government. In the early 1930s, Hoover inveighed against what he considered President Franklin D. Roosevelt's dictatorial tendencies—enlargement of the government, curtailment of economic freedoms, and regimentation (so Hoover believed) of the U.S. people. He also turned attention to the foreign threat. In a trip to Europe in 1938 he visited Adolf Hitler, whom he adjudged "partly insane." When he went on to Finland, Norway, and Poland, on a sentimental journey to countries he had once helped, he spoke against Hitler; he did the same on return to New York, and soon afterward condemned the Nazi treatment of Jews. He nurtured an even greater abhorrence of the "gangster regime" in Soviet Russia.

After another European war erupted in 1939 and Hitler's armies overran much of Europe, Hoover worked strenuously to prevent U.S. intervention. The British naval blockade and President Roosevelt's political opposition stymied Hoover's efforts to organize another Committee to Feed the Small Democracies. Although he never joined the noninterventionist America First Committee, the former president spoke out against the alleged deceit of aiding Hitler's opponents through such

nonneutral measures as the Destroyers-Bases Deal and Lend-Lease. After Germany's invasion of Russia in June 1941, Hoover claimed to speak for a majority "who do not want to go to bed with Stalin, who fundamentally dislike any British dictation, and who hate Hitler, and yet they are being dragged into war." When the administration embargoed oil against Japan, Hoover became convinced that Roosevelt was doing all he could to "get us into the war through the Japanese back door." Although opposed to Japanese aggression in China, he always viewed Japan as a pro-Western counterweight to Soviet Russia. Through his contacts in Washington he monitored negotiations with Japan, and in late November 1941 he participated in a last-minute attempt through intermediaries to arrange a six-month *modus vivendi* between Tokyo and Washington. His backstage efforts helped fashion a tentative memorandum that seemed acceptable to both President Roosevelt and Japanese diplomats in Washington as late as 5 December 1941.

Hoover ended all public criticism after Pearl Harbor and supported the United States's war effort. In collaboration with diplomat Hugh Gibson, he wrote perhaps his most important book, *The Problems of Lasting Peace* (1942), emphasizing that military success alone would not ensure a peaceful world. Among his fifty proposals were a new international organization that would focus solely on the peaceful settlement of national disputes, gradual disarmament, and a ban on military alliances. When Roosevelt died in April 1945, a pall virtually fell from Hoover's shoulders—he had disliked his Democratic successor that much—and he sought communication with FDR's successor, who was delighted to see him and use his talents. President Harry S. Truman said privately that Hoover politically was to the right of Louis XIV, but he quickly sent the former president on a survey of world food resources. By 1946 Hoover was once again coordinating food relief for thirty-eight countries; the next year, after studying the dire economic conditions in Germany and Austria, he recommended that only by restoring prosperity to former enemies could economic recovery and democratic politics return to Europe. Hoover's report helped rally bipartisan support for the Marshall Plan. The former president also played a key role in establishing the United Nations International Children's Emergency Fund (UNICEF), whose first director was a longtime colleague from Belgian relief, and whose initial $15 million appropriation followed Hoover's favorable testimony to Congress.

As an elder statesman Hoover at times showed surprisingly liberal views. In May 1945 he told Truman that war with the Soviet Union would mean the extinction of Western civilization. He opposed the atomic bombings of Hiroshima and Nagasaki. In 1950 he refused to chair a bipartisan committee to investigate communists in government. "I doubt," he said, "if there are any consequential card-carrying communists in the Government." He nonetheless favored a Fortress America policy—he was against U.S. intervention in the Korean War, and against the expansion of U.S. forces in Germany in the 1950s. In a vision that appealed to agrarian and business interests, especially in the Midwest and Far West, he urged the withdrawal of U.S. troops from Europe, with Europeans caring for their own defenses. Naval and air power alone could protect the United States and other island bastions, such as Great Britain, Japan, Taiwan, and the Philippines. Meanwhile, he believed, the United States would display its banner to the world, the banner of freedom and democracy. Part of the display should consist, he said, of expulsion of the Soviet Union from the United Nations.

Spending his final years in residences in Palo Alto, California, and New York, he liked to say, when asked what ex-presidents did, "We spend our time taking pills and dedicating libraries." By the latter he meant the Herbert Hoover Library in West Branch, Iowa, where he deposited most of his personal and official papers. He also took pride in the vast archival research collections at the Hoover Institution for War, Revolution, and Peace, which he founded at Stanford in 1919 and endowed with more than a million dollars during his lifetime. When he died of cancer in 1964 at age ninety, he was still working on a "magnum opus" about U.S.-Soviet relations after 1933.

J. GARRY CLIFFORD
ROBERT H. FERRELL

See also America First Committee; Clark Memorandum; Commerce, U.S. Department of; Coolidge, Calvin; Destroyers-for-Bases Deal; Germany; Gibson, Hugh Simons; Harding, Warren; Humanitarian Intervention and Relief; Isolationism; Japan; Korean War; Lend-Lease; London Naval Conferences of 1930 and 1935–1936; Manchurian Crisis; Marshall Plan; Open Door Policy; Presidency; Roosevelt, Franklin Delano; Roosevelt Corollary; Russia and the Soviet Union; Stimson, Henry Lewis

FURTHER READING

Best, Gary Dean. *Herbert Hoover: The Post-Presidential Years*, 2 vols. Stanford, Calif., 1983.
Brandes, Joseph. *Herbert Hoover and Economic Diplomacy*. Pittsburgh, Pa., 1962.
Burner, David. *Herbert Hoover: A Public Life*. New York, 1979.
DeConde, Alexander. *Herbert Hoover's Latin American Policy*. Stanford, Calif., 1951.
Fausold, Martin E. *The Presidency of Herbert Hoover*. Lawrence, Kans., 1985.
Ferrell, Robert H. *American Diplomacy in the Great Depression: Hoover-Stimson Foreign Policy, 1929–1933*. New Haven, Conn., 1957.
Gelfand, Lawrence E., ed. *Herbert Hoover: Great War and Its Aftermath*. Iowa City, Iowa, 1979.
Hawley, Ellis W., ed. *Herbert Hoover, Secretary of Commerce*, 1981.
Hogan, Michael J. *Informal Entente: The Private Structure of Cooperation in Anglo-American Economic Diplomacy*. Columbia, Mo., 1977.
Hoover, Herbert. *Addresses Upon the American Road*, 8 vols. New York, 1936–1961.
———. *American Individualism*. New York, 1922.
———. *Memoirs*, 3 vols. New York, 1951–1952.
———. *The Ordeal of Woodrow Wilson*. New York, 1958.
———, and Hugh Gibson. *The Basis of a Lasting Peace*. New York, 1945.
———, and Hugh Gibson. *The Problems of Lasting Peace*. Garden City, N.Y., 1942.
Smith, Richard Norton. *An Uncommon Man, The Triumph of Herbert Hoover*. New York, 1984.

HOOVER INSTITUTION ON WAR, REVOLUTION, AND PEACE

See Think Tanks

HOPKINS, HARRY LLOYD

(*b.* 17 August 1890; *d.* 29 January 1946)

Close political adviser to, and during 1944–1945, special envoy for, President Franklin D. Roosevelt. Born in Iowa, the son of a harness salesman, Hopkins graduated from Grinnell College in 1912. Social work in the slums of New York brought him to the attention of Eleanor and Franklin Roosevelt and subsequently to his appointment as head of the New Deal Federal Emergency Relief Administration in 1933. His success in spending some $9 billion through such relief programs as the Works Progress Administration made him a presidential favorite. Appointed secretary of commerce in 1938, he had to resign in 1940 because of recurrent stomach cancer. Roosevelt thereupon installed him in the White House as speechwriter, doorkeeper, and troubleshooter. Described by another presidential aide as "Death on the way to a frolic," the wisecracking Hopkins stayed five years.

Despite his inexperience, Hopkins soon emerged as the president's principal foreign policy factotum. Equally adept at backstairs intrigue and poker-night tomfoolery, the loyal Hopkins served as sounding board and surrogate. If Roosevelt asked him to jump off the Washington Monument, a columnist once wrote, "the appointed hour would find Mr. Hopkins poised for the plunge. Whether with or without a parachute would depend on what the President seemed to have in mind." At Roosevelt's behest, Hopkins headed a White House staff that directed the war effort. Sent to England in early 1941 to assess British military requirements against Nazi Germany, Hopkins reported: "If courage alone can win—the result will be inevitable." The "catalytic agent between two prima donnas," as Hopkins described himself, he made preliminary arrangements for the first summit between Roosevelt and British Prime Minister Winston S. Churchill. The president named him lend-lease coordinator in March 1941. Following Germany's attack on the Soviet Union in June, Hopkins flew to Moscow, talked to Soviet leader Joseph Stalin and his generals, and recommended immediate lend-lease aid to the Soviets. Returning to London, he then accompanied Churchill to the Atlantic Charter meeting with Roosevelt on 9–12 August 1941. Churchill dubbed the blunt Iowan "Lord Root of the Matter."

A key participant at every wartime conference, Hopkins supported Roosevelt's "grand design" for a liberal postwar international order shaped and supervised by the United States, Great Britain, and the Soviet Union. He pushed hard for a second front in 1942 because Great Britain and the United States could not organize the world "without bringing the Russians in as equal partners." He also predicted the end of colonial empires because "vast masses of people are not going to tolerate it and for the life of me I can't see why they should." Unlike hard-liners in the Department of State, Hopkins believed that friendly relations with Moscow could continue after the war if the Soviets were treated generously. Because he always tried to quickly get more lend-lease aid to the Soviets, they regarded him with special trust and affection. Stalin said Hopkins was the first American who spoke "from the soul." For Hopkins the compromises struck at the Yalta Conference in early 1945 marked the "dawn of a new day....We were absolutely certain that we had won the first great victory of the peace—and, by 'wc,' I mean all of us, the whole civilized human race."

Following Roosevelt's death in April and Germany's surrender in May 1945, President Harry S. Truman sent Hopkins to Moscow to resolve disagreements over the Yalta accords. With instructions to "use diplomatic language or a baseball bat," the emaciated Hopkins warned that U.S. opinion would turn against the Soviet Union if it continued to obstruct free elections in Poland, a symbol of Soviet-U.S. trust. Stalin explained that he could not allow the anti-Soviet London Poles, the most likely winners in an election, to govern postwar Poland; the Soviets had "not easily forgotten" that Poland twice "served as a corridor for German attacks. . . . It is therefore in Russia's vital interest that Poland should be both strong and friendly." Hopkins worked out a compromise whereby a few noncommunists were added to the Polish government, and Stalin accepted the U.S. position on United Nations veto procedures and promised to recognize the Jiang Jieshi (Chiang Kai-shek) regime in China. Hopkins's last diplomatic mission only temporarily delayed the onset of the Cold War. He died of hemochromatosis several months later.

J. GARRY CLIFFORD

See also Cold War; Jiang Jieshi; Churchill, Winston Spencer; Lend-Lease; Roosevelt, Franklin Delano; Truman, Harry S.; World War II; Yalta Conference

FURTHER READING

Adams, Henry H. *Harry Hopkins.* New York, 1977.
McJimsey, George T. *Harry Hopkins.* Cambridge, Mass., 1987.
Sherwood, Robert E. *Roosevelt and Hopkins.* New York, 1948.
Tuttle, Dwight W. *Harry L. Hopkins and Anglo-American-Soviet Relations, 1941–1945.* New York, 1983.

HORNBECK, STANLEY KUHL
(*b.* 4 May 1883; *d.* 10 December 1966)

Asia expert who took a hard line toward Japan in the 1930s. Hornbeck served as chief of the Department of State Division of Far Eastern Affairs (1928–1937) and later as political adviser to the secretary of state (1938–1944). Hornbeck insisted that U.S. policy in East Asia should encourage equal commercial opportunity for all nations as well as preserve the integrity of China (the Open Door Policy). He was an articulate and often acerbic critic of Japan's expansionism during the 1930s and was a strong supporter of Jiang Jieshi's (Chiang Kai-shek's) Nationalist government in China. Hornbeck argued that the imposition of economic sanctions, a U.S. naval buildup, and aid to China would force Japan to halt its aggression. Between 1939 and 1941 the United States gradually implemented these measures. The Japanese attack on Pearl Harbor (7 December 1941) seemed to confirm Hornbeck's assessment of Japan's aggressiveness at the same time that it revealed the failure of his strategy. Forced out of the State Department in 1944, Hornbeck served as U.S. ambassador to the Netherlands (1944–1947). As ambassador Hornbeck reestablished normal U.S.-Dutch relations after the dislocations of World War II, but feeling isolated, he decided to retire. As a private citizen, Hornbeck became an outspoken critic of the People's Republic of China and opposed U.S. recognition of the communist regime.

BARNEY J. RICKMAN III

See also China; Japan; Jiang Jieshi; Open Door Policy

FURTHER READING

Buhite, Russell D. "The Open Door in Perspective: Stanley K. Hornbeck and American Far Eastern Policy." In *Makers of American Diplomacy*, edited by Frank J. Merli and Theodore A. Wilson. New York, 1974.
Burns, Richard Dean. "Stanley K. Hornbeck." In *Diplomats in Crisis*, edited by Richard Dean Burns and Edward M. Bennett. Santa Barbara, Calif., 1974.
Doenecke, Justus D. *The Diplomacy of Frustration: The Manchurian*

Crisis of 1931–1933 as Revealed in the Papers of Stanley K. Horn-beck. Stanford, Calif., 1981.

Hu, Shizhang. *Stanley K. Hornbeck and the Open Door.* Westport, Conn., and London, 1995.

HOSTAGES

See Terrorism

HOT LINE AGREEMENTS

Agreements between the Soviet Union and the United States to establish, and later to improve on, a direct and highly reliable channel of communication between Moscow and Washington. The first hot line agreement was signed in June 1963 with the intention of preventing diplomatic crises from escalating into war. Although the need for better and faster communication had been evident, it was the 1962 Cuban missile crisis that compelled the two nuclear powers to set up a so-called hot line (formally known as the Moscow-Washington Direct Communications Link). As the world came to the brink of nuclear war in October 1962, messages between President John F. Kennedy and Premier Nikita S. Khrushchev took more than six hours to be delivered through regular diplomatic channels, which included the use of Western Union's telegraph service. Both the Department of State and the U.S. military had opposed the idea of any direct communications between the Kremlin and Washington that could circumvent their own bureaucracies, but the crisis demonstrated the need for such a link. The United States raised the issue at the Eighteen Nation Disarmament Committee meeting in December 1962. The Soviets responded favorably to the U.S. proposal, clearing the way for a Washington-Moscow hot line.

The image of the hot line as often portrayed in movies—a red phone with a direct line to the Kremlin within reach of the president's fingertips—is a false one. Actually, the hot line was designed to allow for communication through the written word, primarily to lower chances of a faulty translation and to give leaders more time for decision making. The hot line was staffed by translators at both ends, working twenty-four hours per day, and initially consisted of a teletype system (made in East Germany and Norway to protect U.S. and Soviet communications technology), with operators punching coded messages on tape and transmitting them at a rate of one page every three minutes. Additional U.S.-Soviet agreements, however, led to a gradual modernization of the hot line, as with the 1984 agreement to add facsimile ("fax") transmission capability and the 1987 agreement to establish nuclear risk reduction centers in Washington and Moscow. In the mid-1990s the hot line consisted of computers and fax machines hooked to the Kremlin by two satellite systems and an undersea cable for nearly instantaneous communication. Its U.S. location has always been deep inside the Pentagon, at a windowless complex called the National Military Command Center, where the translators can relay messages to and from the White House in a variety of ways. Every hour the translators check the reliability of the line by sending test messages.

The hot line has been activated at tense moments in U.S.-Soviet relations to register strong protests or to avoid misunderstandings. President Lyndon B. Johnson used the hot line during the Gulf of Tonkin incident of August 1964 to convey a personal message that the United States did not intend to expand the Vietnam War. The Soviets first sent a message on the hot line on 5 June 1967, shortly after the start of the Six-Day War between Israel and several Arab countries. President Richard M. Nixon turned to the hot line during the India-Pakistan crisis in late 1971, the Yom Kippur War in 1973, and in 1974 when Turkey invaded Cyprus. President Jimmy Carter, in a novel move, sent a letter over the hot line early in his administration to try to develop greater rapport with Soviet leader Leonid Brezhnev about Strategic Arms Limitation Treaty negotiations. Carter used it again to protest the Soviet intervention in Afghanistan in 1979. President Ronald Reagan sent several hot line messages during crises in Lebanon, Poland, and the Soviet arrest of a U.S. journalist on spy charges in 1986.

Beginning in the late 1980s, with the decline of superpower conflict, Presidents George Bush and Bill Clinton began to call Soviet President Mikhail Gorbachev or Russian President Boris Yeltsin regularly on conventional, yet secure, telephones rather than communicate through the hot line. Although the Soviet Union collapsed in 1989, there is a general consensus among foreign policy experts that the hot line was worth maintaining as closer links in U.S.-Russian relations continued to unfold.

JEREL A. ROSATI

See also Cold War; Cuban Missile Crisis; Russia and the Soviet Union

FURTHER READING

Blechman, Barry M. "Efforts to Reduce the Risk of Accidental or Inadvertent War." In *U.S.-Soviet Security Cooperation*, edited by Alexander L. George, Philip J. Farley, and Alexander Dallin. New York, 1988.

Webster Stone. "Moscow's Still Holding: Twenty-Five Years on the Hot Line." *New York Times Magazine* (18 September 1988).

HOUSE, EDWARD MANDELL
(*b.* 26 July 1858; *d.* 28 March 1938)

An intimate adviser to President Woodrow Wilson who influenced U.S. foreign policy in the crucial period of

World War I and its aftermath; his influence was second only to Wilson himself. The son of T. W. House, a leading, wealthy Texas citizen, Edward had a privileged youth and met many prominent people who visited the family homes in Galveston and Houston and enjoyed the colorful life of the vast Gulf of Mexico coastal plain near Houston. After his father's death in January 1880, House undertook the management of the family properties. He became a prominent member of society in the late 1880s and early 1890s while pursuing farming and land speculation. House was drawn into state politics through his friendship with James Stephen Hogg, whom in 1892 House helped gain reelection. Hogg rewarded House with the title of colonel. Concerned more with the process of politics than its substance, House proceeded to build his own faction—"our crowd" as he called it—into a powerful force in Texas politics. An ambitious political operator, skilled in organizing and inspiring others, he worked largely behind the scenes, developing ties of loyalty and affection with his close associates and using patronage to rally party workers behind his candidates. Every governor of Texas who served from 1894 to 1906 was a protégé of Colonel House.

At the turn of the century, House became bored with his role in Texas politics, restlessly searching for broader horizons. He sought further wealth through investments in oil and railroads and felt the pull of the East. For years he had summered on Boston's North Shore and gradually began to winter in New York, severing most of his ties with Texas and only occasionally visiting the state. A conservative, sound-money Democrat, he disliked the platform of William Jennings Bryan and in 1904 gave his support to Alton B. Parker, who won the Democratic nomination. Discouraged by the prospects of the Democratic party after Parker's defeat in 1904 and Bryan's in 1908, House turned temporarily from politics to tours of Europe and spiritualism.

In November 1911 House met Woodrow Wilson, with whom he quickly formed a close and long-lasting friendship. He advised Wilson on political matters during Wilson's 1912 campaign for the Democratic nomination and the presidency. After Wilson's election House played a key role in patronage decisions, eventually placing five friends in the cabinet, although he refused any cabinet position for himself. During the winter of 1912–1913 House joined the circle of presidential intimates dedicated to advancing Wilson's political career and to maintaining Wilson's physical and emotional well-being. House was a shrewd political infighter who liked people and understood how to move them. He performed all sorts of political tasks, such as mediating quarrels within the Democratic party, which the president found distasteful, and he catered to many of Wilson's personal needs. Thanks to House's gently deferential manner, his lack of

assertiveness, and his assurances of affection and support, he soon become Wilson's most trusted confidant.

House developed a deep and genuine admiration for Wilson. He believed that inspired leadership could solve the nation's problems and bring its spiritual regeneration, and in Wilson he found an effective political leader who embodied his own moral and political values. The president's first wife, Ellen Axson Wilson, who had a keen insight into her husband's emotional makeup, sought House's advice on both personal and political matters. Her death in August 1914 left Wilson in despair and caused him to lean even more heavily on House for companionship and emotional support. Wilson's second wife, Edith Bolling Galt, whom he met in March 1915 and married in December, was a different sort of person. She was lively and attractive but poorly educated and underestimated House's value as a personal and political adviser. Wilson had imprudently drawn her into his work, showing her House's letters and many important state papers; he encouraged her to believe that her judgment was as good as that of his experienced advisers. House resented Edith's influence. After Wilson's marriage to Galt, the remarkable intimacy between the two men lessened. They remained dependent on one another but the closeness of their early years faded.

In 1913 and 1914, as Wilson pushed his New Freedom agenda through Congress, House served as a high-level political intermediary, helping fuse the needs of many special interest groups into a coherent, moderate legislative program. He collaborated with Wilson in moving the Democratic party away from its traditional advocacy of states' rights and limited government toward an extension of federal authority over the nation. House's visits to the White House excited much speculation, as journalists labeled him a taciturn man of mystery and exaggerated his influence with the president.

In the early summer of 1914, House saw a European crisis developing. When World War I broke out in August, House was the first member of the administration to inform himself about the complexities of the struggle and to grapple seriously with the dangers and opportunities the war posed for the United States. As Wilson began to appreciate the magnitude of the conflict and the difficulties of U.S. neutrality, he turned to House for advice and sent him to European capitals to talk with belligerent leaders. Wilson failed to inform his secretary of state, William Jennings Bryan, of many of House's activities. A longtime anglophile who identified with the Allied cause, House sent back from Europe vivid, detailed letters on every phase of the war. He also dramatized these missions, exaggerating the possibilities for peace and his influence on European leaders.

Prior to U.S. entry into the war in 1917, House undertook two missions to Europe. During the first, from January to June 1915, he visited London, Paris, and Berlin, and learned that the Allies were not prepared to think seriously about ending the conflict. He sympathized with their position and sought to cultivate their goodwill. After the sinking of the *Lusitania* on 7 May 1915, with the loss of U.S. lives, tension heightened between the United States and Germany. House now viewed the war as a struggle between democracy and autocracy and became convinced that U.S. intervention was inevitable. One way or another, House wanted to guarantee an Allied victory. Wilson, on the other hand, viewed U.S. mediation as a way in which to end the war. The president still believed that the United States could remain aloof, and he was not yet willing to use U.S. military power to ensure an Allied triumph.

Wilson sent House on another mission to Europe, although it is clear that the two men had different notions of what was to be achieved. During his second trip, from January to March 1916, House negotiated a memorandum with British Foreign Secretary Sir Edward Grey in which the two conferees agreed that, on a signal from the Allies, Wilson would propose a peace conference to put an end to the war. If Germany refused to attend the conference or, once there, insisted on unreasonable terms, the United States "would probably enter the war against Germany." Because the Allies refused to invoke the House-Grey Memorandum, this scheme was never tested, and the differences between House and Wilson never rose to the surface. On 31 January 1917 Germany announced resumption of unrestricted submarine warfare: all vessels, enemy and neutral, found near British waters would be attacked. On 3 February Washington severed diplomatic relations with Berlin. On 25 February, Wilson learned of a telegram sent to Mexico by German Undersecretary of State Arthur Zimmerman proposing a military alliance. These events, along with the sinking of U.S. ships by German U-boats, ended all hopes for peace and led directly to the U.S. declaration of war against Germany on 6 April 1917.

After U.S. intervention, House continued to be Wilson's closest foreign policy adviser. Bryan had resigned as secretary of state in June 1915, and his successor, Robert Lansing, never won the president's confidence. House consulted with the president over his plans for peace and served as his special diplomatic emissary to the Allied governments. In September 1917 Wilson directed House to assemble a group of experts, eventually known as "the Inquiry," to study U.S. war aims and to plan for peace negotiations. In late October, House traveled to Europe to participate in inter-Allied military discussions and to seek their agreement on war aims. He returned to the United States empty-handed and helped draft Wilson's unilateral statement of aims—the Fourteen Points of 8 January 1918. In the summer of 1918 Wilson assigned House the responsibility for preparing a covenant for a League of Nations, and he and the president exchanged drafts in the ensuing months. In October, when Germany sought peace on the basis of the Fourteen Points, Wilson again dispatched House to Europe to engage in prearmistice negotiations with the Allies. The success of these efforts led Wilson and House to overestimate U.S. influence and to remain convinced that out of the chaos of war a new community of nations would emerge, based on a League of Nations and a sweeping reconstruction of the international order.

As the Paris Peace Conference unfolded, differences emerged between Wilson and House on basic issues of the peace. House was more willing than the president to make concessions on key questions, such as reparations and Allied territorial demands. House's arrogance and ambition gradually became apparent to Wilson and other members of the U.S. delegation. At first, during the drafting of the League covenant, House and Wilson worked together, but a gap became apparent when Wilson returned to the United States in mid-February, and House took his place in deliberations with leaders of the chief wartime powers. House lacked the president's deep commitment to the Fourteen Points, as well as his distrust of the Allies. During Wilson's absence he accepted, despite the president's clear instructions to the contrary, French plans to occupy the left bank of the Rhine and the separation of the covenant of the League of Nations from a preliminary treaty with Germany. In mid-March, when Wilson returned to Paris and became aware of House's concessions, he lost confidence in his intimate adviser. For the remainder of Wilson's presidency, House was sidelined. Wilson rejected House's advice that, to assure U.S. membership in the League of Nations, he compromise with senators critical of the peace treaty. On 28 June 1919—when the Treaty of Versailles was signed—Wilson and House parted and never met again. In the fall, when Wilson became grievously ill, the presidential entourage did nothing to reunite the former friends. House claimed never to have understood why he had lost the confidence of the president.

During the 1920s House made frequent trips to Europe as a private citizen and energetically urged U.S. membership in the League of Nations and the World Court. He also sought to mediate bitter quarrels within the Democratic party and to strengthen the party's organization. In 1932 he supported Franklin D. Roosevelt for the presidential nomination. After Roosevelt's election House attempted to reestablish his role as a presidential confidant. Although House influenced some diplomatic appointments, the president seldom consulted him and he became increasingly critical of the New Deal. His unique career as a confidential adviser ended in frustration.

CHARLES E. NEU

See also Fourteen Points; Grey, Edward; Paris Peace Conference of 1919; Wilson, Thomas Woodrow; World War I

FURTHER READING

Floto, Inga. *Colonel House in Paris: A Study of American Policy at the Paris Peace Conference 1919*. Princeton, N.J., 1980.

Fowler, Wilton B. *British-American Relations, 1917–1918: The Role of Sir William Wiseman*. Princeton, N.J., 1969.

George, Juliette L., and Alexander George. *Woodrow Wilson and Colonel House: A Personality Study*. New York, 1956.

Heckscher, August. *Woodrow Wilson: A Biography*. New York, 1991.

Link, Arthur S. *Wilson*, 5 vols. Princeton, N.J., 1947–1965.

Neu, Charles E. "Woodrow Wilson and Colonel House: The Early Years, 1911–1915." In *The Wilson Era: Essays in Honor of Arthur S. Link*, edited by John Milton Cooper, Jr., and Charles E. Neu. Arlington Heights, Ill., 1991.

Seymour, Charles. *The Intimate Papers of Colonel House*, 4 vols. Boston, 1926–1928.

Weinstein, Edwin A. *Woodrow Wilson: A Medical and Psychological Biography*. Princeton, N.J., 1981.

HOUSE-GREY MEMORANDUM

See Grey, Edward; House, Edward Mandell

HUDSON'S BAY COMPANY

See Fur Trade

HUERTA, VICTORIANO

(*b*. 23 December 1854; *d*. 13 January 1916)

Commander of the Mexican Army (1911–1913), who turned against the government, deposed and arrested the president, and briefly assumed his office. A professional officer, Huerta served in the Mexican army, rising to the rank of general during the dictatorship of Porfirio Díaz, and remained on active duty under President Francisco Indalécio Madero's constitutional government, which replaced Díaz's dictatorship. In September 1912, however, Madero removed Huerta from his command on the grounds of disobedience of direct orders.

Madero's government faced a powerful insurrection that began on 9 February 1913, led by General Félix Díaz (nephew of the dictator) and Bernardo Reyes (Díaz's ex-minister of war). Madero recalled Huerta to active duty to put down the rebellion. Without prior U.S. government authorization, U.S. Ambassador Henry L. Wilson secured a truce between Huerta and rebel Díaz and plotted Madero's overthrow with them—the secret "pact of the embassy." On 17 February, Huerta joined the rebellion, proclaimed himself president, and had Madero arrested. On 22 February, Madero and his vice president were murdered. Ambassador Wilson, calling Huerta Mexico's savior, asked President William H. Taft to recognize the Huerta government. Taft had lost the 1912 election to Woodrow Wilson but was still president until Wilson's inauguration on 4 March. Taft deferred recognition while rebellions sprouted against Huerta. Once inaugurated, President Wilson recalled Ambassador Wilson and asked Huerta to resign on the grounds that he had overthrown the elected constitutional government. Instead, Huerta dissolved the congress and turned to Great Britain for weapons and loans. The U.S. government induced Great Britain to back down, organized the diplomatic isolation of the Huerta government, worked to deny it international loans, and imposed an arms embargo. Huerta refused to resign.

In early April 1914 crew members from the USS *Dolphin* disembarked in Tampico to load gasoline but entered a restricted wharf area without permission and were arrested and held for a brief time. They were released with an apology, but Admiral Henry T. Mayo, the commander of U.S. naval forces off Tampico, demanded that Mexican authorities hoist a U.S. flag and give it a twenty-one gun salute. Huerta refused. In response to this incident, President Wilson ordered the Atlantic fleet to Mexico. To prevent the unloading at Veracruz of a cargo of weapons consigned to Huerta from a German ship and to build up pressure to oust Huerta, Wilson ordered U.S. forces to seize Veracruz. The occupation was preceded by a severe bombardment that resulted in hundreds of Mexican casualties and generated violent demonstrations against the United States in several Mexican cities. U.S. forces occupied Veracruz for seven months.

Wilson and Huerta accepted international mediation. Rebel leader General Venustiano Carranza opposed U.S. intervention in Mexico and refused to accept international mediation while he pursued the war against Huerta. In July 1914, with his forces in broad retreat and still without having reached agreement with the United States, Huerta resigned and fled to Spain and later to Texas. Huerta's primary legacy is that he created the conditions to deepen U.S. intervention during the Mexican revolution.

JORGE I. DOMÍNGUEZ

See also Díaz, (José de la Cruz) Porfirio; Mexico

FURTHER READING

Gilderhus, Mark. *Diplomacy and Revolution: U.S.-Mexican Relations Under Wilson and Carranza*. Tucson, Ariz., 1977.

Grieb, Kenneth J. *The United States and Huerta*. Lincoln, Nebr., 1964.

Quirk, Robert E. *An Affair of Honor: Woodrow Wilson and the Occupation of Veracruz*. Louisville, Ky., 1962.

HUGHES, CHARLES EVANS

(*b*. 11 April 1862; *d*. 27 August 1948)

Secretary of state (1921–1925) in the administrations of Presidents Warren G. Harding and Calvin Coolidge and chief justice of the Supreme Court (1930–1941). A graduate of Brown University and Columbia Law School, Hughes had established a reputation for distinguished public service before he began his tenure at the Department of State, having been a moderately progressive governor of New York (1907–1910), associate justice of the Supreme Court (1910–1916), and Republican presidential candidate (1916). Bewhiskered, intellectually brilliant, and personally reserved (Theodore Roosevelt dubbed him "the bearded iceberg"), Hughes enjoyed the complete confidence of the two presidents he served as secretary of state. A harsh critic of Woodrow Wilson during the League of Nations controversy of 1919–1920, he was nonetheless a bona fide internationalist (albeit a conservative one) who believed that the United States must play a leading role in world affairs. "Foreign policies are not built upon abstractions," he once said. "They are the result of practical conceptions of national interest arising from some immediate exigency or standing out vividly in historical perspective." From that premise he proceeded to conduct the nation's diplomacy.

When the Harding administration took office in 1921, the United States was technically still at war with Germany because the United States had not ratified the Treaty of Versailles. Hughes devised an instrument whereby the United States would enjoy "all rights, privileges, indemnities, reparations, or advantages" accorded to it in the original peace settlement but with all references to the League of Nations eliminated. Upon the signing of this agreement, the Treaty of Berlin, on 25 August 1921, the war with Germany was at last declared at an end.

Serious problems growing out of World War I persisted, however, such as the economic instability in Germany that caused that nation to default on its $33 billion reparations bill to the Allies; the default was partly responsible for the suspension of payments by the Allies on their own $10 billion war debt to the United States. The situation was exacerbated by the highly protective Fordney-McCumber Tariff Act of 1922, which further limited the capacity of the British and French to obtain dollars and therefore make payments. To counter Allied demands for cancellation of their debts and to avert a general crisis, Hughes worked assiduously to establish an international commission to be run not by U.S. officials but by financial experts from the private sector. This approach would both sidestep the League of Nations and avoid formal commitments to any European government, thus shielding the Harding administration from isolationist critics in the Senate. The Dawes Plan of 1924 established a schedule for Germany's reparations payments and reduced the annual installments to a low of $250 million gradually increasing to $600 million; it also provided for a series of loans from Wall Street banks to Germany.

As a result, U.S. investments flowed into the German economy; the Germans accepted the scaled-down reparations obligation to the Allies; and the Allies began to pay back their debt to the United States. Although successful for a time and a credit to Hughes, the Dawes Plan collapsed by 1930 under the strain of the Great Depression.

Hughes's greatest claim to statesmanship rests on an achievement in a wholly different realm of diplomacy—disarmament. Despite Germany's prostration, all of the great powers, including the United States, had continued with their enormously costly naval building programs after the war. The competition was especially worrisome not only because of Great Britain's formidable, first-ranked fleet of capital ships, but also because Japan, the world's third greatest naval power, was becoming an increasing threat to U.S. interests in Asia. In addition, the ongoing Anglo-Japanese alliance of 1902 remained a source of concern; theoretically, a war between Japan and the United States could obligate Great Britain to side with Japan.

Hughes, the internationalist, considered the problem of expanding navies from other perspectives. For example, as an authentic conservative, he believed in balanced budgets; a renewed naval race would place an unconscionable strain on the financial resources of all nations and imprudently make their economies overly dependent on the production of weapons. Hughes also strove to redeem the lives of those 112,000 Americans (not to mention millions of Europeans) who had perished in World War I. Responding to demands at home and abroad for multilateral reductions in military outlays, the secretary (with President Harding's enthusiastic support) invited representatives from eight nations to come to Washington to seek a way to avoid a renewed naval armaments race.

Hughes himself opened the first session of the highly publicized conference, on 12 November 1921. In stunned silence, his audience listened as he told them what must be done to prevent another race in naval armaments similar to the one that had preceded World War I. "We can no longer content ourselves with investigations, with statistics, with reports, with the circumspection of inquiry," he declared. "One program inevitably leads to another, and if competition continues, its regulation is impracticable. There is only one way out and that is to end it now." With these words the secretary of state set in motion what would remain the only successful disarmament agreement in modern history until the 1987–1988 treaty limiting intermediate-range nuclear forces.

The Manchester *Guardian* did not exaggerate when it observed that "Hughes sank in thirty-five minutes more ships than all the admirals of the world have sunk in a cycle of centuries." The so-called Five Power Treaty required the United States, Great Britain, and Japan to scrap, respectively, 846,000 tons, 583,000 tons, and 450,000 tons of warships. The pact also imposed limits of 500,000 tons each for the United States and Great Britain, 300,000 for Japan, and 175,000 tons each for Italy and France (that is, limits based on a ratio of 5:5:3:1.75:1.75) and established a ten-year moratorium on the construction of capital ships. The Nine Power Treaty, signed by those five nations along with China, Belgium, Portugal, and the Netherlands, secured formal recognition of the principle of the "Open Door" in Asia and obliged the British and the Japanese to abrogate their military alliance, while Japan agreed to withdraw from China's Shantung Peninsula and from Siberia.

Notwithstanding his accomplishment in leading the United States and the world community to such meaningful accords, Hughes was unable to realize the internationalist goal of bringing the United States into the Permanent Court of International Justice. In February 1923 he drafted a proposal to that end and sent it to the Senate. Carefully worded to accommodate the views of the small but influential isolationist bloc, the recommendation avoided the implication of formal relations with the League of Nations, made the submission of disputes to the World Court strictly voluntary, and reserved to the United States the right to approve any changes in the court's procedures as long as it was a member. Even with these limitations, the Senate did not accept the proposal until 1926; by then, so many other qualifications had been added that the court itself rejected the petition. Despite repeated attempts to revive the proposition during the next decade, the United States never became a member of the court.

Meanwhile, in 1925, Hughes had decided to resign as secretary of state. Three years later, to the gratification of Republican and Democratic internationalists alike, he accepted a seat on the World Court, where he remained until President Herbert Hoover appointed him chief justice of the Supreme Court. During his eleven years on the high bench he advanced mainly moderately conservative views and staunchly opposed President Franklin Roosevelt's court-packing plan. Although Hughes retired from public life in 1941, Secretary of State Cordell Hull frequently consulted him on matters pertaining to postwar international organization.

Hughes's stewardship of the Department of State was skillful, steady, substantive, and salutary. He conducted a foreign policy that was neither globalist in the Cold War meaning of that term nor isolationist. A conservative internationalist, Hughes helped the United States adjust to its post-Versailles role as a world power.

THOMAS J. KNOCK

See also Coolidge, Calvin; Dawes Plan; Germany; Harding, Warren; Isolationism; League of Nations; Permanent Court of International Justice; Reparations; War Debt of World War I; Washington Conference on the Limitation of Armaments

FURTHER READING
Glad, Betty. *Charles Evans Hughes and the Illusions of Innocence: A Study in American Diplomacy.* Urbana, Ill., 1966.
———. "Charles Evans Hughes: Rationalism and Foreign Affairs." In *Studies in American Diplomacy*, edited by Norman Graebner. New York, 1985.
Hughes, Charles Evans. *The Pathway of Peace.* New York, 1925.
Perkins, Dexter. *Charles Evans Hughes and American Diplomatic Statesmanship.* Boston, 1956.
Pusey, Merlo J. *Charles Evans Hughes*, 2 vols. New York, 1951.

HULL, CORDELL
(*b.* 2 October 1871; *d.* 23 July 1955)

Member of the U.S. House of Representatives (1907–1921, 1923–1931) and the Senate (1931–1933), and secretary of state (1933–1944) for a period longer than any other person who has served in that position. Hull battled to liberalize world trade, led the movement to make President Franklin D. Roosevelt's Good Neighbor Policy a reality, labored to deter Japanese expansion in Asia, and fostered the United Nations. By the time he assumed cabinet rank, the sixty-one-year-old Hull had been in politics for more than forty years. Born in a log cabin in the mountains of middle Tennessee, Hull came from a family that was just beginning to work its way out of poverty. Education was important to the Hulls. They could not afford a store-bought shirt but managed to scrape together the money to send Cordell to a private elementary school. When the family's fortunes improved, Hull was able to attend colleges in Kentucky and Ohio before returning to Tennessee to study law. He was admitted to the bar in 1891.

Although Hull entered the practice of law at the age of twenty, his real love was politics. He gave his first political stump speech when only sixteen. At nineteen he was elected to the Democratic party's state convention, where hard work earned him the chairmanship of his county delegation. In 1892, at the age of twenty, he was elected to the Tennessee legislature, where he served for five years. As would any aspiring politician, Hull captained a company of volunteers that served in the occupation of Cuba following the Spanish-American-Cuban-Filipino War of 1898. He was appointed a circuit judge for middle Tennessee in 1903 and won a seat in the U.S. House of Representatives in 1906. Repeatedly reelected, except in the Republican landslide of 1920, Hull also was elected to the Senate in 1931.

The foreign policy issues and managerial style that characterized his tenure as secretary of state were clearly developed during his congressional years. In Congress,

Hull was meticulous in his research and made it a point not to speak on a subject until he knew as much as or more than any other person who might speak on the same topic. While still in his teens, Hull had become persuaded that the greatest obstacle to free competition was the protective tariff, and, once in Congress, he showed little interest in anything other than tariff and tax questions. Hull initially thought of the tariff as an affront to his constituents, but World War I forced him to think in larger terms; he concluded that a global system of free trade was necessary if there was going to be worldwide prosperity and economic growth. In 1916 and again in 1919, Hull had sought a postwar international conference to discuss ways to remove the old economic policies that had helped bring on the war and to fashion an order that would encourage free trade.

Not surprisingly then, when President-elect Franklin D. Roosevelt approached Hull to be secretary of state, Hull sought and received assurances from the president-elect that as secretary he would have a free hand to negotiate reciprocal tariff reduction agreements. Hull's liberal commercial world view, however, had a far greater impact on U.S. foreign relations than simply negotiating reduced tariffs. In the secretary's mind, there was no significant difference between bloated trusts employing the protective tariff in the United States and Nazi Germany and Imperial Japan militarily imposing economic control over Europe and East Asia. Each group sought to deny hardworking Americans an opportunity to build something worthwhile.

When he spoke about the tariff as a member of Congress, Hull reviled the Republican party for fastening on the country "the sleepless monster of protection, clothed in the livery of the law, [which] has invaded every American home and exacted its 'pound of flesh.'" He declared that the "chief underlying cause of existing economic, financial, and social ills is traceable to this partnership of the government with crime—the protective tariff." As Secretary of State, Hull's diplomatic language was more circumspect but his feelings were no less intense. Hull argued that by seeking to dominate militarily the economic resources of vast regions of the world, the Axis powers would undo the social, political, and economic progress the world had enjoyed for the past five hundred years.

Given the magnitude of the threat Hull perceived in the aggressor nations, a war to stop them became a reasonable alternative, but when he spoke publicly about the threat the aggressor states posed, he stressed the need for nations to abide by the principles of right conduct embodied in such treaties as the Nine Power Treaty to protect China and the Kellogg-Briand Pact to outlaw war. Because of such rhetoric he was labeled an idealist or legalist rather than pragmatic diplomat, but Hull was more practical in conducting diplomacy than his moralistic public rhetoric suggested. He never considered simple military aggression or violation of a treaty a just cause for war and did not advise confronting Japan or Germany when they violated international law. It was only when those nations sought to impose a world economic order that threatened vital U.S. interests that Hull advocated resistance, and then only when he was certain the United States was prepared to mount the force necessary to stop the Axis.

Although he was inflexible where his basic principles were involved, Hull was not confrontational in his style. In political as well as diplomatic negotiations he preferred to avoid discussion of specific issues (which might be difficult to resolve) in favor of finding a common principle that would remove most of the points of disagreement. This technique worked well at a series of Latin American conferences where Hull found common ground on general principles with his Latin American neighbors in the era of the Good Neighbor Policy. His desire to get along, however, did not shelter him from attacks by other members of the Roosevelt administration; Secretary of the Treasury Henry Morgenthau, Jr. and Secretary of the Interior Harold Ickes were two of his most persistent critics. Hull was cautious in an administration filled with bold risk-takers. He was a New Freedom Wilsonian surrounded by economic nationalists who sought to restore prosperity through a planned economy. Moreover, Hull was the southern mountaineer educated at no-name colleges in an administration full of brains-trusters. His tenure of office was a constant fight to keep control of the reigns of foreign policy. An adept political maneuverer, he bided his time when faced with an initial defeat and, more often than not, was successful in eventually undercutting his adversary's position.

For example, as soon as Hull entered office and began planning for his reciprocal trade agreements program, he was blocked by the economic planners who believed that free trade would disrupt their carefully calculated plans for restarting the national economy. Hull took this setback quietly and in 1934 was able to gain passage of the Johnson Act, which authorized negotiation of bilateral trade agreements that would substantially reduce tariffs. Not only did Hull get the legislation he wanted, he made sure that the implementation of that policy would be in his hands, not those of the economic nationalists. In 1934 he also helped secure the formation of the Export-Import Bank to stimulate U.S. foreign trade.

Roosevelt could not afford to alienate his secretary, who was popular both within the Democratic party and across the nation. (Hull was a leading contender for the Democratic nomination for president in 1940 until Roosevelt decided to seek a third term.) Roosevelt, however, found Hull's perpetual caution tiresome. Hull would not venture a recommendation to the president or send an instruction to an ambassador on an important diplomatic issue without examining the subject at lengthy, tedious staff meetings. That these detailed reviews consumed vast amounts of time and energy did not faze Hull. Hard work was his strength. He rarely took a day off and frequently held staff meetings on Sunday mornings. He shunned the diplomatic dinner circuit in favor of working in his study at home. He had no outside interests other than croquet; in fact, while secretary of state he took the time to see only one motion picture (*Sergeant York*, in which he was portrayed). As years went by he took longer and more frequent vacations, but these were actually efforts to control the tuberculosis that was eating away his lungs, an illness that was a well-kept secret in Washington.

Frustrated by Hull's slowness to act, Roosevelt frequently initiated policy without consulting Hull—often by giving some other member of the administration permission to take the initiative. After 1938 the president increasingly relied on Undersecretary Sumner Welles to carry out his diplomatic initiatives—but Hull was not powerless. He jealously guarded his "turf" on reciprocal trade agreements, Pan-American relations, and U.S.-Japanese relations. When another member of the Roosevelt administration tried to alter one of Hull's policies, the secretary exercised his considerable influence to alter or block the new policy or at least limit its impact. Occasionally, and almost always successfully, Hull asked the president to control a fellow cabinet member or some lower-ranking bureaucrat who was challenging the secretary's authority. Hull was shrewd enough to avoid such a head-on confrontation with Welles, who enjoyed unlimited, direct access to the president, but in 1943 Hull secretly used reports of Welles's homosexuality to force his undersecretary to resign. In the ongoing struggle to control power in Washington, Hull could outmaneuver almost everyone, given enough time.

The greatest challenge to Hull's control over foreign affairs involved policy toward Japan during 1937-1941. Throughout the nation and the administration there were calls to stop Japan's war in China. Hull refused to yield to such initiatives, even when put forward by the president, and crafted a policy that avoided any confrontation with Japan while it refused to accept Japan's New Order in East Asia. As Japanese-American relations deteriorated, "hawks" within the administration pushed for economic sanctions against Japan while "doves" urged a conciliatory policy to embolden Japanese moderates. The secretary rejected both approaches and held enough power to make his decision final. But control of policy was becoming more difficult as proliferating Washington agencies sought to impose sanctions against Japan under the guise of economic mobilization at home. By 1941, Japan was consuming almost all of his time. When he was not beating back overzealous bureaucrats or deflecting one of the president's few initiatives in Japanese-American relations, Hull was trying to persuade Japan to abandon its autarkic ways and embrace liberal commercialism. By the end of November 1941, discouraged and exhausted, Hull gave up diplomacy and handed over the issue to the War and Navy departments.

During World War II, Hull's influence declined as diplomatic issues melded with military issues personally handled by the commander-in-chief. Hull continued in office through most of 1944 and worked to help establish the United Nations, but his failing health and hospitalization reduced his influence and made his retirement inevitable. Hull formally left office on 30 November 1944, and a year later he was awarded the Nobel Peace Prize for his efforts in establishing the United Nations.

In his retirement, Hull kept up with international affairs but made no public comments on government policy. He wrote a two-volume memoir that chronicled foreign policy during three Roosevelt administrations but revealed little that was personal about himself. Popular during his lifetime, Hull has not received strong posthumous acclaim: many historians have concluded that Roosevelt acted as his own secretary of state, while others, writing in the Cold War years, have dismissed Hull as an idealist. His humble southern mountain origins also have led some critics to assume that he lacked the stature for the job; but as many people within the Roosevelt administration discovered to their dismay, Hull was a formidable adversary who had considerable influence on the conduct of U.S. foreign relations in the eras of the Great Depression and World War II.

JONATHAN G. UTLEY

See also Free Trade; Good Neighbor Policy; Idealism; Isolationism; Japan; Kellogg-Briand Pact; Kennedy, Joseph Patrick; Pearl Harbor, Attack on; Roosevelt, Franklin Delano; Tariffs; United Nations; Welles, Sumner; Wilson, Thomas Woodrow; World War II

FURTHER READING

Adams, Frederick C. *Economic Diplomacy: The Export-Import Bank and American Foreign Policy*. Columbia, Mo., 1976.

Dallek, Robert C. *Franklin D. Roosevelt and American Foreign Policy, 1932–1945*. New York, 1979.

Gelman, Irwin F. *Secret Affairs: Franklin Roosevelt, Cordell Hull, and Sumner Welles*. Baltimore, Md., 1995.

Hinton, Harold. *Cordell Hull: A Biography*. Garden City, N.Y., 1942.

Hull, Cordell. *The Memoirs of Cordell Hull*, 2 vols. New York, 1948.

Jablon, Howard. *Crossroads of Decision: The State Department and Foreign Relations*. Lexington, Ky., 1983.

Pratt, Julius W. "Cordell Hull, 1933–1944." Vols. 12 and 13 of *The American Secretaries of State and Their Diplomacy*. New York, 1964.

Utley, Jonathan G. *Going to War with Japan, 1937–1941*. Knoxville, Tenn., 1985.

HUMANITARIAN INTERVENTION AND RELIEF

Humanitarian intervention is generally the use of armed force by a state or group of states to prevent or terminate massive human rights violations that the government of the target state commits against its own citizens. Humanitarian relief is the provision of urgent assistance in the form of food, medical supplies, clothing, and the like to people suffering due to man-made devastation and warfare or natural disasters. Few concepts have generated greater controversy or cynicism than humanitarian intervention, because history confirms that humanitarian intervention is inextricably linked to the general and more ominous concept of intervening in another state's internal affairs. In other words, some interventions may be justified based on "humanitarian purposes," when in fact the real motive is to achieve power or maintain an advantage rather than to provide humanitarian assistance to oppressed people.

Until the late 1980s, there were few reservations about the concept of humanitarian relief. On the contrary, the frequent occurrence of natural and man-made disasters has required genuine humanitarian responses to alleviate mass suffering. Although more recent humanitarian relief operations, such as the ones in Bosnia-Herzegovina and Somalia, have drawn widespread criticism, few would dispute that such missions are still the most acceptable facet of the international community's response to human crises.

When Is an Intervention Humanitarian?

There is no scholarly consensus on what constitutes humanitarian intervention. Two sets of arguments are examined here—the specific criteria definition and the legal test. Some scholars and analysts contend there are specific criteria that an armed intervention must fulfill to be classified as humanitarian. These usually include a situation in which the target state's government commits, or contemplates committing, large-scale atrocities against its own citizens; the intervening powers limit the scope of their intervention agenda, in particular to an emphasis on stopping or preventing mass killings rather than on expanding their own influence on the target state; the action is nonconsensual and forceful; there is a preference for multilateral force interventions, sanctioned by the United Nations or by regional organizations; and force is used only as a last resort once nonforcible options have been exhausted.

This list of defining criteria is by no means comprehensive. Some analysts have argued that the first criterion should not be confined to the protection of the target state's citizens, but should also include the protection of any people whose human rights are threatened in the tar-

get area. Among classic examples they point to are the 1964 Stanleyville rescue mission in the Congo, when the United States, Great Britain, and Belgium worked to evacuate more than 1,000 foreign nationals held as hostages by a rebel group, and the 1965 U.S. intervention in the Dominican Republic to protect the lives of U.S. and foreign nationals. The validity of both cases as instances of humanitarian intervention has been challenged. The Stanleyville operation has been criticized as undue interference in the internal affairs of the Congo and as tilting the balance in the Congolese conflict in favor of the Leopoldville government, thus violating the criterion of limited objectives. The Dominican intervention has been criticized for the discrepancy between the professed goals of the operation and the final outcome.

Other analysts have argued that there is an inherent conflict between the criterion of limited objectives and the termination of gross human rights abuses that often result from structural violence. In cases where a regime systematically persecutes its own population, it is highly unlikely that any intervention short of overthrowing the regime will stop the persecution. An example is the 1978–1979 Vietnamese intervention in Cambodia, which led to the overthrow of the genocidal regime of Pol Pot, and the 1979 Tanzanian intervention in Uganda, which led to the overthrow of the brutal dictatorship of Idi Amin. Although both interventions are routinely criticized and rejected as instances of humanitarian intervention, primarily because they also protected the regional interests of Vietnam and Tanzania, no one can seriously argue that either the Pol Pot or the Idi Amin regime exhibited any capacity for humane governance.

Some analysts contend that humanitarian intervention should also include assistance given to national liberation movements. These efforts have not been very successful. Although the UN General Assembly's Declaration on the Granting of Independence to Colonial Countries and Peoples (1960) was the first major step toward the acknowledgment of self-determination as a legal right, the use of force to promote self-determination, let alone any legal entitlement to external assistance in the process, remains highly controversial. The record has shown that the international community is prepared to tolerate, at best, rather than endorse the use of force, particularly in cases where these liberation movements initiate rather than respond to force. Moreover, state practice has exhibited a very restrictive understanding of what constitutes self-determination, associating it almost exclusively with colonial situations.

The second argument centers on the legality of humanitarian intervention and the lessons to be learned from state practice. In this context, a distinction is usually drawn between the periods before and after the establishment of the United Nations in 1945. Two important provisions of the UN Charter are particularly relevant. The first prohibits the threat or use of force, except in cases of individual or collective self-defense. The second advances the promotion of human rights as one of the fundamental purposes of the United Nations.

There is near-universal consensus that before the 1945 Charter, there were few if any legal restrictions on the use of force in interstate relations and hardly any internationally accepted standards on what constituted lawful conduct on the part of a country's ruler toward its citizens. This, however, did not prevent states from both using force and justifying it on humanitarian grounds. What complicated the issue was that those humanitarian uses of force almost invariably involved Western hegemonic powers who intervened in the internal affairs of states they considered "uncivilized." The repeated interventions against the Ottoman Empire, supported by the Concert of Europe during the nineteenth century, are a good example. Undoubtedly, the outcome of several of these interventions increased humanitarian awareness, but the selective nature of these undertakings sustained and reinforced the growing inequality of legal capacities between the enforcers and the target states. This inequality proved to be a major fault line in legitimizing the normative parameters of the international system.

Because there was no conventional law on humanitarian intervention in the pre-UN Charter era, customary law of the time is the only way to assess whether a country had the right to intervene on humanitarian grounds. There is some debate about whether a customary right to intervene on humanitarian grounds was annulled by the UN Charter's prohibition of the threat or use of force. Two criteria, however, are usually offered to indicate the presence of a customary rule of international law—state practice consistent with the rule in question and a perception that there is a legal obligation to abide by that rule. While some states have relied on the first criterion to justify their intervention on humanitarian grounds, the second criterion has proven to be much more elusive. Repeated analyses of case studies have focused almost exclusively on the necessity of intervention rather than on the act of intervention as a legal obligation of the intervening state.

In the post-1945 period, the UN Charter's promotion of human rights and the growing corpus of international human rights law are usually cited to support the legality of humanitarian intervention. International human rights law has indeed legalized noncoercive action in response to human rights violations, including primarily humanitarian relief operations, fact-finding missions, reports, recommendations, and state and individual complaints procedures of the regional human rights systems, especially the European and inter-American ones. In addition, the international community has been legally empowered to intervene in certain cases of extreme and massive human rights violations. Examples include the precedent-setting Security Council Resolution 418 of 4 November 1977, which imposed an arms embargo against the apartheid regime of South Africa, as well as the Genocide Convention of 9 December 1948, which empowered any contracting party to take appropriate action to prevent and suppress genocide.

While these are important developments, two things must be kept in mind. First, despite the international community's empowerment, its response has not been consistent with the enormity of the problem of human rights abuses. Second, there is a gray area between noncoercive action and massive human rights abuses, amounting to genocidal massacres for which the international community has at best a precarious legal basis for action. In the past, responses to matters in this gray area have been determined primarily on the basis of geopolitical considerations rather than human rights.

History of U.S. Intervention

The interventionist tradition in U.S. foreign policy is closely associated with the cluster of ideas known as liberal democratic internationalism. These ideas, fully articulated during the presidency of Woodrow Wilson (1913–1921), include a commitment to national self-determination; a belief in democratic governance, which can also contribute to a more peaceful international system; the promotion of a liberal international economic order to combat the debilitating effects of mercantilism; and the espousal of a system of genuine collective security in which the strong moral leadership of the United States would eradicate the balance-of-power machinations traditionally favored by the European powers.

Two main factors contributed to the popularity of liberal democratic internationalism. These were a growing capacity to project U.S. influence beyond the country's borders and an opportunity to shape the international system after the devastation of World War I. The first effort to project broader U.S. influence was formally launched with the Monroe Doctrine (1823) and in particular with the doctrine's warning to European powers that the United States "should consider any attempt on their part to extend their system to any portion of this hemisphere as dangerous to our peace and safety." While the doctrine also declared that the American continent was off-limits to any future European colonization, it was the warning against European expansionism into any country in the Western hemisphere that primarily reflected U.S. perceptions about its hemispheric role as protectors and moral superiors in relation to the rest of America and its European competitors.

In this context, World War I proved to be an important turning point. The United States realized that hemispheric peace and safety could not be insulated from the events unfolding in Europe. The call to make the world "safe for democracy" signaled an acknowledgment that the world's nations were becoming interdependent and a belief that democratically governed states could best promote their own self interests by pursuing communal welfare in the New World Order. In the process, the United States had to implicitly renounce its policy of noninvolvement in European affairs (another tenet of the Monroe Doctrine).

Despite its considerable appeal, liberal democratic internationalism has generated great controversy among policymakers and scholars. Realist policymakers, such as Richard Nixon and Henry Kissinger, and analysts and commentators, such as George Kennan and Hans Morgenthau, criticized its penchant for incorporating values such as democracy and human rights in the conduct of interstate relations, which introduced a moralizing dimension in balance-of-power calculations. As a result, they said, it contributed to a "naive belief" that promoting democratic values worldwide could take the place of timely and decisive projections of power in protecting the country's vital national security interests. Among their favorite targets were Wilson's performance at the 1919 Versailles Peace Conference and President Jimmy Carter's human rights policies.

Liberal democratic internationalism has also come under attack by circles, such as left-liberal analysts and commentators, that share some of its fundamental beliefs. In particular, they have criticized its failure to consistently act on its moral commitment. Instead of a preponderance of naive idealism, these critics have argued, the U.S. record demonstrates the perennial subsumption of concerns about human rights and democratic governance under realist considerations. They point to a long history of U.S. involvement in Central and Latin American affairs (since the proclamation of the Monroe Doctrine), in European affairs (during World War I), and in world affairs (since World War II). In this process, they detect precious few instances in which the United States has made humanitarian considerations a priority, more so than other concerns.

In this context, the Spanish-American-Cuban-Filipino War of 1898 and the concomitant U.S. "humanitarian intervention" on behalf of the Cuban rebellion against the Spanish monarchy had less to do with the freedom and independence of the Cuban people and more with the U.S. desire to ensure that the colonial possessions of a weakened Spain would not fall prey to the ambitions of predatory European powers. Likewise, U.S. intervention in Haiti in 1915 and in the Dominican Republic in 1916 had less to do with promoting democracy and more with U.S. fears of a European attempt to exert a controlling influence in the affairs of politically corrupt and fiscally irresponsible Caribbean governments.

In a similar vein, the containment of Communism during the Cold War spawned a whole set of interventionary activities of questionable domestic and international legality. The turning point came with the Vietnam War, which had less to do with the Vietnamese people's quest for self-determination and more with Washington's obsession with the domino effect of Communist influence in Southeast Asia. In fact, it has been argued that it was Washington's failure to perceive the Vietnamese conflict as an anticolonial rather than an anticommunist struggle that contributed to the ensuing debacle.

These controversies point to an inherent tension in the liberal democratic internationalist vision. The attempt to incorporate norms relating to the rule of law, to democratic governance, and to human rights in policymaking has sustained the creative tension between the state-centered and society-centered conceptions of order. It is a tension to which the realist vision has paid lip-service, given its exclusive preoccupation with the distribution of power among states and with externally induced challenges to that distribution. The liberal vision, in its efforts to address intrastate as well as interstate concerns, has conspicuously broadened the agenda. In the process, it has transformed issues relating to societal security, such as state repression and failure to meet basic human needs, into issues of legitimate international concern. Thus, part of the liberal internationalist predicament (confusion, according to its critics) stems from the uneasy cohabitation of the aforementioned two conceptions of order.

Post-Cold War Intervention Policy and Challenges

The end of the Cold War and the premature pronouncement of a New World Order triggered the United States's ongoing quest for a sound national security policy with an unwelcome sense of urgency. This goes beyond the painful readjustment associated with a transitional period. For the first time in its history, the United States must operate within parameters that challenge the fundamental premises of the Westphalian system, which emerged in the aftermath of the Thirty Years' War (1618-1648) and was premised on the idea that juridically equal, sovereign states would be the central actors of the international system. In the process, the notions of humanitarian intervention and relief have compounded the growing complexity of the post-Cold War era.

One of the most pressing tasks for U.S. policymakers is to provide a coherent and consistent response to what one analyst has aptly called "the challenge of the weak state," namely a state "that is in the grips of a war of internal fragmentation or that is in any sense ungovernable, either as a consequence of civil strife or overwhelming humanitarian crisis." The more recent prominence of weak states has dealt a serious blow to the notion of the integral state, the fundamental building block of the international system.

The main problem that the international community has to confront—especially in cases of massive civil strife—is the capacity of subnational actors, such as ethnic, religious, and cultural groups, to question not only the legitimacy of the rulers of a certain nation-state, but also the integrity of the nation-state as a frame of reference for resolving the conflict. More ominously, subnational actors have challenged the possibility of coexisting with other forces in the same public space, even when the resulting framework guarantees their privileged access to power. An example of this is the quest of the Bosnian Serbs for a separate Bosnian Serb state, which challenges not simply the legitimacy of the larger unit (Bosnia-Herzegovina), but also the capacity of the international community to provide a solution acceptable to all sides (as the failed initiatives of the European Union, of the CSCE (OSCE) and of the United Nations have amply demonstrated). As crises in several parts of the world have shown, subnational insecurity (the main legacy of weak states) challenges both the relevance of the nation-state and the international community's methods for a credible response.

Any response to civil strife in weak multiethnic states must take into account the following key features and consequences of such conflicts in these areas. First, they are fought by both regular armies and irregular units, such as militias and armed civilians. The latter often exhibit little discipline and also loose links to their central chain of command. This provides the official civilian and military leadership with an added advantage. On one hand, they can reap the military benefits of the irregular units' field operations. On the other hand, they can escape all blame for their transgressions of international humanitarian law, claiming that these units are beyond their control.

Second, genocidal policies, such as ethnic cleansing, are easier to implement in a state with ethnic dispersion. Thus, in a territory like Boznia-Herzegovina, where pockets of one ethnic group are dispersed throughout the territory controlled by another ethnic group, it is entirely possible to have a cease-fire along the frontline (which is often unstable and not clearly demarcated), while warlike activities continue in the interior. These activities can escape monitoring because of their location and their perpetrators, namely paramilitary, "politically irresponsible" units.

Third, these weak-state conflicts often lead to a total breakdown of state institutions and thus social norms and values. Therefore, for any intervention to be effective, it must tackle the root causes of violence. This means that intrastate conflicts require a long-term involvement by the international community to ensure they do not recur. In his 1992 *Agenda for Peace*, UN Secretary General Boutros Boutros-Ghali characterized this type of involvement as post-conflict peace building. This refers to "comprehensive efforts to identify and support structures which will tend to consolidate peace and advance a sense of confidence and well-being among people."

Fourth, these conflicts exhibit an increasing politicization of humanitarian relief operations. This politicization is spawned by the aforementioned decentralized conduct of war and the dispersion of ethnic enclaves throughout the contested territory. Traditionally, the protocol for humanitarian relief operations has been to deliver aid to civilian war victims in an impartial and comprehensive manner, but this is exactly why the combatants challenge humanitarian relief. In their minds, a continued delivery of supplies to the opposing side enhances the opponents' standing and ability to pursue the conflict, undermining the combatants' war aims. The more successful the relief operation is viewed by the international community, the more likely the combatants will perceive it as a weapon of war.

Therefore, the efforts undertaken by the UN Operation in Somalia I (UNOSOM 1) as part of the 100-Day Action Programme for Accelerated Humanitarian Assistance to deliver food and other supplies to the victims were continuously frustrated by rival Somali factions in their quest for territorial control. The extortion, blackmail, and robbery of this international relief effort and repeated attacks on UN personnel and equipment led to the adoption in 1992 of UN Security Council Resolution 794 (Operation Restore Hope), authorizing use of "all necessary means to establish as soon as possible a secure environment for humanitarian relief operations in Somalia."

Finally, the increasing politicization of humanitarian relief operations sooner or later generates the need to protect them with force. As noted earlier, combatants will not look upon a successful provision of relief supplies to their opponents as an impartial gesture. When their ability to continue delivery of these supplies is challenged, the providers must inevitably confront the option to use force. This option can not be credibly exercised without taking sides in the conflict, and this abandonment of neutrality is fraught with potentially ominous consequences.

Thus, in the case of Somalia, the United Somali Congress/Somali National Alliance (USC/SNA) eventually perceived the UNOSOM II efforts to protect the local people and to pursue humanitarianism as subversive, undermining its authority and promoting the process of national reconciliation at its own expense. The ensuing challenge to UNOSOM II's mandate and the 5 June 1993 attacks on UNOSOM II troops led to the UN decision to shed its traditional neutrality and take forceful action against the USC/SNA. This confrontation culminated with the 3 October 1993 incident in which U.S. Army Rangers launched an operation in southern Mogadishu to capture some key aides of USC/SNA leader General Mohammed Farah Aidid. In the process, eighteen U.S. soldiers were killed and seventy-five were wounded. These casualties, coupled with the humiliating treatment to which the bodies of the dead soldiers were subjected, destroyed whatever U.S. consensus existed on the merits of UN peacekeeping operations.

U.S. Intervention Theory in the 1990s

The debate on the merits of humanitarian intervention is nothing new. The issue has become more complex, however, because of the absence of clearly defined U.S. national security interests and the proliferation of actors (particularly at the subnational level) who may adversely affect them. Moreover, the initial pronouncements of a New World Order, with its commitment to collective security and the rule of law, have contributed little analytical rigor to the quest for security. Rather, by reaffirming the legitimacy of societal security on the international security agenda, it has accentuated the tensions inherent in liberal democratic internationalism.

In such a context, the links between humanitarian intervention and relief are being redefined in the process of providing a credible response to humanitarian emergencies. While in the past these concepts were perceived as addressing different sets of humanitarian challenges, they are now viewed as simultaneously complementary and contradictory. This confusion stems from the ways in which the international community has responded to humanitarian crises and is reflected in two key aspects of these responses. First, humanitarian mandates have constantly been redefined and expanded. As the conflicts in Somalia and the former Yugoslavia have shown, the nonforcible task of establishing a secure environment for humanitarian relief operations slowly but steadily changes both the nature of the mandate (from traditional peacekeeping to aspects of post-conflict peace building) and the methods (from nonforcible to forcible measures under Chapter VII of the UN Charter). Second, the U.N. mandate calls for both humanitarian and peace-enforcement activities, and sometimes these activities conflict. For example, the same mandate that enforces peace by imposing economic sanctions also supplies food, medicine, and other supplies through its relief agencies, such as UNICEF and the World Health Organization. Once again, the UN situations in Somalia and the former Yugoslavia illustrate this conflicted mandate.

Perhaps the most disturbing aspect of post-Cold War humanitarian intervention that U.S. policymakers face is the progressive transformation of a relatively basic humanitarian response into a full-blown military engagement to protect the continued delivery of humanitarian assistance. Throughout its history, the U.S. has consistently supported a policy of selective interventionism. The quest for selective interventionism continues despite neoisolationist fears about a creeping indiscriminate interventionism (the latter based on a misreading of the lessons of the U.S. response to recent crises such as Bosnia, Somalia, and Haiti). What has changed in the process is not the selectivity per se, but whether there is a credible role for forcible and nonforcible humanitarian responses to the proliferation of subnational challenges. The impact of these challenges on national, regional, and international security continues to be studied and revealed.

GEORGE ANDREOPOULOS

See also Cold War; Congo; Dominican Republic; Genocide Convention; Human Rights; International Law; Monroe Doctrine; Somalia; Uganda; United Nations; Vietnam War; Yugoslavia

FURTHER READING

Bazyler, Michael J. "Reexamining the Doctrine of Humanitarian Intervention in Light of the Atrocities in Kampuchea and Ethiopia." *Stanford Journal of International Law* 23 (1987).

Boutros-Ghali, Boutros. *An Agenda for Peace. Preventive Diplomacy, Peacemaking and Peace-Keeping.* United Nations General Assembly, 17 June 1992.

———. *Supplement to an Agenda for Peace: Position Paper of the Secretary-General on the Occasion of the Fiftieth Anniversary of the United Nations.* United Nations General Assembly, 3 January 1995.

Bull, Hedley, ed. *Intervention in World Politics.* Oxford, 1984.

Cahill, Kevin M., ed. *A Framework for Survival: Health, Human Rights, and Humanitarian Assistance in Conflicts and Disasters.* New York, 1993.

Damrosch, Lori F., ed. *Enforcing Restraint. Collective Intervention in Internal Conflicts.* New York, 1993.

Deng, Francis M. *Protecting the Dispossessed.* Washington, D.C., 1993.

Falk, Richard A. *Human Rights and State Sovereignty.* New York, 1981.

Franck, Thomas M., and Nigel S. Rodley. "After Bangladesh: The Law of Humanitarian Intervention by Military Force." *American Journal of International Law* 67 (1973).

Human Rights Watch. *The Lost Agenda. Human Rights and U.N. Field Operations.* New York, 1993.

Lillich, Richard, ed. *Humanitarian Intervention and the United Nations.* Charlottesville, Va., 1973.

Scheffer, David J. "Toward a Modern Doctrine of Humanitarian Intervention." *University of Toledo Law Review* 23 (1992).

Smith, Gaddis. *The Last Years of the Monroe Doctrine: 1945–1993.* New York, 1994.

Smith, Tony. *America's Mission: The United States and the Worldwide Struggle for Democracy in the Twentieth Century.* Princeton, N.J., 1994.

United Nations Department of Public Information. *The United Nations and the Situation in Somalia.* New York, 1994.

———. *The United Nations and the Situation in the Former Yugoslavia.* New York, 1995.

HUMAN RIGHTS

Human rights are typically understood to be equal and inalienable rights that each and every person possesses simply by virtue of being human. Americans often regard human rights as a defining feature of their national heritage. The standard civics textbook history of the colonial period emphasizes the pursuit of religious, political, and personal liberty, and presents the Declaration of Independence and the first ten amendments to the Constitution as founding the new nation on the protection of inalienable natural rights. Associated with this personal understanding is a perception of the United States as a model for the world of a society dedicated to the pursuit of political freedom, civil liberties, and individual rights.

Practice, however, has often diverged radically from this comfortable self-understanding. Domestically, the "rights of man" were understood, until well into the twentieth century, as primarily the rights of white males, with special emphasis on property rights. Internationally, the U.S. rhetoric of freedom, democracy, and self-determination has all too often been mixed with the practice of imperialism, intervention, and support for repressive regimes.

An honest assessment of the United States' international human rights record is further complicated by the presence of two competing visions of the ideal, one inward looking and exemplary, the other more outward looking and missionary. The exemplary understanding of the U.S. calling, rooted in the biblical image of the city on the hill, sees America as only a model or beacon. To continue with the religious analogy, the focus is on bearing witness rather than proselytizing. The missionary version, however, considers such a policy in the face of foreign tyranny to be a betrayal of the United States' historic mission and a sacrifice of the rights of other peoples to political expediency. According to this view, to fulfill its role the United States must actively foster the international preservation of human rights.

From Washington to Wilson

President George Washington's Farewell Address, which powerfully combines arguments of realpolitik and republicanism, remains one of the clearest and most often cited statements of the exemplary vision of the U.S. mission. Although Washington stressed the importance of providing "the magnanimous and too novel example of a people always guided by an exalted justice and benevolence," he emphasized above all avoiding foreign political entanglements. Neutrality, even isolation, would allow the United States time to develop its resources to the point at which it could protect itself from any foreign attack. No less important, though, was the fact that isolation would avoid "the insidious wiles of foreign influ-ence," which "history and experience prove" to be "one of the most baneful foes of republican government."

Throughout most of the nineteenth century the exemplary focus on internal rights development predominated. For example, independence of Spain's colonies in Central and South America in the 1820s was greeted with pleasure and satisfaction. The United States, however, remained largely uninvolved in the affairs of these new states—except to assert its own "rights" under the Monroe Doctrine to exclude European influence, thus laying the basis for hemispheric hegemony. Likewise, democratic initiatives, movements, and revolutions in Europe received primarily verbal and symbolic American support.

Beyond the boundaries of the new republic, the United States focused its attention on westward territorial expansion. But this too was seen largely in terms of developing internal economic and political resources, and providing a context for settlers to better enjoy their rights. What today we would describe as the blatant disregard of the rights and interests of the native peoples was at the time widely seen as a realization of the nation's "manifest destiny," the fulfillment of America's civilizing mission, a continuation of the spread of freedom into previously savage territory that had begun with the Atlantic colonies of the seventeenth and eighteen centuries.

As the frontier began to disappear, however, U.S. attention turned increasingly outward. The rapid growth of U.S. international power in the decades after the Civil War made isolationism more an option than a necessity. The missionary dimensions of U.S. expansionism thus began to come to the fore.

The Spanish-American-Cuban-Filipino War was a crucial turning point. The U.S. decision to go to war with Spain in April 1898 involved a variety of conventional national interests, including national pride (offended by the mysterious sinking of the battleship *Maine* in Havana harbor), a growing political and military assertiveness in regional and international affairs, and the pursuit of new markets for trade and investment. But it also reflected outrage over Spanish atrocities in Cuba and a more general sentiment of anticolonialism. Paradoxically, however, the United States acquired not only indirect, quasicolonial rule over Cuba, but its own colonial empire in the Philippines and Puerto Rico. And control over the Philippines was consolidated only through a brutal war against Filipino forces fighting for their independence.

In the following years, as suggested by the labels "Big Stick" and "Dollar Diplomacy," the United States intervened in Colombia, Cuba, Haiti, Mexico, Nicaragua, and Panama to protect U.S. economic and geopolitical interests. Although there were occasional references to fostering democracy, the central concerns of U.S. policy were protecting American investments and lives, acquiring and securing a transoceanic canal, and excluding European powers from this U.S. sphere of influence. The rights of local people and the principle of self-determination were barely considered. Oligarchs and military dictators were acceptable to the United States, perhaps even desirable, if they protected U.S. economic interests and supported U.S. geopolitical objectives. Even President Woodrow Wilson, who is best known for his idealism and his commitment to national self-determination in Europe, authorized military interventions in both Mexico and Nicaragua in 1916.

World Wars I and II

Wilson, however, is much better remembered for his January 1918 speech to Congress in which he enunciated "Fourteen Points" to guide the United States' postwar policy. His emphasis on "the principle of justice to all peoples and nationalities, and their right to live on equal terms of liberty and safety with one another," along with his characterization of what later would come to be known as "the culminating and final war for human liberty," suggested a much more active concern with human rights in foreign policy. His seemingly altruistic efforts to redraw the postwar map of Central and Eastern Europe in greater accord with the principle of national self-determination reflected similar concerns.

Nonetheless, human rights remained a peripheral element of interwar U.S. foreign policy under both Democratic and Republican administrations. It is difficult to point to a single major instance in which the United States sacrificed even minor economic or security objectives in the pursuit of human rights goals. In Central America and the Caribbean, direct U.S. intervention did decline in the 1920s, and Franklin Roosevelt's "Good Neighbor" policy in the 1930s suggested a growing respect, or at least tolerance, for the principle of self-determination. U.S. policy toward Latin America, however, continued to emphasize economic interests and gave little weight to the human rights practices of local governments. For example, during Roosevelt's tenure the Somoza family dictatorship, which would rule Nicaragua for forty years, came to power with U.S. support. In other regions, especially Asia, the standard U.S. policy was political isolationism coupled with the assertive pursuit of economic interests.

This was, however, the norm in the international relations of the era. Human rights, which principally regulate the way in which a state treats its own nationals in its own territory, were almost universally considered by Americans and Europeans to be a matter of domestic jurisdiction, at least among "civilized" (that is, developed, Western, white, and Christian) states. The principles of sovereignty and nonintervention were understood to render the human rights practices of such states largely a protected exercise of sovereign prerogative. Even the Covenant of the League of Nations failed to mention human rights. Therefore, from a comparative perspective what is most notable is that the United States was one of the few countries that gave even sporadic lip service to human rights objectives in its foreign policy.

The place of human rights in international relations began to change during World War II. President Roosevelt's "Four Freedoms" speech to Congress in January 1941 gave an explicit human rights dimension to the war, as a struggle to assure freedom of speech and expression, freedom of religion, freedom from want, and freedom from fear. But it was the end of the war in Europe, as the world's attention gradually shifted from German aggression to the horrors of the Holocaust, that brought human rights into the mainstream of international relations. Most strikingly, human rights were listed as one of the four principal objectives of the new United Nations (UN) organization in both the Preamble and Article 1 of its Charter.

The United States played a leading role in effectuating this change. For example, the United States strongly supported the Nuremberg War Crimes Tribunal, where the novel charge of "crimes against humanity" was introduced into international law. The prominent place of human rights in the UN Charter owed more to the work of nongovernmental organizations (NGOs) and other states than to the official U.S. delegation to the San Francisco drafting conference. Nonetheless, the United States did endorse the idea. Furthermore, it emerged as a leading proponent of international human rights in the immediate postwar years.

The Cold War

The United Nations, and in particular the UN Commission on Human Rights, focused its early human rights work on developing an authoritative statement of international norms. These efforts culminated in the Universal Declaration of Human Rights, adopted by the UN General Assembly on 10 December 1948. Although the Declaration was drafted principally by the French and Canadian members of the commission, the U.S. representative, Eleanor Roosevelt, played a key role in working out the crucial political compromises. She also emerged as one of the most prominent national and international human rights advocates.

This new international attention to human rights did not penetrate very deeply. In 1946, for example, the Commission on Human Rights adopted a resolution affirming its lack of authority to investigate the complaints of human rights violations that were received by the United Nations. Authoritative international human rights norms were undoubtedly emerging, but the international community was unwilling to allow an active international role in implementing these norms.

Work bogged down even in the effort to transform the Universal Declaration of Human Rights, a nonbinding statement of principles, into a legally binding international treaty. (The International Human Rights Covenants were not completed until 1966.) The ostensible cause was a dispute over the relative importance of economic, social, and cultural rights. In fact, though, human rights had largely been transformed into simply another tool to carry on the superpowers' Cold War rivalry. Each side used the United Nations to draw attention to rights on which the other performed poorly—racial discrimination and unemployment in the United States, denials of freedom of religion and freedom of information in the Soviet Union—while ignoring, and even supporting, pervasive human rights violations in their own spheres of influence. Outside the United Nations as well, the United States (and the Soviet Union) had by the early 1950s adopted an almost completely rhetorical and self-interested approach to international human rights.

The cynical abuse of the rhetoric of human rights was strikingly underscored by U.S. and Soviet military interventions in the mid-1950s. In Guatemala in 1954 the United States overthrew the freely elected government of Jacobo Arbenz Guzmán, in part because of its redistributive policies that aimed to better implement economic and social rights. This ushered in thirty years of military rule that culminated in the early 1980s with the systematic massacre of tens of thousands of Guatemalans by the armed forces and semiofficial death squads. Meanwhile, the Soviets not merely embraced and encouraged, but forcibly insisted upon, one-party totalitarian dictatorships in Central and Eastern Europe. For example, Soviet tanks rolled into Hungary in 1956 to put an end to a short-lived experiment in liberal political reforms.

In the United States, anticommunism not only supplanted human rights as a principal foreign policy objective, but also came to be equated with "democracy," and thus, with the struggle for human rights. The United States, presenting itself as the leader of the "Free World," insisted on the "democratic" credentials of repressive anticommunist civilian and military dictatorships. This rhetoric reflected a healthy dose of crude self-interest and convenient self-delusion. But it also rested on a peculiar and deeply rooted American self-understanding.

There has been a strong tendency among Americans to assume that what the United States does is not merely consistent with but is a positive contribution to the realization of human rights. In its stronger forms, this attitude involves virtually equating U.S. foreign policy and international human rights. In the 1980s in particular, this argument appeared regularly in a subtle form, name-

ly, the contention that because communism was the principal threat to human rights in the contemporary world, the U.S. struggle against the Soviet Union was the highest and most authentic form of international human rights policy. In the 1950s and early 1960s, though, the virtual equation of U.S. foreign policy and international human rights—or, as it was more frequently put, "freedom" and "democracy"—was much more unreflective.

Unsavory military dictators were seen as a perhaps unfortunate, but necessary, price to pay to preserve economic and political "freedom" in the world. No leading figure in either political party in the 1950s or early 1960s seriously questioned the view that "freedom" was not merely coincident with U.S. interests, but could also be defined largely as those interests. Republican and Democratic administrations alike, along with the leadership in both houses of Congress, readily accepted systematic violations of basic personal freedoms, civil liberties, and political rights among client regimes. But they reacted strongly against infringements of the right to private property, especially the property rights of Americans. Expropriation of U.S. economic assets almost always was treated as a much more serious problem than denial of the right to vote, violations of freedom of speech and other civil liberties, or even systematic political violence. Only the far left of the U.S. political spectrum even seemed aware of the perverse irony of such policies carried out in the name of freedom and democracy.

Underscoring the implicit equation of U.S. policy and international human rights was a vociferous refusal to allow independent international scrutiny of the domestic human rights practice of the United States. Even if a binding international human rights treaty had been drafted in the early 1950s, the United States would not have ratified it; nowhere near two-thirds, and almost certainly not even a majority, of the Senate would have voted for ratification. In fact, the controversy over the Bricker Amendment, which would have restricted the President's ability to undertake international legal obligations for the United States, and reflected a more general struggle beween Congress and the President over control of foreign policy, was crystallized by congressional fears of an impending international human rights treaty. Senator Bricker explicitly pointed to a possible international human rights covenant as a principal motivation for advancing his amendment. This powerful opposition was a crucial factor in the U.S. decision in 1953 to withdraw from the drafting work in responsibilities of the Commission on Human Rights.

The United States thus operated under a stunning double standard, freely and self-righteously judging the human rights practices of others according to its own often idiosyncratic standards, while no less self-righteously refusing to have its own practices at home judged by others according to mutually agreed-upon international norms. And unlike the interwar period, when all states insisted on their right to be protected from such scrutiny, the United States was increasingly becoming an aberration among liberal democratic states. While the United States was closing itself off from even the possibility of impartial international scrutiny of its human rights practices, the states of Western Europe were drafting and adopting the European Convention on Human Rights, which established what would become a very strong system of regional monitoring and regional judicial enforcement of human rights obligations.

So complete was the U.S. separation from international human rights norms and procedures that even the language of human rights vanished from U.S. policy during the Cold War era. As in domestic politics, where the language of civil and constitutional rights was used to discuss what elsewhere were considered human rights issues, talk of human rights largely disappeared from U.S. foreign-policy rhetoric in favor of the vaguer and more easily manipulated language of freedom and democracy. The immediate postwar attention to human rights, understood in terms of authoritative, impartial, international standards, thus became a brief historical aberration, perhaps best accounted for by postwar euphoria over victory and guilt over inaction in the face of the Holocaust.

Reintroducing Human Rights

Human rights began to reenter U.S. policy debates in the late 1960s. The civil rights movement helped produce a more self-critical understanding of domestic human rights practices. The Vietnam War shattered the convenient equation of U.S. interests and international human rights. Critical, rights-orientated perspectives thus increasingly entered the mainstream of U.S. foreign policy discussions.

The explicit reentry of human rights into U.S. foreign policy, however, came in connection with the treatment of Jews and political dissidents in the Soviet Union. Although ironic, given the role of Cold War rivalry in suppressing and distorting human rights concerns, this was the one human rights issue capable of creating a broad political coalition that included both liberals and cold warriors. The Jackson-Vanick Amendment to the Trade Act of 1974 tied trade liberalization for the Soviet Union to Soviet policies on Jewish emigration. And in 1975 the Conference on Security and Cooperation in Europe (CSE, renamed OSCE in 1993) adopted the Helsinki Final Act. In addition to codifying the postwar political division of Europe, the Helsinki Final Act included important human rights provisions, especially Principle VII: "Respect for human rights and fundamental freedoms." This document, along with follow-up meetings in Belgrade (1977–1978), Madrid (1980–1983), and Vienna

(1986–1989), both emboldened Soviet dissidents and provided the basis for very public western criticisms of Soviet human rights practices. As a result, human rights became a real, although hardly nonpartisan, issue in East-West policies.

Less prominent at the time, but ultimately no less important, was the development of a congressional bloc that advocated broader attention to human rights in U.S. foreign policy. In 1973, Congress recommended linking U.S. foreign aid to the human rights practices of recipient countries. In 1975, over the opposition of the Gerald Ford administration, this linkage was made mandatory: U.S. foreign-aid policy was required to take into account (although not be determined by) the human rights practices of potential recipients. Congress also required the Department of State to prepare annual reports on the human rights practices of countries that received U.S. aid. Such legislation was both nationally and internationally unprecedented.

When Jimmy Carter became president in 1977, the U.S. executive branch also became generally supportive of pursuing human rights in foreign policy. For example, Carter reversed U.S. policy toward the military dictatorships of the Southern Cone of South America. Just a month after entering office, Carter reduced military aid to Argentina and Uruguay by two-thirds and throughout his term successfully opposed new aid to these countries. In addition, the Carter administration pursued a vigorous campaign of public diplomacy against these governments and the military regime in Chile, including support for resolutions critical of these governments in both the United Nations and the Organization of American States (OAS). By contrast, in 1976, Secretary of State Henry Kissinger had publicly reprimanded the U.S. ambassador to Chile for even raising the issue of human rights in private discussions.

In Central America as well, the Carter administration significantly redirected U.S. policy. Military aid to Guatemala was prohibited in 1978 and the U.S. Congress voted against multilateral loans to Guatemala in 1979 and 1980. The United States also moved away from its traditional support of the Somoza family dictatorship in Nicaragua. And when a mass popular revolution forced Anastasio Somoza Debayle to flee his country in July 1979 the United States emerged as the largest foreign donor to Nicaragua (over $100 million in eighteen months), despite concerns about the socialist agenda of the new Sandinista government. In El Salvador the Carter administration attempted to distance itself from some of the more repressive elements of the Salvadoran oligarchy. For example, the United States supported a coup by reformist military officers in October 1979.

But even Carter only partially transformed U.S. international human rights policy. In countries such as Iran and the Philippines, the United States continued to support "friendly" client dictators. In South Africa and Indonesia geopolitical and economic interests easily predominated over human rights concerns. And Chinese totalitarianism came in for surprisingly little official public criticism, especially in comparison to the attacks by U.S. policymakers on Soviet bloc states.

During the Carter years, there was greater public and private anguish over the trade-offs between human rights and other foreign-policy objectives. In addition, a new constituency for international human rights—symbolized and further galvanized by the award of the Nobel Peace Prize to Amnesty International (AI) in 1977—made the traditional subordination of human rights to other foreign-policy concerns more politically contentious than in the past. Nonetheless, Carter's rhetoric, which proclaimed human rights "the heart" and "the soul" of U.S. foreign policy, was only fitfully translated into practice.

Furthermore, even such a partial transformation of U.S. international human rights policy provoked considerable controversy. For example, in June 1979 more than a hundred members of Congress signed a full-page advertisement in the *New York Times* criticizing Carter's policy toward Nicaragua and warning of "another Cuba." And in the 1980 presidential campaign, Ronald Reagan argued forcefully, and with considerable apparent impact, that Carter's international human rights policy was a misguided sacrifice of true U.S. interests.

The Reagan Era

When Reagan took office in 1981, his administration embarked on an aggressive public campaign to reverse the Carter policy. Aid to Nicaragua was suspended and secret funding for a guerrilla war commenced. In neighboring El Salvador, despite the political murders of thousands of civilians by government troops and their paramilitary allies in secret death squads, U.S. aid was not merely continued but increased substantially. Relations with the military dictatorships in the Southern Cone of South America returned to cordiality, and U.S. aid was again extended. Such policy reversals, especially in the context of Reagan's revival of the Cold War against the Soviet "evil empire," led many people both at home and abroad either to hope or to fear that human rights would again be forced to the sidelines in international relations, as in the 1950s and 1960s. Secretary of State Alexander Haig even announced that the Reagan administration would replace the Carter emphasis on human rights with a focus on international terrorism.

This did not, however, occur. The Reagan administration faced a transformed international human rights environment. A growing number of countries, beginning with the Netherlands in 1979, explicitly incorporated human rights into their foreign policies, and most others at least began to use the language of international human rights in their policy statements. At the multilateral level, the human rights machinery of the United Nations was reinvigorated in the late 1970s, under the leadership of a newly revitalized Western European group in the Commission on Human Rights. The subject of human rights simply could not be buried in international relations in the 1980s, whatever the preferences of the Reagan administration.

At home as well, the political environment for human rights had been permanently changed during the Carter years. Human rights NGOs formed in the mid- and late 1970s, such as Helsinki Watch, the Lawyer's Committee for International Human Rights, and the Clearinghouse for Persecuted Scientists of the American Association for the Advancement of Science, became increasingly active in the 1980s. Human rights NGOS increasingly formed lobbying coalitions with organizations sharing their concerns. They also developed more effective linkages with advocates of a stronger U.S. international human rights policy in the Congress, where a semiformal network had developed in the late 1970s.

Human rights advocates in the United States were thus able to mount an unusually vigorous campaign against Reagan's new Cold War vision. They lost more battles than they won. But by the end of the decade, something approximating their vision had become the mainstream view in both Congress and the executive branch and among the general public as well.

Central America was the public focus of the struggle over U.S. international human rights policy in the 1980s. Congress was the central battleground. Congressional human rights advocates devoted considerable energy and attention to Central American policy. And they received substantial support, and prodding, from the NGO community. Leading human rights NGOs, such as Americas Watch and the Lawyers' Committee, cooperated closely not only with each other, but also with regionally based organizations. The Washington Office on Latin America in particular emerged as a focal point of activity. In addition, international human rights NGOs worked closely with organizations that had a more particular or sporadic interest in U.S. international human rights policy, such as the American Civil Liberties Union, which became active on Salvadoran policy in the early 1980s.

The results of these efforts included a legal requirement that the president certify human rights progress in El Salvador before aid could be released in 1982 and 1983. The Reagan administration countered by largely ignoring the facts of massive human rights violations when it issued the certifications. At the end of 1983 Reagan vetoed new legislation requiring further certifications.

Congressional opponents had somewhat more success on Nicaragua. In July 1983 aid was suspended to the

Nicaraguan Contras, who were waging a guerrilla war to overthrow the Sandinista-led government in Managua. The Sandinistas had loose ties to Moscow but were also supported by Canada, France, and many other countries in Western Europe. In June 1985, U.S. "humanitarian" aid to the Contras was resumed and military aid recommenced the following summer. It was suspended again early in 1988.

In accounting for the persistence of human rights advocacy in U.S. foreign policy in the 1980s, it must also be noted that the Reagan administration carried out selected international human rights initiatives on its own. Although not as frequent, consistent, prominent, or forceful as many Carter initiatives, they did reflect a deeper penetration of human rights into U.S. foreign policy that is too easily overlooked when one focuses only on the often vitriolic controversy over Central America.

In its relations with the Soviet Union, the Reagan administration, of course, continued to press the issue of human rights. But in other cases as well, the Reagan administration spoke and occasionally even acted on behalf of international human rights concerns. For example, at the last minute it abandoned its support of the Marcos dictatorship in the Philippines, and then warmly embraced the new civilian government led by Corazon Aquino. Regarding the military dictatorships of the Southern Cone of South America, the administration made private diplomatic overtures on behalf of prominent political dissidents. And when repression deepened in Chile in 1984, Assistant Secretary of State Elliott Abrams, the leading administration spokesman on human rights, condemned publicly the actions of the Pinochet regime.

South Africa, however, presents the clearest example of the deepened penetration of human rights ideas into U.S. foreign policy in the 1980s. Since the early 1960s, the United States had expressed consistently its displeasure with South Africa's policy of systematic, state-sponsored racial discrimination—apartheid—and white minority rule. Democratic and Republican administrations alike, however, were unwilling to take concrete actions beyond a very poorly enforced arms embargo, initiated by the Kennedy administration. Carter had been more critical than most U.S. presidents, but even his policies against South Africa were almost entirely verbal and symbolic.

The Reagan administration replaced the Carter emphasis on public condemnation of South Africa with a strategy of "constructive engagement." The stated objective was to increase U.S. leverage by developing more cordial relations and pursuing common objectives, especially the containment of Soviet and Cuban influence in Southern Africa. Constructive engagement was to be a central example of the efficacy of Reagan's low-keyed approach to human rights. It was also intended to demonstrate the ultimate compatibility of national security and human rights concerns, when the latter were pursued in a less adversarial war in order to effect seeking gradual incremental change.

By 1984, however, the situation in South Africa had become increasingly violent and the white government showed no intention to compromise, let alone move toward black majority rule. Even conservative Republicans in the Congress, who had initially supported constructive engagement, began to desert President Reagan. In November 1984, Republican Senators Richard Lugar (chairman of the Foreign Relations Committee) and Nancy Kassebaum (chairwoman of the Foreign Relations African Affairs Subcommittee) sent a letter to Reagan asking for a review of the administration's South Africa policy. The following month thirty-five conservative members of the House also called on the president to abandon constructive engagement.

In July 1985, a House-Senate conference committee reached agreement on a bipartisan economic sanctions bill, which forced Reagan to issue an executive order imposing sanctions, albeit less extensive ones, in September. Although limited to loans and just a few products, and full of loopholes, this was a historic milestone in U.S. international human rights policy. A bipartisan congressional coalition, backed by a diverse range of NGOs and interest groups, had agreed on relatively strong international human rights action for a cause in no way motivated by Cold War rivalry. In fact, opponents of sanctions invoked Cold War considerations—South Africa's opposition to Marxist regimes in neighboring Angola and Mozambique—to little effect. The following year a Reagan veto of slightly stronger sanctions was overridden.

U.S. international human rights policy in the 1980s certainly was less evenhanded and more politically contentious than under Carter. But the Reagan administration failed to force human rights to the bottom of the foreign policy agenda. Quite the contrary; when George Bush took office in 1989, human rights had a secure (although controversial) and institutionalized place in U.S. foreign policy.

The Post–Cold War Era

During the George Bush and Bill Clinton administrations, the general principle of regular, continuing action on behalf of international human rights received considerable bipartisan support in Congress and from the general public. The new place of human rights in U.S. foreign policy was especially clear in the Bush administration's treatment of Central America, a political litmus test during the Reagan era. Although refusing to go as far as congressional critics and human rights organizations such as Americas Watch would have liked, Bush did step up U.S. pressure on El Salvador to improve its human rights record. He moderated his opposition to Sandinista rule in Nicaragua. And in late 1990, military aid to Guatemala was suspended to protest an upsurge in political violence.

But Bush's tepid response to the Tienanmen massacre of June 1989, in which China's emerging democracy movement was brutally crushed, illustrates the incomplete penetration of human rights into what had become the moderate center of the foreign policy mainstream. The failure of human rights advocates to obtain harshly punitive measures against China from the Congress further illustrates the broader limits of U.S. international human rights policy, as does President Clinton's decision to normalize Sino-American relations, for largely economic reasons.

Human rights policy, of course, never can be identical with foreign policy, which necessarily encompasses a variety of national goals and interests. The real issue is the relative place of human rights when faced with competing economic, political, and security objectives. The Bush administration (especially after 1989) and the Clinton administration went a bit further than their predecessors, but fell far short of the consistent, aggressive policies favored by most national and international human rights advocates. They generally took human rights seriously in the foreign-policy decision-making policy, but gave human rights concerns a relatively low priority.

The United States has tended to respond quickly and publicly to deteriorating human rights situations in countries in the Americas. For example, both Bush and Clinton sustained U.S. pressure on the Guatemalan military to curb political violence, although here too, as made evident by the revelations of continued Central Intelligence Agency (CIA) covert aid directly to the Guatemalan military, the efforts were less than were claimed. When President Fujimori suspended the parliament in Peru in 1992, the U.S. response was rapid and forceful. And the military government in Haiti faced sustained and escalating pressure from the United States, culminating in the arrival of U.S. troops in the autumn of 1994.

In Africa the tendency of the U.S. government has been to adopt a much lower profile, out of both a perception of lesser public interest and a fear of neo-imperial overtones in adopting relatively aggressive U.S. initiatives. Nonetheless, in countries such as Malawi and Kenya the United States has applied some pressure for political liberalization. Furthermore, the United States has generally supported the trend in the 1990s toward multiparty politics on the continent.

In the Middle East, however, other interests have taken priority. Human rights criticisms have been largely restricted to political (although certainly justified) attacks on Iran and Iraq. Much the same has been applied on behalf of political dissidents and ethnic minorities in Burma. But the only high-profile human rights case in the region has been the United States' gradual unlinking of human rights from its economic relations with China.

Perhaps the most striking feature of the 1990s, however, is the minimal public criticism in response to U.S. foreign policy decisions that consider human rights. Whether the final decision is to give priority to human rights or to some other foreign policy objective—peace in the Middle East in the case of Syria, or nonproliferation in relations with North Korea—the legitimacy of raising human rights concerns is rarely questioned. In the mid-1970s, debates often focused on whether human rights concerns even had a legitimate place in U.S. foreign policy. In the 1990s the focus of debate has been instead on the weight to be given to human rights concerns in particular cases.

Nonetheless, it must be emphasized that human rights considerations alone almost never determine important U.S. policy decisions. Without additional interests, it is hard to mobilize sufficient public support. For example, the desire to stop the flow of Haitian refugees and the special links to Haiti felt by many African Americans (including the Congressional Black Caucus) were important factors in building a coalition for sanctions against the military government in Haiti.

The greater emphasis on human rights in U.S. foreign policy undoubtedly owes much to the end of the Cold War. The elimination of the perceived threat of communism has also eliminated a principal ground for supporting repressive governments. As a result, it has been much easier for the United States to act on its often-expressed preference for multiparty democracy, especially in light of the strong internal pressure for political liberalization and democratization in most countries of the Third World and the former Soviet bloc.

The end of the Cold War, however, only removed impediments to a serious international human rights policy. The emergence of human rights as a standard element in foreign-policy discussions across a wide political spectrum reflects a deeper reassessment of the importance of human rights as a foreign-policy goal. This reevaluation has been supported by the growing prominence of human rights in the foreign policies of other countries. It has also been associated with a growing willingness to adopt international human rights standards, most notably in the growing tendency in public discussions to use "democratic" more as a synonym for a regime that protects the internationally recognized human rights of its citizens than one that protects U.S. interests. The United States has even agreed to open its own practices to international Covenant on Civil and Political Rights, which requires submitting periodic reports on a wide range of human rights to an independent international supervisory committee.

The reality and importance of such changes deserve emphasis. But so do their limits. Even where countervailing considerations have been largely absent, there has been considerable controversy over the extent to which the United States should go in supporting human rights abroad. For example, critics of the invasion of Haiti, in both parties, forcefully questioned the wisdom of risking American lives in the pursuit of human rights objectives. (The same questions arose in the protracted debate over possible U.S. involvement in the Yugoslav Civil War.) And where there are countervailing foreign-policy objectives, the relative standing of human rights considerations remains very low indeed. This is perhaps most clearly illustrated by the decision to cut the link between human rights performance and most-favored-nation (MFN) trading status for China.

Nonetheless, in the mid-1990s human rights have been more thoroughly incorporated into U.S. foreign policy than at any other time. In fact, human rights finally seem to have become—in practice, not merely in rhetoric—an enduring, although still subsidiary, objective of U.S. foreign policy.

JACK DONNELLY

See also Amnesty International; Carter, James Earl; Cold War; Fourteen Points; Humanitarian Relief and Intervention; Idealism; Nuremberg, International Military Tribunal at; Realism; Reagan, Ronald Wilson; Self-Determination; United Nations; Wilson, Thomas Woodrow

FURTHER READING

Baehr, Peter R. *The Role of Human Rights in Foreign Policy.* New York, 1994.
Donnelly, Jack. *International Human Rights.* Boulder, Colo., 1993.
Forsythe, David P. *Human Rights and U.S. Foreign Policy: Congress Reconsidered.* Gainsville, Fla., 1988.
———. *The Internationalization of Human Rights.* Lexington, Mass., 1991.
Kaufman, Natalie Hevener. *Human Rights Treaties and the Senate: A History of Opposition.* Chapel Hill, N.C., 1990.
Lawson, Edward, ed. *Encyclopedia of Human Rights.* New York, 1991.
Mower, A. Glenn, Jr. *Human Rights and American Foreign Policy: The Carter and Reagan Experiences.* New York, 1987.
Nichols, Bruce, and Gil Lascar, eds. *The Moral Nation: Humanitarianism and U.S. Foreign Policy Today.* Notre Dame, Ind., 1989.
Shute, Stephen, and Susan Hurley, eds. *On Human Rights (The Oxford Amnesty Lectures, 1993).* New York, 1993.
Shue, Henry. *Basic Rights: Subsistence, Affluence, and U.S. Foreign Policy.* Princeton, 1980.
Staunton, Marie, and Sally Fenn, eds. *Amnesty International Handbook.* Claremont, Calif., 1991.

HUMPHREY, HUBERT HORATIO

(*b.* 27 May 1911; *d.* 13 January 1978)

Outspoken liberal senator from Minnesota (1949–1964, 1971–1978) and vice president (1965–1969), an effective legislative advocate for civil rights and nuclear-arms control, and a sponsor of the Peace Corps. Although anticommunist in domestic politics, he sought improved relations with the Soviet Union during the Cold War and he floor-managed the Senate's ratification of the Limited Nuclear Test Ban Treaty in 1963. Humphrey's close association before 1960 with then-Senate Majority Leader Lyndon Johnson led to his selection as Johnson's vice presidential running mate in 1964. As vice president, Humphrey at first advocated a diplomatic settlement of the war in Vietnam. That stance isolated him within the Johnson administration, which was determined to escalate U.S. military intervention, and Johnson did not consult with him before sending troops into the Dominican Republic in 1965. Seeking to regain his standing within the administration, Humphrey became a highly vocal supporter of the Vietnam War, thereby alienating many liberal Democrats. Competing against opponents of the war, Humphrey won the Democratic nomination for president in 1968, but lost the election because he believed that as vice president he could not oppose Johnson's policies, whereas his successful opponent, Richard M. Nixon, promised to end the costly war.

DONALD A. RITCHIE

See also Johnson, Lyndon Baines; Limited Nuclear Test Ban Treaty; Peace Corps; Vietnam War

FURTHER READING

Humphrey, Hubert Horatio, Jr. *The Education of a Public Man.* 1977. Reprint: Minneapolis, Minn., 1991.
Solberg, Carl. *Hubert Humphrey: A Biography.* New York, 1984.

HUNGARY

A landlocked central European republic bordered by Slovakia, Ukraine, Romania, Serbia, Croatia, Slovenia, and Austria. Present-day Hungary is a successor of the medieval Hungarian kingdom, occupied by the Ottoman Turks in the sixteenth century, and absorbed by the Austrian Habsburgs in 1718.

The arrival of Protestant missionary Stephanus Parmenius Budaeus in the sixteenth century is the earliest known contact between Hungary and the North American continent. As commerce and colonial territories expanded during the seventeenth and eighteenth centuries, the presence of ethnic Hungarians on the American continent increased as well. Hungarian militia fought in the War for Independence, and continued—through immigration in the nineteenth century—to contribute to the growth and prosperity of the emerging global power status of the United States. Although relatively small in number compared to other European immigrant populations, the Hungarian émigré community contributed both to U.S. cultural life and to the political debates that shaped the international system during the twentieth century. The most significant foreign policy intervention by the United States on Hungary's behalf during the whole of the nineteenth century occurred during Hungary's failed attempt to overthrow the Habsburg monarchy in 1848–1849 and declare itself an independent republic.

An abiding faith in the concept of American democracy propagated by visitors to the United States who returned to Hungary in the early 1800s led to tacit U.S. support for the Hungarian revolutionary movement and its leader, Lajos Kossuth. Kossuth organized an initial reform movement in the 1830s which culminated in the creation of an independent opposition party. The party's platform was expressed in a "Proclamation of the Opposition" which in turn led to demands for equality in taxation, fair legal practice, the abolition of serfdom, and the creation of parliamentary government. Russian military intervention provided the necessary leverage for the Austrian monarchy to crush the rebellion. Despite his failure in Budapest, Kossuth became a *cause célèbre* in the United States after a triumphal arrival in New York City in December 1851. He was held in such high esteem that his welcome in Philadelphia prompted a comparison to the arrival of a Hungarian George Washington.

The political repercussions of the Hungarian rebellion, combined with Prussia's crushing defeat of Austria in the war of 1866, led to the "Austro-Hungarian Compromise" of 1867, which granted equal status and a degree of autonomy to Hungary under the auspices of the Dual Monarchy.

In World War I, Austria-Hungary was allied with Germany, Bulgaria, and the Ottoman Empire as one of the Central Powers; indeed it was the assassination of the Austrian Archduke Franz Ferdinand in Sarajevo in June 1914 that precipitated the war. On 16 November 1918, less than two weeks after the armistice was signed ending World War I, the Hungarian republic was constituted out of the deconstructed Habsburg empire. Two years later, in the Treaty of Trianon, and as part of the overall peace settlement, significant areas of Hungarian territory were taken away. For Hungarians this represented an excessive and brutal penalty for Hungary's wartime role. For the United States and the other allies, the implementation of the peace settlement was paramount, and the eradication of Hungary's historical borders an acceptable price for Hungary to pay. In addition, while President Woodrow Wilson's Fourteen Points had stipulated the principle of self-determination in the abstract, was a goal apparently better suited to those nations in Central Europe that had emerged in the winner's circle or had suffered under the Central Powers—most notably Romania, and the newly created Poland and Czechoslovakia. Thus, the Hungarian territory of Transylvania became Romanian.

Throughout the interwar period, Hungary continued to press for a revision of the borders delineated according to the Trianon treaty, and acted through the League of Nations to press its cause upon President Herbert Hoover in 1930. Later, the Hungarian-American émigré community promoted territorial revisionism through a direct petition to President Franklin D. Roosevelt. By the late 1930s, however, it was clear that Hungarian borders were no longer debatable in the United States, particularly following the rise of Nazism in Germany. Alternatively, adherents to the political philosophy of the interwar "reform generation" in Hungary turned once again to their former German allies. Eventually, Hungary found support for territorial changes in its favor in Berlin in exchange for supporting the Hitlerite regime. Beginning in 1938, Germany helped Hungary absorb parts of Czechoslovakia, Romania, Austria, and Yugoslavia. In 1941 Hungary entered World War II on Hitler's side. Later in the war, in March 1944, Germany took over control of its erstwhile ally; in little more than a year, over a half million Hungarian Jews were arrested and sent to concentration camps. Soviet troops occupied most of Hungary during the last months of the war.

The World War II peace settlement required Hungary to give up all the land it had gained in collusion with the Nazis. In November 1945, elections were held and the country reproclaimed a republic. However, while a democratic coalition was initially formed, the Hungarian communists gradually gained control of the government, largely because of the continued presence of Soviet troops. By 1949, communists had eliminated all opposition political parties and declared a People's Republic modeled after the Soviet regime. In 1955, Hungary joined the Warsaw Pact and was also admitted to the United Nations.

In the early 1950s, Hungary experienced more unrest than other Soviet bloc states, sparked by serious economic problems and by growing indigenous pressures for acquiring a higher degree of political freedom. These developments culminated in October 1956 in an insurrection, centered in Budapest, and an attempt by Premier Imre Nagy to end Hungary's obeisance to Moscow, declare itself neutral, and withdraw from the Warsaw Pact. Thereupon, Soviet troops invaded Hungary and brutally crushed the revolution. Both at the time and in the years since there has been extensive debate in the United States over the Eisenhower administration's policy of publicly protesting Moscow's actions while withholding any real support for Hungarian freedom fighters. It has also been argued that the Hungarian people were in part inspired to revolt by the liberationist rhetoric of Secretary of State John Foster Dulles, and did so expecting U.S. support. On the other hand, it must be remembered that the uprising in Budapest coincided with the height of the Suez crisis and also occurred on the eve of the U.S. presidential election. In the final analysis, U.S. policy makers chose to be governed by larger strategic considerations, fears of potential superpower conflict, and the possibility of an escalation that could lead to nuclear war.

An era of direct (although limited) contact between Hungarian representatives and the United States government ceased when it became clear that bipolar strategic considerations were paramount in the nuclear age. By the 1970s, however, Hungary began to open its economy and society to a limited extent according to Premier János Kádár's adoption of the principle of "Socialism with a human face," itself the test of the viability of pacifying an otherwise restless populace with the easing of some social and cultural restrictions, and the adoption of policies which allowed for the introduction of a measure of free markets and emphasized increasing the availability of consumer goods. Kádár's "goulash communism" emerged as a potential pattern for successful—socialist—societal development.

However, as inflationary pressures and the aftershocks of the 1973 oil crisis disrupted the steady flow of Soviet oil to the Eastern Bloc, consumerism was undermined, and political discontent rose. Beginning with the eruption of Polish worker strikes in Gdansk in 1980, the era of artificially high standards of living and commensurate support for the "modernized" socialist political construct started to come to a close. The succession of Mikhail Gorbachev to the General Secretaryship of the Soviet Communist Party in 1985 saw the gradual loosening of Soviet domination of Eastern Europe and a thaw in U.S.-Soviet relations that were fundamental parts of Gorbachev's *perestroika*. Notable—in particular to Hungarians, given the tragedy of 1956—was Moscow's announcement in December 1988 that 50,000 Soviet troops were to be withdrawn from eastern Europe within two years.

Events turned out to have moved much faster, and Hungary played an absolutely crucial role in what, by the end of 1989, became the end of Soviet bloc supremacy in eastern Europe. In May 1989, Hungary began dismantling the barbed-wire fence along its border with Austria. In September it allowed, for the first time, East Germans coming to Hungary to move on to Austria or West Germany without their government's approval. This meant that East Germans, who previously met their West German relatives in western Hungary on Lake Balaton, were now free to board trains in Budapest bound for Vienna, Bonn, or Frankfurt. It also meant that some could take these routes as emigrants, with no plans of returning. Many did exactly that.

In October the party Congress of the Hungarian Socialist Workers' party (HSWP) renounced the "crimes and ideology" of its past, renamed itself the Hungarian Socialist Party, and recast itself in the manner of Western European social democratic parties, calling for free multiparty elections and a more market-based economy. The changes in Hungary were somewhat overshadowed in ensuing months by the more dramatic crumbling of the Berlin Wall and the "velvet revolution" in Czechoslovakia; but they both were quite profound in their own right and arguably at least in part responsible for the changes occurring in the rest of the region.

In the years since, Hungary has been in the forefront of efforts by Central Europeans to become integrated into the West. President George Bush visited Hungary in July 1989, and while offering less tangible support and aid than many Hungarians had hoped for, the visit had great symbolic and political impact. Hungary has been one of the major recipients of U.S. aid in both the Bush and Clinton administrations. George Soros, the Hungarian-born U.S. financier and philanthropist, made Budapest one of the main locales for the work of the Soros foundations.

In 1990, Hungary became the first former communist state to be granted membership in the Council of Europe. In 1991 it reached initial agreement with the European Community on trade privileges, and in April 1994 led the way in applying for full membership in the European Union. With respect to the North Atlantic Treaty Organization (NATO), it is on the "short list" affirmed by President Clinton (Hungary, Poland, the Czech Republic, and perhaps Slovakia) for future membership. The whens and hows of NATO expansion have yet to be clarified; in the interim Hungary has became a member of NATO's Partnership for Peace (PFP) program.

In the meantime, Hungary has been seeking diplomatic solutions to a number of simmering disputes with neighboring countries: with Ukraine, a border issue on which agreement was reached in 1993; with Slovakia, a dispute over a hydroelectric dam on the Danube; with Romania, anger over the violence and repression experienced by the Hungarian ethnic minority. While these and other disputes have deep historical roots, some going back to the Treaty of Trianon, thus far they have been managed and contained through bilateral efforts as well as through the intermediary role played by international institutions, such as the World Court, and regional organizations, such as the Conference/Organization on Security and Cooperation in Europe (CSCE/OSCE).

Internally, the euphoria of the early days of the post-communist era notwithstanding, Hungary continued to face significant political and economic problems. The governing coalition of the Hungarian Democratic Forum (HDF) under Prime Minister Josef Antall held power from 1990–1993. While progress was made in opening up the economy through privatization and more liberal trade policies, this came at the cost of extensive economic dislocation. The International Monetary Fund (IMF) has provided Hungary with substantial loans, but with the usual austerity conditions attached. When Antall died in 1993, the HDF coalition no longer could withstand the opposition's challenges, including those from right-wing and ex-communist groups. A new coalition government was formed in 1994 led by the Hungarian Socialist Party, the successor to the old communist one, led by Prime Minister Gyula Horn.

In foreign policy terms the Horn government has largely continued the commitments and policies favoring Western integration. Domestically, it continues to wrestle with the primary dichotomy between those who have profited from the adoption of market capitalism and those who are dependent upon a nonsustainable level of social expenditure formerly guaranteed by heavy foreign borrowing (under the defunct socialist regime). In addition, the persistent dichotomy between the urban and rural Hungarian populations further complicates the reform process. Budapest's two million inhabitants have benefited most directly and most substantially from the opening of the Hungarian economy to the West, and—with the notable exception of certain larger cities such as Székesfehérvár, Sopron, and a few others with substantial foreign direct investment—have also been the principal direct beneficiaries of employment, income, and goods surpluses brought with modernization and capital inflow.

External contingencies (such as continued levels of investment and consistent levels of trade with the European Union, the United States, and Asia) combined with internal consistency in the pace and substance of reform will determine the success of Hungary's reform program. The United States has shown consistent political support for Hungary's effort to reemerge on the European continent as the "Paris of the East." As is apparent from the difficulty even in France and in Germany to maintain deficit levels consistent with European Monetary Union (EMU) guidelines while confronting record unemployment levels of more than 10 percent, Hungary's immediate task is to persist with economic adjustment while maintaining the support of a populace that in many sectors has realized a short-term relative decline in living standards. During the remaining years of this century, Hungary may continue to pursue a strictly market capitalist model or balance the demands of westernization with the pressures from those at the bottom of the socioeconomic ladder for at least a modicum of support in this postcommunist era devoid of a social safety net.

TIMOTHY W. BAKER

See also Austria; Cold War; Dulles, John Foster; Eisenhower, Dwight David; Russia and the Soviet Union; Soros, George; World War I; World War II

FURTHER READING
Hanak, Peter. *The Corvina History of Hungary*. Budapest, 1991.
Major, Mark Imre. *American Hungarian Relations 1918–1944*. Astor, Fla., 1974.
Radványi, János. *Hungary and the Superpowers: The 1956 Revolution and Realpolitik*. Stamford, Conn., 1972.
Toma, Peter A., and Ivan Volgyes. *Politics in Hungary*. San Francisco, 1977.
Zöld, Ferenc, and Gábor Kelecsényi, ed. *What They Saw in Hungary*. Budapest, 1988.

HURLEY, PATRICK JAY
(*b.* 8 January 1883; *d.* 30 July 1963)

Secretary of war (1929–1933), minister to New Zealand (1942–1943), President Franklin D. Roosevelt's personal representative in the Near and Middle East (1942–1943), and controversial ambassador to China (1944–1945). Born in Choctaw territory in Oklahoma, Hurley fought in World War I as an officer in the Oklahoma National Guard. A flamboyant Republican lawyer and businessman, he served as President Herbert Hoover's secretary of war, adamantly opposing early independence for the Philippines and overseeing the expulsion from federal property of the Bonus Marchers, jobless World War I veterans who encamped in Washington to demand federal assistance. As representative of the Sinclair Oil Company, Hurley negotiated a claims agreement with the Mexican government in 1940, thereby facilitating a general settlement of Mexico's 1938 expropriation of American oil properties. During World War II, Hurley went on several missions to Australia, New Zealand, the Soviet Union, Iran, and China, dealing largely with transportation and economic aid. Named ambassador to China in November 1944, Hurley tried unsuccessfully to mediate between the Chinese Communists and the Guomindang (Kuomintang), relying on a Soviet promise not to support the Communists. Resigning in late 1945, Hurley publicly blamed his failure on Foreign Service officers whom he accused of pro-Communist bias and disloyalty. This charge helped ignite the demagogic campaign about who "lost" China. A supporter of the China Lobby, he ran unsuccessfully for U.S. senator from New Mexico three times, and never again held important public office.

J. GARRY CLIFFORD

See also China; China Hands; China Lobby; Hoover, Herbert; Mexico; Oil and Foreign Policy; Oil Companies; Philippines

FURTHER READING
Buhite, Russell D. *Patrick J. Hurley and American Foreign Policy*. Ithaca, N.Y., 1973.
Kahn, E.J. *The China Hands*. New York, 1975.
Koen, Ross Y. *The China Lobby in American Politics*. New York, 1974.

HUSSEIN, SADDAM

(*b.* 28 April 1937)

President of Iraq since 1979 and, since 1994, prime minister, who emerged as one of the strongest and most controversial leaders in the Arab world. His relations with the United States have gone from antagonism in the 1970s to an alliance of convenience in the 1980s, to wartime foe in the Gulf War of 1990–1991, to continuing adversary in the years since. While Saddam is sometimes accused of being unstable or erratic, it is far more likely that his willingness to take risks and use force is the result of the combination of his personal background, his ruthless opportunism, and the violent character of Iraqi nationalism and politics. His personal history does much to explain his insecurity, his use of violence, and his self-glorification. Although he later claimed descent on his mother's side from Ali (the fourth caliph and, in Shiite Islam, the revered First Imam), Saddam was born the son of a landless peasant from the village of al-Auja, near Takrit in north central Iraq. The full details of his youth are uncertain, but his father either died or abandoned his mother prior to Saddam's birth, and the boy grew up first in the home of his maternal uncle, Khayr Allah Tulfah, who instilled in him a xenophobic and, at that time, anti-British nationalism, and then in that of his stepfather (and paternal uncle), Ibrahim Hassan, who treated him abusively. Saddam completed intermediate school at sixteen but was unable to pass the entrance requirements for Baghdad Military Academy. He never served in the military and had no military training; he was simply appointed general of the army by President Ahmad Hassan al-Bakr in 1976, and he appointed himself field marshal after seizing the presidency in 1979.

In 1957 Saddam joined the Ba'ath Party of Iraq, then a small party with only 300–600 members. In 1958 the Iraqi monarchy was overthrown by General Abdul Karim Qassim, who soon faced plots by Ba'ath and other opposition groups. Saddam is said to have been a member of the Ba'ath squad that machine-gunned Qassim's car in the failed assassination attempt. He then fled to Egypt, where he stayed until February 1963, returning to Iraq after Qassim was assassinated. Between 1963 and 1968 when the Ba'ath took over, Saddam helped reorganize and rebuild the Ba'ath party. He purged left-wing ideologues and controlled Ba'ath security. Saddam joined the security services of the new Ba'ath government and remained closely tied to political and military figures from his home area of Takrit, including his cousin General al-Bakr. These ties, however, did not protect him when his faction lost power; Saddam was imprisoned from October 1964 until he escaped in 1966. On 17 July 1968 he participated in the successful Ba'ath coup led by General al-Bakr and became head of internal security. On 30 July he engineered a "white coup" within the new power structure, expelling a number of the senior officers who had helped him to power. On 9 October 1968 he presided over the arrest of a "Zionist spy ring" that later led to the trial and execution of fourteen men, eleven of whom were Jewish. This was the first in a long series of sweeping arrests of civilians who might threaten the regime. Saddam systematically expanded his power, using his position as head of the security services to eliminate both the Ba'ath party's perceived enemies and his potential rivals within the party. By 1969 he was deputy chairman of the ruling Revolutionary Command Council.

Between 1970 and 1975, Saddam's political energies were focused on three pressing concerns: The first was consolidation of the Ba'ath's power against internal "counter-revolutionary" elements such as those described above. Having been intimately involved in security matters over the years, he was admirably suited to the task of eliminating opposition: he smashed the power of the military faction of the Ba'ath party and at the same time moved to institute party control over the military. He then purged leading civilian opponents and former friends and colleagues. He nipped in the bud a serious coup attempt by Nahdim Kazzar, the head of the security services and a Saddam protege, in June 1973. The second was the nationalization of Iraq's oil, which was in the hands of the Western-controlled Iraq Petroleum Company. As Saddam saw it, Iraq could not develop or modernize if its major source of revenue, oil, was in the hands of the "imperialists." Shrewdly, despite his distaste for communism he drew close to the Soviet Union and signed a Treaty of Friendship and Cooperation on 9 April 1972; two months later he nationalized the IPC. The third was resolution of the perennial Kurdish problem. Saddam's attacks on the Kurds have a long history. He played a leading role in directing the central government campaign against them from 1968 to 1975. He led the efforts to make peace with the Kurds in 1970 and when the peace arrangements failed directed the military effort to crush them in 1974–1975. Unable to defeat the Kurdish rebels, Iraq was forced to make concessions to Iran in order to persuade the shah of Iran to cut off his aid to them. Saddam played a major role in those negotiations, which resulted in the 1975 Algiers Accord. Some feel that the experience left him with a lasting desire for revenge against both the Kurds and Iran and helped inspire his ruthlessness in his effort to make Iraq the preeminent political and military power in the Persian Gulf.

During the 1970s Saddam emerged as the dominant figure among the Iraqi political elite, for whom violence and ruthlessness were the ultimate measures of success; Saddam raised the qualifications to new and more extreme levels. By July 1979 he had enough power within the Ba'ath to force al-Bakr to give up the presidency for reasons of "health," and Saddam took over control of the Ba'ath party and the government. Less than two weeks later, Saddam began the most bloody purge in the history of the party, eliminating most of his opposition. He also began to surround himself with relatives and supporters from the area of Takrit, while using Iraq's growing oil wealth to support grandiose development and public works projects and to make massive new arms purchases. Iraq saw itself poised to become the leading Arab power. It had resources: water and oil. It was neither overpopulated nor underpopulated, and it was led by a ruthless political elite. Its Arab rivals, Egypt and Syria, had problems: Egypt was ostracized for its peace treaty with Israel, while Syria did not have the resources of Iraq.

Iraq's inexorable rise to predominance in inter-Arab affairs has been sidetracked by the Islamic revolution in Iran. Saddam originally attempted to deal with the Iranian Revolution and the Ayatollah Khomeini's rise to power by accommodating the new regime. Khomeini rejected these efforts and attempted to mobilize Iraq's Shiite majority to overthrow the secular Ba'athist regime. This led to repeated border clashes and raised Iraqi-Iranian tensions to a new height. At the same time, Khomeini's revolution had led to low-level civil war in Iran and large-scale purges of the Iranian military, giving the impression that Iran was a weak and divided state, ripe for the opportunism that was one of Saddam's signature characteristics. On 22 September 1980 Iraq invaded Iran, which unexpectedly unified in the face of invasion; even the Iranian Arabs in the southwest for the most part supported Tehran. The Iran-Iraq War dragged on until August 1988, causing the death of nearly one million Iranians and Iraqis. Iraq was able to survive only because it received more than $80 billion in loans, almost half of them from Kuwait and Saudi Arabia.

While Iraq defeated Iran in a series of major battles late in the war, it was unable to obtain any concessions or gains beyond a cease-fire. Baghdad did, however, take advantage of the end of the war to launch a major military campaign against its own Kurdish population, many of whom had rebelled or supported Iran during the war. Iraqi forces attacked Kurdish population centers, sometimes using poison gas. They killed tens of thousands of Kurds, destroyed hundreds of Kurdish villages, and forcibly relocated hundreds of thousands of Kurds or drove them as refugees into Turkey.

By 1989 the cost of the Iran-Iraq War, foreign debt payments, and Baghdad's efforts to continue funding both massive development projects and arms purchases had brought Iraq to bankruptcy. Its financial situation continued to decline in 1990, made worse by declining world oil prices and the recession in the West. This fed Saddam's deep-rooted desire to establish a regional hegemony in the Persian Gulf. He reacted by provoking a crisis with Kuwait over oil quotas and prices, relief for Iraq's debt, and demands for additional aid, access to the Persian Gulf, and control of the Rumalia oil field. At the same time he increased pressure on the other Persian Gulf states to recognize Iraq as the "Guardian of the Gulf" and stepped up his demands that U.S. and other Western military forces leave the area.

Despite major concessions by Kuwait, Saddam launched an invasion of Kuwait on 2 August 1990, proclaimed Kuwait to be Iraq's nineteenth province, and deployed troops on Kuwait's border with Saudi Arabia in a position where they could quickly seize Saudi Arabia's Eastern Province. Like his invasion of Iran, Saddam's invasion of Kuwait involved high risks but was scarcely irrational. Saddam had little historical reason to anticipate the international diplomatic and military resistance he encountered, while a conquest of Kuwait not only offered a potential solution to Iraq's economic crisis but also would give him secure access to a deep-water port on the Persian Gulf and control over Kuwait's massive financial reserves—and 8 percent of the world's oil reserves. Once again, however, Saddam had overreached. He was confronted with nearly unified resistance from the West and the rest of the Arab world. When he refused to withdraw, the United States, working through the United Nations, mobilized a massive military coalition. The result of his adventure was the Gulf War of 1990–1991, and Iraq's decisive defeat by the U.S.-led coalition in February 1991.

His international failures notwithstanding, Saddam Hussein managed to remain through a combination of ruthless tyranny, more purges of the military, reliance on a small elite of Loyalists, and the use of a tribally based bodyguard and carefully selected Republican Guard forces. He put down the Kurdish and Shiite uprisings after the end of the war with Iran. After the Gulf War he reorganized the Iraqi armed forces, and in 1995 still had roughly 50 percent of the military strength he had before the Gulf War. Saddam continued to exploit Arab and Iraqi nationalism, calling Iraq's Kurds "criminals" and continuing to claim sovereignty over Kuwait, despite Iraq's recognition of Kuwait's sovereignty in the 1991 cease-fire accords. He made lavish use of Islamic rhetoric. He used force to put down Shiite opposition in the south and deployed much of his army around the Kurdish security zone in the north. He lambasted neighbors like Saudi Arabia, and particularly Israel and the West. Iraqi agents attempted to assassinate former President George Bush during his visit to Kuwait in April 1993. None of these actions, however, brought him security, popular admiration, or glory. Despite his lengthy efforts to eliminate all opposition, and his new arrests and purges after the Gulf War, Saddam faced several coup attempts following the war, most notably in June 1992 and August 1993. Then in the summer of 1995 Hussein Kamil, Saddam's son-in-law, formerly in charge of much of Iraq's efforts to develop weapons of mass destruction (WMD), defected to Jordan. While Kamil provided extensive information on Iraqi WMD programs, notions that the opposition might mobilize around him proved untenable given his own brutal record. In early 1996 Kamil renounced his defection and returned to Iraq, only to be murdered at Saddam's behest within a few days.

Saddam's political fortunes have come full circle; just as in the early days of the regime when politics was the politics of survival and consolidation, as he enters the mid-1990s still in charge of Iraq Saddam's political energies are focused on pure survival in the face of this country's socioeconomic disintegrations and defections among officials and members of his family. Yet, in spite of these challenges he continues to show a ruthless determination to maintain power, aided considerably by the weaknesses of Iraqi opposition forces in exile and by his ability to manipulate his extended family. In October 1995 he showed he was still in charge by having the Iraqi people vote in a referendum on whether he should remain president for another seven years. The predictable ninety-nine percent (or more) "voted" for Saddam. He also made promises to "liberalize" the politics of the country.

ANTHONY H. CORDESMAN

See also Bush, George Herbert Walker; Gulf War of 1990–1991; Iran; Iran-Iraq War; Iraq; Kurds; Kuwait; Oil and Foreign Policy; Powell, Colin Luther; Saudi Arabia

FURTHER READING

Cordesman, Anthony H. *Iran and Iraq: The Threat from the Northern Gulf.* Boulder, Colo., 1994.
Darwish, Adel. *Unholy Babylon: The Secret History of Saddam's War and Why We Are Fighting It.* London, 1991.
Khadduri, Majid. *The Gulf War: The Origins and Implications of the Iraq-Iran Conflict.* New York, 1988.
Khalil, Samir al-. *Republic of Fear.* New York, 1991.
Makiya, Kanan. *Cruelty and Silence.* N.Y., 1993.
Marr, Phoebe. *The Modern History of Iraq,* Boulder, Colo., 1985.
Miller, Judith, and Laurie Mylroie. *Saddam Hussein and the Crisis in the Gulf.* New York, 1990.
Matar, Fuad, *Saddam Hussein: The Man, the Cause, and the Future,* London, Third World Publishing, 1981.

HYDE PARK AIDE-MÉMOIRE AGREEMENT

A summary of a discussion between President Franklin D. Roosevelt and British Prime Minister Winston S. Churchill, dated 18 September 1944. The conversation took place at the Roosevelt estate in Hyde Park, New York, where they were spending several days following the Second Quebec Conference. The memorandum represents the most candid expression of Roosevelt's plans for the wartime and postwar uses of the atomic bomb. According to the memorandum, he categorically rejected a proposal by the renowned physicist Niels Bohr for the international control of atomic energy. Several months earlier Bohr had approached Churchill and Roosevelt, insisting that a postwar nuclear arms race could only be prevented by enlisting the Soviet leader Josef Stalin in a plan to ban nuclear weapons. Bohr had argued that such a plan could succeed only if it were proposed before the bomb was built and used. He also had informed the president and the prime minister of his suspicion that the Russians already knew about the Manhattan Project, the secret project to build an atomic bomb, and argued that therefore nothing would be lost by adopting his proposal. Churchill had rejected Bohr's idea outright; Roosevelt had listened sympathetically. In the *aide-mémoire*, Churchill and Roosevelt agreed that Bohr should be watched so that he did not leak information, "particularly to the Russians." In a curiously tentative statement, the memorandum further noted agreement that the bomb "might perhaps, after mature consideration" be used against Japan. Finally, the memorandum committed the United States to a postwar atomic energy partnership with the British, one of Churchill's most sought-after goals. In effect, the memorandum suggests that Roosevelt had come around to a complete acceptance of Churchill's view on atomic energy. Roosevelt never shared the memorandum with any of his advisers; they became aware of it only when the British brought it to their attention months after Roosevelt's death.

MARTIN J. SHERWIN

See also Churchill, Winston Leonard Spencer; Manhattan Project; Nuclear Weapons and Strategy; Roosevelt, Franklin Delano; Science and Technology; World War II

FURTHER READING

Hewlett, Richard G., and Oscar E. Anderson, Jr. *The New World: A History of the United States Atomic Energy Commission, 1939–1946.* vol. 1. Berkeley, Calif., 1990.
Sherwin, Martin J. *A World Destroyed: Hiroshima and the Origins of the Arms Race.* New York, 1987.

HYDROGEN BOMB

One of the two basic types of nuclear weapons. It is also commonly known as the thermonuclear bomb, the fusion bomb, or the superbomb. Unlike the original atomic, or fission bomb, which derives its explosive energy entirely from the fission of uranium atoms, the hydrogen bomb derives a substantial fraction of its energy from the fusion of certain heavy isotopes of hydrogen, specifically deuteride, a gray, salt-like material. At very high temperatures—more than 100 million degrees—a complex series of nuclear reactions takes place in this salt, the net result being the production of helium, huge amounts of explosive energy, and a flood of very energetic neutrons. Many of these neutrons impinge in turn on a surrounding blanket of ordinary uranium in which they can, because of their exceptional energy, induce the fission reaction, leading to still more explosive energy. The basic idea of the hydrogen bomb first arose in the 1940s in the course of work on the atomic, or fission, bomb in the Manhattan Project. No specific workable design for the hydrogen bomb was forthcoming, however, until 1951, when Edward Teller and Stanislaus Ulam, scientists at the Los Alamos National Laboratory, came up with the break-through that made a hydrogen bomb a practical possibility. The first experimental device, estimated to weigh many tens of tons, was successfully exploded at Eniwetok atoll in the mid-Pacific in November 1952. Subsequently, scientists in the Soviet Union, the United Kingdom, France, China, and probably Israel also successfully developed hydrogen bombs.

HERBERT F. YORK

See also Atomic Energy Commission; Atoms for Peace; Manhattan Project; National Security and National Defense; Nuclear Nonproliferation; Nuclear Weapons and Strategy; Oppenheimer, Julius Robert; Strauss, Lewis; Teller, Edward

FURTHER READING

York, Herbert. *The Advisers: Oppenheimer, Teller, and the Superbomb.* 1976. Reprint. Stanford, Calif., 1989.

I

IAEA

See International Atomic Energy Agency

ICBMS

See Nuclear Weapons and Strategy

ICELAND

An island nation in the North Atlantic between Greenland and Norway, with historic ties to Scandinavia. Although its population is small, its strategic location makes it an important member of the North Atlantic Treaty Organization (NATO). A possession of Denmark from the fourteenth century until 1918, Iceland established its first significant trade contacts with the United States during World War I, when the island was cut off from its traditional European markets. Until then, Denmark controlled Iceland's trade through a royal monopoly. In 1918 Iceland was granted formal independence through the Danish-Icelandic Treaty of Union, but until World War II it remained united with Denmark through the monarchy, and Copenhagen continued to administer Icelandic foreign policy interests. When Denmark capitulated to the Germans in April 1940, the Danish parliament transferred royal authority to the government in Reykjavík. In 1941 Iceland's regent, Sveinn Björnsson, concluded a treaty with the United States that allowed U.S. forces to take over defense responsibilities of the island, replacing a British occupying force sent there in May 1940. The U.S. military transformed the small airstrip at Keflavík into a major air base for the protection of vital North Atlantic supply routes to Great Britain and the Soviet Union, and the United States became the chief supplier of foodstuffs and other material to the island. In July 1944, when the 1918 treaty with Denmark was formally terminated and Iceland became fully independent, the United States was the first nation to recognize Iceland.

After the end of World War II, Reykjavík requested that all military installations be dismantled and foreign troops withdrawn and declared the new republic an "unarmed neutral." Washington recognized the strategic importance of Iceland's position along the sea lanes between North America and Europe and wanted U.S. naval and air bases in the country. In 1946 an agreement was reached whereby the United States was allowed to station civilian personnel at Keflavík and was granted landing rights and other special privileges for its military aircraft. When Iceland became a founding member of NATO in 1949, its leaders intended to keep foreign troops off its soil during peacetime. By 1951, however, the marked increase in U.S.-Soviet tensions persuaded Iceland to conclude a defense treaty with the United States, which established the Iceland Defense Force, composed entirely of U.S. troops, to man the military base at Keflavík and other outpost facilities. Since the 1951 agreement (expanded in 1954), U.S.-Icelandic relations have been cooperative, despite objections to the security arrangement in some political circles in Reykjavík. The relationship was defined further in 1986, when Iceland's parliament secured rights for Icelandic companies to tender contracts for the shipment of goods to U.S. bases. In October 1986 Reykjavík was the site of a summit meeting between President Ronald Reagan and Soviet leader Mikhail Gorbachev.

DAVID P. AUGUSTYN

See also Denmark; Fisheries; North Atlantic Treaty Organization; Whaling; World War II

FURTHER READING

Cossolotto, Matthew. *The Almanac of Transatlantic Politics, 1991–1992.* Washington, D.C., 1991.
Lundestad, Geir. *America, Scandinavia, and the Cold War, 1945–1949.* New York, 1980.
Scott, Franklin D. *Scandinavia.* Revised edition. Cambridge, Mass., 1975.
Solheim, Olav Bruce. *The Nordic Nexus: A Lesson in Peaceful Security.* Westport, Conn., 1984.

IDEALISM

The concept propounded by many U.S. leaders since the nation gained its independence that the purpose of U.S. foreign policy should be the promotion of universal human ideals. Idealism is usually contrasted with traditional realism, the belief that a nation's foreign policy should be confined to the pursuit of power, prosperity, and security. Although idealism has a rich legacy, it defies easy characterization. The common element is the belief that foreign policy should be guided by such fundamental values as democracy, respect for human rights, the peaceful settlement of disputes, and openness rather than secrecy in international relations. Throughout U.S. history, however, American leaders and the public have often differed among themselves about the relative importance of these ideals, some of which may sometimes be mutually incompatible. Nevertheless, underlying such idealism has been the core belief that the United States has a special mission to reform the system of international relations: power is to be used for a moral purpose. Adlai Stevenson stated this "exceptionalist" version of America's purpose when he averred that "America is much more than a geographical fact. It is a political and moral fact—the first community in which men set out in principle to institutionalize freedom, responsible government, and human equality." Earlier, Woodrow Wilson proclaimed, "America was established not to create wealth but to realize a vision, to realize an ideal—to discover and maintain liberty among men."

This concept of a transcendant national purpose differs from the realist conception against which it is often juxtaposed. Realism—with equally deep roots—argues that morality should be made subservient to raison d'être and national interest, that in a contest between principle and power, power must be paramount. Advocates of realism stress an obligation for the U.S. government to put its national prosperity, power, and international position ahead of the pursuit of universal values or any other grand ideal.

The history of American diplomacy can be largely viewed in terms of a cyclical swing between periods when idealism was held in high esteem and those in which a realist conception predominated in foreign policy. Scholars such as Frank L. Klingberg and Arthur M. Schlesinger, Jr., have argued that these phases have alternated from generation to generation, roughly every twenty or twenty-five years. Perhaps not coincidentally, idealism has tended to dominate in the immediate aftermath of U.S. victory in war and in times of optimism and prosperity, when hopes for an ideal new world order under American leadership were high. Conversely, when international circumstances have been fraught with threat, a realist mood has flourished; U.S. policymakers were then more likely to focus on order and security than on high ideals.

Idealism is not a coherent philosophy. It is painted in many colors. However, within the constellation of diverse ideas associated with it is a rather consistent set of convictions that render idealism a subset of the larger liberal ideology from which it derives. At the risk of being simplistic and selective, the idealist tradition may be said to encompass the Enlightenment's faith in reason, progress, the essential goodness of human nature, freedom and

liberty, and the benefits of equal access to opportunity. Its beliefs are embedded in the Declaration of Independence, which itself was inspired by the liberal ideas of John Locke and Jean Jacques Rousseau. "We fought not to enslave," wrote Thomas Paine, "but to set a country free and to make room upon the earth for honest men to live in." Paine's version of idealism, however, was to be manifested principally through setting an example. "The purity of America was best maintained by avoiding the contamination of international politics," he wrote, in a spirit that was even more fervently argued by President George Washington in his Farewell Address.

It was only with the twentieth century, and most notably with Woodrow Wilson, that idealism came to call for active U.S. leadership in seeking to reform the world. After World War I Wilson championed an idealist American foreign policy dedicated to building "a world safe for democracy" under a rule of law, managed by an international organization, free from barriers to trade, rendered secure by disarmament agreements, and respectful of peoples' right to self-determination. These proposals were never really put to the test and were repudiated almost as soon as they were pronounced. Nazi Germany's and imperial Japan's bids for hegemony and the subsequent chill of the Cold War further discredited the idealist approach and reinvigorated enthusiasm for policies rooted in realpolitik.

Far from eliminating idealism, the Cold War reintensified the idealist-realist debate. Generally speaking, over the course of the Cold War, U.S. leaders inspired by the idealist vision have advocated support for international law, international institutions and organizations (such as the League of Nations and the United Nations), a liberal trade regime, arms control and disarmament, empowering the voice of the people through the spread of democratic governance, collective security as an alternative to balance-of-power jockeying for advantage, and, in general, multilateral approaches to international peace. Needless to say, the advocacy of these approaches has generated strong resistance from realists, who maintain that pursuit of these lofty goals are predicated on naive assumptions about the problems posed by a relentlessly conflictual and anarchical world. Critics have also been quick to warn that a crusading moralism can easily rationalize excessive U.S. involvement in world affairs. Indeed, they caution that in the past interventionism dedicated to reforming the world in America's image has sometimes destructively led to the prostitution of the very ideals that idealists hold most dear—liberty abroad and at home. It was this fear, for example, that led Secretary of State John Quincy Adams on 4 July 1821 to counsel against "going abroad in search of monsters to destroy." Active globalism, however well-intentioned, would, he warned, undermine the values that made

America special and allow it to "become the dictatress of the world" and accordingly "no longer the ruler of her own spirit."

The idealist program reached its height in the policies of Wilson. With the end of the Cold War, a resurgence of idealism and the liberal tradition from which it emanates was visible. With the peaceful and voluntary end of the Cold War, the promise of Europe's unification, an active role of the United Nations in many aspects of international affairs, and meaningful disarmament agreements such as the Intermediate-Range Nuclear Forces (INF) and the Strategic Arms Reduction (START) treaties, it seems to some that many components of Wilson's idealist vision have been vindicated. The spread of democracy and growing recognition that, as Wilson and other U.S. idealists predicted, democracies almost never go to war with one another, has likewise enhanced confidence in the practicality of idealism. Indeed, some idealists have come to favor more assertive U.S. policies, including the use of military force when deemed necessary, to promote, preserve, and protect democracy abroad. Others, however, have joined hands with realists in arguing that even as the world's most powerful state, and even on behalf of promoting U.S. ideals, the United States should resist the temptation to become too involved, especially militarily, in too many places around the globe; it should, instead, practice selective engagement, and act overseas only in those circumstances where U.S. national interests require it.

CHARLES W. KEGLEY, JR.

See also Atoms for Peace; Fourteen Points; Kellogg-Briand Pact; League of Nations; Realism; United Nations Washington Conference on the Limitation of Armaments; Washington's Farewell Address; Wilson, Thomas Woodrow

FURTHER READING

Doyle, Michael W. "Liberalism and World Politics." *American Political Science Review* 80 (1986): 1151–1169.
Hunt, Michael H. *Ideology and U.S. Foreign Policy.* New Haven, Conn., 1987.
Kegley, Charles W., Jr. "The Neoidealist Moment in International Studies: Realist Myths and the New International Realities." *International Studies Quarterly* 37 (June 1993): 131–146.
Klingberg, Frank L. *Positive Expectations of America's World Role: Historical Cycles of Realistic Idealism.* Lanham, Md., 1996.
Osgood, Robert E. *Ideals and Self-Interest in America's Foreign Relations: The Great Transformation of the Twentieth Century.* Chicago, 1953.
Schlesinger, Arthur M., Jr. *The Cycles of American History.* Boston, 1986.

IMF

See International Monetary Fund

IMMIGRATION

Immigration issues deal specifically with the (legal or illegal) entry of foreigners into a new country with the clear intention of establishing permanent residence as well as formally acquiring citizenship. In drafting the U.S. Constitution the nation's founders paid little attention to immigration, let alone the connection between it and foreign relations. Indeed, during the early years of the new Republic neither Congress nor the presidents indicated a strong interest in carving out an immigration policy. The federal government first counted immigrants in the 1820 census and instead of regulating newcomers, permitted the states to regulate the immigrant flow. During the 1790s, and for some time thereafter, the new government focused on alien rights and naturalization criteria, not on controlling the number and type of immigrants. Congress passed several laws defining the rights of aliens and setting down conditions under which resident aliens (immigrants) could become U.S. citizens; and in doing so, senators and representatives had in mind foreign policy considerations.

The Naturalization Act of 1790 was an extremely generous law for Europeans, because it provided that white immigrants could become citizens after two years residence in the United States. No sooner had it been passed, however, when the European crisis triggered by the French Revolution and the subsequent wars between France and Great Britain, and the efforts of both sides to involve the United States, prompted Congress to revise that law and enact new measures governing aliens. Many Jeffersonian Republicans objected to some refugees from the French Revolution entering the United States, while Federalists feared that too many opponents of Great Britain and friends of revolutionary France were migrating to the United States. In particular, Federalists disliked English and Irish radicals, called the United Irishmen, who sought asylum in the United States after the abortive Irish Revolution of 1798. As a result of these anxieties, in 1795 Congress raised the residency requirement for naturalization to fourteen years, and in 1798 the Federalists pushed through Congress several harsh alien acts and a sedition law. Foreign policy considerations clearly influenced these measures, because the Federalists wished to silence both immigrant and native-born critics of their pro-British foreign policy. Although the Alien and Sedition Acts granted the president authority to deport aliens considered to be dangerous, President John Adams did not use that power and, as the threat of war with France receded in 1800, the laws were allowed to lapse. Congress once again modified the residency requirement for naturalization, making it five years, at which it has remained to this day.

From 1800 until the 1880s the nation operated virtually without a federal immigration policy; the individual states regulated the influx of newcomers. State governments passed a variety of measures to guard against paupers and persons entering with infectious diseases and to improve conditions aboard immigrant-carrying vessels, but these measures had nothing to do with foreign policy and did not seriously hinder immigrants from coming to the United States. As a result, between 1840 and the 1920s, millions poured into the United States from Europe. Before 1890 the vast bulk of Europeans were Irish, British, and Germans. By the turn of the century, however, patterns had begun to change and immigrants from southern and eastern Europe dominated the immigration flows. Italians, Jews, Poles, Slavs, Greeks, and Scandinavians entered the United States in growing numbers. They usually avoided the southern states, because they could not compete with cheap black labor and more jobs were available in the industrial north, but immigrants settled nearly everywhere. Whole urban neighborhoods contained great mixtures of immigrants who found jobs in America's expanding industries. About 25 million newcomers were counted during the heyday of this migrant flow, from the 1880s until the 1920s.

As the flow of immigration rose substantially after 1840 and as the Supreme Court declared that the states had limited power to regulate it, Congress finally assumed control over immigration. In 1875 the federal government began receiving immigrants at Castle Garden at the tip of Manhattan in New York City, and in 1892 offshore at Ellis Island. Beginning in 1875 Congress passed a series of laws limiting immigration. In particular, the legislators banned categories of people thought to be undesirable, such as prostitutes, persons likely to become a public charge, anarchists, and those with certain diseases. Congress also required immigrants to pay a head tax and in 1917 imposed a literacy test. By and large these restrictions did not touch foreign affairs issues.

Restrictions on Chinese Immigration

When Congress began restricting immigrants from particular countries, foreign relations with various nations were affected. Congress enacted the first such restriction in the 1880s as a response to the growing anti-Chinese feeling, especially in California. When the Chinese arrived to seek their fortunes in California's gold rush of 1849, they initially caused little stir. Soon, however, American miners objected to the Chinese and convinced California lawmakers to enact a foreign miner's tax. As the Chinese left the overworked mines and sought employment in agriculture, railroad building, and in various occupations in cities, California laborers argued that the Chinese undercut the American standard of living. The Workingmen's Party of the 1870s successfully urged the California legislature to enact a variety of measures restricting the civil rights and economic choices of Chi-

nese immigrants. This did not satisfy anti-Chinese spokesmen, who insisted that the Chinese were an inferior race and who called on Congress to ban all Chinese immigrants. California workers found support among senators and representatives from other states.

When restrictionists put forth bills in Congress in the 1870s, the battle lines were quickly drawn. Congress finally passed a restriction act, but President Rutherford B. Hayes vetoed it on 1 March 1879, in response to protests from the Chinese government and from those who said that Chinese immigrants were desirable workers. In his veto message, Hayes noted that the Burlingame Treaty between the United States and China gave Chinese the right of immigration; thus, the bill was a violation of an agreement between the two countries. Hayes also worried that China might abrogate the principle of extraterritoriality and leave Americans in China without adequate protection.

President Hayes did not oppose immigration restriction, and he sent an envoy to China to seek a modification of the Burlingame Treaty so that the ban could be effected. After brief negotiations, the United States won a new treaty that gave it the right to limit or suspend immigration but not end it completely. With the new agreement in hand, Congress and the president were now free to act. In 1882 Congress suspended most Chinese immigration for twenty years. When China objected that this suspension was unduly harsh, Congress dropped the figure to ten years. When the time period expired, the ban was extended for a second decade. The Chinese Exclusion Act of 1882 covered only laborers; students, diplomats, and merchants still had the right of immigration, although they could not become U.S. citizens because Congress in 1790 had limited that right to "whites," adding in 1870 "persons of African descent." Court decisions subsequently held that Chinese were neither of African descent nor white.

Cutting immigration from China only partly satisfied racist demands and did not end related diplomatic complications. In the 1880s violent outbursts against Chinese workers in western towns and mining camps, including one in Rock Springs, Wyoming, which claimed twenty-eight Chinese lives, prompted protests from the Chinese government. While insisting that the United States had no obligation toward the families of the miners killed in Rock Springs but was solely making a humanitarian gesture, President Grover Cleveland requested and obtained funds from Congress to compensate China for the deaths.

Restrictions on Japanese Immigration

While most Chinese immigration stopped in the 1880s, Japanese immigration was just beginning, to Hawai'i and the West Coast. Once again workingmen's groups led the charge against these newcomers, claiming that the Japanese competed unfairly and drove wages down and that Japanese immigrants were undesirable persons who would never assimilate into the United States. In 1902, when the Chinese Exclusion Act came up for renewal (as it had been in 1892 and was again in 1943) white workers, the Asiatic Exclusion League, and the Native Sons of the Golden West demanded it be extended and that the Japanese be included in the ban. The international circumstances, however, were different. U.S. politicians and diplomats generally held the Chinese government in contempt, as a weak Asian power to be exploited and treated as a second class nation, but Japan was a rising power in Asia, one whose recent modernization had impressed Europeans and Americans with its strength. President Theodore Roosevelt shared some of the restrictionist's attitudes, but he was impressed with the military strength of Japan and its victory in the Russo-Japanese War of 1904–1905. The president could not avoid the issue, however, because the San Francisco school board precipitated an international crisis when it segregated all Asian children into an "Oriental School." The Japanese government quickly protested, saying such segregation violated the rights of Japanese children under the terms of a treaty between the United States and Japan.

Anxious to avoid a confrontation with Japan, Roosevelt sought to find a way to undo the school board's action but at the same time curtail Japanese immigration to the United States. Once the school board received assurance from Roosevelt that action to restrict immigration would be taken, the board members rescinded their regulation. In 1907–1908 Roosevelt concluded an executive agreement with Japan, in which the Japanese government agreed to halt the emigration of laborers to America. This Gentlemen's Agreement avoided insulting Japan openly, as a treaty would have done, but nonetheless accomplished the restrictionists' goal. The Gentlemen's Agreement did not stop the California legislature from enacting other harassing laws against Japanese immigrants.

Restriction against Japanese immigrants became an issue again during the 1920s, when Congress revised U.S. policies and enacted laws creating national origins quotas, covering European nations and favoring the countries of northern and western Europe. Great Britain alone had nearly one-half of the 150,000 slots allotted under the quota system, while Russia and Italy received only a few thousand. These new restrictions accomplished the main goal of nativists and caused little debate about foreign policy issues. In the case of Japan, however, legislators decided that the Gentlemen's Agreement was inadequate. That agreement covered laborers, but originally not their wives; consequently, many Japanese immigrants who lived in the United States before the ban became effec-

tive brought their wives to the United States. In some cases they had married, by proxy, women they had never seen. These "picture brides," as they were called, alarmed some westerners who wanted all Asian immigration halted. Responding to these demands, Congress in 1924 barred all aliens who were "ineligible for citizenship." Because the courts had held that Japanese were not white under the naturalization act of 1870, this provision meant an end to Japanese immigration. The government of Japan once again protested, preferring to have a quota. When Secretary of State Charles Evans Hughes informed Congress of Japanese complaints, the legislators ignored them and overwhelmingly passed the bill ending virtually all Asian immigration.

Mexican Immigration: 1920s–1940s

Foreign policy issues also figured in the 1920s debates about the Western Hemisphere. Representative John Box of Texas and his allies in Congress wanted the Western Hemisphere brought under the quota system. Nativists feared an invasion of Mexicans, who had no immigration quota, now that European immigration was being sharply curtailed causing a labor shortage. During World War I the United States had permitted a temporary influx of Mexican workers, but now patriotic groups, eugenicists who believed Mexicans to be inferior, and labor unions led in calling for restricting Western Hemispheric migration. They used familiar arguments: that Mexicans depressed the U.S. standard of living and that they were innately inferior and a threat to American society. They were not unopposed. Secretary of State Frank Kellogg introduced foreign policy considerations into the debate, arguments against giving quotas to Mexico and other nations in the Western Hemisphere. He raised the concept of Pan-Americanism and asserted that such quotas would harm the good relations between the United States and its neighbors, Mexico and Canada. While his arguments might have swayed some votes, economic issues were paramount. Agricultural interests and mining and railroad employers needed and wanted low-wage Mexican labor and insisted that Mexicans made good workers and were not a drain on the American taxpayer. In the end, by a vote of 60 to 12, the Senate defeated a proposal to place the Western Hemisphere under a quota system; the House never voted on the measure.

Mexicans and nationals from the Western Hemisphere were covered by other provisions, such as bans on those likely to become a public charge, a restriction that became significant during the Great Depression, when the federal government supported efforts by local communities to deport Mexican immigrants rather than allow them to be recipients of relief. Although the Mexican government was not entirely pleased by these actions, it could do little to halt them, and Mexican officials realized that the employment prospects of Mexican immigrants were grim in the United States during the Great Depression. A few Mexican officials believed that the skills that immigrants had learned in the United States could be put to good use in the Mexican economy.

The outbreak of World War II and the accompanying labor shortages transformed the situation. When the U.S. government had suspended immigration regulations during World War I to permit 72,000 Mexicans to work temporarily in the United States, Washington took this step unilaterally, without consulting Mexican authorities. This action caused some friction from Mexico's fear that without binding agreements Mexicans might be deported, as happened during the 1930s. Not wanting to act in a unilateral way again, when agricultural enterprises reported in the early 1940s that they needed laborers to replace those heading for the rapidly expanding war industries, the United States consulted with the Mexican government about beginning a temporary worker program. Mexico at first was wary because its officials did not want to see a repeat of forced repatriation in case the United States decided its people were no longer needed. Once convinced that their nationals were needed to work on U.S. farms, they agreed to establish the Bracero Program, which lasted from 1943 until 1964. This time the Mexican government made certain conditions. Their workers were to be covered by U.S. regulations governing farm workers and they were not to be employed in Texas, a state where anti-Mexican feeling was widespread. The U.S. government agreed to these terms. Because U.S. farm workers were not protected by federal legislation, the first condition was meaningless, and after a few years Mexicans were permitted to work in Texas.

The Bracero Program involved five million participants, mostly on terms negotiated by the two countries, although the United States did import temporary laborers unilaterally when agreements were not in effect. Mexico was willing to negotiate new terms in 1964, but pressure by American churches, labor unions, and a variety of liberal organizations convinced Congress and President John F. Kennedy that the Bracero Program undercut U.S. farm wages and that the program should be terminated. Provisions in the Simpson-Rodino Act of 1986 included clauses allowing the federal government to inaugurate a new temporary worker program, but these were never utilized.

World War II and the Cold War

The immigration restrictions that had culminated in the enactment of the National Origins System during the 1920s began to unravel during World War II, largely because of foreign policy considerations. Even before the hostilities began, Americans had been softening their views toward China, particularly after the Japanese invasion of China in 1937, when American newsreels showed the Chinese as victims of atrocities, and U.S. policymakers moved to aid the Chinese in their war against Japan. When Japan attacked the United States in December 1941, Americans found themselves allied with China in the Pacific war. Prominent Chinese figures also aroused much pro-Chinese sentiment when they visited the United States during the war, the most noted being the triumphant trip of Madame Jiang Jieshi (Chiang Kaishek) in 1943. The wartime alliance with China prompted several congressmen, missionaries, and scholars to urge overturning the Chinese Exclusion Act. President Franklin D. Roosevelt added his support, saying this action would correct a historical mistake and that repeal was essential to the war effort and postwar peace in Asia. Congress responded in 1943, replacing the exclusion acts with a law giving China a small immigration quota.

Similar considerations arose concerning the Philippines, a U.S. possession from 1898 to 1946, and newly independent India. As U.S. nationals, Filipinos had been exempt from the ban on Asians enacted during the 1920s. Responding to racist and economic fears about the impact of Filipino immigration, however, Congress in 1934 had given the Philippines a quota of only fifty immigrants until independence, after which Filipinos would be barred like all other Asians. Because many Filipinos fought alongside Americans in the Pacific war, public sympathy developed for their heroic efforts. After India achieved its independence from Great Britain in 1947, U.S. political leaders also recognized the importance of India in postwar Asian politics. As a result, Congress granted both the Philippines and India small quotas and permitted these immigrants to become U.S. citizens, effective in 1946. These measures had little impact because the quotas granted were so small—105 for China and only 100 each for the Philippines and India—but their enactment was a sign of America's growing realization of the importance of Asia, and they were a prelude to the growing importance that foreign policy issues would play in the development of U.S. immigration laws and policies.

Refugees and Displaced Persons

The national origins quotas had been tightly enforced during the 1930s. Jews and other refugees were desperate to escape Nazism, especially after 1938. While thousands of Jews did manage to emigrate to the United States, many more would have if the quotas and other restrictions had been relaxed. Whatever his personal feelings, President Roosevelt was unwilling to oppose Congress and admit more refugees. After World War II the United States was once again confronted with a refugee emergency, faced with thousands of survivors of the Holocaust, millions of displaced persons in postwar Europe, and a tight system of national origins quotas. The Citizens Committee for Displaced Persons suggested passage of a special provision to enable the United States to receive several hundred thousand displaced persons. President Harry Truman backed the proposal, and, after considerable debate, Congress passed two Displaced Persons Acts in 1948 and 1950 that permitted European nations to "mortgage" their quotas. This legislation, which opened the door for about 400,000 persons, was largely sold on humanitarian grounds and on the need to help U.S. allies in Europe deal with the war's damage and a flood of refugees. The Displaced Persons Acts were the first of many postwar refugee measures.

When Congress renewed its commitment to national origins quotas in passing the McCarran-Walter Immigration Act of 1952, it was vetoed by President Truman, who declared that U.S. allies in Europe were insulted by the quotas and such discrimination made for poor public policy. Congress thought otherwise, and it passed the bill over Truman's veto. The McCarran-Walter Act represented a reform in at least one area: it removed race as a consideration for naturalization and it allowed all Asian nations to have small quotas. The legislators certainly had in mind the Cold War competition with communism that had already emerged, because the Soviet Union constantly harped on U.S. racial policies. When Congress voted to remove the racial ban, it informed peoples throughout the world that they could emigrate to the United States and become U.S. citizens, although the numbers were small. In eliminating the racial requirement, Congress was also giving recognition to the heroism and patriotism of Japanese-American soldiers during the war and to the importance of Japan in the Pacific.

No sooner had the McCarran-Walter Act been passed when President Dwight D. Eisenhower urged another refugee act to help Europe cope with the still-large number of displaced persons. Congress agreed and the Refugee Relief Act of 1953 became law, admitting another 200,000 refugees. Eisenhower also established an important precedent in dealing with the abortive Hungarian Revolution of 1956 and the subsequent flood of Hungarian refugees into Austria. The quota for Hungary was small, but the president utilized a provision of the McCarran-Walter Act to parole in 36,000 Hungarians. Congress had meant for the parole power to be used in individual, emergency cases, but Eisenhower employed it for a large group. He justified his action on the ground that the United States had an obligation to aid the Hungarian freedom fighters and that the U.S. European allies alone could not care for the 200,000 who escaped when the Soviet Union crushed the rebellion. Despite some grumbling in Congress about the president's misuse of the parole power, the legislators passed a bill approving the president's action and permitting these refugees to become resident aliens.

Several additional refugee acts were passed in the 1950s to admit refugees fleeing communism. The fact that Congress was being called upon to make constant adjustments to the National Origins System codified by the McCarran-Walter Act prompted some political leaders to suggest that a new system be put into place. A healthy economy, effective lobbying, and a more tolerant public all made it possible for the Immigration Act of 1965 to scrap the National Origins System. The new policy, effective as a worldwide system in 1979, gave each nation a quota of 20,000 (excluding immediate family members of U.S. citizens) and based immigrant visas upon preferences for family unification, economic needs in the United States, and refugees. Foreign policy certainly played a role in the debate, because many insisted that the United States could ill afford a discriminatory immigration policy in view of its struggle against communism. The refugee provisions, which provided 17,400 slots annually, were in particular part of an anticommunist foreign policy. The law defined refugees as those escaping communism. Many refugees did enter the United States during the Cold War era. These included Soviet Jews who arrived in the late 1970s, and then ceased coming in 1981 when the Soviet Union refused to grant them exit visas, and began arriving again in the late 1980s and early 1990s, when Moscow permitted thousands of Jews and Armenians to leave for the United States, even as the Cold War ended.

The refugee provisions of the 1965 law quickly proved to be inadequate as a legal basis for admitting persons escaping communism, especially in the cases of Cuba and Vietnam. The United States had begun to admit Cubans as refugees after Fidel Castro assumed power in 1959. Several hundred thousands arrived before the 1962 Cuban missile crisis halted the airlift between the United States and Cuba. In 1965 Castro indicated that he might be willing to renew the airlift, and when President Lyndon Johnson signed the Immigration Act of 1965 at the foot of the Statue of Liberty, he declared that the United States was agreeable to receiving all who wished to leave Cuba. Castro responded favorably, and a new airlift carried several hundred thousand Cubans to Florida. It ended in 1973, although a few thousand persons managed to come by boat from that time until a new crisis erupted in 1980. Like President Eisenhower, President Johnson lacked authority to admit so many persons, but Johnson wanted to embarrass the Cuban government and portray the United States as the land of freedom and opportunity. In 1966 Congress sanctioned Johnson's action and passed the Cuban Adjustment Act, which permitted these refugees to become immigrants and eventually American citizens.

Vietnamese and Cuban "Boat People"

If the Cuban exodus proved somewhat surprising, so did the flood of refugees from Vietnam, where the war uprooted several million Vietnamese, Cambodians, and Laotians, sending them to cities like Saigon in search of security. The United States aided these unfortunate people, but government officials gave no thought to admitting them to the United States as immigrants. Then, in 1973 the administration of President Richard M. Nixon negotiated a settlement and withdrew U.S. forces. In 1975 North Vietnam invaded and conquered South Vietnam and these people found themselves at risk. Suddenly the United States faced another immigration crisis. There was wide public sentiment in the United States for taking in refugees from the disastrous war in Indochina. In the spring of 1975 the United States military airlifted tens of thousands of frantic Vietnamese, first to Guam and then to the United States. Others fled by boat or across the Thailand border. In 1975, 130,000 refugees found their way to the United States, where they were processed through refugee camps and into U.S. communities. Persecution and economic hardship in Vietnam, Laos, and Cambodia (where mass killings took place under radical communist rule) between 1976 and 1979 led to another refugee exodus, and the U.S. government accepted thousands more. In 1980 a mass exodus of hundreds of thousands of "boat people" began, and the United States accepted many of them as refugees. The immigration act gave only 17,400 places annually for refugees, clearly less than the flow from Indochina, but once the Ford and then later the Carter administrations had decided to parole these desperate people, Congress granted funds to aid in their settlement and legislation to enable them to become immigrants.

The ad hoc nature of the Cuban and Vietnamese flows suggested to governmental officials that a new refugee policy was needed. The Refugee Act of 1980 increased the "normal flow" of refugees to a more realistic 50,000 annually and provided special programs to monitor their progress and support their adjustment to American life. The "normal flow" was flexible, and subsequently the United States admitted approximately twice that number yearly.

The Refugee Act of 1980 had scarcely been passed when a new emergency arose. Cuban Americans had been visiting their native land at Castro's invitation in 1979 and early 1980, and when Cubans learned of the success of their former compatriots in the United States, many wanted to join their countrymen in Florida. With Castro's permission and the Peruvian governments agreement to admit them thousands crowded the Peruvian embassy demanding visas. Later they were allowed to enter the United States. Castro then declared that he would permit all who wanted to leave to head for America from the Cuban port of Mariel. President Jimmy Carter, thinking of the foreign policy implications, initially said he would welcome all who came. Cuban Ameri-

cans, utilizing every boat they could find in Florida, journeyed to Mariel to pick up the refugees. A startled administration suddenly faced an exodus of more than 100,000 Cubans, while the new refugee act provided for only 50,000. Reports that Castro was dumping prisoners and mentally ill persons into the boats caused more anxiety among governmental officials and an outcry in many of the communities where these people arrived, and the Carter administration used the U.S. Navy to end the exodus. In 1994 when a growing number of Cubans once again tried to travel by boat from Cuba to Florida, the United States intervened and interned them at the Guantanamo Naval Base. Negotiations between the United States and Cuba led to an agreement allowing them to enter the United States, but Castro agreed to halt future "boat people" from leaving for the United States. The Clinton Administration agreed to permit Cubans to apply for America visas in Cuba in an orderly manner. Cubans would be allowed 20,000 visas per year.

The Haitian Influx and the 1980s Debate on Refugees

Cubans were not the only people from the Caribbean trying to come to America. Thousands of Haitians, escaping from poverty and the repressive dictatorial regimes of François Duvalier and his son, Jean-Claude, had been fleeing Haiti for years, often illegally coming to the United States by boat. The congressional Black Caucus and a variety of ethnic groups involved with immigrant settlement urged that these persons, although arriving illegally in Florida, also should be considered refugees, and an embarrassed President Carter agreed. Wanting to avoid using the much-criticized parole power, he created a new category, "Cuban-Haitian Entrants," for those entering from the spring of 1980 until October of that year. While this status allowed the Cubans and Haitians to stay in the United States, they were left in limbo. The administration of President Ronald Reagan later announced that the Cuban entrants would be permitted to become immigrants under the Cuban Adjustment Act of 1966, but he did not include the Haitians. Congress ultimately resolved the Haitians' position when it passed legislation in 1986 that permitted those who had arrived illegally before 1982 to change their status to that of resident aliens. Haitians, along with any from other countries trying to enter without proper papers after 1982, were to be treated as undocumented aliens and subject to deportation.

In addition to rejecting Haitian claims the Reagan administration blockaded Haiti and returned boatloads of refugees trying to escape to the United States. The exception to this was those who came during the Mariel period, when out of embarrassment caused by the media over the government appearing to be racist by allowing

MAJOR SOURCES OF IMMIGRATION BY COUNTRY OR REGION (IN THOUSANDS)

Period	Germany	Asia[1]	Italy	Britain	Ireland	Austria-Hungary	Canada	Mexico	Russia (USSR)[2]	Caribbean	Denmark, Norway; Sweden[3]
1820-1830	8			27	54		2	5		4	
1831-1840	152		2	76	207		14	7		12	2
1841-1850	435		2	267	781		42	3		14	14
1851-1860	952	42	9	424	914		59	3		11	25
1861-1870	787	65	12	607	436	8	154	2	3	9	126
1871-1880	718	124	56	548	437	73	384	5	39	14	243
1881-1890	1453	70	307	807	655	354	393	24	213	29	656
1891-1900	505	75	652	272	388	593	3	15	505		372
1901-1910	341	324	2046	526	339	2145	179	50	1597	108	505
1911-1920	144	247	1110	341	146	896	742	219	922	123	203
1921-1930	412	112	455	330	221	64	925	459	89	75	198
1931-1940	114	16	68	29	13	11	109	22	7	16	11
1941-1950	227	37	58	132	28	28	172	61	4	50	27
1951-1960	478	153	185	192	57	104	378	300	6	123	57
1961-1970	200	445	207	231	42	31	287	443	16	520	45
1971-1980	66	1634	130	124	14	16	115	637	43	760	15
1981-1990	70	2817	33	142	33	14	119	1653	84	893	19
Total	7062	6161	5332	5075	4765	4337	4077	3872	3528	2761	2518

1 Includes Middle East.
2 Includes Finland, Latvia, Estonia, and Lithuania.
3 Includes Iceland.
4 Figure for 1881-1885 only.
5 Figure for 1894-1900 only.

Sources: *Historical Statistics of the United States: Colonial Times to 1970*, U.S. Bureau of the Census, 1975; *Statistical Abstract of the United States, 1993*, U.S. Bureau of the Census, 1993; U.S. Immigration and Naturalization Service

Cubans and not Haitians to immigrate during the same time period (April to October 1980), both were allowed to enter. Clearly anticommunism was an issue in the formulation of this policy, but anti-communism alone does not explain it. The Black Caucus, with some cause, insisted that racism was a factor in the treatment of Haitians. Moreover, the U.S. government feared another Mariel-style exodus in which immigration would slip out of control. A period of change and upheaval in Haiti in 1986–1994, which included intervals of elected government, military coups and rule, and finally the restoration of elected leaders, did not lead to any changes in U.S. policy toward illegal Haitian immigrants, although President Bill Clinton modified the blockade in 1994. In the fall of 1994 President Clinton ordered an invasion of Haiti to restore the constitutionally elected government. This action, at least temporarily, removed the incentive for Haitians to flee for political reasons. Clinton indicated he wanted an elected government in Haiti to take power, which was done. He also noted that Haitians would no longer need to come to the United States for asylum.

While Cold War considerations dictated refugee policy, some organizations and individuals connected to immigrant programs said that anticommunism alone should not be the sole criterion for the admission of refugees. In 1968 the United States had agreed to the United Nations 1967 Declaration on the Status of Refugees, which provided a broader framework for the definition of refugees to include those who had a well-founded fear of persecution based on race, political opinion, religion, or nationality in their homelands, but the Senate's acceptance of the United Nations position had little meaning in actual policy. Practically all refugees from 1968 to 1980 entered under the guise of escaping communism. Proponents of the UN statement urged that legislative provision be made for that broader definition, and they succeeded in including it in the 1980 refugee law, but policy did not change. The United States continued to admit most refugees from communist nations, such as the Soviet Union, Vietnam, and Cuba. Even after the collapse of communism in Europe and the end of the Cold War in 1989–1991, most of those claiming refugee status continued to come from the former Soviet Union, Vietnam, Cambodia and Laos.

Asylum Policy

The vast bulk of refugees entered the United States from other nations under the sponsorship of the U.S. government and refugee organizations, but there was another way for individuals to gain sanction in the United States. If they came to the United States, either legally or illegally, they could then claim asylum under the UN protocol. Prior to enactment of the 1980 Refugee Act, only a few thousand persons won asylum in this manner, and regula-

tions were not well defined. Seeking to clarify asylum procedures, drafters of the 1980 act included a provision for granting asylum to 5,000 persons annually.

While the asylum section of the law seemed to take care of the few thousand such cases each year, it quickly became the center of controversy and raised important foreign policy issues as tens of thousands of persons claimed asylum each year, creating a huge backlog. During the 1980s the Immigration and Naturalization Service (INS) was reluctant to grant asylum to Haitians, Salvadorans, and Guatemalans, with whose governments the United States had friendly relations; granting asylum to their citizens would be an admission that U.S.-backed governments violated the rights of its citizens. The Department of State advised INS that these people were coming to the United States for economic reasons and could not prove, on an individual basis as required by law, that they faced a well-founded fear of persecution if they returned home. In the case of Haiti, U.S. officials no doubt had in mind the pro-American and anti-Cuban votes the Duvalier government had been providing for years in the UN and Organization of American States.

On the other hand, persons from Iran in the United States had a relatively high rate of winning asylum during the 1980s. After the Islamic revolution in Iran overthrew the U.S.-backed government in 1979 and held American officials hostage, U.S. policy became hostile toward that country. Thus, it was easy for INS to declare that Iranians would face persecution if returned to their homeland.

Another indication that fear of uncontrolled borders played a role in asylum policy occurred in the late 1980s, when the INS dealt with claims of Nicaraguans who crossed the Mexican border and asked for asylum. Because the United States actively supported the Contras who were trying to overthrow the left-wing Sandinista Nicaragua government, Nicaraguans seemed more likely than others to receive asylum, but most claims were nonetheless rejected. The government's fear of an invasion of "feet people" was greater than its willingness to accept persons fleeing Nicaragua. As the conflict in Nicaragua was winding down, one INS official in Florida began in 1986 to grant asylum readily on the ground that the U.S. government considered Nicaragua to be a communist state that oppressed its people. This particular crisis ended, however, when an election held in 1990 in Nicaragua overturned Sandinista rule.

The Debate on Illegal Mexican Immigration

One of the more controversial aspects of postwar immigration has been undocumented or illegal immigration. Undocumented aliens first appeared in large numbers during the 1920s when Mexicans slipped by border crossings rather than pay a head tax and be subjected to a literacy test. No one paid much attention to the U.S.-Mexico border at that time. Congress did not authorize a border patrol until 1924, and during its first years it worried mainly about liquor being smuggled into the United States and the possibility that Asians might try to enter illegally. When the Bracero Program was initiated during World War II, it stimulated another flow of undocumented immigration from Mexico. Mexican nationals who found the Bracero quotas filled simply crossed illegally into the United States and easily found jobs on U.S. farms. In some cases undocumented aliens were able to sign on as Braceros once in the United States, even though the Mexican government was supposed to supervise the contracts on its side of the border. In any event there were ample reasons for Mexicans to head north, legally or not. Alarmed by the growing number of undocumented aliens being apprehended in the Southwest and along the U.S.-Mexico border, the Eisenhower administration in 1954 carried out Operation Wetback, which included sweep operations on U.S. farms to catch and deport undocumented aliens. The government also increased the number of Braceros available for growers, who were content to use them instead of undocumented aliens. Thus, the federal government and INS seemed to have the situation under control and believed that the border was secure.

The Bracero Program was terminated at the same time that Congress passed the Immigration Act of 1965. Although that act represented reform, insofar as it abolished the national origins quotas, in at least one respect it made emigration from the Western Hemisphere more difficult. For the first time, the Western Hemisphere had an immigration ceiling of 120,000, and further changes in the 1970s gave Mexico the same 20,000 limit as all other nations. As a result, Mexicans now found it more difficult to obtain a U.S. visa, and they could no longer sign on as Braceros. They came anyway, as undocumented aliens. The Mexican ambassador to the United States had warned about such a result when the Bracero Program was ended but such warnings were ignored.

As the tide of illegal immigration grew after 1965, a variety of U.S. groups, such as the Federation for American Immigration Reform and some labor unions and environmental organizations, warned that immigration was too large and out of control and that undocumented aliens caused unemployment, drained social services, and lowered the American standard of living. Of course, Mexicans were not the only nationals attempting to live and work in the United States illegally. Others, such as the Irish, Dominicans, and Filipinos, arrived on visitors's visas and then stayed on after their permits expired, but most illegals arrived over the U.S.-Mexico border. By the late 1970s more than one million undocumented persons were being caught annually, the vast bulk at the southern

border of the United States. Thus, the U.S.-Mexico border became a matter of controversy between the two nations.

Most debate about undocumented aliens focused on domestic or local issues, but the discussions touched upon foreign policy as well. Proposals to build huge walls, electric fences, or barriers with sharp edges drew protests from church and immigrant-advocate organizations and the Mexican government, which claimed that such devices were needlessly cruel. Mexico assured the United States that it did not approve of unauthorized border crossings, but the Mexican government knew it had a serious unemployment situation at home and that undocumented workers in the United States sent cash back to their families in Mexico. Thus, the United States hesitated to build more formidable barriers along its southern border for fear of harming U.S.-Mexican relations. In 1986 Congress passed the Immigration Reform and Control Act (IRCA), which was supposed to end the undocumented immigration crisis. IRCA prohibited employers from knowingly hiring illegal aliens; and in return for this provision, the law allowed many illegal aliens in the United States at that time to legalize their status. While IRCA might have temporarily slowed undocumented immigration, it did not end it. Illegal migration rose again in the 1990s and the debate was renewed about what to do to control this immigration.

Some observers insisted that the issue of illegal immigration, at least from Mexico, might be relieved when the North American Free Trade Agreement (1992) became fully effective and Mexico witnessed a rising standard of living, a situation that would allegedly reduce pressures for emigration. The complications arising from undocumented immigrants were another of many immigration issues that touched upon foreign affairs. That they were not resolved satisfactorily to all parties was not untypical of how immigration and foreign policy often produced less than perfect results.

DAVID M. REIMERS

See also Alien and Sedition Acts; Cambodia; China; Cuba; Gentlemen's Agreements; Haiti; Human Rights; Immigration and Naturalization Service; Japan; Laos; Mexico; Philippines; Race and Racism; Refugees; Vietnam

FURTHER READING

Calavita, Kitty. *Inside the State: The Bracero Program, Immigration, and the INS.* New York, 1992.

Craig, Richard B. *The Bracero Program: Interest Groups and Foreign Policy.* Austin, Tex., 1971.

Daniels, Roger. *Coming to America: A History of Immigration and Ethnicity in American Life.* New York, 1990.

Divine, Robert A. *American Immigration Policy, 1924–1952.* New Haven, Conn., 1957.

Higham, John. *Strangers in the Land: Patterns of American Nativism, 1860–1925,* 2nd ed. New Brunswick, N.J., 1988.

Hing, Bill Ong. *Making and Remaking Asian America Through Immigration Policy.* Stanford, Calif., 1993.

Hutchinson, Edward P. *Legislative History of American Immigration Policy, 1790–1965.* Philadelphia, Pa., 1981.

Kettner, James. *The Development of American Citizenship, 1608–1870.* Chapel Hill, N.C., 1978.

LeMay, Michael C. *From Open Door to Dutch Door: An Analysis of U.S. Immigration Policy Since 1820.* New York, 1987.

Loescher, Gil, and John A. Scanlan. *Calculated Kindness: Refugees and America's Half-Open Door, 1945–Present.* New York, 1986.

Reimers, David M. *Still the Golden Door: The Third World Comes to America,* 2nd ed. New York, 1992.

Riggs, Fred. *Pressures on Congress: A Study of the Repeal of the Chinese Exclusion Act.* New York, 1950.

Sutter, Valerie O'Connor. *The Indochinese Refugee Dilemma.* Baton Rouge, La., 1990.

Takaki, Ronald. *Strangers from a Different Shore: A History of Asian Americans.* Boston, 1989.

IMMIGRATION AND NATURALIZATION SERVICE

An agency of the U.S. Department of Justice that administers laws on the admission, exclusion, deportation, and naturalization of aliens. Though in 1819 Congress enacted the first immigration law in an effort to collect statistics on immigrants and supervise conditions on passenger ships, state governments regulated the admission of aliens until 1875. New York City was the main port of entry for immigrants, so the New York State Board of Commissioners of Emigration shouldered much of the responsibility. After establishing the short-lived Bureau of Immigration to recruit immigrant labor between 1864 and 1868, Congress assumed more regulatory responsibilities, particularly in response to nativist demands to exclude Chinese prostitutes and laborers. In 1875 Congress enacted the first direct federal regulatory immigration act banning the admission of felons, prostitutes, and coolie labor, and in 1876 the U.S. Supreme Court declared in *Henderson* v. *Mayor* that state regulation of immigration was an unconstitutional infringement of federal power.

Under the Immigration Act of 1882, the secretary of the Treasury assumed responsibility for enforcing federal laws concerning aliens. Both New York officials and charitable groups wanted more federal control of immigration as well as responsibility for administrative expenses to relieve the states. Nativists wanted the federal government to restrict immigrants from eastern and southern Europe who were regarded as inferior to those who arrived before the 1880s. The new law excluded "idiots," convicts, prostitutes, and persons likely to become public charges, and in 1885 the Foran Act forbade the admission of contract laborers. New York and other states handled the reception of immigrants on behalf of the federal government until 1890 when the U.S. Department of the Treasury selected Ellis Island as a reception area. In 1891 Congress placed immigration entirely under federal control and established the Office of the Superintendent of Immigration in the Department of the Treasury. The office set up the Bureau of Emigration. In 1903 Congress transferred the Bureau to the newly established U.S. Department of Commerce and Labor and enacted a law excluding foreign anarchists.

In 1906 Congress expanded the functions of the Bureau to matters relating to naturalization. It renamed the agency the Bureau of Immigration and Naturalization. The Immigration Act of 1907 consolidated all existing legislation on immigration and made the Bureau responsible for advising immigrants about farm and job opportunities. In 1913 Congress divided the agency into the Bureaus of Immigration and Naturalization and transferred them to the U.S. Department of Labor. Because of the nativist movement against immigrants during World War I and the fear of radicalism during the Red Scare, Congress enacted the National Origins Act of 1924, which imposed quotas to limit the admission of immigrants on the basis of country of origin. The law was designed to curb immigration from eastern and southern Europe, the main source of immigrants before World War I. It exempted Canada and Latin American countries from quotas and banned the admission of Japanese and other immigrants ineligible for citizenship. The Bureau of Immigration cooperated with the Department of State to enforce the quotas, and the Bureau of Naturalization administered laws allowing aliens citizenship.

In 1933 President Franklin D. Roosevelt issued an executive order reuniting the two bureaus as the Immigration and Naturalization Service. Throughout the 1930s Congress and others debated whether political refugees and other immigrants threatened national security. In 1940 Congress mandated that all aliens be fingerprinted and that they report their address every year. Also in 1940, President Roosevelt asked that the agency be shifted to the Department of Justice. By becoming part of that department, Roosevelt said the Service could better contribute to national security amid instability in Europe. The transfer was approved by Congress.

Since 1940 the government has relied on the exclusionary power of the Immigration and Naturalization Service to enforce immigration policies. New laws imposed more responsibilities on the Service to deal with displaced persons from war-torn Europe, political refugees from communist countries, and immigrants seeking economic opportunities. The Cold War led to the McCarran-Walter Immigration and Nationality Act of 1952, which retained quotas and other provisions of previous immigration laws and mandated the exclusion of communists. The Immigration Act of 1965 replaced quotas based on national origins with preference based on class. Though no longer collecting addresses annually from aliens, the Service still patrols U.S. borders, screens applicants for preferential visas, and reviews applicants for naturalization. Its effectiveness in this role was debated in the 1990s, especially with regard to illegal immigration.

A. WILLIAM HOGLUND

See also Immigration; Justice, U.S. Department of; Refugees

FURTHER READING

Divine, Robert A. *American Immigration Policy, 1924–1952.* New Haven, Conn., 1957.
Higham, John. *Strangers in the Land: Patterns of American Nativism, 1860–1925.* New Brunswick, N.J., 1957.
Hutchinson, E. P. *Legislature History of American Immigration Policy, 1798–1965.* Philadelphia, Pa., 1981.

IMPERIALISM

A dynamic process through which a political entity subordinates a weaker one, often by conquest and territorial occupation. The expansion of the Western world since about 1500 provides the most frequently cited examples of imperialism, but occasions of forceful expansion are common to all peoples and civilizations. While the terminology used to describe forms of imperialism is inexact and subject to ideological manipulation, it seems clear that the outward thrust of imperialism takes various forms: the forcible extension of a nation's borders; the establishment of a colonial relationship over a conquered territory; or the imposition on other peoples of some form of indirect control.

Throughout their history, the people of the United States have maintained an ambivalent attitude toward imperial possessions. The United States was born in the act of armed opposition to the British empire's claim to exercise sovereign control over its colonies. Yet as British North Americans, such as Thomas Jefferson and John Adams, contemplated the new nation's future, they spoke of creating a new "empire." Later, U.S. citizens deplored the concept of empire as one of European or foreign inspiration. Many in the United States were convinced that their nation represented a unique blending of freedom, happiness, and justice that other peoples should be encouraged to emulate. They believed that their nation's destiny was to expand westward across the North American continent, and did not regard this "Manifest Destiny" as equivalent to the less noble expansion overseas of a British Empire or a French nation.

Expansion and Empire Through the 1890s

During the nineteenth century the United States steadily extended its land frontier. The Louisiana Purchase (1803), the acquisition of Florida (1819), the annexation of the Republic of Texas (1845), and a war with Mexico that won California and New Mexico (1848) stood as landmarks in this movement. During and after the American Civil War, Secretary of State William Seward called for a new wave of expansion. He negotiated the purchase of Alaska in 1867, worked to project U.S. trade across the Pacific, and predicted that Central America would be drawn into the Union. By Seward's time a gradual shift in the pressures impelling expansion can be discerned. An effort to secure foreign markets for agricultural and industrial exports was slowly superseding the drive for farm land, grazing areas, and mineral deposits. By the 1890s these new forces led to an explosion of imperialist activity. In the last quarter of the nineteenth century, the nations of Europe engaged in a frenzy of expansion overseas. Vast areas of Africa, East and Southeast Asia, and the Pacific were swept up in this grab for territory. So marked was this surge into the non-Western world that it was called the "New Imperialism," since it embodied a second wave of expansion moving beyond the European commercial empires of the seventeenth and eighteenth centuries.

By the 1890s, the United States had entered the race for territories overseas with unabashed enthusiasm. Whatever term might best have described the nation's cross-continental expansion through most of the nineteenth century, by 1895 the United States was as committed to imperial expansion as any of the European states. In fact, the story of the new imperialism cannot be told without allotting major attention to U.S. ambitions. The causes and categories used to describe U.S. imperialism are virtually the same as those used to describe the new imperialism of the European states. These include the demands of a commercial and industrial capitalism in search of markets and investment opportunities, an all-consuming nationalism in which the prestige and survival of the state seemed linked to its unbounded expansion, and an ideology of expansion rooted in Social Darwinism and in a self-declared mission to extend "civilization." European and U.S. imperialism extended their sway both by the formation of colonies and by informal strategies, such as drawing residents of other nations into the economic orbit of the industrially more advanced nation, or by forcing a self-serving treaty upon the less powerful state.

Between 1895 and 1900, the United States joined the scramble for imperial possessions on a grand scale. A cluster of well-placed business executives, politicians, newspapermen, and naval officers urged that the nation undertake a conscious program of expansion. This "foreign policy elite" aimed to solidify the U.S. claim to hegemony in the Western Hemisphere based on a broad application of the Monroe Doctrine. They hoped to reinforce U.S. interests in the Caribbean and pressed for the construction of a canal across the isthmus of Central America, while easing British influence out of the Caribbean area. They expected to extend U.S. interests in the Pacific by the annexation of Hawai'i and to insure U.S. trading interests in East Asia. However, a small, diverse, and distinguished group of political and social leaders opposed the cry for empire. The range of anti-imperialist voices included the industrialist Andrew Carnegie, the labor leader Samuel Gompers, the social reformer Jane Addams, and the novelist Mark Twain. Their critique of imperial expansion was diverse, but they seemed to agree that the imposition of a government by force an another people was inhumane and immoral.

By 1898, a bloody rebellion in Cuba against Spanish rule reached a boiling point, giving U.S. imperialists the opportunity for which they had been waiting. They argued that intervention in that conflict was necessary for humanitarian reasons, for the protection of U.S.-owned properties and trade, and for maintenance of U.S. security in the region. The Spanish military aimed to wipe out the Cuban rebels by forcing the rural population into "reconcentration" camps, which, it was hoped, would leave the rebels with no means of support. Disease, starvation, and death spread. Meanwhile, U.S. trade with the island plummeted and U.S.-owned properties on the island were destroyed. On 11 April 1898, President William McKinley led Congress in a declaration of war on Spain. The crisis in Cuba had provided McKinley and the imperialists with a golden opportunity to join the worldwide race for colonies and enhanced influence overseas. After a brief and successful war against Spain, the United States forged a peace treaty that made Cuba a protectorate with a permanent U.S. naval base at Guantanamo Bay and established U.S. sovereignty in Puerto Rico. At the outset of the war, President McKinley had ordered Commodore George Dewey to attack the Spanish naval forces at Manila Harbor in the Philippines. Dewey scored a quick victory. In the peace settlement, the United States claimed sovereignty in the Philippines, providing a base for easier access to the China market. Finally, in 1898, Congress, by a joint resolution of annexation, formalized U.S. control of the Hawai'ian Islands.

Empire in Latin America and Asia

The predominant imperial interests of the United States lay in the Caribbean basin. In 1903, President Theodore Roosevelt, who came to epitomize U.S. imperialism, supported a Panamian rebellion against Colombia, knowing that the rebels would cede land for a U.S.-built canal across the isthmus of Panama. The next year, when chronic disorder and fiscal instability were tempting European powers to intervene in Latin America, Roo-

sevelt developed his Corollary to the Monroe Doctrine. Roosevelt asserted that, when faced with "chronic wrongdoing" by nations in the Western Hemisphere, the United States might be forced, "however reluctantly, in flagrant cases of such wrongdoing or impotence, to the exercise of an international police power." Over the next decade, U.S. troops landed in Cuba (under the frankly imperialistic Platt Amendment), the Dominican Republic, Haiti, and Nicaragua, and in 1914 and 1916, U.S. forces invaded Mexico.

In the Philippines, the U.S. occupation provoked a Filipino insurrection, as rebels under Emilio Aguinaldo shifted their sights from the despised Spanish colonial overlord to the equally hated American usurper. Before the insurrection ended in 1902, more than 5,000 U.S. soldiers and 200,000 Filipinos had died. After this bitter guerrilla war, the U.S. public became less eager to support the extension of direct colonial rule, although the United States did not grant independence to the Philippines until 1946. The nation turned to the methods of informal empire to sustain its interests overseas, especially in East Asia.

When in 1894–1895 Japan challenged and handily defeated China, the weakness of the Manchu regime was exposed to the world. Taking advantage of this feebleness, the leading European powers soon established spheres of interest and leaseholds in China. Lacking power to deter the Europeans, the United States resorted to a statement of principle. In September 1899, Secretary of State John Hay dispatched identical notes to Japan, Italy, Russia, Germany, Great Britain, and France asking that equal trade opportunities for all nations be observed in their various spheres. In spite of the vague responses of the powers, Hay proclaimed their acceptance of the Open Door Policy in China. In 1900, when the rebellious Chinese "Boxers" attacked the foreign embassies in Beijing, the Western powers landed troops, including 2,500 U.S. marines, to rescue their nationals. Fearing the collapse of China, Hay fired off a second Open Door Policy note in which he reiterated the principle of maintaining unrestricted trade in China, and added a call for the powers to respect the "territorial integrity of China." Critics have asserted that the Open Door Policy best describes a peculiar U.S. type of imperialism, one befitting a nation whose industries were propelling it to the forefront of international trade and to whom access to the markets of the world was akin to a natural law of progress.

If the ideology of the Open Door Policy became a constant in U.S. thinking, occasionally it was overborne by a strain of hard-nosed power politics. When Theodore Roosevelt became president in 1901, he put aside the moralistic espousal of an Open Door Policy in China for the politics of realism. He hoped to preserve U.S. economic interests in east Asia, but he was aware that, without military power in that region, it was idle and dangerous to make visionary pronouncements. Meanwhile, China survived foreign military occupation during the Boxer Rebellion because it became clear that it would not passively accept conquest, and because the great powers were not prepared to accept a major war to sustain their ambitions in China. Russia and Japan were the exceptions and were determined to defend their claims in Manchuria and Korea. War came in 1904. Roosevelt was careful not to invoke the Open Door principle even though the war was fought on Chinese soil.

Roosevelt's chief concern was in safeguarding the U.S. empire in the Philippines. In July 1905 his secretary of war, William Howard Taft, concluded a memorandum of understanding with Japanese Prime Minister Tāro Katsura, which conceded that Japan had a special relationship with Korea but also indicated that Japan harbored no designs on the Philippines. Immediately after, Roosevelt was asked to broker a settlement of the Russo-Japanese War. The president agreed and orchestrated a successful agreement at Portsmouth, New Hampshire. In spite of gains scored by Japan, Roosevelt had largely succeeded in maintaining a realistic balance of power in northeast Asia. In November 1908 the Root-Takahira Declaration was signed, pledging the integrity of Japanese and U.S. insular possessions in the Pacific, recognizing the Pacific Ocean as an open avenue of trade, supporting the status quo, and promising equal opportunity in China. It was clear that Roosevelt's policy was not to enunciate principles of supposed U.S. morality; rather it was to defend the exposed interests of the United States in the western Pacific.

In 1909, as President William Howard Taft took office, the United States moved to sustain its informal imperial stake in northeast Asia. To defend U.S. interests in Manchuria and China proper, Taft reasserted the Open Door principle and U.S. interest in maintaining the territorial integrity of China. Showing little concern that this policy offended Japan, Taft encouraged investment in China as a means of expanding U.S. influence there. Secretary of State Philander C. Knox pursued this type of informal imperialism, called "Dollar Diplomacy," by pressing for U.S. participation in a European banking consortium formed to construct a railroad in south central China, and urging a large international loan to enable Peking to purchase the rail lines in Manchuria owned by Japan and Russia. While the United States eventually won participation in the consortium, the Manchurian initiative collapsed. In 1911, in the midst of revolution, a Republic was proclaimed in China. Knox pressed the six-power consortium to provide funds to President Yuan Shikai; of course, each power would impose its demands on China as a price for the loan. "Dollar Diplomacy" was in flower as Taft's presidency came to an end.

Woodrow Wilson and Empire

On 18 March 1913, soon after his inauguration, President Woodrow Wilson repudiated U.S. participation in the consortium loan to China. Clearly, he realized that such massive financial penetration of China was imperialistic to the core; he argued that the loan would violate the proper application of the Open Door Policy. During World War I, Wilson's defense of the Open Door Policy led the United States to declare that it would not recognize any agreement impairing its treaty right in China or infringing on China's territorial integrity. This was done to block Japan's effort to expand that nation's interests in China during the war. Wilson, the moralist, earnestly defended the territorial integrity of China; but, in so doing, he was also acting to preserve U.S. economic interests. Perhaps no other U.S. leader more fully combined or confused morality with the defense of "imperial" interests. After the United States entered the war against Germany in 1917, Wilson limited the application of the Open Door Policy in China. On 2 November, Washington recognized Japan's "special interests" in China based on its "territorial propinquity." Again Wilson the idealist bowed to the politics of realism.

When in April 1917 Wilson brought the United States into the European war, the immediate cause was Germany's attack on U.S. shipping in the face of the U.S. claim to freedom of the seas. More broadly, the United States entered the war in defense of its perceived strategic and economic interests. In January 1918, Wilson's Fourteen Points specified the war aims of the United States. The president linked idealistic principles with pronouncements similar to those upheld by Great Britain in the heyday of empire. Wilson called for an "open" world after the war, with freedom of the seas, equal trade opportunities, the removal of tariffs, and the end of colonialism. This is not to suggest that there was a cynical design in Wilson's program for a liberal peace, any more than there had been in Great Britain's "free trade imperialism" of the nineteenth century. But Wilson's idealism meshed well with the requisites of the U.S. economy. Free trade was likely to benefit the U.S. economy, which had become the world's most productive and also the strongest financial base.

The U.S. victory in World War I bequeathed an unassailable legacy: the United States became the world's leading economic power. During the war years, to meet the need for raw materials, U.S. companies expanded operations in developing nations. Goodyear went into the Dutch East Indies for rubber, Swift and Armour expanded in South America, and Socony established interests in Middle Eastern oil. By 1920 the United States produced about 40 percent of the world's coal and 50 percent of its pig iron. By the late 1920s, the United States was producing 46 percent of total world industrial goods. Based on the considerable loans extended to its wartime allies, the United States had abruptly shifted from a debtor nation to a creditor, with Wall Street replacing London as the world's financial center. Not unlike the British in their era of "free trade imperialism," the United States continued to profess its rejection of political involvement overseas and proclaim its Open Door Policy for trade. This doctrine, however, was selectively applied. It was usually invoked where the United States faced vigorous competition, as in Asia and the Middle East. In Latin America and the Philippines, however, where U.S. capital and trade dominated, something approximating a "closed door" was in effect. The United States showed little interest in establishing formal political control overseas; after all, the country's vast economic power allowed it to dominate the world economy.

World War II and Cold War

As economic depression spread in the 1930s, the markets and investments controlled by U.S. companies overseas declined in value. Political isolationism joined with economic nationalism as the United States further divorced itself from the chaos endemic in the world, although it maintained hegemony in Latin America even as it espoused the Good Neighbor Policy. European powers clung more tightly to their imperial possessions and observers argued that the world was divided into "have" and "have not" nations. The threat of total economic collapse contributed to the rise of fascism in Europe and reinforced military domination of government in Japan. In any case, the U.S. populace were gradually drawn from their neutralism toward overseas crises, especially when war erupted in Europe in September 1939.

The United States entered the war in December 1941, when Japan attacked in the Pacific and Germany declared war on the United States. In opposing dictatorship abroad, U.S. leaders proclaimed that they were rejecting all forms of imperialism. President Franklin D. Roosevelt indicated clearly to his staff that he was strongly opposed to the restoration of a French empire in Southeast Asia. None can doubt the sincerity of this commitment. Those in the United States saw World War II as a war to end all closed economic systems and terminate the repression of imperial control. It is equally true that, if empires and special economic spheres were done away with, the chief benefit would fall to the nation with the strongest economy, the United States. After the Allied victory in 1945, the vast economic and military power of the United States was unrivaled in the world. Europe and Japan were in ruins and the Soviet Union, while militarily strong in Eastern Europe, was in economic disarray. Almost immediately the United States and the Soviet Union grew suspicious of each other's

intentions. Great-power rivalry led the two powers to establish spheres of influence that, for the most part, were coterminous with the territory each had occupied at the end of World War II. Here was a traditional confrontation between states, each of which sought justification in its own ideological world view. The emerging Cold War could also be seen as a confrontation between two rival forms of imperialism.

In the early postwar period, sparring between the United States and the Soviet Union was motivated by strategic calculations intertwined with a concern to sustain international economic interests. In 1946, in the face of Soviet claims of a preponderant stake in the industries of Manchuria, Washington pressed the Republic of China to maintain an Open Door for trade and investment in its northeast provinces. In Iran, U.S. policy sought to safeguard its oil concessions while blocking Soviet oil claims. By 1947 Secretary of State George C. Marshall proposed, in what came to be called the Marshall Plan, to extend grants and loans to those European states which would align with it in an economic bloc. Here was an example of securing a strategic objective by economic means while at the same time ensuring that Western Europe would remain an area open to U.S. trade and investment. Washington was keenly aware that a healthy U.S. economy required areas abroad as markets and for investments. Many in the United States believed as well that a prosperous Western Europe would also be a democratic region akin to the United States in political principles.

U.S. diplomats in the early Cold War years pursued a self-conscious, expansionist, and often unilateral foreign policy. The aim was to hold the line against Soviet expansion; thus the United States moved toward the creation of a series of alliances to pen in the Soviets. Like it or not, what was intended as a defense zone took on some of the characteristics of an imperial sphere of influence. These strategic commitments ran parallel to significant economic change. In a world recently ravaged by war, U.S. businessmen and government officials cooperated to expand U.S. foreign trade. By 1947 the United States accounted for one-third of the world's exports; soon its trade and investments overseas reached $12 billion. The United States continued to preach the Open Door Policy, but other nations complained that they could not compete and that therefore the Open Door doctrine was actually an invitation to U.S. domination. In throwing his own imperial "curtain" over Eastern Europe, Stalin both genuinely saw the Open Door Policy as a threat and also found it quite useful as a pretext. Nevertheless, Soviet actions and intentions notwithstanding, the U.S. foreign aid program of the postwar years was designed in part to keep U.S. trade and investment flowing; U.S. products could not be purchased unless foreigners had dollars to spend on them. Foreign aid became a tool of U.S. diplomacy—a way of curbing revolution, thwarting communism, promoting allies, and stimulating the U.S. economy.

By the 1950s and 1960 the confrontation between the United States and the USSR had shifted in focus to the Third World. This shift came as the United States celebrated the end of the colonial era and the freedom of people in the Third World to determine their political future. Yet in the context of the Cold War the United States began to impose its will on its allies in East and Southeast Asia. Earlier, during the occupation of Japan, General Douglas MacArthur's rule, however noble U.S. intentions may have been, resembled that of an imperial overlord. Elsewhere, as postwar empires collapsed, the United States rushed in to fill the void and block the extension of communism. The United States assumed the role formerly played by Japan in Korea and by France in Vietnam, while Washington pressed the Dutch to desist from forcefully reimposing their will in the East Indies. In South Korea and in Vietnam, revolutionary movements combined nationalism and communist ideology in an effort to expel foreign influence. Washington saw Soviet communism behind these movements and, in the Korean War (1950–1953) and the Vietnam War (1965–1973), found itself fighting against armies that saw themselves as opposing the last vestiges of colonialism.

If, as some would argue, these wars in East Asia were partially the product of U.S. imperialism, the accusation was made more vehemently with respect to U.S. policy in Latin America. Not unexpectedly the most fiery confrontations took place in the Caribbean region. In Cuba, Fidel Castro's revolution challenged sixty years of U.S. informal control of that island, and, in spite of a U.S.-inspired invasion by anti-Castro Cubans in 1961, Cuba's radical experiment survived (with substantial help from the Soviet Union). Thereafter, other revolutions elsewhere in Latin America took Castro as their model. The U.S. response to the spread of radicalism took various forms, from military invasion in the Dominican Republic in 1965, to support for a coup against Salvador Allende Gossens, the elected left-wing leader of Chile, in the early 1970s, and to support for right-wing insurgents in Nicaragua in the 1980s.

By the 1970s, the United States and the Soviet Union found it increasingly difficult to sustain their commitments overseas. For the United States this relative decline of power came as the entire Western world experienced its first substantial economic setback since the end of World War II. In particular, the United States began to count the economic and moral costs of the Vietnam War. Indeed, in his Guam Doctrine of 1969, President Richard M. Nixon asked Asian powers to assume their share of the defense against communism in east Asia; later he called for burden sharing by the United States' European allies. In the late 1980s, the Soviet Union was staggered by the economic expense of the Cold War and the corruption of the communist bureaucracy. There followed a marked easing of tension. By 1989, the dismantling of the Berlin Wall symbolized Soviet weakness and the end of the Cold War.

The 1990s

Toward the end of the twentieth century it is more difficult than ever to define imperialism as it applies to the United States. The era of singular U.S. economic domination, which characterized the period since the end of World War II, is gone. In the mid-1990s, the economically dynamic European Union and Japan, which has become an industrial and financial giant, combined with U.S. interests to create a world in which a handful of economically strong nations with their multinational corporations and banks mold the future of countless peoples. It is as if the financial consortiums of the early twentieth century have renewed themselves in massive proportion. Critics describe the impact of this combination of the wealthy nations of the world on developing nations as "neoimperialism." Such sweeping judgments may or may not be useful. The key point in applying the term imperialism to what in many ways amounts to the operation of the world economy is to judge the degree to which a certain diminished status or dependent economic position is imposed on weaker nations. Certainly the United States is a player in this process; and in the competitive world economy Washington shows little inclination to press for reform. In addition, it is no easy matter to devise a workable and morally acceptable policy for world economic development.

International politics complicates the issue. Despite the end of the Cold War, U.S. forces remained in position in 1996 in many parts of the world even though their presence was no longer justified by the need to oppose world communism. Leaders in the United States claimed that this is necessary to prevent the outbreak of conflicts and maintain stability in troubled regions. Indeed, the United States remained the leading international power, with a unique ability to deploy its military power through the world, as seen in the Gulf War of 1990–1991. While some would brand such actions as a new form of imperialism, others would claim that there is a moral imperative to act against violence and aggression.

As in the founding days of the Republic, the U.S. public and policymakers remain ambivalent toward imperialism. In the early 1990s they heralded the collapse of the Soviet Empire and deplored what they perceived as the imperialistic instincts of mainland China. However, there has been no broad public outcry over U.S. actions to influence events in the Caribbean, Central America, and elsewhere in Latin America. By and large, most U.S. citizens continue to support the maintenance of U.S. troops in outposts around the world, and many accept the apparent benefits of investment opportunities in foreign lands and the relocation of U.S. industrial facilities overseas. Such military and economic policies are not in themselves imperialistic, but in their implementation they threaten to arouse the imperial instinct.

EDMUND S. WEHRLE

See also China; Cold War; Continental Expansion; Cuba; Manifest Destiny; Monroe Doctrine; Open Door Policy; Panama and Panama Canal; Philippines; Roosevelt Corollary; Spanish-American-Cuban-Filipino War, 1898; Seward, William Henry

FURTHER READING

Billington, Ray A., and Martin Ridge. *Westward Expansion*, 5th ed. New York, 1982.

Cain, P. J., and A. G. Hopkins. *British Imperialism*, 2 vols. London and New York, 1993.

Darby, Philip. *The Faces of Imperialism: British and American Approaches to Asia and Africa, 1870-1970*. New Haven, 1987.

Healy, David. *U.S. Expansionism: The Imperialist Urge in the 1890s*. Madison, Wisc., 1970.

Kennedy, Paul. *The Rise and Fall of the Great Powers: Economic Change and Military Conflict from 1500 to 2000*. New York, 1987.

LaFeber, Walter. *The American Search for Opportunity, 1865–1913*. New York, 1993.

———. *The New Empire: An Interpretation of American Expansion, 1860–1898*. Ithaca, N.Y., 1963.

Perkins, Bradford. *The Cambridge History of American Foreign Relations: The Creation of a Republican Empire, 1776–1865*, vol. 1. New York, 1993.

Williams, William Appleman, ed. *From Colony to Empire: Essays in the History of American Foreign Relations*. New York, 1972.

———. *The Tragedy of American Diplomacy*. New York, 1962.

IMPRESSMENT

The British practice, originating in the thirteenth century, of conscripting seamen into naval service. British press gangs were especially active in the eighteenth century, impressing seamen in British ports as well as from British and American merchant vessels on the high seas. Impressment of seamen in colonial American ports often led to violence and was a minor cause of the American Revolution. After U.S. independence, the British continued to impress seamen from U.S. ships, and the practice helped ignite the War of 1812.

During the French Revolution and Napoleonic Wars (1792–1815), the rapidly expanding U.S. merchant fleet relied heavily on British seamen, many of whom were deserters from the British navy. To reclaim these subjects, British warships stopped U.S. merchant vessels on the high seas and impressed or conscripted British seamen into service. This practice sometimes left U.S. ships dangerously shorthanded. Moreover, because it was diffi-

cult to distinguish between British subjects and U.S. citizens (and sometimes press gangs made little effort to do so), many U.S. citizens were caught in the British dragnet. Securing the release of these Americans, which usually had to be accomplished through diplomatic channels, often took years.

The British refused to honor certificates of citizenship issued by the United States (the equivalent of modern-day passports) because British sailors could easily acquire them by theft, purchase, or fraud. Nor were the British willing to exempt naturalized U.S. citizens from impressment. Upholding the doctrine of perpetual allegiance, they held that anyone born in the British Empire owed first allegiance to the Crown regardless of any subsequent obligations that person might take on. This issue was largely theoretical because few British sailors actually took the time and trouble to become American citizens. American merchants, profiting from good relations with Great Britain, actually objected less strenuously to impressment than did other Americans more concerned about the affront to national honor and sovereignty.

Although the British did not claim the right to impress from U.S. warships, overzealous British naval officials occasionally did so, as in the notorious *Chesapeake-Leopard* affair (1807). The United States refused to ratify the Monroe-Pinckney Treaty of 1806 because it did not provide for an end to impressment, and the issue later became one of the leading causes of the War of 1812. After the British repealed the Orders in Council at the beginning of the war, impressment was the only major issue that still divided the two nations. U.S. unwillingness to give up its demands for an end to the practice prolonged the war by two years, although in the end the nation agreed to a peace treaty that did not even mention the issue. The British were careful not to impress any Americans after the War of 1812 (especially during Napoleon's Hundred Days). In the years that followed, the British gradually abandoned the practice altogether because of improved working conditions in the Royal Navy and the larger labor pool upon which the navy could draw for recruits, which enabled it to meet its needs through voluntary enlistments.

DONALD R. HICKEY

See also Chesapeake-Leopard Affair; Great Britain; French Revolution; Monroe-Pinckney Treaty; War of 1812; Napoleonic Wars

FURTHER READING

Burt, A. L. *The United States, Great Britain, and British North America from the Revolution to the Establishment of Peace after the War of 1812*. New Haven, 1940.

Perkins, Bradford. *Prologue to War: England and the United States, 1805–1812*. Berkeley, Calif., 1961.

Zimmerman, James F. *Impressment of American Seamen*. New York, 1925.

INDIA

Located in Southern Asia, surrounded by the Arabian Sea, Bay of Bengal, and Indian Ocean, and bordering Pakistan, China, Nepal, Myanmar, Bhutan, and Bangladesh. Historically, the U.S. relationship with India, the second most populous nation in the world, has been uneasy yet resilient.

During the Cold War, differing international priorities frequently undermined cooperation between the world's two largest democracies. Whatever their differences, however, U.S. and Indian leaders recognized certain common interests. Especially over the last two decades of the twentieth century, they resolved a number of problems and moved toward closer economic, cultural and political ties.

During the nineteenth and early twentieth centuries when India was part of the British Empire, U.S. interests were largely limited to modest levels of trade and missionary activity. The latter played an important role in the introduction of Western technology, agricultural practices, and medical education. U.S. religious groups and liberal intellectuals were attracted to India's nationalist movement, especially as embodied in Mohandas Gandhi's leadership of the Indian National Congress. That attachment to India's political aspirations partially offset the generally negative impression in numerous motion pictures, textbooks, and other popular works, most notably Katherine Mayo's best-selling *Mother India*.

During the early stages of World War II, when the National Congress demanded independence from Great Britain, India became for the first time a major concern of the U.S. government. When the National Congress launched the "Quit India" movement in the summer of 1942, it anticipated U.S. support. President Franklin D. Roosevelt, who believed that U.S. interests in Asia necessitated identification with anti-colonialism, sympathized with the Indian cause and sent a special emissary to India, but in the end he deferred to Prime Minister Winston Churchill whose hard-line approach resulted in the imprisonment of India's leaders until late in the war.

The United States welcomed Great Britain's decision in 1947 to liquidate its Indian Empire, but the U.S. relationship with independent India began with a number of disagreements, especially over India's dispute with Pakistan regarding the status of Kashmir. U.S. sympathy with some form of plebiscite in the Muslim-majority state that was largely occupied by Indian troops was anathema in New Delhi, which consistently refused to compromise its claims to Kashmir. More generally, differences reflected a divergence between India's policy of nonalignment in the emerging Cold War and the U.S. emphasis on containment of the Soviet Union and, later, the People's Republic of China. Also, from the U.S. perspective, India seemed more critical of the West than of the communist powers. The U.S. decision in 1954 to provide military assistance to Pakistan, which was followed by Pakistan's membership in the U.S.-sponsored Southeast Asia Treaty Organization, led India's Prime Minister Jawaharlal Nehru to condemn the United States for bringing the Cold War to South Asia.

Yet Indo-U.S. relations soon changed dramatically as the administration of Dwight Eisenhower adopted a more accommodating attitude toward nonaligned countries. The power of the emerging Afro-Asian world, symbolized in the Bandung Conference of 1955, and the Soviet Union's courting of newly independent countries including India forced Washington toward a more flexible approach. Overcoming congressional resistance, the Eisenhower administration expanded U.S. economic and technical assistance programs. Bilateral assistance, which totaled $283 million in support of India's First Five Year Plan (1951–1956), increased to $875 million in support of the Second Five Year Plan (1956–1961). An exchange of visits by Nehru and Eisenhower symbolized this era of understanding. In the thinking of Eisenhower and other U.S. officials, support of India was vital to U.S. interests in the emerging Third World. India was considered the critical test of whether democratic societies could meet the challenge of economic development. The alternative model was provided by the authoritarian communist regime in China.

Such thinking was central to the foreign policy of the administration of John F. Kennedy, who as a senator had been a leading proponent of assistance to India. Kennedy's appointment of the prominent economist John Kenneth Galbraith as ambassador signified India's importance. Assistance programs expanded (bilateral aid totaling about $1.8 billion between 1961–1965) as did the development efforts of the Ford and Rockefeller Foundations, while the newly established Peace Corps sent thousands of volunteers to India. An unexpected international crisis brought India and the United States still closer. China's attack on India in the fall of 1962 over territory long disputed between the two countries revealed an Indian military weakness and the bankruptcy of a decade's commitment to Sino-Indian friendship. At India's request, the United States rushed military assistance to its beleaguered forces. The situation offered, to optimistic Americans, an opportunity to bring India into the West's camp. After China's withdrawal, the United States unsuccessfully pressed India to resolve differences with Pakistan in return for a formal military assistance program.

The effective working relationship of 1955–1964 unravelled as Indo-Pakistani differences brought renewed bloodshed to the subcontinent. Warfare in 1965 over a territorial dispute in the Rann of Kutch resulted in both sides blaming the United States: India for the U.S. having equipped the Pakistani army for a decade; Pakistan for U.S. neutrality which worked to India's advantage. The Soviet Union played the role of peacemaker, thus strengthening its position on the subcontinent and particularly its influence with India.

Indo-U.S. relations deteriorated steadily. President Lyndon B. Johnson, who was annoyed by India's criticism of the U.S. war in Vietnam and who also shared the opinion of several officials that India had devoted insufficient attention to increasing its food production, adopted a "short-tether" policy on food shipments, limiting exports in ways that many Indians considered insensitive at a time when low yields brought famine conditions. The 1971 Indo-Pakistani crisis over the demands of Bengalis in East Pakistan for autonomy and eventually independence brought the U.S. relationship with India to its nadir. The administration of Richard Nixon, which was determined to stand by Pakistan as an ally who had recently assisted in the "opening" to China, showed no sympathy for the Bengalis who were suppressed by the Pakistani Army or for India which was forced to absorb hundred of thousands of refugees into the already crowded Indian state of West Bengal. As a showdown approached, India entered into a treaty of friendship with the Soviet Union. When India sent its forces into East Pakistan, the Nixon administration "tilted" in favor to Pakistan and sent a U.S. carrier to the Bay of Bengal. U.S. rhetoric and show of strength notwithstanding, India's intervention assured the establishment of an independent Bangladesh. As that nation emerged from the bloodshed, U.S. policy was condemned throughout India.

The legacy of the Nixon administration's actions in 1971 has clouded Indo-U.S. contacts ever since. The U.S. presence and influence in India notably declined afterward, but there has been an underlying resiliency in the relationship. For India, the treaty with the Soviet Union necessitated improved relations with the United States lest India be seen as a part of the Soviet bloc. For the United States, its South Asian policy was in shambles. Pakistan, in many respects, was even more outraged than India over U.S. actions in the 1971 crisis, since it felt betrayed by an ally which provided no substantive support.

Improving relations was not easy since the 1971 crisis was followed by other points of tension. India objected to the U.S. establishment of a naval base at the Diego Garcia atoll in the Indian Ocean, while Americans took exception to India's development of nuclear capability and to Prime Minister's Indira Gandhi's Emergency Proclamation that suspended civil liberties. India's stature as a model of democratic government in the Third World was severely undermined by Gandhi's dicta-torial policies. Yet, at the same time, some contentious issues, such as U.S. ownership of Indian rupees equivalent to $3 billion resulting from the sale of food to India under the PL-480 program and the controversy over the United States supplying uranium for a nuclear power plant at Tarapur (which was criticized in Congress as contrary to nonproliferation policy), were resolved through negotiation. At the same time, Indo-U.S. trade and U.S. investment regained momentum. Cultural interaction remained strong, if largely as a one-way phenomenon marked by considerable U.S. influence on Indian popular culture, media, education, science and technology. Meanwhile, the steadily growing Indian immigrant community in the United States—an outgrowth of major change in U.S. immigration policy in 1964—built what one U.S. official described as a "two-way bridge." And the post-emergency resurgence of Indian democracy served to enhance relations between the world's two largest democratic nations.

During the 1970s détente, and then again with the end of the Cold War, India's strategic importance to the United States declined as a result to the improved U.S. relationships with the Soviet Union/Russia and the People's Republic of China. Ironically, the very success of India—its political stability and the survival of democracy—has served also to make the country of less concern to Americans. At the same time U.S. presidents, beginning with the reviled Nixon, have accorded India greater recognition as a regional power since Pakistan's decline in 1971. In a further irony, as India has gained status, it has also played a less significant role on the international stage than it did in the days of Nehru's leadership of nonalignment. Partly that is a matter of choice, but mostly it is a function of the rise of other prominent international players.

Over recent years, while differences remain over such issues as Kashmir, India-Pakistan relations, and nuclear proliferation, overall the relationship has evolved toward an equilibrium. Of critical importance in this development has been India's liberalization of its policy regarding foreign investment and trade, and the growth of a large Indian middle class as an attractive market. Prime Minister P.V. Narasima Rao, when visiting the United States in 1991, foresaw economic ventures in which "the sky's the limit." The expansion of investment and trade supports Rao's prediction. Hence, the Indo-U.S. relationship, which has been described in terms of "ups-and-downs" or "mutual misunderstanding," shows promise of evolving toward a steadier course, based on firmer interests and, indeed, understanding.

GARY HESS

See also Bangladesh; China; Nehru, Jawaharlal; Nixon, Richard Milhous; Nonaligned Movement; Nuclear Nonproliferation; Pakistan

FURTHER READING

Brands, H. W. *India and the United States: The Cold Peace.* Boston, 1990.

Chary, M. Srinivas. *The Eagle and the Peacock: U.S. Foreign Policy Toward India Since Independence.* Westport, Conn., 1995.

Kux, Dennis. *India and the United States: Estranged Democracies, 1941-1991.* Washington, D.C., 1994.

McMahon, Robert J. *Cold War on the Periphery: The United States, India, and Pakistan.* New York, 1994.

Merrill, Dennis. *Bread and the Ballot: The United States and India's Economic Development, 1947-1963.* Chapel Hill, N.C., 1990.

INDONESIA

Republic located in Southeast Asia, between Malaysia and Australia, and the fifth most populous nation in the world. Comprised of more than 13,000 islands in the Malay archipelago, it was controlled by the Netherlands for much of its history until the twentieth century. Beginning in 1602 the Dutch slowly established themselves as rulers of all the islands of present-day Indonesia, except for the eastern half of the island of Timor, which Portugal ruled until 1975. The Indonesian independence movement began during the first decade of the twentieth century and expanded rapidly between the two world wars. The Japanese occupied Indonesia for three years during World War II and, for their own purposes, encouraged a nationalist movement.

After proclaiming independence on 17 August 1945, Indonesia strove to enlist international support and to oppose Dutch attempts to reimpose colonial rule. Indonesia recognized that the pursuit of an antiforeign nationalistic policy would do more harm than good; international goodwill was critically needed. It sought to present a moderate policy to the world, particularly to the United States, whose support was believed of central importance in efforts to compel the Dutch to relinquish their colonial claims. U.S. diplomatic efforts were instrumental in helping Indonesia to achieve independence.

The Cold War complicated U.S.-Indonesian relations, especially over United Nations efforts to resolve Indonesian-Dutch conflict in 1947 and 1948. The Soviet Union and its allies offered a series of resolutions in condemnation of Western powers in general and of the Dutch and the United States in particular. The United States, expected to play a role in favor of Indonesia, was caught between its disapproval of the Dutch methods and its need to help rebuild Western Europe economically and militarily as a bulwark against Soviet expansion. The United States initially was unable to support Indonesia fully, but after the second Dutch police action in 1948, U.S. policy became outspoken in its criticism of the Dutch action and initiated steps toward the suspension of Marshall Plan aid to the Netherlands.

By 1950 Indonesian political leaders were generally appreciative of the U.S. role in facilitating the achievement of their complete independence. They chose English as the language to be taught in high schools and to be used when a Western language was necessary in higher education. They welcomed U.S. technical assistance and continued to profess a basic friendship for the American people. At the same time they carefully pursued a nonaligned foreign policy, established diplomatic relations with China, and hosted the Afro-Asian summit meeting, also known as the first summit of the Nonaligned Movement, in Bandung in 1955. After the mid-1950s, however, U.S.-Indonesian relations rapidly cooled and came close to a complete rupture in 1965. Indonesian leaders blamed the United States for basing its Asian policy heavily on anticommunism and for its failure to totally support them against Dutch control of West Irian—the western part of the Island of New Guinea, which the Dutch continued to administer despite strong Indonesian protests until the early 1960s. Justified or not, Indonesians assumed that U.S. failure to support their cause against the Dutch in the West Irian dispute was based on the need to maintain an alliance with the Netherlands within the framework of the North Atlantic Treaty Organization (NATO).

In February 1958 an armed insurrection broke out in Sumatra. The following month President Sukarno—Indonesia's charismatic nationalist leader and first president—publicly accused the United States of having provided encouragement and perhaps aid to the rebels. Although the allegation was rejected as untrue, this episode, coming as it did in the wake of Indonesia's repeated failures to settle the West Irian question at the United Nations, only served to heighten Sukarno's distrust of the United States.

Following the establishment of the Federation of Malaysia in September 1963, the United States sought to maintain neutrality toward Sukarno's policy of confrontation with the new state, but Sukarno's continued confrontation prompted the United States to suspend military aid to Indonesia. The United States arranged a temporary cease-fire between the antagonists in January 1964, but when Sukarno's anti-American actions became violent, U.S. aid to Indonesia was virtually halted in March 1964. At that time Sukarno denounced U.S. aid policies as incompatible with Indonesian national interests and labeled the United States as reactionary. The Indonesian Communist party (PKI) inspired boycotts of U.S. films and goods. Increasing harassment of Peace Corps volunteers and United States Information Service (USIS) activities grew unchecked by Indonesian leaders. By 1964 and 1965 Indonesians had nationalized business firms, foundations, and estates of private U.S. groups and severely curtailed or completely halted their activities.

The 1965 coup, the destruction of the PKI and its sympathizers, and Sukarno's fall from power began a new period in cooperative Indonesian-U.S. relations. Considerable controversy exists among historians about the scope and effect of the role played by U.S. officials in efforts by the Indonesian army to crush the PKI after the 1965 coup. President Suharto abandoned the previous anti-imperialist, isolationist foreign policy posture, ended an earlier policy challenging the legitimacy of the neighboring government of Malaysia, and took steps to reestablish relations with the rest of the world. The new government saw that the United States should play a major role in facilitating the rehabilitation and development of the Indonesian economy. For its part the U.S. government indicated its willingness to cooperate fully with Suharto's government. In April 1966 the United States made public an offer of a five-year credit to Indonesia for the purchase of 50,000 tons of rice and 7,500 bales of cotton. American rubber plantations, firms, and oil interests that had been seized by Sukarno's government were gradually returned to their individual owners. In 1967 and again in 1968 the United States continued to assist Indonesia in alleviating acute rice shortages. It also played a leading role in the formation, in the 1966–1967 period, of an international aid consortium. In late July 1969 President Richard M. Nixon paid an official visit to Djakarta, the first by a U.S. president to Indonesia, as part of his trip to five Asian nations.

Suharto's longer term objective was to ensure that Asian affairs were settled by Asians themselves. He maintained diplomatic relations with Hanoi during the Vietnam War. Nonetheless he accepted over the shorter term a strong U.S. presence in Asia. Indonesians were concerned that the U.S. military withdrawal and accompanying Sino-U.S. détente in the 1970s not presage a realignment putting Southeast Asia under strong Chinese influence.

Indonesian diplomacy since the mid-1970s often has been on a parallel and cooperative track with U.S. foreign policy. Key elements include Indonesia's moderating role in the nonaligned movement and the Muslim world; Indonesia's leadership in organizing and guiding negotiations leading to the Cambodian peace settlement of 1991; the participation of Indonesian troops in the United Nations peacekeeping force in Cambodia; Indonesia's role in the Association of Southeast Asian Nations (ASEAN) and the Asian Pacific Economic Cooperation (APEC) forum; and its attempts to mediate a multicountry territorial dispute over the Spatly Islands in the South China Sea that involved China, Vietnam, Taiwan, Malaysia, the Philippines, and Brunei.

U.S. security interests in Indonesia remained strong despite the abatement of the Cold War, primarily because of increased U.S. military commitments and deployments in the Indian Ocean and the Persian Gulf. Since the early 1970s the U.S. Seventh Fleet has moved

warships through the straits between Indonesian islands that connect the Pacific and Indian Oceans. The Seventh Fleet assumed operational responsibility for the Indian Ocean after the Vietnam War. A major portion of the fleet deployed through these passages during the Persian Gulf vessel-reflagging crisis of 1988 and the Persian Gulf War of 1990–1991, signaling that the United States and Indonesia have arrangements for the U.S. Navy's use of the straits. With the withdrawal of the United States from military bases in the Philippines in November 1992, Indonesia's strategic importance increased. To gain new support facilities for U.S. forces, the United States sought access to port and ship repair installations and air bases in several Southeast Asian countries, including Indonesia.

U.S. economic interests in Indonesia are considerable. U.S. exports more than doubled from $795 million in 1985 to $1.9 billion in 1991. Indonesia's population of more than 180 million remains a potentially huge market if Indonesia can maintain the annual economic growth rate (in the six to eight percent range) that it has achieved since 1980. Indonesia has large development programs, based partly on nearly $5 billion in aid it receives annually from aid donor countries and international financial institutions.

U.S. interest in the advancement of human rights and democracy was strong but was a less active component of U.S. policy than other interests. The Department of State has documented Indonesia's major restrictions on political and civil liberties and abuses of human rights in its annual human rights reports. Successive U.S. administrations, however, have not pressed the Indonesian government for changes in these policies. President Ronald Reagan and Secretary of State George Shultz did not raise these issues during their visit to Indonesia in 1986, and Vice President Dan Quayle reportedly made only general statements on human rights during his 1989 visit to Djakarta. Reflecting at least some shift in U.S. policy emphasis, President Bill Clinton raised the issue of Indonesia's authoritarian rule in East Timor when he met privately with President Suharto in July and November 1993 and again during his visit to Indonesia for the 1994 APEC summit.

ROBERT G. SUTTER

See also East Timor; Malaysia; Netherlands; Nonaligned Movement; Sukarno; United Nations

FURTHER READING
American University. *Area Handbook for Indonesia.* Washington, D.C., 1983.
Emmerson, Donald K. *Indonesia's Elite: Political Culture and Cultural Politics.* Ithaca, N.Y., 1976.
Jenkins, David. *Suharto and His Generals: Indonesian Military Politics 1975–1983.* Ithaca, N.Y., 1984.
Leifer, Michael. *Indonesia's Foreign Policy.* London, 1983.

MacDonald, Hamish. *Suharto's Indonesia*. Blackburn, Victoria, 1980.

Ricklefs, M. C. *A History of Modern Indonesia: Circa 1300 to the Present*. Bloomington, Ind., 1981.

World Bank. *Indonesia: A Strategy for Sustained Reduction in Poverty*. Washington, D.C., 1990.

INF TREATY

See Intermediate Nuclear Forces Treaty

INTELLECTUAL PROPERTY

See Copyright and Intellectual Property

INTELLIGENCE

The knowledge—and, ideally, foreknowledge—sought by nations in response to external threats and to protect their vital interests, especially the well-being of their own people. A sound understanding of the world—of its dangers and opportunities—is a core ingredient for effective decision-making by top policy officials. This understanding can be reliably derived only from a thorough gathering and study of information about global personalities, events, and conditions. This worldwide collection of data, along with its close perusal (or "analysis") by experts, lies at the heart of intelligence. More formally, professional intelligence officers define strategic intelligence as the "knowledge and foreknowledge of the world around us—the prelude to presidential decision and action" (*Fact Book on Intelligence*). At this level, the objective is to achieve a global understanding of dangers and opportunities confronting the nation. In contrast, tactical intelligence refers to knowledge and foreknowledge of dangers and opportunities in specific battlefields or theaters of war.

Intelligence is considered both a product and a process. As product, intelligence is the information gathered and analyzed about world or battlefield conditions. As a process, intelligence consists of a series of interactive stages whereby officials plan what information to gather; collect, organize, and analyze it; and, lastly, distribute it to decision-makers. Intelligence also is sometimes thought of in terms of structure and organization; that is, intelligence is the network of secret agencies involved in processing information from around the globe for U.S. decision makers. Finally, intelligence can refer to the three major missions carried out by agencies: the collection and analysis of information; counterintelligence (thwarting enemy intelligence services); and covert action (secret intervention in the affairs of other nations).

Intelligence is widely considered the first line of defense in a nation's efforts to protect itself in a world full of uncertainties. The core assumption is that sound effective foreign policy decisions are most likely to be made if a nation's leaders have the most accurate, complete, and timely information possible about the capabilities and intentions of other nations.

Intelligence gathering is as old as the earliest civilizations. Its beginnings in the United States can be traced to 1776, when the Continental Congress established the first U.S. intelligence service, the Committee on Secret Correspondence. General George Washington, whose secret code number was "711," made use of an effective network of spies led by Paul Revere. Perhaps its most famous agent was young Nathan Hale, who declared, just before the British hanged him for espionage in 1776, "I only regret that I have but one life to lose for my country."

Intelligence activities have figured in every U.S. military conflict since the Revolutionary War. For example, General Ethan Allen Hitchcock, grandson of Ethan Allen, formed a highly successful spy ring in the U.S. Army during the 1840s that helped America win the War with Mexico. The nation's first real detective, Allan Pinkerton, led an intelligence operation in the Civil War that substantially aided the Union Army in uncovering Confederate spies. An active spy for the South, Rose O'Neal Greenhow (alias Rebel Rose), provided information that helped the Confederacy win the Battle of Bull Run.

The involvement of this nation in World War I produced the first serious efforts toward the development of a sophisticated U.S. intelligence capability. The most notable accomplishments are in the field of codebreaking or "cryptanalysis." Early technological breakthroughs came from the inventive minds of Herbert I. Yardley in the Department of State and the husband-and-wife team of William and Elizabeth Friedman in the Army Signals Security Agency. The Navy also had its own codebreaking program. These three independent efforts led to only modest successes during the war, but by the 1930s the efforts to read the communications of other nations (while protecting our own) had reached an impressive level of achievement.

Although World War I stirred efforts in Washington, D.C., to organize more effectively the conduct of U.S. intelligence, only with the onset of World War II did this subject receive the full attention of the president. The attack by the Japanese air force at Pearl Harbor, Hawai'i, on 7 December 1941, caught the United States by surprise and produced extensive destruction of the U.S. Navy's Pacific fleet. It was the most disastrous intelligence failure in American history. On 13 June 1942, Franklin D. Roosevelt ordered the formation of a new intelligence agency, called the Office of Strategic Services (OSS). It vigorously pursued each of the three major intelligence missions against the Axis powers. The U.S. military intelligence services also reached new heights of accomplishment, with remarkable success in breaking both the German and the Japanese secret intelligence, military, and diplomatic codes.

At the end of World War II, President Harry S. Truman further modernized U.S. intelligence capabilities. With the establishment of a Central Intelligence Agency (CIA) in 1947, President Truman hoped to improve the ability of the United States to anticipate dangers to its security, such as had occurred at Pearl Harbor. His goal was to upgrade substantially the collection, analysis, and coordination of information useful to the United States in its external relations.

The Intelligence Community

In the United States, intelligence activities are carried out by a dozen major and several minor intelligence agencies. Collectively, these agencies are called the "intelligence community." They employ over 150,000 people and in 1996 had an annual budget (according to media reports) of approximately $28 billion (down slightly from a high of $30 billion in the 1988–1993 period), most of which has been kept secret.

The most prominent of the U.S. secret agencies are: the CIA, chiefly responsible for strategic analysis and for covert action; the National Security Agency (NSA), the nation's codebreaking and electronic eavesdropping agency; the Defense Intelligence Agency (DIA), which coordinates military intelligence; the military intelligence units, which gather intelligence and provide counterintelligence; the Department of State's Bureau of Intelligence and Research (INR); the National Reconnaissance Office (NRO), which coordinates satellite surveillance; the Federal Bureau of Investigation's intelligence units; the Department of the Treasury (home of the Secret Service, the Internal Revenue Service, and the Drug Enforcement Agency, each with an intelligence component); and the Department of Energy, which tracks the flow of fissionable materials.

Together, these agencies compose the largest information-producing apparatus in the history of the world. The challenging task of coordinating these various entities (each with its own directors, budgets, and bureaucratic turf) falls upon the Director, Central Intelligence (DCI).

Gathering and making sense of information about the world is the primary mission of a nation's intelligence bureaucracy. This "collection and analysis" mission consists of five interacting phases that together make up the "intelligence cycle": planning and direction, collection, processing, analysis, and dissemination.

Managers inside the CIA and other U.S. intelligence agencies initially must decide, in consultation with policymakers, what information should be sought and how. Although seventy-five to eighty percent of the desired information can be acquired through open (public)

sources, some is concealed by foreign governments, which wish to keep their capabilities and intentions private. This information must be gained through secret methods—in a word, espionage. Career professionals in the intelligence field speak of freshly gathered information as "raw intelligence." After this information is analyzed—that is, studied and interpreted—it becomes "finished intelligence." Intelligence managers do not always have a clear idea about what kinds of raw intelligence to procure, and by what means. Policymakers may fail to make their informational needs known, or may also have unrealistic expectations about what information can be uncovered by the secret agencies. Even when good information is gathered and skillfully interpreted, intelligence managers may find it rejected by policymakers who choose to disbelieve or ignore the findings for political or psychological reasons: the ancient practice of killing—these days, ignoring—the messenger who brings bad news.

The initial decision that intelligence managers must make, then, is what information to collect in which countries and by what means. This selection of intelligence targets is known as "setting requirements" or "tasking." During the Cold War, for example, U.S. intelligence agencies viewed the Soviet Union as the chief target for intelligence gathering, an adversary drawing more than sixty percent of every intelligence dollar expended by the U.S. government. The reason for this lopsided resource distribution in a world of some 170 nations was obvious: the Soviet Union bristled with intercontinental missiles that could destroy the United States in thirty minutes. With the end of the Cold War, while this part of the world continues to garner a disproportionate share of U.S. intelligence investment, roughly sixty percent of the intelligence dollar is now spent elsewhere, in response to a long list of real and potential threats now confronting the United States. The CIA and other U.S. intelligence agencies collect information on terrorist activities, the flow of illegal drugs, the spread of fissionable materials and conventional weapons around the world, oil-pricing debates in the Organization of Petroleum Exporting Countries (OPEC), the intricacies of Chinese politics, the state of food and water supplies in various parts of the globe, the quality of computers with military applications in Iran, the fidelity of nations to arms-control agreements, possible violations of United Nations trade sanctions instituted against Iraq, population demographics, immigration patterns, human rights abuses, international energy shortages, the AIDS epidemic in Africa and elsewhere, and debt financing in the developing nations. Many other topics are crowding in line for limited budget resources. Intelligence targets may continue to change over time, depending upon the shifting alliances of nations and changes in world conditions. The copper-

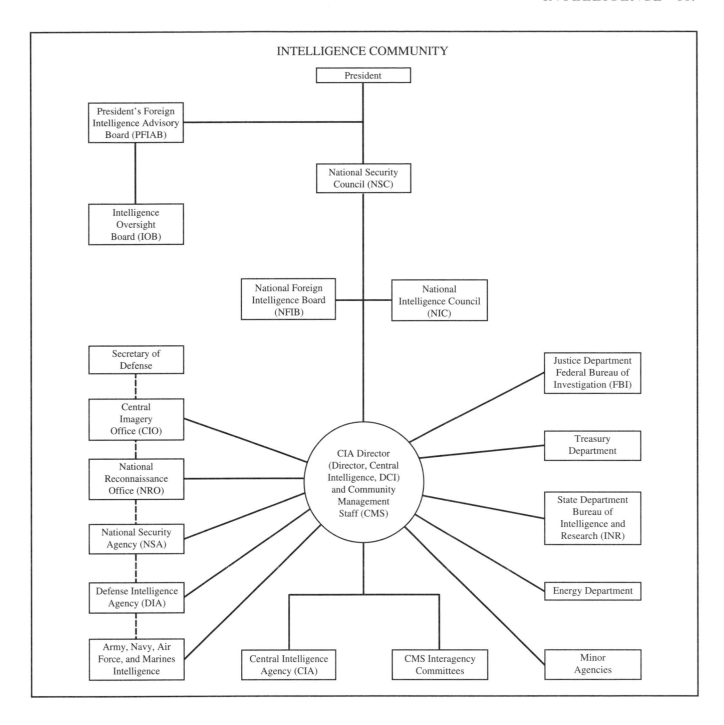

INTELLIGENCE COMMUNITY

producing African nation of Zaire, for example, was once of greater interest to U.S. intelligence professionals before the advent of plastic pipe diminished America's dependence on copper tubing.

The type of intelligence collected is related to the form and timing of the information desired by policy-makers, which in turn determines the degree of specula-tion and richness of factual detail included in an intelli-gence report. Sometimes decision-makers seek what is

called "current intelligence," that is, up-to-the-minute data on events in a certain nation or region—say, what has happened in Moscow during the past two hours. This kind of near-instant appraisal is sometimes vital in times of crisis but it can be difficult to obtain. The objective is to provide a window for policymakers to see events, actions, and situations as instantaneously (in "real time") as possible. Of greatest importance in the domain of cur-rent intelligence is "indications and warning" (I and W) information, which, once detected, provides an early alarm for impending threats to U.S. interests.

Despite the difficulties of collecting current intelligence, especially about nations ruled by totalitarian regimes, U.S. intelligence agencies have received high marks for quickly assembling data during a crisis ("crisis management"), as well as for having on hand extensive maps, economic data, and personality profiles of world figures. Failures sometimes occur, however. When the United States invaded the tiny island of Grenada in 1983, for instance, military personnel had to obtain maps of the island at local service stations. Often decision-makers seek more deeply analyzed predictions about long-range likelihoods in foreign nations, say, information on what is apt to occur in Pakistan over the next two years. This form of information is known as an "estimate" or predictive intelligence. Here the intelligence agencies have enjoyed less success, in large part because predicting the future is a notoriously difficult task. So, too, is penetrating the inner sanctums of terrorist cells, narcotics cartels, and tightly self-contained autocracies like the North Korean regime.

In a third form of intelligence, policymakers desire an in-depth research presentation on a specific topic, such as, say, the state of Russian oil reserves over the next thirty years. This is "research intelligence" or "basic intelligence"—which allows room for detail and the tracing of nuances. Yet, the policymaker—short on time and under pressure to make decisions—is drawn more to current intelligence, often in raw form or presented in a hurried oral briefing.

Collecting Information

For the actual collection of information, intelligence agencies depend on three approaches—the first overt in nature and the second two covert. On the overt side, which accounts for almost all of the information gathered by intelligence agencies, collectors rely on diplomatic reports, newspapers and political periodicals, libraries, media broadcasts, economic and environmental reports, agricultural statistics, scientific and technical journals, and other materials. The CIA's library receives virtually every publication in the world, and its Foreign Broadcast Information Service (FBIS) monitors global radio and television transmissions. In the face of this blizzard of information, the dilemma for overt collectors is less one of having too little data than of sorting out what is genuinely useful to policymakers.

The two methods of covert collection that augment overt sources are human intelligence (HUMINT) and technical intelligence (TECHINT) gathering. HUMINT is classical espionage, using spies and "sources;" TECHINT relies on mechanical devices for collection—satellites, reconnaissance aircraft, wiretaps, and a plethora of other machines with remarkable visual and auditory capabilities. Collection represents the costliest phase of the intelligence cycle, especially the expensive TECHINT platforms in space. Among other things, TECHINT has demonstrated its considerable prowess for spotting foreign military movements and missile installations from afar—an enormously important reason why peace between the superpowers prevailed during the Cold War. In October of 1962, it was a CIA U-2 reconnaissance aircraft that spotted the existence of missile sites in Cuba, providing vital warning to President John F. Kennedy that the Soviets had escalated the Cold War. During the Persian Gulf War in 1991, the combined TECHINT capabilities of the intelligence community provided U.S. battlefield commanders in Kuwait and Iraq with close to real-time data on the location of Iraqi radar, antiaircraft sites, armored vehicles, and other military targets, making a significant contribution to the overwhelming victory of the U.S.-led coalition of United Nations forces.

Yet many experts debate the wisdom of too heavy a reliance on machines. Satellites cannot see through roofs or thick clouds, and cannot attend, as a skillful human spy might be able to, the adversary's key decision meetings. A single HUMINT spy (an agent or asset) might be able to provide invaluable documents stolen from enemy safes, as was the case with the top CIA agent Colonel Oleg Penkovsky of Soviet military intelligence (GRU) during the Cuban missile crisis. The information he provided about the substantially inferior Soviet weapons capabilities compared to the United States in 1962 may have helped to avert a nuclear war between the superpowers. This information allowed President Kennedy to confront the Soviets during the crisis with some degree of confidence that the Kremlin would back down. This also works in reverse, however, as with the damage done by CIA agent turned Soviet spy, Aldrich Ames.

The third phase in the intelligence cycle, called processing, is the least disputatious. The objective at this stage is to prepare raw intelligence for study by analysts. This may mean translating a document into English, decrypting coded data, interpreting photographic material, or transcribing words captured on a wiretap (electronic surveillance). These tasks can be enormously time-consuming and require personnel with specialized training. A professional photo interpreter, for example, may need four hours to decipher fully a single frame of satellite photography.

Throughout the Cold War, NSA employed elaborate listening stations along the perimeter of the Soviet Union to monitor missile tests, military communications, and other activities of Soviet military personnel. Conversations between MIG pilots in midair, for instance, could be plucked out of the air by NSA TECHINT equipment, relayed by satellite to NSA headquarters at Fort Meade, Maryland, and translated from Russian into English by NSA linguists for examination by analysts throughout the intelligence community. After processing comes the central purpose of the intelligence cycle: the conversion of raw, unevaluated data into usable, finished intelligence. This is the marriage of information, overtly or covertly obtained, with thoughtful assessment by experts: in a word, analysis. The analysts are highly educated men and women who specialize on a single country, on broad topics such as the flow of petrodollars, or on quite technical matters such as the diversion of fissionable materials and technology from peaceful nuclear energy programs to the clandestine development of nuclear weapons.

Intelligence analysts prepare their findings according to the formats preferred by policymakers: written reports, oral briefings, or even videotapes (a favorite of President Ronald Reagan, a former Hollywood actor). For policymakers seeking current intelligence, the intelligence agencies produce a number of daily documents, among which the President's Daily Brief (PDB) is preeminent. Written by CIA officers in consultation with the other U.S. intelligence agencies, the PDB circulates only to the president, the vice president, the secretaries of state and defense, and the national security adviser. This document provides a summary of major developments throughout the world that have occurred in the previous twenty-four hours.

Beyond the various forms of current intelligence, the secret agencies also prepare short-range predictions that take the form of Interagency Intelligence Memoranda (IIM). Longer-range projections are called National Intelligence Estimates (NIEs). The NIEs are prepared routinely on different parts of the world, whereas Special National Intelligence Estimates (SNIEs) examine specific topics of interest to policymakers.

The NIE—the showpiece of the intelligence agencies—assesses events and conditions in a specific region or nation and normally makes a prediction. The highly classified document sets down and frequently ranks possible outcomes that might threaten or present opportunities for the United States. The best NIEs are accurate, timely, and dispassionate—the culmination of careful combing and evaluation of data collected by the various intelligence agencies.

The chief supervisors in the drafting of an NIE are a group of senior analysts in the government known, since 1973, as National Intelligence Officers (NIOs). They judge the findings and the conclusions in each NIE, from the reliability of the data and hypotheses to the wisdom of the forecast. The actual initial drafting rests, however, largely with various analysts picked by the NIOs from throughout the government. The NIOs also serve as liaison officers between the intelligence agencies and policymakers in the White House and elsewhere.

The analytic phase has been far from trouble free. Some NIOs have been accused of politicizing the analytic process by becoming too involved personally and politically with decision makers. They have also been criticized for being too slow and cautious in the preparation of NIEs, for failing to work as a team, and for drawing too heavily from CIA sources instead of relying on other major U.S. intelligence agencies for information and interpretation.

The politicization charge is the most troubling, given that the whole purpose of intelligence is to provide policymakers with accurate, unbiased truth about world affairs, insofar as that can be achieved. The biblical injunction, "know the truth and the truth shall make you free," is the chosen motto of the CIA, chiseled in marble in the lobby of its headquarters in Langley, Virginia. While the overwhelming majority of intelligence professionals have kept a respectful distance between themselves and policymakers, so as not to contaminate the purity of intelligence reports, some officials—not only NIOs—have occasionally allowed the needs of their political masters to color their findings. In 1983, for instance, critics concluded that CIA estimates on Central America seemed less like objective analysis than "intelligence to please"—that is, reports meant to reinforce the political views of the Reagan White House against the Sandinista government in Nicaragua. The Iran-Contra Affair of 1986–1987 demonstrated clearly that close personal ties between a CIA director and a president can lead to a disregard for established guidelines protecting U.S. intelligence agencies from partisan and unlawful practices.

With few exceptions, though, U.S. intelligence agencies have had impressive successes in their efforts to understand the world and its threats. Among them have been the accurate monitoring of arms agreements, the flow of petrodollars, OPEC investment strategies, and the rise of political leaders around the globe (anticipating, for example, the emergence of several of the Soviet dictators). The CIA predicted Sputnik in 1957, the Chinese A-bomb in 1964, the Arab-Israeli War of 1967, and the Soviet invasion of Afghanistan in 1979.

The agencies have had their share of failures, too. The most conspicuous was their inability (and everyone else's) to predict the collapse of the Soviet Union in 1990, though the CIA did closely chronicle the USSR's failing economic infrastructure. Earlier, analysts failed to anticipate the placement of Soviet tactical and strategic warheads in Cuba in 1962, or the Soviet invasions of Hungary in 1956 and Czechoslovakia in 1968.

The final, and frequently the most difficult, phase of the intelligence cycle is to place the best intelligence available into the hands of policymakers. The key to success is dialogue between intelligence producers and consumers. The relationship is freighted with difficulties. Policymakers are busy and often think they do not have time to read intelligence reports; sometimes they are ideologues less interested in facts than in acquiring position papers that support their political point of view. Prior to the failed CIA-sponsored secret invasion of Cuba at the Bay of Pigs in 1961, for example, analysts on Cuba in the CIA and INR were never consulted about the chances for success. As declassified documents reveal, these experts would have warned against an invasion, realizing that Fidel Castro, the Cuba leader, enjoyed widespread support among the people of his island nation at that time. Learning from its mistakes, the Kennedy Administration pursued a much closer working relationship with intelligence officials during the tense two weeks of the Cuban missile crisis more than a year later. This time, the CIA and other agencies were given the opportunity to provide valuable information that helped resolve the crisis.

Given the distractions that draw the attention of policymakers away from intelligence reports, the managers of the intelligence agencies with analytic responsibilities find they must market their product, not simply prepare it for reading. One technique is to flood the policymaker with a steady stream of analytic papers on a topic, hoping that eventually he or she may become interested. Another approach is to be provocative. One CIA rule of thumb is that the more provocative the intelligence report, the more likely it is to be read. Sometimes a brief, one-page memorandum has the best chance of making it out of the policymaker's in-box.

Packaging becomes all-important. Innovative methods are used to attract the attention of the policymaker: pictures, graphs, even videotapes often help, depending on the tastes of the particular consumer. Intelligence videotapes were notably popular with President Reagan, especially in portraying international personalities like Soviet Premier Leonid Brezhnev and Colonel Muammar al-Qaddafi of Libya. Videotapes can be costly to produce, however, and are somewhat superficial compared to carefully researched and written analytic reports. Despite these marketing innovations in recent years, a vexing irony of intelligence remains: the American government is prepared to spend nearly $30 billion a year on intelligence gathering and analysis, only to see its top leaders often ignore the results of the intelligence cycle altogether.

Intelligence as Covert Action

At its core, then, intelligence refers to the process of information collection and analysis; it can mean the information itself that is gathered, or the analyzed, finished version of this information. Another usage of the term has to do with the two additional missions assigned to secret agencies: covert action and counterintelligence. Covert action is activity designed to influence secretly affairs in other countries, not just gather information overseas. This mission, which evolved quickly after the creation of the CIA, is also known as "special activities." It is sometimes called the "third option" between sending in the Marines or relying on diplomats to settle international disputes.

Covert actions are usually grouped into four categories: propaganda, and political, economic, and paramilitary (PM) operations. No form of covert action is used more extensively than propaganda, sometimes called psychological warfare or simply "psy war." Especially during the Cold War, as a supplement to overt distribution of information abroad through the U.S. Information Agency (USIA) and other organizations, the CIA secretly provided a flood of supportive propaganda distributed through its vast, hidden network of "media assets": reporters, newspaper and magazine editors, TV anchor people, and other media personnel in foreign countries. By means of political covert action, the CIA has also provided secret financial aid to friendly politicians and other governmental officials abroad. One example is the support provided by the CIA to General Manuel Antonio Noriega, the president of Panama, in return for information on political and military developments throughout Central and South America—before he was apprehended during a U.S. military invasion of Panama in 1989 and convicted in a Miami court for drug dealing. Another approach has been the attempt through secret means to disrupt the economies of U.S. adversaries. The techniques have included contaminating foreign agricultural produce with unpalatable (though nonlethal) chemical substances (as planned for Cuban sugar in 1961, but halted by President Kennedy); encouraging labor unrest (in Chile during the 1960s, among other places); counterfeiting foreign currencies (in Iraq); and a whole range of operations used against North Vietnam during the Vietnamese War, including contaminating oil supplies, dynamiting electrical power lines and oil-storage tanks, mining harbors to discourage commercial shipping (a ploy used against Nicaragua as well during the 1980s), and even trying to control the rainfall over North Vietnam by cloud seeding.

No covert actions have held higher risk or been more contentious than paramilitary, or warlike, operations. They often involve large-scale "secret" wars, as in Laos during the 1960s. A special type of paramilitary operations is the assassination plot. Congressional investigators reported in 1975 that this option had been resorted to infrequently and, at least when directed against heads of state, never successfully—though numerous attempts were made against the life of Fidel Castro and another plot was underway against the Congolese leader Patrice

Lumumba just before he was murdered by a rival political faction in the Congo (now Zaire).

The third major form of intelligence activity is counterintelligence. Like covert action, this mission went unmentioned in the National Security Act of 1947, yet it also grew quickly in importance as the protective side of U.S. intelligence. During the Cold War, the United States became the target of espionage activities conducted by the intelligence services of the Soviet Union and several other nations (including some U.S. allies). To thwart these hostile activities and protect U.S. secrets, the U.S. intelligence agencies established counterintelligence defenses.

The practice of counterintelligence entails both maintaining security and carrying out counterespionage. Security is the passive or defensive side of counterintelligence, involving the creation of static defenses against hostile foreign operations directed against the United States. These defenses include the use of security clearances, polygraphs (lie-detection machines), camouflage, codes, fences, sentries, alarms, badges and passes, watchdogs, curfews, restricted areas, and checkpoints.

Counterespionage is the offensive or aggressive side of counterintelligence. It involves the identification of a specific adversary and a knowledge of the operation he or she is conducting. Counterespionage personnel then attempt to undermine these hostile operations by infiltrating the enemy's intelligence service, a ploy called a "penetration" and carried out by an agent called a "mole." The thrust of the hostile operation is turned back against the enemy, for example, by blackmailing a Soviet espionage agent during the Cold War and forcing him or her to work against the USSR, or at least by using the agent as a conduit for misleading intelligence (a "disinformation" operation). The Soviets used the same approach against the United States, with their most notable success occurring near the end of the Cold War when they recruited CIA officer Ames to spy on their behalf. The information provided by Ames led to the deaths of a dozen or more U.S. agents in Russia and over two hundred blown operations, until his treachery was uncovered by the CIA and FBI in 1994.

Usually the most effective and desirable penetration—for purposes of both counterintelligence and espionage—is the recruitment of an "agent-in-place," a citizen of an adversary nation who is already in the employ of its intelligence service and, ideally, highly placed. Almost as good as the agent-in-place is the defector, although determining whether a defecting agent from a hostile intelligence service is genuine or in reality a double agent can be exceedingly difficult. The *bona fides*, the avowed credentials of several key Soviet defectors, remained in dispute among counterintelligence officials throughout the Cold War. About half of the communist intelligence defectors who came over to the West during the Cold War returned to their homeland, out of homesickness—or, perhaps more likely—because they were false defectors ("deception agents") all along.

Other counterespionage techniques include provocation, surreptitious surveillance, and interrogation. Provocation involves the harassment of adversary intelligence services, such as publishing the names of their personnel or sending a deception agent into their midst. Surveillance of suspected hostile agents can consist of various methods, including audio, mail, physical, and "optical" (photography). Defectors are also interrogated by counterintelligence officers, sometimes while kept incommunicado for long periods of time.

The Domestic Component

Although this discussion chiefly describes the foreign aspects of U.S. intelligence (the only legitimate domain for the CIA and most of the other secret agencies), intelligence has a domestic component as well. Within the United States, the FBI has the primary responsibility for two forms of intelligence activity: the collection and analysis of information about suspected subversives—including terrorists—and monitoring the activities of suspected or confirmed foreign-intelligence agents operating within U.S. borders. Although these are legitimate assignments, in the past the FBI has also engaged in improper domestic "covert actions" or harassment operations against innocent individuals. These harassments, part of a secret FBI Counterintelligence Program (COINTELPRO) during the 1960s, consisted of anonymous threats (including a blackmail threat against civil rights leader Dr. Martin Luther King, Jr.) and scurrilous mailings, along with efforts to ruin the reputations of people in their work place or undermine their marriages. Some of the COINTELPRO targets were clearly unsavory people—including Ku Klux Klansmen who had torched African-American churches in the South—but others were individuals merely exercising their rights of free speech to criticize the Vietnamese War or to advocate civil liberties at home.

At the formal, written (albeit top secret) request of the Nixon White House in 1970, counterintelligence officers in the CIA turned their surveillance arts against Vietnamese War protesters within the United States (in an operation code-named CHAOS)—in clear violation of the agency's 1947 statutory charter. The only proper and sharply limited authority held by the CIA to conduct operations in the United States is in the case of suspected espionage by its own employees. Other U.S. intelligence agencies have also misused their powers by conducting surveillance against American citizens, including the NSA and the DIA—both engaged in surveillance operations against Vietnamese War dissenters during the

1960s. These sad chapters in the history of modern U.S. intelligence underscore another troubling irony of intelligence: it has a capacity to undermine as well as to protect democracy.

Intelligence is frequently discussed in terms of its policy implications and the special difficulties it raises for oversight by Congress, the courts, and the executive branch itself—the question of accountability or policy supervision, so vital in a democracy. Policy refers to what a government decides to do: the decisions it makes. Intelligence policy thus refers to the decisions that governmental officials make about how the intelligence budget will be spent; what countries or groups will be targeted for espionage purposes; what will be the ratio between the use of HUMINT and TECHINT; how much the nation should focus on military tactical intelligence for battlefield purposes, in contrast to the collection of worldwide (strategic) information on economic, demographic, and other trends; how many analysts will be hired to examine what sources of information; when covert action will be used, against whom, and at what level of intrusion; what the nation's counterintelligence priorities are; what defector's bona fides will be accepted; how much information held by U.S. secret agencies can be released to the public without jeopardizing intelligence sources and methods; and how the intelligence agencies can serve decision-makers more effectively. These are the kinds of policy questions that intelligence managers and their overseers must grapple with each day.

In a democracy the people must stand guard against the misuse of this hidden power, which manifests itself in the forms of information upon which important decisions are made, activities that can include war-making and assassination plots, and budgets that have grown immense. This power is made doubly dangerous because the information, activities, and budgets of the intelligence agencies are kept secret and away from scrutiny by the public.

In the years from 1947–1974, U.S. secret intelligence agencies were subjected to little outside scrutiny by the Congress or the courts. Even key members of the NSC had little detailed knowledge of CIA and other agency activities and budgets. This state of minimal accountability changed dramatically in the wake of a series of articles published by the *New York Times* in December 1974. These reports, by journalist Seymour M. Hersh, claimed that the CIA had engaged in unsavory covert operations during the 1960s and early 1970s against the democratically elected government of Chile and, more startling, had resorted to espionage operations at home (the CHAOS program).

These allegations appeared on the heels of the Watergate scandal and, as a result, had a particularly explosive effect. Congress and the president called for special inquiries, which led to a long series of recommended reforms and significant changes in the conduct of intelligence policy. Most notably the senate, relying on its constitutional authority to ensure that the laws it passes are properly carried out, created a permanent intelligence-oversight committee in 1976 and the house created its counterpart in 1977. Presidents Gerald Ford and Jimmy Carter authored executive orders that also brought more stringent rules of accountability on the secret agencies, including the creation by President Ford of an Intelligence Oversight Board attached to the White House. With the Foreign Intelligence Surveillance Act of 1978, the judicial branch was also brought into the oversight process, through the establishment of a special court to review all requests for electronic surveillance against national-security targets in the United States.

A new era of closer accountability had been introduced for the secret intelligence agencies. Operations CHAOS and COINTELPRO, along with the excesses in Chile (among other examples), demonstrated that the casual watchfulness exercised by officials during the early days of the Cold War was insufficient. This more vigorous supervision proved unable to prevent the Iran-Contra abuses, in which officials in the Reagan Administration bypassed the new intelligence-oversight laws to conduct covert actions in Nicaragua prohibited by law. For the most part, though, the new system worked, striking a workable balance between closer accountability by outside supervisors and sufficient secrecy to ensure the effectiveness of U.S. secret agencies.

Throughout the Cold War, U.S. intelligence agencies made monitoring the USSR their first priority. The stunning collapse of the Soviet Union dramatically altered the nature of world politics, however, and caused intelligence managers in the early 1990s to undertake a reexamination of existing perils to U.S. security. Eyeing the new world, they pointed to a fresh set of security threats as well as some dangers that lingered on from the days of the Cold War.

Intelligence officials in recent years have considered the most serious threat to American national security to be the global proliferation of nuclear, biological, and chemical weapons, as well as the spread of conventional armaments.

Countering the flow of narcotics into the United States also presented an ongoing challenge of enormous proportions to the intelligence agencies, as did maintaining a vigilance against terrorist activities of the kind that led in 1993 to the bombing of the World Trade Center in New York City. Other claimants on the time and budget resources of the intelligence agencies included calls for the monitoring of global environmental degradation, closer attention to worldwide economic trends, and industrial espionage (an activity strongly resisted by the intelligence agencies as inappropriate for them). As well, policymakers wanted more collection and analysis of information on ethnic territorial disputes around the world, on the spread of AIDS and other diseases, on foreign nuclear safety problems, on migration and refugee flows, and on the international technology race.

In the place of one large danger—the USSR—had arisen a series of smaller, but still dangerous, threats. The core task of the intelligence agencies had become less a matter of stealing secrets from Kremlin safes and peering into Soviet missile sites from satellites than it was one of trying to help policymakers understand a complex new world of fledgling nations and combustible ethnic rivalries. As the first post–Cold War CIA Director R. James Woolsey put it, although the Soviet Union may have been a large dragon, at last slain, "we live now in a jungle filled with a bewildering variety of poisonous snakes, and in many ways the dragon was easier to keep track of."

LOCH K. JOHNSON

See also Central Intelligence Agency; Cold War; Congress; Covert Action; Cryptology; Cuban Missile Crisis; Iran-Contra Affair; National Security Agency

FURTHER READING

Berkowitz, Bruce D., and Allan E. Goodman. *Strategic Intelligence for American National Security*. Princeton, 1989.
Colby, William, and Peter Forbath. *Honorable Men: My Life in the CIA*. New York, 1978.
Ford, Harold P. *Estimative Intelligence: The Purposes and Problems of National Intelligence Estimating*. Lanham, Md., 1993.
Godson, Roy, ed. *Intelligence Requirements for the 1990s*. Boston, 1989.
Jeffreys-Jones, Rhodri. *The CIA and American Democracy*. New Haven, Conn., 1989.
Johnson, Loch K. *America's Secret Power: The CIA in a Democratic Society*. New York, 1989.
———. *Secret Agencies: U.S. Intelligence in a Hostile World*. New Haven, Conn., 1996.
Mangold, Tom. *Cold Warrior*. New York, 1991.
Miller, Nathan. *Spying for America: The Hidden History of U.S. Intelligence*. New York, 1989.
Powers, Thomas. *The Man Who Kept the Secrets: Richard Helms and the CIA*. New York, 1979.
Prados, John. *President's Secret Wars: CIA and Pentagon's Covert Operations Since World War II*. New York, 1986.
Ranelagh, John. *The Agency: The Rise and Decline of the CIA*. New York, 1986.
Ransom, Harry Howe. *The Intelligence Establishment*. Cambridge, Mass., 1970.
Richelson, Jeffrey T. *The U.S. Intelligence Community*. Cambridge, Mass., 1985.
Shulsky, Abram N. *Silent Warfare: Understanding the World of Intelligence*, 2nd ed. (revised by Gary J. Schmitt). Washington, D.C., 1991.
Smist, Frank J., Jr. *Congress Oversees the United States Intelligence Community, 1947-1989*. Knoxville, Tenn., 1990.
Treverton, Gregory F. *Covert Action: The Limits of Intervention in the Postwar World*. New York, 1987.
Turner, Stansfield. *Secrecy and Democracy: The CIA in Transition*. Boston, 1985.

INTER-AMERICAN DEVELOPMENT BANK

The oldest regional institution for development finance. Prior to the bank's establishment in 1959, the United States repeatedly had rejected proposals for an inter-American bank, but the Cuban revolution fed a sense that more attention needed to be paid to regional development. The Inter-American Development Bank (IADB), headquartered in Costa Rica, focuses much of its resources on social and economic development. With the capital contributed by bank members and with funds raised in international financial markets, the IADB promotes both public and private capital investment in developing countries of the region. The IADB, often in tandem with the World Bank, provides technical assistance to complement its programs and projects as well as cofinancing for their implementation. Like other development banks (Asian Development Bank, African Development Bank, and the World Bank), the IADB is governed jointly by representatives of the donor and recipient nations. As the largest donor, the United States exercises substantial influence in the IADB, including a veto over the bank's concessional lending.

Several pieces of congressional legislation in the 1960s and 1970s required U.S. representatives to the IADB (and in some cases, all development banks) to oppose loans to countries that expropriated U.S. foreign investments without compensation, purchased sophisticated military equipment, failed to take adequate steps to suppress illegal drug traffic, or engaged in gross violations of human rights. Charges that the United States influenced the IADB to stop lending to Chile during the Salvador Allende period (1971–1973) to undermine the economy and bring about the collapse of the socialist government have never been fully substantiated. The IADB has had wide-ranging impact. By the 1980s it had an accumulation of loans worth $25 billion spanning 2,000 different projects. Many Latin American members, uncomfortable with U.S. domination as the largest donor, have sought to strengthen the bank's ties with Japan and Europe.

MARGARET P. KARNS

See also International Bank for Reconstruction and Development; Latin America

FURTHER READING

Sanchez Arnau, J. C., ed. *Debt and Development*. New York, 1982.
Sanford, Jonathan. *U.S. Policy and the Multilateral Banks: Politicization and Effectiveness. Staff Report to the Senate Subcommittee on Foreign Assistance of the Committee on Foreign Relations*. Washington, D.C., 1977.

INTERCONTINENTAL BALLISTIC MISSILES

See Nuclear Weapons and Strategy

INTERMEDIATE-RANGE NUCLEAR FORCES TREATY

(1987)

Arms control agreement signed by the United States and the Soviet Union that eliminated an entire class of inter-mediate- and shorter-range missiles whose deployment had resulted in an unprecedented political crisis within the North Atlantic Treaty Organization (NATO). The Intermediate-Range Nuclear Forces (INF) Treaty repre-sented an historical watershed. It was the only U.S.-Sovi-et nuclear arms control agreement to be concluded in the 1980s and the first to be signed and ratified since the Strategic Arms Limitation Treaty (SALT I) of 1972. Its conclusion signified the approaching end of the nuclear confrontation in Europe and the Cold War more generally.

The origins of the INF Treaty can be traced to the evolving U.S.-European nuclear relationship, in which Western Europe was faced with a Soviet military threat on its borders and depended on the nuclear protection provided by a country an ocean away, the United States. This central geostrategic circumstance, which had con-fronted NATO almost from the start of its existence, became more salient during the 1970s, when U.S.-Soviet nuclear arms control negotiations and agreements focused on stabilizing the balance of their strategic forces while skirting controls on weapons with less than inter-continental range—so-called gray-area systems. Whereas the SALT negotiations succeeded in bringing U.S. and Soviet strategic forces in balance, the exclusion of these gray-area systems from the negotiations created fears of an impending imbalance in these weapons, especially once the Soviet Union began to modernize its intermedi-ate-range nuclear forces in 1976.

As the Soviet Union deployed more accurate and mul-tiwarhead SS-20 missiles, NATO agreed on 12 Decem-ber 1979 to deploy 572 cruise and Pershing II missiles by 1983 unless arms control negotiations would succeed in changing this requirement. Known as NATO's double-track decision, it became highly controversial, especially in Western Europe, where a growing antinuclear move-ment took to the streets to oppose both the pending deployment and the strident anti-Soviet rhetoric and policies of President Ronald Reagan's administration.

Galvanized by European and growing American pub-lic opposition, the Reagan Administration decided in November 1981 to enter into negotiations with the Sovi-et Union on the INF missiles. Largely for propaganda purposes, the administration proposed an agreement eliminating all Soviet and U.S. intermediate-range mis-siles. This "zero option" put the onus for deployment of the cruise and Pershing II missiles squarely on Moscow, which could prevent the deployment only if it agreed to eliminate its SS-20 missiles.

Despite valiant efforts and attempts at ingenious com-promises by Paul Nitze and Yuli Kvitsinski, the U.S. and Soviet negotiators, the INF talks remained deadlocked until late 1983. The Soviet Union refused to cede its advantage in intermediate-range nuclear systems, and the United States and NATO continued to insist that deployment would proceed unless Moscow agreed to the zero option. When in November 1983 the first U.S. mis-siles arrived for deployment in Germany and Great Brit-ain, the Soviet delegation walked out of the INF talks.

INF negotiations resumed in March 1985 in a quite different atmosphere, created partly by the fait accompli of NATO deployments and partly by the accession of Mikhail Gorbachev to power in the Soviet Union a month earlier. From then on the INF negotiations served as a key indicator of the steady rapprochement in U.S.-Soviet relations. The breakthrough came in October 1986 dur-ing an historic summit meeting between Reagan and Gorbachev in Reykjavík, Iceland. The two presidents agreed to eliminate their INF missiles in Europe, although a final deal foundered on disagreements over whether and how to constrain research on the U.S. Strategic Defense Initiative. The Reykjavík meeting, however, set the stage for an agreement in 1987. By March the two countries had reaffirmed their desire to eliminate INF missiles in Europe; in April Gorbachev offered to eliminate shorter-range missiles (with ranges between 500–1,000 kilometers, or 320–610 miles) as well, thus adding a second "zero"; and in July both sides agreed to make the double-zero agreement truly global, affecting not just weapons deployed in Europe, but also those deployed or stored everywhere else.

The INF Treaty, signed by Reagan and Gorbachev on 8 December 1987, provided for the elimination of all ground-based cruise and ballistic missiles with ranges between 500 and 5,500 kilometers (320–3,400 miles) as well as their launchers. U.S. weapons covered by the treaty included 867 ground-launched cruise missiles, Per-shing II, and Pershing IA missiles; the treaty encom-passed 1,836 Soviet SS-20, SS-4, SS-5, SSC-X-4, SS-12, and SS-23 missiles. All of these missiles and their associ-ated launchers were in fact eliminated by June 1991.

The INF Treaty included a number of notable aspects, all of which were incorporated in subsequent nuclear arms control agreements. The treaty was the first agreement actually to mandate reductions in, rather than limitations on, nuclear weapons systems. It was also the first agreement to provide for the elimination rather than the reduction of missiles and launchers, although it did

INTERMEDIATE-RANGE NUCLEAR FORCES (INF) TREATY: WEAPONS TO BE ELIMINATED

At 1 Nov 1987:	Launchers			Missiles		
	Deployed	Non-deployed	Type total	Deployed	Non-deployed	Type total
United States						
LRINF						
Pershing II	115	51	166	120	127	247
GLCM	99	17	116	309	133	442
Sub-total	214	68	282	429	260	689
SRINF						
Pershing I	–	1	1	–	178	178
Total	214	69	283	429	438	867
Soviet Union						
LRINF						
SS20	405	118	523	405	245	650
SS4	79	6	85	65	105	170
SS5	–	–	–	–	6	6
SSC-X-4	–	6	6	–	84	84
Sub-total	484	130	614	470	440	910
SRINF						
SS12	115	20	135	220	506	726
SS23	82	20	102	167	33	200
Sub-total	197	40	237	387	539	926
Total	681	170	851	857	979	1,836

From *Strategic Survey, 1987–1988.* The International Institute for Startegic Studies

not affect nuclear warheads. Whereas previous agreements had relied solely on national technical means for monitoring, this treaty was the first nuclear arms accord to require on-site inspections of declared sites. These inspections were specified to continue for thirteen years after entry into force (until 2001). The treaty also called for continuous monitoring at missile production facilities in each country, another first. Last, the treaty mandated a detailed exchange of data on intermediate and other treaty-designated weapons systems.

The treaty's ratification in the United States proved unexpectedly difficult. Some opponents, former Republican officials, such as Richard Nixon, Henry Kissinger, and Brent Scowcroft, focused on the treaty's possible negative effect on NATO strategy, including the fear that it represented a first step toward the denuclearization of Europe. Others worried that the treaty might not cover "futuristic" systems based on laser and other technologies. Some senators questioned the accuracy of the Soviet data on which the implementation of the treaty rested. In the end, on 27 May 1988, with President Reagan already en route to Moscow for a summit meeting at which the instruments of ratification were to be exchanged, the U.S. Senate voted for the treaty, 93–5. The treaty entered into force on 1 June 1988.

The INF Treaty represented an important milestone along the steady path from East-West confrontation to cooperation. A highly popular achievement, the treaty nonetheless remained controversial among the small elite of U.S. and European defense experts who continued to subscribe to the predominant assumptions of the Cold War. These critics influenced intra-NATO deliberations throughout much of 1988 and 1989, until the crumbling of the Berlin Wall exposed just how esoteric debates about nuclear strategy really had become. What many in the public, but few within the defense elite, seemed to grasp was that the INF Treaty in fact represented an important sign of the Cold War's impending demise. The INF Treaty also set important precedents for subsequent arms control negotiations, including far-reaching reductions in U.S. and Soviet nuclear forces. The treaty's verification provisions, especially mandatory on-site inspections, production monitoring, and detailed data exchanges, provided a benchmark for future arms control agreements.

IVO H. DAALDER

See also Cold War; Conventional Armed Forces in Europe, Treaty on; Gorbachev, Mikhail Sergeevich; North Atlantic Treaty Organization; Nuclear Weapons and Strategy; Reagan, Ronald Wilson; Verification

FURTHER READING

Daalder, Ivo H. *The Nature and Practice of Flexible Response: NATO Strategy and Theater Nuclear Forces Since 1967.* New York, 1991.
Risse-Kappen, Thomas. *The Zero Option, INF, West Germany, and Arms Control.* Boulder, Colo., 1988.
Talbott, Strobe, *Deadly Gambits: The Reagan Administration and the Stalemate in Nuclear Arms Control.* New York, 1985.

INTERNATIONAL ATOMIC ENERGY AGENCY

Established in 1957, following President Eisenhower's "Atoms for Peace" initiative. Through scientific exchanges, technical assistance programs and regulations, this specialized UN agency seeks to control the dissemination of nuclear technology and manage the peaceful use and practical application of atomic energy research and development. The IAEA has been instrumental in facilitating the exchange of scientific and technical information; generating health and safety standards for atomic installations; advising operating officials of nuclear facilities and, most importantly, controlling weapons development through a system of safeguards.

A key to the IAEA's work since 1963 has been the joint U.S.-Soviet recognition of nuclear proliferation's threat and agreement on the principle of on-site inspection of nuclear facilities in countries without nuclear weapons. Despite the Cold War, the two superpowers worked together to create and expand the international nuclear nonproliferation regime centered on the IAEA and the Nonproliferation Treaty (NPT) which entered into effect in 1970.

The IAEA has been particularly valuable to the United States for thwarting other countries' nuclear weapons development, creating rules, and monitoring non-nuclear weapons' states activities through the system of safeguards. Controlling technology is at the crux of IAEA activities and requires working with countries that are exporters and consumers of nuclear technology. The IAEA conducts about 1,800 on-site inspections every year. Technical assistance with peaceful uses of nuclear power is the principal benefit for non-nuclear weapons states that accept the regime's rules.

The IAEA is governed by its General Conference and Board of Governors. The thirty-five board members are elected according to a formula for regional representation and leadership in nuclear technology. As a result, the board is dominated by the thirteen states who are most advanced in nuclear technology and most concerned with promoting international nonproliferation norms.

Until the early 1970s, the IAEA promoted nuclear technology and the use of nuclear power. As fears of proliferation grew after the rise in oil prices and reports of weapons development programs in Israel, Taiwan, South Africa, India, and South Korea, however, efforts shifted to improving safeguards and rules on technology transfer and development. Two supplier cartels that were formed in the 1970s—the Nuclear Suppliers Group and the Zangger Committee—attempted to restrict access to nuclear technology for civilian and military usages. Still, it was important to uphold the transfer side of the NPT bargain of control in return for assistance.

By the end of 1990, the IAEA had constructed safeguard agreements with 104 states; in 1995, 178 states were parties to the Nuclear Nonproliferation Treaty. Iraq was the first member-state and signatory to the NPT to violate its safeguards agreement with the IAEA and the Iraqi case stirred doubts about the effectiveness of the IAEA regime. Following the 1991 Gulf War, the UN Security Council condemned Iraq's non-compliance and established the special commission on Iraq (UNSCOM) to dismantle Iraq's weapons of mass destruction and work with the IAEA in conducting special inspections to monitor Iraqi facilities. The economic sanctions imposed on Iraq at the outset of the Gulf crisis were also then linked to its compliance with IAEA safeguards. This represented the first use of the IAEA Statute's provision (Article XII.C) whereby the agency's director can report instances of safeguards non-compliance to the Security Council for enforcement action. North Korea was similarly found in default of its safeguards commitments in 1992 and in 1993 rejected an IAEA request to inspect sites within its borders that Western intelligence had identified as possible nuclear weapons facilities. The IAEA then concluded that it could no longer determine whether North Korea's nuclear fuel was being used solely for peaceful purposes or whether some had been diverted to a secret weapons program. The UN Security Council debated imposing sanctions in 1994 after inspectors were not permitted to take samples at North Korea's declared nuclear sites. The confrontation eased only after the United States negotiated an agreement to provide $4 billion in energy aid to North Korea in return for a freeze and dismantling of the nuclear weapons program, as well as full and continuous inspections.

The actions against Iraq and North Korea illuminated the double standard under which the IAEA has long operated, singling out countries which are parties to the NPT for enforcement action and adopting the politically expedient course of not challenging non-NPT countries such as India, Israel, and Pakistan. Nonetheless, in January 1992, the UN Security Council affirmed the importance of preventing the proliferation of all weapons of mass destruction and preventing the spread of technology related to such weapons and their production, noting the importance of effective IAEA safeguards and export controls. In May 1995, the Nonproliferation Treaty itself came up for twenty-five-year review and was indefinitely renewed after extensive debate. In return for agreement on indefinite extension, the nuclear weapons states pledged to reduce and ultimately eliminate their nuclear arms as well as to conclude a comprehensive ban on nuclear testing in 1996 and to provide greater sharing of nuclear technology for energy, medicine, and agriculture. There will be yearly assessments of compliance beginning in 1997. South Africa, which gave up its nuclear weapons program in 1992, signed the NPT, and agreed to IAEA inspections, played a key role in securing the consensus on NPT indefinite renewal.

With a limited budget of $60 million that has not changed since the late 1980s, the IAEA has been pressed to meet expanding responsibilities. These include monitoring compliance of Ukraine, Belarus, and Kazakhstan with agreements to dismantle the nuclear weapons they inherited from the former Soviet Union and to return them to Russia, as well as denuclearizing Iraq and inspections of nuclear facilities in South Africa, Brazil, and Argentina which renounced their weapons programs. Critics contend that the IAEA should be more aggressive in inspecting undeclared nuclear facilities and in giving shorter notice to reduce the risk of states' hiding their activities. Although Cold War efforts to prevent the spread of nuclear weapons were largely successful, thanks to cooperation between the two superpowers and the IAEA-based regime, nuclear proliferation has emerged as a major problem of the post–Cold War era that will demand greater efforts by the United States and the IAEA.

MARGARET P. KARNS

See also Atoms for Peace; Iraq; Nuclear Nonproliferation; United Nations

FURTHER READING

Brenner, Michael J. *Nuclear Power and Nonproliferation: The Remaking of Policy.* New York, 1981.
Fischer, David. *Stopping the Spread of Nuclear Weapons: The Past and Prospects.* London, 1992.
Scheinman, Lawrence. *The International Atomic Energy Agency and World Nuclear Order.* Washington, D.C., 1987.
Schiff, Benjamin N. "Dominance without Hegemony: The U.S. Relationship with the International Atomic Energy Agency." In *The United States and Multilateral Institutions: Patterns of Changing Instrumentality and Influence.* Margaret P. Karns and Karen A. Mingst, eds. Boston, 1990.
———. *International Nuclear Technology Transfer: Dilemmas of Dissemination and Control.* Totowa, N.J., 1984.

INTERNATIONAL BANK FOR RECONSTRUCTION AND DEVELOPMENT

Multilateral lending institution, better known (with its subsequently organized affiliates) as the World Bank Group, began operations in June 1946 and has become the single most influential factor in international development lending. By 1995, the number of member countries had grown to 178, capital resources were $300 billion, loans and credits outstanding were $205 billion and annual lending was $25 billion. A staff of 7000, recruited from 121 countries, administered this huge flow of capital and the technical assistance that went with it. The size and complexity of World Bank Group operations and the rapid rise of private flows in borrowing countries have raised questions about its current practices and future direction. Still, the World Bank stands as a prominent example of effectively functioning multilateralism, one that encompasses goals, resources and decision-making. Throughout the World Bank Group's history, the United States has been its prime mover, largest single source of financial support, and since the mid-1970s its most persistent critic. At the same time, the World Bank Group operations, directed toward the peaceful economic improvement of low income countries, have served to advance important objectives of U.S. foreign policy.

At Bretton Woods, New Hampshire, in July 1944, forty-four countries convened to negotiate the Articles of Agreement for the International Monetary Fund (IMF) and the IBRD. Most of the debate centered on the IMF, which in the end emerged as a compromise between U.S. and British views about how to free postwar international payments and trade from the destructive controls and distortions that had contributed to the Great Depression and, indeed, to World War II. The IBRD had received less attention outside the U.S. government in the preparatory work, which led to some uncertainty as to whether it would come up for consideration at the conference. In fact, the proposal for a bank received widespread support. The Europeans emphasized its potential help in reconstruction, and the low income countries emphasized its role in assisting their development. The articles of agreement, generally reflecting the U.S. work-

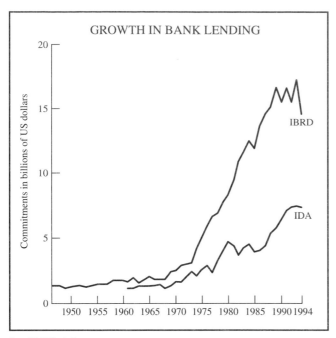

GROWTH IN BANK LENDING

From World Bank Group

ing draft, outlined a new instrument to facilitate the recovery of long-term international lending.

The two Bretton Woods institutions were conceived to have distinct financing responsibilities. IMF funds would provide financing for temporary current account deficits. IBRD funds would provide long-term resources for development. Membership in the IMF was required for membership in the IBRD. Initially the IBRD proved ill equipped to address either of its assigned tasks. A modest amount of useable capital and conservative lending guidelines precluded it from being a significant factor in financing the repair of wartime damage. That task soon fell to the U.S. loan to the United Kingdom and much more to the Marshall Plan. As for development, the wartime planners could only dimly foresee the the magnitude of the task. Part of the reason they did not anticipate the need for large-scale lending was the enormous foreign exchange surpluses accumulated during the war by the Latin American countries and the low-income members of the pound-sterling bloc. In addition, the planners had not predicted the rapidity of decolonization after the war. Only later would the quantum increase in foreign capital and technical assistance that would be needed by the newly independent countries become clear. Yet the structure the planners established for the IBRD proved to be remarkably adaptable.

Structure and Lending Guidelines

Ultimate control of the IBRD rests with its board of governors, which consists of one ministerial representative from each country and meets in plenum only once a year.

The governors delegate their powers to a board of executive directors, which is centered in the bank, meets frequently and gives final approval to budgets and individual projects. The president of the bank is responsible for operating the bank and recommending policies and priorities. All are subject to review and approval by the executive directors of which he is chairman. Headquarters are in Washington, D.C. Nominally, the IBRD is a specialized agency of the United Nations; operationally it is independent.

A country's voting rights, with a slight modification, is proportionate to its capital subscription. In 1995, the industrial countries plus a few others that provide net financing had sixty-five percent of the voting rights; the borrowing countries had thirty-five percent. This principle of weighted voting has been a key element in IBRD expansion, because member countries recognized that continued increases in capital could not be expected for a bank controlled by borrowers. While capital may be subscribed only by member governments, the IBRD depends on private investors for most of its lendable funds. Of its capital subscriptions of $176 billion in 1995, only 6.2 percent was paid-in. This portion alone represents a budgetary expenditure for subscribing governments. The remainder is callable capital, which serves as backing against which the IBRD is able to issue top-rated bonds on world financial markets. Callable capital is a contingent liability that would have to be paid by subscribing governments only in the event that any defaults on IBRD loans could not be covered by the bank's substantial accumulated retained earnings and its paid-in capital. As of 1995 there had been no defaults on IBRD loans, although $2.6 billion are in non-accrual status. Two-thirds of this amount stems from disruptions following the breakup of Yugoslavia. A reserve of over $3.7 billion, out of retained earnings of $15.7 billion, is set aside against the possible losses from these loans.

In effect, the IBRD's financial structure enables it to operate as a unique financial intermediary. Using the strong credit position of its wealthier member governments, it channels funds from private capital markets through the screen of its lending requirements to lower-income borrowing countries whose credit position is not yet strong enough to borrow sufficient funds directly from such markets at reasonable terms.

The IBRD may lend only to governments or for purposes guaranteed by governments, or it may itself guarantee government flotations or private investments. The planners expected that issuing guarantees would be the IBRD's primary function, facilitating the recovery of international lending; in fact, this guarantee capability has been scarcely used. In 1995, the IBRD launched a new program to use guarantees to attract private investment, particularly for large infrastructure projects. The

WORLD BANK FINANCING, 1995
(major recipients)

LOANS (in millions of U.S. dollars)		IDA DEVELOPMENT CREDITS (in millions of U.S. dollars)	
Mexico	19,966	India	22,847
Indonesia	18,575	China	10,061
India	15,508	Bangladesh	7,380
China	13,876	Pakistan	4,967
Brazil	11,336	Ghana	3,444
Turkey	7,482	Tanzania	3,086
Argentina	7,312	Uganda	2,592
Philippines	6,922	Kenya	2,426
Morocco	5,598	Ethiopia	2,129
Russia	4,721	Sri Lanka	1,955

Source: *The World Bank Annual Report, 1995*. The World Bank

IBRD uses its resources mainly to make loans for specific projects that must also include a substantial portion of locally financed resources. Loans are extended over a medium term, usually twenty years, at market-related interest rates, that is, a small premium over the cost of IBRD borrowed funds. Total IBRD loans and guarantees outstanding may not exceed the sum of its subscribed capital, reserves, and surplus. In contrast, commercial banks may lend some ten times their capital resources. Not having such leverage, the IBRD must go back to its members for additional capital when there is a prospective limitation on its lending capacity. The board of governors approved three general increases in capital subscriptions: in 1959, 1979, and 1988.

Until the late 1980s IBRD membership reflected the divisions of the Cold War. The USSR participated at Bretton Woods and then decided not to join. Czechoslovakia and Poland, also participants and then members, resigned in the 1950s. The Republic of China (Taiwan), an original member, represented China, at times only nominally, until 1980 when the Peoples Republic of China took over the country's seat. After the breakup of the Soviet Union, Russia and the other former republics individually joined the IMF and the World Bank Group.

IBRD Affiliates

The IBRD has three affiliates—the International Development Association (IDA), the International Finance Corporation (IFC) and the Multilateral Investment Guaranty Facility (MIGA)—which meet needs outside the scope of the IBRD charter. They are organized similarly. IDA and the IFC have the same president and executive directors as the IBRD, although the votes of executive directors vary in each organization depending on the capital sub-

scribed by the countries they represent. MIGA has the same president and broadly the same though not identical executive directors. Membership in the IBRD is necessary for membership in the affiliates. The World Bank consists of the IBRD and IDA. Collectively, IBRD and its three affiliates are known as the World Bank Group.

When it became apparent that the poorest countries could not service a significant inflow of capital at market terms, the International Development Association was established in 1960 as the soft-loan affiliate of the IBRD. The two organizations have the same management and staff; for operating purposes they are one. IDA is financed, however, through budgetary contributions from its members, mainly the wealthier countries, on the basis of a formula negotiated for each three-year replenishment. IDA credits, as distinct from IBRD loans, are extended on grant-like terms—thirty-five to forty years, ten years grace, 0.5 percent service charge and interest free. Still, these credits must meet the efficiency standards and go through the appraisal procedures applicable to IBRD loans. Eligibility to receive IDA credits is restricted to countries having per capita incomes below $695 in 1993 dollars.

As of 1995 the IDA board of governors had approved ten replenishments of resources, generally at increasing levels in real terms, and each has been politically difficult to negotiate for budgetary and burden sharing reasons. In addition, the IBRD annually transfers a portion of its profits to IDA and repayments of principal on earlier credits generate a mounting volume of funds for new credits. Financing IDA has been the most severe test of the multilateral principle in development assistance; the results are impressive. In 1995, total IDA credits outstanding reached $75 billion and annual commitments amounted to $5.7 billion. Their distribution followed no narrowly identifiable interests of particular donor countries. Geographically, forty percent of the 1995 commitments went to countries in Africa, twenty-five percent to South Asia, nineteen percent to East Asia, mostly to China, and the rest to low-income countries in Central Asia, Eastern Europe, and Latin America.

The International Finance Corporation was established in 1956 as the investment banking arm of the IBRD. The IFC's objective is to expand the role of the private sector in developing countries. In contrast to IBRD loans, IFC investments are not supported by a government guaranty. It makes loans, takes minority equity positions and furnishes advice to help put together private projects, acting as a catalyst for other investors, domestic and foreign. When participations mature and become marketable, the IFC sells them to private buyers at its discretion. It has its own chief operating officer and staff, floats bonds on private markets and is legally and financially independent of the IBRD, although it draws on IBRD expertise and sometimes borrows from it. Capital subscriptions from IFC member governments are fully paid-in. IFC gains financial leverage for operations by being permitted to borrow up to four times its capital and surplus. In 1995, paid-in capital and retained earnings had grown to $3.7 billion.

IFC's role remained modest for a surprisingly long time. Initial capital of $100 million was too small to make an impact. Early replenishments were far from ambitious, as was its leadership, and the IBRD staff did not consciously try to incorporate IFC investment possibilities into country plans. Moreover, the climate for private foreign investment turned unattractive in the wake of the oil industry nationalizations of the early 1970s. A spurt began later in the decade, but it was in the late 1980s, as market reforms and emphasis on the private sector took hold in developing countries and in Eastern Europe, that the IFC began to come into its own. In 1995 alone, financing approved for IFC's own account amounted to $2.9 billion, which covered investments in infrastructure, energy, manufacturing, the development of capital markets and support of privatization. The additional $17 billion in private capital associated with these projects is testimony to IFC's newfound potential to mobilize private domestic and foreign funds for investment.

After an unusually long gestation period during which the concept itself was in dispute, the Multilateral Investment Guarantee Program came into being in 1988 as the first multilateral program to protect private foreign direct investment against noncommercial risks. It offers investors insurance covering expropriation, currency transfers, war and civil disturbance and breach of contract caused by government action; it offers host governments advisory services relating to investment experience and regulations. By 1995, the number of member countries had grown to 128, subscribed capital was $1 billion and contingent liabilities in connection with the guaranty program was $1.6 billion.

Operating Trends

Between 1947 and 1990, annual World Bank lending increased almost fifteen times in real terms. It then stabilized over the next five years as the flow of private capital surged (see graph). Shifts in the purposes for which it lends have been equally dramatic. The organization has carried out the activities of a development institition while retaining important characteristics of a bank—loan appraisals, reflow of funds and earning a profit.

The United States ratified the Bretton Woods agreements in July 1945, to be quickly followed by other signatory countries, which enabled the IBRD to open for business in June 1946. For at least a decade, the U.S. capital subscription, thirty-two percent of the initial capital of $10 billion, was the effective ceiling for lending. Other industrial countries were slow to make the paid in portion of their subscriptions freely available and financial markets were slow to accord them the credit standing to back IBRD bonds. Even with U.S. backing, IBRD bonds as a new type of international issue had to be tested cautiously, first in the United States, then in foreign markets. The bonds gradually received a top financial rating and the low interest rates that went with it, testimony to the work of the World Bank's third president, Eugene Black (1949-1962). Nonetheless, limitations on borrowing capacity dictated prudence in lending, both as to scale and to the type of projects deemed to be bankable.

In 1955, when war reconstruction could be considered accomplished, half of IBRD loans still were made to industrial countries. A decade after that the proportion was one-fourth, although these loans phased out a few years later. Infrastructure projects, for power generation, transportation and ports, received heavy emphasis from the first, a priority that continued well into the 1960s. Lending for agriculture and education, mostly financed by IDA credits, was at an early stage. Over its first two decades, the World Bank in the main held the view that the need to build a physical base for economic expansion should have first call on its resources.

Annual lending in real terms tripled in the 1970s and doubled again in the next decade. This acceleration, initiated and carried forward during the presidency of Robert McNamara (1968-81), sought to make a measurable impact on the developing world at a time when bilateral assistance was slowing down. In 1960, World Bank lending was equal to one-ninth of all bilateral programs; by 1990 it was one-third. A shift to new areas of lending also took place. Partly, this shift reflected the belief, voiced in the U.S. Congress and by private organizations in many industrial countries that economic growth was not enough; it should accompany a spread of material benefits. Foreign assistance, therefore, should do more to advance basic human needs and alleviate poverty. In response, the World Bank devoted a growing proportion of its resources to finance projects in the fields of agriculture and rural development; population, health and nutrition; improvement in urban sewage and water supply; and education. All required more staff time and entailed greater risk than traditional infrastructure projects.

At the end of the 1970s, when the second oil shock unsettled the oil-importing developing economies and helped to bring on the Third World debt crisis, the World Bank Group sought to step into the breach with non-project or balance-of-payments loans. Called structural adjustment lending, these loans aimed at encouraging policy changes necessary to mobilize more resources for investment and use them more efficiently. They have become a continuing feature of the World Bank's development arsenal. Operating results in 1995 dramatize the turn in the World Bank's portfolio. Investments in social overhead together with non-project lending accounted for three-fifths of total loans; traditional lending accounted for one-third. "Poverty reduction," President Lewis Preston could say in 1993, "must be the benchmark against which [World Bank Group] performance as a development institution is judged."

After a half a century of experience, the World Bank Group's activities span the field of development. A sampling makes the point. World Bank Group lending comprises some thirty percent of total official assistance to developing countries. It has an important role in coordinating bilateral programs and it mobilizes capital for the private sector. A vast flow of technical assistance, accounting for ten percent of lending, is supplied with World Bank Group projects or provided as stand alone investments in institutional development. The United Nations Development Program uses the World Bank as executing agent for its pre-investment surveys. Assisting the economic transformation of countries in Eastern Europe and the former Soviet Union has become a major responsibility. The World Bank's research program is used by bilateral aid agencies, regional development banks, and commercial institutions investing abroad. A World Bank facility, financed from its profits, buys up commercial bank debt of very poor countries at a fraction of face value. The World Bank has become the leading financier of environmental projects in the developing world and administers and is responsible for investment projects financed by the Global Environment facility, a multinational program formed to address threats to the atmosphere.

How to adapt most efficiently to the remarkable structural change since the late 1980s in the financing of development is the central issue facing the World Bank Group. Between 1987 and 1994 net long-term private flows to developing countries increased from $25 billion to $173 billion, more than half of which consisted of foreign direct investment; in contrast, official flows, including those from the multilateral banks, went from $43 billion to $54 billion, barely keeping pace with inflation. These record private flows followed development success; they were concentrated on countries in East Asia and Latin America that liberalized their economies, expanded private markets, privatized public enterprises, and generated growth in private savings and production. To support these flows and widen their applicability to additional countries, the World Bank Group needs to devise and use more extensively new forms of lending partnerships with private investors, including guarantees, cofinancing techniques and IFC participations. This will require a marked shift in emphasis from financing state activity to helping countries run a successful market economy.

At the same time, heavy social overhead and infrastructure lending requirements in the poorer countries, notably in sub-Saharan Africa, continue to face the World Bank Group. These investments to alleviate poverty and strengthen the foundations for economic advance are needed not only in their own right but to help prepare these countries to attract private capital and participate more strongly in the world economy.

U.S. Role and U.S. Foreign Interests

The United States has had a prominent role in the World Bank Group from conception, to financing, to evolution of mission. That role followed from U.S. postwar interests as a world power and accompanied other early initiatives toward the same end. By the same token, World Bank lending tends to benefit the foreign policy interests of the United States more than other countries because the World Bank operates on a world scale. This relationship has not been affected by the sharp proportionate decline over the years in financing supplied by the United States. In the IBRD, the U.S. share fell from thirty-two percent in 1945 to nineteen percent in the general capital increase of 1988; in IDA, from forty percent in 1960 to twenty-one percent in the replenishment of 1993. Increased shares from Japan and Germany, as their economies grew, made up the gap. This reduced share in financing did not keep the United States from influencing the World Bank to intensify its efforts in poverty alleviation, improving the environment, and encouraging the private sector, or to be more willing to open its operations to public scrutiny. Largest shareholder or not, the United States did not get its way when it sought to link parochial trade concerns to World Bank lending.

The United States has had a continuing interest in an improvement in living standards in the developing world, including countries in Latin America and Asia it considers of strategic or special political importance. Until budgetary will flagged and public disenchantment set in, the U.S. bilateral assistance program, which early on dominated international development much as the World Bank does now, sought these objectives. They are now encompassed in the World Bank's mission.

There are also problems involving global public goods, not readily susceptible to the efforts of one country, even the United States, for which the World Bank is structured to take the lead. One example is the effect of economic growth on the environment; at issue is whether the World Bank can devise a strategy that makes the cost concerns of lower income countries compatible with the requirements for environmental sustainability. Another is the World Bank population program which is an important element in the effort to avert global disaster inherent in unchecked population growth in the Third World. There is also the example of the World Bank's success, working under the leadership of the IMF, in containing the Third World debt crisis of the 1980s, and the need to have it stand ready to assume similar responsibilities in the future. Finally, a number of new country situations underline the connection between World Bank programs and U.S. strategic concerns. In Russia, the World Bank Group's long-term lending, in conjunction with IMF efforts to help get macroeconomic policies right, is bound to be an important factor in successful economic transition, as it is in Eastern Europe. In a Middle East settlement, the United States must look to the World Bank for leadership in a comprehensive economic program for the Palestinian areas. Much the same will be true for the economic rehabilitation of Bosnia-Herzogovina once peace is secure. In sum, the existence of a multipolar world in the economic sphere has made the objectives of the Bretton Woods conference even more pertinent today. Without a freestanding economic superpower, there is no substitute for efficient multilateral cooperation to deal with development problems, or to satisfy U.S. policy interests associated with those problems.

EDWARD R. FRIED

See also Bretton Woods System; International Monetary Fund; Third World; Third World Debt

FURTHER READING

Bretton Woods Commission. *Bretton Woods: Looking To the Future.* Washington, D.C., 1994.

Gardner, Richard N. *Sterling-Dollar Diplomacy: The Origins and the Prospects of our International Economic Order*, rev. ed. New York, 1969.

Lewis, John P., and Richard Webb. *The History of the World Bank as a Development.* Washington D.C., 1996.

Mason, Edward Sagendorph, and Robert E. Asher. *The World Bank Since Bretton Woods.* Washington, D.C., 1973.

INTERNATIONAL COMMODITY AGREEMENTS

Agreements between producing and consuming governments to regulate trade in primary commodities. The purpose of such agreements is to stabilize or enhance export prices, which is accomplished through the use of buffer stocks or export quotas. International Commodity Agreements (ICAs) have been established because producers of primary commodities, mainly developing countries, face an inelastic demand for their products, with the result that prices tend to be highly sensitive to fluctuations in supply and, hence, unstable. An ICA attempts to regulate price fluctuations by releasing product from buffer stocks during times of scarcity and by reducing the amount of product reaching the market through buffer stock purchases or export controls during times of plenty. A buffer stock requires that a fund be established to buy up stocks during periods of oversupply and slumping prices.

Commodity agreements can be a simple bilateral arrangement between exporters and importers, or they can be more complex multilateral agreements involving varying degrees of national commitments and international structure. Since the 1970s formal efforts to organize markets have occurred in more than one dozen commodities, and completed agreements have been achieved for coffee, sugar, rubber, olive oil, cocoa, tin, jute and jute products, wheat, and tropical timber. The success of these agreements has varied. In the main, the United States has been suspicious of ICAs, owing to its support for free international markets and opposition to government intervention in the international economy.

Commodity controls originated in the 1920s and saw development during the decades of the 1930s and 1970s. In the former period, the Great Depression produced a drop in the price of commodities and stimulated attempts to manage international markets through political cooperation. In the latter period, sharp constraints on supplies of commodities, particularly petroleum, emboldened producers and led to the actions of the Organization of Petroleum Exporting Countries (OPEC), as well as efforts in the United Nations Conference on Trade and Development (UNCTAD), to create an international regime for the management of various other commodities. Prior to the efforts of the 1970s, commodity agreements and other issues of international trade were handled mainly in bilateral relations. An exception was the World Economic Conference of 1927, which recommended multilateral ICAs, and ICAs were again promoted by the World Economic Conference of 1933. Despite these efforts to promote multilateral management of commodities, bilateralism and protectionism remained the dominant international policies of the 1930s.

When World War II erupted in 1939, concerns increased for commodity controls to address problems of shortages and uncertain markets. For example, the United States established the Commodity Credit Corporation, which, on occasion, resorted to the purchase of entire crops to ensure stable supplies. The end of World War II brought a resurgence of international organization and with it an increasing concern for the economic prospects of developing countries. These developments created political conditions favorable to the formation of ICAs, which combined with the economic conditions of the 1970s to promote the commodity arrangements that continue into the 1990s.

Spurred by OPEC's success, UNCTAD adopted the Integrated Program for Commodities (IPC) in 1974, intended to create a comprehensive trading arrangement for some eighteen commodities in lieu of fragmented case-by-case agreements that tended to be disadvantageous to exporters, especially developing countries. The central institution of the IPC was the Common Fund, which, with assistance from oil-exporting developing countries, was intended to mobilize funds for stockpiling commodities, both to take supplies off the markets when excesses were putting downward pressure on prices and to release supplies at times of shortage. Negotiations for the Common Fund were difficult and not completed until 1980, and it took nine years to receive necessary ratifications and enter into force. In actuality, however, the Common Fund has had much less impact than its planners hoped. Meanwhile, individual commodity agreements were established for various products from the mid-1970s onward.

The recession of the early 1980s, combined with the collapse of commodity prices, produced an unfavorable environment for ICAs. A further difficulty was created by the opposition of conservative governments in several developed countries that opposed the market interventionism inherent in ICAs. Under President Ronald Reagan the United States was philosophically opposed to ICAs, but it joined the coffee, sugar, and jute ICAs during President Jimmy Carter's administration. Generally, the United States has supported the use of buffer stocks but not export restrictions in ICAs, and it has encouraged commodity exporters to participate in General Agreement on Tariffs and Trade (GATT) multilateral trade negotiations as a means of strengthening their economies.

GILBERT R. WINHAM

See also General Agreement on Tariffs and Trade; New International Economic Order; Organization of Petroleum Exporting Countries; United Nations Conference on Trade and Development

FURTHER READING

Chimni, B. S. *International Commodity Agreements: A Legal Study.* New York, 1987.

Corea, Gamani. *Taming Commodity Markets: The Integrated Programme and the Common Fund in UNCTAD.* New York, 1992.

Finlayson, Jock A., and Mark W. Zacher, *Managing International Markets: Developing Countries and the Commodity Trade Regime.* New York, 1988.

INTERNATIONAL DEBT

In accounting terms, a nation's international debt comprises the total stock of claims on domestic residents or governmental entities held by foreigners. Obligations may include not only debts incurred by borrowing but also investments from abroad in the equity of commercial enterprises at home. The nation's net debtor-creditor status, or international investment position, is the balance of all external obligations less reverse claims on foreigners. International debt has long played a prominent role in the foreign relations of the United States. Indeed, the country was born in debt as a result of foreign borrowing by the fledgling U.S. government to help finance the American Revolution. Over time, however, the policy significance of international debt has shifted dramatically, as the United States evolved from a debtor nation in the nineteenth century to the world's largest creditor throughout most of the twentieth century and then, quite swiftly, back to debtor status again during the decade of the 1980s.

The United States began life as a debtor, a natural result of being a relatively undeveloped and capital-poor colonial domain at the fringe of the world economy, then centered in Europe. To help finance the Revolutionary War, the Continental Congress raised loans in France, Spain, and Holland. Subsequent arrearages in interest payments, which cast doubt on the creditworthiness of the new U.S. government, led Alexander Hamilton, the first secretary of the treasury, to call for a full funding of all public obligations, domestic as well as foreign, in 1790. Although controversial, his program was adopted after lengthy congressional debate, and some $75 million of state and federal debts were duly converted into long-term securities redeemable in specie (gold or silver). Hamilton's purpose was to assure a high rating to the public credit and attract foreign capital. A measure of his success could be seen in 1803 when the federal government, which had been nearly bankrupt in the 1780s, had no trouble raising some $11.25 million on short notice, mostly from European lenders, to underwrite the Louisiana Purchase.

The Nineteenth Century

Foreign debt gradually increased throughout the nineteenth century, although the pace of capital inflow was periodically slowed by recurrent financial or political crises. Major defaults on state government bonds in the 1840s and again in the 1870s, following enthusiastic waves of borrowing in the 1830s and during Reconstruction to finance canal and railway building, temporarily soured foreign investors and roiled Washington's relations with key European governments. Tensions with Great Britain, already high for other reasons, were particularly aggravated by the widespread interest arrears that built up after the panic of 1837. In all, nine states failed to meet their foreign obligations in whole or in part. Consequently, in 1842 the federal government itself found it impossible to float a loan in London, not because its own credit was poor, but because it had declined to assume the indebtedness of the states. Much the same pattern was repeated in the 1870s, when seven states repudiated some or all of their foreign liabilities. In each instance, however, most of the defaulted loans were ultimately settled, leading to renewed market access, although to this day Mississippi, which refused to resume payments in the 1840s, is still listed in London as a bad debtor.

In the latter part of the century much European capital, particularly from Great Britain, was invested in private ventures of various kinds, including utilities, mining, and cattle raising. Especially helpful was the Resumption Act of 1875, pledging a renewal of specie payments for U.S. paper currency, greenbacks, which did much to restore the confidence of foreign lenders. Also helpful, of course, was the rapid development of the U.S. economy, which simply offered too many attractive investment opportunities to ignore. Overall, foreign credit accounted for a comparatively small share of domestic capital formation. Nevertheless, by the turn of the century, the United States had become by far the world's greatest debtor nation. In 1914, the total of foreign capital invested in the U.S. economy exceeded $7 billion.

Meanwhile, from the 1870s onward, U.S. capital began to move abroad, at first slowly and then more rapidly, as growing enterprise at home increasingly sought out new markets and sources of supply overseas. In contrast to the bulk of foreign investment in the United States, which was largely portfolio in nature, purchases of bonds or bank loans, U.S. capital outflows were more tilted toward direct investment, involving overt management and control; foreign acquisitions exceeded portfolio lending by a ratio of two to one and were heavily concentrated in Latin America and Canada. The net debtor position of the United States peaked at around $3.3 billion in 1896, the year of the first recorded public offering of foreign securities in the U.S. capital market.

Dollar Diplomacy

By the turn of the century, more money was flowing out of the United States than was coming in. By 1914, as invest-

ments abroad continued to accelerate and foreign inflows slowed, U.S. net liabilities were down to less than $2.2 billion. Not surprisingly, as U.S. financial interests in the Western Hemisphere expanded, they became increasingly entangled with political concerns, particularly during the first two decades of the twentieth century, the heyday of what came to be known as the policy of dollar diplomacy. President Theodore Roosevelt laid the groundwork for the policy in 1904 with his Roosevelt Corollary to the Monroe Doctrine (1823), asserting a right of intervention in financially unstable Latin American nations that might be vulnerable to European control. Henceforth, the United States itself would assume the responsibility of seeing to it that backward states in the hemisphere honored their external financial obligations. The approach was developed following an Anglo-German blockade of Venezuela in 1901, ostensibly intended to force the Venezuelan government to make good on defaulted loans and clearly motivated by a desire to promote U.S. financial predominance in the Caribbean region, as well as to safeguard the newly built Panama Canal. The Roosevelt Corollary was first implemented in the Dominican Republic in 1907 when, to ensure collection of foreign debts, U.S. loans were exchanged for the right to choose the head of Dominican customs, the country's major revenue source.

Dollar diplomacy was further extended, although not without controversy, by the administrations of both Republican William Howard Taft (1909–1913) and Democrat Woodrow Wilson (1913–1921). Defended by Taft as a means of "substituting dollars for bullets," the approach was applied most forcefully in Nicaragua, which was of special interest to Washington because of its potential as the site of an alternative canal route. When the Nicaraguan government resisted demands to use U.S. banks rather than European banks to refinance its foreign debt, the Taft administration helped to engineer a successful rebellion and then, in 1911, negotiated a debt refunding with payment to be secured by a customs receivership under U.S. protection. Similar pressures, at times accompanied by overt military occupation, were also brought to bear in Guatemala, Haiti, and Honduras, as well as again in the Dominican Republic and Nicaragua, despite explicit repudiation of dollar diplomacy as an official policy by President Wilson in 1913. In fact, it was not until 1933, with the signing of the Montevideo Treaty outlawing overt interventions in the hemisphere, that Washington finally laid the Roosevelt Corollary formally to rest. In place of Theodore Roosevelt's "big stick," President Franklin D. Roosevelt proposed the Good Neighbor Policy, which emphasized hemispheric solidarity.

World War I and the Interwar Period

World War I was a financial watershed, rapidly transforming the United States from a debtor to a creditor nation.

With the opening of hostilities in Europe 1914, inflows of capital ceased altogether, and many foreign-owned assets were liquidated to help finance the protracted conflict. Conversely, outflows soared to feed an insatiable appetite for capital abroad. U.S. banks, once intermediaries in bringing resources to the United States, now used their tested skills and contacts to facilitate a massive reverse flow of funds back across the Atlantic. Washington pitched in as well, extending numerous loans directly to allied European governments to underwrite purchases of arms and munitions. International lending was popularized through so-called liberty loan campaigns, under which federal government purchases of foreign bonds were financed by matching sales of dollar-denominated securities to the U.S. public. By the time the armistice was declared in 1918, foreign authorities owed Washington more than $10 billion, private U.S. claims abroad had more than doubled, and investments in the United States were down by half. Even excluding intergovernmental debts, the country was now a net creditor of nearly $4 billion, second only to a severely weakened Great Britain, which actually liquidated or lost about fifteen percent of its foreign holdings during the war years. Almost overnight, the United States had become the world's dominant financial power, in effect, banker to the world.

Capital exports continued to grow during the 1920s, especially after 1925 when European stability seemed assured, until they were abruptly cut off by the global economic crisis in 1931. As a result of the wartime loan experience, the U.S. investing public had developed a taste for international claims. Creditor optimism was assured by the speed with which all the bond issues that had been publicly floated during the war were either repaid or refunded soon after hostilities ceased, except for two Russian loans totalling $75 million that, along with all other czarist debt, were repudiated by the new Soviet government. With an almost reckless disregard for risk, U.S. banking interests competed eagerly to market the obligations of a diverse range of borrowers. In the twelve years from 1920 to 1931, no less than $11.5 billion of foreign bonds were sold in the United States, primarily for the benefit of governments or government-controlled corporations in Europe (forty percent), Canada (thirty percent), and Latin America (twenty percent). On the eve of the Great Depression, the U.S. creditor position was up to $22 billion ($10.5 billion excluding war debts).

For its part, the federal government expressed a reluctance to become systematically involved, either diplomatically or militarily, in the lending boom of the 1920s. Officially, the policy of dollar diplomacy was dead. In this new era of self-conscious isolationism and economic liberalism, Washington preferred to leave the allocation of capital, as much as possible, strictly to the market-

INTERNATIONAL INVESTMENT POSITION OF THE UNITED STATES 1976–1994 (U.S. bilions of dollars)	
Year	Net Position (+ = creditor, - = debtor)
1976	+175.9
1977	+190.5
1978	+228.4
1979	+342.9
1980	+392.5
1981	+374.3
1982	+378.9
1983	+363.0
1984	+321.4
1985	+132.8
1986	+ 45.0
1987	- 11.1
1988	-134.5
1989	-250.3
1990	-251.1
1991	-355.1
1992	-515.7
1993	-545.3
1994	-680.8

Source: U.S. Department of Commerce

place. In practice, however, given the circumstances of the time, finance and foreign policy simply could not be disentangled. Inevitably, the federal government was drawn in to playing an active role in the management of critical debt problems during the period, first in Europe in the 1920s and then in Latin America in the 1930s.

In Europe, there were actually two problems, the twin dilemmas of Allied war debts and German reparations. Even before World War I had ended, it was already clear that the debts of the European governments, as initially contracted, were simply too large to service satisfactorily over any reasonable period of time. Once peace was restored, both Great Britain and France argued strongly for a cancellation of wartime obligations. Washington resisted, however, insisting on at least partial debt repayments. In President Calvin Coolidge's words, "They hired the money, didn't they?" At most, the government would consider a possible revision of terms based on the debtors' diminished capacity to pay. In 1922 the World War Foreign Debt Commission was set up by an act of Congress to negotiate specific agreements to stretch out loan repayments and lower interest charges; over the next few years some remarkably generous accords were worked out with a number of European governments. In

1925 Italy's interest rate was reduced to 0.4 percent and four-fifths of its debt was cancelled. The following year France's interest rate was reduced to 1.6 percent with three-fifths of its debt cancelled. Despite such concessions, Washington's adamancy fed considerable anti-U.S. feeling in Europe, which, in turn, reinforced isolationist sentiments in the United States.

Moreover, complicating the war-debt dilemma was the issue of German reparations, which had been imposed over President Wilson's objections during the peace negotiations in 1919. Under the Treaty of Versailles, Germany was obliged to transfer the equivalent of $33 billion to the victorious Allies in compensation for wartime damages, a sum, as economist John Maynard Keynes accurately predicted in his *Economic Consequences of the Peace* (1919), that turned out to be well beyond the capacity of the enfeebled Weimar Republic to pay. Much of the decade of the 1920s was taken up by efforts to scale back Germany's obligations to more realistic levels. While the United States did not ratify the Versailles Treaty and had waived all claims to reparations, Washington nonetheless had little choice but to become deeply involved in the search for a satisfactory solution. In part, this was simply a reflection of the newfound financial power of the United States, but mostly it was due to the insistence of the Allies on tying their own debt repayments to their reparations claims on Weimar. No more money would be remitted to the United States, they warned, than they themselves received from Germany.

Two factors enabled the Weimar Republic, for a time, to keep up a flow of payments to the Allies. One was the 1924 Dawes Plan, worked out by a special commission appointed by President Coolidge, which effectively reduced and rescheduled most of Germany's overdue obligations. The Dawes Plan was underwritten by a foreign loan totaling some $200 million. The other factor was the outpouring of private capital from the United States, much of which went directly to a variety of German borrowers. In effect, a kind of financial recycling operation was in effect, with funds flowing from the United States to Germany, then onward to the European Allies in the guise of reparations, and then back across the Atlantic again in repayment of war debts. Fragile as the process was, it worked successfully as long as the U.S. lending boom persisted.

Unfortunately the boom ended, first faltering after the 1929 stock market crash, then ceasing altogether after the start of the global monetary crisis in 1931, triggered by the failure of Austria's Credit-Anstalt bank. Consequently, the financial recycling operation soon collapsed. An effort to again reduce and reschedule Germany's reparations burden under the Young Plan provided only temporary relief. In 1931 President Herbert Hoover finally proposed a worldwide moratorium on all interallied debts and reparations. Although initially intended to be temporary, the moratorium soon became permanent as, one by one, Germany and the Allies (with the notable exception of Finland) all defaulted on their foreign obligations. In the end, U.S. taxpayers paid the price for the excessive burden imposed on Germany.

Once the defaults began, they quickly spread beyond Europe to engulf other borrowers as well, including no fewer than fourteen nations of Latin America. While feelings of resentment toward the seemingly ungrateful Europeans ran deep, the Latins were regarded more as victims of circumstances beyond their own control, in need of assistance rather than criticism. Hence, as the decade progressed, the administration of President Roosevelt gradually became quite actively involved in the restructuring of Latin American debts, often negotiating directly with borrowers over the heads of private investors; settlements were ultimately reached, the last after World War II began, that were highly favorable to debtors. Obligations were substantially reduced, and interest rates eased considerably. In effect, the administration concluded that hemispheric solidarity had to take precedence. The Good Neighbor Policy would have to prevail over the interests of private creditors.

World War II and Beyond

World War II brought new demands on Washington for financial assistance, but, chastened by its earlier war-loan experience, the government this time elected to provide aid in the form of lend-lease, an euphemism for outright gifts, so that no large burden of indebtedness would remain after the end of hostilities. Once victory was assured, on the other hand, and especially after the Cold War with the Soviet Union began, sizable amounts of money were loaned to West European governments to help promote economic recovery, starting with a massive $3.75 billion loan to Great Britain in 1946 and reaching a high point with the even more substantial Marshall Plan from 1948 to 1951. First proposed by Secretary of State George Marshall in 1947, the Marshall Plan took the form predominantly of grants but also included loans and conditional aid, assistance extended in support of intra-European trade. In all, some $12.5 billion was provided to the Europeans to underwrite their postwar reconstruction effort.

Although private capital outflows were practically nonexistent in the immediate postwar years, owing to the lingering effects of the collapse of financial markets and widespread defaults of the 1930s, it was only a matter of time before U.S. investors would again begin to look abroad for profitable opportunities. Direct investments, particularly in Europe, began to recover after the mid-1950s; portfolio lending, first in the form of bond sales and later as bank credits, began to take off in the early 1960s. By the start of the 1970s, outflows rivaled the pace of the 1920s. Once more, the United States had become banker to the world, and once more, it was only a matter of time before the country would find itself enmeshed in critical problems of debt.

One problem, evident even before the end of the 1960s, derived from the special role that the U.S. dollar had come to play in the international monetary system after World War II. Because the dollar, alone among currencies, was directly convertible into gold for central banks, it became the world's favored reserve asset and, through deficits in the U.S. balance of payments, the principal source of growth of international liquidity that governments used to maintain fixed exchange rates. Overall, throughout the early postwar years, the rise of U.S. overseas claims greatly exceeded increased foreign obligations. By 1970, in fact, the country's net investment position at $70 billion stood nearly three times higher than at the end of World War II. The dilemma, however, was that while the bulk of U.S. claims was long-term in nature, a much larger share of the country's liabilities was short-term. By the mid-1960s the sum of liquid dollars abroad had already grown to exceed the value of U.S. gold reserves stored at Fort Knox. In effect, therefore, the country had a liquidity problem. The challenge for Washington was to keep dollar holders from mounting a run on the bank.

Much of the 1960s was taken up with efforts to cope with this challenge to the dollar. At one level, various defenses were erected to fend off any possible attack on U.S. gold reserves, including a network of reciprocal credit arrangements with more than a dozen foreign central banks. Additional resources were also raised through special bonds sold to dollar-rich governments abroad. At another level, efforts were made to reduce the flow of U.S. money into foreign hands by limiting capital outflows, first by means of taxes, for example, the Interest Equalization Tax of 1963, and later via direct controls, for example, the ostensibly voluntary capital-export restrictions of 1965, made fully mandatory in 1968. None of these measures sufficed to stem the tide, owing to a worsening balance of payments deficit caused by, among other things, inflationary monetary and fiscal policies at home and accelerated spending for the Vietnam War abroad. On 15 August 1971 President Richard Nixon threw in the towel by terminating the convertibility of the dollar, in effect removing the central linchpin of the postwar monetary system. After a year and a half of uncertainty, in 1973 the dollar and all other major currencies began to float freely.

A second major crisis erupted a decade later, in August 1982, following a financial breakdown in nearby Mexico. Throughout the 1970s, and especially after the hike of oil prices inspired by the Organization of Petroleum Exporting Companies in 1973, U.S. banks led the way in promoting a new wave of foreign lending, in particular to developing economies in Latin America or else-where in the Third World. In a process reminiscent of the recycling operation of the 1920s, now known as petrodollar recycling, surplus funds deposited by oil exporters flowed from the international banking system to oil importers, who used the money to pay their bills to OPEC, who deposited their receipts back to the banks again. As in the 1920s, the lending boom was almost reckless in its apparent disregard for risk. As in the 1920s, the fragile process soon collapsed, once the boom ended.

Even prior to the 1980s, of course, it was not uncommon for some developing countries to experience occasional difficulties in servicing external obligations. Earlier debt problems, however, had been relatively few in number and small in scale. Mexico's crisis, on the other hand, involved one of the Third World's largest debtors and triggered a wave of near defaults in more than three dozen other nations, which threatened bankruptcy for many international lenders and chaos in global financial markets. For Washington the challenge was now twofold, averting a U.S. banking crisis while also preserving economic and political stability in debtor countries. Policy evolved through three distinct phases before the challenge could be considered safely resolved: first an emphasis of rescheduling of obligations to ease severe cash flow strains; then, in 1985, a call for new lending by banks and international institutions to support debtor growth, the Baker Plan, named after Secretary of the Treasury James A. Baker; and in 1989, a proposal for negotiated reductions of debtor liabilities, the Brady Plan, named after Baker's successor at the Treasury, Nicholas F. Brady. In subsequent years, beginning with Mexico, agreements were reached with virtually all major Third World borrowers to write down a significant portion of debt burdens.

By the 1990s, however, yet another potential debt problem began to emerge, much closer to home, reflecting the country's dramatic shift back to net debtor status again after years of financial dominance. The creditor position of the United States, so slowly accumulated over decades of foreign lending and investment, peaked in 1980 at approximately $390 billion and then abruptly declined as capital inflows began to exceed outflows for the first time in nearly a century. By the late-1980s external obligations were already greater than claims, as the United States became the world's largest debtor. By 1992 net liabilities exceeded one-half trillion dollars. What will this mean for the country's future conduct of foreign affairs? Where will the resources come from to maintain a presence on the world stage? Will policy have to be constrained by a need to maintain the confidence of international creditors? Questions like these ensure that the issue of debt will remain at the center of U.S. foreign relations for years to come.

BENJAMIN J. COHEN

See also Brady Plan; Dawes Plan; Dollar Diplomacy; Foreign Direct Investment; Lend-Lease; Marshall Plan; Roosevelt Corollary; Third World Debt

FURTHER READING
Aldcroft, Derek Howard. *From Versailles to Wall Street, 1919–1929.* Berkeley, Calif., 1977.
Cohen, Benjamin J. *In Whose Interest? International Banking and American Foreign Policy.* New Haven, Conn., 1986.
Lissakers, Karin. *Banks, Borrowers, and the Establishment: A Revisionist Account of the International Debt Crisis.* New York, 1991.
Madden, John Thomas, Marcus Nadler, and Harry Charles Sauvain. *America's Experience as a Creditor Nation.* New York, 1937.
Nearing, Scott and Joseph Freeman. *Dollar Diplomacy: A Study in American Imperialism.* New York, 1925.

INTERNATIONAL JOINT COMMISSION

Created by the Canada-U.S. Boundary Waters Treaty of 1909 to prevent disputes over the use of boundary waters between the United States and Canada. (Boundary waters include those along which a boundary runs, as well as upstream and downstream transboundary waters and tributaries to and from boundary waters.) The IJC functions as an administrative, quasi-judicial, arbitral, and investigative body. Although the IJC has absolute authority in certain narrow judicial areas, it is best known for its advisory work, which is governed by specifically worded references provided by both national governments soliciting advice on water quality, water levels, and air quality domains. The IJC is composed of three Canadian and three U.S. commissioners, supported by small technical staffs in Washington, D.C., in Ottawa, by a staff and at its Great Lakes office in Windsor, Ontario.

JOHN E. CARROLL

See also Canada

FURTHER READING
Carroll, John E. *Environmental Diplomacy: An Examination and Prospective of Canadian-U.S. Transboundary Environmental Relations.* Ann Arbor, Mich., 1983.
———, *International Environmental Diplomacy.* Cambridge, 1990.
Spencer, Robert, John Kirton, and Kim Richard Nossal, eds. *The International Joint Commission Seventy Years On.* Toronto, Ont., 1981.

INTERNATIONAL LABOR ORGANIZATION

An autonomous institution established in 1919 within the League of Nations and subsumed as a specialized agency of the United Nations in 1945. Its purpose is to foster voluntary cooperation among its member states in promoting full employment, recognition of the right to collective bargaining, labor-management cooperation, improvement of labor conditions, increased living standards, and overall economic and social stability. International Labor Organization (ILO) conventions and recommendations deal with all aspects of work life. A blacklist documents member states' violations of ILO-set labor standards. ILO member states are represented in the International Labor Conference and governing body by tripartite delegations composed of one worker, one employer, and two government delegates, which makes the ILO the only international governmental organization to mandate the representation of nongovernmental groups. In the 1970s the ILO agenda focused heavily on the Arab-Israeli conflict and labor issues in the Occupied Territories. The United States withdrew for two years (1978–1980) charging that this focus politicized the ILO while excluding labor issues within communist countries.

MARGARET P. KARNS

See also United Nations

FURTHER READING
Haas, Ernst B. *Beyond the Nation-State: Functionalism and International Organization.* Stanford, Calif., 1964.
Jenks, Clarence Wilfred. *Social Justice in the Law of Nations: The ILO Impact After Fifty Years.* New York, 1970.
Strong, David and Patricia Mei Yin. "The International Labour Organization and the Welfare State: Institutionalized Effects on National Welfare Spending, 1960–1980." *International Organization* 47 (Spring 1993):235–262.

INTERNATIONAL LAW

Once commonly referred to as the law of nations, international law is the law of the modern international system of independent nation-states. International relations depend on a legal order that serves as a common framework for intercourse between states and for their common enterprise. The law provides concepts and principles, institutions and procedures, by which states maintain diplomatic relations, carry on trade, and resolve differences. International law brings order and stability, warrants expectations and reliance, promotes friendly relations, and places restraints on hostile inaction. It does so for the powerful, as well as for the weak. As eighteenth-century French philosopher Jean-Jacques Rousseau said in another context, "The strongest is never strong enough always to be master unless he transforms forces into right and obedience into duty." Contrary to common impression, international law works. All states observe almost all international law and almost all of their international obligations almost all of the time.

International law consists principally of customary law built by state practice and international agreements, mostly treaties, voluntarily agreed to. Since World War II multilateral treaties generally open to all states have made new law, for example, the United Nations Charter and international human rights covenants. Some multilateral treaties have codified what had been customary law, for example, conventions on the law of the sea and on diplomatic immunities. That international law is essential to the international state system is evidenced by the mass of law and the many law-related institutions, the thousands of treaties now in force, the thousands and thousands of persons involved in concluding them, and the untold numbers engaged daily in carrying out their provisions.

International law is a complete if still primitive legal system. It establishes the character of the international system as a network of independent states. It prescribes how law is made and implemented and determines the relation of international law to national laws. It defines the status, rights, and duties of states; it regulates relations between states; between states and other entities (notably intergovernmental organizations such as the United Nations); and between states and individuals, including their own inhabitants. International law provides for the peaceful settlement of disputes, for example, by arbitration or resort to the International Court of Justice. Like the law of every developed national society, international law includes basic principles of property, contract, and tort. The law also prescribes responsibility for states to respect foreign nationals and their property and limits the exercise by a state of jurisdiction over individuals outside its territory. The law also addresses the problems of the commonage—the law of the sea, the air, and outer space, and the growing law of the environment.,

Traditionally, the values of the international system have been state values, commitment to the right of every state to be left alone, to keep its territory inviolate, and to preserve its political independence. To that end, the twentieth century saw the development of law to prohibit war and other uses of force between states and to control the use and spread of armaments. By law, states established institutions for maintaining peace, such as the League of Nations and the United Nations, and bodies for settling disputes, such as the Permanent Court of International Justice and its successor, the International Court of Justice.

The second half of the twentieth century also saw the growth of cooperative arrangements to promote other common values, for example, international financial institutions (the World Bank and the International Monetary Fund), other specialized agencies (United Nations' Educational, Scientific, and Cultural Organization, the Food and Agriculture Organization, and the World Health Organization), the General Agreement on Tariffs and Trade (GATT) and its successor the World Trade Organization, and their regional counterparts.

The end of World War II saw international law move from its primary devotion to state values to an increasing concern for human values. By international law, states have sought to safeguard the human rights of individuals (and groups) in their own countries against their own governments, beginning with general pledges in the UN Charter and the Universal Declaration of Human Rights, then by a growing body of international covenants and conventions. The system, however, has remained a liberal system, not a welfare system, and resisted legal obligations to establish a new economic order, encouraging assistance to the less developed world on a voluntary basis.

John Jay, one of the framers of the U.S. Constitution, wrote, "The United States, by taking a place among the nations of the earth, (became) amenable to the law of nations." International law became a part of the law of the United States automatically without provision to that effect in the Constitution and without any formal act by Congress or the president. The Constitution assumes the applicability of international law to the United States, in the clause that confers on Congress the power to define offenses against the law of nations. The Constitution expressly declares treaties of the United States to be the supreme law of the land. The federal government must itself respect U.S. obligations under international law; it also must secure compliance by all who exercise official authority in the United States, including states and municipalities and their officials, and by citizens whose acts might impinge on U.S. obligations.

Other references to international law and treaties punctuate the U.S. Constitution. The president has the power to make treaties, with the advice and consent of the U.S. Senate. The judicial power of the United States extends to cases arising under the laws of the United States, interpreted to include international law and treaties of the United States.

All branches of the federal government deal with the rights and obligations of the United States under international law. Congress enacts laws to fulfill U.S. obligations under its treaties or under customary law, to define and punish international crimes (piracy, genocide), and to authorize or approve executive agreements, such as trade agreements. U.S. rights and duties under international law are primarily the responsibility of the president, as part of his foreign affairs power. Within the executive branch, questions of law, including international law, are ultimately determined by the attorney general and the Department of Justice. In largest part, however, and in daily operations, questions of international law are decided by the Department of State as part of its responsibility for U.S. foreign relations. The Department of State's legal adviser and their office (consisting of about a hundred officers) advise the secretary of state and the department. Questions of international law frequently arise for other departments, notably the Departments of Defense and Commerce, and their determinations of law may be coordinated by the legal adviser of the Department of State and, if necessary, resolved by the attorney general.

Since international law is part of the law of the United States, it is the business of both federal and state courts. International law was prominent in early prize cases arising out of hostilities at sea and in other maritime cases that reached the Supreme Court early in the nineteenth century. Congress has given the federal courts jurisdiction of cases under the laws (including international law) and treaties of the United States. In addition, Congress gave the federal courts special jurisdiction over suits by aliens arising in tort for violations of international law, and recently courts have entertained such suits against foreign officials for torture, extrajudicial killing, or disappearance. State courts may have jurisdiction over cases involving issues of international law under their own constitutions and laws, but international law limits the jurisdiction of courts by principles of sovereign and diplomatic immunity. The courts have limited their own role by a reluctance to pass on "acts of states."

International Law in U.S. Foreign Policy

Like all nation-states, the United States conducts its foreign relations and determines its foreign policy in the context of the international political system and in the light of international law. Like all nation-states, the United States, generally and ordinarily, conforms its behavior and its policies to what international law requires. More than most nation-states, the United States has a traditional, cultural commitment to the rule of law. In its early days, as a new small state, the United States found security in the law of nations. International law helped prevent or resolve disputes and regulated warfare when war came (limited war with France in 1800; full war with Great Britain in 1812). The United States relied on international law to avoid entanglement in European affairs, to protect its interests in Canada vis-à-vis Great Britain, including the *Caroline* Affair (1837), and in Latin America, to maintain European neutrality during the American Civil War.

In principle, respect for international law remained central to U.S. foreign policy even after it became a major power. In the Calvo Clause controversy in the 1880s, the United States insisted that Mexico respect the traditional rules that protected U.S. investments in Mexico against expropriation without prompt, adequate, and effective compensation. Violations of international law by Germany were declared to be the basis for U.S. entry into World War I under the Doctrine of Neutral Rights, the obligation of a belligerent not to take the lives of nonre-

sisting civilians on the high seas. U.S. relations with its neighbors in the Americas between the world wars were sometimes seen by them as governed not by the rule of law but by power and sphere-of-influence politics, but the United States insisted that it was acting in accordance with law, although it took advantage of the inadequacies of international law at the time on regulating the threat or use of force.

After World War I, the United States resisted adopting new law or joining international bodies or arrangements that might limit U.S. freedom of action, that might obligate the United States to take military or economic measures, or that might subject U.S. actions to judgment and decision by international organs. President Woodrow Wilson's efforts to have the United States join the League of Nations were frustrated by the U.S. Senate, which riddled its consent to ratification with destructive reservations. Later, the United States refused to accept the jurisdiction of the Permanent Court of International Justice. Between the world wars, the United States sponsored the Kellogg-Briand Pact (1928), which outlawed war as an instrument of national policy and joined other nations in establishing limitations on naval power, but it did not join efforts to enforce them against violation by Nazi Germany or Fascist Italy.

The end of World War II brought another attempt to establish a new legal order. The United States led its Allies in adopting the UN Charter to prohibit the use of force between states and to establish the United Nations organization to maintain international peace and security, as well as to promote social welfare and human rights around the world. The United States also joined the Rio Treaty and the Organization of American States to bring law and order into its relations in the Western Hemisphere. In the United Nations, however, the United States, no less than its big power allies, insisted on having a permanent seat and a veto in the Security Council, the organ charged with maintaining international peace and security and having the authority to make legally binding decisions.

In the early postwar years, the United States maintained its commitment to the rule of international law. It provided leadership in developing the United Nations, and it accepted the compulsory jurisdiction of the International Court of Justice with reservations probably intended as modest, although later interpreted as extravagant. It was active in international financial institutions, sought international agreement on trade and for stability in the law of the sea, and supported programs for promoting an international law of human rights.

Inevitably, however, U.S. respect for and reliance on international law suffered in times of international tension. During the Cold War, the United States remained committed to law and proclaimed that commitment as the hallmark in its ideological struggle with world communism. It led the defense of South Korea against aggression. It joined in establishing the North Atlantic Treaty Organization (1949) and acted in collective self-defense arrangements in conformity with the UN Charter. During the Cold War, however, the United States sometimes acted to meet the needs of its national security as it saw them, with less than scrupulous regard for law. Several military actions by the United States, particularly in Central America, were widely condemned as violations of international law, for example, the invasion of Grenada (1983) and military measures against Nicaragua (including support for the Contras), which the International Court of Justice found to be illegal. U.S. military involvement in Vietnam in the 1960s and early 1970s also was widely condemned as illegal. The United States sought to impose its export control laws on European companies selling to the USSR, as in the 1981–1983 pipeline controversy, an attempt to apply U.S. law extraterritorially, which even friendly countries considered illegal. Later, countries objected on similar grounds to U.S. law (the Helms-Burton Act) that sought to penalize those who "traffic" in property in Cuba that had belonged to U.S. nationals. During the Cold War the United States was more likely to exaggerate the sins of its adversaries and condone those of its allies. In one instance, however, the United States was compelled to invoke international law even against its friends, when it joined the Soviet Union to compel Great Britain, France, and Israel to terminate their invasion of Suez after Egypt had seized the Suez Canal (1956). The U.S. decision probably reflected fear that the Soviet Union might intervene by force and risk wider war. East and West largely respected international norms during the Cold War, and during periods of détente they concluded the Helsinki Accords (1975) and important strategic arms limitation agreements.

The end of the Cold War provided new opportunities for the United States to promote the rule of law. It joined in efforts to revive the Security Council and led the successful effort to repel Iraqi aggression against Kuwait in 1990–1991. It supported broad interpretations of the UN Charter to justify Security Council action in Somalia, Haiti, and the former Yugoslavia, including the establishment of an international tribunal for war crimes in the former Yugoslavia.

Both during the Cold War and since, the United States has remained reluctant to enter into new agreements or arrangements that would limit its freedom of action in important political or economic matters, might subordinate its freedom of action to decisions of international bodies, or entrust important interests to binding determination by judicial bodies. After ten years of negotiation leading to apparent agreement, President Ronald Reagan refused to ratify the 1982 Convention on the Law of the Sea because of the institutions it established to regulate deep-sea-bed mining. The United States turned to the International Court of Justice in its attempt to obtain the release of its hostages in Tehran (1980), but it would not accept adjudication of matters which it deemed of vital national interest, particularly those relating to war and peace. When the court decided to exercise jurisdiction over U.S. actions in Nicaragua, the United States refused to participate in the case and terminated its declaration, accepting the court's compulsory jurisdiction.

The United States has not always resisted the temptation to use force that is not likely to lead to major war, sometimes in response to suspected state terrorism, such as punitive air strikes on Libya (1986) and on Iraq (1993) or the invasion of Panama (1990) to capture General Manuel Noriega. U.S. attitudes to the international law of human rights are an instructive example of ambivalence in U.S. foreign policy. The United States has promoted the international law of human rights and has monitored the human rights obligations of other states. Acts of Congress deny arms sales and economic assistance to states guilty of consistent patterns of gross violations of internationally recognized human rights, but the United States has resisted adhering to international covenants and conventions, and to its few ratifications of such agreements it attached reservations that limited U.S. obligations and international scrutiny of human rights conditions in the United States. For example, when the United States finally ratified the International Covenant on Civil and Political Rights (1992), it refused to assume an international obligation to respect some human rights. In fact, it refused to adopt international human rights standards where they are more protective than those of U.S. domestic law. It has not agreed to respond to individual complaints before the Human Rights Committee.

International Law in U.S. Law

The Constitution is silent on its hierarchical relation to international law. The framers of the U.S. Constitution may have assumed that since the United States is subject to the law of nations, the Constitution must itself be subordinate to international law. Indeed, in 1920 Justice Oliver Wendell Holmes, in dictum, appeared to read Article 6 of the Constitution as implying that U.S. treaties are not subject to constitutional limitations (*Missouri* v. *Holland*). In 1957, however, a plurality opinion of the Court (by Justice Hugo Black) declared that the United States "can only act in accordance with all the limitations imposed by the Constitution" (*Reid* v. *Covert*). Senator John W. Bricker of Ohio unsuccessfully sought to have the Constitution amended to affirm explicitly that a treaty is valid only if its provisions are consistent with the

Constitution. Although courts have not had occasion to rule, scholarly opinion is uniform that treaties as well as principles of customary international law, which are internationally binding on the United States, are valid as law in the United States only if they are consistent with the Constitution.

Subject to the Constitution, then, both customary international law and treaties are the law of the United States and have the status of federal law. Article 6 of the Constitution declares explicitly that treaties are the supreme law of the land; international law is also supreme over state law. However, as regards customary law for much of U.S. history, state courts applied international law as part of the common law they inherited from Great Britain, and even some federal courts treated international law as as part of the law of the state in which the court sat. In 1964, however, the Supreme Court ruled that international law in the United States has the status of federal law and is binding as such on the states and on their courts (*Banco Nacional de Cuba* v. *Sabbatino*). Issues of international law, then, are federal questions subject to review by the Supreme Court of the United States, and the Supreme Court's determinations of international law, like its interpretations of a treaty, are federal law binding on the states, as well as on the federal government.

As federal law, principles of international law and provisions in treaties of the United States have been held to have the same status as other federal law under the Constitution. Therefore, a treaty of the United States is equal in status to an act of Congress. Where fairly possible, the courts construe laws of the United States to be consistent with U.S. treaty obligations, but where inconsistencies cannot be interpreted away, the courts will give effect to the act of Congress if it is later in time, although that places the United States in violation of its international obligations. There appears to be no instance in which Congress enacted law inconsistent with principles of customary international law, or where new principles of customary law developed that were inconsistent with an earlier act of Congress; but, while not unanimous, scholarly opinion suggests that here too the "later in time" should prevail.

The Constitution does not explicitly forbid Congress to violate international law or U.S. treaty obligations; by contrast, the Constitution requires the president to "take care that the laws be faithfully executed," and "the laws," it is accepted, include customary international law, as well as self-executing treaties that make law for the United States. The Congress of the United States has rarely adopted legislation that would cause the United States to be in violation of international law or obligation; the record of the executive branch is not as favorable. The continuing struggle between Congress and the president as to their respective authority in the conduct of U.S. foreign affairs, notably as to their war powers or the control of covert activities, sometimes tends to inhibit action, including acts questionable under international law.

Constitutional justifications for executive branch violations of international law are not easy to come by. It is sometimes argued that the Constitution has given the president control of foreign affairs and authority to make foreign policy; his actions in that regard are therefore of constitutional character, not unlike the powers of Congress. By analogy with the principle that courts will give effect to an act of Congress in the face of an earlier treaty obligation, it is argued the courts ought not enjoin the president from exercising his constitutional authority even in the face of an international obligation, despite the "take care clause." Sometimes the courts seem to treat such action as raising issues that are not justiciable. In fact, however, the courts will order the executive branch to respect self-executing treaty obligations that are the law of the land, and it is not obvious why they should not enjoin the executive branch from violating customary international law. The argument, moreover, may explain why the courts might not enjoin the president. It does not make the president's actions constitutional; it does not meet his obligations to take care that the laws be faithfully executed.

Foreign relations are national relations, and the states of the United States have no direct role in making foreign policy. The Constitution expressly prohibits states from making treaties; they can make an agreement or compact with foreign states only with the consent of Congress. The courts have interpreted the Constitution as permitting state agreements or compacts with foreign countries even without the consent of Congress on matters of local import, such as cultural cooperation between Louisiana and Quebec or with France, that have no significant implication for national foreign policy. The Constitution has been construed as prohibiting states to discriminate against foreign commerce or to burden such commerce unduly. In 1964 in *Sabbatino* the Supreme Court established that the determination of international law is a federal question, so that Supreme Court determinations are binding on the states. In a unique case in 1968, the Supreme Court held that states cannot adopt laws that interfere with U.S. foreign policy (*Zschernig* v. *Miller*).

It is difficult to summarize or to characterize simply the place of international law in U.S. foreign policy. In general and in principle, the United States, law-ridden in its domestic life, is committed also to the rule of law, to order and stability in its international relations. Therefore, U.S. foreign policy favors respect for established international law and for the treaties to which it is party. An essential isolationism and deep reluctance to limit its freedom of action in matters it deems of great moment have led to some uses of force of questionable legality and have engendered resistance to extending the domain of the law, to assuming additional international obligations, to accepting international scrutiny, and to submitting important interests to international adjudication or other third party judgment. The end of the Cold War and the changed world order at the end of the twentieth century promise no major change in these regards.

Louis Henkin

See also Anzus Treaty; Bricker Amendment; Calvo Clause; Caroline Affair; Cold War; Constitution; Contras; Curtiss-Wright Case; Executive Agreements; Grenada Invasion; Gunboat Diplomacy; Helsinki Accords; Human Rights; Humanitarian Intervention and Relief; Korean War; Law of the Sea; North American Free Trade Agreement; North Atlantic Treaty Organization; Paris Peace Conference of 1919; Permanent Court of International Justice; Reciprocal Trade Agreement Act; Rio Treaty; Southeast Asia Treaty Organization; Strategic Arms Limitation Talks and Agreements; Supreme Court and the Judiciary; United Nations; War of 1812; Washington Conference on Limitation of Armaments

FURTHER READING

Henkin, Louis. *Foreign Affairs and the Constitution.* 2nd ed. Oxford, 1972.
——. *How Nations Behave: Law and Foreign Policy,* 2nd ed. New York, 1979.
——. *International Law: Politics and Values.* Boston, 1994.
Oppenheim, Lassa. *International Law.* Multivolumes. 9th ed., ed. by Sir Robert Jennings and Sir Arthur Watts. London, 1992.
Restatement of the Law, the Foreign Relations Law of the United States. Two vols. rev. and enl. ed. "As adopted and promulgated by the American Law Institute at Washington, D.C., May 14, 1986." St. Paul, Minn., 1987.
Schachter, Oscar. *International Law in Theory and Practice.* Boston, 1991.

INTERNATIONAL MONETARY FUND

One of the most powerful and controversial international organizations, established at the Bretton Woods Conference in 1944 with the objective of ensuring the effective and efficient functioning of the post–World War II international monetary system. This objective became a broad mandate for seeking to influence the exchange of capital between and among sovereign countries. The international monetary system embraces such vital economic rules and procedures as the mechanism by which countries make and receive payments for all forms of international transactions, techniques of exchange rate management, and the manner in which countries adjust disequilibriums in their respective balance of payments positions, that is, their policy responses for dealing with

either an excess of earnings from overseas transactions relative to overseas expenditures or vice versa. The International Monetary Fund (IMF) was created to assure the smooth functioning of the fixed exchange rate system agreed upon at Bretton Woods, and, more generally, the IMF makes short-term loans to assist countries with the effects of domestic policy adjustments taken in the effort to reduce their balance of payments deficits.

In the spring of 1973, the nature and functions of the IMF underwent a sweeping change. The fixed exchange rate standard formally collapsed in the wake of repeated turmoil in the foreign exchange markets, most of which reflected declining confidence in the value of the U.S. dollar. The major industrial countries mutually agreed to abrogate indefinitely the unequivocal obligation of IMF member countries to keep exchange rates fixed. Under the new arrangements, countries had the option of either seeking to maintain a fixed exchange rate or allowing their exchange rates to float on the basis of supply and demand in the foreign exchange market. Ironically, although the IMF was established to reinforce a system of fixed exchange rates, it would find itself with a greater degree of importance and influence in a world of floating exchange rates than ever before. By the late 1970s, IMF officials were becoming intensively involved in drafting blueprints for domestic economic austerity and reform programs for a steady and growing number of less developed countries (LDCs) facing long-term and serious balance of payments deficits.

The IMF has served several major objectives of postwar U.S. international monetary policy, including making sufficient foreign exchange available from the late 1950s through the mid-1960s to a limited number of industrial countries with balance of payments deficits, thus easing the pressures on these countries to adopt growth-retarding domestic economic policies; negotiating international monetary reform in the mid-1960s; providing foreign exchange to non–oil producing LDCs hurt by the two oil price shocks in 1973–1974 and 1979–1980; designing market-oriented adjustment policies for LDCs suffering an international debt crisis in the 1980s; and recommending reform policies in the formerly communist countries in transition to market-based economies.

IMF Activities

The IMF began operations in 1946 with thirty-nine members. At year end 1995, it was truly a universal organization with 181 member countries. Its original lending resources of less than $8 billion grew to a little more than $200 billion in 1996, the result of new members and periodic calls for additional pay-ins of currency subscriptions by existing members. As the price of joining the IMF, each country is assigned a quota for contributing a specific amount of its currency. This subscription, which is

USE OF IMF CREDIT AND LOANS
(millions of SDRs*)

	1995	1994
General Resources Account	16,967.9	4,979.5
Stand-by arrangements	14,382.1	1,829.3
Extended Fund Facility	1,965.2	900.3
Compensatory and Contingency Facility	8.9	308.0
Systemic Transformation Facility	611.7	1,941.8
Structural Adjustment and Enhanced Structural Adjustment Facilities	1,431.5	910.5
TOTAL	18,399.4	5,890.0

*Special Drawing Rights, an international reserve asset which is the IMF's unit of account. (In 1995, Special Drawing Rights on average equalled 1.43 U.S. dollars)

Note: 1995 figures include major loans to Russia and Mexico

Source: International Monetary Fund

calculated on the relative size of a country's economy and value of its international transactions, determines a member's relative voting power, as well as the amount it can borrow from the IMF's lending facilities. The United States is assigned the largest subscription, thereby receiving the largest single share of the total weighted vote and the largest ability to borrow.

Despite an impressive record of international lending, the IMF is not a development institution. Its Articles of Agreement declare it to have the principal operational function of lending money on a relatively short-term basis. Specifically, its duty is to facilitate the efforts of countries that are in the process of undertaking a correction in their balance of payments deficits. Inevitably, such efforts induce some painful reductions in domestic aggregate demand and consumption as the means to the specific ends of reducing imports and inflation while increasing exports. The fiscal prudence and monetary conservatism that dominate the financial ministries and central banks of large industrial countries dominate the IMF. Its lending philosophy is summed up in this brief 1984 statement of the managing director: "No country can live permanently beyond its means."

Since the mid-1970s the amount and terms of IMF lending have become critical factors in the domestic economic performance of many borrowing countries in Asia, Latin America, Africa, Eastern Europe, and the former Soviet Union. The IMF generally attaches substantial conditions to lending and can require member countries to adopt restrictive domestic economic policies. Understandably, most borrowing countries wish to avoid, delay, or minimize the implementation of such policies. Austerity measures inflict short-term social dislocations and, on occasion, foment political unrest. Although the relatively poor borrowing countries angrily denounce the severity of these measures, the industrialized countries of the North, which control the IMF, view them as embodying the kind of sound, domestic economic policy discipline which will lead a "free spending" country to policies encouraging sustainable, low inflationary growth and a stronger balance of payments position.

History, Organization, and Operating Rules

The IMF had its genesis in circumstances similar to those that gave rise to the General Agreement on Tariffs and Trade (GATT). Competitive devaluations were among the beggar-thy-neighbor policies adopted by many countries during the Great Depression in an effort to export unemployment and stagnation from one's own country to others, but which ended up being mutually impoverishing. Most of the large industrialized countries devalued their currencies' exchange rates at least once with the expectation that this would make their products cheaper and more competitive overseas and make their imports more expensive and less desirable, an economic phenomenon that does occur, except when all countries are simultaneously devaluing their currencies. The result was a sharp drop in the volume of international trade, which deepened and prolonged the depression.

The Bretton Woods planners were determined to devise a stable international monetary system that would promote worldwide economic recovery and growth. To do so, it was felt that the new system needed to minimize exchange rate instability, yet avoid the inherent growth-retarding effects of the pre–World War I gold standard. The U.S. delegation, led by U.S. Secretary of the Treasury Harry Dexter White, successfully advocated relatively limited and stringent lending terms by the IMF. On the other hand, economist John Maynard Keynes, Great Britain's chief negotiator, advocated more extensive and generous lending facilities, no doubt expecting his country to become an international borrower, not a creditor country like the United States.

The Articles of Agreement established the following priority objectives for the IMF: to promote international monetary cooperation and exchange rate stability; to facilitate the expansion and balanced growth of international trade; and to assist in the establishment of a multilateral balance of payments system with a minimum of restrictions on international commerce and capital flows. The IMF was empowered to supervise and enforce the established rules and procedures of the international monetary system. It was also given the financial resources to provide short-term funding necessary to help any member country correct a balance of payments deficit without resorting to measures destructive of national or international prosperity, such as repeated currency devaluations, trade barriers, or capital controls. From the beginning, a formal link was established between a country's willingness to adhere to domestic and international policies acceptable to the IMF's officials and its ability to borrow from the Fund.

The ultimate power in the IMF resides in the governments of the industrialized countries that pay in the most foreign exchange and therefore control a majority of the weighted votes. The senior decision-making forum in the IMF is the board of governors. It is composed of one representative and one alternate from each member country. Governors are selected by their governments, and in most cases they are either the minister of finance or the head of the national central bank. Established in 1974, subsequent to the adoption of the floating exchange rate system, the Interim Committee is a ministerial level advisory group that analyzes the performance of the international monetary system. It is composed of twenty-four governors who represent the same constituencies as the executive directors. It has become an influential body because of its procedural advantages: it brings together a smaller number of senior officials than the full board of governors. The joint IMF–World Bank Group Development Committee is also a ministerial level advisory group to the board of governors; its mandate is to provide input on the economic needs of poor countries.

Because the board of governors meets only once a year in the joint IMF–World Bank Group annual meetings, the day-to-day decision-making rests with the twenty-four executive directors comprising the executive board. The executive directors are posted permanently to the IMF and meet in formal session several days a week at the IMF's Washington, D.C., headquarters to consider

IMF Quotas in 1996 (million SDRs*)		
Country	Quota	Percentage
TOTAL	145,318.80	100
United States	26,526.80	18
Japan	8,241.50	6
Germany	8,241.50	6
United Kingdom	7,414.60	5
France	7,414.60	5
Saudi Arabia	5,130.60	4
Italy	4,590.70	3
Canada	4,320.30	3
Russia	4,313.10	3
China	3,385.20	2
Others	65,739.90	45

*Special Drawing Rights, an international reserve asset which is the IMF's unit of account. On May 29, 1996, SDR 1.00 equaled US $1.43455.

Source: International Monetary Fund

general policy, review ongoing country lending programs, and discuss issues relating to member countries. The executive directors operate on an informal consensus-making basis, rather than formally casting votes to determine a majority view. Eight of the directors represent a single major national contributor; in order of voting power and financial commitment, they are the United States, Japan, Germany, France, the United Kingdom, Saudi Arabia, Russia, and China. The other sixteen executive directors speak for and cast the weighted votes for each of several countries, numbering as many as twenty-five in some cases. The IMF carries out its functions with a staff of more than 2,000 international civil servants headed by a managing director, who by tradition has always been a European.

Membership in the IMF has implications for the economic policy behavior of sovereign countries. Members are obligated to follow certain positive economic policy guidelines, for example, to inform other members of the means to be used in determining the value (exchange rate) of their currency in relation to others and avoid imposing restrictions on the conversion of their currencies into other currencies. The Articles of Agreement charge that the IMF "exercise firm surveillance over the exchange rate policies of its members" to help assure a stable international exchange rate system. Operating on the assumption that exchange rates are merely a reflection of underlying domestic economic conditions, surveillance has come to involve a candid examination and evaluation of all aspects of a country's economic performance.

The surveillance function is implemented mainly through IMF staff reports sent to the board of governors for consideration. The reports reflect information gleaned from periodic consultations by staff economists with economic policy officials of each member country. Surveillance is also conducted in a multilateral context through regular discussions on the global economic outlook held by the executive board. The IMF has no legal power to force countries to undertake the economic policy changes recommended in the surveillance exercise, but failure to respond positively to such recommendations would weigh heavily against the ability of a country to gain approval when it sought to borrow from the IMF.

Lending Facilities and Rules

The IMF lends to member countries only in situations specifically connected to balance of payment problems, in effect, shortages of foreign exchange earnings relative to overseas spending needs and obligations. As stipulated in an official publication of the IMF, it will supply a country with convertible foreign exchange on a limited-term basis "to allow it to put right what has gone wrong in its economic life, with a view to stabilizing its currency and strengthening its trade." Lending commitments can come from any of several facilities, most of which have been created since the 1970s in response to the ever-growing complexity and severity of the international economic problems confronting LDCs. Total IMF lending in 1995 of the equivalent of about $27 billion was more than three times the totals for each of the previous two years. (Net reimbursements were smaller because of steady repayments to the Fund of previous borrowing.) This upsurge in gross lending, caused mainly by large drawings by Mexico and Russia, pushed cumulative IMF disbursements and undrawn commitments from all lending facilities to about $60 billion at the end of 1995. Both annual disbursements and cumulative outstanding credit hit their peak in the mid-1980s, also the peak of the LDC debt crisis.

The basic right to borrow foreign exchange from the IMF is the first credit tranche, an amount up to the equivalent of twenty-five percent of the country's paid-in quota. Approval is automatic in this case, as long as a member country can demonstrate a balance of payments problem. Access may next be made, one at a time, to three upper credit tranches, each of which is also equal to twenty-five percent of the country's quota. Conditions attached to approval of loans from the second, third, and fourth credit tranches get progressively steeper. The basic criterion that borrowers must meet in getting loan requests approved is that they will adopt the kinds of corrective economic policies that will make it likely that they will be able to solve their balance of payments difficulties in a reasonable period of time. Only in this way

can the required assumption be made that the borrower will be able to repay the IMF within the stipulated terms of three to five years.

Conditional borrowing requires a country to present the IMF's executive directors with a specific program of reform. Typically, a program includes measures such as reduced government expenditures and a depreciation of its currency to a level appropriate to the country's relative competitiveness. If approved, a conditional loan is made under a so-called standby arrangement, whereby a line of credit can be disbursed in installments for up to three years on the condition that the borrower keeps its promised economic reforms in place and attains certain quantitative objectives, for example, a stipulated percentage reduction in its budget deficit. The extended fund facility allows the IMF to provide assistance to members to borrow in amounts greater than available in credit tranches and have up to ten years for repayment.

A number of special lending facilities address the LCD's structural and longer-term balance of payments problems that go beyond the cyclical deficits that the IMF was originally designed to finance. Credit limits in every case are calculated as some specified percentage of the borrower's quota in the IMF. The Structural Adjustment Facility (SAF) provides low-interest loans to support the macroeconomic and structural adjustment programs of developing countries with protracted balance of payments problems. Countries seeking to borrow from the SAF must first develop a satisfactory policy framework paper that lays out appropriate performance goals and structural reforms, in cooperation with the professional staffs of the IMF and World Bank Group. Lending also takes place through the Enhanced Structural Adjustment Facility, which operates under procedures similar to the SAF, but it provides larger amounts of funding to support more ambitious adjustment measures. At year-end 1995, sixty-one countries had extended lending programs through the IMF. Twenty-six countries had standby arrangements with the IMF, nine had extended fund facility arrangements, and twenty-six were drawing from the Enhanced Structural Adjustment Facility.

The IMF also operates the Compensatory and Contingency Financing Facility. Compensatory financing provides financial assistance to members experiencing severe but temporary declines in export earnings below their five-year trend line, for reasons beyond their control. Typical causes would be a drop in worldwide prices of commodities or export shortfalls, due to a crop freeze. Separately, contingency financing assists members with active borrowing arrangements at the IMF to maintain the momentum of policy reforms when they are faced with unforeseen adverse external shocks, such as increases in import prices and upward movements in interest rates.

The newest lending program, begun in 1993 to operate on a temporary basis, is the Systemic Transformation Facility. It is especially designed to assist member countries that are in the early stages of transition from communist, centrally planned economies to market-based economies. Such countries tend to experience immediate and severe balance of payments strains caused by disruptions to traditional trade and payments arrangements, mainly declines in export earnings. Twenty transition countries were drawing from this facility by the end of 1995.

The Fixed Exchange Rate Standard

The first decade of the IMF's existence was marked by relative inactivity. The physical devastation after World War II in Western Europe was so serious that the region's financial needs far exceeded the limited, highly conditional lending facilities of the IMF. Following the IMF's policy decision in 1948 that it would not lend to countries receiving Marshall Plan assistance, IMF lending dropped to a trickle. In the first half of the 1950s, lending averaged less than $100 million annually. A significant level of lending did not materialize until the latter part of the decade when France and Great Britain borrowed heavily.

The relative strength of the U.S. economy in the immediate postwar period caused the quick elevation of the dollar to the status of the world's preeminent currency, acceptable in every country for settlement of any kind of international transaction. Ownership of the world's key currency accorded the United States significant influence in international monetary relations, in general, and the operation of the IMF, in particular. At a minimum, the United States had enough voting power to block acceptance of any significant proposal under consideration in that institution. Acceptance of U.S. economic leadership was further guaranteed when the United States began running balance of payments deficits in 1950. Europeans accepted the deficits, because the net dollar outflows to Western Europe served to build up depleted governmental and commercial financial reserves in these countries.

As the U.S. deficits grew and began to generate annoyance and concern in many countries in Western Europe, the management of the international monetary system moved from U.S. domination to decision by committee. The Group of Ten industrial countries was formed in 1961 as the result of the establishment of the General Agreements to Borrow, an agreement to provide the equivalent of a $6 billion supplement to the IMF's resources. The latter were deemed to have insufficient amounts of nondollar currencies to lend to the United States. There was a growing expectation that it would eventually need to borrow from the IMF in connection with its increasingly large balance of payments deficits.

The United States would need to borrow nondollar currencies that could then be used to buy dollars being sold in the foreign exchange market.

Within five years, the Group of Ten would serve as the forum for preparing a contingency plan for creating and distributing additional reserve assets after the presumed termination of the U.S. balance of payments deficit. If dollars ceased to flow abroad, this would eventually constrain international economic growth through what is termed a shortage of international liquidity. To the extent that a balance of payments deficit country lacks reserve assets, it must accelerate efforts to restore equilibrium by restraining aggregate demand. The outcome of the negotiations held to deal with the issue of liquidity was an agreement on special drawing rights (SDRs). SDRs are a man-made form of monetary reserve that can be created whenever there is a consensus by IMF members that the international monetary system as a whole needs additional reserve assets. Two such determinations have been made, in 1969 and in 1978. To date, the IMF has created and distributed SDRs with a cumulative value of about $30 billion.

SDRs are allocated to members of the IMF on a pro rata basis that matches the relative size of their IMF quota, not on the basis of need. Countries with a balance of payments problem may use any SDRs in their possession to acquire the foreign exchange they need to finance imports or to stabilize the value of their currencies in the foreign exchange market. The IMF acts as the intermediary to designate a second member country, one with a strong balance of payments position, to swap a given amount of foreign exchange in exchange for the equivalent amount of SDRs. A country using SDRs does not have to repay them. This attractive attribute has created periodic demands by less developed countries for a large SDR allocation to be distributed exclusively to them, in order to ease their balance of payments burdens. The large industrial countries have opposed and prevented this initiative on the grounds that the international monetary system as a whole is not experiencing a shortage of reserves.

U.S. Use of IMF Assets

The only significant IMF borrowing by the United States occurred in November 1978. A major financial package was assembled at the time by the U.S. government in the effort to reverse a precipitous decline in the dollar's exchange rate. An important element of this package was a war chest of foreign currencies that could be sold for dollars in the foreign exchange market in an effort to equalize supply and demand. In order to convince speculators that selling dollars had now become financially risky, the U.S. government announced that it was borrowing the foreign currency equivalent of $3 billion from the IMF and that it was selling $2 billion equivalent of its SDR holdings at the IMF to acquire additional balances of strong currencies. The resulting purchases of dollars, along with the domestic tightening in U.S. monetary policy, was a great success. The dollar quickly reversed its downward course, and the resulting change in investor sentiment led to a prolonged period of stability in the dollar's exchange rate.

Because the IMF lends to other countries most of the dollars that the United States pays in as its quota, the IMF's holdings of dollars at any given time is usually lower than the U.S. quota. The difference is known as the reserve tranche. Under IMF rules, therefore, the United States has had automatic access to large sums of foreign currencies at the IMF. Any future run on the dollar could prompt a heavy drawing on its resources, if the U.S. government were so inclined.

Floating Exchange Rates

The international monetary system has adhered to a floating exchange rate regime since 1973. In theory, the central concern of the IMF, loans to assist countries to maintain fixed exchange rates while they correct relatively minor, cyclical balance of payments disequilibriums, had disappeared. After the industrial countries came to rely on constant exchange rate changes as a primary means to the end of achieving equilibrium in their current accounts, their need to borrow from the IMF steadily dissipated. All of the IMF's lending after 1978 has gone to LDCs and to countries in transition from communist to market-oriented economies. The extraordinary balance of payments and external debt problems of the LDCs placed the IMF in the eye of a procession of distinct and severe international financial storms occurring from the mid-1970s through the early 1990s. The oil shocks and the debt crisis imposed unprecedented needs for external credits on LDCs. As the level of the IMF's available lending resources declined, it became necessary to attach increasingly severe conditions on its loans to LDCs. The most controversial period in the IMF's history was at hand.

The swift and large escalation in oil prices implemented by OPEC in the fall of 1973 and January 1974 triggered tremendous economic dislocations: a mammoth disequilibrium in the global balance of payments picture, as oil exporters developed large surpluses while oil importers suffered large deficits; a reduction in economic growth; and an increase in inflation in oil-importing countries. The IMF quickly advocated intensified international economic cooperation in lieu of unilateral actions. In order to meet the surging demand for borrowed capital, IMF officials began lobbying for a major increase in quotas and moved to establish a new series of lending facilities. The first was the Oil Facility. Funded by borrowing from oil exporting countries, it quickly started making loans specifically to ameliorate the damage inflicted by higher oil prices on the balance of payments of oil-importing countries.

The second OPEC oil shock of 1979–1980 accelerated an unsustainable trend that had begun five years earlier after the first oil shock: heavy borrowing from commercial banks by a small number of advanced, relatively creditworthy developing countries. The two sides needed each other. The nonoil LDCs needed capital inflows to finance suddenly enlarged current account deficits. Banks were flush with petrodollars, currency deposited by the major oil exporting countries. Oil importing countries faced the choice between slower growth or heavy borrowing to offset what was an overnight leap in their oil import bills. Most countries had no choice other than to accept lower growth rates and fewer imports. Official development assistance did not increase very much, and bank lending, which did increase rapidly, went to only the most creditworthy LDCs; hence, only a few countries were able to exercise the option of heavy borrowing.

The stronger LDCs, principally Brazil, Mexico, and Argentina, might have been able to continue the rapid run-up in their external indebtedness for many more years, had they not been hit from all sides by the fallout of the industrial countries sliding into serious recession in 1981. With rising interest rates increasing the costs of servicing their debts and demand for their exports sagging in the economically depressed industrialized countries, the LDCs found themselves on the road to being unable to repay their outstanding debts. Mexico shocked the world in August 1982, when it went public with its inability to continue repaying the principal and interest on its loans. The so-called international debt crisis was now officially a matter of public record, and the IMF was on center stage in dealing with it.

The IMF began to shift its behavior, acting less like a friendly credit union lending to an in-group of industrialized countries and more like a highly conservative financial intermediary. It altered its basic approach to lending, because it decided that protecting its assets had become the priority. Instead of lending to prevent the need for a country suffering balance of payments deficits to devalue, the IMF regularly demanded that LDCs seeking loans, other than the first credit tranche, must reduce the value of their currencies as part of a reform package. More than ever before, the IMF demanded a growing number of specific changes in national policy as the prerequisite for the ability to borrow.

As the IMF tightened conditions for lending, the concept of conditionality became a major bone of contention in international economic relations between North and South. To be eligible to borrow, countries were now called upon to meet an almost standardized list of quantitative performance criteria and structural reforms. The most often repeated demands were a depreciation of what usually was an overvalued exchange rate, a reduction of the budget deficit, a decrease in the rate of growth of the money supply, a reduction in the rate of new credit creation, curbing the subsidization of key consumer goods like bread and heating fuel, and reduced government ownership of so-called parastatal companies.

The reduced aggregate demand and real incomes that invariably follow in the wake of compliance with imposition of austerity measures, all things being equal, will lead to improvement in the merchandise trade balance. This accomplishment reduces a country's need to borrow additional money from commercial banks, increases its ability to repay old loans, and generally promotes an easing of the debt crisis. In pursuing this policy track, however, the IMF opened itself to a torrent of criticism from one side for a lack of flexibility, failure to understand that many of the LDCs' problems originated from external factors and were not their fault, and alleged violations of the terms of its own charter. The Articles of Agreement state that one of the IMF's goals is to provide members "with the opportunity to correct maladjustments in their balance of payments without resorting to measures destructive of national or international prosperity." The so-called lost decade of the 1980s for Latin America added fuel to the harsher critics' arguments that the IMF had allowed itself to become first and foremost a debt collector on behalf of creditor governments and commercial banks. Critics with a different view criticized the IMF as wasting taxpayers' money to bail out the commercial banks from their own mismanagement, that is, their excessive lending to LDCs. Officials of the institution are quick to counter with the argument that it does not impose its will on any sovereign country; if a country does not wish to comply with reform demands of the IMF, it simply need not borrow.

An objective assessment of the IMF's role in the debt crisis is complicated by the fact that its policy actions differed considerably over time. In the early months of the crisis, the belief was widespread that the LDC debtors were only experiencing a short-term liquidity squeeze and merely needed an infusion of new loan capital to tide them over a brief problem. Two of the largest loans in the IMF's history were arranged for Mexico and Brazil in 1982–1983. Because the IMF did not believe that these loans met all of these countries' borrowing needs, senior IMF officials became catalysts in convincing commercial banks to make additional commitments. This effort was a factor in the IMF becoming the dispenser of the seal of approval attesting that a debtor government had adopted appropriate, that is, austerity, policies. Until new commercial bank lending to most LDCs ceased in the late 1980s, being able to secure a standby agreement with the IMF became a precondition for being given access to either new borrowing or a rescheduling of debt repayment from commercial banks.

The relationship between the LDCs and the IMF soon became strained. In the late 1980s, neither the IMF nor the banks were providing net new liquidity to the major debtors; in both cases, repayments exceeded new disbursements by a large margin. By this time, most of the major debtor countries had ceased borrowing from the IMF in order to avoid what were viewed as overly damaging and wholly inappropriate policies for a situation that suggested to some the need for the LDCs to grow out of their debt problems.

A major new phase in the IMF's role in abating the debt crisis was ushered in during 1989 with the initiation of the Brady Plan, named for former U.S. Treasury Secretary Nicholas F. Brady. In return for continued economic reforms, debtor countries would either be given access to new commercial bank loans, or their existing commercial bank debt would be reduced. The IMF and the World Bank Group helped to support debt reduction by lending debtor countries the funds to retire a portion of their external debt by directly buying it back from commercial banks at a deep discount from its face value. Under the Brady Plan, the IMF and the World Bank Group also provided financial resources to allow debtors to collateralize, or guarantee, bonds used to convert relatively short-term loans into long-term debt at lower interest rates or at lower face value.

The IMF found itself caught in the middle of the intense high stakes economic debate and foreign policy issue that erupted in late 1993, which concerned the disbursement of additional loans to Russia. Despite the growing threat from extremist political parties to the perceived centrist administration of Boris N. Yeltsin, the IMF temporarily suspended all further lending activities to that country. IMF officials acted because of the repeated failure of the Yeltsin administration to resume implementing reforms originally promised to the IMF and the failure to achieve key performance indicators, such as reduction in the budget deficit as a percentage of gross national product and abatement of inflation. As the economic situation in Russia appeared to deteriorate and political extremists attracted a greater following, the pressures intensified on the IMF to release more funds, even if such an action was not fully consistent with the IMF's internal requirement that there be reasonable expectation of on-time, full repayment, that is, good prospects that a country's balance of payments would gradually improve. Apparently in response to the urging from the governments of many of the large industrialized countries, in April 1994 the IMF approved a second drawing from the Systemic Transformation Facility equivalent to about $1.5 billion to support Russia's economic reform and stabilization program. One year later, the IMF approved a standby credit, equivalent to approximately $6.8 billion, following the Russian government's announcement of a new stabilization and adjustment program.

The IMF had become the principal coordinator of the industrialized countries' multilateral economic assistance package to Russia mainly at the suggestion of the U.S. government, which did not wish to be the one to impose vigorous lending terms, since the IMF had acquired considerable expertise in designing economic reform programs for LDCs during the 1980s. Except for the greater strategic importance of Russia, a country with 30,000 nuclear warheads, the basic economic issues in this case are the same as with Latin America. In both instances, the core question is whether economic austerity and free market reforms are the best possible economic prescriptions for countries in balance of payments distress? If they are, should they be pursued, even if there are potentially serious social and political consequences?

The deep gulf between advocates of gradualism and cold turkey adaptation of free market doctrine in reforming a country in economic transition has caused a major escalation of the debate over the relevance of the old rules of the IMF at a time of new problems in the global economy. Critics increasingly suggest that the long-term economic assistance orientation of multilateral development banks is far more relevant to the contemporary needs of LDCs and countries in economic transition than is the IMF's relatively short-term balance of payments perspective. The IMF's supporters, however, still applaud the fact that its charter effectively requires borrowing countries to accept the need for economic discipline and officially precludes the IMF from thinking and acting like a development agency.

STEPHEN D. COHEN

See also Balance of Payments and Balance of Trade; Brady Plan; Bretton Woods System; International Debt

FURTHER READING

Dell, Sidney Samuel. *On Being Grandmotherly: The Evolution of IMF Conditionality.* Princeton, N.J., 1981.

De Vries, Margaret Garritsen. *The IMF in a Changing World, 1945–1985.* Washington, D.C., 1986.

Gwin, Catherine, and Richard E. Feinberg, eds. *The International Monetary Fund in a Multipolar World: Pulling Together.* New Brunswick, N.J., 1989.

International Monetray Fund. *Annual Report.*

Johnson, Mary Elizabeth. *The International Monetary Fund, 1944–1992: A Research Guide.* New York, 1993.

Sidell, Scott R. *The IMF and Third World Political Instability.* New York, 1988.

Stiles, Kendall W., ed. *Negotiating Debt: The IMF Lending Process.* Boulder, Colo., 1991.

INTERNATIONAL RED CROSS AND RED CRESCENT MOVEMENT

A humanitarian organization that assists casualties of war, political prisoners, and victims of natural disasters; known until 1986 as the International Red Cross. The International Committee of the Red Cross (ICRC), which provides wartime emergency services; the League of Red Cross and Red Crescent Societies, which offers relief from natural disasters; and the 152 national Red Cross and Red Crescent societies together constitute the International Red Cross and Red Crescent Movements. In 1859 Jean Henri Dunant, a Swiss businessman, directed impromptu efforts to care for Austrian and French soldiers wounded in battle at Solferino, Italy, during the Second War of Italian Independence. His example inspired a group of Swiss citizens to organize the ICRC in 1863. The Geneva Convention of 1864, a multilateral treaty, called for the formation of national Red Cross societies to provide neutral assistance to wounded soldiers. The ICRC maintained the authority to grant legal recognition to new societies. Clara Barton, an American humanitarian, lobbied to gain support for the convention in the United States. In 1882 President Chester A. Arthur overcame traditional U.S. resistance to permanent alliances, and the United States subscribed to the treaty. Subsequent conventions expanded Red Cross activities to include aid to wounded seamen, prisoners of war, and noncombatants. In 1906 "Red Crescent" was adopted to designate societies in Muslim countries. The unprecedented mobilization of national organizations during World War I led to the creation of the League of Red Cross and Red Crescent Societies in 1919 to facilitate peacetime operations. After the founding of the League, national organizations continued to contribute financially to ICRC activities. The committee has relied on voluntary contributions from around seventy governments, though, for ninety-five percent of its funding.

ICRC visits to prisoner of war camps gained notoriety in World War II. Increasingly, states became reluctant to assume the political costs that would be engendered if they blocked these visits. Although the Geneva Conventions did not provide protection for civilians until 1949, the ICRC committee received repeated condemnations during the war for its decision not to oppose publicly the Nazi death camps. The Berne government, fearing a German challenge to Swiss neutrality, exerted enormous pressure on the ICRC to ensure the organization's silence.

The twenty-five member committee remains entirely composed of Swiss nationals, but most states have accepted the ICRC's assertion of independence from any external authority, including the Swiss government. While the United States has been a strong supporter of most Red Cross and Red Crescent ministrations, it refused to ratify a 1977 protocol to the Geneva Conventions that strengthened the ICRC's power to monitor the conduct of belligerents in wars of national liberation. In 1987 the administration of President Ronald Reagan rejected the treaty in order to avoid further legal restrictions on the conduct of U.S. military operations. Despite such obstacles, the committee continues to enjoy tremendous international prestige. In 1990 the ICRC received observer status at the United Nations. At the same time, though, warring factions in civil and international conflicts during the mid-1990s have increasingly disregarded Red Cross and Red Crescent neutrality, leading to the deaths of ICRC representatives in Afghanistan, Somalia, and Bosnia.

CHARLES D. MCGRAW

See also Geneva Conventions; Humanitarian Intervention and Relief

FURTHER READING

Bossier, Pierre. *From Solferino to Tsuchima: History of the International Committee of the Red Cross.* Geneva, 1985.

Forsythe, David F. "Choices More Ethical Than Legal: The International Committee of the Red Cross and Human Rights." *Ethics and International Affairs* 7(1993):131–151.

Pryor, Elizabeth Brown. *Clara Barton: Professional Angel.* Philadelphia, Pa., 1987.

INTERNATIONAL TRADE AND COMMERCE

Trade is the act of exchanging goods and services through barter or sale. International trade is simply the extension of a country's economic activity outside its borders to the international arena. Specialization and exchange are fundamental aspects of trade between countries, just as they are significant in economic relations within countries.

Trade between countries encounters political impediments much greater than those existing in internal trade, namely, the attempts by citizens to restrict the benefits of economic exchange to themselves and their fellow citizens. Thus, nationalism and the trade restrictions imposed by the state are important elements of any examination of international trade. In the first half of the twentieth century, such restrictions were so onerous as to almost stop trade altogether, while in the second half of the century they have been the subject of a lengthy and coordinated effort by trading countries to liberalize the flow of goods and services in the international economy. The result is that trade cannot be examined independently of trade policy. Thus the field of international trade is a blend of the disciplines of economics, politics, and law.

Trade and Regulation

An examination of the origins of trade must go back to the beginnings of human history. The earliest forms of trade among our primitive ancestors served not only to acquire scarce commodities between groups with differing expertise or resources, but also as a means of communication. The communication function should not be underestimated. Without the knowledge of other communities that came from trade, it is difficult to see how human history could have evolved as it did.

Trade lay at the center of state revenue and state power for many of the ancient and medieval powers. Nowhere was this clearer than in ancient Athens. Contrary to Aristotle's belief that self-sufficiency was crucial to the *polis*, Athens was dependent on trade and developed, at least in part, through commercial activity with its neighbors. Athens exported silver and olive oil throughout the Mediterranean region and in turn imported the grain necessary to feed its population.

As early as the classical period, it was recognized that the role of trade was to create wealth. Trade created wealth as the product of specialization, division of labor, and exchange. The Greeks used their wealth to create a remarkable civilization, and then misused it in the Peloponnesian War to destroy their civilization. But trade also allowed the Greeks to become familiar with a wider world and thus begin the process of broader societal interaction. Moreover, trade permitted the concentration of the Greek population in the cities and thus formed one of the building blocks of modern society. Finally, trade among the ancient Greeks created what the economist F. A. Von Hayek called "a self-generating order" that permitted humans to organize into larger and more complex social arrangements than ever before.

Trade has thus played an important role in the transition from the ancient to the modern world. Historians have noted that international trade is intimately related to the course of human development. For example, there were trade routes from Asia and North Africa to Greece and then Rome, which broke down after the fall of the Roman Empire. From the sixth to the eighth centuries, social and physical communication between these areas and Europe and among the European communities themselves was severed, trade was disrupted, and the period often referred to as the "Dark Ages" settled in Europe. Trade recovered very slowly and from its resurgence the modern trading world has developed. Just like the Greeks, the modern trade regime has used trade to increase wealth.

Any discussion of the history of trade would not be complete without a discussion of the regulation of trade. As John Condliffe, author of *Commerce of Nations*, has argued, trade is ancient, but the regulation and taxation of trade are nearly as old. As soon as traders began to profit from trade, authorities began to intervene to control and tax the traders. In the beginning, the means of regulating trade were as primitive as the trade itself. The earliest method was the imposition of tolls, which were payments or tribute exacted by local leaders for permis-

WORLD MERCHANDISE EXPORTS BY PRODUCT, 1980–1992
(in percent)

	1980	1985	1992
All products[1]	100.0	100.0	100.0
Agricultural products	14.7	13.7	12.2
Mining products	27.6	21.9	12.2
Manufactures	54.0	61.2	72.8
Machinery and transport equipment	25.8	31.0	37.3
Textiles	2.7	2.7	3.2
Clothing	2.0	2.5	3.6

WORLD EXPORTS OF MERCHANDISE AND COMMERCIAL SERVICES, 1992
(in percent)

	1970	1980	1992
Merchandise	81.0	83.0	79.0
Commercial Services	19.0	17.0	21.0

[1]Including unspecified products.

Source: *International Trade: 1993 Statistics.* ©1993 by GATT, Geneva

sion to pass through territory, or to trade, or for protection—indeed, tolls were often only one step up from piracy. Although the imposition of tolls had little basis in economic theory, they taught traders an important economic lesson. Where tolls were excessive, the activity was relocated, a lesson modern multinational corporations have learned well.

Tolls were a form of taxation and the ability to tax implied an increased presence of some organized body with taxing authority. From earliest times, tolls were an expression of military control and often political sovereignty. The rule was simple: if you controlled territory, you could exact tolls at will. The result was a hindrance to trade, particularly in Europe in the Middle Ages when the region was divided into many small jurisdictions. The increased size of the political units through the consolidation of nation-states from the fourteenth century onwards stimulated trade across the region.

As trade itself became more sophisticated, so too did the methods of regulation. Tolls were replaced by tariffs, or customs duties, a percentage tax added to the price of imports. The imposition and administration of tariffs are among the oldest functions of government. Adam Smith nicely summed this up when he described customs as simply "customary."

While tolls appeared at times to be random or opportunistic, tariffs tended to reflect organized government policy. Their main purpose was to raise revenue. They did this effectively and by the beginning of the eighteenth century, duties on imported goods had become the main source of revenue in Europe. Another function of tariffs was the protection of domestic producers from foreign competition. Both these functions were elements of a more general policy called mercantilism, which involved a policy of exporting more than was imported. This enabled a state to accumulate wealth and therefore, presumably, power. After the beginning of the twentieth century, governments found more effective means to raise revenues—particularly the direct tax on incomes—and the revenue function of tariffs, as well as the policy of mercantilism, became much less important.

Theory of Trade and Commerce

International trade has a rich theoretical tradition. The basic idea is that if countries are given opportunities to trade abroad, they will increase their wealth by specializing in products they make efficiently, and trading to obtain the rest. This concept is simple and ancient—indeed, the economic value of the division of labor and exchange was well known to the Greek philosopher, Plato. The idea was elaborated by the classical political economists David Ricardo and John Stuart Mill as the theory of comparative advantage, which states that to maximize their welfare, countries should specialize in and export their least-cost products, based ultimately on their relative endowment in the factors of production.

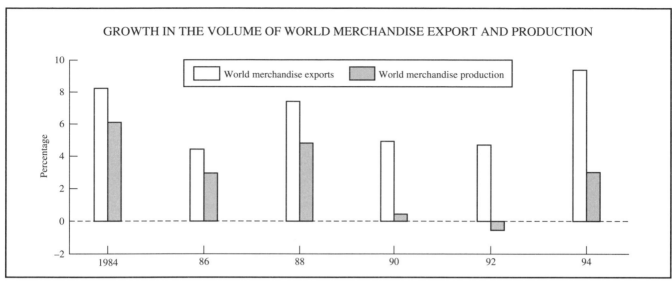

GROWTH IN THE VOLUME OF WORLD MERCHANDISE EXPORT AND PRODUCTION

Source: *International Trade: 1995 Statistics.* ©1995 by GATT, Geneva

Thus a country richly endowed with arable land might specialize in wheat, while a labour-intensive economy might specialize in textiles.

Two assumptions were important to the classical theory of comparative advantage. The first was that prices had to reflect the true costs of products. If a country had a monopoly position on traded goods, then it might be able to apply tariffs and gain a unilateral advantage, much as a monopolist can increase profits by restricting sales and driving up the price. The second assumption was that a country's position in international trade had to be independent of its own trade policy; for example, a country could not effectively use a tariff in order to force a trading partner to drop its own tariffs. These assumptions have been explored by modern strategic trade theorists, whose work has been more receptive to the use of tariffs and other trade restrictions than was the classical theory of Ricardo and Mill. However, one important limitation to the use of tariffs in trade policy is the possibility of retaliation by one's trading partners. Where retaliation occurs, the likelihood is that trade restrictions will lead to a lower level of welfare for all countries.

The theory of comparative advantage has become less accurate in predicting postwar patterns of trade in manufactured products. After the 1960s, the proportion of manufactured products in total world trade rose to about 60 percent, which is significant because it represents the breaking of an historic link between manufactured goods and primary products. This link had effectively limited the growth of trade in manufactured goods to increases in trade in primary products. Breaking this link allowed for a rapid expansion of trade, which has occurred especially among advanced industrial countries. However,

these developments could not be easily explained by the theory of comparative advantage, since industrial nations often trade the same kinds of products (for example, automobiles) with each other. Such intra-industry, as opposed to inter-industry, trade has been explained by showing that trade in manufactured goods is essentially an extension of a country's domestic activity across national frontiers. Consequently, products that are exported tend to be products that are already manufactured for domestic consumption.

An alternative to the classical trade theory rooted in Ricardo and Mill is the theory of the German economist Friedrich List that focuses on nationalism and national development. List attacked the notion that trade on the basis of comparative advantage would maximize the economic welfare of nations. Instead, List proposed a model of national development that emphasized rapid industrialization for developing countries. Trade protectionism was a necessary policy to promote such industrialization. List's philosophy was not well received in already industrialized England, but the developing countries of his day, notably Germany and the United States, effectively incorporated List's thinking into their trade policies. Until recently, most modern developing countries also pursued policies consistent with List's ideas, for they used high tariffs and other measures to protect import-competing industries and promote industrialization. Furthermore, List's philosophy has found some support in the United States in recent years, where trade analysts have argued that the United States should abandon its ideological opposition to government intervention in the economy, and instead use government policies to improve the country's trade performance with other countries.

Since midcentury, the idea of freer trade has been in the ascendency, and in the last decade it has become much more popular with developing countries than it ever was in the past. In theory, free trade could be practiced unilaterally by any country, although the only country ever to do so was Great Britain in the nineteenth century. In practice, free trade has relied on reciprocity, which could be defined as a fair or equivalent exchange of concessions. The intellectual basis for twentieth-century trade liberalization has been the theory of bargained exchange, whereby countries have reduced their own tariffs and other trade restrictions in exchange for similar reductions by other countries. These exchanges cannot be explained in classical trade theory, since that theory would view tariffs as promoting inefficiency, and hence the main beneficiary of a tariff reduction would be the country lowering the tariff, and not its trading partner. Instead, the concept of bargained exchange and reciprocity has provided a convenient mechanism for countries seeking to liberalize trade to mobilize necessary political support for that policy.

Antecedents to Modern Trade Philosophy

No discussion of international trade and commerce would be complete without a discussion of international trade agreements. Much as regulations evolved along with trade, so did agreements about trade evolve. Thus, as trade is an ancient phenomenon, so too are trade agreements and thus trade policy. For example, archaeologists have discovered tablets, perhaps the earliest known examples of written history, chronicling external relations of the Egyptian royal family which make reference to a commercial treaty between Egypt and Babylonia. These tablets have been dated at around 2500 B.C.

There has thus historically been a close relationship between trade and commercial agreements or treaties. These agreements started as simple arrangements about how commercial relations would be conducted. It has been argued that, along with war and its conduct, trade and commercial treaties provided the major base for modern diplomacy. International trade today continues to promote a diplomatic function, but it is diplomacy based on the values of shopkeepers, not of warriors—values such as common sense, desire for continuity, and the search for mutual gain.

Trade agreements have historically been conducted between self-interested actors who have used the regulation of trade to promote their own interests. This continues to be true in the 1990s. It became clear as trade increased in scope and intensity that international agreements could alleviate some of the negative effects of competitive national regulations. Once this was recognized, formal agreements became commonplace and by the nineteenth century treaties of commerce and navigation were in existence between all the largest trading countries.

The history of international trade and trade agreements over the past two centuries has reflected contradictory tendencies toward either protectionism or free trade. In the late eighteenth century, protectionism was the norm in the countries of Europe. But after the Napoleonic Wars, Great Britain led a move towards free trade. Great Britain was able to do this because it was in a better economic position than Europe. The Napoleonic Wars had left Great Britain unscathed—much the same position the United States found itself in after World War II—thus its economic strength was much greater than that of the other countries of Europe, which had suffered tremendous costs fighting the wars.

The British economy became the dominant economic force and Great Britain became the world's creditor country. Trade with the United States and the colonies was substantial, but trade with Europe was hampered by high tariffs on the continent and the protectionist Corn Laws in Great Britain which restricted grain imports from Europe. British efforts to promote liberalism in Europe were met with demands that Great Britain itself reduce or eliminate duties on grain. These demands, combined with domestic pressure for general political reform in Great Britain, led to the 1846 repeal of the Corn Laws, followed by administrative measures that put free trade into practice.

The movement toward free trade spread to the European continent, in part due to the French free-trade movement led by the economist Michel Chevalier. Chevalier attempted to convince the French government to follow the British example but had little success until the opportunity arose to incorporate a tariff negotiation into a commercial and political treaty with Great Britain. The result was the Anglo-French (or Cobden-Chevalier) treaty of 1860, which was instrumental in opening the French market to British manufacturers and demonstrated that trade agreements could be an effective means of trade liberalization. The Cobden-Chevalier treaty stimulated a series of liberalizing agreements throughout Europe. Thus, in Europe by the third quarter of the nineteenth century, Adam Smith's notion of an international economic system based on free exchange was as close to realization as it had ever been.

This period of free trade did not last long however. Rapid technological improvements in the mid-1850s meant that increasingly the comparative advantage in grain cultivation was shifting toward the New World. At the same time, a slump occurred in European industrial production. International competition for grains and manufactured goods became severe and in all countries there were pressures to implement protectionist policies against imports. The European governments succumbed to the pressure one by one. Austria-Hungary raised tariffs in 1876, followed quickly by Italy and Germany. France responded to German protectionism with restrictions of its own. The United States did not join in the European momentum toward free trade. It had remained firmly protectionist throughout the nineteenth century and avoided the trend toward free trade in midcentury, primarily due to the Civil War. Thus, by the end of the century, Great Britain was the only major nation still practicing free trade.

The depression that began in the 1870s triggered a period of protectionism that lasted for more than half a century. Protectionism, nation-building, and nationalism in Europe around the turn of the century exacerbated the tensions in that area. The beginning of World War I continued the movement toward protectionism and away from the free trade regime of the mid-1800s.

Breakdown: The Interwar Years

Economists have had great difficulty sorting out the consequences of World War I. What can be said, however, was that four years of war broke up an imperfect but workable equilibrium between internal economic policies, trade, and payments that had existed under the gold standard of the nineteenth century.

Although they were overshadowed by the more visible conferences on disarmament and reparations, there were a number of attempts in the 1920s and 1930s to restore economic confidence and open up the international trading system. These economic conferences included the International Financial Conference in 1920, the Genoa Conference of 1922, a conference on customs formalities in 1923, and the World Economic Conferences of 1927 and 1933. The early conferences sought to restore the prewar level of trade, which had fallen by almost half its volume after the war. Rather than the reduction of trade barriers per se, the initial emphasis was to reestablish a payment mechanism, for without some system of monetary exchange, trade was impossible.

There is no one action or policy that can be said to have caused the depression of the 1930s. But it is generally agreed that the breakdown of the international economic system deepened the depression within national economies, and it is understood that the breakdown was associated with several failed attempts to create a more cooperative approach to international economic activity.

Perhaps the most important failure was the failure of the Geneva Convention on Import and Export Prohibitions and Restrictions, resulting from the World Economic Conference of 1927. Until the General Agreement on Tariffs and Trade (GATT) was negotiated in 1947, the Geneva Convention was the most ambitious attempt to promote international cooperation on trade ever negotiated. The convention banned "prohibitions" on exports and imports, and created a common set of rules regarding the use of quantitative restrictions. The convention did not deal specifically with tariffs, but it nevertheless represented an important effort to instill confidence in multilateral trade management.

The convention was to come into force when eighteen countries had signed it. Although it was signed quickly by the most important European trading countries, it failed by one country to get the necessary eighteen signatories, and support for the convention unravelled. An important opportunity to build confidence in international trade management was lost.

The United States emerged from World War I as the largest trading nation in the world. It is to be expected, then, that actions undertaken by the United States would have major implications for the international economic system. One particular action had a devastating effect. In 1930 the United States passed the Smoot-Hawley Act which raised U.S. tariffs to historically high levels. The act itself did not represent a dramatic change in U.S. policy, since high tariffs already existed, but it represented a fundamentally important step in the process of gradual and widespread closure of national boundaries to foreign imports.

The Smoot-Hawley Act was the product of a number of factors in the United States. First, it was the product of protectionist values that were widespread in society at the time. Second, the legislation was the product of increased nationalism and a reaction or perhaps overreaction to nationalist economic policies in Europe. Third, an important factor in the passage of the Smoot-Hawley Act was the nature of the political process in the United States. First, the act was written in congressional committees by members of government who were unable to understand the complexity or the implications of the legislation. Second, the process was vulnerable to pressure from well-organized and vocal special-interest groups who were demanding protection. In the face of this pressure, Congress essentially granted protection to all those groups that demanded it.

The process leading to the Smoot-Hawley Act was closely watched by the governments in Great Britain and Europe. With its passage, they moved quickly to retaliate. The 1930s became characterized by a complicated series of retaliatory moves and countermoves. Great Britain ended its historic policy of free trade in 1931 and in 1932 negotiated the Ottawa agreements which resulted in a tariff preference area in the British Commonwealth.

The competitive and protectionist actions of the United States, Great Britain, and the continental European powers completed the breakdown of the international trade system by the mid-1930s. The impact of raising tariffs and implementing other protectionist measures was devastating—world trade declined by approximately two-thirds from 1929 to 1934. It took years to repair the damage. These economic actions, combined with the rise of fascism and nationalism, made World War II almost inevitable.

The GATT Regime

Although the 1930s had been a decade of protectionism and retaliation, one important action premised the establishment of a liberal international economic regime after World War II. This action was the passage of the Reciprocal Trade Agreements Act (RTAA) in the United States in 1934, following the initiative of Secretary of State Cordell Hull.

RTAA was essentially just an amendment to the Smoot-Hawley Act, but it produced a revolution in U.S., and perhaps even international, trade policy. The main change in terms of U.S. politics was that tariff-setting power was transferred from Congress to the president. Congress had shown itself unable to manage tariffs and to withstand the pressure from constituents for protection. From the standpoint of the international community, RTAA was important because it implicitly accepted that setting tariff rates would no longer be a unilateral policy, but rather a matter to be settled by negotiation.

After the passage of RTAA in 1934 the United States began to pursue reciprocal trade agreements with other countries. Although twenty-one agreements reducing a significant number of tariffs were concluded, circumstances at the time were not favorable and RTAA could not undo the damage done by the Smoot-Hawley Act and the resulting retaliatory measures. Liberalization efforts effectively ceased during World War II but the process initiated by RTAA was not wasted. The bilateral agreements reached under RTAA program were generally successful in increasing the flow of trade, but more importantly for the postwar period, the program provided a body of experience in trade liberalization that was integrated into the postwar international trade regime.

After World War II the leadership of the international economic system fell to the unrivaled economic power of the United States. This leadership role was not resisted by the countries of Western Europe because in general the economic principles the United States was pursuing were also their principles. The security problem increasingly posed by the Soviet Union and the devastation of the war made the European countries amenable to an American leadership role in the immediate postwar years.

Any system in which one country is dominant is likely to reflect the values of that country. The trade system set up after World War II was no exception. This system combined three aspects of U.S. values: (1) a traditional suspicion of government; (2) a belief in the importance of economic growth for peace; and (3) a newfound realization that free trade, not protectionism, was the route to prosperity. Although not tremendously popular in Europe, trade liberalization was ideologically attractive to the United States and served the U.S. national interest since the United States was positioned to benefit greatly from it. Thus, partly because of the predominant role of the United States, trade liberalization became the goal of the Western economic regime. Because the European countries were in no position to argue, they went along with the U.S. conception of how the postwar international economic regime should look. But the trade regime thus incorporated seeds of discontent and controversy that would blossom after Europe regained its equilibrium.

Despite the depression, there had been many bilateral agreements negotiated in the interwar period. Following the war these agreements were brought together into a multilateral contract known as the General Agreement on Tariffs and Trade (GATT). The role of GATT was to provide structure to the trade-agreements process. GATT was created as a set of trading rules and was implemented in 1947 to accompany multilateral tariff-reduction talks that were held in 1948. It was hoped that the establishment of such rules would reduce the chance of a renewed bout of international protectionism.

Unlike many of the international organizations created in the postwar period, GATT was not intended to be an organization. It established what is usually referred to as a "regime," a term used to refer to a set of principles, rules, or decision-making procedures that shape behaviors in a particular area. Thus, GATT, until its incorporation by the World Trade Organization, was not an organization—participants were not "members" but were "contracting parties." GATT emphasized process over structure, policy over institutions, and pragmatism over idealism.

GATT was organized to promote trade liberalization through international cooperation, and was based on a number of principles. First, it incorporated the principle of nondiscrimination (Article I) so that any advantage granted to one contracting party was accorded to all other contracting parties. This principle was intended to replace the practice of bilateral tariff preferences that were instituted for political reasons prior to World War II and which often reduced the flow of trade. A further form of nondiscrimination was national treatment (Article III), that also obliged countries to treat foreign products (on which customs duties had been paid) the same as domestic products with respect to taxes and other requirements (Article III).

A second principle of GATT was a qualified prohibition against quantitative and other nontariff restrictions to trade (Article XI). A third principle dealt with the process and values adopted by GATT in reducing trade restric-

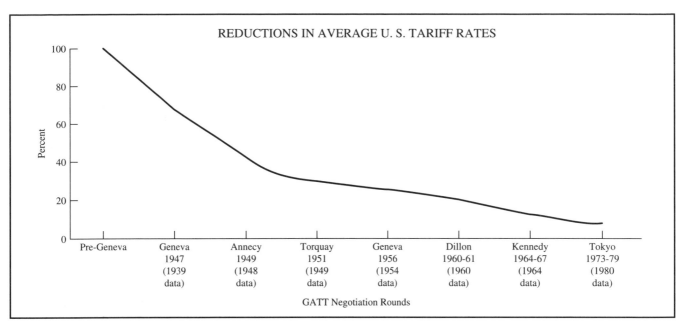

REDUCTIONS IN AVERAGE U. S. TARIFF RATES

GATT Negotiation Rounds

Source: *Protectionism*, Jagdish Bhawati. ©1988 by MIT Press, Cambridge, Massachusetts. Reprinted with permission of MIT Press

tions (Article XVIII). Negotiations were to be carried out "on a reciprocal and mutually advantageous basis" and "directed to the substantial reduction of tariffs."

A fourth principle consisted of safeguards. The GATT plan was that restrictive measures on trade would be changed to tariff protection and then tariffs would be reduced through multilateral negotiations. However, in a situation where this process caused a serious political problem, GATT allowed (Article XIX) a country to *raise* tariffs temporarily to allow the adjustment of the domestic market. The safeguards were included so that problems in particular industries did not jeopardize the entire liberalization process.

A fifth principle was "commercial considerations." This meant the utilization of free market processes rather than government intervention. In this, state-controlled enterprises were called upon to act in accordance with market principles and thus avoid subsidies and other market-distorting policies.

Multilateral negotiation was the main mechanism for decision making in GATT. In effect, GATT simply incorporated the bilateral negotiation process established by the RTAA and multilateralized it. However, GATT could do little to punish countries that did not follow up their contractual agreement. Like most international bodies, GATT procedures for carrying out rules were weak. Article XXII provided that contracting parties involved in a dispute would be obliged to consult with each other. If the dispute continued, Article XXIII enabled a judicial-like panel to be established to hear the dispute. The panel's report would be submitted to the

GATT Council for adoption, and the council would then attempt to get all contracting parties to carry out their obligations. This process had its limitations, because GATT is simply a contract and had no power to enforce liberalization. Despite this lack of enforcement power, however, statistics indicate there has been compliance for the majority of GATT panels.

Changes in Trade Patterns: 1945–1995

The competitive protectionism of the interwar period, as well as the compartmentalization of national economies during World War II, combined to drive world trade volumes to a fraction of their pre–World War I levels. Following World War II, national economies rebounded as countries recovered from the war. Furthermore, governments made a concerted effort to create more liberal trading policies. For example, as a result of GATT negotiations, average tariff rates in the United States fell from a postwar high of about 100 percent to less than 10 percent by 1980. Both war recovery and tariff reductions led to a sharp resurgence of world trade.

GATT Negotiation Rounds

From the late 1940s to the early 1970s, the volume of world trade grew by an annual average of 7 percent, while the growth of world production averaged about 5 percent. In the next decade, trade and economic production slowed to an annual average growth of 2.8 percent and 2.5 percent respectively. In 1982, trade and production volumes declined sharply from the previous year, but then by 1984 annual growth averages rebounded to over 8 percent for trade and more than 6 percent for world output. For the remaining seven years to 1992, the annual average growth of trade was 5.4 percent, while annual growth in world output was 2.5 percent. Over the forty-five-year period, both trade and growth were buoyant, and world trade consistently led world output in advances as well as declines. This supports the argument that trade is an engine of economic growth.

The early postwar period was characterized by the economic hegemony of the United States. In 1950 the United States accounted for almost 17 percent of world trade, and this share was about one and one-half times the share of the next leading nation, Great Britain. Through the decade of the 1950s, U.S. preponderance increased in world trade, and by 1960, U.S. trade was 20 percent of overall world trade. This figure was more than twice as large as that of the next leading nation, Great Britain, and it was roughly equal to the combined total of the three leading European economies, namely Great Britain, France, and West Germany.

During the 1960s the position of the United States began to change. The enormous trade surplus of the United States—which had led to the accumulation of gold reserves in the 1950s—dissipated during the 1960s and turned to a trade deficit in 1971. By 1972 the United States had lost its commanding trade position, and its trade in that year was only approximately 20 percent larger than its next nearest competitor, West Germany. Even more important was the establishment of the European Community (EC) and its effect on U.S. leadership in world trade. When the EC was created in 1958, it and the United States accounted for roughly the same volume of international trade. Since then, due to economic growth in Europe and the growth in membership of the EC itself, the trade volume controlled by the EC has surpassed that of the United States. For example, in 1973 U.S. exports of $68 billion were approximately 13 percent of world trade, but they were dwarfed by the combined exports of EC members of $205 billion. In terms of external trade alone, the EC accounted for over $93 billion in exports, over one-third larger than U.S. exports.

Since the 1970s, world trade has undergone changes of structure and composition. On the first point, due to increasing levels of direct foreign investment and the resulting greater role of multinational corporations in the world economy, a growing proportion of international trade is carried out between parent firms and their subsidiaries in foreign countries. Such trade is known as intra-firm trade, and analysts have estimated that intra-firm trade may account for as much as 50 percent of U.S. imports. The implication of intra-firm trade is that the prices set on goods being traded across national boundaries may not conform to real values, but rather are artificial prices (that is, "transfer" prices) that are manipulated to minimize the firm's exposure to tariffs and other taxes applied by governments. Intra-firm trade calls into question the assumption that international trade occurs between disinterested parties, and it therefore creates difficulties in planning and administering national trade policies.

The composition of trade has also changed since the 1970s. Agriculture, which has represented a falling proportion of trade in this century, continued to decline between 1980 and 1992. Mining products also declined substantially. By contrast, the proportion of manufactured products, of which machinery and transport equipment constituted about one-half, grew substantially. Textiles and clothing trade also increased, reflecting in part the increasing participation of developing countries in the world economy.

As distinct from merchandise goods, commercial services are also an important component in international trade. Although the proportion of services relative to goods has grown in developed economies like the United States in recent decades, the proportion of services in international trade has remained stable; see Table 2. Service trade was liberalized in the GATT Uruguay Round negotiation which concluded in 1994, and it is likely the result will be an increase in service trade in the coming years.

U.S. Multilateral Trade Policy

Trade policy encompasses a wide variety of subjects, ranging from tariffs and quantitative restrictions, technical standards, customs procedures, and licensing schemes, to investment or export incentives, trade remedy procedures, subsidies, and government procurement. Most of these subjects have found their way on to multilateral trade agendas. Including the Uruguay Round, there have been eight multilateral trade negotiations since 1947. In the first six negotiations—the original GATT negotiations, 1947; Annecy, 1949; Torquay, 1951; Geneva, 1956; the Dillon Round, 1960–1961; and the Kennedy Round, 1963–1967—tariff reductions were the main focus. The focus broadened in the following two negotiating rounds, the Tokyo Round, 1973–1979, and the Uruguay Round, 1986–1994.

The dominant position of the United States provided a liberalizing force in the postwar international economic system. While the United States could define the system, its leading position meant it had to allow trade benefits to accrue disproportionately to its trading partners. In effect the United States absorbed the economic problems in the system. But by the 1970s, it was no longer able (or willing) to play this role.

Although the Kennedy Round began changing the balance of the GATT negotiations because the six European Common Market countries negotiated as a single actor, it was the Tokyo Round that redefined both international and U.S. trade policy. The 1970s was a difficult decade in which to negotiate a trade agreement. Problems of inflation, recession, and the OPEC energy crisis created a climate of international economic uncertainty. As well, the relative position of the United States had declined. Internal divisions over the war in Vietnam, the first American trade deficit in the century (1971), and major political scandal over the Watergate incident all contributed to a less assertive U.S. position in the Tokyo Round. The U.S. decline was matched by an increasing European role. In 1973 Great Britain, Ireland, and Denmark joined the EC, making it the largest trading entity in the world. It is of great significance to the world economy that the United States made a fundamental decision to meet the reality of a unified Europe through liberal rather than isolationist policies.

The Tokyo Round arose out of the recognition that a number of trade problems had accumulated since the conclusion of the Kennedy Round in 1967. In particular, the longstanding dispute between the United States and the EC regarding agriculture needed resolution. As well, the increasing use of nontariff barriers, which were contrary to the GATT prohibition against quantitative restrictions, was a matter that needed multilateral attention.

The Tokyo Round changed the process and substance of the GATT talks. It represented a major overhaul of the international trade system and was the main focus of trade policymaking in the 1970s. The results fell into three areas: (1) six codes dealing with nontariff measures; (2) tariff reductions; and (3) revisions to GATT articles particularly relating to developing countries. The six codes updated and expanded GATT's trade law and were the most important part of the agreement. They covered customs valuation, import licensing, technical standards for products, subsidies and countervailing measures, government procurement, and antidumping. In general, the codes represented a change in GATT from encompassing statements of broad principles to detailed regulations regarding trade.

The Tokyo Round produced only modest results in agriculture, which was of particular concern for the United States and one of the reasons for initiating the talks in the first place. Politically, however, the negotiation was considered a success. The purpose of the negotiation was to increase the openness and certainty of trade rules, and it did this. The Tokyo Round also completed the transition from a hegemonic economic system led by the United States to one managed by a U.S./EC partnership. This was a tremendous change in international economic-political relations.

The New Protectionsim

In trade policy, the liberalizing effects of trade negotiations have always been balanced by domestic pressures for protectionism. These pressures increased in the 1980s, and there were numerous indications that trade policy in developed countries, and especially the United States, had become more nationalistic and self-serving. One indication is that all leading nations were increasingly motivated to develop certain high-tech industries that appeared to have especially high growth and export potential. Such industries include microelectronics, aviation, biotechnology, communications, and computing. These industries usually needed government promotion and protection in the domestic economy and, even more important, support of strong-arm government policies to open foreign markets.

Another indication of increasing protectionism was the expanded use of unfair trade remedies and unilateral measures, such as U.S. Section-301 legislation. Unfair trade remedies include mainly antidumping duty actions, which are extra duties levied on those products that are sold more cheaply into foreign markets ("dumped") than they are sold in their home market. Anti-dumping duties are provided by importing governments to domestic competing industries on the basis of a legal petition and as a result of an administrative proceeding that establishes both the existence of dumping and the extent of injury to domestic producers. The incidence of antidumping duty actions increased sharply in the 1980s, to the point where they became a serious impediment to trade in some industries.

Unilateral measures are best exemplified by Section-301 in U.S. trade law, which gives the U.S. government the power to determine whether a foreign trade practice is unreasonable or discriminatory, and to remedy that situation through negotiations with the foreign country, backed up with the power to employ sanctions such as new trade restrictions. Section-301 is not legal under GATT, but nevertheless it has been used on several occasions by the United States, often to pressure foreign countries to open their markets to U.S. and other nations' products. The use of unilateral measures is widely condemned among trading nations.

A third indicator of the new protectionism was the increasing criticism leveled at GATT during the 1980s. One such criticism was that trading countries should focus less on GATT rules than on trade results, that is, ensuring that actual trade flows reflected a balanced and "fair" distribution of benefits to all parties. This criticism struck at the heart of the rules-based nature of the GATT system, and was additionally regarded as a licence for strong countries to enforce their own concepts of fairness in trading relations. As with much of the new protectionism, the argument for a trade results philosophy was attenuated by the successful completion of the GATT Uruguay Round negotiation in the early 1990s.

The Uruguay Round

Although efforts to open a new round began almost immediately after the conclusion of the Tokyo Round, the

Uruguay Round was not officially initiated until a GATT ministerial meeting in Punta del Este, Uruguay, in September 1986. The agenda was broken down into fifteen negotiating groups in four major categories: market access, reform of GATT rules, measures to strengthen GATT as an institution, and new issues. In the first category the most important issues were agriculture, which placed the United States in opposition to the EC, and textiles, in which developed countries and developing countries were opposed. In the second category, negotiations were generally intended to make incremental legal changes to GATT and to discuss procedural issues left over from the Tokyo Round. The third category focused on the institutional development of GATT, including dispute-settlement mechanisms, decision-making procedures, relations with other international economic organizations (especially the IMF and the World Bank), and evolution into the World Trade Organization.

Apart from the issue of agriculture, it was the fourth category, namely, services, trade-related intellectual property (TRIPs), and trade-related investment measures (TRIMs), that was most controversial. The issue of including services at all in the GATT regime produced great debate. Services are not goods, but rather processes in which skills and knowledge are exchanged to meet a consumer need. Services now account for more than 50 percent of the gross national product (GNP) of developed countries. The main obstacles to their free exchange have been either the refusal of authorities to grant foreign firms the right to establish in their market, or the protection of local providers. The negotiations worked toward implementing the same principles—transparency, national treatment, and reciprocity—for services as for goods.

The issue of TRIMs was also controversial. It had become apparent in recent years that in many ways investment was interchangeable with trade and that trade liberalization was ineffective without corresponding investment liberalization. Investment, however, has always been strictly regulated in importing countries because of the threat to sovereignty posed by high levels of foreign investment. Rather than trying to change the entire international investment philosophy, the TRIM negotiations targeted specific investment restrictions that had an impact on trade or reduced the flexibility of investment.

TRIPs was a third new issue, although it had been discussed previously in GATT negotiations under the heading of counterfeit goods. Intellectual property rights grant state protection for a specified period for the commercialization of a new idea. There are two main types of intellectual property rights: one covering industrial property, protected by patent law, and the other covering artistic creations, protected by copyright. The United States had repeatedly argued that inadequate protection of intellectual property was a serious barrier to trade. The developing countries, represented most vocally by Brazil and India, also viewed this as a barrier to trade. However, they were initially more concerned with the developed countries' monopolies over products they considered crucial for development, and the potential for developed countries to use protection of intellectual property to maintain a competitive edge over countries lacking research and development infrastructure.

The Uruguay Round was scheduled to conclude in Brussels in December 1990. This deadline was established in part to accommodate U.S. legislation that specified a time limit on the authority of the U.S. government to negotiate. The meeting that was to conclude the round failed, however, due particularly to the issue of agriculture. This was one of the most significant negotiating failures ever recorded in the GATT, and it raised the specter of the breakdown of the cooperative postwar trading system. In response to the Brussels failure, the U.S. Congress extended the president's negotiating authority to permit completion of the round.

There was a significant change in the players involved in this round of talks, as the developing countries were much more involved than ever before. Of the fifteen issues on the agenda, approximately half were issues of contention between developed and developing countries—in particular textiles and agriculture. Along with the increased role of developing countries, the Uruguay Round also saw the appearance of coalition behavior. One of the most important coalitions was the Cairns group, which included agricultural exporting countries from both the developed and developing worlds. This group played an important role bridging the differences between the United States and the EC, and acted to promote liberalization of global agricultural markets.

The negotiations for the Uruguay Round were more strained than previous GATT talks. The disagreement between the United States and the EC over agriculture became bitter and divisive. Until very near the end of the talks, the developing countries were unwilling to allow the agenda (especially regarding TRIPs, TRIMs, and services) to move forward if their interests were not served. Particularly, they were not willing to agree to the liberalization of service regulations, TRIMs, or TRIPs without compensating benefits on textiles and agriculture, and the development of a safeguards code. The cross-sector linkages and the fact that the agreement was treated as one package that all participants were expected to accept, meant that the negotiations were very difficult. Additional problems that militated against a successful conclusion were the broad range of issues discussed, the large number of actors involved, and the technical complexity of the subjects on the table. Given these difficulties it is surprising that the negotiation was successfully concluded at all.

The "Final Act" of the Uruguay Round negotiation was completed on 7 December 1993, and the concluding signing ceremony was held in Marrakesh, Morocco, on 7 April 1994. The final act consisted of 550 pages of legal texts produced by 117 participating countries. Included in the final act is the establishment of a new international trade organization known as the World Trade Organization (WTO), which will encompass the GATT and other trade agreements signed under its auspices. For the United States, the concluding action was the passage of legislation to implement the final act in U.S. law. This action occurred with strong bipartisan support in an exceptional session of Congress on 7 December 1994.

U.S. Regional Trade Policy

On 12 August 1992, Canada, Mexico, and the United States concluded the North American Free Trade Agreement (NAFTA), which came into force 1 January 1994. NAFTA created the world's largest free trade region, encompassing 360 million people. This trilateral agreement extended the bilateral free trade arrangement between Canada and the United States concluded in 1987. Since it has provision for expansion, NAFTA may become a multilateral trade arrangement. It is the first free trade agreement concluded between developed and developing countries which is based on "full reciprocity."

NAFTA is a comprehensive agreement designed to ensure a more stable trade and investment climate. Consistent with GATT principles, it provides for the gradual and complete removal of tariffs among Canada, Mexico, and the United States, and establishes rules and principles for trade. The rules concern subjects reminiscent of the Uruguay Round discussions, including intellectual property, government procurement, services, energy, and dispute settlement. Since Canada, Mexico, and the United States all require export-generated growth to help alleviate their foreign debts and current account deficits, it was important to reach an agreement that ensured that this growth was not achieved through measures detrimental to each other.

Movement toward a NAFTA was effectively started with the implementation of the Canada-U.S. Free Trade Agreement (FTA) in 7 January 1989. Canada had initiated this agreement in an effort to increase and secure its access to the U.S. market, and to improve the competitiveness of its economy. For similar reasons, Mexico requested a bilateral free trade agreement with the United States, and on 7 June 1990, the presidents of both countries issued a joint statement of intent to negotiate such an agreement. Subsequently, Canada requested participation in the talks.

The United States saw the conclusion of a North American free trade agreement as promoting economic goals such as the efficient use of resources and labor, and thus improving competitiveness. It was argued that by establishing free trade and lowering Mexico's trade restrictions, the incentive for industries to locate in Mexico to get access to its market would be reduced. As well, NAFTA was seen as an opportunity to expand the American export market into the rapidly growing Mexican economy. It was believed that NAFTA would create further economic growth in Mexico which would in turn increase Mexican demands for American goods and services.

There was serious concern in the United States about creating stability in Mexico. Economic growth created by NAFTA would alleviate political and social pressures in Mexico and in turn perpetuate economic and political reforms. It was hoped that creating a free trade regime between Mexico and the United States would also make violent political upheaval less likely and decrease the flow of illegal immigrants to the United States.

Although NAFTA is derived from the FTA, it has considerably broadened the scope in some areas (for example, services) and it includes new areas (for example, intellectual property). It is divided into eight main areas: objectives and scope, trade in goods, technical barriers to trade, government procurement, investment and services, intellectual property, institutional provisions (for example, dispute-settlement mechanisms), and general provisions. The agreement allows for the accession of other countries, providing they meet specified criteria and each original party agrees.

NAFTA will provide for the virtual elimination of all tariffs among Canada, Mexico, and the United States. The elimination of tariffs is particularly important in terms of the automobile industry. The Mexican automotive industry had previously been insulated from competition through restrictive legislation, but under NAFTA, Mexico immediately dropped its tariffs by 50 percent and is phasing out the rest over a ten-year period, toward the NAFTA goal of the elimination of all automobile tariffs by 2003. Mexico's acceptance of automobile liberalization was partially offset by Canada and the United States agreeing to significant liberalization of the heavily protected textile industry.

NAFTA obliges each party to extend national treatment or most-favored-nation (MFN) treatment (whichever is better) to many commercial services and the financial sector (after a transition period ending in the year 2000). Indeed, perhaps the most important change from the FTA was the investment chapter, which substantially broadened the definition of "investment," incorporated services into the investment regime, and provided a mechanism for dispute settlement between private investors and host states.

Two issues made the conclusion of a free trade agreement with Mexico particularly controversial in the

United States, namely, environmental practices and labor policies in Mexico. Environmentalists were concerned that corporations would move to Mexico to take advantage of more relaxed environmental laws and that this would result in severe environmental degradation. Similarly, labor activists were concerned about corporations relocating to Mexico to take advantage of lax or nonexistent labor policy on minimum wages, health and safety, and child labor. These concerns led to the conclusion of side agreements in these areas in August 1993, which provided for cooperation and specific dispute-settlement mechanisms.

Another major concern over the conclusion of NAFTA in both the United States and Canada was the impact it would have on employment. There was serious concern that the much cheaper labor costs in Mexico would have a significant negative impact in Canada and the United States. The counterargument is that while jobs would disappear in inefficient sectors, by improving the economy as a whole, the NAFTA regime would result in overall employment increases.

Initially there was concern that regional trade agreements, like NAFTA, threatened the GATT multilateral trade system. However, the successful completion of the Uruguay Round has alleviated much of this concern and today it is commonly believed that regionalism pursued for the purpose of liberalizing trade is unlikely to jeopardize the multilateral trade regime achieved under GATT.

Looking Ahead

The study of international trade is a study of human interaction and development. From the cavemen trading furs for clubs to the agreements dealing with patents in superconductor technology, trade and trade agreements have played an important role in shaping human history. International trade has helped to enhance living standards by utilizing comparative advantage and by providing choice among diverse resources and products. Trade agreements, which originally were simple contracts between two parties, have evolved into complex, often multilateral, legislative agreements designed to promote predictability and stability in international trade and to keep the trade system open to increasing interaction.

Despite the objective of establishing and maintaining a liberal international trade regime, the future will probably see an increase in regulations involving international trade. This results from the increasingly complex nature of the international economy: there are more products, more facets of human interaction, and more participants involved than ever before. The agreement coming out of the Uruguay Round of GATT illustrates both the complexity and the changing nature of international agreements. In addition to traditional discussion about trade in goods, the Uruguay Round included discussion about trade in services and the protection of ideas. This reflects the expanded agenda of trade talks, which complements the expanded roles and expanded number of participants in the process. Not only has the agenda expanded, but the international trade system itself indicates a recent trend toward regional trade agreements, such as NAFTA, taken within the framework of GATT.

The conclusion of the Uruguay Round, the most recent round in the GATT process, does not signify that international trade regulations and relationships have been set in stone. New issues affecting international trade continue to arise—including the relationship between trade and the environment, rules regarding competitive practices, the place of immigration in an international trade regime, and the relationship between international security and trade.

Of the new items on the international agenda, the issue of the environment seems most likely to remain salient in the foreseeable future. Although the environment was not on the agenda of the Uruguay Round, the heated arguments and the necessity of side agreements on labor and the environment in NAFTA illustrate the importance environmental considerations have assumed in the 1990s.

Environment and trade tend to interact at two levels: political and legal. At the political level, environmental issues have been forced on to the trade agenda by citizens who fear that economic pressures will compromise environmental integrity and that this will be legitimized in international trade agreements. At the legal level, environmental concerns become disputes over conflicting national regulations. The dispute between the United States and Mexico over legislation protecting dolphins in the harvesting of tuna illustrates the conflict between national environmental regulations and international prohibitions on trade restrictions. The international trade regime is likely to be plagued by environmental disputes in the future as national legislation diverges widely. If the environmental movement is hijacked by protectionist interests that want to utilize the issue in order to create advantage for themselves, even more disruption will ensue.

The increased interaction among national economies and the increased linkages between domestic and international levels of government in trade ensures that new issues, such as the environment, will continue to arise to challenge the effectiveness of the international trade regime. To maintain a stable and open trading system in the future, the international trade regime must deal with two problems. First, it must deal with the problem of recent tendencies toward economic nationalism possibly leading to self-seeking nationalist actions that completely disrupt the system. And, second, the regime must be able to manage an increasingly large and complex international economic system. The will of major economic actors like the United States to maintain the system, and the flexibility of the system itself, will be crucial for the continuance of a liberal international trade regime.

GILBERT R. WINHAM
ANN GRIFFITHS

See also General Agreement on Tariffs and Trade; Reciprocal Trade Agreement Acts; Tariffs; World Trade Organization

FURTHER READING

Bhagwati, Jagdish. *Protectionism*. Cambridge, Mass., 1988.
Condliffe, J. B. *The Commerce of Nations*. New York, 1950.
Grimwade, Nigel. *New Patterns of Trade, Production and Investment*. London, 1989.
Hufbauer, Gary Clyde, and Jeffrey J. Schott. *North American Free Trade: Issues and Recommendations*. Washington D.C., 1992.
Jackson, John H. *The World Trading System: Law and Policy of International Economic Relations*. Cambridge, Mass., 1989.
————. *Restructuring the GATT System*. London, 1990.
Lawrence, Robert Z., and Charles L. Schultz, eds. *An American Trade Strategy: Options for the 1990s*. Washington D.C., 1990.
List, Frederick. *National Systems of Political Economy*. Trans. G.A. Matile. Philadelphia, 1856.
Morici, Peter, ed. *Making Free Trade Work: The Canada-U.S. Agreement*. New York, 1990.
Ohmae, Kenichi. *The Borderless World: Power and Strategy in the Interlinked World Economy*. New York, 1990.
Ostry, Sylvia. *Governments and Corporations in a Shrinking World*. New York, 1990.
Porter, Michael. *The Competitive Advantage of Nations*. New York, 1990.
Reich, Robert B. *The Work of Nations: Preparing Ourselves for 21st Century Capitalism*. New York, 1991.
Winham, Gilbert R. *International Trade and the Tokyo Round Negotiation*. Princeton, N.J., 1986.
————. *The Evolution of International Trade Agreement*. Toronto, 1992.

INTERNATIONAL TRADE COMMISSION

Semijudicial commission founded in 1916 as the Tariff Commission and renamed as a result of the 1974 Trade Act. The commission (ITC) has six members, of whom no more than three can be members of one political party. Members are appointed by the president for nine-year terms and are subject to confirmation by the senate. A member may serve no more than one full term. Although the commission conducts various studies of trade issues for the U.S. government, its primary role is to determine, or in some cases help to determine, whether a U.S. industry should be protected from imports. The commission carries out this function under three sections of U.S. trade law. Section 201–204 cases allow a U.S. industry to petition the commission to find that growing imports constitute a "substantial cause of serious injury." If the commission finds in the affirmative it makes recommendations to the president for relief. These cases are relatively rare. Section 337 cases involve claims by U.S. firms that foreign products are entering the United States and are infringing on their patents, copyrights, trademarks, or maskworks. If the commission finds that such infringement has occurred, it may issue a cease and desist order and exclude the violating products from the U.S. market. In rare cases, it also has imposed fines in Section 337 cases.

By far the most important role of the commission involves countervailing duty and dumping cases, which occur in large numbers. The Department of Commerce has the responsibility to determine whether foreign governments have provided subsidies on products sold in the United States or whether products have been sold here at less than fair market value. If the Department of Commerce finds that dumping or subsidization has occurred, it determines the percentage countervailing duty or dumping margin (tariff) that should be imposed. The role of the ITC is to determine whether the subsidies or dumping have been sufficient to impose serious injury on an existing U.S. industry.

During the 1970s and 1980s the Congress changed the relevant laws in ways that make it much easier for U.S. industries to file countervailing duty and dumping cases and make it much more likely that the Department of Commerce will find in favor of such industries. As a result, the number of such cases coming to the commission for a finding of injury has increased sharply. The commission has tended to be less supportive of protectionist measures than has the Department of Commerce. During the early 1990s, for example, the Department of Commerce supported rather dubious dumping charges against a large number of foreign steel companies, many of which were located in close allies of the United States such as Canada. Our trading partners were quite angry over this decision, and this issue threatened to become a continuing problem in U.S. foreign economic relations. The ITC, however, reversed the decision of the Department of Commerce in most of the cases, thereby calming what could have been a source of considerable difficulty for the United States. Decisions of the commission may be appealed to the Court of International Trade, which also sits in Washington, D.C.

ROBERT M. DUNN, JR.

See also Commerce, U.S. Department of; International Trade and Commerce; Tariffs

FURTHER READING

Dobson, John M. *Two Centuries of Tariffs: The Background and Emergence of the U.S. International Trade Commission*. Washington, D.C., 1976.
International Trade Commission. *Annual Report*. Washington, D.C.

INTERNATIONAL TRADE ORGANIZATION

International organization proposed as part of a 1945 U.S. plan for a multilateral commercial convention. The ITO was designed to administer and enforce post–World War II rules governing international trade and was to be a United Nations agency open to all UN members. The ITO never came into existence, however, because of opposition in the United States and Great Britain. The Havana Charter, as it was known, was submitted to Congress in 1949, but it was never put to a vote. Opponents included protectionists fearful that the ITO would direct U.S. trade policy and a coalition of American businesses that claimed that the charter contained too many barriers to free trade, including existing systems of trade preference. The General Agreement on Tariffs and Trade (GATT) signed in Geneva in 1947 was intended as a preliminary document to the ITO's establishment. As an executive agreement, GATT did not have to be submitted to Congress for ratification and thus became the main institution for achieving trade objectives in the Bretton Woods system. Plans for the ITO included a permanent secretariat and a conference of all members, each with one vote, plus an eighteen-member executive board. The drafters utilized the structure and terms of the 1934 U.S. Reciprocal Trade Program that established a comprehensive code of behavior for liberalizing trade. Because that program was limited to bilateral trade negotiations, the ITO (and GATT) represented efforts to move toward multilateral adoption and enforcement of trade rules. The ITO's draft charter endorsed broad principles and also contained commitments to avoid particular trade practices and specified circumstances under which exceptions would be allowed.

MARGARET P. KARNS

See also General Agreement on Tariffs and Trade; International Trade and Commerce; United Nations

FURTHER READING

Lenway, Stefanie Ann. *The Politics of U.S. International Trade: Protection, Expansion, and Escape.* Boston, 1985.
Pastor, Robert A. *Congress and the Politics of U.S. Foreign Economic Policy, 1929–1976.* Berkeley, 1980.

INTERNATIONAL WHALING COMMISSION

See Whaling

IRAN

Strategically situated Middle Eastern country bordering the Persian Gulf, Caspian Sea, the former Soviet Union, Afghanistan, Pakistan, Turkey, and Iraq. Rich in oil, Iran has played a key role in U.S. foreign relations as both an ally and an adversary since the end of World War II. After becoming increasingly involved in Iranian affairs during World War II and the immediate postwar period, the United States established a very close relationship with Iran in 1953 that lasted until the 1978–1979 Islamic revolution, a revolution that began an era of considerable hostility between the United States and Iran.

The United States established diplomatic relations with Iran—then known as Persia—in 1856. In the late nineteenth century contact between the two countries consisted primarily of missionary activity and archaeological expeditions. U.S.-Iranian relations gradually expanded in the first few decades of the twentieth century, with the United States acting as a benevolent alternative to Great Britain and Russia, who were vying to control southwestern Asia at that time. In the early 1920s Arthur Millspaugh, a U.S. citizen, was hired by the Iranian government to carry out fiscal reforms, helping to lay the groundwork for a modern economy. Together with a small coterie of teachers, missionaries, and archaeologists working in Iran, Millspaugh helped create a positive image for the United States among Iranians.

In September 1941, with war raging on two fronts in Europe, British and Soviet forces invaded Iran to establish a supply corridor to the Soviet Union. They quickly overpowered the Iranian army and forced Iran's monarch, Reza Shah Pahlavi, to abdicate in favor of his twenty-one-year-old son Mohammad Reza Pahlavi, who ruled Iran for the next thirty-seven years. Following U.S. entry into World War II, the U.S. Army sent troops to Iran in conjunction with this supply operation, initiating a period in which U.S.-Iranian relations grew rapidly in scope and magnitude. By early 1944 some 30,000 U.S. soldiers were stationed in Iran, guarding the supply route against bandits and German agents, expanding and improving Iran's transportation system and oil production facilities, and building plants to assemble aircraft, trucks, and oil drums. The United States sent military missions under the command of General Clarence Ridley and Colonel Norman Schwarzkopf, Sr., to Iran to reorganize and train the Iranian army and gendarmerie. Millspaugh returned to Iran as an economic adviser in 1942, and the United States provided Iran with $8.5 million in lend-lease aid during the war. By 1944 U.S.-Iranian relations had grown sufficiently that a diplomat of ambassadorial rank for the first time was sent to Tehran to head the U.S. embassy.

Relations During the Early Cold War

As the German threat eased in 1944, the Soviet Union began to expand its influence in the areas of northwestern Iran it was occupying and sought oil concessions in those areas from the hapless Iranian government. The

Soviet posture toward Iran grew more menacing in early 1945 and began to be perceived by U.S. policymakers as part of a global Soviet effort to expand its sphere of influence. U.S. officials began to pressure the Soviets to withdraw their troops from Iran in accordance with pledges made during the war by the Allied occupying powers. Soviet leaders demurred, and in December 1945 and January 1946 Soviet-backed rebels in the Iranian provinces of Azerbaijan and Kurdistan proclaimed the establishment of independent states known as the Autonomous Republic of Azerbaijan and the Kurdish People's Republic.

The Iranian government sought backing from the United States and Great Britain and petitioned the newly established United Nations Security Council to demand Soviet withdrawal. U.S. officials issued notes of protest to the Soviet government and strongly supported the Iranian position in the Security Council. In a deliberate show of force, also in part prompted by the related crises in Greece and Turkey, the U.S. battleship *Missouri* was dispatched to Istanbul. Against this backdrop, Iranian Prime Minister Ahmad Qavam traveled to Moscow in March 1946 and negotiated an agreement under which Soviet troops would be withdrawn in exchange for an oil concession, which was subject to approval by the Iranian parliament. The Soviet Union withdrew its troops shortly thereafter and Iranian troops reoccupied Azerbaijan and Kurdistan in December 1946, ending the uprisings in these provinces. The Iranian parliament later soundly defeated a bill establishing the Soviet oil concession, closing one of the first chapters in the Cold War.

As the Azerbaijan crisis was ending, the Department of State conducted a thorough review of U.S. interests in Iran, concluding that Iran was vital to U.S. strategic interests because of its location between the Soviet Union and the Persian Gulf oil fields. Despite this finding, Iran did not receive anything like the large aid package given under the Truman Doctrine to Greece and Turkey. The United States did, however, slowly increase its involvement in Iran in other ways. The military training missions begun during World War II were renegotiated and extended in 1947 and 1948. The U.S. embassy staff grew considerably, enhancing diplomatic, commercial, and cultural interactions between the two countries. The Central Intelligence Agency (CIA) established a station in Tehran, taking over intelligence operations previously conducted by U.S. military attachés and embassy political officers.

By early 1950 unrest had grown considerably in Iran. This unrest was being mobilized by two main organizations: the communist Tudeh (Masses) party, which was closely aligned with the Soviet Union; and the National Front, a coalition of organizations and individuals led by a charismatic member of parliament, Mohammad Mosad-

deq, whose main goals were to nationalize Iran's British-controlled oil industry and democratize its political system. At the same time, the U.S. National Security Council (NSC) was undertaking a major reevaluation of U.S. global strategy, a document that came to be known as NSC-68. The new approach called for a stronger and more global effort to contain the Soviet Union and placed greater emphasis on strengthening countries located along the Sino-Soviet periphery. While NSC-68 was never fully and formally approved, its strategy nevertheless largely took hold. As applied to Iran, this strategy led U.S. policymakers to establish sizable military and economic aid programs and greatly increase the U.S. presence in Iran during the next few years.

In late April 1951 the shah bowed to popular pressure and appointed Mosaddeq prime minister. Mosaddeq then nationalized the oil industry, leading the British to organize a global boycott of Iranian oil exports and make repeated attempts to overthrow him. Under the administration of President Harry S. Truman, the United States played a relatively evenhanded role in the growing confrontation, trying to mediate the oil dispute, pressing both sides to make concessions, continuing to provide limited military and economic aid to Iran, and blocking a September 1951 British plan to invade Iran. At the same time, however, the CIA sharply increased its activities in Iran, taking steps to undermine Mosaddeq's base of support.

By late 1952 many U.S. officials had concluded that Mosaddeq had to be overthrown to resolve the deepening crisis and prevent Soviet influence from growing in Iran. Soon after the inauguration of President Dwight D. Eisenhower in 1953, the administration began to make plans to overthrow Mosaddeq. In February 1953 Kermit Roosevelt, head of the CIA's Middle East operations division and grandson of President Theodore Roosevelt, was put in charge of efforts to organize a coup to overthrow Mosaddeq. Roosevelt traveled to Great Britain and Iran several times in the following months, meeting with British officials, members of the Tehran CIA station, and certain influential Iranians to organize the coup and persuading the shah to support it. In July 1953 the CIA began an extensive covert political action effort to destabilize Mosaddeq's regime. On 16 August the shah dismissed Mosaddeq and appointed Fazlollah Zahedi prime minister. Roosevelt's team of CIA officers then hired large crowds to demonstrate against Mosaddeq and persuaded several top army commanders to deploy their troops in support of Zahedi. After several days of turmoil Mosaddeq was forced to surrender.

In the following weeks Zahedi's forces arrested some 1,400 Mosaddeq supporters and Tudeh members and carried out a purge of the armed forces and government bureaucracy. This wave of repression continued for more than a year, silencing all sources of opposition to the new regime. The CIA assisted this effort by providing the security forces with intelligence and conducting covert operations against certain opposition elements. Within weeks of the coup the United States also provided the new government with approximately $70 million in emergency financial assistance, accounting for roughly one-third of the income Iran had lost since May 1951 because of the oil embargo. U.S. officials also helped resolve the oil dispute, thus permitting Iran to resume oil exports. These various initiatives enabled the post-coup government gradually to consolidate power.

In early 1955 an Eisenhower administration policy review concluded that Iran needed to be transformed into an effective bulwark against Soviet expansionism. This effort had three main components. First, a long-term $600 million economic aid program was established aimed at promoting economic growth and thus presumably reducing unrest. Second, Iran's internal security forces were to be reorganized and strengthened. The most important element of this effort was a CIA initiative begun in late 1953 to establish and train a new intelligence agency, known as SAVAK, which over the next twenty-five years became not just an externally directed intelligence agency but also a powerful, feared, and hated instrument of domestic repression. Third, the United States began to reorganize, train, and reequip the Iranian armed forces and integrate them into the U.S. global defense network through the Baghdad Pact, later known as the Central Treaty Organization (CENTO). In return, the shah cooperated with the United States in a variety of ways, including permitting the CIA to establish electronic intelligence-gathering facilities in northern Iran aimed at the Soviet missile testing sites in Central Asia. These facilities remained operational until after the 1978–1979 revolution, providing the United States with critically important intelligence data.

The U.S. role in the 1953 coup and the U.S. assistance provided to Iran thereafter had a considerable impact on Iranian domestic politics, strengthening the shah and weakening the opposition. By the late 1950s a strong authoritarian regime had been established in Iran. U.S. officials, however, were becoming increasingly concerned that political unrest might reemerge. They began to encourage the shah to carry out reforms. The shah responded by easing restrictions on opposition political activity and undertaking socioeconomic reforms, including an extensive land reform program, a major expansion of educational and health care facilities, and the enfranchisement of women. The more open political environment in this period produced an upsurge of opposition political activity. Unwilling to tolerate meaningful opposition, and with a strong security apparatus in place, the shah cracked down in 1962 and 1963, reestablishing the repressive regime that had existed in the mid-1950s.

Resenting this pressure for reform, the shah also began to distance himself from the United States in the late 1950s and early 1960s, ending the SAVAK training program and certain other joint activities and significantly but cautiously improving his relations with the Soviet Union. Relations between the United States and Iran eased further in the mid-1960s, when Iran's growing oil revenue and pressing needs elsewhere led U.S. policymakers to scale back and eventually terminate the U.S. military and economic aid programs in Iran. Consequently, Iran's relations with the United States evolved from the near-total dependence of the mid-1950s to a much more evenhanded relationship based on mutual interests by the late 1960s.

The Shah: At His Peak, Toward His Demise

The shah, at the pinnacle of his power in the early 1970s, seemingly unchallenged by domestic opposition, and enjoying rapidly growing oil income, began to play an increasingly active role in regional and world affairs. The general thrust of his foreign policy was to combat radical forces in the region and expand Iran's regional and global influence. Toward these ends he became increasingly antagonistic toward Arab radicalism, sending Iranian troops to help suppress the Dhofar uprising in Oman, undertaking covert operations against various radical Arab forces, and establishing a close albeit mostly quiet relationship with Israel. He also worked with Saudi Arabia and other conservative Arab states against radical forces in sub-Saharan Africa. U.S. officials strongly encouraged the shah to undertake these activities, assisting him in various ways.

In the 1970s Iran came to be viewed as a prototype for the Nixon Doctrine—a "regional policeman" that would help defend Western interests against Soviet-sponsored forces. The administration of President Richard M. Nixon therefore initiated a massive arms sales program to Iran, giving the shah permission to purchase any nonnuclear weapons in the U.S. arsenal. At the same time the shah was careful to maintain autonomy from the United States, frequently criticizing the West and pursuing a more independent foreign policy. The most important manifestation of this greater independence was the shah's leading role in raising oil prices within the Organization of Petroleum Exporting Countries (OPEC) from 1971 through 1973—actions that set the stage for the 1973 oil embargo by the Arab members of OPEC. Although as a non-Arab state Iran sold oil to the United States during the embargo, the shah's role in these events helped trigger major U.S. and world recessions.

Despite the shah's aura of omnipotence, domestic unrest grew considerably in Iran during the 1970s. The first manifestation of this unrest was the emergence of several leftist and Islamic guerrilla groups in the early

1970s that attacked symbols of the shah's regime and the U.S. presence in Iran. The security forces suppressed these groups mercilessly, severely weakening them. Realizing that unrest was widespread, the shah also cracked down harshly on moderate opposition elements and placed strict new curbs on the press. As Iran's economy overheated following the oil boom of the early and mid-1970s, unrest grew further, reaching alarming levels by 1977. Moreover, although it was not publicly known at the time, the shah was stricken with cancer in 1974, which as the disease worsened often had the effect of clouding his judgment and undermining his self-confidence.

During his 1976 presidential campaign Jimmy Carter had criticized Iran's poor human rights record and pledged to restrict U.S. arms sales abroad. After Carter was elected the shah became deeply concerned that the United States would again pressure him to carry out domestic reforms and deny him access to advanced weaponry. Once in office, however, Carter failed to press the shah on these matters and lavishly praised him when they met in Washington and Tehran, leaving the shah uncertain about his relationship with the United States.

Reacting to the increasing domestic unrest and the growing concern in the United States and Europe about human rights conditions in Iran, in late 1976 the shah began to signal that he would permit limited political liberalization. In response, several intellectuals circulated open letters criticizing the shah. When no effort was made to stop this dissent, a variety of secular opposition organizations began to emerge. At the same time followers of the Ayatollah Ruhollah Khomeini, the leading Shiite cleric in Iran and a long-time political opponent of the shah, became increasingly active, agitating against the shah's regime through their network of mosques and seminaries. Following the publication of a newspaper article in January 1978 that libeled and criticized Khomeini, the Khomeinists held a large demonstration in Qom that was brutally suppressed by the security forces, resulting in several deaths. In accordance with Shia practice, demonstrations were held forty days later to mourn for those killed, and again the security forces responded violently. Additional demonstrations were held forty days later, establishing a pattern that continued into the summer of 1978. Secular opposition forces joined in these demonstrations, producing a united front against the shah's regime.

U.S. officials reacted to the growing turmoil by expressing strong support for the shah and downplaying the threat to his regime. President Carter made a highly publicized trip to Iran for New Year's Eve of 1977, toasting the shah's Iran as "an island of stability in one of the more troubled areas of the world." Carter and other U.S. officials echoed this theme throughout 1978, publicly praising the shah and dismissing the idea that a revolution was in progress. During the summer and fall of 1978, CIA and State Department officials produced analyses that concluded that the shah would survive the deepening crisis. These statements and analyses conflicted sharply with accounts appearing in the press and emanating from the U.S. embassy in Tehran, and served to reinforce the shah's complacency. Satisfied with these analyses, Carter and his top foreign policy advisers preoccupied themselves with the Camp David negotiations and paid scant attention to Iran. The first clear signal that a major problem existed came in a 1 November cable sent from Tehran by Ambassador William Sullivan. He reported that the shah was considering abdication, claiming that he could only remain in power by governing through the military. A week later Sullivan expanded on this pessimistic assessment in a cable titled "Thinking the Unthinkable," arguing that the shah had little chance of remaining in power. Sullivan's views shocked the foreign policy bureaucracy in Washington and set off a wave of infighting and recrimination but produced no immediate change in U.S. policy.

By early December 1978 the shah's position had become increasingly untenable, and he initiated negotiations with moderate opposition figures aimed at establishing a coalition government that would preserve the monarchy while greatly reducing its powers. U.S. officials publicly continued to express support for the shah, but privately they were deeply divided, with National Security Adviser Zbigniew Brzezinski arguing for a hard-line approach aimed at keeping the shah in power and Secretary of State Cyrus Vance and other State Department officials calling for a dialogue with the opposition aimed at establishing a broad-based coalition government. Moreover, communication between Washington and Ambassador Sullivan was erratic and often confused, leading him increasingly to act on his own. The U.S. foreign policy bureaucracy was thus unable to formulate a coherent policy toward the crisis or even provide useful advice to the shah.

Ayatollah Khomeini and the Islamic Revolution

On 30 December the shah appointed Shahpour Bakhtiar, a moderate National Front leader, to head a coalition government. A few days later the shah privately told Ambassador Sullivan that he was preparing to take a long "vacation" abroad. U.S. officials began to coalesce around a policy of supporting Bakhtiar and shoring up the armed forces, which they viewed as a critical pillar of stability and bulwark against Soviet penetration. They sent U.S. General Robert Huyser to Tehran to maintain liaison with the armed forces and secure sensitive U.S. military and intelligence equipment located in Iran. The Bakhtiar government was quickly denounced by Ayatollah Khomeini and other opposition leaders, rendering it ineffective. Nevertheless, U.S. officials established contact with Khomeini's entourage in Paris, urging them to support Bakhtiar. The shah left Iran for exile in Egypt on 16 January 1979 and the armed forces began to disintegrate. With their efforts to create a friendly government now in ruins, U.S. officials began to engage in damage control, terminating military contracts, trying to safeguard sensitive equipment, and evacuating U.S. citizens from Iran. Khomeini returned triumphantly on 1 February, sweeping Bakhtiar from power and dealing a major blow to U.S. influence and prestige in the region.

Khomeini installed a provisional government headed by Mehdi Bazargan, a long-time National Front leader relatively friendly toward the West. Bazargan and his associates represented only the moderate, secular wing of the revolutionary movement, and they were soon challenged by members of the more radical, Islamist wing. U.S. officials tried to establish a good relationship with the Bazargan government, hoping to protect U.S. interests and end the anarchy. Bazargan reciprocated by maintaining a dialogue with the U.S. embassy and cooperating with it on a variety of matters. At the same time, however, the CIA began to work closely with opponents of Khomeini, both inside Iran and in Europe and the United States. Khomeini and many of his followers had long been extremely suspicious of the United States, believing that the U.S. embassy was working against them. Therefore, with the Bazargan government exercising only limited authority in Tehran, the U.S. embassy staff was in considerable danger in the months after Khomeini's return to Iran. Indeed, Iranian militants briefly seized the U.S. embassy compound on 14 February, holding the ambassador and his staff hostage for several hours until the Bazargan government was able to intervene. Despite this incident, an effective, although distant, working relationship emerged between the two governments in the spring and summer of 1979.

The shah had been seeking asylum in the United States since his departure from Iran in January, working in part through Henry Kissinger and David Rockefeller, both of whom had long personal as well as professional relationships with him and who repeatedly pressed the Carter administration to admit him. U.S. officials demurred, fearing for the safety of U.S. citizens remaining in Iran. In September 1979 the Carter administration was informed that the shah had cancer and urgently needed treatment. Carter therefore agreed to admit the shah in late October, fully realizing the dangers this posed for U.S. embassy personnel and other U.S. citizens in Iran. Several days later, on 4 November, a group of student militants seized the U.S. embassy compound and took some seventy embassy staff members hostage.

Ayatollah Khomeini and the radical Islamist wing of the revolutionary movement immediately praised the hostage-

takers and launched a barrage of criticism against Bazargan and his moderate colleagues, making the hostages pawns in the struggle to control the revolution. Bazargan initially tried to free the hostages, but the unrelenting attacks against him forced him to resign from office two days after the takeover. The successor government was much more radical—although it included a few moderates—and it showed no inclination to release the hostages promptly. The Carter administration began a series of public and private diplomatic efforts aimed at freeing the hostages and imposed a series of economic sanctions on Iran. It also quietly began to make contingency plans for a military operation to free the hostages. Although thirteen female and minority-group embassy staff members were released in mid-November at the request of Palestine Liberation Organization (PLO) Chairman Yasser Arafat, U.S. diplomatic and economic initiatives made little headway. The shah left the United States for Panama on 16 December, but this too had no effect.

In late December 1979 the Soviet Union invaded Afghanistan, sharply increasing tensions in the region and leading the United States to unveil the Carter Doctrine, which voiced a strong reaffirmation of the U.S. commitment to deter and contain Soviet influence in the Persian Gulf region, including through the use of military force. This event put additional pressure on the Carter administration to resolve the hostage crisis. U.S. officials therefore began secret negotiations with the Iranian government through two Paris-based intermediaries. When these negotiations collapsed in early April 1980, Carter decided to break diplomatic relations with Iran and approved a complicated military operation to rescue the hostages. The operation began on 24 April, when eight helicopters carrying Delta Force commandos took off for Iran from the USS *Nimitz* in the Arabian Sea. By the time they reached their initial destination in central Iran, three of the helicopters had malfunctioned, leading the commander to cancel the mission. During refueling one of the helicopters collided with a cargo plane, causing an explosion that killed eight crew members and forced the commando team to abandon the remaining helicopters and evacuate the site. News of the failed rescue mission quickly spread, provoking celebrations in Tehran and intense anguish in the United States. Secretary of State Vance, who had opposed the rescue mission, promptly resigned, and Carter's presidency was severely damaged.

The rescue attempt had been the last viable U.S. option for resolving the hostage crisis, and no new initiatives were undertaken in the following months. In Iran the radical Islamist wing of the revolutionary movement was consolidating its control over the revolution, marginalizing the moderates who had been willing to negotiate with the United States but also making the hostages less valuable in the internecine struggle. Several coup attempts occurred in the summer of 1980 and tension with Iraq escalated sharply, culminating in Iraq's September 1980 invasion of Iran, which the United States at the time officially condemned. The shah died of cancer in late July, obviating the main pretext for keeping the hostages. These events and economic crises led Iran's revolutionary leaders increasingly to regard the hostage crisis as a liability in the summer of 1980. In September they sent a message to U.S. officials through the German ambassador in Tehran that they would release the hostages if certain relatively innocuous conditions were met. It is also widely rumored—but not fully substantiated—that Iranian officials made a deal with members of Ronald Reagan's presidential campaign staff in this period to delay release of the hostages until after the November U.S. presidential election. For whatever reason, negotiations over Iran's proposal dragged on past the 4 November election, culminating only on 19 January—one day before Reagan's inauguration. The hostages were finally released at 12:30 P.M. on 20 January—thirty minutes after Reagan was inaugurated.

The Reagan administration entered office without coherent plans for U.S. policy toward Iran. The hostage crisis had created intense animosity toward Iran in the United States and diplomatic relations between the two countries had been severed, making normal relations impossible. Moreover, Iran had begun to export its Islamic revolution in 1979 and these efforts grew rapidly in the early 1980s, most notably in the Persian Gulf region and in Lebanon, where Iranian Revolutionary Guards began to arm and train Hezbollah (Party of God) and other guerrilla groups. It was these groups that took a number of U.S. citizens hostage in Lebanon and that conducted the October 1983 bombing of the U.S. marines barracks in Beirut, killing 241. Nevertheless, many Reagan administration officials continued to believe that Iran could be useful to the United States in helping to contain Soviet influence and pin down the huge Iraqi military machine to prevent it from attacking Israel. As a result, U.S. policy toward Iran remained confused and contradictory during Reagan's first term in office.

The Reagan administration publicly criticized Iran, continued most of the economic sanctions, and initiated a highly visible campaign called Operation Staunch to block foreign arms sales to Iran. Quietly, however, it decided to eschew efforts to overthrow the revolutionary regime in Tehran and even to facilitate Iran's arms acquisition efforts—most notably by authorizing Israel to sell it advanced U.S.-made military equipment. At the same time the Reagan administration became increasingly supportive of Iraq, expanding diplomatic contacts, providing agricultural export credits, allowing U.S. manufacturers to sell civilian aircraft and other defense-related equipment to it, and making no effort to prevent European and Arab countries from selling military equipment to Iraq. This tilt toward Iraq increased in 1983, after Iranian forces made important battlefield gains.

Using a field station in Frankfurt, West Germany, the CIA expanded its relations with several Iranian exile opposition groups in the early 1980s and gave them financial assistance. Although the CIA's main purpose in working with these groups was to make use of their contacts inside Iran as sources of intelligence, it also helped them in limited ways to carry out propaganda activities and perhaps other covert operations in Iran. The CIA also began to build its own network of agents inside Iran in the early 1980s to provide it with military and political intelligence, including agents in the Iranian foreign ministry, the Iranian navy, and possibly other branches of the armed forces. The CIA and other U.S. government agencies appear not to have provided any assistance to the Mojahedin-e Khalq, the only opposition group that posed much of a threat to the Khomeini regime. In 1982 the CIA and the British intelligence agency together also provided the Iranian government with a wealth of intelligence about the Tudeh party obtained from a Soviet defector, enabling the Iranian government to arrest hundreds of Tudeh members in early 1983, killing many, and effectively destroying this organization.

In the summer of 1985 CIA Director William Casey began to urge President Reagan to approve an initiative to establish informal contacts with Iran, mainly to seek Iranian help in gaining release of several U.S. citizens held hostage in Lebanon. At the same time Israeli officials approached National Security Adviser Robert McFarlane with a plan to sell U.S. arms to Iran in exchange for release of some of the hostages. Reagan approved this plan, and several shipments of TOW anti-tank missiles and other advanced equipment worth some $100 million were sent to Iran during the following year. Three U.S. hostages were released as a result of these efforts, although Lebanese militants seized three others at about the same time. U.S. officials also provided Iran with intelligence about the Iraqi war effort, even though they were simultaneously selling arms and providing intelligence about Iran's war effort to Iraq. NSC staff member Oliver North, a key figure in these events, diverted some of the profits from the arms sales to the Contra rebels fighting against Nicaragua's Sandinista government. In November 1986 information about these activities was published in a Lebanese newspaper and soon became known in the United States. The U.S. Congress and later a special prosecutor investigated these activities and exposed the Iran-Contra affair.

After the Iran-Contra affair came to light, official statements were made that the United States had no hostile intentions toward Iran, but in an effort to distance itself from the fiasco the Reagan administration in fact became much more hostile toward Iran during the next two years. It quickly suspended the arms sales program that had been at the heart of the Iran-Contra affair and presumably stopped providing Iran with intelligence as well. After Iran and Iraq began to attack civilian shipping in the Persian Gulf in early 1987, the United States acceded to a request by Kuwait that it protect and reflag Kuwaiti oil tankers. By the end of the year as many as forty-eight U.S. Navy warships were stationed in the Persian Gulf, and Kuwaiti tankers were sailing under the U.S. flag to discourage Iranian attacks. Because Kuwaiti oil revenue was helping to finance the Iraqi war effort, and as Iraq continued to attack Iranian tankers, this represented a clear U.S. tilt toward Iraq's side in the war. Iran reacted to the U.S. presence in the Persian Gulf with great hostility, laying mines where they could—and eventually did—hit U.S.-flagged Kuwaiti tankers and threaten to attack U.S. warships. The United States also pressed the UN Security Council to impose an international arms embargo on Iran, although this effort was blocked by the Soviet Union.

There were numerous clashes and other incidents between U.S. and Iranian forces in the Persian Gulf over the next fifteen months. The culmination came in July 1988, when the USS *Vincennes* mistakenly shot down an Iranian civilian airliner, killing 290 passengers and crew members. Iran reacted with great fury, and it is widely believed that in retaliation the Iranian government or forces close to it arranged to bomb a Pan Am commercial airliner over Lockerbie, Scotland, in December 1988. Although the Iran-Iraq war ended in July 1988, obviating the need for a large U.S. presence in the Persian Gulf, tension between the United States and Iran remained high for the remainder of Reagan's term.

Prospects for improved relations between the United States and Iran, which did not seem good when George Bush was inaugurated in January 1989, worsened several weeks later, when Khomeini issued an edict pronouncing a death sentence on British author Salman Rushdie, whose novel *The Satanic Verses* had allegedly slandered Islam. After the death of Khomeini in June 1989, however, the Bush administration apparently decided to test whether U.S. relations with Iran could improve under the new regime by making a series of conciliatory gestures. Soon after Khomeini's death, U.S. officials unexpectedly offered to pay compensation to the relatives of Iranians killed in the airliner shot down by the *Vincennes*. Several weeks later, following the execution of a U.S. military officer held hostage by pro-Iranian guerrillas in Lebanon, the Bush administration began negotiations with Iran aimed at securing release of the remaining U.S. hostages. These negotiations produced an agreement in November 1989 under which the United States released $567 million of Iranian assets that had been frozen since 1979. Two

hostages were later released, prompting U.S. officials to issue a public statement thanking Iran for its help. Further agreements were signed during the next two years releasing additional Iranian assets and resolving other minor disputes. The last U.S. hostages were finally released in late 1991, at least partly through Iranian pressure.

Following Iraq's invasion of Kuwait in August 1990, Iran condemned both the invasion and the subsequent U.S.-led military buildup in the region. Although it reestablished diplomatic relations with Iraq shortly after the invasion and permitted a limited amount of cross-border smuggling to occur in violation of the UN trade embargo, Iran remained essentially neutral in the confrontation that culminated in the Gulf War of 1990–1991. U.S. officials were evidently pleased with Iran's benign posture during this period and with its failure to disrupt the post–Gulf War UN trade and weapons embargoes and de facto partition of Iraq.

Despite the release of the remaining U.S. hostages and Iran's benign posture toward Iraq, U.S. relations with Iran grew more tense during the final years of the Bush administration. U.S. officials increasingly expressed their displeasure at Iran's post–Gulf War military buildup, its alleged efforts to develop nuclear weapons, its support for anti-Western Islamist groups throughout the region, its opposition to the Arab-Israeli peace negotiations, its refusal to lift the death sentence decreed for Rushdie, its poor human rights record, and its apparent assassination of Iranian dissidents and other foes living abroad. Moreover, with the breakup of the Soviet Union in 1991 and declining world oil prices, Iran's proximity to the Persian Gulf oil fields became less significant to U.S. national security. The Bush administration therefore made no further effort to improve relations with Iran, leading Iranian officials to complain bitterly that their efforts to improve relations with the United States had not been reciprocated.

The administration of President Bill Clinton was even more hostile toward Iran during its first year in office. In March 1993 Secretary of State Warren Christopher branded Iran an "international outlaw" because of its alleged support for international terrorism and efforts to build nuclear weapons. The Clinton Persian Gulf strategy was dubbed "dual containment," implying that rather than once again trying a regional balance of power strategy of siding with Iran or Iraq against the other, U.S. interests required containing both. The administration contended that it was the Iranian government's policies and not the regime itself that it opposed and that should the regime change its policies, improved relations were possible. Tightened economic sanctions were to be one of the principal components of this strategy. However, the administration had limited success persuading the European allies to do much more than restrict technologies and other exports which had direct military applications.

The problem was compounded by efforts in 1995–1996 by the Republican Congress to claim extraterritoriality for U.S. sanctions and impose penalties including loss of certain trade privileges with the United States on European companies that continued to trade with or invest in the Iranian oil and gas sectors. The Clinton administration thus found its strategy of economic pressure squeezed on the one side by allies who wanted to do less and on the other by the Congress which wanted to do more. Nevertheless the administration claimed that it still was having some impact, adding some economic hardship to an already problematic domestic economic situation within Iran.

Still, though, the Clinton administration tagged Iran as continuing to support terrorism, including links to Hamas in the Palestinian territories and Hezbollah in Lebanon, and seeking to develop weapons of mass destruction. While on the one hand such claims were used to justify continuation of the dual containment strategy, on the other hand critics based their case for more flexibility on the failure of existing policy to have achieved its own stated objectives. What was clear, though, was that U.S.-Iranian relations remained quite antagonistic, with little prospect foreseeable for significant improvement.

Mark J. Gasiorowski

See also Abrams, Elliott; Azerbaijan; Brzezinski, Zbigniew; Bush, George Herbert Walker; Carter, James Earl; Carter Doctrine; Casey, William Joseph; Central Intelligence Agency; Central Treaty Organization; Christopher, Warren Minor; Covert Action; Eisenhower, Dwight David; Gulf War of 1990–1991; Iran-Contra Affair; Iraq; Khomeini, Ruhollah; Kissinger, Henry Alfred; Kurds; McFarlane, Robert Carl; Middle East; Mosaddeq, Mohammad; National Security Agency; National Security Council; North, Oliver Lawrence; NSC-68; Organization of Petroleum Exporting Countries; Pan Am Flight 103; Reagan, Ronald Wilson; Shah of Iran; Terrorism; Truman, Harry S.; Vance, Cyrus Roberts

FURTHER READING

Alexander, Yonah, and Allan Names, eds. *The United States and Iran: A Documentary History*. Frederick, Md., 1980.

Bill, James A. *The Eagle and the Lion: The Tragedy of American-Iranian Relations*. New Haven, Conn., 1988.

Cottam, Richard W. *Iran and the United States: A Cold War Case Study*. Pittsburgh, Pa., 1988.

Gasiorowski, Mark J. *U.S. Foreign Policy and the Shah: Building a Client State in Iran*. Ithaca, N.Y., 1991.

Keddie, Nikki R., and Mark J. Gasiorowski, eds. *Neither East Nor West: Iran, the Soviet Union, and the United States*. New Haven, Conn., 1990.

Kuniholm, Bruce Robellet. *The Origins of the Cold War in the Near East*. Princeton, N.J., 1980.

Motter, T. Vail. *United States Army in World War II: The Middle East Theater, The Persian Corridor, and Aid to Russia*. Washington, D.C., 1952.

Ramazani, Rouhollah K. *The United States and Iran: The Patterns of Influence*. New York, 1982.

Sick, Gary. *All Fall Down: America's Tragic Encounter with Iran*. New York, 1985.

Yeselson, Abraham. *United States-Persian Diplomatic Relations, 1883–1921*. New Brunswick, N.J., 1956.

IRAN-CONTRA AFFAIR

A series of secret foreign policy initiatives conducted by the administration of President Ronald Reagan in the mid-1980s. At the heart of the affair were two different Reagan policies that later became linked: selling arms to Iran in exchange for the freeing of American hostages held in Lebanon; and providing secret military support to the rebel forces, or Contras, who were fighting Nicaragua's leftist Sandinista government. The revelation of these initiatives in the fall of 1986 dealt a blow to the foreign policy credibility and domestic political standing of the Reagan administration. The result was an investigation by a presidential review board, a year-long Congressional investigation, and a seven-year criminal inquiry by an independent counsel. The affair and its aftermath raised a number of questions concerning the foreign policy powers of the executive and legislative branches, the use of secrecy in foreign policy, and responsibility for abuses committed under superior orders.

The principal actors in the affair were Central Intelligence Agency Director William Casey and three officials from the National Security Council (NSC) staff, National Security Adviser Robert McFarlane, his successor, John Poindexter, and NSC aide Oliver North. In 1984, after Congress terminated secret CIA military assistance for the Contras, NSC officials continued to provide them with secret military advice and to raise funds for them from private citizens and foreign governments. In response to questioning by Congress in 1984 and 1985, NSC officials falsely denied that they were providing such assistance.

In an effort to free U.S. hostages held by pro-Iranian Islamic fundamentalist groups in Lebanon, in November 1985 President Reagan secretly approved a U.S. government role in the transfer of U.S. arms (initially TOW antitank missiles Iran wanted for its war against Iraq) from Israel to Iran. The president approved additional sales in late 1985 and early 1986, over the objections of Secretary of Defense Caspar Weinberger and Secretary of State George Shultz, who argued that the sales violated U.S. law, were contrary to the U.S. policy of refusing to bargain with hostage-takers, and contravened the U.S.-led arms embargo against Iran.

When the arms sales came to light in late 1986, administration officials initially said they were intended to cultivate moderates in Iran's government. Officials later acknowledged, however, that the sales were essentially arms-for-hostages swaps. Poindexter admitted destroying the presidential "finding" authorizing the first arms sale, which characterized it as an arms-for-hostage deal, in order to save the president from political embarrassment.

The Nicaragua and Iran initiatives became linked in late 1985, when NSC officials diverted arms sales profits to the Contras. Neither Congress nor the independent counsel found evidence confirming that President Reagan was aware of this diversion. Congressional investigators found that the Contras ultimately received $3.8 million of the $16.1 million generated by the sales. Private intermediaries took an estimated $6.5 million in commissions and profits. The rest of the surplus was spent on secret operations in Central America and the Middle East or deposited, and later frozen, in Swiss bank accounts.

On 1 December 1986, several days after the diversion of funds to the Contras was disclosed, President Reagan appointed a three-member Special Review Board, chaired by former Senator John Tower, to investigate the role of the NSC in the Iran-Contra affair. The board, which was known as the Tower Commission, concluded its review the following February. It attributed the Iran-Contra Affair to the failure of White House officials to follow standard procedures for making and implementing policy decisions. The Board also criticized President Reagan for inadequately monitoring and directing his staff's performance.

In their final report on the affair, the house and senate investigating committees concluded that executive branch officials used secrecy "not as a shield against our adversaries, but as a weapon against our own democratic institutions." According to the report, "officials holding no elected office," who "believed that they alone knew what was right," repeatedly defied Congress's efforts to perform its constitutional foreign policy oversight role. This defiance of Congress "created the conditions for policy failure" and led to "contradictions" between public and secret policies that "undermined the credibility of the United States." The committees concluded that it was the president's policy—not the decision of his subordinates—to sell arms directly to Iran and to use U.S. government resources to keep the Contras intact. The president also "created or at least tolerated an environment" in which senior officials felt justified in evading the law and misleading Congress. "For failing to take care that the law reigned supreme," the final report stated, "the president bears the responsibility."

In Congressional testimony, several key Iran-Contra figures argued that the ends they sought justified the means they employed, that they did not violate any laws, and that their activities were consistent with the president's explicit and implicit wishes. Independent counsel Lawrence Walsh brought criminal charges against fourteen participants in the Iran-Contra affair. Most of the charges related to efforts to conceal the affair when it broke into public view. Of the fourteen people charged, eleven either pleaded guilty or were convicted in trial. The convictions of Oliver North and John Poindexter were overturned when appeals courts ruled that their immunized 1987 congressional testimony had tainted the testimony of several witnesses during their trials. In December 1992 President George Bush pardoned six Iran-Contra defendants, including former Secretary of Defense Caspar Weinberger, whose case had not yet gone to trial, and former Assistant Secretary of State Elliott Abrams.

Walsh came under substantial criticism for the length, cost, and character of his investigation, which closed down in January 1994. In his final report Walsh concluded that efforts to cover up the affair were more concerted than Congress had realized in 1987, that Vice President George Bush and other senior officials were better informed about the Iran arms sales than they said they had been, and that relevant documents were withheld from investigators. The Iran-Contra affair resulted from "executive branch efforts to evade congressional oversight," wrote Walsh, not "rogue operations" by zealous officials.

LEE H. HAMILTON

See also Abrams, Elliott; Bush, George Herbert Walker; Casey, William Joseph; Contras; Iran; McFarlane, Robert Carl; National Security Council; Nicaragua; North, Oliver Lawrence; Reagan, Ronald Wilson

FURTHER READING

Draper, Theodore. *A Very Thin Line: The Iran-Contra Affairs.* New York, 1991.

U.S. House of Representatives Select Committee to Investigate Covert Arms Transactions with Iran, and U.S. Senate Select Committee on Secret Military Assistance to Iran and the Nicaraguan Opposition. *Report of the Congressional Committees Investigating the Iran-Contra Affair.* Washington, D.C., 1987.

Walsh, Lawrence. *Final Report of the Independent Counsel for Iran/Contra Matters.* Washington, D.C., 1993.

IRAN-IRAQ WAR

(1980–1988)

A conflict that began on 22 September 1980 and ended on 17 August 1988, in which the two largest powers of the Persian Gulf region fought for supremacy over the region and its oil. For Iran this was also a holy war against a secular, nationalist Iraq and an effort to extend the reach and reputation of the Islamic forces that had swept the shah of

Iran from power in 1979. In the end, however, both powers lost; the war drained both blood and treasure, but left the Iran-Iraq border where it had been in 1980.

The war began with an Iraqi armored thrust into western Iran and ended when Iran's leaders, their revolutionary zeal exhausted and their regime seemingly on the edge of collapse, signed a cease-fire resolution sponsored by the United Nations. Between these events, however, Iran enjoyed most of the war's small victories. Iraq's initial attack quickly bogged down, and over the next two summers Iran's Revolutionary Guards drove Iraqi troops out of Iran. Iran then chose to continue the war in hopes of toppling Iraq's government—a fateful decision, because it inaugurated a bloody and indecisive war of attrition. Each year's dry season saw Iranian troops charge into increasingly well-prepared Iraqi defensive positions all along the Iran-Iraq border. The attacks spilled enormous amounts of blood, most of it Iranian, but managed only to seize just enough territory to sustain fear throughout the Persian Gulf and among oil-consuming states that sooner or later Iraq's defenses would collapse.

They never did. Rather, Iraq found ways to escalate the war. It began using chemical weapons in 1982 and made more elaborate and skillful use of these weapons as the years went by. Iraq also began firing missiles at Iranian cities in 1982, but this tactic soon backfired. By 1985 Iran had acquired Soviet-made SCUD missiles and responded with attacks on Baghdad that Iraq was unable to match, given the much greater distance from the border to Tehran. In 1984 Iraq initiated the "tanker war," striking tankers servicing Iran's oil terminals with antiship missiles purchased from France the year before. Iran countered with strikes against tankers servicing the gulf sheikhdoms, using armed speedboats, mines, and later Silkworm antiship missiles purchased from China. Neither country's strikes had much effect on gulf oil traffic, but they raised the war's salience among oil-consuming states, and this presumably served Iraq's interest.

For most of the war, however, the world watched from the sidelines. With Iraq on the U.S. list of terrorist states and Iran still holding U.S. diplomats hostage when the war began, U.S. policymakers worried only that a war between equally unpalatable combatants might spread or provide opportunities for Soviet intrigue. As the tide of war turned in Iran's favor, fear of an Iranian victory led the United States to tilt toward Iraq, providing intelligence and dual-use equipment and technology—trucks, helicopters, and other items that, while not weapons, had military relevant uses—to Iraq while supporting it diplomatically in the United Nations. The Persian Gulf sheikhdoms supplied Iraq with money, and Kuwait allowed arms bound for Iraq to enter the gulf through its port. Iraq respond-

ed by adopting more moderate positions toward its neighbors and Israel.

International involvement in the war finally took off in 1987 and helped bring the war to an end the next year. On the diplomatic side, the UN Security Council began to formulate a cease-fire resolution in January 1987; UN Resolution 598 was completed by summer but only Iraq would sign it. On the military side, the U.S., Soviet, and several European navies stepped up their presence in the gulf over the summer and fall to protect oil tankers from increasingly intense Iranian attacks. Over the winter the confrontation between the United States and Iran gradually escalated, with the United States winning most of the naval battles. Still, the confrontation was not without embarrassment for the United States, as when a U.S. navy frigate, the *Stark*, was mistakenly attacked by an Iraqi warplane and the first tanker the United States sought to protect hit an Iranian mine north of Bahrain. Nor in the end was the confrontation without tragedy; on 3 July 1988, a U.S. cruiser mistakenly shot down an Iranian airliner flying across the lower gulf, killing some 290 civilians on board.

As tragic and senseless as it was, this incident added to mounting pressure on Tehran. Over the spring of 1988, Iraq's army had finally begun to win ground battles, while Iraqi SCUD missiles, modified for increased range, finally began hitting Tehran. Iraq's missile attacks produced devastating psychological effects, in part because Iranians feared they were carrying chemical warheads. With their ground forces in disarray, their navy depleted, their people fleeing Tehran, and the United States shooting their airliners from the sky, Iran's revolutionary leadership reluctantly signed UN Resolution 598 on 18 July. The resolution went into effect a month later, bringing an end to the fighting, if not the war.

The war's results were ambiguous. On the positive side, Iran's revolutionary drive was contained, and the balance of power maintained in the Persian Gulf. The U.S. relationship with the sheikhdoms warmed considerably, but U.S. relations with Iraq had also warmed over the course of the war, to the point where the administrations of Presidents Ronald Reagan and George Bush were blind to mounting evidence in the months after the war ended that Iraqi dictator Saddam Hussein was returning to his old and radical ways. Unstinting U.S. efforts to win Saddam's favor may have encouraged him to invade Kuwait—an invasion motivated partly by Kuwait's refusal to write off billions of dollars in loans to Iraq made during the Iran-Iraq war. In these ways the Iran-Iraq war laid the groundwork for the Kuwait crisis of 1990 and Operation Desert Storm.

Thomas L. McNaugher

See also Gulf War of 1990–1991; Hussein, Saddam; Iran; Iraq; Kuwait

FURTHER READING

Bakhash, Shaul. *The Reign of the Ayatollahs*. New York, 1984.

Chubin, Shahram, and Charles Tripp. *Iran and Iraq at War*. London, 1988.

Karsh, Efraim, ed. *The Iran-Iraq War: Impact and Implications*, rev. ed. New York, 1989.

IRAQ

A republic located in the Persian Gulf region, bordered by Kuwait, Saudi Arabia, Jordan, Syria, Turkey, Iran, and the Gulf itself. Like most Middle Eastern states, Iraq did not exist as a sovereign political entity before this century. Iraq was established in 1920, under the Treaty of Sèvres, as a League of Nations mandate to be administered by Great Britain. It encompassed the former vilayets of Basra, Baghdad, and Mosul, three provinces of the Ottoman Empire, which was on the losing side of World War I and was subsequently dismembered. Iraq became a kingdom in 1921; and in 1932, Iraq became completely independent of Great Britain and joined the League of Nations. Subsequently, Iraq was intermittently, if uneasily, pro-Western; but between April 1941 and January 1943 the country was ruled by a pro-Axis junta. Anti-British sentiment surfaced again in the 1940s, although by 1955 Iraq had emerged as the linchpin of an Anglo-U.S. regional security system, the Baghdad Pact.

A military coup in 1958 abolished the monarchy and reversed Iraq's orientation. The new leader, General Abdul Karim Qassim, was an erratic figure, who lacked any institutionalized power base in Iraq. He came to rely on Iraq's Communist Party, chose to align Iraq with the Soviet Union, and withdrew from the Baghdad Pact in 1959. In early 1963, a Baathist coup toppled Qassim. Baghdad recognized Kuwait, which had become independent two years earlier, while Iraq's relations with the U.S. improved. Many suspected a CIA hand in the coup. But the Baath were soon thrown out by a rival group of Arab nationalists. Four years later, in June 1967, Israel delivered a stunning blow to Egypt's Gamal Abdel Nasser and the self-styled Arab nationalist regimes. Although scarcely involved in that brief war, Baghdad cut diplomatic relations with the United States. They would not be resumed for seventeen years.

In 1968, when the Baath again seized power, Iraq again turned to the Soviet Union, becoming the first Arab country to sign a "Friendship Treaty" with Moscow in 1972. For its part, the United States backed Iraq's neighbor and perennial rival, Iran, then ruled by Shah Mohammad Reza Pahlavi, to secure Western interests in the region, above all unimpeded access to oil. U.S.-Iraqi relations remained practically invisible through the 1970s. When the Jimmy Carter administration took office, it offered to renew diplomatic ties. Iraq, however, was not interested. Following the 1979 Iranian revolution, the Carter administration again approached Iraq. But Baghdad remained uninterested in forging serious ties with the United States.

However, over the next decade Iraq's attitude changed dramatically, or so it seemed. In 1979, Saddam Hussein became president after another coup and purge. A year later the Iran-Iraq war began, ostensibly over the Shatt-al-Arab waterway, with an Iraqi thrust across the Iranian frontier in September 1980. But the quick victory Baghdad expected never materialized and a stalemate ensued. In late 1981, Iranian forces began to repulse the Iraqis, driving them from Iranian soil, and as they did, U.S.-Iraqi ties began to improve in line with the old adage, "the enemy of my enemy is my friend."

In early 1982, Iraq was removed from the Department of State list of countries sponsoring international terrorism, allowing Baghdad to qualify for U.S. economic assistance. By the summer, Iran had pushed Iraq back across the border, and for the next six years Iraq was put on the defensive, the threat of an Iranian breakthrough arising after every major Iranian offensive. Despite the seeming convergence of interests, however, U.S.-Iraqi relations were complex and periodically quite troubled. Iraq did not really want close ties to the United States. Conversely, given the brutal, totalitarian nature of the Baghdad regime, along with its use of chemical weapons against Iran from 1983 on, and later against the Kurds, no U.S. administration could be seen to be too close to Iraq. Diplomatic relations were re-established in late 1984, after the U.S. presidential elections. Significant amounts of economic assistance were provided to Iraq, mostly through the Commodity Credit Corporation, which issues short term loans to promote U.S. agricultural exports. The United States also loosened restrictions on dual-use technology exports and provided limited covert military support. Most importantly, it shared satellite intelligence with Baghdad.

Formerly a leading rejectionist state, Iraq now ceased to oppose an Arab-Israeli settlement, and it even came around to making informal approaches to Israel, through Egypt. More generally, in U.S. eyes, Iraq served as the bulwark against an Iranian conquest of the militarily weak oil-rich states of the Arabian Peninsula. Following the revelation of covert U.S.-Israeli arms sales to Iran in late 1986, and in the wake of a major Iranian offensive soon thereafter, the United States decided to make an intense effort to end the Iran-Iraq war. In the summer of 1987, while formally protecting Kuwaiti oil tankers, U.S. warships began to escort neutral shipping in the Persian Gulf. That show of muscle, along with bolder and more effective Iraqi military efforts, and an energetic U.S. diplomatic campaign, finally helped end the war in August 1988.

It was expected that the war's end would bring about a loosening of Baghdad's internal repression and an overall improvement in U.S.-Iraqi relations. But that did not happen. With the war with Iran over, Saddam turned against the Iraqi Kurds, launching massive attacks including the use of chemical weapons. The U.S. Senate pushed for sanctions, but the Ronald Reagan administration headed them off, still preferring the enemy-enemy-friend strategy. Ayatollah Khomeini still ruled in Teheran and he was a bitter, uncompromising opponent of the United States and its Middle Eastern allies, both Arab and Israeli. The George Bush administration began by seeking actively to improve U.S.-Iraqi relations, but in February 1990, serious tensions began to arise as Saddam suddenly called for U.S. forces to leave the Gulf and for the Arabs to liberate Jerusalem. Those tensions culminated in Iraq's invasion of Kuwait six months later, on 2 August 1990.

In invading Kuwait, Saddam sought not only to enhance his popularity at home but also to polarize the Middle East by posing as a champion of Arab causes, exploiting the anti-Western sentiment endemic to the region. The initial U.S. response was both military and diplomatic. Over 200,000 troops were deployed to Saudi Arabia as part of Operation Desert Shield, both to contain possible further Iraqi aggression and to position forces for rolling back the occupation of Kuwait. A broad-based coalition, eventually including twenty-seven countries, was built, which among other things was key to winning passage of a series of United Nations (UN) Security Council resolutions condemning Iraq, imposing comprehensive economic sanctions, and eventually legitimizing military action, which became Operation Desert Storm.

With the U.S. decision to oust Iraq from Kuwait, and Saddam's belief that he could prevail in any conflict by inflicting unacceptably high casualties, war began 16 January 1991. It ended 28 February, after overwhelming demonstrations of U.S. and allied military superiority, yet even so with a unilateral allied cease-fire. As President Bush would explain five years later, he had expected the defeat to cause Saddam's overthrow.

But that did not happen. Instead, as the Kurdish population in the North and the Muslim Shi'ite population in the South rose against the regime after the war, Saddam proceeded to crush them. The Bush administration chose to avert its eyes and U.S. forces did little. However, the ferocity of the repression and, above all, the fear that Saddam would again use chemical weapons against them, caused an exodus of the Kurdish population, which spilled over the Iraqi borders into Turkey and Iran. The Bush administration was obliged to act. It established a safe haven for the Kurds in the North and prohibited Iraqi airplanes from flying there (Operation Provide Comfort).

And as Saddam survived, he soon began rebuilding his military forces. The Bush administration soon realized that it could not tolerate Saddam's remaining in power, but it was not prepared to do a great deal toward that end. Thus, it authorized some low-level covert activities against the regime, pushed additional economic sanctions through the UN, and took the position that it would not agree to lift economic sanctions while Saddam remained in power. The expectation was that such a stance would contribute to prospects for promoting a coup. Thus, there was some irony to the fact that despite the huge boost in his popularity following the Gulf War victory, Bush lost his 1992 reelection bid. Saddam, though, remained in power.

Although during the 1992 presidential campaign President Bill Clinton had criticized Bush for not being tough enough on Iraq, as president-elect, in January 1993, Clinton made the stunning statement that as a Baptist he believed in "death-bed conversions," before explaining the terms under which he was prepared to come to terms with Saddam. He quickly reversed himself, but the new administration still insisted it was "depersonalizing" the conflict, implying it could tolerate Saddam's remaining in power.

Nevertheless, Saddam's operatives tried to assassinate Bush and his entourage when they visited Kuwait in April 1993. The United States retaliated in June 1993, with a strike on Iraqi intelligence headquarters in Baghdad, and otherwise toughened its position. Talk of "depersonalizing" the conflict ended; while at the UN, the United States took the lead in resisting pressure from France and Russia, among others, to begin to lift the economic sanctions. Then in October 1994, as Saddam remobilized substantial numbers of his forces near the Kuwaiti border, the Clinton administration countered by mobilizing U.S. and allied air, naval, and ground forces. Another U.S.-Iraqi confrontation came in August-September 1996.

Even such measures, though, failed to take account of Saddam's vengefulness. Iraq was behind the February 1993 bombing of New York's World Trade Center, yet the issue of state sponsorship was never properly addressed. With the first arrests, a week after the bombing, the Federal Bureau of Investigation (FBI) refused to share information with the national security agencies. It maintained that the bombing was a criminal matter to be handled by law enforcement. Thus, no proper intelligence investigation addressing the question of state sponsorship was ever carried out by the agencies with the expertise to do such an investigation.

Then in January 1995 Ramzi Ahmed Yousef, the figure most responsible for the Trade Center bomb, planned to bomb eleven U.S. airplanes; but while mixing chemicals in a Manila apartment, he started a fire and had to flee, leading to his arrest a month later.

A danger even more ominous than Saddam's bombs soon emerged. In July 1995 Baghdad acknowledged having produced large quantities of biological agents, but claimed to have destroyed them, even though it could produce no credible documentation to support that claim. A month later, Hussein Kamel Hassan, Saddam's son-in-law, who had supervised the development of Iraq's unconventional weapons program, defected to Jordan, producing yet more stunning revelations. Notions that the Iraqi opposition might mobilize around Kamil proved untenable given his own brutal record. In early 1996 Kamil renounced his defection to return to Iraq, only to be murdered at Saddam's behest within a few days.

All this time the United Nations Special Commission on Iraq (UNSCOM) continued to make discovery after discovery of weapons of mass destruction-related materials, installations, designs, and other evidence of what Iraq still had and what it might still be planning to do and develop. Iraq still had significant numbers of missiles and tons of the deadly chemical agent, VX. Moreover, it had progressed much further toward a nuclear bomb than previously thought. The danger existed even of a "nuclear breakout" if Iraq managed to acquire sufficient fissionable material.

With Saddam still in power, still defiant, and still in violation of key UN resolutions, not only was there no prospect for improvement in U.S.-Iraqi relations, the possibility of further troubles down the road could not be precluded.

LAURIE MYLROIE

See also Baghdad Pact; Bush, George Herbert Walker; Gulf War of 1990-1991; Hussein, Saddam; Iran-Iraq War; Kuwait; Middle East; Reagan, Ronald Wilson

FURTHER READING
Freedman, Lawrence, and Efraim Karsh. *The Gulf Conflict: Diplomacy and War in the New World Order.* New York, 1993.
Grummon, Stephen. *The Iran-Iraq War: Islam Embattled.* New York, 1982.
Helms, Christine Moss. *Iraq: Eastern Flank of the Arab World.* Washington, D.C., 1984.
Jentleson, Bruce W. *With Friends Like These: Reagan, Bush and Saddam, 1982–1990.* New York, 1994.
Karsh, Efraim, and Inauri Rautsi. *Saddam Hussein: A Political Biography.* New York, 1991.
Miller, Judith, and Laurie Mylroie. *Saddam Hussein and the Crisis in the Gulf.* New York, 1990.

IRELAND

Island republic located in the North Atlantic Ocean, across the Irish Sea from Great Britain. The extent and concentration of Irish immigration to the United States has been more significant in the relationship between the two countries than any intrinsic importance Irish issues may have had to U.S. national interests. Irish immigrants fled to the United States after the famine in 1845. Collecting principally in the cities of the east coast, they expressed a powerful hatred for British policies in Ireland and supported militant Irish nationalism. In 1858 Irish immigrants founded the Fenian Brotherhood, led by John O'Mahoney, and in 1867 the Clan Na Gael, with John Devoy and Patrick Ford as its dominant figures. These organizations sought not only to foment a rebellion in Ireland, but also to direct U.S. policy in support of Irish independence. The large number of votes of Irish immigrants provided political leverage for these organizations.

The revolutionary government set up by the Irish nationalists sent one of its leaders, Eamon de Valera, to the United States in 1919 to raise funds and gain support for independence. De Valera was successful in raising $5 million from Irish-American organizations but was unsuccessful in getting the Republican and Democratic parties to include a call for Irish independence in their platforms. Nor would President Woodrow Wilson, with his pro-British posture, advance Ireland's claim for recognition at the League of Nations. After Ireland achieved a degree of independence within the British Commonwealth in a 1921 treaty with London, the interest of Irish Americans in the Irish question diminished.

In 1939 de Valera, now prime minister of Ireland, chose a policy of neutrality in World War II. He could not support the United Kingdom while Ireland was partitioned, nor for pragmatic reasons ally with the Germans. David Gray, the U.S. ambassador to Ireland from 1940 to 1947, made every effort to influence de Valera to drop neutrality in order to enlist the Irish resources in the war. Gray supported the British negotiations with de Valera to end the partition of Ireland in exchange for alliance in the war. De Valera refused to abandon neutrality and provoked Gray to try to discredit de Valera among Irish Americans and in U.S. public opinion. Gray arranged for a note to be sent from the United States to Ireland requesting that the diplomatic missions from Germany and Japan be expelled from Ireland on the basis that their potential for espionage constituted a threat to the D-Day invasion. In February 1944 the demand was delivered to de Valera, who flatly rejected it in March. The Department of State released the document to the press, provoking a sharp negative reaction toward Ireland and Irish neutrality.

In 1949, in the context of the Cold War, the United States invited Ireland to become a member of the North Atlantic Treaty Organization (NATO). Ireland objected to joining an alliance with Great Britain while Ireland was partitioned and Ireland declined to join the organization. The administration of President Harry S. Truman was not unduly concerned, because relations with the United Kingdom were more central to U.S. security interests. The United States did include Ireland in the

Marshall Plan, although the £36 million, of which £31.5 million was a loan, was considerably less than what Ireland hoped to get. Nevertheless, the funds constituted fifty percent of state investment in economic development from 1948 to 1951, the year Marshall Plan aid ended. After Ireland's entry into the European Community in 1973 there was a surge of U.S. private investment seeking access to the European market. Since then the United States has become the largest foreign investor in Ireland, and U.S. firms employed twenty percent of the work force in the mid-1990s.

The period from the 1950s through the 1960s included no significant developments in U.S.-Irish relations; immigration had diminished and Irish Americans had moved up the socioeconomic ladder. The connection between the countries was marked by the ethnically symbolic visit of President John F. Kennedy in 1962. A sharp increase in the number of young Irish immigrants in the 1980s, a large number of them illegal, resulted in pressure to reform the 1965 Immigration Act. Legislation passed in 1985 provided five thousand visas to Irish immigrants, later expanded to ten thousand.

The explosion of violence in Northern Ireland in 1969 brought a renewed interest in the region by Irish Americans, who sought to pressure the U.S. government to influence British policy. Irish-American political figures responded to the increasing violence in Ulster with calls for a change in British policy. Presidents Ford, Carter, and Reagan were responsive to the Irish government's request for help in curbing support for IRA violence among U.S. groups. President Clinton allowed Gerry Adams, the head of the Sinn Fein party, to visit the United States in 1994 and supported the efforts of the British and Irish prime ministers in 1994 and 1995 to generate a new approach to peace in Ulster after the IRA declared a cease fire in 1994. President Clinton appointed former Senator George Mitchell of Maine to develop an investment conference in the United States, held in 1995, to encourage American business investment in Northern Ireland. In support of the peace process and American investment, in November 1995, President Clinton became the first American president to visit Northern Ireland.

RICHARD B. FINNEGAN

See also Fenians; Great Britain; Immigration; Marshall Plan; Northern Ireland

FURTHER READING

Brown, Thomas. *Irish-American Nationalism.* New York, 1966.

Cronin, Sean. *Washington's Irish Policy: Independence, Partition, Neutrality.* Dublin, 1987.

Dwyer, T. Ryle. *Strained Relations: Ireland at Peace and the USA at War, 1941–1945.* Dublin, 1988.

Wilson, Andrew J. *Irish Americans and the Ulster Conflict 1968-1995.* Washington, D.C., 1995.

IRON CURTAIN

See Churchill, Winston Leonard Spencer; Cold War

ISOLATIONISM

A set of assumptions which guided U.S. foreign policies for nearly two centuries and which held that Europe's interests differed markedly from U.S. interests, that broad oceans rendered the United States impregnable to attack and made political or military involvement with Europe unnecessary and unwise, and that Americans could shape a world order favorable to U.S. ideals and interests through example, not military action. Avoiding alliances and maintaining neutrality during European wars also became isolationist tenets. Isolationism did *not* mean non-involvement in world affairs, as thriving U.S. foreign trade and imperial conquests indicate.

Despite America's rise to global power, participation in World War I, and alterations in the balance-of-power system that had nurtured an independent U.S. course, isolationism prevailed in the United States until World War II exposed its inadequacies. Shortly after the Japanese assault on Hawai'i catapulted the United States into World War II in December 1941, Senator Arthur H. Vandenberg of Michigan, a self-proclaimed "insulationist", noted in his diary that "my convictions regarding international cooperation. . . took firm form on the afternoon of the Pearl Harbor attack. That day ended isolationism for any realist." Vandenberg's changing views essentially mirrored those of his fellow citizens. Most pre–Pearl Harbor isolationists, including Vandenberg, supported global war against the Axis, voted for U.S. participation in the United Nations, and backed postwar military alliances such as the North Atlantic Treaty Organization (NATO). With the U.S. economy having become the engine of international prosperity and nuclear weapons eliminating geographical security, old-fashioned isolationism had become obsolete.

Isolationist ideas began in the colonial period. Escaping religious persecution and economic hardship at home, settlers inevitably made geographic and moral distinctions between the New World and the Old Colonial leaders eventually argued that the imperial connection with England was one-sided, and that Americans were constantly embroiled in England's wars against their will. The French and Indian Wars usually originated in European quarrels, yet Americans nonetheless had to pay taxes, raise armies, fight, and die. Great Britain did not always appreciate colonial sacrifices. New Englanders captured the strategic French fortress of Louisbourg on Cape Breton Island in 1745, but in the subsequent European peace treaty the British handed back Louisbourg in exchange for French conquests in India. A disgruntled

Benjamin Franklin claimed that Americans had enjoyed "perfect peace with both French and Indians" and that the recent conflict had been "really a British war." He expressed what historian Max Savelle has called "a deep-seated feeling of escape from Europe and a strong tendency. . . to avoid becoming entangled in European conflict, whenever it was in their interest to do so."

Thomas Paine's best-selling *Common Sense* (1776) spelled out the benefits of an independent, isolationist foreign policy. There was not "a single advantage that this continent can reap by being connected with Great Britain." On the contrary, "France and Spain never were, nor perhaps ever will be, our enemies as Americans but as Our being subjects of Great Britain." Paine predicted that U.S. commerce by itself "will secure us the peace and friendship of all Europe, because it is in the interest of all Europe to have America as a free port.... As Europe is Our market for trade, we ought to form no partial connection with any part of it. It is the true interest of America to steer clear of European contentions."

The attractions of U.S. commerce proved insufficient, however, and American leaders during the Revolutionary War had to make an alliance with France to win independence from Great Britain. That alliance brought entanglements, both during and after the war. When French diplomats intrigued to gain U.S. support for France's own revolutionary war against Europe in the 1790s, President George Washington issued perhaps the most famous statement of isolationist principles. In his Farewell Address of 1796, he warned: "Against the insidious wiles of foreign influence... the jealousy of a free people ought to be *constantly* awake." Washington posited the "Great Rule" that "in extending our commercial relations" the United States should have as "little *political* connection as possible" with foreign nations. Like Paine, he extolled American uniqueness. "Europe," said Washington, "has a primary set of interests which to us have none or a very remote relation....Our detached and distant situation invites and enables us to pursue a different course." Then came his most memorable words: "'Tis our true policy to steer clear of permanent alliances with any portion of the foreign world....[but] we may safely trust to temporary alliances for extraordinary emergencies." Washington did not say "no entangling alliances ever," as later politicians sometimes misstated. Nor did he preclude westward expansion. Thomas Jefferson later amended Washington by vowing "peace, commerce, and honest friendship with all nations, entangling alliances with none."

The Nineteenth Century

Following the War of 1812 and successful Latin American revolutions against Spain, President James Monroe's "doctrine" of 1823 admonished European powers not "to extend their system to any portion of this hemisphere" and proclaimed that "the American continents...are henceforth not to be considered as subjects for future colonization by any European powers." Monroe also pledged: "In the wars of the European powers in matters relating to themselves we have never taken any part, nor does it comport with our policy to do so." Secretary of State John Quincy Adams had already warned Americans against intervening abroad "in search of monsters to destroy." America "well knows," Adams had avowed in 1821, "that by once enlisting under any other banners than her own, were they even the banners of foreign independence, she would involve herself beyond the power of extrication, in all the wars of interest and intrigue, of individual avarice, envy, and ambition, which assume the colors and usurp the standards of freedom."

Ironically, the first official use of the term "isolation" to describe American policy did not occur until 1863 when Secretary of State William Seward spurned a joint démarche by France, Great Britain, and Austria against Russia over Poland. Seward praised rejections by earlier administrations of "seductions from what, superficially viewed, seemed a course of isolation and indifference." "Our policy of nonintervention, straight, absolute, and peculiar as it may seem," he wrote, "has. . . become a traditional one, which could not be abandoned without the most urgent occasion, amounting to manifest necessity."

Such isolationist pronouncements suited U.S. circumstances in the formative years. An agricultural country on the periphery of world capitalism, lacking a large army and navy, surrounded by weak neighbors and wide oceans, and indirectly benefiting from British free trade and naval dominance, the young republic could concentrate on internal development. When wars in Europe intruded, Americans could play one power off against another and gain "advantage from Europe's distress." Thus did the United States, during the nineteenth and early twentieth centuries, expand its domain across North America and begin an empire in the Caribbean and the Pacific without abandoning isolationist principles. It removed Native Americans from their lands, fought undeclared naval wars with France and the Barbary Pirates, waged wars against England, Mexico, and Spain, suppressed the Filipino insurrection, used military force in Cuba, Haiti, Panama, Nicaragua, Santo Domingo, and Mexico, all without foreign alliances or sending U. S. troops to Europe. No U.S. soldiers fought on the European continent until Congress declared war on Germany in 1917, and even then President Woodrow Wilson chose to be an "Associate Power" rather than an ally of England and France.

Changes at home and abroad nonetheless eroded the foundations of isolationism. Improvements in transportation and communications shrank the globe, as steamships, railroads, telegraph, cable, radio, automobiles, movies, and airplanes expanded U.S. markets and horizons. The growth of urban industry and finance and increased exports after the Civil War signaled the decline of rural, small-town America with its emphasis on the domestic market. The gradual erosion of British and French power, plus the ambitious emergence of Germany and Japan, diminished the relatively free national security previously enjoyed by the United States. As imperialists carved up Asia and Africa in the 1870s and 1880s and threatened U.S. interests in Latin America and the Pacific, Washington joined the competition and attained world power status following the war with Spain in 1898. Cosmopolitan elites like Theodore Roosevelt challenged isolationist traditions by calling for a big navy, overseas colonies, a Central American canal, and even a large modern army based on universal military training. His Roosevelt Corollary declared that the United States should exercise its role as an "international police power."

President Theodore Roosevelt temporarily abandoned isolationist principles by successfully mediating the Russo-Japanese War in 1905. When Kaiser Wilhelm II of Germany touched off a war scare in 1905 by challenging French claims to Morocco, mainly to prevent an alliance between France and England, Roosevelt interceded again. Convoking an international conference to settle Morocco's future at Algeciras, Spain, in 1906, Roosevelt devised a compromise that substantially favored the French and persuaded the Kaiser to accept it, thereby isolating Germany and strengthening the Anglo-French entente. The Senate, however, approved the Algeciras pact only after disclaiming any "purpose to depart from traditional American foreign policies." Theodore Roosevelt's successors made no attempt to intervene in the more ominous second Moroccan and Balkan crises that preceded the "Great War."

World War I and Its Aftermath

Nor did President Woodrow Wilson intend to reverse traditional policies when he asked Americans to be "impartial in thought as well as in action" once the European war began in 1914. In supervising American neutrality, however, Wilson made choices that eventually put the United States on the side of England and France against Germany. With Great Britain commanding the seas, U.S. exports to Great Britain and France increased from $754 million in 1914 to $2.75 billion two years later; exports to Germany shrank to $2 million in 1916. Credits from private U.S. bankers financed Allied purchases of more than $3 billion in goods during 1914–1917. Wilson sincerely hoped to mediate a "peace without victory," but he interpreted international law flexibly with respect to the Allied blockade and rigidly with regard to German sub-

marine warfare. When the Germans violated America's rights, ideals, and property, and threatened its security with a proposed alliance with Mexico, Wilson asked Congress for a crusade to "make the world safe for democracy," a liberal world order in which barriers to trade and democracy would disappear, in which revolution and aggression no longer threatened world peace. Despite notable exceptions such as Senators George Norris of Nebraska and Robert La Follette of Wisconsin, most isolationists voted for war in 1917 because the United States was arguably fighting on its own volition in defense of its own interests.

Wilson's peacemaking evoked a more negative response. Because joining a League of Nations seemed the sort of open-ended commitment that George Washington had proscribed, isolationist senators rallied to kill it. George Norris thought that the League did not do enough to deter war, that it actually was a device to preserve Great Power dominance. Henry Cabot Lodge asked a key question: "Are you willing to put your soldiers and your sailors at the disposition of other nations?" With regard to Article Ten of the League Covenant, which required member states to preserve the territorial integrity and independence of other members, Senator William E. Borah purported to be "willing to help my neighbor…but I do not want him…[to] decide for me when and how I shall act or to what extent I shall make sacrifice." When senators attached a resolution to Article Ten whereby the United States assumed no obligation to preserve the territorial integrity of another country unless authorized by Congress, President Wilson instructed his followers to vote against any treaty with reservations. Although historians cite medical reasons for Wilson's inflexibility, the president also refused to compromise because he saw the difference between himself and his critics as fundamental: Was it in America's interest to participate in collective security or to seek safety unilaterally? Thus did traditional American nationalism and nonalignment, or isolationism, decide the debate against Wilson?

How much the United States, transformed by World War I into the world's leading economic power and creditor nation, thereafter returned to isolationist precepts remains in dispute. True, Americans hoped to avoid foreign entanglements and concentrate on domestic issues in the 1920s and 1930s. The army of four million "doughboys" who fought in France shrank to a low of 120,000 in 1927; according to the historian Russell Weigley, the U.S. Army "may have been less ready to function as a fighting force than at any time in its history." Within the limits of U.S. power, however, American leaders pursued an active foreign policy befitting their high international status. They worked hard to create a community of law-abiding nations characterized by peaceful and orderly processes, liberal trading practices, and economic and political stability. Washington emphasized nonmilitary means—treaties, conferences, disarmament, economic, and financial arrangements—in its pursuit of world order. America remained isolationist between the wars primarily in the sense that it wanted to isolate itself from war, to scale down foreign military interventions, and to preserve the freedom to make independent decisions on behalf of national prosperity and security. The historian Joan Hoff Wilson's phrase "independent internationalism" better describes American behavior, especially during the 1920s—active on an international scale, but independent in action. Where the United States lacked viable power, such as in Asia or Europe, it moved hesitantly. Where it possessed power, as in Latin America, it acted vigorously.

The shock of the Great Depression, Europe's subsequent default on its debts, and new threats of war after the Manchurian Crisis of 1931 revived U.S. tendencies to look inward and eschew international uncertainties. "Revisionist" historians argued that Germany alone had not precipitated World War I, that business leaders and propagandists had manipulated an unneutral Wilson administration to favor the British, and that the exorbitant costs and meager results did not justify U.S. participation. The best-selling *Merchants of Death* (1934) charged that profiteering manufacturers of armaments had exploited the American economic system to compromise U.S. neutrality. President Franklin D. Roosevelt encouraged Senator Gerald P. Nye of North Dakota to hold hearings during 1934–1936 to assess whether bankers and munitions makers had lobbied Wilson into war. The committee never proved the charge, but did uncover telling evidence that these entrepreneurs zealously supported the Allied cause. Such revelations encouraged Congress to pass a series of neutrality laws in the 1930s, designed, it was often said, to keep the United States out of World War II. No longer did Americans claim the right to travel on belligerent passenger liners such as the *Lusitania*, sunk by a German submarine in 1915. Loans to belligerents were banned, as was the sale of arms and munitions; all other wartime commerce could continue on a cash-and-carry basis with U.S. merchant ships prohibited from war zones.

Although liberals, conservatives, and peace advocates from all regions espoused isolationist principles to some degree, what the historian Thomas N. Guinsburg has called the "triumph of isolationism" by the late 1930s owed much to its strength in the Middle West and Great Plains. The region's insularity, populist-progressive heritage, economic nationalism, cultural, and ethnic composition reinforced isolationist dogmas. Agrarian isolationists such as Henrik Shipstead Nye of Minnesota, and Arthur Capper of Kansas, among others, objected to foreign policies designed by the same urban, financial elites who exploited farmers at home. They opposed taxes for expensive warships that purportedly subsidized eastern steel manufacturers and shipbuilders. They voiced suspicion of war propaganda aimed at arousing patriotic support for foreign adventures that benefited urban business interests, not national security. Such isolationists backed the Ludlow Amendment calling for a national referendum on decisions for war, and they feared that increased presidential authority over foreign affairs, following Roosevelt's ill-fated plan to pack the Supreme Court, would create dictatorship at home. With Roosevelt dependent on progressive isolationist votes for New Deal reforms, isolationists had seized the initiative with neutrality laws that promised to keep the country "out of every foreign entanglement and every European war," as Senator Hiram Johnson smugly put it. When isolationists in Congress easily blocked a presidential effort to repeal the arms embargo in the summer of 1939, Roosevelt complained that "only a great shock like that of 1932" could change public attitudes.

From FDR to Clinton

The spring of 1940 provided such a jolt. Adolf Hitler's blitzkrieg victories over Scandinavia and France created a deep sense of insecurity, including the specter of a direct attack on the United States if Germany destroyed or captured the Royal Navy. British analysts of American opinion noted "a reaction to fear of aggression from Europe as fundamental as the fear of entanglement with Europe which had dominated the preceding months." Americans heard the sounds of German bombs exploding in London, courtesy of Edward R. Murrow of CBS radio. Roosevelt responded by transferring to England fifty old destroyers in exchange for leases to eight British bases from Newfoundland to the Caribbean; in mid-September he obtained passage of the Selective Service Act of 1940, the first peacetime draft in American history. Most isolationists reluctantly supported both measures. Reelected to a third term after promising not to send American boys into any foreign wars, Roosevelt nonetheless inched toward intervention by steps "short of war"—the occupation of Greenland and Iceland in the name of hemispheric defense, Lend-Lease aid to Great Britain, China, and Russia, naval patrols, convoys, economic embargoes, and neutrality repeal. According to Winston Churchill, the president promised to "wage war" against Germany, "but not declare it" and to do "everything" to "force an 'incident.'"

Roosevelt also encouraged guilt-by-association techniques to discredit isolationists. While conceding that many "who shut their eyes to the ugly realities of international banditry" might be "sincere" and "patriotic," he warned in May 1941 that isolationists were playing into Nazi hands and that Americans must ignore "the tender whispering of appeasers that Hitler is not interested in the Western Hemispheres" or "the soporific lullabies that a wide ocean can protect us from him." A cabinet officer smeared the isolationist America First Committee as "anti-democrats, appeasers, labor baiters, and anti-Semites," even though that committee's founders (who included future President Gerald R. Ford and future Ambassadors Kingman Brewster and R. Douglas Stuart) conspicuously barred extremists from membership. One widely disseminated pamphlet identified America First as the "Nazi Transmission Belt." When famed aviator Charles A. Lindbergh proclaimed at an America First rally in September 1941 that the "three most important groups…pressing this country toward war are the British, the Jewish, and the Roosevelt administration," Roosevelt's supporters cried foul and called Lindbergh anti-Semitic. According to the historian Wayne S. Cole, "neither Lindbergh nor America First ever recovered from the staggering blows that statement brought upon them."

Even before the Pearl Harbor attack destroyed America's aura of invulnerability, Roosevelt had signed the Atlantic Charter and reaffirmed Wilsonian principles of collective security, national self-determination, freedom of the seas, and multilateral trade. This revival of Wilsonianism, combined with a determination to avoid Wilson's errors, exemplified a wartime strategy designed to eradicate isolationism. This time Germany would have to surrender unconditionally. There would be no reparations tangle because Lend-Lease would "eliminate the dollar sign." This time the United States would join an international organization to maintain peace, even if it meant paying court to the sensitive Senator Vandenberg, whose allegiance also was swayed by defense contracts for Michigan. Created in 1944, the World Bank and International Monetary Fund promoted a postwar international political economy conducive to U.S. trade and investment. As the only major belligerent untouched by enemy bombers or marauding armies, the U.S. gross national product jumped from $90.5 billion in 1939 to $211.9 billion in 1945. By war's end, according to the historian Thomas McCormick, the United States had become "the global workshop and banker, umpire and policeman, preacher and teacher."

Despite changed commitments and conditions, the fear persisted that the United States might still spurn global leadership. Roosevelt himself never believed that the United Nations (UN) would maintain global peace. He preferred to rely on the "Four Policemen" to keep order after World War II. Hopeful that UN membership would condition U.S. citizens to an international perspective, Roosevelt still feared that public opinion would not permit U.S. troops to stay in Europe for more than a year. Such a scenario did seem possible when new Republican senators such as Joseph McCarthy of Wisconsin and John Bricker of Ohio joined other isolationist-leaning Republicans elected since 1938. Because such Republicans considered dollars spent on the reconstruction of war-torn Europe as "globaloney," the Truman administration found it necessary to "scare hell" out of the American people to gain bipartisan backing for such programs as the Truman Doctrine, Marshall Plan, and the North Atlantic Treaty Organization (NATO). The communist takeover of Eastern Europe, Mao Zedong's successful Communist revolution in China, the Korean War, and a Soviet-American nuclear arms race also encouraged consensus. Former isolationists might grumble over who "lost China" in 1949, question the extent of U.S. military commitments to NATO, and back the Bricker Amendment (requiring Senate approval for all executive agreements), but most became "Asia Firsters" who urged all-out war against Communist China as well as military commitments to Korea, Taiwan, and Indochina. "For isolationists these Americans certainly do get around!" quipped one pacifist.

A Cold War consensus thus emerged by the 1950s in support of global containment, with Soviet Russia and Communist China as unrelenting adversaries. Military strength through nuclear deterrence, plus the willingness to fight limited wars (especially in Asia), became the acknowledged strategy. The "Free World" buttressed U.S. security through a series of alliances and military assistance pacts, while the so-called "Third World" became an arena of competition, peaceful or otherwise, between East and West. Differences within the Cold War consensus were tactical—how much emphasis to put on disarmament negotiations, how much money to spend on foreign aid to which countries, how and where to deploy tactical nuclear weapons, how to undermine Fidel Castro. Even during the Vietnam War, when critics questioned the legitimacy as well as the efficacy of fighting in Asia, the Johnson and Nixon administrations marginalized opponents by labeling them isolationists. "Compared to people who thought they could run the universe," journalist Walter Lippmann shot back, "I *am* a neo-isolationist and proud of it." When George McGovern offered an isolationist alternative by running for president on the slogan "Come home, America" in 1972, however, his crushing defeat at the hands of Richard M. Nixon underscored the strength of globalist Cold War perceptions.

The end of the Cold War, by depriving the United States of its principal adversary, has revived isolationist impulses toward unilateralism and nonintervention. Despite President George Bush's spectacular leadership of a United Nations coalition in the Gulf War of 1991, subsequent crises in Bosnia, Haiti, and Somalia dulled U.S. appetites for collective action. After eighteen Americans died in a UN peacekeeping mission in Somalia and ethnic fighting in the former Yugoslavia threatened to ignite a wider Balkan war, President Bill Clinton issued Presidential Directive 25, which declared that "the United States does not support a standing UN army, nor will we earmark specific U.S. military units for participation in UN operations." As of 1995, the United States ranked 20th among countries making troop contributions to UN operations. Once the world's largest donor of foreign aid, Washington currently contributes 0.15 percent of its gross domestic product, the lowest among twenty-one industrial nations.

Such impulses, however reinforced by pressing economic needs at home, are unlikely to resurrect the isolationist verities of an earlier United States—not in a "high-tech" world where computers instantly communicate between continents and cable television brings wars into U.S. living rooms. In an increasingly interdependent world, "everything is interrelated," Czech Republic president Václav Havel reminded Americans in 1994. "The future of the United States," he wrote, "is being decided in suffering Sarajevo or Mostar, in the plundered Brazilian rain forests, in the wretched poverty of Bangladesh or Somalia." In responding to Havel's plea for "global responsibility," U.S. leaders will weigh his advice against a history of isolationist tradition.

J. GARRY CLIFFORD

See also America First Committee; Borah, William Edgar; Bricker Amendment; Cold War; French and Indian War; Jefferson, Thomas; League of Nations; Lend-Lease; Lindbergh, Charles; Lippmann, Walter; Ludlow Amendment; Marshall Plan; McGovern, George Stanley; Monroe Doctrine; Neutrality Acts of the 1930s; North Atlantic Treaty Organization; Nye, Gerald Prentice; Paine, Thomas; Roosevelt, Franklin Delano; Roosevelt, Theodore; Russo-Japanese War; Seward, William Henry; Truman Doctrine; Vandenberg, Arthur Hendrick; Vietnam War; Washington, George; World War I; World War II

FURTHER READING

Adler, Selig. *The Isolationist Impulse: Its Twentieth Century Reaction.* New York, 1957.

Cole, Wayne S. *America First: The Battle Against Intervention, 1940–1941.* Madison, Wisc., 1953.

———. *Charles A. Lindbergh and the Battle Against American Intervention in World War II.* New York, 1974

———. *Roosevelt and the Isolationists, 1932–1945.* Lincoln, Nebr., 1983.

Cooper, John Milton. *The Vanity of Power: American Isolationism and the First World War, 1914–1917.* Westport, Conn., 1969.

Divine, Robert A. *The Illusion of Neutrality.* Chicago, 1982

Doenecke, Justus. *In Danger Undaunted: The Anti-Interventionist Movement of 1940–1941 as Revealed in the Papers of the America First Committee.* Stanford, Calif., 1990.

———. *Not to the Swift: The Old Isolationists in the Cold War Era.* Lewisburg, Penn., 1979.

Guinsburg, Thomas N. *The Pursuit of Isolationism in the United States Senate from Versailles to Pearl Harbor.* New York, 1982.

Jonas, Manfred. *Isolationism in America, 1935–1941.* Ithaca, N.Y., 1966.

Stromberg, Roland. *Collective Security and American Foreign Policy.* New York, 1963.

Tucker, Robert W. *A New Isolationism.* New York, 1972.

Wiltz, John E. *In Search of Peace: The Senate Munitions Inquiry, 1934–36.* Baton Rouge, Louis., 1963.

ISRAEL

Bordered by Egypt, Jordan, Syria, Lebanon, the disputed territories of Gaza and the West Bank, and the eastern Mediterranean Sea, founded in 1948 as a Jewish state. Israel is a major partner of the United States and a recipient of substantial U.S. foreign aid. Even before its independence on 14 May 1948, efforts to establish a sovereign state in the traditional Jewish homeland had become an issue for U.S. foreign policymakers. Since the turn of the century, the Zionist ideology of bringing Jews back to the land of Israel and creating a Jewish homeland and eventually a Jewish state there motivated Jews around the world. The question of the proper U.S. posture toward the aspirations of the Zionist movement in Palestine confronted presidents from Woodrow Wilson onward, but achieved unprecedented urgency after 1945 because the Nazi Holocaust and the evident inability of Great Britain to maintain the Palestine Mandate accentuated the plight of the stateless Jews. Thus substantial U.S. involvement began during the 1945–1948 period leading up to Israeli statehood. Ever since, the United States has tried to help Israel achieve national security but in ways compatible with good U.S.-Arab relations and access to oil.

The United States has been a significant factor at most key junctures in Israel's history: the initial war to gain independence, 1948–1949; the 1956–1957 Suez Crisis; the crucial weeks before the outbreak of the Six-Day War on 5 June 1967; the Yom Kippur War in October 1973, and ever since as the key external actor in the Middle East brokering various types of Israeli-Arab negotiations. The signings of the 1978 Camp David Accords, the 1993 Declaration of Principles between Israel and the Palestine Liberation Organization (PLO), and the 1994 accord that led to the treaty between Israel and Jordan took place in Washington under the aegis of the U.S. president.

The closeness of the U.S.-Israel special relationship, which has been a fundamental element of U.S. policy, has varied over time; there have been numerous occasions of great tension and a divergence of views between the two parties. A commitment to the security and well-being of the Jewish state has been a cornerstone of U.S. policy for a number of reasons, including a moral and religious identification with the goals of Zionism, in particular after the destruction of European Jewry; general support for Israel as a democracy with shared values; the salient attachment

Israel and its Neighbors 1949-1967

LEBANON

Tyre •
• Kuneitra

Naharlya•
Acre
Safed •
SYRIA

Haifa
Tiberias •
• Ein Gev

Nazareth
Beit Shean

Netanya •
Jenin
Tulkarm

Jordan River

Nablus
WEST BANK
JORDAN

Tel Aviv
Jaffa
Amman

Lod
Ramla
Jericho

Ashdod
Jerusalem

Nitzanim
Bethlehem

Yad Mordecai
Gat
Hebron

Gaza
Ein Gedi

Khan Yunis
Rafah
Nirim
Beersheba
Dead Sea

Gevulot

El Arish •
Revivim

Mediterranean Sea

EGYPT

NEGEV

Eilat • • Akaba

The territory of Israel In the United Nations plan for the partition of Palestine in 1947

Territory beyond the United Nations line conquered by Israel, 1948-1949

– – Israel's boundaries. 1949-1967

Israel and its neighbors clashed in the Suez war of 1956

0   30 miles

0   60 km

From *American Foreign Relations*, Thomas G. Paterson, J. Garry Clifford, and Kenneth J. Hagan, Volume II. ©1995 by D. C. Heath and Company. Reprinted with permission of Houghton Mifflin Company

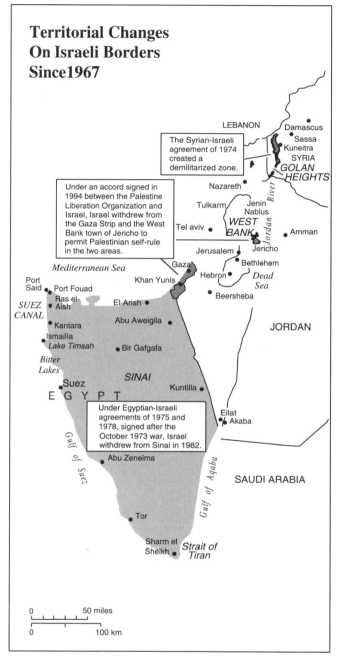

Territorial Changes On Israeli Borders Since1967

LEBANON
• Damascus
• Sassa
Kuneitra
SYRIA
GOLAN HEIGHTS

The Syrian-Israeli agreement of 1974 created a demilitarized zone.

Nazareth

Under an accord signed in 1994 between the Palestine Liberation Organization and Israel, Israel withdrew from the Gaza Strip and the West Bank town of Jericho to permit Palestinian self-rule in the two areas.

Tulkarm
Jenin
Nablus

Jordan River

WEST BANK

Tel aviv •
• Amman

Jerusalem
Jericho

Mediterranean Sea
Gaza
Bethlehem
Dead Sea

Port Said
Port Fouad
Khan Yunis
Hebron •
• Beersheba

Ras el-Aish
• El Arish

SUEZ CANAL

Kantara
Abu Aweigila
JORDAN

Ismailia
Lake Timsah
• Bir Gafgafa

Bitter Lakes

Suez
SINAI

E G Y P T
Kuntilla

Under Egyptian-Israeli agreements of 1975 and 1978, signed after the October 1973 war, Israel withdrew from Sinai in 1982.

Eilat
Akaba

Gulf of Suez

• Abu Zeneima

Gulf of Aqaba

SAUDI ARABIA

• Tor

Sharm el Shelkh
Strait of Tiran

0   50 miles

0   100 km

From *American Foreign Relations*, Thomas G. Paterson, J. Garry Clifford, and Kenneth J. Hagan, Volume II. ©1995 by D. C. Heath and Company. Reprinted with permission of Houghton Mifflin Company

to Israel of the U.S. Jewish community; and the usefulness of Israel at times for U.S. Cold War strategy.

U.S. ties to Israel have often complicated efforts to maintain a coherent Middle East policy because of the frequent juxtaposition of Israeli and Arab interests. This problem gradually diminished, however, with the decline of the Soviet Union and emergence of the United States as the preeminent external power in the Middle East in the early 1990s. But precisely because of the special relationship, the United

States has been in the best position to assist Israel and the Arabs to resolve their longstanding differences, some of which date back to the Arab refusal to accept Israel's creation in 1948 and others which relate to the results of the Six Day War in 1967, when Israel's preemptive strike enabled it to gain control and then maintain the occupation of territory in Sinai, on the West Bank, and the Golan Heights. The effort to bring the Arab-Israeli conflict to a successful conclusion has been a major U.S. policy objective for over 25 years, with

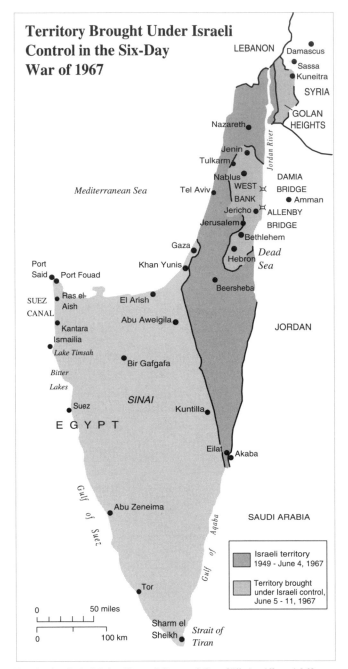

Territory Brought Under Israeli Control in the Six-Day War of 1967

LEBANON
Damascus
Sassa
Kuneitra
SYRIA
GOLAN HEIGHTS
Nazareth
Jenin
Tulkarm
Jordan River
Nablus
Tel Aviv
WEST BANK
DAMIA BRIDGE
Amman
Jericho
ALLENBY BRIDGE
Jerusalem
Bethlehem
Gaza
Dead Sea
Khan Yunis
Hebron
Beersheba
Port Said
Port Fouad
SUEZ CANAL
Ras el-Aish
El Arish
Abu Aweigila
JORDAN
Kantara
Ismailia
Lake Timsah
Bir Gafgafa
Bitter Lakes
SINAI
Suez
Kuntilla
E G Y P T
Eilat
Akaba
Abu Zeneima
SAUDI ARABIA
Mediterranean Sea

Israeli territory 1949 - June 4, 1967

Territory brought under Israeli control, June 5 - 11, 1967

Gulf of Suez
Gulf of Aqaba
Tor
0   50 miles
0   100 km
Sharm el Sheikh
Strait of Tiran

From *American Foreign Relations,* Thomas G. Paterson, J. Garry Clifford, and Kenneth J. Hagan, Volume II. ©1995 by D. C. Heath and Company. Reprinted with permission of Houghton Mifflin Company

"land for peace" a persistent theme. Each newly-elected U.S. president since 1968 has undertaken a major initiative to further the peace process early in his first term, usually in the first year. Few of these initiatives have been successful, but all of the advances toward Arab-Israeli peace have involved a substantial U.S. role.

The Pre-State Period: 1917–1945

There was little U.S. participation in the issuing of the Balfour Declaration in 1917 by the British government, an event which led to an international commitment, through the 1920 League of Nations mandate, to the establishment of a Jewish National Home in Palestine. President Wilson secretly expressed his general support for the British initiative, despite misgivings in the Department of State and on the part of advisers who had counseled restraint. The Mandate was essentially a trusteeship granted to Great Britain over territory that had been under the control of Turkey until the end of World War I. The purpose of fostering a Jewish national home in Palestine was spelled out in the terms of the Mandate.

Wilson's instinctive disposition toward the Zionist cause was not matched by Franklin Delano Roosevelt, who approached the Zionist issue with caution, even as the dimensions of the Holocaust became known. In 1942, the Zionist movement, realizing that a Jewish state could have saved many of the six million European Jews who were being slaughtered by the Nazis, and with the support of much of U.S. Jewry, declared that statehood was the objective. Even as they joined the British to fight Germany, the Palestinian Jews made plans to achieve independence as quickly as possible, developing the necessary political and military infrastructures. As the war in Europe ended, U.S. Jews recognized their relative passivity on behalf of Jewish immigration to the United States during the Nazi period and became much more assertive in their support for the Zionist cause and its urgent realization. President Roosevelt came under strong pressures from the British and the Arabs, who both opposed the Zionist enterprise. As a result he balanced public support for Zionist goals with private assurances of sympathy to Arab leaders such as King Ibn Saud of Saudi Arabia.

Emergence of Israel: 1945–1950

The end of World War II meant that President Harry S. Truman had to confront a series of questions regarding Palestine early in his term. The most pressing question was the plight of Jewish refugees from Nazism who sought refuge in Palestine and the three-way conflict between Jews, Arabs, and British that made the Mandate increasingly unsustainable. The possible consequences of difficult choices led to considerable infighting within the administration, especially as the end of the Mandate neared in 1947 and early 1948. Opposition to policies favoring the Zionists was particularly vigorous from the Department of State and from Secretary of Defense James Forrestal. On the other side were presidential aides such as Clark Clifford and David Niles. Truman, while sympathetic to Jewish aspirations, vacillated as he tried to understand both sides of the issue, particularly the need to maintain good relations with Great Britain, keep oil flowing to Western Europe, avoid alienating the Arab world, and satisfy the domestic pro-statehood constituency among U.S. Jews. He was also conflicted for personal reasons. Though not particularly sympathetic to Jews as a group, he associated with individual Jews for business and political reasons. In addition, he was genuinely moved by the human tragedy of the Holocaust. When the United Nations Special Committee on Palestine in 1947 finally recommended partitioning the territory into a Jewish and an Arab state, the administration supported the idea, despite intense division among Truman's advisers. The General Assembly adopted the partition plan in a tense vote on 29 November 1947.

The period from then to the end of the Mandate in May 1948 was one of severe pressures on Truman, from inside and outside the government. Generally people within the national security apparatus, notably the Department of State and the Pentagon, tended to be anti-Zionist because of their strategic calculations regarding the relative importance of the Arabs and the Jews, while the Zionists had considerable support in Congress and public opinion. Secretary of State George Marshall shared his aides' concerns about American oil interests in the Middle East and was skeptical of the Jews' ability to defend themselves militarily against the anticipated Arab onslaught. Many key people in the Department of State contended that by supporting partition the president was placing crass political considerations, namely the votes of U.S. Jews, ahead of the U.S. national interest. Marshall and his advisers opposed partition and then, as the end of the Mandate approached, opposed the idea of an independent Jewish state. Even so, presidential aides and outsiders with access to the president, such as Zionist leader Chaim Weizmann, generally kept Truman in favor of the statehood for the Jews that was promised in the UN partition resolution. U.S. policy was not always consistent, however, due to continued infighting, which led to a last-ditch attempt to reverse policy through a speech by the United States UN representative in the Spring of 1948.

When the new State of Israel declared its independence on 14 May 1948, Truman was quick to extend de facto recognition, which was welcomed by the Zionists as as a major demonstration of support. Even though Israel was attacked immediately by the surrounding Arab states, the United States remained committed to the arms embargo that had been in place while hostilities escalated during the waning months of the mandate. Truman's support for the nascent Jewish state was undoubtedly due in part to the remarkable campaign by U.S. Zionists, but also reflected the president's own sense of what was right. Had he not been positively oriented toward the idea of Jewish statehood, he could easily have resisted the Zionist pressures.

During Israel's War of Independence, which lasted until January 1949, the United States provided political support in the United Nations and elsewhere, emphasizing the necessity of direct negotiation between Israel and the Arabs to end the conflict and rejected the idea of a solution that would be imposed by the great powers or the United Nations. After Israel's military success, the United States supported the bilateral armistice agreements with the neighboring belligerents (Egypt, Transjordan, Syria, and Lebanon). Then following Israel's first Knesset election in October 1949, the United States extended de jure recognition, sponsored Israel for UN membership, and offered a loan for economic purposes.

As a result of the partition of Palestine and Israel's War of Independence, hundreds of thousands of Palestinian Arabs left their homes and went to Arab-controlled territory, mainly in the Gaza Strip, the West Bank, and Lebanon. There were between 600,000 and 750,000 Palestinian refugees after 1948–1949, roughly equal to the number of Jewish refugees from Arab countries. But while the Jewish refugees were absorbed into Israel, the Arab refugees remained in camps, awaiting the day when they might return to their home towns. Given the enmity that existed between the Arab world and Israel and the prevalent view among the refugees that the Israelis had usurped their homeland, Israel generally refused to allow them to return, fearing that they would constitute a fifth column. Even though the United Nations finally recognized in 1967 that a settlement of the refugee problem was an essential component of a durable and just peace, the issue remained on the negotiating table for decades.

The Early Cold War Years

As the Cold War intensified, the issue of the Middle East became increasingly salient for U.S. policy makers. A recurring question for the administration of President Dwight D. Eisenhower was how relations with Israel might affect relations with the Arabs. Given the administration's emphasis on achieving policy objectives within the Arab world, the period from 1953 to 1961 was one in which Israel had little leverage with the U.S. government. It was a frustrating time for the pro-Israel camp, which failed to stop the Baghdad Pact (an attempt at collective security against the Soviet threat that grouped Great Britain, Iraq, Iran, Turkey, and Pakistan and was seen by Israel as ominous), obtain arms sales, or formalize a U.S.-Israeli alliance. Still, U.S.-Arab hostilities, in large part due to Arab perceptions of U.S. favoritism to Israel, prevented a U.S.-Arab accord. Even after the United States reprimanded Israel for its attack against Egypt in the Suez War of 1956 Washington did not abandon Israel.

One of the ways in which the United States helped Israel was through the provision of aid, a program which began shortly after the birth of the Jewish state, but which was solely economic and then in quite modest amounts for the first twenty years. During the Eisenhower years, economic grants and loans totaled about $150 million per year. Even in the year after the Suez crisis, the United States provided a total of $127 million in loans and grants to Israel.

Eisenhower had surrounded himself with aides and advisers from Secretary of State John Foster Dulles on down, who wanted to enhance ties with the Arab states and had little of the instinctive identification with Israel of Truman's staff. But the United States was often at odds with Egypt, whose president, Gamal Abdel Nasser, opposed the Baghdad Pact in 1955 and then began to seek Soviet arms. Nasser's policies also created great apprehension in Israel. He maintained a tight ban on Israeli-bound shipping through the Suez Canal, a blockade of the Straits of Tiran, Israel's lifeline to the Far East, allowed terrorist raids into Israel from Gaza, and was negotiating for a massive arms deal with the Soviet bloc. An Israeli attack on Egyptian military headquarters in Gaza, a reprisal for the terrorist attacks, gave Nasser a pretext to conclude the arms deal with Czechoslovakia and brought a strong condemnation from the Eisenhower administration.

Yet when Israel—in cooperation with Great Britain and France, and even more concerned about Egypt's arms buildup and terrorist raids launched from Egyptian-controlled territory, initiating the Suez Crisis—attacked Egypt eight days before the 1956 presidential election, Eisenhower was caught off guard and became outraged. After the Israeli victory, which brought the entire Sinai under Israeli control, the administration took a very hard diplomatic line. Eisenhower warned Israel of dire consequences if it did not withdraw from Sinai, including UN condemnation, attacks by Soviet volunteers, suspension of U.S. government aid, and termination of tax deductible private fundraising for Israel. At the time the United States was giving Israel $113 million per year in loans and $50 million per year in grants, both limited to economic aid. The total of $163 million for 1956 dropped to $127 million in 1957. Private giving on a tax deductible basis, largely through agencies such as the United Jewish Appeal and the Jewish National Fund, were only a fraction of the government aid. Since that time private giving to Israel has grown substantially, reaching peaks during years of crisis such as 1967 and 1973 and several hundred million dollars per year into the 1990s.

Prime Minister David Ben-Gurion then agreed to withdraw under suitable conditions, namely a UN force in the Sinai to act as a buffer between the Egyptian and Israeli armies, and guarantees for innocent maritime passage. The mutual suspicion that remained after the confrontation over Sinai created serious tension in the bilateral relationship for the balance of the Eisenhower years.

Furthermore, the U.S. desire to work closely with conservative Arab regimes to combat the possible spread of communism, or even Soviet influence, reinforced the conviction that the United States should not be too close to Israel. The American reluctance regarding Israel was ameliorated somewhat due to hostility between Washington and Nasser's Egypt.

Eisenhower's skepticism about Nasser, combined with his desire to contain Soviet influence in the Middle East, led to the articulation of the Eisenhower Doctrine in 1956–1957. This was an attempt to strengthen bilateral relationships with friendly Arab regimes in order to prevent the advance of communism. Israel was at first suspicious, but eventually went along with the idea. The real test of the Eisenhower Doctrine came in 1958, when he sent marines to Lebanon in the wake of a coup in Iraq.

President John F. Kennedy took a different tack, trying simultaneously to improve relations with Egypt and Israel by providing economic aid to the former and initiating arms sales (Hawk antiaircraft missiles) to the latter. He also was prepared to consider a possible role for Israel in his overall strategy for the region, especially in light of his opposition to Egypt's war in Yemen. These trends advanced under President Lyndon B. Johnson, who arranged to sell Israel offensive weapons such as tanks and Skyhawk fighter-bombers. Under Johnson, U.S. and Israeli interests converged to an increasing extent because of Soviet penetration of key Arab states, such as Egypt and Syria. The Soviet Union became their main arms supplier, stationed advisers in those countries to work with their armies, and worked very closely with them on political matters. U.S.-Israeli economic, military, and intelligence ties were also enhanced during the period leading up to the 1967 war.

The 1967 War

In May 1967, inaccurate information regarding Israeli troop buildups against Syria led Egypt's President Gamal Abdel Nasser to move Egyptian troops into Sinai in place of the UN forces that had been there since 1957 as part of the settlement of the Suez War. He also closed the vital Strait of Tiran, an action that Israel regarded as a casus belli, induced his Syrian allies to mass troops on the border with Israel, and threatened a war of destruction against Israel. At first, the United States urged restraint on Israel and tried to avert war, but was unable to reverse the Egyptian actions or reopen the contested waterway. Finally, Washington gave the green light to Israel, which then struck preemptively on 5 June to destroy the Egyptian air force on the ground. After defeating Egypt and gaining control of the Gaza Strip and the Sinai Desert, Israel repulsed a Jordanian attack and drove the Jordanian army out of the West Bank. The Israeli army confronted the Syrians, defeating them and occupying the Golan Heights. During the war, Israel attacked a U.S. intelligence ship, but claimed that it was a mistake and paid compensation for the casualties.

The brief war of June 1967 marked a significant turning point in U.S.-Israeli relations. Since then the United States has assumed the key external responsibility for seeking solutions to the Arab-Israeli conflict. During the same period, the United States became Israel's major source of weapons. Although the United States backed Israel in 1967 and has since supported Israel, albeit not without major differences, it has been successful in assuming the role of honest broker between the parties. This became increasingly clear after Soviet influence in the Arab world began to decline in 1972.

The Six-Day War radically changed the configuration of power in the Middle East and the primary diplomatic issues. Israel's lightning victory established it as the dominant military power in the region and humiliated the Arab regimes. The occupation of territory as the result of the war and the creation of additional refugees dramatically transformed the issues relating to the achievement of peace between the Arabs and Israel. And the events leading up to the war made outsiders, especially in the United States, more sensitive to Israel's need for secure and recognized borders. The efforts to resolve the effects of that war represent the beginnings of the Arab-Israeli peace process that continued into the mid-1990s. Finally, the Palestinians were able to capitalize on the loss of the West Bank and Gaza to launch a very successful international campaign for the support and recognition their cause.

In the months after the war, the United States was instrumental in the efforts, particularly at the United Nations, to try to resolve the underlying issues of the Arab-Israeli conflict. The result was Security Council Resolution 242, adopted in November 1967, which set out a framework for peace. The resolution called upon Israel to withdraw to secure and recognized borders in exchange for peace and recognition, and proposed a settlement for the Palestinian refugees of the 1948–1949 conflict, as well as the 1967 war. Resolution 242 became the structure within which all subsequent efforts to achieve peace have been carried out.

During the period between the Six-Day and Yom Kippur Wars, the United States worked for the realization of the objectives of Resolution 242. Generally the United States agreed with Israel that it was necessary to conclude peace agreements with the Arab countries and that Israel need not withdraw from territories occupied in 1967 except in the context of such treaties. Despite this general congruence of objectives, there were often disagreements with regard to specific issues, such as the necessity for direct negotiations between Israel and its Arab neighbors, the possible disposition of the occupied territories, and weapons sales in the region. The problem became exacerbated as Israeli ambivalence regarding the possibility of giving up territory, especially in the West Bank and the Golan Heights, increased during the 1970s.

When Richard Nixon came to office in 1969, his strategic view emphasized broad U.S. interests in the Middle East. This orientation required a somewhat more distant relationship with Israel while still continuing the U.S. commitment to maintaining Israeli military superiority. His secretary of state, William Rogers, energetically promoted plans bearing his name in order to coordinate superpower pressure on the parties and flesh out details of a settlement.

Between 1970 and 1973, the implications of the U.S.-Israel relationship for superpower competition became more evident. Increasingly success for their Arab allies became a major concern of the Soviets, while some elements of the U.S. government, notably National Security Adviser Henry Kissinger, urged closer ties with Israel as a counterweight to Soviet actions, particularly arms supplies to Arab antagonists of Israel and the building of political alliances in the Arab world. By 1972, the United States was trying to pursue a multi-pronged policy that involved détente with the Soviet Union, protection of Arab oil producers against Soviet penetration, and military and economic support for Israel. The Nixon administration concluded the first long-term arms deal with Israel for the supply of Phantom jets and sophisticated electronic equipment.

The Yom Kippur War and Its Aftermath: 1973–1977

When the Egyptians and Syrians surprised Israel with their attacks in October 1973, the United States was forced to make some unprecedented decisions. Most notably, the surprisingly rapid expenditure of weapons and the inability of Israel to prevail quickly necessitated a massive U.S. resupply effort of aircraft, tanks, and ordnance as well as the provision of emergency financial aid to Israel. Thus the United States intervened decisively on Israel's side for the first time, but only after hesitation and intense deliberations during the first week of the three week conflict. The war invalidated many key U.S. and Israeli assumptions: that the Arabs would be deterred from war by Israel's military strength, that Israel could defeat its enemies easily, and that the Soviet Union would remain out of the conflict. The stance taken by the United States led Arab oil producers to impose an oil embargo, opened divisions with European allies, and resulted in a brief but dangerous confrontation with the Soviets near the end of the war. After Israel trapped the Egyptian Third Army and surrounded it east of the Suez Canal, the Soviets threatened to intervene themselves in order to prevent a surrender. A Soviet attack on Israel could well have brought the United States into the conflict, thereby creating the possibility of a direct Soviet-U.S. confrontation. When the crisis passed, the ceasefire call and the reiteration of the principles of peace found in Resolution 242 were expressed in United Nations Security Council Resolution 338 which both the United States and the Soviet Union supported.

Kissinger, by then secretary of state, saw an opportunity to utilize Israel's newly revealed vulnerability to make progress toward peace. He sought to achieve a balance in which Israel would remain safe militarily but not achieve a repetition of the decisive military victory of 1967. In addition, Israel's increased dependence on the United States for military and economic aid after the war presumably made it more amenable to Kissinger's objectives. But as Kissinger pushed forward, the United States and Israel diverged. The former was eager to obtain a settlement, in part due to the oil embargo and international tensions, but was not meticulous about the terms. Israel, on the other hand, insisted that the terms be negotiated carefully because of the implications for vital national security interests, even if it meant that the process would take a longer time. The strain in U.S.-Israeli relations was alleviated in part by the development of a step-by-step approach that eventually led to two disengagement agreements, one with Egypt and one with Syria. These agreements provided for the respective armies to pull back from their confrontation positions, thereby lessening tensions and the threat of a renewal of fighting. They also enhanced Kissinger's status and that of the United States in general, brought gains internationally to the United States by improving its ability to work closely with both sides, and entailed new U.S. military equipment and economic aid commitments to Israel. After Kissinger and President Gerald Ford issued a thinly veiled threat to reassess the U.S.-Israeli relationship, the second Egyptian agreement was completed in 1975. It involved painful strategic concessions for Israel in connection with the pullback in Sinai from the Abu Rhodeis oil fields and the key Gidi and Mitla passes, but some political compensation in terms of a "Memorandum of Agreement," which amounted to a virtual U.S.-Israel alliance and provided guarantees about oil supplies, economic and military aid, arms, and innocent passage of Israeli cargoes through the Suez Canal. The United States also pledged not to negotiate with the Palestine Liberation Organization, whose charter denied Israel's right to exist and claimed all of Israel's territory for the Palestinians, until that body accepted UN Resolutions 242 and 338. Despite the pain of the reassessment, the conclusion of Sinai II marked a high point in U.S.-Israel relations. Later in 1975, the U.S. vehemently opposed a "Zionism is Racism" resolution that was adopted by the UN General Assembly.

The Camp David Accords and After

The transition to the Carter administration early in 1977 left the U.S. role in Middle East peacemaking somewhat uncertain. When the United States suggested a bilateral initiative with the Soviets early in October 1977, neither Egyptian President Anwar Sadat nor Israeli Prime Minister Menachem Begin was eager to see the Soviets insert themselves into peacemaking. Hence they accelerated a process that was already underway. On that basis, Sadat stunned most observers and visited Jerusalem in November 1977, inaugurating the first direct Israeli-Arab negotiations. Further negotiations, in which the United States played a relatively minor role, continued for several months without agreement. Finally, in an effort to break the impasse, President Jimmy Carter invited Begin and Sadat to Camp David in September 1978. Carter's intervention in the negotiations proved critical to the achievement of the Camp David Accords and the subsequent Israeli-Egyptian peace treaty. Israel agreed to a staged withdrawal from Sinai to the international border between Egypt and Palestine which had been demarcated in 1906 in exchange for peace, security guarantees, diplomatic recognition, and various types of relationships. The treaty, which took effect in 1979, called for further negotiations on Palestinian autonomy in the coming years. U.S. diplomacy and Carter in particular won widespread praise for the triumph. The exultation was to be short-lived, however, because Carter soon had to come to grips with the implications of the treaty for Palestinian autonomy. After the peace treaty became operative, his posture toward Israeli-Palestinian issues, such as the nature of the autonomy and the building of Israeli settlements in the West Bank, caused a cooling in U.S.-Israel relations and a drop in support from pro-Israel voters. Egyptian and Israeli negotiators, who were supposed to move beyond the treaty to the terms of the autonomy, failed to make significant progress, despite U.S. efforts. Carter also found Begin's hardline positions annoying and feared that Begin was not really interested in moving beyond the treaty itself. Meanwhile the Israelis were concerned with Carter's apparent flirtation with the PLO, which resulted in the firing of the American UN Ambassador Andrew Young for holding unauthorized talks with the PLO representative at the United Nations.

The administrations of Ronald Reagan and George Bush witnessed substantial changes in the U.S.-Israel relationship, highlighted by generally close ties under Reagan and greater tension under Bush. The significance of Israel as a strategic asset to the United States emerged as an important consideration during the Reagan years and was emphasized by U.S. supporters of Israel in Congress, in the Jewish community, and among opinion makers. Reagan generally favored Israel, but his own orientation did not prevent serious differences from erupting. Some of the points of contention included U.S. arms sales to Arab states such as Saudi Arabia, which Israel perceived as threatening its security, the Begin government's policy of settling Israelis in Gaza, the West Bank, and the Golan Heights, and Israel's bombing of Iraq's nuclear reactor in 1981. But by far the most serious confrontation occurred when Israel invaded Lebanon in June 1982 in order to attack the PLO and drive it out of the country. Israel's destructive move through southern Lebanon and on to Beirut caused great consternation within the administration. After the intense Israeli bombing of the city on August 12, Reagan demanded an end to the attacks. Sharp words flew between Washington and Jerusalem. U.S. troops soon went to Beirut as part of a first multilateral force to ensure the safe departure of the PLO's armed personnel. In September, following the mass killings of Palestinians in the Sabra and Shatilla refugee camps by Christian militias while Israeli forces were nominally in control, a second U.S. contingent joined them. Over 200 soldiers from this second U.S. force were killed by a terrorist bomb in October 1983. In February 1984, under intense domestic political pressure, President Reagan decided to withdraw U.S. troops from Lebanon.

During Reagan's second term, the Israeli role in the attempt to trade arms to Iran in exchange for hostages, part of the Iran-Contra Affair, and the 1985 arrest and guilty plea of U.S. naval intelligence analyst Jonathan Pollard for spying on behalf of Israel tested the strength of U.S.-Israel relations. Furthermore, the Palestinian uprising known as the intifada, which began in 1987, accentuated differences between the U.S. and Israeli conceptions of how to deal with the territories. Then, at the very end of the Reagan administration, Secretary of State George Shultz announced that the United States would begin a direct dialogue with the PLO.

President George Bush proved to be much less favorably inclined toward Israel than his predecessor. He carried on a dialogue with the PLO and had a number of confrontations with Prime Minister Yitzhak Shamir, whose tough line on the future of the occupied territories conflicted with the increasing emphasis by the United States on the traditional view that Israel had to be prepared to withdraw from virtually all of the territory occupied since 1967 in order to achieve a genuine peace. A specific controversy was Bush's refusal to extend a $10 billion loan guarantee unless Israel suspended the building of new settlements in the occupied territories.

During the Gulf War in 1991, designed to compel Iraq to reverse its invasion of Kuwait, the effort to build an anti-Saddam Hussein coalition, including several Arab countries, persuaded U.S. policymakers to press Israel not to respond to the provocations coming from Baghdad. When Iraq launched Scud missiles against Israeli population centers, such as Tel Aviv, the United States strongly urged Israel not to respond militarily for fear of disrupting the coalition. The effort succeeded, although Israel endured casualties and property damage as well as the necessity of keeping its population in sealed rooms with gas masks during missile attacks in case any Iraqi chemical weapons had been launched. The United States sent Patriot anti-missile teams to defend against the Scuds, marking the first time that the Israelis had direct-defense help from foreign troops. The Israelis appreciated the Patriots at the time, but later analyses indicated the missiles were not as effective as claimed. The experience of being attacked without being able to retaliate was upsetting to many Israelis, who had to ponder the long-term strategic implications.

After the Gulf War, and with the waning of the Cold War, the administration believed the time was right to move ahead with the Arab-Israeli peace process. The United States took the initiative in convening a peace conference in Madrid in 1992 that provided a format in which the various outstanding issues could be negotiated either bilaterally or multilaterally.

The Israel-PLO Breakthrough

The real opening came during 1993, after Bill Clinton won and Shamir lost to Yitzhak Rabin in 1992 elections in both countries. Rabin's Labor Party dramatically reversed long-standing Israeli policy by negotiating secretly for months with the PLO. The United States was left out of the process, with Norway playing the crucial mediating role. But when Israel and the PLO agreed on a Declaration of Principles (DOP) in September, President Clinton hosted Rabin and PLO Chairman Yassir Arafat for an elaborate signing ceremony on the White House lawn, emulating Carter in conferring the blessing and the backing of the United States to an agreement that had been negotiated directly between the parties. The DOP represented an implementation of the essence of the autonomy plan that had been proposed by Begin and incorporated into the Camp David Accords. Its key feature was the reciprocal recognition of Israel and the PLO, which promised to transform the nature of the peace process. The Clinton administration's image as a strong backer of Israel reportedly contributed to Arafat's determination to deal directly with Israel for terms that were less than he had been demanding. In particular, the DOP did not provide for the establishment of a Palestinian state, but rather left the final status of the disputed territories to a further round of negotiations beginning in 1996.

The signing of the DOP transformed the Middle East peace process, opening up possibilities that previously had been beyond reach. From the perspective of American foreign policy, it was an exceptionally significant step because the regularization of a relationship between Israel and the PLO provided the United States with much greater room to maneuver in its Middle East diplomacy. As a result, the United States backed the process enthusiastically, made its good offices available to both parties, and did whatever it could to promote ties between Israel and the Arab countries. The Clinton administration put its prestige behind the efforts to bring about a comprehensive and lasting peace in the region. Although much of the negotiation went ahead without substantial U.S. involvement, the administration was careful to seal all significant agreements with its imprimatur. Furthermore it helped to broker negotiations between Israel and states such as Jordan and played a central role in the efforts to bring about an elusive peace between Israel and Syria. In succinct terms, the United States was present at every vital juncture and was welcomed by the parties for its interventions along the way.

President Clinton closely identified himself with the post-1993 peace process and backed Prime Minister Rabin and Chairman Arafat energetically. Two 1994 developments, the Cairo Agreement, which fleshed out the intentions of the DOP and provided for Israel's withdrawal from Gaza and Jericho, and the Israel-Jordan Peace Treaty, were largely negotiated between the parties, but certainly with the blessing and backing of the United States. But in 1995, the U.S. role became more obvious and visible. The Israel-PLO interim agreement, which set the terms for substantial Israeli withdrawals from the West Bank and for the elections of the Palestinian Authority's council, was signed in an elaborate ceremony on the White House lawn in September with President Clinton presiding. Known as Oslo II, it represented a large step toward the eventual full implementation of the DOP.

When Prime Minister Rabin was assassinated in November 1995 by a Jewish extremist, President Clinton demonstrated his commitment to Rabin's ideals and to Israel by his moving speech at the funeral. He also made it clear that the United States supported Prime Minister Shimon Peres in his efforts to maintain the momentum of the process that Rabin and Arafat had begun.

Peres lost, however, in the May 1996 elections to Likud leader Benjamin Netanyahu. During the campaign Netanyahu and Likud were highly critical of the Oslo peace process and, implicitly and at times explicitly, of the U.S. role in it. Both because of these policy differences and the Clinton administration's efforts to support and boost Peres's candidacy, relations between the two countries seemed somewhat shaken by the Netanyahu victory.

Nevertheless close and cooperative U.S.-Israeli relations continued to rest on shared interests and common values. Thus whatever the specific and immediate differences may prove to be, cooperation and friendship are likely to prevail.

HAROLD M. WALLER

See also Arafat, Yassir; Bush, George Herbert Walker; Camp David Accords; Carter, James Earl; Clinton, William Jefferson; Cold War; Egypt; Eisenhower Doctrine; Eisenhower, Dwight David; Gulf War of 1990–1991; Holocaust; Kissinger, Henry Alfred; Lebanon; Middle East; Nasser, Gamal Abdel; Nixon, Richard Milhous; Palestine; Palestine Liberation Organization; Reagan, Ronald Wilson; Refugees; Sadat, Anwar El-; Suez Crisis

FURTHER READING

Ben-Zvi, Avraham. *The United States and Israel: The Limits of the Special Relationship.* New York, 1993.

Brecher, Michael. *Decisions in Israel's Foreign Policy.* New Haven, Conn., 1975.

Cohen, Michael Joseph. *Truman and Israel.* Berkeley, Calif., 1990.

Gilboa, Eytan. *American Public Opinion toward Israel and the Arab-Israeli Conflict.* Lexington, Mass., 1987.

Organski, A.F.K. *The $36 Billion Bargain: Strategy and Politics in U.S. Assistance to Israel.* New York,1990.

Quandt, William B. *Peace Process: American Diplomacy and the Arab-Israeli Conflict since 1967.* Washington D.C., 1993.

Reich, Bernard. *Securing the Covenant: United States–Israel Relations After the Cold War.* Westport, Conn., 1995.

Reich, Bernard, and Gershon Kieval, eds. *Israeli Politics in the 1990s: Key Domestic and Foreign Policy Factors.* New York, 1991.

Safran, Nadav. *Israel: The Embattled Ally.* Cambridge, Mass., 1981.

Schoenbaum, David. *The United States and the State of Israel.* New York, 1993.

Spiegel, Steven L. *The Other Arab-Israeli Conflict: Making America's Middle East Policy, from Truman to Reagan.* Chicago, 1985.

Tschirgi, Dan. *The American Search for Mideast Peace.* New York, 1989.

Wilson, Evan. *Decision on Palestine: How the U.S. Came to Recognize Israel.* Stanford, Calif., 1979.

ITALY

A peninsular country located in southern Europe extending into the central Mediterranean Sea, bordered in the north by France, Switzerland, Austria, and Slovenia. The United States has viewed Italy as a source of cultural inspiration and large numbers of U.S. citizens emigrated from this country. Relations have ranged from enmity during World War II to alliance within the North Atlantic Treaty Organization (NATO). Italy became a united nation in 1861. The United States, which had maintained diplomatic relations with several of the states of the Italian peninsula, promptly recognized the Kingdom of Italy. In 1867, prior to the final step in the unification of Italy, the occupation of Rome in 1870, the United States ended diplomatic relations with the Papal States, which had been initiated in 1848.

From the beginning, Italy loomed large in the U.S. consciousness as a source of Western culture and as a place where art and life could be experienced on a different plane. Artists and financiers wintered in Rome or Florence; institutions like the American Academy in Rome were created as the embodiment of this U.S. interest in Italy as a cultural mother lode. The United States had another nongovernmental link with Italy. Beginning in the late nineteenth century, Italians, mainly from the South and Sicily, began migrating to the United States; by the mid-1920s, when immigration was severely limited, 4.5 million Italians had reached the United States. This migration was a cause of embarrassment, bordering on shame, to Italy. The newly arrived Italians, largely removed from a premodern rural environment, struggled for existence in the cities of the industrial Northeast of the United States, where they had a difficult time and enjoyed little prestige. As time went on, however, their voting strength became a factor in U.S. politics.

These two powerful connections outside the traditional area of foreign relations constituted the bulk of U.S.-Italian relations until the 1930s, when the storm clouds of a possible new European war began to gather. President Woodrow Wilson's rejection of Italy's claim to much of the Adriatic coast of the newly created Yugoslavia, as a reward for having entered World War I on the side of the Allies, did cause Italian resentment. The United States nevertheless initially adopted a benevolently tolerant and financially helpful attitude toward the Fascist regime of Benito Mussolini that was installed in 1922. Public opinion in the United States began to turn against the Mussolini regime beginning with the Italian invasion of Ethiopia in 1935. In the early 1930s, however, the U.S. government sought to encourage Mussolini in his position of resistance to the expansion of the dominion of Adolf Hitler's Nazi Germany. Later, when Mussolini clearly threw in his lot with Hitler, the United States adopted a chilly and negative attitude toward the Italian regime, culminating in President Franklin D. Roosevelt's description of the Italian attack on France in June 1940 as a "stab in the back."

The Allied invasion of Sicily in 1943, followed by the removal of Mussolini and the surrender of Italy, truly began the era of intensive U.S.-Italian relations. As in other parts of the Mediterranean, the United States initially was willing, perhaps even eager, to let Great Britain resume its traditional role of hegemoy, but a combination of British exhaustion and differences of views and interests eventually led the United States to assert a dominant role in Italy.

In the early postwar period the United States was quick to display friendliness to Italy over issues such as the fate of Trieste (which did not become a part of communist Yugoslavia) and reincorporation of Italy in the family of nations. Moreover, the United States was the one source of economic assistance to Italy's prostrate economy. The main U.S. objective was to prevent Italy's falling into the Soviet Union's orbit. The United States encouraged the May 1947 expulsion of the communists from the Italian government, and then did its best, through means ranging from Marshall Plan aid to covert action, to ensure that the communists were defeated in the elections of April 1948.

For the next forty-five years the Christian Democrats dominated the Italian government, which remained a loyal ally of the United States, but there were some difficult moments. Italy's entry into NATO was contested both from within and without, from within not just by the discounted communists but by those in the Italian establishment who preferred a more detached and free-wheeling role, and from without by most of the core group of potential NATO members, because inclusion of Italy would mean extending the alliance to the Mediterranean, and Italy would be more of a military liability than an asset. After some temporizing, Italy's great postwar prime minister, Alcide de Gasperi, pushed for Italy's inclusion, and on 4 April 1949, Italy became one of the original signatories of the North Atlantic Treaty.

At times Italy adopted a rhetorically independent position on some major international relationships, particularly with the communist East and with the Middle East. Italy was an early advocate of détente in East-West relations, particularly through trade. In the late 1950s and early 1960s, Italy became a major importer of Soviet oil, raising fears in the United States that Italy would become economically dependent on the Soviet Union and culminating in strong pressure from the administration of President John F. Kennedy to cut back this trade. In 1966 the Italian auto manufacturer Fiat undertook one of the first major Western investments in the Soviet Union since the 1920s, when Vladimir Lenin's New Economic Policy was in force. Italy became more friendly with Arab states as popular attitudes shifted against Israel after the Six-Day War (1967) and especially after the Yom Kippur War (1973). Concerns about energy supply and export markets in the Middle East also contributed to this shift. These developments coincided with and were in part the result of the declining authority of the Christian Democratic party, which felt it necessary to make concessions both to the other coalition parties and to the communist opposition. Nevertheless, Italy continued to make contributions to the alliance and U.S. military requirements. It accepted the role of a U.S. "aircraft carrier" in the midst of the Mediterranean, continuing to provide the United States the generous base rights granted in secret agreements of the 1950s.

Italy's ambivalent position led to occasional clashes with the United States. In the acrimonious dispute over the handling of the hijacking in October 1985 of the Italian cruise liner *Achille Lauro* by Arab terrorists, during which a U.S. citizen was killed, Italy released the chief plotter of this crime. Until the end of the Cold War, Italian foreign policy continued to combine Atlantic loyalty with overtones of independence. The other main theme in Italian foreign policy was the construction of a European community. The United States encouraged this development as part of its Marshall Plan program. Prime Minister de Gasperi was a convinced Europeanist. His successors echoed his beliefs, and Italy became one of the founding members of the European Community. The perennial deficiencies of the Italian state contributed to the overwhelming popularity of European unity in Italy; Europe was seen as delivering benefits that the government in Rome never could.

The end of the Cold War in 1989 came at a time when Italy was becoming increasingly conscious of its prosperity and economic power. It had participated with the leading nations of the noncommunist world in the annual Economic Summits since their inception in 1975, and in 1987 the financial consultations of the Group of Five were expanded, as the Group of Seven, to include Italy. The Italian government began to take a slightly more active role in international affairs, joining in several international peacekeeping efforts. It sent a contingent to the Persian Gulf during the U.S.-led military action against Iraq in 1990–1991, to Somalia in 1992–1994, and to Bosnia in 1995–1996.

The conclusion of the Cold War contributed to the breakup of the postwar alignment of Italian political parties and the disclosure of widespread political corruption. In the elections of 1992 and 1994 Italian voters rejected the traditional ruling parties, especially the Socialists but also the Christian Democrats. The 1994 elections, fought under a new electoral system, brought a right-wing coalition to power for the first time in Italy's postwar history. This government spoke of seeking a higher profile internationally and within Europe. However, despite the participation of a "post-Fascist" party, its only nationalist action was to delay Slovenia's association with the European Union. More open and competitive domestic politics in Italy may make foreign policy a subject for significant debate and could change the heretofore muted style of Italian diplomacy, but it seems unlikely that the Italian government will attempt to play an independent role in world politics. Its interests—and its weaknesses—will probably dictate continued subordination to an integrated Europe, for economic prosperity, and to the transatlantic alliance, for security.

JOHN W. HOLMES

See also Mussolini, Benito; North Atlantic Treaty Organization; World War I; World War II

FURTHER READING

DeConde, Alexander. *Half Bitter, Half Sweet: An Excursion into Italian-American History*. New York, 1971.

Ginsborg, Paul. *A History of Contemporary Italy: Society and Politics, 1943–1988*. New York, 1990.

Hughes, H. Stuart. *The United States and Italy*, 3rd ed. Cambridge, Mass., 1979.

Mack Smith, Denis. *Italy: A Modern History*, rev. ed. Ann Arbor, Mich., 1969.

McCarthy, Patrick. *The Crisis of the Italian State: From the Origins of the Cold War to the Fall of Berlusconi*. N.Y., 1995.

Romano, Sergio. *Guida alla Politica Estera Italiana*, 2nd ed. Milan, 1993.

Spotts, Frederic, and Theodor Wieser. *Italy, A Difficult Democracy: A Survey of Italian Politics*. Cambridge, 1986.

IVORY COAST

See Côte d'Ivoire in Appendix 2

J

JACKSON, ANDREW

(*b.* 15 March 1767; *d.* 8 June 1845)

Military hero and seventh president of the United States (1829–1837). Born in the South Carolina back country the decade before the American Revolution, Jackson came to symbolize the virtues of the frontier and the common person: action, individualism, and the spirit of democracy. A military leader and president who advocated territorial and commercial expansion, his influence on U.S. foreign relations reflected pioneering virtues.

Orphaned at age fourteen when his mother succumbed to fever while nursing Revolutionary soldiers (his father had died before Andrew was born), Jackson studied law in Salisbury, North Carolina, and in 1788 migrated to Nashville to establish his career. He quickly earned a sound reputation as a prosecuting attorney and land speculator. After Tennessee became a state in 1796 Jackson served brief terms in the U.S. House of Representatives and the Senate, but he had little interest in the positions and resigned from both. He became a Tennessee state judge and, in 1802, was elected major general of the state militia.

During the War of 1812 Jackson defeated the Creek Indians, who were allied with the British, at the Battle of Horseshoe Bend, Alabama, on 29 March 1814. The victory broke the power of the Creeks and led to a treaty in which the Indians ceded 23 million acres of territory. Jackson was then named a major general in the U.S. Army, in which capacity he defeated British troops decisively at New Orleans on 8 January 1815. The battle impacted national pride tremendously, and it exercised strategic importance as well. Though a treaty ending the war had been signed at Ghent, on 24 December 1814, Great Britain might not have exchanged ratifications had they won at New Orleans. British forces included officers prepared to form a civil government and a governor's commission denying the legitimacy of the Louisiana Purchase. Louisiana might have been awarded to Spain at the Congress of Vienna.

In 1818, acting on imprecise instructions from Secretary of War John C. Calhoun and President James Monroe, Jackson led U.S. troops into Spanish Florida, where he captured Spanish forts and executed Indians and British subjects Robert Ambrister and Alexander Arbuthnot, whom he accused of inciting Indians to rebel against the United States. When Spain demanded an apology and punishment for Jackson, President Monroe and his cabinet appeared about to turn against Jackson. Secretary of State John Quincy Adams, however, in a note dated 23 July 1818, to Spanish minister Luis de Onís, defended Jackson as acting in self-defense because Spain could not control Indians in its jurisdiction. Adams used diplomatic leverage he gained in this incident to bring about the Adams-Onís Treaty of 1819, in which Spain sold Florida to the United States and agreed to a transcontinental boundary with the United States.

Major issues encountered by Jackson's administration were efforts to purchase Texas from Mexico, negotiations with Great Britain regarding trade with the British West Indies and the Maine-New Brunswick boundary, and a dispute with France over spoliations claims owed the United States. One of Jackson's main goals was the acquisition of Texas from Mexico. In 1829 he named Anthony Butler chargé to Mexico and authorized an offer of up to $5 million for Texas. Butler tried to bribe Mexican officials and was replaced in 1836, though Jackson may have abetted Butler's schemes. When Texas declared independence in 1836, relations between Mexico and the United States deteriorated and Jackson ordered the legation closed.

In U.S.-British affairs, Jackson reopened direct trade with the British West Indies, which had been closed or limited since the American Revolution. After painstaking negotiations, the United States and Great Britain signed a reciprocity treaty in 1830, which admitted U.S. vessels to Great Britain's ports in the West Indies. Jackson sought to settle the Maine-Canada Boundary controversy, an issue since the Treaty of Paris of 1783. The King of the Netherlands arbitrated, and in 1831, he awarded the United States most of the disputed territory. Jackson wished to accept the award, but political opposition to relinquishing any of the disputed territory caused the United States to reject the decision.

Trouble arose with France over U.S. claims for French spoliations of shipping during the Napoleonic Wars. In a treaty signed 4 July 1831, France agreed to pay the United States 25 million francs ($4.6 million) in six annual installments plus interest. When the first installment came due, however, the French Chamber of Deputies declined to appropriate funds. Jackson threatened reprisal, asserting that if the Chamber did not appropriate the funds, he would ask Congress for the power to confiscate French ships and property. The French Chamber passed an appropriation, but demanded that Jackson explain his remarks before any money was paid. Jackson responded that while the honor of his country would "never be stained by an apology from me," he had never intended "to menace or insult the Government of France." France paid the missing installments.

During Jackson's administration, the United States completed a number of commercial treaties and claims negotiations with other nations, including Chile, Denmark, Mexico, Naples, Peru-Bolivia, Portugal, Russia, Spain, Turkey, and Venezuela. Jackson sent Edmund Roberts as a special agent to Southeast Asia to expand U.S. trade there. To demonstrate U.S. strength, the frigate *Potomac* was dispatched to punish the Sumatran town of Quallah Battoo in the East Indies for its depredations on the U.S. trading vessel *Friendship*.

President Jackson pursued a vigorous foreign policy motivated by nationalism and economic expansion. Although he was more forceful in style, Jackson continued the policies articulated by earlier presidents and addressed the same issues.

KENNETH R. STEVENS

See also Adams-Onís Treaty; Canada; France; Mexico; Napoleonic Wars; War of 1812

FURTHER READING

Belohlavek, John M. *Let the Eagle Soar!: The Foreign Policy of Andrew Jackson*. Lincoln, Neb., 1985.

Cole, Donald B. *The Presidency of Andrew Jackson*. Lawrence, Kan., 1993.

Remini, Robert. *Andrew Jackson and the Course of American Empire, 1767–1821*. New York, 1977.

———. *Andrew Jackson and the Course of American Freedom, 1822–1832*. New York, 1981.

———. *Andrew Jackson and the Course of American Democracy, 1833–1845*. New York, 1984.

JACKSON, HENRY MARTIN

(*b.* 31 May 1912; *d.* 1 September 1983)

Democratic senator from the state of Washington who served more than five terms in the Senate (1953–1983). Widely considered one of the Senate's preeminent experts on foreign and defense policy, "Scoop" Jackson was a principal critic of the 1970s policies of détente with the Soviet Union. Jackson was generally regarded as a domestic liberal, supporting and promoting such causes as statehood for Alaska and Hawai'i, advocating the proper use of U.S. natural resources while preserving the environment, and strongly encouraging a U.S. energy policy. He was also known as the "senator from Boeing,"

because of his strong support for the aircraft manufacturer, located in his home state, and its major defense contracts. Yet it was in foreign policy that he gained his greatest recognition.

Jackson, a consistent and leading proponent of a strong defense posture and an amply funded defense budget, served continuously from 1955 until his death in 1983 as a member of the Senate Armed Services Committee. As chairman of the Permanent Subcommittee on Investigations and of the Subcommittee on National Policy Machinery, he was able to conduct oversight on a wide variety of foreign and domestic issues. In 1959 he conducted the first comprehensive evaluation of foreign policymaking since the passage of the National Security Act in 1947.

Two important foreign policy amendments that Jackson helped enact into law reflect his abiding concern with the security challenge from the Soviet Union. Under the 1972 Offensive Arms Pact Agreement, contained within the first Strategic Arms Limitation Talks accords, the Soviet Union was allowed to possess a quantitative advantage over the United States in a series of nuclear weapons categories. Jackson questioned this arrangement and proposed and had enacted into law the Jackson Amendment. Under this amendment, all future nuclear agreements between the United States and the Soviet Union would be at numerical parity. His second major foreign policy amendment, the Jackson-Vanik Amendment, was added to the 1974 Trade Act. The amendment required that U.S. granting of most-favored-nation (MFN) status to communist countries be contingent upon freedom of emigration for their citizens. At the time, the Soviet Union did not have a free emigration policy and imposed barriers to members of its Jewish population who sought to go to the state of Israel or elsewhere. The amendment also reflected Senator Jackson's staunch support of Israel and his desire to promote human rights.

In 1972 and again in 1976, Jackson mounted campaigns for the Democratic party presidential nomination. In both instances, first against George McGovern and then against Jimmy Carter, he was supported principally by those who felt the Democratic party in its post-Vietnam trauma was becoming too isolationist and too soft in its opposition to the Soviet Union and communism. Jackson failed to win the nomination each time, which exacerbated the splits within the party to the point where a number of "Jackson Democrats" (such as Jeane D. Kirkpatrick, Richard N. Perle, Paul H. Nitze, and Eugene V. Rostow) left the party to support Ronald Reagan in his 1980 presidential campaign. Under the Reagan administration, they held important positions in foreign policy and defense.

JAMES M. McCORMICK

See also Democratic Party; Jackson-Vanik Amendment

FURTHER READING

Fosdick, Dorothy. *Henry M. Jackson and World Affairs*. Seattle, 1990.
Garside, Grenville. "The Jackson Subcommittee on National Security." In *Staying the Course: Henry M. Jackson and National Security*, edited by Dorothy Fosdick. Seattle, 1987.

JACKSON-VANIK AMENDMENT

Amendment to the Trade Act of 1974 that linked the granting of most-favored-nation (MFN) status to the Soviet Union and other communist countries to the free emigration of the citizens of these nations. In the early 1970s the administration of President Richard M. Nixon, seeking to expand trade with the Soviet Union in accordance with its policy of détente, pledged MFN status to the Soviet Union. Senator Henry Jackson of Washington and Representative Charles Vanik of Ohio argued that MFN status should not be provided until the Soviet Union and other communist states allowed free emigration. Senator Jackson's motives in proposing this amendment were threefold. First, he was skeptical of détente and the benefits of expanded trade with the Soviet Union. Second, he wanted to alert Soviet leaders to the fact that they would have to improve their human rights and emigration policies if they wanted expanded economic relations with the United States. Third, he was seeking the 1976 Democratic presidential nomination and wanted the electoral support of labor, which was generally opposed to détente and feared cheap Soviet imports, and of Jewish voters, who were deeply committed to Soviet Jewry and were influential in the Democratic party. From the vantage point of the Soviet Union and many other foreign countries, however, the amendment was an example of U.S. interference in their domestic affairs.

The Jackson-Vanik Amendment won Jewish and labor support for Jackson and set back détente and the expansion of trade with the Soviet Union. It also signaled the Soviet leaders that there were important American leaders and constituencies who were unhappy with Soviet emigration policies and would oppose an expansion of trade as long as these policies were in place. The amendment did not, however, increase Jewish emigration from the USSR. Arrivals of Soviet Jews in Israel actually fell from 31,568 in 1972 and 33,364 in 1973 to 16,868 in 1974 and 8,295 in 1975.

The Jackson-Vanik Amendment remained in effect for the duration of the Cold War. Following the initiation of *perestroika* by Soviet president Mikhail Gorbachev, which included dramatic increases in Soviet Jewish emigration, the Soviet Union was granted a waiver of the Jackson-Vanik Amendment and received MFN status. The actual legislation, however, remained on the books. The amendment was also behind a controversy between Congress and the administration of President George Bush over whether to rescind the People's Republic of China's MFN status after the 1989 Tiananmen Square killings and the massive human rights crackdown. Although many members of Congress pushed to rescind, the administration refused. The dispute carried over to the administration of Bill Clinton, which, after considerable discussion, maintained China's MFN status in 1993 and again in 1994.

GARY K. BERTSCH

See also China; Export Controls; Most-Favored-Nation Principle; Russia and the Soviet Union

FURTHER READING

Stern, Paula. *Water's Edge: Domestic Politics and the Making of American Foreign Policy*. Westport, Conn., 1979.

JAMAICA

An island nation of 2.5 million people, located in the northern Caribbean Sea about 160 km south of Cuba, that achieved its independence from Great Britain on 6 August 1962. Columbus claimed the island for Spain in 1494, from which it was seized by Great Britain in 1655. The Treaty of Madrid (1670) confirmed British possession, and Jamaica remained its colony until achieving independence. Jamaica is a constitutional monarchy governed under a parliamentary democracy. The British monarch is head of state, and the two major political parties are the People's National Party (PNP) and the Jamaica Labour Party (JLP). Full diplomatic relations have been maintained with the United States since independence, as has United Nations membership, and an active role in the British Commonwealth of Nations. Jamaica, which participates in the Nonaligned Movement, joined the Organization of American States (OAS) in 1969, and helped found the Caribbean Community and Common Market (CARICOM) in 1973.

The JLP's post-independence assumption of power introduced a decade of cooperation with the United States that accommodated Jamaica's increasingly independent foreign policy. PNP victory in 1972, however, signalled change, as the democratic socialist agenda of Michael Manley's administration strained relations. Over U.S. and OAS objections, Jamaica established diplomatic relations with Cuba in 1972, gravitating more closely to Fidel Castro's government, while distancing itself from the United States. The Manley administration became increasingly pro-Third World and anti-United States, at one point declaring the U.S. ambassador to Jamaica persona non grata. The failure of domestic reforms, brought on, in part, by rigid International Monetary Fund (IMF) fiscal demands, as well as the U.S.'s intransigent anti-PNP posture, contributed to Manley's premature fall from power in 1980. His conservative successor, Edward Seaga (JLP), discarded PNP policies (he distanced himself from Castro and severed diplomatic ties with Havana), and pursued a close alliance with the United States. Increasingly cordial diplomatic relations prevailed thereafter, notwithstanding Manley's return to power in 1989 (he reestablished diplomatic relations with Cuba that year), and the PNP's landslide reelection under P.J. Patterson in 1993. Jamaica participated in the U.S.-led invasion of Grenada in 1983, and championed President Ronald Reagan's Caribbean Basin Initiative (CBI), which granted favorable trade terms under the Caribbean Basin Economic Recovery Act (CBERA). Through the 1980s, Jamaica joined the United States in drug interdiction efforts, while generous IMF, World Bank, and United States Agency for International Development (USAID) loan provisions infused the island economy with significant levels of foreign capital. In 1994, Jamaica agreed to host a U.S. facility for processing Haitian refugees, and provided troops for a U.S.-led, UN-sanctioned invasion of Haiti to oust the military dictatorship and install democratically elected President Jean-Bertrand Aristide. Jamaica's geographical proximity to Cuba and Haiti ensures its continuing importance to U.S. foreign policy. Strategic considerations and the centrality of U.S. trade to the island's economy have fostered close relations between the two nations.

RODERICK A. McDONALD

See also Caribbean Basin Initiative; Cuba; Grenada Invasion; Haiti; Nonaligned Movement; Organization of American States; Reagan, Ronald Wilson

FURTHER READING

Country Profile: Jamaica, Belize, Bahamas, Bermuda, Barbados. London Quarterly.
Manley, Michael. *Up the Down Escalator: Development and the International Economy—A Jamaican Case Study.* Washington D.C., 1987.
Meditz, Sandra W., and Dennis M. Hanratty, eds. *Islands of the Commonwealth Caribbean: A Regional Study.* Washington D.C, 1989.
Stone, Carl. *Class, State, and Democracy in Jamaica.* New York, 1986.

JAPAN

A few hundred miles off the east coast of the Asian mainland and four thousand miles northwest of Honolulu, Japan occupies a volcanic archipelago of four major islands—Hokkaido, Honshu, Kyushu, and Shikoku—as well as many smaller islands, arching from north to south between the Sea of Japan, the East China Sea, and the Pacific Ocean proper. In 1995, Japan was surpassed only by the United States in total gross national product, making the island nation of 125 million people an economic superpower. Issues of trade, national security, and race thinking have, over time, stood at the center of Japanese-U.S. relations.

Contacts between Japan and the United States effectively began in 1854, when, by tactfully yet forcefully negotiating the Treaty of Kanagawa, U.S. Navy Commodore Matthew Calbraith Perry opened the hitherto isolated Japanese nation to foreign penetration. Problems plaguing the Atlantic seaboard's whaling interests and China traders since the late eighteenth century prompted President Millard Fillmore, in 1852, to dispatch Perry's expedition of heavily gunned, steam-powered warships and older sailing ships to open up Japan by agreement, as China had been after the first Opium War (1839–1842), ahead of the United States's British, French, and Russian rivals. Perry's celebrated treaty sought to establish "firm, lasting and sincere friendship" between the United States and Japan. Included were a most-favored-nation (MFN) clause and commitments by Japan to make marine supplies available at the ports of Shimoda and Hakodate, to rescue shipwrecked seamen, and to allow the stationing of a U.S. consul at Shimoda. Perry's treaty lacked any guarantees, however, for actually commencing trade.

In truth, it was Townsend Harris, the first consul general at Shimoda, who opened the door to Japan. On 29 July 1858, Harris concluded a new pact establishing formal diplomatic relations between Japan and the United States. This treaty also opened the ports of Nagasaki and Kanagawa to U.S. shipping, and it approved freedom of trade as a guiding principle while fixing a schedule of import tariffs. Between 1860 and 1863, moreover, Japan agreed to open the ports of Niigata and Hyogo (Kobe) plus Edo (Tokyo) and Osaka for foreign residence, with extraterritorial privileges for Americans virtually to police themselves. The British, French, Russians, and Dutch soon won similar treaties, with extraterritorial rights and even lower import duties. Such provisions were copied into pacts with other nations, spread far and wide, through MFN clauses. Harris was promoted to ministerial rank in 1859 and inaugurated the first U.S. legation in Edo. In 1860, Japanese diplomats traveled to the United States aboard the USS *Powhatan* to exchange ratifications of Harris's treaty and install Japan's first legation in Washington.

Before the century's end, Japan's thrust toward modernization turned imperialistic, exploiting the opportunities the Chinese empire's dwindling control over its ancient tributary provinces afforded. At the same time, the continent-wide expansiveness of the United States carried itself seaborne far into the western Pacific. The

U.S. MINISTERS AND AMBASSADORS TO JAPAN

MINISTER	PERIOD OF APPOINTMENT	ADMINISTRATION
Townsend Harris	1859–1862	Buchanan
		Lincoln
Robert H. Pruyn	1862–1865	Lincoln
Robert B. Van Valkenburgh	1867–1869	A. Johnson
		Grant
Charles E. De Long	1869–1873	Grant
John A. Bingham	1873–1885	Grant
		Hayes
		Garfield
		Arthur
Richard B. Hubbard	1885–1889	Cleveland
John F. Swift	1889–1891	B. Harrison
Frank L. Coombs	1892–1893	B. Harrison
Edwin Dun	1893–1897	Cleveland
Alfred E. Buck	1897–1902	McKinley
		T. Roosevelt
Lloyd C. Griscom	1903–1905	T. Roosevelt

AMBASSADOR

Luke E. Wright	1906–1907	T. Roosevelt
Thomas J. O'Brien	1907–1911	T. Roosevelt
		Taft
Charles Page Bryan	1911–1912	Taft
Larz Anderson	1913	Taft
George W. Guthrie	1913–1917	Wilson
Roland S. Morris	1917–1920	Wilson
Charles Beecher Warren	1921–1922	Harding
Cyrus E. Woods	1923–1924	Harding
		Coolidge
Edgar A. Bancroft	1924–1925	Coolidge
Charles MacVeagh	1925–1928	Coolidge
William R. Castle, Jr.	1930	Hoover
W. Cameron Forbes	1930–1932	Hoover
Joseph C. Grew	1932–1941	Hoover
		F. D. Roosevelt
Robert D. Murphy	1952–1953	Truman
		Eisenhower
John M. Allison	1953–1957	Eisenhower
Douglas MacArthur 2nd	1957–1961	Eisenhower
Edwin O. Reischauer	1961–1966	Kennedy
		L. B. Johnson
U. Alexis Johnson	1966–1969	L. B. Johnson
Armi H. Meyer	1969–1972	Nixon
Robert S. Ingersoll	1972–1973	Nixon
James D. Hodgson	1974–1977	Nixon
		Ford
Michael J. Mansfield	1977–1988	Carter
		Reagan
Michael Armacost	1989–1993	Bush
Walter F. Mondale	1993–Present	Clinton

Sources: *Principal Officers of the Department of State and United States Chiefs of Missions.* ©1991 by Office of the Historian, Bureau of Public Affairs, Washington, D.C.; *The U.S. Government Manual,* Annual. Washington, D.C.

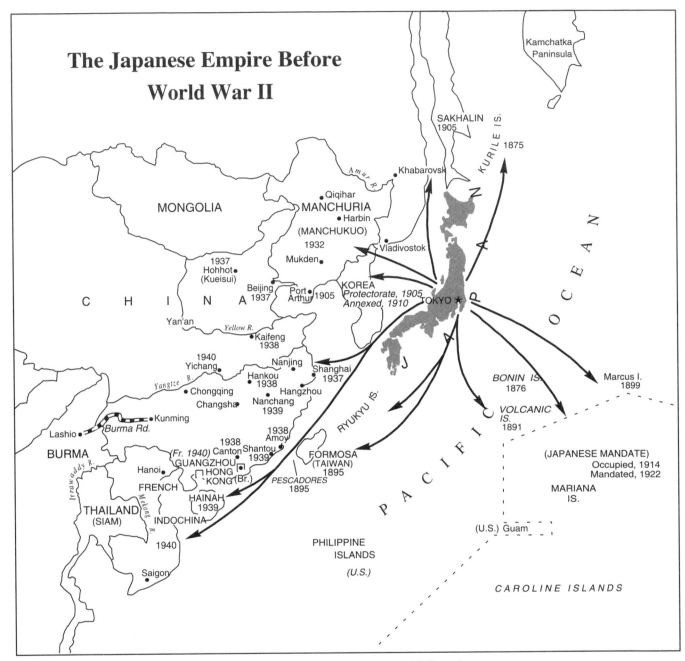

The Japanese Empire Before World War II

MONGOLIA

Amur R.

Khabarovsk

Qiqihar

MANCHURIA

Harbin

(MANCHUKUO)

1932

Mukden

SAKHALIN
1905

KURILE IS.

1875

Kamchatka
Paninsula

Vladivostok

1937
Hohhot
(Kueisui)

Beijing
1937

Port
Arthur

1905

KOREA
Protectorate, 1905
Annexed, 1910

TOKYO ★

C H I N A

Yan'an

Yellow R.

Kaifeng
1938

1940
Yichang

Nanjing

Hankou
1938

Shanghai
1937

Yangtze R.

Chongqing

Hangzhou

Changsha

Nanchang
1939

JAPAN

RYUKYU IS.

BONIN IS.
1876

Marcus I.
1899

Kunming

1938
Amoy

Lashio

Burma Rd.

VOLCANIC
IS.
1891

BURMA

Irrawaddy R.

1938
(Fr. 1940) Canton Shantou
GUANGZHOU 1939
HONG
KONG (Br.)

Hanoi

FRENCH

Mekong R.

HAINAH
1939

THAILAND
(SIAM)

INDOCHINA

1940

Saigon

FORMOSA
(TAIWAN)
1895

PESCADORES
1895

PHILIPPINE
ISLANDS

(U.S.)

(JAPANESE MANDATE)
Occupied, 1914
Mandated, 1922

MARIANA
IS.

(U.S.) Guam

P A C I F I C

O C E A N

CAROLINE ISLANDS

hostility that in due course would grow up between the United States and Japan centered inevitably about their competition for preeminence in China, plus the emotions inflamed on both sides by racist opposition within the United States against East Asian immigrants. Sporadically, for four decades before 1941, the possibility of war excited jingoistic passions and inflammatory outbursts.

Beginning in 1937, Japan's ill-starred effort to conquer China, amplified by Tokyo's entry of 1940 into the Triple Alliance with Germany and Italy, led inexorably to the 1941 attack on the United States at Pearl Harbor, to the spread of World War II into the Pacific, and finally to catastrophic defeat followed by a humiliating military occupation for Japan. The success of China's Communist Revolution in 1949 and some forty years of the Cold War in Asia substantially fueled Japan's recovery through the billions of dollars of goods and services provided to the United States for its anticommunist, containment endeavors. Japan loyally served U.S. policymakers throughout the Korean and Vietnam wars as a strategic forward base and major military supplier. The Japanese "miracle" of the 1970s and 1980s, however, introduced the United States to a chronic imbalance of payments, and Japan to an entirely novel form of economic power often at odds with the United States.

Empires on the Move

During more than two centuries of self-willed isolation after 1639, feudal Japan's warrior lords (*daimyo*) and their aristocratic vassals (*samurai*) had subjected themselves to a shogun, the hereditary overlord of the Tokugawa clan. The emperor at Kyoto, the source of imperial legitimacy, became under the shogunate a powerless figurehead, and was usually bypassed on worldly matters. Yet Japan's weakness was technological rather than cultural, for its society around 1850 harbored a relatively tranquil and literate population of thirty million people.

Japan's modernizers, at first only a handful of nationalistic aristocrats fearful that Japan might succumb, like China, to unequal treaties imposed at foreign command, were girding themselves to overthrow the shogunate and restore the emperor to his ancient power. Their revolution eventually succeeded, though not before their fears were partially realized. Fifteen-year-old Emperor Mutsuhito (1852–1912) became, on 9 December 1867, Japan's highest authority. Taking the name of Meiji for himself, he moved the court from Kyoto to Edo, and renamed the city Tokyo for "eastern capital."

In Emperor Meiji's name, a talented array of youthful *samurai* bureaucrats hurriedly modernized, industrialized, and militarized Japan, to move their extraordinary nation by 1912 into the front ranks of global powers. Clever young Japanese went off to Europe and the United States to learn all they could about modern technology, government, and armed services. Foreign specialists, among them U.S. postal, agricultural, and educational technicians, arrived to instruct the eager Japanese. Nevertheless, throughout the 1870s and 1880s, the government of Japan found itself forced to struggle against its foreign treaties that implied the nation's racial inferiority, confined the economy, and, in varying degrees, hobbled its sovereignty. Japan's efforts collided with new waves of western imperialism in Asia, Africa, and Pacific Oceania.

Leading the way for the United States westward across the Pacific Ocean toward Asia, Secretary of State William H. Seward, an imperial visionary, expanded his nation's sovereignty far beyond the fifty or so volcanic islet "appurtenances" already being gathered up under the "Guano Law" of 1856 (empowering the president to take over guano-rich islands in the Pacific), by arranging, in 1867, to purchase Alaska from Russia and also claiming Midway Island. Seward's dream of a North Pacific commercial empire for the United States rested upon defining Alaska's role as one intended to guard its north-

ern flank along the approach to Asia, next acquiring the Hawai'ian Islands for a midocean base, and one day opening an isthmian canal across Central America for interoceanic shipping and defensive purposes. Economically and strategically, the still independent Kingdom of Hawai'i handcuffed itself to the United States through the reciprocity treaty of 1875 and its 1887 extension, which conceded to the United States the naval rights for Pearl Harbor as a coaling station and repair base in return for a guaranteed market for the islands' sugar crop. Trouble spread throughout the revolutionary Hawai'ian republic after 1893, over the American planters' treatment of Japanese workers, when false rumors of an invasion by Japan's navy ran wild.

During the Spanish-American-Cuban-Filipino War of 1898, Congress annexed the Hawai'ian Islands, and, by the treaty of peace, the United States acquired the Philippine Islands from Spain, together with Guam and Wake islands, to launch unwittingly a fullblown imperial rivalry in the western Pacific between Japan and the United States. In further proof of Manifest Destiny's seaworthiness, the United States obtained sovereignty, in 1899, over the six easternmost Samoan Islands, which it still holds. Japanese anxieties, touched off by the development of the Pearl Harbor naval base, now became secondary to alarms over U.S. steps to fortify Manila Bay in the Philippine Islands. Southeast of Japan, the archipelago lay virtually at China's doorstep and close to the East Indies. East Asia's balance of power was at issue from this point forward.

In the meantime, a series of disputes had erupted between Japan and China over their conflicting claims to the Ryukyu Islands, Formosa (Taiwan), and Korea, which, since 1870, Japan had forcibly opened to commercial penetration. The Tokyo government was employing the methods of the great European powers, notably Great Britain, France, Russia, and Germany, if only to gain parity of access to China's resources and population. Curiously, some U.S. leaders, including Secretary of the Navy Hilary A. Herbert and Minister to China Charles Denby, applauded Japan's victory over China in the Sino-Japanese War of 1894–1895 as evidence of their newly modernized protégé's enlightened progress. A decade later, so did President Theodore Roosevelt, until he thought more carefully about the consequences of Japan's surprising victory in the Russo-Japanese War of 1904–1905 and the subsequent Russian Revolution of 1905.

Open Door Policy, Immigration, and the Rising Sun

China, weakened by decline and rendered helpless from the devastating defeat administered by Japan in the Sino-Japanese War of 1894–1895, tottered on the brink of dismemberment by the great powers. Japan obtained Formosa and an initial foothold in Korea. Germany, Russia, and France wrested leases from China for themselves for ports or inland territories. Great Britain gained control over the port of Weihaiwei (Weihai) on the Shandong peninsula and the new territories adjacent to Kowloon, opposite Hong Kong. The Celestial Empire was fast expiring. In vain, Great Britain appealed to the United States for support to uphold its tradition of equal commercial opportunity for all nations trading in China. Businessmen from the American Asiatic Association, abetted by missionary friends, clamored for governmental help.

Secretary of State John Hay thereupon circulated his famous "Open Door" notes. On 6 September 1899, his first note asked Japan, Russia, Germany, Great Britain, France, and Italy each to sustain a policy of equal trading opportunity within their spheres of interest in China. Hay overrode the evasive replies he received to proclaim adoption for the U.S. Open Door Policy for China. Hay's second Open Door note, dated 3 July 1900, went out during the Boxer Rebellion amid widespread xenophobic violence and the prospect that in retaliation the powers might carve up China. Hay appealed for a solution that would preserve China's "territorial and administrative integrity," protect all treaty rights, and safeguard the principle of equal and impartial trade throughout the Chinese empire.

Hay's policy expressed a U.S. determination to keep the trading door open in China and the country itself intact in the face of foreign threats. Although fragile and insubstantial, his policy commenced before long to carry weight. It would lodge itself in the popular mind at home, like the Monroe Doctrine for the Western Hemisphere, as the righteous and patriotic course for U.S. foreign policy to pursue. Furthermore, Hay's Open Door Policy would become congealed into an almost sloganized resistance on the part of the United States against Japan's drive toward hegemony over the onetime Celestial Empire. To protect their interests and safeguard their nationals, the United States and the other powers stationed troops inside China, with armored cruisers and gunboats patrolling coastal and inland waterways.

After 1905, it became conceivable that Japan might one day challenge the Open Door Policy. The possibility, however remote, induced President Roosevelt to try to keep competition alive between Japan and Russia so that they might moderate each other's ambitions. He evenhandedly softened his support for the Open Door Policy, in the Taft-Katsura Agreement of 1905, to concede Japan's priority inside Korea in return for Tokyo's acceptance of U.S. overlordship in the Philippines. Next, he brought the triumphant but exhausted Japanese and the defeated Russians together for peace talks at Portsmouth, New Hampshire, in August 1905, and proceeded to win a Nobel Peace Prize for himself by settling

the Russo-Japanese War. Over the next five years Japan went ahead, unchallenged this time, to absorb Korea outright, virtually excluding U.S. merchants and investors altogether from Korea and Manchuria.

At the same time, longstanding racist fears in the United States of a so-called "Yellow Peril" reached a climax in the Immigration Act of 1904, permanently excluding any more Chinese, and grew ever more virulent as evidence of Japan's power multiplied. Nothing that missionaries and merchants could affirm about their friendly encounters with the Japanese people could dissuade the mounting popular prejudices against them.

When, in 1904, about 15,000 Japanese arrived, many of them through Hawai'i, Californians shrieked in alarm. Anti-Japanese and anti-Korean leagues sprang up. San Francisco's Board of Education established a segregated Oriental School, in 1906, for Chinese, Japanese, and Korean children, thus touching off an international crisis in the face of Tokyo's outrage. To dampen the hysteria, Roosevelt carefully persuaded Congress to ban Japanese immigration from Hawai'i to the mainland. He also approved a "Gentlemen's Agreement," in March 1907, whereby the Japanese government promised to halt the emigration of laborers to the United States, with Washington promising steps to prevent discriminatory acts against residents of Japanese origin.

In 1908, as a show of strength, Roosevelt ordered the navy's entire complement of sixteen battleships to embark on a goodwill cruise across the Pacific Ocean and around the world. Japan welcomed the "Great White Fleet" at Yokohama with a rousing reception, which featured rows of schoolchildren waving U.S. flags and singing "The Star-Spangled Banner." The two governments promised to respect each other's possessions and to maintain the status quo in the Pacific region, as well as to uphold the integrity of China in keeping with the Open Door principle of equal opportunity for the commerce and industry of all nations.

Nevertheless, the race issue refused to die. In May 1913, California enacted a restrictive alien land law to bar its residents of Japanese origin from owning real estate, and Japan's angry protests immediately prompted a minor war scare. Unresolved during Woodrow Wilson's presidency, California's discriminatory statute increasingly embittered the Japanese. So did Wilson's rejection of Tokyo's plea, at the Paris Peace Conference in 1919, for inserting a racial equality clause into the covenant of the League of Nations. Wilson did not seem to recognize the combination of forces undermining his country's position in Asia.

China's republican revolution of 1911–1912 and World War I afforded Japan golden opportunities for acquiring preeminence in East Asia, along with a seaborne empire among the islands of Pacific Oceania to rival the possessions of the Great Powers. The birth of the Republic of China terminated both the Qing (Ch'ing) Dynasty (1644–1912) of Manchu emperors and the ancient empire of China. China then plunged itself into an indecisive civil war and a prolonged period of domestic turmoil. With the outbreak of World War I in Europe in August 1914, Japan, as Great Britain's military ally since 1902, was encouraged to pursue its own ambitions against Germany's extensive Pacific leaseholds and concessions. President Wilson, preoccupied by Mexico's revolution and his championship of neutral rights, then by his leadership role in the war itself, found little time or energy for Asia's problems.

Japan had plenty of both. Declaring war on 23 August 1914, Japan quickly seized Germany's North Pacific islands and the leaseholds of Jiaozhau (Kiaochow) Bay and Qingdao (Tsingtao) on China's Shandong peninsula. In January 1915, Japan followed up its seizures by brashly presenting China with its Twenty-One Demands, which, if fully conceded, would have reduced China to serve as Japan's protectorate. The Sino-Japanese treaties of May 1915 in fact confirmed Japan's dominance over China's economy. Chinese intellectuals, their pride deeply wounded, called for boycotts of Japanese goods. The Wilson administration merely proclaimed its refusal to recognize any of Japan's inroads against China that threatened the treaty rights of the United States or the Open Door Policy. Isolated by its neutrality, Washington could not even lift a finger against Japan's determination to expand. The Open Door Policy appeared to be little more than a paper tiger.

Suddenly, by the U.S. declaration of war against Germany, 6 April 1917, Japan and the United States became allies. Within a few months, China likewise declared war against Germany, as urged on by the United States and Great Britain, in part to counter Japan at the peace table. As allies, cooperation and friendship became U.S. and Japanese watchwords. Therefore, Secretary of State Robert Lansing, in his agreement of 2 November 1917 with Viscount Ishii Kikujiro, conceded Tokyo's special interests in China owing to Japan's "territorial propinquity," while, just as paradoxically, Ishii guaranteed his nation's support for the Open Door Policy and China's territorial integrity.

Japan's diplomats compounded the dismay of the Chinese by explaining away the Lansing-Ishii Agreement as another example of U.S. perfidy concerning the Open Door Policy for China. Intervening belatedly in 1918, Wilson revived the international banking consortium for Chinese development he had destroyed in 1913. To obtain Japan's agreement, the consortium had to agree, as it had in 1912 at its inception, to stay out of Manchuria. Wilson was thrown back where he had started and where his predecessor, William Howard Taft, had ended—

thwarted in China by Japan. Worse, as the news came out, the Chinese warlords governing at Beijing had already signed protocols confirming Japan's rights as Germany's successor in Shandong. Chinese patriotic frustrations boiled over riotously in the May Fourth Movement of 1919, when Wilson yielded at the Paris Peace Conference to Tokyo's retention of Shandong in order to persuade Japan to join his cherished League of Nations.

Washington Conference, Liberal Japan, and the Manchurian Crisis

Throughout the 1920s, successive Republican administrations headed by Presidents Warren G. Harding, Calvin Coolidge, and Herbert Hoover pursued internationalistic policies and armaments reductions outside the League of Nations, which the United States refused to join. Spurred by President Harding and Secretary of State Charles Evans Hughes, the Washington Conference of 1921–1922 produced an entirely new treaty system for East Asia and the Pacific. Japan's diplomats, led by Ambassador Shidehara Kijuro, proved unexpectedly accommodating. The Five-Power Treaty among Great Britain, the United States, Japan, France, and Italy scrapped large numbers of naval vessels already built or under construction, limited maximum tonnages, and set ratios for the signatory powers for capital ships, including aircraft carriers.

There was more to come. In the Four-Power Treaty, the United States, Great Britain, France, and Japan promised to respect each other's domains and maintain the existing levels of naval fortifications in the western Pacific. Great Britain and Japan ended their now obsolete alliance. Japan agreed to return Shandong to China, and withdraw its troops from Russian Siberia. The Nine-Power Treaties among the Big Five, Portugal, Belgium, the Netherlands, and China guaranteed China's sovereignty, independence, and territorial integrity. The treaty, on paper at least, effectively internationalized the Open Door. For Washington's leaders, the new treaties constituted an unqualified success, since naval equilibrium at low cost was attained, together with an overdue affirmation of Hay's Open Door Policy. Assured by the naval limitations of dominating the western Pacific, Japan withdrew from mainland Asia except for Manchuria and Korea.

Major domestic changes overtook Japan at the same time. The Meiji generation having passed from the scene, new leaders, under the regency established in 1921 for the ailing Taisho Emperor (1879–1926), forswore further imperial expansion. They turned instead toward promoting economic growth through their parliamentary system. Japan's export trade boomed, 40 percent during the 1920s flowing to the United States alone. Although the great Kanto earthquake of 1923 cleared the way for modernizing transportation and the urban infrastructure, rich businessmen and rural landlords, notwithstanding the advent of universal male suffrage, continued to dominate politics through family-controlled alliances called *zaibatsu*. Foreign Minister Shidehara increasingly pursued a conciliatory policy toward both China and the Soviet Union, the communist pariah. The 1928 Kellogg-Briand Pact renouncing war as an instrument of national policy, signed by sixty-two nations, including the United States and Japan, superficially reduced tensions between Washington and Tokyo.

Still, the postwar mood within the United States embodied powerful fears and a prevailing distrust of the world outside. Most naval officers, the Hearst newspapers, and avowed racists growled habitually about the Japanese. The Immigration Act of 1921 adopted a quota system for admitting new entries based upon national origins that favored northwestern Europeans above all others. Although Congress sustained the Gentlemen's Agreement, the latest anti-Japanese campaign over alien land holdings was already sweeping across California. Then, the Immigration Act of 1924 completely closed the gates to any more Japanese, including picture brides, by debarring all persons ineligible to become naturalized citizens of the United States. Infuriated by this blatant discrimination against Asians, the Japanese protested in heated terms. Hughes anguished that the law had "implanted the seeds of an antagonism which are sure to bear fruit in the future."

After 1929, the worldwide depression struck Japan with especially harsh consequences for workers and farmers alike. The towering tariffs of the U.S. Hawley-Smoot-Hawley Act of 1930 aggravated the depression's ravages for the Japanese people, just as worries were spreading over the ambitions vis-à-vis Manchuria of the Chinese nationalist forces of Jiang Jieshi. Swayed by military officers and patriotic zealots, the Japanese people began repudiating liberals and moderates in public life, turning toward a politics of desperation. "Government by Assassination," as it was called, began with an ultranationalist's shooting of Prime Minister Hamaguchi Osachi in late 1930. During 1931–1932, Japan's Kwantung (Manchurian) army seized Manchuria, and the Tokyo government after some hesitation incorporated the puppet state of Manchukuo into its empire.

The Hoover administration lodged its intense disapproval for Japan's conquest through the Wilson-like doctrine of nonrecognition put forward by Secretary of State Henry L. Stimson. Alarms intensified when fighting broke out between Japanese and Chinese forces at Shanghai. The Japanese navy's bombardments of the city infuriated Stimson. He persuaded President Hoover to transfer the U.S. Asiatic fleet from Manila to Shanghai to show some force behind his objections, and to appoint Joseph C. Grew as ambassador in Tokyo as further evidence of his displeasure. Grew soon concluded that U.S. moralizing without a display of power only fortified the aroused militants taking control of Japan's destiny.

To Pearl Harbor: Japanese Militarism, U.S. Sanctions

Upon entering office in 1933, President Franklin D. Roosevelt, preoccupied by problems of economic recovery, continued the Hoover-Stimson policy of refusing to recognize Manchukuo as rightfully Japan's. To increase the pressure, the United States started, in 1934, to build up its navy toward treaty strengths, which alarmed Japan's admirals sufficiently to call upon the Tokyo government to renounce the treaty limitations and resume building warships. The possibility arose now that a war might become unavoidable if, as the margin separating their navies narrowed, the United States persisted through its Open Door Policy in seeking to uphold China's territorial and administrative integrity and opposed Japan's reviving imperial ambitions.

The Japanese public's support, somewhat tenuous at best, for such western ideals as individualism, parliamentary democracy, and economic liberalism, rapidly dissolved against the deepening brutality of the country's economic crisis, the threatening surge of Chinese nationalism, and the powerful appeals of Italian and German fascism. A mystical spirituality religiously shrouded the Showa Emperor (1901–1989), better known as Hirohito, that extolled Asia's solidarity under Japan's leadership. More to the point, the army and navy took control of the government in Tokyo.

Following the lead of the militarists, the cabinet of Prime Minister Hirota Koki launched plans, in 1936, to convert Japan into a garrison state. Hirota rejected European and U.S. demands for restraint, and moved to establish full hegemony over China. Japanese Navy leaders pressed for the formal abrogation of the Five-Power Treaty limitations, and called for a military campaign southward to acquire the natural resources, commercial strongholds, and defensive outposts essential for guaranteeing Japanese ascendancy over China and throughout East Asia.

Next, a clash between Chinese and Japanese troops, at the Marco Polo Bridge west of Beijing in July 1937, unexpectedly marked the opening of the Second Sino-Japanese War. Beijing capitulated almost without a battle. Japanese forces overcame Shanghai behind massive naval and aerial bombardments. When Nanjing fell, the entry of the Japanese army into the city featured a savage brutality against civilians to be memorialized thereafter as the "rape of Nanjing." China's Nationalist government hurriedly withdrew to Chongqing, while Japan stretched a naval blockade along the entire Chinese coastline. In the United States, newspaper headlines bannered these worrisome tidings.

Meanwhile, President Roosevelt and his aides dreaded that Europe's own headlong plunge toward war would once again drag the United States into foreign combat. Roosevelt and the general public feared an interruption in the New Deal's hard-won progress toward domestic recovery. The Neutrality Acts of the 1930s unmistakably expressed the nation's revulsion toward the crusading experience of its 1917–1918 World War I intervention.

Although Stanley K. Hornbeck, who dominated the Department of State's Division of Far Eastern Affairs, repeatedly warned that Japan, if not dissuaded, would descend one day upon the Philippine Islands and overrun the British, French, and Dutch colonies in Southeast Asia, Roosevelt bided his time.

On 12 December 1937, Japanese warplanes attacked two British patrol vessels and sank the USS *Panay*, a Chang Jiang (Yangtze River) gunboat convoying three small Standard Oil tankers. Apologizing for this incident as an error of identification, the Tokyo government paid an indemnity of $2,214,007. Japan's militarists, absorbed in their own designs, may have trusted that their movements against China could never cause hostilities with the United States. But their moves beyond China into Southeast Asia would, in the end, bring about bitter confrontation.

Throughout 1938 and 1939 the Roosevelt administration buttressed both the Chinese and the U.S. positions against Japan. Chinese silver was purchased in huge amounts enabling China to buy military equipment, and technical assistance was extended to the Nationalist armed forces. Secretary of State Cordell Hull levied a "moral embargo" against sales of aircraft to the Japanese. Construction began on two more U.S. Navy aircraft carriers, as well as the doubling of the fleet's air arm. By September 1939, with the Soviet Union neutralized through its pact with Germany and a general European war having broken out again, the United States and Japan remained the only outside powers capable of significantly affecting mainland East Asia's balance of power. There, it was clear, they were competing for China directly against each other.

Once more, war in Europe redounded to Japan's advantage. Germany's lightning victories, in May–June 1940, when first the Low Countries and then France quickly capitulated, created Tokyo's opportunity. A Nazi invasion of England loomed. Europe's resource-laden colonies and holdings in the Pacific region, French Indochina and the Netherlands East Indies in particular, now lay at Japan's mercy. Japan proclaimed its intention to erect a Greater East Asia Co-Prosperity Sphere as Asia's "New Order," which, in actuality, signified Tokyo's slamming shut the United States's Open Door. Hoping to

restrain Tokyo, Washington announced its intention to abrogate the Japanese-American Treaty of Commerce and Navigation of 1911, and, at the same time authorized the construction of two more battleships. Roosevelt, though avowedly trying to stay out of war, levied an embargo against Japan on 25 July 1940, on top-quality scrap metal and most petroleum products including aviation fuel. Shocked though unfazed, Japan insisted on the right to station troops in French Indochina and sent warships there. In September, France's puppet Vichy regime granted the use of three airfields and several seaports in conceding Japan's occupation.

In September 1940, Japan joined Germany and Italy in the Tripartite Pact, and claimed the right to requisition supplies of oil, rubber, tin, and rice from Europe's beleaguered possessions throughout Southeast Asia. Roosevelt expanded the embargo against Japan, on 26 September, to include all scrap iron and steel. Six months later, on 13 April 1941, Japan and the Soviet Union signed a neutrality pact, which freed Japan to move southward. The United States, obviously, was Japan's only likely enemy, especially after Germany's invasion of the USSR on 23 June. Nevertheless, U.S. attention still concentrated itself on Europe and the Atlantic Ocean.

Diplomacy afforded only the slenderest hope in the ever-worsening U.S.-Japanese confrontation. Throughout prolonged negotiations, from early March to mid-July 1941, Secretary of State Hull doggedly upheld the Open Door Policy, to which the Tokyo government could never accede without abandoning its own ambitions for China and the militarists' pan-Asian designs. Ambassador Nomura Kichisaburo failed to impress his superiors with the strength of the U.S. commitment to its traditional stand over China, while Hull believed stubbornly that a posture of firmness based on moral rectitude would deter Tokyo. When Japanese units moved for the first time on 23 July 1941, into southern Indochina, Roosevelt retaliated with an economic blockade. His executive order froze all Japanese assets in the United States, and further curtailed the movement of petroleum supplies to Japan. Japanese military forces could operate for only eighteen months without fresh imports of oil. Financial paralysis gripped the nation's economy.

Japan's army and navy leaders now began to insist on either an early diplomatic breakthrough or waging war to get what they wanted. In September, Prime Minister Konoe Fumimaro half-heartedly appealed for a meeting with Roosevelt. Ambassador Grew urged Roosevelt to receive him, though Hull did not trust Konoe and Hornbeck feared a betrayal of China. Roosevelt instead concentrated on mustering support for Great Britain and the Soviet Union in their hour of gravest peril. He hoped to postpone, if not avoid forever, any final showdown with the Japanese. Neither he nor British Prime Minister Winston Churchill expected the Japanese to move beyond Indochina against the Royal Navy and the guns of Singapore. Although Konoe's overture was never formally rejected, Hull informed Nomura that a number of agreements must first be reached before a summit conference could take place. Neither Roosevelt nor Hull sensed the desperate determination of Japan's high command.

Konoe's government responded with apparent concessions on 23 September, when it tacitly abrogated the Tripartite Pact by promising neutrality for Southeast Asia for as long as Japan could obtain vital resources there. Konoe also demanded a resumption of normal trade relations, including large-scale deliveries of U.S. oil, and a halt in U.S. aid to China. He refused to withdraw from Indochina before peace was reached with China. Japan's terms would require the United States to recognize Japan's overlordship in China and to treat Manchukuo as Japanese. Only by abandoning Jiang's Nationalists might the United States hope to block Japan's expansionist intentions for Southeast Asia. Yet in turn, Japan would become impotent without oil. On 16 October, Konoe resigned, loath to lead Japan into war against the United States.

Although Emperor Hirohito, too, hoped to avert war, he named General Tojo Hideki, the war minister, to the premiership, with instructions to try once more for peace. Tojo, who epitomized the army's militarists, in fact insisted that his chiefs obey the emperor. They consented, but stipulated 1 December for their deadline. If Japan did not reach a diplomatic settlement by that date, they would make war early in December.

Ambassador Nomura and Kurusu Saburo, a special envoy, presented Japan's final terms to Secretary Hull on 20 November 1941. In return for Japan's promise to withdraw its troops from southern Indochina, the United States would have to restore normal commercial relations, supply Japan with a stated quantity of oil, and cease trying to prevent a Japanese victory over China. The United States rejected these overtures on 26 November, dismissing them as mere contrivances to obtain U.S. backing for Japanese hegemony over the western Pacific and East Asia. Japan's fateful decision to attack Pearl Harbor followed. Admiral Yamamoto Isoroku intended to knock out the U.S. Navy's Pacific fleet before Japan's drive into Southeast Asia, designated by now as the Southern Resources Area.

Japan's war orders, pending the outcome of negotiations, had already gone out to the Pearl Harbor striking force. On 8 December 1941 (Sunday morning, 7 December, Hawai'i time), Japan would attack. Ahead lay four years of terrible strife. Both nations would harvest the fruits of their short-sightedness and ignorance of each other.

Allied Victory in the Pacific

Within ninety minutes of the initial attack, Vice Admiral Nagumo Chuichi's carrier force finished its devastation of Pearl Harbor and the outlying installations. The heart of the prewar Pacific fleet lay in ruins as well as most of the first-line military aircraft in Hawai'i. Luckily for the U.S. Navy, its aircraft carriers and submarines were positioned elsewhere, and six of the eight battleships damaged by the attack were later raised from shallow waters and repaired to rejoin the U.S. fleet. On 8 December 1941, as President Roosevelt denounced the "day that will live in infamy," Congress declared war against Japan. Germany and Italy, Japan's Axis allies, declared war on the United States on 11 December, and Congress, the same day, declared war on them. The United States braced itself for a worldwide struggle.

The Pearl Harbors attack unleashed a tidal wave of intolerance against individuals of Japanese origin or descent living in the United States. President Roosevelt authorized the army to "intern" such persons in "relocation" centers throughout the western states. Two-thirds were U.S. citizens. Most were living in California. On an unprecedented scale for the United States, the evacuees suffered losses of careers, properties, and constitutional rights from which a great many never recovered. An official apology, eventually delivered by President Ronald Reagan, would have to wait until 1988, with compensation voted by Congress (at $20,000 each for living survivors) delayed until 1990.

For six months, in late 1941 and early 1942, Japan's forces advanced at will. Hard-driving troops overwhelmed Wake and Guam islands and Great Britain's base at Hong Kong. Other Japanese forces sped through the Philippine Islands and the Malay Peninsula into Thailand, the Netherlands East Indies, and Burma, even entering India. In short order Manila and Singapore, longtime symbols of U.S. and British imperial power in the Pacific, fell. U.S. General Douglas MacArthur promised to return from Australia and liberate the Philippines, where the trapped survivors of Corregidor and Bataan were subjected to the horrors of the Death March. By May 1942, Asia's map had been redrawn. Japan had only to defend the Greater East Asia Co-Prosperity Sphere against inevitable counterattacks in order to absorb its resources and manpower as needed. Tokyo's strategists drew fresh plans to win the China war, as well as to assist Germany by striking at the Soviet Union. They wholly underestimated the vengeful fury and mobilizing capacity of the United States.

In the decisive battle of Midway (3–6 June 1942), U.S. Naval and Marine Corps aviators victoriously reversed the tables by destroying the Japanese carriers' striking power. Midway, which predated the battles of El Alamein and Stalingrad, was followed up by the U.S. invasion of Guadalcanal (August-November 1942) in the Solomon Islands to stem Japan's southward thrusts. Midway proved to be the second turning point of World War II after the Battle of Britain

(August–October 1940). Thereafter, in vain, the Japanese fought desperately to hold onto their farflung oceanic shield of heavily defended islands.

Roosevelt and Churchill, at the Casablanca conference of January 1943, in spite of the priority assigned the European theater following the North African campaign, ordered wide-ranging assaults against Japan. From the South Pacific, MacArthur's forces, in scores of battles, successfully developed an island-hopping strategy up from the Solomons through New Guinea to invade Leyte (17–20 October 1944) in the central Philippines. The Japanese Navy mobilized its remaining strength for an attempted knockout blow. However, in the Battle of Leyte Gulf, the greatest naval battle in history, U.S. and Allied warships and aircraft virtually destroyed Japan's ability to conduct war at sea, although *kamikaze* bombers wreaked a terrible toll in lives and ships. While Admiral Chester W. Nimitz directed gigantic fleets across the central Pacific for sea, air, and land operations, General Joseph W. Stilwell led a reconstituted army of Chinese, Indians, Britons, and Americans back into northern Burma to break Japan's blockade of China. By late 1944, MacArthur and Nimitz had all but shattered Japan's outer defenses.

By early 1945 the end seemed in sight. In savage fighting, Manila was retaken. U.S. capture of Iwo Jima (February–March) and Okinawa (March–June) cost frightful casualties for both sides. Giant B-29 Superfortress bombers incinerated Tokyo and dozens of other Japanese cities. U.S. submarines sank hundreds of enemy ships carrying rice, oil, and other essentials. Roosevelt died in April. On 8 May, the war in Europe ended. Japan hovered towards paralysis, its population slipping close to starvation. On 26 July, the new president, Harry S. Truman, published the Potsdam Declaration demanding Japan's unconditional surrender, threatening utter destruction otherwise. Truman issued orders to prepare to drop the atomic weapon, but still the Japanese government failed to heed the Potsdam Declaration's warnings.

With no Japanese surrender forthcoming, the B-29 *Enola Gay* dropped a uranium bomb onto Hiroshima on 6 August 1945, killing 130,000 people. The nuclear epoch had dawned. Still, Tokyo procrastinated. On 8 August, the Soviet Union declared war against Japan, quickly overrunning Manchuria, northern Korea, and the island of Sakhalin. On 9 August, the United States dropped its second atomic bomb, a plutonium weapon this time, on Nagasaki. In Tokyo, consternation and confusion ruled. The fate of the emperor remained the last obstacle to peace. Secretary of State James F. Byrnes reluctantly conceded that Hirohito might retain his throne subject to the direction of the supreme commander of the Allied Powers. On 14–15 August, a last-minute, diehard coup attempt meant to prevent the emperor from speaking out for peace, failed at the Imperial Palace. Hirohito, the Showa emperor, broadcast the news of Japan's capitulation on 15 August.

In Tokyo Bay, aboard the USS *Missouri*, on 2 September 1945, MacArthur, designated as Supreme Allied Commander, accepted Japan's surrender. The Allied occupation had in fact already begun. The Potsdam Declaration required the demobilizing of Japan's forces and installing a representative government, yet nearly seven million Japanese, mostly military personnel, were still marooned overseas. Roosevelt and Truman had planned only for victory, not for an occupation. MacArthur's directives emerged only after heated debates among the State, War, and Navy Department bureaucracies.

The Occupation and Recovery of Japan

The initial goals of Washington's post-surrender policy were to help put together a peacetime economy sufficient for Japan's civilian requirements, and to impose democratic reforms that would drastically transform Japanese society. U.S. directives for about eighteen months mixed vengefulness with welfare state liberalism.

MacArthur proved omnipotent. His flair for the correct gesture at the right moment disarmed the Japanese. He intended to conciliate them and to assist them to renew their faith in themselves. Carrying out his instructions as he saw fit, he proceeded to install democracy and benevolence from above. He supplied food and inoculations for the hungry and epidemic-threatened population. He canceled naval restrictions against Tokyo Bay fishermen. He promulgated a bill of rights enfranchising women, legalizing labor unions, decentralizing the police, and guaranteeing freedom of speech, press, and religion. He attacked as monopolistic, family-controlled networks of manufacturing and banking. He prepared the way for war crimes trials, like those at Nuremberg for Germany's Nazi leaders. During 1946–1947, an eleven-nation tribunal in Tokyo tried and condemned ex-Prime Minister Tojo Hideki, who approved the attacks on Pearl Harbor and Southeast Asia, as well as six other top officials for atrocities, including Japan's notorious army commanders, Homma Masaharu and Yamashita Tomoyuki. Their executions by hanging quickly followed. Military and civil courts handed down lighter sentences to about four thousand "war criminals." In addition, some two hundred thousand persons, eighty percent of them military, lost their eligibility to hold offices and other political rights. Under MacArthur's prodding, the legislative Diet replaced *Shinto*, the way of the gods, with *Minshushugi*, the way of democracy. Once Emperor Hirohito had renounced his claim to divinity and called in person on MacArthur, he allowed himself to be transformed, dignity intact, into a constitutional monarch.

To spark Japan's recovery, MacArthur called in U.S. bankers and industrialists to rebuild the war-shattered economy along peaceful lines. Inflation was halted by a steep income tax increase and savings stimulated by a tax exemption on interest earned. U.S.-style managerial techniques were introduced, which underscored the necessity for making supervisors familiar with every stage of production, to instill productive cooperation among workers and departments. Japan's eager disciples would continue to teach such techniques to other students for decades to come. However, Japan's stagnant economy and the impact of the Cold War by 1947 sharply altered U.S. policy.

The challenge of Soviet and Chinese communism drove the United States, with its deep-seated aversion to Marxist-Leninist revolutionary doctrines, into a losing effort to uphold China's Nationalists against the Communists led by Mao Zedong. Mao's proclamation of the People's Republic of China, on 1 October 1949, on top of Soviet seizures of power in Eastern Europe, launched decades of all-out efforts by the United States and its allies to halt communism's spread. For the next twenty-five years, which came to include the Korean War and the Vietnam War, studied containment efforts by the United States would contribute markedly to the political and economic rehabilitation of both Japan and Germany.

The peace treaty restoring Japan's sovereignty was signed at a multinational conference in San Francisco on 8 September 1951, with the Soviet Union and communist-bloc nations bitterly abstaining. The pact, hailed as a "Peace of Reconciliation," testified to the successful outcome of the postwar occupation. Simultaneously, Washington and Tokyo concluded a bilateral agreement permitting U.S. troops to remain in Japan for an indefinite period. The two countries signed a treaty on 8 February 1952 authorizing the United States to maintain military installations in Japan for defensive purposes. Inasmuch as Japan's "MacArthur Constitution" renounced war as an instrument of national policy, the United States now assumed full responsibility for its former enemy's security. When the Allied Occupation ended in April 1952, U.S. bases and military personnel remained. Communist China and North Korea had to be walled off, and Japan itself defended.

In 1960, Japan and the United States signed a new security treaty which provided for more consultation by U.S. officials with their Japanese counterparts on issues of defense. But the treaty sparked nationalistic protest in Japan, including riots in Tokyo that forced President Dwight D. Eisenhower to cancel a planned visit. Although Japan ratified the treaty, many Japanese worried that a continuous security pact with the United States might drag Japan into an unwanted war as a U.S. Cold War ally.

By 1952, $2 billion worth of economic assistance had poured in from the United States, while many of the Occupation's reforms were set aside or muted. Once again, a government-business partnership was taking control. During the Korean War (1950–1953), $4 billion more would be spent by the United States in Japan for supplies, facilities, and services to support the conflict. Additional billions would follow later, covering the costs of mounting the defense of Taiwan, and fighting the wars in Indochina. All the while, the Central Intelligence Agency (CIA) spent lavishly to maintain Japan's pro–United States Liberal Democratic Party in power. Huge U.S. outlays for the Cold War sparked Japan's second economic takeoff within a hundred years. Yet, within the United States, Japan's progress toward recovery continued to be popularly underestimated, while the first sign of trade conflict emerged. In early 1961, for example, U.S. textile union members vowed not to work with Japanese cloth to protest growing imports of Japanese-made men's and boys' suits. President John F. Kennedy helped arrange an end to the work boycott and opened negotiations with Japan, which reluctantly agreed in 1962 to limit textile exports to the United States.

Japan's "miracle" years began around 1955. The nation's gross national product (GNP) grew at nine percent per year to 1960, at ten percent per year to 1965, and at more than thirteen percent per year to 1970, raising Japan's ranking to third place in the world behind the United States and the Soviet Union. On a per capita basis, Japan surpassed the United States's GNP by the late 1980s. The Organization of Petroleum Exporting Countries (OPEC) oil embargo, in 1973, struck Japan hard, inducing a drastic shift away from energy-intensive manufacturing. In making steel by innovative means, Japan became the world's foremost exporter of steel. By 1978, of the twenty largest furnaces, none was in the United States and fourteen were in Japan.

The Ministry of Trade and Industry (MITI) orchestrated Japanese steel's spectacular performance with detailed guidance, long-term financing, tax breaks, and incentives to consolidate. Likewise MITI brought Japan's automotive industry to the forefront. In 1956, only 12,000 cars were made in Japan, but in 1989 the Honda Accord outsold Ford's Taurus as the first best seller ever in the United States for a foreign make. Similarly, MITI assisted Japan's consumer electronics and semiconductor memory chips industries to outdistance their U.S. and European competitors. During the Gulf War of 1990–1991, it became evident that the U.S. Defense Department's military hardware heavily depended on Japanese-made computer components.

MITI's bureaucracy comprised an elite directorate of career professionals, unlike their politically appointed, short-term counterparts in Washington. MITI initiated most trade- and industry-related legislation for Japan's Diet (parliament) to approve. Also, MITI's regulatory obstructions neatly impeded access for U.S. manufacturers to Japanese markets, while its insistence on high quality standards for imported products additionally raised competitive barriers.

Trade Conflict and a Troubled Relationship

Export trade for Japan in the postwar years became a critical necessity, due to the nation's need to import oil, food, and other essentials. The United States offered an open and accessible market. An immense trade imbalance commencing around 1970 quickly converted the United States from the world's largest creditor to the world's largest debtor. By 1990 the United States owed $58 billion to Japan, with its total foreign debt nearing $700 billion. In 1987, the U.S. trade deficit with Japan hit $56 billion; in 1993 it soared to $59 billion. In 1960, no Japanese bank ranked among the globe's top ten; by 1990 nine of the ten largest banks were Japanese. In 1995, 149 of the 500 largest companies in the world were Japanese; 151 were American. Japan was also by then the largest provider of foreign aid, which, in addition to humane considerations, served as a valuable wedge into foreign markets. Japan contributed $13 billion to support the United Nations's effort in the Gulf War of 1990–1991. Some observers predicted that a "Pacific Century" was replacing the "American Century."

Widespread Japanese buying into U.S. real estate holdings as well as corporate and government securities excited envy and resentment in the U.S. population, tinged with an undercurrent of lingering racism expressed in what some labeled "Japan bashing." At the same time, Washington's trade negotiators repeatedly pressed for reciprocity of treatment for U.S. goods in Japan or, at least, for a level playing field. Presidents George Bush and Bill Clinton paid personal visits to Japan, attempting, with but marginal success, to persuade its leaders to open the country's trade doors. The Japanese, in turn, found it hard to understand why the rich and powerful United States, suddenly pressed by real economic difficulties, seemed to do little to help itself out of its crisis.

The trade issue between the United States and Japan could be likened by the mid-1990s to a Gordian knot, with neither side able or willing for various reasons to cut through the emotion-charged tangle. On the one hand, both countries are members with sixteen other nations of the Asia-Pacific Economic Cooperation forum (APEC), which has pledged itself to achieve free trade and investment throughout the region by the year 2020. Meanwhile, on the other hand, the United States has often threatened to invoke Super 301, the provision of the 1988 Trade Act that permits naming a country an unfair trading partner and initiating retaliatory measures. The Bush administration in 1989 cited Japan for discriminating against U.S. superconductors, satellites, and wool products, but lifted its "unfair trader" tag in early 1990.

In 1985, the dollar entered upon a decade-long slide against the yen. U.S. automakers and other manufacturers enjoyed a special form of protection in the U.S. market against Japanese competitors, whose imports accordingly became more expensive. As Japan's economy wavered along through a debilitating depression, the rising strength of the U.S. dollar in world markets in the 1990s hinted that a Japanese recovery seemed imminent.

Tortuous and lengthy, the paths from Kanagawa to Pearl Harbor, to Hiroshima and Nagasaki, to the closing years of the twentieth century display but uncertain guideposts for the future. For the United States and Japan alike, the dynamics governing their disparate societies and intertwined memories of past encounters challenge the prospects for discovering a mutually beneficial sense of direction. Both the Japanese and American peoples shared musical favorites from jazz and hard rock to symphonic classics. They enjoyed fast foods, including hamburgers served at hundreds of McDonald's outlets across Japan, with Japanese *sushi* cuisine's popularity rising fast in the United States. They also shared clothing fashions, jeans especially, sports, and movies. But similarities between their popular cultures did not mean an absence of major differences.

Controversies in 1995 and 1996, involving the fiftieth anniversary of the end of terrible war between them, highlighted the uncertainty principle underlying United States-Japan relations. Both at the Smithsonian Institution's Air and Space Museum in Washington and Nagasaki's Peace Park Museum, angry patriotic outcries prompted significant curtailments of the exhibits interpreting the U.S. nuclear bombing of Japan.

Meanwhile in 1995, on Okinawa, where three-fourths of the 136 U.S. bases in Japan were concentrated, three of the 50,000 U.S. servicemen stationed there sexually assaulted a young schoolgirl, prompting anguished outcries to remove all U.S. military bases from Japan. The servicemen were convicted for the attack, but Ambassador Walter F. Mondale was compelled to defend the U.S.-Japan Security Treaty of 1952 as the only real basis for preserving stability in East Asia. On 8 September 1996 Okinawans nonetheless voted ten to one in a nonbinding referendum for a reduction in American military bases on the southern Japanese island.

Prime Minister Hashimoto Ryutaro asserted, moreover, on taking office early in 1996, that his government would soon commence to design a new Japanese foreign policy better suited for the twenty-first century. The Treaty of Kanagawa of 1854, establishing "a firm, lasting, and sincere friendship" may be remembered in the process of rethinking U.S.-Japanese relations.

ARTHUR POWER DUDDEN

See also Boxer Rebellion; China; Cold War; Extraterritoriality; Gentlemen's Agreement; Grew, Joseph Clark; Harris, Townsend; Hay, John Milton; Hawai'i; Hirohito, Emperor; Hiroshima and Nagasaki Bombings of 1945; Hornbeck, Stanley Kuhl; Immigration; Korean War; Lansing-Ishii Agreement; MacArthur, Douglas; Manchurian Crisis; Manifest Destiny; Open Door Policy; Opium Wars; Pearl Harbor, Attack on; Perry, Matthew Calbraith; Philippines; Potsdam Conference; Race and Racism; Roosevelt, Franklin Delano; Roosevelt, Theodore; Russo-Japanese War; Samoa, American; Seward, William Henry; Shidehara, Kijuro; Sino-Japanese War; Stimson Doctrine; Taft-Katsura Agreement; Tojo, Hideki; Truman, Harry S.; Vietnam War; Washington Conference on the Limitation of Armaments; Wilson, Thomas Woodrow; World War II

FURTHER READING

Barnhart, Michael A. *Japan and the World Since 1868.* New York, 1995.

Beasley, W.G. *The Rise of Modern Japan.* 2nd ed. New York, 1995.

Boyle, John Hunter. *Modern Japan: The American Nexus.* Fort Worth, Tex., 1993.

Buckley, Roger. *U.S.-Japan Alliance Diplomacy 1945-1990.* New York, 1992.

Daikichi, Irokawa. *The Age of Hirohito: In Search of Modern Japan.* Mikiso Hand and John K. Urda (trans.). New York, 1995.

Dower, John W. *War Without Mercy: Race and Power in the Pacific War.* New York, 1986.

Dudden, Arthur Power. *The American Pacific: From the Old China Trade to the Present.* New York, 1992.

Emmerson, John K., and Harrison M. Holland. *The Eagle and the Rising Sun: America and Japan in the Twentieth Century.* Reading, Mass., 1988.

Giffard, Sydney. *Japan Among the Powers, 1890-1990.* New Haven, Conn., 1994.

Iriye, Akira. *Pacific Estrangement: Japanese and American Expansion 1897–1911.* Cambridge, Mass., 1972.

———. *After Imperialism: The Search for a New Order in the Far East, 1921–1931.* Cambridge, Mass, 1965.

———. *Power and Culture: The Japanese-American War, 1941–1945.* Cambridge, Mass, 1981.

Iriye, Akira, and Warren I. Cohen. *The United States and Japan in the Postwar World.* Lexington, Ky., 1989.

Ladd, Everett Carll, and Karlyn H. Bowman. *Public Opinion in Americ and Japan: How We See Each Other and Ourselves.* Washington, D.C., 1996.

Lifton, Robert Jay, and Greg Mitchell. *Hiroshima in America: Fifty Years of Denial.* New York, 1995.

Miyoshi, Masao, and H.D. Harootunian, eds. *Japan in the World.* Durham, N.C., 1993.

Neu, Charles E. *The Troubled Encounter: The United States and Japan.* New York, 1975.

Prange, Gordon W., Donald M. Goldstein, and Katherine V. Dillon. *Pearl Harbor: The Verdict of History.* New York, 1986.

Reischauer, Edwin O. *The United States and Japan.* Cambridge, Mass., 1965.

Schaller, Michael. *The American Occupation of Japan: The Origins of the Cold War in Asia.* New York, 1985.

JAVITS, JACOB

(*b.* 18 May 1904; *d.* 7 March 1986)

Republican senator from New York (1956–1981). Born on Manhattan's Lower East Side in 1904, Javits was elected to the House of Representatives in 1946 and to the Senate in 1956. Javits was the chief author of the 1973 War Powers Resolution requiring the president to notify Congress upon sending American forces into hostilities, actual or imminent, and to obtain congressional authorization for their continued deployment after a "trigger" period of sixty days.

The resolution was the result of congressional dissatisfaction with President Richard M. Nixon's policies in the Vietnam War. However, it was not passed until 1973 (and then over Nixon's veto), after a peace agreement ending America's direct role in Vietnam insured that the resolution would not be applied to that conflict. The law received its first real test when Congress claimed it applied to U.S. intervention in Lebanon in 1983. Although President Ronald Reagan disputed its authority and Congress declined to insist upon a U.S. withdrawal, the law's supporters believed that the War Powers Resolution had exercised substantial restraint on the president's use of American forces there. At the time of the Gulf War of 1991, some members of Congress believed that the law also required legislative approval for the dispatch of American forces to the Middle East.

During the Cold War, Javits, a strong believer in a vigorous American global presence, championed such nonmilitary elements of U.S. foreign relations as economic aid and cultural exchange with countries from Western Europe to East Asia. His maiden speech in the House established him as a firm supporter of the state of Israel. He was known as a liberal Republican who often sided with Democrats on domestic issues from civil rights to health care. He was the author of several books.

MICHAEL A. BARNHART

See also Vietnam War; War Powers Resolution

FURTHER READING

Javits, Jacob K., and Rafael Steinberg. *Javits: The Autobiography of a Public Man.* Boston, 1981.

JAY, JOHN

(*b.* 12 December 1745; *d.* 17 May 1829)

Noted politician, diplomat, and jurist during the American Revolution and the early Republic. Born into one of the most prominent families in colonial New York, Jay studied law at King's College (now Columbia University), graduating in 1764, and during the Revolution served as one of New York's delegates to the First Continental Congress. He was elected president of the Second Continental Congress in 1778, negotiated the peace treaty with Great Britain, and, with Alexander Hamilton and James Madison, was one of the authors of *The Federalist Papers* (1787). He became the first chief justice of the United States (1789–1795) and served two terms as governor of New York (1795–1801).

In foreign affairs, Jay held important positions at critical points in America's development. For two years (1780–1782) he represented the United States in Madrid, where he attempted to secure Spanish recognition of U.S. independence, the right of Americans to navigate the Mississippi River, and Spanish military and financial support for the struggling colonies. Treated with disrespect and evasion, Jay was in a foul mood when he arrived in Paris in June 1782, in order to serve with Benjamin Franklin, John Adams, and Henry Laurens as a member of the American peace commission. Although informal peace talks with Great Britain had already begun, Jay, suspicious that France, America's ally, secretly sought to delay independence as well as American territorial interests, assumed a leadership role. He persuaded his fellow commissioners that American interests necessitated violating their instructions from Congress and engaging in direct talks with the British. Jay's suspicions proved justified, and by insisting upon independent negotiations, the Americans achieved significant concessions from the British, as well as recognition of American independence. A preliminary treaty of peace was signed on 30 November 1782, and the Americans affixed their signatures to the Definitive Treaty of Peace on 3 September 1783.

Upon his return to the United States in 1784, Jay succeeded Robert R. Livingston as secretary of foreign affairs under the Articles of Confederation government. He held this position until the implementation of the Constitution in 1789, at which time Jay became chief justice.

As secretary of foreign affairs, Jay's greatest challenges came from Great Britain, which persisted in discriminating against U.S. trade, particularly in the Caribbean. When Adams was sent as minister to London in May 1785, he was treated with disdain by the British, who refused even to reciprocate by appointing a minister to the United States. The United States was unable to win from Great Britain compensation for slaves carried off during the Revolution, the removal of British forts from U.S. territory, or an end to British incitement of Indians along the frontier.

Jay also was confronted with an unfriendly Spanish attitude that precluded agreements on the navigation of the Mississippi River, on conflicting border claims, and commercial matters. In 1786, after the Spanish minister to the United States, Don Diego de Gardoqui, had sought to influence Jay by lavishing compliments and gifts on Mrs. Jay, the two men signed what became known as the Jay-Gardoqui Treaty. In exchange for some commercial concessions, Jay agreed to forgo for thirty years the right of Americans to navigate the Mississippi. Terms of the treaty produced an emotional debate in Congress along sectional lines, which ultimately doomed the treaty. One of the results of the treaty's failure was to entice the shadowy figure of American general James Wilkinson into the employ of Spain in a scheme to detach the southwestern part of the United States and create an independent country.

In 1793, when war with Great Britain seemed possible because of a host of issues, including discriminatory policies, seizure of American ships, impressment of American seamen into the Royal Navy, and Britain's failure to evacuate forts on American territory, President George Washington appointed Jay, then chief justice, to undertake a special diplomatic mission to seek redress of grievances and to avert war. On 19 November 1794 Jay signed the treaty that bears his name. The treaty's significance lay in the fact that for the first time Great Britain signed a commercial treaty, even if a limited one, with an independent United States. The British made few concessions, however. The most important one was a promise to evacuate their forts in the Northwest Territory. When the terms of the treaty leaked out, Americans, particularly Jeffersonian Republicans, denounced it, as did the French. Jay was vilified and burned in effigy because, although he had opened the British West Indies to U.S. trade, the terms were very restrictive. Jay had even accepted a provision that gave up the right of neutrals to trade with belligerents—a right dear to Americans. Nevertheless, after much deliberation, and not without mixed feelings, President Washington signed the treaty.

Jay's Treaty helped give rise to political parties in the United States, as Jeffersonian Republicans (basically pro-French) and Federalists (basically pro-British) differed over how best to preserve the national interest. Angry and feeling betrayed, the French began to meddle in U.S. politics and embarked on a policy of seizing American commercial ships, thereby helping to bring on the Quasi-War with France (1798–1800). Upon his return to the United States in 1795, Jay resigned as chief justice and became governor of New York. Following the Republican electoral triumph in 1800, he retired to his home in Bedford, New York.

THOM M. ARMSTRONG

See also American Revolution; Articles of Confederation; Federalist Papers; France; Great Britain; Jay's Treaty; Mississippi River; Spain; XYZ Affair

FURTHER READING

Bemis, Samuel Flagg. *Jay's Treaty: A Study in Commerce and Diplomacy*, 2nd ed. New York, 1962.

Combs, Jerald A. *The Jay Treaty: Political Battleground of the Founding Fathers.* Berkeley, Calif., 1970.

DeConde, Alexander. *Entangling Alliances: Politics and Diplomacy Under George Washington.* Durham, N.C., 1958.

Monaghan, Frank. *John Jay: Defender of Liberty.* New York, 1935.

Morris, Richard B. *The Peacemakers: The Great Powers and American Independence.* New York, 1965.

———. *John Jay, the Nation, and the Court.* New York, 1967.

JAY'S TREATY

(1794)

The Anglo-American treaty named for John Jay of New York, the first chief justice of the United States and a staunch Federalist selected by President George Washington to embark on a diplomatic mission to England in an effort to avert war. In naming Jay for this mission, Washington had selected a man well-known for pro-British sympathies. Pro-French Jeffersonian Republicans were suspicious of Jay's mission from the very beginning. Although given discretionary power because of his distance from the United States, Jay's instructions precluded him from signing any document contrary to the treaties the United States had with France, which was at war with Great Britain.

The trouble between Great Britain and the United States stemmed from several issues: discriminatory trade policies Britain had pursued since the end of the American Revolution, confiscation of U.S. ships and impressment of U.S. seamen into the Royal Navy, the notion that Great Britain was largely responsible for Indian troubles in the Northwest, failure to evacuate British forts on U.S. soil as required by the peace treaty of 1783, and the contention that the British took slaves when they evacuated U.S. territory. Jay's only point of leverage was the possibility that if the British were intractable, he could negotiate with Danish and Swedish ministers in London about joining an armed neutrality being formed to resist Great Britain's high-handed maritime practices. Jay's bargaining position was undermined by unethical behavior on the part of Secretary of the Treasury Alexander Hamilton, who secretly informed the British minister in the United States that the Washington administration had no intention, given the president's policy outlined in his Neutrality Proclamation of 1793, of joining the Armed Neutrality.

On 19 November 1794, in London, Jay signed a treaty that stipulated the following: (1) peace and friendship would exist between the two countries; (2) British troops and fortifications would withdraw from U.S. territory as determined by the Treaty of Peace of 1783; (3) citizens of both countries, as well as the Indians, would be allowed free passage across the boundaries of the United States and Great Britain by land or water; (4) the Mississippi River would be open to free navigation; and (5) territories of the two nations could trade freely.

Great Britain had, for the first time, signed a commercial treaty with the newly independent United States, though it was limited in scope. Other issues, such as the northeast boundary, debts from before the Revolutionary war, and spoliation claims for maritime seizures would be settled by arbitration. The use of international arbitration to settle differences between nations gained greater prominence as a result of Jay's Treaty.

Jay's Treaty was notable partly for what it did not contain. The British practice of taking slaves when they vacated U.S. territory, impressing U.S. seamen, and interfering with the Indians were not addressed. Regarding British seizure of U.S. ships, Jay conceded on the principle of free ships making free goods, whereby small-navy neutral countries during war could trade with warring parties and not worry about seizure of their ships or their cargoes.

The Senate, when it received the treaty, was fearful of public reaction and voted to keep the treaty's provisions secret during debate. Although neither Washington nor Hamilton liked the terms, they recommended it be approved because it reduced the chances of war with Great Britain. The most objectionable part of the treaty was Article 12, which limited the size of U.S. ships and dictated types of tropical produce that could not be exported to the United States from the British West Indies. To salvage the treaty, the Federalists offered a resolution calling for its passage without Article 12. By a vote of 20 to 10, the treaty was accepted, with the minimum number of votes required for passage. When terms of the treaty leaked out, many Americans protested, as did the French. Jay was vilified in demonstrations and effigies of him were burned. After much deliberation, the president affixed his name to the document.

Having failed to prevent approval of the treaty in the Senate, pro-French Republicans sought to garner enough votes in the House of Representatives to defeat the appropriations necessary for the treaty's implementation. In a resolution introduced by Edward Livingston of New York and passed by a vote of 62 to 37, the House of Representatives called on the president to produce the diplomatic documents relating to the negotiation of Jay's Treaty. After consulting members of the cabinet for advice, the president refused to comply with the request. Debate raged for two months in the House. Washington defended his right to withhold the documents by arguing that the Constitution granted to the executive branch and Senate the power to negotiate treaties. The House, therefore, had no right to request the documents. Support by the president ultimately saved the treaty and the House appropriated the money on 30 April 1796.

Although Washington's decision to proceed with the treaty was probably wise, he left himself vulnerable to criticism from many Americans who had revered him, as well from the French, who saw in the treaty a betrayal of the French alliance and a pro-British move. The French responded by renewing their seizure of U.S. merchant vessels, intervening in U.S. politics, and laying the groundwork for the reestablishment of a French empire in North America.

The treaty helped spawn political parties in the United States: the Federalists and the Democratic Republicans (or simply Republicans). Intense Republican and French attacks on George Washington helped persuade him not to seek election for a third term. In his Farewell Address of September 1796, he not only cautioned against the evils of partisan factions, but advised against foreign entanglements in a clear reference to the French alliance.

Although Jay's Treaty was unpopular, it did postpone war with Great Britain. Such a war, because of strong sentiments both for and against the British, could have split the Union. The treaty brought complete British fulfillment of the provisions contained in the peace of 1783. Deserted by their British friends, Indians in the Northwest lost the Battle of Fallen Timbers and were forced to come to terms in the Treaty of Greenville in August 1795. One of the most indirect consequences of Jay's Treaty was Pinckney's Treaty with Spain in October 1795. Thinking Jay's Treaty might portend an Anglo-American alliance that could threaten their colonies in North America, Spain acceded to most U.S. demands, including unrestricted navigation of the Mississippi, a three-year right of deposit at New Orleans subject to renewal, establishment of the U.S. southwest boundary at the 31st parallel, and a Spanish promise not to encourage Indians along the Spanish frontier to attack U.S. citizens.

THOM M. ARMSTRONG

See also American Revolution; Arbitration; France; Great Britain; Hamilton, Alexander; Impressment; Jay, John; Neutral Rights; Pinckney's Treaty; Washington, George; Washington's Farewell Address

FURTHER READING

Bemis, Samuel Flagg. *Jay's Treaty: A Study in Commerce and Diplomacy*, rev. ed. New Haven, Conn., 1923, 1962.

Combs, Jerald A. *The Jay Treaty: Political Battleground of the Founding Fathers*. Berkeley, Calif., 1970.

DeConde, Alexander. *Entangling Alliance: Politics and Diplomacy Under George Washington*. Durham, N.C., 1958.

Monaghan, Frank. *John Jay: Defender of Liberty*. Indianapolis, Ind., 1935.

JEFFERSON, THOMAS
(*b.* 13 April 1743; *d.* 4 July 1826)

Third president of the United States. Jefferson was also the statesman who more than any other affected the formulation and conduct of early U.S. foreign policy. As minister to France during the period immediately after the recognition of U.S. independence (1784–1789), as secretary of state during the first administration of George Washington (1790–1793), and as president (1801–1809), Jefferson played a critical role in the conduct of foreign policy. His "peculiar felicity of expression," in John Adams's words, often gave his utterances, in official pronouncements and private correspondence, a commanding influence over the hearts and minds of the people of the United States.

Jefferson is the great exemplar, along with Woodrow Wilson, of the national conviction that the United States had rejected the diplomacy of European states and that the destiny of the United States was to lead the world to a new and better diplomacy. He sought to implement "but one system of ethics for men and for nations—to be grateful, to be faithful to all engagements under all circumstances, to be open and generous, promoting in the long run even the interests of both." Against European diplomacy's assertion of the primacy of foreign over domestic policy, he insisted that the objectives of foreign policy were but a means to the end of protecting individual freedom and promoting domestic society's well-being. "However...we may have been reproached for pursuing our Quaker system," Jefferson once explained to a European correspondent, "time will affix the stamp of wisdom on it, and the happiness and prosperity of our citizens will attest its merit." Countering the view that necessity might override legal obligation, Jefferson held that the chief security of liberty lay in the constraints of a written constitution: "free government is founded in jealousy, and not in confidence; it is jealousy and not confidence which prescribes limited constitutions, to bind down those whom we are obliged to trust with power...In questions of power, then, let no more be heard of confidence in man, but bind him down from mischief by the chains of the Constitution."

Jefferson's rejection of the doctrines and precedents of European statecraft went deeper than an insistence on a strict construction of the Constitution. He rejected, in fact, the whole apparatus of the modern state that had emerged in Europe in the eighteenth century. The combination of funded debt, executive power, burdensome taxation, government-supported manufactures, and standing military establishments that characterized the Great Powers in the eighteenth century were thought by Jefferson to constitute the essence of tyrannical government. In the Jeffersonian scheme of things, the United States was meant to escape the corruptions of Europe, something it could not do if it succumbed to the blandishments of the power state.

These considerations go far toward explaining Jefferson's attitude toward war, a primary instrument of European statecraft. War—and the necessities that were regularly alleged to attend its conduct—constantly threatened the very institutions and values that provided its ultimate justification. This was true above all for republics. Hence, for Jefferson, and for Republicans generally, war was the great nemesis. "Of all the enemies to public liberty," James Madison wrote in *Political Observations*, "war is, perhaps, the most to be dreaded, because it comprises and develops the germ of every other. War is the parent of armies; from these proceed debts and taxes; and armies, and debts, and taxes are the known instruments for bringing the many under the domination of the few." This outlook did not prevent the Jeffersonians from embracing what would now be called police actions against either Native Americans or Barbary states; it did, however, make the prospect of war with the Great Powers something to be avoided save in the worst extremity, for war would introduce into the Republic profound forces leading to its corruption.

Although Jefferson abhorred war, he was perhaps the greatest expansionist of the nation's early statesmen; he worked assiduously as secretary of state to gain from Spain the free navigation of the Mississippi River and the recognition of the United States's title to the lower eastern Mississippi Valley. An important desire of his presidency was to bring the Floridas into the Union, which his successful acquisition of Louisiana only whetted. He wished also to break down the mercantilist barriers that restricted U.S. trade, thus assuring an expanding market for U.S. agricultural surpluses. As historian Drew McCoy has observed, Jefferson wished that the United States would "expand through space" rather than "develop through time," a conception of U.S. development sharply at odds with that of Alexander Hamilton, Jefferson's great rival. Most of Jefferson's other diplomatic objectives were derived from his emphasis on territorial expansion and free commerce. He gave an expansive reading to U.S. rights as a neutral, in part because he wished to use neutral rights "to fatten on the follies" of a Europe at war. He was one of the first to articulate the substance of the "No Transfer" doctrine because he recognized that the United States might gain Spanish territories "piece by piece" so long as they remained in the hands of that weak power. He realized that the United States would have much greater difficulty in obtaining the land if it fell to either France or Great Britain.

The great dilemma of Jefferson's statecraft, then, lay in his apparent renunciation of military means to ensure security and to satisfy expansionist ambitions, together with his simultaneous unwillingness to renounce the ambitions that normally led to the use of these means. He wished that the United States could enjoy the fruits of power without falling victim to the normal consequences of its exercise. He had good reasons for harboring both of these aspirations; both grew naturally out of his vision of domestic society. To pursue them together created for him a dilemma with which he wrestled throughout his presidency, forcing him to articulate and ultimately employ a new diplomatic method, sharply opposed to the classical statecraft of Hamilton. "To conquer without war," observed French diplomat Louis Marie Turreau in 1805, was "the first fact" of Jeffersonian politics. How to do so constituted the essence of Jefferson's problem in dealing with the world.

Threats of war and possible alliances represented ways of conquering without war, and Jefferson frequently used these altogether traditional diplomatic means, both as secretary of state and as president. Although he was never averse to securing his aims by conjuring up before his adversary a diplomatic alliance on the enemy's opposite flank, and he often threatened war against Spain, Jefferson was aware that conflict could result; he later saw it come to pass in the War of 1812. The core of his diplomatic method lay elsewhere, in the instrument of "peaceable coercion." By this he meant an ordering of U.S. economic relations that would leave the mercantilist states of Europe no choice but to succumb to U.S. demands. Believing that the European powers would do almost anything to preserve the great advantages they gained from their commerce with the United States, he thought that mere U.S. economic legislation could work his will upon other powers, despite their hostility.

The basic elements in Jefferson's thinking emerged clearly during his years as secretary of state, but their influence on policy was muted by his rivalry with Hamilton over the basic direction of President Washington's administration's foreign policy. With the outbreak of war between Great Britain and France in 1793, Jefferson initially opposed a proclamation of neutrality. He doubted the executive had the constitutional authority to issue one, and he deemed it inexpedient to make known American intentions without first receiving explicit recognition from Great Britain that it would concede, as the price of it, "the broadest privileges" to neutral nations. Washington overruled him on this point, and a proclamation was issued on 22 April 1793 that warned American citizens "carefully to avoid all acts and procedures whatsoever which may in any manner tend to convey…a conduct friendly and impartial toward the belligerent powers." Before Jefferson left office at the end of that year, British seizures of U.S. commerce brought a new crisis in Anglo-American relations. Washington responded not with the commercial sanctions that Jefferson wanted but with the mission to London of John Jay, who succeeded in settling the disputes with Jay's Treaty. Out of office, Jefferson sharply criticized the direction of Federalist diplomacy, which he considered to be in the grip of "Anglomen" and "monocrats."

The Presidential Years

Jefferson's new diplomacy was tested with his election to his first term of the presidency in 1801. The first test occurred immediately, when news arrived of the retrocession of Louisiana from Spain to France in the secret Treaty of San Ildefonso, signed on 1 October 1800. With that treaty, New Orleans threatened to come under the jurisdiction of the French. Observers have long differed over the character of Jefferson's diplomacy to remove the French from the territory. Contemporary defenders of Jefferson saw the acquisition of Louisiana as a great political blessing—even more, as a triumph of statecraft—not only because of what he got but for the way he got it. "We have secured our rights by pacific means," wrote the editors of the administration's most faithful newspaper; "truth and reason have been more powerful than the sword." The administration's critics, both at the time and subsequently, held that the purchase was a piece of pure luck, the unexpected result of the failure of French imperial designs in Haiti, which destroyed Napoléon's imperial scheme and made Louisiana expendable. Others credit Jefferson with playing the diplomatic game to perfection, taking advantage of Europe's distress with well-timed threats of alliance with Great Britain and war with France.

Whereas Jefferson's first term ended on a note of triumph, his second term ended badly. His various projects to secure the Floridas from Spain ended in failure, as did his attempt to gain from England a satisfactory arrangement on the high seas. Worse, the means Jefferson chose to meet the growing crisis on the high seas—an embargo on U.S. shipping, imposed in late December 1807—led to a host of unforeseen and pernicious consequences. His retreat to Monticello in 1809 was a release from a score of accumulated troubles, that broke his health and shattered the people's confidence in his statecraft.

Historians have variously explained the failure of the embargo. One view sees Jefferson as the victim of circumstances beyond his control and the embargo as the inevitable result of the vise in which the French and the British progressively placed the United States. France's victories on land and Great Britain's at sea left the two antagonists without a ready means of striking at one another, and in resorting to sweeping measures of reprisal against neutral commerce they sucked the one great remaining neutral into a vortex that even the wisest U.S. statesman could not have avoided. "The whole world," as Jefferson explained, "is thus laid under interdict by

these two nations and our vessels, their cargoes, and crews are to be taken by the one or the other, for whatever place they may be destined, out of our limits." Though Jefferson's embargo failed, Great Britain's relaxation of commercial restrictions in 1812 showed, according to this sympathetic interpretation, that commercial pressure could be effective.

For other historians, such as Henry Adams, Jefferson's second administration was a study in political pathology; the embargo was merely the culminating episode in a pattern of weakness toward British aggression. Jefferson's problem, Adams held, was that he would not compromise his principles, but would not fight for them either, a contradiction that inevitably reduced him, in Josiah Quincy's expression, to "a dish of skim milk curdling at the head of our nation." Jefferson's dread of war was well known in London and Paris, according to Adams, and it served to invite assaults that might otherwise not have been undertaken. Yet a third interpretation focuses on Jefferson's Anglophobia and his zealous attachment to an overambitious conception of U.S. rights as a neutral nation.

Both the triumph of Louisiana and the failure of the embargo had ironic consequences. In the former case, Jefferson abandoned his constitutional scruples rather than run the risk that Louisiana might be lost as a consequence of adhering to them. The strict interpretation of the Constitution he had once championed was abandoned in the face of the danger—not very great—that Napoléon might abandon the cession unless it was swiftly completed.

The embargo of 1807–1809 led to even more ironic consequences, for its logic was to give a primacy to foreign policy that has remained to this day as onerous as any the nation has experienced. The measures taken to implement the embargo brought much of the economy to a virtual standstill and drove Massachusetts and Connecticut to the verge of rebellion. Great as the financial, political, and moral costs of the embargo were, it proved a failure. Taken to escape the alternatives of national humiliation or war, it led first to humiliation and then, ultimately, to war. The system of war that Jefferson had hoped to reform by the embargo was not reformed despite his commitment to take any and all measures necessary to give effect to the embargo.

The Jefferson Legacy

Jefferson's legacy has always evoked controversy. Some critics find in that legacy an abiding commitment to isolationism. In March 1799 Jefferson wrote to a friend: "I sincerely join you in abjuring all political connection with every foreign power; and tho I cordially wish well to the progress of liberty in all nations, and would forever give it the weight of our countenance, yet they are not to be touched without contamination from their other bad principles. Commerce with all nations, alliance with none, should be our motto." Jefferson would not have expressed himself thus in the early 1790s; he would not have spoken in terms that implied the moral equivalence of "all nations," including France. Then, as secretary of state, he had equated the fate of the French Revolution with that of liberty everywhere. Were France to go down before the might of the First Coalition, he had believed, her defeat could be expected to result in the permanent ascendancy of the enemies of liberty in the United States. The cause of republicanism would be seriously impaired and perhaps even perish.

It was largely out of this same conviction that Jefferson wished to intervene in the conflict, not by abandoning the United States's neutral status but by insisting on a view of neutral rights that would work to France's distinct advantage. The year 1793 marks Jefferson's first attempt—tentative and qualified as it was—to intervene in the great conflict brought on by the French Revolution. The second occurred in 1807–1809 and took the form of the embargo, Jefferson's great experiment in peaceable coercion. In this effort, however, the hope and expectation that informed the first was gone. With the coming to power of Napoléon, Jefferson no longer found moral importance in the European war. A conflict once endowed with profound moral significance, the outcome of which he had identified with the future of liberty, was now viewed as a mere struggle for power between the "tyrant on land" and the "tyrant of the ocean."

Jefferson continued to insist on the moral equivalence of France and Great Britain to the end of their armed struggle. In his view, there was no room for the consideration that the one belligerent—the "tyrant of the ocean"—was defending an international order within which the United States could enjoy a basic security whereas the other belligerent—the "tyrant of the land"—was intent on destroying this order and the security of the states that formed it.

Nor was this refusal to differentiate between the belligerents essentially qualified by Jefferson's occasional bow to balance-of-power considerations. After the British naval victory at Trafalgar and the French defeat of Austria at Austerlitz, he had insisted that "our wish ought to be that he who has armies may not have the dominion of the sea, and that he who has dominion of the sea may be one who has no armies." The "wish" that he expressed in 1806, however, did not inform the policy he pursued in 1807 and 1808. So enraged was he over British transgressions against neutral rights that he no longer troubled himself over the danger that "he who has armies" might gain "the dominion of the sea." He acknowledged his change of attitude by confessing that it was "mortifying that we should be forced to wish success to Bonaparte, and to look to his victories as our salvation." He had

never expected to be placed in this position. "But the English being equally tyrannical at sea as he is on land, and that tyranny bearing on us in every point of either honor or interest, I say, 'down with England' and as for what Bonaparte is then to do with us, let us trust to the chapter of accidents." Dismissing the prospect of danger from Napoléon even in the aftermath of a conquest of Great Britain as "hypothetical" and "chimerical," Jefferson's true policy was to assert neutral rights against Great Britain and otherwise trust to the chapter of accidents to preserve a balance of power.

Although separated by a decade and a half, these two critical episodes illuminate the tension in Jefferson between the desire to reform the international system and the desire to remain separate from it. Reformation could come only as a result of successfully imposing one's will on the system, or, at least, on a significant part of it, but this could prove difficult and dangerous. Whatever their initial intention, those bent on reform, and therefore on intervention, generally have had to resort to the sword. This Jefferson did not want and had no intention of doing. Force threatened the very interests for which he had sought reform. The result of this reasoning could only lead to withdrawal. If the state system could not be reformed, it had to be abandoned. Then Jefferson could speak of the desirability of "Chinese isolation" and of the need to place "an ocean of fire between us and the old world."

Exemplar or Crusader?

Jefferson is perhaps best remembered for his evocation of the mission of the United States. As the "solitary republic of the world" and "the only monument of human rights," the nation was to serve as an example that would allow "the sacred fire of freedom and self government...to be lighted up in other regions of the earth, if other regions of the earth shall ever become susceptible to its benign influence."

After Jefferson left the presidency in 1809, he often expressed skepticism that other lands would become susceptible to the benign influence of the U.S. example. Freedom was a plant, he observed, that could grow and flourish only in a favorable environment. Jefferson did not consistently adhere to this doubt; from time to time his innate optimism manifested itself. Still, his disillusionment over the course of the French Revolution ended the only real "enthusiasm" he ever entertained respecting the imminent prospects for liberty among the nations of Europe. "All their energies," he wrote to Monroe in 1823, "are expended in the destruction of the labor, property, and lives of their people." Thus it was, thus it had always been, and, Jefferson finally came close to believing, thus it always would be. Nor did he think these prospects any better among the peoples of this hemisphere. Writing in 1818 to John Adams, who shared his views on this matter, Jefferson observed that while the peoples to the south "will succeed against Spain...the dangerous enemy is within their own breasts. Ignorance and superstition will chain their minds and bodies under religious and military despotism."

Even if Jefferson had seen the world as being more receptive to the institutions of freedom than he did in his later years, he still would have had strong reservations about taking on the role of crusader for freedom. Any role that went beyond example necessarily incurred the risk of war, which in turn raised the dangers—executive aggrandizement, debt, and taxes—that Jefferson believed would be fatal to republican institutions.

Although Jefferson became increasingly skeptical over the prospects for freedom elsewhere, his skepticism never quite overcame a deeper, congenital optimism. He declared in 1820 that Europe was a region "where war seems to be the natural state of man," but he could write on the same day of his hope that "the disease of liberty is catching." Despite his doubts about the peoples of the south being ready for freedom, he still thought that they might obtain it "by degrees...because that would...bring on light and information, and qualify them to take charge of themselves understandingly."

Jefferson had very important reasons for not abandoning hope in the prospects for freedom in the world. In a world that was ruled by arbitrary power, the fate of free institutions in the United States would never be quite assured, however much the nation might try to isolate itself from the world. For monarchy meant war and, despite the best efforts of the United States, Europe's wars might always spread to the Western Hemisphere. Only a world made up of republics would be a world where peace was truly possible.

What ultimately thrust an unwilling Jefferson onto the world was not political or ideological but commercial motivation. Persuaded that the health and well-being of the Republic required a free trading system, Jefferson believed he could isolate commercial interest from the political entanglement he was determined to avoid. Events were to show that the insistence on preserving an open trading system entailed the need to intervene against those whose efforts were directed to keeping the system closed.

Certainly Jefferson never consciously contemplated the role of crusader. He did not do so in his own day for the most apparent and compelling of reasons. But what of the future day when the United States might "shake a rod over the heads of all" and do so with relative impunity? Why should the United States not do so then, if this might contribute to its security and well-being while striking a blow for the cause of liberty? It was one thing to reject "a war to reform Europe" and quite another to abandon the hope that the international system might ultimately be reformed without war. The former implied a course of action that might always prove disastrous for the United States internally, a prospect that necessarily outweighed that of attempting to replace arbitrary power elsewhere with government based on consent. The latter held out a far different course, promising reformation of the international system at but modest cost. Such a course was in the tradition of "peaceable coercion" and it is difficult to believe that Jefferson would have rejected it.

On the issue of the nation's proper role in the world, then, Jefferson's legacy remains ultimately ambiguous. It is this ambiguity, among others, that lends Jefferson's name to such conflicting uses in the never-ending debates over U.S. foreign policy. Among the statesmen of the early Republic, he is more responsible than any for warning of the hazards that must attend the role of crusader. Yet he is also the statesman who is more responsible than any for evoking the perennial attractions of this role.

ROBERT W. TUCKER
DAVID C. HENDRICKSON

See also France; French Revolution; Great Britain; Hamilton, Alexander; Louisiana Purchase; Spain; Washington, George

FURTHER READING

Adams, Henry. *History of the United States of America during the Administrations of Thomas Jefferson, 1801–1809.* New York, 1986.

Boyd, Julian P., et al., eds. *The Papers of Thomas Jefferson.* 28 vols. Princeton, N.J, 1950–.

Cunningham, Noble E. *In Pursuit of Reason: The Life of Thomas Jefferson.* Baton Rouge, La., 1987.

LaFeber, Walter. "Jefferson and an American Foreign Policy." In *Jeffersonian Legacies,* edited by Peter S. Onuf. Charlottesville, Va., 1993.

Malone, Dumas. *Jefferson and His Time.* 6 vols. Boston, 1948–1981.

McCoy, Drew R. *The Elusive Republic: Political Economy in Jeffersonian America.* New York, 1980.

Perkins, Bradford. *Prologue to War: England and the United States, 1805–1812.* Berkeley, Calif., 1961.

Peterson, Merrill D. *Thomas Jefferson and the New Nation.* New York, 1970.

Spivak, Burton. *Jefferson's English Crisis: Commerce, Embargo, and the Republican Revolution.* Charlottesville, Va., 1979.

Tucker, Robert W., and David C. Hendrickson. *Empire of Liberty: The Statecraft of Thomas Jefferson.* New York, 1990.

JESSUP, PHILIP CARYL

(*b.* 5 January 1897; *d.* 31 January 1986)

International jurist, professor at Columbia University, and author. From the 1920s to the 1940s Jessup was a legal adviser to political leaders, the Department of State, and international organizations. From 1947 to 1953 he served on the U.S. delegation to the United Nations.

In 1949, when he was named U.S. ambassador-at-large, he became a trusted adviser to Secretary of State Dean Acheson. That same year he helped negotiate the settlement of the Berlin crisis and served as editor in chief of the China White Paper. He served on the World Court from 1961 to 1970 and in 1966 wrote an important dissent when the court ruled in favor of South Africa's establishment of apartheid in Southwest Africa.

SHANE J. MADDOCK

See also Permanent Court of International Justice

FURTHER READING

Burke, Lee H. *Ambassador at Large: Diplomat Extraordinary*. The Hague, Netherlands, 1972.
Jessup, Philip C. *The Birth of Nations*. New York, 1974.
McLellan, David S. *Dean Acheson: The State Department Years*. New York, 1976.

JIANG JIESHI

(*b*. 31 October 1887; *d*. 5 April 1975)

Leader of the Republic of China (1928–1949) and later, on the island of Taiwan (Formosa), head of a government in exile. From the 1930s to the 1970s, Americans either loved or hated Jiang Jieshi (Chiang Kai-shek). To some, he ranked as a brilliant Chinese patriot, anticommunist fighter, national hero, and indispensable friend of the United States. To others, he seemed a contemptible and corrupt dictator and an embarrassment to the United States. Despite his undeniable importance to modern China and Sino-American relations, in the United States his historical assessment is still colored by emotions related to the Communist takeover of the mainland in 1949.

Jiang was born in Zhejiang Province, not far from the city of Shanghai. He developed an early interest in the army, attended military schools in China and Japan, and participated in the revolutionary movements led by Sun Zhongshan (Sun Yat-sen) in 1911 and 1913. He also developed links with the Shanghai underworld. By the early 1920s, Jiang had become prominent in the efforts of the army of Sun's Guomindang (Kuomintang) Party to unify China. In 1923 he visited the Soviet Union as a member of a military delegation; the trip, he later claimed, opened his eyes to the evils of communism.

After Sun's death in 1925, Jiang took over the Guomindang and established the Republic of China as the national government in Nanjing (NanKing), with himself as supreme leader. He won his anticommunist reputation when, in a bloody purge, he decimated the Chinese Communist Party, which had previously been an ally in the national unification effort. Jiang's fight against communism became an obsession for him, even overshadowing efforts to resist Japanese aggression against China in the 1930s and 1940s. His policies led many Chinese to look elsewhere for national leadership, and they looked increasingly to the Chinese Communist Party.

During World War II, President Franklin D. Roosevelt publicly praised China under Jiang's leadership as one of the world's four great powers in the wartime alliance and a partner in shaping the peace. Jiang's meeting with Roosevelt and British prime minister Winston S. Churchill at the Cairo Conference of 1943 seemed to confirm this status, although privately Churchill thought the idea of China as a great power was nonsense and Roosevelt had his doubts. Many in the United States, including influential businessmen and politicians, strongly supported Jiang and his American-educated wife, the former Song Meiling, a member of a prominent family and sister of Mademoiselle Sun, who frequently visited the United States as his emissary. Others, however—including General Joseph W. Stillwell, whom Roosevelt sent to China to serve as Jiang's wartime chief of staff—had open contempt for him.

After World War II, the mission of General George C. Marshall and other U.S. efforts to end the Nationalist-Communist dispute ended in frustration and failure. Jiang refused to seek a compromise, such as a coalition government. When the Communists defeated Jiang's Nationalist forces on the mainland in 1949, Jiang moved his government to Taiwan (or Formosa, as it was called in the West at that time), opposite China's Fujian Province. From there he continued to claim to be the legitimate leader of all of China. During the 1950s, his forces staged attacks against the mainland, frequently launching them from the offshore island groups of Jinmen (Quemoy) and Mazu (Matsu). These attacks contributed to making the region one of the most tense areas during much of the Cold War and were partly responsible for serious crises involving those islands in 1954–1955 and 1958. In 1955 the U.S. Senate passed what became known as the Formosa Resolution, which gave the president a blank check to commit U.S. forces to the defense of Taiwan and the Pescadores. Jiang remained a staunch anticommunist ally of the United States, actively supporting it in the Korean War and the Vietnam War.

Jiang never surrendered his dream of recovering the mainland and repeatedly sought to involve the United States in his controversial efforts. Exercising one-man rule and martial law over Taiwan until his death in 1975, he tolerated no opposition, even within his own party. He never reconciled himself to exile, and subordinated the welfare of Taiwan to his dream of returning to the mainland. He branded President Richard Nixon's trip to Beijing in 1972 a betrayal. After Jiang's death, his son, Jiang Jingguo, assumed power on Taiwan.

GORDON H. CHANG

See also Cairo Conference; Chennault, Claire Lee and Anna Chan; China; China Lobby; Formosa Resolution; Jinmen-Mazu Crises; Marshall, George Catlett, Jr.; McCarthyism; Nixon, Richard Milhous; Roosevelt, Franklin Delano; Stillwell, Joseph

FURTHER READING

Fairbank, John K., ed. *The United States and China.* 4th ed. Cambridge, Mass., 1983.

Tucker, Nancy Bernkoff. *Taiwan, Hong Kong, and the United States, 1945–1992.* New York, 1994.

JINMEN-MAZU CRISES

(Quemoy-Matsu Crises, 1954–1955, 1958)

Cold War confrontations in which the United States resisted efforts by the People's Republic of China (PRC) to expel the Nationalists from islands off the Chinese mainland coast.

After their defeat by the Chinese Communists in 1949, the Nationalist forces of Jiang Jieshi (Chiang Kai-shek) fled across the 100-mile-wide Formosan Strait to the island of Taiwan (formerly Formosa), where they

maintained the Republic of China (ROC). In addition to Taiwan and the Pescadores islands, the Nationalists also controlled several small offshore islands, many of them no more than a few miles from the mainland. The most important of these were the islands of Jinmen (Quemoy) and Mazu (Matsu) which, in the 1950s and 1960s, became the focal point of the ongoing civil war between the ROC and PRC and of major Cold War confrontations.

Following the outbreak of the Korean War in 1950, these island groups became important staging areas for Nationalist harassment of the mainland and PRC shipping. They were also potential jump-off points for Jiang's promised reinvasion of the mainland. U.S. policy supported the Nationalists' retention of these sparsely populated and economically insignificant bits of land.

The first crisis began in September 1954, when PRC shore batteries heavily shelled Jinmen, located at the mouth of the Lung River near the port of Xiamen (Amoy). The Nationalists retaliated with air raids against the mainland and strengthened their island fortifications. Over the following months, tensions mounted as it appeared to the United States that the PRC intended to assault and seize all the offshore islands and possibly even attack Taiwan itself. The United States strength-

From *The American Pacific,* Arthur Power Dudden. ©1992 by Oxford University Press. Reprinted with permission of Oxford University Press

ened its security commitment to Jiang with a mutual defense treaty (2 December 1954) and congressional passage of the Formosa Doctrine (28 January 1955), which committed U.S. forces to the defense of Taiwan.

The crisis peaked in April 1955, when the United States threatened to use nuclear weapons in the event of a Communist attack on Jinmen and Mazu. At the same time, Chinese premier Zhou Enlai signaled his government's willingness to negotiate with the United States. The two developments were not directly linked. Secretary of State John Foster Dulles believed, however, that the nuclear threat led the PRC to resolve the crisis. After the United States and the PRC agreed to meet regularly in Geneva, Switzerland, to discuss bilateral issues, tensions quickly subsided in the offshore area.

In August 1958, another U.S.-China confrontation broke out over Jinmen and Mazu. This crisis was shorter but more intense than the first. For several weeks it appeared that the United States might be drawn into a war with China, and possibly with the Soviet Union, which had pledged its support for the Chinese Communists. Beijing was upset with the lack of progress in its bilateral talks with the United States (which had moved to Warsaw) and believed the time had come for the communist world to take a more militant stance against "U.S. imperialism." As in the first crisis, the tensions broke when Washington and Beijing entered talks. Although the United States and the PRC reached no formal understanding about the offshore islands, Beijing unilaterally ended the crisis in the apparent belief that its actions had brought the attention it wanted to the area.

The offshore islands became an issue in American domestic politics in the presidential campaign of 1960, when Democratic candidate John F. Kennedy criticized the Eisenhower administration's handling of the crisis in a televised debate with the Republican candidate, Vice President Richard M. Nixon.

GORDON H. CHANG

See also China; Dulles, John Foster; Formosa Resolution; Taiwan

FURTHER READING

Chang, Gordon H. *Friends and Enemies: The United States, China and the Soviet Union, 1948-1972.* Stanford, Calif., 1990.
Stolper, Thomas E. *China, Taiwan, and the Offshore Islands.* Armonk, N.Y., 1985.

JOHNSON, ANDREW

(*b.* 29 December 1808; *d.* 31 July 1875)

Seventeenth president of the United States (1865–69). Born in Raleigh, North Carolina, and wholly self-educated, Johnson served as a congressman (1843–1853), enthusiastically supporting war against Mexico; as gover-

nor (1853–1857); and as senator (1857–1862). He was the only Southern senator to remain in office when the South seceded from the Union in 1861. In 1864 he was elected vice president, becoming president when Abraham Lincoln was assassinated in April 1865. At odds over domestic issues with the radical majorities in both houses of Congress virtually from the beginning of his presidency, Johnson left foreign relations almost entirely to Secretary of State William H. Seward, who successfully pressed the French to end their military occupation of Mexico, defused the Fenian problem (Irish-American, anti-British provocations on the Canadian border), purchased Alaska from Russia, and laid the groundwork for the favorable settlement of the *Alabama* Claims against Great Britain. Impeached in February 1868 but retaining office by a single vote in the Senate, Johnson retired from the presidency in March 1869. Reentering the U.S. Senate in 1875, he died after attending one brief session.

NORMAN B. FERRIS

See also Alabama Claims; Alaska Purchase; American Civil War; Juárez, Benito; Mexico, War with

FURTHER READING

Latley, Thomas. *The First President Johnson: The Three Lives of the Seventeenth President of the United States.* New York, 1968.

JOHNSON, LYNDON BAINES

(*b.* 27 August 1908; *d.* 22 January 1973)

Thirty-sixth president of the United States (1963–1969) whose administration Americanized the war in Vietnam. Born near Stonewall, Texas, he graduated from Southwest State Teachers College in 1930. Although he taught briefly in public schools, Johnson's career ambitions lay in politics, which he pursued as a legislative aide to Representative Richard M. Kleberg of Texas from 1932 to 1935, and as administrator for Texas of the National Youth Administration from 1935 to 1937. He was elected to the U.S. House of Representatives in 1937 and to the U.S. Senate in 1948. Johnson rose quickly to leadership positions in the Senate, being elected Democratic party whip in 1951, minority leader in 1953, and majority leader in 1955. He sought the Democratic presidential nomination in 1960 but was defeated by Senator John F. Kennedy, who named Johnson as his running mate. Johnson became vice president of the United States on 20 January 1961.

Although he traveled the world to represent the United States as vice president, Johnson did not play a significant role in the foreign policy-making of the Kennedy administration. In 1961 he toured Southeast Asia for the purposes of reassuring pro-Western governments there of

U.S. support and of assessing the threat posed by communism to the region. Upon his return, he advocated a greater commitment of U.S. economic and military resources in the area, particularly to Vietnam. Johnson was sworn in as president on 22 November 1963 following Kennedy's assassination.

As president, Johnson's most important goals were in the field of domestic policy, culminating in the creation of his Great Society reform programs. He did not regard himself as an expert in foreign affairs, which caused him to rely to an extraordinary degree on advisers he inherited from the Kennedy administration—Robert McNamara, Dean Rusk, McGeorge Bundy, and others. Their advice pushed him, for the most part, in directions he already was prepared to go. Johnson shared with his advisers a belief in the Doctrine of Containment that defined the foreign policy of the Cold War era, and regarded the presence and power of the United States as an essential barrier to communist expansion and domination throughout the world.

Johnson's perspective on foreign policy was an outgrowth of his views on domestic politics and opinion. He thought the mood of the American people about foreign affairs was one of "indifference and passivity" that concealed the possibility of "a mass stampede, a violent overreaction to fear, an explosion of panic," such as that which had arisen in the era of McCarthyism. He stressed the importance of presidential leadership in foreign policy and emphasized the need to rely on experienced policy-makers with access to timely information.

Johnson also thought that the principles that guided American life and politics were universally applicable. He once spoke of visiting an impoverished woman in Senegal. "As I looked into her determined eyes," he said, "I saw the same expression that I saw in my mother's eyes when she, the wife of a tenant farmer, looked down on me and my little brothers and sisters, determined that I should have my chance...." He viewed economic development as the solution to the world's problems, which he believed resulted from poverty, ignorance, and disease.

Another lesson that Johnson drew from his experience in politics was the importance of personal persuasion. "I always believed," Johnson commented, "that as long as I could take someone into a room with me, I could make him my friend, and that included anybody, even [Soviet leader] Nikita Khrushchev." For Johnson, face-to-face negotiations could defuse even the most dangerous foreign disagreements.

The Vietnam War

Johnson's most difficult immediate test was the developing conflict in South Vietnam. Despite the presence of more than 16,000 so-called U.S. advisers in the country in November 1963, the political and military situation deteriorated there following the overthrow and death of Premier Ngo Dinh Diem that month. Johnson confirmed the Kennedy administration's commitment to protect South Vietnam against a communist takeover and stepped up U.S. assistance to the Saigon government. Johnson's perception of the struggle, shared by Secretary of State Dean Rusk and Secretary of Defense Robert S. McNamara, as well as by other holdovers from the Kennedy administration, was that the National Liberation Front and Vietcong guerrillas were dependent upon the support of North Vietnam. The "Free World" thus faced a war of communist aggression, in response to which there must be no "appeasement." He developed a strategy designed to persuade the North to discontinue its aid to the communist forces while preventing a rebel victory in the South.

Although applied minimally in the beginning, this strategy led in August 1964 to U.S. aerial reprisal raids against North Vietnamese targets following a series of incidents in the Gulf of Tonkin involving attacks by communist PT boats against U.S. destroyers. Subsequent investigations have cast doubt on the accuracy of the reports of these attacks, as well as Johnson's manipulating of the events and information, but the Gulf of Tonkin Resolution, to which they gave rise, became Johnson's justification for the eventual intervention of U.S. forces in Vietnam.

Following his landslide reelection in November 1964, due largely to his apparent moderation in foreign affairs compared to the views of his opponent, Senator Barry Goldwater, Johnson turned his attention to the worsening situation in Vietnam. As the South Vietnamese government and military neared collapse, he approved plans for a series of reprisal raids against the North, which began in February 1965 in apparent response to a Vietcong attack on a U.S. Air Force barracks at Pleiku. As the administration had planned, these reprisals grew into Operation Rolling Thunder, an ongoing and ascending program of bombing raids against North Vietnam. When these raids brought an increased threat against the U.S. air base at Da Nang, Johnson decided to guard it with a contingent of U.S. Marines, who became the first U.S. combat troops to enter the conflict in Vietnam.

As his administration scaled up U.S. military intervention in the war in Vietnam, Johnson received conflicting advice. The Joint Chiefs of Staff recommended a rapid large-scale buildup, including the introduction of several hundred thousand combat troops and bombing the North Vietnamese capital of Hanoi, while some officials at the State Department pushed for a negotiated settlement of the war. Although he hoped to avoid a full-scale military intervention, Johnson's belief in containment and the domino-like threat to all of Southeast Asia if South Vietnam became communist precluded a negotiated settlement that did not promise to preserve the Saigon government. These views were shared by Johnson's closest advisers, Rusk, McNamara, and National Security Adviser McGeorge Bundy. Johnson thus adopted a strategy of increasing the military pressure on North Vietnam in hopes of bringing about a satisfactory settlement without a full-scale military intervention, which he feared would endanger support for his reform program at home. This approach failed to satisfy his critics, who became more vocal as the size of the U.S. force in Vietnam grew without bringing about a negotiated end to the war.

When a bombing halt in May 1965 failed to produce negotiations, Johnson embarked on a course of escalation, announcing on 28 July 1965 that an additional 50,000 troops would be sent to Vietnam. By the end of the year, the total had reached 184,000 U.S. soldiers, who had substantially taken over the fighting of the war from South Vietnamese forces. A second bombing halt, beginning on Christmas Eve of that year and extending until the end of January 1966, also did not result in negotiations, which seemed pointless to both sides because of their disagreement over the composition of the Saigon government. Johnson thus continued to pursue a course of steadily expanding the U.S. military role in Vietnam.

During 1966, as the size of the U.S. force in Vietnam more than doubled and U.S. bombers flew missions closer to the industrial and population centers of North Vietnam, Johnson attempted to define his administration's long-term goals for peace in Southeast Asia. In February, he met in Hawaii with South Vietnamese leaders Nguyen Cao Ky and Nguyen Van Thieu to discuss the social, political, and economic reconstruction of their country. In October, as part of a two-week Asian tour, Johnson met in Manila with representatives of the Association of Southeast Asian Nations (ASEAN) and issued a Declaration of the Goals of Freedom that called for conquering hunger, illiteracy, and disease as well as maintaining peace and security throughout the region. Johnson's critics nonetheless saw these efforts as insignificant compared to the expanding U.S. military activities in Vietnam.

Johnson also tried to find a formula that would bring about a negotiated settlement of the war. In a speech on 29 September 1967 in San Antonio, Texas, he offered to halt the U.S. bombing of North Vietnam whenever doing so would lead "promptly to productive discussions," provided that the North Vietnamese refrain from taking military advantage of the bombing halt. He also softened U.S. terms by indicating a willingness to admit the Vietcong to political participation in South Vietnam. The San Antonio Plan did not satisfy the North Vietnamese, who insisted that the United States abandon the Thieu regime, and Johnson followed the advice of his senior

staff members, especially National Security Adviser Walt W. Rostow, in continuing to expand the war. By the end of 1967, the U.S. force in Vietnam had passed 500,000, with additional troops scheduled to arrive in the first six months of 1968.

By then, U.S. military leaders were reporting that the war was substantially won. When General William C. Westmoreland, the commander of U.S. forces in Vietnam, returned to the United States in November 1967 he told Johnson and the Congress that victory was almost at hand. The inaccuracy of this assessment became apparent beginning 31 January 1968 when the Vietcong launched their Tet Offensive against cities and hamlets throughout South Vietnam. Although the communist offensive was beaten back quickly in most locations, it fueled doubts about the status of the war and the veracity of the Johnson administration. As the press and public reacted negatively to events in Vietnam, the Tet Offensive shook the faith of Johnson and many of his advisers in the U.S. military's ability to win the war. With Secretary of Defense McNamara preparing to leave office as a result of his dissent from the war, Johnson asked McNamara's successor, Clark M. Clifford, to investigate the best course for the administration to follow in the aftermath of the communist offensive. Clifford, who had been a strong supporter of the Vietnam War, interviewed military leaders in the Pentagon and came away disillusioned. He thus recommended a halt to the U.S. military buildup, a limitation on the bombing of North Vietnam, and a renewed search for a negotiated settlement. Secretary Rusk agreed with these recommendations, as did the so-called Wise Men, Johnson's committee of elder statesmen and military officers who advised him occasionally on questions of foreign affairs.

Johnson announced on 31 March 1968 his decision to limit the bombing of North Vietnam to the region adjacent to the demilitarized zone. Although refusing to compromise on the basic issues of the war, he also offered to begin peace negotiations with North Vietnam and declared that because of his preoccupation with the Vietnam War and other foreign policy issues he would not accept his party's nomination for the presidency in 1968. Negotiations began in May but little progress was made during the remainder of the Johnson administration, even following a further presidential announcement on 31 October that the United States would halt all bombing of North Vietnam. The level of conflict in South Vietnam did not diminish during 1968, due in part to the major battle for Khe Sanh, which Johnson feared as a U.S. Dien Bien Phu, as well as to the concern that the communists might mount another large-scale offensive. Republican Richard M. Nixon won the presidency in 1968 promising to end the Vietnam War. Johnson's Vietnam policy stands as the greatest failure of his administration. He became tormented by his inability to find a formula for victory there, as he was by the war itself. In the end his worst fears came true: the war in Vietnam overshadowed and undermined the domestic achievements of his presidency.

Latin America

Johnson also perceived the threats of revolutionary communism and anti-Americanism in the Western Hemisphere. He sustained the policy of isolating Fidel Castro's Cuba, especially through an economic embargo, to limit its influence in the region. In January 1964 a mob of Panamanians, incensed by a violation of an agreement pertaining to the flying of flags in the Canal Zone, rioted and destroyed U.S. property in the area. U.S. troops clashed with Panamanians, whose government demanded a review of U.S. treaty rights in the zone. Johnson refused to consider the idea at first, but announced in December that Panama and the United States would begin to negotiate a new treaty.

A more serious incident prompted a U.S. military intervention in the Dominican Republic. In September 1963 the elected government of Juan Bosch was overthrown by a military coup and replaced by a new government led by Donald Reid y Cabral. The Reid government, which was even less popular than its predecessor had been, faced widespread dissension that included a dissatisfied military group as well as a small left-wing contingent. The United States did nothing to aid Reid until April 1965, when Bosch supporters in the army rebelled against his government. When Reid's supporters requested U.S. Marines to quell the disturbances, Johnson complied, claiming that U.S. lives were in danger. The president also wanted to keep Bosch from power and feared that the communists might take advantage of the turmoil to gain control of the government and turn the Dominican Republic into "another Cuba." When the intervention proved difficult and more troops had to be sent later, critics saw Johnson's actions as an unnecessary over-reaction to the fear of further communist encroachment in the Caribbean. They also criticized the president for failing to permit the Organization of American States (OAS) to play a role in his initial decision, a mistake that he attempted to rectify by including an OAS peacekeeping force in later stages of the intervention. Order was eventually restored and elections for a new government were held in 1966.

In Latin America, as in Southeast Asia, Johnson tempered his use of military force and aid to military regimes with plans for economic and social development. He attempted to expand U.S. assistance to the region through the Kennedy administration's Alliance for Progress, while focusing on what he regarded as the interdependence of all nations in the Western Hemi-

sphere. In April 1967 Johnson met at Punta del Este, Uruguay, with the leaders of thirteen Latin American states to discuss matters of concern to all nations in the hemisphere and to promote the idea of a partnership in the region to supplant the image of the United States as the "colossus of the north." He also held bilateral conversations that resolved difficulties between the United States and individual states, such as differences over oil imports with Venezuela. Johnson failed, however, to win the increased appropriations from Congress required to put his development plans into effect.

The Cold War

In relations with the Soviet Union, Johnson attempted to ease the tensions of the Cold War, which had grown alarmingly during the Kennedy years but had begun to abate in the final months of the Kennedy administration. He promoted cultural exchanges with the USSR and on 1 June 1964 a Consular Convention was signed in Moscow. Although not ratified until 1967, this agreement was important to Johnson, who thought that reaching agreement on individual issues dividing the United States and the USSR was more likely than seeking a comprehensive agreement to lead to a stable relationship between the two nations.

Johnson tested this theory in negotiations over limiting and controlling nuclear weapons. Following up on the Kennedy administration's Limited Nuclear Test Ban Treaty, he announced in April 1964 that he and Soviet premier Nikita Khrushchev had reached agreement on a cutback in the production of weapons-grade uranium and on allocating more fissionable materials for peaceful purposes. Johnson also pressed the Soviet leaders for a treaty to limit the proliferation of nuclear weapons, a proposal that gained immediacy following the explosion of a nuclear device by the People's Republic of China in October 1964. Although a logical next step, such a treaty involved difficult questions of protecting the security interests of U.S. and Soviet allies, as well as those of neutral nations that were being asked to forgo the development of nuclear arms. A basic agreement was worked out by December 1966, although many important details still needed to be determined. Johnson and Soviet chairman of the council of ministers, Aleksey Kosygin, finally decided during their summit meeting at Glassboro, New Jersey, in June 1967 to submit the treaty to the Geneva Disarmament Conference without resolving their differences on mutual safeguards against violations. The Treaty on the Nonproliferation of Nuclear Weapons was signed on 1 July 1968, but because of hostility in the U.S. Senate following the Soviet invasion of Czechoslovakia in the summer of 1968 was not ratified until March 1969, during the presidency of Richard Nixon.

Following the preliminary agreement on a nuclear nonproliferation treaty in late 1966, Johnson attempted to initiate talks aimed at curbing the strategic arms race. The Soviet Union was installing an anti-ballistic missile (ABM) system around Moscow, which promised to require a similar system in the United States as well as increasingly elaborate offensive weapons systems designed to circumvent the ABMs. Johnson pursued the idea of limiting both the ABM systems and strategic weapons during the Glassboro summit, and he and Kosygin announced their intention to begin arms limitation talks at the time of the signing of the nonproliferation treaty. The Strategic Arms Limitation Talks (SALT) were another casualty of the Soviet action in Czechoslovakia, not beginning until November 1969 in Helsinki, Finland.

The Soviet Union's invasion of Czechoslovakia in August 1968 disrupted improving U.S.-Soviet relations. Faced with anti-Soviet reforms instituted by the liberal government of Alexander Dubcek, the USSR sent its military forces into Czechoslovakia. Johnson had no intention of intervening militarily, a course that would not have found support among the U.S.'s allies. He thus attempted to discourage the Soviets while avoiding actions that might further inflame the crisis or harm U.S.-Soviet relations. In addition to stalling the negotiations concerning nuclear weapons, the Soviet invasion also prevented a second Johnson-Kosygin summit, which had been tentatively planned to take place in Moscow in October 1968.

Johnson viewed European affairs primarily in terms of their effect on U.S.-Soviet relations. He regarded the North Atlantic Treaty Organization (NATO) as essential to the security of Europe and the U.S., and thought that unity within the Atlantic community was the best means of ensuring a cooperative and peaceful Soviet Union. Western unity was threatened in February 1966, when French president Charles de Gaulle announced that he was terminating his nation's participation in the military aspects of NATO. This meant that U.S. troops would have to leave France and that NATO headquarters would have to be moved from Paris. Although irritated by de Gaulle's action, Johnson did not make an issue of de Gaulle's decision, thereby avoiding the impression that NATO was fragmenting.

Another strain on the Western alliance came from economic differences brought about by the postwar recovery of Europe. By 1966, the cost of maintaining a large U.S. force in Europe was exacerbating the balance of payments problem and threatening the U.S. gold supply. England was facing a similar problem and threatening to withdraw its forces from Germany. Despite growing economic pressures, Johnson rejected the outright withdrawal of any U.S. units from Germany. His administration worked out purchase agreements that eased the balance of payments problem and developed a dual-bas-

ing system that rotated U.S. forces in and out of Germany while maintaining the formal presence of all units currently there.

Johnson also worried about the implications for U.S.-Soviet relations arising from the Six-Day War in the Middle East. Tensions were high in the Middle East in the spring of 1967 due to repeated rumors that Israel was preparing to respond to repeated Syrian terrorist attacks by invading that country. The Syrians, backed by the USSR, sought assistance from the president of Egypt, Gamal Abdel Nasser, who wanted to reestablish his leadership of the Arab world. In May the United Nations acted at Nasser's request and withdrew its peacekeeping force from the Sinai Peninsula, whereupon Egyptian troops moved into the area and took up positions on the border of Israel. Despite Johnson's pleas for calm, Egypt closed the Gulf of Aqaba to Israeli shipping on 22 May, forcing the United States to consider joint naval action to keep it open. On 5 June the Israelis acted themselves, attacking Syria and Egyptian forces in the Sinai.

Johnson worked through the United Nations to achieve a ceasefire. Although supporting a negotiated end to the conflict, the Soviet Union became threatening as the Israeli forces humiliated its Syrian allies. Johnson responded by ordering the U.S. Sixth Fleet closer to Syria, a step designed to warn the Soviet leaders against intervention in the war and to signal U.S. support of Israel. A ceasefire took hold on 10 June, with the Israelis occupying territory they had won in the Sinai, Jordan, and Syria. Although Johnson would have preferred a less decisive result, he maintained a steady commitment to Israel based partly on domestic political concerns. He also was successful in his main objective of preventing a wider conflict that might have increased tensions between the United States and the USSR.

Johnson faced one of his worst crises when North Korean naval forces seized the USS *Pueblo*, an electronics intelligence ship gathering information in international waters off the coast of North Korea. Occurring on 23 January 1968, at the beginning of the siege of Khe Sanh and immediately before the Tet Offensive, the capture of the *Pueblo* and its 83 crew members came at a troubled time for the Johnson administration. Johnson feared that it might presage a new North Korean invasion of South Korea and ordered additional U.S. forces to the peninsula. Although he considered military retaliation, Johnson decided that a concerted diplomatic effort was the best way to win the release of the U.S. sailors. The crew of *Pueblo* was returned to the United States after eleven months in captivity.

The Vietnam War has dogged Johnson's reputation for the conduct of foreign affairs, just as it did his presidency. The war epitomized his shortcomings in handling world affairs—oversimplification of issues, ignorance of other cultures, and lack of imagination in seeking foreign policy alternatives. Yet, except for the invasion of the Dominican Republic, these qualities did not prevent Johnson from the effective management of foreign affairs. He maintained U.S.-Soviet relations on an even keel, held NATO together following the departure of France, and acted to prevent a widening of the Six-Day War. Although Johnson's presidency will never be seen as a success in foreign relations, it was not as disastrous as the defeat in Vietnam might make it seem.

After leaving the presidency, Johnson returned to his ranch in Texas, wrote his memoirs, and opened the Lyndon Baines Johnson Presidential Library in Austin. He died at his ranch in Johnson City, Texas.

ROBERT C. HILDERBRAND

See also Alliance for Progress; Antiballistic Missile Treaty; Bundy, McGeorge; Clifford, Clark McAdams; Cultural Diplomacy; Czech Republic; Dien Bien Phu; Dominican Republic; Khrushchev, Nikita Sergeyevich; McNamara, Robert Strange; Middle East; Nuclear Nonproliferation; Nuclear Weapons and Strategy; Panama and Panama Canal; Presidency; Pueblo Incident; Rusk, David Dean; Tet Offensive; Vietnam War

FURTHER READING

Brands, H. W. *The Wages of Globalism: Lyndon Johnson and the Limits of American Power.* New York, 1995.
Conkin, Paul Keith. *Big Daddy From the Pedernales: Lyndon B. Johnson.* Boston, 1986.
Dallek, Robert. *Lone Star Rising: Lyndon Johnson and His Times, 1908-1960.* New York and Oxford, 1991.
Geyelin, Philip V. *Lyndon B. Johnson and the World.* New York and Washington, D.C., 1966.
Herring, George C., *LBJ and Vietnam: A Different Kind of War.* Austin, Tx., 1994.
Johnson, Lyndon B. *The Vantage Point: Perspectives of the Presidency 1963-1969.* New York, 1971.
Kunz, Diane. *The Diplomacy of the Crucial Decade.* New York, 1994.

JOHNSON, URAL ALEXIS

(*b.* 17 October 1908)

Career diplomat (1935–1977) who specialized in Asian affairs. After attending the Georgetown School of Foreign Service, he held various Asian assignments and became deputy assistant secretary of state for Far Eastern affairs in 1951. In 1953 he played a key role in the Korean armistice negotiations. That same year he became ambassador to Czechoslovakia. He was a participant at the Far Eastern Conference meetings in Geneva in 1954, which resulted in the eventual release of U.S. citizens incarcerated by the Chinese Communists. Johnson then served as ambassador to Thailand (1958–1961), where he improved relations with the Sarit government by obtaining more development money for

Bangkok and fostering a close association with Thai leaders. Civil war in neighboring Laos was then threatening Thailand's national security. Johnson made it clear that the U.S. obligation to Thailand under the Southeast Asia Treaty Organization (SEATO) was not dependent on the prior agreement of all other parties to that treaty.

President Kennedy's secretary of state, Dean Rusk, elevated Johnson to deputy undersecretary for political affairs in 1961 and he became Rusk's most trusted subordinate. As a member of Excomm during the Cuban missile crisis of 1962, Johnson was initially a proponent of airstrikes against Cuba but soon came to favor a blockade, partly to give the Soviet Union a chance to save face. Along with Paul Nitze, Johnson in fact drafted the blockade scenario that took into account possible Soviet responses. During the first two years of Lyndon B. Johnson's presidency, he served first as deputy ambassador to Saigon and than as undersecretary of state. He found it stressful to work with President Johnson because of the latter's mounting frustration over U.S. deployment in Vietnam, a commitment that Alexis Johnson never seemed to question.

From 1966 to 1969 he served as ambassador to Japan and sought unsuccessfully to get that country more involved economically in Vietnam. He also failed to make a major dent in the U.S. trade deficit with Japan. But he helped to fashion agreements leading to the reversion from the U.S. to Japan of the Ryuku Islands, including Okinawa, and the Bonins, including Iwo Jima. He returned home to serve as President Richard M. Nixon's undersecretary of state for political affairs (1969–1973) but found it difficult working with Nixon and National Security Adviser Henry A. Kissinger, who sought to weaken the Department of State's influence. He ended his career as ambassador-at-large (1973–1977), spending most of that time as the chief of the U.S. delegation to the Strategic Arms Limitation Talks (SALT). In 1979, President Jimmy Carter withdrew the SALT II treaty from the Senate, a major disappointment for Johnson. Throughout his lengthy career, Johnson was known as a cool, efficient administrator and a staunch anticommunist.

JAMES N. GIGLIO

See also Carter, James Earl; Cuban Missile Crisis; Czech Republic; Japan; Johnson, Lyndon Baines; Kissinger, Henry Alfred; Korean War; Nixon, Richard Milhous; Okinawa; Strategic Arms Limitation Talks and Agreements; Thailand; Vietnam War

FURTHER READING

Ball, George W. *The Past Has Another Pattern: Memoirs.* New York, 1982.
Johnson, U. Alexis, with Jef Olivarius McAllister. *The Right Hand of Power.* Englewood Cliffs, N.J., 1984.

JOHNSON ACT

(1934)

Congressional legislation, named for Senator Hiram Johnson (Republican of California), barring the U.S. government or Americans under government jurisdiction from making loans to, or purchasing bonds from, any foreign government in default on debts owed to the United States. The act reflected the isolationist temper of Congress and general annoyance with the failure of European governments to pay back money borrowed from the United States during World War I. Johnson, one of the "irreconcilables" who had unconditionally opposed American membership in the League of Nations, originally wanted prohibition to apply when debts were in default to U.S. private citizens as well as to the government. President Franklin D. Roosevelt persuaded him to drop the reference to private citizens. Roosevelt signed the Johnson Act on 13 April 1934. Since Great Britain was one of the defaulters, Roosevelt could not lend money to Great Britain to purchase arms in the United States at the outset of World War II. The Lend-Lease Act of 1941, involving no borrowed money, was an answer to the Johnson Act straitjacket.

GADDIS SMITH

See also Isolationism; League of Nations; Lend-Lease; Neutrality Acts of the 1930s; War Debt, World War I

FURTHER READING

Vinson, J. Chalmers. "War Debts and Peace Legislation: The Johnson Act of 1934." *Mid-America* 50, (1968): 206-22.

JOINT CHIEFS OF STAFF

A committee of the highest ranking officers in the U.S. military, responsible for developing national defense strategies, including plans for war and other possible uses of force by the United States. In theory, the Joint Chiefs of Staff (JCS) reflects the truism that air, sea, and land forces should be considered as an integrated single instrument, not as respective bailiwicks of separate branches of the armed forces. The Joint Chiefs are subject to the legal authority of the president and the secretary of defense, whom the JCS advises on issues which might involve the use of military force.

The JCS consists of the Chiefs of Staff of the Army and Air Force and the Chief of Naval Operations, and is headed by a chairperson selected by the president. The chairman regularly participates in meetings of the National Security Council, although he is not an official member of the body. The JCS is served by a Joint Staff made up of military officers from each of the services. The Joint Staff includes the Joint Staff Planners, the Joint Strategic Survey Committee, the Joint Logistics Committee, and a number of other, smaller staff bodies designed to assist the JCS with its planning functions.

Modeled on a comparable British group, the JCS emerged during World War II and joined with the British in 1942 to constitute the Combined Chiefs of Staff. The National Security Act of 1947 established the JCS as a permanent entity within the Department of Defense. Separate legislation in 1949 created the position of JCS chairman; General Omar N. Bradley was the first to hold that position. Other prominent chairmen have included General Maxwell D. Taylor (1962–1964), Admiral Thomas H. Moorer (1970–1974), and General Colin L. Powell (1989–1993).

BENJAMIN FORDHAM

See also Defense, U.S. Department of; Powell, Colin; Taylor, Maxwell Davenport; World War II

FURTHER READING

Betts, Richard K. *Soldiers, Statesmen, and Cold War Crises.* Cambridge, Mass., 1977.
Huntington, Samuel. *The Soldier and the State.* Cambridge, Mass., 1957.
Woodward, Bob. *The Commanders.* New York, 1991.

JORDAN

An Arab state bordered by Syria, Israel, Saudi Arabia, Iraq, and the disputed West Bank, that has maintained a special relationship with the West since its founding as the Emirate of Transjordan in 1921 and, especially since 1957, with the United States. In the eyes of the West, Jordan has historically provided two important assets: its position as a classic buffer state, separating radical Syria from oil-rich Saudi Arabia and equally radical Iraq from Israel, and its tacit cooperation with Israel, especially in maintaining calm along the longest Arab-Israeli border. Jordan is a resource-poor state whose principal sources of revenue have been foreign aid (both directly—from Great Britain, then the United States, and more recently Arab states, Europe, and Japan—into state coffers, and indirectly to support Palestinian and other refugees), workers' remittances, and income from service as a regional entrepôt. Jordan's commercial relations with the United States have been small.

Jordan's first patron was Great Britain, whose mandatory authorities rewarded Abdullah ibn-Hussein, one of the sons of the Sharif of Mecca, for his family's loyalty in World War I by creating for him an emirate (principality) out of the ruins of the Ottoman Empire and then by providing political, economic, and military support. The emirate declared formal independence in 1946, changing its name to the Hashemite Kingdom of Jordan. The United States withheld diplomatic recognition for three years,

CHAIRMEN OF THE JOINT CHIEFS OF STAFF

CHAIRMAN	DATES	ADMINISTRATION
Adm. William D. Leahy, USN (Chief of Staff to the Commander in Chief of the Army and Navy)	1942–1949	F. D. Roosevelt Truman
Gen. Omar N. Bradley, USA	1949–1953	Truman Eisenhower
Adm. Arthur W. Radford, USN	1953–1957	Eisenhower
Gen. Nathan F. Twining, USAF	1957–1960	Eisenhower
Gen. Lyman L. Lemnitzer, USA	1960–1962	Eisenhower Kennedy
Gen. Maxwell D. Taylor, USA	1962–1964	Kennedy L. B. Johnson
Gen. Earle G. Wheeler, USA	1964–1970	L. B. Johnson Nixon
Adm. Thomas H. Moorer, USN	1970–1974	Nixon
Gen. George S. Brown, USAF	1974–1978	Nixon Ford Carter
Gen. David C. Jones, USAF	1978–1982	Carter Reagan
Gen. John W. Vessey, Jr., USA	1982–1985	Reagan
Adm. William J. Crowe, Jr., USN	1985–1989	Reagan Bush
Gen. Colin L. Powell, USA	1989–1993	Bush Clinton
Gen. John M. Shalikashvili, USA	1993–present	Clinton

Source: *The U.S. Government Manual*

however, because of continuing U.S. pique at Great Britain's treaty prerogatives inside the new kingdom as well as concerns about Jordan's role in the Arab-Israeli conflict. Abdullah's British-trained forces, the Arab Legion, were the first troops to attack the fledgling Jewish state following Israel's own declaration of independence. During those years, the U.S. consul-general in Jerusalem had responsibility for Jordan. Washington finally extended *de jure* recognition to Jordan on 31 January 1949. The Truman administration's decision to recognize a sovereign Jordan reflected Great Britain's changed circumstances in the region and the diminished Zionist opposition to U.S. recognition of Jordan. The United States maintained diplomatic representation at the ministerial level until 27 August 1952, when the two countries exchanged ambassadors. Like most countries, the United States did not recognize Jordan's annexation of the territories in the former Mandatory Palestine (the West Bank) that its army captured in the 1948–1949 war with Israel (technically referred to in Jordan as "the union of the two banks"). The United States neverthe-

less supported Jordan's admission to the UN in 1955, without reference to the disputed annexation, largely because of Jordan's pro-West posture in the Cold War.

Until 1957, U.S. diplomats viewed Jordan as essentially a British domain, with protection of the kingdom a British concern governed by the Anglo-Jordanian Treaty of Alliance that provided for British base rights. At times, U.S. officials questioned the viability of the Hashemite state, because Palestinians, including hundreds of thousands of wartime refugees, constituted a large majority of its post-1948 population and were generally hostile to Hashemite rule (though not until the late 1960s did elements of the Palestine Liberation Organization, founded in 1964, and its main constituent group, Yassir Arafat's Fatah movement, take up arms against the Hashemites). Nevertheless, in 1957, the United States assumed Great Britain's role as Jordan's strategic patron. This change followed a brief period of royal eclipse when Jordan's parliamentary leaders, swept up in Nasserist fervor, forced the termination of the Anglo-Jordanian Treaty of Alliance shortly after the 1956 Suez crisis. For the next fifteen years, Amman reaffirmed its role as an anti-communist state under the leadership of a strong monarch. The United States remained Jordan's largest donor of foreign aid and the source of an implicit strategic guarantee against aggression from the kingdom's Arab neighbors.

Two episodes show the strength of the U.S. commitment to Jordan's independence and territorial integrity. First, in April 1957, the twenty-one-year-old King Hussein bin Talal, grandson of the kingdom's founder, successfully outwitted army coup-makers, but still faced open insurrection from his cabinet, fueled by foreign (principally Syrian) scheming. To bolster Hussein on the eve of his declaration of martial law, the Eisenhower administration acquiesced in an urgent request from the king for a public display of support. At that critical moment, the White House declared "the independence and integrity of Jordan as vital"—as explicit an application of the Eisenhower Doctrine as ever was made regarding Jordan—and dispatched ships from the Sixth Fleet to the eastern Mediterranean as a warning against Soviet-supported adventurism. Hussein prevailed.

The second episode came during the Nixon administration, when, in September 1970, as Jordanian troops battled Palestinian *fedayeen* insurgents in a bloody civil war, Syrian armed forces launched a ground invasion across the Derá-Ramtha border. While Jordan's highly regarded ground troops stood a good chance of repelling the Syrians, the introduction of Syrian air support might have tipped the balance. After a stern warning to Syria against any such escalation, ships from the U.S. Sixth Fleet steamed to the eastern Mediterranean, where Israeli officers joined their U.S. counterparts aboard deck in a visual message of American-Israeli support for Jordan. The Syrian air force, under the control of Minister of Defense (and former air force chief) Hafiz al-Assad, stayed out of the fray, and again Hussein prevailed.

Because of its historically pro-Western outlook, its tacit cooperation with Israel in maintaining a quiet border and in fighting Palestinian irredentism, and its sensitive role as a non-Palestinian regime governing a significant share of the world's Palestinian population, Jordan has long figured prominently in American diplomatic efforts to resolve the Arab-Israeli dispute. In 1954, President Dwight D. Eisenhower authorized special envoy Eric Johnston to propose a water sharing plan for the Jordan River Valley that might eventually have led to the resettlement of tens of thousands of Palestinian refugees. Following the June 1967 Arab-Israeli war, the Johnson administration strongly supported efforts that led to the passage of United Nations Security Council Resolution 242, whose two basic provisions called for withdrawal of Israeli forces from territories occupied in the recent conflict and the establishment of secure and recognized borders between the region's states. Jordan was the first Arab country to accept the resolution, affirming its desire to regain through peacetime diplomacy the territory (the West Bank) it had lost through war.

In 1974, following the negotiation of disengagement agreements with Israel on the Egyptian and Syrian fronts, Secretary of State Henry Kissinger proposed a similar accord that would return a strip of territory along the Jordan River, including the city of Jericho, to Jordanian rule. In 1978, the Camp David accords allotted a special role for Jordan in the determination of the Palestinian interim self-governing authority. In 1982, President Reagan enunciated a U.S. policy that envisioned Palestinian self-government "in association with Jordan." For a variety of reasons—ranging from Jordan's reluctance to break Arab ranks to Israel's reluctance to commit itself to withdrawal from the West Bank—all of these initiatives came to naught. They cumulatively confirmed, nevertheless, the idea of some form of "Jordanian option" to resolve the Israeli-Palestinian-Jordanian component of the larger Arab-Israeli conflict.

From the early 1970s, Persian Gulf states have replaced the United States as Jordan's main financial patron; and over time, Amman looked to other countries, such as Iraq, for strategic support to supplement what it viewed as a weakening U.S. commitment. The Amman-Washington strategic connection reached its nadir during the 1990–1991 Gulf crisis and war, when Jordan's attempt at neutrality was viewed by Washington as belligerently pro-Iraqi. Nevertheless, it did not take long before most of the wounds in the relationship healed, as Jordan rehabilitated itself in U.S. eyes by playing a constructive role in the Arab-Israeli peace process and by distancing itself from its Iraqi connection (though Jordan's economy remains strongly tied to Iraq's, highlighted by Jordan's receipt of discounted Iraqi oil). U.S.-Jordan military exercises were resumed in 1993 and, in 1994, the Clinton administration included Jordan on the list of only five countries in the world to receive foreign military assistance, alongside NATO allies Turkey and Greece and "major non-NATO allies" Israel and Egypt.

The convening of the U.S.-sponsored Madrid Peace Conference on October 1991 marked an important stage in the renewal of warm relations between Washington and Amman. At that conference, aspects of the "Jordanian option" were revived in Jordan's role as senior partner in a "joint delegation" with the Palestinians, which facilitated the convening of direct Israeli-Jordanian and Israeli-Palestinian negotiations, under U.S. auspices, immediately thereafter. And despite the diplomatic breakthrough between Israel and the Palestine Liberation Organization in 1993, which led to the Oslo Accords and the establishment of Palestinian self-government in Gaza and Jericho, a form of the "Jordanian option" lives on in the concept of a Palestinian-Jordanian "confederation" as a potential arrangement for the "final status" of the West Bank and Gaza.

Jordan itself responded to the Israel-PLO agreement by accelerating efforts to seek its own accord with Israel. Preliminary negotiations, including an important reaffirmation of U.S.-Jordanian ties by President Clinton, resulted in the Washington Declaration of July 1994, when King Hussein and Israel's Prime Minister Yitzhak Rabin ended their nations' forty-six-year-old state of war. The two countries signed a formal peace treaty, along the Jordan-Israel border, in October 1994, with President Clinton in attendance. The Jordan-Israel treaty settled discrete bilateral disputes over such issues as border demarcation and water resources, outlined terms for the establishment of formal diplomatic relations, and committed the two parties to an ambitious program of bilateral cooperation in economic, social, and cultural fields. Within months, many of those commitments were translated into practical forms of bilateral cooperation underscored by the heavy flow of tourism.

Personality has played an important role in the development of U.S.-Jordanian relations. A single figure—King Hussein—has ruled the Hashemite kingdom since Jordan's parliament approved the bloodless deposition of his ill father in August 1952. Hussein, educated at Victoria College (Alexandria, Egypt) and the British military academy at Sandhurst, has governed as a benign, generally well-respected—although absolute—monarch. His reputation for personal courage and gallantry, combined with his normally moderate and pro-West political leanings (highlighted by his opposition to communism in the 1950s and 1960s and his generally supportive approach to U.S. peace process initiatives since 1967), earned him good favor in Washington. Hussein has met personally with every president since Eisenhower and has come to personify Jordan in the eyes of the U.S. leadership and people alike. This personal link was bolstered by his marriage (his fourth) to the former Lisa Halaby (now Queen Noor al-Hussein), the Princeton-educated daughter of the former chairman of the Federal Aviation Administration. In a clear signal of renewed military ties, the United States dispatched to Jordan an Air Expeditionary Force of 34 aircraft in 1996 to help patrol the ari-exclusion zone in southern Iraq for six weeks and agreed to a no-cost lease of 16 F-16 aircraft to the Jordanian air force.

ROBERT B. SATLOFF

See also Camp David Accords; Egypt; Eisenhower Doctrine; Gulf War of 1990–1991; Israel; Middle East; Palestine (to 1948); Palestine Liberation Organization; Refugees; Syria

FURTHER READING

"The Hashemite Kingdom of Jordan." *Tel Aviv, annual. Middle East Contemporary Survey.*

Dann, Uriel. "The United States and the Recognition of Jordan, 1946–1949," in *Studies in the History of Transjordan.* Boulder, Colo.,1984.

Kaplan, Stephen S. "United States' Aid and Regime Maintenance in Jordan, 1957–1973," *Public Policy,* 23, (Spring 1975):189–217.

al-Madfai, Madiha Rashid. *Jordan, the United States, and the Middle East Peace Process.* New York, 1993.

Satloff, Robert B. *Troubles on the East Bank: Challenges to the Domestic Stability of Jordan.* Washington, D.C., 1986.

JOURNALISM AND FOREIGN POLICY

From the early days of the Republic, the press has played an important and multifaceted role in the development of U.S. foreign policy. Depending upon the issue, the specific newspaper, magazine, or electronic media outlet for which they work, and the nature of their profession during different eras, journalists have helped set the news agenda, informed the public about diplomatic affairs, originated and advocated policies, supported or criticized the government, and even served decision-makers by publishing calculated leaks and trial balloons. Of all their functions and roles, the media's ability to help set the news agenda may be the most important, particularly during the years following World War II. While they may not be able to tell people what to think, they have been singularly successful in telling them what to think about. The intimate relationship between policymaker and the press predates the establishment of the United States. Harold Nicolson, the dean of historians of diplomacy, reported that "The use of the printing press as an ally to diplomacy is as old as Swift and the Treaty of Utrecht." Nonetheless, the arrival of the democratic United States on the international scene raised new issues about the relationship between diplomats and journalists.

A democracy needs an independent press to inform the public about issues it confronts as the ultimate decision-maker, if only at the ballot box. On the other hand, vital matters concerning foreign affairs and war demand secrecy in order to keep putative foreign enemies from learning about one's intentions, capabilities, and even battle plans, and also, allegedly, to keep the nationalistic, passionate, and often poorly informed electorate from pushing its representatives into unwanted and unnecessary crises or wars.

From Washington to Wilson

The problem of establishing the proper balance between a free press and the need to keep national security matters secret has bedeviled citizens and leaders alike since the administration of George Washington. In 1789 Congress passed a statute that required departments to establish regulations for handling their official documents and correspondence, paving the way for censorship and classification. Three years later, supporting the idea of an independent and unencumbered press, Secretary of State Thomas Jefferson wrote to President Washington that "No government ought to be without censors and while the press is free, no one ever will." But where to draw the line? In the wake of news leaks about the Bay of Pigs invasion in 1961, President John F. Kennedy told a group of newspaper publishers, "Every newspaper now asks itself, with respect to every story: 'Is it news?' All I suggest is that you add the question, 'Is it in the national interest?'"

No doubt, Kennedy would have been even more upset with the perceived irresponsibility of the press during Jefferson's time than he was during his own. From the 1790s until at least the 1830s, there was no such thing as an independent press in the United States. Newspapers were little more than fiercely partisan organs representing factions, parties, and individual leaders. Jefferson helped a clerk in his Department of State found the *National Gazette*, which became his faction's personal mouthpiece. Jefferson's rival, Secretary of the Treasury Alexander Hamilton, sponsored the *Gazette of the United States*, among other Federalist journals. In the pages of such newspapers, Hamilton, under the pseudonyms of "Camillus," "Philo-Camillus," and "Pacificus," did battle with Republican leaders such as James Madison, who wrote under the name of "Helvidius" in his party's press. Beholden to their parties, the newspapers made most of their income from government printing contracts, publishing official notices, and printing broadsides and pamphlets. Everyone who could read, and that was not the majority of the population, knew that newspapers were partisan organs. Thus, they played a more important role rallying the party faithful than in altering opinion, especially in areas far from Washington where local leaders often took their cues from what they read in their party's press. In this era before railroads and the telegraph, the newspaper was an essential institution for spreading information about national political issues, even if that information was usually reported subjectively.

In 1795 the Republican *Philadelphia Aurora* published a copy of the controversial Jay's Treaty—the first case of a press leak of an important secret document. Other secret documents leaked to the press included the Treaty of Guadalupe Hidalgo (1848) that ended the War with Mexico, the 1944 Dumbarton Oaks Conference agreement about the United Nations, and sections of the Yalta Conference agreements of 1945. The most famous leak in the history of U.S. diplomacy occurred in 1971 when the *New York Times* and other newspapers published excerpts from the secret Department of Defense history of the Vietnam War, *The Pentagon Papers*. That same year columnist Jack Anderson revealed that the Richard M. Nixon administration was not neutral in a war between

Pakistan and India as it had been proclaiming but had in fact been "tilting" toward Pakistan. For that alleged breach of national security, several White House aides, including G. Gordon Liddy, began to plan to murder or otherwise incapacitate Anderson. The argument heard in 1971, as well as in Hamilton's and Jefferson's day, was not only that national security was jeopardized by the publication of such information, but even more important, such improprieties signaled to foreign leaders that they had to be careful what they said to U.S. diplomats. Their private messages, meant to be hidden in the archives for several generations, might see the light of day instantaneously because of leakers and enterprising reporters. Whatever the merits of that argument, the Supreme Court, at least in 1971 in *The Pentagon Papers* case, permitted the media wide latitude to publish classified materials.

Administration officials often argued against publication of state secrets in order to keep the press and the public from criticizing unpopular policies. Moreover, they themselves selectively leaked materials when it could help them, as was the case with President John Adams in 1798, who released documents relating to the XYZ Affair to his newspapers in order to rally the public against France. The French government retaliated by leaking some of their official documents to friendly Republican papers. However he used them, Adams, along with many of his colleagues, had little respect for the press. The second president felt that "it is impossible that newspapers can say the truth."

In 1798, during the Quasi-War with France, Federalists in Congress pushed through the nation's first sedition act (Act for the Punishment of Certain Crimes), which made it a crime to speak against the president or Congress in a defamatory manner. At least eight Republican editors and printers were convicted under this act, which was the first, but not the last, time that the government limited freedom of speech and the press during wartime. Under the prompting of Jefferson, the Kentucky and Virginia legislatures passed resolutions nullifying the allegedly unconstitutional act in their states, and the act soon became a potent Republican issue in the election of 1800. Not surprisingly, therefore, during the War of 1812, Republican president James Madison, Jefferson's old ally, did not impose censorship. The president's support for freedom of the press did not stop a mob from destroying a printing office in Maryland and killing a journalist, nor did it stop General Andrew Jackson from briefly imposing censorship after he occupied New Orleans in 1815. Prior to the war, assertive western newspapers had been instrumental in inflaming anti-British sentiment in their region.

With the development of the telegraph, railroads, and high-speed printing presses in the 1830s and 1840s, newspapers became less dependent on political patronage for their income. In 1835 the flamboyant James Gordon Bennett founded the *New York Herald*, the first major newspaper with an editorial policy free of party control, and Bennett himself became the first Washington correspondent. Other editors and writers from the new, mass circulation "penny press" developed their own voices and helped popularize the expansionist spirit of the times, with John L. O'Sullivan of the *New York Morning News* the coiner of the phrase Manifest Destiny.

During the War with Mexico (1846–1848), President James Knox Polk sent journalists Moses Y. Beach and Jane McManus Storms of the *New York Sun* to Mexico to try to arrange a surrender. Throughout U.S. history, presidents have employed journalists as private agents, including Woodrow Wilson, who sent William Bayard Hale to Mexico during another crisis, and John F. Kennedy, who made use of ABC's John Scali as an intermediary during the Cuban missile crisis in 1962 and the *Saturday Review*'s Norman Cousins to help with negotiations in the Soviet Union that culminated in a partial nuclear test ban treaty the following year. Although the War with Mexico was the best-covered war up to the time, dispatches from the front sometimes took as long as one month to reach the East Coast because the telegraph had not yet gone farther south than Richmond, Virginia. For the most part, journalists wrote stories strongly supportive of the sometimes controversial military effort, and several war correspondents, including the most famous one of the era, George V. Kendall, participated in combat. During the Civil War most Confederate journalists also fought alongside the troops in gray.

When the Civil War began, President Abraham Lincoln seized control of the telegraph lines in Washington, D.C. In February 1862 he declared all telegraph lines under federal control and ordered the postmaster general to deny the use of mail service to disloyal newspapers. Under the terms of that order, newspapers were seized or suppressed and editors imprisoned. For the most part, the postmaster general did not have to worry about the 500 correspondents who accompanied the Union army. Because of self-censorship, as well as official censorship at the source, they tended to underestimate casualties and report uncritically about strategic and tactical blunders, an important factor in war when presidents are concerned about maintaining high morale on the home front to head off pressure to sue for a premature peace. Despite censorship on both the Union and Confederate sides, Generals Robert E. Lee and William Tecumseh Sherman, among others, reported that they often picked up intelligence about troop movements and battle plans from reading the newspapers. In his second inaugural speech, Lincoln remarked sardonically, "The progress of our arms, upon which all else chiefly depends, is as well known to the public as myself." On the other hand, Lincoln found the war correspondents' accounts in the newspapers useful as a supplement to his own official reports. Moreover, he frequently requested interviews with them when they returned to Washington, in order to learn directly what was going on in the combat theaters. Lincoln and the Departments of War and State, however, were very concerned about foreign journalists at the front, particularly the British. They feared that their dispatches about Union losses and military ineptitude could influence the British public and its leaders as they considered recognition of the Confederacy.

The government simplified all reporters' tasks in 1864, when Secretary of War Edwin Stanton began issuing daily war bulletins. Such official bulletins and briefings continued to dominate the coverage of crises and wars, even the briefings during the Vietnam War that reporters dubbed the "Five O'Clock Follies." Accepting dependable, always available, neatly packaged news items from government officials in time to meet a deadline made a journalist's life easier. Such practices, however, often led to the simple uncritical reprinting of the party line, and the vast majority of news about U.S. foreign relations has come to be little more than the repackaging of press releases from public information officers in the White House and the Departments of State and Defense.

Newspapers played their most significant role in the history of U.S. diplomacy during the period prior to the Spanish-American-Cuban-Filipino War in 1898. Publishers of the sensational mass circulation "yellow press," including Joseph Pulitzer and his *New York World* and William Randolph Hearst and his *New York Journal*, adopted the cause of the Cubans fighting for independence from Spain and helped create strong interventionist sentiment in the United States. Aside from uncritically accepting material from propagandists in the Cuban junta, Hearst himself manufactured stories of Spanish depravities and even sent a correspondent to rescue a Cuban woman from a Spanish prison. The Cuban revolution was a colorful story, made more colorful by Hearst and his colleagues. Historians have debated whether President William McKinley could have won the authority for intervention if there were not a constant barrage of pro-Cuban stories. In early February 1898, one week before the U.S. battleship *Maine* exploded in Havana harbor, Hearst published a letter written by Enrique Dupuy de Lôme, the Spanish minister in the United States, in which the minister criticized President McKinley. The *Journal*'s inflammatory headline read, "The Worst Insult to the United States in Its History." On the way toward war, Hearst's newspaper circulation increased from 150,000 in 1896 to 800,000 by 1898. No wonder once the United States declared war, he ran the headline, "How Do You Like the *Journal*'s War?" That bravado was an exaggeration. While there is no doubt that the yellow press created the Cuban sensation, President McKinley never lost control of the situation. Indeed, observers credit him with being the first president to understand how to work with the press; he handled editors in a masterful manner in 1898 when he skillfully prepared the public for U.S. intervention. During the war McKinley employed military censors at the Western Union office in Key West, Florida, and wire services offices in New York City and centralized the release of military and diplomatic information in Washington. Nonetheless, although Americans thrilled to stories of victories on land and sea, reporters also wrote about scandals in the Quartermaster Corps and serious logistical problems.

Those were minor issues compared to the reports that leaked through censorship in the war fought by U.S. soldiers against Filipino insurrectionists (1899–1902). In their counterguerrilla operations, U.S. troops employed torture and other questionable practices, and military information officers presented inaccurate casualty figures. Unlike the Spanish-American-Cuban-Filipino War, the insurrection in the Philippines did not enjoy widespread support. The journalists' reports from the field helped the influential Anti-Imperialist League in its campaign for U.S. withdrawal from the islands. McKinley was so distressed by those reports that he contemplated prosecuting several publishers for treason.

McKinley's modernization of presidential press relations continued apace through the administrations of Presidents Theodore Roosevelt, William Howard Taft, and Woodrow Wilson. In 1909 the Department of State established the Division of Information, which became the more important Office (later Bureau) of Public Affairs during World War II. With the United States becoming more involved and interested in international relations, U.S. newspapers devoted increasing attention to the subject. In an interesting case of self-censorship in 1908, William Bayard Hale of the *New York Times* obtained an exclusive and highly sensational interview with the flamboyant William (Wilhelm) II of Germany. Alarmed that some of the things the kaiser said might cause an international incident, a representative from the *Times* publisher asked Roosevelt whether the interview should be printed. When the president strongly advised against it, the publisher acceded to his request. In a similar situation in 1961, President Kennedy was successful in convincing the *Times* not to run a story detailing military preparations on the eve of the Bay of Pigs invasion. In general, the *Times* could be trusted not to embarrass the United States, as had been proven during the late 1950s, when columnist James Reston kept information about the existence of the U-2 air reconnaissance flights over the Soviet Union out of the pages of his widely respected newspaper.

Not all publishers, however, were as willing as the semiofficial *Times* to refrain from printing sensitive items. On the eve of the Japanese attack on Pearl Harbor in December 1941, the most important anti-interventionist paper in the United States, the *Chicago Tribune*, revealed information about U.S. mobilization plans. During the war the *Tribune* reported that government cryptographers had broken Japanese codes. The intelligence that Pacific commanders picked up from MAGIC, the name given to the decoding breakthrough, was still vitally important. Fortunately for the United States, the Japanese did not take the *Tribune* report seriously.

The Two World Wars

From 1898 to the end of World War I in 1919, the United States and Great Britain moved toward what historian Bradford Perkins labeled the "Great Rapprochement." After more than a century of quarreling over boundaries, tariffs, and fisheries, the two countries began to align their foreign policies to such a point that when World War I began, there was no chance the United States would go to war against its historic adversary, no matter how the British navy ran roughshod over neutral rights. The vast majority of publishers, editors, and journalists from the most influential newspapers and magazines of the Progressive Era were strong believers in the rapprochement. Their anglophilia showed in the way they covered the score of crises during the ten years preceding World War I, and it continued in their coverage of the war during the period of U.S. neutrality (1914–1917).

Eagerly accepting the propaganda turned out by London's agents in the United States, journalists presented an almost universally favorable picture of British policies. The German government countered by secretly purchasing the *New York Evening Mail* and subsidized U.S. journalists during the war in a vain attempt to influence American public opinion. Similarly, in the period prior to U.S. entry into World War II, the Japanese engaged in an even more unsuccessful attempt to find outlets for their policies through their involvement with the less-than-influential *North American Review*. Although it is not quite the same as purchasing media outlets or buying or bribing journalists, since the 1960s representatives of foreign governments in Washington have spent millions of dollars on public relations firms and lobbyists to plant their arguments in the U.S. media. In 1993, for example, the government of Mexico announced that it planned to spend $50 million on a public relations campaign to ensure passage of the North American Free Trade Agreement (NAFTA).

Undoubtedly, the overwhelmingly favorable treatment the British received in the U.S. press from 1914 through the early part of 1917 contributed significantly in moving the American public from its traditional anti-interventionist stance at the start of the war to being prepared to follow President Wilson's lead into war in April 1917. This was not simply a case of blind anglophilia. Journalists found little positive news to publish about Germany after it invaded Belgium and launched its submarine offensive. There were also reports of some real and many exaggerated atrocities and incredibly clumsy espionage activities in the United States.

As the ultimate break with Berlin approached in late February 1917, Wilson used the press to inflame anti-German sentiment by releasing for publication the Zimmermann telegram. British agents had given him the message they intercepted in which the German foreign minister told his ambassador to Mexico to offer that country an alliance in case of war with the United States. Had Wilson preferred to maintain German-U.S. relations on an even keel, he could have kept the purloined telegram to himself. As President Kennedy later commented, "The press is a very valuable arm of the presidency."

After U.S. entry into the war in April 1917, Wilson established the Committee on Public Information (CPI), or Creel Committee, named after its chair, journalist George Creel, the first in a line of journalists to head government propaganda agencies. During World War II radio commentator Elmer Davis led the Office of War Information, and in 1961 radio and television journalist Edward R. Murrow became chief of the United States Information Agency. Creel's CPI encouraged support for the war effort by controlling and manipulating information that reached the public. It sent the committee's official bulletin of war news to post offices, produced films and newsreels using the Army Signal Corps, and dispatched 75,000 speakers around the country who delivered 750,000 four-minute talks in 5,000 cities, often in movie houses. Those talks encouraged patriotism, hatred for the enemy, and support for the administration's military and diplomatic policies.

The government also established the Censorship Board, on which Creel played an important role, and took control of the telegraph and wireless systems. In June 1917 Congress passed the Espionage Act, which permitted the postmaster general to refuse to mail magazines and newspapers he deemed subversive. The Sedition Act of May 1918 made speaking or writing against the war effort a crime. Under those acts, the government barred certain foreign publications from entry into the country, banned such magazines as the antiwar *Masses* and the *International Socialist Review* and the pro-Irish *Catholic Register*, and sent pacifist Socialist party leader Eugene V. Debs to prison, from where he ran for president in 1920. In addition, a film producer received a ten-year prison sentence for the anti-British sequences he included in his patriotic film about the American Revolution, *The Spirit of '76*. The crude manner in which the Censorship Board flouted the First Amendment, and the CPI's defense of Wilson's agenda, produced a backlash during the interwar period that affected the way President Franklin D. Roosevelt addressed such issues during World War II.

In Europe during World War I, U.S. military authorities established their first formal accrediting procedure. If journalists wanted to go to the front, they had to submit their copy to censors, behave "like a gentleman of the press," and provide a $10,000 performance bond. When correspondents broke the rules, as did United Press International's Westbrook Pegler, they were sent home. For the most part, journalists practiced self-censorship so that they would not have to rewrite their stories once the military censors had reviewed them. The CPI also operated abroad. Woodrow Wilson appointed Edgar Sisson, a former editor of the *Chicago Tribune*, to head a mission to Russia in the fall of 1917. Sisson, who became an ardent anti-Bolshevik, obtained for Wilson a set of documents that "proved" that Vladimir Lenin and his crowd were German agents. Wilson released the Sisson documents to the press in September 1918 and thus helped increase anti-Bolshevik sentiment in the United States. Even after he discovered that the documents were forgeries several months later, he refused to reveal that information to the press, because the notion that Lenin had been working for Berlin fit well with the policy he and his allies had adopted in opposition to the new Soviet Union.

In the first of his Fourteen Points, Wilson suggested that the days of secret documents and secret diplomacy were at an end. In the new era of international relations that was to be launched at the Paris Peace Conference of 1919, there would be "open covenants, openly arrived at." Thus, when journalists arrived at the conference, they expected more access to the negotiations than at previous peace conferences. They were disappointed. Wilson himself abandoned the first of his Fourteen Points when he did not permit the press to enter the conference rooms.

Revelations about British propaganda in U.S. newspapers, the excesses of the Creel Committee, and old-fashioned secret deals at Versailles contributed to the development of isolationist sentiment in the United States during the 1920s and 1930s. Although most of the elite influential media still maintained an internationalist perspective, the powerful *Chicago Tribune* was a fervent advocate of isolationism, as were the many Hearst publications, including the *New York Journal-American*. During the interwar period, one in four Americans read something that was produced by the Hearst publishing empire. Further, while newspapers, magazines, and radio news programs were interested in foreign affairs, especially as the international system was rocked by periodic crises after 1931, the dominant interest then, as it remains today, was in the domestic arena. As late as 1941, when James Reston covered the Department of State for the *New York Times*, he was joined by fewer than ten colleagues when Secretary of State Cordell Hull held press conferences in his private office.

Even newspapers with internationalist leanings were nervous about involving the United States in the European conflict. It was for that reason that the editors of the *New York Times* altered Herbert Matthews's dispatches from the Republican side of the battle lines during the Spanish Civil War when he revealed prematurely that Italians were fighting on the Nationalist side. (Twenty years later Matthews became embroiled in another controversy because of his positive reports about Cuban rebel Fidel Castro, which, in that case, the editors did not alter.) All the same, the overwhelming support of U.S. war correspondents for the Republican side, and especially the volunteer Abraham Lincoln Brigade, contributed to a shift in public opinion in the United States toward the Madrid government.

The influence of the isolationist press on President Roosevelt became manifest in the wake of his Quarantine Speech in the fall of 1937, when he signaled that the administration was prepared to assume a more active role in collective security against aggressors. He had been nervous about giving the speech, fearful of what he perceived to be overwhelming opposition among the public against such a *demarche*. When he scanned the press in a very impressionistic manner the next day, he felt that his caution had been correct; editors strongly opposed any move away from isolationism. It turns out that Roosevelt was wrong and that a majority of editorial writers supported his speech, but he was so concerned about the powerful isolationist sentiment in the nation's press that he allowed his unscientific sampling to convince him not to follow up the Quarantine Speech with action. Throughout modern history, presidents have often read the press in a comparably impressionistic manner. They have often equated public opinion with opinion printed publicly and have seen either public support or opposition to their policies in the pages of a handful of elite newspapers and magazines or in the comments of a few columnists.

As World War II approached, despite the general non-interventionist posture of most editorial pages, U.S. media embraced the British cause. Especially important were Henry Luce's periodicals, which included *Time*, *Life*, and *Fortune*. Luce himself was a one-person China lobby as he promoted stories in his publications that painted a very favorable picture of the Nationalist Chinese and a very unfavorable one of the Japanese, who started the war in Asia in 1937. His depiction of China as a great power and its government as a progressive democracy contributed to the nationwide shock and search for scapegoats when the Communists defeated the Nationalists only four years after the end of World War II.

Radio journalists had come to play an increasingly important role in the United States by the beginning of World War II. Two of the most popular, Raymond Gram Swing and H. V. Kaltenborn, strongly supported U.S. aid to Great Britain. From London, Edward R. Murrow reported on the Battle of Britain. Originally, the British government objected to his live accounts of the bombings, fearing they would demoralize supporters in the United States, but the British soon realized that Murrow's stirring descriptions of Nazi attacks against civilians increased popular sympathy for the cause.

Among those who strongly supported all possible aid to England was the Committee to Defend America by Aiding the Allies. Working closely but secretly with the Roosevelt administration, the committee was headed by a well-respected Republican journalist, William Allen White of the *Emporia Gazette*. In addition to holding conferences, writing articles, and lobbying politicians, members of this committee also took out advertisements in newspapers supporting their position. The practice of placing such ads, along with the names of hundreds, and even thousands, of luminaries who lent their support to the messages they contained, became a major activity of antiwar leaders during the Vietnam War era.

In June 1942 President Roosevelt established the Office of War Information (OWI), which played a role comparable to Wilson's Creel Committee. The OWI replaced the Office of Facts and Figures that had been established the previous October. The new organization provided information about the war and developed campaigns at home and abroad to buttress support for aspects of the war effort. Every two weeks officials from OWI met with media executives, including Hollywood studio heads, to suggest themes to promote the war effort. Few editors or journalists complained about the government recruiting them to engage in propaganda activities.

A new Office of Censorship issued a code of wartime practices for newspapers and radio that was designed to stop them from publishing or broadcasting material helpful to the enemy. For the most part, the office relied on voluntary compliance, but it did censor international communications and communications from war industries and military installations in the United States. This practice did not prevent the enemy from attempting to obtain intelligence from U.S. media. As late as 1945, Nazi propaganda minister Joseph Goebbels pored over U.S. newspapers searching for signs of a decline in morale. Overseas, beginning with the cover-up of the extent of the damages at Pearl Harbor, the U.S. military exercised strict censorship at the source. The high command compelled foreign correspondents, including more than 1,000 in Europe alone, to accept formal accreditation. General Dwight D. Eisenhower, the chief of Allied forces in Europe, was keenly aware of the importance of the war correspondents. He noted: "Public opinion wins war. I have always considered as quasi-staff officers, correspondents accredited to my headquarters." Almost all journalists accepted censorship willingly in World War II, including being forbidden to transmit photographs that graphically portrayed U.S. wounded and dead. Thus, they did not always report about the extent of casualties, delayed for three months before running a story personally embarrassing to General George Patton, and played down incidents of cowardice during the Battle of the Bulge. Serving as cheerleaders for the U.S. military effort, their reports helped keep citizens supportive of Washington's diplomatic, political, and military strategies. This was the last war in which U.S. journalists so docilely accepted censorship.

The Cold War

At the start of the Cold War, the unprecedented involvement of the United States in international relations enjoyed widespread support in the media. For one thing, the early years of the Cold War were also, not coincidentally, the early years of a Red Scare in the United States. It was dangerous for newspapers, magazines, or radio commentators to challenge administration policies after 1947. Those who did so in the face of a widespread anti-Soviet bipartisan consensus could be considered if not communists certainly fellow travelers. One of the first major scandals of the era involved the leaking of State Department documents in 1945 to the editors of the journal *Amerasia*, who were accused of being too friendly with Russians. The establishment media, including such newspapers as the *Times* and the *Herald Tribune* and such news magazines as *Time* and *Newsweek*, rarely presented criticism of Harry S. Truman's foreign policies. The radio and emerging television networks followed suit. Moreover, prominent opinion-makers and government officials enjoyed a symbiotic relationship. Columnists Walter Lippmann and James Reston helped Senator Arthur H. Vandenberg write an important internationalist speech in 1945, Secretary of War James M. Forrestal sent *New York Times* reporter Arthur Krock information he wanted to reach the public, Soviet expert Charles E. Bohlen leaked material to the *Tribune*'s Joseph Alsop, while Undersecretary and then Secretary of State Dean Acheson had a special relationship with Reston. The Truman administration even leaked sections of George F. Kennan's 1946 top-secret "long telegram" from Moscow, which signaled the start of the Cold War, to *Time*. The administration realized that it had to do a strong selling job to convince the public that the United States could not retreat into isolation as it had following World War I. The media were

witting handmaidens to that propaganda campaign, which increased in intensity in 1947 and 1948. Of the way he helped develop U.S. foreign policy during the period, one foreign policy aide complained that "almost 80 percent of your time is...management of your domestic ability to have policy, and only 20 percent, maybe, dealing with the foreign."

The National Security Act of 1947, establishing the Central Intelligence Agency (CIA) and the National Security Council (NSC), further centralized control over foreign policy information in the White House. The McMahon Act of September 1951 and executive orders from Truman and President Eisenhower codified the ways that information about foreign and military affairs could be restricted in the United States. For the first time in U.S. history during peacetime, citizens would not be able to learn in their press about important diplomatic, military, and intelligence activities. Without such information, they could not properly evaluate the efficacy of specific foreign policies and even interventions. Looking back at that era in 1993, former Secretary of the Interior Steward L. Udall claimed: "The atomic weapons race and the secrecy surrounding it crushed American democracy. It induced us to conduct government according to lies. It undermined American morality. Until the Cold War, our country stood for something. Lincoln was the great exemplar. We stood for moral leadership in the world."

At the start of the Korean War in 1950, in part because there was no formal declaration of war, correspondents sent uncensored dispatches from the front about the corruption and ineptitude of the U.S. ally in South Korea, Syngman Rhee, and about instances of U.S. troops indiscriminately shooting at civilians. In December 1950, after complaints from Seoul, Washington announced full censorship in the combat theater. To be sure, readers could find reports critical of official policy in a handful of obscure left-wing journals and newsletters, but most were exposed daily to the mainstream media's messages that supported wholeheartedly not only the effort in Korea but the entire panoply of Cold War policies. Indeed, one wonders how readily the public would have accepted such popular instruments of containment as the Truman Doctrine, the Marshall Plan, and the North Atlantic Treaty Organization (NATO) had the *New York Times* and the Luce publications devoted attention to the often plausible criticisms of those programs that came from both the somewhat disreputable left and the isolationist-nationalist right, represented by such leaders as Senator Robert A. Taft and former president Herbert Hoover.

The public might have been even more critical had it known about the CIA's covert activities. In 1954, as the Eisenhower administration began to plan a CIA-operated coup against the left-leaning, democratically elected government in Guatemala, it informed the publisher of the *New York Times* that Sidney Gruson, its respected Central American correspondent, was a security risk and demanded his recall from the country. The administration knew the charge was not true, although Gruson was not the most faithful cold warrior. The *Times* complied with Washington's request and the knowledgeable Gruson was not on the scene to report how the CIA orchestrated the civil war that brought to power a pro-Western regime.

Like intelligence services in most other countries, the CIA also recruited journalists to serve as part- or full-time intelligence agents and subsidized magazines. Moreover, it often planted false stories in the press to accomplish certain foreign policy goals. For example, intelligence and other officials in President Ronald Reagan's administration operated a disinformation campaign in the media against Libyan leader Moammar al-Qaddafi in order to lay the groundwork for military attacks against Libya. Most journalists who accepted the false stories did not know they were being used by their government.

The way the Korean War started demonstrated another dramatic development in international interactions during the postwar era. The first news to reach Washington about the North Korean invasion came not from the U.S. embassy in Seoul but from a United Press International (UPI) dispatch. The embassy telegram beat the news story to Washington but it was slow in reaching officials in the Departments of State and Defense because it needed to be decoded.

In the 1980s, after the development of information satellites and the Cable News Network (CNN), U.S. diplomats, as well as diplomats around the world, often learned more about crises from electronic media than from their own sources on the scene. During the Gulf War of 1990–1991, Russian KGB officers watched CNN for "intelligence" about diplomatic and military activities, while the U.S. secretary of defense referred to its reports to support his arguments in press conferences. During that same crisis, one U.S. diplomat noted that the best way to get a message to the Russians was over CNN, not through official channels, because "diplomatic communications just can't keep up with CNN." From the late 1970s on, CNN and other U.S. news agencies' reports appeared far more frequently than reports from other countries' news services on television sets around the world. Aware of this phenomenon, CNN founder Ted Turner ordered his news anchors not to use the word "foreign" on their programs, in an attempt to make his network appear less "American." CNN had become a multinational business enterprise, presumably without loyalty to the country in which it was based.

Presidential press conferences represented another dramatic change in the relationship between journalists and foreign policymakers during the postwar era. After the days when a handful of beat reporters crowded into Roosevelt's Oval Office for a mostly off-the-record or deep-background briefing, the presidential press conference became a much larger and more formal and filmed event during the Eisenhower era and live televised press conferences began during the Kennedy administration. Professional diplomats express concern about live conferences because of what a president might inadvertently say or because a president's casual remarks might be interpreted in a way that could have international implications. President Truman once created an international incident when he suggested to reporters in an off-the-cuff manner that he would consider using atomic weapons in the Korean War. When lesser officials spoke live in public, their comments could be amended or even repudiated by the president. When the president misspoke, it was difficult, because of the need to maintain political face, to issue retractions. Ronald Reagan was an exception to the rule. During his tenure administration spokespersons were able to retract or correct the chief executive's statements because journalists had learned not to take seriously everything the sometimes confused president uttered in public. One celebrated case of a press conference misstatement occurred in 1961, when Secretary of Defense Robert S. McNamara blurted out that he had discovered that there was no missile gap and that the Soviets were far behind the United States. He found it impossible to retract his statement, which showed the Russians that the enemy had discovered their awful truth—their missile programs were still rather primitive. McNamara's gaffe helped convince them to work doubly hard to catch up to the United States, since bluffing would no longer work in a crisis.

The televised press conference of the early 1960s reflected another significant change in the relationship between news media and foreign policymakers. From that point on, television began replacing print media as the place where most Americans went for news of foreign affairs. To be sure, opinion-makers and other members of the so-called attentive public still relied heavily on the prestige papers and magazines. Moreover, morning papers like the *New York Times* helped shape the programming of the evening telecasts. Nonetheless, more and more Americans came to rely on thirty-minute telecasts for their news about the world. Compared to a newspaper, whatever appeared on those telecasts (which were actually only twenty-two minutes long if one discounted the commercials) lacked context, depth, and detail. Moreover, television, more than the print media, depended upon interesting visuals to enliven its coverage for the rating wars. Many important foreign policy issues do not often offer interesting visuals. In addition, television cannot cover some issues simply because of economic reasons. In 1992 two fierce civil wars raged in east-central Africa, one in the Sudan, the other in Somalia. In both wars, tens of thousands of children were dying of hunger and disease, but because television concentrated its limited resources and air time on heart-rending pictures from Somalia, it was there that the United States and the United Nations felt compelled to dispatch a humanitarian mission.

The Vietnam War

Of all of the wars in which the United States fought, the war in Vietnam was the one in which the media allegedly played their most nefarious role. According to a widely held belief during the two decades following the war, the media had a good deal to do with the U.S. defeat in Southeast Asia. For one thing, journalists in the combat theater made their reading and viewing public back home believe that U.S. troops were not only losing the war but committing unspeakable atrocities. Further, they allegedly emphasized the corruption and venality of the South Vietnamese regime while ignoring the oppression of the communist North Vietnamese and the brutal behavior of its troops and the National Liberation Front. Television's depictions of dead and wounded American soldiers supposedly helped demoralize television viewers. On the home front, journalists allegedly gave aid and comfort to the enemy by approving of the activities of the antiwar movement while ignoring the silent majority that supported administration policies. When leaders and citizens alike later demanded "no more Vietnams," many included the allegedly defeatist and unpatriotic media under that slogan.

According to almost all scholarly studies on the subject, the charges against the media are false. To be sure, reporters in Vietnam, who operated without formal censorship, were free to criticize political, diplomatic, and military aspects of the conflict. By and large, however, they followed the administration line, at least until 1968 when the public, as well as the leadership, realized that the war was not going well. There were some notable exceptions and it is to those that critics have pointed. In 1962 and 1963, young correspondents on the scene, such as David Halberstam, Charles Mohr, and Neil Sheehan, all of whom supported U.S. involvement in the war, reported about Saigon's failing military and political efforts. For such accurate reporting, several were expelled from the country by the South Vietnamese government, and the Kennedy administration was able to convince publishers to reassign other reporters. That did not stop such journalists as Peter Arnett from covering the self-immolation of Buddhist monks who took that highly mediagenic action to demonstrate their hatred for the Ngo Dinh Diem regime. The Buddhist leadership knew how to attract U.S. attention to their unprecedented act

of opposition, and their activities caused many Americans to question the U.S. commitment to the South Vietnamese regime and led some in the Kennedy administration to look for ways to remove the unpopular president of South Vietnam.

In 1965 CBS television's Morley Safer showed U.S. Marines burning peasant huts, after the administration announced that they were not doing such things. In December 1966 the *New York Times*'s Harrison Salisbury reported from the North Vietnam capital Hanoi about the bombing of civilian structures. In February 1968, because of President Lyndon B. Johnson's well-earned "credibility gap," correspondents failed to emphasize that although the Tet Offensive might have been a psychological defeat for allied forces, it really was a smashing military defeat for the enemy, as the administration proclaimed. Their error was compounded by the impact of CBS anchor Walter Cronkite's pessimistic report from South Vietnam that was broadcast that month and contributed to President Johnson's conviction that he was losing public support for the war. A year later Seymour Hersh revealed the story of the My Lai massacre and the Pentagon cover-up in the *New York Times*.

Most of the time, however, reporters tended to follow the administration line on military progress not only in the field but on the combined U.S. and South Vietnamese attempts to win the hearts and minds of the people. As believers in the tenets of objective journalism as well as supporters of the Cold War containment policies, most dutifully reported what they were told about such progress at daily military briefings, even though they were often skeptical of some reports. Further, as in World War II and Korea, the producers and editors of television news shows rarely presented viewers glimpses of bloody or mutilated U.S. troops. U.S. citizens saw the Vietnam War live, in "real time," on their screens. Film footage was either sent by air to Tokyo or to the United States for later showing by the television networks. Those same networks, with their limited twenty-two-minute news space, centered their Vietnam stories after 1968 around peace negotiations and not around the continuing bloody fighting in Vietnam, thus convincing many viewers that the war was really winding down, which it was not.

On the home front, journalists, even those with an antiwar bias, tended to treat the antiwar movement in an unfavorable light. Although many reporters personally opposed the war, they nonetheless did not approve of mass demonstrations and the young people to their left in leadership positions. Moreover, whatever they thought of mass demonstrations, the need to sell newspapers or attract viewers led them to emphasize the most bizarre and violent of antiwar activists, even when 99 percent of participants were serious and law abiding. Indeed, it was difficult to attract the journalists' attention to mass demonstrations unless they were larger than previous ones or involved colorful activities that would not appeal to middle class people whose support the movement was after. It is not surprising that although a majority of citizens became critical of the war by 1968, a larger number, including many who labeled themselves doves, were even more critical of the antiwar movement that they perceived, through the media's filters, as radical and violent. Unfortunately for the antiwar movement, the more gentle and dignified the demonstration, in general, the less interesting it was to the media.

The myth of the liberal media losing the war in Vietnam was propagated by President Richard M. Nixon's administration, which launched an onslaught against them in November 1969 as an adjunct to his "Silent Majority" speech. Nixon's chief spokesperson was Vice President Spiro T. Agnew, aided by speechwriter Pat Buchanan, who attacked the control of the media by a few elitists in New York and Washington, calling them "nattering nabobs of negativism" who allegedly did not represent the views of the rest of the country. The television networks in particular took seriously the administration's threats against them and, for example, offered meager coverage of the massive 15 November Moratorium and Mobilization demonstration. Nixon earlier had been outraged when reports of his secret bombing of Cambodia were leaked to the *New York Times*. He ordered the first in a series of illegal wiretaps in an attempt to find the source of the leak. That action, which prefigured the more elaborate activities of the "plumbers," became one of the issues in the Watergate scandal that brought down his administration.

The popularly held view that the media played an unpatriotic role in Vietnam, that the war was lost more in the pages of the *New York Times* and on the *CBS Evening News* than in the battlefields, dramatically affected the way that the media were treated in succeeding U.S. military interventions. During the invasion of Grenada in 1983, military authorities kept newspeople at arm's length from the combat. Confronted by opposition to a policy that gave reporters no access to the island for two days after combat had begun, the Pentagon created the Sidle Commission, named after its chair, Major General Winant Sidle, to plan for pool coverage of future interventions. Sidle had been a prominent critic of the media's performance during the Vietnam War, and his committee's reforms did not work well in practice during the invasion of Panama in 1989, when even official pool reporters complained again about their inability to cover the story adequately.

When polled, however, most citizens agreed with the censorship rules. Taking their cue from poll results, much of the mainstream media had to go along with the government's policy as well, in part because they feared more criticism from a public that distrusted them. Indeed, when in late January 1991 more than 100,000 people gathered in Washington to oppose the launching of the air war over Iraq, most newspapers, magazines, and television networks ignored the event. Prior to that demonstration, of the nearly 3,000 minutes of coverage of the Gulf War buildup on network evening newscasts from 8 August 1990 through 3 January 1991, only twenty-nine were devoted to those who opposed the buildup in Saudi Arabia. In part, the media's unwillingness to cover antiwar activities reflected their own mistaken belief that such coverage would give aid and comfort to the enemy, as had been the case in the past. At the least, they knew that Iraqi leader Saddam Hussein and his advisers were watching CNN and U.S. print media for any sign of a weakening in U.S. resolve. Saddam had to be encouraged by the strong minority opposition in Congress he observed on CNN during the debate over the policy of moving from sanctions to armed combat.

More and more from the 1970s through the 1990s, television became a major influence in U.S. and other nations' foreign policies. The technological developments of the minicam, cable systems, and satellites enhanced television's abilities to bring news and interviews from all over the world in real time. Leaders sometimes found it advantageous to use television and television personalities for public diplomacy. In one prominent case in 1977, Egyptian president Anwar as-Sadat explained his peace overtures to Israel over worldwide television first to U.S. news personality Barbara Walters. President Jimmy Carter's Middle East negotiators, who had been deeply involved in trying to resolve the Arab-Israeli dispute, learned about Sadat's astounding announcement that he wanted to go to Jerusalem when they joined millions of other viewers around the world watching the Walters interview on television.

Most important during the Jimmy Carter administration was television's role in the Iranian hostage crisis. The militants who had taken U.S. hostages in Tehran in 1979 inflamed anti-Iranian feelings in the United States by staging frequent flamboyant anti-American parades in front of the occupied U.S. embassy. Had the television networks not covered such activities, the hostage issue might have left center stage, and the hostages might have seemed less important to their captors. According to this line of argument, the Iranians might have been more willing to release them once they had lost their "value," as established by media attention. ABC initially developed the television program *Nightline* to offer late-night coverage of the extended crisis. Other news shows also kept the story alive for more than a year. Carter claimed that any chance he had of winning the 1980 election disappeared on the weekend before election day when television networks ran specials on the first anniversary of the hostage taking, and thus reminded the public of the incumbent's disastrous failure to obtain their release.

Television coverage in the 1980s of spokespersons for another group of hostage takers in Lebanon, and even for hostage families in the United States, kept the pressure on President Reagan's administration to find some way to obtain their release. This pressure contributed to the series of actions that resulted in the Iran-Contra scandal, which almost destroyed an administration when Oliver North and others tried to exchange arms for the hostages. Similarly, in many of the terrorist seizures of airplanes or buildings in the 1980s, television cameras served to keep issues alive, thus increasing the value of whoever the terrorists were holding hostage. Administrations were unable to convince television networks not to cover or emphasize sensational rumors and developments in the various crises.

Lloyd Cutler, one of Carter's aides, expressed concern about the role that television had begun to play in foreign policy. He complained: "Whatever urgent but less televised problem may be on the White House agenda on any given morning, it is often put aside to consider and respond to the latest TV news bombshell in time for the next broadcast. In a very real sense, events that become TV lead stories now set the priorities for the policymaking agenda."

It was not just television news that set the agenda. An enlarged media punditocracy became an important independent player in the shaping of foreign policy. In the past, a handful of columnists and foreign correspondents had exercised occasional influence over U.S. policy, the most famous of whom was Walter Lippmann, whose illustrious career spanned six decades. Indeed, because of his reputed influence, he was often selected by presidents for special briefings, during which they tried to cajole him to include material in his column favorable to their policies. Occasionally, this could confuse other nations, as was the case during the Cuban missile crisis when Soviet leaders mistook a suggestion in a Lippmann column to trade missiles in Cuba for those in Turkey as an official trial balloon. Respected columnists like Lippmann not only affected opinion but occasionally affected decision-makers in a purely personal manner. Many did not like to be criticized by columnists who wrote for prestigious papers. Although presidents might have had the support of most of the country, along with most of the press, over a specific issue, they permitted their egos to become involved when a respected pundit read by everyone who counted in Washington Beltway spoke ill of them. Presidents Johnson and Nixon were two of those most sensitive to slights from the media, especially those that appeared in the *New York Times*.

In many ways, the *Times* itself has been an independent actor in the formation of U.S. foreign policy. In 1989

several columns about the relationship between Libya and German poison-gas makers written by William Safire in its pages led German Chancellor Helmut Kohl to complain, "This Safire fellow has done more damage to German-American relations than any other individual." A Safire column in early 1994 also figured prominently in the decision of Bobby Ray Inman to withdraw his name from consideration as President Bill Clinton's secretary of defense.

It was television and not the print media, however, that most influenced the development of the Persian Gulf War. That war was the first "living room war," in the sense that Americans and viewers around the world observed some of the action in real time. Devising diplomatic and military policies with an eye to the lessons learned during the Vietnam War, the George Bush administration was concerned about the role of the media in affecting opinion about the crisis and the war itself. The Pentagon even went so far as to hold daily briefings at 6 p.m. so that they could not be compared to the "Five O'Clock Follies" during the Vietnam War.

Unlike authorities in the Vietnam War, the administration applied strict censorship to the work of the more than 1,000 journalists who covered the action from Saudi Arabia. Moreover, unlike the Vietnam War, correspondents were not free to travel among the troops at the front lines. Military authorities led small groups of pool reporters to the front and limited severely what they could see. During the war itself, military police arrested eight U.S. newspeople, including three from the *New York Times*, for various transgressions. In addition, they refused to permit correspondents from antiwar publications, such as the *Nation*, the *Village Voice*, and *Mother Jones*, to join the pools. In May 1991 these publications joined twelve other news organizations to complain formally to the Pentagon for its alleged violations of First Amendment rights. Coalition commander General H. Norman Schwarzkopf felt that national security outweighed freedom of the press when he contended that "I don't want to give him [Saddam Hussein] one damn thing that will help his military analysis if I can prevent it." Despite all the planning for the media, the activities of U.S. journalists did occasionally give the Pentagon cause for concern during the Gulf War. For example, during the buildup period in the fall and winter of 1990 and before the imposition of strict censorship, U.S. television journalists broadcast pictures of female soldiers driving vehicles or sometimes not wearing all their clothes in the hot desert sun, two activities that worried culturally different Saudi Arabians. Further, the Saudi royal family was furious when it discovered that film clips of the soldiers' Christmas celebrations, on their holy soil, were also broadcast by U.S. media to the world. More important, one journalist, CNN's Peter Arnett, remained in Baghdad during the war. His reports, censored by his hosts, occasionally played into Iraq's hands by emphasizing civilian bombing damage and raising the specter of U.S. opposition to the bombing campaign. The Bush administration was indeed embarrassed when Arnett, among others, reported the bombing of a shelter in Baghdad that was full of women and children, even though doubts later emerged as to the accuracy of Arnett's report.

Most important, the coverage of bloody battles during the last day of the 100-hour war and the stories of U.S. troops engaging in a "turkey shoot" on the media-dubbed "Highway of Death" was one of the reasons President Bush decided to call a halt to the war before Iraq's Republican Guards had been captured or destroyed. The president and his advisers worried that the public would become upset if it appeared that the United States was participating in something that looked like an atrocity in the newscasts. They also had to worry about the reaction among their Arab allies to films and stories about an apparently needless slaughter of their brethren.

The United Nations coalition was not the only one to encounter problems with the media. Saddam Hussein's attempt to use the media to influence U.S. and world opinion failed miserably. In one instance in late 1990, he appeared to the world with hostages he was holding, including children. Because of his demeanor and that of his "guests," he ended up increasing hostility toward himself and his regime. Further, during the aerial war, his broadcast to international cable networks of pictures and statements by captured allied fliers, several of whom looked as though they had been beaten, also contributed to the revulsion against him.

However one evaluates the impact of the media on the Gulf War, at the least it served as one way for the two sides to talk to one another during the eight months of crisis and war. Marveling at this situation, CNN's Turner commented, "If we had the right technology, you'd have seen Eva Braun on the *Donahue Show* and Adolf Hitler on *Meet the Press*." Whatever one may think of Turner's flippant observation, his network and others came to play an increasingly more important role in international relations. At the very least, all national leaders, particularly those in a democracy, now take into serious consideration how their foreign activities will be affected by television coverage, and to a lesser degree by the print media, along a global information highway. Graphic images of horrifying massacres in Bosnia or Rwanda flickering across tens of millions of television screens may in fact help to determine their foreign activities. The problems posed by the media for George Washington, and indeed even John F. Kennedy, appeared to be far less difficult, even though U.S. journalists and diplomats have always maintained a tenuous relationship.

MELVIN SMALL

See also Committee on Public Information; Hearst, William Randolph; Jay's Treaty; Lippmann, Walter; Luce, Henry; Mexico, War with; Murrow, Edward (Egbert) Roscoe; Public Opinion; Spanish-American-Cuban-Filipino War 1898; Vietnam War; World War I; World War II; XYZ Affair; Zimmermann Telegram

FURTHER READING

Boylan, James. "Journalists and Foreign Policy." In *Encyclopedia of American Foreign Policy*, edited by Alexander deConde. New York, 1978.

Cohen, Bernard C. *The Press and Foreign Policy*. Princeton, N.J., 1963.

Denton, Robert E., ed. *The Media and the Persian Gulf War*. Westport, Conn., 1993.

Graber, Doris. *Public Opinion, the President, and Foreign Policy: Four Case Studies from the Formative Years*. New York, 1968.

Hallin, Daniel C. *The "Uncensored War": The Media and Vietnam*. New York, 1986.

Hilderbrand, Robert C. *Power and the People: Executive Management of Public Opinion in Foreign Affairs, 1897–1921*. Chapel Hill, N.C., 1981.

Hohenberg, John. *Foreign Correspondence: The Great Reporters and Their Times*. New York, 1964.

May, Ernest R. "The News Media and Diplomacy." In *The Diplomats, 1939–1979*, edited by Gordon A. Craig and Francis L. Lowenheim. Princeton, N.J., 1994.

Merk, Frederick. *Manifest Destiny and Mission in American History: A Reinterpretation*. New York, 1963.

Newman, Johanna. *Lights, Camera, War: Is Media Technology Driving International Politics?* N.Y., 1995.

Reston, James. *The Artillery of the Press*. New York, 1967.

Serafty, Simon, ed. *The Media and Foreign Policy*. New York, 1990.

Small, Melvin. *Covering Dissent: The Media and Anti-Vietnam War Movement*. New Brunswick, N.J., 1994.

Tebbel, John, and Sara Miles Watts. *The Press and the Presidency: From George Washington to Ronald Reagan*. New York, 1985.

Vaughn, Stephen. *Holding Fast the Inner Lines: Democracy, Nationalism, and the Committee on Public Information*. Chapel Hill, N.C., 1980.

Winkler, Allan M. *The Politics of Propaganda: The Office of War Information, 1942–1945*. New Haven, Conn., 1978.

JUÁREZ, BENITO PABLO

(*b*. 21 March 1806; *d*. 18 July 1872)

A Zapotec Indian, governor of the Mexican state of Oaxaca (1847–1852), de jure president of Mexico (1858–1861), elected president (1861–1865, 1867–1872), and self-proclaimed president (1865–1867). He fought to reform Mexican institutions and to maintain Mexican independence, resisting intervention by several European powers, especially France, and he sought active U.S. assistance to achieve those ends.

In 1855, as part of a broad process known as "the Reform," Juárez, then minister of justice, sponsored a law to curb the powers of the Roman Catholic Church and the military. In protest against this and other Reform laws, in December 1857 General Félix Zuloaga rebelled with the support of army and church conservatives, seized Mexico city, and proclaimed himself president. The constitutional president, Ignacio Comonfort, resigned. At the time, Juárez was president of the supreme court and, according to the Mexican constitution, next in line for the presidency. With two governments, one conservative under Zuloaga and one liberal under Juárez, civil war ensued. In order to gain resources and political support during the civil war, Juárez sponsored new legislation in 1859 to confiscate church wealth. Entrepreneurs who sought to acquire the church's property backed Juárez, who also enjoyed substantial popular support.

To win U.S. support for his side, in December 1858 the Juárez government signed the Ocampo-McClane Treaty, ceding to the United States the perpetual right of transit across the Isthmus of Tehuantepec and allowing U.S. intervention in that area to protect such transit. The U.S. Senate rejected the treaty, however. In 1859 Juárez appealed to the U.S. government for military assistance against the warships of his conservative opponents. A U.S. naval force intercepted the ships, thereby helping Juárez's liberal government. In December 1860 Juárez's forces recaptured Mexico City.

In June 1861 the Mexican government suspended payments on its foreign debt. In protest, France, Spain, and Great Britain sent a fleet to Mexico. When Mexico then promised to pay its debts, Spain and Great Britain withdrew, but more than 30,000 French troops invaded Mexico and in 1864 installed the Habsburg archduke Maximilian, brother of the Austrian emperor, as emperor of Mexico. The U.S. government protested but, preoccupied with its own civil war, could do little. The Juárez government, which continued to claim its legitimacy, maintained diplomatic relations with both the Confederacy and the Union during the American Civil War, but in August 1861 the Juárez government allowed Union forces to cross Mexican territory to attack the Confederacy. In 1864–1865 Maximilian's government adopted a policy of neutrality toward the Union and the Confederacy. The U.S. government was formally neutral toward Mexico's two governments during these years but favored the Juárez government and refused to establish diplomatic relations with Maximilian's government.

In late 1865, the victorious Union government, belatedly invoking the Monroe Doctrine, demanded French withdrawal from Mexico and blocked Austrian military assistance to Maximilian. Pressured also by the threat of war with Prussia, France withdrew its troops, and in 1867 Juárez's forces recaptured Mexico City. Maximilian was captured, court martialed, and executed by a Mexican army firing squad.

In gratitude for U.S. support, Mexico signed the Seward-Romero Agreement with the United States in July 1868 to settle all property and injury claims outstanding since the Treaty of Guadalupe Hidalgo (1848). To implement this agreement, Mexico paid U.S. claimants more than $4 million, while Mexican claimants were paid about $150,000. Mexico also permitted U.S. troops to enter northern Mexico in pursuit of Mexicans who had violated U.S. territory. As Juárez shouldered the burden of reconstruction, he faced factionalism and uprisings. In November 1871 a rebellion led by General Porfirio Díaz failed, but Juárez died soon after. During his presidency, Juárez succeeded in consolidating Mexican independence and strengthening the power of the central government while improving relations with the United States for the first time since the war between the two countries.

JORGE I. DOMÍNGUEZ

See also Díaz (José de la Cruz), Porfirio; Mexico; Mexico, War with; Monroe Doctrine; Seward, William Henry

FURTHER READING

Miller, Robert Ryan. *Arms Across the Border: U.S. Aid to Juárez During the French Intervention in Mexico.* Philadelphia, 1973.

Olliff, Jonathan C. *Reforma Mexico and the U.S.: A Search for Alternatives to Annexation, 1854–1861.* Birmingham, Ala., 1981.

Schoonover, Thomas D. *Dollars over Dominion: The Triumph of Liberalism in Mexican–United States Relations, 1861–1867.* Baton Rouge, La., 1978.

JUSTICE, U.S. DEPARTMENT OF

The department of the executive branch of the U.S. government with the primary responsibility for the administration and enforcement of federal laws. "The nation's litigator," as the department terms itself, originated in the position of United States Attorney General, authorized in 1789; in 1870 Congress enacted legislation establishing the department with the attorney general as its head. The attorney general supervises most legal counsel employed by the United States, plus a wide range of law enforcement personnel, and furnishes advice on legal matters to the president, the cabinet, and the heads of the government's executive departments and agencies.

Sometimes described as the largest law office in the world, in the mid-1990s the Department of Justice had a staff of nearly 100,000 employees, most of whom are located in Washington, D.C. Its organizational chart includes the Immigration and Naturalization Service (INS), the Drug Enforcement Agency (DEA), and the Federal Bureau of Investigation (FBI). All are well known to the public and all have responsibilities bearing on foreign relations. The DEA is the U.S. government's primary narcotics enforcement agency. Its staff reviews international agreements on drug matters, maintains contact with the Department of State, and assists foreign governments in the preparation of drug-related laws. The

DEA's International Law Section pursues worldwide drug enforcement efforts, including the provision of training to foreign nations in developing policies and procedures and in intelligence gathering.

The controversial Iran-Contra affair of the mid-1980s provides an example of the Justice Department's occasional involvement in foreign policy at a high level. This clandestine initiative by the administration of President Ronald Reagan featured arms sales, direct and indirect, to so-called moderate elements in the Iranian government, with which the United States had no diplomatic relations, and the even more secret transfer of proceeds therefrom to the Contra insurgents fighting the Marxist Sandinista government of Nicaragua. In 1984 Congress had passed the Boland Amendments, which essentially banned U.S. assistance to the Contras. The White House called upon Attorney General Edwin Meese III and the legal counsels of the Department of State and the Central Intelligence Agency (CIA) to rule on the legality of the Iranian segment of the activity. Existing legislation bearing on the subject included the Intelligence Oversight Act, the Arms Export Control Act, the Economy Act (which authorizes CIA purchase of weapons at cost from the Defense Department), and the 1974 Hughes-Ryan Amendment to the National Security Act (which requires a presidential finding and notification to Congress of CIA activity under the Economy Act). Eventually, the Boland Amendments came into play. The attorney general and other senior administration advisers looked at the relevant body of law and found no impediment to undertaking arms sales to Iran. The clandestine efforts proceeded until information on the diversion of funds to the Contras surfaced, and the affair came to a halt in a welter of congressional investigation and public dispute, at which point legal interpretations became irrelevant.

The INS affects the more routine U.S. relations with nations and peoples abroad as few other federal agencies do. For more than a century, it has overseen the entry into the United States of would-be visitors and immigrants after the Foreign Service has screened applicants abroad and issued them visas. INS efforts now center on administration of the Immigration Reform and Control Act of 1986, which concerns illegal immigration, and the Immigration Act of 1990, which modified the provisions of the Immigration and Naturalization Act of 1952 (the McCarran Act). Immigration judges preside nationwide over quasi-judicial hearings on the admissibility of applicants. In a related function, the Board of Immigration Appeals is a quasi-judicial appellate body that sets precedents binding on the INS. The Executive Office for Immigration Review, an office independent of the INS, exercises the delegated authority of the attorney general in interpreting immigration laws. The Office of Immigration Litigation in the Civil Division represents the United States in suits brought against the INS, the Department of State, and other agencies.

The FBI, in addition to its Washington headquarters and fifty-six field offices, assigns staff abroad in certain major U.S. embassies. These offices operate in a liaison capacity on intelligence and criminal matters associated with the bureau's domestic responsibilities, for example, arranging for the extradition of a fugitive criminal.

A number of other components of the Department of Justice have foreign affairs–related responsibilities. Among these is the Foreign Claims Settlement Commission, another independent body within the department; it adjudicates claims of U.S. nationals against foreign governments in nationalization or expropriation cases and advises other agencies on matters relating to international claims. The Office of International Programs works with the Department of State, the Agency for International Development, and the U.S. Information Agency in developing international training and technical assistance.

The Criminal Division's Office of International Affairs coordinates all international evidence gathering, cooperates with the Department of State in negotiating extradition treaties, and participates in UN-sponsored and other committees concerned with international law enforcement. It maintains a field office in Rome. The division's Money Laundering Section evaluates the international implications of legislation in its area of expertise, and the Narcotic and Dangerous Drug Section assists in efforts toward international cooperation against drug trafficking. The Antitrust Division's Foreign Commerce Section; the Civil Division's Commercial Litigation and Federal Programs branches; and the Environment and Natural Resources Division's Policy, Legislation, and Special Litigation Section are among offices that have duties falling at least partially in the international field.

HENRY E. MATTOX

See also Drug Enforcement Agency; Extradition; Immigration; Immigration and Naturalization Service; Iran-Contra Affair; Kennedy, Robert Francis; Supreme Court and the Judiciary

FURTHER READING

Meese, Edwin, III. *With Reagan: The Inside Story.* Washington, D.C., 1992.

U. S. Department of Justice. *Attorneys General of the United States, 1789–1985.* Washington, D.C., 1985.

———. *United States Department of Justice: Legal Activities, 1993–1994.* Washington, D.C., n.d.